D1500672

THE MEDITERRANEAN
AND THE MEDITERRANEAN WORLD
IN THE AGE OF PHILIP II

FERNAND BRAUDEL

The Mediterranean
and the Mediterranean World
in the Age of Philip II

VOLUME I

Translated from the French
by Siân Reynolds

UNIVERSITY OF CALIFORNIA PRESS
Berkeley · Los Angeles · London

A Lucien Febvre,
toujours présent
en témoignage
de reconnaissance
et de filiale affection

University of California Press
Berkeley and Los Angeles, California

University of California Press, Ltd.
London, England

First California Paperback Printing 1995

VOLUME I

Library of Congress Cataloging-in-Publication Data

Braudel, Fernand.
    [Méditerranée et le monde méditerranéen à l'époque de Philippe
II. English]
    The Mediterranean and the Mediterranean world in the age of Philip
II / Fernand Braudel ; translated from the French by Siân Reynolds.
        p.   cm.
    Includes bibliographical references.
    ISBN 0-520-20308-9 (pbk. vol. I : alk. paper). —
ISBN 0-520-20330-5 (pbk. vol. II : alk. paper)
        1. Mediterranean Region—History.   2. Human geography—
Mediterranean Region.   I. Title.
DE96.B713   1995   95-37581
909'.0982205—de20   CIP

First published in France under the title
La Méditerranée et la Monde Méditerranéen à l'Époque
de Philippe II, 1949, second revised edition 1966
© Librairie ARMAND COLIN 1966

English translation by Siân Reynolds copyright © 1972 by Wm. Collins Sons
Ltd. and Harper & Row, Publishers, Inc. Published by arrangement with
HarperCollins Publishers, Inc. and HarperCollins Publishers, Ltd.

Printed in the United States of America
9   8   7   6   5   4   3   2

Contents

Preface to the English Edition   *page* 13
Preface to the Second Edition   14
Preface to the First Edition   17

Part One
THE ROLE OF THE ENVIRONMENT

I. THE PENINSULAS: MOUNTAINS, PLATEAUX, AND PLAINS   25

1. *Mountains Come First*   25
   Physical and human characteristics   25
   Defining the mountains   30
   Mountains, civilizations, and religions   34
   Mountain freedom   38
   The mountains' resources: an assessment   41
   Mountain dwellers in the towns   44
   Typical cases of mountain dispersion   47
   Mountain life: the earliest civilization of the Mediterranean?   51

2. *Plateaux, Hills, and Foothills*   53
   The high plains   53
   A hillside civilization   55
   The hills   58

3. *The Plains*   60
   Water problems: malaria   62
   The improvement of the plains   66
   The example of Lombardy   72
   Big landowners and poor peasants   75
   Short term change in the plains: the Venetian Terraferma   78
   Long term change: the fortunes of the Roman Campagna   81
   The strength of the plains: Andalusia   82

4. *Transhumance and Nomadism*   85
   Transhumance   85
   Nomadism, an older way of life   87
   Transhumance in Castile   91
   Overall comparisons and cartography   94
   Dromedaries and camels: the Arab and Turk invasions   95
   Nomadism in the Balkans, Anatolia, and North Africa   98
   Cycles spanning the centuries   101

II. THE HEART OF THE MEDITERRANEAN: SEAS AND COASTS   103

1. *The Plains of the Sea*   103
   Coastal navigation   103

The early days of Portuguese discovery 108
The narrow seas, home of history 108
The Black Sea, preserve of Constantinople 110
The Archipelago, Venetian and Genoese 115
Between Tunisia and Sicily 116
The Mediterranean Channel 117
The Tyrrhenian Sea 120
The Adriatic 124
East and west of Sicily 133
Two maritime worlds 134
The double lesson of the Turkish and Spanish Empires 135
Beyond politics 137

2. *Mainland Coastlines* 138
The peoples of the sea 138
Weaknesses of the maritime regions 140
The big cities 145
The changing fortunes of maritime regions 146

3. *The Islands* 148
Isolated worlds 149
Precarious lives 151
On the paths of general history 154
Emigration from the islands 158
Islands that the sea does not surround 160
The Peninsulas 162

III. BOUNDARIES: THE GREATER MEDITERRANEAN 168
A Mediterranean of historical dimensions 168

1. *The Sahara, the Second Face of the Mediterranean* 171
The Sahara: near and distant boundaries 171
Poverty and want 173
Nomads who travel far 176
Advance and infiltration from the steppe 177
The gold and spice caravans 181
The oases 185
The geographical area of Islam 187

2. *Europe and the Mediterranean* 188
The isthmuses and their north–south passages 188
The Russian isthmus: leading to the Black and Caspian Sea 191
From the Balkans to Danzig: the Polish isthmus 195
The German isthmus: an overall view 202
The Alps 206
The third character: the many faces of Germany 208
From Genoa to Antwerp, and from Venice to Hamburg: the conditions
    of circulation 211
Emigration and balance of trade 214
The French isthmus, from Rouen to Marseilles 216
Europe and the Mediterranean 223

3. *The Atlantic Ocean* 224
Several Atlantics 224

Contents 7

The Atlantic learns from the Mediterranean 225
The Atlantic destiny in the sixteeth century 226
A late decline 230

IV. THE MEDITERRANEAN AS A PHYSICAL UNIT: CLIMATE AND HISTORY 231
1. *The Unity of the Climate* 231
The Atlantic and the Sahara 232
A homogeneous climate 234
Drought: the scourge of the Mediterranean 238

2. *The Seasons* 246
The winter standstill 246
Shipping at a halt 248
Winter: season of peace and plans 253
The hardships of winter 255
The accelerated rhythm of summer life 256
The summer epidemics 258
The Mediterranean climate and the East 259
Seasonal rhythms and statistics 260
Determinism and economic life 265

3. *Has the Climate Changed Since the Sixteenth Century?* 267
Supplementary note 272

V. THE MEDITERRANEAN AS A HUMAN UNIT: COMMUNICATIONS AND CITIES 276
1. *Land Routes and Sea Routes* 276
Vital communications 278
Archaic means of transport 282
Did land routes increase in importance towards 1600? 284
The intrinsic problem of the overland route 289
Two sets of evidence from Venice 290
Circulation and statistics: the case of Spain 293
The double problem in the long term 295

2. *Shipping: Tonnages and Changing Circumstances* 295
Big ships and little ships in the fifteenth century 299
The first victories of the small ships 300
In the Atlantic in the sixteenth century 301
In the Mediterranean 306

3. *Urban Functions* 312
Towns and Roads 312
A meeting place for different transport routes 316
From roads to banking 318
Urban cycle and decline 322
A very incomplete typology 323

4. *Towns, Witnesses to the Century* 324
The rise in population 326
Hardships old and new: Famine and the wheat problem 328
Hardships old and new: epidemics 332
The indispensable immigrant 334

8 *Contents*

Urban political crises 338
The privileged banking towns 341
Royal and imperial cities 344
In favour of capitals 351
From permanence to change 352

Part Two
COLLECTIVE DESTINIES AND GENERAL TRENDS

I. ECONOMIES: THE MEASURE OF THE CENTURY 355

1. *Distance, the First Enemy* 355
For letter-writers: the time lost in coming and going 355
The dimensions of the sea: some record crossings 358
Average speeds 360
Letters: a special case 363
News, a luxury commodity 365
Present-day comparisons 370
Empires and distance 371
The three missions of Claude du Bourg (1576 and 1577) 374
Distance and the economy 375
Fairs, the supplementary network of economic life 379
Local economies 382
The quadrilateral: Genoa, Milan, Venice, and Florence 387

2. *How Many People?* 394
A world of 60 or 70 million people 394
Mediterranean waste lands 398
A population increase of 100 per cent? 402
Levels and indices 403
Reservations and conclusions 410
Confirmations and suggestions 412
Some certainties 413
Another indicator: migration 415

3. *Is It Possible to Construct a Model of the Mediterranean Economy?* 418
Agriculture, the major industry 420
An industrial balance sheet 427
The putting-out or 'Verlag' system and the rise of urban industry 430
The system prospered 432
An itinerant labour force 433
General and local trends 434
The volume of commercial transactions 438
The significance and limitations of long distance trade 441
Capitalist concentrations 444
The total tonnage of Mediterranean shipping 445
Overland transport 448
The State: the principal entrepreneur of the century 449
Precious metals and the monetary economy 451
Was one fifth of the population in great poverty? 453
A provisional classification 457
Food, a poor guide: officially rations were always adequate 459
Can our calculations be checked? 460

II. ECONOMIES: PRECIOUS METALS, MONEY, AND PRICES   462

  1. *The Mediterranean and the Gold of the Sudan*   463
    The flow of precious metals towards the east   463
    Sudanese gold: early history   466
    The Portuguese in Guinea: gold continues to arrive in the
      Mediterranean   469
    The gold trade and the general economic situation   472
    Sudanese gold in North Africa   474

  2. *American Silver*   476
    American and Spanish treasure   476
    American treasure takes the road to Antwerp   480
    The French detour   484
    The great route from Barcelona to Genoa and the second cycle of
      American treasure   487
    The Mediterranean invaded by Spanish coins   493
    Italy, the victim of 'la moneda larga'   496
    The age of the Genoese   500
    The Piacenza fairs   504
    The reign of paper   508
    From the last state bankruptcy under Philip II to the first under Philip
      III   510

  3. *The Rise in Prices*   516
    Contemporary complaints   519
    Was American treasure responsible?   521
    Some arguments for and against American responsibility   522
    Wages   524
    Income from land   525
    Banks and inflation   528
    The 'industrialists'   532
    States and the price rise   532
    The dwindling of American treasure   536
    Devalued currency and false currency   537
    Three ages of metal   541

III. ECONOMIES: TRADE AND TRANSPORT   543

  1. *The Pepper Trade*   543
    Mediterranean revenge: the prosperity of the Red Sea after 1550 545
    Routes taken by the Levant trade   549
    The revival of the Portuguese pepper trade   554
    Portuguese pepper: deals and projects   556
    Portuguese pepper is offered to Venice   558
    The Welser and Fugger contract: 1586–1591   560
    The survival of the Levantine spice routes   562
    Possible explanations   568

  2. *Equilibrium and Crisis in the Mediterranean Grain Trade*   570
    The cereals   570
    Some rules of the grain trade   571
    The grain trade and the shipping routes   576

Ports and countries that exported grain 579
Eastern grain 583
Equilibrium, crisis, and vicissitudes in the grain trade 584
The first crises: northern grain at Lisbon and Seville 585
The Turkish wheat boom: 1548–1564 591
Eating home-produced bread: Italy's situation between 1564 and 1590 594
The last crisis: imports from the north after 1500 599
Sicily: still the grain store of the Mediterranean 602
On grain crises 604

3. *Trade and Transport: The Sailing Ships of the Atlantic* 606
I. *Before 1550: the first arrivals* 606
Basque, Biscayan, and even Galician ships 607
The Portuguese 608
Normans and Bretons 609
Flemish ships 612
The first English sailing ships 612
The period of prosperity (1511–1534) 613

II. *From 1550 to 1573: the Mediterranean left to Mediterranean ships* 615
The return of the English in 1572–1573 621
Anglo-Turkish negotiations: 1578-1583 625
The success of English shipping 626
The situation at the end of the century 628
The arrival of the Hansards and the Dutch 629
From grain to spices: The Dutch conquer the Mediterranean 630
How the Dutch took Seville after 1570 without firing a shot 636
New Christians in the Mediterranean 640

Abbreviations 643

TRANSLATOR'S NOTE

A full bibliography and index will appear in Volume II. Where possible reference has been made to English editions of books mentioned in the notes.

List of Illustrations

Following page 322
1. Plan of Venice (XVIth Century) *Photo Mas, Barcelona*
2. Constantinople *Photo B. N. Paris*
3. Height and depth above and below sea-level (Figure 1)
4. Atlantic sailing vessel *Photo B. N. Paris*
5. Venetian galleon *Photo O. Böhm, Venice*
6. Merchant's round ship *Photo O. Böhm, Venice*
7. The English take Cadiz, 1596 *Photo B. N. Paris*
8. The Harbour, Barcelona
9. The Venice Arsenal (1500)
10. Sailing ships large and small *Photo B. N. Paris*
11. The Alps between France and Piedmont *Photo B. N. Paris*

List of Figures

1. Height and depth above and below sea-level (*see* Plate 3)
2. The folds of the Mediterranean   27
3. The great canals of the Lombardy plain   73
4. The regularization canals safeguarded half of the Venetian lagoons 79
5. Winter and summer pasture of sheep in Haute-Provence   90
6. Castilian transnumance   93
7. Transnumance in modern times   98

8. The wrecks of boats sailing to Venice from 1592 to 1609   112
9. Captured vessels during the same period   113
10. Sicily and Tunisia cut the Mediterranean in two   114
11. Corfu, lying opposite Otranto, commands the entrance to the Adriatic   124
12. The Mediterranean and the rest of the world   169
13. The implantation of palm groves from the Indus to the Atlantic   172
14. Saharan caravans, fifteenth and sixteenth centuries   183
15. The roads of the German isthmus   204
16. The Alpine barrier   205
17. Lyons and the spice trade   218
18. Marseilles and the internal French market, 1543   221
19. The 'true' Mediterranean, from the olive tree to the great palm groves   232
20. A voyage to Spain that ended up at Tabarka, January, 1597   250
21. Effects of the mistral, 19th April, 1569 and days following   252
22. Seasonal variation of the volume of business at the *Fondaco dei Tedeschi* at Venice   266
23. The road network of the Iberian peninsula in 1546   279
24. Roads over the Tuscan Apennines   280
25. The Great Bazaar at Constantinople   313
26. The heart of Venice   314
27. Population of the towns of Castile   324
28, 29, and 30. News travelling to Venice   366–367
31, 32. Venice: the voyages of the *galere da mercato*   392
33. The population of the Venetian mainland in 1548   397
34. Population of Castile in 1541 and in 1591   406
35. Increase in population, 1541–1591, 1593   407
36. The population of Sicily, 1501–1716   409
37. Baptisms at Florence, 1551–1600   413
38. The exchange rate of the Venetian sequin   472
39. Gold versus silver   473
40. The two ages of American silver   477
41. Spanish 'political' silver in Europe, 1580–1626   479
42. Wheat prices in the Mediterranean and Europe   516
43. Prices at Bursa, 1489–1633   518
44. Rising prices in Paris   520
45. The price rise is felt at Strasbourg before Valencia   523
46. Prices and real wages at Valencia   525
47. Real prices of cereals at Strasbourg, Lwow and Valencia   526
48. Devaluation of moneys of account   528
49. The Sicilian *caricatori* in 1532   580
50. Venice: imported grain and mainland grain   596
51. Sicilian exports   598
52. Sicily after 1593   605
53. A register of marine insurance at Genoa   618–620
54. The increasing number of northern boats at Leghorn, 1573–93   632–633

Facsimile of the *carpeta* of a letter from Philip II's ambassador in Lisbon   461

Preface to the English Edition

This English version of *The Mediterranean* corresponds to the second French edition of 1966. When, in 1964, several English-language publishers suggested to me the possibility of a translation, the original French edition had been out of print for twelve or thirteen years and I would not have wanted to re-issue the book without thoroughly revising it, in order to incorporate in the new edition the results of recent studies and of the extensive research carried out by my pupils and myself since 1949. But I do not think I should ever have found the courage to undertake this major revision had I not been faced with the prospect of a translation. I did not wish to offer the English-speaking public a book which had already had a somewhat tempestuous career. With the mass of books flooding from the presses today, works on history age more quickly than they used to.

The Mediterranean speaks with many voices; it is a sum of individual histories. If these histories assume in the course of research different values, different meanings, their sum must perforce change too. English-speaking historians will see that I have taken note of their work, and that I have given more space than I did in 1949 to the voyages to the Mediterranean of the ships of the northern countries, their merchants and their merchandise, through the narrow gateway of Gibraltar. I have also devoted more attention to what is a major historiographical problem, a zone of formidable uncertainty: the Ottoman empire. After the conquest of the Balkans and especially after that of the southern coast of the Mediterranean, from Syria to Algiers and almost to Gibraltar, that empire covered a good half of the Mediterranean region; it was an Anti-Christendom, balancing the weight of the west. We historians of the west are in exactly the same position as the contemporaries of Philip II, of Gian Andrea Doria or Don John of Austria: we can glimpse the Turkish world from the outside only. The reports sent by ambassadors and intelligence agents to Christian princes tell us something of the workings of that great body, but hardly ever anything of its motives. The secret, or some of the secrets, lie hidden in the vast archives in Istanbul. Access to them is difficult and it is only now that we are seeing some of the results of investigation of these sources, in works which are naturally all breaking new ground. I have done my best to take account of these recent studies – with the greater energy since in many cases (and I am very sensible of the honour) the area of the problem as defined in my book and the hypotheses (they were no more) which I advanced in the first edition had served as the original frame of reference for the research. As I write these lines, I have on my desk the admirable study by M. A. Cook, *Population pressure in rural Anatolia: 1450–1600*, which has just been published by the Oxford University Press. I am touched and flattered by both his criticism and approval of my book.

Today in 1972, six years after the second French edition, I think I can say that two major truths have remained unchallenged. The first is the unity and coherence of the Mediterranean region. I retain the firm conviction that the Turkish Mediterranean lived and breathed with the same rhythms as the Christian, that the whole sea shared a common destiny, a heavy one indeed, with identical problems and general trends if not identical consequences. And the second is the greatness of the Mediterranean, which lasted well after the age of Columbus and Vasco da Gama, until the dawn of the seventeenth century or even later. This 'waning' of the Mediterranean, to borrow the word Huizinga used of the Middle Ages, had its autumnal fruits: Titian and Tintoretto in Venice; Caravaggio and the Carracci at Rome and Bologna; Galileo in Padua and Florence; in Spain, Madrid and the Golden Century; and the rise everywhere of the theatre and music we still love today.

In this brief foreword to a very large book, I should like to express my gratitude to all those concerned in producing the English edition: first of all to Hugh Van Dusen, who perhaps because he had wished for so long to see the book in English has taken the greatest pains to ensure that it has a quality rare I believe in the realm of translations. To Georges Huppert who helped us to find a translator. To Siân Reynolds who agreed to this weighty assignment and has admirably fulfilled the hopes we placed in her: it is no small task to adapt my not uncomplicated style to the vigorous rhythms of the English language. To Oreste Ranum, that great expert on the language and civilization of France, who agreed to read and revise the text and to resolve all the small problems that crop up in any translation. And finally to Richard Ollard, who has with energy and devotion seen the book through the press and presented it to the English-speaking public. To all may I express here my appreciation and warmest thanks.

FERNAND BRAUDEL
Paris, 8th February, 1972

Preface to the Second Edition

It was with much hesitation that I undertook a new edition of *The Mediterranean*. Some of my friends advised me to change nothing, not a word, not a comma, arguing that a work that had become a classic should not be altered. But how could I decently listen to them? With the increase in knowledge and the advances made in our neighbouring disciplines, the social sciences, history books age more quickly now than in the past. A moment passes and their vocabulary has become dated, the new ground they broke is familiar territory, and the explanations they offered are challenged.

Moreover, *The Mediterranean* does not date from 1949, when it was first published, nor even from 1947, when it was defended as a thesis at the Sorbonne. The main outline of the book was already determined if not entirely written by 1939, at the close of the dazzling early period of the *Annales* of Marc Bloch and Lucien Febvre, of which it is the direct result. So the reader should not be misled by some of the arguments in the preface to the first edition. They are attacks on old positions, forgotten in the research world, if not in the teaching world of today, yesterday's polemic chasing shadows from the past.

Thus it soon became clear to me that a new edition would mean an extensive if not a total revision of the text, that it would not do simply to include the maps, diagrams, graphs, and illustrations which material difficulties in 1949 had made it impossible for me to publish. Corrections, additions, and revisions have been in some places considerable, since I have had to take account not only of fresh knowledge but also of what is often more significant, fresh approaches to historical problems. Several chapters have therefore been totally rewritten.

Any work of synthesis, as Henri Pirenne used to say, inspires a new crop of specialized research. Such research did not fail to follow in the wake of my book. It began by following in my footsteps and has now completely overwhelmed me. Many pages would be required to give an account of the immense amount of work that has been accomplished since 1949 in areas directly concerned by this book, with the books and articles published and unpublished of Ömer Lütfi Barkan and his pupils, Julio Caro Baroja, Jean-François Bergier, Jacques Berque, Ramón Carande, Alvaro Castillo Pintado, Federico Chabod, Huguette and Pierre Chaunu, Carlo M. Cipolla, Gaetano Cozzi, Jean Delumeau, Alphonse Dupront, Elena Fasano, René Gascon, José Gentil da Silva, Jacques Heers, Emmanuel Le Roy Ladurie, Vitorino Magalhães Godinho, Hermann Kellenbenz, Henri Lapeyre, Robert Mantran, Felipe Ruiz Martín, Frédéric Mauro, Ruggiero Romano, Raymond de Roover, Frank Spooner, Iorjo Tadić, Alberto Tenenti, Ugo Tucci, Valentin Vázquez de Prada, Pierre Vilar, and lastly the studies undertaken by the group formed by the late José Vicens Vives and his admirable pupils. I have participated, often very closely, in the course of these studies.

And finally I myself have found much to add to the information given in the first edition, in the course of continued research and reading in the archives and libraries of Venice, Parma, Modena, Florence, Genoa, Naples, Paris, Vienna, Simancas, London, Cracow, and Warsaw.

This harvest had somehow to be brought home. And here the insidious questions of method once more raise their heads, as they inevitably must in a book on this scale which takes as its subject the Mediterranean region understood in the very widest sense embracing every aspect of its rich and dense life. Including more material necessarily means rearranging, eliminating old problems only to encounter new ones, the solution of which may be neither easy nor clear-cut. Not only that, but in the fifteen years that separate this new edition from the original draft, the author himself has changed. It was impossible for me to touch this book again without immediately altering the balance of some of the arguments, even the basic approach around which the whole work is structured, the dialectic of space and time (geography and history) which was the original justification of the book. This time I have made explicit and prominent views that were only embryonic in the first edition. I have felt obliged to give more space to economics, political science, a certain idea of civilization, and a more detailed demographic study. I have added many fresh perspectives and I hope I am right in thinking that they have shed new light into the very core of this work.

The basic problem, however, remains the same. It is the problem confronting every historical undertaking. Is it possible somehow to convey simultaneously both that conspicuous history which holds our attention by its continual and dramatic changes – and that other, submerged, history, almost silent and always discreet, virtually unsuspected either by its observers or its participants, which is little touched by the obstinate erosion of time? This fundamental contradiction, which must always lie at the centre of our thought, can be a vital tool of knowledge and research. Relevant to every area of human life, it may take on a variety of forms according to the terms of the comparison.

Historians have over the years grown accustomed to describing this contradiction in terms of *structure* and *conjuncture*, the former denoting long-term, the latter, short-term realities. Clearly there are different kinds of structure just as there are different kinds of conjuncture, and the duration of either structure or conjuncture may in turn vary. History accepts and discovers multidimensional explanations, reaching, as it were, vertically from one temporal plane to another. And on every plane there are also horizontal relationships and connections. The reader will find my feeling expressed more simply and unequivocally in the preface to the first edition, which also describes my original intentions and explains the arrangement of the chapters of the book.[1]

19th June, 1963

---

[1] The maps and diagrams for the second edition were produced to my specifications at the Cartographical Laboratory of the VIe Section of the École Pratique des Hautes Études, under the supervision of Jacques Bertin. I should like to express my thanks to Mlle. Marthe Briata, Mme. Marianne Mahn, A. Tenenti, and M. Keul for assistance in checking the bibliography and reading the proofs.

Preface to the First Edition

I have loved the Mediterranean with passion, no doubt because I am a northerner like so many others in whose footsteps I have followed. I have joyfully dedicated long years of study to it – much more than all my youth. In return, I hope that a little of this joy and a great deal of Mediterranean sunlight will shine from the pages of this book. Ideally perhaps one should, like the novelist, have one's subject under control, never losing it from sight and constantly aware of its overpowering presence. Fortunately or unfortunately, the historian has not the novelist's freedom. The reader who approaches this book in the spirit I would wish will do well to bring with him his own memories, his own vision of the Mediterranean to add colour to the text and to help me conjure up this vast presence, as I have done my best to do. My feeling is that the sea itself, the one we see and love, is the greatest document of its past existence. If I have retained nothing else from the geographers who taught me at the Sorbonne, I have retained this lesson with an unwavering conviction that has guided me throughout my project.

It might be thought that the connections between history and geographical space would be better illustrated by a more straightforward example than the Mediterranean, particularly since in the sixteenth century the sea was such a vast expanse in relation to man. Its character is complex, awkward, and unique. It cannot be contained within our measurements and classifications. No simple biography beginning with date of birth can be written of this sea; no simple narrative of how things happened would be appropriate to its history. The Mediterranean is not even a *single* sea, it is a complex of seas; and these seas are broken up by islands, interrupted by peninsulas, ringed by intricate coastlines. Its life is linked to the land, its poetry more than half-rural, its sailors may turn peasant with the seasons; it is the sea of vineyards and olive trees just as much as the sea of the long-oared galleys and the roundships of merchants and its history can no more be separated from that of the lands surrounding it than the clay can be separated from the hands of the potter who shapes it. 'Lauso la mare e tente'n terro' ('Praise the sea and stay on land') says a Provençal proverb.

So it will be no easy task to discover exactly what the historical character of the Mediterranean has been. It will require much patience, many different approaches, and no doubt a few unavoidable errors. Nothing could be clearer than the Mediterranean defined by oceanographer, geologist, or even geographer. Its boundaries have been charted, classified, and labelled. But what of the Mediterranean of the historian? There is no lack of authoritative statements as to what it is not. It is not an autonomous world; nor is it the preserve of any one power. Woe betide the historian who thinks that this preliminary interrogation is unnecessary, that the Mediterranean as an entity needs no definition because it has long been clearly defined, is instantly recognizable and can be described by dividing general history along the lines of its geographical contours. What possible value could these contours have for our studies?

But how could one write any history of the sea, even over a period of only fifty years, if one stopped at one end with the Pillars of Hercules and at the other with the straits at whose entrance ancient Ilium once stood guard? The question of boundaries is the first to be encountered; from it all others flow. To draw a boundary around anything is to define, analyse, and reconstruct it, in this case select, indeed adopt, a philosophy of history.

To assist me I did indeed have at my disposal a prodigious body of articles, papers, books, publications, surveys, some purely historical, others no less interesting, written by specialists in neighbouring disciplines – anthropologists, geographers, botanists, geologists, technologists. There is surely no region on this earth as well documented and written about as the Mediterranean and the lands illumined by its glow. But, dare I say it, at the risk of seeming ungrateful to my predecessors, that this mass of publications buries the researcher as it were under a rain of ash. So many of these studies speak a language of the past, outdated in more ways than one. Their concern is not the sea in all its complexity, but some minute piece of the mosaic, not the grand movement of Mediterranean life, but the actions of a few princes and rich men, the trivia of the past, bearing little relation to the slow and powerful march of history which is our subject. So many of these works need to be revised, related to the whole, before they can come to life again.

And then, no history of the sea can be written without precise knowledge of the vast resources of its archives. Here the task would appear to be beyond the powers of an individual historian. There is not one sixteenth-century Mediterranean state that does not possess its charter-room, usually well furnished with those documents that have escaped the fires, sieges, and disasters of every kind known to the Mediterranean world. To prospect and catalogue this unsuspected store, these mines of the purest historical gold, would take not one lifetime but at least twenty, or the simultaneous dedication of twenty researchers. Perhaps the day will come when we shall no longer be working on the great sites of history with the methods of small craftsmen. Perhaps on that day it will become possible to write general history from original documents and not from more or less secondary works. Need I confess that I have not been able to examine all the documents available to me in the archives, no matter how hard I tried. This book is the result of a necessarily incomplete study. I know in advance that its conclusions will be examined, discussed, and replaced by others and I am glad of it. That is how history progresses and must progress.

Another point is that by its inauspicious chronological position, between the last flames of the Renaissance and Reformation and the harsh, inward-looking age of the seventeenth century, the Mediterranean in the second half of the sixteenth century might well be described, as it was by Lucien Febvre, as a 'faux beau sujet'. Need I point out where its interest lies? It is of no small value to know what became of the Mediterranean at the threshold of modern times, when the world no longer revolved entirely around it, served it and responded to its rhythms. The rapid decline of the Mediterranean about which people have always talked does not seem at all clear to me; rather, all the evidence seems to point to the contrary. But even leaving this question aside, it is my belief that all the problems posed by the Mediterranean are of exceptional human richness, that they must therefore interest all historians and non-historians. I would go so far as to say that they serve to illumine our own century, that they are not lacking in that 'utility' in the strict sense which Nietzsche demanded of all history.

I do not intend to say much about the attraction and the temptations offered by such a subject. I have already mentioned the difficulties, deceptions, and lures it holds in store. I would add just this, that among existing historical works, I found none which could offer general guidance. A historical study centred on a stretch of water has all the charms but undoubtedly all the dangers of a new departure.

Since the scales were so heavily weighted on both sides, was I right in the end to come down on the side of the unknown, to cast prudence aside and decide that the adventure was worth while?

My excuse is the story of how this book was written. When I began it in 1923, it was in the classic and certainly more prudent form of a study of Philip II's Mediterranean policy. My teachers of those days strongly approved of it. For them it fitted into the pattern of that diplomatic history which was indifferent to the discoveries of geography, little concerned (as diplomacy itself so often is) with economic and social problems; slightly disdainful towards the achievements of civilization, religion, and also of literature and the arts, the great witnesses of all worthwhile history; shuttered up in its chosen area, this school regarded it beneath a historian's dignity to look beyond the diplomatic files, to real life, fertile and promising. An analysis of the policy of the Prudent King entailed above all establishing the respective roles played in the elaboration of that policy by the king and his counsellors, through changing circumstances; determining who played major roles and who minor, reconstructing a model of Spanish foreign policy in which the Mediterranean was only one sector and not always the most important.

For in the 1580s the might of Spain turned towards the Atlantic. It was out there, whether conscious or not of the dangers involved, that the empire of Philip II had to concentrate its forces and fight for its threatened existence. A powerful swing of the pendulum carried it towards its trans-atlantic destiny. When I became interested in this hidden balance of forces, the physics of Spanish policy, preferring research in this direction to label-ling the responsibilities of a Philip II or a Don John of Austria, and when I came to think moreover that these statesmen were, despite their illusions, more acted upon than actors, I was already beginning to move outside the traditional bounds of diplomatic history; when I began to ask myself finally whether the Mediterranean did not possess, beyond the long-distance and irregular actions of Spain (a rather arid topic apart from the dramatic confrontation at Lepanto), a history and a destiny of its own, a powerful vitality, and whether this vitality did not in fact deserve something better than the role of a picturesque background, I was already succumbing to the temptation of the immense subject that was finally to hold my attention.

How could I fail to see it? How could I move from one set of archives to another in search of some revealing document without having my eyes opened to this rich and active life? Confronted with records of so many basic economic activities how could I do other than turn towards that economic and social history of a revolutionary kind that a small group of historians was trying to promote in France to the dignity that was no longer denied it in Germany, England, the United States, and indeed in Belgium, our neighbour, or Poland? To attempt to encompass the history of the Mediterranean in its complex totality was to follow their advice, be guided by their experience, go to their aid, and be active in the campaign for a new kind of history, re-thought, elaborated in France but worthy of being voiced beyond her frontiers; an imperialist history, yes, if one insists, aware of its own possibilities and of what it had to do, but also desirous since it had been obliged to break with them, of shattering traditional forms – not always entirely justifiably perhaps, but let that pass. The perfect opportunity was offered me of taking advantage of the very dimensions, demands, difficulties, and pitfalls of the unique historical character I had already chosen in order to create a history that could be different from the history our masters taught us.

To its author, every work seems revolutionary, the result of a struggle for mastery. If the Mediterranean has done no more than force us out of our old habits it will already have done us a service.

This book is divided into three parts, each of which is itself an essay in general explanation.

The first part is devoted to a history whose passage is almost imperceptible, that of man in his relationship to the environment, a history in which all change is slow, a history of constant repetition, ever-recurring cycles. I could not neglect this almost timeless history, the story of man's contact with the inanimate, neither could I be satisfied with the traditional geographical introduction to history that often figures to little purpose at the beginning of so many books, with its descriptions of the mineral deposits, types of agriculture, and typical flora, briefly listed and never mentioned again, as if the flowers did not come back every spring, the flocks of sheep migrate every year, or the ships sail on a real sea that changes with the seasons.

On a different level from the first there can be distinguished another history, this time with slow but perceptible rhythms. If the expression had not been diverted from its full meaning, one could call it *social history*, the history of groups and groupings. How did these swelling currents affect Mediterranean life in general – this was the question I asked myself in the second part of the book, studying in turn economic systems, states, societies, civilizations and finally, in order to convey more clearly my conception of history, attempting to show how all these deep-seated forces were at work in the complex arena of warfare. For war, as we know, is not an arena governed purely by individual responsibilities.

Lastly, the third part gives a hearing to traditional history – history, one might say, on the scale not of man, but of individual men, what Paul Lacombe and François Simiand called '*l'histoire événementielle*', that is, the history of events: surface disturbances, crests of foam that the tides of history carry on their strong backs. A history of brief, rapid, nervous fluctuations, by definition ultra-sensitive; the least tremor sets all its antennae quivering. But as such it is the most exciting of all, the richest in human interest, and also the most dangerous. We must learn to distrust this history with its still burning passions, as it was felt, described, and lived by contemporaries whose lives were as short and as short-sighted as ours. It has the dimensions of their anger, dreams, or illusions. In the sixteenth century, after the true Renaissance, came the Renaissance of the poor, the humble, eager to write, to talk of themselves and of others. This precious mass of paper distorts, filling up the lost hours and assuming a false importance. The historian who takes a seat in Philip II's chair and reads his papers finds himself transported into a strange one-dimensional world, a world of strong passions certainly, blind like any other living world, our own included, and unconscious of the deeper realities of history, of the running waters on which our frail barks are tossed like cockleshells. A dangerous world, but one whose spells and enchantments we shall have exorcised by making sure first to chart those underlying currents, often noiseless, whose direction can only be discerned by watching them over long periods of time. Resounding events are often only momentary outbursts, surface manifestations of these larger movements and explicable only in terms of them.

The final effect then is to dissect history into various planes, or, to put it another way, to divide historical time into geographical time, social time, and individual time. Or, alternatively, to divide man into a multitude of selves. This is perhaps what I shall be least forgiven, even if I say in my defence that traditional divisions also cut across living history which is fundamentally *one*, even if I argue, against Ranke or Karl Brandi, that the historical narrative is not a method, or even the objective method *par excellence*, but quite simply a philosophy of history like any other; even if I say, and demonstrate hereafter, that these levels I have distinguished are only means of exposition, that I have felt it quite in order in the course of the book to move from one level to another. But I do not intend to plead my case further. If I am criticized for the method in which the book has been assembled, I hope the component parts will be found workmanlike by professional standards.

I hope too that I shall not be reproached for my excessive ambitions, for my desire and need to see on a grand scale. It will perhaps prove that history can do more than study walled gardens. If it were otherwise, it would surely be failing in one of its most immediate tasks which must be to relate to the painful problems of our times and to maintain contact with the youthful but imperialistic human sciences. Can there be any study of humanity, in 1946, without historians who are ambitious, conscious of their duties and of their immense powers? 'It is the fear of great history which has killed great history,' wrote Edmond Faral, in 1942. May it live again![1]

May, 1946

[1] My list of debts is long. To enumerate them all would fill a book. I shall list only the greatest. My grateful thoughts go to my teachers at the Sorbonne, the Sorbonne, that is, of twenty-five years ago: Albert Demangeon, Émile Bourgeois, Georges Pagès, Maurice Holleaux, Henri Hauser to whom I owe my first interest in economic and social history and whose warm friendship has been a constant comfort to me. In Algiers I benefited from the friendly assistance of Georges Yver, Gabriel Esquer, Émile-Félix Gautier, René Lespès; I had the pleasure in 1931 of hearing the marvellous lectures of Henri Pirenne.

I must express my particular thanks to the Spanish archivists who have helped me with my research and were my earliest masters in Hispanic studies, Mariano Alcocer, Angel de la Plaza, Miguel Bordonau, Ricardo Magdalena, Gonzalo Ortiz. I have the happiest of memories of all of them – as I do of our discussions at Simancas, the 'historical' capital of Spain. At Madrid, Francisco Rodriguez Marin gave me a princely welcome. I also wish to thank the archivists in Italy, Germany, and France whom I have inundated with requests in the course of my research. In my acknowledgments I would reserve a special place for Mr. Truhelka, well-known astronomer and incomparable archivist at Dubrovnik, who has been my great companion in my journeys through archives and libraries.

The list of my colleagues and students at Algiers, São Paulo, and Paris who gave me their help is long too, and they are dispersed throughout the world. I would especially thank Earl J. Hamilton, Marcel Bataillon, Robert Ricard, André Aymard, who have collaborated with me in very different ways. Of my companions in captivity two have been associated with my work, Maître Addé-Vidal, Counsel at the *Cour d'Appel* at Paris, and Maurice Rouge, urbanist and historian in his leisure time. I could not forget finally the assistance that the little group around the *Revue Historique* has always unstintingly accorded me – Maurice Crouzet and Charles-André Julien, in the days when Charles Bémond and Louis Eisenmann protected our aggressive youth. In the final corrections to the book I took note of the remarks and suggestions of Marcel Bataillon, Émile Coornaert, Roger Dion, and Ernest Labrousse.

What I owe to the *Annales*, to their teaching and inspiration, constitutes the greatest of my debts. I am trying to repay that debt as best I can. Before the war I only once made contact with Marc Bloch. But I think I can honestly say that no aspect of his thought is foreign to me.

May I finally add that without the affectionate and energetic concern of Lucien Febvre, this work would probably never have been completed so soon. His encouragement and advice helped me to overcome long-lasting anxiety as to whether my project was well founded. Without him I should undoubtedly have turned back once more to my endless files and dossiers. The disadvantage of over-large projects is that one can sometimes enjoy the journey too much ever to reach the end.

Part One

The Role of the Environment

The first part of this book, as its title suggests, is concerned with geography: geography of a particular kind, with special emphasis on human factors. But it is more than this. It is also an attempt to convey a particular kind of history.

Even if there had been more properly dated information available, it would have been unsatisfactory to restrict our enquiries entirely to a study of human geography between the years 1550–1600 – even one undertaken in the doubtful pursuit of a determinist explanation. Since in fact we have only incomplete accounts of the period, and these have not been systematically classified by historians – material plentiful enough it is true, but insufficient for our purpose – the only possible course, in order to bring this brief moment of Mediterranean life, between 1550 and 1600, out of the shadows, was to make full use of evidence, images, and land-scapes dating from other periods, earlier and later and even from the present day. The resulting picture is one in which all the evidence combines across time and space, to give us a history in slow motion from which permanent values can be detected. Geography in this context is no longer an end in itself but a means to an end. It helps us to rediscover the slow unfolding of structural realities, to see things in the perspective of the very long term.[1] Geography, like history, can answer many questions. Here it helps us to discover the almost imperceptible movement of history, if only we are prepared to follow its lessons and accept its categories and divisions.

The Mediterranean has at least two faces. In the first place, it is composed of a series of compact, mountainous peninsulas, interrupted by vital plains: Italy, the Balkan peninsula, Asia Minor, North Africa, the Iberian peninsula. Second, between these miniature continents lie vast, complicated, and fragmented stretches of sea, for the Mediterranean is not so much a single entity as a 'complex of seas'. Peninsulas and seas: these are the two kinds of environment we shall be considering first of all, to establish the general conditions of human life. But they will not tell the whole story.

One one side, to the south, the Mediterranean is a near neighbour of the great desert that runs uninterrupted from the Atlantic Sahara to the Gobi Desert and up to the gates of Peking. From southern Tunisia to southern Syria, the desert directly borders the sea. The relationship is not

[1] Fernand Braudel, 'Histoire et sciences sociales, la longue durée', in: *Annales E.S.C.*, Oct.–Dec., 1958, pp. 725–753.

casual; it is intimate, sometimes difficult, and always demanding. So the desert is one of the faces of the Mediterranean.

On the other side, to the north, lies Europe, which if often shaken by Mediterranean influences has had an equally great and sometimes decisive influence on the Mediterranean. Northern Europe, beyond the olive trees, is one of the permanent realities of Mediterranean history. And it was the rise of that Europe with its Atlantic horizons, that was to decide the destiny of the inland sea as the sixteenth century drew to a close.

Chapters I to III, then, describe the diversity of the sea and go far beyond its shores. After this we shall have to consider whether it is possible to speak of the physical unity of the sea (Chapter IV, *Climate*) or of its human and necessarily historical unity (Chapter V, *Cities and Communications*). These are the divisions of a long introductory section whose aim is to describe the different faces, and the face, of the Mediterranean, so that we may be in a better position to view and if possible understand its multicoloured destiny.

CHAPTER I

The Peninsulas: Mountains, Plateaux, and Plains

The five peninsulas of the inland sea are very similar. If one thinks of their relief they are regularly divided between mountains – the largest part – a few plains, occasional hills, and wide plateaux. This is not the only way in which the land masses can be dissected, but let us use simple categories. Each piece of these jigsaw puzzles belongs to a particular family and can be classified within a distinct typology. So, rather than consider each peninsula as an autonomous entity, let us look at the analogies between the materials that make them up. In other words let us shuffle the pieces of the jigsaw and compare the comparable. Even on the historical plane, this breakdown and reclassification will be illuminating.

I. MOUNTAINS COME FIRST

The Mediterranean is by definition a landlocked sea. But beyond this we must distinguish between the kinds of land that surround and confine it. It is, above all, a sea ringed round by mountains. This outstanding fact and its many consequences have received too little attention in the past from historians.

Physical and human characteristics. Geologists, however, are well aware of it and can explain it. The Mediterranean, they say, is entirely contained within the zone of tertiary folds and fractures covering the Ancient World from Gibraltar to the Indian Archipelago: in fact, it constitutes one section of the zone. Late foldings, some dating from the same time as the Pyrenees, others from the time of the Alps, raised and activated the sediments of a secondary Mediterranean much vaster than the one we know, chiefly enormous limestone deposits, sometimes over 1000 metres thick. With some regularity these violent foldings collided with ancient hard masses of rock, which were sometimes raised (like the Kabylias) or sometimes incorporated into great ranges, as is the case of the Mercantour and various axial ridges of the Alps or the Pyrenees. More often still, they collapsed – to the accompaniment of a greater or lesser degree of volcanic activity – and were covered by the waters of the sea.

Although interrupted by inlets of the sea, the mountains correspond on either side of the straits to form coherent systems. One range formerly linked Sicily and Tunisia; another, the Baetic range, existed between Spain and Morocco; an Aegean range used to stretch from Greece to Asia Minor (its disappearance is so recent in geological terms as to correspond to the Biblical flood) – not to mention land masses like the Tyrrhenides continent of which there remain only a few islands and fragments scattered along the coast to mark the spot, that is, if geological hypotheses have some foundation in reality – for these are all hypotheses.[1] What we can be certain of is the architectural unity of which the mountains form the 'skeleton': a sprawling, overpowering, ever-present skeleton whose bones show through the skin.

All round the sea the mountains are present, except at a few points of trifling significance – the Straits of Gibraltar, the Naurouze Gap, the Rhône valley corridor and the straits leading from the Aegean to the Black Sea. There is only one stretch from which they are absent – but that is a very considerable one – from southern Tunisia to southern Syria, where the Saharan plateau undulates over several thousand kilometres, directly bordering the sea.

Let it be said too that these are high, wide, never-ending mountains: the Alps, the Pyrenees, the Apennines, the Dinaric Alps, the Caucasus, the Anatolian mountains, the mountains of Lebanon, the Atlas, and the Spanish Cordillera. They are impressive and demanding presences: some because of their height, others because of their density or their deep, enclosed, inaccessible valleys. They turn towards the sea impressive and forbidding countenances.[2]

So the Mediterranean means more than landscapes of vines and olive

---

[1] This is not the place for a detailed discussion of this controversial issue. A. Philippson, *Das Mittelmeergebiet*, 1904 (4th ed., Leipzig, 1922) is clearly out of date. For more recent geological explanations, the reader is referred to such classic works as Serge von Bubnoff, *Geologie von Europa*, Berlin, 1927; W. von Seidlitz, *Diskordanz und Orogenese am Mittelmeer*, Berlin, 1931 – a great work of general relevance despite its title; or H. Stille, *Beiträge zur Geologie der westlichen Mediterrangebeite*, hsrg. im Auftrag der Gesellschaft der Wissenschaften, Göttingen, 1927–35; or to monographs such as H. Aschauer and J. S. Hollister, *Ostpyrenäen und Balearen* (Beitr. zur Geologie der westl. Mediterrangebiete, no. 11), Berlin, 1934; Wilhelm Simon, *Die Sierra Morena der Provinz Sevilla*, Frankfurt, 1942, or the recent study by Paul Fallot and A. Marin of the Rif Cordillera, published in 1944 by the Spanish Institute of Geology and Mineralogy (cf. paper given to *Académie des Sciences*, session of 24th April, 1944, by M. Jacob). It would be impossible to compile a complete list of the many works by P. Birot, J. Bourcart, and J. Lecointre. The return to the apparently outdated theory of vanished continents and mountain ranges was suggested to me by Edouard Le Danois, *L'Atantique, histoire et vie d'un océan*, Paris, 1938. Raoul Blanchard's clear and stimulating book, *Géographie de l'Europe*, Paris, 1936, (Eng. translation by Crist, *A Geography of Europe*, London, 1936) stresses the family resemblance of the Mediterranean mountains, for which he suggests the general name of Dinarides. For the Dinarides proper, see Jacques Bourcart, *Nouvelles observations sur la structure des Dinarides adriatiques*, Madrid, 1929. P. Termier, *A la gloire de la terre*, 5th edition, has a chapter on the geology of the Western Mediterranean. As I said I do not here wish to enter into discussion of the geological or geographical problems of the Mediterranean as a whole, for which the reader is referred to the standard works. For the present state of research and an up-to-date bibliography, see P. Birot and J. Dresch, *La Méditerranée et le Moyen-Orient*, 2 vols., Paris, 1953–56.

[2] The dense, compact character of the mountains under the general heading Dinarides is well brought out by R. Blanchard, *op. cit.*, pp. 7–8. M. Le Lannou, *Pâtres et paysans de la Sardaigne*, Paris, 1941, p. 9.

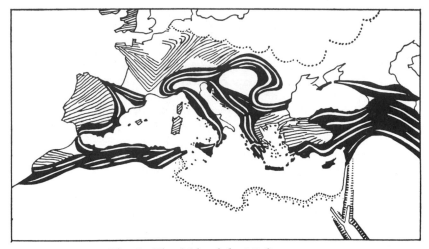

Fig. 2: *The folds of the Mediterranean*

Hercynian blocks banded, Alpine foldings in black; the white lines indicate the direction of the mountain ranges. To the south, the Saharan plateau in white, borders the Mediterranean from Tunisia to Syria. To the east, the tectonic fractures of the Dead Sea and the Red Sea. To the north, the intra-Alpine and extra-Alpine plains are in white. The dotted lines mark the furthest limit of former glaciers.

trees and urbanized villages; these are merely the fringe. Close by, looming above them, are the dense highlands, the mountain world with its fastnesses, its isolated houses and hamlets, its 'vertical norths'.[3] Here we are far from the Mediterranean where orange trees blossom.

The winters in the mountains are severe. Snow was falling thickly in the Moroccan Atlas when Leo Africanus, crossing in winter, had the misfortune to be robbed of clothes and baggage.[4] But any traveller who knows the Mediterranean well will have seen for himself the winter avalanches, blocked roads and Siberian and Arctic landscapes only a few miles from the sunny coast, the Montenegrin houses buried in snow, or in Kabylia the Tirourdat col, the gathering point for tremendous blizzards, where up to four metres of snow can fall in a night. In an hour skiers from Chrea can reach Algiers where roses are in bloom, while 120 kilometres away in the Djurdjura, near the cedar forest of Tindjda, the local inhabitants plunge bare-legged up to their thighs in snow.

The traveller will have seen too the snows that linger until midsummer, 'cooling the eye', as a visitor once put it.[5] The peak of the Mulhacen is

[3] Strzygowski's expression. In Greece, notes A. Philippson, *op. cit.*, p. 42, it is often possible to climb up above the belt of orange and olive trees, pass through all the European zones of vegetation and arrive practically at the point of all-year-round snow.

[4] Leo Africanus, *Description de l'Afrique, tierce partie du Monde*, Lyons, 1556, p. 34.

[5] Président Charles de Brosses, *Lettres familières écrites en Italie*, Paris, 1740, I, p. 100.

white with snow while down below, Granada swelters in the heat; snow
clings to the slopes of the Taygetus overlooking the tropical plain of Sparta;
it is preserved in the crevasses of the mountains of Lebanon, or in the
'ice boxes' of Chrea.[6] These are the snows that explain the long Mediterranean history of 'snow water', offered by Saladin to Richard the Lion-
heart, and drunk to fatal excess by Don Carlos in the hot month of
July 1568, when he was imprisoned in the Palace at Madrid.[7] In Turkey
in the sixteenth century it was not merely the privilege of the rich; in Constantinople, but elsewhere as well, Tripoli in Syria, for instance,[8] travellers
remarked on merchants selling snow water, pieces of ice, and water-ices
which could be bought for a few small coins.[9] Pierre Belon relates that snow
from Bursa used to arrive at Istanbul in whole boatloads.[10] It was to be
found there all the year round according to Busbecq, who was astonished
to see the janissaries drinking it every day at Amasia in Anatolia, in the
Turkish army camp.[11] The snow trade was so important that the pashas
took an interest in the exploitation of the 'ice mines'. It was said in 1578 to
have provided Muḥammad Pasha with an income of up to 80,000 sequins
a year.[12]

Elsewhere, in Egypt, for example, where snow arrived from Syria by

[6] The list could easily be extended to the Mercantour behind Nice; Mount Olympus
'with its greenish crown of snow' (W. Helwig, *Braconniers de la mer en Grèce*, Leipzig,
1942, p. 164); the snows of Sicily noted by Eugène Fromentin, in his *Voyage en
Égypte*, Paris, 1935, p. 156; and 'that terrible snow desert' near Erzurum mentioned
by the Comte de Sercey (*Une ambassade extraordinaire en Perse en 1839–1840*, Paris,
1928, p. 46) apropos of the Armenian mountains. See also the astonishing lithograph
by Raffet of the retreat from Constantine in 1836, which could be a picture of the
retreat from Moscow (reproduced in Gabriel Esquer, *Inconographie de l'Algérie*,
Paris, 1930). Or the details given by H. C. Armstrong (*Grey Wolf, Mustafa Kemal*,
1933, p. 56) of the 30,000 Turkish soldiers surprised by winter in the mountains on
the Russian frontier during the 1914–18 war, who died huddled together for warmth
and were found long afterwards by Russian patrols. On the persistence of snow in
North Africa, a note by P. Diego de Haëdo, *Topographia e historia general de Argel*,
Valladolid, 1612, p. 8 v°: '. . . en las montañas mas altas del Cuco o del Labes (do
todo el año esta la nieve)'. Heavy snowfalls saved Granada in December 1568.
Diego de Mendoza, *Guerra de Granada*, Biblioteca de autores españoles, vol. XXI,
p. 75.
[7] The best book on Don Carlos is still Louis-Prosper Gachard, *Don Carlos et
Philippe II*, 1867, 2nd ed., 2 vols. The question is also raised in Ludwig Pfandl, *Johanna
die Wahnsinnige*, Fribourg-en-Brisgau, 1930, p. 132 ff. The theory advanced by Viktor
Bibl, *Der Tod des Don Carlos*, Vienna, 1918 is unacceptable.
[8] *Voyage faict par moy Pierre Lescalopier*, MS H. 385, Montpellier School of Medicine, f° 44 and 44 v°, published in an abridged version by Edouard Cléray, under the
title, 'Le voyage de Pierre Lescalopier Parisien de Venise à Constantinople l'an 1574',
in *Revue d'Histoire diplomatique*, 1921, pp. 21–25.
[9] Salomon Schweigger, *Ein newe Reissbeschreibung auss Teutschland nach Con-
stantinopel und Jerusalem*, Nuremberg, 1639, p. 126.
[10] Pierre Belon (Belon du Mans), *Les observations de . . . singularités*, Paris, 1553,
p. 189.
[11] G. de Busbecq, *The Turkish Letters*, trans. E. S. Forster, Oxford 1927 (reprinted
1968), Letter I, p. 53, letter III, p. 153.
[12] S. Schweigger, *op. cit.*, p. 125.

relays of fast horses; in Lisbon which imported it from great distances;[13] in Oran, the Spanish *presidio*, where snow arrived from Spain in the brigantines of the Intendance;[14] in Malta, where the Knights, if we are to believe them, would die if snow did not arrive from Naples, their illnesses apparently requiring 'this sovereign remedy',[15] snow was, on the contrary, the height of luxury. In Italy as in Spain, however, snow water seems to have been used widely. It explains the early development of the art of ice cream and water-ice in Italy.[16] Its sale was so profitable in Rome that it became the subject of a monopoly.[17] In Spain snow was piled up in wells and kept until summer.[18] Western pilgrims travelling to the Holy Land in 1494 were none the less astonished to see the owner of the boat presented, on the Syrian coast, with 'a sack full of snow, the sight of which in this country and in the month of July, filled all on board with the greatest amazement'.[19] On the same Syrian coast, a Venetian noted with surprise in 1553 that the 'Mores', 'ut nos utimur saccharo, item spargunt nivem super cibos et sua edulia,[20] 'sprinkle snow on their food and dishes as we would sugar'.

In the heart of the warm Mediterranean these snowy regions impress by their originality. Their massive bulk and their constantly moving population compel the attention of the plains, of the brilliant but narrow creations along the coastline, precisely to the extent, and we shall be coming back to this, that these 'favoured' regions require manpower and, since they depend on trade, means of communication. They compel the attention of the plain, but arouse its fear as well. The traveller tries to go round the obstacle, to move at ground level, from plain to plain, valley to valley. Sooner or later he is obliged to travel through certain gorges and mountain passes of sinister repute, but he resorts to them as little as possible. The traveller of yesterday was almost entirely confined to the plains, the gardens, the dazzling shores and teeming life of the sea.

To tell the truth, the historian is not unlike the traveller. He tends to linger over the plain, which is the setting for the leading actors of the day, and does not seem eager to approach the high mountains nearby. More than one historian who has never left the towns and their archives would be surprised to discover their existence. And yet how can one ignore these conspicuous actors, the half-wild mountains, where man has taken root like a hardy plant; always semi-deserted, for man is constantly leaving them? How can one ignore them when often their sheer slopes come right

[13] J. Sanderson, *The travels of John Sanderson in the Levant (1584–1602)*, 1931, p. 50, n. 3.

[14] B. M. Add. 28 488, f° 12, about 1627.

[15] A. N. A. E. B¹890, 22nd June, 1754.

[16] On ice cream and water-ice, Alfred Franklin, *Dict. Hist. des Arts*, p. 363–364; *Enciclopedia Italiana, Treccani*, article 'Gelato'.

[17] Jean Delumeau, *La vie économique à Rome*, 1959, I, p. 398. For a proposal for a tax on snow, A.d.S. Naples, Sommaria Consultationum, 7, f° 418–420, 19th July, 1581.

[18] Ortega y Gasset, *Papeles sobre Velásquez y Goya*, Madrid 1950, p. 20.

[19] Petrus Casola, *Viaggio a Gerusalemme*, 1494 (edited Milan 1855), p. 55.

[20] Museo Correr, Cicogna 796, *Itinerary of Gradenigo*, 1553.

down to the sea's edge?[21] The mountain dweller is a type familiar in all Mediterranean literature. According to Homer, the Cretans were even then suspicious of the wild men in their mountains and Telemachus, on his return to Ithaca, describes the Peloponnese as covered with forests where he lived among filthy villagers, 'eaters of acorns'.[22]

Defining the mountains. What exactly is a mountain? To take some simple definition – all land in the Mediterranean region over 500 metres for instance – would be to draw a completely arbitrary line. What should be reckoned are the uncertain human boundaries which cannot easily be shown on a map. As Raoul Blanchard warned us long ago, 'It is well nigh impossible even to provide a definition of the mountains which is both clear and comprehensible.'[23]

Can we define the mountains as the poorest regions of the Mediterranean, its proletarian reserves? On the whole this is true. But, in the sixteenth century, there were plenty of other poor regions below the 500-metre level, the Aragon Steppes and the Pontine marshes, for instance. Besides, many mountains are, if not rich, at any rate reasonably prosperous and comparatively well populated. Some of the very high valleys in the Catalan Pyrenees are even able to absorb some of 'their own emigrants, from one village to another'.[24] Many mountains are also rich because of their high rainfall: according to Arthur Young, in the Mediterranean climate, soil is unimportant, 'what does all is sun and rain'. The Alps, the Pyrenees, the Rif, the Kabylias, all the mountains exposed to winds from the Atlantic, have green hillsides where grass and trees grow thickly.[25] Other mountains are rich because of their mineral resources.

[21] Cf. a letter from Villegaignon to the king of France in 1552; 'The entire sea coast, from Gaietta to Naples and from Naples to Sicily, is bounded by high mountains, at the feet of which lies a beach open to all the winds of the sea, as you would say that the coast of Picardy is open to the sea-winds, except that your coast has rivers along which one might retreat, and here there are none', Abbé Marchand's communication, 'Documents pour l'histoire du règne de Henri II', in *Bulletin hist. et phil. du Comité des travaux hist. et scient.*, 1901, p. 565–8.

[22] V. Bérard, *Les Navigations d'Ulysse*, II, *Pénélope et les Barons des îles*, 1928, p. 318–9. Such mountain peoples are still found in modern times. Cf. in the last century the Montenegrin immigrants in America; in the twentieth century the soldiers who fought in the Turkish war of independence, the companions of Mustafa Kemal, whom H. C. Armstrong (*Grey Wolf, Mustafa Kemal, op. cit.*, pp. 117 and 124) has described in picturesque detail: the 'irregulars' of Edhem's Green Army, 'wild-faced men', and Mustafa's bodyguard from the mountain tribe of the Lazzes (on the south coast of the Black Sea), 'wild, black-eyed men . . . as lithe as cats', who were allowed as a special privilege to retain their traditional costumes and dances, in particular the 'Zebek' dance. The Kurds are another example: see the remarks by the Comte de Sercey, *op. cit.*, pp. 216, 288, 297, on their black tents, their oatcakes which contain more chaff than grain, their goats-milk cheese and their way of life in general.

[23] Preface to Jules Blache, *L'homme et la montagne, op. cit.*, p. 7.

[24] Pierre Vilar, *La Catalogne dans l'Espagne moderne*, I, 1962, p. 209. Arthur Young's remark is quoted *ibid.*, vol. II, p. 242.

[25] The Rif and the Atlas 'where the typical meal is a comforting hash of flour, beans and oil', J. Blache, *op. cit.*, p. 79–80.

Others, again, are unusually densely populated as a result of the lowland population having been driven up from the plain, an accident which we find frequently repeated.

For the mountains are a refuge from soldiers and pirates, as all the documents bear witness, as far back as the Bible.[26] Sometimes the refuge becomes permanent.[27] This is borne out by the example of the Kutzo-Vlachs, who were chased out from the plains by the Slav and Greek peasants, and from then on throughout the Middle Ages leading a nomadic existence over the free spaces in the Balkans, from Galicia to Serbia and the Aegean Sea, continually being displaced but also displacing others.[28] Nimble as mountain goats, 'they come down from the mountains to carry away some booty . . .', noted a twelfth-century traveller.[29] Throughout the Peninsula, 'as far as Matapan and Crete, they travel with their flocks of sheep and their black hoods, and the two highest ridges, the Haemus and the Pindus, afford them the best shelter. It is from these two mountains that they come down into Byzantine history at the beginning of the eleventh century.'[30] And it is around these mountains that the nineteenth century finds them still, herdsmen, farmers, and above all drivers of the muletrains which are the chief means of transport in Albania and northern Greece.[31]

Many mountains, then, form exceptions to the rule of poverty and emptiness, of which however there is so much evidence in the writings of travellers and other witnesses in the sixteenth century. The Venetian envoy, crossing the mountains of Upper Calabria on his way to join Don John of Austria at Messina in 1572,[32] found them quite deserted; deserted too were the Sierra Morena in Castile[33] and the Sierras of Espadan and Bernia,[34]

[26] Joshua, II, 15–16. After the failure of his conspiracy in Florence, Buondelmonti seeks refuge in the Tuscan Apennines (Augustin Renaudet, *Machiavel*, 1941, p. 108). The Cretans take refuge in the mountains of the island to escape the corsairs and the Turkish ships (B. N. Paris, Ital. 427, 1572 f° 199 v°).

[27] This opinion was held by Paul Vidal de la Blache, *Principes de géographie humaine*, (English translation by Millicent Bingham, *Principles of Human Geography*, London 1926, p. 65.) Among the examples he gives are the Transylvanian Alps where the Rumanian people was reconstituted and the Balkans, where in the same way but on a smaller scale, the Bulgarian people was reborn, the Caucasus, etc.

[28] André Blanc, *La Croatie occidentale*, 1957, p. 97.

[29] *The Itinerary of Benjamin of Tudela*, trans. and ed. M. N. Adler, London, 1907, p. 11.

[30] Victor Bérard, *La Turquie et l'hellénisme contemporain*, 1893, p. 247.

[31] F. C. H. L. de Pouqueville, *Voyage en Grèce*, 1820, vol. III, pp. 8 and 13; V. Bérard, *op. cit.*, p. 79–83 and 247. On the Wallachians and the Aromani there is abundant literature. For details see J. Blache, *op. cit.*, p. 22; J. Cvijić, *La Péninsule balkanique*, Paris, 1918, p. 115, 178 note 1, 202–3.

[32] Luca Michieli, 25th October, 1572, *Relazioni*, A.d.S. Venice, Collegio Secreta, filza 18.

[33] *Don Quixote*, the Cardenio episode, '*la razon que os ha traido*,' asks the knight, '*a vivir y a morir en estas soledades como bruto animal*'.

[34] *Discorso sopra le due montagne di Spadan e di Bernia* (1564 or 1565), Simancas E° 329. To be read in conjunction I think with the document B. N. Paris, Esp. 177: *Instruccion a vos Juan Baptista Antonelli para que vays a reconoscer el sitio de la Sierra de Vernia* (undated).

in the kingdom of Valencia, about which enquiries were made in 1564, when there were fears of unrest among the Moriscos and of a war that might be carried up into this difficult hill country, where the rebels of 1526 had resisted the German lansquenets. Even more deserted, eternally deserted, are the wild bare mountains of the Sicilian interior, and so many other mountains scattered here and there, whose low rainfall makes them unable to support even pastoral life.[35]

But these are extreme cases. According to the geographer J. Cvijić,[36] the central Balkan mountains (we are free to extend his remarks or not as we choose) are a zone of dispersed habitat, where the predominant form of settlement is the hamlet; in the plains, on the contrary, it is the village. The distinction is valid for Wallachia and, almost absurdly so, for Hungary and the enormous villages of the Puzta; also for upper Bulgaria, where the hamlets, formerly semipastoral, are known by the name of *kolibé*. The distinction still holds for Old Serbia, Galicia, and Podolia. No rule though can ever be more than a rough guide. In many cases it would be difficult to mark precisely, on a map, where the zone of lowland villages – often real towns – ends and the zone of mountain hamlets, consisting of a few houses and sometimes a single family, begins. A detailed study by the same author on the Serbo-Bulgarian borders, between Kumanil and Kumanovo,[37] establishes that it is practically impossible to draw a precise boundary.

And then again, can this interpretation of a Balkan pattern be transposed as it stands to the rest of the Mediterranean world, to nearby Greece,[38] or to the Western countries permeated with maritime culture, where for fear of pirate raids the people withdrew from the plains, which were frequently devastated and unhealthy as well? One thinks of the large hill villages of Corsica, Sardinia, Provence, the Kabylias, and the Rif. One thing at least is certain. Whether settled in tiny hamlets or in large villages, the mountain population is generally insignificant in comparison with the vast spaces surrounding it, where travel is difficult; life there is rather like life in the early settlements in the New World, which were also islands set

[35] Cf. the remarks by Paul Descamps, *Le Portugal, la vie sociale actuelle*, 1935, apropos of the Sierra da Estrela, p. 123–124, with its less developed pastoral life than that of the North.

[36] On this question see the illuminating pages in Vidal de le Blache, *op. cit.*, Eng. trans. p. 303–5. J. Cvijić's opinions are expressed in his book in French, *La Péninsule balkanique*, 1918. Apropos of mountain hamlets, Vidal de la Blache notes: 'Constantine Porphyrogenetes wrote regarding these people, that 'they cannot endure having two cabins near one another', *op. cit.*, p. 303.

[37] 'Grundlinien der Geographie und Geologie von Mazedonien und Alt-Serbien' in: *Petermanns Mitteilungen aus J. Perthes Geographischer Anstalt*, Erganzungsheft no. 162, 1908.

[38] For a delightful portrait of the Greek 'village-town' see J. Ancel, *Les peuples et nations des Balkans*, 1926, p. 110–111. Striking proof is provided by Martin Hurlimann, *Griechenland mit Rhodos und Zypern*, Zurich, 1938, p. 28 for a magnificent photograph of the Greek village of Arakhova, which stands at about 3000 feet, overlooking a landscape of terraced cultivated fields, on the slopes of Mount Parnassus. The village is known for its woven products.

in the middle of wide open spaces, for the most part uncultivable[39] or hostile, and thereby deprived of the contacts and exchanges necessary to civilization.[40] The mountains are forced to be self-sufficient for the essentials of life, to produce everything as best they can, to cultivate vines, wheat, and olives even if the soil and the climate are unsuitable. In the mountains, society, civilization, and economy all bear the mark of backwardness and poverty.[41]

It is then possible, in general terms, to talk of the dilution of the mountain population, and even more, of a partial and incomplete form of civilization, the result of inadequate human occupation. Heinrich Decker has produced a handsome study[42] of the artistic civilization of the Alps; but the Alps are after all the Alps, that is, an exceptional range of mountains from the point of view of resources, collective disciplines, the quality of its human population and the number of good roads. The Alps should hardly be considered typical Mediterranean mountains. More typical are the Pyrenees with their violent history and primitive cruelty. And even the Pyrenees are somewhat privileged; one could make out a case for a Pyrenean civilization, if the word is used in its old, genuine sense. One region, to which frequent reference will be made – the Catalan Pyrenees – saw the rise in the eleventh and twelfth centuries of a vigorous Romanesque

[39] Paul Arqué, *Géographie des Pyrénées françaises*, 1943, p. 48, points out that the area *cultivated* in the French Pyrenees according to the calculations of the Inspector-General Thierry 'is comparable to the area of an average *département*'; a revealing observation.

[40] For Corsica, see the letter of remonstrances from F. Borromeo to the bishop of Ajaccio, (14th November, 1581, ed. Vittoria Adami, 'I Manoscritti della Biblioteca Ambrosiana di Milano, relativi alla storia di Corsica', in *Archivio storico di Corsica*, 1932, 3, p. 81). Through these reprimands, a picture emerges of the itinerant life of the bishop, travelling over the mountains with his little caravan of pack animals. Compare this with the difficulties of St. Charles Borromeo, in the Alps it is true, in 1580, or with those of the bishop of Dax, crossing in winter the snow-covered mountains of Slavonia (his letter to the king, January 1573, Ernest Charrière, *Négociations de la France dans le Levant*, 1840–1860, III, p. 348–352.) Travelling in the mountains near Ragusa in winter is an ordeal 'whose consequences are generally most injurious to the health' and can be fatal (12th November, 1593), document published in Vladimir Lamansky *Secrets d'État de Venise*, 1884, p. 104. Until 1923 it still took three days to bring goods from Vianna do Castelo to the mouth of the Lima (P. Descamps, *op. cit.* p. 18).

[41] René Maunier, *Sociologie et Droit remain*, 1930, p. 728, sees in the agnatic family of Kabylia an example of the patriarchal family, a Roman *gens*, in a much debased form of course. On the economic backwardness of mountain regions, frequently remarked, cf. Charles Morazé, *Introduction à l'histoire économique*, 1943, p. 45–46. On what J. Cvijić calls the 'perfected patriarchality' of the Dinaric regions, see *La Péninsule balkanique*, *op. cit.*, p. 36. I prefer his expression 'mountain islands' (*ibid.*, p. 29). Montenegro, the great fortress, and other high regions, he said, behaved 'from a social point of view, like islands'. On the *zadruga*, another example of economic backwardness, R. Busch-Zantner, *Albanien*, Leipzig, 1939, p. 59.

[42] *Barockplastik in den Alpenländern*, Vienna, 1944. On the social environment in the Alps, see A. Günther's great and controversial *Die Alpenländische Gesellschaft*, Jena, 1930. Some interesting remarks in J. Solch, 'Raum und Gesellschaft in den Alpen' in *Geogr. Zeitschr.*, 1931, p. 143–168.

architecture[43] which survived curiously until the sixteenth century.[44] But it is a different story in the Aurès, the Rif, and the Kabylias.

Mountains, civilizations, and religions. The mountains are as a rule a world apart from civilizations, which are an urban and lowland achievement. Their history is to have none, to remain almost always on the fringe of the great waves of civilization, even the longest and most persistent, which may spread over great distances in the horizontal plane but are powerless to move vertically when faced with an obstacle of a few hundred metres. To these hilltop worlds, out of touch with the towns, even Rome itself, in all its years of power, can have meant very little,[45] except perhaps through the military camps that the empire established for security reasons in various places on the edges of unconquered mountain lands: hence León, at the foot of the Cantabrian mountains, Djemilah, facing the rebellious Berber Atlas, Timgad and the annex at Lambaesis, where the *IIIa legio augusta* encamped. Neither did Latin as a language take root in the hostile massifs of North Africa, Spain or elsewhere, and the Latin or Italic house type remained a house of the plains.[46] In a few places it may have infiltrated locally, but on the whole the mountains resisted it.

Later, when the Rome of the Emperors had become the Rome of Saint Peter, the same problem remained. It was only in places where its action could be persistently reinforced that the Church was able to tame and evangelize these herdsmen and independent peasants. Even so it took an incredibly long time. In the sixteenth century the task was far from complete, and this applies to Islam and Catholicism alike, for they both met the same obstacles: the Berbers of North Africa, protected by the mountain peaks, were still hardly at all, or very imperfectly, won over to Muḥammad. The same is true of the Kurds in Asia;[47] while in Aragon, in the Valencia region or round Granada, the mountains were, conversely, the zone of religious dissidence, a Moslem stronghold,[48] just as the high, wild, 'suspicious' hills of the Lubéron protected the strongholds of the Vaudois.[49]

[43] Cf. the handsome studies by J. Puig I Cadafalc, *L'arquitectura romanica a Catalunya* (in collaboration), Barcelona, 1909–18; *Le premier art roman*, Paris, 1928.

[44] P. Arqué, *op. cit.*, p. 69.

[45] In Baetica, Rome was much more successful in the lowlands, and along the rivers, than on the plateaux, G. Niemeier, *Siedlungsgeogr. Untersuchungen in Niederandalusien*, Hamburg, 1935, p. 37. In the mountainous northwest of Spain with the added difficulty of distance, Rome penetrated late on and with little success, R. Konetzke, *Geschichte des spanischen und portugiesischen Volkes*, Leipzig, 1941, p. 31.

[46] Albert Dauzat, *Le village et le paysan de France*, 1941, p. 52.

[47] Comte de Sercey, *op. cit.*, p. 104: 'One can see however, (since they dance) that the Kurdish women, although Moslem, are not kept in seclusion'.

[48] See below, sections on the Moriscos, (Part II, ch. V and Part III, ch. III).

[49] Lourmarin, Cabrières, Mérindol and about twenty other hill towns in the heart of the Lubéron, where there was abundant wild life – foxes, wolves and boars – were Protestant strongholds, J. L. Vaudoyer, *Beautés de la Provence*, Paris, 1926, p. 238. And there were the Vaudois of the Savoy states and in the Apennines in the kingdom of Naples. 'Catharism', wrote Marc Bloch, 'had dwindled to an obscure sect of mountain shepherds', *Annales d'hist. sociale*, 1940, p. 79.

Everywhere in the sixteenth century, the hilltop world was very little influenced by the dominant religions at sea level; mountain life persistently lagged behind the plain.

One proof of this is the great ease with which, when circumstances did permit, new religions were able to make massive, though unstable, conquests in these regions. In the Balkans in the fifteenth century, whole areas of the mountains went over to Islam, in Albania as in Herzegovina around Sarajevo. What this proves above all is that they had been only slightly influenced by Christianity. The same phenomenon was to recur during the war of Candia, in 1647. Large numbers of Cretan mountain dwellers, joining the Turkish cause, renounced their faith. Similarly, in the seventeenth century, when faced with the Russian advance, the Caucasus went over to Muḥammad and produced in his honour one of the most virulent forms of Islam.[50]

In the mountains then, civilization is never very stable. Witness the curious passage by Pedraça in his *Historia eclesiastica de Granada*, written in the time of Philip IV. 'It is not surprising,' he writes, 'that the inhabitants of the Alpujarras (the very high mountains in the Kingdom of Granada) should have abandoned their ancient faith. The people who live in these mountains are *cristianos viejos*; in their veins runs not one drop of heathen blood; they are the subjects of a Catholic king; and yet, for lack of instruction and following the oppression to which they are subjected, they are so ignorant of what they should know to obtain eternal salvation that they have retained only a few vestiges of the Christian religion. Can anyone believe that if the Infidel were to become master of their land tomorrow (which God forbid) these people would remain long without abandoning their religion and embracing the beliefs of their conquerors?'[51]

A separate religious geography seems then to emerge for the mountain world, which constantly had to be taken, conquered and reconquered. Many minor facts encountered in traditional history take on a new meaning in this light.

The fact that Saint Teresa, who as a child dreamed of being martyred by the Moriscos of the Sierra de Guadarrama,[52] should have established the first monastery of the reformed Carmelite order at Duruelo, although a detail, is worth remembering. The house was the property of a gentleman

[50] Muridism, Cf. L. E. Houzar, 'La Tragédie circassienne', in: *Revue des Deux Mondes*, 15/6/1943, p. 434–435.

[51] Francisco Bermúdez de Pedraça, Granada, 1637 fᵒ 95 vᵒ. Quoted in French translation by Reinhart-Pieter A. Dozy, to whom credit for finding this splendid passage is due (*Histoire des Musulmans d'Espagne*, 1861, II, p. 45, note 1.) However the Abbé de Vayrac (*État présent de l'Espagne*), Amsterdam, 1719, I, p. 165) maintains that the inhabitants of the Alpujarras, although Christians are Moriscos who have retained 'their old way of life, their costume and their particular language which is a monstrous mixture of Arabic and Spanish'.

[52] As a child, St. Teresa set off, with her brother, towards the mountains in the hope of finding martyrdom: Gustav Schnürer, *Katholische Kirche und Kultur in der Barockzeit*, 1937, p. 179; Louis Bertrand, *Sainte Thérèse*, 1927, p. 46–47.

of Avila. 'Quite an adequate porch, a bedchamber with its attic and a small kitchen,' writes the saint, 'was the entire extent of this fine dwelling. After consideration, I thought the porch could be made into a chapel, the attic into a choir, and the bedchamber into a dormitory.' And it was in this 'perfect hovel' that Saint John of the Cross came to live, with a companion, Father Anthony of Heredia, who joined him there in the autumn, bringing a chorister, Brother Joseph. There they lived through the winter snow the most frugal monastic life, but not shut off from the world: 'often they would go barefoot, by the most terrible paths, to preach the gospel to the peasants as if to savages'.[53]

A chapter of missionary history can be glimpsed too from the religious history of Corsica in the sixteenth century. The example is even more significant if we remember that the Corsican people had been converted by the Franciscans several centuries earlier. What traces were left of the first Catholic conquest? Many documents show that by the time the Society of Jesus arrived at the island to impose upon it Jesuit law and the Roman order, the spiritual life of the population had reached an extraordinary state. They found that even those priests who could read knew no Latin or grammar, and, more seriously, were ignorant of the form of the sacrament to be taken at the altar. Often dressed like laymen, they were peasants who worked in the fields and woods and brought up their children in the sight and full knowledge of the whole community. The Christianity of their congregations was inevitably somewhat eccentric. They did not know the Creed or the Lord's Prayer; some did not even know how to make the sign of the cross. Superstitions fell on fertile ground. The island was idolatrous, barbaric, half-lost to Christianity and civilization. Man was cruel, unmerciful to man. Killings took place even in church and the priests were not the last to take up the lance, the dagger, or the blunderbuss, a new weapon that had reached the island towards the middle of the century and enlivened disputes. Meanwhile in the tumbledown churches, the rain-water poured in, grass grew, and lizards hid in the cracks. Let us allow a little for the natural exaggeration of even the best-intentioned missionaries. But the general picture was true. One stroke completes it. This half-savage people was capable of great religious outbursts, of spectacular devotion. When a foreign preacher passed through, the church was invaded by peasants from the mountains, late comers stood outside in the pouring rain, and penitents came to confession until late into the night.[54]

In much the same way, in a Moslem country this time, what we can

[53] E. Baumann, *L'anneau d'or des grands Mystiques*, 1924, p. 203–4.

[54] On the shortcomings of religious observance in Corsica, there is an enormous dossier: the letter from Cardinal de Tournon to Paul IV, 17th May, 1556, asking for the reform of abuses, Michel François, 'Le rôle du Cardinal François de Tournon dans la politique française en Italie de janvier a juillet 1556' in: *Mélanges . . . de l'École Française de Rome*, vol. 50, p. 328; Ilario Rinieri, 'I vescovi della Corsica' in: *Archivio storico di Corsica*, 1930–31, p. 334 ff. Father Daniele Bartoli, *Degli uomini e de' fatti della Compagnia di Gesù*, Turin, 1847, III, 57–58; Abbé S. B. Casanova, *Histoire de l'Église corse*, 1931, p. 103 ff.

glimpse of the Marabout conquest of the Sous mountains, in the sixteenth century, through the hagiographies of the period – notably Ibn 'Askar – gives an idea of the atmosphere of wonderment in which the saints and their admirers moved: 'We find them surrounded by a crowd of schemers, madmen, and simple souls.'[55]

It is not surprising that the folklore of these high regions reveals primitive credulity. Magic practices and superstitions abounded in everyday life, encouraging both religious enthusiasm and downright trickery.[56] A novella by the Dominican Bandello[57] takes us to a little village in the Alps near Brescia, about the beginning of the sixteenth century, where there are a few houses, spring water, the village fountain, great barns for storing fodder, and, among his little flock, a priest, who goes about his duties, blessing the thresholds of the houses, the barns and the cowsheds, preaching the holy word, and setting an example of virtue. One day a peasant girl, coming to draw water from the presbytery fountain, arouses his lust. 'You are in terrible danger,' he goes among his parishioners explaining, 'a great bird – a griffon – an exterminating angel – is about to swoop down on you to punish you for your sins. As soon as it appears, I will ring the church bell, and you must all stand still and hide your eyes.' No sooner said than done. No one moved until the bell rang for the second time. And Bandello does not even think it necessary to protest the truth of his story.

This is of course only a tiny example picked out of the enormous dossier of peasant superstitions which historians have not yet seriously tackled. Widespread, irresistible outbreaks of 'diabolism' swept through the old populations of Europe, holding them enthralled, and nowhere did these outbreaks occur more strongly than in the uplands whose primitive isolation maintained them in backwardness. Sorcerers, witchcraft, primitive magic, and black masses were the flowerings of an ancient cultural subconscious, from which Western civilization could not entirely separate itself. The mountains were the favoured refuge of these aberrant cults, which originated far back in time and persisted even after the Renaissance and Reformation. At the end of the sixteenth century, there were innumerable 'magic' mountains, stretching from Germany as far as the Milanese or Piedmontese Alps, from the Massif Central, seething with revolutionary and 'diabolical' ferment, to the healing soldiers of the Pyrenees, from the Franche-Comté to the Basque country. In the Rouergue, in 1595, 'sorcerers

[55] R. Montagne, *Les Berbères et le Makhzen dans le Sud du Maroc*, 1930, p. 83.

[56] How can we unearth the rich folklore of these mountains? One example is the story of the *teriels*, quoted by Leo Frobenius, *Histoire de la civilisation africaine*, 1936, p. 263 ff. apropos of Kabylia, whose remote life he describes, devoted to great hunts not to agriculture. Perhaps there is somewhere a collection of mountain folksongs? On the religious life of the Alps and the localization of heretical sects, G. Botero, *Le relationi universali*, Venice, 1599, III, 1, p. 76. On the visit of Cardinal Borromeo to Mesolina, *ibid.*, p. 17.

[57] IV, 2nd part, *Novelle*, London edition, 1791, II, p. 25–43. The ancedote is set in the Val di Sabbia, part of the Brescian Pre-Alps.

reign over the mass of the inhabitants and their ignorance'; because of
the lack of local churches even the Bible was unknown. And everywhere
the black sabbath seems to have been a social and cultural reaction, a
mental revolution for lack of a coherent social revolution.[58] The Devil
seems to have been afoot in all the countries of Europe as the sixteenth
century drew to a close, and even more in the first decades of the following
century. He even seems to have crossed over into Spain by the high
Pyrenean passes. In Navarre in 1611, the Inquisition severely punished a
sect of over 12,000 adherents who 'worship the Devil, put up altars to him
and deal with him familiarly on all occasions'.[59] But we must leave this
fascinating topic, as our chief interest for the moment is the problem of
disparity between mountain and lowland, of the backwardness of mountain society.

Mountain freedom.[60] There can be no doubt that the lowland, urban
civilization penetrated to the highland world very imperfectly and at a
very slow rate. This was as true of other things as it was of Christianity.
The feudal system as a political, economic, and social system, and as an
instrument of justice failed to catch in its toils most of the mountain
regions and those it did reach it only partially influenced. The resistance of
the Corsican and Sardinian mountains to lowland influence has often
been noted and further evidence could be found in Lunigiana, regarded by
Italian historians as a kind of mainland Corsica, between Tuscany and
Liguria.[61] The observation could be confirmed anywhere where the population is so inadequate, thinly distributed, and widely dispersed as to prevent the establishment of the state, dominant languages, and important
civilizations.
   A study of the vendetta would lead one towards a similar conclusion.
The countries where the vendetta was in force – and they were all mountainous countries – were those that had not been moulded and penetrated

---

[58] These remarks were suggested to me by Emmanuel Le Roy Ladurie's study, *Les
paysans de Languedoc*, Paris, 1966, p. 407.
   [59] A. S. V. Senato, *Dispacci Spagna*, Madrid, 6th June, 1611, Priuli to the Doge.
   [60] As observed by contemporaries; Loys Le Roy, *De l'excellence du gouvernement
royal*, Paris, 1575, p. 37, writes 'A country covered with mountains, rocks, and forests,
fit only for pasture, where there are many poor men, as is most of Switzerland, is best
suited for democracy . . . The lands of the plain, where there are greater numbers of
rich and noble men, are better suited to an aristocratic form of government'. Jean
Bodin, in *Les six livres de la République* (English translation, *The Six Books of the
Commonwealth*, by Knolles, 1606, facs. edition Harvard, 1962, p. 694) reports that Leo
Africanus was astonished by the robust physique of the mountain folk of Mount
Megeza, while the plain-dwellers were smaller men. 'This force and vigour doth cause
the mountaineers to love popular liberty . . . as we have said of the Swissers and
Grisons'. The Middle Ages in Corsica, says Lorenzi de Bradi, *La Corse inconnue*, 1927,
p. 35, were a great period for liberty. 'The Corsican would not suffer any man to rob
him of the product of his labour. The milk from his goat and the harvest from his field
were his alone.' And H. Taine in his *Voyage aux Pyrénées*, 1858, p. 138, says 'freedom
took root here deep in the past, a gruff and wild sort of freedom'.
   [61] Arrigo Solmi, 'La Corsica' in *Arch. st. di Corsica*, 1925, p. 32.

by mediæval concepts of feudal justice,[62] the Berber countries, Corsica, and Albania, for example. Marc Bloch,[63] writing about studies of Sardinia, points out that during the Middle Ages the island was an 'extensively manorialized, but not feudalized society' as a result of having been 'long isolated from the great currents which swept the continent'. This is putting the accent on the insularity of Sardinia, and it is quite true that it has been a decisive factor in Sardinian history. But the mountains are an equally important factor, just as responsible for the isolation of the people of Sardinia as the sea, if not more so; even in our own time they have produced those cruel and romantic outlaws, at Orgosolo and elsewhere, in revolt against the establishment of the modern state and its *carabinieri*. This moving phenomenon has been portrayed by anthropologists and film directors. 'He who does not steal', says a character in a Sardinian novel, 'is not a man'.[64] 'Law?' says another, 'I make my own laws and I take what I need.'[65]

In Sardinia, as in Lunigiana and Calabria, and everywhere where observation (when it is possible) reveals a hiatus between the society and the broad movements of history – if social archaisms (the vendetta among others) persisted, it was above all for the simple reason that mountains are mountains: that is, primarily an obstacle, and therefore also a refuge, a land of the free. For there men can live out of reach of the pressures and tyrannies of civilization: its social and political order, its monetary economy. Here there was no landed nobility with strong and powerful roots (the 'lords of the Atlas' created by the Maghzen were of recent origin); in the sixteenth century in Haute-Provence, the country nobleman, the '*cavaier salvatje*', lived alongside his peasants, cleared the land as they did, did not scorn to plough and till the ground, or to carry wood and dung on the back of his donkey. He was a constant irritation 'in the eyes of the Provençal nobility, who are essentially city-dwellers like the Italians'.[66] Here there were no rich, well-fed clergy to be envied and mocked; the priest was as poor as his flock.[67] There was no tight urban network so no

[62] For a general picture, see the penetrating but legalistic work by Jacques Lambert, *La vengeance privée et les fondements du droit international*, Paris, 1936. In the same order of ideas, cf. Michelet's remark on the Dauphiné, where 'feudalism (never) exerted the same influence as it did upon the rest of France.' And Taine again: *op. cit.*, p. 138, 'These are the *fors* of Béarn, in which it is said that in Béarn in the old days there was no *seigneur*'. On blood feuds in Montenegro and upper Albania, see Ami Boué, *La Turquie d'Europe*, Paris, 1840, II, p. 395 and 523.

[63] Marc Bloch, *Feudal Society*, (trans. L. Manyon), London, 1961, p. 247. See also his useful remarks on Sardinia, 'La Sardaigne' in *Mélanges d'histoire sociale*, III, p. 94.

[64] Maurice Le Lannou, 'Le bandit d'Orgosolo', *Le Monde*, 16/17 June, 1963. The film was directed by Vittorio de Seta, the anthropological study carried out by Franco Caguetta, French transl.: *Les Bandits d'Orgosolo*, 1963; the novels mentioned are by Grazia Deledda, *La via del male*, Rome, 1896; *Il Dio dei viventi*, Rome, 1922.

[65] *Ibid.*

[66] Fernand Benoit, *La Provence et le Comtat Venaissin*, 1949, p. 27.

[67] For the high Milanese, see S. Pugliese, 'Condizioni economiche e finanziarie della Lombardia nella prima meta del secolo XVIII' in *Misc. di Storia italiana*, 3rd series, vol. xxi, 1924.

administration, no towns in the proper sense of the word, and no gendarmes either we might add. It is only in the lowlands that one finds a
close-knit, stifling society, a prebendal clergy, a haughty aristocracy, and
an efficient system of justice. The hills were the refuge of liberty, democracy, and peasant 'republics'.

'The steepest places have been at all times the asylum of liberty', writes
the learned Baron de Tott in his *Memoirs*.[68] 'In travelling along the coast
of Syria, we see despotism extending itself over all the flat country and its
progress stopt towards the mountains, at the first rock, at the first defile,
that is easy of defence; whilst the Curdi, the Drusi, and the Mutuali,
masters of the Lebanon and Anti-Lebanon, constantly preserve their
independence'[69]. A poor thing was Turkish despotism – ruler indeed of the
roads, passes, towns, and plains, but what can it have meant in the Balkan
highlands, or in Greece and Epirus, in the mountains of Crete where the
Skafiotes defied, from their hilltops, all authority from the seventeenth
century onward, or in the Albanian hills, where, much later, lived 'Alī
Pasha Tepedelenli? Did the Wali Bey, installed at Monastir by the Turkish
conquest of the fifteenth century, ever really govern? In theory his authority extended to the Greek and Albanian hill-villages, but each one was a
fortress, an independent enclave and on occasion could become a hornets'
nest.[70] It is hardly surprising, then, that the Abruzzi, the highest, widest,
and wildest part of the Apennines, should have escaped Byzantine rule,
the rule of the Exarchs of Ravenna, and finally the domination of Papal
Rome, although the Abruzzi lie directly behind the city and the Papal
State ran north through Umbria as far as the Po valley.[71] Nor is it astonishing that in Morocco the *bled es siba*, lands unsubdued by the sultan, should
be essentially mountain regions.[72]

Sometimes this freedom of the hills has survived into our own time and
can be seen today in spite of the immense weight of modern administration.
In the Moroccan High Atlas, notes Robert Montagne,[73] 'the villages which
are ranged along the sunny banks of the mountain torrents, near immense
walnut trees watered by the turbulent Atlas streams, have no *chikhs*' or

[68] *Mémoires sur les Turcs et les Tartares*, (Eng. trans. *Memoirs of the Baron de Tott
on the Turks and Tartars . . .* London 1785, I, p. 398): 'asylum of liberty, or,' he adds,
'the haunt of tyrants.' This was in connection with the Genoese installations in the
Crimea.
[69] *Ibid.*, Preliminary Discourse, I, 11.
[70] Cf. Franz Spunda in Werner Benndorf, *Das Mittelmeerbuch*. 1940, p. 209–210.
[71] A. Philippson, 'Umbrien und Etrurien', in *Geogr. Zeitung*, 1933, p. 452.
[72] Further examples: Napoleon was unable to control the mountains round Genoa,
a refuge for deserters, in spite of the searches organized (Jean Borel, *Gênes sous
Napoléon Ier*, 2nd ed. 1929, p. 103). In about 1828, the Turkish police were powerless
to prevent outbreaks of brigandage by the peoples of Mt. Ararat (Comte de Sercey,
op. cit., p. 95); they seem to be equally unsuccessful today in protecting the mountain's forest wealth from the ravages of the flocks (Hermann Wenzel, 'Agrargeo-
graphische Wandlungen in der Türkei', in *Geogr. Zeitschr.* 1937, p. 407). Similarly in
Morocco: 'In reality, in southern Morocco, the sultan's authority did not reach beyond
the plain', writes R. Montagne, *op. cit.*, p. 134.
[73] *Ibid.*, p. 131.

Khalifats' houses. It is impossible to distinguish between a poor man's house and a rich man's. Each of these little mountain cantons forms a separate state, administered by a council. The village elders, all clad alike in brown wool garments, meet on a terrace and discuss for hours on end the interests of the village. No one raises his voice and it is impossible from watching them to discover which is their president.' All this is preserved, if the mountain canton is sufficiently high and sufficiently inaccessible, away from the main roads, which is a rare case today but was less so in former times before the expansion of road systems. This is why the Nurra, although connected to the rest of the island of Sardinia by an easily accessible plain, remained for a long time out of the reach of roads and traffic. The following legend was inscribed on an eighteenth century map by the Piedmontese engineers: 'Nurra, unconquered peoples, who pay no taxes'![74]

The mountains' resources: an assessment. As we have seen, the mountains resist the march of history, with its blessings and its burdens, or they accept it only with reluctance. And yet life sees to it that there is constant contact between the hill population and the lowlands. None of the Mediterranean ranges resembles the impenetrable mountains to be found in the Far East, in China, Japan, Indochina, India, and as far as the Malacca peninsula.[75] Since they have no communication with sea-level civilization, the communities found there are autonomous. The Mediterranean mountains, on the other hand, are accessible by roads. The roads may be steep, winding, and full of potholes, but they are passable on foot. They are a 'kind of extension of the plain' and its power through the hill country.[76] Along these roads the sultan of Morocco sent his *harkas*, Rome sent its legionaries, the king of Spain his *tercios*, and the Church its missionaries and travelling preachers.[77]

Indeed, Mediterranean life is such a powerful force that when compelled by necessity it can break through the obstacles imposed by hostile terrain. Out of the twenty-three passes in the Alps proper, seventeen were already in use at the time of the Romans.[78] Moreover, the mountains are frequently overpopulated – or at any rate overpopulated in relation to their resources. The optimum level of population is quickly reached and exceeded; periodically the overflow has to be sent down to the plains.

[74] M. Le. Lannou, *Pâtres et paysans de la Sardaigne*, 1941, p. 14, n. 1.

[75] J. Blache, *op. cit.*, p. 12. On this contrast see Pierre Gourou, *L'homme et la terre en Extrême-Orient*, 1940, and the review of the same book by Lucien Febvre in: *Annales d'hist. sociale*, XIII, 1941, p. 73. P. Vidal de la Blache, *op. cit.*, Eng. trans. p. 371–2.

[76] R. Montagne, *op. cit.*, p. 17.

[77] I am thinking in particular of the travels of Sixtus V, in his youth and middle age, as described by Ludwig von Pastor, *Geschichte der Papste*, Freiburg-im-Breisgau, 1901–31, X, 1913, p. 23 and 59. They would make a good map.

[78] W. Woodburn Hyde, 'Roman Alpine routes', in *Memoirs of the American philosophical society*, Philadelphia, X, II, 1935. Similarly the Pyrenees have not always been the barrier one might imagine (M. Sorre, *Géog. univ.*, vol. VII, 1st part, p. 70; R. Konetzke, *op. cit.*, p. 9)

Not that their resources are negligible: every mountain has some arable land, in the valleys or on the terraces cut out of the hillside. Here and there among the infertile limestone are strips of flysch (a mixture of slate, marls, and sandstone) and marls on which wheat, rye, and barley can be grown. Sometimes the soil is fertile: Spoleto lies in the middle of a fairly wide and comparatively rich plain, and Aquila in the Abruzzi grows saffron. The further south one goes, the higher is the upper limit for the cultivation of crops and usable trees. In the northern Apennines today, chestnut trees grow as far up as 900 metres; at Aquila, wheat and barley are found up to 1680 metres; at Cozenza, maize, a new arrival in the sixteenth century, grows at 1400 metres, and oats at 1500 metres; on the slopes of Mount Etna, vines are grown up to a level of 1100 metres and chestnut trees at 1500 metres.[79] In Greece wheat is grown up to a level of 1500 metres and vines up to 1250 metres.[80] In North Africa the limits are even higher.

One of the advantages of the mountain region is that it offers a variety of resources, from the olive trees, orange trees, and mulberry trees of the lower slopes to the forests and pasturelands higher up. To the yield from crops can be added the produce of stockraising. Sheep and goats are raised, as well as cattle. In comparatively greater numbers than today, they used to be plentiful in the Balkans, and even in Italy and North Africa. As a result, the mountains are a source of milk, cheeses[81] (Sardinian cheese was exported in boatloads all over the western Mediterranean in the sixteenth century), butter, fresh or rancid, and boiled or roasted meat. The typical mountain house was a shepherd's or herdsman's dwelling, built for animals rather than for human beings.[82] In 1574, Pierre Lescalopier, when crossing the Bulgarian mountains, preferred to sleep 'under some tree' than in the peasants' huts of beaten clay where beasts and humans lived 'under one roof, and in such filth that we could not bear the stench'.[83]

The forests in those days, it should be pointed out, were thicker than they are today.[84] They can be imagined as something like the National Park of the Val di Corte, in the Abruzzi, with its thick beechwoods climbing up to 1400 metres. The population of the forests included foxes, wolves,

[79] Richard Pfalz, 'Neue wirtschaftsgeographische Fragen Italiens', in *Geogr. Zeitschr.*, 1931, p. 133.

[80] A. Philippson, *Das Mittelmeergebiet, op. cit.*, p. 167.

[81] Victor Bérard, *La Turquie et l'hellénisme contemporain, op. cit.*, p. 103, writes on leaving Albania: 'After three days of goat cheese . . .'.

[82] P. Arqué, *op. cit.*, p. 68.

[83] *Op. cit.*, f° 44 and 44 v°.

[84] There used to be forests on the slopes of Mount Vesuvius. On the forests in general, the observations of Theobald Fischer are still useful (in. *B. zur physischen Geogr. der Mittelmeerländer besonders Siciliens*, 1877, p. 155 ff.) On the forests of Naples, Calabria and the Basilicata, in 1558, cf. Eugenio Albèri, *Relazioni degli ambasciatori veneti durante il secolo XVI*, Florence, 1839–63, II, III, p. 271. Even today there are many remains of the great forests of the past, forest ruins. They are listed for Corsica in Philippe Leca (preface by A. Albitreccia) *Guide bleu de la Corse*, Paris, 1935, p. 15; See also the latter's *La Corse, son évolution au XIXe siècle et au début du XXe siècle*, 1942, p. 95 ff.

bears, and wildcats. The Monte Gargano's oak forests supported a whole population of woodcutters and timber merchants, for the most part in the service of the shipyards of Ragusa. Like the summer pastures, the forests were the subject of much dispute among mountain villages and against noble landowners. Even the scrubland, half forest, can be used for grazing, and sometimes for gardens and orchards; it also supports game and bees.[85] Other advantages of the mountains are the profusion of springs, plentiful water, that is so precious in these southern countries, and, finally, mines and quarries. Almost all the mineral resources of the Mediterranean, in fact, are found in its mountain regions.

But these advantages are not all found in every region. There are chestnut tree mountains (the Cévennes, Corsica) with their precious 'tree bread',[86] made from chestnuts, which can replace wheat bread if necessary. There are mulberry tree mountains like those Montaigne saw near Lucca in 1581,[87] or the highlands of Granada. 'These people, the people of Granada, are not dangerous', explained the Spanish agent, Francisco Gasparo Corso, to Euldj 'Alī, 'King' of Algiers in 1569.[88] 'What could they do to injure the Catholic King? They are unused to arms. All their lives they have done nothing but dig the ground, watch their flocks, and raise silkworms. . . .' There are also the walnut tree mountains: it is under the century-old walnut trees that even today, in the centre of the village, on moonlit nights, the Berbers of Morocco still celebrate their grand festivals of reconciliation.[89]

All told, the resources of the mountains are not as meagre as one might suppose. Life there is possible, but not easy. On the slopes where farm animals can hardly be used at all, the work is difficult. The stony fields must be cleared by hand, the earth has to be prevented from slipping down hill, and, if necessary, must be carried up to the hilltop and banked up with dry stone walls. It is painful work and never-ending; as soon as it stops, the mountain reverts to a wilderness and man must start from the beginning again. In the eighteenth century when the Catalan people took possession of the high rocky regions of the coastal massif, the first settlers were astonished to find dry stone walls and enormous olive trees still growing in the middle of the undergrowth, proof that this was not the first time that the land had been claimed.[90]

[85] Comte Joseph de Bradi, *Mémoire sur la Corse*, 1819, p. 187, 195 ff.
[86] P. Vidal de la Blache, *op. cit.*, (Eng. trans.) p. 141, 147, 221, 222. There are some excellent observations in D. Faucher, *Principes de géogr. agraire*, p. 23. 'The people eat bread from the trees', near Lucca, Montaigne, *Journal de voyage en Italie*, (ed. E. Pilon, 1932), p. 237.
[87] Montaigne, *ibid.*, p. 243.
[88] *Relacion de lo que yo Fco Gasparo Corso he hecho en prosecucion del negocio de Argel*, Simancas E° 333 (1569).
[89] R. Montagne, *op. cit.*, p. 234–5.
[90] Franchesci Carreras y Candi, *Geografía general de Catalunya*, Barcelona, 1913, p. 505; Jaime Carrera Pujal, *H. política y económica de Cataluña*, vol. 1, p. 40. Similarly Belon, *op. cit.*, p. 140, v° notes that there had formerly been terraced fields, abandoned when he saw them, in the mountains round Jerusalem.

Mountain dwellers in the towns. It is this harsh life.[91] as well as poverty, the hope of an easier existence, the attraction of good wages, that encourages the mountain people to go down to the plain: 'baixar sempre, mountar no', 'always go down, never go up', says a Catalan proverb.[92] Although the mountain's resources are varied, they are always in short supply. When the hive becomes too full,[93] there is not enough to go around and the bees must swarm, whether peacefully or not. For survival, any sacrifice is permitted. As in the Auvergne, and more especially as in the Cantal in the recent past, all the extra mouths, men, children, artisans, apprentices, and beggars are expelled.[94]

The history of the mountains is chequered and difficult to trace. Not because of lack of documents; if anything there are too many. Coming down from the mountain regions, where history is lost in the mist, man enters in the plains and towns the domain of classified archives. Whether a new arrival or a seasoned visitor, the mountain dweller inevitably meets someone down below who will leave a description of him, a more or less mocking sketch. Stendhal saw the peasants from the Sabine hills at Rome on Ascension Day. 'They come down from their mountains to celebrate the feast day at St. Peter's, and to attend *la funzione*.[95] They wear ragged cloth cloaks, their legs are wrapped in strips of material held in place with string cross-gartered; their wild eyes peer from behind disordered black hair; they hold to their chests hats made of felt, which the sun and rain have left a reddish black colour; these peasants are accompanied by their families, of equally wild aspect.[96] . . . The inhabitants of the mountains between Rome, Lake Turano, Aquila, and Ascoli, represent fairly well, to my way of thinking,' Stendhal adds, 'the moral condition of Italy in about the year 1400.'[97] In Macedonia, in 1890, Victor Bérard met the eternal Albanian, in his picturesque cavalry soldier's costume.[98] In Madrid, Théophile Gautier came across water-sellers, 'young Galician *muchachos*, in tobacco-coloured jackets, short breeches, black gaiters and pointed

[91] Life in Haute-Provence for example: 'The farm of Haute-Provence' writes Marie Mauron ('Le Mas provençal', in *Maisons et villages de France*, 1943, preface by R. Cristoflour, p. 222) 'which endures long winters, fear of avalanches, and indoor life for months on end, behind the snowy window panes with prospects confined to winter rations, the cowshed, and fireside work'.
[92] Maximilien Sorre, *Les Pyrénées méditerranéennes*, 1913, p. 410.
[93] This surplus population which makes the move to the plains necessary is indicated in the geographical survey by H. Wilhelmy, *Hochbulgarien*, 1936, p. 183. But there are other motives: whether life is agreeable or not, for example, cf. A. Albitreccia in Philippe Leca, *La Corse, op. cit.*, p. 129 who also notes of Corsica: 'in other places the presence of roads encourages emigration; here their absence does so.'
[94] J. Blache, *op. cit.*, p. 88, according to Philippe Arbos, *L'Auvergne*, 1932, p. 86.
[95] The mass.
[96] *Promenades dans Rome*, ed. Le Divan, 1931, I, p. 182–183.
[97] *Ibid.*, p. 126. A similar picture, this time of the Caucasus, is to be found in *Souvenirs* of the Comte de Rochechouart, 1889, p. 76–77, on the occasion of the capture of Anapa by the Duc de Richelieu: the Caucasian warriors, some clad in iron, armed with arrows, are reminiscent of the thirteenth or fourteenth century.
[98] Victor Bérard, *La Turquie et l'hellénisme contemporain, op. cit., passim.*

hats'.[99] Were they already wearing this dress when they were to be found, both men and women, scattered all over sixteenth-century Spain in the *ventas* mentioned by Cervantes, along with their Asturian neighbours?[100] One of the latter, Diego Suárez, who was to become a soldier and chronicler of the events of Oran at the end of the sixteenth century, describes his own adventures, his escape, while still a child, from his father's house, his arrival at the builders' yards of the Escorial where he works for a while, finding the fare to his taste, *el plato bueno*. But some of his relatives, from the mountains of Oviedo, arrive in their turn, no doubt to find summer work on the farms of Old Castile, like so many others. And he has to move on so as not to be recognized.[101] The whole region of Old Castile was continually being crossed by immigrants from the mountains of the North who sometimes returned there. The Montaña, the continuation of the Pyrenees from Biscay to Galicia, provided little sustenance for its inhabitants. Many of them were *arrieros*, muleteers, like the Maragatos[102] whom we shall meet again, or the peasant-carriers from the *partido* of Reinosa, travelling south, their wagons laden with hoops and staves for casks, and returning to their northern towns and villages with wheat and wine.[103]

In fact, no Mediterranean region is without large numbers of mountain dwellers who are indispensable to the life of town and plains, striking people whose costume is often unusual and whose ways are always strange. Spoleto, whose high plain Montaigne passed through in 1581 on the way to Loreto, was the centre for a special kind of immigrant: pedlars and small traders who specialized in all the reselling and intermediary activities that call for middlemen, flair, and not too many scruples. Bandello describes them in one of his novellas as talkative, lively and self-assured, never short of arguments and persuasive whenever they want to be. There is nobody to beat the Spoletans, he says, for cheating a poor devil while calling the blessing of St. Paul upon him, making money out of grass-snakes and adders with drawn fangs, begging and singing in marketplaces, and selling bean meal as a remedy for mange. They travel all over Italy, baskets slung around their necks, shouting their wares.[104]

[99] *Voyage en Espagne*, 1845, p. 65, 106. On the *gallegos*, both harvesters and emigrants, see *Los Españoles pintados por si mismos*, Madrid, 1843. This collection contains: *El Indiano*, by Antonio Ferrer Del Rio, *El segador*, *El pastor trashumante* and *El maragato* by Gil y Curraso, *El aguador* by Aberramar.

[100] At Toledo, at the house of the Sevilian, there are two *mocetonas gallegas*, (Galician girls) (*La ilustre fregona*). Galicians and Asturians do heavy work in Spain, especially in the mines: J. Chastenet, *Godoï*, 1943, p. 40. On *gallegos* as harvest workers in Castile in the eighteenth century, see Eugenio Larruga, *Memorias políticas y económicas sobre los frutos, comercio, fabricas y minas de España*, Madrid, 1745, I, p. 43.

[101] Diego Suárez, MS in the former *Gouvernement-Général* of Algeria, a copy of which was kindly passed on to me by Jean Casenave, f° 6.

[102] See below, p. 484.

[103] Jesús García Fernández, *Aspectos del paisaje agrario de Castilla la Vieja*, Valladolid, 1963, p. 12.

[104] Matteo Bandello, *Novelle*, VII, p. 200–201. Spoletans often served as soldiers, particularly in foreign armies, L. von Pastor, *op. cit.*, XVI, p. 267. On their cunning, see M. Bandello, *ibid.*, I. p. 418.

The people of the Bergamo Alps[105] – in Milan commonly known as the people of the *Contado* – are equally familiar in sixteenth-century Italy. They were everywhere. They worked as dockers in the ports, at Genoa and elsewhere. After Marignano, they came back to work the small-holdings of the Milanese, left abandoned during the war.[106] A few years later Cosimo de' Medici tried to attract them to Leghorn, the fever town where no one wanted to live. Rough men, clumsy, stocky, close-fisted, and willing for heavy labour, 'they go all over the world', says Bandello[107] (there was even an architect to be found working at the Escorial, Giovan Battista Castello, known as *el Bergamasco*[108]), 'but they will never spend more than four *quattrini* a day, and will not sleep on a bed but on straw'. When they made money they bought rich clothes and fed well, but were no more generous for it, nor any less vulgar and ridiculous. Real-life comedy characters, they were traditionally grotesque husbands whom their wives sent to *Corneto:* like the bumpkin in one of Bandello's novellas who has the excuse, if it is one, that he found his wife in Venice, among the women who sell love for a few coppers behind St. Mark's[109].

The picture, as we see, quickly turns to caricature. The mountain dweller is apt to be the laughing stock of the superior inhabitants of the towns and plains. He is suspected, feared, and mocked. In the Ardèche, as late as 1850, the people from the *mountagne* would come down to the plain for special occasions. They would arrive riding on harnessed mules, wearing grand ceremonial costumes, the women bedecked with jangling gold chains. The costumes themselves differed from those of the plain, although both were regional, and their archaic stiffness provoked the mirth of the village coquettes. The lowland peasant had nothing but sarcasm for the rude fellow from the highlands, and marriages between their families were rare.[110]

In this way a social and cultural barrier is raised to replace the imperfect geographical barrier which is always being broken in a variety of ways. It may be that the mountain dweller comes down with his flocks, one of the two annual movements of stock in search of pasture, or he may be hired

[105] M. Bandello, *op. cit.*, II, p. 385–386. It was poverty which obliged the people of Bergamo to emigrate. Sober at home, they were said to be great eaters elsewhere. At least one native of Bergamo could be found in every place in the world. Most of the Venetian subjects in Naples were *Bergamaschi*, E. Albèri, *op. cit.*, Appendix, p. 351 (1597).

[106] Jacques Heers, *Gênes au XVe siècle. Activité économique et problèmes sociaux*, 1961, p. 19. M. Bandello, *op. cit.*, IV, p. 241. Similarly, after the restoration of Francesco Sforza, many peasants arrived in Milan from Brescia.

[107] *Op. cit.*, IX, p. 337–338.

[108] L. Pfandl, *Philippe II*, French trans. 1942, p. 353–354. Both the famous Colleoni and the Jesuit Jean-Pierre Maffee, the author of *L'histoire des Indes*, Lyons, 1603, came from Bergamo.

[109] *Op. cit.*, IV, p. 335. He came from Brescia and had settled at Verona.

[110] Result of personal research. In fact, this opposition between highland and lowland is even more marked further north. Gaston Roupnel reports it in *Le vieux Garain*, 1939, on the Burgundy Côte, around Gevrey and Nuits-Saint-Georges. In 1870 the 'mountain folk' still wear smocks when they come to the lowland fairs.

in the lowlands at harvest time, and this is a seasonal emigration which is fairly frequent and much more widespread than is usually supposed: Savoyards[111] on their way to the lower Rhône valley, Pyrenean labourers hired for the harvest near Barcelona, or even Corsican peasants who regularly in summer, in the fifteenth century, crossed over to the Tuscan Maremma.[112] Or he may have settled permanently in the town, or as a peasant on the land of the plain: 'How many villages in Provence or even in the County of Avignon recall, with their steep, winding streets and tall houses, the little villages of the southern Alps'[113] from which their inhabitants originally came? Not so long ago, at harvest time the people from the mountains, young men and girls alike, would flock down as far as the plain and even the coast of lower Provence, where the *gavot*, the man from Gap, which is really a generic name, is still known 'as typically a hard worker, careless of sartorial elegance, and used to coarse food'.[114]

A host of similar and even more striking observations could be made if one included the plains of Languedoc and the uninterrupted flow of immigrants coming to them from the North, from Dauphiné, and even more from the Massif Central, Rouergue, Limousin, Auvergne, Vivarais, Velay, and the Cévennes. This stream submerged lower Languedoc, but regularly went on beyond it towards wealthy Spain. The procession re-formed every year, almost every day, and was made up of landless peasants, unemployed artisans, casual agricultural workers down for the harvest, the grape harvest, or threshing, outcasts of society, beggars and beggar-women, travelling preachers, *gyrovagues* – vagabonds – street musicians, and shepherds with their flocks. Mountain poverty was the great spur of this journey downwards. 'Behind this exodus', says one historian, 'there lies an obvious disparity of living standards, to the advantage of the Mediterranean plains.'[115] These beggars would arrive, set off again and die on the road or in the hospices, but in the long run they contributed to the human stock of the lowlands, so that for centuries there persisted the aberrant type, the man of the North, taller than average, with fair hair and blue eyes.

Typical cases of mountain dispersion. Transhumance is by far the most important of these movements from the hill to the plain, but it is a return journey. We shall study it later in more detail.

The other forms of mountain expansion are neither as large-scale nor as regular. All the evidence is of particular cases; we shall have to present a series of examples, except perhaps in the case of 'military' migration, for

---

[111] P. George, *La région du Bas-Rhône*, 1935, p. 300: mentions bands of Savoyards going to work at harvest time in the Arles region, in the first years of the seventeenth century.

[112] Grotanelli, *La Maremma toscana, Studi storici ed economici*, II, p. 19.

[113] P. George, *op. cit.*, p. 651.

[114] Fernand Benoit, *op. cit.*, p. 23.

[115] Emmanuel Le Roy Ladurie, *op. cit.*, p. 97 ff.

all the mountain regions, or almost all, were 'Swiss cantons'.[116] Apart from the vagabonds and adventurers who followed armies without pay, hoping only for battle and plunder, they provided regular soldiers, almost traditionally reserved for certain princes. The Corsicans fought in the service of the king of France, of Venice, or of Genoa. The soldiers of the Duchy of Urbino and those of the Romagna, whom their overlords sold by contract, were generally allotted to Venice. If their masters turned traitor, as they did at the battle of Agnadello in 1509,[117] the peasants abandoned the cause of St. Mark to follow them. There were always lords of Romagna to be found at Venice; having broken their ban and committed other crimes, they now sought absolution and restitution of their property from Rome,[118] in return for which they went to the Low Countries to serve the cause of Spain and Catholicism. Or again there were the Albanians, the *pallikares* of Morea, and the 'Anatolian oxen' whom Algiers, and other similar cities drew from the barren mountains of Asia.

The story of the Albanians deserves a study in itself.[119] Attracted by the 'sword, the gold trappings, and the honours',[120] they left their mountains chiefly in order to become soldiers. In the sixteenth century they were to be found in Cyprus,[121] in Venice,[122] in Mantua,[123] in Rome, Naples,[124] and Sicily, and as far abroad as Madrid, where they went to present their projects and their grievances, to ask for barrels of gunpowder or years of pension, arrogant, imperious, always ready for a fight. In the end Italy

---

[116] It would be impossible to list all the known examples. For the predominance of recruitment from poor and mountainous areas in Spain, see Ramón Carande, *Carlos V y sus banqueros*, Madrid, 1949, p. 14 (the high regions of Valencia and the *montes* of León). Th. Lefebvre, *Les Pyrénées atlantiques*, 1933, p. 286, (3000 Giupuzcoans and soldiers from Navarre fought at Pavia). On the Aragonese Pyrenees, see Fernand Braudel, *La Méditerranée* . . . 1st ed., p. 47 and 48.

[117] Piero Pieri, *La crisi militare italiana nel Rinascimento*, 1st ed. Naples, 1934, p. 523.

[118] H. de Maisse to the king, Venice, 6th June, 1583; A.E. 31, f⁰ 29 v⁰ and 30.

[119] For a bibliographic guide see R. Busch-Zantner, *Albanien*, 1939. On the Albanian migrations, caused by famine in the Middle Ages towards the plains of Metohidja and Podrina, cf. J. Cvijić, *op. cit.*, p. 150. On their fantastic success in the Turkish empire in the nineteenth century, *ibid.*, p. 17. In the Bibliotheca Communale of Palermo there is an unpublished memoir by Mongitore Antonino, *Memoria de Greci venuti dall' Albania in Sicilia*, Qq E 32, f⁰ 81. On the Albanian as a great drinker of wine see Bandello, *op. cit.*, IV, p. 350–351. On the Albanians seeking Christendom, any one of a number of documents, e.g. Joan de Pallas, consul at Ragusa to the Grand Commander of León, Naples, 3rd April, 1536, A.N., K. 1632.

[120] Victor Bérard, *La Turquie* . . . *op. cit.*, p. 164.

[121] In Cyprus they were soldiers from father to son. Fr. Steffano Lusignano di Cipro, *Corograffia et breve historia universale dell' isola de Cipro*, Bologna, 1573, (B.N. Paris, 4⁰ G 459).

[122] They made up a considerable section of the Venetian army, cf. the series of documents, published by V. Lamansky, *op. cit.*, p. 549, note.

[123] M. Bandello, *op. cit.*, III. p. 329 ff.

[124] Museo Correr, D. delle Rose, 21, f⁰ 80 on the large Albanian villages in Apulia, 1598. At the beginning of the century they are often feared. They are forbidden (3rd June, 1506) to leave fortified towns and villages carrying arms. Ludwig von Thallóczy, 'Die albanische Diaspora', in *Illyrisch-albanische Forschungen*, 1916, p. 339.

gradually shut its doors to them. They moved on to the Low Countries,[125] England,[126] and France during the Wars of Religion, soldier-adventurers followed everywhere by their wives, children, and priests.[127] The Regencies of Algiers[128] and Tunis refused them, and the lands of the Moldavian and Wallachian boyars also denied them entry. So they hastened to the service of the Sublime Porte, as they had in the first place, and as they were to do on a massive scale from the nineteenth century on. 'Where the sword is, there is the faith'. They were for whoever would give them a living. And, if necessary, 'with, as the song goes, their gun for pasha and their sabre for vizir',[129] they set up on their own account and became brigands. From the seventeenth century on, large numbers of Albanians, for the most part orthodox, spread over Greece where they camped as if in conquered territory. Chateaubriand could not fail to notice them in 1806.[130]

The history of Corsica – outside the island – is no less rich in information. Famous Corsicans are claimed everywhere, with some reason let it be said. 'In Spain, how many islanders achieved fame', exclaims de Bradi.[131] De Lecas, alias Vazquez, was one of Philip II's ministers; this is certainly true, and Cervantes even addressed some verses to him. De Bradi goes on to say that the original Don Juan was a Corsican, of Corsican father and mother. He even gives his name and his parents' names. One feels he is ready to prove that Christopher Columbus was born at Calvi! But without going as far as Don Juan, one can trace many genuine Corsicans who, whether as sailors, dealers, merchants, agricultural labourers – when they were not kings of Algiers,[132] or pashas, or renegades in the service of the Grand Turk – lived around the shores of the Mediterranean.

The inhabitants of the Milanese mountains have provided another longstanding source of immigrants. We mentioned the *Bergamaschi*, subjects of Venice. But every mountain valley in the Alps has its swarm always ready to leave. There is frequently a second homeland where the exiles can meet. The travelling tinkers of the Val Vigezzo traditionally went to France, sometimes settling there permanently, like the Mellerios who are today jewellers in the Rue de la Paix.[133] The inhabitants of Tre-

[125] O. de Torne, 'Philippe et Henri de Guise' in *Revue Historique*, 1931, II, p. 324.
[126] In 1540; G. Lefèvre Pontalis, *Correspondance politique d'Odet de Selve*, 1888, p. 64, 65, 351, 354.
[127] A.H.N. L° 3189, 1565, Inquisition of Valladolid, the curious affair of Guillermo de Modon.
[128] D. Haëdo, *Topographia* . . . p. 121 v°, mentions in Algiers Arnaut Mami and 'un renegado, tambien albanes y arnaut como el', p. 122 v°.
[129] Victor Bérard, *La Turquie* . . . *op. cit.*, p. 26.
[130] *Itinéraire de Paris à Jérusalem* (ed. 1831) I. pp. 111 and 175.
[131] *La Corse inconnue*, p. 44, with a list of Corsicans who achieved fame outside the island.
[132] Like Hasan Corso, J. Cazenave, 'Un Corse roi d'Alger, 1518–1556', in *Afrique latine*, 1923, pp. 397–404.
[133] Giuseppe Mellerio, *Les Mellerio, leur origine, leur histoire*, 1895. On emigration from the Milanese, Alps, see Carlo Antonio Vianello, 'Alcuni documenti sul consolato dei Lombardi a Palermo', in *Archivio storico Lombardo*, 1938, p. 186.

mezzo preferred the Rhineland; from their numbers came the Majnoni and Brentanos, the Frankfurt bankers.[134] From the fifteenth century on, the emigrants from the Val Masino took the road to Rome.[135] They can be found in the apothecaries' shops and bakeries of the Eternal City, and in Genoa too. From the three *pievi* of Lake Como – particularly those of Dongo and Gravedona – men left for Palermo as innkeepers. As a result there is a rather curious link, with visible traces, in the.Val di Brenzio,[136] in the costume and ornaments of the women. For these departures often ended in return journeys. We find a considerable number of typically Milanese surnames in sixteenth-century Naples;[137] however, says the consul G. F. Osorio in 1543, 'these Lombards who come here in thousands to work, as soon as they have earned any money, go back to Milan with it'.[138] Lombard masons – *muratori* – (doubtless from the Alps) built the castle of Aquileia in 1543;[139] when winter came, they went back home. But if we were to follow these masons or stonecutters, the search would lead us all over Europe, and certainly throughout Italy. As early as 1486, *lapicide lombardi* were working on the construction of the Palace of the Doges at Venice.[140]

Even a country as continental and enclosed as Armenia does not escape the inevitable fate of all mountain regions. Without subscribing to the Armenian story that the Murat family, whose real name was Muratjan, originally came from Kara Bagh in the Caucasus[141] – it seems on examination even less likely than a Corsican Don Juan – we have plenty of evidence of the Armenian dispersion in the directions of Constantinople, Tiflis, Odessa, Paris, and the Americas. Armenia played a considerable part too in the rise of the great Persia of the Shah 'Abbās, at the beginning of the seventeenth century. It provided him with, among others, the indispensable travelling merchants[142] who journeyed at that time[143] to fairs in Germany,

[134] A. Vianello, *ibid.*, p. 186.
[135] *Ibid.*, p. 186.   [136] *Ibid.*, p. 187.   [137] *Ibid.*, p. 187.
[138] G. F. Osorio, console dei Lombardi alla camera dei mercanti di Milano, Naples, 27th September, 1543, ed. A. Vianello, *op. cit.*, p. 187.
[139] A.d.S. Naples, Sommaria Partium 240, f° 111–113, 15th January, 1544, with the names of the *muratori*.
[140] A.d.S. Venice, Notatorio di Collegio 13, f° 121, 12th October, 1486.
[141] According to a newspaper article, 'Eriwan, die Haupstadt der Armenier' in *Frankfurter Zeitung*, 9th August, 1940.
[142] Jean-Baptiste Tavernier, *Les six voyages qu'il a faits en Turquie, en Perse et aux Indes*, (Eng. trans. by John Phillips: *The Six Voyages of Jean-Baptiste Tavernier*, London, 1677, Persian Travels, p. 159.)
[143] 'At that time', that is in the seventeenth century. In the sixteenth century, in Constantinople and the eastern Mediterranean, the Armenians' time had not yet come: N. Iorga, *Points de vue sur l'histoire de commerce de l'Orient a l'époque moderne*, 1925, p. 23. In the seventeenth century by contrast, the Armenians were trading as far away as the western Mediterranean. An Armenian ship 'The Merchant Armenian' brought wheat to Leghorn (*Mémoires du Chevalier d'Arvieux*, 1735, I, p. 13). On the role played by the Armenians in the quarrel over the holy places in 1621, cf. Gérard Tongas, *L'ambassadeur L. Deshayes de Cormenin (1600–1632)*, 1937, p. 132. On the present dispersion of the Armenians there are a few words in Werner Sombart, *Vom Menschen*, 1940, p. 178–179.

to the quaysides of Venice, and to the shops of Amsterdam.[144] Others before the Armenians had attempted this connection and had failed. If they succeeded, it is in small part because of their Christianity, and in large measure because they would take on hard work, had great resistance, and were very sober, that is real mountain people. 'When they return from Christendom', notes Tavernier who knew them well, 'they bring along with them all sorts of Mercery-ware and Pedlery-ware of Nuremberg and Venice; as little Looking-glasses, trifles of Tin enamel'd, false Pearls, and other things of that nature; which pays for the Victuals they call for among the Country-people'.[145] It was with large fortunes in ready money that they returned home to Zolpha, the rich Armenian colony of Ispahan, where they led a life as ostentatious as the Persians, dressing their women sumptuously in Venetian brocades and harnessing their horses with gold and silver trappings. True, they had two avenues of trade to choose from and not content with Europe, they dealt with the Indies, Tonkin, Java, the Philippines, 'and throughout the East except for China and Japan'.[146] They might make the journey themselves: Tavernier travelled to Surat and Golconda with the son of a wealthy Armenian merchant of Zolpha – or they could take advantage of the branch set up in the nearby great city by the 'Banyans', the Hindu merchants who formed the advance guard of Asiatic commerce in the Persian capital. Some Armenians even owned ships on the Indian Ocean.[147]

This emigration dating from the end of the sixteenth century and the early seventeenth, explains the Venetian cast of the Armenian Renaissance. But was it not precisely because Armenia extended herself beyond her frontiers to such an extent, both to her advantage and her cost, that she ceased to be a state, if not a human reservoir of great potential, after the fourteenth century? Armenia was lost through her own success.

Mountain life: the earliest civilization of the Mediterranean? The mountains have always been a reservoir of men for other people's use. Mountain life, exported in generous quantities, has contributed to the overall history of the sea.[148] It may even have shaped the origins of that history, for moun-

[144] There exist trading manuals, in Armenian, specially written for the great northern town.

[145] J.-B. Tavernier adds, 'indeed the Armenians are so much the more fit for trading, because they are a people very sparing and sober; though whether it be their virtue or their avarice, I know not. For when they are going a long journey, they only make provision of Bisket, smoak'd *Bufalo*'s flesh, Onions, bak'd butter, Flour, Wine and dry'd Fruits. They never buy fresh Victuals but when they meet with Lambs or Kids very cheap in the mountainous countries'. *The Six Voyages*, Persian Travels, p. 159.

[146] On the wealth and luxury of the Armenians of Zolpha, see J.-B. Tavernier, *op. cit.*, Persian Travels, p. 159.

[147] *Ibid.*, *Travels to India*, p. 16.

[148] The mountains are 'a zone of human emigration', Pierre Deffontaines, Mariel Jean-Brunhes-Delamarre, P. Bertoquy, *Les problèmes de géographie humaine*, 1939, p. 141. On the mountain-plain contrast characteristic of the Mediterranean region, Charles Parain, *La Méditerranée: les hommes et leur travaux*, Paris, 1936, p. 191; Jules Sion, *La France méditerranéenne*, Paris, 1934, p. 44 ff.

tain life seems to have been the first kind of life in the Mediterranean whose civilization 'like that of the Middle East and Central Asia, cloaks and barely disguises its pastoral origins',[149] a primitive world of hunters and herdsmen, of nomads and migrating flocks, with now and then a few crops hastily sown on burnt clearings. This is the life of the high places, the first to be brought under control by man.

Why was this? Perhaps because of the varied distribution of mountain resources, and also because the plains were originally a land of stagnant waters and malaria, or zones through which the unstable river beds passed. The thickly populated plains which today are the image of prosperity were the culmination of centuries of painful collective effort. In ancient Rome, in the time of Varro, people could still remember the time when one had to cross the Velabrum by boat. Human habitation only gradually progressed from the highlands down to the fever-ridden flats with their stagnant pools.

There is no lack of proof of this. Take for example the map of pre-historic settlements of the Lower Rhône in the study by P. George.[150] All the known sites are to be found in the high limestone country overlooking the low-lying delta, to the east and north. It was not until thousands of years later that work began on the draining of the Rhône marshes in the fifteenth century.[151] Similarly, in Portugal, prehistoric sites are not found in the valleys and basins. The mountains on the other hand were populated from the time of the Bronze Age: the deforestation there is not as recent as that of central Europe. In the ninth and tenth centuries, people still lived high up; the places that date back to that period – the age of the kings of the Asturias and León – are almost always the highest villages of today.[152]

The example of Portugal takes us outside the limits of the Mediterranean. But right in the centre is Tuscany: a country of narrow, naturally marshy plains, interspersed with valleys between the hills which rise higher and higher as one travels east or south, Here there are towns. And the earliest and oldest towns are precisely at the highest points, looking down on the slopes that today are covered with vines and olive trees. This is where we find the Etruscan towns, all *oppida*-towns perched on hill tops, *Hochrückenstädte*, as A. Philippson calls them.[153] Pisa, Lucca, Florence,

---

[149] Jules Blache, *op. cit.*, p. 15. The same point is made in P. George, *op. cit.*, p. 352.

[150] P. George, *op. cit.*, p. 237; V. L. Bourilly and R. Busquet, *Histoire de la Provence*, 1944, p. 7: 'In Provence, the earliest settlements have been found on the edges of the Mont Ventoux, on the mountains of the Vaucluse, on the south of the Lubéron, on the right-hand side of the Durance valley and at the point where the Verdon joins it; they seem to be connected with the abundant deposits of flint and hard rocks rolled down by the rivers'. Louis Alibert is of the same opinion, 'Le Génie d'Oc.' in *Les Cahiers du Sud*, 1943, p. 18. 'The essentially mountainous skeleton of the Mediterranean countries favoured the sedentarization and permanent settlement of prehistoric and protohistoric peoples'.

[151] P. George, *op. cit.*, p. 310–322.

[152] H. Lautensach, 'Die ländlerkundliche Gliederung Portugals' in *Geogr. Zeitschr.* 1932, p. 194.

[153] A. Philippson, 'Umbrien und Etrurien', in *Geogr. Zeitschr.*, 1933, p. 455, 457, 461, 462.

and the lowland towns were on the contrary late developments of the Roman period.[154] And around Florence, the marshes remained a threat for a long time to come.[155] Even in the sixteenth century the plains of Tuscany had not been completely drained. In fact, the water level rose dangerously over the region. Marshland spread in the Val di Chiana and on the edge of the plain flooded by Lake Trasimene. Fever increased in the Maremma and in the wheat-growing plain of Grosseto where all the efforts of the Medicis' policy failed to develop intensive wheat culture for export.[156]

So the contrast between plain and mountain is also a question of historical period. We have learned from agrarian studies to distinguish in central and western Europe between old and new soils, *Altland* and *Neuland*, as German historians and geographers call them, the former acquired by neolithic farmers, the latter opened up by mediæval and modern colonization. Old soils and new soils: in the Mediterranean one might almost call them mountain and plain.

2. PLATEAUX, HILLS, AND FOOTHILLS

This sketch of the mountain regions is necessarily incomplete. Life cannot be reduced to such a simple outline. The mountains are full of variety, in relief, history, customs, and even cooking. In particular, there is alongside the high mountains that half-mountainous region of plateaux, hills, and foothills that in no way resembles – indeed all its features clearly distinguish it from – the real mountains.

The high plains. Plateaux are large, high, open plains, where the soil, at least in the Mediterranean, is dry and therefore hard, occasionally interrupted by river gorges. Roads and tracks are comparatively easy to establish. The plateau of Emilia, for example, hardly a plateau at all – almost a plain – is criss-crossed with roads and has always been the seat of outstanding civilizations, of which Bologna is the prime symbol. Asia Minor, with its precious tertiary overthrusts (without which it would have been as wild as its neighbours, Kurdistan and Zagros),[157] with its caravans, caravanserais, and stage-post towns, is the centre of an unrivalled history of communications. Even the high Algerian plateaux are like an uninterrupted chain of steppes, from Biskra and the Chott-el-Hodna basin to the Moulouya in Morocco.[158] In the Middle Ages, a great east-west thoroughfare linked these markets and this main artery, before the rise of Bougie, before Algiers and Oran were founded, and the Saracen sea became important in the tenth century,[159] was the physical embodiment of what was known as Africa Minor, between Ifriqiya and Morocco.

---

[154] A. Philippson, *op. cit.*, p. 457.
[155] Alfred von Reumont, *Geschichte Toscana's*, Gotha, 1876, p. 366–367.
[156] *Ibid.*, p. 368 ff.
[157] A. Philippson, *Das Mittelmeergebiet*, p. 20.
[158] And beyond; E.-Félix Gautier has frequently stressed the role of this backbone of North Africa, in among other works, *Le Passé de l'Afrique du Nord*, 1952, p. 115.
[159] Georges Marçais, in *Histoire d'Algérie*, by Gsell, Marçais and Yver, 1927, p. 121.

As for the two pre-Apennine plateaux that extend westward more or less over Umbria and Tuscany, and eastward over Apulia, should we follow Philippson[160] and describe them as the vital theatres of the history and cultural development of the peninsula? Undoubtedly they played a significant role, simply because along these plateaux ran the all-important roads. To the west, on the tuff plateaux of southern Etruria, Rome lost no time in building the Via Flaminia, the Via Amerina, the Via Cassia, the Via Clodia and the Via Aurelia. In the sixteenth century their outlines were still there almost unchanged. Apulia, a vast limestone plateau,[161] not too high, facing eastwards towards Albania, Greece, and the East, is equally accessible to traffic. It is crossed by two parallel strings of towns: one on the coast, from Barletta to Bari and Lecce; the other five miles inland, from Andria to Bitonto and Putignano.[162] From antiquity Apulia has been a centre of habitation between the sea and the almost deserted interior of the Murge. And it was already a cultural centre. Its character as a communications region opened it to western influence – it was Latinized without difficulty[163] – as well as to constant influences by sea from the east, from Greece and Albania; so much so that at certain points in its history Apulia gave the impression of literally turning its back on the rest of the peninsula. It clearly bears the mark of man's continual intervention.[164] In the sixteenth century, wealthy Apulia was a grain-store and an oil reservoir for the rest of Italy. People came from all around in search of foodstuffs. They came in particular from Venice, which was always hoping to gain control of the region – and did twice in 1495 and 1528 – but also from the other towns on the Adriatic, Ragusa, Ancona, Ferrara.[165] Through the intermediary of the little archipelago of the Tremiti and the good offices of the Frati della Carità who lived there, the contraband passage of wheat persisted throughout the sixteenth century.[166]

The finest example of these busy plateaux, however, is in the centre of the Spanish peninsula, the plateau of the two Castiles, Old and New, chequered with roads or rather tracks,[167] which were none the less inundated with people on the move, swarming with caravans of *arrieros*. The carters, whose adventures Cervantes describes, only played a minor role by comparison.[168] These unending processions of beasts of burden, mules and

160 'Umbrien . . .' *art. cit.*, p. 450.
161 Jules Sion, *Géogr. Univ.*, VII, 2, 1934, p. 326.
162 P. Vidal de la Blache, *op. cit.*, (Eng. trans.) p. 136.
163 N. Krebs, 'Zur politischen Geographie des Adriatischen Meers', n *Geogr. Zeitschr.*, 1934, p. 375.
164 I am thinking for example of the *trulli*, but even more of the irrigation system of the plateau-plain, the 'acquedotto pugliese'. Fritz Klute, *Handbuch der geogr. Wissenschaft*, Berlin, 1914, p. 316, provides a good diagram of it, but what is its history?
165 According to A.d.S. Naples, Dipendenze della Sommaria, Fascio 417, fasc. I°, 1572.
166 A.d.S. Naples, Sommaria Consultationum, II, 237–241.
167 Georg Friederici, *Der Charakter der Entdeckung und Eroberung Amerikas durch die Europäer*, I, Gotha, 1925, esp. p. 174–179.
168 In 'The Man of Glass', *The deceitful marriage and other exemplary novels*, Signet classics, 1963, p. 162.

donkeys invisible inder their loads, journeyed over the Castiles from north to south and from south to north. They transported anything that could be sold along the way, wheat and salt, wool and wood, earthenware and pottery from Talavera, as well as passengers.

This carrying trade enabled Castile to maintain the links between the peripheral regions of the peninsula which surround it and in places separate it from the sea. It was this, and not Castile unaided, as has been said,[169] 'which made Spain'. This traffic determined and, it could be said, revealed the basic economy of the country. So it was that for a long period the movement of caravans was directed to the east coast, first to Barcelona, which therefore among its other functions was responsible for selling Spanish wool; then to Valencia, which reached the peak of its fortunes in the fifteenth century,[170] especially in the reign of Alfonso the Magnanimous (1416–1458); and eventually to Málaga and Alicante, which were the great wool ports in the sixteenth century. In his work on the *Grosse Ravensburger Gesellschaft*, A. Schulte suggests that if Valencia declined at the end of the fifteenth century, it was because Castilian traffic, restored in all its vigour under the ordered regime of the Catholic Kings, turned to the North and its thriving towns, Medina del Campo, Burgos, Bilbao, through which Spain made links with powerful northern Europe. This is a reasonable argument that takes account of the movement throughout the area, the caravan traffic to which reference must be made if we are to understand either Spain as a whole or Castile itself with its north–south alignments of towns situated along the transhumance and transport routes – the very same roads taken by the Reconquest; Castile, that was so quickly and effectively brought under control by its kings, and ruled, after Villalar, with that 'rod of iron' mentioned by a Venetian ambassador in 1581[171], for ease of communication is one of the first conditions of effective government. Castile for all these reasons became the heart, the centre of gravity of Spain.[172]

A hillside civilization. Where mountain and plain meet,[173] at the edge of the foothills – in Morocco known as the *Dir* – run narrow ribbons of flourishing, established ways of life. Perhaps it is because between 200 and 400 metres they have found the optimum conditions of the Mediterranean

---

[169] Ortega y Gasset, *España invertebrada*, Madrid, 1934, Similar remarks can also be found in the works of Unamuno, Machado, and Pidal.

[170] A. Schulte, *Geschichte der grossen Ravensburger Gesellschaft*, 1923, notably I, p. 285 ff. and p. 295.

[171] E. Albèri, *Relazioni*, I, V (Francesco Morosini), p. 293.

[172] P. Vidal de la Blache, *États et Nations de l'Europe*, 1889, p. 358.

[173] M. Sorre, *Les fondements biologiques de la géographie humaine*, Paris 1943, p. 386: 'The climate of the foothills and the lowest plateaux is more encouraging to effort, at least in the Mediterranean, than that of the lowlands'. There is a good outline in André Siegfried, *Vue générale de la Méditerranée*, 1943, of the 'mountain fringes' the 'revermonts', to use an expression from the Jura; by these I mean all the foothills, including the curious line of the Piedmonts, that zigzag line which is so important, especially in Andalusia: see G. Niemeyer, *op. cit.*, p. 109.

habitat, above the unhealthy vapours of the plain, but within the limits between which the *coltura mista* can prosper. The mountain's water resources also allow irrigation and the cultivation of the gardens which are the beauty of this narrow region.

In Morocco, on leaving the Atlas for the *Dir*, which lead to the great plains of the west, one finds at the entrance of every valley irrigation channels and along with them the gardens and orchards admired by the Père de Foucauld. Similarly the traveller from the North receives his first impression of Italy, that is of the real Mediterranean, only some time after crossing the Alps, when he reaches the first foothills of the Apennines whose gullied hillsides stretch from Genoa to Rimini dotted with delightful oases. Arriving in spring, he is greeted by a green landscape already bright with flowers, and cultivated fields where white villas stand among vines, ash, and olive trees, while in the Po valley, the bare trees, poplar, willow, and mulberry, still seem to be in the grip of winter. For *coltura mista*, the combination of orchard, market garden and sometimes sown fields, is often localized at the level of the foothills. 'At this altitude (between 200 and 400 metres)', notes Vidal de La Blache,[174] 'is situated the series of *castelli romani* around the Roman campagna, and the ancient *oppida* bordering the unfrequented fringe of the Pontine marshes (it still was unfrequented in Vidal's time) upon the slopes of the Volscians and the age-old cities commanding the almost deserted approaches to ancient Etruria. . . . Gardens fill the foreground, grey mountains the background. The *oppida*, old fortified enclosures, found a foothold on the parts of the mountain spurs which are not cultivable. Urban life is not indigenous there. Instead there is a rather puissant cantonal life. . . . In this crisp pure air, there is both preserved and constantly replenished a race of men which formerly furnished this same Rome with the best of its legionaries, and to-day the labour supply for cultivating the campagna.'

The same kind of hillside landscape overlooks the Adriatic, along the edge of the Dinaric Alps, from around Istria up to Ragusa or Antivari.[175] A narrow strip of Mediterranean life borders the mountains almost as far as the coast, running inland with the contours of the land, reaching as far as Postojna by the Carniola gate, as far as Livno by the Prolog col, or to Mostar in Herzegovina by the fever-ridden valley of the Narenta. In spite of these incursions, this is basically a ribbon phenomenon, quite unlike the vast expanse of Zagora, the *Karst* highland, which is as wide at the latitude of Ragusa as the Alps on a level with Munich, and forms a barrage on the side of the Balkan subcontinent.

It is difficult to imagine a more striking contrast. To the east, the vast

---

[174] *Op. cit.*, p. 149–150.
[175] On the whole of this question see J. Cvijić's book *La Péninsule balkanique*, Fr. trans. 1918, which is full of insights. For descriptive colour see R. Gerlach, *Dalmatinisches Tagebuch*, Darmstadt, 1940. For a geographical description, Milojević, *Littoral et îles dinariques dans le Royaume de Yougoslavie* (Mém. de la Soc. de Géographie, vol. 2), Belgrade, 1933.

mountain ranges, ravaged by the rigours of winter and the catastrophic droughts of summer, a land of herds and unsettled existence, which ever since the Middle Ages, and perhaps before (particularly Herzegovina and Montenegro), has poured its men and animals down on the foothills, towards Moravian Serbia with its poorly drained fluvial beds, towards Sumadija whose forests were formerly impenetrable, towards Croatia-Slavonia to the north and as far abroad as Sirmia. One could hardly imagine a region more primitive, more patriarchal and, whatever the charms of its civilization, in fact more backward. In the sixteenth century this was a combat region, a frontier zone facing the Turks. The *Zagorci* were born soldiers, bandits or outlaws, *hajduk* or *uskok*, 'nimble as deer', their courage was legendary. The mountain terrain lent itself to their surprise attacks, and any number of folk songs, the *pesma*, glorify their exploits: the beys they trounced, the caravans they attacked, and the beautiful maidens they carried off. That these wild mountains should spill over towards Dalmatia is not surprising. But the invasion showed none of the anarchy of the East and North. It was disciplined and carefully filtered by the lowlanders. The flocks of the *Zagorci* met a well-organized resistance: they might overrun Lower Albania, but not the narrow fields and gardens of the coast. They managed to penetrate in only a few places, in particular by way of the Narenta valley. As for the men, they were tamed by the new environment. The brigand became the gendarmes' auxiliary. A possible colonist, he might be directed towards the islands and, even more likely, through the efforts of Venice, towards Istria, where there were more empty fields than anywhere else.[176]

For here, the invader had come face to face with an exceptionally stable and well-ordered civilization, unused to movement, or at any rate to the massive migration and wild flights of the mountain region, a closely knit rural civilization, patiently constructed by hacking out terraced gardens, orchards, vineyards, and fields where the hillside was not too steep. A series of urbanized villages and small towns with narrow streets and tall, closely packed houses was installed in the hollows, the *draga*, the promontories, the isthmuses of the coast. Here the people were hard-working and level-headed, comfortable, if not rich. For like anywhere else in the Mediterranean, only a modest living could be made. It was maintained by battling with nature, with the vast threatening Zagora, and with the Turks; in addition there was always the struggle against the sea. All this required coordinated activity, not people who were free to behave as they pleased. The peasant of Ragusa from the thirteenth century on was in the situation of a colonial settler, of a peasant in semi-slavery. In the

[176] The preceding remarks on 'metanastasic' movements are based on J. Cvijić. His pupils have pursued this problem of emigration from the Slav mountains, e.g., J. Mal, *Uskoke seobe i slovenske pokrajine* (The migrations of the Uskoks and the Slovene regions), Lubljana, 1924, shows how this migration was used in the organization of the Turkish, Venetian and Austrian military zones. R. Busch-Zantner, *op. cit.*, p. 86, draws attention to the Albanian pressure which determined the Serbian migrations towards the north – Albanian and not Turkish pressure.

fifteenth century a cadastral register reveals the similar situation of the peasants round Spalato. In the sixteenth century around the Venetian towns of the *altra sponda*, the fearful farmers had to have the protection of the soldiers. Work gangs of peasants would set off in the morning and return at night under the protection of the troops.[177] This would hardly encourage individualism or peasant unrest, of which there is however some evidence.[178]

The whole of Dalmatian society moreover was dominated by hierarchy and discipline. One has only to think of the role of the noble families of Ragusa. Even in recent times an entire leisured class of *Sjor* or *Signori* existed above a proletariat of humble gardeners and fishermen. 'A fisherman', says Cvijić, 'fishes for himself and for a *Sjor* with whom he is closely associated. The *Sjor* considers him as almost one of his household and the fisherman refuses to sell his fish to anyone else.' 'These societies are so stable,' Cvijić goes on to say, 'that they are as if petrified, fixed once and for all.' This is both true and false, for what we have here is a stable kind of humanity rather than a stable society. In fact, socially, the peaceful foothills develop, change, and progress, particularly when the foothills are in Dalmatia, or on the edge of the Catalan massif, which we might equally well have taken for our example. Their case is complicated by the fact that they do not, like the *castelli romani*, overlook a narrow and limited plain, but onto the sea, which makes their position at the same time easier and more complicated. For the Dalmatian strip is linked by the Adriatic to Italy and the world: it is wide open to outside influence. Venice, which dominated it politically in the sixteenth century, penetrated it with its triumphant civilization, without even trying.

The hills. We meet the same problem when we turn to the hills, particularly the hills of tuff or tertiary limestone which man occupied early and soon brought under control: the hills of Languedoc; the hills of Provence; the hills of Sicily; the hills of Montferrat, those 'islands' in northern Italy; the Greek hills whose classical names are famous; the hills of Tuscany, with their celebrated wines, their villas, and villages that are almost towns, set in the most moving landscape in the world; the *Sahels* of North Africa, well-known in both Tunisia and Algeria.

Between the sea and the Mitijda, up against the miniature Massif

---

[177] J. N. Tomić, *Naselje u Mletackoj Dalmaciji*, Niš, 1915, vol. I, 1409-1645, a short study of the bonds of personal and economic dependence of the peasants in the Venetian possessions in Dalmatia. This regime tended to spread to the islands and the Istrian interior. The Turkish peril caused human losses which Serbian immigration from Bosnia and Herzegovina could no longer compensate. It led to the organization of compulsory militias against attacks, whether from Turks, corsairs, or bandits. On Venetian Dalmatia in the sixteenth century, V. Lamansky, *op. cit.*, especially p. 552 for the exodus of Dalmatian soldiers as far abroad as England, and their employment in the fleet and army of Venice, as well as on foreign boats, where they were attracted by better conditions than were to be found in the Venetian fleet.

[178] Documents read at the Archivio di Stato at Venice, reference not noted.

Central of the Bouzareah, the Sahel of Algiers is the basic component of the *Fahs*, the Algiers countryside.[179] It is an urbanized countryside, divided among the estates of the Turks of Algiers, and shares the dialect of the nearby town, a narrow 'oasis' among the 'nomadic' dialects[180] that surround the urban centre. These hills, cultivated, equipped, and drained – the canals from the Turkish period have been rediscovered in our own day[181] – are lush and green. The gardens, the pride of many Mediterranean towns, are magnificent here, surrounding the white houses with trees and running water. They won the admiration of a Portuguese captive, João Carvalho Mascarenhas, in 1627.[182] His admiration was not feigned: Algiers, a corsair town that grew like the American colonies, was also a town of luxury and art in the Italian fashion at the beginning of the seventeenth century. With Leghorn, which grew up in the same way, it was one of the richest towns of the Mediterranean, and one of the most disposed to convert its wealth into luxury.

A superficial reading of these examples might suggest that the problems here were of a simple nature and above all particular to these regions. The fresh evidence produced in René Baehrel's recent work on Lower Provence in the seventeenth and eighteenth centuries[183] should warn us against such a notion. Viewed in detail, this fragile economy of terraced crops on the hillside is infinitely complex and variable with the passage of time. Between its low retaining walls the bank of earth, known as the *restanque*, or more often *oulière*, is broader or narrower depending on the slope of the hillside. 'Vines were planted on the edge of the *oulière*, trees more or less everywhere'; between vines and trees grew wheat, oats mingled with vetch (for the mules), and above all vegetables ('lentils, peas, *farouns*'). These crops were forced to compete with each other according to market prices; they also had to compete with the produce of neighbouring regions and be incorporated into the richness or poverty of a larger-scale economy than their own. Around Vicenza at the end of the sixteenth century the countryside was all of a piece, made up of 'uninterrupted gardens', although it covered plains, valleys, and *monti*.[184] In the interior of Bas-Languedoc, on the other hand, there are innumerable barren hills that are not worth the trouble of making *rompudes* (clearings).[185] A stony *pech* is often abandoned when times are hard. For the expenditure of human effort on terracing crops does not always pay.

[179] H. Isnard, 'Caractère récent du peuplement indigène du Sahel d'Alger', in *2e Congrès des Soc. sav. d'Afrique du Nord*, 1936.
[180] On this subject cf. G. Millon, 'Les Parlers de la région d'Alger, in *Congrès des Soc. sav. d'Afrique du Nord*, 1937.
[181] M. Dalloni, 'Le problem de l'alimentation en eau potable de la ville d'Alger', in *Bulletin de la Soc. de Géogr. d'Alger*, 1928, p. 8.
[182] Bernardo Gomes de Brito, *Historia tragico-maritima*, Lisbon, vol. VIII, 1905, p. 74.
[183] René Baehrel, *Une croissance: la Basse-Provence rurale, fin du XVIe siècle – 1789*, Paris, 1961, p. 125.
[184] Marciana Library, Venice, 5838, C II, 8, f° 8.
[185] E. Le Roy Ladurie, *op. cit.*, p. 223 ff.

In short, we should not exaggerate the importance of the hillside civilizations, relatively few in number. Sometimes they hold the longest established human population of the Mediterranean, and the most stable landscapes. Some people, Lucien Romier for one,[186] have seen the focal point of Mediterranean civilization, its only creative source, in the hills; but this claim carries with it dangers of oversimplification. We should not be so led astray by the examples of the hills of Tuscany or Languedoc that their clear waters make us forget the other springs which have nourished the great Mediterranean body.

3. THE PLAINS

It is even more easy to be mistaken about the role of the plain in the Mediterranean. If we say mountains, it suggests austerity, harshness, backwardness, and a scattered population. If we say plain, it suggests abundance, ease, wealth, and good living. In the period we are studying, and with reference to Mediterranean countries, the suggestion is likely to be misleading.

There are certainly plenty of plains in the Mediterranean, large and small, installed between the Pyrenean and Alpine foldings, often resulting from a collapse followed by silting up: the age-long work of lakes, rivers, or seas. It is hardly necessary to stress that, whether they are great or small (and only about ten are of any significant size, regardless of their resources), whether they are near or far from the sea, the plains have a totally different aspect from the highlands surrounding them. They do not have the same light, the same colours, the same flowers, or even the same calendar. When winter lingers on in Haute-Provence or in 'Daufiné', it 'lasts no more than a month' in Lower Provence, 'so that even in that season, one may see roses, pinks and orange blossom'.[187] The ambassador de Brèves who, on 26th June, 1605, went with his travelling companions to see the cedars of Lebanon, was astonished by the differences effected by the altitude: 'Here [on the mountains of Lebanon] the vines were only just beginning to flower, as were the olive trees, and the wheat was just turning yellow; and at Tripoli [on the coast] the grapes were growing, the olives were already big, the wheat had been harvested, and all the other fruits were well advanced.'[188] A Flemish traveller, Peter Coeck of Alost, accompanies with illustrations his report in 1553 of the difficulties he encountered besides the 'rain, wind, snow, and hail', crossing the mountains of Slavonia. 'When one reaches the lowland countryside', everything improves: 'Greek women

---

[186] *Plaisir de France*, 1932, p. 119–120: 'the spirit of the Midi was formed on the hills' and not 'on the mountain sides which were then too poor and at periods deserted'. On the people of the hill country, see Isabelle Eberhardt, *Notes de route*, 1921, on the Tunisian Sahel (p. 221), or Marcel Brion on Tuscany and 'its landscape of human dimensions', *Laurent le Magnifique*, 1937, p. 282

[187] Anon. (Claude de Varennes), *Voyage de France, dressé pour l'instruction et la commodité tant des Français que des étrangers*, Rouen, 1647, p. 136.

[188] *Op. cit.*, p. 56–57.

. . . bring to sell to travellers all sorts . . . of useful supplies and provisions such as horse shoes, barley, oats, wine, bread or round loaves baked in hot embers.'[189] Similarly, Philippe de Canaye in 1573 was glad to reach the smiling plains of Thrace after the snow-covered mountains of Albania.[190] Many others have like him rejoiced at the pleasant sight of the warm plains that appear so welcoming.[191]

Or so they appear. They must have been easy to bring under control when they were of small proportions.[192] Man immediately took possession of the rising ground, strategic hillocks, the fluvial terraces,[193] and the foot-hills of the mountains; here he established his large, compact villages, sometimes even towns. But at the lowest point of the basin, always threat-ened by the waters, a dispersed habitat was often the rule. This is how Montaigne saw the plain of Lucca, and Pierre Belon the plain of Bursa; this is how we can still see the plain of Tlemcen, which was already being farmed in Roman times: in the centre, gardens and irrigated fields; on the borders, orchards and vineyards; further away the range of famous villages – the same spectacle that Leo Africanus had before his eyes in 1515.[194] And as if by virtue of Thünen's law of circles, the largest estates of extensive culture were situated farthest from the centres of popula-tion.[195]

When they were larger, the Mediterranean plains were far more difficult to conquer. For a long time they were only very imperfectly and tempor-arily taken over by man. Only recently, towards 1900,[196] was the Mitidja, behind Algiers, finally claimed for cultivation. It was not until after 1922 that Greek colonization eventually triumphed over the marshes in the plain of Salonica.[197] And it was on the eve of World War II that work

[189] B. N. Estampes (Od. 13, pet. in-fol): *Les moeurs et façons de faire des Turcz . . . contrefaictes par Pierre Coeck d'Alost l'an 1533.*

[190] Philippe de Canaye, sieur de Fresne, *Le Voyage du Levant,* 1573, ed. H. Hauser, 1897, p. 40.

[191] Cf. V. Bérard, *La Turquie . . .,* p. 93: for the contrast between Albania with its mountains, its 'violent, earth-stirring' rivers and its passes guarded by *dervendjis*; and Macedonia with its peaceful waters and wreaths of mist. Cf. Paul Bourget, *Sensations d'Italie,* 1891, p. 89–90, for the transition from Tuscany to Umbria; Tuscany may be wild but the air is pure, while over the chestnut trees and vineyards of Umbria hangs the pall of mist and fever.

[192] On the early occupation of the small plains, I agree with H. Lehmann, 'Die geographischen Grundlagen der kretisch-mykenischen Kultur', in *Geogr. Zeitschr.,* 1932, p. 337. Similarly in the Middle East, it is reasonable to suppose that the smaller oases were the first to be settled by man.

[193] Pierre Vilar, *op. cit.,* I, p. 223.

[194] *Op. cit.,* p. 243 ff. G. Marçais, 'Tlemcen, ville d'art et d'histoire', in *2e Congrès des Soc. savantes d'Afrique du Nord,* vol. I, 1936.

[195] G. Neimeyer, *op. cit.,* p. 28. A far-reaching observation. The rural space is organized as a function of and starting from the urban settlement, whether town or village.

[196] On this point see Julien Franc, *La Mitidja,* Algiers, 1931, and E.-F. Gautier, 'Le phénomène colonial au village de Boufarik', in *Un siècle de colonisation,* Algiers, 1930, p. 13–87.

[197] J. Ancel, *La plaine de Salonique,* 1930.

was finished on the draining of the Ebro delta and the Pontine Marshes.[198] In the sixteenth century, then, the big plains were not all rich, far from it. By an apparent paradox, they frequently presented a spectacle of misery and desolation.

Let us take them in turn. The Campagna Romana: a semi-desert, in spite of a further attempt at settlement begun in the fifteenth century. The Pontine Marshes: a roaming ground for a few hundred shepherds and a refuge for herds of wild buffalo; the only abundance here was of wildlife, all kinds of game including wild boars, a sure index of minimal human habitation. The regions of the lower Rhône valley were equally deserted, hardly affected by the few riverside 'improvements' of the previous hundred years.[199] The plain of Durazzo was completely empty; it still is today. Even the Nile delta was only very thinly populated.[200] And the mouth of the Danube was as it has remained to this day, an incredible marshland, a tangled amphibious world, with floating islands of vegetation, muddy forests, fever-infested swamps and, living in this hostile environment where wildlife thrives, a few wretched fishermen. In 1554 Busbecq was passing through the plains beyond Nicaea in Anatolia where there were no villages or houses; it was here, he noted that 'we saw also the famous goats from whose fleece or hair . . . is made the well-known cloth known as camlet', which tells us he was nearing Ankara.[201] The inland plains of Corsica, Sardinia, and Cyprus at the same period were a scene of desolation. On Corfu, the *provveditore* Giustiniano travelled over an almost deserted plain in 1576.[202] The marshes at Biguglia and Urbino in Corsica were a festering sore.[203]

Water problems: malaria. But we need not complete the list of plains that had not reached prosperity in the sixteenth century. For a plain to become rich required prolonged effort and the solutions to two if not three problems. First, there was the problem of flooding. Mountain regions are sources of water: that water normally collects in the plains.[204] In winter,

---

[198] On the Ebro delta, E. H. G. Dobby, 'The Ebro Delta', in *Geogr. Journal*, London, May 1936. On the Pontine marshes, Schillmann, 'Die Urbarmachung der Pontinischen Sümpfe', in *Geogr. Wissenschaft*, 1934.

[199] P. George, *op. cit.*, p. 296–299, 310–322, 348. From the twelfth to the sixteenth century, the Camargue became increasingly unhealthy, p. 606.

[200] J. Lozach, *Le Delta du Nil*, 1935, p. 50.

[201] *Op. cit.*, p. 46. Another example near Adrianople where 'a large area of flooded country is formed where the rivers converge', *Turkish Letters*, p. 88. In Ignacio de Asso, *Hist. de la economia política de Aragon*, 1798, (re-ed., 1947) cf. details of the 'pantanal' of Benavarre (p. 84), the plains of Huesca (p. 72–3) of Saragossa (p. 94 ff.) and Teruel (p. 186).

[202] B.N. Paris, Ital., 1220, fol. 35.

[203] Philippe Leca, *La Corse . . . op. cit.*, p. 213 and 270; J. de Bradi, *op. cit.*, p. 25.

[204] In the rainy season, the plains become lakes or fields of mud (J. J. Tharaud, *La Bataille à Scutari*, 1927, p. 53, on the Albanian plains); the Boyana overflows its banks to make mud-flats and marshes, (*ibid.*, p. 148).

which is the rainy season, plains tend to flood.[205] To avert disaster their inhabitants must take precautions, build dams and dig channels. Even so, there is not a plain in the Mediterranean today, from Portugal to Lebanon, that is not threatened by the danger of flood waters. Even Mecca disappears under torrential rains in some winters.[206]

In 1590 widespread floods submerged the Maremma in Tuscany devastating the sown fields. At that time the Maremma was, with the Arno valley, the chief grain supplier of Tuscany. The Grand Duke was obliged to go to Danzig (for the first time) in search of grain, without which it would not have been possible to bridge the gap. Sometimes violent summer storms alone can produce similar disasters, for water from the mountains rushes down very quickly, almost as soon as it has fallen. Any river bed dry in summer can become a foaming torrent in winter, within a few hours. In the Balkans the Turks built high hog-backed bridges without piles, to give as free a passage as possible to sudden rises in the water level.

When the waters reach the flats, they do not always run smoothly to the sea. Waters from the Alban and Volscian hills form a stagnant stretch about 30 kilometres wide, the Pontine Marshes. The reasons for this are the flatness of the plain, the slow flow of water, and the high line of sand dunes barring the way to the sea. In the case of the Mitidja, the plain, which is bordered to the south by the Atlas, is literally shut off on the north by the hills of the Sahel, only imperfectly breached by the Oued El Harrach and the Oued Mazafran, to the east and west of Algiers. In fact there is almost always stagnant water at these low levels. And the consequence is always the same: 'Acqua, ora vita, ora morte': here water is synonymous with death. Where it stands it creates vast stretches of reeds and rushes. At the very least, in summer it maintains the dangerous humidity of the marshes and river beds, from which come the terrible swamp fevers, the scourge of the plains in the hot season.

Before the use of quinine, malaria was often a fatal disease. Even in a mild form it led to a reduction in the vitality and output of its victims.[207] It

[205] As they were in 1940 in the south of Spain; in January 1941 in Portugal, in February 1941 in Syria; in October 1940 in the Ebro basin (newspaper reports). There were floods at Córdoba on 31st December, 1554 and 1st January, 1555, Francisco K. de Uhágon, *Relaciones históricas de los siglos XVI y XVII*, 1896, p. 39 ff.

[206] Gen. Éd. Brémond, *op. cit.*, p. 17; by the same author, *Yémen et Saoudia*, 1937, p. 11, note 6.

[207] There are countless useful works on malaria. For a bibliographical guide, see Jules Sion, 'Étude sur la malaria et son évolution en Méditerranée' in *Scientia*, 1938, and M. Sorre, *Les fondements biologiques de la géogr. humaine*, 1942, as well as the excellent article by M. Le Lannou, 'Le rôle géographique de la malaria' in *Annales de Géographie*, XLV, p. 112–135. It would be interesting to be able to measure and chart the rise of malaria during the last world war in the Mediterranean when there was a shortage of quinine. For its history, the most important works are: Angelo Celli, 'Storia della malaria nell' agro romano' in *M.R. Ac. dei Lincei*, 1925, 7th series, vol. I, fasc. III; Anna Celli-Fraentzel, 'Die Bedeutung der Malaria für die Geschichte Roms und der Campagna in Altertum und Mittelalter' in *Festschrift B. Nocht*, 1927, 2 pl., 1 map, p. 49–56; 'Die Malaria im XVIIten Jahrhundert in Rom und in der Campagna, im Lichte zeitgenössischer Anschauungen' in *Arch. f. Gesch. der Medizin*, XX, 1928,

wore men out and led to frequent appeals for labour. It is a disease that directly results from the geographical environment. Plague, carried from India and China by long-distance travellers, although greatly to be feared, is only a passing visitor to the Mediterranean. Malaria is permanently installed there. It constitutes the 'background to Mediterranean pathology'.[208] We now know that it is directly linked to the anopheles and haematozoa of the *plasmodium* species, the pathogenic agents of malaria of which the anopheles are only the carriers. Of the country round Aiguesmortes, in about 1596 Thomas Platter said, 'it is so infested with mosquitoes in summer that it is pitiful'.[209] This is the malarial complex known to biologists and connected in fact with the overall geography of the Mediterranean plains, which are the only region seriously and persistently infected, mountain fever being insignificant in comparison.[210]

In order to conquer the plains, then, the unhealthy water had to be dealt with and malaria reduced.[211] The next task was to bring in fresh water for the necessary irrigation.

Man has been the labourer of this long history. If he drains the marshes and puts the plain under the plough, if he manages to produce his food from it, malaria retreats. The best remedy against malaria, says an Etruscan proverb, is a well-filled pot.[212] But if the drainage and irrigation channels are neglected, if the mountains are too quickly deforested, altering the conditions of the flow of the streams, or if the population of the plain falls and the peasant's hold on the land is relaxed, then malaria spreads again and paralyses everything. The plain will soon be reduced to its original marshy state: it is an automatic counter-improvement. This was

p. 101–119; 'La febbre palustre nella poesia' in *Malariologia*, 1930. On malaria in the Crimea, cf. Comte de Rochechouart, *Mémoires, op. cit.*, p. 154.

Some details for the sixteenth century: Cyprus had such a bad reputation for fever that in transport contracts signed with pilgrims to the Holy Land, sea captains had to agree not to put into Cyprus for more than three days, Reinhold Röhricht, *Deutsche Pilgerreisen nach dem Heiligen Lande*, 1900, p. 14. According to G. Botero, *op. cit.*, there are fever-ridden swamps near Salses, p. 5; unhealthy towns are Brindisi, Aquileia, Rome, Ravenna, Alexandria in Egypt, I, l, p. 47. Albenga on the Genoese coast possesses a very rich plain 'ma l'aria n'è pestilente', p. 37. At Pola, the townspeople leave the town in summer because of fever and return in winter, Philippe Canaye, *Le voyage du Levant, op. cit.*, p. 206. Was it malaria from which the queen of Spain suffered at Segovia in August, 1566? (Celestin Douais, *Dépêches de M. de Fourquevaux, ambassadeur de Charles IX en Espagne, 1565–1572*, Paris, 1896–1904, III, p. 10); Philip II had an attack of fever in Badajoz, M. Philippson, *Ein Ministerium unter Philipp II*, Berlin 1895, p. 188.

[208] M. Sorre, *op. cit.*, p. 388. In September, 1566, all of Spain was racked with fever (Fourquevaux to the queen, Segovia, 11th September, 1566, Douais, *op. cit.*, III, 18.)
[209] *Journal of a Younger brother*, trans. Seán Jennett, 1963, p. 89.
[210] Jules Leclercq, *Voyage en Algérie*, 1881, was struck by the ravages wrought by malaria in the lowlying regions of Algeria and wrote, p. 178: 'If Europeans cannot live in the valleys, why do they not build mountain villages'?
[211] One of the problems arising from choosing Ankara as the Turkish capital, in quite recent times, was the malaria prevalent in the neighbouring plain: Noëlle Roger, *En Asie Mineure*, 1930, p. 46.
[212] Quoted by M. Sorre, *Fondements biologiques*, p. 344.

apparently the case in ancient Greece. It has also been suggested that malaria was one of the causes of the decadence of the Roman Empire. This theory is perhaps somewhat exaggerated and too categorical. Malaria progresses when man relaxes his efforts, and its dreaded return is as much a consequence as a cause.

It does seem, however, that there have been in the history of malaria, periods of greater and lesser virulence.[213] There may well have been an increase in marsh fevers at the end of the Roman Empire. That there was another increase towards the end of the fifteenth century is attested by Philipp Hiltebrandt, who unfortunately does not give his sources. Fresh pathogenic elements made their appearance at this time. Along with the *treponema pallidum*, the recently discovered Americas contributed to the old Mediterranean world *malaria tropicalis* or *perniciosa*, which had hitherto been unknown. Pope Álexander VI himself was possibly one of its first victims in 1503.[214]

It is very difficult to pronounce with certainty. Antiquity and the Middle Ages must have witnessed a disease something like *malaria tropicalis*, but it was certainly less dangerous, since Horace crossed the Pontine Marshes without harm in spite of mosquito bites;[215] and more particularly, since in September, 1494, the army of Charles VIII – 30,000 men at the lowest estimate – encamped safely around Ostia, in a particularly dangerous site. But these examples are hardly sufficient to formulate, let alone to solve the problem. We need far more precise documentation of the history of malaria than we possess at the moment. Was it malaria or dysentery that decimated Lautrec's troops in July, 1528, in the flooded countryside around Naples?[216] We need precise knowledge of the regions that were seriously affected by it in the sixteenth century. We do know that Alexandretta, which served as a port for Aleppo from 1593, had to be abandoned later because of fever. We know that Baiae, on the gulf of Naples, which in Roman times was a resort for leisured high society, and which was described as a charming place by Petrarch in a letter to Cardinal Giovanni Colonna in 1343, was deserted by its population, fleeing from fever, in the sixteenth century. But we have only incomplete records of even these particular cases. Of Alexandretta we know that the town was later reoccupied by English and French consuls, and that it has survived; but how? and under what conditions?[217] As for Baiae, is it not because it was already in decline, at least two generations before Tasso

[213] W. H. S. Jones, *Malaria, a neglected factor in the history of Greece and Rome,* London, 1907.

[214] P. Hiltebrandt, *Der Kampf ums Mittelmeer,* 1940, p. 279. Leo X, who was fond of hunting, also seems to have succumbed to an attack of malaria (Gonzague Truc, *Léon X,* 1941, p. 71 and 79). And did not Dante himself die of malaria, as Guido Cavalcanti had twenty years before? (L. Gillet, *Dante,* 1941, p. 340.) As far as we know, that is.

[215] P. Hiltebrandt, *op. cit.,* p. 279.

[216] Bernardo Segni, *Storie fiorentine . . . dall'anno 1527 al 1555,* 1723, p. 4.

[217] J. B. Tavernier, *The Six Voyages,* p. 55, mentions the 'standing pools' of Alexandretta, in 1691.

landed there in 1587, that fever was able to take such a firm grip?[218] On the other hand we should note that about twenty years before Columbus, in 1473, the Venetian fleet, which was operating along the Albanian coast during the first siege of Scutari, was decimated by fever and had to put into Cattaro to recover. The *provveditore* Alvise Bembo died; Triadan Gritti came close to death. Pietro Mocenigo decided to go to Ragusa 'per farsi medicar'.[219]

Nevertheless one cannot escape the impression that there was a fresh outbreak of malaria in the sixteenth century. Perhaps it was because at this time man was running ahead of the enemy. During the whole of the sixteenth century, as indeed of the fifteenth, he was in search of new land. Where was there a more promising prospect than in the shifting marshes of the plains? And precisely the greatest danger lies in the first disturbance of infested regions. To colonize a plain often means to die there: we know how many times the villages of the Mitidja had to be resettled at the beginning, before the plain was won over from fever in the painful struggle of the nineteenth century. The internal colonization which was carried out throughout the Mediterranean in the sixteenth century also took its toll. It was particularly marked in Italy. If Italy took no part in the great movement of colonization of distant territories the reason is perhaps partly to be sought in her preoccupation with reclaiming all available land within her own frontiers, from the flooded plains to the mountain peaks. 'Italy is cultivated right up to the mountain tops,' wrote Guicciardini at the beginning of his *History of Italy*.[220]

The improvement of the plains. To conquer the plains has been a dream since the dawn of history. The vessel of the Danaides might be a folk-memory of the introduction of perpetual irrigation into the plain of Argos.[221] The inhabitants of the shores of Lake Kopaís began to encroach

---

[218] K. Eschmid, in Werner Benndorf, *Das Mittelmeerbuch*, Leipzig, 1940, p. 22. A propos of the extension of malaria, what lies behind the following remark by Stendhal (*Promenades*, II, 164) 'M. Metaxa, I believe, a celebrated doctor and man of wit, has drawn a map of the places affected by fever'?

[219] A.d.S. Venice, Brera 54, f° 144 v°.

[220] Francesco Guicciardini, *La historia d'Italia*, Venice, 1568, p. 2 (Peaceful Italy) 'cultivata non meno né luoghi più montuosi et più sterili, che nelle pianure, et regioni sue più fertili'. Cf. the astonishing observations of Montaigne, *op. cit.*, p. 237, around Lucca, since about fifty years ago, (1581) vines have been taking the place of 'woods and chestnut trees' on the mountains, p. 248; and 'this method they have of cultivating the mountains right up to the peak'. I am not therefore in agreement with Michelet's eloquent remarks, *La Renaissance*, Paris, 1855, p. 31–32. Ph. Hiltebrandt, *op. cit.*, p. 268, sees the problem in the same light as I do. The Italians took part in the great discoveries – Venezuela is after all, little Venice – but the Italian population was not short of space at this period; the bourgeoisie was not interested in the world beyond the Mediterranean horizon; and finally, the Peninsula was not troubled by the religious disturbances which drove Englishmen and Dutchmen overseas.

[221] Herbert Lehmann, 'Die Geographischen Grundlagen der kretisch-mykenischen Kultur,' in *Geogr. Zeitschr.*, 1932, p. 335.

upon its marshy edges at a very early date.[222] The network of underground canals covering the Roman Campagna, of which archaeologists have found traces, dates back to Neolithic times.[223] We know too of the primitive works of the Etruscans in the narrow plains of Tuscany.

Between these early attempts and the vast 'improvements' of the nineteenth and twentieth centuries mentioned above, the struggle was never abandoned although it may have been relaxed at times. Mediterranean man has always had to fight against the swamps. Far more demanding than the problem of forest and scrubland, this colonization is the distinguishing feature of his rural history. In the same way that northern Europe established itself or at any rate expanded to the detriment of its forest marches, so the Mediterranean found its New World, its own Americas in the plains.

Throughout the sixteenth century, as indeed in the fifteenth, many improvement schemes were under way with the limited means available to the period: ditches, trenches, canals, low-powered pumps. In the following century Dutch engineers perfected more efficient techniques.[224] But the Dutch engineers had not yet made their appearance in the period under discussion. The inadequacy of means therefore limited the undertakings. The marsh was attacked sector by sector, which led to many failures. In Venetia, in the Adige Valley, Montaigne in 1581 came across 'an infinite expanse of muddy sterile country covered with reeds',[225] formerly ponds that the Signoria had tried to drain, 'to put under the plough . . . ; they lost more than they gained by trying to alter its nature', he concluded. Similarly whatever the 'press' of the period – the official chroniclers – might say, the enterprises of Grand Duke Ferdinand in the Tuscan Maremma and the hollow of the Val di Chiana were not a success.[226]

In the Maremma the grand dukes, from Cosimo on, tried to create a grain-producing region (the equivalent on a grander scale of what Genoa attempted in the eastern plain of Corsica). To this end measures to encourage population were taken, advances were offered on capital and yield,

[222] August Jardé, *Les Céréales dans l'Antiquité grecque*, 1925, p. 71, references to Strabo. A. Philippson, 'Der Kopais-See in Griechenland und seine Umgebung,' in *Zeitschr. der Gesellschaft für Erdkunde zu Berlin*, XXIX, 1894, p. 1–90. P. Guillon, *Les Trépieds du Ptoion*, 1943, p. 175–195.

[223] M. R. de la Blanchère, 'La malaria de Rome et le drainage antique,' in *Mélanges d'Arch et d'hist.*, published by the French School at Rome, II, 1882, p. 94 ff.

[224] Was the first of these 'Hollanders', these northerners, the engineer – or *dijkmeester* – whom the *nuncio* sent to Ferrara at the request of the Pope in 1598, and who seems to have been thinking of using windmills to drain the water. *Correspondance de Frangipani*, published by Armand Louant, 1932, Vol. II, Brussels, 13th June, 17th June, 25th July, 13th August, 1598, p. 345, 348, 362–3, 372.

[225] Montaigne, *op. cit.*, p. 138.

[226] A. von Reumont, *Geschichte Toscana's*, I, p. 358 ff. On the same subject, O. Corsini, *Ragionamento istorico sopra la Val di Chiana*, Florence, 1742; V. Fossombroni, *Memorie idraulico-storiche sopra la Val di Chiana*, Florence, 1789; Michelet, *Journal inédit*, p. 169–170. In the sixteenth century there was an unsuccessful attempt to improve lake Castiglione, A. von Reumont, *op. cit.*, I, p. 369.

manpower was recruited and here and there drainage schemes carried out. Grosseto on the Ombrona was then becoming a port for the export of grains to Leghorn. The reasons for the semi-failure of the scheme were spelled out long ago by Reumont in his *History of Tuscany*.[227] The grand dukes were pursuing two contradictory ends. They were creating a grain-producing plain, which entails great outlay, and setting up a monopoly of the purchase of the grain for their own advantage, that is for selling at a low price. What they should have done was to throw the market open to the competition of all the Mediterranean buyers. For these improvement schemes were expensive and the return on them, the *utilità*, was not always worth the outlay. In 1534 the Orators of Brescia pointed out to the Venetian Senate that 'to divert and contain the waters requires infinite expense; so much so that several of our citizens have been ruined through wanting to further such enterprises. Besides the initial expense of bringing the water, there is the continual cost of maintenance, so that when it is all reckoned there is very little difference between expense and profit.'[228] In this case evidently the people of Brescia were producing arguments and pleading poverty to avoid paying too many taxes, but it is nevertheless true that improvement schemes were large undertakings which required much financing. Ideally they were undertaken by governments.

In Tuscany it might be an 'enlightened' government that took charge of them, or as in 1572, a prince from the ducal family, the future Grand Duke Ferdinand who was interested in possible improvements in the marshy Val di Chiana.[229] It was on the initiative of the Duke of Ferrara that what came to be called the *grande bonifica estense* was set up in the Valle di Ambrogio in 1570, in the heart of the vast marshy region of the Po delta. It was hindered by subsidence and the return of the infected waters and finally condemned by the same *taglio* of Porto Viro that in 1604 gave permission for Venice to divert the course of the river Po to the south via the open breach.[230] At Rome it was the pontifical government;[231] at Naples, the viceroy who initiated an official project for draining the great marshes

---

[227] I, p. 366 ff.

[228] A. Zanelli, *Delle condizioni interne di Brescia, dal 1642 al 1644 e del moto della borghesia contro la nobiltà nel 1644*, Brescia, 1898, p. 242–3.

[229] A. von Reumont, *op. cit.*, I, p. 363–364. Still in Tuscany, in about 1550, there was a scheme to improve the marshes of Ansedonia (G. Venerosi Pesciolini, 'Una memoria del secolo XVI sulle palude di Ansedonia' in *La Maremma*, VI, 1931)· H. Wätjen notes that in the reign of the Grand Duke Ferdinand, a major preoccupation in Tuscany was the draining of the marshes, *Die Niederländer im Mittelmeergebiet*, 1909, p. 35. On an improvement plan for the Sienese Maremma proposed to the king of France in 1556, cf. Lucien Romier, *Les origines politiques des guerres de religion*, 1913–1914, II, p. 397–398.

[230] Hansjörg Dongus, 'Die Reisbaugemeinschaft des Po-Deltas, eine neue Form kollektiver Landnutzung', in *Zeitschift für Agrargeschichte und Agrarsoziologie*, October 1963, p. 201–202; C. Errera, 'La bonifica estense nel Basso Ferrarese', in *Rivista Geogr. Ital.*, 1934, p. 49–53.

[231] On the improvements in the papal states in the time of Pius V, Pastor, *op. cit.*, XVII, p. 84.

of Cherranola and Marellano near Capua.[232] At Aquileia it was the Imperial government.[233] In Turkey from the little we can see, it seems that land improvement was the work of enterprising noblemen who created new villages of serfs – *čiftliks* – particularly from the seventeenth century on, in the low-lying marshy regions as well as in the Durazzo plain or on the edge of the Vardar.[234] These are large villages, easily recognizable from the hovels clustering around the tall master's house, that towers and watches over them.

In the West, too, a series of improvements were the result of individual initiatives by wealthy capitalists. It was they who in the sixteenth century established rice fields in the lowest parts of Lombardy which developed so quickly that they were certainly exporting their produce to Genoa in 1570, and perhaps even earlier. A former patrician of Venice – struck off the list of nobles, as the result of injustice, according to him, but still possessed of a good fortune – tried to lay sacrilegious hands on the Venetian lagoons. The authorities were alerted and became worried. Could anyone seriously be thinking of transforming the lagoons into cultivable land? Were not changes in the level to be feared? The enterprise was classified as undesirable.[235]

The capitalists led the way in lower Languedoc too, with the great drainage works beginning in 1592 and carried on with more or less energy and success until about 1660–1670. Identical works had been begun near Narbonne in 1558, when they began to drain the pools. But at the end of the century with the first embankments around Lake Launac, the movement gained speed. Provençal engineers, specialists in hydraulics and disciples of Adam de Craponne, lent their assistance. A 'group' (Bernard de Laval, Dumoulin, Ravel) directed this operation and the following ones, also in the Narbonne area. It was Laval, lord of Sault who provided the original sum of money, and later the 'supplements'.[236]

These improvement schemes arose in reply to the needs of the towns, whose population in the fifteenth and sixteenth centuries was steadily

[232] B. N. Paris, Esp. 127, f° 20 v° and 21. This was a scheme which was considered by the 'Camera' in 1594, but eventually abandoned. However the Count of Olivares was very interested in it. The authorities were prepared to farm out the works.

[233] On a possible drainage scheme at Aquileia, Giacomo Soranzo to the Doge, Vienna, 7th August, 1561, G. Turba, *Venet. Depeschen*, 13, p. 191.

[234] At any rate this is how I interpret the book by Richard Busch-Zantner, *Agrarverfassung, Gesellschaft und Siedlung in Südosteuropa*, Leipzig, 1938, whose argument is somewhat obscured by the wealth of material. As I see it, for him, unlike Cvijić, the *čiftlik* is not an ancient type of village dating back to the Middle Ages (p. 104–5) but a recent type, set up in the sixteenth century and becoming more widespread in the seventeenth. It is therefore a village born of modern colonization and improvement. It is generally situated right down in the plains, near the waters of lakes and valleys and frequently exposed to flooding (p. 124). Ömer Lütfi Barkan agrees with my interpretation.

[235] R. Cessi, 'Alvise Cornaro e la bonifica veneziana nel sec. XVI', in: *Rend. R. Acc. Lincei, Sc. Mor., St. e Fil.*, VIth series, vol. XII, p. 301–323. Reviewed by F. Braudel, in *Ann. d'Hist. Sociale*, 1940, p. 71–72.

[236] E. Le Roy Ladurie, *op. cit.*, p. 442 ff. Adam de Craponne, 1519–1559, built the canal named after him which irrigated the Crau in about 1558, between the Durance and the Rhône.

increasing. The urgent need for a food supply impelled the towns to develop crop cultivation all around them either by taking over fresh ground or by extending irrigation. This gave rise to many disputes but also to some fruitful agreements. 'We should achieve a good supply of water by diverting the Oglio,' say the Orators of Brescia in 1534, 'but it would lead us into endless litigation with the people of Cremona, not to mention the risk of assassination of which we have already had some experience.'[237] In 1593 the Rectors of Verona, with the support of Venice, had the works of the, Mantuans to retain the waters of the Tartaro demolished; this was followed by long-drawn-out wrangles.[238] In Aragon in the eighteenth century the towns were still involved in disputes, each trying to obtain the precious sources of irrigation from its neighbours.[239] On the other hand, from the fifteenth century on, riverside communities cooperated with each other on the drainage works of the Lower Rhône valley, works which would in any case have been unthinkable without the capital provided by Italian immigrants and the labour force from the Alps.[240]

Whether pursued in cooperation or in competition, the efforts made by the towns were successful. They created, within reach of the central markets, the vegetable gardens and wheatfields they needed. A Venetian ambassador passing through Castile concluded that it was cultivated only around the towns. The wide *paramos* where sheep grazed and the *secanos* reserved for wheat, yellow plains where even the houses built of earth can hardly be distinguished from their background, appeared to him to be stretches of barren countryside. Around the Castilian towns on the other hand he had seen the green patches of irrigated land. At Valladolid, orchards and gardens bordered the banks of the Pisuerga. In Madrid itself, Philip II could only extend the Prado by buying up vineyards, gardens and orchards: we have the deeds of sale to prove it.[241] At Toledo, the Vega 'striped with trees and crops' is under the town walls. The same link between town and agricultural effort is found in Provence. New land was brought into cultivation in the sixteenth century at Mandelieu, Biot, Auribeau, Vallauris, Pégomas, Valbonne, Grasse, Barjols, St. Rémi, St. Paul de Fogossières, and Manosque. Market gardens were developed all along the Durance valley.[242] In lower Languedoc '*orts* and irrigated

---

[237] A. Zanelli, *op. cit.*, p. 243.

[238] A.d.S. Venice, *Annali di Venezia*, 11th April, 1593 ff.

[239] I. de Asso, *op. cit.*, p. 72–73.

[240] P. George, *op. cit.*, p. 292–294.

[241] Purchases in the direction of the Vega Gate, towards the new Segovia bridge, beyond Manzanares, around the Real Casa de Campo which Philip II had converted. See in particular Simancas, Patronato Real, deeds of sale, nos. 3142 to 3168.

[242] Pierre Imbart de la Tour, *Les origines de la Réforme*, I, Melun, 1949, p. 218. We still have to distinguish between genuine improvement and the colonization of new land in general. The movement towards land reclamation began in France, as it did in England, in the middle of the XVth century (René Gandilhon, *Politique économique de Louis XI*, 1940, p. 147). The improvement schemes in the Savoy domains are described somewhat briefly in the rather derivative work by F. Hayward, *Histoire des ducs de Savoie*, 1941, II, p. 40.

meadows in fact form only a minute proportion of the land holdings, as in Spain': they are 'well-watered, restricted to the urban belts where the *seigne* is situated – the draw well which alone accounts for 30 per cent of the value of a garden'.[243]

A large-scale transfer of urban investment to the countryside was therefore taking place.[244] The search for new land for cultivation became of public concern from the end of the century. Olivier de Serres, in his *Théâtre d'Agriculture*,[245] gives full instructions on converting marshy land. But the task was only tackled piecemeal. The striking fact about the history of the whole undertaking is the incredibly long time it took to bring the plains to life. Yet the work, hardly complete in the sixteenth century, had begun hundreds of years previously. This is true of all plains: of Murcia and of Valencia, of Lerida, Barcelona and Saragossa, of the Andalusian plain and the Po valley, the *campagna felice* of Naples and the Conca d'Oro of Palermo or the plain of Catania. Every generation contributed its strip of land rescued from the waters. One of the merits of the government of Pietro di Toledo at Naples was to have drained the marshy *Terra di Lavoro* near the city, between Nola, Aversa, and the sea, and to have made of it, according to one chronicler, 'la più sana terra del mondo', with its canals, its trenches, its fertile crops, and its drained fields.[246]

The small plains were the first to be conquered. The plains of the coastal massif of Catalonia had been claimed by man for his precious crops as early as the high Middle Ages. The digging of the *cequies* dates back traditionally to the reign of Hacam II. There is nothing to prove that they are not older still. It is quite certain however that Lerida, which was reconquered in 1148, had already been made fertile by the Clamor canals; that Tortosa had its irrigation channels from the time of the Arabs; that Camarasa, when it was reunited with the County of Barcelona in 1060, also had its water trenches. Following the example of the Moslems, the counts of Barcelona for their part set up the irrigation system of the territory covered by the town itself, and of the Llobregat plain. It is to one of them, Count Mir (945–966), that the famous *rech* of the Barcelona county is attributed – the *rego mir* – as well as the construction of another canal, from the Llobregat to Cervello. The legacy was received, preserved and continually added to by later generations.[247]

There was a similar progression in the case of the plain of Saragossa, an important zone of *tierras de riego*, 'irrigated lands'. The foundations were already established when the Moslems were expelled from the town in 1118. But after the original operation, the works were developed and

[243] E. Le Roy Ladurie, *op. cit.*, p. 86–87.

[244] This is surely one aspect of the economic crisis of Barcelona – its bourgeoisie invested its money in land, not wishing to risk it any further in maritime ventures.

[245] Drainage by hen's foot trenches' (*pieds de gélines*), Olivier de Serres, *Pages choisies*, 1942, p. 64.

[246] 'Vita di D. Pietro di Toledo' in *Archivio Storico Italiano*, IX, p. 21–22.

[247] F. Carreras y Candi, *Geografía General de Catalunya*, Barcelona, 1913, p. 471–472.

extended. Thus the Grand Canal was projected in 1529, work began on it in 1587, and it was finally completed in 1772, at a time when the entire plain of Aragon, under the influence of the agronomists of the age of enlightenment, was revising and completing its irrigation network.[248]

The example of Lombardy. But the best example of these progressive conquests – because it is the clearest to see – is that of Lombardy.[249] Let us leave aside the higher regions: on one side the Alps, unproductive above 1500 metres, stony masses with terraced pastures and forests between 700 metres and 1500 metres; on the other, the Apennines, whose raging torrents rush down to the plains in winter, rolling stones and boulders in their swirling waters, but in summer dry up completely so that there is no water either for irrigation or consumption. As a result the Apennines above 1000 metres are as barren as the Alps above 2000 metres; in summer they afford only a few tufts of grass fit for goats and sheep.

Between these two ramparts, lower Lombardy is a complex of hills, plateaux, plains and river valleys. The hills are the region of vines and olives, and even citrus fruits grow near the great Alpine lakes. There are 'plateaux' in the true sense of the word only in the North. First a plateau without irrigation, a rectangular block defined to the south by a line joining Vicolungo and Vaprio, on the Adda, covered with barren stretches of scrubland and given over to growing mulberry trees; a low, irrigated plateau comes next, forming a triangle whose southern side runs from Magenta on the Ticino to Vaprio on the Adda, and where wheat, mulberry trees, and pastures are plentiful.

The most interesting feature of the Lombardy lowlands is the vast alluvial plain, between this plateau and the foothills of the Apennines, in other words the bottom of the bowl, the classic zone of rice fields, pasture lands, and equally important, of artificially created prairies. The selling price of hay has even been used as the basis of an attempt to show the general movement of prices in Milan in the sixteenth century.[250]

Man has entirely transformed this plain. He has flattened the land, eliminated the swamps and made intelligent use of the water brought by the rivers from the Alpine glaciers. The regulation of the water began in at least 1138 with the works of the Benedictine[251] and the Cistercian monks, at Chiaravalle Abbey. In 1179, work began on the *Naviglio Grande* which was finished in 1257 by the *podestà* Beno Gozzodini. The waters of the Ticino were now brought to Milan by an artificial river nearly 50 kilometres

[248] Esp. I de Asso, *op. cit.*, p. 94 ff.

[249] The following relies particularly on the remarkable article by S. Pugliese, 'Condizioni economiche e finanziarie della Lombardia nella prima meta del secolo XVIII', in *Misc. di st. it.*, 3rd series, vol. XXXI, 1924, p. 1–508, which contains in the opening pages not only a good geographical description of Lombardy but also much information relating to the sixteenth century.

[250] A. Fanfani, 'La rivoluzione dei prezzi a Milano nel XVI e XVII secolo', in *Giornale degli economisti*, July, 1932.

[251] E. Lucchesi, *I Monaci benedettini vallombrosani in Lombardia*, Florence, 1938.

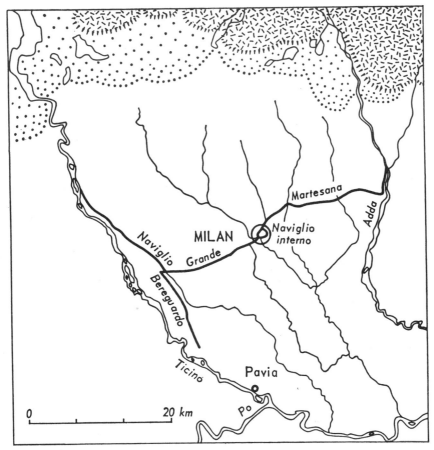

Fig. 3: *The great canals of the Lombardy plain*

From Charles Singer, *History of Technology*, 1957, vol. III. The dotted area indicates morainic deposits and hills preceding the Alps.

long which could be navigated and used for irrigation. Before 1300 the Basca *roggia* was diverted from the Sesia; later it would be tapped to feed the Biraga, Bolgara, and other *roggie* that irrigated the Novarese and Lomellina. In 1456 Francesco Sforza built the Martesana canal, over 30 kilometres long, bringing the waters of the Adda to Milan. It was widened in 1573 to make it navigable. Since Ludovic the Moor had already linked it with the *Naviglio Grande*, in 1573 the two great lakes of Lombardy, Lake Como and Lake Maggiore, were brought into communication at the very heart of the state.[252] Milan now became an important waterways centre, which enabled it to receive wheat, iron, and in particular wood, at less

[252] S. Pugliese, *art. cit.*, p. 25–27.

expense, and to ship off to the Po and Ferrara the large artillery pieces made in its foundries – in fact to compensate for its major disadvantage of being a town surrounded by land.[253]

Even this evidence, which only concerns waterways, shows how slow the process of land reclamation was. It was accomplished in stages, each one corresponding to the installation of different social groups, so that the three Lombardies were encapsulated one within the other, each representing a different group of people. Upper Lombardy, the mountainous, pastoral region, which in the north comes close to the zone of the *brughiere*, is the country of small peasant proprietors, poor but free, devoting their lives to producing all their needs from their land, including the poor wine of their vineyards. Lower down on the well-watered plateau of the upper plain, the region of springs (*fontanili*) and grassy meadows, begins the ecclesiastical and noble property. At this level, a little higher than the plain itself are to be found the castles, the tenant farmers, and the monasteries shaded by their tall trees. Lower down again are the rice fields belonging to the capitalists.[254] Their revolutionary initiative resolved the problem of cultivating the flooded fields. Economic progress was assured – but at the price of social misery.

Rice growing in Lombardy meant the enslavement under terrible conditions of workers who were unable to voice any effective protest since they were not organized. Rice fields do not require labour all the year round, but large numbers of casual workers for a few weeks, at the times of sowing, transplanting, and harvest. This kind of agriculture depends entirely on seasonal migration. It hardly requires the landowner to be present except for paying wages and overseeing the gangs at work. Centuries later Cavour would go to his property in Leri in nearby lower Piedmont, personally settling wages and rising at dawn to supervise the labourers.[255]

This is true of almost all the crops grown in the plain. Land which is easy to work, where the furrows can be drawn up with a line, lends itself to the regular employment of oxen or buffaloes, animal mechanization. It is only at the season of harvest and grape gathering that it calls for the massive recruitment of mountain labourers. After a few weeks of work these

[253] G. de Silva to H.M. 17th April, 1573, Simancas E° 1332.

[254] A. Schulte, *op. cit.*, I, 252, thinks that rice-growing was introduced to Lombardy from Spain before 1475. Rice was exported to Germany for the first time by a native of Basel, Balthasar Irmi. On the introduction of rice by Louis XII, Marco Formentini, *Il Ducato di Milano*, Milan, 1876, II, p. 600 ff. On the problem in general, S. Pugliese, *art. cit.*, p. 35.

[255] Maurice Paléologue, *Un grand réaliste, Cavour*, 1926, p. 21. On the larger question of the need of the plains for agricultural labourers, cf. the example of Languedoc (Georges Lefebvre, *La Grande Peur de 1789*, Paris, 1957, p. 17); at the time of the French Revolution the agricultural labourers of Bas-Languedoc came from the Causses and the Black Mountain. Another example is that of Thrace whose labourers come from Upper Bulgaria and did so in the seventeenth century too according to Herbert Wilhelmy, *Hochbulgarien*, Kiel, 1936, p. 325. Thessaly, (which we know exported grain via Vólos) relied on central Greece and even Attica for its labour force, Vandoncourt, *Memoirs on the Ionian Islands*, 1816, p. 215. On these two Balkan examples see R. Busch-Zantner, *op. cit.*, p. 94.

labourers return home. They are the true rural proletariat. But the peasant farmer who settles in the plain is often in very much the same situation.

The Spanish enquiry of 1547[256] on property in Lombardy indicates that the peasants possessed less than 3 per cent of the land in the fertile lower region, while the poor land on the hills was very largely in their hands. Nothing could indicate better than these figures the conditions of life in the plain. Here the peasant lived off very little, in deplorable conditions of health and hygiene. He had masters and what he produced went to them. Often a newcomer, a simple man from the mountains, he might be cheated by the landowner or his steward. In many ways he was a kind of colonial slave, whatever his precise position in law.

Big landowners and poor peasants. We were comparing the converted plains of the Mediterranean with the cleared forests of northern Europe. Like any other comparison this one has its limits. In the new towns in the forest clearings of the North there grew up a more free civilization on the American pattern. One of the problems of the Mediterranean, and one of the causes of its traditionalism and rigidity, was that (apart from a few regions where colonization encouraged agrarian individualism[257]) newly-acquired land remained under the control of the wealthy. A pick and an axe might be enough in the North, as it was later to be in America, to make the soil productive. In the Mediterranean rich and powerful landowners had an essential role to play, increasingly so as small-scale improvements were abandoned in favour of extensive, long-term schemes. The goal could only be achieved by holding ranks under a discipline possible only through a rigid social order. How could Egypt or Mesopotamia have been cultivated by independent peasant farmers in the sixteenth century? In Spain the traveller passing from the *secanos* to the *regadios* – from the dry to the irrigated zones – left behind a relatively free peasant to find a peasant slave. Spain had inherited all the great irrigation networks from the Moslems after the Reconquest, taking them over intact along with the labour force of *fellahin* who were necessary to keep them in good order. The Lerida plain was still being worked by *fellahin* in the sixteenth century; *fellahin* were farming the Rioja in the Ebro valley; and *fellahin* were to be found in Valencia, Murcia, and Granada: *fellahin* or, more accurately Moriscos, whose Spanish masters cared for and protected them in the same spirit as they would their livestock and exactly as they were to protect their slaves in the New World.

The plains were the property of the nobleman.[258] One has to go down to the Portuguese *veigas* to find the houses of the *fidalgos*, the *solares* with

---

[256] S. Pugliese, *art. cit.*

[257] P. George, *op. cit.*, p. 354.

[258] To the nobleman and even more, to large estates even when the plain had not been improved. This was so almost up to the present day (R. Pfalz, *art. cit.*, in *Geogr. Zeitschrift*, 1931, p. 134): before the recent improvements, 38 per cent of the land of the *Campagna* had belonged to four big landowners; while 'in general the mountain regions are the reserve of smallholders' (*ibid*). Jules Sion, *La France Méditerranéenne*

their great coats of arms.[259] The vast low-lying plain of the Sienese Maremma, a real fever trap, is, like its neighbour the Tuscan Maremma, dotted with noblemen's castles. Their anachronistic silhouettes of tower and keep conjure up a whole society, the crushing presence of the feudal landlords who dominated the country without even living there, for these residences were only their temporary abodes. Most of the year the masters lived in Siena, in the huge town houses still standing today, palaces into which Bandello's lovers find their way, with the ritual complicity of the servants, up staircases leading to the great attics where sacks of grain are stored, or along corridors leading to the rooms on the ground floor, always a little neglected.[260] We can follow them into the houses of these old families to relive the comedies and tragedies whose dénouement would take place in secret in the old castle in the Maremma, far from the town gossip and family control. Isolated from the world by fever and the sultry heat, what better place could there be for putting to death, according to the custom of Italy and the century, an unfaithful wife – or one suspected of being so? The climatic explanation would have delighted Barrès. But was there not also an element of social complicity, which allowed the murderer almost total impunity in the low lands where he was absolute master? Was the plain the rich man's fief to do as he liked with?

'In the plain,' writes Robert Montagne[261] of the Moroccan Sous of today, 'the distance between rich and poor increases rapidly. The former own gardens, the latter work in them. The irrigated fields yield in plenty cereals, vegetables, and fruits. Another source of wealth is olive and argan oil, which is transported in goatskins to the northern towns. The greater proximity of markets encourages the introduction of foreign produce, so that the life of a *notable* in the Sous plain tends to become similar to that in the other provinces where the Maghzen has always reigned. But at the same time, the life of the labourers in the gardens, the *klemmas*, becomes increasingly wretched.' This seems to have been the rule in the Mediterranean plains. A considerable distance separates rich from poor; the rich are very rich and the poor very poor.

1934, p. 143, makes a further distinction. 'The regions where there are the largest number of holdings are the hilly areas where farming is relatively archaic and the yields (today) are poor; large estates are the rule in the plains with their superior yields, particularly the lands recently reclaimed at great expense from the marshes'. On this subject, see G. Niemeyer's information, *op. cit.*, p. 29–30 and 59, on the contrast between Córdoba, an old centre with large estates and Carlotta, a new town founded in the eighteenth century, where the land was divided up into many holdings. I personally think that a considerable role was played by the monocultures which took over in the plains (wheat for instance in the past) and tended to lead to the creation of large estates.

[259] P. Descamps, *Le Portugal. La vie sociale actuelle*. Paris 1935, p. 14. Near Vieira, in the Minho 'the mountains are democratic; lower down, by the time one reaches Vieira, one finds the *fidalgos* belonging to ancient noble families. There are still *solares* at Vieira and in a few parishes'.

[260] M. Bandello, *op. cit.*, I, Novella 12.

[261] *Op. cit.*, p. 48.

Large estates have remained the rule in the plains. Here, the seignorial system – which is often the façade for large estates – found natural conditions for survival. In Sicily, in Naples, in Andalusia, the entailed estates of the noble landowners have been handed down undiminished right up to the present day. Similarly, in the great eastern plains of the Balkans, in Bulgaria, Rumelia, and Thrace, in the grain and rice producing regions, the Turkish regime of large estates and serf-villages took strong root, whereas it more or less failed in the mountains of the West.[262]

There are many exceptions according to locality and circumstances, such as the early Roman Campagna, or the present day peasant democracy of Valencia, or those of Ampurdán and Roussillon. 'These plains,' writes Maximilien Sorre of the latter two[263] 'have always been the land of small and medium-sized farms.' For 'always', read 'in modern times'. In fact we do not know what was happening in these lowland districts before the agrarian troubles of the fourteenth century, above all before the great collective irrigation schemes, even those undertaken for example by the Templars of Mas Deu, in the Roussillon basins of the Réart and Cantarane. What is clear is that we have a rule and a number of exceptions – not the only rule nor the only exceptions. In Provence 'it is rare to find a rural proletariat, except in the plain of Arles, which is divided into a number of great estates'.[264] In Catalonia there was a prosperous peasantry, at least after 1486.[265] Perhaps if an overall explanation is to be flexible enough, we shall have to reconsider at length the deceptively simple notions of small property and large estate (large or powerful?); to distinguish between plains according to their size and whether they have been divided up or not; and, above all, there should be research to discover whether – and with what logical explanation – there have been successive alterations in the system of property owning and farming: whether land has been subdivided, brought back under one holding, only, perhaps, to be divided up again. In one place it may be the size of the population; in another the implantation of new crops, the introduction of tools, or their continued use; elsewhere the extended impact of the nearby towns that has continually upset the geographical and social order of the lowlands; while in other regions, the tyranny of the wheatfields and the swing-plough (according to Gaston Roupnel), and the use of oxen has helped to maintain the established order and the power of the rich. This is the great

---

[262] J. Cvijić, *op. cit.*, p. 172. On the Bulgarian peasant, his work and his comparative well-being in the fifteenth century, his carts drawn by yoked oxen or buffaloes, see Ivan Sakazov, *Bulgarische Wirtschaftsgeschichte*, Berlin-Leipzig, 1929, p. 197; the peasant of the plain, much more than either mountain dweller or townsman, is attached to his environment. On the Nile delta, J. Lozach, *op. cit.*, p. 38. On the desolation there in the sixteenth century, *ibid.*, p. 50.

[263] *Pyrénées méditerranéennes*, p. 245. NB in the Camargue, which is an analogous case, the great estates owned before the Revolution, by the Knights of Malta, J. J. Estrangin, *Études archéologiques, historiques et statistiques sur Arles*, 1838, p. 307.

[264] F. Benoit, *op. cit.*, p. 26.

[265] Pierre Vilar, *op. cit.*, I, p. 575 ff.

value of the pioneering work of Emmanuel Le Roy Ladurie[266] on the peasants of Languedoc, between the fifteenth and the eighteenth centuries. Who would have thought, before his research, that this rural order was to such an extent the result of a combination of social, demographic, and economic circumstances, and therefore constantly subject to change and alteration? The problem will now be to find out whether the timetable of the successive peasant orders of the Languedoc is applicable to the other coastal regions and if we shall find some of them ahead, some lagging behind, but the majority keeping pace. We are far from knowing the answer at the moment.

Short term change in the plains: the Venetian Terraferma. We can attempt to follow these short-term changes in one example at least: Venice.

The low-lying regions of the Venetian countryside, which are also the richest and most populated, were the object of frequent improvements beginning before the end of the fifteenth century. We can guess at their scale without unfortunately knowing their geographical extent or their precise chronology. These costly schemes that began so early do not usually seem to have brought any advantage to peasant farmers or village communities.

At first sight there could be nothing more reasonable than the usual course of these improvement schemes, kept to an unvarying programme over a period of centuries, under the prudent procedures, generally governed by precedent, of the Venetian administration, which after 1566 was in the hands of the *Provveditori ai beni inculti*.[267] Every improvement, every *ritratto*, established for a defined area of obviously marshy land a programme of various hydraulic works: dykes built or to be built (*argile*), entry points for water (*presi*), and canals and trenches for distributing irrigation streams (*scalladori*). Sometimes small craft used the canals that had already been constructed and a toll was established, which partially recouped the expense. But in the short term, the owners of the land had to pay for these costly installations, at the rate of one or two ducats per *campo*,[268] depending on whether the land was cultivated, and whether it bore vineyards or only trees. If a landowner was unable to pay his contribution when it fell due, half of his property was exacted in payment, which indicates that the debt per *campo* was not insignificant.

The *ritratto* was sometimes the responsibility of one of the city's

[266] See above, note 58.
[267] Daniele Beltrami, *Forze di lavoro e proprietà fondiaria nelle campagne venete dei secolo XVII e XVIII*, 1961, p. 67, gives the date as 1574; until there is more evidence I incline to the date 1566 given by Andrea da Mosto, *Archivio di Stato di Venezia*, 1937, vol. I, p. 168: the *Provveditori* appear to have been introduced then with the responsibility of supervising crops and drainage and promoting agricultural activity by the setting up of land 'companies'.
[268] A little over one third of a hectare, but the *campo* varies from one region to another; in the Vicentino it is equivalent to 3862 sq. metres, D. Beltrami, *op. cit.*, p. 53, n. 2.

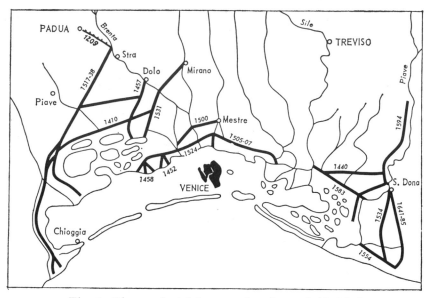

Fig. 4: *The regularization canals safeguarded half of
the Venetian lagoons*

The sketch map is oriented to the northwest. These works safeguarded the Venetian
lowlands and the lagoons that surround the town. But the northern part of the lagoon
has been largely filled in by deposits from the small rivers, the Piave and Sile, which
can become torrential. All this region is covered with stagnant water. To the south,
however, the Brenta was finally brought under control by successive works and the
lagoon is tidal from Chioggia to Venice. From Arturo Uccelli, *Storia della tecnica dal
Medio Evo ai nostri giorni*, 1945, p. 338.

communities (the *communità* of Este,[269] for example, or that of
Monselice[270]; or it might be the property of a real syndicate of landowners
who might have access to advances from the Venetian treasury at low
interest rates (4 per cent); or, finally, the Venetian administration might
take a hand in the enterprise, reserving the right, once work was completed,
to sell any land that might fall to its share; the judgment sometimes took
place on the Rialto. Each *ritratto* was divided, as ships were, into 24
'carats', or shares, and each carat was allocated in turn at public auction,
or as we might say under the hammer of the official appraiser; the documents stipulate 'con la baccheta in terra del su in giù'.

Did all these impressive rules mean anything? One can glimpse something of the true situation here and there from setbacks or even real
catastrophes. A *communità* might not be able to borrow enough to complete its works, so it would sell half the *ritratto* to its citizens, and the other
half to any buyer who would pay the starting price (the auctioneer started

[269] Senato Terra 32, 16th September, 1560; 29th November, 1560.
[270] *Ibid.*, 27, before the 9th May, 1558.

from the highest price and then lowered the bids). It was frequent to find syndicates being set up by landowners who were *consorti* or *caratadori* (carat buyers). These were real merchant associations: it is not surprising to find the great names of the patrician families of Venice at their head. One document (15th February, 1557)[271] mentions a Hieronimo Dolfin (of the banking family) who with his associates was negotiating for the *ritratto* of the San Biasio valley, near Lendinara, between the lower Adige and the lower course of the Po, a project that was still at a standstill, however, at the beginning of 1561.[272] Two years later we find another patrician, Alessandro Bon, who has 'intrapreso a sue spese col permesso della Signoria, la bonifica di tutte le valle che sono tra Po e Bacchiglione';[273] his plans came up against the resistance, the 'unexpected obstacle of the *communità* of Rovigo'. We can only guess at this stage whether these were always large concerns: we do not know and only research into this area can provide the answer. However we know that when there was an accident, as on the 5th November, 1554, when a dyke burst near Rovigo, 30,000 *campi fertilissimi* were flooded; and as the breach was inadequately repaired, 40,000 *stara di formento* were likely to be short at the next harvest, as they had been at the previous one.[274] Therefore large interests were at stake and a great deal of money. On 11th December, 1559, one initiator of schemes, who unfortunately remained anonymous, proposed to build at his own expense a series of *ritratti*; he would take only one *campo* in ten in return.[275] Who was hiding behind this man of property?

Beyond these small details we know very little about the real situation of peasants and landowners in the Veneto, while we now have (by an accident of research) abundant information about the peasants of the Languedoc and their masters.[276] There is still a great deal of research to be done before we shall come near the truth, and then we shall have to weigh the evidence very carefully. What is the real significance, in relation to the overall variety of types of farming, of this effort at land improvement, the long-term triumph of the rice fields, starting perhaps in 1584, which was to assure the well-being of the patrician classes and the favourable balance of payments of the Signoria in the seventeenth century, with the added profits of silk production?[277] In any case, these vast projects are out of all proportion to the works of the *canalistes* of the Languedoc. Similarly, after the end of the sixteenth century, there opened in Venice for the beneficiaries of ground rent a period of even greater prosperity than any experienced by land-owners of Languedoc round Montpellier or Narbonne. When Venetian wealth moved into the hinterland of the Terraferma, it exploited it skil-fully. But we do not know enough for certain about these episodes in Venetian land history. All we know is that the peasants went into debt,

---

[271] Senato Terra 25.   [272] *Ibid.*, 32.   [273] *Ibid.*, 67.
[274] *Ibid.*, 23.   [275] *Ibid.*, 31.
[276] See above, n. 266 and 58.
[277] Domenico Sella, *Commerci e industrie a Venezia nel secolo XVII*, 1961, p. 87 ff.

that the economy often remained archaic, that the communal lands were diminished. It would make a rewarding subject for research.[278]

Long term change: the fortunes of the Roman Campagna. Long term change is obviously easier to estimate. The Roman Campagna is a very good example of continuous large-scale change.[279] The peasant took possession of it in Neolithic times. Thousands of years later, under the Empire, the *agro romano*, which was then inhabited over all its area, was provided with large aqueducts. Malaria was not a great problem at this time. Disaster came with the Ostrogoths in the fifth century, when the aqueducts were breached. Only a century or two later could land reclamation be taken in hand again. Ostia rose from its ruins. The eleventh century brought another setback and further disasters; afterwards, once again, agricultural life began to prosper in the fourteenth and fifteenth centuries. Ostia was raised again, this time owing to the activity of Cardinal d'Estouteville. In the fifteenth and sixteenth centuries there grew up great noble estates with big farmhouses built like castles: the *casali*, which can still be seen today on the side of the main roads. Their massive dimensions are a sign of the insecurity of the plain, threatened by bandits always ready to come down from the mountains. These big, 'colonial' farms practised rotation of crops – wheat was their chief produce – and large-scale stock-farming. Their labour came from the Abruzzi mountains. But how permanent was this possession of the plain?

In the sixteenth century the situation was not very brilliant. The cardinals had their 'vines' in the Campagna, but they were situated on open hillsides, like the Casino of the Borghese on the Palatine. Benvenuto Cellini, who liked to hunt outside Rome, gives a detailed account of a long illness from which he only recovered according to him, by a miracle, and which seems to have been a particularly severe attach of malaria.[280] We should imagine the Campagna at this time with many waste stretches, swamps, and wild areas which were not much more than hunting grounds. Moreover, a vigorous and expanding pastoral community was coming down from the different parts of the Apennines and knocking at the gates of the city, as in the far-off days of its early existence. Notarial acts in Rome towards 1550 mention many stock dealers, among them Corsican immigrants.[281] Competing with foreign wheat as well, the agriculture of the plain deteriorated rapidly. In the eighteenth century things got even worse. De Brosses has left a harrowing account of the troubles of the plain, of the negligence of the

---

[278] On this vast problem see the pioneering work of Daniele Beltrami, *Forze di lavoro e proprietà fondiaria nelle campagne venete dei secoli XVII et XVIII*, 1961.

[279] I have followed the outline given by M. Sorre, *Les fondements biologiques de la géographie humaine*, p. 379 ff. See also, C. de Cupis, *Le Vicende dell'agricoltura e della pastorizia nell'agro romano e l'Annona di Roma*, Rome, 1911; Pfalz, art. cit., p. 133–134, and particularly Jean Delumean, *op. cit.*, II, p. 521 ff.

[280] *Vita de Benvenuto Cellini scritta da lui medesimo*, English trans. Symonds, *The Life of Benvenuto Cellini*, London, Phaidon, 1949, p. 156–162.

[281] C. Trasselli, 'Notizie economiche sui Corsi in Roma (secolo XVI) in *Archivio storico di Corsica*, X, Oct–Dec., 1934, p. 576 ff.

landowners and the fevers that ravaged it.[282] 'The beginning of the nineteenth century finds the *agro romano* in a more lamentable condition than
ever.'[283]

The strength of the plains: Andalusia. More commonly the fortunes of the
plains were less troubled. Or perhaps they seem so to us because we know
less about them. All the same there have been, between Roman times and
our own, considerable variations in the occupation and exploitation of
land in lower Tunisia, where there is abundant evidence of antique splendour. The same can be said of lower Syria or Macedonia, deserted for
centuries and only revived since 1922, or the amazing Camargue, which has
still not finished surprising us.

Whatever the truth, these great plains represent the essential agricultural
history of the Mediterranean, the last, the most difficult, and the most magnificent of its successes – that is if one does not look too closely at the high
cost in human terms of reclaiming them from the marshes. Each conquest
was a great historical achievement, rich in consequences. So much so that
one should always ask oneself whether behind any great event there is not,
as an underlying cause, one of these important agricultural triumphs.

The most dazzling example of such success is that of the plains of lower
Andalusia. In the sixteenth century this was one of the richest regions of the
Mediterranean. Between the ancient Castilian shelf to the north and the
forbidding mountains that form the Baetic Cordillera to the south, roll
the gently undulating Andalusian plains with their meadows, sometimes, in
the west, reminiscent of the fields of Flanders, their vineyards and vast
olive orchards. Like all the other plains, it was conquered only gradually.
In early Roman times, all the lower Guadalquivir was a marsh[284] comparable perhaps to the lower Rhône Valley in primitive times, or to the
Mitijda before it was colonized by the French. But Andalusia, or Baetica,
was fairly rapidly to become the heart of Roman Spain, a garden of towns
that soon became too brilliant and overpopulated.

For the wealth of towns is the opposite of the wealth of plains. They
specialize in a few products that bring profit, and depend in part on foreign
goods for their daily bread. The Andalusian towns exported oil, grapes,
wine, cloth, and manufactured goods and lived off North African wheat.
Whoever owned the wheat had the towns more or less at his mercy. The

[282] *Lettres d'Italie, op. cit.*, I, p. 312–313. On the emptiness of the Roman Campagna.
'Today only peasants from the Sabine hills and the Abruzzi come from time to time to
sow a few fields in the *campagna* and then go away again until harvest time'. The
explanation President de Brosses gives of the causes of depopulation and particularly the responsibility of Sixtus V calls for some correction. Pastor thinks that if
fever was on the increase it was possibly because of deforestation: the campaign against
bandits in the time of Sixtus V was in fact accompanied by the systematic burning of
the brushland which afforded them cover.
[283] M. Sorre, *op. cit.*, p. 398.
[284] Note the impression made on E. Quinet, *Mes vacances en Espagne*, 1881, p. 320,
by the 'marshes' of the Guadalquivir. In fact these were the wet *latifundia* of the Maris-
mas where half-wild bulls were reared, a vast region of flowery meadows in springtime.

Vandals, with their complicity, seized control of the wheat[285] in the fifth century. When Byzantium chased them out in the next century, Andalusia fell under its power. Later it offered no resistance to the conquering Arabs. Every time it was 'conquered', Andalusia became the jewel in the new crown. It was the centre of an expanding Moslem Spain, which did not reach much of the northern part of the Iberian peninsula, but spread over North Africa, with whose coastline, rugged population, and turbulent history it was closely identified. In this garden of towns, there were two great metropolises: Córdoba and later Seville. Córdoba was the centre of learning for all Spain, and the entire Western world, whether Christian or Moslem, and both towns were capitals of art and centres of civilization.

Hundreds of years later, in the sixteenth century, this pre-eminence was still marked. And yet it had taken a long time to heal the scars caused by the Christian Reconquest in the thirteenth century. It had created in Andalusia, especially to the south, many desert regions which colonization, first military then pacific, had only gradually reclaimed. In the sixteenth century, the long labour of reclamation was still going on[286]. But even so Andalusia was still a splendid land: 'granary, orchard, wine-cellar and stable of Spain',[287] the object of the ritual praise of Venetian ambassadors in their *Relazioni*. To the blessings of its soil the sixteenth century added another gift: America was given to Seville in 1503 for almost two centuries. America, or rather the *Casa de la Contratación*, the fleets that sailed to the West Indies and those that brought back silver from Mexico or Peru, the trading colonies overseas, thriving and active. All this was given to Seville exclusively as a legal monopoly. Why? In the first place so that the profitable trade could be more jealously controlled – the rulers' chief consideration. Secondly because the route to America depended on the trade winds and Seville stood at the gateway of the trade winds. But behind this singular good fortune did there not also lie the weight of a town in a privileged position, so well served by the boats going down the Guadalquivir and by the famous carts pulled by four oxen? It was the great wine- and oil-producing plain that in part accounted for Seville's trade. It was for wine and oil from its slopes that the northern ships came from Brittany, England, Zeeland, and Holland, and not merely for salt from San Lucar – much prized for salting cod – and the produce of the Indies.

[285] E. F. Gautier, *Genséric, roi des Vandales*, Paris, 1932, p. 109.
[286] On these questions see the detailed study by Georg Niemeyer, *op. cit.*, p. 37. 56–57, for the ravages caused by the Reconquest beyond the Guadalquivir. The systematic colonization of Andalusia was hardly begun until the time of Charles III. It was first undertaken with German settlers (p. 57). For the gaps still remaining in 1767, see figure 8, p. 62 of the same work. There was only one episode of colonization in the sixteenth century: Mancha Real, founded in 1540 in the steppe of Jaen. NB the important observation p. 100, on the significance of age – and therefore of history – in the system of property-owning, accompanied by a comparison of an old community, Córdoba, with a new one, Carlotta, founded in 1767. For the export of oil from Seville, 60,000 to 70,000 quintals, see Pedro de Medina, *Libro de grandezas y cosas memorables de España*, 1548, f° 122
[287] G. Botero, *op. cit.*, p. 8.

Andalusia's wealth encouraged – not to say forced – her to look outwards. In the sixteenth century, Seville and the Andalusian hinterland, still half-Moslem and hardly half-Christian, were engaged in sending their men to settle whole areas of Spanish America. These areas still bear the mark of their origins. Carlos Pereyra has perfectly described it. Spain sent all her sons down to this southern region opening onto the sea.

We should therefore be rather wary of Pierre George's vivid phrase describing these plains as 'farming cells' near the sea. In fact these cells are far from being shut in on themselves. If they extend their influence, it is generally because the economy of the great sea expanses comes to their assistance, or more precisely takes them into its service and condemns them to producing crops for export. Olives and vines prospered in lower Andalusia in the sixteenth century simply because they were favoured by the enormous trade of Seville. Similarly, at the other end of the Mediterranean, almost outside our area, the expansion of wheat-growing in Moldavia and Wallachia in the time of Michael the Brave, at the end of the sixteenth century, and the strengthening of the feudal system which it produced, were connected with the demand created in the Black Sea by a grain trade then in a period of full expansion. There are other examples, outside the sixteenth century this time: the cotton and tobacco which led to the improvement of the plain of Salonica; madder, introduced to the County of Avignon in the eighteenth century, for which low-lying regions were drained and the last marshes eliminated; or the vines which in 1900 made the Mitidja healthy at last.

There is little room for doubt: the land improvement schemes of the plains could only be financed by an influx of big profits from trade, long-term and large-scale trade. And that, in concrete terms, meant the proximity of a big trading town with openings to the outside world and a stock of capital – a town that could afford to carry the risks and responsibilities of the undertaking. And it is precisely in the regions near big cities – Venice, Milan, Florence – that all the sixteenth-century improvement schemes we have mentioned have been situated. Similarly, under the influence of Algiers, towards 1580, a thriving agriculture was set up in the Mitidja. It may have been short-lived, for the plain had not at that stage totally eliminated the unhealthy swamps, but it began to produce for the expanding town and the luxurious houses of the Turkish and renegade corsairs – at a cost in human life we can only surmise – meatstock, milk and butter, beans, chick peas, lentils, melons, cucumbers, poultry, and pigeons. It provided the boats in the port with wax, leather and large quantities of silk. It had fields of wheat and barley; and Haëdo, who perhaps had not been to see it for himself, came to the conclusion that it must be a garden of Eden. Valencia was another city which accounted for the gardens surrounding it, and also provided them with manure. 'If the streets of Valencia are not paved,' writes an eighteenth-century traveller,[288] 'it is because their refuse mixed with the excrement with which they are only

[288] Baron Jean-François Bourgoing, *Nouveau voyage en Espagne*, 1789, III, p. 50.

strewn for a few moments, is carried at frequent intervals outside the walls to fertilize the adjoining countryside, and the people are convinced that if they were to pave them, they would deprive the great orchard, which surrounds Valencia on all sides, of one of the principal sources of its fertility.'

Any plain that is claimed for agriculture becomes an economic and human power, a force. But it is obliged to live and produce for the outside world, not for its own sake. This is both a condition of its importance and a cause of its subordination and its troubles. We shall see this in the case of Andalusia, which even before 1580 was forced to import northern wheat.[289]

4. TRANSHUMANCE AND NOMADISM:
TWO MEDITERRANEAN WAYS OF LIFE

We have left to the last a description of the multiple problems of transhumance and nomadism, the regular movement of men and flocks which is one of the most distinctive characteristics of the Mediterranean world. We cannot attempt a total explanation of these continual migrations without looking eastwards and southwards beyond the Mediterranean peninsulas and without bringing into our discussion the pastoral life of the vast desert regions, which is why this topic – one not easily identified with any geographical region – has been postponed until now.

Transhumance.[290] There are several kinds of transhumance: geographers distinguish between at least two, possibly three.

[289] See below, I. p. 585 ff.

[290] To the historical dossier on transhumance we should add the documents relating to the grazing lands of the *presidios* in Tuscany (Sim. Secretarias Provinciales de Napoles, legajo no. 1, 25th January, 1566; 20th February, 1566; 5th March, 1566; 15th March, 1566). A letter from the Duke of Alcalá to the prince of Florence (copy, Simancas, 1055, f° 37) and the prince's reply (*ibid.* f° 66) on the subject of taxes imposed by the Tuscans on the migrating flocks which came to the *presidios* on the coast. An undated document in Italian, addressed to Philip II (probably in the same year 1566) mentions the attractions for sheep farmers of the grazing lands of the warm region of the *presidios* on the coast. The tax levied by the Tuscans on the way out towards these grazing lands was 10 lire per 100 head of stock, *di pecore, capre e altro bestiame* (Simancas, E°. 1446, f° 45). On the location of these pastures, cf. 24th August 1587, A.d.S. Naples ,Sommaria, fasc. 227. On the immense importance of the 'aduanero' of Foggia for transhumance, see B.N. Paris, Esp. 127, f° 61 and 61 v° (towards 1600) and the reference to the lengthy lawsuit of one of the customs farmers, the Marquis de la Paluda, whose excesses led to an action at law.
There is a great deal of geographical literature on the subject. Cf. the theory suggested by Deffontaines on the origins of transhumance (in the 4th edition 1935, of Jean Brunhes, *Géographie humaine*, p. 184); P. George, *op. cit.*, (355 ff.); Jules Blache's book, already mentioned, esp. p. 18 ff., 21, 31; P. Arqué, *op. cit.*, p. 43. An excellent summary of the problem in the Mediterranean, with a map showing the position in 1938 for the whole region, can be found in the article by E. Müller, 'Die Herdenwanderungen im Mittelmeergebiet', in *Peterm. Mitteilungen*, 84, 1938, p. 364–370 which gives a bibliography with particular mention of the great books by J. Frödin, *Zentral-*

In the first place there is 'normal' transhumance: sheepfarmers and shepherds are in this case people from the lowlands; they live there but leave in summer, which is an unfavourable season for stockraising on the plain. For these purposes, the mountains simply provide space. And even this space may often be the property of the peasant farmer from the plain, if more usually it is rented out to the mountain dweller. Arles in the sixteenth century, and possibly for four or five centuries previously,[291] was the capital of large-scale summer transhumance, controlling the flocks of the Camargue and especially of the Crau, sending them every year along the routes of the Durance valley to the high pastures of the Oisans, the Dévoluy, the Vercors, and even to the Maurienne and Tarentaise. This was a real 'peasant capital': it was where the 'capitalists' lived[292] – the top sheep farmers were still known by that name in recent times – and it was where notaries drew up and registered contracts.

'Inverse' transhumance in the sixteenth century was, for example, the kind found in Spanish Navarre. Flocks and shepherds would come down from the highlands, the *euskari*. The lowlands served only for marketing purposes, that is when there was a market. This transhumance was a frantic rush down from the mountains in winter – cattle and men hurried to escape the cold of the mountains and flooded into lower Navarre like an invading army. All doors were padlocked against these unwelcome visitors, and every year saw a renewal of the eternal war between shepherd and peasant, first on the way down, until the flocks reached the open plains or the wide grazing lands of the Bardenas Reales, and then on the way back. The Bardenas Reales are a stony steppe on the borders of Aragon, where winter rains provide rather meagre grazing.[293]

This inverse transhumance is also found in Calabria, where shepherds and flocks crowd into the narrow coastal strip during winter and spring. 'On the morning of Easter Day,' explains the Bishop of Catanzaro in June, 1549, 'some priests would go to the sea front, where there were many flocks, and were in the habit of celebrating mass on an altar made up of *formes* of cheese, afterwards blessing the cheese and the flocks and giving communion to the shepherds. The priest was then given all the cheese used to make the altar. I punished the priests who had held these services

---

europas Almwirtschaft, 2 vols., 1941, and Merner, *Das Nomadentum in Nord-West-lichen Afrika*, Stuttgart, 1937. The difficulty lies not only in cataloguing the different types of transhumance, but also in establishing its boundaries, the points at which it gives way in the North to the Alpine type of pastoral life and in the South to the nomadism of the Sahara, which amounts to a definition of the boundaries of the Mediterranean region. The recent studies by X. de Planhol (for full references see notes 301, 325–327) are decisive on this point.

[291] J. J. Estrangin, *Études archéologiques historiques et statistiques sur Arles*, 1838, p. 334 ff.

[292] Fernand Benoit, in *Encyclopédie des Bouches-du-Rhône*, vol. XIV, p. 628. On the role of the 'capitalists' see the brief but informative notes by Albitreccia, *op. cit.*, p. 256 ff.

[293] G. Desdevises du Dézert, *Don Carlos d'Aragon, Prince de Viane, Étude sur l'Espagne du Nord au XVe siècle*, 1897, p. 27.

and . . . forbade any others under pain of terrible penalties to dare to hold them in the future'.[294]

These are the two basic types of transhumance. There is also a third, less important, mixed type, which combines both summer and winter transhumance, where dwelling and starting point are halfway between summer and winter pastures. It is still practised in the Corsican Chataigneraie today.

In fact it is impossible to do justice to this complex phenomenon by rigid classification. Transhumance implies all sorts of conditions, physical, human, and historical.[295] In the Mediterranean, in its simplest form, it is a vertical movement from the winter pastures of the plain to the summer pastures in the hills. It is a way of life combining the two levels, and at the same time a source of human migration. These men may belong to one village or another, one rural – or non-rural – group or another; they may be simply shepherds, or they may, during one of their stays, hastily cultivate the earth, sometimes burning the scrubland in autumn to make crops grow more quickly;[296] they may have their homes in the hills or on the plains; they may or may not have fixed dwellings. In short there are many variations on the theme, but they are imposed by local conditions and are virtually unavoidable. One anecdote deserves mention. Coron, on the Greek coast, was in 1499 still a Venetian outpost. The Pasha of Morea wanted to prevent the Albanians and Greeks of the little town from sowing crops or grazing flocks on the territory of the Grand Turk. The *Rettori* of Coron merely replied *dolcemente*, 'Our flocks may go to your land in summer, but your flocks come to ours in winter.'[297]

Topographical relief and season are the two factors that broadly determine what can and should happen in particular cases. In 1498,[298] at carnival time, some *stradiots* carried out a raid near Pisa. Their haul was not surprising in winter near the sea: 300 head of large stock, buffaloes and cattle, 600 sheep, some mares, and some mules. Another raid near Zara, against the Turks, in January, 1526, resulted in 2500 animals being carried off.[299] A final example occurred in December, 1649,[300] when Morlachian raiders, led by a new chief, seized '13,000 head of cattle' near the coast of Dalmatia.

Nomadism, an older way of life. Transhumance, so defined, is simply one form of the Mediterranean pastoral way of life, alternating between the grazing lands of the plains and the mountain pastures; it is a regulated and on the whole peaceful form, the result of a long period of evolution. Transhumance even in its most disruptive forms only concerns a specialized population: the shepherds. It implies a division of labour, a settled form of agriculture with crops to maintain, fixed dwellings, and villages. The

[294] Buschbell, (article; reference mislaid) p. 7, note 1.
[295] Jules Blache, *op. cit.*, p. 22 ff.
[296] M. Le Lannou, *op. cit.,* p. 62.
[297] M. Sanudo, *Diarii*, II, column 577.
[298] M. Sanudo, *op. cit.*, I, column 898, Pisa, 1st March, 1498.
[299] *Ibid.*, XL, p. 816, Zara, 1st February, 1526.
[300] *Recueil des Gazettes*, year 1650, p. 88, Venice, 26th December, 1649.

villages may lose a part of their population according to the season, either to the plains or the mountains. Many documents of the sixteenth century mention these half-empty mountain villages, where only women, children, and old men remain.

Nomadism, on the contrary, involves the whole community and moves it long distances: people, animals, and even dwellings. But unlike transhumance, it has never been a way of dealing with enormous flocks of sheep. Even its largest flocks are scattered over a vast area, sometimes in very small groups. Today nomadism – which no longer exists around the Mediterranean in its residual state, it is true – consists of the knot of about ten people who might be seen round a fire at nightfall in one of the outer suburbs of Beirut; or at harvest time in Algeria, a few camels, sheep and donkeys, two or three horses, some women dressed in red, and a few black goat-skin tents amidst the stubble; or in the plain of Antalaya, in Pamphylia to the south of Taurus, about twenty tents, sometimes, but not often arranged in a horse shoe, the relic of a tradition which is slowly disappearing.[301]

Transhumance and nomadism seem to be activities dating from different ages. Is nomadism really an older way of life? Under our own eyes, throughout the desert and semi-desert zone that surrounds the south Mediterranean and continues into central Asia and beyond, the sedentarization policies of present-day governments have converted the old nomadism into a modified pastoral way of life (in the Sahara and Tripolitania, in Syria, in Turkey, and Iran), a way of life that is really transhumance, a division of labour. So the chronological order seems probable. One might add that in the context of the mountain regions of the Mediterranean, it looks as if inverse transhumance was practised earlier than what geographers call 'normal' transhumance.

This classification – nomadism, inverse transhumance, so-called normal transhumance – seems convincing. But things never happen as simply as an *a priori* model would suggest. The past has been richer in catastrophes and brutal revolutions than in slow evolution. Unfortunately catastrophes in these areas are less well-known than in the political arena.

In fact, when pastoral structures are studied in detail, inverse transhumance and normal transhumance often seem to operate simultaneously. In Haute-Provence[302] in the fifteenth and sixteenth centuries farmers from the upper regions (the richest and most numerous) and from the lower used the same pastures. In these conditions it is the system of property owning alone that distinguishes the two kinds of transhumance. This leads us out of the geographical context into the social context of property owning and even into politics. For the movement of flocks offered fiscal resources which no state could ignore, which it would hasten to organize

---

[301] Xavier de Planhol, *De la plaine pamphylienne aux lacs pisidiens. Nomadisme et vie paysanne*, 1958, p. 194.

[302] Th. Sclafert, *Cultures en Haute-Provence, Déboisements et Pâturages au Moyen Age*, 1959, p. 133 ff., esp. maps on p. 134–5.

and always protect. Between the Abruzzi and the Apulian Tavoliere, inverse transhumance was established as early as Roman times and explains the textile industries of Taranto. It survived under a fairly liberal system until 1442–1447, when Alfonso I of Aragon[303] organized it on authoritarian lines, with privileged and compulsory sheep routes, the *tratturi*, connecting tracks (*tratturelli*), resting pastures (*riposi*), and winter pastures, and, in addition, rules stipulating that wool or beasts had to be sold at Foggia and nowhere else, with payment exacted all along the line, naturally. Once this system was in place it changed little and was to be protected from the obstinate and regular encroachment along the routes by peasants, planting vines, olives and, in particular, wheat.

In 1548, over an area of 15,000 *carri* (one *carro* equals over 58 acres) situated in Apulia, royal grazing lands represented just over 7000 *carri*; besides this the authorities recovered 2000 *carri* in ploughed fields to which they were more or less entitled. The flocks which then averaged a million head of sheep, went up to an average of 1,300,000 head for the next ten years. And this number increased again, since in 1591 official records speak of 2,881,217 sheep, while regularly following years of high cereal prices (in 1560, 1562, 1567, 1584, 1589–1590, and 1591) the land through which the flocks moved was let out to peasants for six-year periods – the wheat yield from these fields fertilized by the passage of the flocks reached record figures of 1 to 20 or 1 to 30. This led to exciting 'candle-stick' auctions[304] at Naples between would-be purchasers. Big interests were at stake: those of the taxation system for which the Apulian customs duties were an 'irreplaceable jewel', those of the wool and meat merchants, and those of the big sheep-farmers who were increasingly becoming distinct from the mass of small farmers. 'A *villano* of this province of the Abruzzi,' says a report addressed to the Catholic King, 'will have 10, 15, 20, or 30,000 sheep, which he brings every year to this customs post [in Apulia] to sell wool and beasts. Then when he has packed his saddlebags with gold crowns he goes home to bury his money; sometimes he dies leaving his treasure still in the ground.'[305] However, in the seventeenth century, and even more in the eighteenth, there was some concentration of property and an increase in the size of the flocks of the rich sheep farmers, and it *looks* as if the lowlands had the advantage: this is only an impression for which there is little verifiable evidence.[306] At any rate it gives an idea of the complexity of the problem.

[303] Josef Ivanic, 'Über die apulischen Tratturi in ihrer volkswirtschaftlichen und rechtlichen Stellung' in *Illyrisch-albanische Forschungen*, 1916, p. 389, ff.

[304] A.d.S. Naples, Sommaria Consultationum, 2, f°s 12 v° to 15, 13th March, 1563; 11, f°s 61 v° and 64 v°, 10th October, 1591. In 1561, the revenue from the *dohana delle pecore de Puglia* came to 164,067 ducats; in 1564 it was 207,474 ducats; in June, 1588 it was 310,853 (*ibid.*, 2, f°s 78–83, 8th October, 1564, and 9, f°s 426, 4th June, 1588).

[305] G. Coniglio, *Il Viceregno di Napoli nel secolo XVII*, 1955, p. 28.

[306] G. M. Galanti, *Nuova descrizione storica e geografica delle Sicilie*, vol. II, Naples, 1788, p. 287, 303, 305, and even better, A.d.S. Naples Sommaria Consultationum 41, f°s 99 to 101, 17th October, 1637.

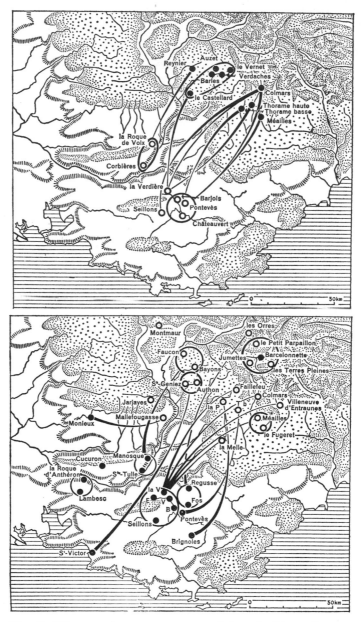

Fig. 5: *Winter and summer pasture of sheep in Haute-Provence towards the end of the fifteenth century*

Taken from Thérèse Sclafert, *Cultures en Haute-Provence*, 1959, p. 134 and 135, where the abbreviated place names are given in full.

The same duality is found in the Vicenza region – the *Vicentino*. The unpublished work of a sixteenth-century scholar, Francesco Caldagno,[307] describes it as a *habitatissimo* region, with no land uncultivated, a continuous garden sprinkled with big villages, almost towns, with their markets, commerce, and 'fine palaces'. It has everything: wood, which arrives in waggons or by water, and charcoal; the farmyards are stocked even with peacocks and 'turkey-cocks'. On the rivers and streams there are countless mills, sawmills, etc. In the irrigated meadows, thousands and even 'tens of thousands' of animals graze. Calves, kids, and lambs are abundant, and in summer this entire animal population is sent 'alli paschi della montagna'. This was normal transhumance which always stirred up trouble with the mountain dwellers about the letting and use of the high pastures; so there were quarrels with the Grisons about the 'Mandriole', a mountain rented by the *Vicentini*, which is hardly surprising. The men of Grisons had to drive their stock to the southern Alps and towards Venice,[308] where they sometimes settled as butchers. But the *Vicentino* had its own mountain people, in the section of the Alps known as the *Sette Communi*, with their woodcutters, their trappers, and also their crops and their own flocks, notably at Galio which possessed between 50,000 and 60,000 sheep. In summer they stayed on the pastures of the *Sette Communi*, in autumn they went down and scattered over the countryside of the Vicentino, the Paduvano, the Polesino, the Trivigiano, the Veronese, and even the Mantovano. This is proof that the vigorous pastoral life arising from the Vicentino plains did not have the monopoly of the area available for grazing. Everyone had his share.

Transhumance in Castile. Castilian transhumance is a good example upon which to test all our definitions. It has been described a hundred times. We are familiar with its conditions, its constraints, and its complexities.

We should immediately distinguish between 'long-distance transhumance' which can lead to treks of 800 kilometres, and short or very short-distance transhumance. We shall only be concerned here with the long-distance variety, which depended on the illustrious sheep-farming 'syndicate' of the *Mesta*, whose letters of privilege went back to 1273. As an eighteenth-century naturalist wrote, Spain has 'two species of sheep: the first kind, whose wool is ordinary, spend their lives in one place, do not change pastures, and return every night to the sheepfold; the others, which have fine wool, travel every year, ànd after spending summer in the mountains go down to the warm meadows of the southern parts of the kingdom, such as La Mancha, Extremadura, and Andalusia. This second species is known as the "itinerant sheep".'[309] Like all distinctions this is only approximate; the term 'itinerant sheep' should really be restricted to

[307] Marciana, 5838, C II, 8.

[308] A.d.S. Venice, *Cinque Savii*, 9, fº 162, 2nd March, 1605.

[309] Guillaume Bowles, *Introduction à l'histoire naturelle et à la géographie physique de l'Espagne*, trans. from the Spanish by the Vicomte de Flavigny, Paris, 1776, p. 470.

those that travelled, their precious fleeces smirched with red clay in the winter, to the 'utmost extremities' of Castile along the main roads, the *cañadas* on which there were a dozen royal tolls. But there was a subsidiary pastoral traffic along the secondary roads (*cordeles, veredas*). These flocks outside the main stream of circulation varied according to the season. They were known as *ganados travesios*, or *riberiegos*, or *merchaniegos* when they were on their way to the sheep fairs (*mercados*). A long, painstaking struggle was carried on by the royal authorities to extend their control beyond the main routes. It explains the sharp rise, until 1593–1599,[310] of taxation on sheep, but this is not our problem.

Our problem is to visualize this large-scale transhumance according to the *cañadas*, the map of which we have reproduced from Julius Klein's classic book,[311] repeated movements along the axes north-south and south-north. No uncertainty is possible. In spite of the vast range of movements (often horizontal, or through breaches in the mountains) what we have here is not a case of nomadism, since the sheep are accompanied by professional shepherds and by them alone, the *rabadanes*, master-shepherds and under-shepherds, armed with slings and long crooks, taking with them only their mules, a few horses, their cooking pots, and their dogs. There is no sign of an entire population on the move. We can even say without hesitation that this was a case of inverse transhumance. The fine-wool flocks travelled from the northern highlands to the southern plains. Flocks and farmers (both big and small) hailed from the North and particularly from the four big 'sheep cities' that upheld in the Cortès the powerful interests of the *Mesta*: León, Segovia, Soria, Cuenca. The whole system depended moreover on the capacity of the summer pastures, i.e. the northern ones: in the South, the vast empty plains of Extremadura, of La Mancha and of Andalusia allowed unlimited expansion.[312] So if the Castilian flocks did not cross the symbolic Portuguese frontier, it was not merely because of the opposition of their vigilant neighbours but also because they did not need the space, although the Castilians grumbled about the restriction.

This said, we are not for the moment concerned with the multiple quarrels between peasant farmers and shepherds (which were particularly marked when the flocks went back up to the hills); nor with the distinction between long-distance and short-distance flock movements. The question of the folded flocks, *estantes* or *travesios*, involves towns outside the orbit of the *Mesta*, such as Salamanca, towns, that is, where there was a local aristocracy of landed gentry and farmers. Neither are we concerned with the disputes between the *Mesta* pressure group and jurisdiction hostile

---

[310] Modesto Ulloa, *La hacienda real de Castilla en el reinado de Felipe II*, 1963, p. 222 and the excellent chapter p. 215–223.

[311] Julius Klein, *The Mesta: a study in Spanish Economic History 1273–1836*, 1920. See A. Fribourg, 'La transhumance en Espagne' in *Annales de Géographie*, 1910, p. 231–244.

[312] Jacob van Klaveren, *Europäische Wirtschaftsgeschichte Spaniens im 16. und 17. Jahrhundert*, Stuttgart, 1960, p. 200 ff.

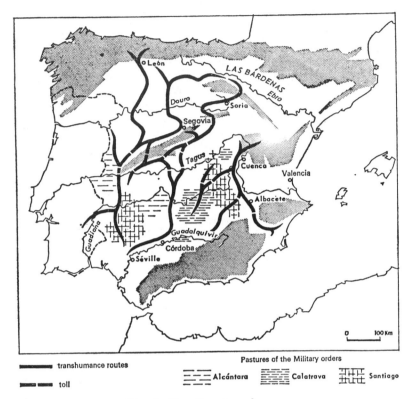

Fig. 6: *Castilian transhumance*

According to Julius Klein, *The Mesta, a Study in Spanish Economic History 1273–1836*, Cambridge, 1920, p. 18-19.

to its judiciary privileges; nor with the fight over the tolls between the state, the towns, the high nobility, and the Church. Yet all these well-known factors, taken together, indicate the complexity of the system of transhumance, based as it was on other systems and only comprehensible in the light of a long process of earlier evolution. Sheep-breeding meant more to the Iberian economy, says one historian, 'than the olives, grapes, copper, or even the treasures of Peru'.[313] And he is right. We should see in this much more than the generalization of the *merino* sheep, in the fourteenth century, the result of crossbreeding between Spanish sheep and sheep imported from North Africa. A whole combination of circumstances and the concurrence of the international situation were necessary

[313] Roberto S. Lopez, 'The origin of the merino sheep' in *Jewish Social Studies Publication*, vol. 5, New York, 1953, p. 161–168.

for the establishment (and rise until about 1526 perhaps) of the *Mesta*. If it had not been for the European crisis of the fourteenth and fifteenth centuries, the attraction of the probable low price of Castilian wool, the well-known drop in exports of English wool, and the thriving textile industry of the Italian towns, the great rise of sheep farming in Castile and its millions of itinerant sheep would have been impossible and unthinkable.[314]

In short, the case of Castile with its spectacular expansion leads to unambiguous conclusions. Any transhumance presupposes complicated internal and external structures and weighty institutions. In the case of Castilian wool, it involved towns and markets like Segovia; Genoese businessmen who bought up wool in advance and, like the Florentines, possessed vats where the fleeces could be washed, not to mention the Castilian agents for these big merchants, the transporters of the bales of wool, the fleets that sailed from Bilbao for Flanders (controlled by the Consulate of Burgos), or the consignments sent off to Alicante or Málaga, destined for Italy; or even to take an everyday detail, the indispensable salt which had to be bought and transported to the grazing lands for the flocks. It is impossible to explain Castilian transhumance outside this wide context, of which it was both product and prisoner.

Overall comparisons and cartography. The analysis of any example, whether important or not, seems to lead to similar conclusions.

1. All the cases studied in any detail show that transhumance is markedly institutionalized, protected by safeguards, rules, and privileges, and somewhat outside society, as is shown by the situation of the shepherds, who are always a race apart. Some studies, relating to southern Germany it is true,[315] underline this 'untouchable', outcast aspect of the shepherd, and this in itself is revealing. And one admirable description of the lives of the migrating shepherds of present-day Provence[316] takes the reader into a totally separate world and civilization.

Obviously precautions on behalf of or against transhumance may vary from region to region, but they are always there. Around Arles, in the Crau, some of the regulations were abused to the advantage of 'foreign flocks'; the municipal council deliberated the question in 1633 and authorized the captain of the watch to organize the necessary inspections and to levy a special tax to reimburse himself. The Parlement of Aix endorsed the ruling. We need not press the point: an order had been established.[317] At Naples at the beginning of the seventeenth century.[318] the principal office outside the big city was that of the customs officer at Foggia. It was he who distributed grazing lands, issued summonses, levied the rents for pastures. Or in his absence, the administration was represented by a

[314] Jacob van Klaveren, *op. cit.*, p. 200 ff.

[315] Wolfgang Jacobheit, *Schafhaltung und Schäfer in Zentraleuropa bis zum Beginn des 20. Zahhunderts*, Berlin, 1961.

[316] Marie Mauron, *La transhumance du pays d'Arles aux grandes Alpes*, 1952.

[317] J. F. Noble de la Lauzière, *op. cit.*, p. 461, 1632.

[318] B.N. Esp. 127 f° 61 and 61 v°, undated, beginning of the seventeenth century.

president of the Camara who went to the district twice a year, *al modo de la Mesta*, says an anonymous report. Whether fair or not, this comparison is symptomatic. Similarly in Aragon, pastoral life was governed by a Mesta with its privileges like that of Castile, but so far its archives have not tempted a historian.

2. Secondly, all transhumance is the result of a demanding agricultural situation which is unable either to support the total weight of a pastoral economy or to forgo the advantages it brings, and which therefore offloads its burdens according to local possibilities and the seasons, to either the lowland or the mountain pastures. Any logical study should therefore begin with this basic agricultural situation. It is this situation that determines the separation between shepherds and peasants. A first step towards understanding the large-scale pastoralism of which the Tavoliere of Apulia is the terminus and the Abruzzi the centre of departure, would be to note the positions at both high and low levels of the settled peasantry. In the case of Castilian transhumance we have noted the dominant role of the North and its entrenched peasant farmers. In the Vicentino we should think of the *paese habitatissimo* of the lowlands. And under our very eyes, in North Africa and Turkey or in Iran, we have the example of a rise in population and advances in agriculture breaking up a formerly pastoral way of life. What is happening today happened in the past too.

3. The only way to see beyond a series of particular instances is to project all known cases of transhumance on to a map of the whole Mediterranean region. This is possible for our own period, and was done in 1938 by Elli Müller, whose map we have reproduced, expanded, and simplified.[319] For the past, we have to reconstruct it from successive fragments. The transhumance routes – about 15 metres wide – bear different names in different regions: *cañadas* in Castile, *camis ramaders* in the Eastern Pyrenees, *drayes* or *drailles* in Languedoc, *carraïres* in Provence, *tratturi* in Italy, *trazzere* in Sicily, *drumul oilor* in Rumania. The remaining traces of this network indicate an overall geography whose message is clear. In the Mediterranean region in the sixteenth century, transhumance was confined above all to the Iberian peninsula, the South of France, and Italy. In the other peninsulas, the Balkans, Anatolia, North Africa, it was submerged by the predominance of nomadism or semi-nomadism. Only one sector of the Mediterranean possessed a sufficiently rich agriculture, large population, and vigorous economy to have been able to contain pastoral life within strict boundaries.

Outside this area everything becomes more complicated. But the skein of contradictions is not explained so much by geography, which is important of course, as by historical precedent.

Dromedaries and camels: the Arab and Turk invasions. History provides some far-reaching explanations. To the east and to the south the Mediterranean suffered two invasions, in fact two series of prolonged upheavals

[319] See below, fig. 7.

that altered everything. These were the two 'gaping wounds' spoken of by Xavier de Planhol: the Arab invasions which began in the seventh century and the Turkish invasions which began in the eleventh: the latter coming from the 'cold deserts' of Central Asia, accompanied or reinforced the spread of the camel; the former, coming from the 'warm deserts' of Arabia, aided, if not explained, by the spread of the dromedary.[320]

The two beasts of burden differ from each other in spite of obvious similarities and possible confusion. The West persisted in confusing them, not without some excuse: Savary in his *Dictionnaire de Commerce* (1759) defined the dromedary as 'a double camel,' which is certainly not the case. They are two quite different animals: the camel, originating in Bactria, is unaffected by cold or height; the dromedary, from Arabia, is an animal of the sandy deserts and warm zones. It is practically useless for climbing mountain paths or withstanding low temperatures. Even during the cool nights of the Sahara or Arabian deserts its master takes care to have its head sheltered under the canvas of the tent. Hybrids obtained by crossing camels and dromedaries in Turkestan towards the tenth century, played only a local role.

The ecology of the two animals is of capital importance. A fairly large frontier zone separates their respective habitats, stretching between a line running along the southern edge of the Zagros and the Taurus (which is the decisive boundary) and a more hypothetical line running from the eastern tip of the Black Sea to the south of the Caspian Sea and the bend of the Indus.[321] Very roughly, this zone is the Iranian plateau, cold during winter. The dromedary did penetrate into this zone, of course, and participated in the active caravans that in the sixteenth century centred around Ispahan.[322] The dromedary even got as far as India and fetched prices there equal to or slightly higher than the horse[323], proof that it was something of a stranger there. In fact, neither the plateaux of Anatolia nor the Iranian highlands were really open to it, and if the Arab conquest failed in Asia Minor, if it was never very assured in Persia, the reason is largely to be sought in the inferiority of the dromedary.

In any case, the two zones each have a separate history.

From Syria to the Maghreb the Arab invader disregarded the high lands. He left alone to their fate the old, dry mountains of the interior, facing the desert, which man had colonized early in time, such as the Aurès in North Africa; and he skirted the edge of the deserted mountains bordering the sea, where an abundant rainfall accounts for the thick forests of

[320] Apart from his thesis, quoted above note 301, the articles by Xavier de Planhol are essential reading: 'Caractères géneraux de la vie montagnarde dans le Proche-Orient et dans l'Afrique du Nord' in *Annales de Géographie*, 1962, no. 384, p. 113–129; and 'Nomades et Pasteurs', I and II in *Annales de l'Est*, 1961, p. 291–310, 1962, p. 295–318. I am indebted to these excellent studies.

[321] This is based on the information in Emil Werth, *Grabstock, Hacke und Pflug*, 1954, esp. p. 98.

[322] British Museum, Royal 14 R XXIII, f⁰ 22 (About 1611).

[323] J. Savary des Brulons, *Dictionnaire universel de commerce*, 1759, I, column 804.

antiquity long respected by man. The forests, therefore, served as refuges for the native populations fleeing before the Arab conquerors. From the eighth to the ninth century the Maronites and Druses settled in Lebanon; they cleared the ground and set up their states. In North Africa the Kabylias were settled from the tenth century, and particularly from the eleventh century on, after the great push forward of the Hilalian nomads.[324] 'Bedouinization' following the Arab conquest spread all over the land in between these mountains, whether early or lately settled, like a flood cutting off the mountain tops as islands. So an often archaic way of life was isolated in these high places, of which some characteristics (the ox as a pack animal, irrigated valley crops, grain stored in the attics, troglodyte dwellings where men and animals huddle together) have persisted up to or very nearly up to our time.

In the mountains of Asia Minor, and to a lesser extent in the Balkans (where there were many exceptions), the invasion of the Turkish camel drovers meant violent upheavals, often without intermission, but of a completely different nature. An aggressive form of nomadism became established, wherever it was possible, up as far as the highest regions of the mountainous zones, above the upper limits of the forest. Perhaps it was because of 'what the term *yayla* – summer stay – means in the Turkish language and culture, where the notions of coolness, icy running water, and luxuriant pastures combine to form an image of Paradise'.[325] As soon as spring arrives there is a great move to leave 'winter quarters, *pirelendi* . . . flea-ridden . . . and full of vermin', and above all to get away, to take to the road. A Turkish proverb, freely translated, says 'a *Yürük* [a nomad, walker] does not need to go anywhere, but needs to be moving'.[326] obeying traditional urges as much as, if not more than geographical necessities.

The vast history of this nomadism is confused and difficult to disentangle. It has its own imbroglios, but it is also at odds with the eternal opposition of the settled peasants; it has to overcome, or go round, or break through the barriers they set up, and often to yield before their silent advance. In Asia Minor from the thirteenth to the fifteenth century the nomadism of the shepherds was gradually rejected, regularly eliminated from the plateaux and hollows of the interior, and pushed out to the mountainous margins and peripheral plains, 'almost deserts', which had relapsed into 'unhealthiness and neglect' for centuries, 'a plague-ridden brushland in summer': the plains of Cilicia, of Pamphylia, the valleys of the Meander and the Gediz. In the sixteenth century the Turkish government was constantly disciplining the *Yürüks*, forcing them to settle by land concessions, and condemning the most recalcitrant to work in the mines or fortifications, or deporting them, to Cyprus for example, which was Turkish after 1572.

But the task was never-ending. If nomadism declined in western Anatolia,

[324] X. de Planhol, *art. cit.*, in *Annales de Géog.* 1962.
[325] X. de Planhol, *art. cit.*, in *Annales de Géog.* 1962, p. 121.
[326] X. de Planhol, *De la plaine pamphylienne, op. cit.*, p. 202.

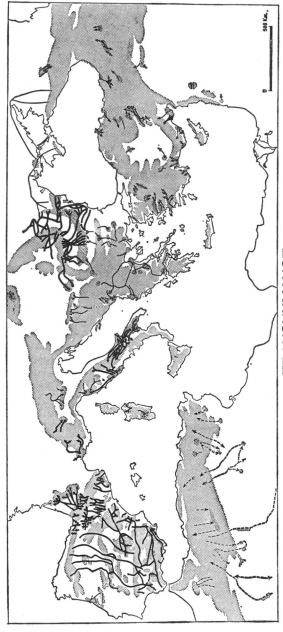

TRANSHUMANCE

Winter pastures ◯ Transhumance routes ⌇ Directions of Transhumance ⌇

Normal (flocks belonging to inhabitants of the plains)

Inverse (flocks belonging to inhabitants of the mountains)

Normal and inverse

Double (flocks belonging to inhabitants of intermediary zones)

500 Km.

Fig. 7: *Transhumance in modern times*

From Elli Müller, 'Die Herdenwanderungen im Mittelmeergebiet', in *Petermann's Mitteilungen*, 1938.

it prospered in the East, where the nomads coming from Asia bear the generic name of Turkmenes. To this day, in the Anatolian steppes, the Turkmenes roam between Aleppo and Damascus; and the problem of their settling at one end or the other of their journey still remains. Starting in the sixteenth century, and particularly in the seventeenth, Ottoman governors and tax collectors gave a great deal of attention to the Turkmene nomads, who had never been troubled during the grand period of Turkish expansion earlier. What interested the Sublime Porte was collecting taxes and recruiting cavalry. The bitter struggles against the Persians led to the withdrawal towards Iran of the Shiite tribes; the Sunnites on the other hand advanced westwards and renewed the nomad stock of the *Yürüks*. So we find a tribe which was in 1613 in Karaman, to the southeast of Konya, seventy years later as far up as Kutahya. There were even groups that crossed over to Rhodes. There was one final renewal. The gaps left to the east were to be filled again, as the Kurds broke out of their isolation in the mountain tops. In the nineteenth century they 'start up again the great north-south migrations between the high Anatolian plateau and the southern Piedmont of Taurus', proof that there are cycles in the nomadic way of life, with astonishing halts, periods of integration and settlement and new departures.[327]

Nomadism in the Balkans, Anatolia, and North Africa as witnessed by western observers. It is, of course, an over-simplification, if a permissible and even necessary one, to explain everything in terms of invasions – the invasions of the seventh century and their consequences and those of the eleventh century and their consequences. The dromedary was already to be found in the Sahara and North Africa before the Arab invasions and the camel had reached Anatolia before the first Seldjuk advance. But the explanation is on the whole correct. The Mediterranean, where the hot and cold deserts cutting through the continental mass of the Ancient World come together, witnessed the survival – though attenuated and domesticated by the stubborn resistance of the peasantry – of the 'natural' nomadic way of life from Asia.

The survival of these ancient patterns of living completes the portrait of the Mediterranean peninsulas in the sixteenth century – the Balkans, Anatolia, North Africa – where transhumance, as defined by western sources, was pushed aside, driven to marginal areas, or considerably modified. This perspective is essential to the understanding of some of these 'mountain islands', independent but isolated, regarded with suspicion and having very little access to the outside world, such as the Jebel Druz, a self-governing enclave from which 'raids . . . on Moors, Turks and Arabs'[328] were launched without warning, or Kabylia – the kingdom of

[327] The preceding details are all taken from X. de Planhol, 'Géographie politique et nomadisme en Anatolie' in *Revue internationale des Sciences sociales*, XI, 1959, no. 4.
[328] François Savary, comte de Brèves, *Relations des voyages de monsieur . . . tant en Terre Saincte et Aegypte, qu'aux Royaumes de Tunis et Arger*, 1628, p. 37.

Cuco as the Spanish texts call it – which had its independence but not freedom of movement. Its rulers sought in vain, notably at the little beach of Stora (near the present-day site of Philippeville), to make contact with the Spaniards.[329] In North Africa the pattern was relatively simple. Every summer, the long-distance nomads would drive their flocks to the sea; at the approach of winter, they would return to the South and the Sahara. When the flocks returned to the lowlands they had left the previous autumn, these mountain people would pause for a while in their travels. There was nothing of the sort in Anatolia, as we have seen, nor in the Balkans, where transhumance and nomadism both intermingled and clashed. In the eastern part of the Peninsula, the Turkish government more or less deliberately installed colonies of nomads, the *Yürüks* of Asia Minor, in the hope of persuading them to adopt a sedentary way of life and thereby strengthen the Turkish military defences. And they were by no means the only nomads in the vast Balkan peninsula.

These clear departures from the Italian or Spanish pattern did not escape western observers, either in the sixteenth century or later. The movements of the nomadic (or rather semi-nomadic) shepherds made similar impressions on Diego Suárez,[330] the soldier-chronicler of Oran, on the Fleming Busbecq, on that admirable traveller Tavernier, on the enquiring mind of the Baron de Tott, and on Chateaubriand's English contemporary, Henry Holland. The most vivid description is Holland's recollection of his meeting in 1812 with the rough shepherds of Mount Pindus,[331] who were driving their flocks over what was then the semi-deserted plain of Salonica or along the shores of the Gulf of Arta, a sort of inland sea with shallow waters. Every year when summer came they would set off back to the mountains. These were certainly nomads since they took with them women and children. Behind the long procession of sheep, whose speed dictated that of the rest, came the convoy of horses, up to a thousand at a time, all laden with household goods and camping materials, tents – and young children sleeping in baskets. There were even priests accompanying their flocks.

They were nomads too whom Busbecq[332] saw near Ankara, in the region of the angora goats and the fat-tailed sheep known in North Africa as Barbary sheep. 'The shepherds who look after these flocks spend day and night in the fields, and take their wives and children about with them in wagons which serve them for houses, though they sometimes put up small tents. They wander over wide stretches of country seeking out the plains or high ground or valleys according to the time of year and the available pasture.' On the borders of Armenia and Chaldea, 'four leagues from the

[329] Fernand Braudel, 'Les Espagnols en Algérie, 1429–1792', in *Histoire et Historiens de l'Algérie*, 1931, p. 245–246.

[330] See below, p. 177.

[331] Henry Holland, *Travel in the Ionian Isles, Albania, Thessaly, Macedonia during the years 1812 and 1813*, London, 1815, p. 91–93.

[332] *Op. cit.*, p. 47.

city of Erivan', writes Tavernier[333] towards the middle of the seventeenth century, 'are high mountains where the Natives that inhabit the hot and sun-burnt Countries towards *Chaldea* come twenty thousand together to seek out good pasturage for their Cattle and about the end of Autumn return again into their own country'.

Again there can be no doubt in this case. In the following century the Baron de Tott saw the same Turkmene nomads, but his account may puzzle us a little. 'The people,' he writes, 'who in the winter inhabit the centre of Asia and who stretch even into Syria in the summer to feed their flocks with their arms and baggage are thought to be wandering tribes, but are in fact no more so than the Spanish shepherds who follow their sheep during eight months of the year throughout all the mountains of Andalusia.'[334]

This brings us to the question of a useful definition and it can be quickly answered. The confusion between the *rabadanes* of Castile and the Turkmene shepherds is possible, though only on first sight, if one remembers the enormous distances travelled by the 'itinerant' flocks of the *Mesta*. The Turkmenes do not travel greater distances, but they take their families and dwellings with them and that is the difference. Besides the discussion centres round the use of the word 'nomad'. We might bear in mind that the learned word 'nomadism' does not appear in Littré's dictionary and that he only gives an example dated 1868 for 'transhumance'. The words 'transhumant' and 'transhumance' are of recent derivation: the Bloch-Wartburg dictionary (1960) gives the earliest use of the words as 1803. While the word 'trashumante' is found in the writing of Ignacio de Asso as early as 1780 [335], it does not seem to be a very ancient word on the other side of the Pyrenees either, and *trashumancia* still does not exist. But this is straying from the argument.

Cycles spanning the centuries. Throughout the present chapter we have noted the extremely slow pattern of oscillation, whether from nomadism to transhumance or from mountain dwelling to settling in the plain. All these movements require hundreds of years to complete. While a plain is coming to life, overcoming its dangerous waters, organizing its roads and canals, one or two hundred years may pass by. Similarly from the time when a mountain region begins to lose its population until the moment when the economy of the plains has absorbed as many waves of immigration as it can use, another one or two centuries may have passed. These are processes which span the centuries and can only be grasped if the chronological field of study is extended as far as possible.

History usually only concerns itself with the crises and high points of these slow movements. In fact, these points are only reached after immense preparation and are followed by interminable consequences. It sometimes

[333] *Op. cit., Persian Travels,* p. 14.
[334] *Memoirs of the Baron de Tott,* II, 349.
[335] *Op. cit.,* p. 109, 112, 251, 295.

happens that in the course of their slow process these movements gradually change direction. One may find periods of construction and deterioration alternating indefinitely. A mountain region for instance may achieve prosperity, only to lose it all or lose itself in its own success. When this history is not confined to mere accident or local progress, it appears that these extremely slow-moving 'geographical' cycles, if one may use the term, obey a very rough synchronism. So as the sixteenth century comes to an end, we find an explosion of liberation from the Mediterranean mountains which were in all cases overpopulated and subject to strain. The diffuse war which results is swallowed up in the interminable masked social war-fare known as banditry – an ill-defined word if ever there was one. From the Alps to the Pyrenees, the Apennines or any other mountains, Moslem or Christian, a common destiny seems to emerge along these long mountain chains separated by the sea.

In this almost motionless framework, these slow-furling waves do not act in isolation; these variations of the general relations between man and his environment combine with other fluctuations, the sometimes lasting but usually short-term movements of the economy. All these movements are superimposed on one another. They all govern the life of man, which is never simple. And man cannot build without founding his actions, consciously or not, on their ebb and flow. In other words, geographical observation of long-term movements guides us towards history's slowest processes. Consciousness of this has directed our observation both in this and in following chapters.

CHAPTER II

The Heart of the Mediterranean:
Seas and Coasts

Let us now leave the mainland and turn to the sea. Our journey will take us in turn to the different stretches of water within the Mediterranean, to the coastal strips, and to the islands. Our progress will be guided by these geographical units, but again our chief concern will be to select for analysis and comparison identical elements within them and by so doing to make the units themselves more intelligible.

I. THE PLAINS OF THE SEA

We shall of course have to measure these expanses of water in relation to human activity; their history would otherwise be incomprehensible if indeed it could be written at all.

Coastal navigation. The sea in the sixteenth century was an immensity of water: man's efforts had only conquered a few coastal margins, direct routes, and tiny ports of call. Great stretches of the sea were as empty as the Sahara. Shipping was active only along the coastline. Navigation in those days was a matter of following the shore line, just as in the earliest days of water transport, moving crab-wise from rock to rock,[1] 'from promontories to islands and from islands to promontories'.[2] This was *costeggiare*,[3] avoiding the open sea – what Pierre Belon calls 'les campagnes de mer', 'the fields of the sea'. More precisely, according to the galley accounts of a Ragusan vessel,[4] it was a matter of buying one's butter

---

[1] Éric de Bisschop, *Au delà des horizons lointains*, I, Paris, 1939, p. 344. To quote Cervantes: '*navegando de tierra a tierra con intencion de no engolfarnos*', *Novelas ejemplares*. This was a voyage from Genoa to Spain.

[2] Peter Martyr to the Count of Tendilla and the Archbishop of Granada, Alexandria in Egypt, 8th January, 1502, letter no. 231, re-edited by Luis Garcia y Garcia, *Una embajada de los Reyes Católicos a Egipto*, 1947, p. 55, note.

[3] *Costeggiare*, to hug the shore, also means to go carefully: the Doge of Venice advises the Duke of Ferrara to go *costegiando*, A.d.S., Modena, Venezia 77 IX, f° 43, J. Tebaldi to the Duke, Venice, 29th April, 1526. The opposite, to go straight ahead, is *s'engoulfer*, to plunge in, to go *a camin francese*. The Captain General of the Sea, Tommaso Contarini, writes from Corfu, 10th July, 1558 '. . . . *La notte, si comme le scrissi, levatomi me ne venni qui a camin francese, senza tochar alcun loco . . .*'. A.d.S. Venice, Provveditori da Terra e da Mar, 1078. Another expression but less precise is *venire de lungo*. A.d.S. Venice Senato Mar. 19, f° 34, 28th December, 1517, grain ships, loaded at Cyprus . . . '*sono venute de longo a Venetia senza tocar Corphù*'. cf. the Spanish expression *a largo mar*, *CODOIN*, LV, p. 8 (1628).

[4] Archives, Ragusa, exact reference mislaid. See Bertrand de la Borderie, *Le Discours du Voyage de Constantinople*, Lyons, 1542, p. 6; Pierre Belon (*op. cit.*, p. 85) passed

at Villefranche, vinegar at Nice, oil and bacon at Toulon. Or as a Portuguese chronicler puts it, of travelling from one seaside inn to another, dining in one and supping in the next.[5] Thomé Cano, the Sevilian, said of the Italians, 'They are not sailors of the high seas.'[6] Sailing in the Adriatic, Pierre Lescalopier was 'amusing himself watching the mummers' on Mardi Gras in 1574 at Zara; two days later, on February 25th, he passed in front of St. John of Malvasia and dined on the 26th at Spalato.[7] This is how the princes and notables of this world would have travelled, from one coastal town to the next, taking time for festivities, visits, receptions, or rest while the crew was loading the boat or waiting for better weather.[8] This is how even the fighting fleets travelled, doing battle only in sight of land.[9] The word that springs to mind as one studies the itineraries or *Arti di navigare* of the period, which are from beginning to end a description of the coastal route, is the humble word 'tramping'.

On exceptional occasions the ship might lose sight of the coast, if she was blown off course; or if she embarked on one of the three or four direct routes that had long been known and used. She might be going from Spain to Italy by the Balearics and the south of Sardinia, which was often called 'sailing by the islands'. Or from the straits of Messina or Malta, she might be aiming for Syria, by way of Cape Matapan and the coasts of Crete and Cyprus.[10] Or she might take the direct route from Rhodes to Alexandria in Egypt, a swift crossing with a favourable wind[11] and one which was undertaken in the Hellenic period. In 1550 Pierre Belon went 'straight through' from Rhodes to Alexandria. But these could hardly be

so close to Magnesia Point, 'that we might have thrown a stone from our ship on to the land'. On ships unable to leave the coast, *Saco de Gibraltar*, p. 134–136.

[5] J. de Barros, *Da Asia, Dec.*, I, book IV, ch. XI, (edited A. Baião, p. 160): '*jantando em un porto e ceando em outro*'.

[6] Damião Peres, *História de Portugal*, 1928–1933, IV, p. 214; Thomé Cano, *Arte para fabricar . . . naos de guerra y merchante . . .* Seville, 1611, p. 5 v⁰. Escalante de Mendoza, 1575, distinguishes between the '*marineros de costa y derrota y otros de alta mar*'. Neither those who sail from Biscay to France, nor those who sail 'to all the Levant' count as sailors of the high seas; Henri Lapeyre, *Une famille de marchands: les Ruiz*, 1955, p. 194.

[7] *Op. cit.*, p. 25.

[8] Cf. the voyage made by the Archdukes Rudolph and Ernest (E. Mayer-Loewenschwerdt, *Der Aufenthalt der Erzherzöge R. und E. in Spanien, 1564–1571*, Vienna, 1927) or that made by Cardinal Camillo Borghese (A. Morel Fatio, *L'Espagne au XVIe et au XVIIe siècle*, 1878, p. 160–169) who in 1594 called at Leghorn, Savona, Palamos, Barcelona, '*costegiando la riviera de Catalogna*'. Marie de Medici took twenty-two days to get from Leghorn to Marseilles, 13th October–3rd November, 1600, Agrippa d'Aubigné, *Histoire universelle*, ed. for *Société de l'Histoire de France* by A. de Ruble, 1886–1897, IX, p. 338–339.

[9] La Prevesa, Lepanto . . . but also La Hougue, Aboukir, Trafalgar. Is it only in our own time that wars are lost in mid-ocean? R. La Bruyère, *Le drame du Pacifique*, 1943, p. 160.

[10] Paul Masson, *Histoire du commerce français dans le Levant au XVIIe siècle*, 1896, p. 487–488. It is the old Marseilles route, but with the difference that in the thirteenth century, only a small number of vessels reached Syria from Messina without putting in there on the way.

[11] Belon, *op. cit.*, p. 81 v⁰ ff.

called authentic high sea routes. Ships were not really taking to the open sea when they sailed from one island to another, seeking shelter from the north wind on the east–west passage; or taking advantage on the north–south passage, on the Rhodes–Alexandria crossing which is after all quite short, of the wind which in one season blew from the north and in the other from the south. The venture might be repeated on shorter trips, crossing from one side of a bay to the other. But in January 1571, when a Venetian galleon, *Foscarini e Panighetto*, coming from Candia, ran into fog on the other side of Corfu and was obliged to advance blind with no land in sight, the crew was seized with despair[12].

The importance of the shore was such that the coastal route was scarcely different from a river. The owner of land on the coast might exact toll from all passing boats, which might be justified if the sum corresponded to a real service in the port. But this was not the case when the Dukes of Monaco and Savoy, both owners of an absurdly small portion of the coast-line and most anxious therefore to have a share in the rich traffic passing under their noses, claimed the right to collect payment from all ships for the mere privilege of sailing past their land. Woe betide any sailing ship stopped by their galleys.[13] The 2 per cent duty at Villefranche, as a result of French bad temper, almost turned into a diplomatic incident under Louis XIV. Nothing shows better than this the extent to which shipping was tied to the coast. The possession after the treaty of Cateau-Cambrésis of the *presidios* of Talamona, Orbetello, Porto-Ercole, and S. Stefano on the Tuscan coast, made it possible for Philip II to interrupt shipping between Genoa and Naples at will.[14] The role played by La Goletta on the

[12] Ugo Tucci, 'Sur la pratique vénitienne de la navigation au XVIe siècle' in *Annales E.S.C.*, 1958, p. 72–86.

[13] Simancas E° 1392, Figueroa to the king, Genoa, 30th April, 1563; the Duke of Monaco stopped three *escorchapines* coming from Tortosa laden with wool, because they had not paid the passage dues. The merchandise was intended for Spanish merchants in Florence. The Duke claimed that his privilege had been confirmed by Charles V. A.d.S. Genova, L. M. Spagna, 10–2419: a Savoyard galley in October, 1588, captured boats carrying oil, actually off the Genoese riviera, a mile from land, because they had not paid the Villefranche duty. On the Villefranche duty which goes back to 1558, see Paul Masson, *Histoire du commerce français dans le Levant au XVIIe siècle*, 1896, p. 72–73, and *Histoire du commerce français dans le Levant au XVIIIe siècle*, 1911, p. 192–193: *C.S.P.* VII, p. 229, 25th June, 1560; A. N., Marine B 31; Genoa, Manoscritti no. 63, 1593; A.d.S. Florence, Mediceo 2842, 11th August, 1593; A.N., Foreign Affairs Bl, 511, Genoa, 17th June, 1670; *Lettres de Henri IV*, VI, p. 126.

[14] The possession of Piombino alone (an independent state with its own ruling family, Piombino was to be occupied by Cosimo de' Medici from 1548 to 1557) was considered to enable one to interrupt all Italian shipping. It is true that if Genoa should for any reason break with Spain, Piombino would be the only port suitable for linking Italy and Spain. Leghorn did not then possess a good port and Monaco was *poco capaz* (Instructions from J. de Vega to Pedro de Marquina, Buschbell, *art. cit.*, p. 338, September, 1545). Many documents referring to Piombino in Arch. Hist. Nacional, Madrid, Catalogue no. 2719, H. Lippomano to the Doge, (A.d.S. Venice), Madrid, 26th January 1587: the Grand Duke of Tuscany was prepared to give a million in gold for the possession of the *presidios*, or even for a single one. Philip II refused 'perché tra le altre cose con haverebbe dalle parte di Catalogna et da tutte li rive di Spagne fino a Napoli alcun porto di conto . . .'.

Barbary coast immediately becomes clear. A lookout post was sufficient to halt or impede the procession of coastbound ships.

If the practices of navigation on the high seas did not reach the Mediterranean, it was not for lack of technical competence. Mediterranean mariners knew how to handle the astrolabe and had used the lodestone for a long time; or could have if they had wanted to. Indeed the Italians had been the forerunners and instructors of the Iberians on the routes to the New World.[15] Mediterranean – or 'Levantine' ships as they were known in Spain – yearly made the voyage from the inland sea to London or Antwerp. They were familiar with Atlantic waters. Ships from the Mediterranean even made direct crossings to the New World; the *Pélerine* of Marseilles, for instance, which in 1531 sailed to Brazil and back only to be captured by Portuguese ships at Málaga[16] at the end of the run. In November, 1586, the galleon of the Grand Duke of Tuscany on arriving at Alicante allowed herself to be chartered for the 'Indies'; she carried munitions for the fortress at Havana and brought back merchandise left behind by a vessel that had been unable to make the crossing.[17] In 1610 two Tuscan vessels were unloading cargoes carried directly from the Indies.[18] Ragusan ships may have rounded the Cape of Good Hope[19] not long after Vasco da Gama; they certainly reached the New World.

If Mediterranean sailors persisted in using the old coastal routes, apart from the few direct crossings mentioned above, it was because the old ways fulfilled their needs and suited the complexities of its coastline; it was impossible to sail far in the Mediterranean without touching land. And a coastline always in sight is the navigator's best aid and surest compass. Even a low-lying coast is a protection against the sudden and violent Mediterranean winds, especially off-shore winds. When the *mistral* blows in the Gulf of Lions, the best course even today is to keep close to the coast and use the narrow strip of calmer water near the shore. So the lodestone was not essential to Mediterranean life. In 1538, unlike the Spanish galleys, the French galleys did not use it.[20] Again they could have if they had wanted to.

[15] Richard Ehrenburg, *Das Zeitalter der Fugger*, 1922, I, 373, Paul Herre, *Weltgeschichte am Mittelmeer*, 1930, p. 229–231.

[16] P. Gaffarel, *Histoire du Brésil français au XVIe siècle*, 1878, p. 100–101.

[17] A.d.S. Venice, H° Lippomano to the Doge, Madrid, 19th November, 1586.

[18] A.d.S. Florence, Mediceo 2079, f°s 337 and 365. The ships were probably Italian. For a direct voyage from Brazil to Leghorn, but probably by a Portuguese, ship, see Mediceo 2080, 29th November, 1581. There is also mention of a ship sent 'alle Indie' by the Grand Duke Ferdinand to discover new lands, dated 1609, in Baldinucci *Giornale di ricordi*, Marciana, VI, XCIV. Could there be an error of a year in the date? The Grand Duke Ferdinand was in agreement with the Dutch to colonize part of Brazil at the beginning of the seventeenth century, Giuseppe Gino Guarnieri, *Un audace impresa marittima di Ferdinando I dei Medici, con documenti e glossario indo-caraibico*, Pisa, 1928, p. 24, notes.

[19] J. Cvijić, *La péninsule balkanique*, 1918, p. 377.

[20] Édouard Petit, *André Doria, un amiral condottiere au XVIe siècle, 1466–1560*, 1887, p. 175. Belon writes, *op. cit.*, p. 92, 'the ancients had more difficulty in navigating than we do now ... and usually did not lose sight of land. But now that everyone

Besides, sailing close to shore was more than a protection against the elements. A nearby port could also be a refuge from a pursuing corsair. In an emergency the ship could run aground and the crew escape by land. This was how Tavernier escaped a corsair in 1654 in the Gulf of Hyères; he even had the luck not to lose the ship in the incident.

'Tramping' also made it possible to take on cargo. It gave ample opportunity for bargaining, and for making the most of price differences. Every sailor, from captain to cabin-boy would have his bundle of merchandise on board, and merchants or their representatives would travel with their wares. The round trip, which could last several weeks or months, was a long succession of selling, buying, and exchanging, organized within a complicated itinerary. In the course of the voyage, the cargo would often have completely altered its nature. Amid the buying and selling, care was always taken to call at some port, such as Leghorn, Genoa, or Venice, where it was possible to exchange spices, leather, cotton, or coral for metal currency. Only the big specialized salt and grain ships had any resemblance to the destination-conscious shipping of today. The others were more like travelling bazaars. The calls at port were so many opportunities for buying, selling, reselling, and exchanging goods, not to mention the other pleasures of going ashore.

There was the further advantage of the almost daily renewal of supplies, rations, water, and wood, which was the more necessary since the boats were of small capacity and on board rations, even drinking water, quickly deteriorated. Frequent stops were made to 'faire aiguade et lignade', 'to take on water and wood', as Rabelais says.

This slow-motion shipping, if we can call it that, governed the geography of the coastal regions, in the sense that for one big ship capable of by-passing ports we must reckon dozens of boats and small sailing vessels that were processionary by vocation. In the same way that along land routes, such as the Roman roads in the western countries, daily halts led to the remarkably regular establishment of villages, along the coastal sea routes, the ports are found a day's voyage apart. Where river estuaries were unsuitable because of sandbanks, they grew up on the sheltered shores of bays. In between them there was practically nothing.[21] Sometimes on a

---

knows the virtue of the Lodestone, navigation is easy'. And he mentions the use corsairs made of the lodestone. But the corsairs of course were the very ships which did need to sail away from the coast, in order to surprise other vessels by coming from the open sea. The compass is supposed to have arrived in the Mediterranean from China in the twelth century. But is this certain? F. C. Lane, 'The Economic Meaning of the Invention of the compass' in *The American Historical Review*, vol. LXVIII, No. 3, April, 1963, p. 615.

[21] Cf. Bisschop's remarks, *op. cit.*, p. 332, on the arid and unwelcoming coast of Mediterranean Spain; Siegfried's note, *op. cit.*, p. 319, on the dry and often deserted coasts of the Mediterranean. Similar remarks in R. Recouly, *Ombre et soleil d'Espagne*, 1934, p. 174; hundreds of kilometres without seeing towns or villages. These coasts are deserted but also without shelter: so the coast of Spain from Cape Palos to Cape Salon affords no shelter, apart from Valencia and Alicante, except from offshore winds (*Instructions Nautiques*, no. 345, p. 96). Along the *entire* Mediterranean Spanish

coast where the hinterland was sparsely populated, like North Africa, a port, with its indispensable source of water, might exist as a meeting point for boats and fishermen, without a town having grown up around it: proof, if it were needed, that the functions of a port are not sufficient to create a town.

This is more than the picturesque sideshow of a highly coloured history. It is the underlying reality. We are too inclined to pay attention only to vital communications; they may be interrupted or restored; all is not necessarily lost or saved. Everyday coastal shipping has untiringly spun threads connecting the different areas of the sea which may pass unnoticed in the great movements of history.

The early days of Portuguese discovery. Finally, it is of some interest to watch how the Portuguese, at the beginning of the fifteenth century, tackled the immense problem of navigation on the high seas, in the Atlantic, which was entirely new to them. At the time of the expedition against Ceuta in 1415, the inexperience of the Portuguese had been obvious. It was only with great difficulty that they had managed to master the currents of the Straits of Gibraltar.[22] The chronicler de Barros says quite clearly that his compatriots were familiar with the declination and the astrolabe, but until 1415 'they had not been accustomed to venture far on the high seas'.[23] One historian has even said of the early Portuguese discoverers, following the endless African coastline, that in the lifetime of Henry the Navigator they were still 'primarily timid and fearful coast-huggers, with no spirit of adventure'[24] – Mediterranean sailors, in fact, despite their experience of the ocean. However, once the caravels had been perfected – the revolutionary ships developed in 1439–1440 to meet the difficulties encountered on the return voyage from Guinea of a head wind and contrary currents – they had to take to the open sea and make for the Azores in order to reach Lisbon, steering a vast, semi-circular course.[25] After that they began to take to the sea in earnest and very quickly made up for lost time.

The narrow seas, home of history. The Mediterranean is not a single sea but a succession of small seas that communicate by means of wider or narrower entrances. In the two great east and west basins of the Mediterranean there is a series of highly individual narrow seas between the land masses,

---

coast, there is no natural protection against sea-winds (*ibid.* p. 1.). On the bare mountainous coast of Provence, see Honoré Bouche, *Chorographie, ou des descriptions de la Provence . . .* 1664, p. 18.

[22] Richard Hennig, *Terrae Incognitae*, 2nd edition, 1953, III, p. 261.

[23] João de Barros, *Da Asia*, Dec. I, book I, ch. 2, Venice 1551, p. 7.

[24] Georg Friederici, *Der Charakter der Entdeckung und Eroberung Amerikas Durch die Europäer*, 1936, II p. 23.

[25] Vitorino Magalhães-Godinho, *L'Économie de l'Empire portugais aux XVe et XVIe siècles. L'or et le poivre. Route de Guinée et route du poivre*, Paris, 1958. Typed thesis, Sorbonne, p. XLVIII ff.

each with its own character, types of boat, and its own laws of history;[26] and as a rule the narrowest seas are the richest in significance and historical value, as if man had found it easiest to impose himself on the Mediterranean in a small compass.

Even today, these seas still maintain their local life, with the picturesque survival of old sailing vessels and traditional fishing boats.[27] At Sfax, in the Sea of the Syrtes, one can still see the *mahonnes* with their triangular sails, and the sponge fishers' boats, the *kamaki*, manned by men from the Kerkenna and Djerba islands who still fish with a trident, a vision from the past.[28] Théophile Gautier had just passed Cape Malea and the Greek islands and calm waters were coming into sight when suddenly 'the horizon was filled with sails; schooners, brigs, caravels, argosies, crossing the blue water in all directions'. The narrow seas have kept their elusive enchantment to this day.[29] The survival of these archaic forms of transport, of circuits that have been in existence for centuries is in itself a subject for reflection. Their importance now as in the past lies in short trips, collecting small cargoes. Their security lies in the narrow and familiar compass in which they operate. Difficulties begin only when they embark on long voyages, if they have to leave their native sea and sail out past dangerous headlands. 'He who sails past Cape Malea,' says a Greek proverb, 'must forget his homeland.'[30]

Linked by shipping routes which made large-scale trade possible, these narrow seas were far more important in the sixteenth century than the two great basins, the Ionian Sea to the east, and the western Mediterrnanean bounded by Sardinia, Corsica, Europe, and Africa. Both of these, particularly the former, were maritime Saharas; trading vessels would either skirt the edges of these expanses or cross as fast as they could.

The maritime activity of the Mediterranean was carried on at the edges of these two forbidding stretches, in the security of the narrow seas: to the east, the Black Sea, only partly Mediterranean; the Aegean or Archipelago Sea (in the sixteenth century even in French it was known by the Italian word *Arcipelago*); in the centre the Adriatic and the seas between Africa and Sicily which do not have a particular name; to the west the Tyrrhenian Sea, the true Sea of Italy, the 'Etruscan' sea between Sicily, Sardinia, Corsica and the west coast of Italy; and in the far west, between southern Spain and North Africa, another sea without a name, the 'Mediterranean Channel', which could have as its eastern boundary a line running from Cape Matifou near Algiers to Cape de la Nao, near Valencia, and which joins the Atlantic at the Straits of Gibraltar.

[26] Y. M. Goblet, *Le Temps*, 30th April, 1938.
[27] The multicoloured boats of the Aegean with their raised bulwarks (W. Helwig, *Braconniers de la mer en Grèce*, Fr. trans. 1942, p. 133). In the sea around the Balearics elegant schooners can still be seen carrying oranges, R. Recouly, *op. cit.*, p. 179.
[28] Emmanuel Grévin, *Djerba l'île heureuse et le Sud Tunisien*, 1937, p. 35.
[29] Théophile Gautier, *Voyage à Constantinople*, 1853, p. 36 Cf. the present day port of Cavalla (M. N. 'Kawalla die Stadt am weissen Meer', *Kölnische Zeitung*, 16th July, 1942); sailing boats laden with tobacco, olives, and dried squids . . .
[30] Cdt. A. Thomazi, *Histoire de la Navigation*, 1941, p. 23.

Even within these seas smaller areas can be distinguished, for there is hardly a bay in the Mediterranean that is not a miniature community, a complex world in itself.[31]

The Black Sea, preserve of Constantinople. The far-off Black Sea, limit of Mediterranean shipping, was ringed round by wild lands, with a few exceptions, both uncivilized and de-civilized. Great mountains bordered it to the south and east, hostile mountains through which the roads made their difficult way from Persia, Armenia, and Mesopotamia to the great centre of Trebizond. To the north by contrast rolled the great Russian plains, a land of passage and nomadism, over which a jealous guard was still maintained by the Crimean Tartars in the sixteenth century. It was only in the following century that the Russian outlaws, the Cossacks, were to reach the shore of the sea and begin their piracy at the expense of the Turks. Already in the sixteenth century, the Muscovites were taking advantage of the winter to make 'courreries' towards its shores.[32]

The Black Sea at this period, as indeed throughout its history was an important economic region. In the first place there was the produce of its own shores: dried fish, the botargo and caviar of the 'Russian' rivers, the wood indispensable to the Turkish fleet, iron from Mingrelia[33], grain, and wool; the latter was collected at Varna and loaded along with hides on to the great Ragusan vessels; the grain was cornered by Constantinople. Secondly, there was the merchandise transported through the Black Sea; goods passing through to Central Asia and Persia and goods brought by caravan in transit to Constantinople and the West. Unfortunately we do not know a great deal about this two-way trade with the East in the sixteenth century. One has the impression that Constantinople monopolized the long-distance trade as well as the domestic trade of the Black Sea, acting as a screen between this Mediterranean extremity and the rest of the sea. Almost on its doorstep, the Black Sea was the supplying region without which the mighty capital could not survive, for it was only inadequately provided for by the tribute of the Balkans (mostly sheep) and

[31] For individual descriptions, cf. on the bay of Naples, *Instructions Nautiques*, no. 368, p. 131; on the gulf of Vólos, with its many islands, Helwig, *op. cit.*, p. 16; on the gulf of Quarnero, H. Hochholzer, 'Die Küsten der Adria als Kultur-Siedlungs-und Wirtschaftsbereich', in *Geogr. Zeitschr.*, 1932.

[32] Dolu to the bishop of Dax, Constantinople, 18th February, 1561, E. Charrière, *op. cit.*, II, p. 650–652: on the subject of the Muscovite raids on Tana. The Muscovites took advantage of the frozen rivers, returning home in the spring (cf. *ibid.*, p. 647–648 and 671–672, 5th February and 30th August). For Russian sea pirates, cf. a reference in 1608: Avisos de Constantinople, 12th June, 1608, A.N. K 1679. The Pasha of the Sea thought of sending galleys out against them, but galleys, he was told, would be powerless against their small boats. It would be better to send '*caiches que son barcos medianos*'. In 1622 there were raids on Black Sea ports by Cossacks in the service of Poland; and Kaffa, 'the capital of Tartary' was sacked, Naples, *Storia, Patria*, XXVIII, B. 11, f[os] 230 and 230 v°; 1664 J. B. Tavernier, *op. cit.*

[33] Mingrelia, notes Tavernier (*op. cit.*, Persian Travels, p. 114) in 1664 is always on good terms with Turkey 'because the greatest part of the Steel and Iron that is spent in *Turkie* comes out of Mingrelia through the Black Sea'.

the wheat, rice and beans brought in by the fleets of Alexandria, along with spices and drugs. Pierre Belon[34] mentions the butter that was carried from Mingrelia to Constantinople 'in the freshly flayed and undressed hides of oxen and cows', probably on board one of the innumerable Greek *caramusalis* that plied the Black Sea, although they were better suited to the short journeys in the Archipelago than to this dangerous sea,[35] which was often rough and shrouded in fog. In October, 1575, a single storm sank a hundred of these little ships laden with grain.[36]

In the sixteenth century the Black Sea was attached to Constantinople, just as in former times it had been the preserve of Miletus, of Athens, and after 1265 of the Italians and Genoese[37] who installed themselves at Tana and Kaffa in the protected site in the south of the Crimea,[38] sheltered by the mountains of the peninsula from the peoples of the northern steppe; they also settled in Constantinople (only leaving in 1453 and then not altogether), and were only dislodged from their Crimean ports by the Turks later on, in the last quarter of the fifteenth century. Kaffa was taken in 1479. There followed a major realignment of the land routes leading to the sea. They no longer went to the Crimea but to Constantinople instead. In the Moldavian lands the routes leading to Kilia and Cetatea Alba were replaced by the great trade route towards Galatz which thereafter tapped the trade of the Danube and, beyond it, that of Poland.[39]

From then on the Black Sea became the recognized granary of the enormous Turkish capital. The Ragusans, however, continued to make their way in, at least until the 1590's, loading up whole boats at Varna with fleeces and hides: *montinini*, *vacchini*, and *buffalini*. They managed to do the same thing on the Sea of Marmara, at Rodosto.[40] Perhaps to avoid customs expenses? In any event, at the end of the sixteenth century the Ragusans abandoned both ports almost simultaneously under what circumstances we do not know. The Black Sea was more completely closed to the west than ever, at any rate closed to shipping: for there seems to have been a victory of land routes over sea passages at this time, as we shall see. Was it simply that Constantinople locked the door, to put an end to the

[34] Pierre Belon, *op. cit.*, p. 163.
[35] 'That furious sea . . .', 19th May, 1579, E. Charrière, *op. cit.*, III, p. 799. The ships of the Black Sea were often badly ballasted. Cf. the wreck of a ship carrying planks, Tott, *Memoirs*, *op. cit.*, II, p. 170.
[36] Avisos de Constantinople, 17th, 18th, 24th October, 1575, Simancas E° 1334.
[37] The Black Sea was opened to the Italians towards 1265, by the political decline of Byzantium: G. Bratianu, *Études byzantines*, 1939, p. 159.
[38] A. Philippson, 'Das Byzantinische Reich als geographische Erscheinung', in: *Geogr. Zeitschr.* 1934, p. 448.
[39] I. Nistor, *Handel und Wandel in der Moldau*, 1912, p. 23.
[40] The question of Western trade in the Black Sea is a large subject. For Ragusan trade, see below p. 318. From time to time, Venice continued to send ships as far as the Black Sea (H. F° to the Doge, Pera, 25th May, 1561, A.d.S. Venice, Seno. Secreta, Const. Fza 3C, refers to a small Venetian ship which set out for Mingrelia). Note (A.d.S. Florence, Medicео 4274) that in the capitulation project between Florence and Constantinople, the Florentines demanded freedom of shipping in the Black Sea, 1577.

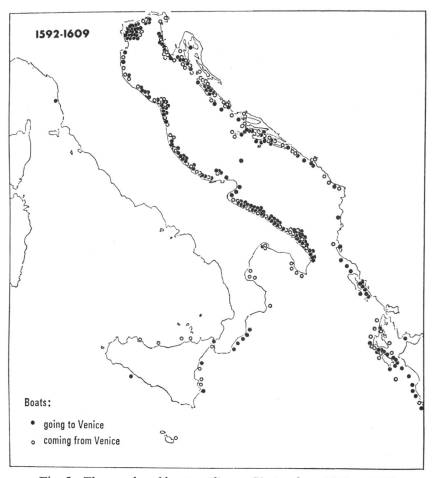

1592-1609

Boats:

● going to Venice
○ coming from Venice

Fig. 8: *The wrecks of boats sailing to Venice from 1592 to 1609*
(From A. Tenenti, *Naufrages, Corsaires et Assurances maritimes à Venise*, 1959). They indicate the importance of the coastal route.

rôle of the Black Sea as the 'turntable of international trade' at the end of the Middle Ages?[41] Or perhaps the closure had other more distant origins. The Black Sea was the terminus not only of the roads that met at Trebizond or Sinope, but also of what is generally known as the silk route. Now it seems fairly clear that this route was interrupted from the fourteenth century on. The trade that had made it rich turned towards Persia. Turkestan certainly suffered from the change. Meanwhile, in the middle of the sixteenth century, the Russians advanced along the Volga. The

[41] G. I. Bratianu, 'La mer Noire, plaque tournante du trafic international à la fin du Moyen Age', in: *Revue du Sud-Est Européen*, 1944, p. 36–39.

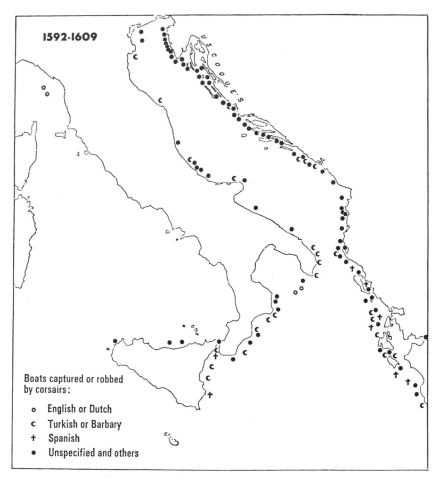

1592-1609

Boats captured or robbed
by corsairs:

o English or Dutch
c Turkish or Barbary
+ Spanish
• Unspecified and others

Fig. 9: *Captured vessels during the same period, from the same source*

khanate of Kazan, an eastern parallel to the kingdom of Granada, enriched by the caravan traffic and long coveted by the Russians, fell into
their hands half-ruined as a result of troubles it is difficult to assess, which
may or may not have followed the interruption of the Turkestan route.
Ivan the Terrible took Astrakhan in 1556. This time the door was shut and
bolted, in spite of the Turkish attempt of 1569–70, the great unknown event
of history.[42]

[42] Cf. below, II, Part III, ch. 3, section 2. On the question of a canal linking the
Don and the Volga, cf. its previous history. J. Mazzei, *Politica doganale differenziale*,
1931, p. 40; even more useful is W. E. D. Allen, *Problems of Turkish power in the
Sixteenth century*,1963, p. 22 ff.

Sicily and Tunisia cut the Mediterranean in two

Fig. 10: *Sicily and Tunisia cut the Mediterranean in two*

The Archipelago, Venetian and Genoese. The archipelago, 'the most hospitable sea of the globe', is a succession of barren islands and even poorer coasts. This too can only be understood in connection with a great town. In classical times it was the parade ground of Athens. Later it became the basis of Byzantine sea-power, which through its control of this sea was able to preserve the Aegean and then drive out Islam which had installed itself briefly in Crete in the ninth century. Through this sea too, communication with the West by the seas of Greece and Sicily and the routes of the Adriatic, was safeguarded, before Venice in turn rose to greatness.

Centuries passed, and the Archipelago became Venetian and Genoese. The two rival cities divided between them its principal islands. They installed upon them their patricians, guardians of the empire, landowners, planters, merchants too, in fact colonial aristocracies which remained separate from the Orthodox populations. These might become 'Latinized' in their habits, but would never be assimilated to the foreign invader. It was the usual story, and it ended with the mutual solidarity of the colonial settlers. When Venice supplanted Genoa in Cyprus in 1479, the planters of both colonial powers came to an agreement without too much difficulty: an obvious and inevitable case of class discipline.

In the Archipelago, the Latins defended their positions with greater ease and, above all, efficiency than they had in the Black Sea, with means that were for a long time superior to those of the attacker. However Negropont (Euboea) was captured in 1479; Rhodes fell in 1522; Chios was occupied in 1566 without a shot fired; Cyprus after an easy landing and two sieges, at Nicosia and Famagusta, in 1570–72; and Crete in 1669, after a twenty-five year war.

But the struggle for the Archipelago was by no means confined to a series of pitched battles. It also took the everyday form of a social war. More than once the Greek 'natives' betrayed their masters, at Cyprus and later at Crete. The Archipelago collaborated in the Turkish victory, and even before that victory Greek sailors had been tempted by employment in the fleet of the Grand Turk, whose crews often came from the Archipelago. The Cretans were perhaps the readiest to join the fleet of the Grand Signior at the beginning of each summer for the campaign that was about to begin. The recruiters would find them in the taverns of Pera, near the Arsenal;[43] this was over a century before Crete fell into Turkish hands.

Constantinople could also offer the Greeks, besides employment in its armies, the profits of Black Sea and Egyptian voyages. In the gigantic task of supplying the capital, there was a place for the grain-bearing *caïques* and *caramusalis*,[44] for the *gerbe* carrying horses and wood, indeed for all

[43] J. W. Zinkeisen, *Geschichte des osmanischen Reiches in Europa*, 1840–1863, III, p. 29 ff.

[44] Robert Mantran, *Istanbul dans la seconde moitié du XVIIe siècle*, 1963, lists the types of Turkish boats whose names are recognisable: *firkata* (frigate), *zaïka* (caïque) *kalyon* (galleon), p. 318, note 2; should we distinguish between the *caïque*, the Greek boat *par excellence* which transported wheat in the Aegean and the Sea of Marmara, and the *caramusali*, *Haramürsel*, in the Sea of Marmara only, 'from the name of the

the Greek sailing vessels of the Archipelago. To all this could be added the attraction of religion: Constantinople was the Rome of the Orthodox Church.

And in the first decades of the sixteenth century there began a fresh phase of Greek expansion over the whole of the Mediterranean. The career of the Barbarossas, sailors from Lesbos converted to Islam, who settled first in Djerba then at Djidjelli, and provided transport for Spanish Moslems who wanted to leave the Peninsula, later becoming corsairs and, finally, after 1518, rulers of Algiers – this whole episode was not an accident. Neither was the career of Dragut, another Greek whom we find in the 1540s on the Tunisian coast and in 1556 installed at Tripoli in Barbary, in place of the Knights of Malta whom the Turks had expelled five years earlier.

Between Tunisia and Sicily. It will be difficult to denote with precision the role played by the ill-defined sea between Africa and Sicily, with its deep waters full of fish, its reefs of coral and sponges, and its islands, often uninhabited because they are so small: La Favignana, Marettimo, and Levanzo at the western tip of Sicily; Malta, Gozo, and Pantelleria in the middle of the sea; and Tabarka, La Galite, Zembra, Djerba, and the Kerkenna Islands near the Tunisian coast. Its boundaries correspond to those of the ancient geological 'bridge' stretching from North Africa to Sicily: to the east a line drawn from Tripoli to Syracuse, to the west a line from Bône to Trapani. The essential axis of this sea is north–south, from Sicily to Africa. Ships travelling from east to west, from the Levant to the Atlantic, passed through, but this traffic was generally diverted to the north towards the main route passing through the Straits of Messina. Moreover, in the Sicily–Africa sector, this traffic did not have the frequency of the north–south currents.

These currents have dictated its history, making the whole complex shift sometimes to the south, sometimes to the north, with the tide of events. The whole region was Moslem with the Aghlabids, and so, from 827, when the conquest began, to 1071, when Palermo was recaptured, a citadel of Islam; then it was Norman, or on the way to being so from the eleventh century, for the Norman advance from Naples to Sicily did not stop at the reconquest of the island; it spread southwards by war, privateering, trade, and even emigration to the African territories. The Angevins and Aragonese were later to continue this policy dictated by proximity. Several times they attacked the African coast; levied tribute from the emirs of Tunis; held Djerba from 1284 to 1335. Meanwhile Christian merchants settled everywhere, particularly in the *souks* of Tunis and Tripoli, and obtained privilege upon privilege. Christian soldiers, and in particular the Catalan mercenary, later to be master of Sicily (the Sicilian Vespers took place in 1282), found adventures in Africa almost as profitable as in

---

port near Izmit (Nicomedia) where it is built' p. 488–489: a boat with a half-deck, three sails and oars? Western texts do not agree.

the East. As early as the twelfth century Catalan sailors were frequenting the coral reefs of Tabarka.

Political circles in Palermo and Messina were, even in the sixteenth century, continually suggesting projects of African conquest to the vanity and colonial ambitions of the viceroys of Spanish Sicily: first to Juan de la Vega, later to the Duke of Medina Celi, later again to Marcantonio Colonna. These projects translated the dimly felt necessity of uniting the shores and islands of this intermediary region, of bringing together Sicily's wheat, cheese, and barrels of tunny fish, and the oil from Djerba, the leather, wax, and wool of the southern lands, and the gold dust and black slaves of the Sahara trade; the need to control the whole maritime complex and ensure the policing of the coasts, the security of the tunny-boats and the safe fishing of the Barbary coral reefs by fishermen from Trapani, half-Catalans whose boats though poorly armed did not hesitate to attack the vessels of the Barbary corsairs in the sixteenth century, and finally the need to protect from the corsairs the *caricatori* of Sicilian wheat which were often threatened from the south, for piracy here as elsewhere often tended to re-establish a natural balance which had been disturbed by history.

It is customary when discussing Sicily to keep looking to the North, towards Naples, and to regard their two histories as fundamentally opposed, the rise of Naples leading to the decline of Palermo and vice versa. It is even more important to emphasize its links with North Africa, that is the value of this maritime world which our imperfect knowledge or lack of attention has left without a name.

The Mediterranean 'Channel'. The most westerly part of the Mediterranean Sea is an independent, narrow passage between the land masses, easily accessible to man, the Mediterranean 'Channel' as one geographer, René Lespès, has called it. It is a separate world, lying between the Straits of Gibraltar to the west and an eastern limit running from Cape Caxine to Cape de la Nao, or even from Valencia to Algiers. The east–west passage is never easy for shipping; to sail eastwards is to enter the great stretch of the western Mediterranean; to go westwards is to come to the even vaster expanse of the Atlantic, by way of the Straits which are themselves dangerous because of frequent fog, powerful currents, reefs, and sandbanks along the shores. All straits, like projecting headlands, cause an alteration in currents and winds. Here it is particularly marked and the passage is always a complicated operation.

By contrast the north–south journey is comparatively easy. The sea does not act as a barrier between the two great continental masses of Spain and North Africa; but rather as a river which unites more than it divides, making a single world of North and South, a 'bi-continent', as Gilberto Freyre has called it.[45]

Like the corridor between Sicily and Africa, this channel was one of the

[45] *Casa Grande e senzala*, Rio de Janeiro, 5th ed. 1946, I, p. 88; Paul Achard, *La vie extraordinaire des frères Barberousse, op. cit.*, p. 53.

conquests of Islam in the Middle Ages; a late conquest – in the tenth century – at the time when the caliphate of Córdoba was reaching the peak of its short-lived glory. The success of the Ummayyads ensured that wheat, men, and mercenaries would be brought over from the Maghreb, and that the produce of the Andalusian cities would be exported in return. The free, or at any rate easy, access to this strip of water meant that the centre of Andalusian maritime life passed from Almeria, with its bustling ship-yards, vessels, and silklooms, to Seville, where Mediterranean shipping concentrated in the eleventh century. It brought so much wealth that the port on the Guadalquivir soon began to rival in splendour the old continental capital, Córdoba.

Similarly, Moslem supremacy in the Mediterranean led to the rise or expansion of great sea-towns on the African coast: Bougie, Algiers, and Oran, the last two founded in the tenth century. And twice, the 'African Andalusia', under the Almoravids and then the Almohads, rescued the real Andalusia from Christian pressure, in the eleventh and twelfth centuries.

Right up to the end of Islam's hold on the Iberian Peninsula – until the thirteenth century at least and after – the 'Channel' remained in Saracen hands from the approaches of Algarve in Portugal to Valencia and even the Balearics. Islam held this channel even longer than the Sicilian Mediterranean, well after Las Navas de Tolosa in 1212, at least until the capture of Ceuta by Dom João of Portugal and his sons in 1415. From that day the passage to Africa was open and the Moslem community left in Granada was condemned; only the long Castilian disputes prolonged its existence. When the war of Granada began again for the last act of the *Reconquista* in 1487, Ferdinand and Isabella used ships from Biscay to blockade its coast.

After the conquest the Christian victors were drawn into taking the southern coast of the Ibero-African channel, but their efforts lacked the conviction and coherence that would have best served Spanish interests. It was a tragedy for Spanish history that after the occupation of Melilla in 1947, of Mers-el-Kebir in 1505, of the Peñon de Velez in 1508, of Oran in 1509, of Mostaganem, Tlemcen, Ténès and the Peñon of Algiers in 1510, this new war of Granada was not pursued with more determination, that this thankless but vital undertaking was sacrificed to the mirage of Italy and the comparatively easy gains in America. Spain's inability, or un-willingness, to develop her initial success, which was perhaps too easy ('It looks,' wrote the royal secretary, Hernando de Zafra, to their Catholic Majesties in 1492, 'as if God wishes to give Your Highnesses these African Kingdoms.'), her failure to pursue the war on the other side of the Mediterranean is one of the great missed opportunities of history. As an essayist wrote,[46] Spain, half-European, half-African, failed to carry out her geographical mission and for the first time in history, the Straits of Gibraltar 'became a political frontier'.[47]

[46] Gonzalo de Reparaz, *Geografiá y política*, Barcelona, 1929, *passim*.
[47] Émile-Félix Gautier, *Les siècles obscurs du Maghreb*, 1927, p. 280.

Along this frontier there was constant warfare, a sign that the essential links had been severed here as well as between Sicily and Africa. Crossing the channel had become difficult. This is easy to see in the case of supplying Oran, which was a precarious undertaking throughout the sixteenth century. From the great 'central station' of Málaga, the *proveedores* organized convoys and chartered ships and boats to send to the *presidio*.[48] They generally sent them in winter, taking advantage of breaks in the weather long enough for the short crossing. Even so the corsairs managed to capture supply ships, which they would then in the normal process of bargaining, offer to sell back at Cape Caxine. In 1563, when the *presidio* was besieged by troops from Algiers, the ships that ran the blockade were *balancelles* and brigantines from Valencia and Andalusia. These small boats were like those that 'in the old days', as an enquiry in 1565 says,[49] used to sail from Cartagena, Cadiz, or Málaga carrying caps from Córdoba and cloth from Toledo to the North African ports: or like the fishing-boats which on the other side of Gibraltar continued to sail the Atlantic, manned by a race of sailors from Seville, San Lucar de Barrameda, or Puerto de Santa Maria, who would fish as far away as Mauritania, and on Sundays go ashore to hear mass in one of the Portuguese *presidios* on the Moroccan coast;[50] or the little boats from Valencia that carried to Algiers rice, Spanish perfumes, and, despite the prohibitions, contraband merchandise.[51]

At the end of the century this now-quiescent part of the sea was aroused abruptly by a dramatic challenge, but not from Spain's traditional rivals: the sailors of Marseilles who had always frequented the Barbary ports, or the sailors of Leghorn, new arrivals after 1575, who were attracted by Tunis and lingered there but who sometimes voyaged as far as Larache[52] and the Moroccan Sous.[53] The new element was the massive invasion by northern ships, especially after the 1590s. These foreigners had to pass through the Straits twice, on the way in and out. On the way out they were expected and a watch was kept for them. Did the Hollanders, as has been claimed,[54] discover a new way of passing through the Straits, which they afterwards taught their pupils, the corsairs of Algiers? It is possible if not altogether certain. In any event, the Spaniards put a great deal of effort into keeping watch and even preventing ships from passing through, using galleys in the calm summer days and galleons in the stormy winter months. From Cape St. Vincent on the Portuguese coast to Cartagena

[48] According to the documents in the series Estado Castilla, at Simancas. Cf. below, II, Part II, ch. 7, end of section 1.

[49] 14th Mars, 1565, Simancas E° 146.

[50] R. Ricard, 'Les Portugais au Maroc', in: *Bulletin de l'Ass. Guillaume Budé*, July, 1937, p. 26.

[51] D. de Haëdo, *Topographia . . . op. cit.*, p. 19 v°.

[52] F. Braudel and R. Romano, *Navires et marchandises à l'entrée du port de Livourne, 1547–1611*, 1951, p. 45.

[53] *Ibid.*, p. 45.

[54] J. Denucé, *L'Afrique au XVIe siècle et le commerce anversois*, 1937, p. 12.

and Valencia,[55] and even as far as Mers-el-Kebir, Ceuta, and Tangier, to Larache, which was occupied on 20th March, 1610, and La Mamora, occupied in August, 1614, we must imagine these lookout posts, alerts, patrols, and battles, often with no glory attached, which persisted until the eighteenth century.[56] The rulers of Spain, her sailors, and advisers were always dreaming of a final solution: to install on Gibraltar itself reinforced cannons which would be sure to hit the ships;[57] to fortify the little island of Perejil off Ceuta;[58] or on the advice of the mad and brilliant adventurer in the service of Spain, the Englishman Anthony Sherley, to take Mogador and Agadir, and thereby hold Morocco, the Catholic King becoming 'absoluto señor de la Berberia'[59] – and this in 1622!

But the struggle was never resolved. The enemy, English, Dutch, or Algerian, would pass through the Straits by stealth, taking advantage of a calm night in winter,[60] or by force, seldom leaving a ship in the hands of the adversary, more often giving the patrol ships a battering with his superior vessels and artillery. An unspectacular or at any rate little-known war, this great Mediterranean drama was fought out at the very gateway to the sea, almost outside its waters. We shall have more to say about it.

The Tyrrhenian Sea. The vast Tyrrhenian Sea – the 'channels of Corsica and Sardinia', as it is called in the sixteenth-century documents – open to neighbouring civilizations and bordered by rich and populous lands, could not fail to have an eventful history.

Earliest times show an area divided among the Etruscans who ruled Tuscany, the cities of the Greek Empire and Sicily, the separate world of Marseilles and its empire, and finally the Carthaginians, who had settled in western Sicily and on the coasts of Sardinia and Corsica, where there were also Etruscan settlements. Roughly speaking the Etruscans controlled the central area; the others its extremities: the Greeks of the South held the route to the Levant; the Carthaginians the route which went from Panormos (Palermo) to Africa by way of Drepanon (Trapani); and lastly the Greeks of Marseilles the route linking the Etruscan sea to the West, just at the point where ships have to wait for favourable winds to cross the Gulf of Lions on the way to Spain.

This early situation already shows what were to be the permanent

[55] Philip II to the Adelantado of Castille, S. Lorenzo, 4th September, 1594, Simancas E° Castilla 171, f°, 107, knew that the Adelantado who was with his ships at Ceuta intended to patrol the coast as far as Cape St. Vincent, and wanted him to go on to Lisbon.
[56] Ustariz, *op. cit.*, p. 260–261 (1724).
[57] A.d.S. Venice, Alvise Correr to the Doge, Madrid, 28th April 1621. It would be unlikely to succeed, notes the Venetian 'because of the great distance between one side of the Straits and the other'.
[58] Xavier A. Flores, *Le 'Peso Politico de todo el mundo' d'Anthony Sherley, 1963*, p. 176.
[59] *Ibid.*, p. 111.
[60] A.d.S. Venice, H° Lippomano to the Doge, Madrid, 19th November, 1586, on the crossing made by Amurat, corsair king of Algiers 'on a dark night'.

features of the Tyrrhenian: the value of the central 'lake' and the importance of the gateways to it. It gives some indication of the reasons why this sea, too vast and open, could never be under the control of one single power, economy, or civilization. Except under the levelling hegemony of Rome, no navy ever maintained a position of supremacy in the sea, neither the Vandals whom Byzantine brought to heel, nor the Saracen fleets since Italy eluded them in the end, neither the Normans nor the Angevins, the former meeting opposition from Byzantium, the latter from both Islam and the Catalans. And Pisa found herself up against the competition of Genoa.

In the sixteenth century, the first place belonged to Genoa, mistress of Corsica. But this position of supremacy had its weaknesses: Genoa was increasingly relying on foreign ships for transport, the first sign of decline. In addition she found herself faced with the Spaniards, who had captured several strong positions in the Tyrrhenian Sea. The trail had been blazed by the Aragonese, who had seized Sicily in 1282 and then in 1325, despite prolonged Genoese resistance, Sardinia, which they needed for communication with Sicily. Catalan expansion – and this was one of its original features – progressed due eastwards from the Balearics by way of Sardinia and Sicily. In these islands, the Catalans installed real maritime colonies, Alghero in Sardinia and Trapani in Sicily.

This expansion was victorious but exhausting. Coming late in time, it had to struggle to find a place for itself, combining piracy with shipping. Barcelona, where it had originated, gradually abdicated the leadership to Valencia, and it was the Valencians who led the successful conquest of the Kingdom of Naples under Alfonso the Magnanimous (1455). The Valencian act, however, was over almost as soon as it had begun, since the crown of Aragon was soon to fall under the control of Castile. At the time of the Italian wars, further change came to the Tyrrhenian: the Castilians replaced the Aragonese as soldiers and officials, both in Naples and in Sicily.[61] From now on Spain with her galleys and *tercios* brought to bear on the Tyrrhenian the full weight of a maritime, military, continental power. It was not a merchant power, however. From the time of Charles V, and in spite of ancient commercial privileges, exports of Catalan cloth to Sicily and Sardinia actually declined. The Emperor, there as elsewhere neglectful of Spanish interests, let the Genoese merchants flood the market with their own textiles. Does this mean Genoa took her revenge and regained her supremacy?

The answer is not so simple. Towards 1550 Genoa forfeited some of her maritime activities, in the Tyrrhenian and elsewhere, to the Ragusans. With their merchantmen, the latter took over the transport of Sicilian wheat and salt and the long distance voyages to Spain, the Atlantic, and the Levant. The Tyrrhenian Sea would almost have become a Ragusan lake if

[61] R. B. Merriman, *The Rise of the Spanish Empire*, 1934, IV, p. 248, 434. Was it, as R. Konetzke suggests, the fault of the Aragonese, too preoccupied with their own minor affairs, *op. cit.*, p. 148? I am reluctant to accept this explanation.

it had not been for the presence of Marseilles (at first modest, it was to become important after the 1570s), and the later rise of Leghorn, which was both a creation and a revival, for Leghorn represented both Pisa and Florence. It also represented the calculated policy of Cosimo de' Medici, who took an early interest in Genoese Corsica.[62] Lastly through the wide passage between Sicily and Sardinia came the disturbing invasion of the Barbary corsairs, who often surprised the coastal areas, far to the north, of Savona, Genoa, Nice, and even Provence. The Tuscan barrage on Elba, at Portoferraio, gave warning of them more often than it stopped them.

This divided and composite sea, the Tyrrhenian, was too closely implicated in the general life of the Mediterranean to have a very distinct identity of its own. But by enabling it to live almost entirely off its own resources, its diversity gave it a certain autonomy. The grain that went to feed its towns and those regions that were either too densely populated or too pastoral to feed themselves, came from Sicily, and until 1550 from Provence – at least it was shipped from Provence, but often came from Burgundy or even further away. Salt came from Trapani; cheese from Sardinia; *vino greco* or *latino* from Naples; salted meat from Corsica; silk from Sicily or Calabria; fruits, almonds, and walnuts, as well as barrels of anchovy or tunny from Provence; iron from Elba; money and capital from either Florence or Genoa. The rest came from outside: leather, spices, dye-woods, wool, and before long salt from Ibiza.

Of these two sets of relationships, internal and external, the internal pattern was the richer. It explains the close intermingling of peoples, civilizations, languages, and arts. It also explains why this stretch of the sea, with its comparatively calm, sheltered waters should have been predominantly a region of small ships. In one year, from June, 1609 to June, 1610, the port of Leghorn alone received over 2500 barques and small vessels[63] – an enormous figure. Only small ships could sail up the Tiber to Rome and its river port Ripa Grande,[64] perhaps carrying the furniture and belongings of a bishop arriving at the Court of Rome, or the casks of *vino greco* that some church official had taken the care to have shipped from the kingdom of Naples. All the statistics, those of Leghorn which are very rich for our period, those of Civitavecchia, Genoa, or Marseilles reveal the immense importance of these short-distance links: from Cape Corse to Leghorn, or Genoa for the transport of wood; or from Rio on Elba to the Tuscan port for iron. It was all carried in these small vessels, barques, *saëtes*, *laudi*, *luiti*, tartans, frigates, *polaccas*.[65] At Genoa the customs registers divided incoming vessels into two classes, *venuta magna* and *venuta parva*, depending on whether the boats had a

---

[62] Giovanni Livi, *La Corsica e Cosimo dei Medici*, Florence, 1885.

[63] A.d.S. Florence, Mediceo, 2080.

[64] Jean Delumeau, *Vie économique et sociale de Rome dans la seconde moité du XVIe siècle*, I, 1957, p. 128.

[65] Danilo Presotto, '*Venuta Terra*' et '*Venuta Mare*' nel biennio 1605–1606, typescript thesis, Faculty of Economics and Commerce, Genoa, 1964, p. 31 ff.

capacity of more or less than 150 *cantara* (about 30 tons). In a year the port of Genoa received a few dozen 'big' ships and one or two thousand 'small' ones: 47 big and 2283 small ships in 1586; 40 and 1921 in 1587;[66] 107 and 1787 in 1605.[67] (These figures which underestimate the total number relate only to ships paying entrance duty, from which the numerous ships carrying wheat, oil, and salt were exempt.)

Tramping was of course an everyday activity in all these narrow seas, indispensable to the fortunes of trade. But in the Tyrrhenian Sea it was operated on an exceptional scale. This, combined with the documentation, itself exceptional, which we have for the region, makes it possible to see clearly here what we can only guess at in other places: the considerable role played by small cargo boats in economic exchanges. It was not unusual for the master of a Corsican boat to arrive at Leghorn with a few casks of salted meat and a few cheeses,[68] which he would then sell in the streets of the city, regardless of the protests of the local shopkeepers.

However, small boats would not do for everything. If Carthage, in the 'Sea of Sicily', Marseilles at the extreme edge of the Tyrrhenian Sea, and, much later, Genoa were able to play such great roles, it was because they had found a solution, as Vidal de La Blache has pointed out,[69] to the great problem of sailing westward, exposed to the east wind, the dangerous *levante*, and the *mistral*. This required a different kind of ship. At the time of the Median wars both Carthage and Marseilles used for these voyages vessels that were rather heavier than those of other navies, hence their success. Centuries later, at the end of the Middle Ages, it was thanks to a technical innovation, the amplification of the lateen rig, that Genoa was able to find a more effective answer to the problem of long-distance shipping than her rivals. She gained so much from her discovery that from the end of the thirteenth century she was sending her sailors through the Straits of Gibraltar, as far as Flanders.[70]

Genoa retained her preference for heavy ships. In the fifteenth century she was sending on the long run from Chios or Pera to Flanders ships and vessels of which some were over 1000 tons. 'What a pity that you did not see the *Fornara*,' wrote a captain to a friend in Florence in 1447, 'tu avresti avuto piacere maxime a vedere questa nave che ti parebbe in magnificenza'.[71] There was no ship of greater tonnage at the time. On St. Martin's day 1495, the two great 'Genoese ships', which arrived before the port of Baiae 'and there appeared and dropped anchor without entering the port', could have reversed the situation in favour of the French unaided according to Commynes, 'for these two ships alone would have sufficed to take Naples again; for the two ships were fine and tall, one being three thousand *botte* and the other two thousand five hundred *botte*; being

[66] Giovanni Rebora, *Prime ricerche sulla 'Gabella Caratorum Sexaginta Maris,'* typed thesis, Faculty of Economics and Commerce, Genoa, 1964, p. 31.
[67] Danilo Presotto, *op. cit.*, p. 53.   [68] A.d.S. Florence, Mediceo 2080.
[69] *Principles of Human Geography*, p. 432.   [70] See below p. 299.
[71] Jacques Heers, *Gênes au XVe siècle*, 1961, p. 275.

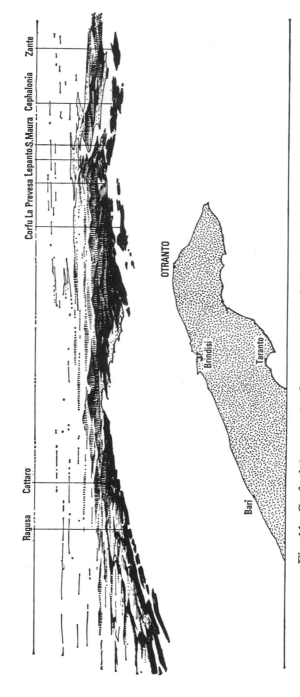

Fig. 11: *Corfu, lying opposite Otranto, commands the entrance to the Adriatic*
Note the positions of the great naval encounters: La Prevesa, 1538; Lepanto, 1571. Sketch by J. Bertin.

Ragusa   Cattaro   Corfu La Prevesa Lepanto S. Maura Cephalonia   Zante

OTRANTO

Brindisi

Taranto

Bari

called by name the Gallienne and the Espinole . . .'.[72] But neither of them intervened to the extent of moving from Baiae to the nearby city. These details are more relevant to the central problem than they might seem. For one often finds that power, supremacy and zones of influence in a maritime region can be a matter of technical superiority in details such as the sails, oars, helms, shape of hull, and tonnage of the ships.

The Adriatic.[73] The Adriatic is perhaps the most unified of all the regions of the sea. It provides material for all the problems implied in a study of the Mediterranean as a whole.

Longer than it is wide, it is in effect a north–south passage. To the north it is bordered by the flat stretch of coastline from Pesaro and Rimini to the gulf of Trieste, where the plain of the Po meets the Mediterranean. To the west it is bounded by the Italian coast, often low and marshy, although only a short way inland, overlooking the *Sottovento*, runs the ridge of the Appenines from which a series of mountain buttes project towards the sea, one, the Monte Gargano, conspicuous by its oak forests. To the east it meets a string of rocky islands, the Dalmatian islands, immediately behind which rise the barren mountains of the Balkan land mass, the unending white wall of the Dinaric Alps, forming the edge of the great *karst* plateau behind the Dalmatian coast. Lastly, to the south, the Adriatic opens into the Ionian Sea through the Strait of Otranto between Cape Otranto on the Italian side and Cape Linguetta in Albania. The channel is narrow: the charts give its width as 72 kilometres. As early as the third century B.C. the *lemboi* could cross it in a day, under full sail with a favourable wind.[74] So could the frigates that in the sixteenth century carried dispatches for the viceroy of Naples to the Italian coast from Corfu and Cephalonia and vice versa. A Spanish report indicates that 'dende Cabo de Otranto se veen las luces de la Velona'.[75] From an aeroplane flying towards Athens, today's traveller can see simultaneously the Albanian coast and Corfu, Otranto, and the Gulf of Taranto; little apparently separates them.

This narrowing at the southern end is the essential characteristic of the basin: it gives it unity. Control of that narrow passage amounted to control

[72] *Mémoires de Messire Philippe de Comines, augmentés par M. l'abbé Lenglet du Fresnay*, ed. London and Paris, 1747, IV, p. 103. The ships had a capacity of 2100 and 1750 tons at most, and in fact probably 1500 and 1250.
[73] Mapa del Mar Adriatico, 1568, Sim. E°, 540. There is an enormous literature on the subject: cf. the few lines in Le Danois, *op. cit.*, p. 107; A Philippson, *op. cit.*, p. 40–41; J. Boucard, 'L'histoire récente de l'Adriatique' in *C.R.S. de la Soc. géologique de France*, no. 2, March, 1925. H. Hochholzer, *art. cit.*, in *Geogr. Zeitschr.*, 1932 p. 93–97, gives some precise measurements: from Venice to the Straits of Otranto the Adriatic measures 700 kilometres; its area – 140,000 square kilometres – is therefore only one-sixth as big again as the Gulf of Finland. Reduced to a circle it would have a diameter of 492 kilometres. Its continental and island coasts measure respectively 3887 and 1980 kilometres a total of 5867 kilometres. Except for the Venetian and Albanian littoral, there is a submarine contour of –10 metres all round the coast.
[74] Maurice Holleaux, *Rome, la Grèce et les monarchies helléniques*, 1921, p. 176–177.
[75] B.N. Paris, Esp. 127, f° 7. Early XVIIth century.

of the Adriatic. But the problem was to know which was the best vantage point for keeping watch over the straits. The key positions were not the active ports of Apulia, Brindisi, Otranto and Bari, which were occupied by Venice, twice but not for long, in 1495 and 1528, and which she thought of occupying again in 1580 for the sake of her trading interests.[76] The Turks too held Otranto briefly, after the sack of 1480 which outraged Italian Christendom. But the gateway to the Adriatic could not be controlled from the Italian side. The Peninsula is here 'more than waist-deep in the sea'; it was the Balkan coast opposite which commanded the Adriatic, as was noted by Saint-Gouard, French ambassador at Madrid, who wrote to Charles IX, on 17th December, 1572, 'If it is true that the Grand Turk is building a fort at the entrance to the gulf of Quatero [Cattaro], in order the easier to take the said Quatero, then I hold him to be master of the Adriatic and to have it within his power to make a descent on Italy and thereby surround it by land and sea.'[77]

In fact the key position was further south, on Corfu. And Venice had possessed the island since 1386. It was here that shipping concentrated, in the shelter of the east coast, poor but mountainous and therefore a protection.[78] To enter or leave the Adriatic usually meant sailing past Corfu. This island, as a sententious text of the Senate (17th March, 1550) says, was the 'heart' of the Venetian State 'regarding shipping as much as any other aspect'.[79] The Signoria therefore devoted much attention to it,[80] sparing no expense in fortifying the island, spending such large sums of money, says a document of 1553,[81] 'che chi potesse veder li conti si stupiria'. Fresne-Canaye, who was there in 1572, admired the huge fortress towering above the little Greek town that was the island's capital; its 700 pieces of artillery were said to have a firing range reaching to the Albanian coast. However he was astonished to find that the Turks had been able to lay waste the island, under its very walls, the previous year, with 500 horsemen.[82] It is less astonishing if one reads further in the 1553 document, which is the report of a *bailo* on his appointment to Corfu. All the expense would be wasted, he said, if the fortifications of the old fortress were not brought up to date with modern methods of siege and warfare. Work had hardly begun on this, and what there was was ineffective, in spite of the 200,000 ducats that had been spent on it. When was it to be completed? Not very soon, apparently, since a report made in 1576[83] was still complaining about the inadequacy of the fortress. The enemy, without 'putting hand to

[76] E. Albèri, *Relazioni degli ambasciatori veneti*, II, V, p. 465.
[77] B.N. Paris, Fr. 16,104.
[78] On the lack of ports of the west coast, *Instructions nautiques*, no. 408, p. 32.
[79] A.d.S. Venice, Senato Mar, 15, f° 2.
[80] On Venice's determination to fortify Corfu because of the threat from the Turks: bishop of Dax to the king, Venice, 29th July and 12th August, 1559, E. Charrière, *op. cit.*, II, p. 599–600.
[81] V. Lamansky, *op. cit.*, p. 610–611.
[82] P. Canaye, *op. cit.*, p. 190–192, year 1573.
[83] V. Lamansky, *op. cit.*, p. 611.

sword' could come and set up his artillery right on the counterscarp! Similar complaints flood from the pens of Venetian officials throughout the second half of the century: the impressive defences installed by the Signoria are out of date, incapable of preventing pirate raids; the mountains have no water, so cannot serve as a refuge, and the unfortunate population of Corfu has to take shelter as best it can in the fortress and even in the trenches, at risk of its life; the Turks are free to invade the deserted countryside and abandoned villages. The result was that Corfu, which had 40,000 inhabitants before the 'war of 1537', had only 19,000 in 1588.[84] It is true that Venice relied principally for the island's defence on her galleons with their gilded prows that patrolled the Archipelago and the 'Gulf'.

In fact, with Corfu and her fleet, Venice controlled the entrance to the Adriatic and indeed the entire Adriatic. For the key position at the northern end of the sea was the city itself: the meeting point of sea routes and the continental land routes that in spite of the Alps linked central Europe with the Adriatic and the Levant. Venice's mission was to provide this link.

So she was Queen of the Adriatic, of her 'gulf' as she called it. She would seize any ship when she pleased and police the sea with skill or brutality, depending on the circumstances. Trieste was an annoyance, so she demolished its saltworks in 1578.[85] Ragusa was an annoyance, so she sent galleys into the waters of Ragusa Vecchia to pounce upon the grain ships supplying the city; she incited the allies of the Holy League against the city in 1571; in 1602 she gave support to the rebel Ragusan subjects on the island of Lagosta, famous for its fishing;[86] she was still taking her rival's ships in 1629.[87] Ancona was an annoyance, so she tried to wage a tariff war against her.[88] Ferrara was an annoyance, so she contemplated seizing the port. The Turks were an annoyance; she did not hesitate to attack them whenever she could do so without too much risk.[89]

[84] Correr, D. delle Rose 21, f° 29.

[85] Felice Toffoli, 'Del commercio de Veneziani ai tempi della Repubblica, con accenni a Trieste', 1867, p. 24, extract from *Osservatore Triestino*, May, 1867.

[86] Serafino Razzi, *La storia di Raugia*, 1595, ed. 1803, p. 260.

[87] A.d.S. Venezia, *Cinque Savii alla Mercanzia*, Busta 4, copy (extracts from the history of Gio. Batta Nani). There had been countless previous incidents. Cf. the letter from the Rector of Ragusa to the Ragusan consul at Venice (16th January, 1567) on the subject of goods seized by the Count of Corzola who wanted to be paid a 10 per cent customs duty (Archives, Ragusa L.P., I, f° 34, A.d.S. Venice, *Cinque Savii*, Busta 3 copy, 10th August, 1597).

[88] Venice, *Cinque Savii alla Mercanzia*, Busta 3, the Five Wise Men to the Doge, 29th December, 1634, copy. The opposition to Ancona and its leather trade took the form of abolishing customs duties (between 1545 and 1572) on gall-nuts coming from Upper and Lower Romania.

[89] In 1559, there was a serious incident at Durazzo: the *provveditore* Pandolfo Contarini pursued some Turkish corsairs who took refuge in Durazzo; the Venetian bombarded the town. Cf. Campagna, *La vita del catholico . . . Filippo II*, 1605, II, XI, p. 82–83, and the bishop of the Dax to the king, 30th April and 20th May, 1559, E. Charriere, *op. cit.*, II, p. 573–575. In 1560 this time peacefully, she made the Turks give up 'trente et trois cazalz' which they had usurped near Sebenico (Dolu to the bishop of Dax, Constantinople, 21st September 1560, E. Charrière, *op. cit.*, II, 625–628).

128 *The Role of the Environment*

The golden rule, the 'ben noto principio', is quite explicit as laid down by the *Cinque Savii alla Mercanzia:* 'ogni merce che entra nell' Adriatico o esce dall' Adriatico deve toccar Venezia', all goods carried in the Adriatic must pass through Venice,[90] according to a typically urban policy of authoritarian concentration of trade.[91] Only the Signoria had the right to grant exemptions if she saw fit, and she rarely saw fit.[92] For her it was a way of regulating traffic according to what she judged to be her interests, to defend her fiscal system, her markets, her export outlets, her artisans, and her shipping. Every action, even the apparently trivial seizure of two small boats from Trieste carrying iron,[93] was part of an overall calculated policy. In 1518, in order to ensure her monopoly, Venice insisted that merchant vessels could not leave Crete, Napoli di Romania, Corfu, or Dalmatia without leaving a deposit guaranteeing that their merchandise would be brought to Venice. On paper this looked foolproof. But Istria had been omitted from the ruling, and the breach was sufficient to ensure the free passage of inferior quality textiles – *rasse, sarze, grisi* – made in Istria and Dalmatia, which were sold in large quantities at the Recanati fair.[94] So we know that in this game of cops and robbers, there was opposition from skilful smugglers on the sea as well as on the overland and river routes; between Venice and Ferrara a contraband trade was carried on that all the controls were powerless to prevent. Venice's smaller neighbours were obliged to submit to her conditions, but whenever possible they resorted to trickery.

As for her more powerful neighbours, they raised their voices and invoked counter principles. The Spaniards had quarrels of precedence with the Republic and frequent disputes about captured vessels. 'For many years now this Signoria of Venice has claimed without any foundation that the gulf belongs to her', wrote Francisco de Vera, Philip II's ambassador at Venice, 'as if God had not created this part of the sea, like the rest, for the use of all'.[95] The Venetians never tired of replying that they had bought the Adriatic not with their gold but with their blood, 'spilt so generously'.

The Signoria was evidently unable to prevent her larger neighbours from opening doors and windows on to the Adriatic and using them.

[90] A.d.S. Venice, *Cinque Savii* 9, f° 175.

[91] This policy is quite clear regarding the salt works of the Adriatic which were almost all under Venice's thumb; or even salt imported from further away. It was doubtless a necessary policy: in 1583–85, for three years, Venice's maritime export trade was worth 1,600,000 ducats 'dentro del colfo fin a Corfu' and 600,000 outside it (A.d.S. Venice, Papadopoli, codice 12, f° 22 v°.) This figure comes from a contemporary source and is based on the 'datio della uscita' of 5 per cent on merchandise. On salt, which was in effect a supplementary form of currency in the Adriatic, cf. Fernand Braudel, 'Achats et ventes de sel à Venise (1587–1793) in *Annales E.S.C.* 1961, p. 961–965, and the accompanying map. Through the salt, Venice had the custom of the Balkan stock-farmers.

[92] A.d.S. Venice, *Cinque Savii*, 13th May, 1514: permission to load and transport directly to Alexandria in Egypt, oils, almonds, walnuts, and chestnuts.

[93] A.d.S. Venice, *Senato Mar*, 186, 6th March, 1610.

[94] *Ibid.*, 19th and 20th June, 1520.

[95] Francisco de Vera to Philip II, 7th October, 1589, A.N. K 1674.

The Turks were at Valona in 1559, the Spanish in Naples; the Papacy at Ancona and later at Ferrara in 1598 and Urbino in 1631; the House of Austria was at Trieste. From 1570 Maximilian II was talking of asking Venice for 'negotium liberae navigationis'.[96] This was an old demand previously formulated by the Papacy. In the turmoil preceding the battle of Agnadello, Julius II had proposed, in February, 1509, to absolve the Venetians if they would grant free shipping rights in the Adriatic to all subjects of the Church,[97] and the same claims were untiringly advanced afterwards.

Finally there was Ragusa with her fleet of merchantmen. The tenacious republic of St. Blaise played on its double status as protegée of the Papacy and vassal of the Sultan. This neutral position was useful: in a hostile Mediterranean, Ragusan ships almost always passed unharmed. So Venice had Ancona and Ragusa for the present and Trieste for the distant future as enemies whom she could not afford to ignore. The two former took advantage of Venice's difficulties at the beginning of the century during the pepper and spice crisis. But Venice survived the crisis. And in any case her rivals were obliged to her for marine insurance, cash remittances, and transport. They often acted as her servants and could cause her little inconvenience except on short voyages from one side of the Adriatic to the other. This was minor traffic: iron from Trieste taken to be sold in Italy, western textiles, wool and wine from Apulia taken to Dalmatia without passing through Venice. The Venetian authorities tried to punish subjects of the Signoria who dealt in this 'black market'. But since they frequently reiterated threats and punishments, it appears that these were neither very effective nor dictated by extreme necessity.[98]

After all these were only routine police actions. Venice was not only on the lookout for smugglers and rivals; she was also on her guard against corsairs attracted by the very abundance of trade in the Adriatic: wheat, wine with high alcohol content, oil from Apulia and Romagna, meat, cheese from Dalmatia, not to mention the ships carrying the rich long-distance exports and imports of the Signoria. Against these pirates Venice waged a sporadic but never-ending war: driven from one area, the corsairs would reappear with monotonous and obstinate regularity in another.

[96] The Emperor to Dietrichstein, 2nd May, 1570, P. Herre, *Europäische Politik im cyprischen Krieg 1570–73* 1902, p. 148; on the quarrels and negotiations between Vienna and Venice, see G. Turba, *op. cit.*, XII, p. 177 note (23rd November, 1550) XIII, p. 148 (9th June, 1560). Germany 'did not have free passage through the Adriatic until the reign of Charles VI' cf. Krebs, *art. cit.*, p. 377–378, and J. Kulischer, *Allgemeine Wirtschaftsgeschichte*, 1928–1929, II, 236–7.
[97] A. Le Glay, *Négociations diplomatiques entre la France et l'Autriche durant les trente premières années du XVIe siècle*, I, 1845, p. 232.
[98] E.g. A.d.S. Venice, *Cinque Savii*, 2, 26th February, 1536, when Venetian ships carrying goods loaded in the Levant for Venetians and foreigners which often went to unload directly at the towns of the *Sottovento*, were formally forbidden to do so. On Apulian wines transported to Dalmatia, cf. the report of Giustiniano, 1576, B.N. Paris, Ital. 220 f° 72, copy. And as early as 5th October, 1408 there was a formal prohibition on exporting grain outside the 'gulf' (*Cinque Savii* 2).

The fifteenth century had seen the last glorious years of Catalan privateering, based on Sicily. Venice had learned to arm a few big merchantmen against this if necessary, and to hunt down or at least neutralize the enemy. Retrospectively this privateering with big ships seems more spectacular than dangerous.[99]

Turkish piracy was on the increase in the sixteenth century;[100] it entered the Adriatic through the Albanian ports of Stapola, Valona, and Durazzo. It became a serious threat with the appearance of the Barbary corsairs[101] and even more so with the arrival of Turkish armadas, preceded and followed by pirate ships. However we should not exaggerate this threat. On the whole, until the last quarter of the sixteenth century, Turks and Barbaresques made few incursions into the 'gulf' itself.[102] It was not until after 1580 that there was a definite change in the Adriatic as elsewhere. A Venetian report of 1583 describes this change: for some time, and particularly since the Apulian coast has been fortified with watchtowers whose artillery is capable of protecting both the coast and boats seeking the shelter of their cannons, the corsairs have taken to carrying out their raids further north and have invaded the gulf. They have been making short and frequent attacks and thus escaping the notice of the galleys.[103]

To these hazards another, much worse, was gradually added. It had appeared before the middle of the century:[104] this was the constant piracy of the Uskoks of Segna and Fiume. These towns, a rendezvous for Albanian and Slav adventurers, were only a stone's throw from Venice and her rich flow of traffic. These lightweight enemies were few in number it is true, about a thousand men, says the *provveditore* Bembo in 1598;[105] 400 of them were in the pay of the Emperor and 600 'sono li venturieri che altro non fano che corseggiare et del bottino vivono'. A handful of men, but they were protected by the Emperor and were continually reinforced by the arrival of Balkan outlaws, 'per lo più del paese del Turco'. In any case there was little the Venetian ships could do against these tiny boats rowed at high speed, so light that they could use the shallowest channels between the islands where the galleys dared not follow them for fear of running aground. Such robbers were practically immune from any

[99] Numerous references, e.g. A.d.S. Venice, Senato Terra 4, f° 123 v°, f° 124, 27th September, 1459; Senato Mar 6, f° 89 v°, 28th September, 1459. For Genoese piracy too, see Senato Mar 6, f° 196 v°, 16th June, 1460.

[100] For one of the first appearances of the Turkish corsairs, A.d.S. Venice, Senato Mar 18, f°, 119 v°, 9th September, 1516; it was the corsair *Curthogoli* with 12 to 15 sails at the entrance of the gulf.

[101] In 1553 as the result of a false manoeuvre, two Venetian galleys fell into the hands of 12 Barbary galliots off Valona, Giuseppe Cappelleti, *Storia della Repubblica di Venezia del suo principio al suo fine*, Venice, vol. VIII, 1852, p. 199.

[102] But it had been getting worse since 1570, Museo Correr, D. della Rose, 481, 1st October, 1570: the corsairs got away with 76,000 ducats worth of wine and oil.

[103] V. Lamansky, op. cit., p. 600–601.

[104] Giacomo Tebaldi to the Duke of Ferrara, Venice, 28th March, 1545. A.d.S. Modena, Venezia XXIV, 2383/72 '*Quelli diavoli Scochi hano preso certi navilii richi et impicato tutti quelli v'erano dentro, com'intesero ch'erano venetiani*'.

[105] Correr, D. delle Rose, 21, f° 78.

pursuer. It would be easier, says a Venetian senator, to stop the birds flying through the air with one's hands than to stop the Uskoks on the sea with galleys.[106] If one of the latter should fall into a big ambush (600 men) it was lost; this was what happened on 17th May, 1587, at the mouth of the Narenta (Neretva).[107] If a ship ran aground it fell a prey to them.

Encouraged by their success, these *diavoli*, these robbers, these 'persone . . . uniti per rubbare', as the Venetians called them, held nothing sacred. Everything was fair game to them. Even the Turks threatened massive reprisals. Even Ragusa was to take up arms against them one day. Venice lost her temper, blockaded Fiume or Segna, sometimes even burning 'the mill-wheels' and 'hanging the captains'. But these actions had little effect. The city behind this adventure was neither Segna nor Fiume (the latter only briefly tried to commercialize the products of piracy but without success) but Trieste, the great centre for selling and reselling, whether Turkish slaves whom the Grand Duke of Tuscany bought for his galleys, or fine cloths of gold and camlets stolen from the Venetians. As an enemy Trieste was formidable. Behind her lay the archdukes, the Habsburgs of Vienna and indirectly of Spain. Italian and Venetian merchants travelled to Carniola and Croatia and to Styria in vain. The trade of the hinterland fell increasingly into the hands of the growing community of travelling peasant merchants and pedlars, who were in touch with the privateers and external commerce. It was against this multiple threat that Venice sought to maintain her privileges. She could hardly do so without difficulty, compromises, and surprises.

All these characteristics and the others from which one could easily compile a book on the Adriatic are a testimony and proof of the unity of the 'gulf', a unity that was as much cultural and economic as it was political, and whose predominant flavour was Italian. The gulf was Venetian, of course, but in the sixteenth century it was more than this, it was the sphere of a triumphant Italian culture. The civilization of the peninsula wove a brilliant, concentrated web along the east coast of the sea. This is not to suggest that Dalmatia was 'Italian' in the sense that apologists of racial expansion would have understood it. The entire sea-coast of the *Retroterra* is today inhabited by a Slav population.[108] And so it was in the sixteenth century in spite of superficial appearances. At Ragusa at the time, Italianism was a commodity: Italian was the commercial language of the entire Mediterranean. But fashion and snobbery entered

[106] Correr Cigogna, 1999 (undated).
[107] A.d.S. Venice, Papadopoli 12, f° 25.
[108] Cf. the evidence of, among many others, H. Hochholzer, *art. cit.*, p. 150. While we may discount the exaggerations in Attilio Tamaro's *L'Adriatico golfo d'Italia*, 1915, the value and talent of his studies 'Documenti inediti di storia triestina, 1298–1544' in *Archeografo triestino*, XLIV, 1931, and *Storia di Trieste*, 2 vols, Rome, 1924 should be acknowledged. Some interesting points are touched on by Bozzo Baldi, *L'isola di Cherzo*, pref. R. Almagliâ, fasc. 3, Studi geografici pubblicati dal Consiglio Nazionale delle Ricerche, 1934; the bases of Italianism on the island were both social and economic: large estates and shipping.

into it as well. Not only was it considered desirable that the sons of noble families should go to study at Padua, and that the secretaries of the republic should be as fluent in Italian as in Latin (the archives of Ragusa are almost all in Italian), but the ruling families, who governed trade and politics, unhesitatingly invented Italian genealogies for themselves. In fact, of course, these haughty *gentes* were descended from some mountain Slav, the Italianized names betray their Slavonic origins, the coastal population continued to be drawn from the mountains, Slavonic was the spoken language, the familiar tongue of the women and the people, and even, after all, of the elite, since the registers of Ragusa frequently record strict orders to speak only Italian at the assemblies of the Rectors; if an order was necessary, clearly Slavonic was being spoken.

On the basis of this knowledge it is certain that the Adriatic of the sixteenth century was attracted by the sophisticated civilization of the nearby Peninsula, and drawn into its orbit. Ragusa was a town of Italian art; Michelozzo worked on the Palace of the Rectors. And yet of the towns of the *altra sponda*, it was the one least influenced by Venice, since except for a brief period it had always been independent. At Zara, Spalato, the island of Cherso and elsewhere, abundant documents record the names of schoolmasters, priests, notaries, businessmen, and even Jews who had come from the Peninsula, ambassadors and architects of the Italian civilization that was grafted on to this region.[109]

But the Adriatic was not exclusively Italian. Strictly speaking it is not orientated north–south but north-west and south-east; it was the route to the Levant, with long-established trade and relations, open too as we shall see to the illnesses and epidemics of the East. Its civilization was profoundly complex. Here eastern influence could already be felt and Byzantium lived on; elements which combined to give this frontier zone its own originality. Its Catholicism was a fighting religion, faced with the threatening Orthodox world up in the mountains and with the immense Turkish peril. If, in spite of this mixed experience, Dalmatia remained loyal to Venice, as Lamansky noted long ago, it was because its loyalty lay basically beyond the Signoria, with Rome and the Catholic Church. Even a town like Ragusa, so awake to her own interests, firmly embedded in both the Orthodox and the Turkish world, surrounded that is by heretics and heathen, was remarkable for her fervent Catholicism. Her religious foundations would be as fascinating to investigate as her economic structure; interest played a part – and why not? – in some of her greatest religious outbursts. Her loyalty to Rome protected her on her threatened frontier, as was shown during the terrible crisis of 1571. And with the great economic withdrawal of the seventeenth century, after the splendours of a Renaissance which like those of Venice and Bologna, developed late, her sons found magnificent careers in the Church, travelling all over the

[109] Antonio Teja, 'Trieste e l'Istria negli atti dei notai zaratini del 300' in *Annali del R. Ist. Tech. Rismondo*, 1935; Silvio Mitis, *Il governo della repubblica veneta nell'isola di Cherzo*, 1893, p. 27.

Christian world, even to France, merchants and bankers of the old days turned princes and servants of the Church.

Geography, politics, economics, civilization, and religion all combined to make the Adriatic a homogeneous world, extending beyond the coasts of the sea and into the Balkan continent to the final frontier between Latin and Greek worlds. On the other side, to the west it was responsible for a subtle dividing line along the Italian peninsula. We are usually only conscious of the very marked opposition between northern and southern Italy. But the east–west division between Tyrrhenian and Levantine Italy, while less obvious, is no less real. Throughout the past it has acted as a hidden force. For a long time the east took the lead over the west of the peninsula; but it was the west, Florence and Rome, that produced the Renaissance, which would only reach Ferrara, Parma, Bologna, and Venice with the end of the sixteenth century. Economic advance followed a similar pendulum movement: When Venice was in decline, Genoa's fortunes rose; later Leghorn was to become the leading town of the peninsula. These swings from east to west, Adriatic to Tyrrhenian, were to determine the fate of Italy and of the whole Mediterranean on either side of the peninsula which acted as the beam of an enormous balance.

East and west of Sicily. The narrow seas are the active parts of the Mediterranean, teeming with ships and boats. But the vast empty stretches of water, the solitary wastes, are also part of the general structure of the sea.

In the sixteenth century the Mediterranean, which is so small by present-day standards of travel, contained enormous, dangerous and forbidden stretches, no-man's-lands separating different worlds. The Ionian Sea is the largest of these hostile areas, prolonging over the sea the desert of Libya and thus creating a double zone of emptiness, maritime and continental, separating East from West.[110]

On the other side of the channel of Sicily another wide sea stretches from the Sicilian and Sardinian shores to the Balearics, Spain, and the Maghreb. This sea, which we might call the Sardinian Sea, is also difficult to cross with its inhospitable coasts and sudden blasts from the *noroît* and the *levante*. The east–west passage bristles with obstacles.

It is true that some of the earliest ships had overcome these obstacles and linked East with West; in the North, travelling from east to west and vice versa, they kept close to the Balkan coastline and the Neapolitan shore, using the Straits of Messina in preference to the Sicilian Channel, which was a more risky route. This was the Christian shipping route. The Islamic route, less convenient and less frequented, passed diagonally through the Sicilian Channel. This was the path taken by the Turkish armadas, from the Albanian coast to Valona, from Valona to the shores of Naples and Sicily, and from Sicily to Bizerta or sometimes as far as Algiers. It was never as busy as the first.

[110] A. Philippson, 'Das byzantinische Reich als geographische Erscheinung' in *Geogr. Zeitschr.*, 1934, p. 441–455.

To the south the obstacle was avoided by following the African coast, which, since there are reports of Christian privateers, must have been quite a busy area for shipping.[111] The pirates' best course was to appear from the open sea and surprise ships coming from Egypt, Tripoli, Djerba, and sometimes from Algiers. At the beginning of the sixteenth century Venetian galleys were still operating the *muda* of the Barbary coast, which they reached by way of the coast of Sicily. At the end of the century, English and Dutch ships in their turn followed the coast of North Africa from Gibraltar to the Sicilian Channel, which they too crossed diagonally to reach the Sicilian coast and then the Greek coasts on the way to Crete, the Archipelago, and Syria. This was doubtless to avoid Spanish inspections at the Straits of Messina.

All these itineraries went the long way round the Ionian Sea and the Sea of Sardinia and avoided crossing them. They constituted the chief link between the eastern and western Mediterranean, or if one prefers between East and West, and are of capital importance to history. Alongside them we should take account of the overland traffic across Italy. The peninsula acted as a channel between two arms of the sea. Ancona and Ferrara were linked with Florence, Leghorn, and Genoa. Venice exported goods to Genoa and the Tyrrhenian. To the traffic passing through Messina and the Sicilian Channel must be added what was carried from one coast of Italy to the other by the unending flow of mule trains. This additional traffic would not of course look very significant to us either in volume or value if exact statistics could be obtained. But in the sixteenth century it was decisive. It contributes to the unity of the Mediterranean region and of this book. What kind of unity is it?

Two maritime worlds. To claim that the considerable obstacles between the two halves of the Mediterranean effectively separated them from each other would be to profess a form of geographical determinism, extreme, but not altogether mistaken. It is true that the waves of human emigration from one side of the sea to the other were constantly brought face to face with the difficulties of both overland and maritime routes. General Brémond, in a book which has something of the verve of Émile-Félix Gautier, has pointed out that the Arab invasions from the seventh to the eleventh century did not significantly alter North Africa in human terms, that the invaders were few in number and therefore the more easily absorbed. This is a transposition of Hans Delbrück's thesis of the Germanic invasions of the fifth century, but let that pass: what interests us is the obstacle nature has placed in the path of human migrations from east to west or west to east, whether by land or sea. It is as if they came up against a finely meshed filter.

There were of course in the sixteenth century natives of the Levant

[111] Instructions of Pandolfo Strozzi to the general of the galleys sent out on a pirate raid, Leghorn, 1st April, 1575, A.d.S. Florence, Mediceo 2077, f° 540 and v°. The raid was to take the following route: Messina, Cape Passero, Cape Misurata, for near the latter African cape passed the ships travelling from the Levant to Tripoli, Tunis, Bône, and Algiers.

living on western shores: Greeks at Leghorn, Cypriots in the Balearics and Cadiz, Ragusans in all the big ports, Levantines and Asians in Algiers. The Barbarossas and the janissaries of Algiers came from the Aegean and Asia Minor.[112] Conversely, traces of Latin colonization have survived in the East, and the legion of renegades even more than the counting houses of the merchants led to a fresh colonization of the Turkish world. But these minor grafts were of little real importance. The two halves of the sea, in spite of trading links and cultural exchanges, maintained their autonomy and their own spheres of influence. Genuine intermingling of populations was to be found only inside each region, and within these limits it defied all barriers of race, culture, or religion.

All human links between different ends of the Mediterranean, by contrast, remained an adventure or at least a gamble.

For example, the Phoenicians long ago settled in Carthage and from there extended their influence westwards triumphing over the long distances of the Mediterranean far west with their great ships. And the Ancient Greeks landed at Marseilles, which they too used as a base for expeditions. Similarly, the Byzantines for a while controlled Sicily, Italy, North Africa, and Baetica. The Arabs in the seventh, eighth, and ninth centuries seized North Africa, Spain, and Sicily. All these great victories were either short-lived or followed by the severing of connections between the advance parties and the country of origin: this was the fate of Marseilles, Carthage, and even of Moslem Spain which in the tenth and eleventh centuries received all its cultural nourishment from the East, its poets, doctors, professors, philosophers, magicians, and even its redskirted dancers. Then it was cut off from the source and, thrown together with Berber Africa, began to evolve a western way of life. The men of the Maghreb who then travelled to the east, either as pilgrims or to study, were astonished to find themselves 'almost in a foreign world'. 'There is no Islam in the East,' exclaims one of them.[113] This history was to repeat itself at the end of the sixteenth century, when the Africa of the Turkish Regencies freed itself from the Ottoman hand.

It is confirmed in the opposite direction by the symmetrical history of the Crusades and the Latin kingdom of Jerusalem. There is no need to labour the point.

The double lesson of the Turkish and Spanish Empires. Each sea tends to live off itself, to organize the shipping circuits of its sailing vessels and small

---

[112] On migrations from one basin of the sea to the other, cf. two Greeks condemned in the auto-da-fé of Murcia on 14th May, 1554 (A.H.N. Lo. 2796). Greeks travelling to Madrid (Terranova to H.M., Palermo, 20th December, 1572, Simancas E° 1137). Numerous documents on Greeks at Leghorn on the sixteenth century. A Greek from Cadiz was taken prisoner by the Turks of Algiers in 1574, D. de Haëdo, *op. cit.*, p. 175 v°. A Cypriot at Majorca, 19th February, 1589, Riba y Garcia, *El consejo supremo de Aragon en el reinado de Felipe II*, 1914, p. 285. Greeks serving in the Spanish navy: Tiepolo to the Doge, 19th August, 1560, *Calendar of State Papers* (*Venetian*) VII, 247.
[113] J. Sauvaget, *Introduction à l'histoire de l'Orient musulman*, 1943, p. 43–44.

136   *The Role of the Environment*

boats into an autonomous system. This was also true of the two grea
basins of the Mediterranean, east and west. They communicated and hac
links with each other but tended to organize themselves into closed cir·
cuits, notwithstanding a certain number of contacts, alliances, and rela·
tions of interdependence.

This is underlined only too clearly by sixteenth-century politics. What a
marvellous geopolitical map one could draw of the western half of the
Mediterranean between the middle of the fifteenth and the middle of the
sixteenth century, with arrows showing the old and new directions of
Spanish imperialism, the positions it seized and exploited in order to gain
control of the western sea. For it did gain control. And after 1559, with the
demobilization of the French fleet and the loosening of ties between the
French king and the Sultan, the western sea became incontestably Spanish.
The Moslems only held one coast, and that not the best, North Africa.
They only held it by virtue of the corsairs, and their authority, kept in
check by the defensive line of Spanish *presidios*, was constantly threatened
from within and without. In 1535 Charles V was victorious against
Tunis; in 1541 he was defeated, but only just, before Algiers; this setback
could be rectified. At Madrid the *Consejo de Guerra* had permanently on
its files a plan for attacking the city of the *re'īs*, which, one day, might
be suddenly put into execution. It very nearly was in the time of Don John
of Austria and again in 1601 with the surprise attempt by Gian Andrea
Doria.

The Ionian Sea, the 'Sea of Crete', was by contrast the Ottoman sea.
The Turks, masters of the coasts of the eastern Mediterranean after the
occupation of Syria in 1516 and Egypt in 1517, found it necessary to gain
control of the sea by creating a strong armed fleet.

These two different Mediterraneans were vehicles, one might almost say
they were responsible for the twin empires. Zinkeisen has said as much of
Turkey. Is it not also true of Spain?[114] The two halves of the Mediter-
ranean were in the sixteenth century two political zones under different
banners. Is it therefore surprising that the great sea battles in the time of
Ferdinand, Charles V, Sulaimān, and Philip II should repeatedly have
taken place at the meeting point of the two seas, in the frontier zones? –
Tripoli (1511, 1551), Djerba (1510, 1520, 1560), Tunis (1535, 1573, 1574),
Bizerta (1573, 1574), Malta (1565), Lepanto (1571), Modon (1572),
Coron (1534), Prevesa (1538).

[114] The aim of Ferdinand the Catholic in 1509–11, at the time of the great expeditions of Pedro Navarro, was not merely to put out of action the pirate ports of the
Maghreb, or to open the way for a new war of Granada of which Africa would be the
prize (Isabella and not he, had foreseen and dreamed of that.) It was above all to set
up a shipping route with coastal bases from southern Spain to Sicily which was rich
in grain. Oran was taken in 1509, and the Spanish Armada was already taking Tripoli
in Barbary in 1511. The speed with which it was accomplished indicates the object of
his mission (Fernand Braudel, 'Les Espagnols et l'Afrique du Nord', in *Revue Africaine*, 1928). Lucien Romier thought there was a similar intention to be detected in
Charles V's campaign against Provence.

Politics merely followed the outline of an underlying reality. These two Mediterraneans, commanded by warring rulers, were physically, economically, and culturally different from each other. Each was a separate historical zone. Physically the East had a more continental climate, with sharper extremes, worse droughts than the West, higher summer temperatures and therefore if that is possible more bare and desert lands (*fauves* as Théophile Gautier would have said). Its maritime regions were correspondingly more animated. The prominent role played in communications by the Aegan Sea deserves mention. It is worth emphasizing the ease of navigation in the East, particularly since it seems to be little known. A document of 1559 is quite explicit. An adviser wanted the Republic of St. Mark to fit out a certain number of galleys at Cyprus as in the other Venetian islands. There would then be no difficulty in having them cross over to Crete: the crossing could be made before St. Gregory's day (12th March), the traditional date of the sortie of the guard at Alexandria and Rhodes. For, he says, 'li boni tempi usano in quelle parte più a bon hora che in queste', the good weather begins earlier there than here.[115] Could this be the reason for the advance that the Turkish fleet always seemed to have over its rivals? Should the swiftness of its attacks be attributed to the early fine weather in the Aegean? In a period when the rhythm of the seasons determined that of war, this could be important.

Beyond politics. The economic and cultural differences between the two zones became increasingly marked in the sixteenth century, while their respective positions were being reversed. Since the thirteenth century the East had gradually lost one by one her supremacy in various fields: the refinements of material civilization, technical advance, large industry, banking, and the supply of gold and silver. The sixteenth century saw her final defeat, in the course of an unprecedented economic upheaval when the opening up of the Atlantic destroyed the age-old privilege of the Levant, which for a time had been the sole repository of the riches of the 'Indies'. From that point on, every day saw a widening of the gap between the standard of living of the West, which was going through a revolution in technical and industrial progress, and the eastern world of low-cost living, where money coming from the West would automatically rise in value and acquire higher purchasing power.

But this difference in level in a way recreated the economic unity of the two seas, indeed it made it absolutely necessary, overcoming all barriers, including political ones, and using any means, including piracy. Differences in voltage determine electrical currents; the greater the difference, the greater the need for currents. For the easterners, it was essential to be associated with the superiority of the West, to share in its wealth whatever the price: from the West they wanted precious metals, in other words American silver, and they were obliged to follow the progress of European

[115] V. Lamansky, *Secrets d'État de Venise*, St. Petersburg, 1884, p. 563–564, Venetian report of 1559.

technical advance. In return, developing western industry had to find markets for its surplus production. These are big questions and we shall come back to them later. For it was the interaction of such pressing needs, such disturbances and restorations of economic balance, such necessary exchanges, which guided and indirectly determined the course of Mediterranean history.[116]

2. MAINLAND COASTLINES

The Mediterranean has always seemed the chosen country of seafarers. This has been said time and time again, as if a coastline had only to be irregular in order to be populated, and populated by sailors. In fact, the Mediterranean has never been inhabited by the profusion of sea-going peoples found in the northern seas and the Atlantic. It has only produced them in small numbers and in certain regions.

The peoples of the sea. This was bound to be the case, since it could not support more. The Mediterranean waters are hardly more productive than the lands. The much vaunted *frutti di mare* are only moderately abundant,[117] its fisheries provide only a modest yield, except in such rare spots as the lagoons of Comachio, the coasts of Tunis and of Andalusia (where there is tunny fishing).[118] The Mediterranean which is a deep sea, formed by geological collapse, has no shallow shelves, no continental platforms where submarine life could thrive down to a depth of 200 metres. Almost everywhere a narrow ridge of rocks or sand leads straight from the shore to the deep gulfs of the open sea. The water of the Mediterranean, which is geologically too old, is apparently, according to oceanographers, biologically exhausted.[119] There are no long-distance fishing fleets except for coral, which is not for consumption. There is nothing here comparable to the long journeys of northern trawlers towards Newfoundland and Iceland or the North Sea fishing grounds. In February, 1605,

[116] On the great East-West contrast during the ancient Roman period – which confirms my argument – see G. I. Bratianu, *Études byzantines*, 1939, p. 59–60, 82–83. Jacques Pirenne, *Les grands courants de l'histoire universelle*, 1944, I, p. 313. Pierre Waltz, *La Question d'Orient dans l'Antiquité*, 1943, p. 282.

[117] R. Pfalz, *art. cit.*, p. 130, n.l. notes that in 1928, 10,280 quintals of fish were caught off the Genoese coast while the town needed 20,000 quintals. The Italian fisherman's earnings are a quarter those of a French fisherman and an eighth of those of an English fisherman and yet fish is no dearer in France or England than in Italy.

[118] On tunny fishing see Philip II to the Duke of Alva, 4th May, 1580, (*CODOIN*, XXXIV, p. 455) 19th May, 1580, (*ibid.*, p. 430) 18th April, (*ibid.*, XXXII, p. 108), A. de Morales, *Las antigüedades de las ciudades de España*, Madrid, 1792, f° 41 v° says that in 1584 tunny fishing brought into Andalusia 70,000 ducats to the Dukes of Medina Sidonia and Arcos. With picturesque details: at the time of the catch, '*tocase a tambores y hazese gente para yr a su tiempo a esta pesqueria con el atruendo y ruydo que se aparaja una guerra.*' Fishing at Conil from May to June, the sea is red with blood. Pedro de Medina, *Libro de grandezas y cosas memorables de España*, enlarged edition by D. Perez de Messa, 1595, p. 108.

[119] E. le Danois, *op. cit.*, p. 197–198.

when there was a shortage of fish, the Signoria of Genoa tried to limit consumption during Lent.[120]

The scarcity of fish explains the scarcity of fishermen and consequently that of sailors, which always acted as an unseen brake on the grand projects of Mediterranean powers. Between political dreams and reality there always lay this obstacle: the shortage of men capable of building, equipping, and handling the fleets. It is to this that we can attribute the difficult rise of Leghorn. It took a lifelong effort, that of Cosimo de' Medici to provide the new port with the sailors she needed, and he had to search for them all over the Mediterranean. A whole set of circumstances had to be united before the Turks could build their fleet, or the corsairs establish their base at Algiers. Equipping the galleys of all the armadas that were fighting in the Mediterranean was above all a problem of manpower. If it had not been for the slaves, prisoners of war, and convicts brought from their cells and chained to the oars, how could enough oarsmen have been found for the galleys? From the middle of the century on documents complain of the shortage of volunteers for the galleys, the *buonavoglia*; times are not hard enough for men to come forward and sell themselves as they used to, argues a Venetian admiral, Cristoforo da Canal in 1541.[121] Venice even had to introduce a militia system of compulsory service in her Cretan galleys, and after 1542–1545 had to use *condannati* in her own galleys. There was not only a shortage of oarsmen; crews were equally hard to come by. The documents stress the incompetence and poor organization of Venice: if this or that was put right, if the pay was better, sailors from Venetian possessions would not leave to go and serve on foreign boats, on the Turkish armadas, or even those of the western sea. This may well be true. What is even more certain is that there were not enough sailors to man all the boats in the Mediterranean; and while they naturally went where conditions were best, no country in the sixteenth century could boast of having more men than it needed.

This is why at the end of the century the Mediterranean states and towns were enlisting or trying to enlist sailors from the North. In 1561 a Scottish Catholic brought a galley into the service of Spain.[122] A document dating from after the Invincible Armada shows Philip II and his advisers actually trying to recruit sailors from England.[123] At Leghorn it was a distinct feature of the policy of Ferdinand de' Medici to call on sailors not only from the Mediterranean but also from northern Europe.[124] Algiers was to follow suit after the end of the sixteenth century.[125]

From the better-equipped North the Mediterranean borrowed not only

---

[120] Danilo Presotto, *op. cit.*, p. 364.
[121] Alberto Tenenti, *Cristoforo da Canal*, 1962, p. 82.
[122] Letter patent from Philip II, 1st October, 1561, in favour of the Scotsman, Chasteniers, who fitted out a galley against the Infidel, B.N. Paris, Fr. 16103, f°s 69 and 69 v°.
[123] A.d.S. Florence, Mediceo (full reference not available).
[124] G. Vivoli, *Annali di Livorno*, IV, p. 10–11.
[125] *Ibid.*, IV, p. 10.

men but new techniques; for example the 'cog', or *Kogge*, a heavy cargo vessel, originally a single-masted square-rigged ship, which could brave the worst winter storms. It was the Basque pirates of Bayonne who first demonstrated its qualities to the Mediterraneans.[126] It became the typical roundship both in the Baltic and the Mediterranean in the fourteenth and fifteenth centuries. In return, the voyage of the *Pierre de la Rochelle* to Danzig some hundred and fifty years later introduced the surprised Danzigers to a new type of ship, the carrack, incontestably a southern invention, derived from the cog but with an increased number of masts and multiple sails – a Mediterranean tradition – combining both square and lateen rig. It was a southern boat, but from the Atlantic regions, for it seems to have been the Biscay shipbuilders who developed it before it became the typical merchantman of the Atlantic and the Mediterranean in about 1485.[127]

It looks as if the Atlantic led the way in developing technical progress in navigation. One champion of northern superiority has gone so far as to claim that the Mediterranean, an inland sea, never developed any types of boat of more than local importance.[128] It was, however, the sailors of the Mediterranean who originally initiated direct and regular shipping between the inland sea and the Atlantic. They led the way in the fourteenth century, but were gradually overtaken as time went on. First of all on the Atlantic part of the trip, if one remembers the important role played in the fifteenth century and even earlier by the sailors of Biscay and their *balaneros*, the Bretons, the Flemish hookers, which monopolized trade between Spain and the Low Countries from 1550. Then on the whole trip from the end of the fifteenth century until 1535, English ships in large numbers appeared in the Mediterranean and after an interruption, began to use the route again permanently in about 1572, preceding the Dutch convoys by a good fifteen years. After this it was inevitable that the Mediterraneans would finally lose, to the sailors from the North and the Atlantic, the struggle for world domination begun at the end of the fifteenth century.

Weaknesses of the maritime regions. If there were relatively few sailors in the Mediterranean it was because the coastal regions that traditionally produce sailors – and by their activity give the illusion of a Mediterranean whose warm waters breed a race of seafaring men – were few in number too: the Dalmatian coast; the Greek coasts and islands; the Syrian coast (but this was in such decline in the sixteenth century that it can be discounted: the correspondence of Venetian *baili* in Constantinople between 1550 and 1560 mentions only one ship from Beirut); the coast of Sicily (especially the west); some parts of the Neapolitan shore; the coast of Cape Corse; and finally the almost adjacent coastal regions of Genoa,

---

[126] F. C. Lane, *Venetian ships and shipbuilders of the Renaissance*, 1934, p. 37–38.
[127] *Ibid.*, p. 42.
[128] B. Hagedorn, *Die Entwicklung der wichtigsten Schiffstypen*, Berlin, 1914, p. 1–3 and 36; references in F. C. Lane, *op. cit.*, p. 41.

Provence, Catalonia, Valencia, and Andalusia. In all a small portion of the Mediterranean coastline, and of these regions how many could boast the crowded streets and close-packed *campanili* of the Genoese Riviera?[129]

Often the activity of a long seaboard can be accounted for by a few tiny but active ports some distance apart. The island of Mezzo[130] narrow and defenceless, off Ragusa, provided the port with most of the captains for her big merchant vessels. Perasto,[131] at the end of the century, could only claim 4000 men *da fatti* (eligible to bear arms) but 50 ships both large and small. In fact, the *Perastani* were exempt from all taxes in return for policing the long gulf of Cattaro, whose entrance they guarded on behalf of Venice: thanks to them the *golfo* was *sicurissimo de mala gente*. In the kingdom of Naples we may imagine the tireless but inconspicuous activity of a string of small ports, such as Salerno[132] or Amalfi,[133] whose names are famous, or on the Calabrian coast, S. Maffeo del Cilento,[134] Amantea,[135] Viestris,[136] or Peschici.[137] The last-named, a busy shipbuilding centre according to the Neapolitan documents of the *Sommaria*, was rarely idle, since it had the business of the Ragusan boatbuilders. Huge ships were launched from its beaches, one weighing 6000 *salme*, about 750 tons, in July, 1572.[138]

Whether populous or not, these maritime provinces were overwhelmingly situated in the North, along the Mediterranean peninsulas; behind them there generally lay wooded mountains. The southern mountains because of the dry climate were poorly off for forests and therefore for shipyards. The woods near Bougie were an exception. But for them how could there have grown up in the thirteenth and fourteenth centuries a navy which was still very active in the time of Ibn Khaldūn? And cannot the decline of the maritime activities of the Syrian coast be attributed to the exhaustion of the forests of Lebanon? In Algiers not only did the sailors come from overseas, but also, in spite of the use made of the forests behind Cherchel, the timber for building the boats; their oars were brought over from Marseilles.

In the case of all the prosperous seaports, we know either from documents (the arsenal accounts among others, when these have survived, as they have in Leghorn and Venice), from tradition, or from treatises on navigation, the source of the wood used for shipbuilding. Ragusa, which

[129] *Instructions Nautiques*, no. 368, p. 66–70; Andrea Navagero, *Il viaggio fatto in Spagna*, 1563, p. 2 (1525): The roads between Genoa and Rapallo were terrible but the countryside was well populated.
[130] V. Lisicar, *Lopud. Eine historische und zeitgenössische Darstellung*, 1932; (Lopud is the island of Mezzo.)
[131] Museo Correr, D. delle Rose, 21, f° 17 (1584) f° 19 (1586) f° 70 v° (1594).
[132] A.d.S. Naples, Sommaria Partium volume 559, f° 158, 9th October, 1567, for example.
[133] *Ibid.*, 532, 5th November, 1551.
[134] *Ibid.*, 560, f° 209, 10th June, 1568.
[135] *Ibid.*, 543, f° 128, 10th January, 1568.
[136] *Ibid.*, 575, f° 40 17th July, 1567.
[137] *Ibid.*, 577, f° 37–39, 10th October, 1568; f° 89–93, 21st January, 1569.
[138] *Ibid.*, 596, f° 193–6, July, 1572.

like Portugal specialized in the construction of merchantmen, took its timber from the oak forests of the Monte Gargano (also known as Sant'Angelo). This is in fact the reason, according to a treatise written in 1607,[139] for the Ragusans' superiority over the Portuguese, who, if they had a Monte Sant'Angelo, would have the finest galleons in the world. The Turkish *caramusalis* were made out of great plane trees, an excellent wood which behaves particularly well in water.[140] Galleys, which were expected to have a long life, required a range of different woods for the different parts of the boat: oak, pine, larch, ash, fir, beech, and walnut.[141] The best oars were apparently made from the wood brought to Narbonne by way of the Aude and its canal.[142] Much could be made of the travelling diary of the Ragusan who crossed southern Italy between April and August, 1601,[143] in search of timber to fell for the construction of a ship; or of the documents concerning permission to fell trees in the forests of Tuscany, first given to and then withdrawn from the Spaniards;[144] or the purchases made by Genoa, again in Tuscany,[145] or by Barcelona at Naples,[146] although Barcelona relied principally on the oaks and pines of the Catalan Pyrenees, which were renowned for galley-building.[147] Or one might search for contracts like the one signed with the *Sommaria* by Pier Loise Summonte, 'fornitore delle galere regie' (built in Naples) – whereby he undertook to convey from Calabria to Naples timber that was to be felled in the forests of Nerticaro, Ursomarso, Altomonte, Sandonato, and Policastrello.[148]

But clearly what matters is the overall situation, not the exceptions. And that situation was one of scarcity of wood as can be deduced from a reading of the Venetian or Spanish documents, of marked deforestation in the western and central Mediterranean region, reported notably in Sicily and Naples (the very place where one of the great shipbuilding efforts for Philip II's navy was centred). Above all there was a shortage of oak, which was used to construct ships' hulls. After the end of the fifteenth century it was becoming rare and Venice passed a series of draconian measures to save what was left of her forests from destruction.[149] The problem became even more pressing for the Signoria in the following century. Although Italy still possessed large reserves, there was a great deal of timber felling throughout the sixteenth century. We know that deforestation advanced quickly: the Monte Sant'Angelo for example was considered a precious exception. The Turks were better off, with the vast

[139] Bartolomeo Crescentio Romano, *Nautica mediterranea* . . ., 1607, p. 4.
[140] *Ibid.*, p. 4.   [141] *Ibid.*, p. 7.
[142] Fourquevaux, *Dépêches*, I, p. 12, timber from the forests of Quillan.
[143] Archives of Ragusa, Diversa de Foris X, f° 81 v° ff: Conto di spese di me Biasio Vodopia . . .
[144] A.d.S. Florence, Mediceo 4897 bis., f° 6 and 6 v° 15th January, 1566.
[145] *Ibid.*, 2840, f° 3, 23rd July 1560.
[146] Simancas E° 1056, f° 185, 22nd August, 1568.
[147] *Geografía general de Catalunya*, p. 336.
[148] A.d.S. Naples, Sommaria Partium, 562, f° 83, 10th September, 1567.
[149] F. C. Lane, *op. cit.*, p. 219 ff.

forests of the Black Sea and those of Marmara, in the gulf of Nicomedia (Izmit[150]) almost opposite the arsenal of Constantinople. After Lepanto, Venice made strenuous representations to the Holy League that all the experienced seamen among the Turkish prisoners be put to death, in spite of the handsome sum of money they represented. For, she said, being short of neither timber nor money, the Turk would have no difficulty in building more ships as long as he could 'rihaver li homini'.[151] Only men were indispensable.

Mediterranean sea powers gradually began to look elsewhere for what their own forests could not provide. In the sixteenth century northern timber was arriving in Seville in boatloads of planks and beams. For the building of the Invincible Armada, Philip II tried to buy, or at any rate had marked for felling, trees in Poland. Venice was finally obliged to countenance what regulations had previously strictly forbidden all her subjects to do: to buy abroad, not only timber, but ships' hulls which were then rigged at Venice, or even completed ships. Between 1590 and 1616 she received in this way eleven boats from Holland, seven from Patmos, four from the Black Sea, one from Constantinople, one from the Basque country, and one from the Straits of Gibraltar.[152] There is no doubt that this timber crisis offers one explanation of the development of techniques and maritime economies in the Mediterranean.[153] It is not unconnected with the reduction in tonnages, the rising cost of construction, and the success of northern competitors. But other factors were also involved, such as price movements and the high cost of labour, for everything did not depend upon raw materials.[154]

In any case, if maritime civilizations originally grew up near coastal mountains, it was not only because of their forests but also because they formed a natural barrier affording many sheltered places[155] against the

[150] Robert Mantran, *Istanbul dans la seconde moitié du XVIIe siècle*, 1962, p. 445 note 2 and passim.
[151] V. Lamansky, *op. cit.*, p. 83–89 Simancas E° 1329, Venice, 25th November, 1571. Venice's efforts do not seem to have been successful. Even if this policy had been adopted it is doubtful whether it would have had much effect: a letter from the French ambassador at Constantinople, dated 8th May, 1572, reports that in five months the Turks have already built 150 ships, complete with artillery and crews. E. Charrière, *op. cit.*, III, p. 269.
[152] F. C. Lane, *op. cit.*, p. 232.
[153] C. Trasselli, 'Sul naviglio nordico in Sicilia nel secolo XVII', unpublished article, to appear in forthcoming tribute to Vicens Vives.
[154] A study of the cost price of ships would be difficult but possible. There is some valuable information on the price of northern timber in *Dispacci scritti al Senato dal Secretario Marco Ottobon, da Danziga dalli 15 novembre 1590 sino 7 settembre 1591*, copy in A.d.S. Venice, Secreta Archivi Propri, Polonia 2.
[155] *Instructions Nautiques* no. 368, p. 7. Very bad weather is rare on the coast between Nice and Genoa. On the port of Rosas, sheltered and safe from all winds except the south which rarely blows, cf. *Instructions* no. 345, p. 135. On the permanent calm of the port of Antibes, cf. *Instructions* no. 360 p. 175. The mistral blows strongly at Valencia (that is in the gulf of Valencia). It is not dangerous to shipping near the shore, but on the open sea it can force ships to seek shelter in the Balearics: *Instructions* no. 345, p. 12.

relentless north wind, the great enemy of Mediterranean shipping. 'Get under sail with a young south wind or an old north wind', says a proverb of the Aegean.[156] A further explanation is that emigrants from the mountains would naturally go down to the sea, and the tempting waters might well be the best, or the only, way of reaching another part of the coast.[157] So an association might grow up between a sea-going way of life and the mountain economy, which would then interact and complement each other,[158] leading to the extraordinary economic combination of ploughed fields, market gardens, orchards, fishing, and sea-going. On the Dalmatian island of Mljet, a traveller reports that even today the men divide their time between farming and fishing,[159] as they do in the other Dalmatian islands. The same is true of Pantelleria where in addition to the fishing, vines, and orchards, an excellent race of mules is bred. This is the traditional wisdom of the old Mediterranean way of life where the meagre resources of the land are added to the meagre resources of the sea. If it is disappearing today it rarely does so without provoking distress: the Greek fishermen of the Pelion region, 'increasingly drawn to the sea, have to give up their gardens and cottages and move their families to the harbour streets'. But once removed from the traditional balanced pattern of their former way of life, they swell the ranks of the sea poachers who fish with dynamite in spite of government prohibitions.[160] For the sea alone is not rich enough to feed her fishermen.

Neither is the land, on these barren mountains, and this explains the considerable role played by the old rural villages in the economic development of the neighbouring coast. Overlooking the waters of Catalonia the white houses of the villages can be seen through the trees. It is the people of these villages who tend the terraced hillsides of the great massif and produce their horticultural miracles. There is often corresponding to the hill village a fishing village down by the sea, sometimes built out over the sea: Arénys de Mar below Arénys de Mount, Caldetes below Lievaneres, Cabrera below Cabrils.[161] On the Genoese Riviera too the old villages up on the hill often have their fishing port, their *scala* down by the water,[162] and throughout Italy, and not only Italy, there are hundreds of examples, with a continual coming and going of donkeys between the two levels. The seaside village is often more recent in date, an offshoot of the rural village with which it remains closely associated. Its existence is brought about by the economy of the coastal massifs, the terrifying poverty of their

[156] Werner Helwig, *Braconniers de la mer en Grèce*, Fr. trans. 1942, p. 199.
[157] Even today, some parts of the Ligurian coast can only be reached by sea, R. Lopez, 'Aux origines du capitalisme genois', in *Annales d'hist. écon. et soc.*, IX, 1937, p. 434, no. 2. Similarly the railway and road continue to avoid the 'costa brava' of Catalonia.
[158] Cf. the amusing passage on Sicily in Paul Morand, *Lewis et Irène* 1931, p. 17.
[159] E. Fechner, in: Benndorf, *Das Mittelmeerbuch*, p. 99.
[160] Werner Helwig, *op. cit.*, passim.
[161] Pierre Vilar, *op. cit.*, I, p. 249.
[162] On the processions of donkeys between the two levels see P. Vidal de La Blache, *Principles of human geography*, p. 137.

way of life, which even the combination of the two villages cannot transform into plenty. At Rosas, or at San Feliu de Guixols in Catalonia it was still possible quite recently (in 1938) to see food sold in the market in characteristically tiny quantities: a handful of vegetables, a quarter chicken for example.[163] In 1543, the inhabitants of Cassis, sailors and pirates if necessary, blamed poverty for forcing them 'to traffic on the sea and to catch fish, not without great risk and peril',[164] Hundreds of villages on the Mediterranean coast owe their existence to the poverty of the usually mountainous barren hinterland.

The big cities. These seaside villages were the basic unit, but they were not enough to create an active coastal region. A big city was indispensable with its supplies of yards, sail-cloth, rigging, pitch, ropes, and capital; a city with its tradesmen, shipping offices, insurance agents, and all the other services an urban centre can provide. Without Barcelona, and its craftsmen, Jewish merchants, even its soldier adventurers and the many resources of the Santa Maria del Mar quarter, the maritime expansion of the Catalan seaboard would have been incomprehensible. Such success required the intervention, discipline, and imperialism of the big city. It was in the sixteenth century that the Catalan seaboard first awoke to a *historically* visible maritime life. But its expansion only began two centuries later with the rise of Barcelona. Then for three hundred years the procession of ships from the little ports of the Catalan seaboard plied ceaselessly back and forth on t he Barcelona 'beach', where sailing ships from the Balearics would also put in to harbour as well as boats from Valencia which was always something of a rival, Biscay whalers, and the constant flow of boats from Marseilles and Italy. But when Barcelona lost her independence, after the long struggle against John of Aragon, twenty years later in 1402 suffered the equally grave loss of her Jewish community, her *judería*, and finally when her capitalists gradually stopped putting their money into risky investments, preferring the regular income from the *Taula de Cambi*[165] or investing in land near the city, then began the decline of the great merchant city and the Catalan seaboard dependent upon it. So great was its decline that Catalan trade practically disappeared from the Mediterranean and the shores of the county were left undefended when they were ravaged by French corsairs at the time of the wars between

[163] The same observation could be made of the 'starving Ligurian coast' mentioned by Michelet.
[164] A. C., Cassis, B.B. 36. *Biens communaux* 24th–25th September, 1543. It appeared from the rest of the inquiry that 'the vines are plentiful but yield little, the olive trees sometimes produce nothing for up to five years because of the drought; the land is in general impossible to plough . . .'. Cf. Jules Sion's perceptive remark: 'Provence very nearly became one of the regions of the Mediterranean where the scarcity of good land and the patterns of settlement on the coast led the inhabitants of the littoral to live like the Barbary pirates', *France Méditerranéenne*, 1934, p. 110.
[165] A. P. Usher, 'Deposit Banking in Barcelona 1300–1700' in *Journal of Economics and Business,* IV, 1931, p. 122.

the Valois and the Habsburgs – and later by the equally dangerous Algerine corsairs, who all but settled in the wastes of the Ebro delta.

Marseilles, Genoa and Ragusa played similar predominant roles in the lives of the small ports surrounding them. There were even cases where the dependencies were not on the same coast as the metropolis,[166] for example Venice's hold over the Istrian coast, the Dalmatian coast, and the distant Greek islands. Marseilles too attracted not only the swarming population of the Provençal coast, which was completely at her service, but also a large proportion of the sailors from Cape Corse. And Genoa used Ragusan cargo vessels.

The attraction of the big cities is the more understandable in that sailors in the Mediterranean have always been wanderers ready to migrate. In 1461, the Venetian Senate expressed anxiety at the shortage of crews and cabin boys and asked for details: the sailors 'go to Pisa . . . where they are well paid . . . to our loss and another's gain'. Many of these sailors left because they had debts to pay or heavy fines imposed by the *Cinque Savii* or the *Signor de nocte* – the night police of Venice.[167] As the result of a legal dispute in 1526, the accounts have survived of the ship *Santa Maria de Bogoña*, which sailed in the Atlantic, stayed for a while at Cadiz, and put in at Lisbon and the island of São Tomé before arriving at Santo Domingo with her cargo of Negro slaves.[168] This takes us out of Mediterranean waters, but among the *marineros* and *grumetes* (cabin boys) on board her could be found sailors from Lipari, Sicily, Majorca, Genoa, Savona, some Greeks, and a man from Toulon – a real rendezvous for adventurers. At the Hague in 1532, there were similar complaints that the sailors, 'always ready to move away', were leaving Holland and Zeeland for Lübeck.[169] In 1604 a group of Venetian seamen, 'being no longer able to live on the ships of the Signoria because of the low wages', fled to Florence and no doubt to Leghorn.[170] These were daily occurrences of minor importance, but when circumstances lent a hand, they might become indices of large-scale change.

The changing fortunes of maritime regions. This constant flow of migrations completes the picture of the maritime regions. On the whole it is a straightforward one. They were directly concerned in the fortunes of the Mediterranean as a whole, and they thrived, stagnated, declined, or revived according to the state of those fortunes.

[166] So when one tries to estimate the size of the maritime population of an island like Corsica, as Jean Brunhes does, *op. cit.*, p. 69, it seems to me unwise not to take into account Corsican sailors outside the island. Marseilles still has a large population of Corsican sailors today.

[167] A.d.S. Venice, Senato Mar, 7, f° 2 v°.

[168] Archivio General de Indias, Seville, Justicia, legajo no. 7. The lawsuit was in 1530. My attention was kindly drawn to this document by my colleague Enrique Otto. The sailors' origins are presumed from their surnames.

[169] R. Häpke, *Niederländische Akten und Urkunden*, 1913, I, p. 35.

[170] Domenico Sella, *Commerci e industrie a Venezia nel secolo XVII*, 1961, p. 24, n. 1.

Take once more the example of Catalonia. Outside forces were largely responsible for her original rise; it was thanks to the teachings and techniques brought over by Italian immigrants from Genoa and Pisa after the eleventh century that Catalonia developed a thriving maritime economy, two hundred years before the glorious reign of Peter the Great, *Pere lo Gran.* History sooner or later takes back her gifts. By the sixteenth century the decline of Catalonia, already perceptible in the fifteenth, had become evident. Her shipping activity was reduced to sending a few boats to Marseilles or the Balearics. Only rarely did one of her ships venture as far as Sardinia, Naples,[171] or Sicily, or to the African *presidios.* At the very end of the sixteenth century a few voyages began again between Barcelona and Alexandria. But until then activity was at such a standstill on the Catalan seaboard that when Philip II decided in the Grand Council of 1562 to build a great armed fleet, he was obliged to place orders in Italy. And in an effort to revive the arsenal of Barcelona he brought in experts from the boatyards of San Pier d'Arena, in Genoa.[172]

These abrupt declines, so frequent in the Mediterranean, where so many sea-going populations rose and fell in turn, can generally be explained as follows. The seashore provinces, always short of men, could not survive for long what we would call periods of prosperity, and which were in fact periods of hard work and strain. To a very large extent, maritime life was a proletarian life, which wealth and the accompanying inactivity regularly corrupted. A *provveditore* of the Venetian fleet said in 1583, the seaman is like a fish, he cannot stay long out of the water without going rotten.[173]

And as soon as signs of strain appeared they were often exploited and aggravated by competition. The presence of Biscay *balaneros* in the port of Barcelona in the first years of the fourteenth century is an early sign of either strain or competition. And in the context of Genoese history, so is the proliferation of Ragusan sailors and merchantmen hastening to the service of the *Dominante* in the sixteenth century. But this astounding good fortune exhausted in turn the resources of the little world of Ragusa, which consisted of a few kilometres of coastline and some unimportant islands. Between 1590 and 1600 a few incidents were enough to compromise the prosperity which had previously seemed unshakeable.

That does not mean to say that in periods of depression maritime life disappeared altogether from those regions which had previously been thriving. At such times it would subside into a modest everyday form, in which it was almost indestructible. So in the sixteenth century the coasts of Syria and Catalonia lapsed into a quiet rhythm of reduced activity,

---

[171] At the beginning of the sixteenth century the Neapolitan documents I have consulted mention Catalan merchants living in Naples more frequently than Catalan ships such as that of Joanne Hostales, which took on a cargo of wheat in Sicily and transported it to Naples (April-May, 1517, A.d.S. Naples, Dipendenze della Sommaria, fascio 548). After the middle of the century these mentions become very rare.

[172] Simancas Eº 331, Aragon, 1564: a list of sixteen experts, carpenters, caulkers, and masters of galleys, sent from Genoa to Barcelona *'para la fabrica de las galeras'.*

[173] V. Lamansky, *op. cit.,* p. 564.

while there was also a decline in shipping off the shores of Sicily, Naples, Andalusia, Valencia, and Majorca. As far as the last region is concerned there is a clear connection between its decline and the destructive advance of the Barbary pirates. Nonetheless it continued to survive and to provide more material for an active coastal trade than our usual sources of information would suggest. The swift frigates of the privateers which at the end of the century provided the means of effective Christian revenge, from Alicante, Almeria, an old maritime centre, and Palma on Majorca, did not spring from nowhere.

Only a few minor incidents in the background of history indicate the existence of this inconspicuous activity. We have already mentioned the coral fishermen of Trapani, who ventured, in spite of the Barbary corsairs, to the reefs on the African coast. The documents of the French Consulate at Tunis which was set up in 1574, frequently mention Sicilian barques and also small barques from Naples.[174] By contrast, it is interesting to note the absence of Neapolitan coral fishermen, those of Torre del Greco for instance, from the Sardinian reefs where they had been regular visitors in the fifteenth century. Were there serious reasons for their absence? Perhaps not, for there was no shortage of Neapolitan boats either at Rome or Civitavecchia, Leghorn or Genoa.

There was a similar profusion of balancelles, barques, and brigantines on the shores of southern Spain, sailing to North Africa. A document of 1567 records the presence at Algiers of a series of Valencian seamen who, since they were free, must have been there to trade.[175] At the end of the century some other Valencians joined the exciting operations that organized the escape of captives from the prisons of Algiers. Some of their accounts are as thrilling as anything out of Cervantes.[176]

In fact, the apparent death of a coastal region may be no more than a change in the rhythm of its life. It may pass in turn from coastal trading to long-distance voyages, that is for the historian, from an unrecorded to a recorded existence, vanishing again from his attentive gaze every time it lapses into its obscure everyday life. It is as if a regular law has determined the life cycle of the populations and the sea.

3. THE ISLANDS[177]

The Mediterranean islands are more numerous and above all more important than is generally supposed. Some of the larger ones are miniature continents: Sardinia, Corsica, Sicily, Cyprus, Crete, and Rhodes. The

---

[174] For the Sicilian boats see P. Grandchamp, *La France en Tunisie, à la fin du XVIe siècle*, Tunis, 1920, p. 32, 36, 46, 63, 81, 95; for the Neapolitan *ibid.*, p. 30, 31, 33.

[175] 24th January, 1560, A.N., K. 1494, B. 12, no. 18.

[176] See Vol. II, Part II, Ch. 7, section on Christian privateers.

[177] On islands see the curious and striking article of Ratzelian inspiration by Franz Olshaussen, 'Inselpsychologie' in *Kölnische Zeitung*, 12, VII, 1942. The starting point of his remarks is the case of the Chilean island Mas a Tierra, which was the original Robinson Crusoe's island.

smaller ones may combine with neighbouring archipelagos to form families of islands. Large or small, their significance lies in providing indispensable landfalls on the sea routes and affording stretches of comparatively calm water to which shipping is attracted, either between islands or between island and mainland coasts. To the east lies the Aegean archipelago, so scattered over the sea as to be inseparable from it;[178] in the centre the group of islands between Sicily and Africa; in the north the Ionian and Dalmatian islands, which string out like a convoy of ships along the Balkan seaboard, in the sixteenth century flying the flag of St. Mark. There are really two separate flotillas here: one in the Ionian Sea consisting of Zante, Cephalonia, Santa Maura, and Corfu; the other in the Adriatic, with the Dalmatian islands running from Meleda and Lagosta in the south to Quarnero, Veglia, and Cherso behind Istria in the north. Between the Ionian and Dalmatian convoys runs quite a long stretch of coastline including the inhospitable Albanian shore and the little territory of Ragusa. But taken all together, the islands provided a stopping route from Venice to Crete; from Crete a busy trade route linked Cyprus and Syria. These islands, running along the axis of her power, were Venice's stationary fleet.

The western groups of islands are equally important: near Sicily, Stromboli, the Egades, the Lipari islands; further north, the Tuscan archipelago where in the middle of the sixteenth century Cosimo de' Medici built the fortress of Portoferraio on the island of Elba; off the coast of Provence, the Iles d'Hyères and the Iles d'Or; further west, in the open stretch of the western Mediterranean, the Balearics, Majorca, Minorca, Ibiza – the salt island – and the scarcely accessible rock of Formentera. This group has always been of considerable importance: an entire shipping sector revolved around it.

These are the large or fairly large islands. To list the little ones and the very tiny ones (some of which are famous like the islet of Algiers, the islands of Venice, Naples, and Marseilles) would be quite impossible. There is hardly a stretch of the Mediterranean shore which is not broken up into islands, islets and rocks.[179] To rid the coasts of corsairs waiting for a good chance, or taking on fresh water, is called in the correspondence of the viceroys of Sicily, 'limpiar las islas', 'cleaning up the islands', that is checking the moorings of a few dozen islets which were all classic places for an ambush.

Isolated worlds? Whether large or small, these islands of all sizes and shapes make up a coherent human environment in so far as similar

[178] And vice versa, if one thinks of the etymology of the word *archipelago*.
[179] A small example, the islands and islets in the Straits of Bonifacio: *Instructions Nautiques*, no. 368, p. 152 ff. Over a larger area, the islands and islets of the North African coast: *Instructions*, no. 360, p. 225, 231, 235, 237, 238, 241, 242, 244, 246, 247, 257, 262, 265, 266, 267, 277, 282, 284, 285, 287, 291, 297, 305, 308, 309, 310, 311, 313, 314, 331.

pressures are exerted upon them, making them both far ahead and far behind the general history of the sea; pressures that may divide them, often brutally, between the two opposite poles of archaism and innovation.

Sardinia is an average example. In spite of its size it was quite clearly not of key importance in the sixteenth century, whatever the geographers of the period and Sardinian chroniclers of all periods might say. It was too lost in the sea to play an important role, too far from the enriching contacts that linked Sicily, for example, with Italy and Africa. Mountainous, excessively divided, a prisoner of its poverty,[180] it was a self-contained world with its own language,[181] customs, archaic economy, and pervasive pastoralism – in some regions remaining as Rome must have found it long ago. This archaic character of the islands (Sardinia and others), their strange capacity of preserving for centuries antique forms of civilization and mixtures of folklore has been so often remarked upon that there is no need to describe it at length.[182]

But simultaneously with this isolation and in striking contrast, some accidental change of ruler or of fortune may bring to the island's shores an entirely different civilization and way of life, with its dress, customs, and language, which the island may receive and preserve intact over several centuries, bearing living witness to forgotten revolutions. 'Isolation' is a relative phenomenon. That the sea surrounds the islands and cuts them off from the rest of the world more effectively than any other environment is certainly true whenever they are really situated outside the normal sea routes. But when they are integrated into shipping routes, and for one reason or another (often external and quite gratuitous reasons) become one of the links in a chain, they are on the contrary actively involved in the dealings of the outside world, less cut off from them than some inaccessible mountain areas.

To come back to the example of Sardinia, in the Middle Ages it was drawn into the sphere of Pisa, then of Genoa; their solicitude was accounted for by its gold mines. In the fourteenth and fifteenth centuries Catalan expansion found a foothold there on its way east. Catalan is still spoken today in Alghero on the west coast, and scholars have detected a curious Hispano-Gothic architecture there. In the sixteenth century and even before no doubt, the island was the Mediterranean's leading exporter of

[180] E. Albèri, *op. cit.*, I, III, p. 267, the low cost of living, the 'brutta' population. In 1603, its population consisted of 66,669 households, i.e. 266,676 inhabitants using a coefficient of 4. Francesco Corridore, *Storia documentata della populazione di Sardegna*, Turin, 1902, p. 19–20.

[181] On 'Sardinian' and its three dialects, Ovidio and Meyer Lübke, in *Grundriss der romanischen Phil.*, ed. G. Groeber, 2nd ed., p. 551.

[182] We know for instance that Chios, which was under Turkish rule after 1566, remained Catholic long afterwards, earning the title of 'little Rome' of the Levant. Chateaubriand remarked on its Italian character as late as the nineteenth century. And conversely, Malta, the island of the Knights, and Pantelleria have retained their Arab population and dialects to the present day. One is also tempted to mention the curious linguistic analogy of the Crimea, where Gothic dialects persisted until the time of Luther; but the Crimea is not an island, and our evidence in this case is not complete.

cheeses.[183] And so through Cagliari the island was in touch with the rest of the western world; boats and galleons loaded with her *cavallo* or *salso* cheese sailed to the neighbouring coast of Italy, Leghorn, Genoa, and Naples; even to Marseilles, in spite of competition from rivals, the cheeses of Milan and the Auvergne; and even to Barcelona. Another way of being integrated into Mediterranean life in the sixteenth century was to be constantly harassed by the attacks of the Barbary pirates. The piracy was not always successful: corsairs were sometimes captured, though not very often. More numerous were the Sardinians, fishermen or inhabitants of the coast, who, carried off by the Barbary pirates, every year swelled the ranks of the unfortunate captives or the rich renegades of Algiers.

Sardinia then, which has been described as impenetrable, had windows opening outwards from which it is sometimes possible to glimpse, as from an observatory, the general history of the sea. One historian, P. Amat di S. Filippo, has investigated the prices of Moslem slaves at Cagliari in the sixteenth century.[184] He discovered a striking drop in prices after 1580, which naturally corresponds to a considerable increase in the number of slaves on the market at Cagliari. This is because before 1580 the only slaves for sale on the island were a few Barbary pirates who had either been wrecked on Sardinian shores or had been captured by the inhabitants during one of their raids.[185] After 1580 prisoners for auction came from another source. They were brought in by Christian pirate vessels, especially by the light frigates from Almeria and Alicante, for which Cagliari was a convenient stopping place. So Sardinia was in her own way affected by the revival of active Christian privateering, a sort of counter-offensive launched against the Barbary corsairs and based in the Balearics, southern Spain, Naples, and Sicily. It might be argued that this was more true of Cagliari than of the whole of Sardinia; that Cagliari was somewhat isolated and faced seawards, having little to do with the rest of the island. There is some truth in the argument: but Cagliari was after all a Sardinian town, linked to the nearby plain, the mountains, and the whole of the island.

Precarious lives. All islands have towns like this, affected by the general life of the sea, and at the same time (if only because they handle imports and exports) looking inward to that world which the historian, pre-occupied as he is with texts concerning political history, does not notice at first glance: the withdrawn and insecure way of life, the biology isolated as under a bell jar of which naturalists have long been aware.[186] There is

[183] There was a regular link with Leghorn. For the export of Sardinian cheeses to Valencia, Simancas E° 335, 6th September, 1574, f° 46.

[184] Pietro Amat di San Filippo, 'Della schiavitù e del servaggio in Sardegna' in *Miscellanea di storia italiana*, 3rd series, vol. II, 1895.

[185] Stefano Spinola to the Marquis of Mantua, Genoa, 30th April, 1532, A.d.S. Mantua, A. Gonzaga, Genova 759, bad weather drove ashore on the Sardinian coast two galleys, four galliots and a *fuste* whose Turkish sailors almost all escaped.

[186] P. Vidal de la Blache, *Tableau de la géographie de la France*, 1908, p. 25-6. Théodore Monod, *L'hippopotame et le philosophe*, 1943, p. 77.

hardly an island that does not possess, alongside its human peculiarities, its animal and vegetable curiosities that are sooner or later revealed to the outside world. In his description of Cyprus which appeared in 1580, the Reverend Father Stefano[187] (who claimed to be descended from the Royal House of Lusignan) describes 'the peculiar herbs' and 'perfumes' of the island: white *apium*, a sort of water-celery, which is eaten 'crystallised in sugar', *oldanum* which is used to make the liqueur of the same name, the tree known as the 'Cyprus tree' (black cypress), similar to the pomegranate tree, which flowers in clusters like the vine, and whose distilled leaves produce the orange dye that is used to colour the tails of gentlemen's horses, 'as is customarily seen there'. It is also surprising to find that cotton seeds were mixed with chopped straw as fodder for the animals. And what a wealth of medicinal herbs! Among the curious beasts there were 'wild cattle, donkeys, and boars', and the 'vine' birds, buntings, of which thousands of barrels were exported to Venice and Rome, pickled in vinegar.

But extraordinary fauna and flora can never be taken to indicate abundance. None of the islands was assured of the future. The great problem for all of them, never or only partly solved, was how to live off their own resources, off the soil, the orchards, the flocks, and if that was not possible, to look outwards. All the islands with a few exceptions (Sicily in particular) were lands of hunger. The extreme cases were the Venetian islands in the Levant: Corfu,[188] Crete,[189] or Cyprus, which were constantly threatened by famine in the second half of the century. It was a catastrophe when the *caramusalis* did not arrive on time, with their providential cargoes of grain from Thrace, when the stocks of wheat and millet in the stores of the citadels had been exhausted. In fact a black market was organized around these Levantine islands, hence the endless prevarications of the officials reported in inquiries.

The situation was not as precarious as this everywhere.[190] But the

---

[187] Fr. Steffano di Lusignano, *Description de toute l'isle de Cypre*, Paris, 1580, p. 223 v° ff.

[188] Corfu was also short of meat: Philippe de Canaye, *Le voyage de Levant*, 1573, published by H. Hauser, 1897, p. 191. On Corfu in 1576, see the account of Giustiniano, B.N. Paris, Ital. 1220, f° 35 ff: 17,000 inhabitants. The island had fertile but uncultivated plains and could only produce enough grain to last it four months, but exported wine, oil, and flocks to the mainland.

[189] Even in the eighteenth century, Crete was short of grain (Tott, *Memoirs*, II, p. 221). Crete seems at that period to have been an island primarily exporting oil and soap, (*ibid.*, p. 221). For the grain from the caramusalis some of which was brought in illegally, see Hieronimo Ferro, 6th October, 1560, A.d.S. Venice, Seno. Secreta Const. Fza 2/B, f° 274. Without help from her neighbours, Crete would only have been able to provide for one third of the year; hence the frequent shortages and constant anxiety: the harvest was poor on Crete, and there is no grain worth buying, explains Giacomo Foscarini, *provveditore* general of the kingdom of Candia, to the Council of Ten (Candia, 15th November, 1574, A.d.S. Venice, Capi del Consiglio dei Dieci, Lettere, Ba 286, f° 5). In 1573 there was scarcity on Zante, Philippe de Canaye, *op. cit.*, p. 184.

[190] Particularly, and this may seem paradoxical, on the poorer and more backward islands, which had fewer inhabitants and above all were not exploited by crops grown for export. So Sardinia could sometimes afford the luxury of exporting wheat. G. Riba

Balearics could hardly support their military or merchant towns,[191] particularly since little progress had been made towards farming the land. The clearing of stones from the fields of Minorca in the plain behind Mahon, was not completed until the eighteenth century.[192] They had to rely on cereal imports from Sicily and even North Africa. On Malta, too, food was short. In spite of the many privileges permitting the island to import wheat from both Sicily and France, Malta was always in difficulties, so much so that in the summer the galleys of the Knights would stop grain ships coming from the Sicilian *caricatori*, exactly like the corsairs of Tripoli.

As well as the threat of famine there was also the risk from the sea, which in the mid-sixteenth century was more warlike than ever.[193] The Balearics, Corsica, Sicily, and Sardinia, to take the islands we know best, were besieged territories. They had constantly to be defended, watch towers had to be built, fortifications erected, extended, and equipped with artillery, either pieces sent in from outside or cast on the spot by the primitive methods of bell founders.[194] And of course garrisons and reinforcements had to be placed along the coast, as soon as the fine weather arrived and with it the campaign season. It was not easy for Spain to hold Sardinia, or even to be certain of an island as nearby as Minorca.[195] Charles V, after the sack of Mahon in 1535, envisaged, to forestall further danger, nothing less than the evacuation of the entire population of Minorca to the larger island, Majorca.[196] The case of Elba, in the Tuscan archipelago, was equally tragic. The island was brutally surprised in the

y Garcia, *op. cit.*, p. 317–318 (1587) or p. 320 (1588). But in bad years, the island suffered shortages like the others (V.R. of Sardinia to H.M., Caller, 22nd September, 1576, Simancas E° 335, f° 356.) In Corsica, the export of grain, which had been declared free for five years in 1590, soon had to be suspended because of poor harvests. A. Marcelli, 'Intorno al cosidetto mal governo genovese dell'Isola', in *Archivo storico di Corsica*, 1937, p. 416.

[191] E. Albèri, I. III, p. 226, does state that Majorca was self-sufficient; this was in about 1558. At the time the island's population was between 45,000 and 90,000 (30 towns with 500 to 600 households each). But there were lean years too. Cf. 1588 and 1589, for example, when the island was unable to obtain grain from Oran. G. Riba y Garcia, *El Consejo supremo de Aragon*, p. 288–289.

[192] Pierre Monbeig, 'Vie de relations et spécialisation agricole, Les Baléares au XVIIIe siècle' in *Ann. d'hist. éc. et. soc.* IV, 1932, p. 539.

[193] Viceroy of Majorca to H.M., 20th December, 1567: '. . . que todo el año estan cercadas de fustas de moros de manera que muy pocos bateles entran o salen que no se pierdan y este año se han tomado siete o ocho bergantines y toda su substancia se va en Argel . . .'. On this besieging of the Balearics, see also 10th January, 1524 in *Tomiciana* VIII p. 301, M. Sanudo, *op. cit.*, VI, p. 236, 16th March, 1532.

[194] Ciudadela, 10th July, 1536, A.N., K. 1690. Cuidadela after the raid of the Barbarossas. Cf. also on the subject of the founder whose castings went wrong, *ibid.*, Majorca, 29th August, 1536.

[195] On the defence of Sardinia, cf. below, the construction of watchtowers. On troops stationed on the island during the summer, see for example the documents: 8th September, 1561, Simancas E° 328; 25th July, 1565, *ibid.*, E° 332, 6th August, 1565 and 5th July, 1566.

[196] Information given to me at Simancas by Federico Chabod. On Minorca, cf. Cosme Parpal y Marqués, *La isla de Menorca en tiempo de Felipe II*, Barcelona, 1913.

sixteenth century by the advance of the Barbary corsairs and became a maritime frontier under constant enemy attack. Its coastal towns – the large villages along the sea front – fell into abandon. The population had to flee to the mountains of the interior, until Cosimo de' Medici undertook the fortification of Portoferraio in 1548.

These disadvantages explain the historical poverty at the heart of all the islands, even the richest among them: and more pronounced of course in the others, in Corsica and Sardinia where, as we have noted, the economy was primitive and predominantly pastoral; or in the mountains of Cyprus where, as in the mountains of Crete, there stretched one of the most characteristic no-man's-lands of the Mediterranean, the refuge of the poor, bandits, and outlaws. In the interior of even Sicily, rich Sicily, what do we find but a land without roads, rivers without bridges, and poor sheep farming, whose stock was of such low quality that in the seventeenth century Barbary sheep had to be brought over to improve it?[197]

On the paths of general history. A precarious, restricted, and threatened life, such was the lot of the islands, their domestic life at any rate. But their external life, the role they have played in the forefront of history far exceeds what might be expected from such poor territories. The events of history often lead to the islands. Perhaps it would be more accurate to say that they make use of them. Take for example the role played by the islands as stages in the dissemination of crops: sugarcane, which was brought from India to Egypt, passed from Egypt to Cyprus, becoming established there in the tenth century; from Cyprus it soon reached Sicily in the eleventh century; from Sicily it was taken west; Henry the Navigator had some brought from Sicily to send to Madeira, which was the first 'sugar island' of the Atlantic; from Madeira, sugar growing quickly moved to the Azores, the Canaries, the Cape Verde islands and beyond, to America. The islands played a similar role in the dissemination of silkworms, and generally in most cultural movements, some of which were extremely complicated. It was by way of Cyprus and the sumptuous court of the House of Lusignan, that there came to the West, more slowly than the light of some stars reaches the earth, the costumes of the ancient bygone China of the T'ang dynasty. The long pointed shoes and the hennins, which date a period of French history so well that they immediately suggest the frivolous court of Charles VI and the *Très Riches Heures* of the Duke of Berry, had been fashionable in China in the fifth century. And this distant heritage was passed on to the West by the kings of Cyprus.[198]

We should not really be surprised. The islands lay on the paths of the great sea routes and played a part in international relations. To their ordinary day-to-day existence was added a chapter in the history of great events. Their economies often suffered the impact of these events, since

[197] B. Com. Palermo, Qq D. 56, f° 259–273, a series of curious and interesting letters.
[198] G. Bratianu, *op. cit.*, p. 269 ff.

they could offer no resistance to some demands. How many islands were invaded by foreign crops, whose justification lay solely in their position on Mediterranean or even world markets? Grown for export only, these crops regularly threatened the equilibrium of the island's economy. They were often responsible for the threat of famine mentioned above. We can see this in an exaggerated form, blindingly clearly in the islands of the 'Mediterranean Atlantic': Madeira, the Canaries, São Tomé, which were all literally ravaged by the monoculture of cane sugar, as colonial north-east Brazil was to be later. Madeira, which was originally a timber island, rapidly lost the major part of its forest cover to the sugar mills and their need for fuel. This revolution was carried out entirely in the interest of a Europe which was clamouring for the precious sugar, and not in the interests of the islanders themselves. For the tragedy of sugarcane is that wherever it is grown it prevents the growing of other crops in rotation and restricts the space available for food crops. This new arrival completely upset the old balance and was the more dangerous since it was protected by a powerful capitalism which in the sixteenth century was lodged in many quarters, in Italy, Lisbon, and Antwerp. And it was impossible to offer resistance. In general the island populations were unable to withstand this drain on their resources. In the Canaries, sugar was almost certainly as responsible as the brutalities of the first conquerors for the disappearance of the indigenous natives, the Guanches. And it was the sugar plantations which generalized the use of slave labour, leading to the enslavement of the Berbers of the African coast, whom Christian pirates from the Canaries would carry off in their raids, and particularly to the slave trade in Negroes from Guinea and Angola which in the middle of the century, again because of sugar, reached the shores of the American continent. These are examples from the Atlantic. But there is no shortage of strictly Mediterranean examples. Take the wheat-growing invasion of Sicily; until 1590 and even after, Sicily was the Canada or Argentina of the western countries of the Mediterranean. Chios produced mastic, both the resin and the drink;[199] Cyprus, cotton, vines, and sugar;[200] Crete and Corfu, wines;[201] Djerba, olives. These single-crop economies were the result of foreign intervention, artificial and often harmful to what is expressed by the German term *Volkswirtschaft*.

At Cyprus this was to be proved in 1572 when the Turks captured the

[199] L. F. Heyd, *Histoire du Commerce du Levant au Moyen Age*, 1885–6 p. 336. Th. Gautier, *Voyage à Constantinople*, p. 54; J. W. Zinkeisen, *op. cit.*, II, p. 901, n. 2. Girolamo Giustiniano, *La description et l'histoire de l'isle de Scios*, 1606. On the island of Chios after the Turkish conquest of 1566, and its towns with their deserted streets and ruined palaces, cf. Jacobus Paleologus, *De Rebus Constantinopoli et Chii*, 1573. On gum mastic, cf. J. B. Tavernier, *op. cit.* p. 118.

[200] And sometimes wheat. As for the gold and silver threads of Cyprus, I am inclined to agree with J. Lestocquoy (in *Mélanges d'histoire sociale*, III, 1943, p. 25) that this was only a trade description. Cyprus also exported casks of ortolans: J. B. Tavernier, *op. cit.*, Persian Travels, p. 80.

[201] Baron de Busbecq, *Lettres*, Paris, 1748, p. 178, drank at Constantinople 'much wine from the isle of Crete'.

island from Venice. The wealth of the island under Venetian rule had been the vineyards, the cotton plantations, and the fields of sugarcane. But whose wealth? It had belonged to a Venetian and Genoese aristocracy whose sumptuous mansions can still be seen today in the old quarter of Nicosia; certainly not to the natives of the island, Orthodox Greeks. So the Turkish conquest unleashed a social revolution. We have a curious account of it from an English sailor in 1595. A Cypriot merchant had told him the history of the island, pointing out the ruined palaces of the former Genoese and Venetian noblemen, whom the Turks massacred as just retribution, according to our witness, for the extortionate demands they made on the peasants.[202] Indeed, at the time of the invasion, the Venetians were abandoned by the Greeks both in the countryside and the towns. During the Turkish attack on Nicosia in 1570, 'the inhabitants, of all social conditions, . . . almost all remained sleeping in their houses'.[203] It is true that the departure of the Venetians was followed by a drop in exports of cotton, raw and spun alike, and by such a marked deterioration of the vineyards that Venice was able to arrange to buy back the precious leather flasks used for the manufacture of wine, as they were no longer of any use on the island. But this does not necessarily mean the decline of Cyprus. There is no evidence that Turkish rule led to a fall in living standards for the inhabitants of the island.[204]

Crete and Corfu afford matter for similar reflections. Here, as in Cyprus, we must imagine a countryside converted by man for the cultivation of the vine, producing raisins and the wine known as malmsey. On Corfu, the vines spread from the hills and mountains to the plains, the *pianure*, which were easier to cultivate.[205] They drove out the wheat, but in the exclusive production of one crop there is always the possibility of surplus production and a slump. On Crete vines were torn up on official orders in 1584, to

[202] R. Hakluyt, *The principal navigations* . . . London, 1600, p. 309. On the complicity of the near-serf peasants in the Turkish conquest, cf. Julian Lopez to H.M., Venice, 26th October, 1570, Relacion de Venecia, 28th September, 1570 Simancas E° 1327. Cardinal de Rambouillet to Charles IX, Rome, 5th November, 1570, E. Charrière, *op. cit.*, III, p. 124. There was unrest on Chios in 1548-9, when the inhabitants wishing to be free from the *Mahona* offered the island to Cosimo de' Medici, who prudently refused it (Doroni, *L'isola di Chio offerta a Cosimo dei Medici*, Rassegna Nazionale, 1912, p. 41-53). There is a fascinating book to be written some time on the subjects of Venice and Genoa and their social and economic exploitation. Rich sources on this subject in the precious collection of V. Lamansky, *op. cit.*

[203] A.d.S. Venice, *Annali di Venezia*, Famagusta, 8th October, 1570.

[204] On the fate of Cyprus under the Turks, it is important not to forget that in the Venetian period, the island was empty and had only a small population (towards 1570, 180,000 inhabitants, of whom 90,000 were serfs and 50,000 *villani liberi*, 'e il restante è nelle città et terre', B.N. Paris, Ital. 340, f° 55. The Turks began resettlement with Anatolian peasants (H. Kretschmayr, *Geschichte von Venedig*, 1920, III, p. 62). The peasants were then all allotted the same status, that of subjects, the old distinctions being abolished. There was a collapse of the Latin clergy. Many Cypriots became Turk to escape the *Kharadj* ('carage'). But nothing is ever simple; Italian civilization persisted. J. B. Tavernier writes towards 1650 'they were all clad after the Italian manner, both Men and Women'. (*op. cit.*, p. 80).

[205] Museo Correr, D. delle Rose, 21, f° 32 v°.

cries of anger as may be imagined. The victims went so far as to declare that they would make 'no distinction between being subjects of Venice or of the Turks'.[206] This 'colonial' economy evidently had its successes and failures. Many conditions had to be fulfilled before the system could work properly, bringing together vine growers, landowners, sailors, merchants, and distant customers. The wine and raisin trade had in fact long been established over a wide area. Even in England malmsey wine was known and appreciated as a luxury which was in the sixteenth century the equivalent of port today. 'He was so moved and dejected,' says Bandello of one of the characters in his *Novelle*, 'that she went to fetch him a glass of malmsey.'

A final example of monoculture is Djerba, off the southern coast of Tunisia. The Venetian islands were the wine islands; Djerba was the oil island. In circumstances far from clear, while mainland Tunisia was losing the groves of olive trees that were so plentiful in Roman times, Djerba succeeded in keeping hers. This preserved wealth meant that even in the sixteenth century the island was economically important.[207] It had become an oasis of olive oil between Tunisia and Tripoli, which were in general, particularly in the South, rancid-butter countries. The island's oil was of excellent quality, cheap, and suitable for all uses, even the treatment of cloth and fabrics, an oil that was easy to export, as Leo Africanus remarked at the beginning of the century. After 1590 it was to Djerba that the English went for the oil that had previously been supplied to them by Spain.

But geography only records Djerba as a low-lying island with tidal channels,[208] and the history of events only mentions it as the battlefield for the actions of 1510, 1520, and 1560. Yet in the last of these battles the oil played a part. The Christian fleet had anchored at Djerba, instead of pressing on to Tripoli. If it allowed itself to be surprised there by the armada of Piāle Pasha, of whose approach it had been warned, it was because the Christian ships had delayed at the island, taking on merchandise, in particular olive oil; as the report of the *visitador*, Quiroga, established after the disaster.[209]

As long as they did not impose too crippling a monoculture, however, these large-scale activities formed the vital wealth of the islands, if only because they ensured the returns necessary for their survival. They provided them with well-earned reputations. Ibiza was the salt island; the

[206] Marciana, 7299, 9th June, 1584. On the troubles in Candia after 1571, there are several documents, especially in the *Annali di Venezia*, 20th August, 22nd August, 30th August, and 16th September, 1571.
[207] On Djerba as well as olive trees there grew palm trees, apple trees, and pear trees. From this point of view too it was an unusual island. And Djerba as an island conservatory harboured Jewish communities said to date from the persecutions of Titus; above all it was a small Kharijite world, like the Mzab, the repository of ancient ritual and extremely old types of architecture.
[208] *Instructions Nautiques*, no. 360, p. 338, 359–363.
[209] See Vol. II, Part III, Ch. 2, section on Djerba expedition & note 61.

salt of Naxos was also famous, as was its wine 'both White and Claret';[210] Elba was the iron island. And there was Tabarka, the coral island, domain of the Lomellini, an island with several other resources: the exporting of grain and hides, and the ransoming of prisoners who took refuge there. There were the famous fisheries of La Galite on the Barbary coast; or the fisheries of the Dalmatian island of Liesena, which it suddenly lost when the shoals of sardines, according to a document of 1588, just moved off one day to the rock of Pelagosa.[211] Rhodes was able to exploit its position, which assured it, first in the time of the Knights and then in the time of the Turks, after 1522, of 'domination over all the other islands and the admiralty of the whole Mediterranean'.[212] Patmos, in the Archipelago, for want of anything better, bred 'the most troublesome of all the islanders, after Samos', and lived off raids 'both on Christians and Turks'.[213]

Emigration from the islands. But the commonest way in which the islands entered the life of the outside world was by emigration. All the islands (like the mountains, and many Mediterranean islands are mountains anyway) exported their people.[214]

We need hardly dwell on the Greek migrations which affected the entire Archipelago, including the large island of Crete. But it is doubtful whether they were ever as important in the sixteenth century as the movements from the island of emigrants *par excellence*, Corsica. The population, too great for the island's resources, swarmed in all directions, and there can hardly have been an event in the Mediterranean in which a Corsican did not participate.[215] There were even Corsicans at Genoa, the hated *Dominante*: one must take bread where one can find it. There were Corsicans at Venice. They were already to be found in the fifteenth century, working on the land of the Tuscan Maremma; in the sixteenth century the peasants of Niolo, who were being harassed by Genoa, went to colonize such fever-ridden lands in Italy and even Sardinia, where they often made their fortunes.[216] Corsicans were numerous at Rome, where some of them were established as stock dealers[217] and their boats frequented the Roman port on the Tiber, Civitavecchia and Leghorn.[218] In Algiers there were hordes

[210] J. B. Tavernier, *op. cit.*, Persian Travels, p. 120.
[211] Museo Correr, D. delle Rose 21, fº 29.
[212] Comte de Brèves, *op. cit.*, p. 18.
[213] *Ibid.*, p. 15.
[214] Even today: for example the inhabitants of Djerba scattered throughout North Africa and indeed the whole world; or the gardeners from Malta and Mahon, P. Vidal de la Blache, *Principles of Human Geography*, p. 153.
[215] There was even a Sylvestre Corso on the lists of bombardiers of Goa in 1513, Fortunato de Almeida, *Historia de Portugal* 1926–29, III, p. 267.
[216] R. Russo, 'La politica agraria dell'officio di San Giorgio nella Corsica (1490–1553)' in *Riv. st. ital.*, 1934, p. 426.
[217] Carmelo Trasselli, *art. cit.*, in *Archivio storica di Corsica*, 1934, p. 577.
[218] At Leghorn, Mediceo 2908. Cf. the many Corsican boats carrying wine which arrived at Rome, Hº de Torres to Zuñiga, Rome, 29th and 30th January, 1581, *Cartas y Avisos*, p. 33.

of Corsican immigrants, especially the *Capocorsini*. When Sampiero passed through the town in July, 1562, in the course of the dramatic voyage that was to take him to Constantinople, his compatriots rushed to the port to salute him as 'their king', according to a Genoese account.[219] How monstrous that this Sampiero, enemy of Genoa, friend of France, going to the Sultan to beg help for his compatriots, should have been popular and loved by his own people!

Who were these Corsicans at Algiers? Some of them were prisoners. Others, sailors and merchants, did business in the port. More than one settled there among the richest renegades of the town: Hasan Corso was after all one of the 'kings' of Algiers. In about 1568, a Spanish report[220] estimates that there were 6000 Corsican renegades out of a total renegade population of 10,000 in Algiers. The town was swarming with Corsican middlemen, effective agents for the ransoming of captives, according to Genoese documents, but also unofficial agents for foreign powers. There was the mysterious Francisco Gasparo Corso, for instance, who in theory was a resident of Valencia but spent the year 1569 in Algiers, where he had been sent by the viceroy of Valencia. He had conversations there with Euldj 'Alī, trying to persuade him, at the somewhat critical period of the war of Granada, of the best interests of the Catholic King. Who was he exactly, travelling under a name which is hardly one at all? We know that he came and went between Valencia and Algiers, with a brigantine and authorized merchandise, that is, other than the 'contraband' forbidden by Spanish law: salt, iron, saltpetre, gunpowder, oars, arms. He had one brother in Algiers, one or several others at Marseilles, another at Cartagena, and his correspondence with them thus covers the whole of the western Mediterranean. We might add to confuse matters even further, that in a legally sound declaration, drawn up before an impromptu lawyer in the prisons of Algiers, a Spanish prisoner accused Gasparo Corso of dealing in contraband and of being a double agent.[221] We cannot elucidate this little mystery, but might bear in mind the distribution of this extraordinary island family around the Mediterranean.

Other Corsicans were at Constantinople, Seville, and Valencia. But their favourite town, in the sixteenth century as today, was Marseilles, which

[219] He was to arrive at Constantinople in January, 1563. For his call at Chios, A.d.S. Genoa, *Sezione Segreta*, n.g. 5th June, 1563.

[220] Simancas Eº 487.

[221] On Francisco Gasparo, see above Ch. I, n. 88. On the family and Francisco see the Count of Benavente (who had a very poor opinion of Corsicans) to H.M., Valencia, 13th November, 1569, Simancas Eº 333. *Information hecha en Argel a Iº de junio 1570 a pedimo del cap. don Geronimo de Mendoça*, 13th June 1570, Simancas Eº 334. Don Jeronimo de Mendoça to H.M. Valencia, 7th June, 1570, Simancas Eº 334. Count of Benavente to H.M., Valencia, 8th July, 1570; Francisco is probably a double agent '. . . Estos son criados en Francia y tratan alli en Argel y Valencia y tienen su correspondancia en Marsella'. Finally letters from Francisco's brothers from Marseilles, dated 24th and 29th, July, with news from the Levant of no great interest (copy A.N., K 1553, B. 48, no. 77).

must have been almost half-Corsican, at least round the docks, if the documents we have are anything to go by.[222]

The Genoese rulers of the island cannot be either blamed for or absolved of this emigration. The obvious fact in the sixteenth century was that the Corsicans did not take kindly to Genoese rule. Whether or not this attitude was justified, it is quite unreasonable to attribute the exodus entirely to French intrigues and Valois gold. This is not to deny for a moment that there was a definite liaison between the island and France, or to doubt the overwhelming evidence of repeated journeys by French envoys and the dispatch of frigates, gunpowder and money to the island. France's policy towards Corsica was almost identical with that pursued more single-mindedly and with more resources, but less success, by Cosimo de' Medici. The point is – and it brings us back to our original subject – that if French policy succeeded, almost without trying, in stirring up the people of the Corsican mountains, it was less by virtue of any preconceived plans than because of the crucial link between a France that was rich in land and an island that was rich in men. France was open to Corsican emigration as the largest and most fruitful field for expansion, while Italy at the time was too populous itself and indeed regarded Corsica as a land to be colonized for its own use.

This is not to mention the considerable advantage to the Corsicans of the protection of the king of France which was very effective at sea. When they settled in Marseilles they became subjects of the French king, and as such participated in the rising fortunes of the port after the 1570s. In the seventeenth century we find Corsicans established in the *Bastion de France*, facing Tabarka, the Genoese island of the Lomellini, on that shore which one of their documents calls 'la costa che guardano li Francesi in Barberia'.[223] It is curious that on this coral-fishing coast the Corsicans should find their old enemy the *Dominante*, in the form of the fortress of Tabarka, before which Sanson Napollon was to perish in his attack of May, 1633.

Islands that the sea does not surround. In this Mediterranean world, excessively compartmented as it was, where human occupation had left vast empty stretches unfilled, not counting the seas, one might argue that there were places that were fully as much islands as those surrounded by the sea, isolated places, peninsulas – the word itself is significant – like Greece or other regions which were cut off on the mainland side and for whom the sea was the only means of communication. Bounded to the north by the mountain barrier marking its frontier with Rome, the kingdom

[222] On the Lenche and the great question of the coral, see besides P. Masson, *Les Compagnies du Corail*, 1908, the book by P. Giraud, *Les origines de l'Empire français nord-africain . . .*, 1939. On the role played at Marseilles by Thomas Corso, on behalf of the Corsican insurgents, many references in the correspondence of Figueroa, the Spanish ambassador at Genoa, and particularly Figueroa to the king, Genoa, 9th January, 1566, Simancas E° 1394.

[223] *Le Bastion de France*, Algiers, 1930, no. 1.

of Naples could be called an island in this sense. In the textbooks we find mention of the 'island' of the Maghreb, *Djezirat el Moghreb*, the Island of the Setting Sun, between the Atlantic, the Mediterranean, the Sea of the Syrtes, and the Sahara; a world of sudden contrasts, as Émile-Félix Gautier has pointed out.

One might say of Lombardy that it was in a way a continental island between the Alps and the Apennines, between rustic Piedmont and the half-Byzantine world of Venice. It would hardly be an exaggeration to say that Portugal, Andalusia, Valencia, and Catalonia were a series of peripheral islands attached to the Iberian mass through Castile. Note how Catalonia, opening on to the sea, was quick to trim her sails to the winds of history, at times looking to France, under the Carolingians and again later in the age of troubadours and courtly love; at other times towards the Mediterranean, in the thirteenth, fourteenth, and fifteenth centuries; and finally in the eighteenth century towards the backward regions of the Peninsula, as yet not industrialized. As for Spain itself, Maurice Legendre has described it as a *plusqu'île*, more-than-an-island, by which he meant to emphasize its inaccessibility and original character.

At the other, eastern end of the Mediterranean, Syria was another island, a halfway house between sea and desert, a source from which many things were to flow: men, techniques, empires, civilizations, and religions. It gave the Mediterranean the alphabet, the art of glassmaking, purple dyes for cloth, and the secrets of dry-farming in Phoenician times; it provided first Rome and then Byzantium with emperors; its ships ruled over the Phoenician sea, the first, or almost the first Mediterranean in history; and finally in 1516 – as in 634 – it was through its conquest of this vital region that triumphant Islam (Arabs in the seventh century, Turks in the sixteenth) reached the stage of history.

We are now taking great liberties with the concept of insularity, of course, but in the interests of a better explanation. The Mediterranean lands were a series of regions isolated from one another,[224] yet trying to make contact with one another. So in spite of the days of travel on foot or by boat that separated them, there was a perpetual coming and going between them, which was encouraged by the nomadic tendencies of some of the populations. But the contacts they did establish were like electric charges, violent and without continuity. Like an enlarged photograph the history of the islands affords one of the most rewarding ways of approaching an explanation of this violent Mediterranean life. It may make it easier to understand how it is that each Mediterranean province has been able to preserve its own irreducible character, its own violently regional flavour in the midst of such an extraordinary mixture of races, religions, customs, and civilizations.

[224] A. Philippson, *op. cit.*, p. 32: 'Jedes Land ist ein Individuum für sich'. This is what J. W. Zinkeisen, *op. cit.*, III, p. 7, says the bigger islands in the Archipelago: '. . . jedes für sich eine eigene Welt'.

The Peninsulas. The vital force of the sea does not carry in its wake only those fragments of land we call the islands, those thin ribbons we call the mainland coasts. It has repercussions reaching far into the land masses, effortlessly drawing into its orbit all the regions that look seawards, and none more than the vast peninsular blocks, particularly since they present to the intervening seas coasts of exceptional activity. The peninsulas are independent land masses: the Iberian peninsula, Italy, the Balkan peninsula, Asia Minor, North Africa, the last apparently attached to the African continent, but in fact separated from it by the width of the Sahara. What Theobald Fischer said of Iberia, 'It is a world in itself', is true of the other peninsulas, comparable worlds composed of identical pieces: the ever-present mountains, plains, plateaux, coastal strips, and strings of islands. Natural correspondences suggest themselves between both landscapes and ways of life. The words 'Mediterranean climate' or 'Mediterranean sky' conjure up brilliant images, almost all relating to these great land masses which are all, though in varying degrees, caught up by the sea. It is through these countries, especially Italy and Spain, that western travellers regularly get their first glimpse of the Mediterranean. And it would certainly be a mistake to follow them in letting such first impressions blind us to all but these privileged shores, as if they constituted the entire Mediterranean. They are certainly an essential part, but not the whole.

For between the peninsulas lie rather different intermediate regions: along the Gulf of Lions, Lower Languedoc and the lower Rhône valley forming a Dutch landscape; on the Adriatic, lower Emilia and the Venetias; further east, north of the Black Sea, the bare open lands that run from the Danube delta to the edge of the Caucasus; and lastly, in the south this time, the endless ribbon of blank coastline, where it is often difficult to land, stretching from southern Syria to Gabès and Djerba in Tunisia, the long barren front of a *foreign* world looking on to the Mediterranean.

Nonetheless, the peninsulas are the Mediterranean regions which are richest in men and in potential. They are key actors, who have always played leading roles, in turn gathering strength and then expending it. They are almost persons, to rephrase Michelet on France, but persons who may or may not be conscious of themselves. Their unity is obvious, but they do not have the coherence or self-confidence of say France under the Valois, nor the vehemence of its outbursts of political and national passion: for example, in 1540 when Montmorency, who favoured collaboration with the Habsburgs, was thrown from power;[225] or during the continuous crisis from 1570 to 1572, which the Massacre of Saint Bartholomew stopped but did not resolve; or even more striking, the crisis at the end of the century which led to the overwhelming triumph of Henri IV.

---

[225] No study exists of this national sentiment. Cf. the fine passion of Rabelais, *Gargantua*, ed. Les Belles Lettres 1955, p. 137, 'Par Dieu, je vous metroys en chien courtault les fuyards de Pavie'. And in the *Quart Livre*, ed. Les Belles Lettres, prologue, p. 11. 'Ce tant noble, tant antique, tant beau, tant florissant, tant riche royaume de France'.

But perhaps these peninsular units, defined as they are by nature, did not need to be willed into existence by men with the same passion as the more artificial unit of France.

Nevertheless, there is strong evidence of Spanish nationalism. In 1559 it lead to the debarring from high office of Philip II's non-Spanish advisers and inspired the much-repeated Spanish opinions of the Frenchmen of the day: unreliable, quarrelsome, argumentative, easily discouraged at the first setback, but impatient to wipe out a defeat or a concession. This Spanish nationalism was far from homogeneous or even widely expressed. It was only gradually as the years of greatness piled up one after another, that it came into the open, found its themes, and was enticed by the mirage of the idea of empire. In this composite form nationalism became widespread, not in the reigns of Charles V and Philip II, who were its architects, but late in the seventeenth century, when the empire was already in decline, in the reign of the 'Planet' king, Philip IV, and his adviser, the Count Duke of Olivares, in the age of Velásquez, Lope de Vega, and Calderon.

There was no such coherence in Italy. And yet there too appeared an undeniable form of nationalism, or at any rate a pride in being Italian, in the sense that every Italian firmly believed that he belonged to the most civilized of societies with the most glorious of heritages. Was the present so unworthy either? 'From morning to night we hear that the New World was discovered by the Spanish and Portuguese, whereas it was we, the Italians, who showed them the way,' writes Bandello at the beginning of one of his *novelle*.[226] The historian di Tocco has given us an exhaustive account of the complaints and anger aroused in the Italian patriots (ahead of their time) by the end of peninsular liberty after the treaty of Cateau-Cambrésis, and the final victory of the Spaniards.[227] And how can one ignore the many dreams of unity: the passionate appeals of Machiavelli; or Guicciardini's presentation of the years he had just lived through as a single pageant of Italian history?[228] Rare as they are, these are unmistakable signs of feelings of national consciousness and unity.

Another and even more important sign (for national identity is not confined to politics) was the spread of the Tuscan language. Similarly the Castilian language spread over the whole Iberian peninsula in the sixteenth century, and became the language of literary expression used by Aragonese writers from the time of Charles V. It was in Castilian that an Aragonese nobleman, a contemporary of Philip II, kept his family record book.[229] It even reached literary circles in Lisbon in the great period of Camoëns. At the same time it was adopted by all the upper classes throughout Spain, and with it, not only the literary themes of Castile, but also its religious themes and forms of worship. Witness the curious story of St. Isidore, the

[226] M. Bandello, *op. cit.*, II, p. 208.
[227] Vittoria Di Tocco, *Ideali d'indipendenza in Italia*, 1926, p. 1 ff.
[228] A. Renaudet, *Machiavel*, 1942, p. 10.
[229] *Algunes efemerides* by Miguel Pérez de Nueros, in: Fro. Belda y Pérez de Nueros, marqués de Cabra, *Felipe Secundo* (1927), p. 30 ff.

peasant saint of Madrid, who displaced, even in Catalonia, the traditional peasant saints, St. Abdon and St. Sennen, who were the patrons of many confraternities. Statues of them still stand in all old churches, but the peasants of Catalonia forsook them in the seventeenth century for the new arrival.[230]

This directs attention to the coherence of the historical areas within the peninsular boundaries. These boundaries were by no means impassable. It is mistaken to talk of 'electric' frontiers, such as Ramón Fernandez imagined surrounding Spain. Such frontiers never existed, along the Pyrenees or the Alps, any more than along the Danube, in the Balkans, or on the mountains of Armenia, an outstanding region for roads and ethnic mixtures, the Taurus mountains, the Atlas and the Sahara, south of North Africa. Nevertheless, the peninsulas are bordered on the mainland side, from which they project, by obstacles that have hindered relations and exchanges. This in turn should not be underestimated. Paraphrasing Metternich's famous remark, Augustin Renaudet said of Italy in the sixteenth century, with its many divisions and uncertain contours, in the direction of Piedmont for instance, that it was merely a geographical expression.[231] But is that so insignificant? It is a representation of a historical entity within which events had similar repercussions and effects, and were indeed in a sense imprisoned, struggling against but not always overcoming the barriers of its frontiers.

For Gioacchino Volpe this is more or less what is meant by Italian unity. The same could be said of Iberia. The dramatic history of the Moslem conquest and the reconquest which lay at the centre of its life for seven centuries was trapped within its frontiers. This was what forged its basic unity, and enabled it to transform its borrowings from outside: to accept Gothic art from Europe, but to overlay it with the embellishments of the plateresque and Moorish art; later to take over the Baroque, from which it produced the *churriguerismo*. Just as North Africa, when invaded by Islam, lent it its own particular accent and gradually allowed itself to be 'de-Islamized, de-Orientalized, Berberized' by its Marabouts.[232]

The high barriers closing off the peninsulas have made each of them a marginal world with its own characteristics, flavours, and accents.[233]

Every time the political unity of a peninsula has been achieved, it has announced some momentous change. In ancient times the unification of Greece by the Macedonians and the unification of Italy round Rome had far-reaching consequences. At the beginning of the sixteenth century

[230] *Geografía general de Catalunya*, p. 426 ff.

[231] A. Renaudet, *L'Italie et la Renaissance italienne* (Lecture given at the Sorbonne, Sedes, 1937, p. 1).

[232] Augustin Berque, 'Un mystique moderne' in *2e Congrès des Soc. sav. d'Afrique du Nord*, Tlemcen, 1936 (Algiers 1938) vol. II, p. 744. Similar observation by R. Montagne, *op. cit.*, p. 410.

[233] On the orginality of the Balkans arising from their Eurasian situation cf. Busch-Zantner, *op. cit.*, p. IV; their foreignness to westerners, *ibid.*, p. 111. On the unity of Asia Minor, a second Iberian peninsula cf. Ulrich von Hassel, *Das Drama des Mittelmeers*, 1940, p. 22.

Ferdinand and Isabella set about forging the unity of Spain: it was to be an explosive force.

For if the peninsulas have been partly cut off from the continental mainlands of Europe, Asia, and Africa, they have made up for it by their accessibility from the seaward side, so that when strong they have been able to launch aggression, but when poorly defended they have been easily conquered.

Is this the reason for their curious tendency to join together in pairs? Although Italy once dominated all the others in the days of Rome, because she was mistress of the sea, her exceptional achievement was never repeated. In general, conquests from peninsula to peninsula were not so far-reaching. They were more often comparable to the boarding of one ship by another: for example the action that enabled Asia Minor to seize the vast Balkan peninsula at the end of the fourteenth century and beginning of the fifteenth, preparing the way for the great Turkish conquest; or the even more rapid triumph of North Africa over the Iberian peninsula at the beginning of the eighth century. So there came into being, sometimes for long periods, the bi-continents mentioned earlier: Anatolia and the Balkans, first at the time of Byzantium and then under the Turkish Empire; North Africa and Iberia in the Middle Ages, a solid association[234] but one which the break of 1492 damaged for centuries (it was such a fruitful association, however, that it never totally vanished). In the century to which this book is devoted, two further boarding actions occurred: between Spain and Italy, whose union, sealed in 1559, was to last a century in spite of the intervening space of the western Mediterranean and the hostilities it encountered;[235] and between the Balkans and the masterless boat that was North Africa, for the Turks, as we know, only partly controlled it.

These liaisons and partnerships, successively created and destroyed,

---

[234] 'North Africa will always be controlled by the Iberian peninsula and its islands', P. Achard, *Barberousse, op. cit.*, p. 53, no. 1. 'The Iberian world appears inseparable from the Atlas lands, up to and including the Canaries and even the large islands in the western Mediterranean, Sardinia and Corsica', P. Vidal de la Blache, *Tableau géographique de la France*, p. 28. 'Andalusia . . . appears as an extension of the *Maghreb*', George Marçais, *Histoire du Moyen Age*, III, 1936, p. 396 (in *Histoire générale by* Gustave Glotz).

[235] Von Hassel, *op. cit.*, p. 20–22, sees Spain's intrusion into Italy as more dynastic than political in character (in the sense of a dynastic policy). This is questionable. For the cultural links see the works of Benedetto Croce. For Spain's contribution to the institutional framework, see Fausto Niccolini, *Aspetti della vita italo-spagnuola nel Cinque e Seicento*, Naples 1934. On literary relations, Hugues Vaganay, 'L'Espagne et l'Italie' in *Rev. Hispanique*, vol. IX, 1902. Leopold von Ranke, *Les Osmanlis et la monarchie espagnole pendant les XVIe et XVIIIe siècles*, 1839, p. 383–387. W. Platzhoff, *Geschichte des europäischen Staatensystems*, 1928, p. 32, sees the Treaty of Cateau-Cambrésis as sealing Italy's fate. What this list of books does not perhaps sufficiently convey is that the Italian peninsula found it necessary to remain attached to Spain for both economic reasons (American silver) and military reasons (protection against the Turks). It would be inaccurate simply to talk as Stendhal does (*Promenades dans Rome*, II, p. 191) of the 'invasion (of Italy) by Spanish despotism'.

summarize the history of the sea. By turns conquerors and conquered, the peninsulas were preparing, during the quiet periods of their existence, explosions to come. For example, before the conquest of Spain in the eighth century there was an increase in the population of the Maghreb; similarly, much later, before the Turkish conquest of the Balkans, Asia Minor was becoming progressively overpopulated and there seems to have been a transition from a nomadic way of life to a semi-sedentary one, which in itself is significant. By contrast, all conquests lead to exhaustion. When the Roman Empire had completed the monstrous conquest of all the lands of the Mediterranean, the Italian population began to decline. So political supremacy passed from one peninsula to another and along with it supremacy in other fields, economic and cultural. But these transfers did not all take place simultaneously. It was seldom that one peninsula combined preeminence in all fields at any one time. So it is impossible to classify these constantly changing societies in relation to each other. Can we say that certain peninsulas were more powerful, more brilliant, or more advanced than others? It is difficult to give an answer. Take the Maghreb, for instance. It has not always been the eternal laggard described in the books of Émile-Félix Gautier; it has had its moments of splendour, even of supremacy. One could hardly dismiss the civilization of Carthage as trivial, nor the conquests of Spain in the eighth century, Sicily in the ninth century, and Egypt in the tenth. From a religious point of view, North Africa in the time of Apuleius and St. Augustine was the stoutest pillar of the Christian church and Latin culture. Italy at the time was incomparably less well endowed.[236]

An interesting hypothesis, hastily formulated on the occasion of some important excavations on Malta by L. M. Ugolini,[237] suggests that Mediterranean civilization may not have originated in the East, as has always been supposed, but in the West, in Spain and North Africa, well before the second millennium preceding the Christian era. From Spain and North Africa this civilization might then have spread to Italy and the East. Then and only then would the movement have flowed back westwards. Even if the suggested route is not correct it is pleasant to imagine this relay race along the coasts and roads of the sea, the torch passing from island to island, peninsula to peninsula, returning after hundreds or thousands of years to places where it burnt once before, but never with the same flame.

This is fanciful perhaps, but in the long night of the past, one physical law seems to have operated more or less regularly. It is easy to imagine and even probable that the life of the sea, a vital force, would first of all have taken control of the smallest and least weighty fragments of land, the islands and coastal margins, tossing and turning them at its will, as the northern waves toss the shingle.[238] Growing more powerful and compelling, this force would draw into its orbit the larger land masses, the penin-

[236] E. Albertini, in *Mélanges Paul Thomas*, Bruges, 1930.
[237] L. M. Ugolini, *Malta, origini della civiltà mediterranea*, Rome, 1934.
[238] A. Philippson, *Das Mittelmeergebiet, op. cit.*, p. 37.

sulas, elevating the history of the sea to a higher level. And the greatest moments of all would be when it was strong enough to attract towards it the great continental blocs: moments that saw Caesar in Gaul, Germanicus beyond the Elbe, Alexander on the Indus, the Arabs in China, or the Moroccans on the Niger.

At such moments, the historical Mediterranean seems to be a concept capable of infinite extension. But how far in space are we justified in extending it? This is a difficult and controversial question; but if we are seeking to explain the history of the Mediterranean, it is perhaps the fundamental question we should be asking.

CHAPTER III

Boundaries: the Greater Mediterranean

This chapter presents several difficulties. The reader however, may not immediately become aware of them. He is invited to undertake journeys that will lead him far away from the shores of the Mediterranean. He may be willing to make them. But this implies a willingness to accept what may seem to be an excessive extension of the field of study. To claim that there is a *global* Mediterranean which in the sixteenth century, reached as far as the Azores and the New World, the Red Sea and the Persian Gulf, the Baltic and the loop of the Niger, may appear an unwarranted exaggeration of its boundaries.

It also disregards the conventional boundaries. Those drawn by geographer are the most familiar and the most restrictive: for him the Mediterranean region stretches from the northern limit of the olive tree to the northern limit of the palm tree. The first olive tree on the way south[1] marks the beginning of the Mediterranean region and the first compact palm grove the end. The geographical definition accords great importance to climate, which is undeniably a potent factor in the lives of men. But our Greater Mediterranean would disappear if we accepted these limits. Nor would we locate it by accepting the rather different boundaries allowed by the geologist and the biogeographer. They both consider the Mediterranean zone as a long ribbon, a mere linear feature on the earth's great crust; for the geologist it is the long belt stretching from the Atlantic to the Indian Ocean, a combination of tectonic fractures and recent foldings; for biogeographers, it is the narrow zone between certain parallels of latitude where certain plants and animals are typically found from the Azores to the distant Kashmir valley.

A Mediterranean of historical dimensions. To meet the historian's demands, however, the Mediterranean must be accepted as a wide zone, extending well beyond the shores of the sea in all directions. We might compare it to an electric or magnetic field, or more simply to a radiant centre whose light grows less as one moves away from it, without one's being able to define the exact boundary between light and shade.

For what boundaries can be marked when we are dealing not with plants and animals, relief and climate, but men, whom no barriers or frontiers can stop? The Mediterranean (and the accompanying Greater

[1] Felix Platter (*Beloved Son Felix, Journal of Felix Platter*, translated by Seàn Jennett, London, 1961, p. 40) reached Montélimar on 26th October, 1552 'and by evening the market town of Pierrelatte, where I first saw olive trees. They were heavy with fruit, some green, some red and half ripe, and some black and fully mature. I tried them all and found them nasty and very sour.'

Fig. 12: *The Mediterranean and the rest of the world*

Following the orientation of this map, rotating it as we go, we shall be looking in turn at each of the different world horizons of the Mediterranean: the Sahara, the Atlantic, the Indian Ocean, and Europe. The unusual orientation has been chosen to illustrate how the great Sahara desert dominates the sea, stretching from the shores of the Mediterranean to the tropical forests of Africa. The Mediterranean both acts as a frontier between these deserted lands and southern Europe (which reaches to the forests of the North) and, along with the Red Sea and the Persian Gulf punctuates them. The dotted area corresponds to the zones of early human settlement, emphasizing by contrast the emptiness of the mountainous peninsulas of the Mediterranean. Land and sea communications, whose routes and stages leading in every direction the reader will imagine, created the movement in space which we have called the Greater Mediterranean. Map drawn by J. Bertin.

Mediterranean) is as man has made it. The wheel of human fortune has determined the destiny of the sea, expanding or contracting its area. Rome succeeded in converting the Mediterranean world in the strict sense into what was almost a closed system, setting up as it were locks on all the routes into and out of it, and thereby abandoning (perhaps mistakenly) the possibility of controlling the outer limits of Europe, of allowing free access to the Indian Ocean or the depths of Africa, and of establishing free and profitable relations with these distant civilizations. But this policy of lock-building, which was only relatively effective in any case, has been the exception rather than the rule in Mediterranean history. The rule has been that Mediterranean civilization spreads far beyond its shores in great waves that are balanced by continual returns. What leaves the sea comes back and then departs once more. Pieces of eight, the small silver coinage struck in Castile from American metal, flooded the Mediterranean markets in the second half of the sixteenth century; but these pieces *de a ocho reales* also turned up in India and China. The circulation of man and of goods, both material and intangible, formed concentric rings round the Mediterranean. We should imagine a hundred frontiers, not one, some political, some economic, and some cultural, When Goethe went to Italy, he reached the Mediterranean, not, as he says, when he crossed the Brenner Pass or later in the Tuscan Apennines. He had already reached it when he arrived at Ratisbon, the outpost of Catholicism on the great cultural frontier of the Danube, or even, further north again, right at the start of his journey, in Frankfurt, the city of the *Römer*.

If we did not consider this extended zone of influence, the greater Mediterranean, it would often be difficult to grasp the history of the sea. The focal point of trade, of riches accumulated, changing hands sometimes to be lost forever, the Mediterranean can be measured by its wider repercussions. Its fortunes are often easier to read on its outer margins than at the very heart of its bewildering activity. If it was thwarted in one sector, the economic life of the sea found the necessary compensation in another, according to a law of equilibrium which was not always apparent to contemporary observers, and which a few historians think they may have glimpsed. In the fifteenth century the Turkish advance was disturbing the countries of the Levant: western commerce concentrated more than ever on North Africa.[2] Similarly in the sixteenth century, certain economic pressures drew the Mediterranean towards southern Germany and central and eastern Europe. Again, this was doubtless a form of compensation. The survival of Italy until 1620, and even after, would have been unthinkable had it not been for the ventures to the north and north-east. Venice was for many years a gateway to these opportunities. The first signs of decline in the Mediterranean, a decline that was only relative in any case, appeared in the long distance connections, between the Atlantic and the inland sea. In short, the sea's history is recorded in its various forms on the land masses and wide seas that surround it, whether distant or close at hand.

[2] Robert Brunschvig, *La Berbérie Orientale et les Hafsides*, 1940, I, p. 269.

I. THE SAHARA, THE SECOND FACE OF THE MEDITERRANEAN

On three sides the Mediterranean touches the great chain of deserts stretching uninterrupted across the entire width of the Ancient World, from the Atlantic coast of the Sahara to northern China. On three sides: south of the Libyan coast lies the Sahara; east of the Anti-Lebanon lies the Syrian desert, close to 'one of the largest nomadic civilizations in the world';[3] north of the Black Sea stretch the south Russian steppes, the threshold of Central Asia. Along these vast fronts, an abundant caravan traffic entered into contact with Mediterranean trade, becoming both essential to it and in turn dependent on it. Contact was made not only at the important centres, like Egypt and Syria, through which all the fabulous trade of the Levant passed in the sixteenth century, but all along the desert frontiers. Oran, which the Spanish conquest of 1509 had virtually cut off from its hinterland, was still in mid-sixteenth century the centre of a minor trade in black slaves, which was nevertheless important enough to cause the local authorities some concern.[4]

Mediterranean history, then, has felt the pull of its desert pole as well as that of its European pole. The Mediterranean is attracted towards these desolate shores and attracts them in turn; the original and paradoxical quality of this extraordinary sea is that it confronts a desert continent with its vast stretches of water, even by its links with the Red Sea and the Indian Ocean separating one desert from another by water.

The Sahara: near and distant boundaries. The chain of deserts between the Atlantic and China is divided in two by the high Iranian plateaux: to the west lie the warm deserts; to the north and east the cold deserts. But there is a continuity between these barren spaces and their caravan traffic; in Anatolia and Iran, the camel replaces the dromedary of the central and western deserts.

Of these it is clearly the Sahara in the wide sense (the entire range of warm deserts as far as Iran and Arabia), that primarily concerns the Mediterranean. The route over the steppes of southern Russia leads to the great cold deserts of Central Asia, but reaches the Mediterranean as it were by the back door, only sporadically playing a leading role, for instance, in the thirteenth and fourteenth centuries, the period of the splendours of the 'Mongolian route'.[5]

The Sahara, in the wide sense, African and Asian, is contained within two sets of boundaries, one close to, the other very far removed from the

[3] Jacques Weulersse, *Paysans de Syrie et du Proche Orient*, 4th ed., 1947, p. 61.

[4] This information was provided by Felipe Ruiz Martín; I have mislaid the precise reference. On the traffic in Negroes of caravans travelling to Tlemcen and Mostaganem, Diego Suárez, Manuscript B.N., Madrid, chapter 35.

[5] Maurice Lombard, 'Le commerce italien et la route mongole' in *Annales E.S.C.*, 1948, p. 382: 'The continental route to the Indies, prospected by the Italians two centuries before the sea passage was opened up by the Portuguese.'

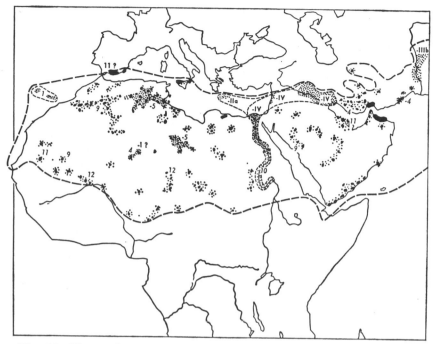

Fig. 13: *The implantation of palm groves from the Indus to the Atlantic*

The Roman numerals indicate millennia, the Arabic numerals centuries. A minus sign preceding a numeral means B.C. The Italic numerals indicate the date not of the first appearance of the palm groves but their first recorded existence. The map is taken from the provisional *Atlas* of cultivated plants to be published shortly, by J. Hémard-inquer, M. Keul, and W. Randles. It demonstrates the extremely slow progress of man's effort of creation; palm-groves and roads are clearly linked to each other throughout the vast zone of the date-palm, from the Indus to the Atlantic.

Mediterranean. A brief survey of these boundaries is the first step towards the characterization of our subject.

On the Mediterranean side, although the transition is rarely very sharply marked, the demarcation line is easily established as it coincides with the northern limit of the long zone throughout which the compact palm groves are scattered, running uninterrupted from east to west, from the Punjab – through Iraq, Syria, lower Egypt, Tripolitania, and the various southern slopes of the Atlas – to the Atlantic Ocean. As a rough limit, this line is as reliable as any that could be drawn from the indices of aridity.[6] The sketch map (Fig. 13) shows it clearly. The whole of this region of palms and palm groves was slowly created by man.

But where is the southern and eastern limit of this great expanse?

[6] Fritz Jaeger, 'Trockengrenzen in Algerien' in *Pet. Mitt. Ergänzungsheft*, 1935, and *Naturwissenschaft*, Berlin XXIX, 31st October, 1941. The 100 millimetre isohyetal line passes between Lahgouat and Ghardaïa, and between Biskra and Touggourt.

Thousands of miles from the Mediterranean it is clear. To find it we must make an imaginary journey to the loop of the Niger, the Upper Nile, the mountainous land of Abyssinia, the Red Sea, Arabia, Iran, the Indus, Turkestan, India, and the Indian Ocean. The striking thing about this desert world is its colossal dimensions. The journey from one town to another, which in the Mediterranean would take a day or a week, would take weeks and months here. The Venetian Giacomo Soranzo describing Persia in his report of 1576,[7] suggests in one sentence its vast emptiness: 'one can travel through this land for four months without leaving it'. The calendar of distances given in the learned book written a century ago by Aloys Sprenger[8] also makes it quite clear: on going from the Mediterranean to the Sahara all the distances grow longer, the scale changes completely. The supreme importance of transport is increased and comes to dominate everything else. On these endless journeys, notes Didier Brugnon, one must 'be guided by the compass and astrolabe as at sea'.[9] The predominance of waste lands forces societies and economies into a perpetual movement that is more burdensome than elsewhere. The extreme mobility of the population, the range of pastoral movements, the ancient thriving caravan traffic, and the activity of the towns are all responses, or attempted responses, to this pressing demand. The towns exhaust themselves in the effort. If 'deserted villages' are one of the characteristics of Western Europe, deserted towns are the most striking feature of the history of the dry countries. In a few years the sand from the dunes can bury a capital city, its houses, streets and aqueducts.[10] The devouring landscape is like the 'unharvested sea' of Homer; man passes through it 'only as a pilgrim and a sojourner'[11] and can halt there only for a brief moment. 'It is a waterless sea', vaster in area than the Mediterranean itself.

Poverty and Want. Immensity and emptiness: poverty and destitution. 'I can lock my hunger in the coils of my entrails,' writes an Arab poet, 'as firmly as a skilful spinning-girl holds in her hand the threads her fingers twist.' It was one of the companions of Muḥammad, Abū Huraira, who said of the Prophet, 'He went out of this world without once feasting on barley bread.'[12] Even in the heart of the richest countries, in Baghdad, how many poor men, like the humble folk in the *Thousand and One Nights*, have dreamed of a buttered cake made with white flour! Not even black bread is eaten everywhere, or the coarse couscous – the *maach* – of the poor people of the Maghreb: often all there is is the rough cake of

---

[7] E. Albèri, *op. cit.*, III, 2, p. 199.
[8] Aloys Sprenger, *Die Post- und Reiserouten des Orients*, 1864.
[9] Didier Brugnon, *Relation exacte concernant les caravanes en cortège des marchands d'Asie*, Nancy, 1707, p. 73.
[10] Marguerite van Berchem, 'Sedrata, une ville du Moyen Age ensevelie sous les sables du Sahara algérien' in *Documents Algériens*, 11th September, 1953.
[11] Arnold Toynbee, *A Study of History* (abridged version, vols. I–VI by D, C. Somervell), London, 1960, p. 166.
[12] Quoted in General Édouard Brémond, *Berbères et Arabes*, 1942, p. 37.

coarsely ground grain, the primitive *kessera*, made with barley, rarely with wheat.

A poor land, without water: here there are few springs, streams, plants, or trees. The sparse vegetation is graced with the name of 'pasture land'. Wood is extremely scarce. So here in the arid zone begin the clay houses, the endless string of towns that from India to tropical Africa are 'mud encampments'. Stone buildings, when they exist, are masterpieces of an exceptional kind; built by a technique of piling stone on stone without any timber work. In the absence of wood what must the precious cedar-wood caskets have been worth in Islam? Think by contrast of the handsome furniture of Renaissance Italy, the chests and writing desks decorated with gold and iron work wrought by the craftsmen of Toledo. Here the problem was not, as in the Mediterranean, the building of ships and galleys, but everyday cooking, the humble camp fire, lit between two stones. Everything was fuel for it: a few sprigs of brushwood, dry plants, straw or esparto-grass, the bark of palm trees, 'the dung of camel, horse or ox, which is dried in the sun'.[13] Even the privileged cities were not immune from this scarcity. For fuel the people of Cairo used dried dung, or the 'straw' from sugarcane, or the very rare and costly wood brought by ships and galleys from Asia Minor to Alexandria. The situation was always precarious. In November, 1512,[14] even the officers' kitchens ceased to function for lack of fuel – for where could one find fuel near Cairo?

In this hostile territory, this 'ἀνοικουμένη', plants, animals, and men have in spite of everything survived, as if nature abhorred not only a physical but a biological vacuum, or so one geographer has said.[15] In fact, in the course of the vast oscillations and climatic catastrophes of the quaternary period, man, like all other living things, was often surprised, trapped, and forced to adapt as best he could – residual populations are found among the Arabs of Arabia as well as alongside the Tuareg. In any case, apart from the oases, which rarely covered a large area, men have only been able to survive in small groups. Without the flocks of sheep even this would have been impossible. For thousands of years the deserts have been the homeland of the horse, the camel, and the dromedary. In the Sahara the dromedary is predominant. 'Man is a parasite of the camel,' as is often said. And the great history of the deserts begins with the beast of burden. However, 'by making it possible for man to lead a nomadic existence, so that there was less localized human settlement, the dromedary encouraged man to make use of vegetation over an ever-increasing and diverse area,' and according to one expert,[16] was 'the intermediary agent responsible for the persistence of the desert'. This seems very possible.

---

[13] *Le voyage d'Outremer*, by Jean Thénaud, Paris, 1884, p. 7. In Cairo, '. . . wood is extremely dear, and one has to pay a lot of money for a small quantity of it', *ibid.*, p. 209–210.

[14] *Journal d'un bourgeois du Caire, Chronique d'Ibn Iyâs*, transcribed and annotated by Gaston Wiet, I, 1955, p. 266.

[15] Konrad Guenther in: *Geographische Zeitschrift*, 1932, p. 213.

[16] Vincent Monteil, see below, note 29.

At best the camel driver can hardly make a living from the milk, butter, and cheese of his flocks: he rarely eats their flesh. He knows all the 'famine foods': the Tuareg of the Aïr[17] use over twenty wild plants, notably the seeds of the *drinn*, the *mrokba*, wild *fonio*, *cram-cram*, *tawit*, the rhizomes and young shoots of the *berdi*.[18] Their neighbours, if that is the right word, the Tibu, 'get their bread from the fruit of the *dûm*'.[19] To these may be added what can be caught by hunting. In the sixteenth century there were still wild sheep, donkeys, oxen, camels, gazelles, and antelopes, and in the Iranian Fars, the hunting of bustard and partridge led to heated contests.[20] 'Between Babylon and Aleppo,' writes a seventeenth-century traveller,[21] 'there is nothing but sandhills, caper-bushes and tamarisks which provide food for the camels . . . and I saw no other wild beasts save donkeys, horses, gazelles and stags, which sometimes met the *cafila* [caravan] in such large numbers, that they prevented us from moving on.' In the heart of the Syrian desert the favoured game is the rat, whose flesh is considered a delicacy.[22] That this life is hard will be easily imagined; that it has its own charms, with the aid of poetry and illusion, must also be accepted. A modern Iraqi writer has said, 'anyone who has tasted the food of the Bedouins will never escape from its spell'.[23]

The nomads are tied to the grazing lands, obliged to move from one source of water to another. During the dry season no flock can wander more than 50 kilometres from a well. The crossing of the *tanezroufts* is a difficult undertaking during which the camels must carry reserves of straw and water. And of course conflicts arise over the possession of even the poorest grazing grounds. These lands, apparently *res nullius*, are in fact entailed by traditional property rights, firmly established, but which have to be fought for, hence the disputes and raids. But it was even more profitable to attack settlers. Syria and Egypt in the sixteenth century could put up little resistance against these raids, these insect bites. Peter Martyr of Anghiera, the humanist whom Ferdinand and Isabella sent to the Sudan, and who reached Egypt in 1502, immediately recognized this. If the innumerable nomads, 'semper versans, semper in motu', had not been divided among themselves, they could easily have seized the lands of the Nile.[24] For one successful punitive expedition against them, how many returned empty-handed or with the meagre bounty of a few prisoners, Bedouin women and children![25] Every day, or at least whenever they felt

[17] [18] [19] Jacques Berque, 'Introduction' in *Revue Internationale des Sciences sociales*, XI, 1959, no. 4, p. 504–505. The issue is devoted to nomads and nomadism in the arid zone.
[20] Jacques Berque, *art. cit.*
[21] Anon., *Brième description d'un voyage fait en Levant, Perse, Indes Orientales, Chine*, (undated) (seventeenth century) B.N. Fr. 7503, n.a.
[22] H. Pohlhausen, *Das Wanderhirtentum und Seine Vorstufen*, 1954, p. 109.
[23] Jacques Berque, *art. cit.*, p. 509.
[24] *Une embajada de los Reyes Católicos a Egipto*, Trans. with an introduction and notes by Luis Garcia y Garcia, 1947, p. 90–92.
[25] *Journal d'un bourgeois du Caire*, I, p. 27 (Nov., Dec., 1468), p. 112 (July, 1507).

like it, the nomads would arrive at the gates of Aleppo,[26] Alexandria,[27] or Cairo. In November 1518, a garrison had to be sent to Aqaba in order to protect the baggage of the pilgrims 'from the Bedouin raids, which are constantly increasing'.[28]

Seen from the inside, through field studies, all these desert societies, so simple at first glance, reveal their complicated organizations, hierarchies, customs, and astonishing legal structures. But from the outside, they seem a handful of human dust blowing in the wind. By comparison, societies which in the Mediterranean seemed so unsettled, mountain society in particular, suddenly appear weighty and established.

Nomads who travel far. We should in any case distinguish between two types of nomad among the peoples of the desert. First there are the mountain nomads, who move within a short radius; they go down to pass the winter in the desert. This is even today the practice of the Oulad Sidi Cheikh south of Oran, the Tuareg of the Ajjers or the Hoggar, and the Regueibat, who go to 'the cliffs of Zemmur' in the Spanish Sahara. Secondly, there are the nomads who pass the summer away from the Sahara, on the neighbouring steppes; they often cover very large distances, like the Rwalla, who travel to the Mediterranean from the Syrian desert; or the Beni Larba who, following the rhythm of the seasons, pass to and fro on the 800-kilometre journey between Laghouat and the high plateaux of Tiaret which they reach in May and June; or, this time moving away from the Mediterranean, the Moors who journey to the banks of the river Senegal in the dry season.[29]

We shall here be concerned only with these wide-ranging nomads, who regularly return with the seasons to the Mediterranean.

Every winter the Mediterranean is invaded by Atlantic depressions bringing rain. To the south and east these rains extend beyond the shores of the sea. In the region of Mecca, the winter rains from the Mediterranean are brief and sometimes violent. 'I have seen more than three feet of water in the streets of Jiddah,' writes General Brémond. The rainfall is far from regular of course. These downpours (one rain every two years, in some of the furthest regions, every four years), create steppes providing pasture, immense grazing lands, but where the grass is widely scattered and soon disappears. Even in the wide depressions of the *oueds*, the tufts are often 20 to 40 metres apart. The grass, which grows in the winter, gradually dries up from the south to the north, from the end of spring. It vanishes before the advance of the flocks, leading them on to the shores of the Mediterranean, which they reach after harvest time. But the sheep are

[26] Alonso de la Cueva to H.M., Venice, 6th June, 1609, A.N. K 1679, '*los Arabes que corrian la campaña robando todos los pasageros*'.
[27] Daniele Badoer to the Doge, Pera, 8th April, 1564, A.d.S. Venice, Senato Secreta Costantopoli, 4 D.
[28] *Journal d'un bourgeois du Caire*, II, p. 266.
[29] Vincent Monteil, 'L'évolution et la sédentarisation des nomades sahariens', in *Revue Internationale des Sciences Sociales*, 1959, p. 600.

content to eat even stubble and dry grass. At the end of summer they return to the regions where the new grass will grow.

These journeys have many difficulties; over the long stages advantage must be taken of the first rains of autumn or the last rains of spring, for the rainy season in the Mediterranean begins before and finishes after the winter. There may be and often are delays, and always stages of the journey on which there is no possibility of any grazing, unavoidable treks across dead lands. In a dry year (1945 was particularly disastrous) the southern pastures dry up well before time. The sheep die in thousands along the roads, the humps of the camels shrink dangerously and the nomads go beyond their usual trails in search of the life-giving grass.

In the sixteenth century nomad shepherds were arriving in far larger numbers than today on the Mediterranean shores. The barrier that the coastal settlers had established and have consolidated since was still very fragile at that period. The nomads were quite at home in Asia Minor and Syria. Pierre Belon saw them in summer near Adana.[30] Throughout the Maghreb the great nomad trails bisected the country from south to north, particularly across the Tunisian steppe, where they met no obstacle, or across the great, dry, exposed plateaux behind Oran to the west. Every year, towards the end of July, Diego Suárez saw the *Uled Abdala* arrive at Oran, where he was garrisoned for so long; they had sown some of the coastal fields in the preceding autumn and were trying to protect their harvest against raids from neighbouring tribes. The soldier-chronicler, who had seen the Arabs with their camels charging the Spanish arquebusiers, had also observed them in peacetime, closely enough to be familiar with their way of cooking, of preserving meat fried in its own fat, eating *alcuzcuz* (couscous) and drinking the sour milk that they called *lebent*.[31]

In Tunisia, there was a similar pattern. If Don John of Austria captured Tunis without a struggle in October 1573, it was because the nomads had already left the shores of northern Tunisia. In August, 1574, on the other hand, the Turks took the town and fortress of La Goletta, because the nomads were on their side and served them as auxiliaries for earthworks and transport. History was repeated over the centuries. As early as 1270 the nomads serving in the Tunisian army threatened in the late season (just after the death of St. Louis) 'to return as was their custom, to the southern pastures'.[32]

Advance and infiltration from the steppe. These large-scale movements of nomads from the steppe to the coast, then from the sea back to the desert, inevitably acted as one of the pressures on Mediterranean history, or perhaps one should say, one of its rhythms. All would be well if the migrations had the regularity of the tides of the sea. But there were a

[30] Belon, *op. cit.*, p. 163.
[31] Diego Suárez, *Historia del Maestre último que fue de Montesa* . . ., Madrid, 1889, p. 46, 284–295.
[32] R. Brunschvig, *op. cit.*, I, p. 61.

hundred causes, apart from intermittent droughts, for the machinery to go wrong and for the nomad to be dissatisfied with the land he was allotted; hence a hundred opportunities for disputes with permanent settlers. Basically nomadic life requires grazing lands; but it may also possibly seek land to grow crops on, even towns that will act as victualling centres and form the basis of its political structures.

Take an example. In about the 1550's the desert of southern Tunisia witnessed the somewhat confusing history of the little state of the Shābbiyya.[33] The Shābbiyya were originally a simple nomadic tribe. Through circumstances we know little about, they succeeded in reaching Kairouan, to the north, very nearly the true Mediterranean of olive trees and fields of barley and wheat; and, what was more, a holy city, which was another strong attraction. The Shābbiyya settled there, taking advantage of the disorder and decadence of the Hafsids, masters of Tunis and its kingdom since the thirteenth century, but suffering from the economic decline of North Africa and foreign intervention, first by Christians then by Turks. Controlling only the city of Kairouan (they had tried in vain to capture the big urban villages of the *Sahel* to the east with their potential taxpayers), the Shābbiyya were easily dislodged when the Turks and Dragut entered the city in 1551. The Shābbiyya State, torn from its roots, died away within a short time. Its dynasty disappeared into the west, say the sources without details, leaving a trail of holiness behind them; and that was all; they had come from nowhere and adapted to a sedentary life for only a brief moment before vanishing again into the darkness.

This was a story often repeated. Around Tripoli in the sixteenth century other nomadic states sprang up in similar conditions, and vanished as quickly without having time to bear fruit. In fact, were not the great ventures of the Almoravids, the Merīnids, and the Hilalians, which strikingly altered the Moroccan world, basically similar feats, differing only in scale? The Almoravids travelled in a few years from the banks of the Senegal to the heart of Spain, right up to the walls of the Valencia of El Cid: as spectacular a success as one could wish for a nomadic civilization.

But alongside these stirring and violent events there were silent invasions too. Take Anatolia at the end of the Middle Ages.[34] When Marco Polo travelled through it, the peasants had risen up against the towns where their Greek landlords lived. When they went over to Islam and opened their ranks to Turkish nomads, when the towns finally went over to Islam as well, the great transformation we have already mentioned was being accomplished. A nomadic world was gradually adapting to a peaceful, sedentary way of life.[35] The nomad found roots for himself. He who would not adapt to the almost tropical agriculture of the oases sometimes let himself be domesticated by the settled populations of the Mediterranean,

[33] Charles Monchicourt, 'Études Kairouannaises', in *Revue Tunisienne*, 1932–1936.
[34] Carl Brockelmann, *Geschichte der islamischen Völker*, 1939, p. 284.
[35] See above, p. 166.

bowing to their simple, often rudimentary methods of agriculture. Morocco provides examples of this.

In the course of the centuries, then, there have been many moves from the steppe to the Mediterranean. Today, sedentarization has made great strides. The obstacles to invasion from the steppe have therefore been greatly reinforced. But they were not enough to prevent the Saharan tribes in 1912 from emulating the feat of the Almoravids with Aḥmad al-Hiba, the 'Blue Sultan', son of the Marabout Mā al-'Ainain. They entered Marrakesh in triumph, but the French army soon drove them back into the desert.[36] In 1920 and 1921, in southern Algeria this time, the French authorities had the foresight to place in camps the great Larba tribe which was dying of hunger and had lost two thirds of its flocks. Left to themselves what might these starving people have done? Similarly in 1927 in the Nedj, that automatic accumulator of the nomadic peoples of Arabia, as T. E. Lawrence called it, the swelling hordes of unemployed desert tribes were threatening to explode. 'Had it not been for the control of the English police,' wrote Alfred Hettner,[37] 'the Arab invasions would have begun all over again,' particularly since they could have drawn on reinforcements from Syria as in the past. Because of the relatively abundant rainfall on the mountains of Lebanon, the Syrian lands were and still are a great centre for nomadism.

These are dramatic examples, but one could give others. From 1940 to 1945, North Africa, deprived of its normal means of transport, saw an increase in nomadic transport, on a larger scale, notably more to the north, than in the years before the war. When lorries were abandoned for lack of petrol, grain began to circulate once again as in the old days, in the great double saddlebags of the camels, bags made of goatskin or camelskin, hand-sewn by the women of the desert. This increase undoubtedly contributed to the spread throughout North Africa of the great epidemics of former days, above all of exanthematous typhus.

So the relations between Bedouin and settler do not simply take the form of continual conflict. The Bedouin is often called into the house he covets. Agriculture in the Mediterranean as it has been and is practised, leads to the rapid exhaustion of the soil, wearing it out more thoroughly than the often-blamed depredations of the sheep and goats of the nomads. The handing over of these lands to the flocks for grazing may then be a way of meeting the need to rest them. 'The nomad and the settler are, to be sure, irreconcilable enemies,' writes one geographer,[38] 'but at the same time they are complementary: indeed they urgently require each other. By his absurd determination always to plough the same field – absurd, that is, in a dry land – the farmer who has ventured beyond the Tell opens up a way for the shepherds; but once they have established their empire,

---

[36] Henri-Paul Eydoux, *L'Homme et le Sahara*, 1943, p. 101.
[37] 'Der Islam und die orientalische Kultur', in *Geogr. Zeitschrift*, 1932, p. 402.
[38] R. Capot-Rey, in *Revue Africaine*, 1941, p. 129, in a review of the book by Jean Despois, *La Tunisie Orientale, Sahel et Basse Steppe*, 1940.

security is assured and transport has become regular and easy, the nomad is drawn into a settled way of life, as he is today in the Tunisian steppe.' Improvements in agriculture such as the installation of modern techniques of rotation and transfer of crops are undoubtedly eliminating the nomadic life. The cultivation by colonial settlers of the high plateaux of Tiaret, their conversion into wheat lands has for decades now kept away almost all the camel-drovers who used to flock there.

But the conflict between the Mediterranean and the neighbouring desert is something more than plough versus flock. It is the clash between two economies, civilizations, societies, and arts of living. Russian historians see all invasions from the steppe as preceded by a change in the structure of its civilizations, their transition from primitive to 'feudalized' societies.[39] The part played by certain explosions of religious mysticism in the victorious expeditions of Islam is well known, as is that played by demographic explosions. The nomad profits by all the failures and weaknesses of the settler, in agriculture certainly, but also in other ways. Without the intentional or unintentional complicity of the settled civilizations these dramatic oscillations would be incomprehensible.

Gautier thinks that North Africa in the sixteenth century was more than usually overrun with nomads.[40] The Peninsula was then witnessing a series of crises, an economic crisis with the disturbance of Saharan trade, and the crisis of foreign invasion with the Portuguese, Spanish, and Turkish conquests. The last-comers restored order in the central and eastern Maghreb, not without opposition, for the prolonged troubles had created a precarious and revolutionary situation. Having taken refuge as far away as the Tuat oases, the Andalusian exiles were later to help the religious centres of the desert to preach holy war and take action. One of the great events of history was the withdrawal of the Marabout centres to the south, which was so marked from the fifteenth to the eighteenth century.[41] There followed the improbable spectacle of order being restored in Morocco by the Sharifs of the Sous, by the desert in fact. In the regencies of Algiers, Tunis, and Tripoli, the troubles at the end of the sixteenth century were linked with the unrest among the *Alarabes* as the Spanish texts call them, that is Arab nomads, often allied with the *moros* of the towns against the Turkish invader. This explains the extent of the unrest that was endemic during the last ten years of the sixteenth century all along the south shore of the Mediterranean, from Gibraltar to Egypt. So the nomad seems to have played a role of increasing importance in North Africa, but perhaps it would be more true to say that the whole region was caught up in the movement of the times, nomadic life as much as the rest. In the end, though, the nomad was to prove no match for the Turkish arquebuses and artillery or the cannon of the Moroccan Sharifs. He might still here

[39] B. Grekov and A. Iakoubowski, *La Horde d'Or*, French, trans. 1939.
[40] An impression gained not so much from his books which do not go into detail on this point, as from personal conversations with him in Algiers.
[41] Robert Montagne, *Les Berbères, op. cit.*, p. 410.

and there carry off a local victory, make successful surprise attacks, and rally whole areas to the dissident cause. But he no longer had the last word. Militarily, the rules had changed. The nomad, until then always victorious, unrivalled in horsemanship, was defeated by gunpowder. This was as true of the nomads of Kazan on the Volga or the Mongols of northern China, as of the tribes of Africa and the Middle East.[42]

The gold and spice caravans. We must distinguish between the everyday history of nomadism and the great caravan trails, long-distance voyages from one side of the desert to the other, linking the Mediterranean on one side to the Far East, and on the other to the *Bled es Soudan* and Black Africa. They were as different from the first as long-distance shipping from coastal trade. The caravans served merchants, and therefore towns and active economies in a world context; they were a luxury, an adventure, a complicated operation.

The sixteenth century inherited them; it used an instrument which it had not created, preserved it intact, and passed it on to later generations who did not appreciably modify it. The descriptions by Gobineau, G. Schweinfurth,[43] René Caillé, Brugnon,[44] and Flachat,[45] are all very similar to those of Tavernier; they even agree, *mutatis mutandis*, with the account of the anonymous Englishman who in 1586 followed the sumptuous caravan of pilgrims to Mecca.[46] It formed at 'Birca', three leagues from Cairo, twenty days after Ramadan, and consisted of up to 40,000 mules and camels and 50,000 people, the merchants anxious to protect their goods walking at the head, sometimes selling along the wayside the silk, coral, tin, grain, or rice that they would for the most part exchange at Mecca, and the pilgrims, free of possessions, looking only after their own persons, coming behind. This procession of rich and poor had its military commander, the 'captain' of the caravan, and some guides; at night, the latter would carry dry-wood torches to light the way, for they preferred to journey between two o'clock in the morning and sunrise, to avoid the heat of the day. An escort was provided against Arab raids on the Red Sea coast: 200 spahis and 400 soldiers, plus field artillery, some six pieces drawn by twelve camels, which served to terrify the Bedouin and make a noise at the triumphal entry to Mecca, 'to make triumph', as the narrator calls it.

It was clearly an enormous caravan, half-religious, half-commercial, and moving quickly: this one covered the difficult journey from Cairo to Mecca in forty days. On every occasion we must imagine vast numbers of

[42] René Grousset, *L'Empire des steppes*, 1941, p. 11.
[43] G. Schweinfurth, *Im Herzen von Africa*, Leipzig, 1874, p. 50 ff.
[44] Didier Brugnon, *Relation exacte . . .*, *op. cit.*, see above note 9.
[45] Flachat, *op. cit.*, I, 345, (1766) talking of caravans setting out from Bochorest (Bucharest): at night '. . . the great bowl of fire which a man from the caravan carried in front of us'.
[46] R. Hakluyt, *op. cit.*, II, p. 200. *A description of the yeerely voyage or pilgrimage of the Mahumitans, Turkes and Moores into Mecca in Arabia.*

182   *The Role of the Environment*

pack animals (the victualling of the Turkish army sometimes required the requisitioning of 30,000 to 40,000 camels) and large numbers of travellers, bound by the strict discipline of the convoy, living by their own means, asking little from the country they journeyed through apart from the water and fuel necessary for cooking and caring for the animals. The mounting of these costly and powerful operations therefore required profitable commercial dealings: in the Sahara there was traffic in salt, slaves, fabrics, and gold; in Syria a luxury trade in spices, drugs, and silk. And these were all regular trades.

It is probable that the overall volume of the Sahara trade increased in the fifteenth and sixteenth centuries even after the great Portuguese discoveries and in spite of them. Certainly after the 1460s Portuguese settlement on the coast of Guinea diverted some of the Sahara trade in that direction, hence the evident gold crisis to which we shall return later. Nevertheless, the great Sahara trails continued to transport the precious metal in the sixteenth century towards North Africa and Egypt[47] and consequently to draw a compensating flow of goods and men towards the south. It would be tempting to explain by irregularities in the export of gold the advance by Salīh Re'īs, 'king' of Algiers as far as Ouargla in 1556. Or the much more important expedition, since it crossed the Sahara from one side to the other, led by Jawdhar Pasha with his Moroccans and Spanish renegades[48] in 1591 to Timbuktu. Does this expedition explain the fact that three years later, in 1594, the Englishman Madoc saw thirty mules arriving at Marrakesh, laden with gold?[49]

These glimpses reflect the fragmentary nature of our information. Nor is it easy to establish with precision what trading was carried on in the upper reaches of the Nile Valley, the natural commercial route linking Abyssinia and Egypt. It was by this route that the ostrich plumes arrived in Turkey to decorate the helmets of the janissaries and spahis.[50] It was also one of the gold routes; in the sixteenth century we have evidence of this. In the seventeenth century Tavernier mentions it as such.[51] In the time of Philip II, while Europe was adapting to the regime of American silver, it seems that Turkish Islam was still living off African gold. One cannot say that Turkey received this gold in large quantities, however,

[47] Vitorino Malgahães-Godinho, *L'économie de l'Empire portugais, aux XIVe et XVe siècles*, typed thesis, Sorbonne, 1958, p. 14 ff. According to the Portuguese sources, the gold from Tacrour, that is the western Sudan, furnished two caravans a year which carried the metal in 'great quantities' by way of Fezzan to Egypt, *ibid.*, p. 43.

[48] Emilio Garcia Gomez, 'Españoles en el Sudan', in *Revista de Occidente*, 1935, p. 93–117: the entry to Timbuktu, 30th May, 1591, J. Béraud-Villars, *L'Empire de Gao. Un État soudanais aux XVe et XVIe siècles*, 1942, p. 144.

[49] Roland Lebel, *Le Maroc et les écrivains anglais aux XVIe, XVIIe et XVIIIe siècles*, 1927; J. Caille, 'Le Commerce anglais avec le Maroc pendant la seconde moitié du XVIe siècle. Importations et exportations,' in *Rev. Afr.*, 1941.

[50] Belon, *op. cit.*, p. 98, 189 v° and 190; N. Iorga, *Ospiti romeni in Venezia*, Bucarest, 1932, p. 150.

[51] The Nile route, one of the gold routes, J. B. Tavernier, *op. cit.*, *Travels in India*, p. 156.

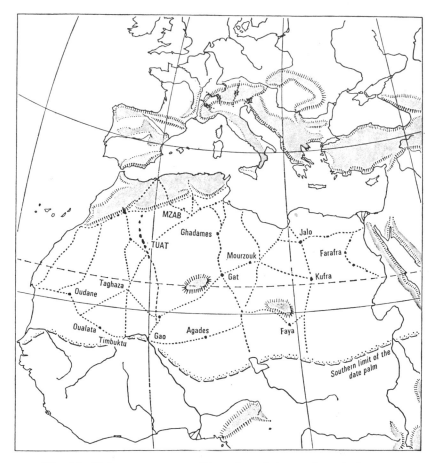

Fig. 14: *Saharan caravans, fifteenth and sixteenth centuries*

Map taken from Vitorino Magalhães Godinho, *Os descobrimientos e a economia mundial*, 1963, which has more particular reference to the fifteenth century. The routes across North Africa towards Oran and Tunis are barely outlined. The rise of Algiers only occurred in the last decades of the sixteenth century. Naturally the routes from the Maghreb to Black Africa were subject to change and variation in activity. Towards Abyssinia, the Nile was the principal route.

since increasingly it was importing precious metal from Christendom. All the same it is curious that Turkey should stand out as a gold area at the end of the sixteenth century, compared with Persia under the Safavids, a silver area.[52]

In the Middle East there were two basic caravan zones: one corresponding to the Mecca routes, setting out either from Syria or Cairo; the other

[52] Hakluyt, II, p. 171 (1583).

running from Aleppo to the Tigris.[53] The Euphrates, according to Tavernier, was not considered for shipping because of its mills, at least until 1638, when the Turkish army was to use it as a communications route.[54] The Tigris was only navigable below Baghdad.[55]

Both sets of routes led towards the Indian Ocean, one in the direction of the Persian Gulf, the other to the Red Sea, ending at the Egyptian ports of Tor and Suez, and further on at Jiddah, the pilgrim port and the terminus of shipping routes linking the Red Sea with India and the East Indies.[56] These links had been in existence for centuries, and their prosperity, dating from the twelfth and thirteenth centuries, was still buoyant in the sixteenth. They provided the link between shipping and the caravan traffic and although from time to time there were delays, missed connections, and threats of competition, the system always righted itself somehow and continued to run efficiently.

That is not to say that the Mediterranean and its extension towards the Indian Ocean were at all 'a single living organism', as Jacob Burckhardt eloquently but exaggeratedly puts it. Geography undoubtedly dictated the routes in advance, because of the narrow land passage separating Syria and the Persian Gulf, and the even more narrow isthmus of Suez. But natural advantages did not dictate everything, and in any case the crossing of these desert lands was always to be an obstacle, overcome only by great effort.

By these means two separate economies were brought into contact, both deriving great advantages from the encounter but both accustomed to an independent existence. Before and after Vasco da Gama the Indian Ocean was an independent and virtually self-sufficient world. Its grain came from Diu, cotton fabrics from Cambay, horses from Hormuz, rice and sugar from Bengal, ivory, slaves, and gold from the southern African coast. The Indian Ocean sought only luxuries from outside: from the Pacific, silks, porcelain, copper, tin, and spices; from the West, textiles and especially silver coins. Had it not been for the continual tipping of the scales by silver pieces, the trading activity of the Indian Ocean would not have

[53] At the end of the nineteenth century there were still Nestorian boatmen on the Tigris, natives of the village of Tell Kel, near Mosul, Edouard Sachau, *Am Euphrat und Tigris*, 1900, p. 24. In the seventeenth century the journey up the Tigris was difficult: the boats had to be hauled by men and it took sixty days to get from Basra to Baghdad, J. B. Tavernier, *op. cit.*, p. 189.
[54] J. B. Tavernier, *op. cit.*, Persian Travels, p. 58.
[55] W. Heyd, *Histoire du commerce du Levant*, French trans. by Furcy-Raynaud, 2 vols., 1885–1886, reprinted 1936, II, p. 457.
[56] A. Philippson, *op. cit.*, p. 46–47, notes the large volume of shipping in the Red Sea and the navigational hazards it encountered: from May to October, the north winds are so strong that it is only possible to sail from Jiddah to Tor or Suez when the prevailing wind drops, and even then only with the aid of an off-shore wind. On the competition between the Red Sea and the Syrian routes, see W. Heyd's classic *Histoire du commerce du Levant, op. cit.*, and the still useful study by O. Peschel, 'Die Handelsgeschichte des Roten Meers' in *Deutsche Vierteljahrschrift*, III, 1855, p. 157–228. On the difficulties of caravans in the Suez Isthmus, Belon, *op. cit.*, p. 132.

allowed itself to be diverted so easily. In the Mediterranean there was a demand for pepper, spices and silk; a feverishly eager demand. But if there had not been a passionate thirst for silver metal in India and China, that demand might well have gone unsatisfied. The Levant trade resulted from great tensions; it was anything but natural and free-flowing. It presupposed a series of efforts and stages without which the operation would hardly have been possible at all. One violent shock would be enough to upset the whole system. One has only to think how many times a sack of pepper from India, or a sack of cloves from the East Indies, must have been handled before it reached a shop, first in Aleppo, then in Venice, and finally in Nuremberg.

The oases. Nomadism, both of men and flocks, the long processions of caravans, or the wandering tribesmen: to the westerner these are the most striking features of the arid regions.

But the desert is not all movement. To forget this would be to disregard its permanent towns and the precious land surrounding them, the achievement of expert rural civilizations, created by the careful use of water, from rivers, springs, or wells. This victory won thousands of years ago by the men of the Middle East, starting no one knows exactly where or when, but very far back in time, in Egypt, Mesopotamia, and Iran, as well as in Turkestan and on the banks of the Indus, was passed on and explained to succeeding generations, was further developed and enriched in the process, and spread towards North Africa and the southern Mediterranean.

The oases were only tiny islands in the desert. Egypt in the sixteenth century was a double ribbon of cultivated fields, with a delta as yet unconquered by man. Mesopotamia, in the days of its antique splendour, consisted of 20,000 to 25,000 square kilometres of fertile gardens;[57] next to nothing on a map. But the oases were points where population concentrated, agricultural towns in a real sense, whose streets ran parallel with the irrigation canals. We can get a glimpse of what they must have been like from the orchard-gardens of present-day southern Algeria, enclosed within mud walls, with their thrifty water regulations, their watchful guardians, and their organization which is even more tyrannical than that of the Mediterranean plains. The close discipline of the Lombardy rice fields was mild compared to the regulations of the Code of Hammurabi. Even in Valencia and other regions where irrigation imposed its strict laws, there was still room for semi-freedom. But an oasis imposes total discipline, and, like the true plain, it requires and consumes large numbers of men.

In their hostile climate man quickly becomes exhausted; he is subject to a series of endemic diseases, including malaria. In Egypt Pierre Belon's face was so covered with mosquito bites that he thought he had measles.[58] So life there has required a constant replenishment of human stock.

[57] According to Hermann Wagner, 'Die Überschätzung der Anbaufläche Babyloniens' in *Nachrichten K. Ges. Wissensch.* Göttingen, Ph. hist. Klass, 1902, II, p. 224–298.
[58] Belon, *op. cit.*, p. 107.

186 *The Role of the Environment*

Well before it reached America, black slavery was commonplace in the oases of the Sahara as well as in Egypt, which throughout its history has maintained constant contact with the Sudan and Abyssinia, hence the Negro blood which is evident in so many *fellahin* of the banks of the Nile. As for Mesopotamia, it seems to have drawn tribute from the mountains bordering it to the north and east. In the Middle Ages it was virtually a branch of Persia, which found it an ideal terrain for the flowering of its civilization, its great capitals, and places of pilgrimage. It has been said that the Turks ruined the Persian gardens of Mesopotamia by their neglect. In fact, once it had been snatched from Iran, Mesopotamia was cut off from its indispensable source of manpower. The Bedouin no longer found it difficult to drive his flocks to the edges of this moribund land and to begin, with his crude methods, his apprenticeship as a farmer.

This is a suitable moment to point out the vulnerability of the gardens – whether in the plains or the oases – in that they had constantly to be re-created and protected against their tireless enemies: in the case of Meso-potamia, the sand, the silting up of the canals, the bursting of dykes, as well as the near-primitive nomads from the neighbouring steppe, from whom, as if from locusts, the gardens had to be defended. Even at the end of the nineteenth century, there was not a village in Mesopotamia without its watchtowers and sentinels to give warning of invasion by the shep-herds.[59] But in any case, would the Bedouin ever have been able to adapt to the tropical regime of the oasis with its predominantly vegetable diet? He belongs to the athletic type of nomad, long-legged and broad-chested, the *Brustrasse* according to German anthropologists. The oasis-dweller is of the *Bauchrasse*, a peasant, with a belly like Sancho Panza's, swollen with vegetable foods. Compare the role played in the history of the Fergana by settlers of Iranian origin. It was they, it appears, who improved the valley of the Syr Daria, cleared the hillsides, which were often covered with dense forests, drained the marshes with their thick reed beds; it was they and not the colourful tribes of nomads and semi-nomads moving all around.[60]

Undoubtedly the oases, great and small, were centres of power. Acquired early, they were the fertile islands on which grew up that 'eastern civiliza-tion' of which Islam was merely a renewal, thousands of years after its first appearance. They were its first 'paradise gardens' with their trees, springs, and roses. If it was not always here that many serviceable plants and agricultural implements like the plough were first discovered, it was certainly here that all these things were very early put to use. That does not mean, as Alfred Hettner has declared, that the oases were the cradle of the East. Geographers, it seems to me, have too often insisted on select-ing one or other of the two opposed and complementary elements of desert life, as a basis for their explanations, as if they could be separated; as if the nomad did not need the stability of the towns and the towns the wanderings of the nomad, above all as if both were not associated elements

[59] E. Sachau, *op. cit.*, esp. p. 43–44.
[60] V. Nalivkine, *Histoire du Khanat de Khokand*, Paris, 1889.

in a history that transcends either one of them, and, in particular, necessary elements for the understanding of the great and unique history of Islam, child of the desert.

The geographical area of Islam. For 'Islam is the desert', declares the essayist Essad Bey,[61] it is the emptiness, the ascetic rigour, the inherent mysticism, the devotion to the implacable sun, unifying principle on which myths are founded, and the thousand consequences of this human vacuum. In the same way, Mediterranean civilization grew up under the determining influence of the emptiness of the sea: one zone peopled by ships and boats, the other by caravans and nomad tribes. Islam, like the sea and like the desert implies movement. Bazaars and caravanserais, as Vidal de La Blache said, are as characteristic of its civilization as mosques and minarets.[62] The desert owes its undeniable human homogeneity to this mobility. 'Bring together a Manchou and a Bass-Arabian Tartar,' wrote Baron de Tott, 'and you will search in vain the interval of fifteen hundred leagues that separate their countries; the climate differs but little; the government is the same. . . .'[63]

But we should be wary of oversimplifying something so complex. Islam is the sum of human realities implied by the desert, harmonious or discordant, the whole family of geographical problems we have noted: the great caravan trails; the coastal zones, for Islam lived off these *Sahels*, fringes of settled civilization along the shores of the Mediterranean, the Persian Gulf, the Indian Ocean, or the Red Sea, and also bordering the countries of the Sudan; the oases and their accumulated power, which Hettner thinks was the essential factor. Islam is all that, a long road cutting through the strong and rigid mass of the Ancient World. Rome, when she achieved the unity of the Mediterranean, did no more.

Islam is also the historical chance that from the seventh century on made it the unifying force of the Ancient World. Between the densely populated blocks, Europe in the large sense, Black Africa, and the Far East, it held the key passes and made a living from its profitable function of intermediary. Without its consent or will nothing could pass through. Within this solid world whose centre lacked the flexibility provided by shipping routes, Islam was what Europe triumphant was later to be on a world scale, a dominant economy and civilization. Inevitably this supremacy had its weak points: the chronic shortage of manpower; imperfect technology; internal quarrels, of which religion was a pretext as much as a cause; the congenital difficulty experienced by the first Islam, of gaining control of the cold deserts, or at any rate of containing them at the level of Turkestan or Iran. This was the weakest link in the chain, near or behind the gates of Dzungaria, between the double threat from Mongol and Turk. As the ultimate weakness, Islam soon became the prisoner of its own

[61] *Allah est grand*, Paris, 1937, p. 11.
[62] *Op. cit.*, p. 469.
[63] *Op. cit.*, Preliminary Discourse, Vol. I, p. 4.

success, of the comfortable conviction of being at the centre of the world, of having found all the right answers and not needing to look for any others. Arab navigators were familiar with both profiles of Black Africa, the Atlantic and the Indian, suspected that the ocean connected the two but did not bother to find out.[64]

At this point, in the fifteenth century, there came the resounding Turkish triumph: a second Islam, a second Islamic order, this time linked to the land, the horseman, and the soldier, a 'northern' Islam, which through possession of the Balkans thrust deep into Europe. The first Islam had reached Spain at the end of its career. The heart of the Ottoman adventure was to lie in Europe and in a seatown which was to triumph over them and betray them too. Istanbul's determination to impose settlement, organization, and planning was European in style.[65] It involved the sultans in outdated conflicts, hiding from them the true problems. In 1529 the failure of the Turks to dig a Suez canal, although it had been begun; their failure in 1538 to commit themselves entirely to the struggle against the Portuguese, indulging instead in a fratricidal war with Persia in the middle of no-man's-land; their failure in 1569 to conquer the Lower Volga and to reopen the silk route, instead wasting their substance in futile wars in the Mediterranean when they should have been trying to break out of that charmed circle: lost opportunities, every one.[66]

2. EUROPE AND THE MEDITERRANEAN

From the Black Sea to the Straits of Gibraltar, the Mediterranean's northern waters wash the shores of Europe. Here again, if he wants to establish boundaries, the historian will have more hesitation than the geographer. 'Europe, a confused concept,' wrote Henri Hauser. It is a twofold or even threefold world, composed of peoples and territories with whom history has dealt very differently. The Mediterranean, by its profound influence over southern Europe, has contributed in no small measure to prevent the unity of that Europe, which it has attracted towards its shores and then divided to its own advantage.

The isthmuses and their north–south passages. The land mass of Europe, lying between the blue waters of the Mediterranean and the other, northern Mediterraneans, the Baltic, the North Sea, and the English Channel, narrows progressively to the west. It is intersected by a series of north–south routes, natural isthmuses that are still decisive influences on ex-

[64] Richard Hennig, *Terrae Incognitae*, 2nd ed., 1956, IV, p. 44 ff.

[65] 'European in style' to the historian that is. To a European traveller, the German, Salomon Schweigger, who passed through Turkey in 1577 (*Eine neue Reissbeschreibung auss Teutschland nach Konstantinopel und Jerusalem*, 4th ed., Nuremberg, 1639), the opposite seemed to be true: 'the habit of nomadic life, which is one of the distinctive features of the Asiatic peoples, is still characteristic of the Turks today', quoted by Ivan Sakazof, *Bulgarische Wirtschaftsgeschichte*, Berlin–Leipzig, 1929, p. 206.

[66] As is explained in a brilliant and original manner in W. E. D. Allen's essay *Problems of Turkish Power in the Sixteenth Century*, London, 1963.

changes today: the Russian isthmus, the Polish isthmus, the German isthmus, and the French isthmus.

To the west the Iberian peninsula is also intersected by routes, but this time running from west to east, from the sea to the ocean: the routes from Barcelona to Navarre and the Basque provinces by way of the Ebro; the important passage from Valencia to Medina del Campo and Portugal; or the short cuts overland from Alicante and Málaga to Seville[67] by which one can avoid the Straits of Gibraltar. These Spanish routes are not our present concern. Their orientation puts them in a very different category, and the perennial question raises itself: is Spain wholly European? So let us come back to the geologists' line from the Bay of Biscay to the Caucasus. We shall consider only the routes to the north of this line as presenting the real problem of Europe's relationship to the Mediterranean, or rather, the series of real problems.

For this northern half of Europe was far from a homogeneous territory although it contrasted violently with the Mediterranean landscape. Compared with the orchards and vineyards of the South, it was the land of thick forests,[68] open plains, meadows, and wide navigable rivers, only rarely producing the food-bearing trees and plants that were the safeguard of Mediterranean life. It was, over vast expanses, the land of wheeled traffic, so that Dantiscus, the Polish ambassador, travelling from Antwerp to Bruges and Calais in the autumn of 1522, naturally writes: 'ex Antwerpia per currus ut hic fieri solet', 'from Antwerp by wagon as is the custom here'.[69] The South by contrast was the land of muletrains. The future queen of Spain, Elizabeth of Valois, and her suite, arriving at the Spanish frontier in January, 1560, with their carriages and belongings were transferred to pack animals that carried them to the interior of the Peninsula.[70] The same thing had happened in 1502, half a century earlier, on the occasion of the first visit to Spain of Philip the Fair.

The North was the land of beer and drinks made from fermented grain, as Germany already was in Tacitus's time. In the sixteenth century the first breweries were set up at Konstanz;[71] the Dominicans introduced beer to Lorraine; it was soon to reach England, as the popular song said, along with hops, as one might expect, and the Reformation.[72] Marco Ottobon,

[67] Gonzalo Menéndez Pidal, *Los caminos en la historia de España*, Madrid, 1951, p. 85. On the Málaga–Seville route for example, see Theodore de Mayerne Turquet, *Sommaire description de la France, Allemagne, Italie et Espagne*, 1629, p. 309.
[68] Cf. Jean Brunhes' evocative description of the forests of northern Europe and the bare slopes of the South, *Géographie Humaine*, 4th ed., p. 51.
[69] Dantiscus to the king of Poland, London, 12th October, 1522, Czartoryski Library, 19, folios 33–34.
[70] L. Paris, *Négociations . . . relatives au règne de François II*, 1841, p. 187.
[71] Friedrich Wielandt, *Die Bierbrauereui in Constanz*, 1936. The first brewer, Jacob Wuederfranck came there from Budwitz.
[72] As a popular song of the time had it G. M. Trevelyan, *History of England*, London, 1943, p. 287, note 1):

> 'Hops, Reformation, bays and beer,
> Came into England all in one year.'

the secretary sent from Venice to Danzig during the winter of 1590–1591 to purchase grain, was astonished, the following summer, by the arrival of two hundred Dutch ships, all in poor condition and inadequately equipped, calling to pick up second-rate grain, 'gli grani per birra'.

For a man from the Mediterranean these were strange countries (not only Poland), where wine was a luxury, to be had only at unbelievable prices. When he was briefly imprisoned in the Low Countries, Bayard, although without fortune, kept a good table, but 'he might in a day spend twenty crowns on wine'.[73] A foreigner in these parts, if he came from a Mediterranean country, would consider the people coarse and unrefined barbarians. Often good 'barbarians', showing great religious devotion (whether Germany before Luther[74] or Normandy in the time of François I,)[75] and honest too (the same Ottobon said of Poland that one could travel there 'l'oro in mano senza pericolo di essere offeso'). And then there was the great advantage that living was much cheaper there than in Italy. In Danzig our Venetian observed, 'for two *thaler* per person per week, I may say that I have a banquet morning and evening'.[76]

But we should beware of generalizations. The Mediterranean was not the exclusive domain of the pack animal, nor northern Europe the undisputed zone of beer and wheeled traffic. In France, and elsewhere too, much transport was by pack animal. Frequently carriages could only be used near towns, within the small radius of urban traffic centres, exceptional areas that can be found well inside Mediterranean lands too. And the Mediterranean had its own backward regions, of primitive religion and cheap living.

Europe, it must be repeated, is diversity itself. Civilization reached it at varying times, along different roads. It travelled up from the South in the first place and bore a heavy Mediterranean influence; later on it moved eastwards along the parallels, from the Christian West, both by sea (as Lübeck imposed her order on the Baltic) and by land (the extensive, though slower, spread of the influence of Magdeburg).

Within Europe, then, the Mediterranean is confronted by a series of different regions, societies, and civilizations resembling each other neither in origin nor in cultural and economic status. They are of different com-

[73] 'La très joyeuse et très plaisant Histoire composée par le Loyal Serviteur des faits, gestes et triomphes . . . du bon chevalier sans paour et sans reprouche, le gentil seigneur de Bayart', published by J. C. Buchon, Coll. 'Le Panthéon littéraire', 1886, p. 106.
[74] Don Antonio de Beatis, *Voyage du Cardinal d'Aragon (1517–1518)*, translated from the Italian by M. Havard de la Montagne, Paris, 1913, p. 74.
[75] A.d.S. Mantua, Series E, Francia 637, the dean of Bayeux to the Marquis of Mantua, Bayeux, 16th April, 1529: 'che a dir il vero li vescovi di qui son havuti in maggior reverentia che in Italia'.
[76] The copies of Marco Ottobon's correspondence make up the series: Dispacci scritti al Senato dal Secretario Marco Ottobon da Danzica delli 15 novembre, 1590 sino 7 settembre, 1591, A.d.S. Venice, Secreta Archivi Propri, Polonia. The register is not paginated. The letters referred to here are those of 13th and 22nd December, 1590.

plexions, different ages, and have felt the pull of Mediterranean attraction in varying ways.

By and large, we should distinguish between *at least* four European groups, corresponding to the routes running north and south through the isthmuses, four skeins of history, each tied more or less securely to the warm sea, the source of prosperity, but also linked to each other, which does not simplify the observer's task.

The Russian isthmus: leading to the Black and Caspian Seas. It would be easy to say, and almost to prove, that in the sixteenth century there was no Russian isthmus, no isthmus, that is, playing a connecting role and bringing large exchange movements to the Mediterranean. The whole of southern Russia was a deserted land, crossed only by the bands of Tartar nomads, whose swift horses carried them to the northern edge of the Caucasus or to the shores of the Caspian Sea, as well as towards Moscow – which they burnt in 1571[77] – or into the lands of the Danube, which they ravaged unmercifully.[78] At the end of the eighteenth century Russian settlers were again to find an immense waste land, empty except for a few nomadic brigands raising their camels and horses.[79]

The raids of the brigands did not people the vast steppes (where there was not a single town) any more than the ships of the corsairs peopled the sea. But they made it dangerous country. Based in the Crimea, which its relief protected on the mainland side, and supported by the Turks who had several strongholds on the peninsula including Kaffa, these southern Tartars proved impossible for the 'Grand Duke' to subdue as he had those of Kazan and Astrakhan. For the Turks had armed them with arquebuses and artillery, thus neutralizing the only advantage that the Russians could

[77] R. Hakluyt, *op. cit.*, I, 402. Paolo Lamberti to the Venetian ambassador at Paris, Rouen, 11th August, 1571, *C.S.P.*, p. 473–474: Moscow burnt down, 150,000 people massacred including Flemish, English, German, and Italian merchants living there. The capture of Moscow made it impracticable for years afterwards to carry on the trade with Narva in which ships freighted at Dieppe had been engaged on Lamberti's account. Karl Stählin, *Geschichte Russlands von den Anfängen bis zur Gegenwart*, 1923, vol. I, p. 282–283, explains the improbable casualty figures (800,000 dead, 130,000 taken prisoner).

[78] In the time of J. B. Tavernier (*Les Six Voyages*, I, p. 310 (omitted from Eng. trans.)) the raids were still carried out by handfuls of horsemen. 'I have remarked . . . that travelling from Paris to Constantinople I met between Buda and Belgrade two bands of these Tartars, one consisting of sixty horsemen, the other of eighty. . . .' On the role played by these 'irregulars' behind the Turkish armies, cf. J. Szekfü, *État et Nation*, Paris, 1945, p. 156–157: their terrible winter sojourns; they lived off the land, with their wives, children, and flocks. The chronology of their exploits was closely followed in Venice (A.d.S. Venice, *Annali di Venezia*, 9th October, 1571, 7th March, 1595; Marciana 7299, 15th April, 1584; 5837 C II.8, 11th January, 1597; Museo Correr Cicogna 1993, f° 135, 23rd July, 1602 etc.); in Poland, Czartoryski Museum, 2242, f° 256, 1571; Johann Georg Tochtermann, 'Die Tartaren in Polen ein anthropogeographischer Entwurf', in *Pet. Mitt.*, 1939. Any attack on Poland by the Tartars provoked a sharp reaction, as in 1522, *Acta Tomiciana*, VI, p. 121; and in 1650, *Recueil des Gazettes, nouvelles ordinaires et extraordinaires*, by Théophraste Renaudot, p. 26–36.

[79] *The Memoirs of the Baron de Tott*, . . . I, 327–328.

have had over them.[80] In return, the Tartars after their raids would provide all the Turkish houses and villages with Slav servants and workers. Large numbers of Russian and sometimes Polish slaves arrived by their good offices in Constantinople, where they fetched high prices.[81] These dealings in human cattle were on such a scale that in 1591 Giovanni Botero spoke of them as one of the reasons for the low population of Russia.[82] The shortage of men possibly explains why the Russians did not attempt to take the shores of the Black Sea in the sixteenth century; they contented themselves with a few counterraids in winter into these empty lands, when the frozen rivers allowed troop movements. At the beginning of the seventeenth century the Russian outlaws, the Cossacks, like the Uskoks or Haiduks, were to arm light vessels and disturb Turkish shipping on the Black Sea. As early as 1602 some 'Polish' Cossacks met a galley at the mouth of the Danube.[83]

If the Russians had as yet only slight connections with the South, it was partly because they had not made any serious efforts in that direction; because they were attracted, through the primitive northern lands, by the economic expansion of the Baltic[84] and by the European countries facing them on the western front, Poland and Germany. Lastly, it was because they tended to focus on the Caspian Sea, which led them towards Persia: they faced southeast, rather than due south.

Russia was not yet Europe,[85] but it was becoming Europeanized. Along the western routes, over the Alps and the lands of Bohemia and Poland, there came to Moscow the Italian architect-masons, builders of the onion-shaped domes. From the West came the precious secrets of gunpowder. The Poles were always protesting the danger of such exchanges.[86] When the Tsar seized Narva, and held it from 1558 to 1581,[87] thus acquiring a window on to the Baltic, the king of Poland was alarmed at the fresh possibilities this opened up to the Muscovites. The only way to keep them in check would be to leave them 'in their barbarism and ignorance'. So the Danzigers did well, wrote King Sigismund to Queen Elizabeth, on 6th December, 1559, to stop English ships going to 'the Narve'.[88] The quarrel dragged on and extended to others besides the English. In June, 1570, a French ship from Dieppe, the *Espérance*, was seized on its way to

---

[80] G. Botero, *Relazioni univ.*, II, p. 39–40; W. Platzhoff, *op. cit.*, p. 32, is too inclined to see Tartary as an inactive buffer-state between Turks and Russians. On the Tartars' chariots, their horsemen, and the countless Russian horsemen who could use the arquebus, E. Albèri, *Relazioni*, III, II, p. 205, 1576.

[81] G. Botero, *ibid.*, I I, p. 34. On this subject see the important texts published in V. Lamansky, *op. cit.*, p. 380–381, note 1, 382, 383.

[82] G. Botero, *ibid.*, II, p. 34.

[83] Museo Correr, 1993, 11th September, 1602.

[84] L. Beutin, in *Vierteljahrschrift für S.u.W. Geschichte*, 1935, p. 83, apropos of the book by Axel Nielsen, *Dänische Wirtschaftsgeschichte*, 1933.

[85] P. Herre, *Europäische Politik in cyprischen Krieg*, 1902, p. 152.

[86] A. Brückner, *Russische Literaturgeschichte*, 1909, I, p. 51.

[87] Walter Kirchner, *The Rise of the Baltic Question*, 1954, p. 70–73.

[88] R. Hakluyt, *op. cit.*, I, p. 237–238.

Narva by Danziger pseudo-corsairs.[89] In 1571 the Duke of Alva warned the German Reichstag against exporting cannon and munitions which would be used to arm the enemies of Germany, and perhaps of all Christendom.[90] These and other details show that the centre of gravity of the Russian economy was gradually moving north, but the south, in the wide sense, and in particular the southeast continued to be important to it.

In Moscow there were Greek, Tartar, Wallachian, Armenian, Persian, and Turkish merchants.[91] Above all there was the flow of traffic along the Volga. Downstream went soldiers, artillery, and grain; upstream in return came salt and dried sturgeon.[92] After the Russian occupation of Kazan and Astrakhan in 1551 and 1556,[93] the entire waterway was seized and regular trade was only disturbed at long intervals by raids from Cossacks or Nogais Tartars.[94] So when the Turks, supported by the Tartars, tried to advance into Astrakhan (with the intention of digging a canal from the Don to the Volga so as to be able to supply their troops, who were engaged against Persia, by way of the Caspian Sea),[95] their expedition ended in the rout of 1569–1570 in the face of stiff Russian resistance. For this southern feeler was Moscow's means of contact with the nomads of the southeast, with Persia and with her old monetary economy. It was from these southern provinces that the Tsar could exact tribute in money; the northern provinces enriched his treasury often only with furs and hides.[96] These furs, incidentally, led to substantial Russian trade with the Balkans, Constantinople, and Persia,[97] Turko-Russian relations having improved after 1570, with the Novosiltsov diplomatic mission.[98]

More interesting for general history was the English attempt between 1556 and 1581 to establish a connection not with the Black Sea (there was little point in aiming at a Turkish lake and a well-guarded one) but with

---

[89] Charles IX to the town of Danzig, Blois, 16th October, 1571. Danzig Archives 300, 53630.

[90] J. Janssen, *Geschichte des deutschen Volkes, seit dem Ausgang des Mittelalters*, 1885, p. 313, n.l.

[91] J. von Hammer, *Histoire de l'Empire Ottoman depuis son origine jusqu'à nos jours*, 1835–1839, VI, p. 118: The Sultan wrote to the Tsar in 1558, to recommend some Turkish merchants going to Moscow to buy furs, R. Hakluyt, *op. cit.*, I, p. 257.

[92] R. Hakluyt, *op. cit.*, I, p. 364.

[93] F. Lot, *Les Invasions barbares*, II, 1937, p. 36; W. Platzhoff, *op. cit.*, p. 31, dates the capture of Kazan in 1552; Werner Philipp, *Ivan Peresnetov und seine Schriften zur Erneuerung des Moskauer Reiches*, 1935; Heinrich von Staden, *Aufzeichnungen über den Moskauer Staat*, published by F. Epstein, Hamburg, 1930, important for the incorporation of the two Tartar towns of the Lower Volga.

[94] As it was in July, 1568 , R. Hakluyt, *op. cit.*, I, p. 394.

[95] Some useful details in the correspondence of the Venetian *bailo*, Constantinople, 30th April, 1569, 8th January, 1570, A.d.S. Venice, *Annali di Venezia*; cf. W. E. D. Allen, *op. cit.*, p. 26 ff.

[96] E. Pommier, 'Les Italiens et la découverte de la Moscovie', in *Mélanges d'Archéologie et d'Histoire publiés par l'École Française de Rome*, 1953, p. 267.

[97] Nicolay (Nicolas de), *Les quatre premiers livres des navigations et pérégrinations orientales*, Lyons, 1568, p. 75, the low price of furs in the 'Besestan'.

[98] J. von Hammer, *op. cit.*, VI, p. 340–341.

the Caspian Sea. This was an effective attempt to get round the Mediterranean, not by a sea passage, as the Portuguese had succeeded in doing in
1498, but by a mixed route, over land and sea.[99]

English ships, in fact, disappeared from the Mediterranean towards the
middle of the century, and with them went the advantages that Oriental
trade had brought English merchants, who became all the more anxious to
participate in the profitable commerce of the Indies, the monopoly of the
Mediterraneans and Iberians. The association of Merchant Adventurers
in London began sending explorers and ships towards the Arctic regions in
the hope of finding a new northern passage as Magellan had a southern.
It was one of these boats, Chancellor's, which in 1553 landed by chance
in St. Nicholas Bay, not far from Archangel. This chance was soon turned
to profit and the resources of the region – whale blubber, wax, furs, flax,
hemp, seal's teeth, timber, and cod – were soon on the way to England,
in return for textiles and money.

The Muscovy Company quickly realised that the original project
could be achieved by going overland through Russia, and that by way of
the Caspian Sea they could reach the spices, pepper, and silk. In 1561 an
English agent arrived in Persia with his merchandise and regular voyages
were soon established. For a few years all the marvels of the East travelled
up the Volga, to be loaded on to London vessels in St. Nicholas Bay. For
a few years only, it is true. The project eventually collapsed for political
reasons and because after 1575, the English again had access to the direct
Mediterranean route. The long trips to the Caspian Sea and Persia lost
their attraction. But they did continue: the Russians did not give up
Persia, their chief eastern ally;[100] when later they were driven out of Narva
in 1581, they became interested in Archangel, the last window left to them
in the great North,[101] and soon the Dutch were sending ships there.[102]

To return to the English venture: the volume of goods concerned was
not large (enough though to bring good profits to English merchants and
some anxiety to Spaniards in London), but it provides us with information
about Mediterranean life in general, the difficulty of shipping between the
Atlantic and the inland sea, and then the reopening of the Mediterranean
to the northerners. It was through Russia that for a few years Anglo-
Mediterranean trade tried to open a passage for itself. In the minds of its
originators, the scheme was to have been even more ambitious. It was to

[99] An excellent description is I. Lubimenko, *Les relations commerciales et politiques
de l'Angleterre avec la Russie avant Pierre le Grand*, 1933, Bibliothèque de l'École des
Hautes Études. A summary is given in Karl Stählin, *op. cit.*, I, p. 279, ff. *Ibid.*, p. 228,
thirty years before the English, Genoa, through Paolo Centurione, had tried to use
the Russian routes leading towards Asia, to get round the Turkish geographical
monopoly of the Levantine trade.
[100] Horst Sablonowski, 'Bericht über die soviet-russische Geschichtswissenschaft in
den Jahren 1941–1942' in *Historische Zeitschrift*, 1955, vol. 180, p. 142.
[101] 'Russia and the World Market in the Seventeenth Century. A discussion of the
connection between Prices and Trade Routes' by Arne Öhberg Vadstena, in *Scandinavian Economic History Review*, vol. III, no. 2, 1955, p. 154.
[102] Jacques Accarias de Serionne, *La richesse de la Hollande*, London, 1778, I, p. 31.

capture by the back door Portuguese trade on one side and Syrian on the other. As late as 1582, there was talk in London of an Anglo-Turkish agreement that would have resulted in diverting the spice trade to the Caspian Sea by way of the Black Sea, by concentrating it on Constantinople. This was a grandiose scheme for a monopoly that would in this case have been shared by England, a scheme that could not be realised, however, for more than one reason. Curiously enough, Père Joseph was later, in 1630, to think of using the Russian detour[103] – certainly not by agreement with the Turks, but on the contrary by using this route to bypass their positions and commercial privileges. This scheme like the previous one underlines the usefulness of the Russian isthmus as a route to the Levant, and the relevance to Mediterranean history of the continental interior. Compare the role played by the same routes during the Middle Ages,[104] in some curious Italian schemes, preceding the English venture,[105] and following it in the eighteenth century;[106] when circumstances allowed, they were capable of disturbing shipping through the entire Mediterranean.

And since these routes determined the rhythm of the Russian economy, they linked it with the life of the rest of the world. This is proved by a recent study of price movements in the Russian state in the sixteenth century.[107] Russian prices varied according to the general European fluctuations. Since this connection is established, we may suppose, venturing to the limits of prudence, that the great recession of the seventeenth century must have been partly responsible for the disorganization of Russia, which was during that period troubled by social unrest and exposed to external setbacks, at least after 1617.[108] In spite of these trials and in spite of the raids up and down the Volga by bands of Cossacks attacking the occasional *staritza* (caravan), the great route was constantly stirring with river craft, pack animals and, in winter, sledges.[109]

From the Balkans to Danzig: the Polish isthmus.[110] What we have called the Polish isthmus did not lead, or no longer led, in the sixteenth century, to the Black Sea but to the Balkan Peninsula; it clearly turned to the west

[103] P. J. Charliat, *Trois siècles d'économie maritime française*, 1931, p. 19.

[104] W. Heyd, *Histoire du commerce du Levant au Moyen Age* (French trans.) (1885–1886, reprinted 1936), I, p. 66 ff.

[105] E. Pommier, *art. cit.*, p. 253 ff.

[106] Paul Masson, *Histoire du commerce français dans le Levant au XVIIIe siècle*, 1911, p. 396.

[107] A. G. Mankov, *Le mouvement des prix dans l'État russe au XVIe siècle*, 1957.

[108] B. Porchnev, 'Les rapports politiques de l'Europe occidentale et de l'Europe orientale à l'epoque de la Guerre de Trente Ans', *Congrès International des Sciences Historiques, Rapports*, IV, Stockholm, 1960, p. 142, lays emphasis on the peace of Stolbova, 1617, which consecrated the Swedish success.

[109] *Recueil des Voyages de l'abbé Prévost*, *Voyage des ambassadeurs du Holstein*, trans. by Wicquefort, vol. II, 1639, p. 76–77.

[110] I have not had time to use the valuable information in the article by M. Malowist, 'Die Problematik der sozialwirtschaftlichen Geschichte Polens vom 15. bis zum 17. Jh.', in *La Renaissance et la Réformation en Pologne et en Hongrie, Studia Historica*, 53, Budapest, 1963.

and led from the Baltic to the Danube, and in a roundabout way to Constantinople (perhaps beyond). Does this mean that the Black Sea when it passed from Genoese into Turkish hands, lost its attraction for Poland? Yes and no. While the Turkish occupation of Kaffa in 1475, Kilia in 1484, and Bialograd in 1484,[111] interrupted a previously thriving commerce, we should also take account of the crises of Middle Eastern trade. The insecurity of the southern roads, because of the Tartars, also played a part. So there was a decline in the long-distance overland trade which since the thirteenth century had brought to Poland from the Black Sea, particularly from Kaffa, the produce of the Levant, chiefly spices and pepper.

But the old link survived; towards the middle of the seventeenth century we still find Tavernier talking of wagon transport from Warsaw to Kaffa, a journey requiring fifty days.[112] But these ancient roads and the busy ones which gave Poland direct access by way of Moldavia, to the Balkans and to both Turkish and Levantine merchandise, should not be overestimated. If the country of Poland was, curiously, a kind of free-trade area or rather an area of free passage with a minimum of duties and tolls, it was also a vast expanse, 'twice as big as France', as the report on Poland by Monseigneur de Valence to Charles IX and Catherine de Medici pointed out in 1572.[113] Overland carriage was of course exorbitantly expensive. Between Cracow and Vilna a *last* of grain could easily double in price.[114] Waterways had therefore to be used as much as possible and advantage taken of regular traffic (such as that of salt); otherwise trade had to be confined to light but costly goods. There were many obstacles.

Above all Poland was, like Muscovy, caught up in the dominant Baltic economy behind which lay the demands of the markets of the Low Countries, which bought wheat, rye, and forest products. Amsterdam, from a distance, dictated prices and their fluctuations.[115] In these circumstances, the role of Danzig was both enlarged and limited. 'This side of the Denmark straits' it was the best situated and most prosperous commercial centre. One should buy there, noted a Venetian[116] in 1591, and not in the neighbouring smaller centres of Königsberg or Elbing, 'because of the greater reliability of the persons with whom one deals, who are richer and

[111] The name of the town (the White City) is the same in Rumanian (Cetatea Alba), in old Slavonic (Bialograd) and in Turkish (Aqkerman). It was captured on 7–8th August, 1484 by the Turks, N. Beldiceanu, 'La campagne ottomane de 1484, ses préparatifs militaires et sa chronologie', in *Revue des Études Roumaines*, 1960, p. 67–77.

[112] J. B. Tavernier, *op. cit.*, Persian Travels, p. 115.

[113] Czartoryski Museum, Cracow 2242, f° 199, Report of Jean de Monluc, bishop of Valence.

[114] Roman Rybarski, *Handel i polityka handlowa Polski w XVI Stulecin*, Poznan, 1928, p. 14.

[115] W. Achilles, 'Getreide, Preise und Getreidehandelsbeziehungen europäischer Räume im 16. und 17. Jahrhundert', in *Zeitsch. für Agrargesch. und Agrarsoziologie*, April, 1959.

[116] Letters of Marco Ottobon, quoted above, A.d.S. Venice, Secreta Archivi Propri Polonia 2.

less barbaric than elsewhere'. It was also relatively easy to reach Danzig for settling bills at the St. Dominic's Fair, which was held in the town itself, or the St. Bartholomew's fair at Gniezno, or the St. Michael's Fair at Poznán (Posen). Besides, there were the financial facilities of Nuremberg which were effective in Vienna, Breslau, Cracow, and Danzig itself.

But between, on one hand, the underdeveloped economy of Poland and the neighbouring regions which Danzig exploited in the name of the sacrosanct principle of 'freie Handel und Commercien', and, on the other, Amsterdam, which dominated it, the town played a limited role, that of an intermediary in a system that continually dwarfed it. Its role was to buy grain (and other products but chiefly grain) at the winter fairs that were held at Torun (Thorn) and Lublin. It was there that nobles would sell their harvests (threshed during the winter and transported after the thaw, in April–May). At Danzig they were bonded, the quality was supervised, and all speed was made to sell them, for at best this was last year's grain, and it was impossible to keep it in store any longer. 'Sono bisognosi di danaro', adds Ottobon, they need cash for new purchases, reinvestments, and even advance payments, in cash, on Nuremberg, on which they normally received a commission of 3 per cent. Could this be the reason for the very modest profits the Danzigers received according to the Venetian who spent seven months among them? Moreover, were they not in fact caught between the demands of the sellers of the grain and those of the buyers, the English, Dutch, French, Portuguese, Spanish and later Mediterranean purchasers? They were in effect at the mercy of anyone who could provide them with the indispensable metal currency which alone enabled them to manipulate the still archaic markets of Poland and the neighbouring countries. Marco Ottobon said as much when he defined the two major conditions for the prosperity of the Danzig grain market: firstly the previous year's harvest, since only year-old grain was offered for sale and secondly Portuguese, or rather Iberian demand, which dominated the market not only because of the relatively short voyage involved and the advantage of payment in cash, but also by its volume. Exports to the Mediterranean, except during the crisis years at the end of the century, bore no comparison with the massive shipments to the Iberian peninsula.[117] Finally, if Danzig was content to assume what amounted to the role of broker, and let her navy decline, it was because her small percentage was levied on enormous quantities of grain passing through the town, almost 80,000 tons in 1562.[118] At all events, Poland's economy was trained on this key port. Danzig was the window through which she saw the world, not always to her advantage obviously.

The country's centre of gravity gradually shifted to the north. In 1569 Lithuania and Poland, previously linked only by the shared crown, were

[117] M. Malowist, 'The Economic and Social Development of the Baltic countries from the 15th to the 17th centuries' in *Economic History Review*, 1959, p. 179, n.2.

[118] M. Malowist, 'Les produits des pays de la Baltique dans le commerce international au XVIe siècle' in *Revue du Nord*, April–June, 1960, p. 179.

formally united. In 1590 the capital was transferred from Cracow to Warsaw.[119] The sudden rise to fortune of a city which in the fifteenth century had been a modest ducal market town is a sign of a powerful economic and consequently political upheaval. It was against Sweden and Russia that during the last years of the century Poland was to wage a 'Spanish-style' struggle, lost in advance, which recalls the attempt made by Philip II at the end of his reign to overcome simultaneously both France and England.

Politics and economics led in the same direction, as is proved by the figures for Polish trade revealed by the research of R. Rybarski.[120] The balance of payments was favourable to Poland, and the accumulation of capital profited the nobility, the *szlachta*, which took good care to sell its wheat, rye, livestock (cattle fattened during the winter and known as gentlemen's cattle), and to make a good profit from everything, even from the sales of beer manufactured cheaply for peasant consumption. Everything conspired to make Poland open her doors – and she did open them – to luxury trade, to the foreign merchants who frequented her towns and her fairs and to the itinerant retailers of Scottish origin, the *Szkoci*,[121] who followed the Court from place to place, protected by great noblemen, rather like the *Mascates* in old colonial Brazil, protected by their clients, the big landowners, who were 'most generous and exceedingly splendid',[122] just as in Poland.

Two southern trading connections now call for comment, one nearby and quite active, the other further away and more difficult to control.

Near home, the chief trade was the regular flow of wine from Moldavia and Hungary to a Poland that had virtually no vines left. The arrival of the new wine was an annual occasion for festivity. To guard against cheating by tavernkeepers, all wine shops in Cracow had to display on their boards either a shock of straw or a green branch according to whether the wine they sold was Moldavian or Hungarian.[123] Wine arrived at Lwow from Wallachia, where it was produced by Hungarian colonies settled in the South.[124]

This nearer trading region also provided, notably from Moldavia, meat on the hoof, mostly cattle, for the numerous sheep of the plains were regularly requisitioned for the insatiable appetite of Constantinople. Moldavian cattle were the exchange currency of a country which could thereby acquire, either from the towns of Transylvania, or in Poland, locally-made everyday textiles and the iron tools indispensable to the peasant – ploughshares, coulters, scythes, sickles, nails – as well as string, rope, halters and harnesses.[125] These exchanges took place at the frontier

[119] Domaniewsk i ,'Die Hauptstadt in der Geopolitik Polens' in *Geopolitik*, May, 1939, p. 327.
[120] *Op. cit.*, p. 246, 248.   [121] *Ibid.*, p. 208, 228.
[122] The expression is Anthony Sherley's (1622), X. A. Flores, *op. cit.*, p. 80.
[123] Cracow Archives, Senatus Consulta (1538–1643), 1213, f° 3, 17th December, 1540.
[124] I. N. Angelescu, *Histoire économique des Roumains*, I, 1919, p. 311.
[125] *Ibid.*, p. 300–301.

fairs, especially at Snyatyn, Sipeniti, and Lintesti.[126] But the white Moldavian cattle were also exported to Germany, Venice, and, according to one historian, to Danzig, from where after the fifteenth century they travelled to England. In 1588 the English ambassador at Constantinople concluded an agreement whereby English cloth would be exchanged for 'white cattle', which were to be transported by way of Danzig to England.[127]

These Moldavian cattle would be joined on the road leading north by cattle from Podolia, Ruthenia, Volhynia, Lithuania, and even Poland, all regions which were poorly served by normal communications, which confined their cereal-growing to their own needs and exported cattle. The cattle had the advantage of providing their own transport, in long convoys travelling towards the towns of the West, from Poznán to Leipzig and even Frankfurt-am-Main. According to R. Rybarski,[128] between 40,000 and 60,000 head of cattle left Poland every year. Documents relating to the Turkish-Polish frontier mention, possibly with a little exaggeration, hundreds of thousands of animals; the impression they give is certainly one of enormous numbers of livestock, rather like colonial America, in a somewhat similar setting: wide spaces little touched by man, great swamps, huge forests, endless journeys, and endless convoys of half-wild animals.

To the south, beyond Cracow, Lwow, and Galatz, avoiding Hungary with its frequent wars, a long trade route ran to the Balkans and beyond, to Constantinople. In one direction travelled furs, hides, a little amber, textiles, either cheap Polish fabrics or luxury goods, in which case they were being re-exported, iron, and possibly base-alloy coinage.[129] In exchange, Armenian or Jewish merchants (especially after 1550) and Turkish or Greek merchants (a Greek merchant of Constantinople, Andrea Carcacandella[130] obtained the right in 1534, with the Sultan's support, to trade freely throughout Poland) would send horses, but more often spices and silks. A dispute on St. Thomas's Eve in 1538 at Cracow has left us an account of the dealings of a Polish merchant, Stanislas Zijemijanij, returning from Turkey with forty pieces of camlet, 'petias czambeloti integras', valued at 10 florins each; 34 small pieces, at 4 florins; 102 pounds of mace; 24 pounds of nutmeg.[131] As far as one can tell, the dispute arose between him and his creditor who had apparently advanced him goods and money before his departure from Cracow.

In 1530 and 1531 we find Armenian merchants from Kamieniec bringing saffron and rice of Turkish origin[132] to the fair of Lublin. In 1548 Lublin obtained the privilege of testing various *res aromaticae* imported from Greece and Turkey.[133] The little town then entered a period of prosperity of which its fairs provided the evidence. It was a convenient halt on the

[126] I. N. Angelescu, *op. cit.*, p. 317. [127] *Ibid.*, p. 317.
[128] R. Rybarski, *op. cit.*, p. 62–64.
[129] X. A. Flores, *op. cit.*, p. 81 (1622).
[130] R. Rybarski, *op. cit.*, p. 286.
[131] Cracow Archives, 437, f° 69–70, 1538, Feria Sexta vigilia Thomae Apostoli. See also 437, f° 86, 1539, Feria sexta die S. Antonii.
[132] R. Rybarski, *op. cit.*, p. 153. [133] *Ibid.*, p. 153.

way to Danzig, between Lwow to the south, and Warsaw, and had the advantage of being a town without the rights of a 'staple', a *Sklad,* unlike Lwow, which had its privileges and defended them. Goods could come in and out of Lublin as merchants pleased. At Lwow they had to stop and be put on sale.

To the latter town, where Jewish, Levantine, and Italian merchants concentrated, came the southern trade too. In 1571 an agent of the firm of Hureau, merchants originally from Valenciennes and established at Antwerp, went from Danzig to Lwow and then on to Constantinople.[134] In 1575 an Italian in the service of one of his compatriots established at Cracow was buying malmsey wine and muscatel at Lwow. These precious beverages like the sweet Greek wine that was drunk in the town must have come from the shores of the eastern Mediterranean.[135] And fairly regularly there passed through Lwow what was called the 'Polish caravan', on its way to Constantinople, a collection of merchants and carriers, stopping at the *hans* of the towns, sometimes benefiting from the protection of the authorities, sometimes not, sometimes halting in the open countryside around campfires. But we do not always know what was being transported to the Bosporus in those heavy wagons drawn by oxen[136] or horses.

Along these difficult roads travelled the Bologna merchant, Tommaso Alberti, who has left an all too brief account of his journeys. He reached Constantinople by sea; he left there on 26th November, 1612, passed through Adrianople and crossed the Dobrudja. Since the carters were Turkish, they deserted him on the day of *Beïram,* which they went to celebrate in a nearby village. The interminable Rumanian plains left the traveller with the impression of a 'sea on dry land'. It was easy to lose oneself if the tracks of preceding vehicles were not there to show the way. He arrived with the snow at Jassy. Six days later he was at Lwow, sold his goods there, bought others and in the spring set off back to Constantinople with sixty wagons each drawn by six horses. On 23rd May, 1613, a wagon overturned during the weary crossing of the Balkans. 'Inside it there were thirty sacks of Spanish *reales,* each sack containing 500 *reales,* sables, and other goods.' Everything was recovered and on 1st June the convoy entered Constantinople, which our merchant left again on 21st. He reached Lwow again on 27th July, then went on to Cracow and Prague, Nuremberg and Milan, arriving back in Bologna on 25th October.[137]

In spite of these picturesque details and the obvious deficit of the Polish balance of trade towards the south, the volume of this traffic was not in any way comparable to the lateral trade links between Poland and her

---

[134] Émile Coornaert, *Les Français et le commerce international à Anvers, fin du XVe–XVIe siècle,* I, 1961, p. 187. On this firm see also K. Heeringa, *Bronnen tot Geschiedenis levantschen Handel,* S'Gravenhage, 1917, I, 1, no. 35 and Alberto Tenenti, *Naufrages, corsaires et assurances maritimes à Venise (1592–1609),* 1959, p. 560.

[135] Cracow Archives, 447, f° 22–23, 1575, Feria quinta post festum S. Jacobi.

[136] I. N. Angelescu, *op. cit.,* p. 326 ff.

[137] Tommaso Alberti, *Viaggio a Constantinopoli, 1609–1621,* Bologna, 1889.

neighbour Germany, with Frankfurt-am-Oder, Nuremberg which bought furs, or Silesia, with its tariff disputes caused by the ambition, sometimes thwarted, of the merchants of Wrocław (Breslau).[138] Nor can it be compared to the diagonal trade links leading via Breslau, Leipzig, Nuremberg, Augsburg, and southern Germany towards Italy and Venice and back again. In June, 1564, the Signoria of Venice granted a whole consignment of arms to an agent of the Polish Crown, including 100 corselets, 500 arquebuses, and 30 halberds.[139] From Italy[140] came an endless flow of artists, merchants, and artisans, three of whom set up a brickworks in Cracow in 1533.[141] Then there were luxury or pseudo-luxury articles. There was manufactured[142] at Venice and Naples a kind of loosely woven silk which was given body by soaking it in a preparation. It was known as 'robba per Polonia'! Towards 1565[143] there were between fifteen and twenty 'botteghe d'Italiani' for the whole of Poland, including that of the Soderini, an extremely rich merchant family. But as the century advanced, men and merchandise from Italy became more plentiful – a movement analogous to that which we shall find in southern Germany, as if at the end of the century, the invasion of central and eastern Europe by Italian men and goods was compensating for the northerners' invasion of the Mediterranean. Italian merchants were everywhere in Poland and they were there to stay, at Cracow, Lwow, Warsaw, Lublin and Sandomir. The great period of Italian presence was from the end of the sixteenth to the middle of the seventeenth century.[144] The ledger belonging to one of these merchants, dated 1645,[145] reveals his activities at the Polish fairs, notably Lublin. He lists the moneys handled, the prices, quantities, carriage and a bewildering list of fabrics of every origin sold at Lublin: a taffeta, 'verdegaio a onde', from London, a velvet 'verde piano' from Florence, a 'caravaccia nera' from Naples, a 'raso azuro piano' from Venice, a 'rosa seccha' material and a 'raso nero' from Lucca. The names are not easy to identify and the stated origins are not necessarily genuine. But they are evidence, like the memoirs of Tommaso Alberti, of the Italian presence well after the sixteenth century. The same remarks could be made of neighbouring Transylvania, where merchants, workmen, architects, masons, stone cutters, and soldiers from Italy were all clearly active.[146]

The preceding outline helps to explain the overall situation of Poland.

[138] R. Rybarski, *op. cit.*, p. 197 and 323.
[139] A.d.S. Venice, Senato Terra, 40, 13th June, 1564.
[140] Jan Ptasnik, *Gli Italiani a Cracovia dal XVI secolo al XVIII*, Rome, 1909.
[141] Cracow Archives, 151, 24th December, 1533.
[142] R. Rybarski, *op. cit.*, p. 180.
[143] *Relazione di Polonia* by Paolo Emilio Giovanni (1565) in *Scriptores Rerum Polonicarum, Analecta Romana*, 15, p. 196.
[144] Hermann Kellenbenz, 'Le déclin de Venise et les relations de Venise avec les marchés au Nord des Alpes' in *Decadenza economica veneziana nel secolo XVII*, 1961, (Fondazione Giorgio Cini), p. 156.
[145] Cracow Archives, Ital. 382.
[146] S. Goldenberg, 'Italians and Ragusans in the economic life of Transylvania in the sixteenth century' (in Rumanian) in *Revista de Istorie*, 1963, no. 3.

What it lacked, in the sixteenth century, was not dynamism, of which there is plenty of evidence, but an active and far-reaching monetary economy. If the Polish state was so fundamentally fragile, and the king 'more to represent than to wield power',[147] the reason is to be sought in the social and political order of the 'republic', and the impossibility of centralizing sufficient reserves of money, and therefore of having a modern army. On the Turkish and Tartar borders frontier defence was left to Cossacks, 'bandoleros agregados de todas naciones', groups of bandits from all nations as a Spanish text says,[148] adding: 'a warlike people, always moving and unsettled, cruel, capable of the greatest endurance but also the most rascally in the world'. At any rate, they were a people free to act as they pleased, not a modern army. In January, 1591, the payment of the soldiers stationed on the Muscovy borders raised difficult problems for the Diet meeting at Warsaw. The soldiers meanwhile were living off the land and devastating it, regardless of which side of the frontier it lay,[149] as has also been the case in some of the richest countries of the West.

Economic considerations explain why Polish policy, dictated by trade, was predominantly concerned with the North, as we have noted, and quarrelled with Muscovy as much over Narva and the Baltic as over the undefined frontiers between the two countries. Consequently, Poland pursued a pacific policy towards the South. The Turks and the Poles were in no hurry to come to blows. The allies of the League in 1572 were wasting their time trying to persuade Poland to advance against the Grand Turk. The Turks for their part furthered the election of the Duke of Anjou as king of Poland. In 1590, on the eve of the Turko-Hungarian War, the English intervened to arrange an amicable settlement between Turkey and Poland. The latter could be conciliatory without prompting. In January, 1591, following a complaint by the Grand Turk about exactions made by Polish Cossacks, the king, with the consent of the barons of the Diet, agreed to pay, or rather to give 'cento timpani de zibellini', valued at the considerable sum of 30,000 florins. It is true that in order to pay for it, a tax of a florin per head was immediately levied, for the year 1591, on all the Jews in the kingdom.[150]

So there was peace in the south, which is not sufficient to explain the curious spread through Poland of fashions in costume and sumptuous tents from Turkey, of which one can still see examples in museums. It is possible that commercial exchanges with the South have been under-estimated.

The German isthmus: an overall view. By the German isthmus we mean all of central Europe in the widest sense, between France on the west side and Hungary and Poland on the east; between the North Sea and the Baltic

[147] X. A. Flores, *Le 'peso politico de todo el mundo' d'Anthony Sherley*, p. 79.
[148] *Ibid.*, p. 81.
[149] Marco Ottobon to the Doge of Venice, Torun, 12th January, 1591 and Danzig, 1st February, 1591. A.d.S. Venice, Secreta Archivi Propri, Polonia 2.
[150] *Ibid* , Danzig, 1st February, 1591.

to the north and the Adriatic and Tyrrhenian to the south. The whole forms a remarkable complex of countries, exchanges, and trade routes as a glance at the map taken from F. von Rauers[151] will show.[152]

We can limit this area by drawing two lines, one from Genoa (or even Marseilles) to London, the other from Venice to Danzig; these are somewhat arbitrary lines, of course, but we are looking for a general picture. This great block of central Europe is bounded to the north and south by its seacoasts: the North Sea, the Baltic, and the Mediterranean. To be more accurate, these crucial seas are an extension of it. We should certainly prolong it beyond the northern seas to take in Sweden (which was investigated with some curiosity by Venetian traders at the end of the sixteenth and the beginning of the seventeenth century),[153] Norway, and above all England, which although caught up in the great Atlantic adventure, was nevertheless firmly moored to Europe. One of the most important of England's trading activities was in cloth, which was exported depending on circumstances by way of Emden,[154] Hamburg,[155] Bremen or Antwerp[156] (and on occasion Rouen). So England – and cloth is merely the best example – was for the time being associated to the continent, and to the particular zone we are concerned with here. It was certainly an active zone, the outstanding example perhaps of an economy based on land transport, the equivalent of what the fairs of Champagne must have been in the twelfth and thirteenth centuries – an early and potentially explosive form of north–south contact.

Taken as a whole this area is curiously proportioned: narrow towards the south in northern Italy, it widens out to become an immense continental expanse on the other side of the Alps. A letter sent by the king of Poland, on 25th July, 1522, to Antwerp, where Dantiscus, his ambassador to Charles V, was impatiently waiting for it, did not arrive until 12th September, taking almost fifty days.[157] Or to take another dimension: Marco Ottobon, travelling from Venice to Danzig, in winter it is true (1590), was on the road for thirty-nine days including halts.[158] There was certainly no common measure between the linked plains of Piedmont,

[151] 'Karte der alten Handelsstrassen in Deutschland' in *Petermann's Mitteilungen*, 1906.
[152] For a bibliography, the best guide is Hermann Kellenbenz, *art. cit., supra*, note 144.
[153] A.d.S. Venice, *Cinque Savii*, 142, f° 6 and 6 v°, 28th August, 1607. Alberto Tenenti, *Naufrages, corsaires et assurances maritimes à Venise 1592–1609*, 1959, mentions two Venetian boats sailing to Sweden, 1591 and 1595, p. 23 and 159. Giuseppe Gabrielli, 'Un medico svedese viaggiatore e osservatore in Italia nel secolo XVII' in *Rendiconti della R. Academia dei Lincei*, 7–12th November, 1938.
[154] B. de Mendoza to Philip II, 10th May, 1559, *CODOIN*, XCI, p. 356, 364.
[155] J. A. van Houtte, 'Les avvisi du fonds Urbinat . . .' in *Bulletin de la Commission Royale d'Histoire*, LXXXIX, p. 388, 24th September, 1569.
[156] Feria to Philip II, 10th May, 1559, *CODOIN* LXXXVII, p. 184; 90,000 pieces of English cloth were brought to Antwerp by the *flota de paños*.
[157] Johannes Dantiscus to King Sigismund, Antwerp, 18th September, 1522, Czartoryski Museum, 274, no. 16.
[158] See note 76.

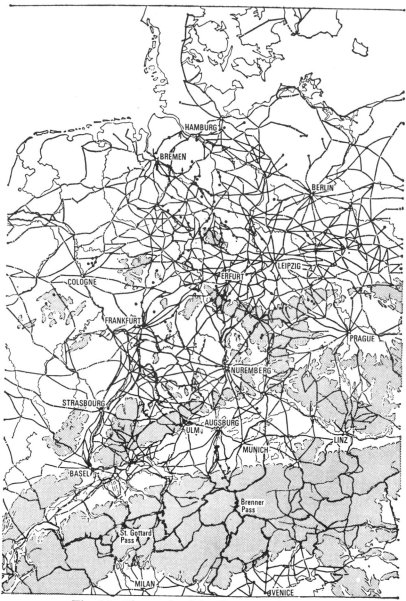

Fig. 15: *The roads of the German isthmus*

This map, taken from F. von Rauers, and reproduced here on too small a scale, nevertheless very clearly shows the density of the road network in Germany in the sixteenth century and the major trans-Alpine routes. A similarly complicated network must be imagined to the west of the map, in France; it has here been reduced to a minimum. The black spots represent the villages of the transporters and carriers. They are much in evidence on the Alpine routes and indicate the importance of the major roads. This map also shows the Prague–Linz connection which is not mentioned in the text: for an excellent documentation see the article by Josef Janaček, 'Die Handelsbeziehungen zwischen Prag und Linz im 16. Jahrh.' in *Historisches Jahrbuch der Stadt Linz*, 1960.

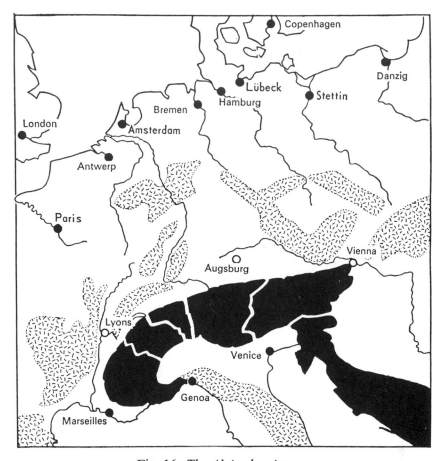

Fig. 16: *The Alpine barrier*

This deliberately schematic map shows the narrow area of northern Italy compared with the lands beyond the Alps. Northern Italy is ringed around with mountains to the west, north, and east (the Dinaric Alps). The great Alpine routes (Mont-Cenis, Simplon, St. Gotthard, Brenner, Tarvis, and a few others) break through the barrier. The map indicates major rivers only below the point at which they become generally navigable.

Lombardy, and Venezia, with easy access to their seaports, and the vast continental countries north of the Alps. In the South the roads converge; in the North they fan out over a wide area. The Alps thus divide central Europe 'by a long and wide barrier'[159] and the two fragments on either side are both geographically and historically of very unequal importance.

The 'German isthmus' then consists in succession of Italy, particularly

[159] Jean-François Bergier, *Les foires de Genève et l'économie internationale de la Renaissance*, 1963, p. 17.

northern Italy, the Alps, then the immense plains and plateaux of central Europe, between the Meuse or the Rhine on one side, and the Oder and the Vistula on the other. Italy needs no introduction. This book will have much occasion to come back to her cities and landscapes so decisive in Mediterranean history. But we should devote some space here to the Alps, the magic mountains where nothing ever seems impossible. Their mountain walls presented an obstacle to Central Europe: they were very soon breached. Travelling was difficult: spontaneous solutions appeared. The Alpine societies and villages seem to have existed for the express purpose of organizing the crossing of the mountains and furthering the progress of this profitable traffic in both directions, south and north.

The Alps. This is because the Alps are contained within a three-dimensional geometry relating together societies and economies from different levels: hamlets and villages at the upper limit of arable land; compact villages in the deep valleys; small towns on the banks of the rivers, with perhaps a firm of 'Lombards' and a few artisans' workshops; and finally, on the outer edges, near the plains and waterways, where traffic begins to move quickly again, are to be found the cities of the *piedmont*: Geneva, Basel, and Zurich; Salzburg, Villach, and Klagenfurt; Susa, Vercelli, Asti, Como, Bergamo, Brescia, and Verona; often towns that held fairs: (Zurzach, Hall, Linz, Bolzano), frequently the centres of transport firms (Chur, Chiavenna, Plurs), and always 'halfway' towns between south and north, where the mountain dweller would find necessary, everyday goods, 'ordinary fabrics for clothing, metal for tools and above all salt, which plays an essential role in stock farming'.[160]

So there was a flow of traffic proper to the Alpine regions along which men, beasts, flocks, and goods daily moved. A different kind of traffic was superimposed onto these everyday movements, using the same men and the same means of transport, and penetrating the whole network through and through. These crossings would have been impossible without the waggoners' and carriers' villages, each jealously guarding the profits it derived from the trade route. Primolano in the Brenta valley, in the Vicenza Alps, was in 1598 a *viletta* numbering barely fifty hearths, whose 'inhabitants almost all live off the wages they get by transporting goods in their carts'.[161] Hundreds of other villages were in the same situation. Convention ruled that all the villages along a route, either when it was being set up or when it was already established, should cooperate, dividing the labour among them, settling the stages, undertaking to ensure the safe passage of travellers and goods and sometimes, on payment of a supplementary sum, providing them with continuous transport, day and night. The Septimer route[162] is a good example, and far from the only one.

---

[160] J.-F. Bergier, *op. cit.*, p. 31.

[161] Marciana 5838, C II, 8. f° 37. Report by Francesco Caldogno 1598.

[162] Aloys Schulte, *Geschichte des mittelalterlichen Handels und Verkehrs zwischen Westdeutschland und Italien*, I, 1900, p. 37 ff.

Thereafter, these coordinated movements seem to have run very smoothly. Even winter did not interrupt them: it offered the relative ease of
sledges.[163] On 16th December, 1537, a transporter-entrepreneur of Vercelli
took charge of 132 bales of merchandise at Geneva, promising to deliver
42 at Ivrea on the following 4th of January, 'saulve le temps'. Marco Dandolo, who was travelling to France to represent the Signoria of Venice,
crossed the Mont-Cenis in a litter in December 1540.[164] True, he retained
an unpleasant memory of it, as did Girolamo Lippomano, who crossed it
in April, 1577: 'The horses and mules plunged up to their bellies in snow
and were only able to extract themselves with great difficulty', but, he
adds, 'a countless throng of travellers passed through there, on their way
to Italy, France, England, and many also bound for Spain'. The village
of Novalesa, which had no crops or vines, provided unofficial guides who
were never short of work. A strange land was this miserable mountainous
Savoy, he thought, 'which sees the sun only three months of the year,
gets a yield from its wheatfields of only two to one', and that as far as
Lanslebourg, where downhill trips were made by sledge, or even as far
as St. Jean de Maurienne.[165]

From these familiar accounts, and so many others and from Aloys
Schulte's patiently collected evidence about the Middle Ages,[166] what
conclusions should we draw? That the twenty-one Alpine passes were all
usable – given favourable circumstances. Scores of successes, of semi-
successes, attempts, and failures are recorded: there is a whole comparative
history and an immense range of archives to explore. Naturally the towns
and the merchants played their part. It was the merchants of Milan, who,
in the thirteenth century, constructed the then revolutionary St. Gotthard
route; they were later, in order to reach the upper Rhine valley, to use the
Splügen, Maloja, and Septimer passes, which political history was to make
famous in the seventeenth century at the time of the occupation of the
Valtellina. These routes, too close together for comfort, competed with or
replaced each other according to political and financial circumstances
and even as a result of route disturbances far from the Alps. When in
1464,[167] Lyons obtained royal authorization to receive pepper and spices
directly, Aiguesmortes and the Rhône route lost their privileged position
to the Mont Genèvre, the Mont-Cenis, and the Little and Great St.
Bernard passes. Any quarrel, large or small, repays close study. In 1603
when Venice had concluded a political alliance with the Grisons, the route
from Morbegno to Chiavenna was completed, and it was to claim, to the

[163] J.-F. Bergier, *op. cit.*, p. 131.
[164] Marco Dandolo to the Doge, Lyons, 12th December, 1540; B. N. Ital. 1715 fº 11 copy.
[165] 'Voyage de Jérome Lippomano' in Collection of unpublished documents on the history of France, *Relations des ambassadeurs vénitiens*, compiled by N. Tommaseo, 1838, vol. II, p. 274–275.
[166] See above, note 162.
[167] Marc Brésard, *Les foires de Lyon aux XVe et XVIe siècles*, 1914, p. 44 and 168.

advantage of Bergamo, part of the trade going towards Milan; a small detail that again reveals Venice's vigilance over Alpine traffic.[168]

These changes did not happen overnight. Geography distributed both obstacles and permanent advantages that were difficult to bypass. There was, for example, the need to connect with the waterways, lakes, and rivers, the Isère, the Lac du Bourget, Lake Geneva, Lake Constance, the Rhône, the Rhine, the Inn, or to the south, the Italian lakes which had their role to play, and particularly a river like the Adige, where the chains put in place by successive administrations could not prevent floating logs or transport in small boats. These were permanent advantages, but they operated against each other. Statistics for transport from Antwerp to Italy show the clear superiority in 1534–1545[169] of the St. Gotthard pass, which benefited from its central situation; it was a gateway either to Genoa or Venice. The Brenner in the east was the other great crossing point. It was the lowest of all the Alpine passes (1374 metres) and had the advantage of using two divergent waterways, the Inn and the Adige, and of leading to Venice. It was also a route accessible to the heavy German wagons – *carretoni* – as they were known south of the Alps – which would travel down after the grape harvest for the new wine from Venezia, and even from Istria, an enormous trading operation repeated every year unless Venice forbade it (as in 1597[170]) which was, however, rarely. Usually she permitted it, preferring for her own consumption the full-bodied wines of the Marches or the islands. With the aid of the wine trade, the Brenner was from the beginning of the sixteenth century, and even more at the end, one of the most active Alpine routes, but its preeminence was not unchallenged. From 1530 the Archbishop of Salzburg[171] had transformed the Tauern route, previously merely a *Saumweg*, or mule-track, into a passable road for wheeled traffic; the Provincial States of the Tyrol, who defended the Brenner, and for good reason, opposed this competition, trying, in vain as it happened, to draw Ferdinand, King of the Romans, into outright opposition. This example is sufficient to indicate the flexibility of the Alpine routes: man constructed them, maintained them and if the need arose, he could divert them.

The third character: the many faces of Germany. Beyond the Alps lay green Europe, with its forests, its wide and busy waterways, and its carriage roads; so cold in winter! In 1491 there was so much snow that the merchants of Nuremberg could travel from their hometown to Geneva by sledge.[172]

One can look at Germany from south to north along the lines of longi-

[168] Hermann Kellenbenz, *art. cit.*, p. 124–125.

[169] Wilfrid Brulez, 'L'exportation des Pays-Bas vers l'Italie par voie de terre, au milieu du XVIe siècle', in *Annales E.S.C.*, 1959, p. 469–70.

[170] A.d.S. Venice, *Cinque Savii*, 21, f° 45, 25th October, 1597.

[171] Otto Stolz, 'Zur Entwicklungsgeschichte des Zollwesens innerhalb des alten Deutschen Reiches' in *Viertelj. für Sozial-und Wirtschaftsgeschichte*, 1954, p. 18, note 40.

[172] J.-F. Bergier, *op. cit.*, p. 131.

tude, or from east to west along the latitudes. These are different ways of approaching it, but it is a land of many faces.

The longitudinal view looking northward from Italy brings into prominence south Germany, which for our purposes stretches as far as Cologne, Frankfurt, and Nuremberg. Thoroughly Italianized, a customer for the wines of the southern Alps, it had for centuries been in contact with the cities of the Peninsula, Genoa, Milan, Florence, Venice above all, but also Rome, Naples, and Aquila, the saffron town, as well as all the towns along the road. This Germany culminated towards the southeast in the *Fontego dei Todeschi*,[173] a sort of miniature Germany, with both controls and privileges, an enormous building on the Grand Canal, facing the Square and Bridge of the Rialto, which was to be rebuilt in great magnificence after the fire of 1505. German merchants were allotted their own offices[174] and could store their goods there. Sometimes the *Fontego* would be piled to the roof with fustians (the revolutionary fabrics made with linen warp and cotton woof). In the *Fontego* too were to be found copper, tin, silver, and ironware. Spices, pepper, drugs, cotton, the *Südfrüchte*, were redispatched to the North.[175]

Venice was also full of German travellers, famous and not so famous: pilgrims about to leave for the Holy Land, merchants learning the trade like Jacob Fugger, artists like Albrecht Dürer, students, or the servants of students on their way to the University of Padua, one of whom, Bernard Müller of Dillingen, with his arquebus on his back, the Venetian police thought it prudent to arrest.[176] There were soldiers too, although after the Treaty of Cateau-Cambrésis in 1559, the great days were over (on this side of the Alps) for the Swiss mercenaries and the lansquenets of Würtemberg. Often they were humbler folk: baker's men, servants, artisans in the wool industry, waiters at inns and taverns, who competed in the profession with natives of Florence or Ferrara.[177] Venice naturally had her German inns, the *White Lion* and the *Black Eagle*,[178] as did other Italian towns: there was *Il Falcone* at Ferrara in 1583, or the *Tre Rei* at Milan.[179] Southern Germany grew up and matured in the shadow of the greatness of northern

[173] *Fontego* is a Venetian form of *Fondaco*, as is *Todeschi* for *Tedeschi*. The classic book by Henry Simonsfeld, *Der Fondaco dei Tedeschi und die deutsch-venetianischen Handelsbeziehungen*, Stuttgart, 1887, reflects the mediocrity of the documents that have survived.

[174] A small detail: on 30th November, 1498, '*prudentes mercatores Henricus Focher et fratres*', requested that the chambers they had occupied '*jam diu*' and which they had gone to great expense to furnish, be attributed to them permanently; since their request had the blessing of the Sovereign Pontiff and the King of the Romans, they received satisfaction. They were of course the Fugger family. A.d.S. Venice, Notario di Collegio, 14–1.

[175] Not only from Venice and the Veneto but from the whole of northern Italy. Fritz Popelka, 'Südfrüchte vom Gardasee nach Graz' in *Blätter fur Heimatkunde*, 1951.

[176] A.d.S. Venice, Senato Terra, 88, 16th August, 1583. The document mentions two German inns: *Il Falcone* at Ferrara; *I Tre Rei* at Milan.

[177] Henry Simonsfeld, *op. cit.*, II, p. 263 ff. Bandello, *op. cit.*, VII, p. 169.

[178] R. Röhricht, *Deutsche Pilgerreisen nach dem Heiligen Land*, Berlin, 1880, p. 11.

[179] See above note 176.

Italy, but also not uncommonly derived advantage from its limitations. Within the partnership, Germany was entrusted with secondary tasks: working cotton, the ersatz textile of the fourteenth century, cheap fabrics, the working of iron, copper, and leather. Without its constant support, neither the trade of Genoa and Venice, nor the economic activity of Milan would have been conceivable. 'Germans and Venetians,' wrote Girolamo Priuli in 1509, 'we are all one, because of our ancient trading partnership.'[180] 'Germans and *Italians*' would have been more accurate.

This shared life lies behind the extraordinary spread of Italian civilization towards the north, recognizable today simply from the façades of the houses.[181] It also resulted in an obvious exploitation of the North by the South. But there were times when south Germany stood to gain from crises in Italy. It was by Protestants, fleeing from Italy, that the brocade and silk velvet industry was brought north to Nuremberg.[182] In the fourteenth century bankruptcies in Florence had brought some profit to German merchants. German civilization too advanced, spread southwards and very quickly invaded the upper Adige valley, extending beyond Trent, the episcopal seat, as the Venetian who was received there by the bishop in 1492 could not fail to observe. The three tables were 'quadre, more germanico'; the meal began with salad, according to German custom, meats and fish were offered on the same dish, with whole-meal wheaten bread in the Bavarian style.[183]

Let us look at Germany along the latitude lines now, starting from the Rhine. The further east one goes, the more Germany appears to be a new country, still undeveloped. In the fifteenth century and during the first decades of the sixteenth, the swift rise of the mining industry created a string of new but short-lived towns, springing up quickly but soon falling into decline in the face of competition from American silver, after 1530, or rather 1550, unless the mid-century recession alone was responsible. During the subsequent recovery which was to last until the end of the century and beyond, Germany, and more generally Central Europe, was to see an industrial revival on all fronts, of which the linen cloth industry of Bohemia, Saxony, and Silesia was the most important item but not the only one. So it is not true that Germany (any more than her neighbours) went into decline in the years after Luther's death in 1546.[184] The Peace of Augsburg (1555), which was long-lasting, brought substantial benefits. And even very far to the east, the health and vigour of the towns tell their own story. Pierre Lescalopier in 1574 admired the German towns of

---

[180] Quoted in H. Kretschmayr, *Geschichte Venedigs*, 1905–1920, II, p. 467.

[181] E. Hering, *Die Fugger*, 1939, p. 204–205. Cf. in Augsburg the Venetian architecture along the banks of the Lech; and the Genoese-style house fronts along the Wertach.

[182] Josef Kulischer, *Allgemeine Wirtschaftsgeschichte des Mittelalters und der Neuzeit*, 1958, II, p. 251.

[183] Marciana, Ital. VII, 7679, f° 30, 1492.

[184] Or even decadence as John U. Nef has called it, 'Silver Production in Central Europe', in the *Journal of Political Economy*, 49, 1951.

Transylvania and the first one he came to, Brasov, 'which the Saxons call Coronestat', gave him the illusion of 'arriving at Mantua so fair is the town, the walls of the houses shining with paint'.[185]

These two views have shown us two Germanies. There is yet another bordering the Low Countries on the shores of the North Sea, at Emden, Bremen, and Hamburg. These towns derived profit from the Atlantic trade which reached them, from their proximity to the Low Countries (first to Antwerp and then to Amsterdam), from their high economic voltage and also from the discord that was to result from it. Hamburg, the most vigorous of them, was just embarking on her long career which even the Thirty Years War did not interrupt.[186] Her merchants profited by the revolt of the Netherlands, being neutral or, as a correspondent of President Viglius wrote, 'being ambidextrous, they make therefore great gain and profit'.[187] Moreover, the Low Countries and that part of Germany which bordered the North Sea, were on the verge of winning a great prize that was to stir Germany to the depths. On the shores of the Baltic, an ancient order, colonial in more ways than one, maintained its handsome façade.

These successive images are brought together in the already dated interpretation (1908) proposed by the historian Johannes Müller.[188] His view was that the centre of the different Germanies, formerly at Cologne on the Rhine, moved eastward to Nuremberg, a city lying at the heart of central Germany, halfway between East and West, halfway between the Italianized South and the North already touched by the breath of the modern world and the Atlantic. Nuremberg: not Augsburg, the town of the Fuggers. This presents something of a temptation to the historian. In his recent book, Jean-François Bergier also falls into this trap. 'Southern Germany,' he writes, 'at the dawn of modern times, became the true centre of gravity of the western world, ahead of northern Italy, the Low Countries, Lyons or even Marseilles in France, ahead even of Imperial Vienna.'[189] This is clearly an exaggeration. But we should beware of seeing at the beginning of modern times only the noisy successes and innovations of commercial capitalism at Lisbon, Seville, and Antwerp, on the privileged shores of the sea. The upsurge of the sixteenth century penetrated Europe to its continental depths.

From Genoa to Antwerp, and from Venice to Hamburg: the conditions of circulation. As we have seen, Mediterranean life was caught up and pro-

---

[185] *Voyage fait par moy Pierre Lescalopier* . . ., Bibliothèque de la Faculté de Médecine, Montpellier, MS, H.385, f° 49 v°, see Ch. I, note 8. The passages omitted from Edmond Le Cleray's edition have been carefully reproduced by Paul I. Cernovodeanu, in *Studii si materiale de Istorie Medie*, IV, Bucharest, 1960.
[186] Günther Franz, *Der Dreissigjährige Kreig und das deutsche Volk*, Jena, 1940, p. 16.
[187] Dr. Gehr van Oestendorp to President Viglius, Bremen, 30th January, 1574, published by Richard Häpke, *op. cit.*, II, p. 308–309.
[188] Johannes Müller, 'Der Umfang und die Hauptrouten des nürnbergischen Handelsgebietes im Mittelalter' in *Viertalj. für Sozial und Wirtschaftsgeschichte*, 6, 1908, p.1–38.
[189] J.-F. Bergier, *op. cit.*, p. 155.

longed northwards by an overland traffic exceptional for the period. That is not to say that the zone north of the Alps between Lyons and Vienna was a scene of bustling activity and modernity, but certainly it was animated by a flow of energy more marked perhaps than in France, particularly if we include Lyons, the city serving the Alps, and the Rhône valley in the central rather than the French part of Europe. Clearly it was a zone with many modern features. Numerous firms grew up, with their roots in the Italian towns, the Low Countries, and the Iberian peninsula. The big family firms, inclined to be inward-looking and often of monstrous size (Fugger, Hochstetter, Welser, Affaitati) gave way to firms that were smaller, but more numerous, and above all, more active than the general histories of the period would suggest: the della Faille in the Netherlands, on whom a book has recently appeared,[190] the Torrigiani, Bartolomeo Viatis (and his associate Fürst) at Nuremberg and Breslau, the Pestalozzi, Bartolomeo Castello at Vienna, the Montelupi at Cracow,[191] to name only a few Italian firms in foreign countries towards the end of the century. Many more names could be added to the list.[192]

A new practice appeared. Firms would work on a commission basis, relying on other merchants who agreed to represent them and act as their agents. It reduced operating costs. 'The enormous increase in the number of smaller-scale merchants', one historian has said,[193] 'constitutes the new and important element in the commercial development of the sixteenth century.' This trend was becoming widespread throughout Central Europe. At the same time, some firms began to specialize in transport, which became a separate activity. We have records of big transport firms at Hamburg and Antwerp: Lederer,[194] Cleinhaus,[195] Annoni,[196] and many others, often of Alpine origin. At Lyons[197] and Venice too, similar developments occurred. An undated Venetian document of the seventeenth century says, 'The merchandise which is transported from Venice to Lombardy[198]

[190] Wilfrid Brulez, *De Firma della Faille en de internationale Handel van vlaamse Firma's in de 16e Eeuw*, 1959.

[191] Noted in the correspondence of Marco Ottobon, 1590–1591, for reference see above (note 76). Bartolomeo Viatis parted from his business associate in 1591. Bartolomeo Castello 'mercante conosciutissimo qui (at Vienna) et de molto negocio in Ongaria'.

[192] Hermann Kellenbenz, *art. cit.*, p. 131 ff.

[193] Wilfrid Brulez, *De Firma della Faille*, p. 53–55, 106–108, 363–365, and in the excellent summary in French at the end of the book, p. 580–581.

[194] Some kerseys sent by the Ragusan firm of Menze to Ragusa 'per via d'Amburgo in condotta di Lederi', Ragusa Archives, Diversa de Foris XV, f° 119, v° 120, 24th June, 1598.

[195] On the Cleinhaus and Lederer firms, cf. Wilfrid Brulez, *op. cit.*, p. 577, and index references.

[196] Wilfrid Brulez, *op. cit.*, p. 467.

[197] R. Gascon, *op. cit.*, (unpublished) quotes 'Letters of carriage' granted to merchants of Lyons.

[198] Museo Correr, Cicogna, 1999, Aringhe varie (undated). The Mantua route, according to this statement, was used *al tempo de la peste* which might mean the plague of 1629–1630 or that of 1576. The alternative does not help to date the document.

and Germany is entrusted to the transporters [*conduttori*] who undertake
on payment of an agreed sum to deliver it to the stated destination in good
condition and within a specified period agreed by both parties.' These
conduttori themselves relied on the services of the *spazzadori* who conveyed the loads by boat, wagon, or pack animal from inn to inn, the inn-
keeper providing them with the necessary animals and vehicles.[199] A final
detail: these *conduttori*, and no doubt the *spazzadori* too were not Venetians, but 'foreigners' from the Alps and perhaps the North. In any case
there was certainly a division of labour, rationalization, and specialization.
Similarly it was in the sixteenth century that the letter post was organized,
and it was not confined to the great and celebrated Tassis family, who
had the monopoly of delivering letters in the Habsburg domains.[200] This
led to increased trading activity, more accessible to merchants who might
be setting up in business with few liquid assets.[201] Similarly, still in this
central area, there grew up a textile industry on capitalist lines and connected to distant markets, which was to be of decisive importance;[202]
such was the linen industry of Saxony,[203] Silesia, and Bohemia which has
already been mentioned.[204] Taking advantage of the wars in the Low
Countries, industries producing silk fabrics and semi-luxury articles[205]
made great advances in Germany, as in the Swiss cantons.

Long-distance trade was inevitably confined to goods whose value was
sufficient to defray the cost of transport: copper, silver, hardware, pepper,
spices, cotton from the Levant (of which Venice continued to be the chief
importer, re-exporting it to the north), silk, the *Südfrüchte*, and finally
and above all, fabrics, which were always of primary importance. In one
direction traffic was in English kerseys ('one of the most important foundations of trade in the world', as a Venetian document was already saying in
1513)[206] linen, serges (from Hondschoote then from Leyden), grosgrain
(from Lille), 'mixed' fabrics (fustians, burats, bombazines) and linens

[199] *Ibid.*, goods bound for Lombardy went by boat as far as Este; for Germany, they
went by boat to Porto Gruaro.
[200] Josef Kulischer, *op. cit.*, II, p. 377.
[201] Wilfrid Brulez, 'L'exportation des Pays-Bays vers l'Italie par voie de terre au
milieu du XVIe siècle' in *Annales E.S.C.*, (1959), p. 465.
[202] Arnost Klima, 'Zur Frage des Übergangs vom Feudalismus zum Kapitalismus
in der Industrieproduktion in Mitteleuropa (vom 16. bis. 18. Jahrh.)', in *Probleme der
Ökonomie und Politik in den Beziehungen zwischen Ost- und Westeuropa* vom 17
Jahrhundert bis zur Gegenwart, hgg. von Karl Obermann, Berlin, 1960. The transition
to modern times was accomplished through the textile rather than the mining industries p. 106–107.
[203] G. Aubin and Arno Kunze, *Leinenerzeugung und Leinenabsatz im östlichen
Mitteldeutschland zur Zeit der Zunftkäufe. Ein Beitrag zur Kolonisation des deutschen
Ostens*, Stuttgart, 1940. G. Heitz, *Ländliche Leinenproduktion in Sachsen, 1470–1555*.
Berlin, 1961.
[204] Arnost Klima, *art. cit.*, note 202 above, and G. Aubin, 'Aus der Entstehungs-
geschichte der nordböhmischen Textilindustrie' in *Deutsches Archiv für Landes-und
Volksforschung*, 1937, p. 353–357.
[205] Hermann Kellenbenz, *art. cit.*, p. 114.
[206] A.d.S. Venice, Senato Mar, 18, f° 35, 8th July, 1513.

from the German and Swiss towns. In the other direction, from
Italy, came velvets, taffetas, high-quality woollen cloth, silken cloth
woven with threads of silver or gold, and luxury fabrics. The Antwerp
firm della Faille was to set up a branch at Venice and another at Verona,
which bought raw silk and spun it on the spot with such care that the quality
of their products was unequalled.[207] The firm's accounts certainly do not
give the impression of a falling-off in trade, quite the reverse.

The movement of goods led to movements of money, from north to
south and south to north.[208] The great event of 1585, the promotion of
Frankfurt-am-Main, previously known for its trade fairs, to the rank
of currency-exchange fair, was well-timed. This event was followed by
others, the founding of the Bank of Amsterdam in 1609 (to be of world
importance), the Bank of Hamburg in 1619, and the Bank of Nuremberg
in 1621.[209] By then these lines of communications were beyond the pioneer
stage and routes, means of transport, and stopping places were all but
settled.

Emigration and balance of trade. Can any positive conclusions be drawn
from all these transactions, whether political or not, and from these circumstances at which we can only guess? We can, I think, offer two general
observations: first, there was a definite balance of trade in favour of the
South. Second, there was a tremendous influx of Italian merchants to all
parts of Germany, probably dating from about 1558;[210] this compensating
flow does not seem to have dried up before the German disasters of the
Thirty Years War.

A balance of trade unfavourable to the North was wholly to be expected. The towns, merchants, and artisans of the North were as if under
apprenticeship, looking for guidance to the towns of the South. Southern
businessmen were for a long time able to exploit local ignorance and backwardness. What the Nuremberg merchant was to Central Europe, holding
it in the palm of his hand, the Milanese or Venetian merchant was to
Nuremberg itself and to other German towns. All apprenticeships have
to be paid for, usually over a long period. Southern goods, more plentiful,
and above all, more expensive per unit were bound to outweigh products
imported from the North. Of this imbalance and of the cash payments
resulting from it we have tangible evidence. In Venice and Florence there
were always bills of exchange (on northern countries) available for buyers,
as the Genoese well knew, often using this method in order to pay in the
North sums of money laid down in their *asientos* with the king of Spain.
This is evidence of a trading balance that undoubtedly favoured Italy, or

[207] Wilfrid Brulez, *op. cit.*, p. 579.
[208] G. Aubin, 'Bartolomäus Viatis. Ein nürnberger Grosskaufmann vor dem
Dreissig-jähren Kriege' in *Viertelj. für Sozial und Wirtschaftsgeschichte*, 1940, p. 145 ff.
[209] R. Fuchs, *Der Bancho publico zu Nürnberg*, Berlin, 1955, 86 p. (*Nürnb. Abh. zu
den Wirtschafts- und Sozialwissenschaften*, Heft. 6). The date 1621 is given in J. Savary
des Brulons, *Dictionnaire universel de commerce*, V, p. 373.
[210] See note 218.

at any rate these two key cities. Even more tangible proof is provided by the repeated complaints of German towns in the seventeenth century. Towards 1620 (i.e., quite late) the merchants of Augsburg were reproached for sending 'great sums of good money to Italy'.[211] A similar charge was later levelled at the Frankfurt merchants.[212] And there are other examples.[213] When the Dutch reached Venice, their balance was still, in 1607, in deficit, according to the *Cinque Savii.*[214]

So Germany, and the North in general, contributed to Italian prosperity, offering it support and advantages and admitting it to open association with its own economic activity. The latter was still thriving during the first decades of the seventeenth century. Augsburg reached the peak of its active prosperity in 1618,[215] Nuremberg witnessed the rise of its banking business until 1628.[216] And Venice continued to act as a clearing house for compensatory payments, as an Italian merchant (from Cremona) shortly put it, 'auf Frankfurt gezogen und . . . gen Venedig remittiert', drawn on Frankfurt and paid to Venice.[217]

And secondly there was the immense operation of the invasion of German towns by Italian merchants, Venetians in the forefront after 1558.[218] Until then, the German merchants of the *Fondaco* had had the monopoly, north of the Alps, of purchases destined for Venice, except for horses, arms, and victuals.[219] During the second half of the sixteenth century, the old ruling fell into disregard, and Venetian merchants were increasingly to be found in German marketplaces. These were more likely to be Venetians from the mainland than from Venice itself, a new generation of traders. This was the case of Bartolomeo Viatis, from Bergamo, who went to live in Nuremberg at the age of twelve, in 1550, and fought his way to the top place, alongside the Kochs.[220] He dealt on a large scale in linens, products from the Levant, ostrich feathers and chamois hides; he owned several offices at the *Fondego dei Todeschi* and, on the occasion of Marco Ottobon's mission to Danzig, he disregarded his own interests and put his credit, which was great, at the disposal of the Signoria of Venice. When he died in 1644, rich in years and descendants, he left a fortune valued at over a million florins. Not all Italian merchants achieved this spectacular success, but their assets often represented large sums, whether in Cologne (in spite of many bankruptcies) or Nuremberg, Prague[221] or Augsburg, and the two towns which were on the rise, Frankfurt and Leipzig.

[211] Hermann Kellenbenz, *art. cit.*, p. 119.
[212] *Ibid.*   [213] *Ibid.*
[214] A.d.S. Venice, *Cinque Savii*, Risposte, 1602–1606, f°s 189 v° – 195, 1st January, (1607).
[215] Hermann Kellenbenz, *art. cit.*, p. 135.   [216] *Ibid.*, p. 147.
[217] *Ibid.*, p. 152; the Italians were the principal exchange dealers at Nuremberg in 1625, p. 149.
[218] *Ibid.*, p. 128.   [219] *Ibid.*, p. 128, p. 143 ff.   [220] *Ibid.*, p. 144.
[221] Josef Janacek, *History of Commerce in Prague before the battle of the White Mountain* (in Czechoslovakian), Prague, 1955.

Clearly these immigrant merchants helped their towns to adapt to a Germany which in the sevententh century was gradually finding 'its new cardinal points', based roughly on the new Frankfurt–Leipzig line, midway between north and south, and the Hamburg–Venice axis. The battle waged by Italian merchants against local merchants, and even more against Dutch dealers – the Calvinists against whom the Leipzig riots of May, 1593, were directed[222] – was to last a long time. In Frankfurt in 1585 when the exchange fairs were set up, out of eighty-two firms who applied for this change in the town's status, twenty-two were Italian.[223] This was a phenomenon of the end of the century and of the beginning of the next. A Dutch report of 1626, to the States General of Holland, pointed out that the Venetians provided, not only their neighbours, 'but even Germany, at far less cost than the Dutch, with all the goods of the Levant'.[224] At Cologne, Frankfurt, Nuremberg, and Leipzig, the presence of the Italian merchants which was already more noticeable after 1580, was maintained well after 1600. In 1633 when the Swedes took Nuremberg, the Venetians ran up the banner of St. Mark to protect their shops, proving at any rate that they were still there.[225] And in 1604, Venice, which had preserved almost intact the monopoly of supplying the German fustian industry with cotton, still required five times as much transport for the journey to Germany as for the return trip.

So Italy, and through her the Mediterranean, kept the door open for a long time, on the wide spaces of northern Europe, and remained firmly entrenched at Antwerp, a financial centre that maintained its role uninterrupted, in spite of (or possibly because of) the festering war of the Netherlands. In 1603 the mission of B. C. Scaramelli[226] restored good relations with England. Soon, in 1610,[227] friendly relations were established between Venice and Amsterdam. In 1616 the proconsuls and senators of Hamburg asked Venice to send a consul to the city.[228] As early as 1599, Sebastian Koch, the Hamburg consul at Genoa, offered to represent at the same time the interests of the Danziger captains.[229] In short, although an overall description can sometimes be deceptive, it seems probable that this central trade area kept doors open on both sides, well after the beginning of the seventeenth century.

The French isthmus, from Rouen to Marseilles. The French isthmus can be

[222] Ernst Kroker, *Handelsgeschichte der Stadt Leipzig*, 1926, p. 113, 19–20th May, 1593.
[223] A. Dietz, *Frankfurter Handelsgeschichte*, vol. III, 1921, p. 216.
[224] Haga to the States General in Heeringa, *Bronnen tot Geschiedenis levantschen Handel*, I, 1, no. 251, p. 532–533.
[225] B. Benedetti, *Intorno alle relazioni commerciali della Repubblica di Venezia et di Norimberga*, Venice, 1864.
[226] A.d.S. Venice, Dispacci, Inghilterra, 2.
[227] P. J. Blok, *Relazioni veneziane*, 1909; A.d.S. Venice, *Cinque Savii*, 3, f° 35, 7th February, 1615, Edigio Overz is recognized as consul of the Netherlands.
[228] *Ibid.*, 144, f° 74, 30th April, 1616.
[229] Genoa, 28th February, 1599, Gdansk Archives, 300–353, 147.

visualized as based on the roads leading from Marseilles[230] to Lyons,[231] then through Burgundy[232] to Paris, and beyond it to Rouen. But a detailed examination will reveal the inadequacies of this over-simple outline.

There were four routes one could take from Lyons to Marseilles: the Rhône itself, which at Beaucaire met the main road to Spain via Montpellier and Narbonne; the main road, chiefly used by mule-trains, running along the left bank; a second road forking east and passing through Carpentras to Aix; and lastly a road leading over the Alps, by the Croix-Haute pass and Sisteron, again to Aix-en-Provence.

Between Lyons and Paris there were three routes: one going by Roanne used the Loire, at least as far as Briare,[233] then went on to Orléans; and two branches separating at Chalon, one passing through Dijon and Troyes, the other through Auxerre and Sens.

In addition, this network was linked, in the east and north, to the roads of Central Europe. Two roads led from Lyons to Italy via Grenoble or Chambéry; they met up again at the Mont-Cenis and beyond at the 'pass of Susa' which was the gateway to Italy for both merchants and soldiers. Susa was one of the busiest roadposts of the Alps, with a constant procession of mule-trains or 'great wagons' arriving and leaving. From Lyons too, one or two roads led towards the Rhine, over the Jura, and two roads led to Antwerp, one via Lorraine and the other via Champagne.

That the road network of the French isthmus should have been drawn towards the East, attracted by its busy flow of traffic, is an important observation in support of which at least two examples can be cited. First, it can be calculated that Lyons was still receiving a large proportion of its pepper and spices by way of the Mont-Cenis, at least between 1525 and 1535, while Marseilles was still a modest port. And second, the importance of the Antwerp connection[234] is strikingly revealed by a map showing the distribution or redistribution through Antwerp of goods belonging to French merchants, which were brought to the Scheldt port by land and sea, or bonded there, and were sometimes of other than French origin, of course. But the connection is clearly established.

The French network was also drawn towards the southwest and Spain. We have already mentioned the Beaucaire route. An active route also ran from Lyons to Bayonne, crossing the Massif Central by Limoges where it met the main road from Paris to Spain. This great road starting in the capital in the Rue St.-Jacques, was not only the ancient pilgrim route to Santiago de Compostela, but the most active thoroughfare of France in the second half of the sixteenth century. Evidence for this is suggested by

[230] From the collection *Histoire du commerce de Marseille*, vol. III, 1951, edited by Joseph Billioud, p. 136 ff.
[231] On Lyons, besides René Gascon, see R. Gandilhon, *La politique économique de Louis XI*, 1941, p. 236, and, towards 1573, Nicolas de Nicolay, *Description générale de la ville de Lyon*, 1883 edition.
[232] H. Drouot, *Mayenne et la Bourgogne*, 2 vols., 1937, I, p. 3 and 4.
[233] The Briare canal, begun in 1604.
[234] Emile Coornaert, *Les Français et le commerce international à Anvers*, 1961.

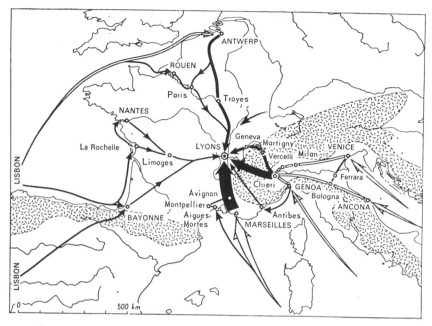

Fig. 17: *Lyons and the spice trade, according to accounts between 1525 and 1534*

From R. Gascon, 'Le siècle du commerce des épices à Lyon, fin XVe–fin XVIe siècle', in *Annales E.S.C.*, July–August, 1960. Note the predominance of the routes from Marseilles and from Chieri, over the Alps, in the concentration of traffic at Lyons.

Frank Spooner's book.[235] The whole of the Atlantic west coast was caught in the toils of Spanish silver, for which Bayonne, because it was a frontier station, was one of the principal entry points, though not the only one. The other was Rennes, because of the voyages made by Breton boats carrying the grain that fed Lisbon and Seville. There was no comparison between the West, rich in silver coins, and poor Burgundy reduced to copper pieces.[236]

This Spanish silver route was for many years a source of profit to Lyons. Lyons, like Geneva the creation of Italian capitalism – not merely the brainchild of Louis XI – the city of fairs among the silk looms, amassed the metal currency that was to swell the assets of the Italian merchants in France. It was a door that long stood wide open for this flight of currency. This role was the culmination of a wide range of activities. One of the great turning points in French economic history was to be when the financial

[235] Frank Spooner, *L'économie mondiale et les frappes monétaires en France, 1493–1680*, 1956, p. 275 ff.

[236] Henri Hauser, 'La question des prix et des monnaies en Bourgogne pendant la seconde moitié du XVI siècle', in *Annales de Bourgogne*, 1932.

centre of the country was transferred from Lyons to Paris.[237] This was a change as important and as difficult to explain as the transfer of Antwerp's supremacy to Amsterdam. In short, any discussion of the French isthmus is bound to lead eventually to discussing the whole of France; as we have already hinted.

After this brief summary, we can return to the Rhône corridor which particularly concerns the Mediterranean. There was a large volume of trade going down the river. Orange, built some distance from the Rhône, was thinking in 1562 of constructing a canal as far as Camaret[238] in order to reach the river traffic. The chief cargo was grain, particularly grain from Burgundy, which was transported in casks (as in Tuscany, another wine-growing region) and directed towards Arles. For this reason, Provence was for a long time a leading grain exporter to the Mediterranean countries. Grain from Provence often enabled the king of France to put pressure on Genoa. After 1559, by contrast, there is no sign of export on this scale, with a few exceptions, such as the small boats that sailed from Avignon to Rome with their loads of grain. Does this mean that after that date the grain from the Rhône valley and Provence was all for home consumption? These river boats also carried, alongside the casks of grain, *brocz* of mineral coal (probably from the Alès basin) which gave Marseilles the privilege of being possibly the only Mediterranean town to use coal for fuel in the sixteenth century.[239]

The river traffic was paralleled by overland traffic also going towards the sea. This time the load was books, for the most part from the presses of Lyons, which were exported in packs to Italy and Spain; and cloth of every origin, English[240] and Flemish, woollen cloth from Paris and Rouen. These were old, established currents of trade, which increased in the sixteenth century, to the advantage of the cottage industry of western and northern France which drove everything before it, Catalan as well as Italian goods. Crowds of pedlars and country merchants would flock to the towns and fairs of the South. At Pézenas and Montagnac in Languedoc, fabrics from the North alone would fill pages and pages: 'cloth from Paris and Rouen, scarlet, black, yellow, violet, or ash-grey' . . . linens from Auvergne, Berry, Burgundy, and especially from Brittany 'to clothe the poor, line cloaks and make sheets and mattresses for the hospitals'.[241]

[237] Frank Spooner, *op. cit.*, p. 279.
[238] A. Yrondelle, 'Orange, port rhodanien', in *Tablettes d'Avignon et de Provence*, 9–16th June, 1928, off-print 1929. The mention of the year 1562 comes from the Communal Archives of Orange.
[239] Coal could also be used by lime-burners, blacksmiths, and in the manufacture of arms, Achille Bardon, *L'exploitation du bassin houiller d'Alais sous l'ancien régime*, 1898, p. 13 and 15. Marseilles imported iron castings from Catalonia. Archives of Bouches-du-Rhône; Admiralty of Marseilles, B IX, 14. The first recorded consignment was 300 balls of iron from Collioure, 2nd May, 1609 (pages of register unnumbered). So there must have been foundries there.
[240] According to the *portate* of Leghorn, A.d.S. Florence, Mediceo, 2080. See also Jakob Strieder, 'Levantinische Handelsfahrten', *art. cit.*, p. 13, where I think there is some confusion over the term *kersey* (carisee).
[241] E. Le Roy Ladurie, *op. cit.*, p. 125.

River traffic and mule-trains cooperated on the journey up river. The small boats of the Rhône carried great quantities of salt for the northern countries. From the time of Louis XI the capitalists of Montpellier had been interested in this lucrative trade, which later even the Wars of Religion did not disrupt.[242] By water, too, went raw wool from Languedoc or Provence, or verdigris from Montpellier. Along the land routes, which were often in poor condition and full of potholes, went everything Marseilles had to send to the interior: spices, pepper, drugs, wool and leather from the Barbary coast, cheeses from Sardinia, barrels of fish, sometimes cases of dates, oranges from Hyères,[243] Turkish carpets, silks, rice from the Levant, steel from Piedmont, alum from Civitavecchia, and malmsey wine.[244] It is possible to compile this list from the chance survival of a Marseilles register dated 1543.[245] It also indicates the towns which as direct customers for this trade made up the economic zone of Marseilles, centred on the axis of the Rhône as far as Lyons. Some goods were dispatched to Toulouse, but this was rare. And very few went as far as Paris; on the whole the Marseilles trade was appropriated by a series of intermediate inland towns. Its volume decreased the further north one went – at Arles, Beaucaire and Pézenas – to disappear altogether when it was swallowed up in the activity of Lyons. This was probably true of all other Mediterranean towns: none of them was in a position at that time to control to the end of the journey the goods it sent inland.

There can be little doubt of the modest scale of Marseilles trade, as it appears from the 1543 register. Yet at this period the city was the unchallenged mistress of the Provençal coast. The neighbouring ports were at her service, some bringing grain from Arles, others ferrying the indispensable casks from Fréjus just before the fishing season. From this time on, it exercised a strong attraction over Cape Corse. But the rise of Marseilles cannot have preceded the capitulation of 1569, or more decisive still, the 1570–1573 war, which immobilized Venice, and greatly disrupted its relations with the Levant. This crisis made Marseilles' fortune, increasing the voyages of her merchant fleet and at the same time swelling the volume of traffic along the Rhône corridor, since some of the German trade, for instance, was diverted via Lyons and Marseilles.[246] Towards 1580 the barques and galleons of the Phocaean city were sailing over the entire Mediterranean.

Clearly the fortunes of Marseilles were not entirely sustained by the

[242] J. F. Noble de la Lauzière, *Abrégé chronologique de l'histoire d'Arles*, 1808, p. 393, 420.
[243] Archives of Bouches-du-Rhône, Admiralty of Marseilles B IX, 198 *ter*.
[244] N. de Nicolay, *op. cit.*, p. 164, 175, 188–189.
[245] See note 243.
[246] Jakob Streider, *art. cit. passim.*; cf. also the article by Karl Ver Hees in *Viertel für S. u. W. Gesch.*, 1934, p. 235–244 on the German firms operating at Lyons, (Lyons municipal archives, H.H. 292, no. 14); in all there were 73 firms, 24 from Nuremberg, 35 from Augsburg, 6 from Ulm, 6 from Strasbourg, 1 from Konstanz, 1 from Cologne, not counting agents for third parties, of course.

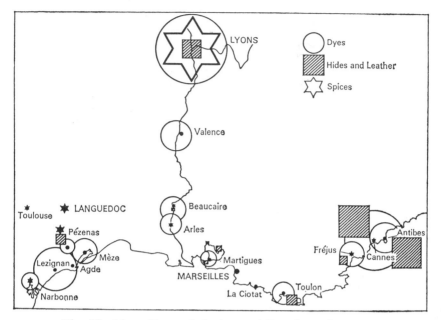

Fig. 18: *Marseilles and the internal French market, 1543*
Very approximate quantities.

roads of the isthmus.[247] They also prospered from sea traffic: the Marseilles barques were at the service of Genoa, Leghorn, Venice, and the ports of Spain and Africa. Like the Ragusan boats they made a living from the sea and its commercial exchanges, the more so since there was no Colbert in the sixteenth century, no strong French industry behind Marseilles. But

[247] The Netherlands faced the important and pressing problem of their communications with the Mediterranean, especially between 1500 and 1580. The following example of a Piedmontese initiative is far from providing a solution to the problem, but it does perhaps shed some light on a point of detail. There was an agreement in 1575 between the Duke of Savoy, Emmanuel-Philibert and the Government of the Netherlands (P. Egidi, *Emmanuele Filiberto*, 1928, II, p. 127) whereby all duties on goods exchanged or in transit were reduced by half. In previous years the Duke of Savoy had tried to enlarge the horizon of his states by treaties with Geneva and the Valtellina (*ibid.*, p. 127). At the same time, he was trying, with the help of the Spaniard, Vitale Sacerdoti, to establish relations with the Levant and the Indies and to this end to reach an agreement with the Turks. We might note that these early negotiations were begun in 1572, at a time when Venice (the War of the League lasted from 1571 to 1573) was having difficulty in maintaining her commercial position. Emmanuel Philibert's attempts were unsuccessful however; success depended on the assistance of the Jewish merchants, so he attempted to protect and attract them, but was unable to overcome the opposition of Rome and Spain on this point (1574). Nevertheless this was in embryo a far-reaching commercial policy centred on the idea of diverting in the direction of Piedmont, as Pietro Egidi points out, and Nice, a part of the great transcontinental trade flow that passed by the Savoy states either on the French side or on the Milanese side (*ibid.*), p. 127.

there was already France, France and her markets. And there was a main road right down through the middle of France making Marseilles one of the gateways through which English cloth and Flemish serges reached the Mediterranean. The civil disturbances after 1563 did not interrupt these trade currents. There was no prolonged crisis or disruption until after 1589, which is a reason, if indeed one is needed, to revise our overall judgments on the internal French crisis.[248]

But a great continental road is not only a trade route. The French axis was not only the channel along which salt travelled northwards or textiles southwards, but also the route taken by the victorious advance after the 1450s of the French language, which penetrated the south of France, the language and civilization of the *Langue d'Oc*, down to the shores of the Mediterranean itself.[249] It was also the route used by the throngs of Italian immigrants of all conditions: merchants, artists, workmen, artisans, labourers, hundreds, thousands of Italians, brilliant and quarrelsome. We can well imagine them sitting down to eat at the French inns, whose abundant fare threw into ecstasies even Girolamo Lippomano himself, the ambassador of opulent Venice. At Paris, he said 'there are innkeepers who can give you meals at all prices: for one teston, for two, for a crown, for four, ten or even twenty per person, if you wish!'[250] These Italians were responsible for whole chapters of history: the draining of the lower Rhône valley; the growth of the bank and bourse of Lyons; and in general for the Renaissance and the art of the Counter-Reformation, powerful advance-posts of Mediterranean civilization.

The French isthmus had its ups and downs. It drew towards it all the active sectors of the western world in the twelfth and thirteenth centuries, through the supremacy of the fairs of Champagne. Then followed a long period of eclipse. But at the end of the Hundred Years' War, the route became active again[251] after about 1450, or perhaps 1480. The occupation of Provence and Marseilles gave royal France a large Mediterranean seaboard, and French influence in the sea increased.

This influence was in the first place that of a great political power: but it was quickly followed by a fresh flowering of French culture, still modest in the century of the Renaissance and the Baroque but discernible in many small details that foreshadowed what was to become an overwhelming influence – in, for instance, the raptures of the ladies of the Spanish court, when the 'Queen of Peace', little Elizabeth of Valois, whom Philip II had just married, unpacked her trunks; or in the way French fashions took hold of even Venice, which was the capital of masculine and feminine elegance until the seventeenth century;[252] or in the pains taken by the

[248] See Part II, Chapter VI.
[249] A Brun, *Recherches historiques sur l'introduction du français dans les provinces du Midi*, 1923, cf. the review by Lucien Febvre, in *Revue de Synthèse*, 1924.
[250] Edmond Bonaffé, *Voyages et voyageurs de la Renaissance*, 1895, p. 92 (1577).
[251] Yves Renouard, 'Les relations économiques franco-italiennes à la fin du Moyen Age' in *Cooperazione intellettuale*, Sept.–Dec., 1936, p. 53–75.
[252] H. Kretschmayr, *op. cit.*, II, p. 378.

Marquise de Gast, at Naples, to win over the Grand Prieur who visited her in 1559: 'Madame la Marquise', wrote Brantôme, who was present, 'greeted him in the French fashion, then the visit commenced. She asked her daughters to keep him company in the French manner, and to laugh, dance, play and talk, freely, modestly, and correctly as you do at the French court.'[253] The French song began to have its champions in the South; early enough not to compete with Italian opera which was to become popular everywhere at the end of the century. These are small signs, apparently superficial. But is it so unimportant that in sixteenth-century Italy, it should already be the Frenchman, as we may imagine him with his gesticulations, his extravagant manners, and his hectic social life, exhausting and wearing out his lackeys, who served as a model for polite society?[254]

Europe and the Mediterranean. The European isthmuses, as we have seen, provided the essential lines along which Mediterranean influence was transmitted, each line forming the axis of a different sector of the continent possessing greater or lesser autonomy; for the Mediterranean was confronted not with a single Europe, but with several Europes, faces of the continent whose communications with each other along the transversal routes were often poor and little used.

But the north–south routes, although important, by no means totally conditioned the mass of countries and peoples they passed through. Distance and frequently relief made this impossible. The barriers lying between the Mediterranean and northern Europe played their negative role. So southern influence did not spread through the North in waves, although that might be the image that first comes to mind. When it penetrated deeply into a region, it was along narrow channels running northwards with the great trade routes and reaching with them the most distant lands. It is sometimes to these distant lands that we must go to explain the history of the sea.

But these channels, often running into lands that were completely foreign – the Russian lands, for example – were only linear extensions of the Mediterranean into a Europe where the influence of the sea was felt in very varying degrees. Strong Mediterranean influence was only present, through the many ramifications of these vital arteries, at a relatively short distance from its shores. This is where we shall find the zone which can properly be said to be impregnated with Mediterranean culture: a privileged but imprecise zone; for its boundaries may vary depending on whether one is thinking of religious, cultural, or economic factors. One example from economic history might make this clear. We earlier mentioned Marseilles, and by implication all the trading ports on the Mediterranean coast, whose services were relayed over a certain area by other urban centres. In western and central Europe the line joining these inland centres would run from Lyons to Geneva, Basel, Ulm, Augsburg, Vienna, Cracow, and Lwow. One cannot fail to be struck by the fact that these are all towns which

[253] Brantôme, *Mémoires*, ed. Mérimée, XII, p. 263.
[254] Gonzague Truc, *Léon X et son siècle*, 1941, p. 127.

are a curious mixture of North and South, towns whose interests and inclinations attracted them both to the Mediterraneans of the North and to the great *Mare Internum*. It cannot be denied that the median axis was deeply scored, an essential hinge on which the European complex turned. Is it any more possible to deny that Europe, which in the last analysis was to be hostile to the Mediterranean, began to the north of these towns of mixed culture: the Europe of the Reformation, the Europe of the new countries with their aggressive advance,[255] whose arrival was in its way to mark the beginning of what we call modern times?

I do not wish to give too schematic a picture. Europe also meant the northern seas, the Atlantic Ocean, and after the Great Discoveries, an all-conquering Atlantic, linked by Magellan to the Pacific and by Vasco da Gama to the Indian Ocean.

3. THE ATLANTIC OCEAN

It may seem paradoxical to end a chapter on the boundaries of the Mediterranean region with the Atlantic itself, as if it were merely an annex of the inland sea. But in the sixteenth century the ocean did not yet have a fully independent existence. Man was only just beginning to take its measure and to construct an identity for it with what could be found in Europe, as Robinson Crusoe built his cabin from what he could salvage from his ship.

Several Atlantics. The Atlantic in the sixteenth century was the association and more or less literal coexistence of several partly autonomous areas. There was the transversal ocean of the English[256] and French, of which the Gulf Stream with its storm-shaken routes was the usual axis, and Newfoundland the first landfall. The Spanish Atlantic was the ellipse whose outline is marked by Seville, the Canaries, the West Indies, and the Azores: its ports of call and its driving forces.[257] The Portuguese Atlantic[258] was the great triangle of the central and southern part of the ocean, one side running from Lisbon to Brazil, the second from Brazil to the Cape of Good Hope, and the third, the route followed by sailing ships returning from the Indies, from St. Helena along the African coast.

These different Atlantics, linked to national histories, have had no difficulty in finding historians. There is another Atlantic which has been neglected, possibly because it links together these particular sectors, and whose full significance will only become apparent in the comprehensive history of the Atlantic that has yet to be written. Yet it is the most ancient of all, the Atlantic of the mediæval and even classical navigators from the Pillars of Hercules to the Cassiterides, that narrow sea with its frequent

[255] Cf. Marc Bloch's eloquent description of the old towns of the south and the new towns of the north, in *Revue historique*, 1931, p. 133.

[256] D. A. Farnie, 'The commercial Empire of the Atlantic, 1607–1783' in *Economic History Review*, XV, 1962, no. 2, p. 205–206.

[257] Pierre Chaunu, *Seville et l'Atlantique*, 1959, 3 vols.

[258] Frédéric Mauro, *Le Portugal et l'Atlantique au XVIIe siècle 1570–1670*, 1960.

wild storms, which lies between the coasts of Portugal, Spain, France, Ireland, and England, in fact the simple north–south route rivalling the land routes of the European isthmuses. From this one followed all the other Atlantic oceans of the fifteenth and sixteenth centuries. It was the nursery of Atlantic exploration.

It was a treacherous sea indeed and one where voyages were difficult. The Bay of Biscay, with its long swells and furious waters, enjoys a bad reputation which is as justified as that of the Gulf of Lions in the Mediterranean. No ship could be sure, on leaving the Mediterranean, of not missing the entry to the Channel to the northeast, although it is so wide. Charles V's younger brother Ferdinand found himself in 1518 quite unintentionally lying off the wild coast of Ireland, with the fleet that had brought him from Laredo.[259] Coming from the North, like Philip II in August, 1559, one was by no means sure of a straight passage to the ports of the Cantabrian coast.[260] The ambassador Dantiscus, who was for so long Poland's representative at the court of Charles V, experienced this voyage, from England to the Peninsula, in December, 1522. He declared that nothing in the Mediterranean or the Baltic could be compared with the horrible violence of the 'Sea of Spain'. 'If I were to gain the empire of the world for the price of that voyage, I should never enter upon such a perilous venture,' he said.[261]

It was indeed through the perils of the nearby Atlantic and the Bay of Biscay that the 'empire of the world' was purchased. On these rough seas Europe underwent her hardest-won apprenticeship of the sea, and prepared to conquer the world.

The Atlantic learns from the Mediterranean. How did these 'Atlantics' influence the Mediterranean, and how did the inland sea affect these great expanses?

Traditional historiography makes no distinction between these Atlantics, regarding them on the whole as the Mediterranean's chief enemy, a vast stretch dominating a smaller one. This is something of a simplification. One exaggeration deserves another. It would be equally reasonable to say that the Mediterranean for a long time dominated its immediate neighbour and that its decadence can be explained, among other reasons by its loss of this control. It is worth repeating that history is not made by geographical features, but by the men who control or discover them.

In the sixteenth century the Mediterranean had clear prerogatives in the western Atlantic. The prosperous trade of the ocean was beneficial to the inland sea; at all events it took part in it. Barrels of cod from Newfoundland; sugar from the islands (Madeira, São Tomé); sugar and dye-woods from Brazil; gold and silver from Spanish America; pepper, spices, pearls, and silks from the Indian Ocean, shipped round the Cape of

---

[259] Laurent Vital, *Premier voyage de Charles Quint en Espagne*, 1881, p. 279–283.
[260] Vol. II, Part III, Ch. 1, section 3.
[261] Czartoryski Museum, Cracow, 35, f° 35, f° 55, Valladolid, 4th January, 1523.

Good Hope – the Mediterranean had a share in all these foreign riches and new trades. During the sixteenth century it was very far from being the neglected and impoverished world that the voyages of Columbus and Vasco da Gama are supposed to have ruined. On the contrary, the Mediterranean shaped the Atlantic and impressed its own image on the Spanish New World. One historian reviewing the first edition of this book, regretted that the donkey, the symbol of everyday life in the Mediterranean, was not given more space.[262] To see peasants riding past on burros in Mexico, he said, is to be irresistibly reminded of a Mediterranean landscape. If so, there are plenty of other occasions! The cereals sown as soon as possible, the vines quickly planted in Peru and Chile, the mule-trains of the *arrieros*, the churches, the Plaza Mayor of the Spanish towns, the flocks brought over from the Peninsula, which soon propagated themselves in the wild state, the astonishing flowering of the colonial Baroque: this whole new civilization had roots in the Mediterranean.[263]

These connections and exchanges were effected during the century by ships which were either Atlantic or Mediterranean, and that is an important problem in itself. But it cannot give a complete picture of the interests involved. It would be an exaggeration to suppose that every time an Atlantic ship or trader entered the Mediterranean another point was lost. At the end of the century the rise of Naples, for instance, as a centre for the purchasing of northern products and for the export of Mediterranean goods, was entirely due to their arrival; and the Dutch ships that transported Spanish wool directly to Venice were partly responsible for the spectacular boom at the end of the sixteenth century in the city's cloth industry.[264] In short, it is not easy to draw up a balance sheet of the credits and debits of both sides.

The Atlantic destiny in the sixteenth century. For our purposes it would be more useful to outline a history of the Atlantic from the point of view of its relations with the Mediterranean.

From the beginning of the century until 1580, the Iberians, that is men of the Mediterranean, controlled the part of the ocean between Seville and the West Indies – 'Seville's Atlantic', as Pierre Chaunu has called it. They also controlled the great Portuguese ocean from Lisbon. Apart from a few French privateers practically no other ship ventured into these well-guarded waters. No other power interrupted or diverted their economic growth. By way of the isthmus of Panama, the Sevilian Atlantic joined up with the sea route to Peru, as far as Arica, the port for the Potosi mines. After 1564 the Manila galleon regularly crossed the Pacific from Acapulco to the Philippines and effectively linked up with the Chinese

[262] Robert Ricard, in *Bulletin Hispanique*, 1949, p. 79.
[263] Charles Verlinden, 'Les origines coloniales de la civilisation atlantique. Antécédents et types de structures' in *Cahiers internationaux d'Histoire*, 1953. This article summarizes the author's other articles, p. 382, note 4.
[264] See below, p. 292-293.

economy.[265] The Portuguese had from the start sent their ships to India, then beyond to the East Indies, China, and Japan.[266] They also organized the great slave trade between Africa and America, not to mention the clandestine export of silver from Potosi by way of the overland routes of Brazil and, even more, by Buenos Aires and the little boats of the Rio de la Plata.[267]

This added up to an immense and complicated system, drawing on the economy of the whole world. There were a few mishaps, a few difficult patches, but on the whole this Iberian-dominated economy maintained itself until 1580 and even longer. Proof of this is to be found in the rise in consignments of silver arriving at Seville as well as of the various goods returning from the 'Indies': leather, Brazil-wood, cochineal – the last figuring among 'royal merchandise', the profits from which were fought over by merchants. Another proof is the vast series of examples of marine insurance at the Consulate of Burgos, where for a considerable period the premium rate was lower for the Atlantic than the Mediterranean.[268] And Lisbon kept her position in the spice trade well after 1600. Finally, when the skies darkened with the first signs of Protestant privateering, the two giants, Spain and Portugal, joined forces. Who would have suspected in 1580 that this was the association of two monumental weaknesses?

But there were shadows, and serious ones, on this optimistic scene: the near Atlantic, the north–south Atlantic, was very soon lost. This route had been pioneered by Mediterranean sailors several centuries earlier. In 1297 Genoese galleys had made the first direct voyage to Bruges, and they were followed about twenty years later by the Venetian *galere da mercato* (some time between 1310 and 1320, probably in 1317) and many other ships.[269] This move coincided (without necessarily being its consequence or cause) with the end of the prosperity of the fairs of Champagne. It brought many Italian merchants to the Netherlands and England; they settled there as if in conquered lands. This maritime triumph immediately brought supremacy to Italy; with her colonies in the Levant and her counting houses in the North, she was able to detach herself from the backward economies surrounding her, now the most advanced and richest of all. Another unexpected consequence was the bringing to life of the European Atlantic seaboard, or at any rate of some parts of it, Andalusia and Portugal, which was to prepare the way for the Age of Discovery.[270]

[265] Pierre Chaunu, *Les Philippines et le Pacifique des Ibériques*, (*XVIe, XVIIe, XVIIIe siècles*), *Introduction méthodologique et indices d'activite*, 1960.
[266] C. R. Boxer, *The great ship from Amacon*, Lisbon, 1959.
[267] Alice Piffer Canabrava, *O commercio portugues no Rio da Prata, 1580–1640*, São Paulo, 1944.
[268] According to the preliminary conclusions of the unpublished work by Marie Helmer on insurance at Burgos.
[269] Renée Doehaerd, *Les relations commerciales entre Gênes, la Belgique et l'Outremont*, Brussels–Rome, 1941, I, p. 89.
[270] G. de Reparaz (hijo), *La época de los grandes descubrimientos españoles y portugueses*, 1931, p. 90.

When the slow but powerful economic advance of the mid-fifteenth century began, it was again the Italian system, both continental and maritime, which drew most profit from it. Venice and Genoa dominated the English and Flemish markets. It was not until the sixteenth century that this system began to decline. In about 1550[271] trade between the North Sea, Portugal, and Andalusia was taken over by northern ships. Twenty years later at the time of the Anglo-Spanish crisis of 1568–1569,[272] the Iberians had virtually to abandon the northern route. Once launched on their career, the northern sailing vessels were soon to take the road to Gibraltar and to achieve the conquest of the Mediterranean which they had only partially accomplished before 1550. But their progress was slow. An old Spaniard (he was 87), relating his memoirs in 1629, remembered a time when the English were hard put to maintain fifteen men-of-war.[273]

Overall, these years meant a series of direct or indirect losses for the Mediterranean, but they were not necessarily disastrous for the Mediterranean countries. Spain and Portugal were marshalling their strength to maintain their great Atlantic routes as chief priority. The case of Viscaya is revealing. It provided the best ships of the *Carrera de Indias*, its galleons set off for the Indies, but its *zabras*, by contrast, which before 1569 had carried wool and silver from Spain to Antwerp, became increasingly rare on the northern routes. But the vital link between Seville and the North was maintained despite these fluctuations. For the northerners bringing grain, fish, wood, iron, copper, tin, gunpowder, woollen cloth, linen, hardware, and ready-made ships, the Spanish trip was worth it for the salt, wine, and silver they could bring back. The Peninsula was well able to pay for their services.

So there were overall losses, but they were compensated within a world system that was wide open to Italian merchants. They were in Lisbon and Seville from the very start. It was the Genoese who launched Seville on her career and set up the indispensable and slow circulation of capital, without which nothing could have been accomplished anywhere on either side of the Atlantic.[274] The Spanish economy provided a basis for their activities as well as for the more discreet but still important contribution of the Florentines. The Italian capitalists, Venetians and Milanese, joined in and held the key routes to the Low Countries. Italian merchants of every origin were to be found at Antwerp, Nuremberg, and even at the other end of the world, at Hormuz or Goa. In short the Mediterranean was not out of the picture at all. Or rather it was never out of any picture. Through the Genoese it even controlled the imperial finances of Spain, and through the

[271] From 1549, A. Ballesteros, *Historia de España, y su influencia en la historia universal*, 1927, IV, 2, p. 180.
[272] See below, p. 482 ff.
[273] *CODOIN*, LV, p. 7–8.
[274] André-E. Sayous, 'Le rôle des Génois lors des premiers mouvements réguliers d'affaires entre l'Espagne et le Nouveau Monde', in *C.R. de l'Académie des Inscriptions de Belles Lettres*, 1930.

so-called Besançon fairs,[275] the entire movement, at the summit, of capital in Europe.

The system was to prove long-lived. There was to be no major disaster for the Mediterranean, before the Dutch ships of Cornelius Houtmann rounded the Cape of Good Hope, in 1596 on the outward trip and 1598 on the return journey. Only then was the system touched in its vitals at the moment when, give or take a few years, the secular trend was being reversed. In such reversals the most spectacular achievements are usually the first to suffer. But in this case there was no sudden change. The most indicative dates are perhaps 1620–1630, when the Portuguese *marranos* were installed at the heart of Spain's finance, those only semi-converted *novos christãos* who were often the straw men of northern capitalism. They took up a decisive position alongside the Genoese *hombres de negocios*. On 8th August, 1628, off Matanzas, near Havana, the *armada y flota* of New Spain was surrounded and captured by the Dutch vessels of Piet Heyn.[276]

These late dates lessen, to my mind, the importance conventionally attached to the year 1588, the year of the Invincible Armada. There are several good reasons why this should be so. First, Spain was still capable, after the failure of 1588 – occasioned by winds and storms and the absence of skilled pilots along the sandbanks of the North Sea quite as much as by the enemy – of launching two more expeditions against England, in 1597[277] and in 1601,[278] as well as fostering a diversionary war in Ireland which was a drain on Elizabeth's financial resources.[279] Second, the failure occurred during a period of general prosperity when it was still possible for a wound to heal over. Third, English privateering slowed down of its own accord; it had clearly dealt the enemy some very nasty blows (the sack of Cadiz in 1596 affected Spain's prestige even more than her wealth), but gradually the islands and the Spanish coast took up arms – English privateering was an industry where profits were becoming harder to find as an English historian has shown.[280] George, Earl of Cumberland, for example, after fifteen years of financing expeditions against the Spaniards was finally overwhelmed by debts and forced to retire to his estates: 'My thoughts must turn from intercepting of Carracks to sowing of corn, from rigging ships to breeding sheep.' Fourth, while England may have prepared the way for Spain's collapse, she did not immediately gain from it. An important detail to be noted is that she signed a peace treaty with the Catholic King in 1604, six years after France, and five years before the United Provinces.

This corresponds to the impression given by the Spanish documents of

[275] See below, p. 379, 504 etc.
[276] Huguette et Pierre Chaunu, *op. cit.*, V, p. 169 and 170, notes 10, 11, and 12.
[277] A. Ballesteros, *Historia de España* . . ., vol. IV, p. 169.
[278] *Ibid.*, p. 200.
[279] George Macaulay Trevelyan, *History of England, op. cit.*, p. 361.
[280] L. Stone, 'Anatomy of Elizabethan Aristocracy' in *Economic History Review* 1948, p. 17.

the end of the century. The struggle against England was often waged in the lonely deeps of the ocean. The English, who controlled the Channel, would leave it before the squadrons of the Adelantado of Castile were ready for them at Lisbon or Cadiz; they could easily sail to the Canaries or the Azores, even up to the Straits of Gibraltar with its guard of galleys, galleons, and Spanish troops. It was not until after the return of the English ships, at the very end of the summer, that the Spanish ships would sail up from Gibraltar to El Ferrol. Their mopping-up operations usually took place in an empty sea. There were, it is true, some encounters – sometimes harmless. In November, 1602, for example, six Spanish galleons left Lisbon, 'to patrol the waters of Corunna'; they did indeed meet some enemy ships, which, better armed and bolder in manoeuvres than the Spaniards, let them approach, fired a few cannon shots, then 'set sail and ran away, as if in game', *quasi scherzando*, as a Venetian account describes it.[281] It was a costly war, but not a mortal one. And it was not always pointless. The Straits of Gibraltar were passed by force by English and Dutch ships. But they did not find it easy. The English ships, according to representatives of the Levant Company, would go through in winter for more security, 'when the water in the straits is very rough and when they are unlikely to meet the Spanish patrol galleons, which are at their moorings'.[282] And every year the fleets from the New World would return with more and more riches, as if 'the hand of God was guiding them'. This was what really mattered to Spain and her Mediterranean associates.

A late decline. So this final voyage, in search of a Greater Mediterranean complements the others. The narrow sea set between the great land masses was until 1600 the scene of a thriving, flexible, and powerful economy. It was not abandoned by history, suddenly, bag and baggage, at the end of the century. The retreat was not sounded until later. The general outline of our subject has now been sketched. It is time to block in the main lines and look more carefully at the detail.

[281] Contarini to the Doge, Valladolid, 24th November, 1602.
[282] Domenico Sella, *op. cit.*, p. 10, note 5.

CHAPTER IV

The Mediterranean as a Physical Unit: Climate and History

> ... the wanderings of Ulysses, ever under the same climate.
> J. de Barros, *Asia*, I. IV, p. 160.

It would be difficult to recognize any unity in this dense, composite, and ill-defined world we have described at such length other than that of being the meeting place of many peoples, and the melting-pot of many histories.[1] Nevertheless it is significant that at the heart of this human unit, occupying an area smaller than the whole, there should be a source of physical unity, a climate, which has imposed its uniformity on both landscape and ways of life. Its significance is demonstrated by contrast with the Atlantic. The ocean too is a human unit and one of the most vigorous of the present day world; it too has been a meeting place and a melting-pot of history. But the Atlantic complex lacks a homogeneous centre comparable to the source of that even light which shines at the heart of the Mediterranean. The Atlantic, stretching from pole to pole, reflects the colours of all the earth's climates.

The Mediterranean of the vines and olive trees consists, as we know, only of a few narrow coastal strips, ribbons of land bordering the sea. This falls very short of the historical Mediterranean, but it is of great importance that the Mediterranean complex should have taken its rhythm from the uniform band of climate and culture at its centre, so distinctive that it is to this that the adjective 'Mediterranean' is usually applied. Such a force operating at the centre could not fail to have far-reaching repercussions, since it affects all movements into and out of the Mediterranean. Nor is this climate merely confined to the coastal strips, for since they surround the whole sea, it is also the climate of the waters in between. That identical or near-identical worlds should be found on the borders of countries as far apart and in general terms as different as Greece, Spain, Italy, North Africa; that these worlds should live at the same rhythm; that men and goods should be able to move from one to another without any need for acclimatization: such living identity implies the living unity of the sea. It is a great deal more than a beautiful setting.

I. THE UNITY OF THE CLIMATE

Above the Mediterranean of land and water stretches the Mediterranean of the sky, having little or no connection with the landscapes below and,

[1] Paul Valéry, 'Réflexions sur l'acier', in: *Acier*, 1938, no. 1.

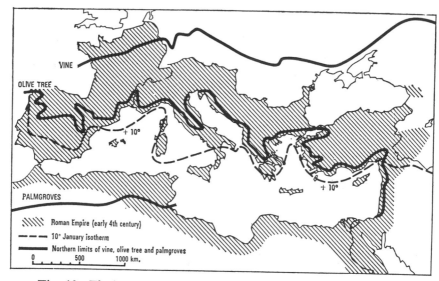

Fig. 19: *The 'true' Mediterranean, from the olive tree to the great palm groves*

The limit of the palm groves refers only to *large*, compact groves. The limit for the date-palm growing isolated or in small clumps is much further north (see Fig. 13, p. 172).

in fact, independent of local physical conditions. It is created by the breath of two external forces: the Atlantic Ocean, its neighbour to the west, and the Sahara, its neighbour to the south. The Mediterranean itself is not responsible for the sky that looks down on it.[2]

The Atlantic and the Sahara. Within this open-ended area, two forces are at work, turn by turn: the Sahara brings dry air, clear light, the vast blue sky; the Atlantic, when it is not spreading clouds and rain, sends in abundance that grey mist and moist air which is more widespread than one would think in the Mediterranean atmosphere during the 'winter semester'. The early Orientalist painters created an enduring false impression with their glowing palettes. In October, 1869, Fromentin, leaving Messina by boat, noted, 'grey skies, cold wind, a few drops of rain on the awning. It is sad, it could be the Baltic.'[3] Earlier, in February, 1848, he had fled towards the Sahara from the persistent grey mists of the Mediterranean winter: 'there was no interval that year', he wrote, 'between the November rains and the heavy winter rains, which had lasted for three and a half months with hardly a day's respite'.[4] All natives of Algiers must at one time or

[2] Emmanuel de Martonne, *Géographie Universelle*, vol. VI, I, 1942, p. 317, '. . . it is not the breath of the Mediterranean which gives Provence its skies'.
[3] *Voyage d'Égypte*, 1935, p. 43.
[4] *Un été dans le Sahara*, 1908, p. 3.

another have had occasion to see newcomers aghast at the torrential downpours over the city.

The rains have always been a fact of life throughout the region. In Florence, notes a diarist for the entry 24th January, 1651,[5] the inclement weather has lasted five months, 'per avere durato a piovere quasi cinque mesi'. The previous year,[6] Capua had been swamped by torrential rains. In fact there was hardly a winter when the rivers did not burst their banks and the towns were not subjected to the terrors and destruction of flooding. Venice suffered more than most, of course. In November, 1443,[7] her losses were enormous, 'quasi mezo million di ducati'; on 18th December, 1600, there was an identical disaster, the *lidi*, the canals, the houses, the private stores at street level, the public stores of salt, grain, and spices all suffering great damage, 'con dano di un million d'oro', which is also evidence that prices had risen in the meantime.[8]

In winter, or more precisely between the September equinox and the March equinox, the Atlantic influence is predominant. The anticyclone over the Azores lets in the Atlantic depressions that move one after another into the warm waters of the Mediterranean; they come in either from the Bay of Biscay, moving quickly over Aquitaine; or, like ships, they enter the Mediterranean by the Straits of Gibraltar and the Spanish coasts. Wherever they enter they cross the Mediterranean from west to east, travelling quickly. They make the winter weather most unsettled, bringing rain, causing sudden winds to spring up, and constantly agitating the sea, which when whipped by the *mistral*, the *noroît* or the *bora*, is often so white with foam, that it looks like a plain covered with snow, or 'strewn with ashes' as a sixteenth-century traveller described it.[9] Above Toledo, the Atlantic humidity contributes in winter to bring those turbulent and dramatic skies of storm and light painted by El Greco.

So every year, and often violently, the Atlantic banishes the desert far away to the south and east. In winter rain falls over the Algerian provinces and sometimes in the heart of the Sahara. Rain falls even on the mountains of western Arabia. The anti-desert is not the Mediterranean, as Paul Morand once wrote, but the Atlantic Ocean.

Around the spring equinox, everything changes again, rather suddenly, at about the time when, as the calendar of the Maghreb says, the season for grafting trees arrives, and the first notes of the nightingale are heard.[10] Of real springtime there is little or none; perhaps a short week that suddenly brings out leaves and flowers. As soon as the winter rains are over, the desert begins to move back and invade the sea, including the surrounding mountains, right up to their peaks. It moves westwards, and above all

[5] Baldinucci, *Giornale di ricordi*, 24th January, 1651, Marciana, Ital., VI, XCIV.
[6] *Recueil des Gazettes*, year 1650, p. 1557, Naples, 2nd November, 1650.
[7] A.d.S. Venice, Cronaca veneta, Brera 51, 10th November, 1443.
[8] Marciana, Cronaca savina, f° 372, 18th December, 1600; there was similar constant rain ('per tre mesi continui') at Christmas 1598, *ibid.*, f° 371 and 371 v°.
[9] Peter Martyr, *op. cit.*, p. 53 note.
[10] *Annuaire de monde musulman*, 1925, p. 8

northwards, passing beyond the furthest limits of the Mediterranean world. In France, the burning air from the south every summer warms the southern Alps, invades most of the Rhône valley, crosses the basin of Aquitaine as a warm current, and often carries the searing drought through the Garonne region to the distant coasts of southern Brittany.[11]

Torrid summer then reigns uncontested in the centre of the Mediterranean zone. The sea is astonishingly calm: in July and August it is like a millpond; little boats sail far out and low-lying galleys could venture without fear from port to port.[12] The summer semester was the best time for shipping, piracy, and war.

The physical causes of this dry, torrid summer are clear. As the sun moves further north, the anticyclone of the Azores increases in size again. When their passage is blocked, the long chain of Atlantic depressions is halted. The obstacle is removed only when autumn approaches; then the Atlantic invasion begins again.

A homogeneous climate. The *extreme* limits of such a climate could be said to lie far from the shores of the Mediterranean, if they are extended on one side, over Europe, to the regions touched by the Saharan drought in summer, and in the other direction to the regions in Asia and Africa, even in the middle of the vast steppes, which are affected by the rain of the Atlantic depressions. But to set such wide limits is clearly misleading. The Mediterranean climate is neither one nor the other of the forces we have described; it is precisely the zone where they overlap, a combination of the two. To overemphasize either of its components would deform the Mediterranean climate. To extend it too far to the east or south would turn it into a steppe or desert climate, to take it too far north would bring it into the zone where the west winds predominate. The true Mediterranean climate occupies only a fairly narrow zone.

Indeed, it is not easy to define its limits. To do so would require taking note of the smallest details, not necessarily physical, for climates are not measured only by the usual gauges of temperature, pressure, wind, and rainfall, but can be traced in thousands of signs at ground level, as has been suggested by André Siegfried of the Ardèche,[13] by Léo Larguier of the border between Languedoc and Lozère,[14] and J. L. Vaudoyer of the transitional zones between the different parts of Provence.[15] But these are points of detail. In general, the geographer's well-known observation must be accepted without question: the Mediterranean climate lies between the northern limit of the olive tree and the northern limit of the palm grove.

[11] E. de Martonne, *op. cit.*, p. 296.
[12] Ernest Lavisse, 'Sur les galères du Roi', in *Revue de Paris*, November, 1897.
[13] *Vue générale de la Méditerranée*, 1943, p. 64–65. English translation by D. Hemming, *The Mediterranean*, London, 1948, p. 87.
[14] Léo Larguier, 'Le Gard et les Basses Cévennes', in *Maisons et villages de France, op. cit.*, I, 1943.
[15] *Op. cit.*, p. 183. For the Volterra region, see Paul Bourget, *Sensations d'Italie*, 1902, p. 5.

Between these frontiers we may count the Italian (or rather Apennine) peninsula, Greece, Cyrenaica, Tunisia, and, elsewhere, a few narrow coastal strips rarely more than 200 kilometres wide. For the mountain barriers soon loom up. The Mediterranean climate is often the climate only of a coastal fringe, the riviera, bordering the sea, a ribbon as narrow as the coastal strip in the Crimea where figs, olives, oranges, and pomegranates all grow freely,[16] though only in the southern part of the peninsula.

But this narrow framework, by reason of its very narrowness, provides undeniable homogeneity, both from north to south and from east to west.

From north to south the entire coastal riviera forms only a thin lengthwise band on the globe. Its widest point from north to south is the distance of 1100 kilometres from the northern end of the Adriatic to the coast of Tripolitania, and that is an exception. In fact the greatest widths vary on an average between 600 and 800 kilometres for the eastern basin and 740 kilometres between Algiers and Marseilles. The entire area, both land and sea, forms a long belt straddling the 37th and 38th parallels. The differences in latitude are not great. They are sufficient to explain the contrasts between the northern shores and the southern, the latter being the warmer. The mean difference in temperature between Marseilles and Algiers is 4°C. The 10°C. January isotherm on the whole follows the general shape of the sea, cutting off southern Spain and southern Italy, regions that have more in common with Africa than with Europe. In general, all parts of the Mediterranean experience what is perceptibly the same 'geometrical' climate.

From east to west there is some variation owing to the fact that moisture from the Atlantic is less pronounced and also later in arrival the further east one travels.

These variations are all worthy of note. At a time when climatologists are attentive to detail, the Mediterranean is rightly regarded by them as a complex of different climates that are to be distinguished one from another. But that does not disprove their fundamental, close relationship and undeniable unity. It is a matter of some importance to the historian to find almost everywhere within his field of study the same climate, the same seasonal rhythm, the same vegetation, the same colours and, when the geological architecture recurs, the same landscapes, identical to the point of obsession; in short, the same ways of life. To Michelet, the 'stony' Languedoc interior recalled Palestine. For hundreds of writers, Provence has been more Greek than Greece, unless, that is, the true Greece is not to be found on some Sicilian shore. The Iles d'Hyères would not be out of place among the Cyclades, except that they are greener.[17] The lagoon of Tunis recalls the Lagoon of Chioggia. Morocco is another, more sun-baked Italy.[18]

---

[16] Comte de Rochechouart, *Souvenirs sur la Révolution, L'Empire et la Restauration*, 1889, p. 110; vines from Madeira and Spain had taken to the soil of the Crimea.
[17] Jules Sion, *La France Méditerranéenne*, 1929, p. 77.
[18] J. and J. Tharaud, *Marrakech ou les seigneurs de l'Atlas*, 1929, p. 135.

Everywhere can be found the same eternal trinity: wheat, olives, and vines, born of the climate and history; in other words an identical agricultural civilization, identical ways of dominating the environment. The different regions of the sea are not, therefore, complementary.[19] They have the same granaries, wine-cellars and oil presses, the same tools, flocks, and often the same agrarian traditions and daily preoccupations. What prospers in one region will do equally well in the next. In the sixteenth century all the coastal regions produced wax, wool, and skins, *montonini* or *vacchini*; they all grew (or could have grown) mulberry trees and raised silkworms. They are all without exception lands of wine and vineyards, even the Moslem countries. Who has praised wine more highly than the poet of Islam? At Tor on the Red Sea there were vines,[20] and they even grew in far-off Persia, where the wine of Shīrāz was highly prized.

With such identity of production, it follows that similar goods can be found in any country bordering the sea. In the sixteenth century there was grain from Sicily and grain from Thrace; there was wine from Naples, *greco* or *latino*, the latter more plentiful than the former,[21] but there were also the many casks of wine shipped from Frontignan; there was the Lombardy rice, but also rice from Valencia, Turkey and Egypt. And to compare goods of modest quality, there was wool from North Africa and wool from the Balkans.

The Mediterranean countries, then, were in competition with each other; at least they should have been. They had more goods for exchange outside their climatic environment than within it. But the sixteenth century was a time when the total volume of exchange was small, the prices modest and the distances travelled short. Arrangements had somehow to be reached between neighbours, between regions that were rich or poor in manpower, and the chief problem was the supply of food for the towns, constantly on the lookout for all kinds of foodstuffs and in particular those that could be transported without too much spoilage: sacks of almonds from the Provençal coast, barrels of salted tunny or meat, sacks of beans from Egypt, not to mention casks of oil and grain, for which, of course, demand was greatest. So identical production did not restrict exchanges within the Mediterranean as much as one might expect, at least during the sixteenth century.

In human terms the unity of the climate[22] has had many other consequences. At a very early stage it prepared the ground for the establishment of identical rural economies. From the first millennium before Christ the civilization of the vine and the olive tree spread westwards from the eastern

[19] A. Siegfried, *op. cit.*, p. 148, 326.
[20] Belon, *op. cit.*, p. 131.
[21] A.d.S. Naples, Sommaria Consultationum, 2 f° 223, 2nd October, 1567. In the preceding years, good or bad, the kingdom of Naples had produced: *vini latini 23,667 busti; vini grechi, dulci et Mangiaguera, 2319 busti*.
[22] 'Similarity of climate . . . encourages penetration into regions similar to those left behind, in order that life may continue in accustomed ways,' P. Vidal de la Blache, *op. cit.*, p. 179.

part of the sea. This basic uniformity was established far back in time, nature and man working to the same end.

As a result, in the sixteenth century, a native of the Mediterranean, wherever he might come from, would never feel out of place in any part of the sea. In former times, it is true, in the heroic age of the first Phoenician and Greek voyages of antiquity, colonization was a dramatic upheaval, but not in later years. To later colonial settlers their journey simply meant finding in a new place the same trees and plants, the same food on the table that they had known in their homeland; it meant living under the same sky, watching the same familiar seasons.

On the other hand when a native of the Mediterranean had to leave the shores of the sea, he was uneasy and homesick; like the soldiers of Alexander the Great when he left Syria and advanced towards the Euphrates;[23] or the sixteenth-century Spaniards in the Low Countries, miserable among the 'fogs of the North'. For Alonso Vázquez and the Spaniards of his time (and probably of all time) Flanders was 'the land where there grows neither thyme, nor lavender, figs, olives, melons, or almonds; where parsley, onions, and lettuces have neither juice nor taste; where dishes are prepared, strange to relate, with butter from cows instead of oil . . .'.[24] The Cardinal of Aragon, who reached the Netherlands in 1517 with his cook and his own supplies, shared this opinion. 'Because of the butter and dairy produce which is so widely used in Flanders and Germany', he concluded, 'these countries are overrun with lepers.'[25] A strange land indeed! An Italian cleric stranded at Bayeux in Normandy in the summer of 1529 thought himself 'for del mondo'.[26]

This explains the facility with which the Mediterranean dweller travelled from port to port; these were not true transplantations, merely removals, and the new occupant would feel quite at home in his new habitat. In striking contrast was the exhausting process of colonizing the New World carried out by the Iberians. Traditional history has preserved, with more or less accuracy, the names of those men and women who were the first to grow wheat, vines, and olives in Peru or in New Spain. Not without

[23] A. Radet, *Alexandre le Grand*, 1931, p. 139.
[24] Alonso Vázquez, *Los sucesos de Flandes* . . . extracts published in L. P. Gachard, *Les Bibliothèques de Madrid* . . ., Brussels, 1875, p. 459, ff., quoted by L. Pfandl, *Jeanne la Folle*, Fr. trans. by R. de Liedekerke, 1938, p. 48, Cf. the following from Maximilien Sorre, *Les Fondements biologiques de la géographie humaine*, 1943, p. 268: 'one of the peculiarities of the peoples who lived on the periphery of the Mediterranean world, which most astonished the Ancients, was the use of cows' butter: those accustomed to olive oil viewed this with shocked surprise. Even an Italian, like Pliny, had the same reaction, forgetting that after all the use of olive oil had not been established in Italy for so very long.'
[25] Antonio de Beatis, *Itinerario di Monsignor il cardinale de Aragona . . . incominciato nel anno 1517* . . . ed. L. Pastor, Freiburg-im-Breisgau, 1905, p. 121. Food at the very least 'corrompedora dos estômagos' says a Portuguese observer, L. Mendes de Vasconcellos, *Do sitio de Lisboa*, Lisbon, 1608, p. 113. This referred to the 'nações do Norte e em parte de França e Lombardia'.
[26] The dean of Bayeux to the Marquis of Mantua, A.d.S., Mantua, Gonzaga, Francia, series E, f° 637, 1st June, 1529.

courage, battling against the hostile nature of the climate and soil, these Mediterranean expatriates tried to build a new Mediterranean culture in the tropics. The attempt failed. Although there were occasional successes the rural and alimentary civilization of their native lands could not be transplanted to the soil of Spanish and Portuguese America, a zone of maize, manioc, pulque, and before long of rum. One of the great trans-Atlantic supply operations from Spain and Portugal was devoted to maintaining artificially in the New World the alimentary civilization of the Mediterranean: ships laden with flour, wine, and oil left Seville and Lisbon for the other side of the ocean.[27]

Yet it was Mediterranean man who almost alone of Europeans survived the transplantation to a new land. Perhaps it was because he was already accustomed to the harsh conditions of one climate, that of the Mediterranean, which is not always kind to the human organism, and was hardened by his struggle against endemic malaria and the regular scourge of plague. Perhaps too it was because he had always been schooled in sobriety and frugality in his native land. The deceptively welcoming climate of the Mediterranean can sometimes be cruel and murderous. It is the filter that has prevented men from distant lands from settling on the shores of the warm sea. They may arrive as conquerors, yesterday's barbarians, today's men of property: but how long can they resist the 'scorching heat of summer and . . . the malaria'?[28] 'The masters come and go,' wrote Walter Bauer of Sicily, 'the others remain, and it is a romance without words',[29] always the same.

Drought: the scourge of the Mediterranean. The disadvantage of this climate for human life lies in the annual distribution of rainfall. It rains a good deal: in some places there is exceedingly high precipitation.[30] But the rains fall in autumn, winter, and spring, chiefly in autumn and spring. It is broadly the opposite of a monsoon climate. The monsoon climate fruitfully combines warmth and water. The Mediterranean climate separates these two important factors of life, with predictable consequences. The 'glorious skies' of the summer semester have their costly drawbacks. Everywhere drought leads to the disappearance or reduction of running waters and natural irrigation: the Mediterranean countries are the zone of the *oueds* and the *fiumari*. It arrests the growth of herbaceous vegetation: so crops and plants must adapt to drought[31] and learn to use as quickly

[27] François Chevalier, 'Les cargaisons des flottes de la Nouvelle Espagne vers 1600', in *Revista de Indias*, 1943.

[28] P. Vidal de la Blache, *op. cit.*, p. 182; Bonjean, in *Cahiers du Sud*, May, 1943, p. 329–330.

[29] In O. Benndorf, *op. cit.*, p. 62, Colette, *La naissance du Jour*, 1941, p. 8–9.

[30] 4 metres a year in the Gulf of Cattaro.

[31] See the article by Schmidthüser, 'Vegetationskunde Süd-Frankreichs und Ost-Spaniens' in *Geogr. Zeitschr.*, 1934, p. 409–422. On deforestation, see H. von Trotha Treyden, 'Die Entwaldung der Mittelmeerländer' in *Pet. Mitt.*, 1916, and the bibliography.

and profitably as possible the precious sources of water. Wheat, 'a winter plant',[32] hastens to ripen and complete its active cycle by May or June – in Egypt and Andalusia by April.[33] The olives of Tunisia are ripened by the autumn rains. From earliest times dry-farming seems to have been practised everywhere, empirically[34] and not only on the initiative of the Phoenicians. From earliest times irrigation in all its diverse forms seems to have penetrated the Mediterranean regions from the East. Today (cf. K. Sapper's map),[35] the limit of the *Kunstbewässerung* is appreciably the same as that of the Mediterranean climate. Many plants, both herbaceous and shrub, which had adapted in the course of evolution to a dry climate, came to the Mediterranean along the same paths as the hydraulic techniques. As we have noted, during the first thousand years before Christ, the culture of the vine and olive spread from the eastern regions of the sea to the West.[36] The Mediterranean, by its climate was predestined for shrub culture. It is not only a garden, but, providentially, a land of fruit-bearing trees.

On the other hand the climate does not favour the growth of ordinary trees and forest coverings. At any rate it has not protected them. Very early the primeval forests of the Mediterranean were attacked by man and much, too much, reduced. They were either restored incompletely or not at all; hence the large area covered by scrub and underbrush, the debased forms of the forest. Compared to northern Europe, the Mediterranean soon became a deforested region. When Chateaubriand passed through Morea, it was 'almost entirely bereft of trees'.[37] The traveller crossing from the bare stones of Herzegovina to the wooded slopes of Bosnia enters a different world, as Jean Brunhes has noted.[38] Almost everywhere, wood was expensive,[39] often very expensive indeed. At Medina del Campo 'richer in fairs than in *montes* [i.e., wooded mountains]', the humanist Antonio de Guevara, reflecting on his budget, concluded, 'all told, the wood cost us as much as what was cooking in the pot'.[40]

Another consequence is the scarcity in the Mediterranean zone of true pastures. As a result there are few of the cattle so useful to the rich farming, necessarily based on the use of manure, practised in the northern countries where the soil is so washed by the rain that it loses its fertile elements – of which the Mediterranean drought is, it is true, a better guardian. Cattle are only found in really large numbers in Egypt and in the rainy Balkans, on the northern margins of the Mediterranean, or on high lands where

---

[32] According to Woiekof, quoted in Jean Brunhes, *Géographie humaine*, 4th ed., p. 133.
[33] G. Botero, *op. cit.*, I, p. 10.
[34] André Siegfried, *op. cit.*, p. 84–85; Jean Brunhes, *op. cit.*, p. 261.
[35] 'Die Verbreitung der künstlichen Feldbewässerung', in *Pet. Mitt.*, 1932.
[36] M. Sorre, *Les foundements biologiques . . . op. cit.*, p. 146.
[37] *Itinéraire de Paris a Jerusalem*, 1811, p. 120.
[38] *Géographie humaine*, 4th ed., p. 51, note 1.
[39] Even at Constantinople, Robert Mantran, *Istanbul dans la seconde moitié du XVIIe siècle, Essai d'histoire institutionelle économique et sociale*, 1962, p. 29.
[40] *Biblioteca de Autores Españoles* (B.A.E.), XIII, p. 93.

more rain falls than elsewhere. Sheep and goats (the former raised for their wool more than for their flesh) could not compensate for the deficiency in meat rations. Rabelais' monk of Amiens, 'quite angry, scandalized, and out of all patience', who with his travelling companions is contemplating the beauties of Florence has the following to say, 'Now at Amiens,' he explains, 'in four, nay five times less ground than we have trod in our contemplations, I could have shown you above fourteen streets of roasting cooks, most ancient, savoury and aromatic. I cannot imagine what kind of pleasure you have taken in gazing on the lions and Africans (so methinks you call their tigers) near the belfry, or in ogling the porcupines and estridges [ostriches] in the Lord Philip Strozzi's palace. Faith and truth, I had rather see a good fat goose at the spit.'[41] Apropos of the Mediterranean a geographer once wrote jokingly to me, 'Not enough meat and too many bones.'[42]

To the northerner, even in the sixteenth century, the livestock of the Mediterranean seemed deficient, the cattle often skinny and the sheep weighing little. 'In 1577, Montmorency and his army ate 8000 sheep brought from all over lower Languedoc. Their average weight "l'ung portant l'autre" was 30 *livres* per beast, or about 12 modern kilos. This was next to nothing and the animal was almost worthless: 4 *livres* each or a little over an *écu* for a sheep . . .'.[43] At Valladolid, for 11,312 sheep slaughtered between 23rd June and 5th December, 1586, an average yield of 11·960 kilogrammes of meat per beast has been calculated (26 Castilian pounds). Similarly for 2302 cattle slaughtered during the same period, the meat per beast was 148.12 kilogrammes (322 Castilian pounds).[44] So the weight of the stock was low; the same was true of horses. There were some very fine horses in the Mediterranean, Turks, jennets from Naples, Andalusian chargers, and Barbary horses from North Africa, but they were all saddle horses, fast and nimble, and went out of fashion during the following century which was to see the popularity of the heavy horses, asses, and mules of the North. Increasingly, for the mails, for the carriages then coming into fashion, for the artillery's gun-carriages and limbers, the strength of the horses was becoming a decisive factor. Dantiscus, who landed on 4th December, 1522 at Codalia on the Cantabrian coast, set off towards León with six pack horses 'non tamen tam bonis', he wrote, 'ut sunt apud nos qui plumbum ferunt ex Cracovia in Hungariam . . .'.[45] The comparison with the horses which transported lead from Cracow to Hungary is too spontaneous to be mistaken. Besides what fodder was there for horses in the south? Oats had only just made their appearance in cer-

---

[41] *Le Quart livre du noble Pantagruel*, Urquhart & Motteux trans., 1904, ed., p. 49.
[42] Letter from Pierre Gourou, 27th June, 1949.
[43] E. Le Roy Ladurie, *op. cit.*, p. 118–119.
[44] B. Bennassar, 'L'alimentation d'une ville espagnole au XVIe siècle. Quelques données sur les approvisionnements et la consommation de Valladolid', in *Annales E.S.C.*, 1961, p. 733.
[45] Dantiscus to the King of Poland, Valladolid, 4th January, 1523, Czartoryski Library, no. 36, f° 55.

tain regions, such as Languedoc[46] and human mouths competed with the horses for barley. Pity the French horses, who once over the Spanish border began to whinny with dismay, according to Barthélemy Joly, for now they would be on a diet of 'short and unappetizing straw'.[47]

Without suggesting that it explains everything, we might note that if the swing-plough, which did little more than scratch the surface of the earth, survived in the Mediterranean countryside, it was not only because of the fragility of the thin layer of loose topsoil, but also because the teams of oxen or mules were not strong enough. Shallow ploughing, the *raies*, were done as often as seven or eight times a year.[48] It would have been better, as time was to prove, to plough more deeply, as in the North, where the wheeled plough with swivelling fore-carriage was a great instrument of progress. In Languedoc, the *mousse* or pseudo-plough imitated from the North, could not fulfil this role and was little used.[49] The poor *aratores* of Languedoc 'untiringly scratched the surface of the fallow fields in vain: they bear no comparison' with the hefty *charrueurs* of the Ile-de-France or Picardy.[50]

The truth is that the Mediterranean has struggled against a fundamental poverty, aggravated but not entirely accounted for by circumstances. It affords a precarious living, in spite of its apparent or real advantages. It is easy to be deceived by its famous charm and beauty. Even as experienced a geographer as Philippson was dazzled, like all visitors from the North, by the sun, the colours, the warmth, the winter roses, the early fruits. Goethe at Vicenza was captivated by the popular street life with its open stalls and dreamed of taking back home with him a little of the magic air of the South. Even when one is aware of the reality it is difficult to associate these scenes of brilliance and gaiety with images of misery and physical hardship. In fact, Mediterranean man gains his daily bread by painful effort. Great tracts of land remain uncultivated and of little use. The land that does yield food is almost everywhere subject to biennial crop rotation that rules out any great productivity. Michelet again was the historian who best understood the basic harshness of all these lands, starting with his own Provence.

There is one visible sign of this poverty: the frugality that has never failed to impress the northerner. The Fleming Busbecq, when in Anatolia, wrote in 1555, 'I dare say that a man of our country spends more on food in one day than a Turk in twelve. . . . The Turks are so frugal and think so little of the pleasures of eating that if they have bread, salt, and some garlic or an onion and a kind of sour milk which they call *yoghoort*, they ask nothing more. They dilute this milk with very cold water and crumble bread into it and take it when they are hot and thirsty . . . it is not only palatable and digestible, but also possesses an extraordinary power of quenching the

---

[46] E. Le Roy Ladurie, *op. cit.*, p. 181.
[47] Barthélemy Joly, *Voyage en Espagne*, p. 9.
[48] E. Le Roy Ladurie, *op. cit.*, p. 78.
[49] *Ibid.*, p. 80.   [50] *Ibid.*, p. 79.

thirst.'[51] This sobriety has often been noted as one of the great strengths of the Turkish soldier on campaign. He would be content with a little rice, ground meat dried in the sun, and bread coarsely cooked in the ashes of the camp fire.[52] The western soldier was more particular, perhaps because of the example of the many Germans and Swiss.[53]

The peasants and even the city-dwellers of Greece, Italy, and Spain were hardly more demanding than these Turks, whose frugal habits were noted only a century ago by Théophile Gautier, who was amazed that the sturdy *caïdjis*, with bulging muscles from their heavy work as oarsmen, could spend the whole day on board their *caïques*, eating almost nothing but raw cucumbers.[54] 'In Murcia,' wrote Alexandre de Laborde in his *Itinéraire descriptif de l'Espagne* (1828), 'one cannot find a servant girl during the summer, and many of those who have a position leave it when the fine weather comes. They can then easily find salad, some fruit, melons and especially red peppers, and these provisions are sufficient to keep them.'[55] 'I invited everyone to supper,' writes Montaigne, adding (the incident took place at the Baths of Lucca), 'because in Italy a banquet is the equivalent of a light meal in France.'[56]

Commines on the other hand went into raptures over the abundant fare of Venice. He had the excuse of being a foreigner. And Venice was Venice, a town privileged for food. Bandello himself was dazzled by the markets of the town, by the 'abbondanza grandissima d'ogni sorte di cose da mangiare',[57] and he is a reliable witness. But this luxurious market in a rich and well-situated town created, as we know, great problems of supply, and cost the Signoria much anxiety and vigilance.

Has the very small part played in Mediterranean literature by feasts and banquets ever been remarked? Descriptions of meals – except of course princely tables – never suggest plenty.[58] In Bandello's novels, a good meal means a few vegetables, a little Bologna sausage, some tripe, and a cup of wine. In the Spanish literature of the Golden Age an empty stomach is a familiar character. Witness the ultra-classical Lazarillo de Tormes or his brother in *picardía*, Guzmán de Alfarache, eating a crust of hard bread without leaving a crumb for the ants.[59] 'May God save you from the plague coming down from Castille,' the same Guzmán is told, 'and from

[51] *The Turkish Letters*, p. 52–53.
[52] G. Botero, *op. cit.*, II, p. 124.
[53] When he was required by Philip II to supply food for the Spanish and German soldiers crossing from Italy to Spain, the Grand Duke of Tuscany preferred to keep the salt meat, of which there was not enough to go round, for the Germans. The Spaniards had arrived first, but would not raise an uproar if they had to be content with rice and biscuit. Felipe Ruiz Martín, Introduction to *Lettres marchandes échangées entre Florence et Medina del Campo*, Paris, 1965.
[54] *Voyage a Constantinople*, 1853, p. 97.
[55] P. 112.
[56] *Journal de voyage en Italie*, Collection 'Hier' 1932, vol. III, p. 242.
[57] *Op. cit.*, III, p. 409.
[58] *Ibid.*, IV, p. 233, p. 340, VI, p. 400–401. Except in northern Italy.
[59] Mateo Aleman, *Vida del picaro Guzmán de Alfarache*, I, part I, 3, p. 45.

the famine coming up from Andalusia.'[60] And we may remember Don Quixote's bills of fare, or the proverb: 'If the lark flies over Castille, she must take her grain of corn with her.'[61]

Although the gardens, orchards, and seafoods may provide varied additions, they supply what is essentially a frugal diet even today, 'bordering on malnutrition in many cases'.[62] This frugality results not from virtue or indifference to food as Busbecq would have called it, but from necessity.

The Mediterranean soil too is responsible for the poverty it inflicts on its peoples, with its infertile limestone, the great stretches blighted with salt, the lands covered with *nitre*, as Pierre Belon called it,[63] its rare deposits of loose soil, and the precariousness of its arable land. The thin layers of topsoil, which only the modest wooden swing-plough can scratch, are at the mercy of the wind or the flood waters. They are enabled to survive only by man's constant effort. Given these conditions, if the peasants' vigilance should be distracted during long periods of unrest, not only the peasantry but also the productive soil will be destroyed. During the dis-disturbances of the Thirty Years' War, the German peasantry was deci-mated, but the land remained and with it the possibility of renewal. Here lay the superiority of the North. In the Mediterranean the soil dies if it is not protected by crops: the desert lies in wait for arable land and never lets go. It is a miracle if it is preserved or reconstituted by the labour of the peasants. Even modern figures prove this. Apart from forests, pastures, and specifically nonproductive land, cultivated land in about 1900 represented 46 per cent of the whole in Italy, 39.1 per cent in Spain, 34.1 per cent in Portugal, and only 18.6 per cent in Greece. On Rhodes, out of a total of 144,000 hectares, 84,000 are still uncultivated today.[64] On the southern shores of the sea the figures are even more disastrous.

But how much do even the cultivated lands yield? Very little, unless there are exceptional conditions (of irrigation for instance) and for this the climate is responsible.

Harvests, in the Mediterranean, more than elsewhere, are at the mercy of unstable elements. If a south wind blows just before harvest time, the wheat dries before it has completely ripened and reached its normal size; or if already ripe, it drops from the ear. To avoid this disaster in Spain, the peasants would often reap in the cool of the night, for the dry grain would fall to the ground during the day.[65] If floods lay waste the lowlands in winter, the sowing is endangered. If there are clear skies too early in spring, the crop that has already ripened is attacked by frost, sometimes irremediably. One can never be certain of the harvest until the last moment. At the end of January, 1574, it looked as if there would be a good harvest

[60] *Ibid.*, part II, 2, p. 163.
[61] Bory de Saint-Vincent, *Guide du voyageur en Espagne*, p. 281, quoted by Ch. Weiss, *L'Espagne depuis Philippe II*, 1844, vol. II, p. 74.
[62] M. Sorre, *op. cit.*, p. 267.
[63] *Op. cit.*, p. 137 v°.
[64] Charles Parain, *La Méditerranée, les hommes et leurs travaux*, 1936, p. 130.
[65] Alonso de Herrera, *op. cit.*, 1645, ed., p. 10 v° (particularly true of barley).

on Crete; there had been plenty of rain and more seed than usual had been sown. But, adds our source, may not these fine hopes be dashed in countries like this, subject to 'pestilential fogs which blight the grain?'[66] The violent winds from the south that are dreaded in the Archipelago often ruined ripe harvests on Corfu[67] and are still feared today throughout the cereal growing area of North Africa; this is the *sirocco*, against which there is no remedy and which in three days can destroy a whole year's work. One other item can be added to the list of dangers to the fields of the Mediterranean: the plague of locusts, a greater threat in the past than it is today.[68]

In the sixteenth century it was rare for a harvest to escape in turn all the dangers that threatened it. Yields were small, and in view of the limited space devoted to cereal growing, the Mediterranean was always on the verge of famine. A few changes in temperature and a shortage of rainfall were enough to endanger human life. Everything was affected accordingly, even politics. If there was no likelihood of a good barley crop on the borders of Hungary (for, in the Mediterranean, barley was the equivalent of oats in the North), it could be assumed that the Grand Turk would not go to war there that year; for how would the horses of the *spahis* be fed? If wheat was also short – as sometimes happened – in the three or four main sources of supply for the sea, whatever the plans of war drawn up during winter or spring, there would be no major war at harvest time, which was also the season of calm seas and great naval campaigns. So immediately brigandage on land and piracy on sea would redouble in vigour. Is it any wonder then, that the only detail of daily life that regularly finds its way into diplomatic correspondence concerns the harvests? It has rained, it has not rained, the wheat has not sprouted; Sicily promises well, but the Turkish harvest was poor, the Grand Turk will certainly not let any wheat out. Will this year be a year of scarcity, of *carestia*, of dearth?

The letters written by the majordomo Francisco Osorio to Philip II in 1558 informed the king at great length, in his northern exile, of the weather over the Peninsula. This citizen of Valladolid pays great attention to the colour of the sky, the state of the harvest and the price of bread. On 13th March, 1558, '. . . for two days now,' he writes, 'the weather here has been clear with plenty of sun and wind. It has not rained since the middle of January. The price of bread has risen somewhat and a "pragmatic" has been instituted to fix the price in future. Since it was published the other day, the sky has become cloudy. This surely brings hope of rain

[66] A.d.S. Venice, 22nd January, 1574, Capi del C° dei X, Lettere B^a 286, f°s 8 and 9.
[67] G. Botero, *Dell'isole*, p. 72.
[68] G. Vivoli, *Annali di Livorno*, 1842–1846, III, p. 18, an invasion of Tuscany by locusts (1541); at Verona, August, 1542 and June, 1553, Ludovico Moscardo, *Historia di Verona*, Verona, 1668, p. 412 and 417; in Hungary, Tebaldo Tebaldi to the Duke of Modena, Venice, 21st August, 1543, A.d.S. Modena; in Egypt, 1544 and 1572, Museo Correr, D. delle Rose, 46, f° 181; on Cyprus, 13th September, 1550, A.d.S. Venice, Senato Mar; 31, f° 42 v° to 43 v°; in the Camargue, 1614, J. F. Noble de la Lauzière, *op. cit.*, p. 446.

in April. In Andalusia and Extremadura, as in the kingdom of Toledo it has rained and the weather is very favourable: the price of bread there has fallen greatly.'[69] On 30th October, 1558, he writes: 'The wheat harvest was abundant; there is a moderate amount of wine throughout the kingdom, sowing is well advanced everywhere. On the 26th it snowed all morning, with big flakes. Afterwards it rained heavily, which will be of great advantage to the sowing. From the weather here I am sure that it cannot be very warm in Brussels. The price of bread throughout the kingdom has fallen.'[70]

That Philip II should be kept minutely informed of the variations in the weather from seedtime onwards; that the price of bread should rise and fall depending on the rainfall; that these details should be found in a series of letters where one searches in vain for any other precise details of economic history: all this is very revealing of the state of the Mediterranean food supply in the sixteenth century. It was no mere 'economic' problem, but a matter of life and death.

For famine, real famine when people died in the streets, was a reality. In 1521, relates the Venetian Navagero, 'there was such famine in Andalusia that countless animals died and the countryside was deserted; many people died also. There was such drought that the wheat was lost and not a blade of grass could any longer be found in the fields; that year the breeds of Andalusian horses for the most part died out and they have not been restored to this day [1525].'[71] This was an extreme case. But we constantly find *carestia* recorded as the years go past; every government went in search of grain and had to organize public distributions to prevent people from dying of hunger, in which it was not always successful. During the second half of the century a particularly serious crisis affected the whole Mediterranean between 1586 and 1591, and this crisis opened up the Mediterranean to the northern ships. Even in a normal year life was never very comfortable or luxurious. Think of the Tuscans who at the end of the sixteenth century, with all their ploughed lands, vineyards, and mulberry trees, 'con tutto ciò non raccolgono vettevaglie per un terzo dell'anno'![72] Or think of the sentence in Guzmán's story, 'it was a lean year because of the drought. Seville suffered greatly from it, for the city is sorely strained even in prosperous years. . . .'

A double constraint has always been at the heart of Mediterranean history: poverty and uncertainty of the morrow. This is perhaps the cause of the carefulness, frugality, and industry of the people, the motives that have been behind certain, almost instinctive, forms of imperialism, which are sometimes nothing more than the search for daily bread. To compensate for its weaknesses, the Mediterranean has had to act, to look

---

[69] *CODOIN*, XXVII, p. 191–192.
[70] *Ibid.*, p. 194–195.
[71] Andrea Navagero, *Il viaggio fatto in Spagna* . . ., Venice, 1563, p. 27–28.
[72] G. Botero, *op. cit.*, I, I, p. 40; Marco Foscari, *Relazioni di Firenze*, 1527; E. Albèri, *op. cit.*, II, I, p. 25.

further afield and take tribute from distant lands, associating itself with their economies: in so doing it has considerably enriched its own history.

2. THE SEASONS

The sea's climate, with its two clearly defined seasons, regulates Mediterranean life into two phases, year in, year out, sending the Mediterranean people by turns to their summer then to their winter quarters. The countless records we have of the quality and nature of the weather can be classified without reference to the year: only the months matter here, and almost invariably we find the same story. The 'gates of the year' open and shut at the appointed time. Gates of the year: this is the name by which solstices and equinoxes are known in Kabylia. 'Every time a new season arrives for men, bringing its chances with it: barley bread or famine.'[73]

The winter standstill. Winter begins early and finishes late: its arrival is dreaded and its departure viewed with disbelief. It is expected ahead of the calendar, as wisdom counsels: 9th September, 'essando hormai il fine dell' estate', says a Venetian Senate document; then on 20th September: 'venendo hora il tempo del inverno'; 23rd September: 'approximandose el tempo del inverno'.[74] What lies behind such concern? In this case a desire not to be surprised by winter, to lay up in good time the *galee grosse*, the *navi* and the light galleys, and to dismiss all unnecessary troops. Now was the time when everyone looked to his personal health, which might be affected during the slightest indisposition by the 'malignità de la stagione'. The roll begins of disasters, trials, restrictions, and abandoned activities, for this was the 'stagione horrida', hard on men and things alike: the season of continual rain, 'di e note', floods sparing neither countryside nor town, heavy falls of snow, storms, tempests at sea, and the cold, cruel to all and particularly to the poor, 'incommodo omnium et maxime pauperum'.[75] The hospitals would be filled with poor folk. And one never knew what might happen, even when the trees were in blossom again, or the plains around Montpellier were blue with wild hyacinths.[76] On 15th April, 1594, at Bologna, five days after Easter, 'there fell heavy snow, after the beginning of a fine spring, with all the trees in bloom. God protect us!'[77] On 23rd May, 1633, at Florence, after rain on the 21st, it suddenly grew so cold that fires had to be lit, 'come per li gran freddi di gennaio', and the mountains were covered in snow.[78]

Most affected by this enforced retirement was country life.[79] The peasant

---

[73] Jean Servier, *Les Portes de l'année*, 1962, p. 13.
[74] A.d.S. Venice, Senato Mar 18, f° 45 v°; 23, f° 97; 31, f° 126.
[75] *Ibid.*, 4, f° 26, 12th December 1460.
[76] *Félix et Thomas Platter à Montpellier*, p. 33, January, 1593.
[77] Galiani, *Cronaca di Bologna*, Marciana, 6114, CIII, 5.
[78] Giovanni Baldinucci, *Quaderno di ricordi*, Marciana, VI–XCIV.
[79] '. . . winter was always the most feared season when one had to survive as best one could', M. Le Lannou, *op. cit.*, p. 52.

perforce must rest, said Aristophanes, while Zeus waters the earth.[80] During clear spells he sows barley (unless he has already done so in October), wheat in December, and at the beginning of spring, maize. In the sixteenth century maize had only just been introduced from America. And these are light duties, which do not call for the mass labour of summer, or the help of one's neighbours, work *por favor*, as they say in Portugal. Even if one adds sowing vegetables and a little ploughing, winter is still a time of leisure and festivities. In Christian countries there is the killing of the pig in December, mentioned in Boccaccio's tales.[81] In January in the mountains of Kabylia, at the winter solstice the feast of the *Ennayer* is celebrated, marking the separation of the sun's cycles, when copious meals lasting long into the night use up precious reserves. This extravagant feasting is to propitiate the coming year.[82]

Cut off by snow, most of the mountain ranges are abandoned for the lowlands by flocks and shepherds. The mountain dwellers who stay at home will have sold at the autumn fairs the young animals they can no longer feed. This is still so today on the borders of the Pyrenees[83] and it was no doubt for the same reason that calves and lambs were being sold cheaply at the Baths of Lucca, when Montaigne passed through in 1581.[84] The mountains deserted by the shepherds were usually avoided by the traveller. In the snowy highlands one might risk losing life and posessions: 'Sire,' writes the French ambassador from Constantinople, 12th February, 1578,[85] 'the snows here have been so continuous and so heavy for fifty days that they have held me besieged and kept me from leaving last week as I had resolved.' Gédoyn 'the Turk', French consul at Aleppo in 1624 describes the hazards of his journey through the Balkan mountains in winter: he narrowly avoided freezing to death or falling prey to bears and wolves.[86] In the Moroccan Atlas, explains Leo Africanus, the merchants bringing dates from the South after October are often caught in extraordinary blizzards of mountain snow. No one escapes them. Even the trees are buried under a great snowy shroud.[87]

Winter journeys were difficult in the lowlands too; with the constant rain, the rivers might overflow their banks, carrying away the bridges 'to such a degree', related Bandello at the beginning of one of his tales, 'that our Mantuans who have estates on that side of the Po cannot make use of the supplies or goods of their lands'.[88] In October, 1595, the river rose so high that 'the Ferrarans up in arms were preparing to open a breach in the

---

[80] See the classic passage in Taine, *La philosophie de l'Art*, 20th ed., II, p. 121.
[81] 8th Day, *Novella VI*.
[82] Jean Servier, *op. cit.*, p. 287, ff.
[83] P. Arqué, *Géographie des Pyrénées françaises*, p. 43.
[84] *Voyage en Italie*, p. 227–237.
[85] E. Charrière, *Négociations de la France dans le Levant*, III, p. 713.
[86] *Le Journal et les lettres de Gédoyn 'le Turc'*, published by Boppe, Paris, 1909, p. 37–38 '. . . and left me alone in the wood full of bears, wolves and other wild beasts, as their footprints freshly made in the snow clearly showed'.
[87] *Description de l'Afrique, tierce partie du monde*, p. 33–34.
[88] *Op. cit.*, I, XVI, p. 360.

dykes on our side', writes a Venetian.[89] Another time it was the Tiber that overflowed. In 1598 it carried away half the 'Aemilius' bridge, which had already been repaired in 1575.[90] In 1594 it was the Arno. That year in Tuscany once again the waterways were all frozen over and the fruit trees damaged by frost.[91] During some particularly cold winters the canals froze in Venice.[92] At best, sixteenth-century travellers would have to face waterlogged roads full of potholes, impassable during the continuous snow and rain, such as the Spanish roads in February, 1581,[93] for example, or those of the Balkans in December, 1592,[94] or more recently, roads 'so muddy that it is difficult to discern the colour of the traveller's clothes'.[95]

Shipping at a halt. The sea also becomes hostile in the winter, so much so that in the past it brought shipping to a standstill. In Roman times ships were laid up by order between October and April, a step counselled by the prudence of the navigators.[96] From the sea voyages of the Apostle Paul, we learn that the *Boniportus* of Crete was not suitable *ad hiemandum*,[97] and that the Alexandrian ship that was to carry Paul had wintered at Malta.[98] Centuries later similar stipulations are found in the maritime codes of medieval towns, in the *Constitutum Usus* of Pisa of 1160,[99] when inactivity was compulsory between St. Andrew's Day and the Kalends of March ('tempore hyemali post festum Sancti Andreae . . . ante kalendas Martii'), in the maritime statute of 1284 at Venice,[100] in the maritime statue of Ancona of 1387.[101] Legislators maintained for centuries the precautions and prohibitions dictated by experience. Until the end of the eighteenth century sailors of the Levant put to sea only between the feasts of St. George (5th May) and St. Dmitri (26th October).[102]

But after 1450, shipping gradually began to triumph over the obstacles

[89] Museo Correr, Dona delle Rose, 23, f° 449 v°.
[90] Stendhal, *Promenades* . . ., ed. Le Divan, 1932, II, p. 258.
[91] G. Mecatti, *Storia cronologica* . . . II, p. 790.
[92] G. de Silva to Philip II, Venice, 2nd January, 1573, Simancas E° 1332; the Bosporus apparently froze over during the reign of Constantine V (Copronymus), 718–775, G. Botero, *op. cit.*, p. 105.
[93] Mario to the Cardinal of Como, Elvas, 19th Feb., 1581, A. Vaticanes, Spagnia 26, orig. f° 124.
[94] Ragusa Archives, *Lettere di Levante*, 38, f° 27 v°.
[95] A. Boué, *La Turquie d'Europe*, 1840, IV, p. 460.
[96] J. M. Pardessus, *Collection de lois maritimes*, I, p. 73, 179, for reference to Pliny's *Natural History*, II, 47; Robert de Smet, *Les assurances maritimes*, 1934, p. VI; A. Schaube, *Handelsgeschichte* . . ., 1906, p. 152–154; Walter Ashburner, *The Rhodian Sea Law*, Oxford, 1909, CXLVIII, E. de Saint-Denis, 'Mare clausum' in *R.E.L.*, 1947.
[97] *Acts of the Apostles*, XXVII, 12.   [98] *Ibid.*, XXVII, 13.
[99] J. M. Pardessus, *Collection de lois maritimes*, IV, p. 1837, p. 578.
[100] *Ibid.*, VI, p. 46.   [101] *Ibid.*, V, p. 179.
[102] Jean Chardin, *Journal du Voyage en Perse*, 1686, I, p. 110 ff. Victor Bérard, *Les Navigations d'Ulysse*, II, *Pénélope et les Barons des îles*, 1930, notes p. 33, n. 1: 'It is curious that the Moslems should have adopted for the payment of leases, rents, etc. those dates which had been in use by the Christians under the Greek Empire, i.e., St. George's Day, 5th May, and St. Demetrius' Day, 26th October.' A. Boué, *op. cit.*, III, p. 120.

of winter weather. Even so these were only partial victories still involving great risk. Spectacular wrecks occurred every year to remind men of winter's powers. So much so that Venice in 1569 brought back the old prohibitions in a milder form it is true, since now they forbade sea voyages only between 15th November and 20th January, 'su'l cuor dell' invernata'.[103] It was clearly impossible to turn the clock back in such matters. The new laws were so little observed that the Signoria had to repeat them in 1598.[104] All the same, the measure is symptomatic, indicating the yearly toll that winter took of shipping even at this period. On 1st December, 1521, a 'Greek' wind sank many ships in the Adriatic, one laden with grain in the very port of Ragusa;[105] on 11th November, 1538, a single storm drove thirty-eight of Barbarossa's galleys on to the coast, where they were broken up by the raging seas, the survivors were killed and the cargoes looted by the Albanians;[106] on 9th November, 1544, seven Ragusan ships fell victim to a storm; in January, 1545,[107] the *greco tramontana* sank fifty vessels in the Adriatic, including three Venetian ships on their way to Syria with over 100,000 ducats on board;[108] on 29th December, 1570, during the 'greatest misfortune' of the Adriatic, two ships laden with grain sank right inside Ragusa harbour.[109] There are countless similar episodes, for example, the entire fleet of Spanish galleys lost in the bay of La Herradura in October, 1562; a hundred ships and twelve galleys driven on to the coast by the raging sea before Constantinople in October, 1575![110]

Anyone sailing in winter knew he was at the mercy of the elements, had to be on the alert, and could expect to see hoisted on bad nights the storm lamps, the 'fanales de borrasca' mentioned by Guzmán de Alfarache.[111] The voyages, being longer and more eventful than in summer, became less frequent during the stormy season. Even in the early nineteenth century, there were fewer departures from Venice and Odessa after October.[112] They were rarer still in the sixteenth century.

On clear days small boats might venture out over short distances, of course, on voyages lasting a few hours. Bigger ships, offering greater resistance to the winter, could accomplish even in bad weather voyages that were the more profitable because of the season. But there was clearly an overall reduction in shipping. As for the galleys, they remained completely inactive in port, under the *volte* of the arsenals, well-sheltered and drawn up out of the water, while the oarsmen languished with little work to do. Marcel Mauss, who studied the effect of winter on religious and social life (among Eskimos, it is true), would have been amused by a

---

[103] J. M. Pardessus, *op. cit.*, V, p. 71–72, law of 8th June, 1569.
[104] *Ibid.*, V, p. 81, law of 18th June, 1598.
[105] S. Razzi, *La storia di Raugia*, p. 121.
[106] *Ibid.*, p. 141.   [107] *Ibid.*, p. 156.   [108] *Ibid.*   [109] *Ibid.*, p. 169–170.
[110] Dispatch from Constantinople, 17th, 18th, and 20th October, 1575, Simancas E° 1334.
[111] M. Aleman, *op. cit.*, II, Part 2, IX, p. 219.
[112] Comte de Rochechouart, *Mémoires, op. cit.*, p. 75, 103.

passage from Chateaubriand's *Itinéraire*. According to him, the French Capuchin friars 'have their principal residence at Napoli [the Rumanian town in Morea] because the galleys of the beys spend the winter there . . . ordinarily from the month of November until the feast of Saint George, which is the day when they put out to sea again: they are full of Christian prisoners who need to be instructed and encouraged, and this task is undertaken with as much zeal as profit by Father Barnabas of Paris, who

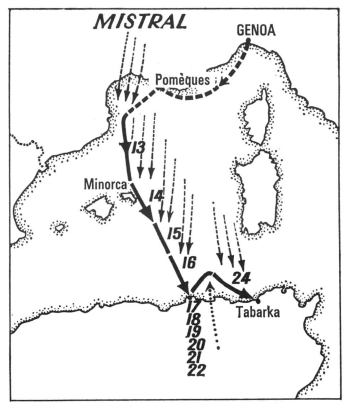

Fig. 20: *A voyage to Spain that ended up at Tabarka, January, 1597*

Cesare Giustiniano embarked at Genoa on a galley belonging to the Republic. He put in at Pomègues, a little island opposite Marseilles and had crossed the Gulf of Lions when the *mistral* surprised his ship near Cape Creus. Instead of reaching Spain, where he was to represent the Republic as ambassador to Philip II (that is just after the financial crisis of 1596, which had so severely affected Genoese businessmen), he was driven due south by the storm. The galley came to shore at a deserted bay on the African coast, between Djidjelli and Collo and stayed there for six days without harm. It was impossible to return to the northern route, and the ship was obliged to make for the Genoese island of Tabarka. The galley was damaged, and it was on board a merchantman that Cesare Giustiniano sailed first to Sardinia, and finally to Spain. From the correspondence of Cesare Giustiniano, A.d.S. Genoa, Lettere Principi.

is at present Superior of the House of Athens and Morea'.[113] This was in 1806, when galleys had practically disappeared in the West, but for those that survived at Malta and in the East, geographical determinism continued to exert just as much influence as it had in the time of Sulaimān the Magnificent.

In the sixteenth century the armadas, *fuste*, or galleys of the corsairs, were also obliged to put into port for the winter. In one month of December (possibly in the year 1580) 'all the corsairs', according to Haëdo, 'wintered off Algiers or had their boats laid up in the port'.[114] Similarly, in December, 1579, again from Haëdo's account, the Re'is Mami Arnaut took up winter quarters 'en el rio de Bona',[115] on the river at Bône, in the Seybouse estuary.

As for the naval squadrons, the Spanish government was only too eager to use them in the off-season, when it could be sure that the Turkish armadas would be in port. The corsairs did the same, whenever they thought it worth the risk; the perils of the seas were after all no more formidable than an encounter with a large armada in summer. But the sailors in the service of Spain were continually protesting against these winter voyages. 'My zeal in the service of Your Majesty obliges me to say,' the Prince of Melfi wrote in August, 1561, 'that to have the galleys sail in winter is to risk losing them, in particular along the Spanish coastline, which has so few ports. Even if the ships escape, the gangs will be lost . . . and will be in no condition to serve at the proper time [next season].' He was then Philip II's naval commander, and was taking his precautions.[116]

Galley warfare was indeed impossible during winter, a fact that the professionals had to keep explaining to their political masters who remained deaf to their advice. Don Garcia of Toledo, who was also 'general de la mar' to Philip II explained his reasons for not sending his fleet against the Corsican uprising in 1564 as Genoa had requested. 'It is a fact, clearly established,' he wrote[117] to the Spanish ambassador at Genoa, Figueroa, 'that all sea expeditions during winter are a complete waste of money. . . . We shall squander money without the least return as has already happened on many occasions and will happen again until the end of time if anything is undertaken at this time of year.' In addition (the troops on board had come from the engagement of the Peñon de Velez and were tired), there was a risk of compromising the spring operations for the sake of chasing after a shadow, or as he put it 'of catching the pigeon by the tail when we might catch it by the head'. Even if this was to be a mere display of force it would be dangerous. Crossing the channel of Piombino 'is a terribly long, uncertain and perilous undertaking'.

[113] *Itinéraire* . . ., p. 157.
[114] P. Diego de Haëdo, *Topographia* . . ., Valladolid, 1612, p. 174.
[115] *Ibid.*, p. 124.
[116] Simancas E° 1051, f° 131.
[117] Simancas E° 1054, f° 20 a similar case, this time concerning a voyage to La Goletta, viceroy of Naples to H.M., Naples, 24th January, 1562, Simancas E° 1052, f° 12.

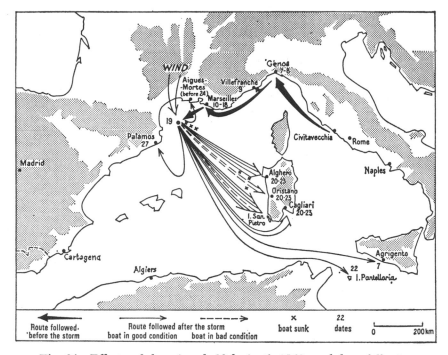

| Route followed, before the storm | Route followed after the storm boat in good condition → boat in bad condition --->| × boat sunk | 22 dates | 0   200 km |

Fig. 21: *Effects of the mistral, 19th April, 1569, and days following*

The squadron of galleys of the Grand Commander of Castile, Don Luis de Requesens, was making for the coast of Spain. Its intention was to reach the shore of the kingdom of Granada, whose frontier lay southwest of Cartagena, and where the Moriscos had risen on Christmas night of the previous year. The galleys were to intercept the Barbary raids that provided the insurgents with men and arms. The *mistral* surprised the squadron in the Gulf of Lions and drove most of the galleys towards the coast of Sardinia. Note the voyage made against the wind by one galley which reached Aigues-mortes; the arrival on 27th of Don Luis de Requesens' galley at Palamos, where he was preceded by soldiers who had left the squadron at Marseilles and were on their way to Spain on foot; the two courses that led one galley to Pantelleria and the other to Agrigento, where she arrived on 7th May. This map is based on the many documents that I have examined and summarized at Simancas, from which J. Gentil da Silva and Jacques Bertin have drawn up the geographical projection reproduced here. It would also have been possible to provide a map of the discovery and communication of the event. In fact, Genoa seems to have been Spain's chief source of information about the accident.

Galleys that failed to observe the rule were courting disaster. They lay too low in the water to resist the heavy swell and winter storms.[118] It is easy to guess why Charles V tried to take Algiers by surprise in October, 1541. But he fell a victim to the season he had chosen, the time of year 'which the Moors call *Cassem*, which means section and marks the passage

[118] P. Dan, *Histoire de Barbarie*, 1637, 2nd edition, p. 307. Victor Bérard, *op. cit.*, p. 34, n. 1.

from the fair season to the foul'.[119] In January, 1554, the French galleys, under Piero Strozzi, left Marseilles for the Roman shore, accompanied by small boats carrying grain. A squall sank several of these boats and one of the galleys; the others were scattered and returned to Marseilles without oars or sails.[120] We shall have more to say about the Herradura disaster in the open bay near Málaga where the Spanish fleet was swallowed up in October, 1562. The Málaga corridor, exposed to the east winds, was terribly dangerous throughout the winter, more so possibly than the Gulf of Lions. Dangerous in winter, and even in spring, for in April 1570, two galleys were driven aground at Málaga, and three others driven out to sea.[121] Wrecks are recorded in 1566.[122] The following year, in February, 27 ships and barques, almost all from Flanders and carrying arms and salt meats, sank off Málaga.[123] And the Gulf of Lions lived up to its reputation: in April, 1569, the gale that scattered the twenty-five galleys of the Grand Commander of Castile, sailing towards the coast of Granada, and could well have brought total disaster, was so powerful that some of the galleys were driven on to the Sardinian coast while one, that of Ambrosio Negron, did not touch land before Pantelleria.[124] In bad weather, in short, it was best to stay in port, or like Carlo Doria in January, 1603, one might be forced to return to port. He tried in vain to leave the 'beach' of Barcelona, on to which he was several times driven back, with broken masts and yards, and having lost 300 oarsmen.[125]

Winter: season of peace and plans. Bad weather thus forced a truce in the great maritime wars. There was an equally regular truce on land, for campaigning was impossible 'with winter on one's back'.[126] Hostilities might not officially come to a halt, but they clearly lost much of their impetus. This was so of the dramatic Persian War from 1578 to 1590, and of any war in the Mediterranean or para-Mediterranean regions. 'The approach of the day of Kasim (St. Demetrius' day, 26th October) ordinarily marks the end of the Turkish campaigns on land and sea,' notes Hammer in his invaluable book on the Ottoman Empire.[127] For war had to live off the land. It had to bide its time – and this was the crucial factor – until the harvest was either over or about to start. Still in Turkish territory, the

[119] Paul Achard, *La vie extraordinaire des frères Barberousse*, 1939, p. 231.
[120] C^or M^or to the king, Rome, 8th January, 1554, *Corpo Diplomatico Portuguez*, VII, 298–299.
[121] Fourquevaux to Charles IX, Córdoba, April, 1570, C. Douais, *op. cit.*, II, p. 214
[122] C. Duro, *La Armada española desde la unión de Castilla y Aragón*, 1895–1903, II, p. 104. Is this perhaps an error for 1567?
[123] Pedro Verdugo to Philip II, Málaga 19th March, 1567, Simancas E° 149, f° 277–278.
[124] Franc° de Eraso to Philip II, 16th May, 1564, Simancas E° 1446, f° 131.
[125] Contarini to the Doge, Valladolid, 11th January, 1603, A.d.S. Venice.
[126] *Mémoires de Guillaume et Martin Du Bellay*, published by V. L. Bourrilly and F. Vindry for the 'Société de l'Histoire de France', vol I, 1908, p. 39.
[127] *Histoire de l'Empire Ottoman*, vol. VII, p. 268–9, (the date 30th November is given in error).

historian Zinkeisen writes apropos of the siege of Belgrade by the Turks in 1456, 'During the month of June, just as the wheat was beginning to ripen, the Ottoman army set out to besiege Belgrade.'[128] The calendar was commander-in-chief.

In short, the 'winter semester' was a calm and peaceful period. National wars were halted, and so were minor wars, except for a few sudden alarms, for, both on land and sea, bad weather made surprise attacks particularly worthwhile. It was during the winter that Protestant bands came up close to the frontier of Roussillon in 1562; in September 1540, that corsairs from Algiers tried to take Gibraltar by surprise, with the result that their retreat was harassed by the *mistral*; it was often at the end of winter that the *ponentini* with galleons or reinforced galleys went privateering on the stormy seas of the Levant.

During the months when there was 'nothing to report', only tongues and pens were busy. On 20th March, 1589, the Spanish consul at Venice, Juan de Cornoça, wrote: 'We have no news of the Turk, winter has closed the roads . . . we have never been so short of information before'[129] – real information, that is, for there was nothing to stop rumours and false reports. Winter, by slowing down or preventing voyages, became the season *par excellence* of false reports and the time too when boasts could be made with impunity. 'Now that it is winter,' the nuncio wrote of the Imperials, 'they let the French brag as they are wont to do. . . .'[130]

For the governments themselves it was a time for making plans and holding great councils. Staff work increased out of all proportion. Winter was the time of bulging files. One might almost call them winter files, to be used with caution by historians. For there was all the time in the world to discuss, predict, and finally to draw up plans in black and white. 'This is what we should do if such and such happens; but if the Turk or the king of France . . .' and so on and so on, filling pages and pages. These grandiose schemes and brilliant plans which historians analyse with so much respect and conviction were often dreamed up by the side of a blazing log fire or brazier, in a cosy room, while outside, in Madrid (or wherever it was) the *cierzo*, the snowy wind from the mountains, was howling. Nothing seemed too difficult or dangerous. Plans to blockade the Netherlands, to deprive them of salt, to buy up all the Hanseatic grain they lived on, to close the Spanish ports to them, were all winter plans. In 1565–1566, after the great failure of the Turks at Malta, the feeling of insecurity that persisted into the early autumn led to a suggestion that 12,000 men, both Italians and Spaniards, should be sent to La Goletta.[131] How would they be lodged in the tiny *presidio*, even with the enlargements made in the 1560s? Well, they would be lodged under the walls, on the Cape Bon side, which on the map looked a reasonable suggestion. It was all arranged, and as so often, never put into execution. Summer, from this point of view, was not neces-

---

[128] *Op. cit.*, II, p. 81–82.   [129] A. N., K, 1674, orig.
[130] Innsbruck, 8th January, 1552, *Nuntiaturberichte aus Deutschland*, I, XII, p. 140.
[131] See Vol. II, Part III, ch. 2, section 3.

sarily a more reasonable but it was a more realistic time of year; to be more accurate, in summer events took their own course without always responding to the control of governments.

But there was one positive activity in winter, the only one: negotiations diplomatic talks, and pacific resolutions. From this point of view winter provided a salutary breathing-space. In any case, it is a fact that all the peace treaties studied in this book date from the winter months, that they were signed before the upheavals and irreparable events of summer. The Treaty of Cateau-Cambrésis was the result of discussions during the winter of 1558–1559, and was signed on 2nd and 3rd April, 1559. The Turko-Spanish truces were all in midwinter, that of 1581 was signed on 7th February, the peace of Vervins on 2nd May, 1598. The Twelve Years' Truce was signed at the Hague[132] on 9th April, 1609. Only the Anglo-Spanish peace treaty signed on 28th August, 1604,[133] is an exception to the rule. But this one was virtually a certainty from the time of Elizabeth's death in March, 1603, before the voyage to England by Don Juan de Tassis, Count of Villamediana (June, 1603). It is far from our intention to reduce the complex workings of diplomacy to the mere sequence of the seasons. But the date of these agreements has some importance. When do they occur? At the beginning of winter, there had hardly been time for discussion; at the very end of winter, there had been fierce debate; was it not fear and apprehension of the coming summer, with its enormous military expenses which made governments reasonable?

The hardships of winter. The Mediterranean winter, then, was a time of peace and rest. Pleasant enough indeed, one might suppose, remembering the traditional images: the January sunshine claimed in advertisements for the Côte d'Azur; or the flocks of migrating birds, alighting exhausted on the lands of the South to which they appeared as manna from heaven, especially in Egypt, whose fields Pierre Belon[134] saw 'quite white' with birds, in the days no doubt when one could pick up quails in the fields like fruit.

In fact, winter in the Mediterranean, as in Europe, is not so gentle. In the towns particularly it was a time of great hardship for the poor. On 6th November, 1572, Gian Andrea Doria wrote to Don John of Austria,[135] 'Your Highness must know that as there is no grain harvested on the territory of Genoa, and very little of any other kind of food, there is in consequence great poverty, not only in the mountains but in the city itself. It is so great that the poor find it difficult to survive, especially in winter when the need for clothing is added to the lack of bread, and there is no possibility of work.' 'So,' concludes the letter, 'it will be possible to collect at Genoa for next spring, voluntary prisoners for the manning of

[132] A. Ballasteros, *op. cit.*, IV, I, p. 200.
[133] *Ibid.*, p. 201.
[134] Belon, *op. cit.*, p. 101 v°, 'whose fields and meadows become white, principally with storks.'
[135] Simancas E° 1061, f° 133.

ten galleys.' A damaging document both for the Genoa of the bankers and for the Mediterranean winter.[136]

I would not go so far as to claim that the Mediterranean winter is bitterly cold. But it is less warm than is commonly supposed and often wet. Above all it is a stranger, arriving suddenly after six months of sunshine, and the inhabitants are always ill-prepared for its coming. Every year it is as if the cold airstreams take the sea by surprise. It is a fact that Mediterranean houses, built to an open design, with tiled instead of wooden floors, which may be more or less well heated, or indeed heatable, are not built for keeping out the cold; they only offer protection against the heat. Ferdinand of Aragon used to say that contrary to the generally held opinion, one should spend summer in Seville and winter at Burgos:[137] it might be colder there, but at least there was some protection. And many travellers shivering in the icy rooms of a house in Algiers or Barcelona must have thought they had never felt so cold as in the Mediterranean!

The accelerated rhythm of summer life. With the coming of the luxuriant spring, often wet, with 'impetuous' winds . . . 'which bring the trees out in bud',[138] the short-lived spring (almond and olive trees are in flower within a few days), life takes on a new rhythm. On the sea, in spite of the dangers, April is one of the most active months of the year. In the fields, the last ploughing is being done.[139] Then follows the rapid succession of harvests, reaping in June, figs in August, grapes in September, and olives in autumn. Ploughing begins again with the first autumn rains.[140] The peasants of Old Castile had to have their wheat sown towards mid-October, so that the young plants would have time to grow the three or four leaves that would help them withstand the winter frosts.[141] In the space of a few months some of the busiest pages of the farmer's calendar are turned. Every year he has to make haste, take advantage of the last rains of spring or the first of autumn, of the first fine days or the last. All agricultural life, the best part of Mediterranean life, is commanded by the need for haste. Over all looms fear of the winter: it is vital to fill cellars and granaries. Even in town houses, provisions are put by in a safe place,[142] wine, grain, and the essential firewood for heating and cooking. Before the approach of winter, towards September, in order to pay for the indispensable pastures and the year's expenses, the Spanish shepherds in Medinaceli and

---

[136] Winter created misery in Aragon, C. Douais, *op. cit.*, III, p. 36, 13th February, 1567.

[137] G. Botero, *op. cit.*, I, p. 10 '. . . che il Re Ferdinando diveca che d'estate bisognava dimorare in Siviglia come d'inverno a Burgos, che è fredessimi città ma con mirabili ripari contra il freddo . . .'.

[138] Leo Africanus, *op. cit.*, p. 37.

[139] Joan Nistor, *Handel und Wandel in der Moldau bis zum Ende des XVI. Jahrunderts*, 1912, p. 9.

[140] J. Sauvaget, *Alep. Essai sur les origines d'une grande ville syrienne, des origines au milieu du XIXe siècle*, 1941, p. 14.

[141] Jesus García Fernández, *Aspectos del paisaje agrario de Castilla la Vieja*, Valladolid, 1963, p. 25.

[142] M. Bandello, *op. cit.*, I, p. 279, and passim.

elsewhere would sell their fleeces in advance to the merchants. In May they would have to hasten to deliver them to their pressing creditors. But the half-million ducats advanced meant security for the winter.[143] The buried silos of the Arabs of the Oran region, and the 'trenches' of the Apulian and Sicilian peasants were another way of providing for the future.[144]

With summer's coming, war sprang to life in all its forms: land warfare, galley warfare, pirate attacks at sea, and brigand raids in the countryside. The roads grew busy with traffic. On land the traveller's chief enemy was now the heat. But he could travel by night or in the early morning.[145] At sea the warm air from the Sahara brought fine weather, and, equally important, stable atmospheric conditions. In the Aegean Sea the Etesian winds blow regularly from north to south between May and October[146] until the early autumn storms.[147] Baron de Tott says that in June between Crete and Egypt, 'the winds which at that season are trade winds, from West and North, without ever raising the sea, enable the mariner to calculate the moment of his arrival in Egypt'.[148] These were the same winds that had already given Pierre Belon in 1550 a successful voyage from Rhodes to Alexandria. The length of the trip was predictable, and crossings throughout the summer months were relatively calm and reliable. The old Prince Doria used to say, 'In the Mediterranean, there are three ports: Cartagena, June, and July.'[149]

Shipping was more active in these calm summers since harvest time increased trading. The peak periods were at reaping, threshing, fruit picking, and the grape harvest. The appearance of the new wines was a great trading occasion. At Seville at least, *la vendeja* was a kind of wine fair set at a fixed date, 'from the 7th to the 19th October . . . the season known as *la vendeja*', wrote the Duke of Medina Sidonia in 1597.[150] It was for the wines of Andalusia as much as for salt, oil, and overseas goods that the northern boats came to Spain. Cervantes, in the *Coloquio de los Perros*,[151]

[143] R. Carande, *Carlos V y sus banqueros*, Madrid, 1943, p. 57 ff.
[144] Diego Suárez, MS. in B.N. Madrid, Ch. 34.
[145] A. Boué, *op. cit.*, IV, p. 460, Granvelle to Cardinal Riario, Madrid, 15th June, 1580, A. Vaticanes, Spagna, 17, f° 135.
[146] P. Vidal de la Blache, *op. cit.*, p. 428.
[147] G. Hartlaub, *op. cit.*, p. 20.
[148] *Memoirs* (English trans.), II, p. 224.
[149] P. Achard, (*op. cit.*, p. 204) wrongly quotes Mahon for Cartagena, G. Botero, *op. cit.*, p. 7. On the security of Cartagena harbour, *Inst. naut.*, no. 345, p. 95.
[150] The Duke of Medina Sidonia to Philip II, S. Lucar, 20th November, 1597, Simancas E° 178. On the importance of the wine trade at Seville, G. Botero, *op. cit.*, I, p. 10, '. . . che si dice che quando non entrano in Siviglia 4000 arrobe di vino al di, bisogna che il Datio fallisca'.
[151] *Novelas ejemplares*, Madrid, 1914, II, p. 261. It is really incorrect to translate 'vendeja' by 'vendange' (grape-harvest): the word really means sale or market, as explained by Marcel Bataillon, 'Vendeja' in *Hispanic Review*, XXVII, no. 2, April, 1959. The confusion is understandable since the 'market' was essentially one of wines. A document from the beginning of the seventeenth century (B.N., Paris, Fr. 4826, f° 5) says explicitly '. . . the fleet of the wine-harvest (vendange) being about to leave France to go to the ports of Spain for the whole month of July.'

describes the tricks of a woman of easy virtue whose accomplice was an *alguazil* (of course). She specialized in exploiting 'Bretons' (i.e., Bretons, Englishmen, and northerners in general). With one of her friends she would go 'in search of foreigners, and when *la vendeja* came to Seville and Cadiz, their prey arrived too; no Breton escaped their clutches'.

Throughout the Mediterranean the grape harvest was an occasion for merrymaking and licence, a time of madness. At Naples the grape harvesters challenged anyone they met, man or woman, monk or priest. This led to various abuses. Pedro de Toledo, viceroy of Naples, champion of *onestità* and enemy of these pagan customs, even issued an edict against such troublesome habits.[152] We are not told whether the measure was successful. Is there any way of fighting the combination of summer and new wine, of preventing collective revelry, at the fig harvest in one place,[153] or the gathering of the mulberry leaves at another, the plain of Murcia, for instance?[154] At Ragusa, a prudent city and obliged to be so more than others, the wine harvest was a time of alarms and alerts for the authorities; there was greater supervision than usual of the guard and the walls; foreigners were searched for arms, particularly the Apulians in August, 1569; 'li pugliesi', say the Rectors, 'quali intendiamo essere molti nella città et scandalosi . . .'.[155]

Summer was also the season for good catches for the fishermen. Tunny in particular depends on seasonal variations. It was in summer that the *madragues*, the tunny nets, were set to work, and that the Duke of Medina Sidonia, who had the monopoly of the Andalusian *madragues* in the time of Philip II, had recruiters drum up the labour he needed. He levied them like a private army. It was at the turn of the season (just before and just after winter) that the fabled fisheries of the Bosporus took place.[156] It was at the end of winter, too, in April, 1543, that there arrived at Marseilles just before the fishing season boatloads of empty barrels sent from Fréjus ready for salt fish: 1800 on the 17th, in three boats; 200 on the 21st; 600 on the 26th; 1000 on 30th April.[157]

The summer epidemics. But the hot weather also caused fresh outbreaks of the endemic diseases that only temporarily subsided in winter. Baron de Tott notes that the plague 'begins its ravages in the spring and usually lasts until the beginning of winter'.[158] The same could be said of all the

[152] 'Vita di Pietro di Toledo' in *Archivio storico italiano*, IX, p. 22.
[153] In Kabylia, J. Leclercq, *De Mogador a Biskra*, 1881, p. 194.
[154] A. Morel Fatio, *Ambrosio de Salazar*, Toulouse, 1901, p. 16.
[155] Ragusa Archives, L. P. 2, f° 26 & v° 27, 30th August, 1569.
[156] G. Botero, *op. cit.*, p. 105, at the beginning of winter and the beginning of spring. *Description du Bosphore.* . . . Collection des Chroniques nationales, Buchon, vol. III, 1828.
[157] Archives of Bouches-du-Rhône, Admiralty of Marseilles, Register of landing certificates for merchandise. Unloading of vessels: B IX 14 (1543), f° LXV v° and LXVI, LXVII v°, LXIX, LXX.
[158] I, p. 23. On summer fevers, Fourquevaux to the queen, 20th July, 1566, Douais, *Dépêches* . . ., II, 7–8, (Fourquevaux was confined to bed, but no details are given);

Mediterranean epidemics, except exanthematous typhus, which was endemic in North Africa, but which regularly abated at the approach of summer. As usual the towns were the most threatened. Every summer Rome was a graveyard of fever. So the cardinals took refuge in their country houses, their *vigne*, which were not merely an ostentatious luxury, despite Scarron's opinion of them.[159] When the cardinal de Rambouillet, ambassador of the king of France, arrived in Rome in July, 1568, 'my lord cardinals of Ferrara and Vitelli' had left the city 'to escape the heat',[160] and so had many others. Sixtus V himself was later to concede to his health to the extent of passing every summer in his villa, which was not in fact very well situated, near Santa Maria Maggiore, in a hollow of the Esquiline,[161] or in the new pontifical palace that had been built on the Quirinal.[162] At the height of summer, even in recent times, Rome was 'the empty, the hot, the fever-discredited' city.[163]

Everywhere, in Rome, Avignon, Milan, and Seville, the rich, whether nobles or bourgeois, laity or clerics, abandoned the hot cities. Philip II, in the Escorial, sought not only solitude, but coolness and relief from the pitiless Castilian summer.[164] Who is better qualified to describe this summer migration of all men of means than Bandello, their table companion, entertainer, and chronicler? How sweet it is in the heat of summer to be in a garden at Milan, near the Porta Beatrice; to eat mellow fruits and drink 'un generoso e preziosissimo vino bianco'.[165] 'Last summer,' he relates, 'to escape the heat which is excessive in Milan, I went . . . with Lord Alessandro Bentivoglio and his wife, Lady Ippolyta Sforza, to their residence, on the other side of the Adda, to the Palace, as they call it, and I stayed there for three months.'[166] Another time, he was on the other side of Brescia, at San Gottardo, and had occasion after the meal to talk of the 'beffe che da le donne, o a le donne si fanno'.[167] Another time, the little society in which one of the novels is set picnics near Pinaruolo, in a meadow of sweet-smelling grasses, while cool and clear water runs nearby in the canal. Elsewhere the little court is held beneath some olive trees, but still near springs of running water. In just such a setting three hundred years earlier the tales of the Decameron had been told.

The Mediterranean climate and the East. The seasonal rhythm of the desert is the reverse of that of the Mediterranean. For there the slowing down or ceasing of activity occurs in summer rather than in winter. The overwhelming heat of summer brings everything to a standstill. After October–

G. Mecatti, *op. cit.*, II, p. 801 (in Hungary in 1595); N. Iorga, *Ospeti romeni, op. cit.*, p. 87, J. B. Tavernier, *op. cit.*, Persian Travels, p. 34, at Smyrna the plague 'usually reigns in the months of May, June, and July'.
[159] *Roman comique*, Part I, 1651, Part II, 1657; ed. Garnier, 1939, p. 64.
[160] B.N. Paris, Fr. 17, 989.
[161] L. von Pastor, *op. cit.*, X, p. 37.   [162] *Ibid.*, p. 47.
[163] Rainer Maria Rilke, *Letters to a young poet*, trans. Snell, London, 1945, p. 25.
[164] Louis Bertrand, *Philippe II à l'Escorial*, 1929, p. 170.
[165] *Op. cit.*, VIII, p. 208.   [166] *Op. cit.*, VIII, p. 175.   [167] *Ibid.*, VIII, p. 165.

November, after the date harvest life and commerce start afresh.

Tavernier, it is true, tells us that caravans arrived at Smyrna in February, June, and October,[168] but Smyrna and Asia Minor are outside the true desert zone. As for the camels that arrived in Egypt in September–October,[169] had they come very far? It was in April, May, and June that the great caravans reached Cairo.[170] De Sercey (a witness from the nineteenth century) claims that it is impossible to cross the desert between Baghdad and Aleppo during the summer. Towards 1640 the caravan traffic from Hormuz operated from the 1st December until March.[171] South of Oran the November caravans are still in the twentieth century the most important,[172] and this renewed activity is reminiscent of the Mediterranean in the month of April.

So the desert begins to wake up just as everything is going into hibernation further north and west. The flocks that left the steppe in summer return to the renewed pastures and, like the caravans, take to the desert roads again. The time of uncertainty is over, life becomes easier, more prosperous, and more industrious at the same time. The archaeologist Sachau was astonished to see people at work at Kut al 'Amara, in winter, repairing the canals and growing vegetables.[173] In fact this was perfectly normal, the accustomed rhythm of life on the steppes.

Seasonal rhythms and statistics. We should look a little more closely at these great problems which have for the most part escaped the attention of historians. Can we use statistics? They are very incomplete and inadequate for the sixteenth century, but it is worth looking at them.

I have already shown from the Marseilles registers of 1543 that the consignments of empty kegs 'for salt fish' from Fréjus marked the importance of the month of April, just before the fishing season.

There follows a record of marine insurance policies taken out at Ragusa for the year 1560.[174] This record reveals the importance of the months of April and May. Boats were insured – as of course one would expect – just before the long voyages began.

---

[168] *Op. cit.*, I, p. 73: Paul Masson, *Le commerce français du Levant au XVIIe siècle*, p. 419.

[169] Belon, *op. cit.*, p. 136.

[170] João de Barros, *Da Asia*, I, libr. III, Ch. III and VIII.

[171] According to La Boullaye Le Gouz, quoted by P. Masson, *op. cit.*, p. 373.

[172] Isabelle Eberhardt, *Notes de route*, 1921, p. 7.

[173] Sachau, *op. cit.*, p. 74–77.

[174] Ragusa Archives, Diversa di Cancellaria 145, f°s 165, 165 v°, 172–173, 174 v°, 175, 176, 176 v°, 177, 177 v°, 180, 180 v°, 188 to 192 v°, 196 to 197, 201 v° to 203; 146, f° 6 v°, 7, 12, 12 v°, 13, 13 v°, 14 v°, 17 v°, 24, 33 v°, 40, 40 v°, 43, 43 v°, 46 v°, 47, 47 v°, 48 to 49 v°, 50 v°, 104 v° to 107, 133 v°, 134, 145 v° to 148, 150 to 153, 155 to 161 v°, 164 to 165, 167 to 168, 170 v° to 171 v°, 174, 182 to 183, 193 to 194, 198 v° to 203, 208 to 209, 211 v° to 213, 215 v° to 218, 226 to 229. Insurances are not written up separately as the reference numbers show, but mixed up with other documents. They are not found as a separate item until the first register of the series *Noli e securtà*, beginning in January, 1563.

Number of Marine insurance policies at Ragusa in 1560

Jan.	Feb.	Mar.	April	May	June	July	Aug.	Sept.	Oct.	Nov.	Dec.
9	6	5	14	20	2	1	5	6	4	7	6

Recorded by month □ = one policy (from Ragusa Archives).

The records of the *portate* of Leghorn[175] give details of the cargoes landed at the port with the name of the boat and her port of origin. These files enable us to locate the arrivals of silk between July and October; the arrivals of pepper from Alexandria between January and July or August; and cheeses from Sardinia after October. These are small seasonal movements that would all repay study. The Leghorn calendar is not absolutely identical with that of other ports, not even with that of Genoa, its nearest neighbour.[176]

But I do not think it is possible to use these documents to establish definite economic variations according to the season. The Leghorn statistics do not offer such a simple answer because they are sixteenth-century statistics, incomplete and with no standardization of measures. It is impossible, for example, to calculate the gross tonnage of goods unloaded there in any single month, which would be the most valuable information they could give. The *portate* of Leghorn record the arrival of boats of very different capacities: barques, gondolas, *galionetti, scafi,*

[175] The *portate* of Leghorn, to which I shall make frequent references essentially compose the registers Mediceo 2079 and 2080 in the A.d.S. Florence. F. Braudel and R. Romano, *Navires et marchandises à l'entrée du port de Livourne*, Paris, 1951, *passim.*
[176] The research in progress on the traffic entering the port of Genoa, by Giovanni Rebora and Danilo Presotto, will no doubt when complete give information on the seasonal variation in shipping movements.

leuti, feluccas, saëtes, *navicelloni*, *caramusali*, tartans, galleons, and *navi*,* the last two categories (galleons and *navi*) being the largest cargo ships in the series. Simply to count every ship named as a single unit would lead to very unrealistic figures: one might as well add up kilos and tons. To classify them by category would not mean very much either, except for *navi* and galleons, and that is what we shall try to do here. If this method is adopted, the following figures will be obtained:

Arrivals at Leghorn in 1578, 1581, 1582, 1583, 1584, and 1585

Year	Ships of every description † arriving between 1st April and 30th September (summer semester)	Ships of every description † arriving between 1st October and 31st March (winter semester)	Total
1578	171	126	297
1581	84	107	191 *
1582	199	177	376
1583	171	171	342
1584	286	182	468
1585	147	160	307
TOTAL	1058	923	1981

* Not 181 which appears in error in F. Braudel and R. Romano, *op. cit.*, appendix table 1.
† Excluding galleys.

Monthly record of the shipping traffic at Leghorn for the same dates*

Year	Jan.	Feb.	Mar.	Apr.	May	June	July	Aug.	Sept.	Oct.	Nov.	Dec.
1578	27	40	40	49	24	27	30	26	15	6	7	6
1581	13	4	5	9	7	15	20	23	10	29	27	29
1582	27	27	33	38	29	44	52	19	17	17	37	36
1583	22	18	21	37	22	28	27	33	24	39	38	33
1584	57	36	31	36	46	55	46	72	31	21	30	7
1585	34	27	17	20	33	17	25	28	23	18	37	28
TOTAL	180	152	147	189	161	186	200	201	120	130	176	139

* Excluding galleys.

These figures are clearly incomplete and imperfect. It is not easy to work from the information they provide. According to the monthly statistics three months appear to have been more active than the others: April, at the end of winter, the time for necessary stock clearance; July and August, after the grain harvest. The two least active months were September

* The word *nave* (Italian, plural *navi*) was used in ship lists of the sixteenth century for any roundship over about 100 tons (F. C. Lane, *Venetian Ships and Shipbuilders*, p. 254). (Translator's note.)

Navi *and galleons entering Leghorn for the same dates*

Year	Jan.	Feb.	Mar.	Apr.	May	June	July	Aug.	Sept.	Oct.	Nov.	Dec.	Total
1578	9	7	3	3	4	2	1	3	—	4	3	4	43
1581	11	4	3	4	6	3	—	4	2	8	4	3	52
1582	5	1	4	6	—	3	1	1	4	2	4	6	37
1583	—·	2	5	1	1	3	—	3	—	2	1	3	21
1584	8	2	6	3	6	2	2	1	2	5	2	2	41
1585	1	7	9	2	—	2	3	—	—	2	2	3	31
Total by month	34	23	30	19	17	15	7	12	8	23	16	21	
Total of other ships	146	129	117	170	144	171	193	189	112	107	160	118	

and October. On our table, April totals 189 arrivals; July, 200; August 201, but September 120; October 130; there is a perceptible drop.

The records of *navi* and galleons refer to large cargo ships and long distance voyages. The activity of these ships is to be distinguished from that of boats of smaller tonnage. The latter worked in April, July, and August, the *navi* and galleons reached their lowest figures in July and their highest in January: 34; March: 30; February and October: 23. The massive arrival of northern ships was to accentuate this discrepancy in the Leghorn shipping.[177] Over short distances grain could be carried in small boats in July and August, as the *portate* indicate, while the long-distance voyages were undertaken by the big ships, in which all merchandise from far countries was carried.

In the western part of the sea, to which the Leghorn statistics refer, and probably throughout the whole Mediterranean, the obstacle of winter had been partly overcome, both over long and short distances. The time was past when a law of Rhodes forbade all marine insurance during winter, on the assumption that there were not, nor should there be, any winter voyages. The arrival of the northern 'cog' in the fifteenth century seems to have marked the beginning of the Mediterranean victory over bad weather. The Venetian galleys already risked putting out in the winter season, and the development was pursued throughout the sixteenth century, so that Tavernier could write in the seventeenth century, 'there is no Sailing at all times upon the *Indian* as upon the *European* seas'.[178] In the sixteenth century only the galley and its derivatives were unable to put out to sea in very bad weather. For other ships, especially the great roundships used by merchants, the risk was still substantial but was no longer enough to prevent them from leaving. And technical progress was reducing the risk every day. The time was drawing near when the galley

[177] J. B. Tavernier, *op. cit.*, Persian Travels, p. 2, 'The *English* or *Holland* fleets, that usually arrive at *Lighorn* either in the Spring or in Autumn.'
[178] J. B. Tavernier, *The Six Voyages*, Travels to India, p. 15.

The Role of the Environment

264 The Role of the Environment

itself would disappear, giving way to the ship of the line that could both sail and fight in bad weather. The Tripolitanian corsairs from the sixteenth century on, used roundships for winter privateering and only fitted out their galleys in summer.[179]

About these difficult problems the Leghorn *portate* can tell us little. Moreover they relate only to arrivals in the port. A good half of the shipping traffic, the departures, remains unrecorded.

We shall hardly fare better with records of the voyages made by German pilgrims from Venice to the Holy Land between 1507 and 1608, a total of about thirty trips, described in the valuable and erudite collection of records by Röhricht.[180] But these are voyages which are at least comparable with each other, and they provide examples from the whole of the century.

The pilgrims would set off in June or July, in the middle of the fine season. Of twenty-four known cases there was one departure in May (20th May); ten in June; eleven in July; one in August, and one in September. They would arrive at Jaffa or Tripoli in Syria in July, August, or September. Of the twenty-three known arrivals, one was in June; seven in July; eleven in August; ten in September; one in October; none in November; and one in December. From the coast to Jerusalem and back, including two or three days in Jerusalem, the pilgrimage was extremely rapid, taking from three weeks to a month. The pilgrims would then re-embark, generally on the same ship that had brought them. Departures from Jaffa, Beirut, or Tripoli in Syria were usually in August (out of twelve cases, there was one in June; six in August; two in September; three in October). It was usually in December that the pilgrims set foot in Venice once more (of thirteen arrivals, four were in November; seven in December; one in January; and one in February).

From these few figures useful information can be sought about the comparative length of the journey in summer and winter, on the outward and return voyage.

The return journey took almost double the time of the outward trip. Was this simply due to the season? Or was there some difficulty connected with the prevailing wind in following the route in the opposite direction? The latter explanation is not convincing. An examination of the figure of seventy-three days recorded for a voyage in the year 1587 shows that this relates to an outward, not a return journey, but one that was *not* made in summer. The ship left Venice on 29th September, 1587 and only arrived at Tripoli on 11th December.[181]

It would be a mistake to rely too heavily on the meagre statistics we have given. At least they establish that winter voyages took longer than those made in summer. The figures confirm the hypotheses and observations of contemporaries. For greater certainty we have drawn up a final

[179] P. Masson, *op. cit.*, p. 41, Tripoli in 1612.
[180] *Deutsche Pilgerreisen*, Gotha, 1889.
[181] *Ibid.*, p. 286–287.

table in which only the outward and return voyages made by the same ships, or what appear to have been the same ships, have been included.

Length of Voyages: Venice–Holy Land

Outward journey		Return journey	
1507	50 days	1507	86 days
1507	46	1507	152
1517	29	1519	79
1520	72	1521	92
1521	43	1523	101
1523	49	(18 days stay at Cyprus)	
1523	57	1523	90
1546	39	(Including journey from	
1549	33	Jerusalem)	
1551	35	1527	80
1556	40	1553	79
1561	47	1561	112
1561	62	1581	118
1563	26	[1587	73]
1565	40	1608	65
1565	38	Average length – 93	
1583	26	days.	
1587	40		
1604	49		
1608	44		

Average length to nearest
whole number – 43 days)

Length of voyages made by same ships on outward and return journeys

Outward journey		Return journey	Relation R/O
1507	50 days	86 days	1·72
1517	29	79	2·7
1521	43	92	2·1
1523	49	101	2·06
1523	57	90	1·57
1608	44	65	1·47
Averages	45 days	85·5 days	1·9

The difference in length between outward and return voyages is almost the same as that of the average lengths in the table above (43 to 93 days).

Determinism and economic life. It is only too clear that these calculations, which appeared in the first edition of this book, are not adequate to solve the problems we are dealing with. Since then I have analysed the statistics of the Leghorn *portate*, but they do not add anything to this debate.[182] There are in existence other harbour records: at Barcelona, where access to the archives is difficult; at Ragusa-Dubrovnik where the figures are in

[182] F. Braudel and R. Romano, *Navires et marchandises a l'entrée du port de Livourne*, 1951.

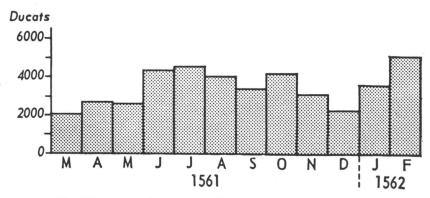

Ducats

Fig. 22: *Seasonal variation of the volume of business at the*
Fondaco dei Tedeschi *at Venice*

The figures above are according to the dues paid to the Signoria. This document, like
many others one could quote, does not reveal any marked seasonal fluctuations that
might point to a possible falling-off of trade during winter. N.B., a point of detail: the
Venetian year began on 1st March.

order and easily accessible only after 1563,[183] and at Genoa, where the
overwhelming mass of documents has discouraged researchers;[184] but
in any case I doubt whether a systematic study of these records would
take us very far. The impression one has, whether rightly or wrongly, but
I suspect rightly, is that the seasonal determinism that so clearly affects
rural life has continually been thwarted by the will of man, particularly
in the towns. Winter on the sea was an obstacle, but small boats could
conquer it over short distances, and large merchantmen on long voyages,
even if they had to throw overboard bales of wool or barrels of grain
during a storm; and sometimes they sped over the waves, for a while at
least 'a sembianza di veloci delfini'.[185] Winter in the mountains was
certainly an obstacle, particularly in the Alps, but we have seen that there
were regular crossings nevertheless.

Winter was clearly a quiet season, as plenty of unmistakable evidence
shows. Perhaps the most unexpected is that of the banks of Naples, which
regularly in winter invested their clients' money in government bonds
whereas in summer they used it to buy up the many agricultural products
of the kingdom, a profitable avenue for speculation.[186] But winter was also

[183] See above note 174.
[184] But two young historians, Danilo Presotto and Giovanni Rebora have begun
a systematic analysis of the customs documents at Genoa, Manuscript thesis at
Facoltà di economia e commercio of Genoa.
[185] Museo Correr, D. delle Rose, 45, 1st January, 1604, the account by Lamberto
Siragusano who left Alexandria in Egypt, in winter accompanied by a Marseillais,
Theodolo, who had joined his ship. At first all went well: the sails were filled and they
sped 'like dolphins', but there was a sudden storm off the coast of Asia Minor near
Satalia.
[186] A.d.S. Naples, Sommaria Consultationum (mislaid reference).

the season of domestic crafts, when looms were busy. On 8th December, 1583, Baltasar Suárez, the Spanish merchant of Florence who was to become a relation by marriage of the Grand Duke, complained to his correspondent at Medina del Campo, Simón Ruiz, that he had not enough wool (he had just received some and sold it at a good price): 'I am much disturbed,' he wrote, 'to see such opportunities pass by, for this is the most industrious season of the year, and without wool, we are all held up.'[187] To achieve a good winter production was also the concern of the urban authorities, if they were wise. As the *provveditore* of the *Arte de Lana* said in Florence in October, 1604, the artisans must be helped at all costs 'now that the cold weather and long nights are here and they need light and clothing, besides food . . .'.[188]

So there were many exceptions: human life responds to the commands of the environment, but also seeks to evade and overcome them, only to be caught in other toils, which as historians, we can reconstruct more or less accurately.

3. HAS THE CLIMATE CHANGED SINCE THE SIXTEENTH CENTURY?

Should we dare to put a final question which means opening a thick file of often unreliable documents and admitting to the argument a large body of journalistic literature of doubtful inspiration? And yet, everything changes, even the climate. Nobody now believes in the invariability of the elements of physical geography. The variations, infinitesimal though they are, of the lines of longitude, are now accepted. Gerhard Solle[189] claims that the mass of the eastern Alps is moving towards Bavaria, at a negligible rate, it is true (one centimetre a year), but it is enough, at certain weak points to cause avalanches, landslides, sometimes major disasters noted in Alpine history. For many years the attention of geographers has been drawn to historical changes in the Mediterranean coastline. Some of them, of course, using precise examples such as the island of Delos, have concluded that the coastline is quite unchanging.[190] On the other hand, there is the work of Theobald Fischer, R. T. Günther, and A. Philippson. The basic problem is to decide whether observed changes are strictly local in character or not. According to the studies by Agostini Arrigo[191] and Dina Albani[192] there have been

[187] B. Suárez to Simón Ruiz, Florence, 8th December, 1583, A. Provincial, Valladolid.
[188] A.d.S. Florence, Mediceo, 920, f° 355. This reference is taken from an unpublished work by Maurice Carmona (C.N.R.S. report).
[189] 'Gebirgsbildung der Gegenwart in den Ost-Alpen' in *Natur und Volk*, 69, p. 169–176.
[190] M. L. Cayeux, in *Annales de Géographie*, XVI, 1907.
[191] *Ricerche sul regime dei litorali nel Mediterraneo*, Rome, 1936.
[192] *Indagine sulle recenti variazioni della linea di spaggia delle coste italiane*, Rome, 1935. Cf. the references of A. Philippson, *op. cit.*, p. 22–23, and the studies by C. Cold, *Küstenveränderung im Archipel*, Munich, 1886, and Theobald Fischer, *Beiträge zür physischen Geogr ıphie der Mittelmeerländer besonders Siziliens*, Leipzig, 1877.

alternating periods during which the Mediterranean beaches have in turn been hollowed out and filled up. In the same way there have been successive unaccountable phases of erosion and sedimentation along the shores of Taormina on the east coast of Sicily, each phase lasting roughly fifteen years. Since the middle of the nineteenth century, the sea has gradually encroached upon the land, whether along the African coastline or the shores below Monte Gargano or around the delta of the Nile. There have been a few instances of movement in the opposite direction and a general aggravation of the situation after 1900. There is nothing to prove that this trend of the sea encroaching upon the land will not be reversed one day. It is tempting to look here for some form of cyclical change, such as Le Danois attempted to trace in the Atlantic Ocean.[193]

Perhaps it is also true of climate: 'everything changes and climates with the rest'.[194] But if they do change, it may be because of man's intervention. In one place climatic change might be the result of large-scale deforestation, in another the result of neglected irrigation, or abandoned crops which can be disastrous in arid regions.[195] Theobald Fischer is convinced that the Sicilian climate became more dry after the Moslem conquest. If so, who was responsible: man or the elements? Goetz, in his valuable *Historical Geography*,[196] mentions a drying-up of surface springs that may have preceded the Moslem conquest, in which case the southern conquerors would have brought with them a solution to the water crisis by their expert methods of irrigation.

In any case, there is a growing body of contemporary literature which accepts that there have been and still are climatic changes in operation. The Arctic ice cap has apparently retreated since 1892–1900[197] while the desert has made advances in both northern and southern Africa.[198]

In the past, on the contrary, all the books and studies were agreed on the immutability of the climate. We cannot regard their arguments as absolutely convincing. We are told, following Partsch,[199] that the Djerid in southern Tunisia has hardly changed its course, since Nefta and Tozeur, on its banks, correspond to the ancient Roman towns of Nepta and Thusurus. We are also told[200] that the flooding of the Nile in ancient times was comparable to its present-day flooding. It has been said that the flora of Minoan Crete (from the evidence of Cretan art), lilies, hyacinths, crocuses, and campions, corresponds exactly to the present-day spring flora of the Mediterranean,[201] or that the reforestation of pinewoods

---

[193] Ed. Le Danois, *L'Atlantique*, 1938, p. 162.
[194] Th. Monod, *L'hippopotame et le philosophe*, *op. cit.*, p. 100.
[195] A. Philippson, *op. cit.*, p. 134–135.
[196] *Historische Geographie*, 1904, p. 188.
[197] As a very general reference, Walther Pahl, *Wetterzonen der Weltpolitik*, 1941, p. 226–227.
[198] Ferdinand Fried, *Le tournant de l'économie mondiale*, 1942, p. 131.
[199] Quoted by A. Philippson, *op. cit.*, p. 133–134.
[200] Fritz Jäger, *Afrika*, 1910, I, p. 53.
[201] Herbert Lehmann, in *Geog. Zeitschr.*, 1932, p. 335–336.

around Valladolid in the sixteenth century can almost entirely be explained by human initiative.[202]

These statements and others of the same nature cannot be taken as definite proof. They reveal in the first place an inadequate grasp of the problem. The location at any time in the past of a climate apparently identical with that of the present day proves nothing either way about periodical variations of the climate. The real problem is to establish whether or not there has been periodicity, and recent writings incline towards the hypothesis that there has. 'A periodicity of about thirty years is not unlikely,' concludes an expert in these matters;[203] and of course there may well be other underlying cycles of long or short duration.

So the climate changes and does not change: it varies in relation to norms which may after all vary themselves, but only to a very slight degree. This seems to me to be of capital importance. To François Simiand's A and B phases,[204] shall we historians one day add phases of greater drought or humidity, heat or cold? Take what Le Danois says of the year 1450, or Gaston Roupnel's protest against 'the historian [who] refuses to grant historical existence to the serious climatic disturbances which transformed the conditions of life in Europe between the thirteenth and fifteenth centuries'.[205]

This is the area of debate. As far as the Mediterranean is concerned we shall confine ourselves to a few general conclusions and one or two hypotheses.

Climatic variations are likely. Their character and duration remain to be noted. In the Alps, in any case, traces of them are visible. According to U. Monterini[206] the mountain regions became drier and warmer after about 1300; after about 1600, on the other hand, they grew increasingly colder and wetter and the glaciers moved back down as a result. In about 1900 a new phase began. The Alps began to dry up again and the glaciers retreated, as we know, over the whole area. In the Hohe Tauern the present shrinking of the glaciers has uncovered high gold mines that were worked in the time of the Romans and again in the Middle Ages.[207]

This takes us a long way from the thirty-year periods accepted by Emmanuel de Martonne. But is this climatic history of the Alps scientifically based? We are not in a position to say. Glaciologists do not usually see the problem as straightforwardly as this (including the early writer, Walcher, *Nachrichten von den Eisbergen in Tyrol*, Vienna, 1773). Further, is it permissible to claim that the Alps have registered not only variations in their own climate, but also those in the climate of the entire Mediterranean, or indeed that one series is in any way linked to the other? The

[202] Bartolomé Bennassar, *Valladolid au siècle d'or*, Paris, La Haye, 1967.
[203] Emmanuel de Martonne, *Géographie Universelle*, VI, I, 1942, p. 140.
[204] Ignacio de Asso, *op. cit.*, 1798, p. 78 mentions a drought lasting about twenty years at Huesca.
[205] *Histoire et destin*, 1942, p. 62.
[206] *Il clima sulle Alpi ha mutato in età storica?*, Bologna, 1937.
[207] Hans Hanke, in *Frankfurter Zeitschrift*, 23rd January, 1943.

present day climate seems to suggest that it is, since the glaciers are in retreat in the Caucasus as well as in the Alps,[208] while to the south of North Africa the Sahara is enlarging its territory. The historical consequences of this theory may be imagined. It is curious to say the least that in about 1300, that is about the same time as the assumed rise in Alpine temperature, German colonists should have settled on the very high slopes of the south face of the Monte Rosa.[209] It is equally curious that in about 1900, under similar conditions and particularly during the [inter-war] years, there has been a flow of emigrants from the Italian mountain villages to the highest points of the Alps and the northern Apennines, for example in the Apuan Alps and the Val Venosta, where new, permanent villages have grown up between the 1500 and 2000-metre level, in the zone of the so-called *Stavoli* (*abitazzione di mezza stagione*).[210]

If it is agreed that there are some grounds for this argument, and that in about 1600 the weather did indeed become colder and wetter, it would also explain the frosts which were so disastrous for the olive trees[211] and the frequent flooding, for example the floods that ruined the fields of Tuscany in 1585 and 1590, not to mention the spread of marshland and consequently of malaria, creating overall conditions of increased difficulty for human life. The roots of the social crisis caused by the food shortage that dominated the end of the century may have lain in an alteration, even a very slight one, in the atmospheric conditions. This takes us to the utmost limits of prudence, but it cannot be discounted. There is no shortage of explanations, both economic and demographic, for the end-of-century crisis. But who is to say that the climate did not play its part on this occasion, and that it is not, in general, a variable factor in history? It is difficult to prove it of course, but a few examples support the argument.[212]

There was a great deal of flooding during the sixteenth century in the Rhône valley: in July, 1501, the Rhône flooded at Lyons; in 1522 the Ardèche; in February, 1524, the Drac and the Isère; in August, 1525, the Isère; in October, 1544, the Gier at Vienne; in November, 1544, the Rhône and the Durance; in November, 1548, the Rhône and the Durance; on

---

[208] B. Plaetschke, 'Der Rückgang der Gletscher im Kaukasus' in *Pet. Mitt.*, 1937.

[209] N. Krebs, in *Geogr. Zeitsch*, 1937, p. 343.

[210] R. Pfalz, in *Geogr. Zeitsch.*, 1931. The same observation is made by Denijer, in *Ann. de Géogr.*, 1916, p. 359, the clearings of the high villages in the Dinaric Alps.

[211] In Provence the olive trees were killed by the mistral in 1507, 1564, 1599, 1600, 1603, 1621–1622. P. George, *op. cit.*, p. 394. René Baehrel, *Une croissance: la Basse–Provence rurale (fin du XVIe siècle – 1789)*, 1961, p. 123, gives a different chronology: 'The disastrous winters' for the olive trees were: 1570, 1594, 1603, 1621, 1638, 1658, 1680, 1695, 1709, 1745, 1748, 1766, 1768, 1775, 1789. At Verona, in 1549 '*per il gran freddo si secarrono quasi tutti gl'olivi, le vite e altri alberi*', Lodovico Moscardo, *op. cit.*, p. 416. At Pépieux, (Aude, near Carcassonne) in 1587, there was snow and the olive trees were hit by frost, J. Cunnac, *Histoire de Pépieux*, Toulouse, 1944, p. 73. In Tuscany, the olive trees were frozen in 1594, G. Mecatti, *Storia cronologica . . .* II, p. 790.

[212] The following is taken from Maurice Champion, *Les inondations en France*, 1861, III, p. 212 ff.

9th September, 1557, the Rhône flooded at Avignon; on 25th August, 1566, the Durance and the Rhône flooded the region round Avignon; on 2nd December, 1570, there was one of the worst floods of the Rhône of the period, particularly at Lyons; in 1571, the Rhône flooded again; the same thing happened in October, 1573 (Beaucaire was flooded); in September, 1579, the Isère flooded at Grenoble; on 26th August, 1580, the Rhône at Avignon; in 1578 the Rhône flooded at Arles and the waters covered part of lower Languedoc from October to February; in 1579 there was flooding at Arles; in 1580 flooding at Arles again (it was said that the Rhône had never been seen so high in living memory) on 5th January, 1581, there was flooding at Avignon from both the Rhône and the Durance, recurring on 6th February; in 1583 the Rhône covered the Camargue; on 18th September, 1586, the Rhône flooded at Avignon; on 6th November, 1588, the Gier flooded; in 1590 there was another disastrous flood at Avignon.

These records might give the impression that there was increased flooding towards the end of the century. But the Rhône floods are not, from our point of view, a very good indicator of the vicissitudes of the Mediterranean climate. Yet it does seem, if contemporary accounts are to be believed, that the rainfall increased in the later decades of the century. In his *République Séquanoise* of 1592 Louis Gollut blamed the deforestation caused by the iron founders and land owners who wanted to have more 'subjects . . . and taxes'. He adds, '. . . for twenty-six years now the rains have been more frequent, longer and more abundant'.[213] This was in the Dôle region. At Aix in 1599–1600, Du Haitze wrote in his manuscript history,[214] 'the cold weather and snow lasted until the end of June, and it did not rain between that month and December. The rains came then in such abundance that the land seemed drowned.' In Calabria, according to the so-called *narrazione* of Campanella: '*ed entrado l'anno* 1599, *venne nova, che in Rome prodigiosamente aveva inondato il Tevere, e non si potettero celebrar le feste di Natale, e in Lombardia il Po; e in Stilo* [a place in Calabria] *non si poteron celebrar, la Simana Santa, gli ufficii divini per le molte gran pioggie che allagavano tutte le chiese . . .*'.[215] When a man from Ferrara, an eyewitness of the flooding of the Tiber,[216] arrived, it was not long before they were talking in the mountains of miraculous omens, foreshadowing the end of the world, the more so since a century was ending, and even the most well-balanced heads were a little swayed by the *mutazione di secolo*. The following year, in June, 1601, torrential rain fell on the Balkans, ruining the crops and causing catastrophic floods 'like those of the Po and of the large rivers of Lombardy', according to one

---

[213] *Mémoires historiques de la République séquanoise*, Dole, 1592, in-folio, book II, ch. XVIII.
[214] Quoted by Ch. de Ribbe, *La Provence au point de vue des bois, des torrents et des inondations avant et après 1789*, 1857, p. 20.
[215] *Archivio storico italiano*, IX, p. 622.
[216] *Ibid.*, p. 624.

witness,[217] the rain falling so heavily said another, that it was feared 'the air was corrupted'.

These are the facts. What conclusion should be drawn? That the climate of the Mediterranean altered towards the end of the century? The events we have listed are one thing, such a conclusion quite another, as must be immediately acknowledged. A thorough re-examination of the whole question is needed to provide more of the concrete data which only research will bring to light. The problem still remains and it is one that we cannot ignore, even if in the present state of knowledge we cannot provide an answer. Historians are by no means the only people who will be able to do so. If our efforts can at least establish that they have a contribution to make to this discussion they will not have been in vain.

Supplementary note. I have not changed anything in the argument of the preceding section which when it was first published in 1947 provoked a certain amount of controversy. The reader may be surprised: at the time I was considered imprudent by some critics. Gustav Utterström[218] in a recent article in 1958 was kind enough to find me timid in retrospect. This is the way of the research world and I should be the last to complain.

What matters is that over the last fifteen years research has been going into these vital problems. Few others are as important. Through variations in the climate a force external to man is asserting itself and claiming its part in the most everyday explanations. Today such variations are accepted.

Following the simple method of my original research – which was a collection of descriptive details – I have completed the evidence. It relates above all to the increased rigours of the end of the century: the continual rain, the disastrous floods, the bitter and *unusual* cold. The chronicle of Luis Cabrera de Córdoba, for example, notes of the winter of 1602–1603 that 'the cold and frosts have been so general this year throughout Spain, that there is not a single locality where there have not been complaints about the rigours of the weather. Even from Seville and other seaside towns, especially Seville, they have written that the Guadalquivir has frozen over, a thing which had never before been seen. What a difference from last year, when we hardly noticed the winter. . . .'[219] At Valencia[220] there were successive frosts in 1589, 1592, 1594, 1600, and 1604. As for the constant rain, floods, and snowfalls, and visions of the end of the world, there are many reports for the whole of the Mediter-

[217] Francisco de Vera to the king, Venice, 30th June, 1601, A.N., K. 1677. Constantinople, 3rd and 4th June, 1601, *ibid.*

[218] 'Climatic Fluctuations and Population problems in Early Modern History' in *Scandinavian Economic History Review*, 1955.

[219] Luis Cabrera de Córdoba, *Relaciones de las cosas succedidas en la Corte de España desde 1599 lasta 1614*, p. 166, Valladolid, 25th January, 1603.

[220] J. Castañeda Alcover, *Coses envengudes en la ciutat y regne de Valencia. Dietario de Mosen Juan Porcar, capellan de San Martin (1589–1629)*, Madrid, 1934, I, p. 3, 4, 10, 41, 71.

ranean in the last years of the century as well as for many years of the next. The recent study by Emmanuel Le Roy Ladurie mentions similar occurrences: 'the Rhône froze right over so hard that it bore mules, cannons and carts in 1590, 1595, 1603, possibly in 1608, in 1616 and in 1624.' At Marseilles, the sea froze in 1595, and in 1638, 'when the water froze round the galleys'. The series of frosts that killed the olive trees of Languedoc occurred in 1565, 1569, 1571, 1573, 1587, 1595, 1615, and 1624.[221] 'These massacres of the olive trees eventually discouraged planters'[222] in Languedoc and no doubt elsewhere as well. It seems certain that it became colder between the last years of the sixteenth century and the early years of the seventeenth than it had been before.

It rained more. From 1590 to 1601, a historian observes, concerning Languedoc: 'late and persistent snow in the spring, extreme cold spells in the summer, torrential rainfall over the Mediterranean accompanied by famine and the famous "invasion" of the inland sea by northern grain'.[223] On the other hand from 1602 to 1612 and even later, there was 'seemingly a breath of warm air and light',[224] and the dry weather returned, or at any rate the rainfall was more unevenly distributed. Many prayers were offered for rain at Valladolid in 1607, 1617, and 1627;[225] at Valencia in November, 1615, '*havia molts mesos que no ploguia*'; in October and November, 1617,[226] '*no caiga un solo chaparron*'. We may not agree with Ignacio Olagüe that Spain then entered into a period of drought that prepared the way for her decadence.[227] But it is quite possible that the countryside of La Mancha was greener in the time of Cervantes than in later years.[228]

The rainfall mechanism in Europe (including the Mediterranean) depends on the paths taken by the Atlantic depressions, which may go either north by way of the Channel, the North Sea and the Baltic (all the year round); or south, by way of the Mediterranean between the autumn equinox and the spring equinox. Utterström suggests that in the sixteenth century this double stream was blocked in the north by periods of intense cold and the resulting buildup of anticyclones of high pressure. Since the northern passage was obstructed, the Mediterranean route was more open than usual in compensation. But is there any reason why one path should open when the other is half-closed? And what was the length of the oscillations if indeed they occurred?

These are really points of detail, short-term explanations. Recent research has taken the matter much further, pursuing two promising lines of investigation: first, the establishment of serial indices; and second, the extension of the field of observation to cover not only the Mediterranean but the Mediterranean plus Europe or even better, the entire globe. I am

[221] E. Le Roy Ladurie, *op. cit.*, p. 48.
[222] *Ibid.*, p. 46. [223] *Ibid.*, p. 39. [224] *Ibid.*, p. 37.
[225] B. Bennassar, *Valladolid au XVIe siècle.*
[226] J. Castañeda Alcover, *op. cit.*, p. 222 and 324.
[227] Ignacio Olagüe, *La decadencia de España*, 1950, vol. IV, ch. XXV.
[228] Ignacio Olagüe, 'El paisaje manchego en tiempos de Cervantes' in *Annales Cervantinos*, III, 1953.

thinking in particular of the pioneering works of Dr. D. J. Schove[229] in England; of the geographer Pierre Pédelaborde,[230] and the historian Emmanuel Le Roy Ladurie.[231]

To extend and classify our information, to apply a prepared grid to all the evidence, so that each descriptive detail should fit into a particular category – humidity, drought, cold, and heat, according to the season and the year – will mark progress from the picturesque to a more genuine quantitative history. Then to record series of comparable events: the dates of grape harvests, the dates of arrival on the market of the first new oil, of the first wheat and the first corn; the information provided by the felling of trees, flow of rivers, flowering of blossom, the first ice on a lake, the first or last icefloe in the Baltic, the advances and retreats of the glaciers, the variations in sea level – will establish chronological records of all climatic variations, whether short or long term.

The second step is to incorporate these problems and this information into comprehensive theories and reports. The 'Jet Stream' theory will perhaps suffer the fate of so many other general explanations. It will hold the stage for a time, perhaps a long time. According to this hypothesis there is a continuous air current over the northern hemisphere, a ring of air moving at variable speeds, about 20 or 30 kilometres above the earth's surface. If it increases speed it swells and moves down the globe, like a hat that is too big for its wearer; if it slows down, it forms meanders and retracts back toward the North Pole. So if our observations were correct, the Jet Stream would have increased speed at the end of the sixteenth century, and moving nearer to the Equator and therefore to the Mediterranean, would have brought rain and cold weather south with it. Our hypotheses would be demonstrated, of course, if there was an unbroken chain of evidence, which no one will be able to claim. In the terms admitted in the present discussion of the subject, there may have begun in the middle of the sixteenth century, perhaps a little earlier or later, what has been called, in the words of Dr. Schove, 'the Little Ice Age' that continued throughout the century of Louis XIV.

Important questions still remain to be answered. Was the change we have suggested part of a long-term phase? If so, the sixteenth century would have marked the beginning of a long period of inflowing cold and rain. I mention here, without for a moment regarding it as proof of anything, a curious remark on the level of the *commune* at Venice, that is, of the average water level which makes a black mark on the side of the houses bordering the canals. One document claims that this level has regularly

---

[229] For an introduction to his many works, see his contribution to 'Discussion: post-glacial climatic change' in *The Quarterly Journal of the Royal Meteorological Society*, April, 1949.

[230] *Le climat du Bassin Parisien; essai d'une méthode rationnelle de climatologie physique*, 1957.

[231] In particular his three brilliant articles: 'Histoire et climat' in *Annales*, 1959; 'Climat et récoltes aux XVIIe et XVIIIe siècles', *ibid.*; 'Aspect historique de la nouvelle climatologie' in *Revue Historique*, 1961.

risen since 1560, over three consecutive centuries.[232] If this observation is true – and some clear evidence is called for – we should still have to know whether the water level in the Venetian lagoon is determined entirely by atmospheric precipitation rather than by local circumstances. But the detail is worth remembering.

A further question remains. What would be the hypothetical effect of this Little Ice Age on life in Europe and the Mediterranean? Will the historian disclaim responsibility for a series of problems relating to rural life, public health, and communications, consigning them to a different area of research? In these areas prudence would suggest the need for some kind of large-scale collective research, which has not so far been attempted. It is tempting to make an instant diagnosis and say that at the end of the sixteenth century there was more stock farming and less wheat growing, but this we are not entitled to do. Rain and cold, by persistently visiting the Mediterranean, dislocated certain patterns, but to a degree that still escapes us. Man too must take his share of responsibility, the extent of which is still to be determined. As Le Roy Ladurie has shown, the progressively later dates of the grape harvest can be attributed to man's preference for the higher alcohol content of riper fruit.[233]

It is clear—and this is one of the greatest advances in this area—that the history of climate is the same throughout the northern hemisphere. The case of the Mediterranean is linked to a series of problems on the same scale. The present-day retreat of the Alaskan icefields, which are restoring to our eyes ancient forests crushed beneath their original advance; the series of exact dates when the cherry trees blossom in Tokyo (each marked by a ritual feast); the concentric rings of trees in California: all these and other 'events' are linked together in climatic history. Whether or not there is a Jet Stream, there is certainly a common source for all climatic change. The 'early' sixteenth century was everywhere favoured by the climate; the latter part everywhere suffered atmospheric disturbance.

---

[232] Correr, D. delle Rose, 20. I make only brief mention of this immense question and the immense bibliography that has arisen around it, since the publication of Luigi Cornaro's *Trattato di acque del Magnifico Luigi Cornaro, nobile Vinitiano*, Padua, 1560. The best guide is to be found in Roberto Cessi, 'Evoluzione storica del problema lagunare' in *Atti del convegno per la conservazione e difesa della laguna e della città di Venezia*, 14–15th June, 1960, (Istituto Veneto), p. 23–64.

[233] *Op. cit.*

CHAPTER V

The Mediterranean as a Human Unit: Communications and Cities [1]

To pass from the true Mediterranean, as defined by its climate, to that greater Mediterranean where its influence is felt, is to pass from a physical unit to that human unit with which this book is concerned. This human unit is not merely the result of nature, or more particularly of the waters of the Mediterranean. The sea is everything it is said to be: it provides unity, transport, the means of exchange and intercourse, if man is prepared to make an effort and pay a price. But it has also been the great divider, the obstacle that had to be overcome. The art of navigation may perhaps have been born far back in time, in the stretches of calm water between the Aegean islands and the coast of Asia Minor, or in the nearby Red Sea; we shall never know for certain. It is at any rate accepted that at the dawn of history long ages elapsed before man learned to master the sea. Gradually the small boats overcame it, creating their own links and building by degrees the coherent entity that was to be the Mediterranean of man and history, for built it was and by the hand of man. Even today, when the Inland Sea is by modern standards of travel little more than a river, easily bridged by airways, the human Mediterranean only exists in so far as human ingenuity, work, and effort continually re-create it. The different regions of the Mediterranean are connected not by the water, but by the peoples of the sea. This may seem obvious, but it is worth saying in an area that has attracted so many bewildering formulas and descriptions.

I. LAND ROUTES AND SEA ROUTES

The Mediterranean has no unity but that created by the movements of men, the relationships they imply, and the routes they follow. Lucien Febvre wrote, 'The Mediterranean is the sum of its routes,' [2] land routes and sea routes, routes along the rivers and routes along the coasts, an immense network of regular and casual connections, the life-giving blood-stream of the Mediterranean region. We may be tempted to linger over its picturesque aspects, to accompany Cervantes along the Spanish cart tracks from *venta* to *venta*, to follow the voyages of merchant or pirate vessels as we read their log books, to go down the Adige aboard the *burchieri*, the heavy cargo boats working below Verona, or to embark 'upon the water to go to

---

[1] This chapter was originally entitled 'Routes et Villes, Villes et Routes' in tribute to Lucien Febvre's comment on first being shown these pages.

[2] *Annales d'hist. soc.*, 11th January, 1940, p. 70.

Venice' at Fusina on the edge of the lagoon, with Montaigne's belongings.[3]
But the essential task before us is to measure the relationships this network
implies, the coherence of its history, the extent to which the movement of
boats, pack animals, vehicles and people themselves makes the Mediterranean a unit and gives it a certain uniformity in spite of local resistance.
The whole Mediterranean consists of movement in space. Anything entering it – wars, shadows of war, fashions, techniques, epidemics, merchandise
light or heavy, precious or commonplace – may be caught up in the flow
of its life blood, ferried over great distances, washed ashore to be taken
up again and passed on endlessly, maybe even carried beyond its shores.

The routes are of course the channels of this movement. But they are
more than mere ribbons over the land, lines across the sea, caravans on
the road to Aleppo, the long processions of horses, mules, and camels on
the Stambulyol (the road to Istanbul along the Maritsa) or the wagons
Busbecq saw in 1555, carrying to Constantinople men, women, and children captured by the Turks in Hungary.[4] There would be no routes if
there were no stopping-places: a harbour; an open roadstead; a caraven-
serai or a *Han*; in western Europe it might be a lonely inn, or in the old
days a fortified castle. For the most part, these halts, the resting places
without which no route could survive, were the towns, the busy centres
towards which the traveller hastened his steps and where he arrived with
joy, perhaps with a feeling of thankfulness, like Guzmán de Alfarache
entering Saragossa,[5] staring in amazement at the grand monuments, the
efficient administration, and, perhaps more than anything else, the abundance of good things: 'tan de buen precio todo,' he says, 'que casi daba de
si un olor de Italia.' He had all the more reason to hasten since in many
cases Mediterranean roads did not run from village to village, for these
were more likely to be removed some distance from the road for safety.
The traveller in Bulgaria and Anatolia, even today, passes through countryside that appears much more deserted and depopulated than it actually is.[6]
We should imagine the great trade route to the East as something like
today's *autostrada*, a great crosscountry highway linking towns but very
rarely passing through villages.

The Mediterranean as a human unit is the combination over an area of
route networks and urban centres, lines of force and nodal points. Cities
and their communications, communications and their cities have imposed
a unified human construction on geographical space. Whatever its shape,
its architecture, or the civilization that illuminates it, the Mediterranean
town creates roads and is created by them. Vidal de La Blache has said the
same of the American town;[7] the Mediterranean region in the sixteenth
century (and it must be extended to its maximum when we are talking of
towns) was unique in its immensity. In the sixteenth century no other

[3] *Journal du Voyage en Italie* (coll. 'Hier', 1932), p. 132.
[4] *Op. cit.*, p. 67–68.   [5] *Op. cit.*, II, 3, I, p. 331.
[6] A. Philippson, *Das Mittelmeergebiet*, p. 219.
[7] *Op. cit.*, p. 475.

region in the world had such a developed urban network. Paris and London were just on the threshold of their modern careers. The towns of the Low Countries and southern Germany (the latter bathing in the reflected glory of the Mediterranean, the former stimulated economically by merchants and sailors from the South), further north the industrious but small towns of the Hanseatic League, all these towns, thriving and beautiful though they might be, did not make up a network as closely knit and complex as that of the Mediterranean, where town followed town in endless strings, punctuated by great cities: Venice, Genoa, Florence, Milan, Barcelona, Seville, Algiers, Naples, Constantinople, Cairo. The last three were over-populated: Constantinople was said to have a population of 700,000,[8] that is double the size of Paris and four times the size of Venice. And to this list should be added the large number of minor towns that nevertheless took part in international exchanges, playing a role more important than the size of their population would suggest. Perhaps the animation and activity of these small Mediterranean towns helps to explain why the Far East, although its cities were more densely populated, more bursting with people than the Mediterranean capitals, did not in fact possess as dynamic an urban network. The cities of the East often merely housed enormous masses of people and lacked the driving force of the great city; they were the expression of Asia's overpopulation rather than of her economic organization.[9]

The Mediterranean is an urban region: an observation that must have been made thousands of times and is certainly no startling discovery. But we should mark its consequences. The prevailing human order in the Mediterranean has been one dictated primarily by towns and communications, subordinating everything else to their needs. Agriculture, even on a very modest scale, is dictated by and directed towards the town; all the more so when it is on a large scale. It is because of the towns that man's life has taken on a faster rhythm than it would under natural conditions. It was thanks to the towns that trading activities came to predominate over all others. The history and the civilization of the sea have been shaped by its towns. Ferdinand Lot[10] rightly maintained against Gautier that even the Moslem invasions were connected to the towns. All roads lead to them. The story of the Mediterranean has often been determined by the triumph of one route, one city, over another route and another city, even in the sixteenth century, when the city states seemed to be losing ground to empires and territorial states, although appearances did not yet correspond to reality.

Vital communications Mediterranean communications consisted, in the first place, of shipping routes and, as we have seen[11], for the most part in the

[8] G. Botero, *op. cit.*, I, p. 106, and II, p. 118, 'almost twice the population of Paris', Jacques Bongars in Anquez, *Henri IV et L'Allemagne*, 1887, p. xxiv.

[9] Konrad Olbricht, 'Die Vergrosstädterung des Abendlandes zu Beginn des Dreissigjährigen Krieges', in *Petermanns Mitteilungen*, 1939.

[10] F. Lot, *Les invasions barbares et le peuplement de l'Europe*, 1937, I, p. 110.

[11] Cf. above, p. 103 ff.

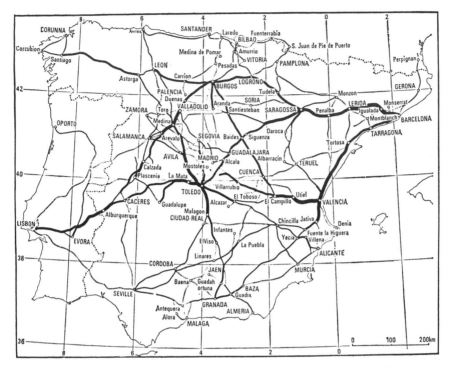

Fig. 23: *The road network of the Iberian peninsula in 1546*

From Gonzalo Menéndez Pidal, *Los caminos en la historia de España*, 1951. The roads are marked with lighter or heavier lines according to the number of times they are mentioned in the Guide by the Valencian Juan Villuga (Medina, 1546). This 'weighting' reveals that Toledo was the traffic centre and therefore the most diversified city of the Peninsula. Other large crossroads were Barcelona, Valencia, Saragossa, Medina del Campo. Madrid's hour of greatness (it was to be the capital after 1556) had not yet struck.

sixteenth century these were coastal routes. Then there were the many land routes: some running along the coast from port to port, like the endless succession of roads, tracks, narrow and hazardous paths, running uninterrupted from Naples to Rome, Florence, Genoa, Marseilles, then through Languedoc and Roussillon, to the Spanish littoral, Barcelona, Valencia, Málaga. Others run at right angles to the coast, for instance the natural routes of the Nile or the Rhône valley, the roads leading to the Alps or the caravan trails from Aleppo to the Euphrates, or from North Africa, to the Sudan. To these could be added the many 'isthmus roads' as Bérard called them, such as the south–north road that ran from Syria through the Cilician Gates, passing over the Taurus and through Anatolia before arriving at Constantinople, either directly by Eskisehir or via the detour to Ankara; or the roads crossing the Balkans, roughly

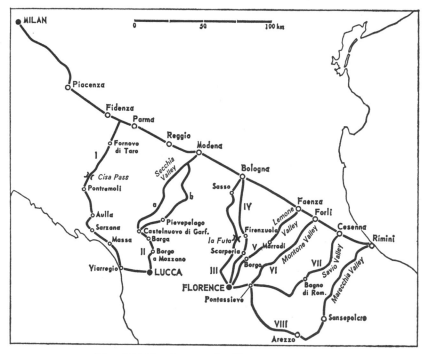

Fig. 24: *Roads over the Tuscan Apennines*

The highway from Rimini to Milan, the old Via Aemilia, bounds the eastern edge of the Apennines. The many roads running at right angles to it leading to Lucca and Florence give some idea of the number of transversal roads throughout the peninsula. The road from Bologna to Florence via La Futa corresponds to the great *autostrada* of the twentieth century. The document on which this map is based lists only the trans-Apennine roads from Florence and Lucca.

from east to west, from Salonica to Durazzo, Valona or Cattaro, from Üskub to Ragusa, from Constantinople to Spalato (whose sudden economic rise at the end of the sixteenth centuty is discussed below); or the series of roads crossing Italy, from the Adriatic to the Tyrrhenian: the road from Barletta to Naples and Benevento, the most important of these southern highways (by the Ariano Pass[12]); further north is what one might call the commercial axis of Tuscany – from Ancona to Florence and Leghorn – and the Genoese axis, from Ferrara to Genoa; finally, in the west, the roads crossing Spain from Barcelona to the Bay of Biscay, from Valencia to Portugal, from Alicante to Seville. Crossing an isthmus from one side to the other could mean taking one of several roads. So between Lombardy and the Romagna on one side, and Tuscany on the other, sixteenth-

[12] Gino Luzzatto, *Storia economica di Venezia dell'XI al XVI secolo*, Venice, 1961, p. 42. There is mention of buffalo hides being transported along this route from Barletta to Naples – Naples, 22nd May, 1588, Ragusa Archives, D. de Foris, VII, f° 245.

century travellers had the choice of eight routes, all difficult since they crossed the Apennines: the most convenient one, and the only one accessible to artillery, was the furthest south, running from Rimini, through the valley of the Marecchia, to Arezzo and Sansepolcro.[13]

To complete the list we should add the river routes, often on the outskirts of the Mediterranean world: for instance the active waterways of the northern Italian plains, the Adige, the Po and its tributaries the Adda, the Oglio and the Mincio;[14] the 'Russian' rivers; all the Portuguese waterways; the Guadalquivir as far as Seville, and above Seville as far as Córdoba;[15] the Nile, only half-Mediterranean, whose enormous quantities of fresh water spill out beyond its delta 'all clouded and yellow'[16] into the sea; or the true Mediterranean waterways, such as the Ebro with its flat-bottomed boats carrying passengers and Aragonese grain to Tortosa, the lower reaches of some of the rivers in Valencia and Granada,[17] and in Italy the lower Arno, the lower Tiber, which was open to sea-going boats as far as Rome and was the home of the curious river boats with lateral rudder and two raised ends that served as steps for disembarking on the steep banks of the river.[18]

All these routes, which could be marked on a map following the road guides of Estienne,[19] Turquet,[20] and L'Herba,[21] provided a framework for the general life of the sea. They differed very little in the sixteenth century from the roads along which the Roman Empire advanced or from those of the Middle Ages. But whatever their pattern, whether varying or not over the centuries, they have always both reflected the range of Mediterranean economic systems and civilizations and governed their fate.

What were the fortunes of the routes? Trades, cities, and states might

[13] Arnoldo Segarizzi, *Relazioni degli ambasciatori veneti*, Florence, III, part 1, 1927, 10–13.
[14] G. Botero, *op. cit.*, I, p. 50.   [15] *Ibid.*, p. 9.
[16] Comte de Brèves, *Voyages . . . op. cit.*, p. 229.   [17] *Ibid.*, p. 5.
[18] Belon, *op. cit.*, p. 103.
[19] Charles Estienne, *La Guide des Chemins de France*, 2nd ed., 1552; *Les voyages de plusieurs endroits de France et encore de la Terre Saincte, d'Espaigne, d'Italie et autres pays*, 1552. Further editions with variants, Paris, 1553, 1554, 1555, 1556, 1558, 1560, 1570, 1583, 1586, 1588, 1599, 1600; Lyons, 1566, 1580, 1583, 1610; Rouen, 1553, 1600, 1658; Troyes, 1612, 1622, 1623, for details see Sir Herbert George Fordham, *Les routes de France, Catalogues des Guides routiers*, 1929, and *Les guides routiers, itinéraires et Cartes Routières de l'Europe*, Lille, 1926.
[20] Théodore Mayerne de Turquet, *Sommaire description de la France, Allemagne, Italie, Espagne, avec la Guide des chemins*, Geneva, 1591–2, 1618, 1653; Lyons, 1596, 1627; Rouen, 1604, 1606, 1615, 1624, 1629, 1640, 1642.
[21] Giovanni de l'Herba, *Itinerario delle poste per diverse parti del mondo*, Venice, 1561. Other guides of the same period: Guilhelmus Gratarolus, *De Regimine iter agentium vel equitum, vel peditum, vel mari, vel curru seu rheda*, Basel, 1561; Cherubinis de Stella, *Poste per diverse parti del mondo*, Lyons, 1572; Anon., *Itinerarium Orbis Christiani*, 1579; Richard Rowlands, *The Post of the World*, London, 1576; Anon., *Kronn und Ausbundt aller Wegweiser . . .*, Cologne, 1597; Matthias Quadt, *Deliciae Galliae sive Itinerarium per universam Galliam . . .*, Frankfurt, 1603; Ottavio Codogno, *Nuovo Itinerario delle Poste per tutto il Mondo . . .*, Milan, 1608; Paulus Hentznerus, *Itinerarium Germaniae, Galliae, Angliae etc.*, Noriberg, 1613.

rise and fall. Disturbances and alterations of routes have rightly had their place in all the great historical explanations. According to Philippson[22] the introduction of direct sea-passages in the eastern basin of the sea, after the third century B.C., brought about the ruin of certain regions of Greece dependent on revenue from ships putting in to port there. The decline of Rome at the end of her career has been variously explained, in the past by the theory that precious metals flowed away along the routes of the Near East following the violent capture of certain key points, and by the more recent suggestion that it was the result of the increased activity of the Danube–Rhine axis which developed to the detriment of the general movement of goods in the Mediterranean.[23] When that general movement fell under the control of Islam in the eighth and ninth centuries the centre of gravity of the entire Mediterranean shifted eastwards, depriving the Christian West of the vital network of sea-routes. Finally, to stop at the period of this book, the Great Discoveries, by opening up the way to the Atlantic and the rest of the world, struck the thriving Mediterranean routes a blow in the back, and in the long run reduced the prosperity of the whole sea. I am even more convinced now than when I wrote the first edition of this book of the importance of these communications. They are the infrastructure of all coherent history. But it will be no easy task to estimate the precise role they played.

Archaic means of transport. At first sight there does not seem to have been any revolutionary change, between 1550 and 1600, in either land or sea transport. There were the same boats as before, the same convoys of pack animals, the same imperfect vehicles, the same itineraries, the same cargoes. There was some improvement in roads and navigation, in the speed and regularity of the mails, the cost of transport fell, but these changes were never of revolutionary proportions. Proof of this is provided by the way the small towns, that is the secondary halts, survived the political and economic transformations of the century. If they survived, it was not, as Stendhal thought, because the big cities were unusually tolerant and allowed the small towns to live their own lives. It was because they defended themselves, and, above all, because the cities could not do without them, any more than the traveller along a road could do without somewhere to change his horses or lay his head. The life of these intermediary places was linked to the arithmetic of distances, the average speed of travel along the roads, the normal length of voyages, all measures that did not substantially change during a century which was not outstanding for its technical progress, which still used the old roads (Rome's ancient splendour survived into the sixteenth century with her roads[24]) and boats of small tonnage (the giants of the Mediterranean were rarely over a thousand tons); which still called on the pack animal more often than the wheeled

[22] *Das Mittelmeergebiet*, (4th ed.), p. 222–223.
[23] André Piganiol, *Histoire de Rome*, 1939, p. 522.
[24] Jean Delumeau, *Vie économique et sociale de Rome*, I, 1957, p. 81 ff.

vehicle.[25] The latter was not unknown in the century of Philip II, but its progress was slow, almost negligible, if indeed it progressed at all in the years between 1550 and 1600. It is worth remembering that in 1881 the wheeled vehicle was still unknown in Morocco;[26] that it only appeared in the Peloponnesus in the twentieth century; and that its appearance has always led to the adaptation of old roads and the creation of new, amounting almost to a revolution, as Cvijić has said of nineteenth-century Turkey[27].

So we should not anticipate: in the sixteenth century, Spain was not yet the country of mule-drawn carriages jingling with bells; nor was Italy the country of the famous *vetturini* of the Romantic period. Here and there vehicles were to be seen (some more or less sophisticated, others still primitive), drawn by horses, mules, oxen, or buffaloes. There were wheeled carts along the Stambulyol, in the countryside around Bursa,[28] in the Constantine region (where they were seen by Leo Africanus)[29] on the Brenner route,[30] throughout almost all of Italy. Casks of wine were conveyed by cart round Florence;[31] Cervantes ridiculed the carters of Valladolid,[32] and when the Duke of Alva invaded Portugal[33] in 1580 he commandeered many *carros* for his army's use. The removal of the court of Philip II from Valladolid to Madrid in 1606 was accomplished by ox-cart.[34]

Wheeled traffic was certainly used then near the big cities, and in the rear of armies which required massive transport. But was it frequent elsewhere? In Naples in 1560 it was suggested that grain should be brought overland from Apulia, instead of by sea as was usual, in order to avoid the long voyage round the south of Italy: but between the city and the grain-producing region it would be necessary to provide transport and to this end 'procurar', says the letter of Philip II to the Duke of Alcala, viceroy of Naples, 'de adereçar los caminos que vienen de Pulla de Asculi', to set about improving the roads that lead over from Apulia in the region of Ascoli; and to do so, and this is the point, 'de manera que pudiendose carretear como se hace en Alemania y otras partes, se trayga el trigo por ellos a Napoles,' in order that carts may travel along them, as is the practice in Germany and other places and the grain may therefore be transported along these roads to Naples.[35] 'Como se hace en Alemania': so the wheeled

[25] Jules Sion, 'Problèmes de transports dans l'antiquité', (review of the book by Lefebvre des Noëttes, *L'attelage, Le cheval de selle à travers les âges*) in *Annales d'hist. econ. et soc.*, 1935, p. 628 ff.

[26] Jules Leclercq, *De Mogador à Biskra: Maroc et Algérie*, 1881, p. 21.

[27] *La Péninsule Balkanique*, 1918, p. 195.

[28] Busbecq, *Lettres* (ed. Abbé de Foy), Paris, 1748, p. 103, but this is only an anecdote.

[29] *Description de l'Afrique tierce partie . . .*, 1830 ed., II, p. 16–17.

[30] E. von Ranke, *art. cit.*, in; *Vj. für Soz. und W. Gesch.*, 1924, p. 79.

[31] B. N. Florence, Capponi, 239, 26th January, 1569.

[32] *Novelas ejemplares*, The man of glass (Signet Classics, 1963, p. 162).

[33] *CODOIN*, XXXIV, 1st May, 1580, p. 442; 4th May, 1580, p. 453.

[34] Franceschini to the Doge of Genoa, Valladolid, 31st May, 1606, A.d.S. Genoa, Spagna 15.

[35] Philip II to the viceroy of Naples, Toledo, 13th October, 1560, B. Com. Palermo, 3 Qq. E 34, f°s 8–11.

cart was not yet in general use in southern Italy; it was considered a German fashion there, even if by the end of the century it seems to have conquered the road from Barletta to Naples,[36] described in official reports of 1598 and 1603, however, as imperfect and unfinished in spite of, or because of, the projects of the papal town of Benevento which would have liked to gain control of all the traffic along this road.[37] Even in France at the end of the century carriage roads were not very frequent.[38] Over large areas the pack animal was still the chief means of transport. In the seventeenth and eighteenth centuries the road network of the Ottoman Empire, object of much admiration in Europe, consisted of narrow paved tracks, one metre wide, for horsemen, on either side of which flocks and pedestrians had beaten out footpaths ten times the width.[39] On such roads there was little or no wheeled traffic.

Did land routes increase in importance towards 1600? And yet traffic continued to flow along these poor roads and even increased in volume towards the end of the century. Both cause and consequence of this increase was the rise in the numbers of mules, at any rate in the European peninsulas: in Spain an agriculturalist contemporary of Charles V, Alonso de Herrera,[40] considered this phenomenon a terrible calamity; in Italy, especially in Naples, in order to save horse-breeding, rich Neopolitans were forbidden, under pain of severe penalties, to use mules to pull their carriages;[41] in Cyprus after 1550 the breeding of mules of both sexes led to a disastrous drop in the number of horses;[42] in Andalusia draconian measures were introduced to save the horse;[43] in the Balkans during the Turko-Hungarian War of 1593–1606 mules were among other spoils of war seized by the Christians.[44] Haëdo also mentions a Moor travelling from Algiers to Cherchel astride a mule.[45] In 1592 she-mules were sent from Sicily for the works at La Goletta.[46]

The triumph of the mule in the sixteenth century is undeniable although it was bitterly opposed by governments in the name of wartime requirements. It seems to have had the same importance in the Mediterranean as the increased number of horses (both for ploughing and transport) in

[36] 22nd May, 1588, Ragusa Archives, D. de Foris, f° 245.
[37] *Arch. st. ital.*, IX, p. 460 and 460 n.l; 468 and 468 n.l.
[38] Albert Babeau, *Les voyageurs en France*, 1885, p. 68–69 (travels of Paul Hentzner, 1598).
[39] Victor Bérard, *Pénélope . . . op. cit.*, p. 307. Chateaubriand, *Itinéraire, op. cit.*, p. 7.
[40] *Libro de Agricultura*, 1539, p. 368 ff. of 1598 edition (first edition 1513).
[41] *A. st. ital.*, IX, p. 255, 2nd May, 1602.
[42] V. Lamansky, *Secrets d'État de Venise*, p. 616, 7th December, 1550.
[43] On the reasons for the decline of horse breeding, *Cria de los cavallos*, Granada, Simancas E° 137.
[44] Guiseppe Mecatti, *Storia cronologica della città di Firenze*, II, p. 802–803, in 1595.
[45] D. de Haëdo, *Topographia . . .*, p. 180.
[46] Duke of Terranova to the king, Palermo, 22nd April, 1572, Simancas E° 1137.

Elizabethan England.[47] The mule was more than an agricultural implement, as Herrera explains at length in his writing on Spain. It was a marvellous pack animal, strong and docile. Rabelais, who took an interest in everything, refers to this in the *Quart Livre*: 'mules are more powerful, more robust and more hard-working than other animals'. As against 600,000 mules used for ploughing, Herrera estimated that 400,000 were used in Spain for 'cavalry',[48] that is for transport. With a little imagination, this increase in mule traffic can be compared to what was to happen in the eighteenth century in Spanish and Portuguese America, where man conquered the empty interior by means of endless processions of mules.

The further question arises: was the mule responsible for an increase in the volume of land traffic at the expense of sea traffic?

Erbalunga, a large seaside village on Cape Corse, built half over the water, almost became a small town during the period when its function was to provide a few sailing boats to carry goods round the Cape. In the seventeenth century a road was opened across the neck of the Cape and the short overland route quickly replaced the long sea passage. After this Erbalunga rapidly declined.[49] This small local example is a warning, if one is needed, against the widely held belief that the superiority of waterways over land routes was a foregone conclusion.

It was certainly not true of news and letters, which were mainly carried overland. Waterways were only rarely used for dispatches. Nor was it true of precious goods, for land transport (undoubtedly a luxury) was a possibility open to them. So at the end of the sixteenth century raw silk from Naples came to Leghorn *by land*, and from there, *still by land*, travelled to Germany[50] and the Low Countries.[51] It was by land too that serges from Hondschoote travelled in the other direction, to Naples, where over sixty specialized firms handled their redistribution between 1540 and 1580.[52]

Finally, at the very end of the century there was a new and important increase in land traffic in the eastern Mediterranean. Ragusa, which had previously made her living from a variety of different shipping trades, some local, others long-distance, (among them the Black Sea trade) now abandoned these activities and withdrew into the Adriatic. It was not that the hides and wool of the Balkans had stopped coming into the city, but now they came from the great centre at Novi-Pazar, by overland routes, which had replaced the sea routes. Similarly, the striking fortune in the seven-

---

[47] G. Trevelyan, *History of England*, p. 287.
[48] A. de Herrara, *op. cit.*, p. 368.
[49] 'Notizie', in *Archivio storica di Corsica*, 1932, p. 296–297.
[50] *Arch. st. ital.*, IX, p. 219: valuable merchandise travelling from Naples to Florence overland. On the Naples–Germany link via Florence after 1592. G. Vivoli, *op. cit.*, III, p. 198 and 350. On porterage, cf. the negative evidence put forward by J. Perret, *Siris*, 1941, and the reply by André Aymard, in *R.E.A.*, 1943, p. 321–322.
[51] Wilfrid Brulez, *De Firma della Faille*, p. 578.
[52] Émile Coornaert, *Un centre industriel d'autrefois. La draperie-sayetterie d'Hondschoote (XVIe–XVIIIe Siècles)*, 1930, p. 252–253, n. 3.

teenth century of Smyrna[53], perched at the very end of the Asia Minor peninsula, can be interpreted as a victory for the overland route. For Smyrna captured part of the rich traffic of Aleppo (notably the Persian trade) possibly because it provided a point of departure further to the west for the sea voyage to the western Mediterranean.

The same movement explains the Spalato venture, which some Venetian scholars mention because it was closely connected with some incidents concerning Turkey.[54] Venice possessed on the *altra sponda*, in Balkan territory, a series of lookout posts and towns as well as two useful commercial links: the first with Cattaro, by way of which Venetian postal communications with Constantinople and Syria were operated in winter; the second with the estuary of the Neretva (Narenta), outside Venetian territory this time: large numbers of small boats carried to Venice the merchandise brought to the estuary by caravan – wool, hides, and beef on the hoof from the Balkan peninsula. It was almost certainly because of the threat to this traffic (from Uskok piracy and later from the competition of Ragusa and Ancona which regularly stole trade from Venice in spite of her claim to the monopoly of the Venice–Neretva route), that attention began to be paid, after 1577 and particularly after 1580, to a suggestion made by Michael Rodriguez, a Jew living in Venice who was said to be of extraordinary intelligence. He suggested that the port of Spalato should be developed – at the time the little town had fallen into decay but still possessed an excellent harbour and had links with the Balkan interior – and that a system of protected convoys be set up between Spalato and Venice. The plan was not realized until after 1591 because of opposition from an influential senator, Leonardo Donato, who was hostile to any risky enterprise: at least that is what Nicolò Contarini says and it may well be true. It could also be that until 1591 Venice did not feel any pressing need to take such a step.

But once this solution had been adopted, it soon had considerable

[53] Smyrna had been an important centre since 1550, Belon, *op. cit.*, p. 89; the Ragusans went to load cotton there; Paul Masson, *Histoire du Commerce français dans le Levant au XVIIe siècle*, 1896, p. 125; J. B. Tavernier, *op. cit.*, Persian Travels, p. 32; Guillaume de Vaumas, *L'éveil missionnaire de la France*, 1942, p. 102; P. Henri Fouqueray, *Histoire de la Compagnie de Jésus en France des origines à la suppression*, 1925, IV, p. 342, ff; Gérard Tongas, *Les relations de la France avec l'empire ottoman durant la première moitié du XVIIe siècle et l'ambassade de Philippe de Harlay, comte de Césy, 1619–1640*, 1942, p. 208; Baron de Tott, *Mémoirs, op cit.*, II, p. 365.

[54] The following is taken from an unpublished history by Nicolò Contarini, V. Lamansky, *op. cit.*, p. 513–515. The episode is also mentioned in passing by H. Kretschmayr and F. C. Lane. There is a great deal of unpublished evidence: A.d.S. Venice, Papadopoli, Codice 12, f° 23; in 1585, 16,000 *colli* of various merchandise were shipped from the Neretva to Venice, proof that this large detour was preparing the way for the rise of Spalato. Other references: *Cinque savii*, 138, f° 77 v° to 79 v°, 16th June, 1589; *ibid.*, f° 182, 24th September, 1592; *ibid.*, 139 f° 54 and v°; 23rd November, 1594; Marciana, Notizie del mondo 5837, 25th January, 1596; Museo Correr, D. delle Rose, 42 f° 35 v°, 7th September, 1596; *ibid.*, 21, 1598, 1602, 1608; *Cinque Savii*, 12 f° 112, 2nd September, 1610. On the construction of the 'lazzaretto' of Spalato, A.d.S. Venice, Senato Zecca, 17th and 22nd April, 1617.

consequences. The Venetians built a completely new town at Spalato: custom houses, warehouses, and hospitals in which merchandise was disinfected and persons quarantined 'for epidemics are rife amongst the Turks'. They repaired the city walls and fortifications. The Turks for their part put the roads leading to Spalato in good order and fixed certain dates for journeys so that merchants could travel in large bands 'known there as caravans', Contarini thinks it necessary to add. Immediately riches and abundance poured into the Dalmatian port. Since piracy was increasing on the sea, the new overland route attracted merchandise from very distant places. Goods that had previously been carried by sea from Syria, Persia, and India were now, after an extraordinary overland journey, arriving at Spalato. The Venetian initiative virtually caused a revolution in transport. 'So', says Contarini, 'there began to arrive in Venice from Spalato . . . silks, spices of various sorts, carpets, wax, wool, hides, camlets [*ciambellotti*], cottonstuffs, and all the things that are produced or made for men's use by the lands of the East.'[55] In return Venice sent her cloths of gold or silver. Great merchant galleys (shorter and lower in the water than those which used to make the voyage from Venice to Southampton,[56] but well protected against the small boats of the Uskoks), were used for the brief journey from Spalato to Venice.

Venice's rivals and enemies knew from then on that to hurt Venice they would have to strike Spalato. From the summer of 1593 the Ragusans, whose carrying trade was threatened by the new link, began a policy of disparaging the Venetians to the Turks. An ambassador whom they sent to the Pasha of Bosnia in May 1593 was instructed to condemn the enterprise, 'di biasmarla', and to explain that 'the whole aim and desire of the Venetians was to attract to this port the Turks and other vassals of the Grand Turk, so as to be able to seize them in time of war. . . .'. In 1596[57] at the time of the troubles of Clissa (the small Turkish possession which the Uskoks seized by treachery and which the Turks recovered fairly quickly, but only by diverting resources to the town that were really needed for the war with Hungary), when the Imperials and the Pope were trying to draw Venice into the war against the Turks, and there were many disturbances in the Venetian possessions in Dalmatia following the Clissa war, the Duke of Olivares, viceroy of Naples, tried to provoke an uprising in Spalato, or at any rate was certainly responsible for some plotting there. The year of the Clissa war was one of many troubles for Venice and many difficulties for the port of Spalato. Nothing better reveals how important this capture of the overland route from the Levant had become to Venice.[58]

It was no mere temporary success, but a permanent link. Spalato became the headquarters for relations between Dalmatia and Venice, relations for which there are some statistics: an average of 11,000 *colli* of merchandise

---

[55] V. Lamansky, *op. cit.*, p. 514.
[56] F. C. Lane, *op. cit.*, p. 27.
[57] V. Lamansky, *op. cit.*, p. 504 ff.
[58] *Ibid.*, p. 514.

were dispatched annually between 1586 and 1591; 16,460 *colli* from 1592 to 1596; 14,700 from 1614 to 1616; 15,300 from 1634 to 1645.[59] Of course *colli* (which simply means large bundles) cannot be accepted as a regular unit of measurement; neither has the Spalato traffic been properly distinguished from the total volume of Dalmatian trade with Venice (although the *Cinque Savii* mention in July, 1607, 12,000 *balle* (*balla* = *collo*) of merchandise from Spalato alone, 'beside sums of money in cash', 'oltre li contadi in bona suma'.)[60] The documents reckon the horses of the caravans in hundreds and soon a throng of merchants was arriving at Venice, coming even from Bursa,[61] Armenians, Jews, Greeks, Persians, Wallachians, people of 'Bogdiana' and Bosnia.[62] The care with which Venice defended these close connections, for instance during the plague that struck Spalato during the summer of 1607,[63] the strengthening of a commercial link with Morea – are all signs that the Balkan connection had become stable, was no longer an expedient but a permanent solution.

As for the precise reasons why Venice was able to capture this trade, it is quite clear that piracy, whether by Uskoks, Christians or Moslems, was largely responsible. Nicolò Contarini, in his *History*, says in so many words that the increase in piracy throughout the Mediterranean determined the prosperity of the *scala*.[64] But the corsairs were not the only reason. The growing and unusual favour 'cosa non più usata', says Contarini, with which the overland route was viewed can and must have other causes. It raises the question of costs and commercial conditions at a time when business was affected by the rise in prices and possibly by an increased volume of trade. To take costs: security must have been a consideration here, as we shall see at the end of the century from the effects of marine insurance premiums which so handicapped Venetian ships in spite of their poorly paid crews and low-cost freighting.[65] Should we consider the possibility that the cost of caravan transport was low in Turkish territory, a region where the effects of the general price rise were felt much later than in the West?[66] The observations of some Turkish historians suggest that this might be a factor.[67]

In any case there is no lack of evidence, at the end of the century and the beginning of the next, of the increase in road traffic in the Balkans. To take Ragusa, commercial papers for 1590–1591[68] on the eve of Spalato's

[59] Domenico Sella, *op. cit.*, p. 2 and 55.
[60] *Cinque Savii*, Riposte 141, f°s 28 and 29, 19th July, 1607.
[61] *Cinque Savii*, 4, f° 1083, 19th September, 1626.
[62] *Ibid.*, 19 f°s 103 and 104, 20th May, 1636.
[63] See above, note 60.
[64] V. Lamansky, *op. cit.*, p. 514.
[65] See below p. 291, and Domenico Sella, *op. cit.*, p. 41 ff.
[66] See below Fig. 43, p. 518.
[67] Notes taken from Professor Lütfi Gučer's contribution to the Colloquium of June, 1957, at the Giorgio Cini Foundation.
[68] The Rectors to O. de Cerva, Ragusa, 20th May, 1593, Ragusa Archives, *Lettere di Levante*, 38, f° 113. There was certainly an increase in land traffic around Oran, Diego Suárez, *op. cit.*, p. 36, 47, 50, 86, 275, 314.

rise to fortune, reveal the extent of her traffic with the interior; as does the construction of a new bazaar near the town for Turkish merchants. In 1628 a more spacious quarantine building was set up at the end of the port.[69] This detail, insignificant in itself, suggests, when taken together with others, that these overland communications must have eliminated or at least reduced the halts in Syria and Egypt and the long sea voyages from the East to Italy; they furthered the movement westwards of merchants and merchandise from the Levant. The *Fontico dei Turchi* in Venice at San Giovanni Decollato dated from 1621.[70] Ragusa also witnessed the arrival of large numbers of Jewish and Turkish merchants.[71] So if the seventeenth century saw a recurrence of outbreaks of plague, particularly in Italy, and also in the Balkans, according to Jorjo Tadić,[72] there was perhaps a connection of cause and effect between these outbreaks and the revival of overland transport.

The intrinsic problem of the overland route. The increased road traffic in the Balkans in itself raises problems of wider relevance, problems relating both to long-lasting structures and to the immediate situation. These problems appear with clarity at the end of the sixteenth century, but we find them occurring earlier and recurring much later. Competition between different means of transport is common to all ages. But we historians of the early modern period have often mistakenly assumed that a sea or river route automatically took precedence over a land route. A road challenged by a waterway we have at once dismissed as doomed to decline. In fact, wheeled vehicles and pack animals offered more resistance to competition than we have credited them with and were not ousted so easily.

It is undeniable, for instance, that the prosperity of the German isthmus was due, among other things, after the fifteenth century, to the increased speed and modernization of wheeled vehicles. Renée Doehaerd has even maintained[73] that Antwerp's 'landward' fortune at the end of the fifteenth and beginning of the sixteenth centuries was the result of a determined takeover of wheeled traffic, whereby Antwerp gained access to the fast flow of goods through Germany and so, indirectly, to Italy, or Poland. This rise of Antwerp forms a contrast with the 'seaward' fortune of Bruges in the previous centuries, simply as a port on the way north for the triumphant advance of the Mediterranean ships. Indeed, between northern Europe and the Mediterranean, sea routes and overland routes clearly

[69] Dr. M. D. Grmek, 'Quarantaine à Dubrovnik' in *Symposium Ciba*, April, 1959, p. 30–33.

[70] Giuseppe Tassini, *Curiosità Veneziane*, 1887, p. 277–278. The Turkish merchants at Venice had been regrouped before this date, Senato Terra 67 (15th May, 1575). On Armenian and Turkish merchants, see the many references in *Cinque Savii*, 3, 4, 13, 15, 17, 18, 19 (from 1622 to 1640).

[71] Ragusa Archives, *Diversa di Cancelleria*, 192 to 196.

[72] In his letter of 7th November, 1963, mentioned earlier.

[73] Renée Doehaerd, *Études anversoises. Documents sur le commerce international à Anvers, 1488–1514*, I, 1963, *Introduction*, p. 66.

coexisted and competed with each other, the cargoes often, if not always, being divided into the heavy and cheap on one hand and the light and costly on the other,[74] the whole system operating over an immense area, both more extensive and easier to assess than the Balkans. I do not now think, as I did when I wrote the first edition, that the Atlantic route and the 'invasion' by northern ships which will be discussed later, immediately and permanently eclipsed the great German and French roads running down to the Mediterranean at the end of the sixteenth century. Some evidence on this point has been produced by Wilfrid Brulez in his book on the Antwerp firm of the della Faille.[75] When trading with Italy between 1574 and 1594 the della Faille firm preferred the Alps to the sea nine times out of ten. It is of no small importance that they should have chosen the former rather than the latter. A close look at the figures shows that they were simply guided by their own interests. The overland route was not without its disadvantages, but it was relatively reliable and the average profits it procured (16·7 per cent) were greater than those yielded by the long sea passage (12·5 per cent) where there were wild fluctuations from 0 (or rather a minus figure) to 200 per cent. The overland route was much steadier (maximum profit 30 per cent).

This particular example concerns luxury goods, of course. There is no evidence that an overall comparison between the Atlantic shipping route and the roads crossing Europe from north to south would show that the former carried (or did not carry) more merchandise than the latter (it certainly did in weight, but whether it did in value is more doubtful). At all events traffic continued to flow along the roads from Istanbul to Spalato, Hamburg to Venice, or Lyons to Marseilles. It was perhaps only in the seventeenth century that the sea passage was to become more important with the advance of the northern ships, the generalization of marine insurance and the establishment, again in the North, of powerful commercial firms.

These general observations are made with a purpose. They will not in themselves solve our Mediterranean problems, but they may shed some light upon them.

Two sets of evidence from Venice. From the preceding paragraphs we can certainly conclude that during the second half of the sixteenth century there was an increase in land traffic and that some abandoned roads were even revived and brought back into use. What about traffic by sea during the same period? There does not seem to have been any corresponding drop in shipping to offset the increased volume of trade on the roads, quite the contrary. The general upward trend seems to have maintained a certain balance between the two.

This can be illustrated by the case of Venice. At the same time as the

[74] Jacques Heers, 'Il commercio nel Mediterraneo alla fine del secolo XIV a nei primi anni del XV', in *Archivio storico italiano*, 1955.
[75] *Op. cit.*, p. 578.

Spalato venture, and even earlier, there was clearly a large reduction in the Venetian fleet. It is undoubtedly one of the factors that have led to talk of the decline of Venice. Domenico Sella puts it at about 1609.[76] Alberto Tenenti sees hints of it from 1592 on.

They are perhaps unduly pessimistic, for in fact the volume of traffic in the port remained the same until at least 1625, according to the figures given by Sella himself: 1607–1610, an average of 94,973 *colli* of which about 15,000 came from the Dalmatian ports and the routes over the Balkans; in 1625, 99,361; in 1675, 68,019; in 1680, 83,590; in 1725, 109,497. Foreign ships must have compensated for the deficiencies of the Venetian fleet. Tenenti's research has shown that this was indeed the case.[77] In his book he analyses the losses at sea registered in the presence of two Venetian notaries: Andrea Spinelli and Giovan Andrea Catti, both shipping specialists, who between them covered practically all possible clients. As soon as a disaster was known, the interested parties would come to register the insurance policy in order to claim their compensation. For eighteen crucial years (1592–1609) covering the turn of the century, this record of disasters lists over a thousand cases, of which about 660 (or almost 37 a year) correspond to wrecks or captures by pirates, the rest to 'accidents' or mishaps of varying gravity.

This unusually detailed survey establishes both the decadence of the Venetian navy, about which we already knew, and the increase in the numbers of northern ships arriving at Venice, either on the way from the western waters, or returning there, in other words, already engaging in trade with the Levant. We can certainly talk of Venice's decline *as a seapower*, but not of a decline in the traffic entering and leaving the port, which is our present concern. A small and unexpected detail is that the insurance rates did not budge during these difficult years,[78] at least until 1607, for Venetian ships.[79] This means one of two things: either the wily financiers, Genoese or Florentine, who controlled insurance in Venice and virtually constituted lobbies, were blind to their own interests and insured merchandise, ships, and freight out of pure philanthropy, or our calculations are mistaken. Let us suppose, and it is not a totally unreasonable supposition, that the average insurance rate was 5 per cent. For the underwriter to balance out gains and losses, he would need to set twenty voyages without incident against one total disaster. For the sake of argument, all ships are assumed to be equivalent to each other, and the disaster befalling the

[76] Domenico Sella, *op. cit.*, p. 72.
[77] Alberto Tenenti, *Naufrages, corsaires et assurances maritimes à Venise,* (*1592–1609*), 1959.
[78] *Ibid.*, p. 59 and 60, fixed rate of insurance at Ragusa, Iorjo Tadić, letter of 7th November, 1963, quoted above.
[79] *Cinque Savii*, 141 ,f° 32 to 33 v°, 24th September, 1607. The premium rates for Syria were 8, 9, or 10 per cent for the outward voyage and the same for the return. In 1593 and 1594, the rates (for a single outward trip or a single return trip) were regularly 5 per cent, A.d.S. Venice, *Miscellanea*, Carte Private 46. Were the *Cinque Savii* exaggerating in order to get permission to ship silver to Syria?

twenty-first as total. Obviously this is an oversimplification: in the first place because disaster was never total for the underwriter since he was re-insured; second, he would have a legal claim to any goods salvaged; third, if he reimbursed the victim, he would usually secure a reduction on the total insurance payment; and fourth, if gain and loss balanced, he would meanwhile have been collecting the interest on the sums received for as long as the insurance had been held. These points complicate the problem, but not impossibly so. In short, and this is my point, it is not absurd to suppose that wrecks were compensated by many safe and successful voyages. For 37 boats lost, there were perhaps 740 voyages a year.[80] In fact, the port of Venice was busier than has been supposed; shipping there was far from sluggish in those latter years of the sixteenth century which are supposed to have been disastrous. In 1605, it is true, Venice possessed only 27 big ships,[81] but if the ratio of small to big ships was the same as elsewhere, she should have possessed over 200 small ships (10 to 1). At any rate, in the *ancorazzo* list (1st September, 1598–1st September, 1599),[82] I have noted 46 *marciliane*, probably Venetian, and there were even smaller ships. True, this *ancorazzo* for 1598–1599 only lists two hundred effective payments, but each payment could refer to more than one voyage, and barques were exempted. Some conclusive research even on a point of detail would resolve the problem here. The question is: how many voyages could one payment represent? But even in our present imperfect state of knowledge, we can say that despite the increased traffic on the main roads of the Balkans, it is perhaps incorrect to assume that shipping in the Adriatic and Mediterranean had declined, slowed down, or disappeared On the contrary, I am inclined to think that Mediterranean trade had reached a large volume by the end of the century. How could piracy, which is reported to have been a profitable occupation, otherwise have prospered? At Ragusa, it is true, the number of Ragusan vessels declined, but a few registrations picked at random from the chancellery of the little town show an Englishman, a Frenchman from Marseilles, even a Catalan, the last certainly a sea captain.[83] New ships had taken over from the old.

There was no outright victor in the competition between sea and land communications, at least in the sixteenth century: general prosperity brought benefit to both. And on the whole the respective positions held by each method of transport remained fairly constant; at any rate the relative value of goods carried did.

Venice offers a little more evidence on the subject of rivalry between shipping and overland routes through the chance survival of a register of bales of wool arriving from 'the west', i.e., Spain, from 1508 to 1606.[84] The bales that came all the way by sea are listed separately from

---

[80] It is of course an optimistic hypothesis.
[81] Tenenti, *op. cit.*, p. 567.   [82] *Ibid.*, p. 563 ff.
[83] Ragusa Archives, *Divers di Cancellaria*, 192 to 196, especially 192 (f° 139, 30th May, 1604, f° 176 v°, 14, 1604, the Catalan); 194 (f° 44 v°, 2nd May, 1605).
[84] Museo Correr, Prov. Div. C 989 (Mercatura e traffichi III).

those that came overland using the roads crossing Italy. The choice of the first route was encouraged by the virtually free entry granted in 1598 to wool arriving by sea. These direct shipments were carried in Dutch vessels. And yet, in spite of these advantages and these superior ships, the overland route, via Genoa and particularly via Leghorn, held its own and even had the advantage over its rival. Why was this? The reason is not hard to guess. In the first place there was the force of habit, and of established interests. We know that the Genoese and Florentines had the monopoly of purchases in Spain; that there was a line of payments (in fact of a sort of credit by remote control) running all the way from Medina del Campo to Florence and back, as the correspondence of Simón Ruiz[85] bears witness; that Venetian merchants bought wool on a commission basis, that is, on credit on Florence and that the first choice of wool stayed in Florence, the second choice going to Venice for processing. The role played by Florence as a go-between explains the frequent use made of the land route; it is just possible that the large total quantities of wool arriving at Venice at the end of the century correspond to the premature collapse of the Florentine woollen industry, which would have liberated raw materials.

This, then, is a good example, although obviously insufficient in itself to decide the matter, of the non-elasticity of competition between the two categories of routes and of the complexity of the factors present. But it is possible to detect a constant structural relationship which can be retained as a working hypothesis.

Circulation and statistics: the case of Spain. Another example, over a larger area this time, is that of Castile, which was surrounded by a series of customs posts, along both coastal and inland frontiers, the latter sometimes well inside Castilian territory. The *puertos secos*, dry ports (inland), were the thirty-nine customs posts, on the frontiers of Navarre, Aragon, and Valencia, commanding access to the principal and secondary roads of Castile; the *puertos altos*, the high ports, were on the borders of Navarre and Aragon, the *puertos bajos*, the low ports, controlled traffic on the Valencia side. The *puertos de Portugal*, about forty-six in number, some of very minor importance, controlled overland routes to Portugal. Along the two sea frontiers, in the Bay of Biscay and the coast from Valencia to Portugal, were on one hand the *diezmos de la mar*, seized by royal authority in 1559[86] (they had previously belonged to the descendants of the Constable of Castile): and on the other hand, the many customs privileges emanating from the vast fiscal complex of the *Almojarifazgo Mayor* of Seville, an institution that had already existed in the time of the Moorish kings and that controlled all entries by sea, sometimes from posts situated

---

[85] Felipe Ruiz Martín, *Lettres marchandes échangées entre Florence et Medina del Campo*, 1965, p. CXVI ff.
[86] Modesto Ulloa, *La hacienda real de Castilla en el reinado de Felipe II*, Rome, 1963, p. 187.

inland, but more often from a string of ports (Seville, Cadiz, San Lucar de Barrameda, Puerto de Santa Maria, Málaga, etc.). To these ancient privileges was added the *Almojarifazgo de Indias*, which only concerned merchandise arriving from the Indies, that is America, or going there.

So Castile was surrounded by customs posts, represented at Simancas by an enormous body of papers and statistics that have been made more accessible by the recent work of Ramón Carande[87] and Modeste Ulloa.[88] Do they provide us with a scale on which to measure the relative proportions of land and sea transport? The answer is yes and no. They ought to because of their relative continuity and great volume; the scale of documentation is sufficient to balance out errors. But on the other hand, the fiscal system of Castile does not distinguish as it should one set of figures from another, so their value to us is reduced. Above all, the region under observation, Castile, is a better guide to the Atlantic, which dominated her entire economic life, than to the Mediterranean on which she turned her back. In any case, we shall only seek from these documents some indication of ranking order and comparison.

The first conclusion that suggests itself is that traffic – and customs duties – increased considerably. (1) If the revenue of the *Almojarifazgo de Indias* in 1544 is represented by 100, in the average year between 1595 and 1604 it reached 666; it had increased more than sixfold in 50 years, a calculation that is confirmed by the research of Huguette and Pierre Chaunu. (2) If that of the *Almojarifazgo Mayor* is represented by 100 in 1525, it reached almost 300 in 1559, 1000 in 1586–1592, and (inflated value) perhaps 1100 in 1602–1604.[89] (3) As for the *diezmos de la mar*, if 1561 is 100, they stood at over 300 in 1571; 250 in 1581; 200 in 1585; a little over 200 in 1598. Clearly it was in southern Spain, as one would expect of course, that the main force of the increase in shipping during the century was felt. (4) The *puertos secos*: 100 in 1556–1566; 277 in 1598. (5) The *puertos de Portugal* show a slower rate of increase: 100 in 1562; 234 in 1598; but they were in a region notorious for smuggling.

However, in order to measure the comparative increase in customs duties from land and sea routes, the index of 100 should be placed in about 1560, since the series are of varying length. At that date this gives 38 million *maravedis* of customs duties for overland traffic, 115 million for all maritime traffic, or a ratio of 1 to 3. If the same calculation is made in 1598 it gives a result of 97 million *maravedis* to 282 million: the ratio 1 to 3 is maintained. It seems then that there was no structural change in the relationship between the different modes of transport in Castile in the second half of the sixteenth century. They advanced at the same pace and would yield very similar curves on a graph. This is rather clearer evidence than our previous examples of a comparative stability in the relations

[87] Ramón Carande, *Carlos V y sus banqueros, La hacienda real de Castilla*, 1949, p. 292 ff.
[88] *La hacienda real . . .*, p. 137–200.
[89] Simancas, Escrivania Mayor de Rentas, 1603–1604.

between the two kinds of traffic. On the whole their relative proportions did not vary greatly.

The double problem in the long term. We can hardly draw conclusions let alone generalize from a few particular examples in time and space. Any solution in this area – where research has persistently revealed not so much the actual volume of either kind of traffic as the ways they have developed, or seemed to develop, relative to each other – could only result from an enquiry spanning a much longer period than the fifty years of this book, a period of several centuries, at least from the fifteenth to the seventeenth or eighteenth, and covering a wider area than the Mediterranean, vast and various though it is. The tempting hypothesis suggested by Hermann van der Wee[90] provides a summary of the area of debate. He proposes that in the fifteenth century there was an increase in the volume of shipping in Europe and the Mediterranean from Venice to Bruges; that it was only in the sixteenth century that this outside impetus brought to life a 'trans-continental' economy, in which both shipping and overland routes developed at the same pace. In the seventeenth century the areas where economic life continued to thrive were once more predominantly the ports and the coastline, and it was not until the following century that sea and land traffic again advanced in step.

I am prepared to accept that there may have been fluctuations of this order. They provide us at any rate with a framework for investigation. Our century, the sixteenth, according to this theory, hedged its bets. One would therefore assume *a priori* that any increase in road traffic would on the whole be accompanied by an increase in shipping and *vice versa*. We should expect to find the sea route predominating only in the fifteenth century with the Italian ships, and in the seventeenth with the Dutch. If this theory is correct, of course, local research ought to confirm it. But it is hardly likely that such a pattern would be reproduced clearly everywhere at the same time. The age of Dutch supremacy did not automatically suppress the activity, and even the revival of some overland routes. In the registers of the *Cinque Savii*[91] one can read under an entry dated 8th May, 1636, 'che molte mercancie che venivano per via di mare habbino preso il camino di terra da Genova o Livorno'. So land routes were still holding their own in some places even in 1636. We should only accept the simplifications of overall theories when there is unmistakable evidence to support them.

2. SHIPPING: TONNAGES AND CHANGING CIRCUMSTANCES

We have records of thousands of Mediterranean ships; we know their names, their approximate tonnage, cargoes, and itineraries. But it is not easy to introduce order and meaning into this mass of detail. The reader

[90] *The Growth of the Antwerp Market and the European Economy*, 1963, II, p. 311 ff.
[91] A.d.S. Venice, *Cinque Savii*, 4a, f° 44, 8th May, 1636.

will, I hope, forgive me for tackling the problem from various angles, in the first place for widely extending the chronological field of observation, making frequent reference to the fifteenth and seventeenth centuries; secondly, for treating the Atlantic as one with the Mediterranean. The reasons for taking these unexpected steps should emerge from the following discussion, and three or four general rules which must be stated at the outset should help to clarify the problem.

1. Mediterranean shipping was not fundamentally different from Atlantic shipping. Techniques, insurance rates, intervals between voyages might differ, but the basic instrument, the wooden ship propelled by the wind, had the same technical limitations. It could not exceed a certain size, number of crew, surface of sail, or speed. Another unifying feature was that no new type of ship appeared in the ocean without examples appearing fairly soon in the Mediterranean. Even at Venice, a city that had her own types of boat and did not readily change them, there were caravels when Marino Sanudo was a young man, at the end of the fifteenth century, and galleons and *bertoni* before the end of the sixteenth. Even the Turks were by then using the ocean-going galleon,[92] 'navis gravis, navis oneraria', the heaviest of all merchant vessels, explains Schweigger, a German traveller who saw them at Constantinople and elsewhere in 1581.[93]

2. In the Atlantic as well as in the Mediterranean, boats of small tonnage were in an overwhelming majority. They loaded quickly, were off at the first puff of wind; proletarians of the sea, they often sold their services cheaply. Two Capuchin friars were returning, in June, 1633, from Lisbon to England: the master of a *naviguela* of Honfleur (35 tons) carrying salt and lemons, offered to take them to Calais[94] for 8 *livres* per passenger. In April, 1616, the Venetian ambassador Piero Gritti, travelling to Spain, preferred to board a Provençal felucca, a small two-masted boat, at Genoa; he wanted a fast crossing, and reserved places for his family on a big ship sailing to Alicante.[95] The felucca, wrote Père Binet in 1632, 'is the smallest of all oarships'.[96]

The small ships then were in a majority, their names varying according to port, region, or period: *grippi* or *marani* or *marciliane*, in the Adriatic, feluccas or tartans in Provence, barques as port statistics sometimes call them with no further detail. These little boats, mostly under 100 and even under 50 tons, plied in the Atlantic as well as in the Mediterranean. There were ten of them for every large merchantman, according to Valencia statistics for 1598 to 1618.[97] When we find that there were thirty-one *navi* (i.e., large merchant ships) at Venice in 1599[98] we must imagine several hundred small boats surrounding them.

[92] R. Mantran, *op. cit.*, p. 489.   [93] S. Schweigger, *op. cit.*, p. 241.
[94] B. M. Sloane 1572, f° 50 v° and 51, 2nd July, 1633.
[95] A.d.S. Venice, Dispacci Spagna, Po. Gritti to the Doge, Genoa, 30th April, 1616.
[96] R. P. Binet, *Essay des merveilles de nature et des plus nobles artifices* (1657 ed., p. 97).
[97] According to the unpublished research work of Alvaro Castillo Pintado.
[98] Museo Correr, D. delle Rose, 217.

3. It must be accepted once and for all that we shall never have complete knowledge of tonnages in the sixteenth century, let alone the average tonnage that would enable us, where we know the number of ships entering or leaving a port, to calculate their total tonnage. I have suggested the figure of 75 tons,[99] based on statistics from the Andalusian ports. This figure is probably much too high. The recorded tonnages are in any case never very precise. Experts calculated them from the ship's measurements (height, breadth, and length). When a boat was being hired out to another state, the figure was of course exaggerated, quite openly when the customer was Spain. Even if we assume honesty all round, we still have to translate *salme, stara, botte, cantara, carra,* into our own measures. This is an area full of pitfalls: if anything it is even worse than trying to convert nominal prices into grammes of silver. The 'nominal' tonnages of the sixteenth century dropped suddenly at Seville, a source of several problems for Huguette and Pierre Chaunu. I once worked briefly on some French consular documents (A. N. series B III) that recorded the arrivals of boats with their cargoes at a series of foreign ports in the eighteenth century this time. Several times the same boat – same master, same name, identical details of route followed and cargo carried – was described in these official papers as being of different tonnage from one port and one consulate to another. In short, all our calculations must be approximate, with the disadvantages that implies.

4. The bulk of the evidence undoubtedly relates to big and very big ships. This takes us not to the borderline between medium and large tonnages, but to the upper limit, around 1000 or even 2000 tons. The Spanish *proveedores* were not usually likely to put an embargo on some Breton fishing smack of about 30 tons, or a caravel that would hold a maximum of only ten horses, as they did in 1541,[100] for instance, before the Algiers expedition.

It was the larger ships they were after and in fact the latter accepted the situation with more equanimity than they expressed, for the Spanish state reserved bounties for them, allowed them good freight rates and generous supplies.

At this period a ship of 1000 tons was a giant and a rarity. On 13th February, 1597, Thomas Platter,[101] the medical student from Basel who had just completed his studies at Montpellier, was in Marseilles. In the port he had eyes only for an enormous Genoese ship that had just been seized by the Marseillais, 'It was one of the largest ships ever launched in the Mediterranean; it was like a great house of five storics rising from the

[99] Based on Simancas E° 160. See below p. 304. Incidentally of great interest to the history of technical progress is A. Delatte, 'L'armement d'une caravelle grecque du XVIe siècle, d'après un manuscrit de Vienne', in *Miscellenea Mercati*, vol. III, 1946, p. 490–508. It is a study of the proportions of the various parts of the vessel in relation to its tonnage. I am indebted to Hélène Bibicou for the translation of this difficult text.

[100] Simancas, Guerra Antigua, XX, f° 15, 15th September, 1541. The transport of horses required a tonnage of at least 20 tons per horse.

[101] Thomas Platter, *Journal of a Younger brother*, p. 117.

middle of the sea. I estimated that its capacity must be at least fifteen thousand quintals [about 750 modern tons]. It had eight or ten sails on two masts of prodigious height, one of which I climbed by means of rope ladders. From that height I could see far and wide including the Château d'If, which has a windmill similar to those in the town.' This example is one of hundreds of similar descriptions.

5. The problem facing us if we wish to establish even an approximate average tonnage, in order to build up a general picture, is the relation of these very large tonnages to the rest. It should be borne in mind from the start: (a) that record tonnages did not rise continuously, unless the impressive figures found in the fifteenth century, which are equal to achievements of the eighteenth century, are incorrect, and I am quite sure this is not so;[102] (b) that big ships were linked to long distances: they monopolized these interminable voyages for a long time. In addition, behind them there were always states with their requirements and resources, cities, and invariably rich shipowners; (c) that these large merchantmen usually carried heavy, bulky cargoes whose price per unit was low and which logically required water transport. So they offered cheap freighting facilities; (d) that before the revolution brought about, quite late, by naval artillery, these floating fortresses spelt security. They might be exposed to the hazards of bad weather like any frail barque, but they could resist an enemy attack. What pirate would seek an encounter with the large crews, soldiers, slingers, and archers they had on board? The big ship was the rich man's best policeman. The two big ships which the Signoria of Venice was slowly and very expensively fitting out in June, 1460, had to be, and that was why they were built, 'spavento a tutti' a bogey to all pirates;[103] (e) that vessels of great tonnage did not eliminate all competition, despite the backing of rich men and commercial cities, and despite the attraction they had for spendthrift governments (the French king had a ship built at Le Havre in 1532 of 'smisurata grandezza tal che si stima dover esse innavigabile';[104] (f) that there were certainly times when the big ships appropriated all transport. The early fifteenth century was a time of monopolies, whether legal or actual, and the sixteenth century was to reintroduce them on the passage to Spanish America and the Portuguese Indies. But if for one reason or another these monopolies were thrown open, there was a host of small and medium-sized ships waiting to rush in. *This comeback by boats of small tonnage almost always seems to have occurred during a period of trade expansion.* If we find big ships alone, business is probably bad; if we find big ships accompanied by little ships, business is certain to be good. This indicator shows every sign of being

[102] According to Louis Dermigny, *La Chine et l'Occident. Le Commerce à Canton au XVIIIe siècle, 1719–1833,* 1964, the tonnage of the great Indiamen was less than 2000 tons; the *Hindustan,* in 1758 had an official capacity of 1248 and in fact displaced 1890, vol. I, p. 202 ff., p. 212 and 213.

[103] A.d.S. Venice, Senato Mar 6, f° 185, 30th June, 1460.

[104] B.N. Paris, Ital., 1714, f° 109, J. A. Venier to the Doge, Rouen, 22nd February, 1532, copy.

reliable, but it will be discussed further. The reader is asked to accept it provisionally.

Big ships and little ships in the fifteenth century. The prosperous career of the big ships in the Mediterranean had begun in the fifteenth century. Mediterranean vessels were already sailing from one end of the Mediterranean to the other and pressing on to London or Bruges, the longest voyages as a rule being undertaken by the Genoese. This gave Genoa a head start in the race for big ships.[105] the more so since she virtually specialized in the transport of bulky goods, notably alum from Phocaea in Asia Minor and wines from the islands of the Levant – which she shipped direct to Bruges and England. The Genoese carrack, which approached 1000 tons, often more, was for a long time the rational solution to a difficult technical problem.

Venice followed suit but much later. In the first place she was nearer than Genoa to the Levant, where much of her activity was centred; second, her system of *galere da mercato*,[106] efficiently organized by the state, regulated traffic into particular voyages; there were galleys to Tana, Trebizond, Romania, Beirut, Alexandria, Aiguesmortes, Flanders, Barbary, and the *trafego* (both the Barbary and Egyptian coast). This system meant that difficulties and risks were shared and direct voyages from the Levant to Bruges, in the Genoese manner, were forbidden; all goods had to pass through Venice, providing the Signoria with the dues on which she lived. There is also the possibility that the connection with the trade axis of central Europe was more vital to Venice than to Genoa. In short, if this complicated system, which was constantly under review, survived, it was because it had been introduced in about 1339 as a result of difficulties arising from the recession of the fourteenth century, and consequently soon came to mean that the most hazardous routes were sub-sidized. In any case, the *galere da mercato* hardly reached 200 to 250 tons at the end of the century.[107] Moreover they only carried luxury com-modities, such as pepper, spices, expensive fabrics, silks, malmsey wines. This being so, it was wisest to spread the risks between several loads. Only the Flemish galleys, returning from the North would load, besides the kerseys and amber, bales of wool, lead and tin from England, otherwise they would have returned empty. However, it was the experience of long voyages to the Black Sea on one hand, and to England on the other, that led to the increased tonnage of the galleys (in the fourteenth century they were only about 100 tons burden) and then to their increased numbers.

[105] Jacques Heers, *Gênes au XVe siècle, Activité économique et problèmes sociaux*, 1961, p. 278.
[106] I have drawn on the early chapters of the unpublished work by Alberto Tenenti, and Corrado Vivanti on the Venetian system of *galere da mercato*, which forms the basis of an article by the same authors 'Le film d'un grand système de navigation: les galères marchandes vénitiennes XIVe–XVIe siècles' in *Annales E.S.C.*, XVI, 1961, no. 1, p. 83–86.
[107] Gino Luzzatto, *op. cit.*, p. 41 ff.

Beside the *galere da mercato*, a private or only partly controlled shipping sector existed at Venice. These were the roundships, 'cogs', which handled in particular the transport of the bulky bales of cotton from Cyprus or Syria.[108] Cotton had become an important textile as early as the thirteenth century, compensating for insufficient woollen production, and was to be much demanded with the development of fustians (linen and cotton mixture). The cotton was transported annually in two *mude:* one, the larger, in February (about half a dozen ships); the other, in September, might consist of only two ships. The large bales required roomy carriers. A document from the *Notatorio di collegio*[109] dated 1st December, 1449, lists the names and tonnages of six roundships that were to make up the *muda* of the following February: 1100, 762, 732, 566, 550 and 495 *botte*, or between 250 and 550 tons. These were very respectable tonnages even for the fifteenth century.

Another advantage of the big ships was that they could defend themselves against pirates. A Catalan roundship of 2800 *botte* (about 1400 tons) in August, 1490,[110] gave chase to the Barbary galleys, which took refuge in the port of Syracuse. In 1497[111] Sanudo mentions a Venetian *nave* of 3000 *botte*, a French 'barque' of 3500, a Genoese *nave* the *Negrona*, of 4000. Two years later, in 1499,[112] he gives some measurements of the Venetian ships that were to join the French fleet. The average tonnage of the thirty ships (including seven foreign ones) was 675 *botte*, or about 338 tons, an average that will seem abnormally nigh to any historian of the sixteenth century. By way of comparison, in July, 1541,[113] 52 ships listed at Cadiz and Seville, just before Charles V's expedition against Algiers, amounted to a total of just over 10,000 tons, or an average of 200 tons per ship. So it must be accepted that the fifteenth century had tonnages as high as anything in the eighteenth century; some of the Indiamen[114] which then carried the trade 'to China' were only in the region of 2000 tons.

The first victories of the small ships. At some point between the fifteenth and sixteenth centuries, there was a reduction in the number of big ships and a rapid extension of boats of smaller tonnage. This movement can be traced to the middle of the fifteenth century and indeed to Venice, where in 1451 there is already mention in a Senate debate[115] of the demand for

[108] Gino Luzzatto, *op cit.*, p. 76.

[109] A.d.S., Notatorio di Collegio, 355, f° 104 v°, 1st December, 1449. In the same series: 372, f° 108 v°, 12th April, 1450 (915, 1150, 1100 *botte*): 97, f° 29 v°, 11th June, 1461 (2500 *botte*) 343, f° 87, 18th February, 1471; 368, f° 96, 8th June, 1471 (a new *nave* of over 1000 *botte*).

[110] A.d.S. Mantua, A° Gonzaga, Series E, Venezia 1433, G. Brognolo to the Marquis of Mantua, Venice, 7th August, 1490.

[111] *Op. cit.*, I, p. 684, 26th June, 1497; p. 802–803, October, 1497.

[112] *Ibid.*, II, p. 1244 ff. Similar sample: Correr, D. delle Rose, 154, f° 69, 1499.

[113] The list was drawn up at Málaga in July, 1541, Simancas Guerra Antigua, XX, f° 10.

[114] Louis Dermigny, *op. cit.*, vol. I, p. 202 ff.

[115] A.d.S. Venice, Senato Mar, 4, f° 28 v°, 16th January, 1451.

small boats for the voyages to Syria and Catalonia; 'et ad viagia Sirie et Cathallonie omnes magis desiderant naves parvas'.

Small ships from the Atlantic became numerous in the Mediterranean after this, Basque, Portuguese and Spanish invaders 'che prima non solevano passar il stretto de Zibilterra', according to a curious Senate debate dated 21st October, 1502;[116] something one does not expect to hear at that date. Venice, if we are to believe her, was on the brink of unspeakable disaster. Her fleet of big ships which had previously numbered 300 (an exaggeration) 'dal 1420 sino al 1450', had dwindled to 16, each with a capacity of at least 400 *botte* and for the most part indeed fit only for scrap; besides these big ships there were few small ships, even including the Dalmatian caravels and the *marani*.

There was no lack of explanation for this crisis: the heavy dues placed on shipping; the absurdly low freight rates; the prohibition placed on loading salt from Languedoc in the *mar de Lion*, the authorization granted to foreign ships to load wines directly at Crete; and then there were those intruders, who had crossed the Straits of Gibraltar and 'are enriching themselves at the expense not only of the *cittadini* but also of the State which they now imperil, of the *mude* of the galleys and of our roundships'. These intruders were the small ships.

Similar developments occurred in the Atlantic, the English Channel, and the North Sea, as Aloys Schulte reported in his marvellous book on the *Grosse Ravensburger Gesellschaft* where one can find information about everything if one is prepared to look for it.[117] The great roundships or *naus* of Genoa and other Mediterranean cities were overtaken by the light and elegant caravels, the new young hope of the world. Andrea Satler wrote from Bruges in 1478, 'Die kleinen haben die grossen Schiffe ganz vertrieben'. The difference between the two categories was enormous. In 1498 four roundships loaded 9000 quintals of merchandise at Antwerp; 28 caravels between them could only take 1150.

The victory of the light sailing vessel over the great ships of the Mediterranean, of the swifter, cheaper boats over the great giants that took an age to load and worked with the monopolists' privileges, marked the beginning of a great transformation both in the Atlantic and the Mediterranean. It was to last until about the 1530s, slowed down towards 1550 (at least in the Mediterranean), started again after the 1570s, and lasted until after the end of the century.

In the Atlantic in the sixteenth century. The problem of Atlantic shipping in the sixteenth century is usually approached from the wrong angle. To set it in perspective, we should consider separately from the rest the two great Iberian monopolies: the *Carrera de Indias*, based in Seville, and the long shipping route between Lisbon and the East Indies.

On these favoured routes the little ships of the explorers soon dis-

[116] Museo Correr, D. delle Rose, 2509, 21st October, 1502, *in rogatis*.
[17] *Op. cit.*, III, p. 413.

appeared. Of Columbus' three ships, the *Santa Maria* was a vessel of 280 tons, the *Pinta* 140, and the *Nina* only 100. Fifty years later, the 1552 regulations would not accept any ships below 100 tons, with a minimum crew of thirty-two men, on the American convoys; a decision by Philip II on 11th March, 1587, raised the minimum to 300 tons.[118] But at the end of the sixteenth century there were few ships over 500 tons on the West Indies route, for 400-ton sailing ships had difficulty crossing the bar at San Lucar de Barrameda, on the Guadalquivir below Seville. It was only in the second half of the seventeenth century that galleons between 700 and 1000 tons were to become common,[119] and the acute problem arose of transferring the *Casa de la Contratación* and the monopoly of the West Indies trade from Seville, which the ships could no longer reach, to Cadiz.[120]

At Lisbon, where there was unimpeded access to the harbour, vessels of large tonnage were not uncommon in the sixteenth century. The *Garça*, which in 1558 carried the viceroy Constantino de Bragança to the Portuguese Indies, was a vessel of 1000 tons; in fact at the time she was the largest ship ever seen on the Indies route.[121] In 1579, according to a Venetian ambassador, the *navi grandissime* at Lisbon were of over 2200 *botte* (over 1100 tons).[122] This figure was often exceeded at the end of the century. The carrack *Madre de Dios*, wihich Clifford seizcd in 1592[123] and brought back to Dartmouth, could not apparently be taken to London because of her draught. She was over 1800 tons, could carry 900 tons of merchandise plus 32 pieces of ordnance, and 700 passengers. From stem to stern, she measured 166 feet, and her breadth at the widesț point, on the second of her three decks, was 46 feet 10 inches; she drew 31 feet of water, her keel was 100 feet long, her mainmast 120 feet high and ten feet round. The admiration of the English was not lessened by the publication on 15th September of the lengthy list of goods she carried, which were to be put up for auction. Forty years later the Portuguese were still building ships as big as this. A traveller[124] in 1604 admired a carrack of 1500 *toneladas* under construction in the port of Lisbon. 'The Portuguese used to make many more of them. The amount of wood which goes to make one is quite incredible: a forest of many leagues would not suffice for two. Three

[118] Huguette and Pierre Chaunu, *Séville et L'Atlantique*, 1955, vol. I, p. 127, n. 3 on the regulations of 13th February, 1553, and 11th March, 1587; the upper limit was also controlled: 400 tons in 1547 and 550 in 1628 for ships travelling in fleets.
[119] J. Kulischer, *Allgemeine Wirtschaftsgeschichte des Mittelalters und der Neuzeit*, 1928 (reprinted 1958), II, p. 385.
[120] Albert Girard, *La rivalité commerciale de Séville et de Cadix au XVIIIe siècle*, 1932.
[121] Barradas in: Bernard Gomes De Brito, *Historia tragico-maritima*, 1904–1905, I, p. 221.
[122] *Journal de voyage de . . . Zane* (1579) unpublished, P.R.O. 30.25.156., f° 32 v°.
[123] Alfred de Sternbeck, *Histoire des flibustiers*, 1931, p. 158 ff. Abbé Prévost, *Histoire générale des voyages*, 1746, vol. I, p. 355. Did Cervantes base the details of the Portuguese carrack in *La española inglesa* on this incident (*Novelas Ejemplares*)?
[124] B. M. Sloane, 1572.

hundred men working on a single ship can hardly finish it in a year. The iron to provide nails and other necessary metalwork weighs 500 tons. These carracks were formerly of 2000–2500 tons. For the mast they choose eight of the greatest and tallest pine trunks and bind them together with hoops of iron; it requires a crew of nine hundred men.'

As late as 1664, Varenius in his *Geographia Generalis*, recognized that the Iberians built the biggest ships: 'Hodie maximae sunt naves Hispanorum seu Lusitanorum quas vocant carracas.'[125] But long before that date the heavy vessels had already lost the battle against the light Dutch ships.

The decline of the giants and the spread of small sailing vessels had begun in the sixteenth century. The latter especially calls for our attention. The ships used in the great English naval exploits of the sixteenth century, whether for voyages of discovery or privateering, were often under 100 tons.[126] In 1572, Drake was aboard the *Pasca* a vessel of only 70 tons;[127] the *Primrose* of London[128] in 1585 was of only 150 tons burden. In 1586 Cavendish's three ships were respectively 140, 60, and 40 tons.[129] In 1587, Spain was given information about fourteen ships standing in the river at London. They were all between 80 and 100 tons.[130] Even in 1664 France possessed in all a few thousand ships over 30 tons, of which scarcely 400 were more than 100 tons and only 60 over 300 tons.[131] Most of her shipping links with the Baltic, for example, were worked by ships of between 30 and 50 tons. In the sixteenth century as in the seventeenth, seas and oceans were populated by small sailing ships. Between 1560 and 1600 the arsenals of Lübeck built two thousand four hundred ships, according to Baasch's research and calculations; their average tonnage was 60 *Lasten*, or 120 tons.[132] And yet we have records of some big ships from Lübeck: the *Grande Barque*, 600 tons, master 'Roqueresbart', was in the bay of Cadiz in spring 1595; the *Joshua* of 300 tons was at the same time at anchor at San Lucar.[133] The Hanseatic towns sent down to Spain large ships that were either hired or bought by the Sevillians for the trips to the New World, and by the Portuguese for Brazil and the Indian Ocean: the *filibote La Esperanza*, 160 tons, from Hamburg, master John 'Neve', equipped with 20 pieces of artillery, which called at Cadiz in March, 1595, was intended for Brazil by the 'contratadores de la provision de la frontera de la corona de Portugal'.[134]

[125] B. Varenius, *Geographia Generalis*, Amsterdam, 1664, p. 710.
[126] V. G. Scammell, 'English merchant shipping at the end of the Middle Ages: some East Coast evidence' in *Economic History Review*, 1961, p. 334, the average tonnage was still 42 tons in 1572.
[127] John Harris, *Navigantium atque itinerantium bibliotheca*, London, 1746, I, p. 115.
[128] R. Hakluyt, *The Principal Navigations*. . . . II, part 2, p. 112–113.
[129] J. Harris, *op. cit.*, I, p. 23.
[130] *La Armada Invencible*, documents published by Henrique Herrera Oria, Valladolid, 1929, p. 24.
[131] P. Charliat, *Trois siècles d'économie maritime française*, 1931, p. XXX.
[132] J. Kulischer, *op. cit.*, II, p. 1572.
[133] Simancas E° 174.   [134] *Ibid.*

The average that Baasch gives, 120 tons, must therefore be an indication of a large number of small vessels that were quite ready to undertake the voyage to Spain. A ship list of 1538 numbers forty ships, boats and shallops, then in the ports of the Asturias, with an average tonnage of 70 tons.[135] In 1575, 1578, and 1579 a record[136] of foreign vessels arriving in Andalusia gives the total figure for 800 ships as 60,000 tons, i.e., a modest average per vessel of 75 tons.

The figures are naturally higher when they include the big foreign ships requisitioned for troop transport, such as those listed in 1595 in three registers drawn up in the ports of San Lucar and Cadiz. The average tonnage of the first group, twenty-eight ships, listed on 29th March, 1595,[137] was about 200 tons; for the second group, thirty-seven ships entered in the inventory on 3rd August and including some or all the ships from the first group,[138] the total tonnage was 7940 tons, the artillery consisted of 396 cannons, and the crews of 665 men in all; on average then each ship had a capacity of 214 tons, carried ten pieces of artillery and about twenty men (eighteen to be precise). To simplify, we may say that a piece of artillery corresponds to about 20 tons, a seaman to 10. The total tonnage of the final group of ships[139] was 8360 tons, or an average of 154 tons per vessel, which is lower not because it was autumn shipping, but because this time the register included all the ships that had entered the port, from the *urcas*, the hookers, that is big ships of northern type, to the little sailing ships that the text describes curiously as *filibotes* (from the same root as *flibustar* to privateer, cf. English, to filibuster): the *Golden Dog* of Stockholm, 80 tons; the *Fortune* of Dunkirk, the *Saint Mary* of Stockholm, the *Saint Peter* of Königsberg, the *Charity* of Dunkirk, the *Hunter* of Stockholm, to name only the first few entries on this list of northern ships, from Norway, Denmark, the Hanseatic towns, and those of the Low Countries that had remained loyal to Spain, ships that in both Seville and associated ports had taken over since 1586 from the English and Dutch vessels banned by the Catholic King from all Peninsular ports – ships laden with sails, timber, planks, beams and grain, which in order to evade the English patrols in the Channel sometimes sailed round the north of Scotland.

[135] Simancas Guerra Antigua, XI, unnumbered; in 1538, *ibid.*, f° 56, *Relacion de los naos y carabellas que se han hallado entrados los puertos deste reyno de Galicia*, records of the sardine boats travelling to Cartagena and Barcelona, of Portuguese caravels, one carrying sugar, another hides, carried off ` rom Ireland. Amongst these pygmies was a carrack of 1000 tons at Vivero 'que a comun opinion es el major navio que ay desde Levante a Poniente'.

[136] Simancas E° 160.

[137] *Relacion de los navios que se han detenido en el baya de Cadiz y puerto de San Lucar de Barrameda y de sus partes, bondad, gente de mar y artilleria en 29 de março*, 1595. Simancas E° 174.

[138] *Relacion particular de los navios que estan detenidos en los puertos de Cadiz, San Lucar, Gibraltar, Huelva*, Simancas E° 174.

[139] *Relacion de las urcas y filibotes que han entrado en este puerto de San Lucar de Barrameda desde los 3 de octubre hasta los 21 del dicho de 1595 y en la baya de la ciudad de Cadix y lo que viene en cada uno dellos.* Simancas E° 174.

But the English and Dutch vessels, once banned from the Peninsula, took to privateering with renewed gusto, scouring the Atlantic, looting poorly guarded coasts and attacking the great unwieldy ships on the Indies route.

In these encounters the little ships often came off best because of their greater speed and manoeuvrability, and also because of their artillery, for as a contemporary of Richelieu[140] was to explain much later in 1626, unlike the old days, a vessel of 200 tons can today 'carry as much cannon as a vessel of 800 tons . . .': this invention 'the quintessence of the sea', made it possible for the small ships, like insects, to attack the huge and unwieldy ships of the Iberians. If they captured one of these floating fortresses they were as likely as not to burn it after stripping it, for it would only hinder them in their swift pirate raids. When he was consulted in 1594, Prince Gian Andrea Doria advised the Indies fleets to use smaller and faster ships in the future.[141] The Spanish admiralty, schooled by experience, even before the capture of the *Revenge* in 1591,[142] undoubtedly set about building lighter vessels. Lippomano recounted this in his report to the Venetian Senate, and the Spanish ambassador there sent a summary to Philip II:[143] 'The Catholic King is resolved to continue the enterprise of England, and hopes to execute his design by remedying the faults of the past and building ships which shall be lighter, better suited to the Ocean and fitted with longer and lighter cannon.' Philip underlined the words 'ships which shall be lighter, better suited to the Ocean' and wrote in the margin, 'I think we are indeed working backwards and it would be well to remind Pedro Menéndez Márquez of it'. So if the problem had not been solved just after the defeat of the Invincible Armada, it had at any rate been noted in high places.

Similar developments appeared in merchant shipping; the small ships were driving out the large, peacefully or with violence. In August, 1579,

[140] Chevalier de Razilly to Richelieu, Pontoise, 26th November, 1626, B.N. Paris, n.a., 9389, f° 66 v°.

[141] *CODOIN*, II, p. 171, 12th May, 1594.

[142] The captured vessel (Henri Hauser, *Prépondérance espagnole*, 2nd ed. 1940, p. 148 and 154; R. Hakluyt, ed. Dent & Sons, 1927, vol. V, p. 1 ff.) may have been taken as a model by the Spaniards. But it is doubtful since the *Revenge* went down during a storm not long after being captured, Garrett Mattingly in *American Historical Review, IV*, no. 2, January, 1950, p. 351. In any case at some time towards the end of the sixteenth century English techniques reached Spain and the Mediterranean. Ragusan shipbuilders (Simancas, Contaduria Mayor de Cuentas, Segunda época 904, 20th February, 1590) were building galleons of the English type, *Indice de la Colección de documentos de Fernández de Navarrete que posee el Museo Naval*, Madrid, 1946, no. 641. The document is wrongly situated between 1570 and 1580. For a much later and more correct date: Gregorio de Oliste to Philip III, Naples, 13th January, 1604: he is actively concerned 'de la fabrica de los 12 galeones que V. M. me mando hazer mediante el asiento', Simancas Napoles, Estado, 1100, f°s 8. Several references A.d.S. Naples, Sommaria Consultationum, 14 (f°s 229–233); 29 (f° 44–45); 30 (f° 31, 38–46, 49–53, 58–80, 158–159, 221–225).

[143] Reported by Frco. de Vera to the king, Venice, 29th July and 5th August, 1589, A.N., K.1674.

the *Govierno* of Viscaya was debating the question.[144] It was a very small state, but had an important Atlantic coastline. Traditional regulations gave preferential loading conditions to large ships (as against small), and to national ships (as against foreigners): so there was a long discussion in the *Govierno*. We learn from this that all the iron from Viscaya went out in small boats; for these could load and unload where big ships could not even attempt to go, 'en muchos puertos de Francia y Galicia por ser pequeños y de poca agua'.[145] Big ships might be held up waiting for a complete load, since their great holds had to be filled. Small ships sailed more frequently, spreading the risk. A big ship might provide an unpleasant surprise. After one of these, Marco Ottobon the Venetian secretary who was chartering ships in Danzig in the summer of 1591, to carry grain to Venice, gave preference to ships of 120 to 150 *lastri* (240 to 300 tons) 'of which there are many; they do not hold a great quantity, but as a result the grain is not so likely to perish on the way, . . . and, since we are not insured, the potential loss will be smaller'.[146] And above all 'questi vasselli di mediocre grandezza espediscono più presto che li grandi'.[147] they 'expedite' their trips more quickly than the big ships. Another significant point was that grain could be loaded straight into the holds, *a rifuso*, which eliminated the need for sacks or barrels. Small ships offered every advantage.[148]

In the Mediterranean. The Atlantic situation has been described at some length, since it casts light on the history of sea transport in the Mediterranean, foreshadowing or confirming its development.

To simplify the problem a little, let us deal straight away with a technical revolution, chiefly concerning Venice it is true, but then Venice was Venice, so it was of no small importance. The galley, which had faced strong competition in the fifteenth century, was to be practically eliminated, during the first thirty years[149] of the sixteenth century by the roundship (*nave*): the large merchantman replaced the long powerful oarship, although the latter did not disappear for some time, for reasons that are not altogether clear. In Bandello's time[150] the Beirut galleys were still a typical feature of Venetian life. Galleys worked the route to the Barbary coast until 1532, the Egypt route[151] at least until 1569 when two galleys

[144] Fidel de Sagarminaga, *El gobierno . . . de Viscaya*, 1892, I, p. 73.
[145] Antonio de Quintadueñas to Simón Ruiz, Rouen, 16th April, 1565, quoted by Henri Lapeyre, *Une famille de marchands, les Ruiz. Contribution a l'étude du commerce entre la France et l'Espagne au temps de Philippe II*, 1955, p. 212, n. 169.
[146] Final report by Marco Ottobon on his return from Danzig, 1591. See Ch. 3, note 76.
[147] *Ibid.* Letter to the Provveditori alle Biave, Danzig, 7th July, 1591.
[148] On all these problems (tonnages, carvel, or clinker built ships, the names of ships and small craft) see the text and notes of Henri Lapeyre, *op. cit.*, p. 206 ff.
[149] Frederic C. Lane, *Venetian Ships and Shipbuilders of the Renaissance*, 1934, p. 26.
[150] *Op. cit.*, VI, p. 71.
[151] Until 1564, according to F. C. Lane, 'The Mediterranean Spice Trade' in *American Historical Review*, vol. XLV, p. 581.

made the voyage to Alexandria and Syria.[152] At the end of the century the galley was still in service on the Venice–Spalato run,[153] since this short trip required a ship which could choose her own course and which would have the means on board – cannon and men – to meet the threat from pirates.

The galley's immediate successors were larger ships, which then held the front rank for some time, maintaining an average size of about 600 tons,[154] carrying wines to England, grain and salt within the Mediterranean, and taking over the voyages to Syria.

In 1525 the Venetian ambassador Navagero sailed from Genoa to Spain in a new Genoese roundship of between 15,000 and 16,000 *cantars*, that is (at 89 kilograms to the *cantar*), between 1300 and 1400 tons;[155] in 1533, a Ragusan roundship of 1200 *botte* (600 tons) was captured, then released again by the Turks in the port of Chios;[156] in 1544 the biggest ship on the Mediterranean (the claim may not be true) was on fire in the bay of Messina. She too was a vessel of 1200 *botte*;[157] on 8th March, 1565, a large Venetian roundship was requisitioned in the port of Alicante, a vessel of 6500 *salme* (approximately 975 tons), with 60 pieces of ordnance on board.[158] A Genoese merchantman of 450 tons and a Portuguese vessel of 225 tons were requisitioned on the same occasion.[159] A series of registrations of roundships, for the most part newly built, in the registers of the *Sommaria* of Naples,[160] for the years 1561, 1568, and 1569, yields ten reliable tonnage figures (five of which were Ragusan vessels). In decreasing order, in tons, they are: 1000, 700, 675, 450, 300, 270, and 190. In 1579, in the port of Leghorn[161] the register of roundships gives the following tonnages: a *nave* from Marseilles on her way to Venice to fetch silk, 90 tons; a hooker heading for Naples, 195 tons; a Venetian *nave*, 165 tons; a Spanish *nave* sailing to Alicante, 165 again; and lastly, a Ragusan ship, the *Santo Spirito et Santa Maria di Loreto*, captain Antonio di Veglia, on her way to Genoa to unload there her cargo of salt and wool, 1125 tons. In 1583, in the fleet which the Marquis de Santa Cruz led to the Azores, there were three Catalan roundships each of 733 tons, seven Ragusan roundships of 726 tons, four Venetian ships of 586, two Genoese of 449 (the figures quoted are averages calculated from the total tonnage given for each group.)[162]

[152] J. Lopez to the king, Venice, 2nd July, 1569. Simancas E° 1326.
[153] Dr. Jules Sottas, *Les Messageries maritimes à Venise aux XIVe et XVe siécles*, 1936, p. 136.
[154] F. C. Lane, *op. cit.*, p. 47.
[155] Navagero, *op. cit.*, p. 1.
[156] S. Razzi, *La Storia di Raugia*, 1903, p. 128.
[157] *Ibid.*, p. 156.
[158] 8th March, 1565, Simancas E° 486.
[159] *Ibid.*
[160] A.d.S. Napoli, Sommaria Partium: 540, f° 51; 546, f° 229 v°; 559, f° 267 v° and 268; 560 f° 73, f° 115 v°, f° 185; 562, f° 55 v°, f° 237 v°; 561, f° 101 v°; 594, f° 28 v° (the 1000-ton *nave* (800 *carri*) under construction at Ragusa); 595, f° 161 v° and 162.
[161] 6th May, 1579. A.d.S. Florence, Mediceo, 1829, f° 67.
[162] A.d.S. Venice, Senato Dispacci Spagna, Zane to the Doge, 15th July, 1583, the figures can be found in Museo Correr, Donà delle Rose, 154, f° 101.

We find mention in 1591 of a Ragusan ship of 375 tons;[163] in 1593 of a *nave* of 450 tons built at Antibes;[164] in October, 1596, a Ragusan round-ship of 750 tons[165] entered Cartagena, carrying gunpowder and arquebus matches; in the same year, the Turks sold back to the Ragusans for the sum of 60,000 aspers a roundship of 350 *botte*, or about 175 tons, captured the previous year by Cigala;[166] off Trapani in 1599 lay a Ragusan *nave* of 240 tons;[167] in 1601 another of 600 tons, laden with salt, the *Santa Maria di Montenegro*.[168]

This is a far cry from the record of the fifteenth century. There was evidently a crisis in heavyweight shipping at Venice, Ragusa,[169] and indeed throughout the Mediterranean, where the fortunes of the little boats were in the ascendant. At Venice the prohibitive rise in prices made it impossible for private citizens to undertake construction of big ships after about 1573 following the Turco-Venetian war. An official document makes this clear.[170] 'From 1573 to the present day [4th November, 1581] prices have risen so much, as everyone knows, that it is only very rarely that anyone will risk building big ships; at present we have only seven left.' From then on big ships could only be built with the assistance of the state bounties which rose steadily: for ships over 500 *botte*, they were 2700 ducats; in 1581 they went up to 3500, later to 4000, 4500, which entirely covered the cost of building a ship of 400 tons. After the 1590s subsidies towards building ships of 800 to 1000 *botte* went up to eight, nine, or ten thousand ducats.[171] This was the end-of-century crisis we have already mentioned. On Crete there was a similar crisis, says the *provveditore* Foscarini on leaving office in 1577.[172] In the past, the Cretans used to sail great galleons, lateen-rigged: 'erano scuole, nelle quali si facevano de' buone marinari', it was a school for making good mariners, who would be able to handle galleys, instead of these *navili* that have been introduced 'navigando alla vela quadra'.

It was not only in Crete that these small ships appeared. Sooner or later the whole Mediterranean was to become familiar with them: the *vascelli quadri* of Leghorn, for instance, in which an English seacaptain

[163] 31st May, 1591, Ragusa Archives, Diversa de Foris, V, f° 15.

[164] 2nd June, 1591, A. Civico, Genoa, Consolato Francese, 332.

[165] Miguel de Oviedo to the king, Cartagena, 19th October, 1596. Simancas E° 176.

[166] 4th March, 1596, Ragusa Archives, D. de Foris, IV, f° 85.

[167] Trapani, 10th May, 1599, Ragusa Archives, D. de Foris, VIII, f° 25 v°.

[168] The Duke of Maqueda, viceroy of Sicily, to the Jurados of Trapani, 21st August, 1601, Ragusa Archives, D. de Foris, f° 203 and 203 v°, a vessel of 4000 *salme*.

[169] Iorjo Tadić (letter dated 7th November, 1963).

[170] A.d.S. Venice, Capitolari, II C 112, 4th November, 1581, quoted by G. Luzzatto, 'Per la storia delle construzioni navali a Venezia nei secoli XV e XVI' in *Miscellenea di studi storici in onore di C. Manfroni*, Venice, 1925, p. 397.

[171] G. Luzzatto, *ibid.*, p. 392 ff.

[172] V. Lamansky, *op. cit.*, p. 560.

[173] Simancas Guerra Antigua, XX, f° 13.

[174] *Ibid.*, f° 10.   [175] *Ibid.*, f° 15.   [176] *Ibid.*, f° 9.

[177] *Ibid.*, XLVI, f° 204.   [178] *Ibid.*, LIII, f° 206.

Average Tonnages of Ships Listed or Requisitioned
in Spanish Ports: 1551–1554

Ports	Dates	No. of ships	Average tonnage in *Toneladas*
Cadiz[173] expedition against Algiers	27th June, 1541	12	170
Cadiz and Seville[174] (*naos* and *urcas*) expedition against Algiers	July, 1541	52	202
Malaga[175] expedition against Algiers	14th Sept., 1541	24	170
Cadiz, San Lucar, Puerto de Santa Maria[176]	(1550) probably 1541	27	190
Seville[177] 'las naos que estan en el rio de Sevilla'	April, 1552	23	267
All the ports of Guipuzcoa and Biscay[178] (new ships)	1554	31	237

Roberto Torton was the great expert.[179] Never absent from the shipping trade, they took widely differing forms in different regions. In the Adriatic the *marciliane* predominated, ousting the *grippi*, small galleys that in Sanudo's time[180] took twenty-two days to bring the new wine from Candia to Venice, or the *marani*, which were originally used in the fifteenth century to carry firewood and building stone from Istria, and which were later employed on longer voyages. The *marciliane* were rounder than the *navi*, but similarly rigged: square-sterned, with a massive prow. From about 1550 they had worked the route from Apulia carrying grain and oil. Of smaller tonnage than the *nave*, they were carrying most of the Adriatic trade by the end of the sixteenth century, and began to move further afield, to the Venetian-held islands. In 1602 Venice possessed seventy-eight *marciliane*, some four-masted, with a capacity of up to 140 or 150[181] and even 240 tons.[182] A significant detail is that the Duchy of Ferrara, whose ports were accessible only to *marciliane*, did not attempt to enlarge them.[183] But the Signoria was to begin putting obstacles in the path of these boats in 1589,[184] and in 1602 they were forbidden to sail to Zante. By 1619 their number had dropped to thirty-eight.[185] This is proof that Venice was determined to protect her big ships from any challenge. As late as 1630–1632, Stochove in his voyage to the Levant, mentions the Venetian

---

[179] Giuseppe Vivoli, *Annali di Livorno*, Leghorn, 1842, III, p. 425.
[180] *Diarii*, LIII, p. 522.
[181] According to Auguste Jal, *Glossaire nautique*, 1848.
[182] F. C. Lane, *op. cit.*, p. 53; Casoni, 'Forze militari' in *Venezia e le sue lagune*, 1847, p. 195.
[183] Alfredo Pino-Branca, *La vita economica degli Stati italiani nei secoli XVI, XVII, XVIII, secondo le relazioni degli ambasciatori veneti*, Catania, 1938, p. 209.
[184] 4th November, 1589, Council of Pregadi, A.d.S. Venice, Busta 538, f° 884.
[185] F. C. Lane, *op. cit.*, p. 52, n. 52, p. 53, n. 57.

merchant ships[186] 'so heavy and unwieldy that they cannot sail in a light wind and are often three or four months arriving at Constantinople. The Provençal vessels on the contrary are small and light, so that they can take advantage of the least breath of wind to be on their way. . . .'.

The fortune of Marseilles after the 1570s had many causes, the flow of French, English, and German goods along the Rhône route, the lack of competition from Venice during the years 1570–1573 when she was at war with the Turks, the privileges that, for better or worse, the *entente* between the French king and the Turks and Barbary nations brought her. It was also the result of the design of the vessels of Marseilles and of Provence, *navi*, galleons, tartans, saëtes, or simply barques, as they are called in the Leghorn shiplists. We should not be misled by these names: a 'nave', the *Sainte-Marie-Bonaventure* is mentioned in 1597[187] as having a capacity of 700 cantars (about 60 tons); a 'navire', the *Sainte-Marie Bonaventure*, (this was the commonest name for boats from Marseilles), was 150 tons. The *nave* captured at Trapani on 5th May, 1596 by Pedro de Leyva was not a big one, 'inventaque sunt in ea coralla . . . et alia'.[188] We do not know the tonnage of the 'galleons' from Marseilles which were working to Tripoli in Syria in 1591:[189] the galleon *La Trinité*, master Nicolas Sicart (5th April, 1591) or the galleon *La Foy*, master George de Bellet (5th April, 1581) or the galleon *Saint-Victor* which was loading at Alexandretta (7th May, 1594). They were in no way comparable to the splendid galleons of the Duke of Provence in the old days[190] In 1612 a Venetian consul in Syria mentions boats from Marseilles of 60 *botte*.[191] Often, as the master of one Marseilles ship said, this would only be a *galeonetto*, carrying beans, hides, and cheeses between Cagliari and Leghorn.[192] Marseilles saëtes at the end of the century were between 30 and 90 tons.[193] A *nave* of 3000 *salme* (450 tons) was built at Antibes during the summer of 1593, but we should note that she was partly owned by a Genoese, Giovanni Battista Vivaldo.[194]

The barques, tartans, saëtes, galleons, and *galionetti*, *navires* and

[186] *Voyage du Levant*, p. 26.

[187] Pierre Grandchamp, *La France en Tunisie à la fin du XVIe siecle*, 1920, p. 88.

[188] B. Com. Palermo, 3 Qq D 77, no. 9, 26, 32.

[189] A Com. Marseilles, series HH unclassified.

[190] Or to the Marseilles galleon of 450 tons that sailed to Constantinople in 1561 carrying alum and called at Chios, Report from the Levant, 12–14th April, 1561, Simancas E° 1051, f° 55.

[191] A. Civico Genoa, September, 1594, Consolato Francese, 332. On the small size of the Marseilles ships, see the records of the '*saettie francese*' which arrived at Venice between 1581 and 1585, A.d.S. Senato Terra, 96. There was a total of thirty-seven arrivals: six in 1581, nine in 1582; seven in 1583; nine in 1584; six in 1585. The largest was 164 *botte* (about 82 tons), the smallest 54 *botte* (27 tons). Leaving aside the four vessels whose tonnage is given in *stara* (440, 440, 460, 305) the average tonnage of the other 33 is slightly over 90 *botte* or 45 tons.

[192] 14th February, 1590, P. Grandchamp, *La France en Tunisie à la fin du XVIe siécle*, 1920, p. 30–31.

[193] 6th August, 1596, *ibid.*, p. 81.

[194] 2nd June, 1591, A. Civico Genoa, Consolato Francese, 332.

navi of Marseilles, gradually invaded the sea in the sixteenth century. There was not a port in Spain, Italy, or North Africa where they were not to be found unloading their goods on to the quayside. From the 1560s Venice was obliged to use their services. Throughout the Mediterranean they would sail in fleets, attracting the fury of the big ships. If in 1572[195] a Ragusan merchantman seized a *nave* from Marseilles, looted and sank her, drowning her entire crew down to the cabin boy, was it not perhaps from vindictiveness as much as search for gain? For the business of the great Ragusan carrying ships was suffering from the transport crisis. They were still sailing the sea, from the Levant to the West, from Sicily to Spain. In the wake of Philip's armadas, they were even to venture into and perish in the Atlantic at the end of the century. But after ten or twenty years, Ragusa, like Venice, indeed more than Venice, withdrew into the quiet waters of the Adriatic.

There was nothing mysterious about these changes. They were dictated in every case by time and circumstance. Marseilles at the end of the century had many ships, but they were all of only moderate size, whereas in a petition to François I in 1526 she had declared that her port was equipped with 'grosses nefz, navires, galions' for trading with Syria, Egypt, and Barbary.[196] So in the course of the century the port had changed. When Ragusa, which according to an eyewitness, in 1574[197] still owned the biggest ships in the Adriatic, re-entered the shipping world after a long period of eclipse during the eighteenth century, it was with a fleet consisting of dozens and dozens of small boats which from 1734–1744 appeared on the routes both within and outside the Adriatic: *navi*, polaccas, frigates, *marciliane*, feluccas, pataches, *vacchette*, *tartanelle*, *trabaccoli*. As one might expect, names, forms, fittings, and ships had changed.[198]

In fact, in the sixteenth century small boats sprang from everywhere responding to the expansion of trade. There were the light craft of the Greek Archipelago as well as the barques of Provence (not only from Marseilles). There were the eight *caramusali* which paid their *ancorazzo* at Venice[199] in 1559, and of which at least five were captained by masters from Mitilíni (Lesbos); more important were the ships from the North, the *bertoni*, as they were often called. These penetrated into the Mediterranean in two waves, before 1550 and after 1570, with the curious gap of twenty years between the first invasion and the second.

But the true dimensions of the problem only emerged gradually. Everything played its part: rising prices, rising living standards, return freights, and changed circumstances. So argued an anonymous Venetian[200] in a document which is not dated but is certainly from the beginning of the

[195] See Vol. II, Part II, ch. 7, note 144.
[196] *Histoire du Commerce de Marseille*, vol. III, p. 193.
[197] P. Lescalopier, *op. cit.*, p. 26.
[198] Josip Luetić, *O pomortsvup Dubrovačke Republike u XVIII stoleču*, Dubrovnik, 1959, p. 190.
[199] Museo Correr, D. delle Rose, f° 217.
[200] *Ibid.*, f° 8 ff.

seventeenth century. In the old days, he says, with honest folk 'di modesto guadagno', things were better. Unlike nowadays when everyone is guided by self-interest, 'What costs 100 ducats today could be had for 25 then'. The result is that there are no more big Venetian ships: the French, English, and Dutch are invading the port, 'con loro navili minori'; they overpay for goods and ruin everyone else's business. If only they could be banned from Cyprus, whose salt and cotton are a godsend as ballast, the *savorna* of the return trip! Those were the days, when there were big ships and voyages that lasted five months! This account – much abridged – reflects the way in which a Venetian without stirring from his native city could appreciate the loss in long distance trades and monopolies that the Mediterranean had suffered; appreciate also the general price rise that persisted uninterrupted for so long.

But in fact Venice's economy did not decline at the same time as her navy. The throng of little boats that invaded the Mediterranean in the sixteenth century were, on the contrary, a sign of the sea's prosperity, of its ability to enlist and pay for the services of the proletarians of the Atlantic. We shall have more to say about this important problem.[201]

3. URBAN FUNCTIONS

The cities of the Mediterranean, however illustrious, were subject to the same regular processes as all urban communities. Like any other towns, they owed their existence to the control over physical space they exercised through the networks of communications emanating from them, the meeting of different transport routes, their continual adaptation to new conditions and the ways in which they developed slowly or rapidly. They were human hives, whose inhabitants might travel far from home. We may find a Ragusan at Potosi, another at Diu,[202] and thousands more scattered throughout the world. There was proverbially and probably literally a Florentine in every corner of the world. We have records of a Marseillais in Transylvania,[203] some Venetians at Hormuz,[204] and a Genoese colony in Brazil.[205]

Towns and Roads. Without markets and roads there would be no towns: movement is vital to them. The heart of Constantinople was its 'bazes-tan'[206] with its four gates, its great brick arches, its everyday foods and its precious merchandise, its slave market, where men stood to be handled like animals at a fair, the buyers spitting on their faces and rubbing

[201] See below p. 606 ff.
[202] See Vol. II, Part II, ch. 6, *Civilizations*, note 15.
[203] N. Iorga, *Ospiti romeni in Venezia (1570–1610)*, 1932, p. 75.
[204] Ugo Tucci, 'Mercanti veneziani in India alla fine del secolo XVI' in *Studi in onore di Armando Sapori*, 1957, p. 1091 ff.
[205] Gilberto Freyre, *Casa Grande et senzala*, Rio de Janeiro, 1946, vol I, p. 360.
[206] Brantôme, *Mémoires*, XI, p. 107.

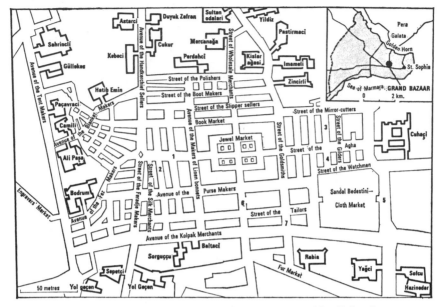

1. Street of the Sellers of ladies' garments   2. Street of the Cloth designers and printers   3. Street of the Honey-sellers
4. Street of the Agate Merchants   5. Street of the Han of the Cloth Merchants   6. Street of the Ribbon Makers   7. Passage of the Chief Tailor

Fig. 25: *The Great Bazaar at Constantinople, sixteenth–seventeenth
centuries*

The great bazaar was the heart of the commercial activity of Constantinople, more or
less on the same site as the Great Bazaar of today. It consisted principally of two
Bedesten-s (the word is a corruption of *Bezzazistan*, hence the frequent use of *Bazestan*
and a variety of different spellings: the root of the word is *bez*: linen, and it originally
meant the bazaar of the linen merchants). The old *Bedesten* was built by Muhammad
the Conqueror after the fall of Constantinople. This was the central building with its
four gates and two main streets, marked Jewel Market. The new one was the *Sandal
Bedesteni*, (from sandal: a mixed silk fabric). Around these two great buildings ran a
series of streets of shops and artisans. The names printed in heavy type mark the
courtyards of the *han-s* (usually known in the West as *Khans*). These were the strictly
controlled warehouses where supplies of food for the Seray and the city were kept.
Wholesalers would sell their merchandise there. The plan was drawn up by Osman
Ergin (1945) and is reproduced in Robert Mantran's book on Constantinople to which
I have made frequent reference.

to see whether the merchants had powdered them or not.[207] It did not
matter whether the bazaar was at the centre of the city – and then it was
always situated in the lowest part, as if everything should naturally flow
down into it – or outside the city, as was the case in the Dinaric zone of
Turkish colonization, where all the towns, Mostar, Sarajevo, etc. had
'exobazaars',[208] as Tangier did in the quite recent past.[209] Whatever its

[207] Philippe de Canaye, *Le voyage du Levant*, p. 114.
[208] Richard Busch-Zantner, 'Zur Kenntnis der osmanischen Stadt' in *Geographische
Zeitschrift*, 1932, p. 1–13.
[209] J. Leclercq, *op. cit.*, 1881, p. 21.

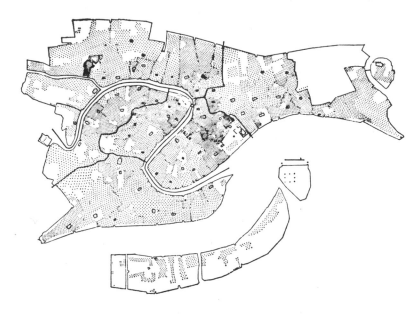

POPULATION IN 1586
Each dot represents 10 inhabitants

SHOPS IN 1661
Each dot represents 1 shop

site or form, a bazaar, a market, or a town is the meeting place of a number of movements. To Algiers came the donkeys hidden under their enormous loads of wood from the nearby Atlas Mountains, entering the city at Bab-el-Oued, the northern gate;[210] camels from the *Mitidja* or the distant south were lodged in front of Bab-Azoun, the southern gate; the harbour was teeming with pirate and merchant vessels, laden with rancid butter from Bône, linens, woollen cloths, and wood from Marseilles, oil from Djerba, perfumes from Spain, not to mention Christian merchandise stolen from ships all over the sea, or ransom money paid by Valencia, Genoa, and other places. On all this the city of Algiers was built and nourished. Every town is founded on movements which it absorbs, uses for its own purposes, and then retransmits. The evocative images of economic life are images of movement, routes, and voyages, even to the bills of exchange, which sixteenth-century authors compare to ships, or ships' cargoes, travelling with more or less security, whence the *agio*, a form of marine insurance which is, as they say, proportionate to the risk.

Interruption in its communications might lead to a town's stagnation or death. This was the case of Florence in 1528. Her links with the South had been severed since the sack of Rome in 1527, so she was losing every week the 8000 ducats her Roman clientele had brought her, as well as the 3000 she earned from sales to Naples.[211] There was trouble in the north too, where all communications with France were blocked by Genoa and all the roads to Germany blocked by Venice. Florence was therefore obliged to cut down her production of *panni garbi*[212] *o fini o d'oro* and to make use of roundabout smugglers' routes in order to survive and to continue exporting goods, by sea to France and Lyons, to beyond Asola,

(Opposite) Fig. 26: *The heart of Venice*

The two maps (facing) taken from D. Beltrami, *Storia della popolazione di Venezia* 1954, pp. 39 and 53, raise the same problem: the organization of an urban area. The reader should take his bearings from the Grand Canal, through the centre of which runs a line separating the various quarters of Venice; then the tiny square representing the bridge of the Rialto, the only one which crosses the Grand Canal; St. Mark's Square; to the north-east the white patch representing the Arsenal; to the South the island of San Giorgio and the Giudecca separated from the rest of the city by the wide channel of the Zattere; the point between the Grand Canal and the Zattere corresponds to the Customs House. The six quarters of the city are San Marco; San Polo, on the right bank of the Grand Canal, to the left of the Rialto; Castello (the Arsenal); S. Croce (the third quarter on the right bank); Cannaregio on the northern side, containing the ghetto; Dorsoduro. The centre of the city lies between the Rialto and St. Mark's. Beyond the bridge, in the middle of the black patch of shops in the second diagram, the Rialto square (white) was the daily meeting place of the merchants. The ghetto, to the north-west of the city, has an abnormal density of population because of the measures of segregation. The quarters are divided into parishes whose boundaries are more visible on one diagram than the other, varying from place to place.

---

[210] D. de Haëdo, *op. cit.*, 178 v°. There were two market days a week in Algiers to which the people of the neighbouring plains and mountains flocked in large numbers.
[211] A. Pino Branca, *op. cit.*, p. 257.   [212] *Panni garbi:* best quality cloth.

to Mantua and even to Trieste; by land to Germany. The strength of territorial states with control over a wide area lay in being able to interrupt at will the communications of the city-states, thus upsetting from a distance the delicate balance of their economies. Genoa accused France of aiding the Corsican rebels, but, wrote Fourquevaux indignantly in February, 1567, if France wanted to harm Genoa, she need not use such indirect methods. She could simply prohibit the use of silks and other Genoese goods at home and forbid the merchants of Provence to trade with Genoa and her riviera which they furnished with grain and wine.[213] In 1575, at the time of the Genoese troubles, one of the first actions of Spain, fearing the worst, was to cut off supplies of Sicilian grain.[214]

Along the roads, all goods, material and immaterial, flowed into the cities. We have already mentioned Augsburg, a city half-German, half-Italian; architecturally it even has its Genoese quarter along the Lech and its Venetian quarter along the Wertach. The Florentine Renaissance was the result of the flow into the city of artists from all over Tuscany; the Renaissance in Rome was the result of the flow of Florentine and Umbrian artists into the Eternal City. Without this dispersed community, wandering from village to village, city to city, completing a half-finished fresco in one place, painting a picture or a diptych in another, adding a dome to a church abandoned by its original architect, the Italian Renaissance would have been very different. Later the architectural elements of what was to be known as the Italian Baroque were brought south by the masons and stone-cutters of the Alps,[215] who travelled long distances to practise their craft, leaving behind them models of ornament and decoration that were to be used by generations of sculptors in village or city.

As one would expect, a map of the cities closely corresponds to a map of the roads. The axis running from Taranto by Bari to Ancona, then on to Bologna, Modena, Pavia and Piacenza, finishing at the Po, is a string of towns. Another road system, more curious and less frequently noted, links Medina del Campo, Valladolid, Burgos, and Bilbao, four outstandingly active cities: the great fair-centre; the capital of Philip II (until 1560); the headquarters of the wool trade, and lastly, the seaport with its sailors and carriers. The road passed through them like an assembly line, distributing tasks.

It is clear that in the western Mediterranean the great cities were all near the sea, the greatest route of all; inland they were less frequent, being served only by the overland roads, which carried less traffic. But in the south and east of the Mediterranean, the great inland cities of Islam are a clear response to the demands of the roads through the desert.

A meeting place for different transport routes. Large towns, which all stand at crossroads, did not necessarily grow up because of them (although

[213] To the queen, 13th February, 1567, Douais, *Dépêches . . .*, III, p. 36–37.
[214] The Duke of Terranova to the king, Simancas E° 1144, 28th August, 1575; E° 1145, 18th February, 1576.
[215] Jacob Burckhardt, *Geschichte der Renaissance in Italien*, 1920 ed., p. 16–17.

Piacenza, for instance, was certainly born of the meeting of the Po and the Via Aemilia). But it is to them that they owe their survival. 'They derive their importance from their geographical situation', as the textbooks say. The place where two routes meet may imply a change of transport, a compulsory halt. At Arles the flotillas of the Rhône met the coasters of Martigues, Bouc, and the Provençal coastline which carried all traffic to Marseilles. At Verona the Adige became navigable, taking over from the mule-trains and wagons that had come over the Brenner pass. The caravans reached the sea at Tripoli in Barbary, Tunis, or Algiers. Aleppo owed its existence less to the resources of its site than to the need for an intermediate stage between the Mediterranean and the Persian Gulf,[216] where as Jacques Gassot[217] said, the merchandise of the Indies could meet the 'cloth, kerseys, and others coming from the West'. It was here that the caravans from Baghdad would stop, in front of the mountains of Lebanon, and other caravans of mules, horses, and little donkeys would take over, the same ones that carried western pilgrims to and fro on the neighbouring route from Jerusalem to Jaffa.

All ports, by definition, stand where land and water meet. Every one stands at the end of a road or inland waterway – usually a road in the Mediterranean. The mouths of the rivers are hazardous to shipping, since they carry alluvial deposits into a sea with no tides. Another factor is the mountain barrier lying directly behind the Mediterranean coastline; so there are hardly any ports without some breach of the relief on the landward side. Genoa is accounted for by a series of breaches in the nearby Apennines, and particularly the Dei Giovi pass; the city's fortunes have been closely linked with this pass. Standing on a wild and jagged coast, where tiny fishing villages had been perched for centuries, it was for a long time a very minor town, little more than a village. It had a sheltered site of course at the head of the gulf, but it was cut off from the rest of the mainland and had little contact with the great trade route of the Middle Ages, the Via Francigena, which ran from north of the Apennines to Rome. Genoa only reached the first rank in the eleventh century, when Saracen supremacy on the sea was declining and northerners with commercial interests in Europe, who were also experts in constructing mountain roads (especially the people of Asti) came down to Genoa to seize the profitable shipping trade, Genoa was born of this advance from the interior and of the opening up of the road over the Dei Giovi pass.[218] The overland route continued to play an important part in the city's fortunes. Alongside the *Venuta di mare* there were always the *Venuta di terra* and profitable trade in both directions. Genoa owed her existence not only to ships but also to the mule-trains which inside the city had to use the brick paths reserved for them, running like lanes in the middle of the paved streets.

[216] Baron de Tott, *Memoirs on the Turks and Tartars*, II, p. 365.
[217] *Le discours du voyage de Venise à Constantinople*, 1547, p. 31.
[218] Renée Doehaerd and Ch. Kerremans, *Les relations commerciales entre Gênes, Belgique et l'Outremont*, 1952, I, p. 77–78.

Like Genoa, all ports face both ways. Marseilles had her connection with the route down the Rhône; Algiers her relationship with the central Maghreb; while Ragusa, although indisputably a town born of the sea, was a permanent presence in the Balkan peninsula, the coast and interior of which she had thoroughly prospected. At one time Ragusa had been interested in the Serbian silver mines and had provided supplies for the extraction centres as well as surrounding towns and fairs, Üskub, Prilep, Prizren, and Peć.[219] In the sixteenth century her overland trade was sub-stantially expanded eastward.[220] Her merchants travelled through Bosnia and Serbia, as far as Vidin; they were active in the Danube provinces; at Üskub, the point of departure for journeys to Constantinople,[221] they formed a closely knit colony. They found their way into Bulgaria, which had previously been closed to them by the activity of Genoese merchants from the Black Sea; they could be found at Belgrade, selling English woollen cloth to the Turkish officers returning from the Hungarian war; at Adrianople, welcoming Christian ambassadors passing through; and of course they were at Constantinople. The astonishing influence of Ragusa in the sixteenth century was closely linked with these trading colonies established throughout the Balkan interior; with the hundreds of shops where her merchants sold, for cash or credit, English kerseys, woollen cloth from Venice and Florence; with the journeys made by traders who bought skins and wool directly from the shepherds; some of their long, narrow account books are preserved in the archives of Ragusa.

Ragusa's entire activity would have been impossible had it not been for the roads, terrible roads in many cases, which ran northwards to Sarajevo, or over the Montenegrin and Albanian mountains to Üskub, the chief gateway to the East. Ragusa lay where two movements met: the flow of traffic of the Balkan interior; and the shipping traffic using the unlimited sea routes along which Ragusans in the sixteenth century travelled to all the countries of the Mediterranean without exception, sometimes to India, often to England, and in at least one case, to Peru.

From roads to banking. Roads and the exchanges they permitted led to the gradual division of labour by which the towns grew up, painfully distin-guishing themselves from the surrounding countryside. though only at the price of an unremitting struggle. This struggle in turn had its effect inside the towns, organizing their different tasks, transforming them inter-nally, according to patterns that were regular only in the very broadest sense.

The starting point of this process, with its many variants, was naturally commercial activity, ever-present, all-important and the source of all

[219] A. Mehlan, 'Die grossen Balkanmessen in der Türkenzeit' in *Viertalj. für Sozial-und Wirtschaftsgeschichte*, XXXI, 1938, p. 20–21.

[220] J. Tadić, *Dubrovcani po juznoj Srbiji u XVI stolecu Glasnik Skop nauc dro* VII–VIII, 1930, p. 197–202.

[221] L. Bernardo, *Viaggio a Costantinopoli*, Venice, 1887, p. 24, 1591.

economic organization. This was obviously the case of Venice, Seville, Genoa, Milan, and Marseilles, quite indisputably so in the case of the last-named, whose industry consisted only of some textiles[222] and soap manufacturing. It was clearly true of Venice, too, which exported her own woollen cloth and silks to the East, but alongside them the woollens and velvets of Florence, Flemish cloths and English kerseys, fustians from Milan and Germany, and from Germany also linens, hardware, and copper. As for Genoa, the mediæval proverb said: *Genuensis ergo mercator*, a Genoese, therefore a trader. So our systems of classification use the term 'commercial capitalism' to describe the agile, already modern and indisputably effective form taken by economic life in the sixteenth century. All activity did not necessarily contribute to its advance but much depended on its dynamism and magnetism. The imperatives of large-scale, long-distance commerce, its accumulation of capital, acted as driving forces. It was in the space defined by a commercial economy that industrial activity was kindled at Genoa, Florence, Venice, and Milan, particularly in the new and revolutionary textile industries, cotton and silk. The classic theory of Paul Mantoux was already true of the sixteenth century: industry is created and fostered by commerce. Perhaps this was truest of all of the Mediterranean where exchange, transport, and reselling were activities central to life.

Thriving commercial activity favoured and furthered the spread of many movements, including the germs of industrial activity, as the wind scatters seeds. These seeds did not always fall on good ground, however. In 1490 a Florentine, Pietro del Bantella, introduced to Ragusa the 'arte di fabricare i panni alti di lana';[223] In 1525 the art of silk making was imported into the city by Nicolò Luccari, a local man.[224] Neither of these industries prospered: Ragusa was content to produce some textiles for her own consumption, and to dye or re-dye some of those that passed through her hands. Similar attempts were made to introduce the silken and woollen industries to Marseilles in about 1560, and, according to Botero, in the case of silk[225] the lack of suitable water prevented their success.

In very general terms it can be said that industrial functions are called into existence by commercial activity,[226] which creates the demand for them; they therefore presuppose a certain level of economic maturity (among many other conditions of course). The industrial centre of southern France was Montpellier,[227] a town behind which lay a rich past, a mass of acquired wealth, capital available for investment, and invigorating contacts with the outside world. Colbert's dream for seventeenth-century

[222] Scarlet manufacture – Council of 20th November, 1575, A. Com. Marseille, BB. 45, f° 330.
[223] Giacomo Pedro Luccari, *Annali di Rausa*, Venice, 1605, p. 120.
[224] *Ibid.*, p. 139.
[225] G. Botero, *op. cit.*, I, p. 35.
[226] Marc Bloch, in *Mélanges d'histoire sociale*, I, p. 113–114.
[227] Francesco Guicciardini, *Diario del viaggio di Spagna*, Florence, 1932, p. 46. For a comparison: Nîmes in 1592, P. George, *op. cit.*, p. 621–622.

France – a native textile industry to supply the French trade with the Levant – had already been realized elsewhere through force of circumstance. Venetian industry first developed in the thirteenth century; but as her commercial activity increased at a much faster rate during the same period, this mediæval industry came to appear insignificant beside the volume of external trade. The real industrial growth of Venice came much later in the fifteenth and especially in the sixteenth centuries, as there was a gradual shift from counting house to workshop, a shift not consciously intended but urged and dictated by the general situation. Venice was tending to become an industrial port, and it was possibly only the outstanding successes of France and northern Europe in the following century that prevented the transformation from running its full course.[228]

If large-scale industry is the second stage of a town's economic life cycle, banking is perhaps the third. From a town's earliest beginnings all forms of economic activity are undoubtedly under way, finance like any other. But it is not usually until a later stage that money-dealing becomes established as an activity in its own right. Economic functions remain confused during the early period. The Florentine firm Giucciardini Corsi, who advanced money to Galileo, also had interests in Sicilian grain and in the cloth and pepper trade; the Capponi, whose great ledgers have survived, not only issued and received bills of exchange but also transported wine and handled shipping insurance; the Medici, more than half of whose interests lay in banking, owned silk workshops in the fifteenth century.

This many-sidedness was a long-established rule; to engage in several activities was a sensible way of spreading risks. Dealings in money, that is private loans (more or less disguised since the Church forbade usury), money openly advanced to cities and princes, investments (*accomandite* as they were known in Florence), marine insurance, all purely financial transactions, are difficult to separate from other forms of commerce. It is only in Amsterdam towards the end of the eighteenth century that we see them emerging in their most sophisticated form.

Even in the sixteenth century, though, financial transactions had already reached a high level, producing in ever larger numbers the quasi-specialist bankers known in Spain as *hombres de negocios*. In eighteenth-century France they would have been called 'financiers' in the service of the state. This phenomenon though was only to be found in a few established merchant cities that had reached full maturity; Venice, where banks and bankers dated back to the fourteenth and even the thirteenth century; Florence, whose great merchant firms had held sway in Europe and the Mediterranean, from England to the Black Sea, since the thirteenth century; and most of all, Genoa, which, in spite of what Michelet said[229] was

---

[228] *Decadenza economica veneziana nel secolo XVII*, Colloquy of Giorgio Cini Foundation (27th June–2nd July, 1957), 1961, p. 23–84.

[229] *Le Banquet*, p. 17, quoted by Th. Scharten, *Les Voyages et les séjours de Michelet en Italie*, Paris, 1934, p. 101.

not 'a bank before it was a town', but where the *Casa di San Giorgio* operated the most sophisticated credit machinery of the Middle Ages. A detailed study[230] has shown that the city was already modern, ahead of its time, in the fifteenth century, daily handling endorsements of bills of exchange and *ricorsa* agreements, an early form of the art of kite-flying, to use modern bankers' jargon. Genoa's early role as intermediary between Seville and the New World, her official alliance with Spain in 1528 did the rest: she became the leading financial city of the world, in the period of rising inflation and prosperity that characterized the second half of the sixteenth century – the century of Genoa, the city where commerce was beginning to appear a rather inferior activity. The *Nobili Vecchi* might occasionally speculate, on a grand scale, in alum, or woollens or in Spanish salt; but on the whole they left trading very much to the *Nobili Nuovi*, themselves devoting their energies to speculation in gold and silver, government bonds, and loans to the king of Spain.

However, in apparent contradiction with this simple picture, many financial centres, *piazze*, sprang up in Europe in towns that were of recent origin. But if we look more closely at these sudden, and quite considerable developments, we shall find that they were in fact ramifications of Italian banking which had by then become traditional. In the days of the fairs of Champagne it was already the bankers from Siena, Lucca, Florence, or Genoa who held the moneychanger's scales; it was they who made the fortune of Geneva in the fifteenth century and later those of Antwerp, Lyons, and Medina del Campo. They were on the scene again in 1585, when Frankfurt-am-Main created the exchange fairs. To the uninitiated their dealings were clearly suspect, if not downright diabolical. A Frenchman in 1550 was amazed by these 'foreign [i.e. Italian] merchants and bankers', who would arrive empty-handed 'without bringing from the said countries anything beside their persons, with a little credit, a pen, ink and paper, and skill in handling, turning and diverting the said exchanges from one country to another, according to the information they have of the places where money is dearest'.[231]

In short, throughout Europe a small group of well-informed men, kept in touch by an active correspondence, controlled the entire network of exchanges in bills or specie, thus dominating the field of commercial speculation. So we should not be too taken in by the apparent spread of 'finance'. There were many differences and degrees between the *piazze*; some were predominantly commercial, others industrial, others partly financial. In 1580, when Portugal joined Spain, Spanish businessmen were astonished by the technical backwardness of the exchange of Lisbon, which was entirely commercial. Investments in Marseilles were still coming from Lyons, Montpellier, and Genoa at the beginning of the seventeenth century. Ragusa, which was commercially so prosperous, was financially dependent on the Italian cities: in the seventeenth century her entire

---

[230] Jacques Heers, *op. cit.*, p. 74 ff.
[231] B.N. Paris, Fr. 2086, f°s 60 v°, 61 r°.

fortune lay in government stocks either in Naples, Rome, or Venice. The case of Venice is even more revealing. A long report by the *Cinque Savii*, in January, 1607,[232] indicates that all 'capitalist' activity, as we should call it, was in the hands of the Florentines, who owned houses in the city, and the Genoese, who provided silver, between them controlling all exchanges. By 'drawing' on Venice, Genoese and Florentines speculated 'on the exchanges' (chiefly at the so-called Besançon fairs, in fact held at Piacenza) with the plentiful money of Venetian investors. They thus 'captured' the available currency in the city. The Piedmontese, Giovanni Botero, grasped the situation when in 1589 he compared Genoa to Venice, giving his preference to the latter. At Genoa the fortunes of the money-dealers were extremely far advanced, but it was to the detriment of the city's other gainful activities. Her industry (textiles and shipbuilding) was sluggish; the *arti* of course meant life or death to the ordinary people of Genoa, whose level of income was low. Alongside her great rival, Venice remained a less developed town, where all the economic functions were still carried on. Her people were therefore less wretched than those of Genoa and the difference between rich and poor was less marked.[233]

Urban cycle and decline. If urban life advances by stages, it also deteriorates by stages. Towns rise, thrive and decline according to the pulses of economic life. In their decline, they are forced to abandon, sector by sector, the sources of their strength. Was it a coincidence that at Genoa the first warning sign (the presence of Ragusan cargo ships) concerned transports, the primary source of a city's wealth, while at the other end of the scale, it it was her banking activities, the latest in time to develop, which held out the longest? At the lowest ebb of their fortunes, in the eighteenth century, Genoa and Venice were still banking centres. Was Barcelona's misfortune, in the sixteenth century at any rate, not a consequence of her past, the price she had to pay for a fortune acquired too quickly and not consolidated on the banking level, in spite of what has been said? It was lack of liquid currency, exchange facilities, *giro*, wrote Capmany[234] that paralysed the town in the sixteenth century.

By stretching this argument to its limits might it not be possible to say that the development of the industrial phase in a city's life often indicates some difficulty in its trading functions, that industry is in a sense a response to a decline in trade? Whether or not this is a permissible assumption, it may be regarded as symptomatic that industry flourished most in cities far from the sea, cities that were prevented by their position from fulfilling all the functions of communication centres, in Lucca, for instance, the home of silk weaving, Milan, Como, or Florence herself. Industry flourished also in towns whose communications or merchandise were

[232] A.d.S. Venice, *Cinque Savii*, Risposte 1602–1606, f° 189, v°, 195.
[233] *Op. cit.*, I, p. 38.
[234] Antonio de Capmany y de Montpalau, *Memorias históricas sobre la Marina, Comercio y Artes de la antigua ciudad de Barcelona*, Madrid, 1779, p. 205 ff.

Plan of Venice (XVIth Century). (Palace of the Marquises of Santa
Cruz, Ciudad Real). Note the Rialto, still made of wood at this time,
the beginnings of the Arsenal, the island of San Giorgio, the Guidecca
and the Zattere

Constantinople. View of part of the city from the Golden Horn (XVIth
Century), B.N. Paris C 4 093

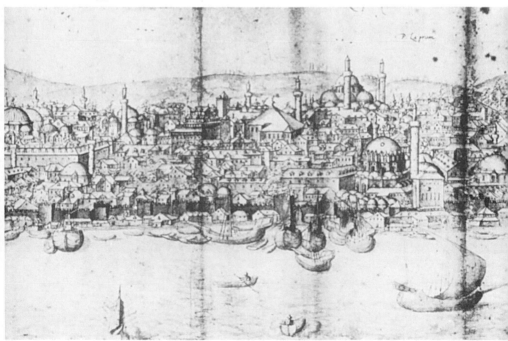

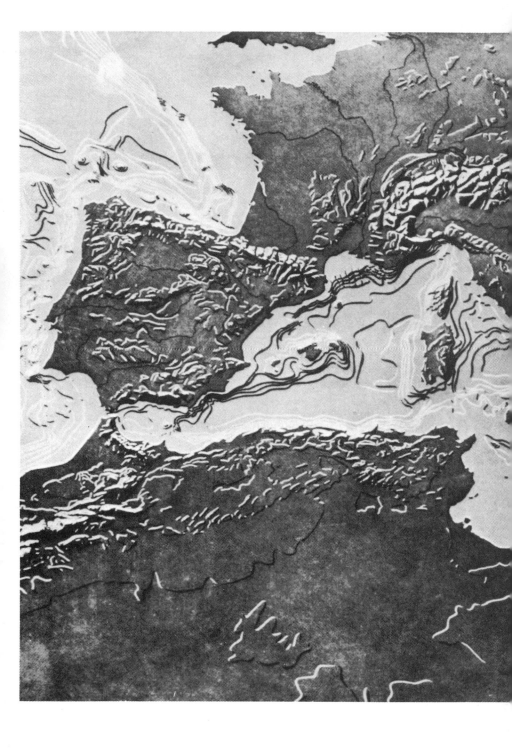

Height and depth above and below sea-level shown at 500 metre
intervals (map by Jacques Bertin)

Atlantic sailing vessel. Either the small ship La Cordeliere or the
Mareschalle, which caught fire on 10 August 1512, in the Goulet de
Brest, B.N. FR 1672, f°9 v°

Venetian galleon. Bas-relief on the tomb of Alessandro Contarini
(1555), Cathedral of Saint Anthony, Padua

Merchant's round ship. Bas-relief on the tomb of Alessandro
Contarini (1555), Cathedral of Saint Anthony, Padua

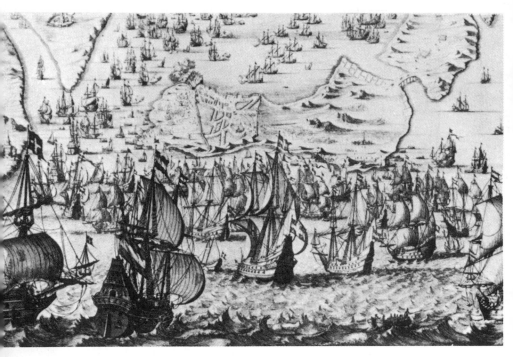

The English take Cadiz, 1596. B.N. Paris, 13 702

Opposite page The Venice Arsenal (1500). From the great plan by Jacopo di Barbaro

The Harbour, Barcelona. The mole is shown so this must be a late drawing, probably the early XVIIth Century. Note the galley towing a round ship. The Arsenal appears at the bottom of the picture.

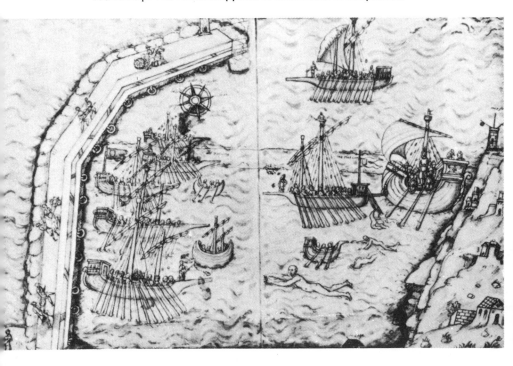

Sailing ships large and small. A huge Portuguese vessel is attacked off Malacca by several small English and Dutch ships (14 October 1602). J. Th. de Bry, *Indiae orientalis pars septima*, Frankfurt, 1606, pl. XII B.N. Res. G 412

The Alps between France and Piedmont. How the mountain barrier between France was depicted in the XVIIth Century. 'Desseing de l'attaquement du paz et destroict de Suze Piemont, emporte par le Roi', 1629. B.N., Est., Id 24 fol. Louis XIII's victory showed that Italy, relinquished in 1559, was still within France's reach

threatened in the sixteenth century, such as Florence or Venice. Is it possible to go even further and say that banking increases in importance when commerce and industry are in difficulty; that one type of activity can only develop to the detriment of others and not necessarily in harmony with them? My intention in raising these questions is not to attempt an overall interpretation, but to indicate, very briefly, the full complex of problems posed by urban dynamism.

A very incomplete typology. The typology of towns outlined above is necessarily incomplete. They led complicated lives. Every town was contained within a certain economic framework. At local level this implied a system of relationships with the surrounding countryside and the neighbouring towns, within which the town might play a dominant or subordinate role. At national or international levels, it implied systems of relationships, depending on distances within the Mediterranean or even the Greater Mediterranean region. Finally there was political change. In the sixteenth century political change destroyed the old independence of the city-state, undermined the foundations of its traditional economy, creating and imposing new structures.

An historian[235] who is completing a work on the typology of the towns of Castile in the sixteenth century has established the following distinctions: bureaucratic towns, such as Granada and Madrid – the latter growing so fast that the machinery for supplying food for its unproductive population was always breaking down and one might see, according to some correspondence in 1615 'bread lacking for days on end, and the people in the streets, money in hand, searching and begging for it "per l'amor di Dio" ';[236] commercial towns, such as Toledo, Burgos, and Seville; industrial towns (in the sense that modern industry grew up there with the capitalist forms of the *Verlagssystem*, which were not peculiar to Germany) such as Córdoba and Segovia; towns whose industrial production was largely in the hands of artisans, such as Cuenca; agricultural towns, dependent on the surrounding countryside, not to say invaded by it, such as Salamanca or Jerez de la Frontera; clerical towns like Guadalajara; a sheep-farming town like Soria. There were also several military towns, which in the sixteenth century were as difficult to distinguish from other towns as warships from ordinary merchantmen. This classification gives some idea of the complexity of the problem. There still remains the distinction to be made between towns of the first and second rank, whatever their type, and the need to study the interaction (within a specifically European structure) between a big city and less important neighbouring towns.

There is the additional problem that no sooner does a town appear to

[235] Felipe Ruiz Martín, Professor at the University of Bilbao, who has communicated to me the outline of his forthcoming book.
[236] A.d.S. Venice, Dispacci Senato Spagna, Fo. Moro to the Doge, Madrid, 1615.

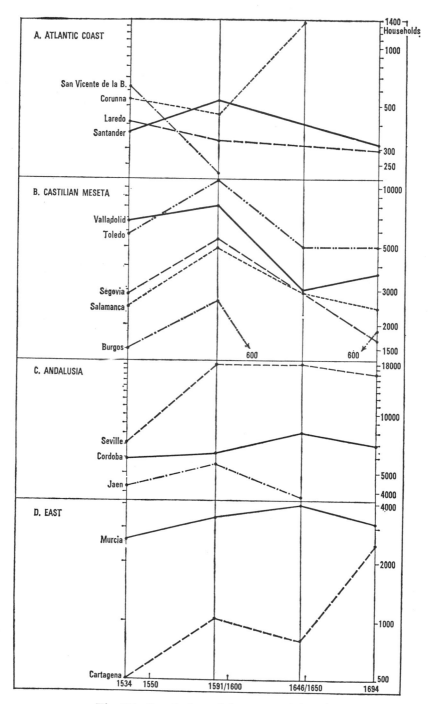

Fig. 27: *Population of the towns of Castile*

fit into a classification than it changes its nature. Seville, which was late to develop financially (although the city did possess banks), could be described equally as a city of bureaucrats, rentiers, and artisans; it was a luxury city, requiring for its maintenance a proletariat whom we can imagine herded together in houses shared by several poor families, as in the Triana quarter where lye and soap were manufactured.[237]

Salamanca was a rural town, but it was also, of course, a great intellectual centre. Padua, another renowned university town, was also a big agricultural centre. In the past (before 1405), during the struggle against Venice, the lords of Carrara, who controlled the town, had 'in order to make goods costly to their rival' placed taxes on all hens, capons, geese, eggs, pigeons, vegetables, and fruit leaving the city. With that conservatism of which the cities show so much evidence, these taxes, although contrary to Venice's interest, were maintained until 1460[238] long after Padua had submitted to the republic of St. Mark.

However, Padua remained plunged in her rural pursuits, and Bayard and his companions in 1509 saw the city engaged upon agricultural tasks: 'every day much hay was harvested', relates the *Loyal Serviteur*, 'and in that quarter the loads were so great that they almost had to be forced through a gateway'.[239] The same sight could be seen at Brescia, where the San Stefano gate which led to the Broletto offered such a narrow opening that 'quando vi si trova qualche carro di feno o paglia o legne, per lì non ponno transitar gli uomini'.[240] A similar situation, if not an identical sight could have been found at Lucera, a small Apulian town that held active fairs. It was also plagued by the captains appointed by the Marquis del Vico, of whom the town had great cause for complaint. Not only did they kill, steal, and gamble, but ultimate insult, they 'have sent a large number of pigs before the appointed date into the territory of the town, to the inconvenience of the other *cittadini* . . . not to mention the great damage which the said pigs have caused to crops, water, and pastures'.[241] So pigs were reared in large numbers inside the city walls. These scenes from agricultural life, frequently in conflict with the arts of military defence or the honesty of those in power, show how open sixteenth-century towns were, whatever the cost, to their surrounding countryside. How else could they have survived?

4. TOWNS, WITNESSES TO THE CENTURY

We should now turn our attention to the points of resemblance between these widely-differing towns, each of which had its own particular balance

[237] Cf. the admirable series of documents at Simancas, Expedientes de Hacienda, 170, where there can also be found the census (*padrón*) of the town in 1561.
[238] A.d.S. Venice, Senato Terra, 4, f° 138, 22nd March, 1460.
[239] *Le Loyal Serviteur, op. cit.*, p. 42.
[240] A.d.S. Venice, Senato Terra 27, Brescia, 5th March, 1558; the problem had come up earlier, *ibid.*, 24, Brescia, February–March, 1556.
[241] A.d.S. Naples, Sommaria Consultationum 2, f° 75 v° and 76, 7th July, 1550.

of activities, to see what features they had *in common*, in so far as they were subject to general conditions applying equally or almost equally well to all parts of the Mediterranean during the second half of the sixteenth century. For those we know most about the evidence concurs: the urban population was rising: despite the crises in their daily life, of which there was no shortage, *in the long term*, they were healthy, since they were still growing; at any rate they overcame crises and difficulties; however all towns without exception saw their liberties being whittled away by the extension of the territorial states, which were expanding even more rapidly than the towns, surrounding them, subjugating them, or even chasing them from acquired positions. A new political and economic age was beginning. From this point of view the Mediterranean was ahead of its time.

The rise in population.[242] We only know a thousandth part – if that – of the evidence that historians might be able to unearth concerning the movement of urban populations in the sixteenth century. However it is possible to give a fairly reliable picture of the overall situation. For a more precise idea of this see the graph (Fig. 27) showing the shift in the urban population of the cities of Castile.[243] Its message is clear: all the curves – with a few exceptions that merely prove the rule – distinctly show a steady rise until the final years of the sixteenth century.

A very similar graph could be produced from the figures for Italy[244] and both European and Asian Turkey.[245] We may safely assume that the situation was broadly the same throughout the Mediterranean, both Moslem and Christian. The increase in population was a fundamental characteristic of the 'long sixteenth century' both in Europe and the Mediterranean, the basis on which everything or almost everything else depended.

All categories of towns shared in this increase, from very small and modest communities to important towns and great cities, whether characterized by industrial or artisan production, by bureaucracy or commerce. There was no discrimination, as there was later to be in the seventeenth century regression,[246] which was characterized by the rise or stability of certain privileged cities, such as Paris, London, Madrid, and even Constantinople, while all the other towns were touched by the decline in population. It should not be surprising then to find increased activity in the sixteenth century in all the towns, to see building yards, both publicly

[242] See the long bibliographical note below p. 394, note 193.
[243] It will need to be revised in the light of the sources in the archives at Simancas, which have so far not received adequate attention. Let us hope that we shall soon see the results of Felipe Ruiz Martin's research.
[244] The great milestone in this area has been the publication of the third and final volume of Karl Julius Beloch's *Bevölkerungsgeschichte Italiens*, Berlin, 1961.
[245] To be found in the revolutionary line of research pursued by Ömer Lütfi Barkan.
[246] E. Hobsbawm, 'The Crisis of the 17th Century' in *Past and Present*, 1954, no. 5, p. 33–53, no. 6, p. 44–65.

and privately owned, opening at Verona as well as Venice, Pavia as well as Milan; to find increased artisan production at Cuenca as well as Segovia; active shipyards on the Mandracchio of Naples as well as on the beaches of Sorrento or Amalfi. This was a period of general prosperity in which *all* the urban centres had a share. The hierarchy of the towns, their mutual relationships and mutual behaviour, therefore, remained almost unchanged. A map of urban standards of living in the kingdom of Granada in 1591, imperfect though it may be since it is based on fiscal records (*millones*), gives an indication of this interurban geography which was hardly to alter.[247] The great cities remained in their dominating positions, with the advantages of high prices, high wages, and many customers for their shops, while satellite towns surrounded them, looked towards them, used them, and were used by them. These planetary systems, so typical of Europe[248] and the Mediterranean, were to continue to function virtually unimpeded.

Nevertheless, conspicuous changes, which could not be ignored, did take place: they too followed a fairly logical pattern.

In the first place an increase in population always works both ways: it may be a source of strength or of weakness, stability or insecurity. Many ancient evils persisted and were sometimes aggravated: the sixteenth century had neither the courage nor the strength to eradicate them. Secondly, the cities were no longer undisputed rulers of the world. Their reign, which had lasted throughout the early rise of Europe and the Mediterranean, from the eleventh to the fourteenth century, was beginning to be challenged at the threshold of modern times by the territorial states which had developed slowly during the previous centuries but which modern times suddenly projected to the centre of the stage. Finally, the rural population was still in the majority. In the sixteenth century the population of the countryside may have risen less quickly than that of the towns that it supplied. The latter certainly shot up, even if the rise cannot be exactly measured.[249] So the towns were reaching a peak, possibly even overreaching it. When the population declined in the seventeenth century, as in Venezia where figures are available,[250] the towns declined more rapidly than the surrounding countryside. Had the picture changed by the eighteenth century? M. Moheau[251] claimed that rural France was then growing faster than urban France. These rapid comparisons may help

[247] Alvaro Castillo Pintado, 'El servicio de millones y la población del Reino de Granada en 1591' in *Saitabi, Revista de la Facultad de Filosofía y Letras de la Universidad de Valencia*, 1961.
[248] Otto Brunner, *Neue Wege der Sozialgeschichte Vorträge und Aufsätze*, Göttingen, 1956, p. 87, and F. Braudel, 'Sur une conception de l'Histoire sociale' in *Annales E.S.C.*, April–June, 1959.
[249] Earl J. Hamilton, *El Florecimiento de capitalismo y otros ensayos de historia ecónomica*, 1948, p. 121–122.
[250] Daniele Beltrami, *Forze di lavoro e proprietà fondiaria nelle compagne venete dei secoli XVII e XVIII*, 1961, p. 5 ff.
[251] M. Moheau, *Recherches et considérations sur la population de la France*, 1778, p. 257–258 and table p. 276.

us to understand the decisive yet fragile fortunes of the towns in the sixteenth century.

Hardships old and new: Famine and the wheat problem. The sixteenth century was not always kind to urban communities. Famine and epidemics waged a continuous onslaught on the towns. Because of the slowness and prohibitive price of transport and the unreliability of the harvests, any urban centre could be exposed to famine at any time of year. The slightest pressure could tip the balance. When the Council of Trent met for the third and last time in 1561 (and although the town was on the great Brenner–Adige route, the route taken by the Bavarian grain which sometimes served Verona), the first problem facing the delegates to the Council and their staff was the difficult question of supplies, about which Rome was justifiably anxious.[252] Both in the Mediterranean regions and outside famine was a commonplace hazard. The famine in Castile in 1521 coincided with the beginning of the war against France and the rising of the *Comuneros* at home. Nobles and commoners alike were panic-stricken by the lack of bread during that year which was known in Portugal as the year of the Great Hunger. In 1525 Andalusia was devastated by a terrible drought. In 1528 famine brought terror to Tuscany: Florence had to close her gates to the starving peasants from surrounding districts. In 1540 the same thing happened. Again Florence was about to close her gates and abandon the countryside to its fate, when the region was saved by the arrival of ships at Leghorn carrying grain from the Levant; but that was something of a miracle.[253] In 1575, in the Rumanian countryside, which was normally rich in cereals, the flocks died by the hundred; the birds were surprised in March by snowdrifts five feet deep and could be caught in the hand. As for the human inhabitants, they would kill their neighbours for a piece of bread.[254] In 1583 the scourge swept through Italy, particularly in the Papal States where people starved to death.[255]

More often, however, famine did not attack entire regions, but struck only the towns. The striking feature of the famine in Tuscany in 1528 was that it extended to the entire countryside surrounding Florence, and as we have remarked, the peasants flocking to the city found the gates closed against them. Similarly at Perugia in 1529 there was no grain at all for a radius of fifty miles. These were still rare catastrophes. In normal times the peasants would obtain from their own land almost all the frugal fare on which they survived. Urban famine on the contrary, within the city walls was an extremely frequent occurrence in the sixteenth century. Florence, although it certainly does not lie in a particularly poor region, experienced 111 famines between 1375 and 1791, as against sixteen very

[252] The prelates of the Council to Borromeo, Trent, 7th August, 1561, Susta, *op. cit.*, I, p. 67–68 and note 68–69.
[253] G. Vivoli, *op. cit.*, III, p. 15 and 24, n. 17.
[254] N. Iorga, *Ospiti romeni in Venezia, op. cit.*, p. 35.
[255] G. Mecatti, *op. cit.*, II, p. 766.

good harvests over the same period.[256] Even the wheat ports, such as Messina and Genoa,[257] suffered terrible famines. Every year, even at the beginning of the seventeenth century, Venice had to part with millions in gold to secure the city's food supply.[258]

Because of their requirements and their resources, the towns were the great customers for grain. A whole book could be written on the grain policy of Venice or Genoa. The latter was always quick to seize any opportunities of obtaining supplies, and in the fifteenth century turned towards France, Sicily, and North Africa: the former engaged in the grain trade of the Levant, negotiated with the Turks, from 1390 on, which did not prevent her from applying to other sources, such as Apulia and Sicily. Venice also had permanent regulations: notably, in 1408, 1539, 1607, and 1628[259] she prohibited the export of any grain outside her 'gulf'.

In the sixteenth century there is hardly a town of any importance which does not possess what is in Venice known by the strangely modern-sounding name of the Grain Office (the files of which for the years we are interested in have been lost). This was a remarkable institution.[260] The Office controlled not only grain and flour entering the city, but also sales in the city markets: flour could only be sold in two 'public places', one near St. Mark's, the other at the 'Rivoalto'.[261] The doge was to be kept daily informed of the stocks in the warehouses. As soon as he discovered that the city had reserves only for a year or eight months, the College was duly informed, provision was made by the Office, on the one hand and on the other by the merchants to whom sums of money were immediately advanced. The bakers were also supervised: they had to provide the public with loaves made from 'good grain', white, whose weight might vary according to the abundance or otherwise of supplies, but whose price per unit remained constant, as was the rule in almost every town in Europe.

Such a Grain Office was not necessarily to be found in every town – there was only one Venice – but under different names and different organizations there were grain and flour offices almost everywhere. At Florence the *Abbondanza* was transformed by the Medici (who took over the external supply of grain) but it survived, at any rate to perform minor functions, after the *bando* of 1556, which is usually regarded as the end of its activity.[262] At Como the task fell to the *Consiglio Generale* of the Commune, the *Ufficio d'Annona*, and the *Diputati di provvisione*.[263] When

[256] *Almanacco di economia di Toscana dell'anno 1791*, Florence, 1791.

[257] In 1539 for example, Rosario Russo, *art. cit.*, in *Rivista storica italiana*, 1934, p. 435; and again in 1560, Simancas E° 1389, 19th June, 1560. In Messina in 1577, Simancas E° 1148, 9th May, 1757.

[258] A. Serra, 'Breve tratatto delle cause che possono far abondare li regni d'oro argento dove non sono miniere', in A. Graziani, *Economisti del Cinque e Seicento*, Bari, 1913, p. 164.

[259] A.d.S. Venice, *Cinque Savii . . .*, Busta 2.

[260] B.N. Paris, fr. 5599.   [261] i.e., Rialto.

[262] G. Parenti, *Prime ricerche sulla rivoluzione dei prezzi in Firenze*, 1939, p. 96 ff.

[263] Giuseppe Mira, *Aspetti dell'economia comasca all'inizio dell'età moderna*, Como, 1939, p. 239 ff.

there was no separate institution, grain policy was in the hands of officials either of the town's government or the administration. At Ragusa, whose poor location made her well acquainted with food shortage, the Rectors of the republic themselves handled it. At Naples it was the viceroy in person who controlled it.[264]

When famine threatened, the measures taken were everywhere identical. To the sound of trumpets it was forbidden to take grain out of the town, the guard was doubled, searches were conducted and available supplies were inventoried. If the danger increased sterner measures were taken: The number of mouths to feed was reduced, the city gates were closed, or else foreigners were expelled, the normal course at Venice, unless they had brought enough grain into the city to feed their staff or household.[265] The Protestants were expelled from Marseilles in 1562,[266] a double gain for the city, which was opposed to the Huguenots. At Naples during the famine of 1591 the University bore the brunt of the disaster. It was closed and the students were sent back home.[267] After that, rationing was generally introduced, as in Marseilles in August, 1583.[268]

But naturally before taking any other steps the town would make every effort to find provisions at any price, in the first place from its usual sources. Marseilles usually turned to the interior and the gracious bounty of the king of France, or applied to 'her very dear and beloved friends', the consuls of Arles, even to the merchants of Lyons. And in order to reach the grain of Burgundy beyond Lyons and to convey it down river to Marseilles, the boats on the 'Shomne and the Rhosne' (the Saône and the Rhône) had to be able, in spite of the increased waters, to pass 'the bridges . . . without grand danger'.[269]

At Barcelona in August, 1557, the Inquisitors begged Philip II to allow them to be sent, at least for their personal use, a little wheat from Roussillon.[270] The Inquisitors of Valencia in the following year[271] asked permission to import wheat from Castile, a request that was repeated in 1559. Verona, expecting a poor harvest, asked the Serenissima for permission to buy wheat in Bavaria.[272] Ragusa turned to the Sanjak of Herzegovina; Venice asked the Grand Turk for authorization to load grain in the Levant.

[264] See below, p. 346.
[265] Simancas E° 1326, 29th September, 1569–1st October, 1569.
[266] Council of 13th December, 1562, BB, 41, f° 25 ff.
[267] Giuseppe Pardi, 'Napoli attraverso i secoli' in *N.R.St.*, 1924, p. 75.
[268] Measures were asked for to control the fishermen of the 'cartier St. Jehan' who 'go out of the port and take with them more bread than is necessary', 7th August, 1583, A. Comm. Marseilles, BB 45, f° 223.
[269] Alexandre Agulftequi(?) to the consuls of Marseilles, Lyons, 11th November, 1579, Arch. Comm. Marseilles.
[270] 28th August, 1577, A.H.N. Barcelona Inquisition, libro I, f° 308.
[271] 12th October, 1558, Valencia Inquisition, libro I, A.H.N.
[272] A.d.S. Venice, Capi del Consiglio dei X, Ba 594, f° 139 projected purchase, 23rd June, 1559; the same request 16th May, 1560, *Ibid.*, f° 144.

Every time this meant negotiations, expeditions, large expenditure, not to mention promises and extra payments to the merchants.[273]

If all else failed, the last great resource was to turn to the sea, to watch out for grain ships, seize them, then to pay the party concerned for the cargo later, not without some discussion. Marseilles one day seized two Genoese barques which had imprudently strayed into her port; on 8th November, 1562, she ordered a frigate to board all ships carrying grain that it found off the coast of the town.[274] In October 1557, the local authorities made ships carrying wheat from Apulia and the Levant unload at Messina.[275] The Knights of Malta, who were not well off for supplies, regularly watched the Sicilian coast. Their behaviour there was hardly different from that of the Tripoli corsairs. They paid up, it is true, but they boarded ships in the same manner as pirates. And nobody was more skilled at this unpopular practice than Venice. As soon as her food supply was endangered, no ship loaded with wheat was safe in the Adriatic. She had no compunction in posting one or two galleys off Ragusa Vecchia, which would then under the very noses of the Ragusans seize ships carrying grain loaded by the *sectors* at Vólos, Salonica, or in the neighbouring ports of Albania. Or she would seek out grain ships along the Apulian coast and make them unload at Corfu, Spalato, or directly at Venice. It is true that she had been unable to maintain the foothold she had twice obtained in Apulia and had lost this providential granary and oil and wine cellar. That did not inhibit her from returning to help herself whenever necessary, either peacefully or by using force. Her behaviour was the source of persistent, quite justified, and completely ineffective protest from Naples, backed up by Spain: the ships seized by Venice were usually those that Naples had chartered for her own supplies. Venice's captures were likely to provoke riots in a city swarming with poor people.[276]

All this proved a great financial burden. But no town could escape its crushing weight. At Venice, enormous losses had to be registered at the Grain Office, which on the one hand gave large bonuses to merchants and on the other often sold the grain and flour it had acquired at lower than normal prices. It was even worse at Naples, where fear made the authorities not merely liberal, but prodigal. At Florence the Grand Duke made

---

[273] At Marseilles. Council of 4th May, 1572, a commission of 6 sous per consignment to the merchants, BB 43, f° 144 ff. Arch. Comm. Marseilles.

[274] A. Comm. Marseilles BB 41, f° 1 ff.

[275] Pietro Lomellino to the Signoria of Genoa, Messina, 8th October, 1557, A.d.S. Genoa, Lettere Consoli, Napoli, Messina, 1–2634.

[276] In August, 1607, food shortage caused a revolt at Naples, *Archivio storico italiano*, IX, p. 266. Another famine was a determining factor later in the Messina uprising of 1647. Many references: 23rd, 26th, 27th December, 1559; 2nd January, 1560, Sim. E° 1050 f° 3; 28th January, 1560, E° 1324, f° 72; 5th November, 1562 E° 1324, f° 154; 16th December, 1562, *ibid.*, f° 147; 8th April, 1563, f° 110; 18th March, 1565, A.d.S. Venice Senato Secreta Dispacci Napoli, no. 1; 7th February, 1566, Sim. E° 1555, f° 25; 18th January, 1570, Sim. E° 1327; 3rd March, 1571, Sim. E° 1059, f° 68; 28th February, 1571, *ibid.*, f° 60.

up the difference. In Corsica, Ajaccio borrowed from Genoa.[277] Marseilles which kept a tight hold on the purse strings, also borrowed, but always looking ahead, would forbid grain to enter the town just before the harvest, and would exhaust the remaining stocks when there were any. This was the practice of many towns.

These policies were difficult to enforce and never reliable. The result was suffering and disorder: suffering for the poor, sometimes for a whole town; disorder for the institutions and the very foundations of urban life. Were these narrow units and mediæval economies adequate for the pressures of the new age?

Hardships old and new: epidemics. One could draw an incomplete but eloquent map showing the incidence of plague, the dreaded visitor to the Mediterranean. If the plague years were marked alongside every town they touched, no city would escape even this brief survey and fail to score. Plague would appear as what it was: a 'structure' of the century. The cities of the East suffered its blows more often than the others. At Constantinople, the dangerous gateway to Asia, it was permanently installed, for this was the great centre for epidemics which then spread to the West.

The visitations of epidemics, combined with famine, led to the perpetual renewal of the population. Venice was stricken by an outbreak of plague in 1575–1577 so terrible that 50,000 people died, a quarter or a third of the population.[278] Between 1575 and 1578 there were 40,000 deaths at Messina. In 1580 after the plague, there spread throughout Italy a deadly epizootic, the disease *del montone* and *castrone*,[279] which indirectly threatened human life. The figures given by contemporaries often indicate by their exaggeration the terror these sufferings inspired. Bandello talks of 230,000 victims at Milan, in the time of Ludovico Sforza![280] In 1525, if we are to believe another source, nine-tenths of the population of Rome and Naples perished;[281] in 1550 half the population of Milan again fell victim;[282] in 1581 the plague was said to have left only 5000 people alive in Marseilles,[283] and to have killed 60,000 in Rome.[284] The figures are not exact, but they undoubtedly show that a quarter or a third of the inhabitants of a town could suddenly vanish at a time when imperfect knowledge of hygiene and medicine afforded little protection against infection.[285] And they concur with the familiar accounts of streets littered with corpses, the death cart passing every day carrying

[277] 1527, Mario Branetti, 'Notizie di Fonti et Documenti' in *Archivio storico di Corsica*, 1931, p. 531.
[278] H. Kretschmayr, *op. cit.*, III, p. 41.
[279] G. Mecatti, *op. cit.*, II, p. 764.
[280] M. Bandello, *op. cit.*, V, p. 167. Salvatore Pugliese, *Condizione economiche e finanziarie della Lombardia nella prima metà del secolo XVIII*, 1924, p. 55, mentions the figure of 100,000 dead in 1524.
[281] G. Vivoli, *op. cit.*, III, p. 268.
[282] *Ibid.*   [283] *Ibid.*   [284] *Ibid.*
[285] 'Un picciol popolo è facilmente consumato da una pestilenza', G. Botero, *op. cit.* II, *Proemio*, (p. 1), unnumbered in 1599 edition.

so many bodies that they could not be buried. Such visitations could completely destroy and transform a town. When the plague finally left Venice in 1577, quite a different city with a new set of rulers emerged. There had been a complete changeover.[286] A *frate di San Domenico* preaching in Naples in March 1584 – was it purely a coincidence? – maintained that 'for some time, Venice had been acting imprudently for the young men had taken over from the old' ('poiche i giovanni havevano tolto il governo a vecchi').[287]

The wounds healed more or less quickly. If Venice never entirely recovered after 1576[288] it was because the secular trend was to turn against her in the seventeenth century. Plague and other epidemics were only serious, in fact, during periods of food shortage and material difficulty. Famine and epidemics went hand in hand, an old truth with which the West had long been familiar. Every town had long tried to protect itself against disease, using disinfectants based on aromatic herbs, destroying by fire the belongings of plague victims, enforcing quarantine on persons and goods (Venice was a pioneer in this respect), recruiting doctors, introducing health certificates, the *cartas de salud* in Spain, *fedi di sanità* in Italy. The rich had always sought their salvation in flight. At the first signs of disease they would flee to neighbouring towns, or, more often, to their precious country houses. 'I have never seen any town more surrounded by farms and country houses,' wrote Thomas Platter[289] arriving at Marseilles in 1587. 'The reason for this is that when plague comes, as frequently happens because of the great number of people who come here from all countries, the inhabitants take refuge in the country.' For 'inhabitants', read 'rich', for the poor always remained inside the diseased town, besieged, regarded with suspicion, and liberally provided with food from outside in order to keep them quiet. This was an old conflict, as René Baehrel has noted,[290] a source of lasting class hatred. In June, 1478,[291] Venice was hit by plague; as usual, looting immediately began in the town. The house of a member of the Ca' Balastreo was completely sacked, as was the warehouse of the Ca' Foscari and at 'Rivoalto' the office of the merchant consuls. This was because 'hoc tempore pestis communiter omnes habentes facultatem exeunt civitatem, relictis domibus suis, aut clausis, aut cum una serva, vel famulo . . .'. In 1656 at Genoa, according to the *Capucin Charitable*, the situation was word for word the same.[292]

---

[286] See above note 278.

[287] Marciana, Ital., 7299, *Memorie publiche dal anno 1576 al 1586*, 18th March, 1584.

[288] On the plague of 1576, see the admirable study by Ernst Rodenwaldt, 'Pest in Venedig 1575–1577, Ein Beitrag zur Frage der Infektkette bei den Pestepedimien West-Europas' in *Sitzungsberichte der Heidelberger Akademie d. Wissenschaften, Mathematischnaturwissenschaftliche Klass*, Heidelberg, 1953, p. 119 ff.

[289] *Op. cit.*, p. 125.

[290] René Baehrel, 'La haine de classe en temps d'épidémie' in *Annales E.S.C.*, 1952, p. 315–350, and esp. 'Économie et Terreur: histoire et sociologie' in *Annales hist. de la Révolution Française*, 1951, p. 113–146.

[291] A.d.S. Venice, Senato Misti, 19, f° 72 v° and 73, 3rd June, 1478.

[292] Père Maurice de Tolon, *Préservatifs et remèdes contre la peste ou le Capucin Charitable*, 1668, p. 60 ff.

However, the great epidemics of the early seventeenth century at Milan and Verona in 1630; Florence in 1630–1631; Venice in 1631; Genoa in 1656; and even London in 1664, seem to have been of a much more serious order than those of the previous century. During the latter half of the sixteenth century the towns seem to have suffered comparatively mildly. Explanations immediately spring to mind: the increased damp and cold and the introduction of more direct links between Italy and the East. But why should the incidence of plague have increased in the East at the same time?

Plague was not the only disease that attacked sixteenth-century towns. They were also afflicted by venereal diseases, sweating sickness, measles, dysentery, and typhus. Illness did not spare the armies either, towns as it were, on the move, which were even more vulnerable. During the Hungarian War (1593–1607) a kind of typhus, known as the *ungarische Krankheit*[293] decimated the German army but spared the Turks and Hungarians; it spread through Europe as far as England. The towns were natural centres for the spread of these infectious diseases. In 1588 an influenza outbreak can be traced from Venice, where it laid low the entire population but did not destroy it, emptying the Grand Council – which the plague had never done – to Milan, France, Catalonia, and then, with a leap, to America.[294]

This prevalence of epidemics made a significant contribution to the insecurity of life in the towns, to the 'social massacres' of the poor which did not end, and even then not completely, until the eighteenth century.

The indispensable immigrant. Another regular feature of Mediterranean towns is that the urban proletariat cannot maintain itself, let alone increase without the help of continuous immigration. The town had the capacity, and the obligation, to attract, besides the eternal mountain immigrants who provided labour of all kinds, a throng of proletarians or adventurers of every origin, a source of supply to meet its demand. Ragusa recruited her labour force from the nearby mountains. In the registers of the *Diversa de Foris*, one can read countless copies of contracts of domestic apprentices, who engage themselves for one year, or two, three, or seven, at the average wage in 1550 of three golden ducats a year, the wages often being payable on expiry of the contract. One *famulus* might undertake to serve his master *in partibus Turcicorum*; all obtained board and clothing and the promise that they would learn their master's trade[295] or receive a payment in gold on the expiry of their five-, eight- or ten-year contracts.[296] Although the texts do not tell us, one wonders how many of these apprentices were not boys from the town but sons of peasants from Ragusan territory, or even *Morlachi*, who were more or less Turkish subjects?

[293] *Op. cit.*, II, p. 14.
[294] Pare P. Gil, *Libre primer de la historia cathalana* . . ., f° 81 r°.
[295] Ragusa Archives; see also the series Diversa di Cancellaria, 137.
[296] *Ibid.*, 146 f° 32 v°, 140, 187 v°, 205, 213 v°, 215, etc.

At Marseilles the typical immigrant was the Corsican, and particularly the *Capocorsino*. At Seville the standard immigrants (not counting those attracted by voyages to the Indies, who came from everywhere), the permanent proletariat were the Moriscos. They came from Andalusia and became so numerous in the city that by the end of the century the authorities feared uprisings no longer in the mountains but in the city itself, in conjunction with English landings.[297] At Algiers the new arrivals were Christians, who swelled the ranks of the corsairs and the prisoners: Andalusian or Aragonese fugitives (arriving at the end of the fifteenth and the beginning of the sixteenth century), artisans, and shopkeepers, whose names can still be found in the present day quarter of the Tagarins;[298] even more were Berbers from the nearby mountains of Kabylia who had already provided the original ethnic base of the city. Haëdo describes them as wretched folk, digging the gardens of the rich, their ambition to get if possible a place in the militia as a soldier: only then will they have enough to eat. Throughout the Ottoman Empire, there was not a single town, in spite of state controls and suspicious corporations that did not receive a continuous stream of immigrants from the poor or overpopulated countryside. 'This clandestine and desperate labour force was a bonus for the rich, who obtained cheap servants for their gardens, stables, and houses . . .'. These wretched people even competed with slave labour.[299]

At Lisbon, where there was a constant flow of immigrants, those worst off were the black slaves. In 1633 they numbered over 15,000 out of a total population of 100,000, and would all walk through the streets of the city on the festival of *Nuestra Señora de las Nieves*, Our Lady of the Snows, an occasion upon which they dressed in loin cloths and colourful fabrics. 'Their bodies are well made and more beautiful than white men's,' remarked a Capuchin friar[300] 'and a naked Negro is more handsome than a clothed white man.'

The immigrants to Venice came from neighbouring towns, (and what a disappointment it was to be ignored, to go unnoticed there, as Cornelio Frangipane, a mid-century writer relates at some length)[301] and from the nearby mountains and countryside (Titian came from Cadore). If the people of Friuli – the *Furlani* – were good recruits for domestic and heavy labour, and agricultural work outside the town, the criminal elements, and there were some, all or almost all came from the Romagna and the Marches. 'Tutti li homeni di mala qualità,' says a report dated May, 1587,[302] 'o la maggior parte di loro che capita in questa città sono Romagnoli e Marchiani.' Undesirable and usually clandestine visitors, they would enter the city at night by regular passages, using the services of some *barcaruol* who could not refuse his boat to men often armed with firelocks,

[297] A.d.S. Florence, Mediceo 4185, f° 171–175.
[298] D. de Haëdo, *op. cit.*, p. 8 v° (on the Kabylians) p. 9 (on the Andalusians).
[299] Ömer Lütfi Barkan, unpublished lectures given at École des Hautes Études, p. 11.
[300] B.M. Sloane 1572, f° 61, July–August, 1633.
[301] B. Gerometta, *I forestieri a Venezia*, Venice, 1858, p .9.
[302] A.d.S. Venice, Senato Terra, 101, May, 1587.

de roda, and who forced him gently or otherwise to carry them to the Giudecca, Murano, or some other island. To forbid entry to these visitors would have kept down crime, but it would have required constant vigilance and local spies.

The Venetian empire and the surrounding regions also provided a crop of immigrants: Albanians, quick to quarrel, dangerously jealous; Greeks, honourable merchants of the 'Greek nation'[303] or poor devils who prostituted wives and daughters to overcome the initial difficulties of settling in the town, and who developed a taste for this easy living;[304] *Morlachi* from the Dinaric mountains. The Riva degli Schiavoni was not only a point of departure. Towards the end of the century Venice became even more oriental with the arrival of Persians and Armenians,[305] of Turks too, who from the middle of the sixteenth century had been quartered in an annex of the palace of Marco Antonio Barbaro[306] until the *fontico dei Turchi* was established in the seventeenth century. Venice also became a halfway house, which might be more or less temporary, for Jewish families of Portuguese origin who were travelling from northern Europe (Flanders or Hamburg) towards the East.[307] Venice was also the refuge of exiles and their descendants. The descendants of the great Scanderbeg still lived there in 1574: 'the race survives . . . in respectable circumstances'.[308]

These indispensable immigrants were not always unskilled labourers or men of little aptitude. They often brought with them new techniques that were as indispensable as their persons to urban life. The Jews, driven out by their religious beliefs not their poverty, played an exceptional role in these transfers of technology. Jews expelled from Spain, at first retail merchants in Salonica and Constantinople, gradually built up their businesses until they were competing successfully with Ragusans, Armenians, and Venetians. To these two great eastern cities they brought the art of printing, the woollen and silk industry,[309] and, if some statements are to be believed, the secret of manufacturing gun-carriages.[310] These were useful gifts! It was also a handful of Jews who, when expelled from Ancona by Paul IV, made the admittedly relative fortune of the Turkish port of Valona.[311]

There were other valuable immigrants, itinerant artists for instance

---

[303] G. Hernandez to the king, Venice, 17th June, 1562, Simancas E° 1324, f° 136; N. Iorga, *op. cit.*, p. 136. Alongside the Greeks were Armenians, Circassians, and Wallachians.

[304] M. Bandello, *op. cit.*, IV, p. 68.

[305] Nicolò Crotto to Antonio Paruta, Angora, 2nd May, 1585; Cucina to Paruta, Venice, 16th April and 25th June, 1509. A.d.S. Venice, *Lettere Com.* 12b, and N. Iorga, *op. cit.*, p. 19.

[306] G. d'Aramon, *op. cit.*, p. 3.

[307] F. de Vera to Philip II, Venice, 23rd November, 1590, A.N., K 1674.

[308] P. Lescalopier, *op. cit.*, p. 29.

[309] G. Botero, *op. cit.*, I, p. 103.

[310] J. W. Zinkeisen, *op. cit.*, vol. III, p. 266.

[311] G. Botero, *op. cit.*, I, p. 99.

attracted by expanding towns which were extending their public buildings; or merchants, particularly the Italian merchants and bankers, who activated and indeed created such cities as Lisbon, Seville, Medina del Campo, Lyons and Antwerp. An urban community needs all sorts and conditions of men, not least rich men. Towns attracted the wealthy just as they attracted the proletariat, though for very different reasons. In the complex process, much discussed by historians, of *inurbamento*[312] it is not only the poor *contadini* who flock to the nearby town, but also the noblemen, the rich, landed proprietors. The brilliant work of the Brazilian sociological historian, Gilberto Freyre, affords a valuable comparison. The first Brazilian towns eventually attracted the *fazendeiros*, house and all. There was a total removal to the town. In the Mediterranean, too, it is as if the town absorbed both lord and manor at once. A lord of Siena would have his country seat in the Maremma and his *palazzo* in Siena, as Bandello has described it for us, with its hardly-used ground floor and its state rooms where silk was making its triumphant first appearance.

These palaces are the visible evidence of a chapter of history which preceded a new exodus from the towns by the rich, the return to the fields, orchards, and vineyards, the 'bourgeois' search for fresh air, which was so evident at Venice,[313] Ragusa,[314] Florence,[315] Seville,[316] and generally in the sixteenth century. This was a seasonal emigration: even if he frequently visited his country house, the lord who had built his palace in the city was now a city-dweller. The country house was merely another luxury, and often a question of fashion. 'The Florentines,' wrote the Venetian ambassador Foscari in 1530, 'go out into the world. When they have made 20,000 ducats, they spend 10,000 on a *palazzo* outside the city. Each follows his neighbour's example . . . and they have built so many palaces, all so magnificent and sumptuous, outside the city, that together they would make a second Florence.'[317] There was a similar pattern at Seville. The *novelas* of the sixteenth and seventeenth centuries make frequent mention of the villas outside the city and their splendid feasts. Much the same were the *quintas*, with their trees and running waters outside Lisbon.[318] These fancies and caprices might give way to more reasoned decisions of greater consequence.

In the seventeenth and even more in the eighteenth century, what happened in Venice was a reconversion of rich city-dwellers to the virtues of real estate. Venice in the time of Goldoni let her most beautiful urban palaces fall into decay while all expense was concentrated in the villas

---

[312] I am thinking in particular of J. Plesner's book, *L'émigration de la campagne libre de Florence au XIIIe siècle*, 1934.
[313] H. Kretschmayr, *op. cit.*, II, 194.
[314] N. de Nicolay, *Navigations et pérégrinations orientales, op. cit.*, p. 157, on the Ragusan houses at Gravosa with their groves of orange and lemon trees.
[315] See note 317.
[316] Mateo Aleman, *De la vida del picaro Guzman de Alfarache*, 1615, I, p. 24 and 29.
[317] Quoted by G. Luzzatto, *op. cit.*, p. 145.
[318] B.M. Sloane, 1572.

on the banks of the Brenta. Only the poor remained in the city in summer, the rich were on their estates. Fashions and fancies, here as always when the rich are concerned, are only part of the story. Villas, country houses, where the landlord lived side by side with his farmhands, *bastides* as they were called in Provence, were so many steps towards a social takeover of the countryside by the money of the towns. This was a large-scale movement which did not spare the fertile lands of the peasant farmers. At Ragusa, where so many peasant contracts are preserved in the official registers, in Languedoc, in Provence, there can be no doubt about it. The map of the Provençal *commune* on the banks of the Durance which appears in Robert Livet's thesis, shows it at a glance. The land surrounding the village of Rognes was from the fifteenth century, even more later on, riddled with *bastides*, each surrounded by a fairly large estate: in the sixteenth century they belonged 'to *forains*, that is, landowners who did not live at Rognes. For the most part they were from Aix', the new rich of Aix-en-Provence.[319]

So there was an alternating ebb and flow between town and countryside. In the sixteenth and seventeenth centuries the flow was from country to town, even where the rich were concerned. Milan, becoming a city of nobles, changed its character. At the same time, the Turkish landowners of the *čiftliks* abandoned their villages and their serfs for the neighbouring cities.[320] At the end of the sixteenth century, many Spanish noblemen left their lands to go and live in the cities of Castile, particularly Madrid.[321] The change in climate between the reign of Philip II and Philip III, attributable to so many variations, was not unconnected with the arrival of the Spanish nobility in the urban centres where until then they had only temporarily taken up residence. Does it explain the so-called feudal reaction under the successor of the Prudent King?

Urban political crises. These problems, the grey history of the towns' day-to-day existence, do not have the dramatic allure of the political conflicts into which the progress of the century unmercifully plunged them one after the other. But we should not exaggerate this spectacular aspect of history. Above all, we should beware of judging it according to the feelings of the people of the time, who were either executioners or victims, beware of judging it as harshly as Pisa judged Florence for example, but should aim to understand the process that crushed, or appeared to crush them. For although the states triumphed, the cities survived, and remained as important after as they had been before their chastening.

Chronicles and political histories recount an interminable catalogue of urban catastrophes. Their casualties were not merely institutions, habits, local vanity; but economies, the creative skills, the happiness even of urban communities. But what collapsed was not always very solid in the

[319] R. Livet, *op. cit.*, p. 157.
[320] R. Busch-Zantner, *op. cit.*, see below Vol II, Part II, ch. V, Societies, section on *čiftliks*.
[321] L. Pfandl, *Introducción al siglo de oro*, Barcelona, 1927, p. 104–105.

first place; conflicts were often resolved without recourse to violence, without apparent drama, and the new and sometimes bitter fruit was a long time ripening.

For the first signs we have to go back to the beginning of the fifteenth century, at least in Italy, which here again was remarkably ahead of the times. Within the space of a few years Verona fell to the Venetians in April, 1404;[322] in 1405 Pisa surrendered to Florence;[323] in November, 1406, Padua was taken by Venice,[324] which then captured Brescia in 1426 and Bergamo in 1427, on the borders of the Milanese; these cities now became the western outposts, constantly on the alert, of the Venetian *Terraferma*.[325]

Years passed: internal crises, undying quarrels, the economic difficulties that preceded and followed them caused even Genoa to totter. In forty years, from 1413 to 1453, fourteen revolutions broke out in the city.[326] The prize was tempting: the king of France seized it in 1458; then the Sforza in 1464; Genoa liberated herself from her masters, then recalled them, first the Sforza then the kings of France. Meanwhile her empire in the Black Sea was slipping away. Nearer home she lost Leghorn. Miraculously she recovered in spite of these blows,[327] almost giving herself to France and François I, then under Andrea Doria going over to Spain in 1528; adopting then an oligarchic constitution.[328] But even before that date, she was strong enough to defend her possessions and seize those of others. In 1523 the Genoese militia took Savona; from 1525 to 1526[329] the conqueror relentlessly attacked her prey, demolishing the breakwater, filling up the harbour, then after an abortive revolt by the town, which would willingly have delivered itself up to the Turks,[330] knocking down its towers in 1528, with the intention of building fortresses.[331] But by then much greater catastrophes had taken place.

The year 1453 saw the fall of Constantinople; symbolic in more ways than one; in 1472 Barcelona capitulated to the troops of John II of Aragon; in 1480 the king of France peacefully gained control of Provence and Marseilles; Granada fell in 1492, These were the years of the collapse of the city-states, too narrowly based to resist the onslaught of the territorial states who were henceforth to play the leading roles. At the beginning of the century some towns had captured other towns, enlarging their territory: Venice was building up the *Terraferma*, Milan the Milanese, Florence was becoming Tuscany. But from now on the conquerors were

[322] H. Kretschmayr, *op. cit.*, II, p. 251.
[323] G. Vivoli, *op. cit.*, II, p. 52.
[324] H. Kretschmayr, *op. cit.*, II, p. 254.
[325] *Ibid.*, p. 337–338.
[326] A. Petit, *André Doria . . ., op. cit.*, p. 6.
[327] *Ibid.*, p. 32–33.
[328] *Ibid.*, p. 261 ff.
[329] Cf. note 331.
[330] P. Egidi, *Emanuele Filiberto*, 1928, p. 114.
[331] Scovazzi and Nobaresco, *Savona*, according to a review in *Rivista Storica*, 1932, p. 116.

the Turks, the Aragonese, the king of France, the joint monarchs of Aragon and Castile.

Now and again the cities made a comeback, but only very briefly: Pisa was conquered in 1406, became free in 1494; subjugated again in 1509, she was abandoned by her inhabitants who emigrated en masse to Sardinia, Sicily, and other regions.[332] Elsewhere new fires were kindled. In 1521 at Villalar the proud and vigorous cities of Castile were brought to heel. In 1540 it was the turn of Perugia, which yielded to the Pope in the course of the *Guerra del Sale*, an inglorious fiscal war.[333] At the same period, towards 1543, the catastrophic debts of the Neapolitan towns were responsible unaided for the suspension of their last remaining liberties.[334] Aquila in the Abruzzi was a mutilated corpse, at least since Philibert of Chalon had deprived it in 1529 of its precious *castelli* and tolls for forty miles around.[335] At the beginning of the seventeenth century, Alonso de Contreras,[336] who commanded a handful of Spanish soldiers garrisoned there, shamelessly insulted the local magistrates. This quarrel of precedence could perhaps be described as one of the last sparks of the fires that had raged for over two centuries.

What disappeared in the course of this prolonged crisis? The mediæval town, the city state, mistress of her own fate, set in the centre of her surrounding gardens, orchards, vineyards, wheatfields, and nearby coasts and roads. And she vanished as historical landscapes and realities do, leaving behind extraordinary survivals. The Venetian *Terraferma* remained a federation of towns with their liberties, tolls, and semi-independence. The same was true of Lucca, which we can see through the eyes of Montaigne, without smiling too much at the military vigilance of the tiny republic. Better still let us stop at Ragusa. At the height of the sixteenth century, Ragusa was the living image of Venice in the thirteenth century, one of the city-states of which formerly there were so many along the trading shores of Italy. The old urban institutions were in place, intact, and the precious documents which correspond to them are still today in perfect order. When as historians we complain that sixteenth-century documents are never in the right place, we may blame negligence, fires, destruction, and pillage, for they have all played their part. But we should also blame, far more, the transition from the city-state to the territorial state, with all the institutional upheavals it brought. At this moment in time the city-state with its meticulous discipline was no longer in control and the territorial state had not yet replaced it – except perhaps in Tuscany where the 'enlightened despotism' of the Medicis hastened the transition.

[332] G. Botero, *op. cit.*, p. 39.
[333] On Perugia cf. the studies by Tordi and A. Bellucci and *Archivio storico italiano*, vol. IX, p. 114 ff.
[334] *Arch. storico italiano*, vol. IX, p. 47.
[335] On this minor episode of urban history see the studies by Leopoldo Palatini, Visca, and Casti.
[336] *Les aventures du capitaine Alonso de Contreras, 1582–1633.* Published by Jacques Boulenger, 1933, p. 222 ff.

But at Ragusa, the unchanging city, everything is in remarkable order in the Palace of the Rectors: judicial papers, registers of certificates, property deeds, diplomatic correspondence, marine insurance, copies of bills of exchange. If there is any chance of understanding the Mediterranean in the sixteenth century it is in this unique city, which has the added advantage that Ragusan merchantmen sailed the whole sea, from Islam to Christendom, from the Black Sea to the Pillars of Hercules and beyond.

But was what is so perfectly preserved at Ragusa reality or illusion? Ragusa agreed to pay tribute to the Turk. This was the condition on which she saved her trading posts scattered throughout the Balkans, her riches, and the precise mechanism of her institutions. She was neutral, and therefore in a good position during the troubled years of the century. She was heroically and skilfully neutral let it be said: she could stick to her guns, plead her çase, and offer prayers to Rome and Christendom, for was she not a fervently Catholic city? To the Turks she spoke firmly. The master of a Ragusan ship which was quite unjustifiably captured by the corsairs of Algiers complained, shouted, and argued so much that one day his captors threw him into the sea with a stone around his neck.[337] Even neutrals cannot always have everything their own way.

There can be no doubt of the illusion in the case of Lucca, a thinly disguised Spanish protectorate in the Milanese. It was the only town in Italy, said Cervantes with candour, where the Spaniards were loved.[338]

But these exceptions merely prove the rule. The cities were unable to survive intact the prolonged political crisis of the fifteenth and sixteenth centuries. They had suffered major upheavals and had to adapt themselves. They might, like Genoa, in turn surrender, betray, negotiate, lose their identity only to recover it, give or sell themselves to another power; or they might struggle, as Florence did, with more passion than lucidity; or, as Venice with a superhuman effort managed to do, they might struggle and what was more stand firm. But they all had to adapt; it was the price of survival.

The privileged banking towns. The victorious states could not take control of and responsibility for everything. They were cumbersome machines inadequate to handle their new superhuman tasks. The so-called *territorial economy* of textbook classification could not stifle the so-called *urban economy*. The cities remained the driving forces. States that included these cities had to come to terms with them and tolerate them. The relationship was accepted the more naturally since even the most independent cities needed the use of the space belonging to territorial states.

Even the whole of Tuscany could not support unaided the super-rich Florence of the Medici. It did not produce even a third of the city's annual consumption of wheat. The apprentices in the shops of the *Arte della Lana* came from the Tuscan hills, but also from Genoa, Bologna, Perugia,

[337] D. de Haëdo, *Topographia* . . ., p. 173 v°.
[338] *Novelas ejemplares*, 'Licenciado Vidriera', I, p. 263, (Eng. trans., p. 150).

Ferrara, Faenza, Mantua.[339] Until about 1581–1585 investments of Florentine capital (the *accomandite*) flowed all over Europe, and even as far as the East;[340] colonies of Florentine merchants were present on almost all the important exchanges, much more influential in Spain than has usually been assumed, predominant at Lyons, in a commanding position even at Venice at the beginning of the seventeenth century.[341] After the accession of the Grand Duke Ferdinand in 1576 there was a more explicit search for new outlets, not the least amazing of which were the cruises of the San Stefano galleys or the agreements with the Dutch to exploit Brazil or the Indies.[342]

The great cities of the sixteenth century with their agile and dangerous capitalism were in a position to control and exploit the whole world. Venice cannot be explained simply by her *Terraferma* or her empire of shores and islands, although she exploited them with tenacity. She lived in fact off the great Turkish Empire, as the ivy draws its nourishment from the tree to which it clings.

Nor did Genoa rely upon her poor rivieras, east and west, to feed her rich appetite, or upon Corsica, a precious but awkward possession. The real drama of the fifteenth and sixteenth century did not lie in the political fortunes of the city, which were merely a consequence and frequently a façade. The real drama was that Genoa lost one empire only to gain another. And the second in no way resembled the first.

Genoa's first empire was essentially composed of trading colonies. In this connection we must leave aside for a moment Werner Sombart's theory on the feudal and agricultural expansion of the mediæval Italian towns, culminating in the consolidation of vast territorial domains, which is undoubtedly true of Syria, Crete, Cyprus, Chios, where the Genoese remained until 1566. But Genoa made her real fortune from the colonies she had settled beyond Constantinople, at the edge of the Byzantine empire, at Kaffa, Tana, Soldaia, and Trebizond. These were her overseas trading stations. Tabarka, on the North African coast, built up by the Lomellini, was to be another, draining away to Genoa the fabulous rewards of coral fishing, still thriving in the sixteenth century, a strange citadel of trade.

Genoa's second empire looked westwards and was based on very ancient centres, old and powerful merchant colonies which merely had to be maintained – in Milan, Venice, Naples. At Messina in 1561 the Genoese colony received a large share of profits from the wheat, silk, and spice trades. Officially according to a consular document, this amounted to 240,000 crowns a year.[343] Ten, twenty, or thirty of these colonies were scattered all around the Mediterranean.

But the empire that compensated Genoa for her losses in the East at

[339] According to Maurice Carmona's unpublished thesis on Florence and Tuscany in the seventeenth century.

[340] Maurice Carmona, 'Aspects du capitalisme toscan aux XVIe at XVIIe siècles' in *Revue d'Hist. moderne et contemporaine*, 1964.

[341] See above, esp. p. 322.   [342] See above p. 106 and note 4.

[343] The consul Raffaelo Giustiniano to the Doge and governors of Genoa, Messina, 3rd June, 1561, A.d.S. Genoa Lettere Consoli, Messina, 1–2634.

the end of the fifteenth century was built up in Spanish territory, at Seville, Lisbon, Medina del Campo, Valladolid, Antwerp, and America. Its founding charter at Seville was the 1493 convention signed between Genoa and the Catholic Kings;[344] it recognized the right of Genoese colonies to elect a consul of their own nation, *consulem subditorum suorum*, and to change him when they wished. These western colonies that were to affect so profoundly and penetratingly the financial and fiscal affairs of Spain on the eve of her American greatness, were quite separate from the others; in fact they were colonies of bankers. Genoa compensated for her commercial defeat in the east by a financial victory in the west.

It was through the art of *cambios* that the Genoese were to set up Sevilian trade with America; that they were very early to seize control of the great monopolies of salt and wool; that they were to have a stranglehold on the government of Philip II himself from mid-century on. Was this a triumph for Genoa? One cannot entirely say so. This financial empire, whose net spread over the whole of the western world with the setting up of the Piancenza fairs in 1579, like the London Stock Exchange in the nineteenth century, was the creation of the great patrician families, the *Nobili Vecchi*, rather than of the city of Genoa, which they had firmly held an unhappy captive since 1528. Despite the new nobility, popular feeling, and the great opportunity of 1575, she did not succeed in shaking off their hold. This extraordinary financial aristocracy devouring the known world was the greatest enterprise undertaken by any city in the sixteenth century. Genoa seemed to lead a charmed life. She had no fleet of her own, at least no adequate fleet: but benefited from the timely arrival of Ragusan cargo vessels and the barques of Marseilles. She lost her Black Sea colonies, then Chios, which had been the centre of her trading operations in the Levant in 1566. But the register of the *caratti del mare* from 1550 to 1650 indicates that she was still receiving silk from central Asia and white wax from Russia and the 'Khazaria' just as she had in the thirteenth and fourteenth centuries.[345] The Turks no longer negotiated 'wheat treaties' with her, but she still consumed Turkish grain on occasion. The seventeenth century saw an economic regression, but Genoa remained powerful and aggressive, declaring herself a free port in 1608.[346] These miracles were all brought about by money, no simple miracle itself. Everything flowed into this city of the rich. A few *carati* of a Ragusan ship[347] were bought, and it was at the service of the *Dominante*. A little money was invested at Marseilles and the barques of the whole Provençal coast were offering their services. Why should silk not come to Genoa from the depths of Asia? The price was only a little precious metal.

[344] A.d.S. Genoa, Giunta di Marina, Consoli nazionali ed esteri, 1438–1599.

[345] R. di Tucci, 'Relazioni commerciali fra Genova ed il Levante' in *La Grande Genova*, November, 1929, p. 639.

[346] G. Vivoli, *op. cit.*, IV, p. 23.

[347] Nicoloso Lomellino for example, owned 8 *carati* of the Ragusan ship *Santa Nunciata*, whose master was V° Basilio, Ragusa Archives Diversa de Foris, XII, f° 135, 4th May, 1596.

And Genoa, after about 1570–1580, was the centre for the redistribution of American silver, controlled by the financial lords, the Grimaldi, the Lomellini, Spinola, and so many others. The money they did not invest in their tall and splendid palaces in Genoa, they placed in land or fiefs at Milan, Naples, in the *Montferrato inferiore* (the poor mountains around Genoa did not offer very safe investments) or in government bonds in Spain, Rome, or Venice.[348] In Spain where the people instinctively disliked these haughty merchants, and where Philip II on occasion treated them as subordinates and had them seized[349] – the list of their misdeeds remains to be compiled. Marxist historiography[350] has listed the ravages of the commercial capitalism of Nuremberg in Bohemia, Saxony, and Silesia, and holds it responsible for the economic and social backwardness of these regions which were cut off from the outside world, communicating with it only through these unsuitable intermediaries. Similar charges could be levelled against the Genoese in Spain. They blocked the development of Spanish capitalism – the Malvenda of Burgos and the Ruiz of Medina del Campo were only of secondary importance and Philip II's financial advisers, from Eraso and Garnica to the Marquis of Auñón, with his newly acquired titles, prebends, and prevarications, were all nondescript men, who could be, and were, bought.

So while the territorial states and empires acquired lands in plenty, they were unable to exploit unaided the resultant huge economic units. This incapacity again opened the door to the towns and the merchants. It was they who behind the façade of subordination were making their fortunes. And even where the states could most easily become masters, in their own territory with their own subjects, they were often obliged to make shifts and compromises. Certain towns were always in a privileged position, for example, Seville and Burgos[351] under the Catholic King; Marseilles and Lyons under the Most Christian King. And so on.

Royal and imperial cities. It is not astonishing then, if despite the annexations of the territorial states, the cities of the sixteenth century, favoured both by the tide of economic advance and by the functions that the states themselves abandoned to them, should have attracted men and wealth, in some cases to an extraordinary degree.

We might stop to consider the case of Madrid; it was a late capital, supplanting Valladolid in 1560, and yielding the first place to it again, with a bad grace, from 1601 to 1606. But Madrid was to come into its own only under the prodigal and powerful reign of Philip IV (1621–1665). We might

[348] Museo Correr, Report of Santolone on Genoa, (1684).
[349] J. Paz and C. Espejo, *Las antiguas ferias de Medina del Campo*, 1912, p. 139–141 are right to single out as exemplary the arrest in November, 1582 of the Prince of Salerno who refused to go to the Fair of Medina del Campo.
[350] Laszlo Makkai, *art. cit.*, see below, p. 386, note 151.
[351] On Burgos, A de Capmany, *op. cit.*, II, p. 323–324, and the important observations by R. Carande, *op. cit.*, p. 56.

also look at Rome, on which an illuminating book has now been written,[352] but Rome was very much an exception. As cities that had made pacts with the devil, the territorial state, Naples and Constantinople are certainly more typical. They made their pacts very early, Naples from the time of the creation of the *Reame*, and certainly after the innovating reign of Frederick II (1197-1250),[353] the first 'enlightened despot' of the West; and Istanbul after 1453, before the map of Europe showed a strong England, under the Tudors, a France restored under Louis XI, or the explosive Spain of the reign of Ferdinand and Isabella. The Ottoman Empire was the first territorial state to establish itself as a major power and in a way – by the sack of Otranto in 1480 – it began the wars of Italy fourteen years before Charles VIII. Finally, Naples and Constantinople were the two most densely populated cities in the Mediterranean, urban monsters, monumental parasites. It was not until later that London and Paris emerged as great cities.

Parasites: for a state concentrates money and resources and capital cities live off this concentration; they are both its servants and, in no small degree, its *rentiers*. Sixtus V was unrealistic in wanting Rome, the urban parasite *par excellence*, to become a productive city.[354] Proof that the change was not called for is the fact that in the seventeenth century Rome was still a city living off others' earnings and still growing effortlessly[355] without having been subjected to the stern discipline of productive labour.

Naples had no equivalent in Christendom. Her population – 280,000 in 1595 – was twice that of Venice, three times that of Rome, four times that of Florence, and nine times that of Marseilles.[356] The whole of southern Italy flocked to the city, both the rich, often very rich, and the hopelessly wretched poor. The size of the population was one reason why so many luxury goods were produced there. Neapolitan goods in the sixteenth century were what would be called fancy goods today: lace, braids, frills, trimmings, silks, light fabrics (taffetas), silken knots and cockades of all colours, and fine linens. These goods travelled as far as Cologne[357] in large quantities. The Venetians claimed that four-fifths of the workers of Naples lived off the silk industry, and we know that the *Arte di Santa Lucia* enjoyed a great reputation over a wide area. Pieces of so-called Santa Lucia silk were even resold at Florence. In 1642 the proposal of sumptuary laws in Spain, which would have threatened Neopolitan exports of silk and silken goods, endangered the annual fiscal income of

[352] Jean Delumeau, *Vie économique et sociale de Rome dans la seconde moitié du XVIe siècle*, Paris, 2 vols., 1959.
[353] Georges Yver, *Le commerce et les marchands dans l'Italie au XIIIe et au XIVe siècle*, 1903, p. 1–5 and passim.
[354] J. Delumeau, *op. cit.*, p. 365 ff.
[355] K. Julius Beloch, *op. cit.*, III, p. 577.
[356] Joseph Billioud, *Histoire du commerce de Marseille*, 1951, p. 551, III, only accepts that there were 30,000 to 45,000 inhabitants in the city, while Marseilles herself claimed to have 80,000, Arch. comm. de Marseille, BB 45, f° 207, 23rd March, 1583.
[357] L. von Ranke, *art. cit.*, p. 93.

335,220 ducats.[358] But there were many other industries either already established in the city or which the vast labour force could have attracted there.

Peasants from throughout the provinces of the vast, mountainous, and pastoral kingdom flocked into the city. They were attracted by the *arti* of wool and silk; by the city's public works begun in the time of Pietro di Toledo and carried on long after him (some buildings were still unfinished in 1594)[359]; by domestic employment in the households of nobles, for it was becoming the fashion for aristocrats to live in the·city and display their wealth; if all else failed, they could always rely upon the countless religious establishments with their throngs of servants and hangers-on. By seeking employment in the city, which was to be had 'in all seasons',[360] the peasants automatically released themselves from heavy feudal obligations to an overlord who might have inherited or bought, as Genoese merchants frequently did, his title and estates, which were always on the market. As the proverb says, 'the city air brings freedom' – but not necessarily happiness or a full stomach. So the city continued to grow: 'for thirty years', says an account written in 1594,[361] 'the number of houses and inhabitants has been growing, the city has increased its circumference by two miles and the new quarters are full of buildings almost equal to the old'. But even in 1551 speculators were interested in the open land on either side of the new wall built from the Porta San Giovanni a Carbonara to Sant'Elmo, near the gardens of the Prince of Alife.[362]

Inevitably the outstanding problem in a conurbation of this size was its food supply. Through the Prefect of the *Annona* (provisions) whom he appointed after the 1550s (and who was in fact a minister of supply, in charge of purchases, maintaining stock, resale to bakers and to the itinerant oil merchants), the viceroy personally controlled this strictly municipal service.[363] The city could not have subsidized such an operation, which always ran at a loss. A document dated 1607, which seems reliable, indicates that the city spent at least 45,000 ducats a month, while her income was under 25,000.[364] Grain and oil were often retailed at a loss. Loans made up the difference, but unfortunately we do not know under what conditions. The secret of Naples's existence lies hidden in part in this deficit which was 3 million in 1596 and 9 million in 1607.[365] Was it the budget of the Kingdom (which was not improving with the years) that made up the difference? Or the strength of an economy which was still simple and robust? Or was it the arrival of northern ships[366] that stimulated

[358] A.d.S. Naples, *Sommaria Consultationum*, 31, f° 110, 111, 7th February, 1624.
[359] *Archivio storico italiano*, vol. IX, p. 247.
[360] *Ibid.*   [361] *Ibid.*
[362] A.d.S. Naples, *Sommaria Consultationum*, 1, f° 79–84, 27th February, 1551.
[363] For further details on the position occupied by this Prefect in the Neapolitan executive body, the Tribunal of S. Lorenzo, see Bartolomeo Capasso, *Catalogo ragionato dell'Archivio municipale di Napoli*, 1876, I, p. 120.
[364] *Archivio storico italiano*, vol. IX, p. 264, n. 1.
[365] B. Capasso, *op. cit.*, p. 51.
[366] Wilfrid Brulez, *op. cit.*, p. 576.

economic activity in Naples, and by bringing her wheat and fish from the North, made her daily life a little easier? This life was always beset by problems, even the supply of drinking water (brought from the springs of Formale in 1560),[367] the upkeep of the streets, or the traffic in the harbour. The breakwater which protected moored ships was by the end of the century so encumbered by refuse, by residue from sewers, and earth unloaded there by the builders of houses and public monuments, that in 1597 serious consideration had to be given not to cleaning it, but to replacing it with a new breakwater.[368] Naples was excessive in every respect. She consumed 40,000 *salme* of Apulian wheat a year, besides her other supplies, and in 1625 she imported the unbelievable quantity of 30,000 cantars of sugar (1500 tons) and 10,000 cantars of honey, re-exporting a large amount in the form of *siropate*, *paste*, and *altre cose di zucaro*, but needless to say it did not go into the mouths of the poor.[369]

We can have very little idea of all this activity. We know that the Spanish authorities thought of curbing the growth of the vast city[370] but without deciding any precise measures. Was it after all wise to suppress the 'safety valve' indispensable to the continuous simmering of the great kingdom?[371] Naples then remained an overpopulated and disquieting city. Order could never be maintained and at night the only law was that of the strong and cunning. Certainly, even if one allows for the bragging of Spanish soldiers who were always ready to let their pens run away with them,[372] it was the most astonishing, most fantastically picaresque city in the world. It was a more hard-working city than its very bad reputation gives it credit for, but that reputation was not undeserved. On one occasion action had to be taken against the vagabonds who were overrunning the town[373] and on another against the many organized bands which were already the training-grounds of the *lazzaroni*.[374]

Naples corresponded to the dimensions of southern Italy and the *Reame*; Istanbul was cast in the image of the immense Turkish empire which was so rapidly created. The city as a whole developed at the same rate as the empire. It numbered perhaps 80,000 inhabitants after the conquest in 1478; 400,000 between 1520 and 1535; 700,000 according to westerners

[367] A.d.S. Naples, Sommaria Consultationum, 1, f° 235 v°, 4th November, 1560.

[368] *Ibid.*, 13, f° 373 v°, 20th June, 1597.

[369] On Apulian grain *ibid.*, 5, 13th April, 1576; on sugar and honey *ibid.*, 33, f° 13, 135–137, 4th February, 1625.

[370] On attempts by the Spanish authorities to curb the expansion of Naples, G. Botero, *op. cit.*, I, p. 114; 22nd March, 1560, Sim. E° 1050, f° 23; 1568, Sim. S.P. Napoles, I; *Arch. st. ital.*, vol. IX, p. 247; B.N. Paris, towards 1600, Esp. 127. f° 17 and 19 v°; Guiseppe Pardi, *art. cit.*, p. 73, and Giuseppe Coniglio's essential book, *passim*.

[371] Felipe Ruiz Martín, 'Fernando el Catolico y la Inquisición en el Reino de Nápoles' in *V Congreso de la Corona de Aragon*, October, 1952.

[372] In particular Miguel de Castro, *Vida del soldado español Miguel de Castro* (Coleccion Austral), 1949, and also *Les aventures du capitaine Alonso de Contreras (1582–1633)*, *op. cit.*, esp. p. 17–20.

[373] Simancas, Napoles Est° 1038, 1549.

[374] Felipe Ruiz Martín, *art. cit.*, p. 320.

at the end of the century;[375] it foreshadowed the development of London and Paris in the seventeenth and eighteenth centuries, as privileged cities whose political preeminence permitted every kind of economic paradox, chief among which was the ability to live well above their income and the level that their internal production permitted. And indeed, like London and Paris and for the same reasons, Constantinople did not decline. The reverse occurred, in fact, during the seventeenth and eighteenth centuries.

Constantinople was not a town; it was an urban monster, a composite metropolis. Its site made it a divided city and this was the source both of its greatness and its difficulties, certainly of its greatness. Without the Golden Horn – the only safe harbour between the Sea of Marmara, which was exposed to bad weather and often rough, and the Black Sea which had a well deserved reputation as a 'punishing sea' – without the Bosporus, neither Constantinople nor its successor Istanbul would have been conceivable. But it also meant that the urban area was interrupted by successive stretches of water, and extensive sea fronts. A population of boatmen and ferrymen manned the thousands of barques, *caïques, perames, mahonnes*, lighters, and 'door-ships' (for the transport of animals from Scutari to the European side). 'Rumeli Hisar and Besiktas, to the south of the Bosporus, are two prosperous villages of ferrymen,'[376] the latter for goods, the former for passengers. For this endless, exhausting work by which the essential unity of the city was achieved, there were always vacancies. Pierre Lescalopier who arrived at Constantinople in the spring of 1574, noted: 'In the "parmes" [*perames* or ferry boats] there are Christians [slaves] who are earning their ransoms, with their masters' permission.'[377]

Of the three cities, Constantinople, or Stambul, or Istanbul, was the largest. It was the triangular city between the Golden Horn and the Sea of Marmara, shut off on the landward side by a double wall 'not in very good condition either'[378] where 'round about, there are ruins in quantity'.[379] It had a circumference of 13 to 15 miles[380] while Venice had only 8. But this urban enclosure was full of trees, gardens, squares with fountains,[381] 'meadows', and promenades, and counted over 400 mosques with lead roofs. Around each one was an open space. The Mosque of Sulaimān the Magnificent, the Sulaimānīye with 'its esplanade, its *medreses*, its library, its hospital, its *imaret*, its schools and gardens, constitutes a whole quarter in itself'.[382] Finally the houses were clustered together, low-lying, built,

---

[375] For these figures and a discussion of their reliability, see Robert Mantran, *Istanbul dans la seconde moitié du XVIIe siècle. Étude d'histoire institutionnelle, économique et sociale*, 1962, p. 44 ff.
[376] *Ibid.*, p. 84.
[377] *Voyage faict par moy Pierre Lescalopier* . . ., f° 35.
[378] G. d'Aramon, *op. cit.*, p. 93.
[379] P. Lescalopier, *Voyage* . . ., f° 31 v°.
[380] G. d'Aramon, *op. cit.*, p. 25.   [381] *Ibid.*, p. 93.
[382] R. Mantran, *op. cit.*, p. 40 and Ömer Lütfi Barkan, 'L'organisation du travail dans le chantier d'une grande mosquée à Istanbul au XVIe siècle' in *Annales E.S.C.*, vol. 17, 1962, no. 6, p. 1093–1106.

'in the Turkish fashion', of wood, 'earthen walls',[383] and half-baked bricks, their façades 'daubed in pastel colours, pale blue, pink and yellow'.[384] The streets 'are narrow, twisting and uneven',[385] not always paved and frequently sloping. People travelled along them on foot, on horseback, but rarely on wheels. Fires were frequent and did not spare even the Seray. In autumn, 1564, a single outbreak destroyed 7500 wooden shops.[386] Inside this great city lay another, the Bedesten ('bazestan'), 'like the St. Germain Fair', as Lescalopier put it, admiring the 'great staircases of fine stone and the beautiful shops selling haberdashery and cotton fabrics embroidered with gold and silk . . . and all manner of beautiful and charming things'.[387] Another was the 'Atbazar', the horse market.[388] Finally, the most sumptuous of all, the Seray, at the southern end of the city; a succession of palaces, kiosks, and gardens. Istanbul was predominantly a city of Turks, their white turbans outnumbered the others: 58 per cent of the population, in the sixteenth as in the seventeenth century. But there were also a number of Greeks with blue turbans, Jews with yellow turbans, as well as Armenians and Tziganes.[389]

On the other side of the Golden Horn, Galata occupied the ribbon running along the southern shore between the Arsenal of Kasim Paşa with 'about a hundred vaulted stone arches each long enough for a galley to be built there under cover . . .',[390] and further to the south the second Arsenal of Top Hane 'where they make powder and artillery'.[391] Galata was the port frequented exclusively by western ships; here were the Jewish commission agents, the shops, and warehouses, the famous cabarets where wine and *arak* were served; behind on the hills were the Vines of Pera, where, first among the western envoys, the French ambassador had his residence. It was the city of the rich, 'quite big, populous, built in the French style', inhabited by merchants, Latin and Greek, the latter often very rich, dressing in the Turkish style, living in grand houses, adorning their women with silk and jewels. These women, rather too given to coquetry, 'appear more beautiful than they are, for they paint their faces as much as possible and spend all their wealth on clothes, many rings on their fingers, and jewels for their head-dresses, most of which are false'.[392] Galata and Pera together, which travellers took for the same place, 'form a town comparable to Orléans'.[393] The Greeks and Latins were not masters there, far from it, but they were free to live and worship there as

---

[383] P. Lescalopier, *Voyage* . . ., f° 32.
[384] R. Mantran, *op. cit.*, p. 29.   [385] *Ibid.*, p. 27.
[386] E. Charrière, *Négociations* . . ., *op. cit.*, II, p. 757–759; cf. Tott, *Memoirs, op. cit.*, I, p. 15. For a list of twenty-two fires between 1640 and 1701, R. Mantran, *op. cit.*, p. 44 ff.
[387] P. Lescalopier, *Voyage* . . ., f° 33 v°.
[388] *Ibid.*, f° 33 v°.
[389] R. Mantran, *op. cit.*, p. 44 ff.
[390] P. Lescalopier, *Voyage* . . ., f° 37 v°, remarks that the 'arches' at the Arsenal at Venice are only about thirty in number and 'no more than wooden piles'.
[391] *Ibid.*, f° 37 v°.   [392] *Ibid.*, f° 38.   [393] *Ibid.*, f° 36 v°.

they pleased. Notably 'the Catholic religion is practised in this city in all freedom, including the Italian processions of flagellants and at Corpus Christi, the streets are decorated under the surveillance of two or three janissaries, to whom a few aspers are given'.[394]

On the Asian side, Scutari (Üsküdar)[395] was almost a third city, different from the other two. It was the caravan terminus of Constantinople, the point of arrival and departure for the great routes across Asia. The number of caravanserais and *hans* alone were a sign of this, as was the horse-market. On the sea front there was no sheltered harbour. Goods had to pass by quickly and trust to luck. A Turkish town, Scutari was full of gardens and princely residences. The sultan had a palace there, and it was a great spectacle when he left the Seray and took a frigate to the Asian side 'to enjoy himself'.[396]

A description of the whole would not be complete without mentioning the most important suburb of Constantinople, Eyüp, lying at the point where the Sweet Waters of Europe meet the Golden Horn, together with the long strings of Greek, Jewish, and Turkish villages on both sides of the Bosporus, villages of gardeners, fishermen, sailors, where the summer residences of the rich soon appeared, the *yali-s* with their stone basements and two storeys made of wood; their 'many unlatticed windows' opened on to the Bosporus where there was no indiscreet neighbour.[397] These 'houses for leisure and gardens'[398] can, not unreasonably, be compared with the villas in the countryside around Florence.

The whole formed a vast conurbation. In March, 1581, eight ships from Egypt laden with wheat only provided food for a single day.[399] Records dated 1660–1661, and 1672–1673[400] give us some idea of the city's appetite which was much the same as in the previous century. Its inhabitants daily consumed 300 to 500 tons of grain, which provided work for its 133 bakers (in Constantinople itself, out of 84 bakers, 12 made white bread); in one year almost 200,000 cattle, of which 35,000 went to make the salt or smoked meat, *pastirma*; and (one has to read the figures two or three times before one can believe them) almost 4 million sheep and 3 million

---

[394] P. Lescalopier *op. cit.*, f° 37.

[395] R. Mantran, *op. cit.*, p. 81 ff. There are many travellers' references to the horses of Scutari.

[396] Cf. P. Lescalopier, *Voyage* . . ., f° 32 v° and 33.

[397] R. Mantran, *op. cit.*, p. 85.

[398] P. Lescalopier, *Voyage* . . ., f° 32.

[399] Salazar to H.M., Venice, 5th March, 1581. Simancas E° 1339; '*Qne 8 naves que avian llegado de Alexandria cargados de grano no havian bastado para mas de un solo dia.*'

[400] R. Mantran, *op. cit.*, p. 181 ff. The documents in the Turkish collection of the Bibliothèque Nationale at Paris have been analysed for me by Halil Sahili Oglou. See the very good article by L. Gucer, 'Le commerce intérieur des céréales dans l'Empire Ottoman pendant la seconde moitié du XVIe siècle' in *Revue de la Faculté des Sciences Économiques de l'Université d'Istanbul*, vol. XI, 1949–1950, and the valuable study by Walter Hahn, *Die Verpflegung Konstantinopels durch staatliche Zwangswirtschaft nach türkischen Urkunden aus dem 16. Jahrhundert*, 1926.

lambs (the precise figures are 3,965,760 and 2,877,400); plus the barrels of honey, sugar, rice, sacks and skins of cheese, caviar, and 12,904 cantars of melted butter, brought by sea, i.e., about 7000 tons.

These figures, too precise to be accurate, too official to be entirely false, give some idea of the order of the operation. Without doubt, Constantinople drew continually on the inexhaustible riches of the empire, under a system organized by a meticulous, authoritarian and *dirigiste* government. The supply zones were chosen to suit the convenience of methods of transport, prices were fixed, and if necessary requisitioning was enforced. Strict regulations fixed the points where merchandise could be unloaded on the quays of the port of Constantinople. It was at Un Kapani, for instance, that grain from the Black Sea was unloaded. But of course all trade did not flow along these official channels. By its very size the city exercised an enormous power of attraction. We should note the role played in the grain trade by the big merchants who exploited the small transporters of the Black Sea, and that played by the Greek and Turkish captains of Yeni Köy, on the European shore of the Bosporus, or of Top Hane, near the quays of Galata, who amassed huge personal fortunes, acted as intermediaries and transporters, and were involved on more than one occasion in the contraband passage of grain to the West from the islands of the Archipelago.[401]

So Constantinople consumed the thousand products of the empire as well as the fabrics and luxury goods of the West; in return the city gave nothing or virtually nothing, except for the bales of wool and hides of sheep, oxen, and buffalo that passed through the port. It would bear no comparison with the great export centres at Alexandria, Tripoli in Syria, and later Smyrna. This capital enjoyed the privilege of the rich. Others worked on her behalf.

In favour of capitals. But one cannot launch inconsiderately into a prolonged indictment of huge cities. Or if one does, one would have to say immediately that there are perfectly good reasons for them and the historian might equally well enter a plea of not guilty on behalf of these admirable political and intellectual instruments, They are the hothouses of every civilization. Furthermore, they create an order. And this order was sadly lacking in some flourishing regions of Europe: in Germany which no town was able to control because of the immense area involved; in Italy, torn between its various urban 'poles'. Cities created by national or imperial units in turn create these units: London and Paris, for instance. Was their achievement so negligible?

The Spanish peninsula lacked a forceful capital. To make the wilful, arbitrary, and 'geometric' move from Valladolid to Madrid was not perhaps the wisest of decisions. The historian J. Gounon-Loubens[402]

[401] R. Mantran, *op. cit.*, p. 184, 189.
[402] J. Gounon-Loubens, *Essais sur l'administration de la Castille au XVIe siècle,* 1863, p. 43–44.

claimed long ago that Philip II's greatest mistake was not to have made his capital city Lisbon, where the Prudent King stayed from 1580 to 1583, then leaving it for good. He might have made it a city comparable to Naples or London. This argument has always impressed me. Philip II's court at Madrid is a foretaste of those governments that were later to set up their capitals in 'selected towns'. Philip II in the Escorial foreshadows Louis XIV at Versailles. But although it is rather a temptation to rewrite history, it is after all only a game, a method of argument by which we attempt to familiarize ourselves with an immense subject that sometimes evades our grasp.

In the sixteenth century these rather special cities, the capitals, began to emerge, but they were only to come into their own in the following century; perhaps because in the midst of a general economic recession the modern state was the only unit that could prosper in the face of adversity. From the end of the sixteenth century signs of decline were visible and a distinction was beginning to appear between those towns whose bread was assured whatever the circumstances and the others who lived entirely from their own labours. The latter were already experiencing stoppages resulting from the reduced current of economic life. The flow was beginning to decrease and the wheels to turn more slowly.

From permanence to change. However a venture into the dynamics of urban history takes us outside our original subject. The intention of this first book has been to concentrate on the constant and stable features, the well-known regular statistics, the recurrent phenomena, the infrastructure of Mediterranean life, its clay foundations and peaceful waters – at least we imagine them to be peaceful. Cities are like motors, turning over, warming up, exhausting themselves then setting off again. Their very breakdowns introduce us to that world of movement which will be the subject of Part II of our book. Their message is one of evolution and changing conditions which hints at their approaching destiny: that decline proclaimed by so many signs at the end of the sixteenth century and accentuated in the seventeenth century. Between 1500 and 1600 we might say that the urban motors had started well; but long before the turn of the century, their accelerators had jammed. Breakdowns and suspicious noises were beginning to occur although they had not yet ground to a halt.

Part Two

Collective Destinies and General Trends

My intention in the first part of this book was to explore, using the concept of geographical space, all the permanent, slow-moving, or recurrent features of Mediterranean life.

In the pursuit of a history that changes little or not at all with the passing of time, I have not hesitated to step outside the chronological limits of a study devoted in theory to the latter half of the sixteenth century. I have taken evidence from witnesses of every period, up to and including the present day. Victor Bérard discovered the landscapes of the *Odyssey* in the Mediterranean under his own eyes. But often, as well as Corfu, the island of the Phaeacians, or Djerba, the island of the Lotus-Eaters, one can find Ulysses himself, man unchanged after the passing of many centuries.[1]

From this long-term perspective the second book takes us to a history closer to the individual: the history of groups, collective destinies, and general trends. This is a *social history*, whose subject is man, human beings, and not 'things' as Maurice Halbwachs would say, or to put it another way, what man has constructed from things.

This second book has, in fact, to meet two contradictory purposes. It is concerned with social structures, that is with mechanisms that withstand the march of time; it is also concerned with the development of those structures. It combines, therefore, what have come to be known as *structure* and *conjuncture* the permanent and the ephemeral, the slow-moving and the fast. These two aspects of reality, as economists[2] are well aware – indeed it is to them that we owe the original distinction – are always present in everyday life, which is a constant blend of what changes and what endures.

But it will not be easy to convey this complex spectacle in a single attempt. The chapters that follow share the task among them, tackling in turn the problems relating to economic systems, states, societies, civilizations, the indispensable instruments of exchange, and lastly the different forms of war. But the reader should not be misled. They are all contribu-

---

[1] Gabriel Audisio, *Sel de la mer*, 1936, p. 177 ff.
[2] Jean Weiller has put his point of view in 'Les préférences nationales de structure et le déséquilibre structural' in *Revue d'Économie politique*, 1949, and returned to the question several times, notably in *Problèmes d'Économie Internationale*, vol II, 1950, and *L'Économie internationale depuis 1950*, 1965. A useful summary in the collective work *Sens et usage du terme structure dans les sciences humaines et sociales*, 1962, Mouton, p. 148 ff.

tions towards a unique, comprehensive view of the subject, impossible to achieve from any one vantage point.

These subdivisions are both convenient and necessary. They may not altogether satisfy the intellect, but any schema is of value as long as it allows for the best possible explanation with the minimum of repetition.

CHAPTER I

Economies: The Measure of the Century

The first problem is to discover the measure, the economic dimensions of the sixteenth century. The aim of this chapter can be compared with Lucien Febvre's aim in the last section of his *Rabelais*:[1] to take stock of the intellectual apparatus of sixteenth-century man, to take its measure so as to eliminate those false and distorting solutions to the problems facing the historian which so flagrantly ignore the possibilities and the intellectual level of the age. We shall find it equally valuable to discover, very broadly, what the economic apparatus of the sixteenth century was, what limits it imposed upon man's achievement, before studying what man actually constructed – or tried to construct – from these beginnings in the Mediterranean.

I. DISTANCE, THE FIRST ENEMY

Today we have too little space, the world is shrinking around us. In the sixteenth century there was too much and it could be both an advantage and an obstacle. Of all the commonplaces about the Mediterranean in which literature abounds, that it is a 'sea within the measure of man' is one of the most deceptive – as if the measure of man could be taken once and for all. The Mediterranean was certainly not within the measure of sixteenth-century man; it was only at the cost of much effort that he mastered its immense area, much as twentieth century man has found it difficult to master the Pacific.

For letter-writers: the time lost in coming and going. To have an idea of the problem, we have only to listen to the complaints of men tackling the details of their own lives. Letter writers have bitter words to say about delays in the mails, 'lo que se pierde en ir y venir', as the Empress confided to her brother, Philip II.[2] Calvin writing to del Vico, whose letter he was late answering,[3] confessed: '. . . when I think how long my letters will spend on the way, I do not know how I can have been so remiss in carrying out my duty several times'. If a letter arrives quickly, its recipient is astonished. 'To come from as far as Valencia to Granada,' writes the humanist Antonio de Guevara to a friend, 'your letter must have had swift carriers for it was sent on the Saturday and arrived here on the Monday.' A letter from the Constable of Castile reached him at Vallado-

---

[1] *Le problème de l'incroyance au XVIe siècle. La religion de Rabelais.* 1st edition, 1942, 2nd edition, 1947, p. 361 ff.

[2] 28th May, 1568, *CODOIN*, XXVII, p. 6.

[3] 19th July, 1558, *Lettres de Jean Calvin*, published by Bonnet, 1854, p. 207.

lid, again in record time: 'If it had been a trout it would still have been fresh.' The image was one that pursued him, for several years later he wrote to the Marquis de los Velez, 'your letter arrived here very quickly, fresher than the salmon which they brought us from Bayonne'.[4] These are the exceptions which as always prove the rule.

Statesmen and ambassadors, whom we usually imagine with weighty matters on their minds, are often preoccupied by the arrival or delays of the mail. On 24th February, 1575, Don Luis de Requesens writes from Antwerp to Don Diego de Zuñiga, Philip II's ambassador at Paris: 'I do not know how your Lordship fares for letters from Spain; for myself, I have heard nothing from the king concerning the affairs of the Netherlands since 20th November last . . . His Majesty's service has suffered greatly by it.'[5]

The arrival or imminent arrival of the mails could become an obsession. Even the ordinary post did not have a fixed hour, sometimes not even a fixed day. 'I am waiting for the regular Flanders mail to go past at any hour,' notes Chantonnay in December, 1561.[6] This obsession was not of course peculiar to the ambassadors of the Catholic King. It is a waste of time, writes the Cardinal de Rambouillet to Charles IX,[7] to hasten to send us letters, 'because of the knavery and negligence of the postmasters in carrying Your Majesty's dispatches . . . which is such and so great . . . that the said dispatches often spend a month or six weeks on the road between the Court and Lyons. So that when I receive them, the time when I could have availed myself of them and had occasion to execute the orders contained in them is often, to my very great sorrow, past . . .'. We find similar complaints from Fourquevaux. 'Five or six couriers, bearing the king's arms,' he writes from Madrid in January, 1567,[8] 'natives of the said Lyons, who sometimes carry the regular mail for Rome, say that they are in the service of Monsieur de Nemours when they are on the road. This is an order to get better treatment from the postmasters.' But they would carry money and dispatches for bankers of any nationality. One of them for example, 'came with all speed these last days to the 'gennevois'[9] attached to this [the Spanish] court, to bring them letters from other 'gennevois' bankers living in the said Lyons'. Meanwhile the letters of the king of France stayed on the road. Another time, the correspondence suffers because of the 'masters of the Landes'[10] and uncommon delays always result. Longlée, Henri III's agent in Spain, indicates in February, 1584, that he has been without news of his government for two weeks[11] but 'that

---

[4] Antonio de Guevara, *Epistres dorées, morales et familières traduites d'espagnol en français par le seigneur de Guterry*, 1558, p. 79, 40, 63; in Spanish in *Biblioteca de autores españoles (B.A.E.)*, 1850, vol. XIII, p. 86, 96, 103.
[5] A.N., K 1337, B 38, no. 15, copy.
[6] To Philip II, Poissy, 21st December, 1561, A.N., K 1495, B 13; no. 105, original.
[7] Rome, 30th January, 1570, B.N., Paris, Fr 17 989, f° 142.
[8] 5th January, 1567, *Dépêches de Fourquevaux*, III, p. 31.
[9] i.e., Genoese.
[10] Longlée to Villeroi, Barbastro, 8th December, 1585, ed. Albert Mousset, *op. cit.*, p. 211.
[11] The same to the same, Madrid, 1st February, 1584, *ibid.*, p. 17.

many [letters] have remained at Burgos coming from the direction of Valladolid'. All kinds of accidents and incidents were possible. It might be that two ordinary mails failed to make the connection;[12] or that the normal routes had been interrupted; or that the couriers, forwarned of brigands, refused to travel at night. Every time, this would mean unexpected delays in distant places. The viceroy of Naples is without instructions, the government of the Prudent King does not know what is happening in the Netherlands; and the Venetian ambassador at Madrid remains sixty days without news from Italy.[13]

These were no doubt exceptional cases, resulting from human error, local circumstances, or bad weather, but it was an 'exception' frequently repeated, which aggravated an already tense situation. The struggle against distance might remain a matter of constant vigilance, but it was also one of chance and luck. At sea a favourable wind and a spell of fine weather might make the difference between taking six months for a voyage or completing it in a week or two. Pierre Belon sailed from the Sea of Marmara to Venice in thirteen days, a journey which frequently took half a year.[14] Similarly on land, where the differences are less remarkable, a war, a state of alert, roads flooded by heavy rain, or passes blocked by a snowfall could mean that even the most liberal estimates would be exceeded. Distances were not invariable, fixed once and for all. There might be ten or a hundred different distances, and one could never be sure in advance, before setting out or making decisions, what timetable fate would impose.

In fact, men of the sixteenth century were resigned to every kind of delay. A letter travelling from Spain to Italy was as likely to go by Bordeaux and Lyons as by Montpellier and Nice. A letter sent to Henri IV by Monsieur de Villiers, his ambassador in Venice in April 1601, arrived at Fontainebleau by way of Brussels.[15] During the 1550s the King of Portugal's ambassadors at Rome often sent their letters by way of Antwerp.[16] This was because the length of the journey depended less on the distance travelled than on the quality and frequency of the mails. And after all everyone was used to it. Three or four days' delay was neither here nor there. At the end of 1587, when the 'Prince of Béarn's' Protestants were occupying the Limousin, regular communications between Bernardino de Mendoza in Paris and Philip II's government were interrupted. Dispatches

---

[12] Villeroi to J. B. de Tassis, Paris, 31st January 1584, original A.N., K 1563.

[13] A.d.S., Venice, Senato Dispacci Spagna, P° Priuli to the Doge, Madrid, 19th November, 1612.

[14] Pierre Belon, *Les observations . . .*, p. 78.

[15] Eugène Halphen, *Lettres inédites du roi Henri IV à M. de Villiers*, 1887, p. 25.

[16] Or the letter from Fr. Jorge de Santiago to the king, sent from Bologna, 28th May, 1548, 'Porque pola via de Frandes que sera mais em breve por ser posta, escrevemos carta comun a Vossa Alteza . . .', *Corpo diplo. port.*, VI, p. 254. Cf. the lines from J. Nicot to the King of France, Lisbon, 28th May, 1561: 'News has come from Alexandria to Flanders, and from there here that there is great disturbance and mutiny in the Indies . . .,' E. Falgairolle, *Jean Nicot, ambassadeur de France au Portugal au XVIe siècle, Sa Correspondence inédite*, 1887, p. 148.

had to be sent by new routes, along which unfortunately there was no organized postal service, 'por donde no hay postas'. In the margin of the letter informing him of these circumstances, Philip II wrote, 'it is more important that the letters should travel by a safe route than that four or five days be gained, except on occasions when speed is essential'.[17]

The dimensions of the sea: some record crossings. The available figures vary a great deal. What is more they only rarely form coherent series. The best one can say is that some notion of 'pure' distance can be obtained by noting exceptional crossings which give, as it were, the minimum dimensions of the sea.[18]

The fastest speeds, 200 kilometres or more per day, were hardly ever attained except by sea,[19] in fair weather and preferably in well-manned galleys, such as the one Don John of Austria sent from Messina in June 1572, which reached the Catalan coast (Palamos) in six days.[20] This was at a crucial moment: Don John's object was to obtain at all costs the cancellation of Philip II's order to remain inactive at Messina with a large part of the fleet. The galley sailed alone and was well armed: according to a Tuscan correspondent she sailed 'sempre per golfo senza toccar terra',[21] straight ahead all the time without putting in to land, so it must have been a direct crossing. The feat was not unique. Two years earlier, and in winter, Gian Andrea Doria had crossed from Genoa to Palamos in five days; the distance and the speed were less but the obstacles overcome were comparable.[22] And sixty years earlier Cardinal Cisneros had made the 200 kilometre crossing from Oran to Cartagena in a single day, Wednesday 23rd May, 1509. This was a miraculous voyage, 'como si tuviera el viento en la manga',[23] as if he had had the winds at his command 'up his sleeve'. This was near the speed of the 'providential' voyages from Rhodes to

[17] B. de Mendoza to Philip II, Paris, 28th November, 1587, A.N., K 1566, marginal note in Philip's hand.

[18] To deduce daily speeds from times taken for the overall journey is not easy, since we rarely know the exact route followed. I have got around this obstacle by calculating speeds based on the distance as the crow flies by sea, and on land, on present-day distances. This has the obvious disadvantage of underestimating distances actually travelled.

[19] Except for the incredible relay races between Rome and Venice, a distance of over 400 kilometres, of which there were three between 1496 and 1530, according to Pierre Sardella: time taken one and a half days, an hourly speed of 10 to 15 kilometres. The average time for the journey was four days. See the tables in Pierre Sardella, *op. cit.*, and the table reproduced on p. 362.

[20] See below, Part III, Ch. IV. Nobili to the prince, Barcelona, 24th June, 1572, A.d.S. Florence, Mediceo, 4903.

[21] G. del Caccia to the prince, Madrid, 30th June, 1572, A.d.S., Florence, Mediceo, 4903.

[22] Leonardo Donà to the Senate, Madrid, 21st December, 1570, in *La corrispondanza da Madrid dell' ambasciatore Leonardo Donà, 1570–1573*, ed. Mario Brunetti and Eligio Vitale, 1963, I, p. 167.

[23] L. Fernandez de Retaña, *Cisneros y su siglo*, 1929–1930, I, p. 550. A similar time, two days, for the voyage from Oran to Valencia was achieved by the Venetian galleys in October, 1485, A.d.S., Mantua, Genova 757, 3rd November, 1485.

Alexandria, which, according to Belon[24] took less than three days and nights – and in ordinary merchant vessels.

On land, with some exceptions, record speeds fell short of those achieved by sea, but were a more regular occurrence, so that for postal communications the overland route, although more expensive, was preferred to the sea route. The fastest speeds in Europe were probably reached by the couriers working for the postal service organized by Gabriel de Tassis on the Italy–Brussels route, via the Tyrol; this was a route that had been carefully planned, halts were kept to a minimum, and, particularly in the Eifel, well-known shortcuts were regularly used. The itinerary in itself was a record. And its 764 kilometres were covered in five and a half days, that is at about 139 kilometres a day.[25] This falls short of the exceptional speeds reached by sea, but exceeds by far the usual speed for the overland route. By way of comparison, the sensational news of the St. Bartholomew Massacre (24th August, 1572) travelled from Paris to Madrid at rather less than 100 kilometres per day: it reached Barcelona on 3rd September and was only known in the Spanish capital on the evening of the 7th.[26]

On the other hand, the rate at which important news travelled can be a good indication of record speeds, for it often travelled on wings.

The capture of Nicosia, 9th September, 1570, was known in Constantinople on 24th September; in Venice, via Ragusa, on 26th October and in Madrid on 19th December.[27]

News of Lepanto, 7th October, 1571, reached Venice on 18th October, Naples on 24th, Lyons on 25th, Paris and Madrid on 31st.[28]

The Turco-Venetian peace treaty, agreed secretly on March 7th, 1573, and announced at Venice on 4th April[29] was known at Rome on 6th April, Naples on 8th, and Palermo and Madrid on 17th.[30]

[24] *Op. cit.*, p. 93 v°. Various examples: A. Thomazi, *Histoire de la navigation*, 1941, p. 26; Victor Bérard, *Pénélope . . ., op. cit.*, p. 181; G. de Toledo to the king, Sobre Denia, 16th July, 1567, Sim. E° 149, f° 22; '. . . por tener por mucho mas breve el camino de la mar que el de la tierra.' This conviction led Don Garcia into mistakenly thinking when he left Sicily for Spain, that it was not worth while informing the king by land: but he left on 27th June, and did not arrive at Denia until 16th July. On the higher costs of the overland route we have the revealing example of present day costs: surface transport from America to Genoa is cheaper than the transport of the same goods on the shorter distance to inland areas of Italy.

[25] E. Hering, *Die Fugger*, 1940, p. 66. On the services of Thurn and Tassis, see map 102, *Zur Geschichte der deutschen Post (1506–1521)* in Putzger's *Atlas.*

[26] St.-Gouard to Charles IX, Madrid, 14th September, 1572, B.N., Paris, Fr. 16105. Paris–Barcelona: 1001 kilometres; Paris–Madrid 1060.

[27] Fourquevaux to the king, Madrid, 19th December, 1570, *Dépêches . . .*, II, p. 307.

[28] And not on 8th November, the date given in R. B. Merriman, *The Rise of the Spanish Empire*, New York, 1918, IV, p. 145; C. Douais, *Dépêches de Fourquevaux*, II, p. 97; Nobili to the Prince, 16th November, 1571, A.d.S., Florence, Mediceo, 490.

[29] G. de Silva to the king, Venice, 4th April, 1573, Sim. E° 1332.

[30] 7th April, 1573, *CODOIN*, C II, p. 72–81; 8th April, 1573, Sim. E° 1332; 17th April, 1537, Palmerini B. Com. Palermo, Qq D 84; 23rd April, A. Vat. Spagna 7, f° 198–199; Candia, 25th April, Capi del C° dei X Lettere Ba 285, f° 165; Philip II to G. de Silva, Madrid, 25th April, 1573, Sim. E° 1332; 22nd May, news of the treaty

News of the capture of La Goletta and Tunis, 25th August, 1574, reached Vienna on 1st October, just as Pierre Lescalopier was arriving there, having left Istanbul on a diplomatic mission and crossed Bulgaria, Wallachia, and Transylvania before arriving exhausted in the Habsburg capital. The news gave him reason to reflect. He had seen this victorious Turkish armada leaving Constantinople on the previous 15th May, only two weeks before his own departure.[31] How much it had accomplished while he had been on the road!

The length of these journeys as measured in waves of communication around Nicosia, Lepanto, Venice, and Tunis provides at best only approximate measurements. From our first example it would appear that the Mediterranean was ninety-nine days long – but this is surely too much. In fact, the news took some time to reach the outside world from Nicosia on the besieged island, and we may be sure that Venice was in no hurry to pass word on to the West. Any measurements must in fact be treated with caution and cannot be regarded as accurate when confined to a single figure. We must remember what we are measuring. The speed of news and the passage of letters is only one aspect of the battle against distance.

Average speeds. Our task becomes very much harder when we leave the question of record speeds for averages. Even when supported by documents, how can average speeds mean very much when we know that the length of any one voyage could vary from twice to three, four, even seven or ten times the shortest time recorded? The essential point to note here is this very variety, the wide range of times taken to travel the same journey: it is a *structural* feature of the century. The modern transport revolution has not only increased the speed of travel to an extraordinary degree; it has eliminated (and this is also important) the uncertainty imposed in the past by the elements. Today bad weather merely means a certain amount of inconvenience. Only in exceptional circumstances does it affect timetables. In the sixteenth century all timetables were completely dependent on the weather. Irregularity was the rule. A Venetian ambassador on his way to England in January 1610 waited for fourteen days at Calais facing a sea so rough that no ship dared put out.[32] To take another, very minor incident, the ambassador Francesco Contarini, travelling from Venice to take up his post at the Turkish capital in 1618,[33] took six hours to cross the wide but shallow river Maritsa, and then not without difficulty. In June, 1609, a Venetian ship bound for Constantinople had to stand for eighteen days

---

was published at Constantinople, G. Mecatti, *Storia cronologica della Città di Firenze*, Naples, 1755, II, p. 753.

[31] *Voyage faict par moy Pierre Lescalopier*, f° 41 and 64 v°.

[32] London, Public Record Office, 30/25 f° 65, Francesco Contarini to the Doge, Dover, 26th January, 1610. Copy.

[33] London, Public Record Office, 30/25 f° 46: Voyage of Francesco Contarini to Constantinople.

off the open beach of Santa Anastasia in the shelter of Chios, waiting for the bad weather to abate.[34] We should therefore beware of reading too much into these strange averages with their specious finality. Their only advantage is that they carry a simple message, speak to the imagination, and help us to see back into the days before the modern transport revolution, of whose tremendous effects we are not always aware. To consider average speeds is to discover what the prospect of a journey meant to a contemporary of Philip II.

The sea-crossing from Constantinople to Alexandria took about a fortnight including calls at port, a week not counting stops.[35] It was only two days' sail from the castles of the Hellespont to the island of Chios.[36] In October or November, 1560, a Ragusan roundship left Messina and reached Alexandria 'fra novi giorni', and this time is not presented as a record.[37]

The sea-crossing in the central zone varied according to the season, the ship, and the route. The same boat that sailed from Malta to Tripoli in Barbary in nine days, took seventeen days to return from Tripoli to Messina.[38] In April, 1562, a *nave* made the trip from Tripoli to Sciacca on the south coast of Sicily in six days.[39] A series of voyages from Tunis to Leghorn (one in 1600, two in 1608, eight in 1609, two in 1610) took the following times: six, seven, eight, nine, nine, nine, ten, eleven, twelve, thirteen, fourteen, fourteen, and twenty days, i.e., an average of about eleven days. The two fastest crossings – six days and seven days – as if to confound expectations were accomplished by a *nave* in January 1600, and by a barque in July, 1609.[40]

We have little information about the length of crossings from Marseilles to Spain on the one hand and North Africa on the other. They were often undertaken in secret. Using the royal galleys, the French king's ambassador d'Aramon took a week to sail from the Balearics to Algiers, in fair weather (at least after the second day).[41] Two voyages in 1609 and one in 1610 on the Algiers–Leghorn route lasted respectively thirteen, fifteen, and five days:[42] five to fifteen – so one voyage was three times as long as the other.

The difference could be very great over long distances. A Venetian roundship sailed in October–November, 1570,[43] from Crete to Otranto in

---

[34] Tommaso Alberti, *Viaggio a Constantinopoli*, published by Albert Bacchi della Lega, Bologna, 1889, p. 13.
[35] Belon, *op. cit.*, p. 93 v°.
[36] *Ibid.*, p. 85.
[37] Ragusa Archives, Diversa di Cancellaria 146, f° 46 v°, 8th January, 1561.
[38] 25th January–3rd February–10th April–27th April, 1564, Simancas E°, 1393.
[39] 16th–22nd April, 1562, Simancas E° 1052, f° 26.
[40] A.d.S., Florence, Mediceo 2079, f° 212, 271, 274, 296, 297, 302, 304, 308, 311, 320, 323, 333, 405, 408. A Spanish text of December, 1595 (B.N., Madrid, MS 10454. f° 34), however, states that one can cross from Sicily to Africa in a few hours; the galleys of Gian Andrea Doria sailed in a day from La Favignana to La Goletta (see below II, Part III, ch. 4, Lepanto, section 3. But these were galley times.
[41] N. de Nicolay, *Navigations, pérégrinations et voyages* . . ., Antwerp, 1576, p. 12.
[42] A.d.S., Florence, Mediceo 2079, f°s 305, 306, 345.
[43] Cadiz, 2nd June, 1561, Simancas E° 140.

Elasticity of news
(after Pierre Sardella)

I	II	III	IV	V	VI	VII	VIII
Alexandria	266	19	89	65	55	17	323
Antwerp	83	13	36	20	16	8	200
Augsburg	110	19	21	11	12·	5	240
Barcelona	171	16	77	22	19	8	237
Blois	345	53	27	14	10	4½	222
Brussels	138	24	35	16	10	9	111
Budapest	317	39	35	18	19	7	271
Burgos	79	13	42	27	27	11	245
Calais	62	15	32	18	14	12	116
Candia	56	16	81	38	33	19	163
Cairo	41	13	10	7	8	3	266
Constantinople	365	46	81	37	34	15	226
Corfu	316	39	45	19	15	7	214
Damascus	56	17	102	80	76	28	271
Florence	387	103	13	4	3	1	300
Genoa	215	58	15	6	6	2	300
Innsbruck	163	41	16	7	6	4	150
Lisbon	35	9	69	46	43	27	159
London	672	78	52	27	24	9	266
Lyons	812	225	25	12	13	4	325
Marseilles	26	7	21	14	12	8	150
Milan	871	329	8	3	3	1	300
Naples	682	180	20	9	8	4	200
Nauplia	295	56	60	36	34	18	188
Nuremberg	39	11	32	20	21	8	262
Palermo	118	23	48	22	25	8	312
Paris	473	62	34	12	12	7	171
Ragusa	95	18	26	13	14	5	280
Rome	1053	406	9	4	4	1½	266
Trano	94	14	30	12	12	4	300
Trento	205	82	7	3	3	1	300
Udine	552	214	6	2	2	1½	133
Valladolid	124	15	63	29	23	12	191
Vienna	145	32	32	14	13	8	162
Zara	153	28	25	8	6	1	600

Column I shows the places in communication with Venice; Column II, the number of cases observed; Column III the number of normal cases; Column IV the maximum time (in days); V, the weighted arithmetical average (in days); VI the normal time in days; VII the minimum time in days; VIII the normal time as an expression of the minimal time (min. = 100), in other words, the relation between the minimum time and the normal time.

twelve days; another, in May–June, 1561,[44] sailed almost the entire length of the Mediterranean from Crete to Cadiz in a month. But in July 1569, two galleys from Algiers reached Constantinople only after seventy-two days at sea. A roundship that left Alexandria on 7th January, 1564, arrived at Messina on 5th April; her voyage had lasted eighty-eight days. The 'normal' figure in the fifteenth century for the Venice–Jaffa voyage

[44] 2nd June, 1561, Simancas E° 140. That is 80 kilometres a day.

was of the order of forty to fifty days, according to one historian.[45] But the average time for the voyage from Venice to the Holy Land that emerges from Röhricht's figures, discussed in a previous chapter[46] was very much longer.

The *portate* of Leghorn[47] have some information to give us. For five voyages from Alexandria to Leghorn (two in 1609, one in 1610, two in 1611) they give the following figures: twenty-three, twenty-six, twenty-nine, thirty-two, and fifty-six days, i.e., an average of thirty-three days. For eight voyages (five in 1609, three in 1610) from Cartagena or Alicante to Leghorn we have the following figures: seven, nine, nine, ten, fifteen, twenty-five, thirty, and forty-nine days, i.e., an average of nineteen days. One might therefore say, *with a modicum of truth*, that the voyage from Spain to Leghorn to Alexandria could take about fifty-two days,[48] but we cannot call this figure an average.

Talking in averages then, we may draw the very general conclusion that the Mediterranean crossing from north to south could be expected to take one or two weeks; and that it was likely to be a matter of two or three months if one were sailing from east to west or vice versa. We might add moreover that these were to remain the dimensions of the sea throughout the seventeenth century and even later.

Letters: a special case. It would clearly be more useful to have a homogeneous series of measurements than these rather unsatisfactory approximations. And we have a very ample one in the letters (yet again) sent by governments, ambassadors, merchants, and private citizens. Between 1497 and 1532, Marino Sanudo, who was always well informed of the actions of the Signoria of Venice, kept a faithful record of the arrival of letters and news, which provides us with a total of 10,000 usable figures. This huge mass of material has been subjected to statistical analysis by Pierre Sardella[49] and the results are summarized in the table on p. 362 and the map on p. 366. Even so, one has to be a little careful in interpreting information that relates only to news *arriving* at Venice and beware of reading too much into it.

Quite clearly, the area measured is heterogeneous, and far from *isotropic*. If one took the distance from Venice to Paris as a radius and described a circle with Venice as its centre, one would be in theory defining an *isotropic* circular area within which news (like light, but slower) would travel at an identical speed from all points on the circumference to the centre. But of course what we have is nothing of the sort. News was held up by natural obstacles, such as the Alps, the Straits of Dover, the sea. Fast speeds depended on the goodwill, calculation, and needs of men. During the period 1497 to 1532, Venice hung on the decisions of the French

---

[45] Dr. Sottas, *op. cit.*, p. 183.   [46] See above, p. 265.
[47] That is the harbour records of the arrivals of boats and merchandise.
[48] A.d.S., Florence, Mediceo 2080.
[49] *Nouvelles et spéculations à Venise*, 1948.

king, on any rumours and news from France, and from Paris these precious packets raced towards her.

Our maps and averages impose an artificial regularity on the journeys travelled by these dispatches. In fact, their movements were extremely unpredictable: the very wide range of times taken (see column VIII, relation of normal to minimum times) would be even wider if one compared minimum times with maximum times. A surprising detail is that the coefficient of irregularity seems to be in inverse proportion to the distance travelled. It also increases, but that is to be expected, when a sea-crossing is involved. So it is not astonishing that Zara should hold the record (a ratio of 1 to 6), since it falls into both categories: it was near Venice, but separated from her by the unpredictable Adriatic crossing.

In short, this table provides us with a basic framework for comparison and verification. Its only disadvantage (or advantage, depending on which way one looks at it) is that all the times it establishes are relatively fast ones. They testify to the vigilance and indeed the means available to a city as rich as Venice. They correspond to an alert system of communications. For Venice, the news from Paris, Valladolid, or Constantinople was not a matter of curiosity but of essential information.

If we look to other records we nowhere find the same briskness. Letters from every city in Europe piled up on the desks of Philip II. It was customary to record on the back of the last page (*la carpeta*),[50] the dates of dispatch and of arrival, as well as the equally interesting but infrequently noted date of sending the reply. Hundreds of thousands of examples are therefore available for statistical analysis. Philip II, apart from his few well-known voyages to Córdoba, Lisbon, Saragossa, Barcelona, or Valencia, hardly stirred from the centre of Castile after his return from the Netherlands in 1559. If there is sometimes uncertainty as to the whereabouts of his correspondents or the route followed by the letters, these are points that can usually be cleared up.

I was tempted to use these data to compile a set of measurements comparable to Pierre Sardella's, again with Venice as the centre of the coordinates. From a sample of forty cases at the end of the century, the correspondence of Spain's representatives at Venice, the shortest time taken on the Madrid–Venice route (which can be assumed roughly equal to the Valladolid–Venice route of Sanudo's day) is twenty-two days (as against twelve days recorded by Sanudo) and the longest time eighty-five days (omitting one aberrant case of 145 days). The arithmetical average (unweighted) is forty days (as against Sardella's weighted average of twenty-nine days). Over the distance Constantinople–Venice, 16 recorded cases during the same years give a minimum length of twenty-nine days, a maximum of seventy-three and an average time of about forty-one-and-a-half days.[51] These figures are nearer, but still higher than Sardella's (which

[50] See below at the end of the chapter the reproduction of a *carpeta*.

[51] The preceding calculations are based on the correspondence of Spaniards living in Venice between 1589 and 1597 preserved (before the war) in the Archives Nationales,

were of course obtained from a much larger number of examples). Should we conclude that at the end of the sixteenth century communications along the length of the Mediterranean were still as difficult and hazardous as they had been at the beginning? More evidence is needed before we can say so with certainty.

What we can say is that in both sets of calculations, mine and Sardella's, Venice figures as very roughly a halfway point between Madrid (or Valladolid) and Constantinople. The sum of the average time taken over each half – forty and forty-one-and-a-half days according to the Spanish figures, twenty-nine and thirty-seven days, according to Sanudo's – gives us a Mediterranean world either eighty or sixty-six days long, a figure certainly greater than the arbitrary time of fifty-two days obtained by adding the Alexandria–Leghorn time to the Leghorn–Cartagena time.[52] Of course they are not strictly comparable since the distance from Alexandria to Cartagena is not the same as the distance, also reconstructed, from Constantinople to Venice to Madrid. But we shall have to accept that we cannot measure the sea with any great degree of accuracy even with the valuable aid of the correspondence of statesmen and merchants.

News, a luxury commodity. News, a luxury commodity, was worth more than its weight in gold. 'No courier', wrote his agent at Venice to the Duke of Ferrara, 'will accept less than a ducat per letter'[53] and this was between two neighbouring cities, Venice and Ferrara. At the beginning of the sixteenth century the tariff between Venice and Nuremberg[54] varied according to the time taken: four days, 58 florins; four days and six hours, 50; five days, 48; six days, 25 (we might note in passing that the fastest speed recorded for this trip by Sardella is two days longer than the last). These were evidently ultra-fast communications available only to rich merchants, in that early part of the sixteenth century when it is probably true to say that price differences between one market and another were greater than ever. It was worth paying even large sums of money to be able to send an

---

Paris, K 1674, 1675, and 1676, and at Simancas E° 1345. I have taken some examples from the Lettere Commerciali, 12 *ter* A.d.S., Venice. N.B. the journey from Ragusa to Constantinople took about a month in winter. The average length suggested in a contemporary estimate (A.d.S., Venice, Papadopoli, Codice 12, f° 26 v°, about 1587) is over-optimistic: in summer the voyage from Constantinople to Cattaro took about 16 or 17 days . . . '*Da Cataro poi a Venetia con le fregate ordinarie secondo i tempi ma ut plurimum in otto giorni*', a total then of 24 or 25 days. On the Venice–Madrid route, here are some figures taken from the correspondence of two Venetian ambassadors at Madrid, P° Priuli and P° Gritti: on 19th November, 1612, P° Priuli had been without news for 60 days; two letters received at Madrid on 5th and 9th December, 1612, had taken respectively 18 and 27 days, both having been sent from Venice by express courier; in 1616 and 1617 ,the times taken by letters to reach Gritti were: 33, 45, 21, 27, 26, 20, 20 days . . ., A.d.S., Venice, Senato Dispacci.
[52] See above p. 363 and note 48.
[53] A.d.S. Modena, Cancellaria Ducale d'Este, Venezia, 77. VI/10. J. Tebaldi to the Duke of Ferrara, Venice, 19th January, 1522.
[54] K. O. Müller, *Welthandelsbräuche 1480–1540*, 2nd impression, 1962, p. 29.

Figs 28, 29, and 30: *News travelling to Venice*

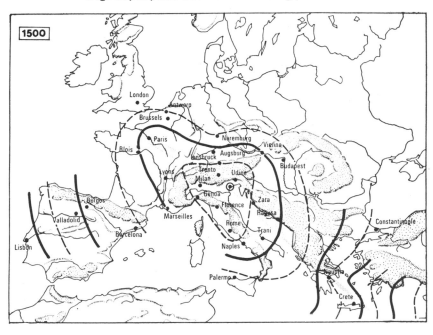

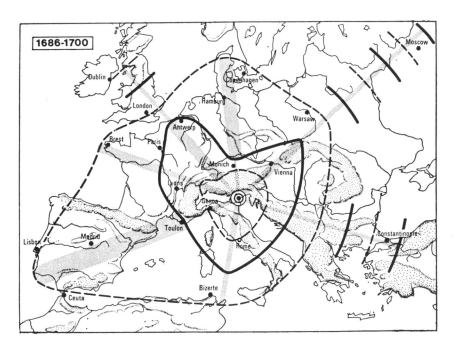

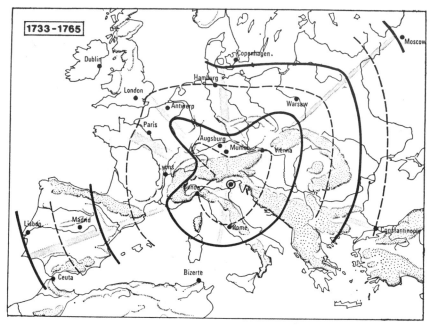

The isochronic lines representing intervals of *one week*, give a broad indication of the time required for the dispatch of letters which in all three diagrams are travelling *towards* Venice.

The first map is based on the research of Pierre Sardella (Cf. p. 363, note 49) about 1500, to be precise 1496–1534. The second and third maps are based on the evidence of Venetian *avvisi* in the Public Record Office at London where they were analysed for me by Frank Spooner.

The width of the shaded lines increases with the average speed of communications.

The differences from one map to another may seem very marked in certain directions. They are a result of the varying frequency of communications, depending on the urgency of the circumstances. Generally speaking, communication seems to be as slow on the third map as on the first while the second shows noticeably shorter delays. But it cannot be regarded as definite proof. Theoretically speeds should be compared over distances defined by comparable isochronic lines. But such distances cannot be ascertained with sufficient accuracy. However if one imagines the maps as being superimposed on each other, they are very roughly equivalent, an extension in one direction being compensated by a reduction in another. Needless to say, the step from areas expressed in square kilometres to daily speeds should only be taken with extreme caution.

order off at top speed. Later on the situation became more settled. The correspondence of Simón Ruiz during the second half of the sixteenth century gives the impression that the rapid dispatch of orders and information was no longer as important as it had been in the past.[55] Only

[55] The exception that confirms the rule is that the Genoese sent special couriers from Madrid to Antwerp, in order to profit from the 'largezza' in the North. V. Vázquez de Prada, *op. cit.*, I, p. 36.

rich bankers or governments could afford such luxuries, the price of which continued to rise throughout the century. On July 14th, 1560,[56] Chantonnay, who was then Philip II's ambassador at the French Court, sent a courier from Chartres to Toledo and back; in all he covered 179 stages and was paid a total of 358 ducats (2 ducats a stage). This was an enormous sum of money, much more than the annual salary of a professor at the University of Padua or Salamanca! The stages must have been about 10 or 12 kilometres each and if the courier covered them at a rate of 18 leagues a day[57] it is clear that we have briefly glimpsed a journey accomplished in record time. Rich men could buy superhuman achievements.

In the end we must acknowledge the paradox of measuring the delays imposed by distance by studying the dispatch of letters. Even at their slowest these precious goods moved faster than any other travellers.

This is one argument against undertaking a systematic analysis of the postal records of Philip II's bureaucracy or a study of the letters of the merchant Simón Ruiz (about 100,000).[58] For neither operation is likely to produce anything very new. Letters depended both on regular and irregular mails, and the former were the more important statistically. Any survey of correspondence would sooner or later lead us to the regular postal services, whose official times we already know. The Tassis firm undertook to transport letters from Rome to Madrid in twenty-four days, between 1st April and the end of September; in twenty-six days during the winter season. It is somewhere near these figures that we can locate not the average time taken by the letters of merchants and ambassadors[59] (for the promises of the postmasters were only rarely kept) but the upper limit of normal speeds. Using these times as a guide, we can, with the help of surveys such as Valentin Vázquez de Prada's[60] (of the Madrid–Antwerp route) calculate and predict the actual range of speeds.

A second and very considerable reason why we should refrain from plunging into this morass of calculations is that again, taking Venice as a centre and using the *avvisi* which Venetians sent in an unending stream and which are still preserved in manuscript in the *Archivio di Stato*, the *Marciana*, and even the Public Record Cffice in London – one can produce maps of communications in the seventeenth and eighteenth centuries very similar to that deduced from Sanudo's information. Frank Spocner

[56] Simancas *Consejo y Juntas de Hacienda*, 28; in a list of Chantonnay's expenses, entry dated 14th July, 1560.

[57] Francés de Alava to the king, 6th March, 1567, A.N., K 1507, n° 70, quoted by H. Forneron, *Histoire de Philippe II*, 1881, vol. II, p. 219, n. 1. This courier was sent by the Netherlands rebels to Montigny, who was then i n Spain, see V. Vázquez de Prada, *Lettres marchandes d'Anvers*, 1960, I, p. 40.

[58] Henri Lapeyre, 'El Archivo de Simón y Cosme Ruiz' in *Moneda y Credito*, June, 1948.

[59] British Museum, Add. 14009, f° 38, Consulto de Consejo de Italia, Madrid, 2nd October, 1623.

[60] V. Vázquez de Prada, *Lettres marchandes d'Anvers*, I, p. 241–242.

has produced two maps covering the periods 1681–1701 and 1733–1735, which establish the zones covered by Venice's information system.[61] The speeds at which news travelled are on the whole similar to the speeds of 1497–1532, a little faster than this in the seventeenth century and a little slower in the eighteenth.

The conclusion is therefore plain to see. One might have hoped to find in these records a 'conjunctural' measure of physical distance, peculiar to the sixteenth century, but we can see even without completing our analysis that distance was a constant; that this is yet another structural feature persisting over long periods of time. However man tackled the obstacle of distance, splintering the oars of close-manned galleys, driving the post-horses to death, or apparently flying over the waves under a fair wind, he always met with passive resistance and distance took a daily revenge for his most strenuous exploits. We may still be curious, as contemporaries were, to hear of record speeds: the news of Charles IX's death travelled from Paris to Cracow in thirteen days, as Sully himself[62] tells us and the 'king of Poland' forsook his subjects the next day . . .; news of the birth of a grandson for François I took only two days to reach Lyons from Fontainebleau (420 kilometres)[63] and a Turkish *estafette* on one occasion covered the distance between Istanbul and Erzurum in eighteen days exhausting many of its horses en route,[64] 'con far creppar molti cavalli'. All these records and many more tell us something and it is useful to be able to compare them with everyday average speeds.[65] But the essential point to bear in mind is that both average and record speeds remained sensibly the same before and after the sixteenth century. Goods, boats, and people travelled as fast, or as slowly, in the days of the Avignon Popes[66] or to Venice during the first half of the fifteenth century,[67] as they did in the age of Louis XIV. Major change and advance did not occur before the end of the eighteenth century.

[61] Calculations and maps by Frank Spooner based on my information. A map of relative distances in the sixteenth century could be drawn up, cf. R. Gascon, *op. cit.*, notably p. 308, for one centred on Lyons.

[62] *Mémoires du Duc de Sully*, (re-edited) 1822, I, p. 68.

[63] R. Gascon, *op. cit.*, (typescript) p. 318.

[64] A.d.S., Venice, the *bailo* to the Doge, Constantinople, 8th August, 1605.

[65] R. Gascon, *ibid.*, p. 308, gives the following (average) speeds for the sixteenth century: goods travelled at 17 to 44 kilometres a day (44 on the road from Lyons to the Low Countries through Amiens; 17 on the road to Burgos across the Massif Central); travelling up the Saône, 14 to 25 kilometres a day, and down the Rhône as much as 90. Between Roanne and Tours, transport was swift, 65 kilometres per day. Average speed of travellers on horseback, 40 kilometres a day, in the mail coach 90. Fast couriers to Italy between 170 and 200.

[66] Yves Renouard, 'Comment les Papes d'Avignon expédiaient leur courrier' in *Revue historique*, 1937; see in particular the table on p. 59 (off-print): these speeds, writes the author, 'are as far as we know the fastest of the period'. N.B. also their high price, *ibid.*, p. 29. For conclusions similar to those of this paragraph see Armando Sapori, *Studi di storia economica*, 3rd ed., 1955, p. 635–636.

[67] Frederic C. Lane, *Andrea Barbarigo, merchant of Venice (1418–1499)*, 1944, p. 199 ff.

Present-day comparisons. 'Taking all factors into account', writes an economist,[68] 'one is led to the conclusion that the area corresponding to the "world" economy in Roman times could be travelled from end to end in about forty to sixty days, using the fastest means of transport; it was an area which extended from the Pillars of Hercules to the borders of the Parthian kingdom and from the mouth of the Rhine to the edge of the African desert. Today [in 1939] it again takes from forty to sixty days to travel the area covered by the modern world economy, using normal goods transport and omitting territories which are economically insignificant and lack means of transport'.

I would not personally endorse these measurements nor the figures offered by the same writer for the speed of road travel in the Roman period, in the region of 50 kilometres a day.[69] But we cannot hope for precise measurements; at most we shall discover an order of magnitude. In this respect the Mediterranean was still broadly speaking the same size in the sixteenth century as it had been in Roman times, that is, over a thousand years earlier. Or to put it another way, the Mediterranean in the sixteenth century was comparable, *mutatis mutandis*, to the entire globe in 1939. It was vast, immeasurable, and its reputation as a 'human' area was earned only by contrast with those other monsters which sixteenth-century man was just beginning to tackle – the Atlantic Ocean, not to mention the Pacific. These were truly monsters, alongside which the Mediterranean was more like a domestic animal, but certainly not the 'lake' it has become in the twentieth century, the sunny resort of tourists and yachts where one can always reach land within a few hours and along whose length the traveller could be transported in the Orient Express. To understand what it was like in the sixteenth century, one must mentally magnify its area to a maximum and draw on remembered images from travellers' tales of the days when months, years, even a whole lifetime, could be spent on a voyage.

Twentieth-century parallels are not hard to find. Take for instance, the journeys of the Tartar merchants described by Aldous Huxley in his *Jesting Pilate*. They travel over the Himalayas to Kashmir and India, first filling their purses with gold coins, ten-rouble pieces from before the Russian revolution, according to Huxley.[70] Romantic characters: in their precautions I am reminded of voyages to Syria in the sixteenth century, the land at the far end of the Mediterranean where two mutually suspicious worlds met face to face. Bills of exchange were of no value here. All transactions were settled either by barter or by cash payments. Merchants had to arrive at the rendezvous armed with gold or silver like these present-day Tartars.

Will the reader suspect me of a facile paradox if I say that I was curiously reminded of France during the Wars of Religion by the spectacle of China

---

[68] Ferdinand Fried, *Le tournant de l'économie mondiale*, 1942, p. 67–68.
[69] *Ibid.*, p. 66–67.
[70] *Jesting Pilate. The diary of a journey*, London, 1927, p. 36–38.

in the first decades of this century, with its monstrous civil wars, foreign invasions, massacres, and famines, and its towns set in the midst of a vast countryside, defensive towns, surrounded by walls whose gates were closed at night? A band of partisans could, by slipping between the towns, make its way unchallenged from upper Szechwan right down to Shantung. It was in a similar setting that France under the last of the Valois saw her strength ebb away, as she was overrun by bands of adventurers, French or foreign. All wealth is consumed in the end, and yet if any nation was wealthy in the sixteenth century it was France – a land flowing with plenty! Giovanni Botero[71] calculated to his astonishment the number of soldiers, whether officially recruited or not, who must have been living there, plundering the immense kingdom, the vast land of sixteenth-century France. A Venetian document of the same period mentions 'the flood of foreigners under arms now entering France'.[72]

This may seem an odd digression. But it is one way of conveying the notion of almost unlimited space, a rather difficult concept for the modern imagination to apply to the Mediterranean. It is not enough merely to repeat the expressions used by German economic historians: *Welttheater* and *Weltwirtschaft* – perfectly legitimate terms though they are – which are readily applied both to the historical and the living Mediterranean to convey its self-sufficiency, a 'world-economy' with its diameter of sixty days' travel, troubling the rest of the world and particularly the Far East only for luxury goods. Our object is to discover the dimensions of this world, and the way in which these dimensions have determined both its political and economic structure. We shall find that a constant effort of the imagination will be needed.

Empires and distance. An understanding of the importance of distance leads one to view in a fresh light the problems of administration in sixteenth-century empires.

And, in the first place, there was the enormous Spanish empire, which depended on what was for the period an unprecedented combination of land and sea transport. It required not only continual troop movements but the daily dispatch of hundreds of orders and reports. The policy of Philip II necessitated these troop movements, transfers of bullion and bills of exchange, all fundamental concerns that in turn help to explain a great many of Philip's actions and in particular why France was of key importance to him. It has always been customary to say of France that she was surrounded by Habsburg possessions. But if their empire could threaten her from without she could threaten it from within, and who shall say which was the greatest peril? France under François I and Henri II had been hostile and closed to Spain; except for his swift passage through in 1540, Charles V all his life gave France a wide berth. Between 1559 and 1589, on the other hand, for thirty years, the road through France was

[71] G. Botero, *op. cit.*, II, p. 8 ff.
[72] A.d.S. Venice, *Annali di Venezia*, f° 185, 26th September, 1578.

more than half-open to the services of Philip II's diplomatic and financial staff. And if the Prudent King did not himself set foot outside Spain, sitting at the centre of his web, it was for many reasons, the financial and economic predominance of Castile and the vital link with America, for example, but it was also because the French frontier was no longer completely closed to his envoys.

So to look over Philip II's shoulder as he deals with his papers, means constantly being aware of the dimensions of France, for him an intermediary zone; it means becoming familiar with the postal services, knowing which routes have regular stages and which have not; noting the delays in the mails caused here and there by the civil wars; measuring their extent, duration, and relative importance; and also learning the detours taken by money, particularly bills of exchange on their way to banking centres.

A state had indeed to wage not one but many struggles against distance. The Spanish Empire, which was poorly situated from the point of view of its European and world possessions, expended the better part of its energy in these struggles. And yet it was better adapted than any other to these necessary tasks and better organized to deal with them. Although much criticized, the Spanish Empire was equal or indeed superior to other leading states for transport, transfer, and communications. It is curious, to say the least, that from the 1560s on, it employed a sort of specialist in troop and goods transport, in the person of Francisco de Ibarra, about whom and his emulators it would be interesting to know more.

Historians have paid too little attention to the gigantic tasks demanded of the Spanish administrative machine. They have noticed only the 'delays' of *el rey papelero*, the bureaucratic king 'with feet of lead', 'himself both master and secretary, which is a great virtue . . .' as the bishop of Limoges wrote of him in 1560,[73] and 'wholly devoted to his affairs, never losing an hour for he is all day among his papers',[74] the overworked king who even a quarter of a century later was still unwilling to abandon his superhuman task in spite of the protests of Cardinal Granvelle[75] who wished in vain for innovations.[76]

So we must distinguish between the different kinds of 'delays' in Spain. There were delays resulting from the mail: reports were delayed on the way in and replies and instructions were delayed on the way out. No government could escape these delays and Spain was particularly vulnerable. But over equal distances Spanish communications were on the whole a match for anyone's. If they had weaknesses they were shared. The

[73] Communication from bishop of Limoges to the cardinal of Lorraine, 27th July, 1560, in L. Paris, *Négociations . . . relatives au règne de François II*, I, p. 49.

[74] *Ibid.*, p. 562, the bishop of Limoges to the cardinal of Lorraine, 26th September, 1560.

[75] Martin Philippson, *Ein Ministerium unter Philip II, Kardinal Granvella am spanischen Hofe*, (1579–1586), 1895, p. 76.

[76] Memorie politiche dal 1576 al 1586, Marciana, 7299, 18th March, 1584, '*Che il Re di Spagna haveva molti ministri che desiderano novità come il Cardinale Granvella et don Joan di (Idiaquez)*'.

Turkish Empire, for instance, was also a sum of delays laid end to end. It took sixteen or seventeen days to travel from Constantinople to the Adriatic, to Cattaro or Spalato, at full speed.[77] In the Black Sea, the *Mar Maggiore*, both itinerary and the length of voyage were extremely unpredictable. In the Aegean, or the White Sea, as the Turks called it, the fastest times recorded seem ridiculously slow. Even in 1686 it was considered worthy of note (in December, it is true) that a Turkish galley should have sailed from Constantinople to Negropont in eight days.[78] Sulaimān Pasha's fleet took two months to cross the Red Sea in 1538.[79] Some of these distances remained invariable, requiring the same time for centuries. Pegolotti in the *Pratica della Mercatura* (1348) says that it takes twelve to thirteen days to travel from Trebizond to Tauris on horseback, thirty to thirty-two days by caravan. In 1850, Goedel, the Austrian consul at Trebizond, claims that the same route takes twenty-seven to thirty days by caravan 'when the road is in good repair'.[80]

A second source of delay was the deliberation and discussion preceding the dispatch of orders. Here all the contemporary evidence is in agreement: French men and Italians felt temperamentally alien when they set foot in this land of phlegmatic Spaniards who were as long in making up their minds as they were skilful at dissembling. That does not mean to say that the image, though familiar, is necessarily correct. The view of a nation that a foreigner may form and express is frequently as unshakeable as it is misleading. But it does seem that the dilatoriness of the Spanish government, or as the bishop of Limoges called it, 'the lengthiness of this country'[81] is beyond question. When news of Drake's exploit at Cadiz was brought to Rome in 1587, the Pope exclaimed 'that his Majesty was a man of little vision who never made up his mind until the occasion had passed'. At Paris, 'this remark has not only been much repeated, but it has also been published along with the added jibe that the queen of England's spinning wheel is worth more than the king of Spain's sword'.[82]

This was malicious talk no doubt. However, if we turn once more to diplomatic correspondence, it seems that the French government, for example, was more prompt in the execution of its affairs. But was this necessarily the fault of the king in Madrid who insisted on reading everything? Spain lay at the centre of an empire whose boundaries stretched much further than those of France (or England). Philip II had to wait for

[77] A.d.S., Venice, Papadopoli collection, Codice 12, fᵒ 26 vᵒ (1587), the average time taken by the letters of the Venetian *bailo*, according to a contemporary statistician, to travel between Constantinople and Cattaro.

[78] London, Public Record Office, 30/25, 21, Venice, 14th December, 1686.

[79] Florence, Laurentiana, Ashb. 1484. 'La retentione delle galee grosse della Illustrissima Signoria di Venetia . . .'.

[80] Details and reference to Pegolotti in W. Heyd, *Histoire du commerce du Levant*, II, p. 120, note 3.

[81] 3rd July, 1561, B.N., Paris, Fr. 16103, fᵒ 3 vᵒ: 'la tardità con quale caminano qua tutti i negotii', G. de Nobili to the Duke, Madrid, 20th March, 1566, A.d.S. Florence, Mediceo 4898, fᵒ 41.

[82] B. de Mendoza to J. de Idiaquez, Paris, 16th July, 1587, A.N., K 1448.

reports to arrive from very distant places before taking decisions. At this point both kinds of delay met together. The Spanish bureaucratic machinery turned over at its own deliberate pace, but also suffered from the delays of shipping in the Atlantic, the Indian, and even the Pacific Oceans; in fact, it had to respond to the workings of the first economic and political system that spanned the known world. This was one reason why the pulses of Spain beat at a slower pace than others. After 1580 and the annexation of Portugal, these pulses beat even slower. Let us pause to reflect with Sassetti, the Florentine who travelled to the East Indies in 1585 and has left us his valuable correspondence: if people had any idea, he wrote from Cochin on 27th January, 1585, to his friend Piero Vettori at home in Florence, what the seven-month voyage is like, 'living off ships' biscuit and brackish water, confined in a small space with 800 or 900 other people, all suffering from hunger, thirst, sea-sickness and discomfort',[83] few would be eager to sail to the Indies. But there it is, when one sees a boat one is filled with the urge to sail on it. And the king of Spain's orders had to endure the seven months of this voyage and many more besides.

So there can be no doubt: Spain waged an unremitting struggle against the obstacle of distance, one that tells us more than any other source about the 'measure of the sixteenth century'.

The three missions of Claude du Bourg (1576 and 1577). A small example will illustrate the point. It concerns a French adventurer, Claude du Bourg, a rather shadowy and puzzling figure. Was he a genius or merely an accentric? Perhaps one day someone will find out from the many unpublished documents in the Bibliothèque Nationale.

It is not so much his character that here concerns us though, as the three rather curious trips he made to Spain: the first in May, 1576, the second in September–October of the same year, and the third in July–August, 1577. On the first two occasions he was acting on behalf of the Duke of Alençon, and no doubt in his own interests too, negotiating in the prince's name the possibility of his marriage to one of the Infantas, Philip II's daughters, whose dowry would have consisted of the Netherlands; on the third occasion (one has to look twice before believing it), Claude du Bourg was acting in the name of Henry of Béarn, soliciting a loan from the Catholic King as well as his help in arranging the marriage of Henry's sister to the Duke of Savoy. Each of these extraordinary missions raises the most complicated problems, and to cap it all, they provoked the fury of the French ambassador, Saint-Gouard.

On the first occasion our hero was sent home with a rather noncommittal letter for his master and a gold chain worth 400 ducats for himself. The second time the King tried to avoid him, 'I did not think that Claude du Bourg was going to come back, especially after your letters of 30th

[83] *Lettere edite e inedite di Filippo Sassetti*, ed. Ettore Marcucci, Florence, 1855, p. 279.

July and 13th August' he wrote to his ambassador at Paris on 4th October, 1576. But the unwelcome visitor had arrived at Barcelona on 2nd September. To stop him and to avoid at the least an unpleasant incident with the French ambassador, when everything had to be done by letter, was a question of speed in the expedition of orders. Zayas wrote two or three times, but Claude du Bourg did not heed him, slipped through the net and 'when I was on my way from the Escorial to the Prado,' writes Philip II, 'he stepped out in front of me at Galapagar on the morning of 22nd September and gave me a letter in the hand of the Duke of Alençon dated 19th August, and proposed more openly than on his first visit, that a marriage should be arranged between the Duke and one of my daughters, the Infantas. I made reply to him through the Duke of Alva'. At this point the story ceases to interest us.

That a lone figure, and, what is more, an undesirable one, should have been able to slip right across Spain, and although remarked by the security services, escaped all checks and controls, finally stepping out in the path of the Prudent King himself is an exploit that can be attributed entirely to the rate at which information travelled in the sixteenth century.[84]

Distance and the economy. Every activity had to overcome the obstacle of physical distance. It is with a constant awareness of the problems of distance that the Mediterranean economy with its inevitable delays, endless preparations, and recurrent breakdowns must be approached.

Even bills of exchange, which were privileged goods, did not escape the general rule of passive resistance. The time taken to reach other exchanges was regularly added to the usance specified on the bill itself. At the beginning of the century the times allowed from Genoa[85] were five days for Pisa, six for Milan, ten for Gaeta, Avignon, and Rome; fifteen for Ancona, twenty for Barcelona, thirty for Valencia and Montpellier; two months for Bruges; three for London. Sums in specie travelled even more slowly. When, during the latter half of the century the arrival of the fleet at Seville became the predominant factor in the European, Mediterranean, and world economy, it was possible to trace the route taken by each annual consignment of silver swelling the stock of currency and circulating from one western financial centre to another according to a very long-drawn-out

[84] There are numerous documents at Simancas concerning the incident: 2nd June, 1576, K 1541; 3rd October, 1576, K 1542 no. 4 A; 3rd October, *ibid.*, no. 3; 4th October, *ibid.*, no. 4; 8th October, 1576, *ibid.*, no. 11; 12th October, 1576, *ibid.*, no. 15; 13th October, *ibid.*, no. 16; 14th October, *ibid.*, no. 17; 15th October, *ibid.*, no. 19; 17th October, no. 20; 18th October, no. 21; 18th October, no. 22; 21st October, K 1542; 23rd October, no. 30; 25th October, 30th October, no. 35; 18th November, 19th December, 1576 (no. 64); Henri (of Navarre) to Philip II, Agen, 3rd April, 1577, 29th April, 1577, K 1543, no. 38 A; Philip II to M. de Vendôme, 8th April, 1577, K 1542, no. 62; 2nd July, no. 52; 12th July, no. 45, 2nd August, K 1542; 4th August, 1577, no. 59, 12th August, no. 61; 17th August, no. 62; 19th August, no. 69.

[85] K. O. Müller, *op. cit.*, p. 39. The extra days were counted *after* the arrival of the bills.

timetable, as José Gentil da Silva's diagrams suggest.[86] Merchandise encountered similar difficulties: it took time to prepare, spent more time in warehouses and changed hands with varying degrees of slowness. Wool from Spain was imported by Florence: many months passed between the purchase of the fleeces and the finishing of the cloth,[87] and it might even be years before it reached customers in Egypt, Nuremberg, or elsewhere in its finished form. We have already mentioned as typical the case of the wheat and rye of Poland, which was sold a full year after being harvested and consumed up to six or twelve months later, sometimes later still if it was sent to the Mediterranean.[88]

Moreover, merchandise sometimes had to wait for the arrival of other goods from distant places. At Aquila in the Abruzzi the thriving saffron trade attracted a large concourse of merchants every year. But saffron was not the only merchandise which had to be at the rendezvous; it had to be packed in linen bags (eight bags to a load), and the bags were in turn wrapped four by four in a leather pouch. In addition, payment was effected in copper bars used by the Aquila mint which struck small coins, *cavali* and *cavaluzzi*. So the saffron market was dependent on the arrival of linen cloth and copper plate from Germany, bales of leather from Hungary,[89] and vice versa. The two streams had to meet. Similarly in the Levant, spices, pepper, drugs, silk, and cotton had a rendezvous with silver coins and woollen cloth from the West. Along the route that led from Ragusa to Venice and from Venice on to Antwerp and London we have intermittent records of the exchange of goods which was the livelihood of the merchant family, the Gondola, of Ragusan origin, with branches in Ragusa itself, Ancona, Venice (later apparently at Messina), and finally in London, which was the centre of operations. They handled the exchange of raisins, *uve passe*, or *curanti*, as they were called in anglicized Italian, imported from the Levant, and rosaries (*paternosters*) not a very successful line, for the kerseys manufactured in the English countryside. Both shipping and overland routes were used, via Ancona or Venice, but the transactions took so long that in 1545 in order to settle outstanding payments the firm had to resort to the Lyons exchange through the good offices of the Salviati.[90]

Delay in transit was a universal evil. Goods, money, and bills of exchange travelled in all directions, passed each other on the road, met up or had to wait for each other. Every commercial centre drew its livelihood from the complex and ever-changing circulation of goods, money, and bills of exchange, or to be precise from their mutual compensations. And these

[86] J. G. da Silva, *Stratégie des affaires à Lisbonne entre 1595 et 1607*, 1956, p. 92, plate V.

[87] Federigo Melis, *Aspetti della vita economica medievale*, 1962, p. 455 ff. considers the problem at the end of the fourteenth century. It had hardly changed by the sixteenth century.

[88] See above, p. 197.

[89] K. O. Müller, *op. cit.*, p. 49.

[90] Ragusa Archives, Diversa di Cancellaria 131, f°s 1 to 6.

goods, money, and bills of exchange were caught up in a slow-moving flow that kept them a long time on the way. A merchant would naturally want to recover his capital as soon as possible, his vital stake in a game that was always ready to start again. There can be no doubt that the collapse of private banks in the sixteenth century was the result of their being too ready to place their clients' money in commercial circuits that moved too slowly. If there was a panic or an emergency, payments could not be made within a few days, for the money was still on the road, a prisoner of the mortal delays of distance.

Time was money, as every merchant, 'with ink-stained fingers' – from the endless number of letters he wrote – well knew. The expression was already in the air. In March, 1590, Baltasar Suárez, the Spanish merchant living in Florence expresses his irritation at the delay of a galleon that will cost him dear 'por el tiempo que pierde la mercaderia'.[91] Prudence therefore counselled that he should divide his outgoings (whether in money or merchandise) between several circuits with different timetables, or between several ships on a single route, and most important of all, that he choose the quickest circuit which would return his money and profits as soon as possible. In the early seventeenth century merchants preferred the overland Venetian routes to the convenient waterway of the Po. The waterway was indeed, as a speaker at Venice remarked,[92] 'always more advantageous and convenient than the road which is dangerous, inconvenient, and expensive'. But all along the river there were too many private rights. Boats had to stop for examination and the exaction of levies, above all wasting time; it was this last factor which tipped the balance.

And time was something no one could afford to waste. If a merchant of Venice in the fifteenth century prefers to deal in Syrian cotton,[93] it is because the whole business can be concluded within six or seven months, a much shorter interval than that allowed by the long voyages of the England or Flanders galleys. Only the really large-scale capitalists of the period, the most skilful and the most fortunate – the Genoese – were able to arrange for payments to be made across the Atlantic from Seville.[94] This was an immense operation – but for the even more extraordinary establishment of regular commercial links between Lisbon and the Indian Ocean, the Portuguese state with all its credit had to intervene, and the king turn pepper merchant, and indeed it soon proved unequal to the task. Inevitably the longer the distance over which trade is carried out, the more money has to be invested and the longer it will spend en route. Merchant shipping from Seville to America or from Lisbon to Asia would have been impossible if it had not been for the previous concentration of capital, in the fifteenth century, in southern Germany and Italy.[95]

[91] B. Suàrez to Simón Ruiz, Florence, 30th March, 1590, Archivo Ruiz, Archivo histórico provincial, Valladolid.
[92] Arringhe varie, Museo Correr, 1999 (undated).
[93] F. C. Lane, *op. cit.*, p. 101–113.   [94] See above, p. 228, note 274
[95] Hermann Van der Wee, *op. cit.*, II, p. 319 ff.

These long-distance trades called for great feats. Feats of endurance by the participants: in July, 1602, a great ship from the Indies came to shore a few miles from Lisbon, with the equivalent of more than 2 'millions in gold' on board, but of her crew there survived only thirty men. It was this exhausted ship that the English privateers seized without difficulty under the noses of the defending galleys.[96] In September, 1614, there was a similar occasion (without the final blow of total loss this time), when a ship from 'the Indies' arrived off Lisbon, carrying 'a million' on board, and sixteen survivors left of the original 300 men who had embarked on her.[97] The extreme case is of the return of a Manila galleon to Acapulco, on the Pacific, without a single living soul on board,[98] but still carrying all her treasure; the ghost ship sailed into port on her own.

It also required great feats of money raising, as we shall see later. Immense resources had to be made available, as the wild fluctuations of the commercial centres regularly reveal. Venice in March, 1464,[99] had sent off all her liquid currency with the Syrian galleys. Her stocks of silver, her *arzenti* were all at sea, 'sono navegati per questi navi di Siria', leaving the city bled white and temporarily paralysed. A similar spectacle was to be offered by Seville a hundred years later, although this was at the height of the city's fortune. The 'Indies' fleet had not even left (it crossed the bar at San Lucar between 24th and 29th March, 1563)[100] before Simón Ruiz' correspondent was writing to him from Seville on 15th February:[101] 'for several days now, one has not been able to borrow a single *real* at any price on the market'. All the available money had gone on last-minute purchases of merchandise to send abroad; the mercantile community at Seville would have to wait for the return of the fleets before it again had an 'abundance' (*largezza*) of metal currency. The previous year, in 1562, when the fleet was late, merchants who were already in debt had to borrow at any

[96] Museo Correr, Cicogna, 1933, f° 162 and 162 v°, 30th July, 1602.

[97] A.d.S., Venice, Dispacci Spagna, F. Morosini to the Doge, Madrid, 22nd September, 1614.

[98] *Diario de Gregorio Martin de Guijo, 1648–1664*, ed. M. R. de Terreros, 1953, 2 vols, vol II, p. 76. Concerning the long voyages to the 'east Indies', François Pyrard wrote at the beginning of the seventeenth century, '. . . there arrived at Goa four great carracks . . . their number had been five on leaving Lisbon, but they did not know what had become of the fifth . . . In each carrack there had embarked up to a thousand persons, and when they arrived at Goa, there were not three hundred in each ship, and half of them were ill'; *Voyage de François Pyrard, de Laval, contenant sa navigation aux Indes orientales . . .*, 1619, II, p. 385 (*sic* for 285) quoted from another edition and in slightly different terms by Stefan Stasiak, *Les Indes portugaises à la fin du XVIe siècle d'après la Relation du voyage fait à Goa en 1546 par Christophe Pawlowski, gentilhomme polonais*, Lwow 1926, p. 33, note 122. See also the *Lusiads* V, 81–82.

[99] A.d.S., Mantua, A° Gonzaga, Series E, Venezia 1431, Giovanni de Strigi to the Marquis of Mantua, Venice, 17th March, 1464.

[100] Huguette and Pierre Chaunu, *Séville et l'Atlantique*, III, p. 36.

[101] Geronimo de Valladolid to Simón Ruiz, Seville, 15th February, 1563, A. P. Valladolid.

price they could get: 'For a month now', states an official letter,[102] 'people have had to borrow at interest at a loss of over 4½ per cent and all into the pockets of foreigners . . .'. And now payments at the Fair of Medina del Campo are about to fall due: would that his Majesty would graciously extend the date and save the merchants!

Fairs, the supplementary network of economic life. Commercial centres were the indispensable motors of economic life. They countered the obstacle of physical space and launched streams of traffic that triumphed as best they could over distance, travelling as fast as the century allowed. They were seconded in their task by other activities, chief among them the fairs, which we can consider almost as towns, temporary commercial centres, differing as towns do, very much among themselves, some of minor, others of moderate, a few of exceptional importance, the latter developing in time from trade fairs to exchange fairs.[103] But nothing could be taken for granted here. The fairs of Champagne died out in the fourteenth century, to be resurrected at Chalon-sur-Saône, Geneva, and later at Lyons. In northern Italy and the Netherlands, countries where there was intense *urban* activity, fairs although still glittering occasions in the sixteenth century, began to decline. When they survived, as at Venice, it was largely as a façade. At Ascensiontide the spectacular fair held in St. Mark's Square and known as *La Sensa*[104] (from the religious festival), was the scene of much festivity and the celebrated marriage of the doge to the sea. But this was no longer the heart of Venice, which now beat on the *piazza* and the bridge of the Rialto.

In this constant dialogue between the towns (or commercial centres) and the fairs, the former since they operated without interruption (at Florence the exchange rates were quoted every week on Saturdays) were bound in the long run to count for more than the fairs, which were exceptional gatherings. Or so one would assume, but evolution is never a simple affair. Surprises and about-turns were still possible. The establishment in 1579 of the exchange fairs (known as the Besançon fairs) at Piacenza in northern Italy was the event of the century from the point of view of the history of capitalism. For many years the relentless 'heart' of the Mediterranean and entire western economy beat here at Piacenza. We shall have more to say about this crucial event. It was not, in fact, Genoa, a city, but the discreet quarterly meeting of a few businessmen at Piacenza that dictated the rhythm of the material life of the West. Only paper

[102] Simancas, Consejo y Junta de Hacienda, 46, Prior and Consuls of Seville to H.M., Seville, 2nd July, 1562.
[103] This was true first of the fairs of Champagne and later of many others, cf. Robert Henri Bautier, 'Les foires de Champagne' in *Recueils de la Société Jean Bodin*, V, *La foire*, 1953, p. 97–145.
[104] This fair of the *Sensa*, mentioned by M. Sanudo, *op. cit.*, I, column 959 (May, 1498), and noted in Mantuan correspondence, attracted foreign merchants to the city, A.d.S., Mantua, Venezia 1431, de Strigi to the Marquis, Venice, 10th May, 1461. Historians of Venice may have underestimated it.

changed hands, and not a penny of currency, reports a Venetian observer with only a little exaggeration.[105] And yet everything – new arrivals and returns, arterial blood and veinous blood – culminated at this vital 'pole', from which flowed drafts and remittances, debts and letters of credit, settlements and returns, gold and silver, the symmetrical or asymmetrical transactions upon which all trade depended.

But at a more humble level local fairs had a part to play: a similar one in kind to that played by the more illustrious fairs, Lyons, Medina del Campo, Frankfurt, and later Leipzig. Recent research has uncovered more details of the history of these innumerable regional fairs, the fairs of Lanciano,[106] Salerno,[107] Aversa, Lucera, Reggio in Calabria, in the kingdom of Naples, the fairs of Recanati and Sinigaglia in the papal states, the interconnected fairs of Lombardy,[108] not to mention the fairs authorized by Venice at Bergamo or Brescia, the Bolzano fairs in the Tyrol that became so prosperous in the seventeenth century,[109] or in Syria the seaside fair at Jeble and the caravan fair of Mzerib (El Muzeirib) held inland, 100 kilometres south of Damascus, in the middle of the desert.[110] And then there were the tiny fairs, hardly more than weekly markets, dynamic points scattered throughout western Europe and the Balkans.[111] In New Castile alone, in about 1575–1580, twenty-two fairs were still regularly held[112] and there were dozens in Portugal.[113] All, even the humblest, were like hastily assembled towns where previously there had only been, as there was at Medina del Campo, a street – La Rua – and a market place; or a vacant lot outside the town as at Lanciano.[114] The fairs would mean a fortnight, three weeks, or at most, a month of feverish activity. At Darroca in Aragon the principal fair began on the feast of Corpus Christi; on this occasion the Brothers of the Trinity would bring out of their church the miraculous wafers that had once been transformed into flesh and blood ('et ciò si vede chiarissimamente', said some young Venetian travellers with conviction in May, 1581). The fair, which lasted a week, attracted a large number of mule dealers, selling beasts for ploughing, saddle or draft,

[105] Museo Correr, Donà delle Rose 181 f° 62, report of the 'zornalier del giro di banco' (of the Rialto) Giovan Battista Pereti (?), July, 1604: 'et il più delle volte non vi è un quatrino di contati . . .'.
[106] Corrado Marciani, Lettres de change aux foires de Lanciano, 1962.
[107] Armando Sapori, Studi di storia economica medievale, 1946, p. 443 ff., on 'La fiera di Salerno del 1478'.
[108] Giuseppe Mira, 'L'organizzazione fieristica nel quadro dell'economia della Bassa Lombarda alla fine del Medio Evo e nell' eta moderna' in Archivio storico lombardo, 1958.
[109] Giulio Mandich, 'Istituzione delle fiere veronesi (1631–1635) e riorganizzazione delle fiere bolzanine' in Cultura Atesina, 1947.
[110] Robert Brunschvig, 'Coup d'oeil sur l'histoire des foires à travers l'Islam' in Recueils de la Société Jean Bodin, V, La foire, 1953, p. 58, 59.
[111] J. Cvijić, op. cit., p. 196–197, and Mehlan, 'Die grossen Balkanmessen in der Türkenzeit' in Vierteljahrschrift für Sozialgeschichte, 1938.
[112] See below note 122.
[113] Virginia Rau, Subsidios para o estudo das feiras medievais portuguesas, 1943.
[114] Corrado Marciani, op. cit., p. 4.

the latter capable of pulling 'those carts which in Spain always have only two wheels'[115] – a detail we may note in passing.

After the fair everything returned to normal. The stands were dismantled and moved on somewhere else like Count Potemkin's villages. Merchants, merchandise, wares, and pack animals would travel on from one town to the next. One fair would end and another would begin. The seven or eight Flemish merchants who left the 'August' fair at Lanciano in September, 1567, were still in time, as they had hoped, for the second Sorrento fair which began on the 21st of the month.[116] One Speranza della Marca, whom a Neapolitan document mentions in April, 1567,[117] 'and associated agents', 'in giro per il Regno', no doubt visited all the fairs selling haberdashery, silk-stuffs, *zagarelle*,[118] gold and silver thread, combs, and caps. Perhaps he satisfied every kind of customer by selling those Spanish hats which an imitative fashion had introduced to Naples.

The fairs were always a rendezvous for the wealthy merchants who were familiar with bills of exchange and credit machinery (whole bundles of bills of exchange have been found at Lanciano),[119] and imported spices, drugs, and rich fabrics. But even at Lyons, in March, 1578,[120] according to the innkeepers, 'for every merchant who comes to the fair on horseback and who can afford a good lodging and has money to spend, there are ten more on foot who are grateful for a room at the humblest inn'. The fairs also drew modest pedlars, genuine representatives of country life offering its products for sale: livestock, bacon, barrels of salt meat, leather, skins, cheeses, new casks, almonds, dried figs, apples, modest local wines and celebrated vintages such as the *mangiaguerra*, barrels of anchovy or sardines, and raw silk. The vital function of such fairs in the broad kingdom of Naples, whose picturesque side we have just glimpsed was to bring into contact the great trade routes and the country paths, muletracks, and 'capillaries' of trade that wound down from the mountains behind Lanciano 'following the beds of the streams'. They clearly gave a tremendous fillip to exchange and circulation, and in fact to a whole series of transactions whether in money or kind, a vast movement that benefited from exemption from tolls, for one of the obstacles posed by distance was the number of customs posts, city tolls, and barriers.[121]

We find the same picture wherever we look. Tendilla,[122] a town in New Castile in the province of Guadalajara, was not exactly famous in 1580. What geographer could locate it from memory at the foot of the Sierra de

---

[115] Voyage of Franceso Contarini, May, 1581, P.R.O., 30, 25, 157, f° 66 vo.
[116] A.d.S., Naples, Sommaria Partium 566, f° 216 v° and 217, 2nd September, 1567.
[117] A.d.S., Naples, Sommaria Partium, 528, f° 204.
[118] Little ribbons.
[119] Corrado Marciani, *op. cit.*, p. 1 and 9–10.
[120] R. Gascon, *op. cit.*, p. 284, A. Communales Lyons, BB 101 f° 58.
[121] Jacob van Klaveren, *op. cit.*, p. 198 and Regla, in *Historia Social de España*, by J. Vicens Vives, III, p. 351.
[122] Noël Salomon, *La campagne en Nouvelle Castille à la fin du XVIe siècle, d'après les 'Relaciones Topograficas'*, 1964, p. 119–120.

la Calderina which looks down on it from the north, on the banks of the Guadiana which runs on from there to Ciudad Real, Badajoz, and Portugal? At this period with its 700 households it was a large seignorial village of about 3000 inhabitants. But one of its two fairs, the St. Matthew's Day Fair just at the end of winter was for a whole month of the year the scene of extraordinary activity. It was a well-timed fair. All winter long the weavers had been working at their woollen cloth and this was the first fair of the year, 'feria de coyuntura que todo el imbierno se han labrado los paños, y ser la primera del ano'. Merchants came from all the neighbouring towns, even the *mercaderes gruesos* of Madrid, Toledo, Segovia, and Cuenca, as well as Biscayan linen cloth and thread merchants and the Portuguese 'in greater numbers here than in any fair in Castile'. The concourse of people and the number of stalls are reminiscent of the Alcayceria[123] at Granada – and what a wealth of goods: cloths of every description and every origin, silks, spices, drugs, brazil-woods, ivory, goldwork, as well as more everyday goods. The Count of Tendilla annually received for his part 1,200,000 *maravedís* from the *alcabala* or sales tax, not a heavy one, about 3 per cent – which means that the total volume of business transacted at the fair must have been 40 million (40 *cuentos*) *maravedís*, over 100,000 ducats. So the fairs were a way of breaking into the ordinarily closed and inward-looking regional economies and made possible the establishment, or at least the beginnings, of a 'national market'.

Local economies. The Mediterranean region was sprinkled with half-enclosed local economies, both large and small, with their own internal organization, their innumerable local measures, costumes, and dialects. Their number is impressive. The islands of Sardinia and Corsica, for example, were virtually outside the main flow of Mediterranean trade. The Sardinian peasant[124] was never offered any incentive to increase his production, to experiment with new crops or change his methods; he was used to burning off the stubble (*narboni*) and did not leave fields fallow. Some parts of the island, even in 1860, Orosei and Posada on the east coast and Gallura to the north, had no wheeled vehicles and all trade 'is conducted on horseback'.[125] In this island which was more pastoral than agricultural in the sixteenth century, money was often unknown. The Jesuit fathers who had been settled at Cagliari since 1557 were overwhelmed with gifts in kind: poultry, bread, kids, perhaps a capon or a sucking pig, good wines, and calves. 'But', says one of their letters,[126] 'the alms we receive in money never amount to 10 crowns.'

---

[123] J. Caro Baroja, *Los Moriscos del Reino de Granada*, 1957, p. 95, note 189, description of the Alcayceria, with its silks and fabrics, after Bermúdez de Pedraça.

[124] M. le Lannou, *op. cit.*, p. 56.

[125] M. le Lannou, *op. cit.*, p. 13, after Alberto della Marmora, *Voyage en Sardaigne ou description physique et politique de cette ile*, 2nd ed. 3 volumes, Paris, Turin, 1839–1860.

[126] Miguel Battlori, 'Ensenyament i finances a la Sardenya cincentista' in: *Historic Studies in Honour of I. Gonzáles Llubera*, Oxford, 1959, off-print, p. 4, 5.

In Corsica every *pieve* was an island within an island, having no contact with the next valley over the mountains. The people of Cruzzini, Bocognano and Bastelica, behind Ajaccio regard each other as foreigners[127] and are obliged to produce everything for themselves, to cover the entire range of their needs (perhaps this is why lard is used as well as olive oil?). Their garments were made of peasant cloth woven at home and the islanders protested when Genoese merchants tried to keep this cloth for their shops. They also protested that the *Dominante* (but was she really responsible?) did not encourage internal trade within the island, *di luogo a luogo*.[128] In fact, geographical factors, relief, and the poor communications were to blame for the lack of contacts. The island remained almost entirely outside the orbit of a monetary economy: taxes could be paid in wheat, chestnuts, silkworm cocoons, oil, or pulses; the master who taught reading and writing was usually paid two *bacini* of grain a year (between 20 and 40 litres). Given these conditions, a Corsican historian of the sixteenth century explained, regarding the food shortage of 1582, 'in spite of such great scarcity, grain did not rise above 4 *scudi* a *mera*, for the island was also poor in money; had there been plenty of money, the price would have risen to over 8 *scudi* . . .'.[129]

Sicily, although a rich island, was equally poorly served in the regions of the interior. The islanders paid taxes for the building of road links, but the government used the money for other things, so the Sicilian interior had no properly maintained roads until the eighteenth century. As late as 1726 special privileges were offered to any merchants who undertook to set up shop in the inland region.[130] So it is not surprising that in the sixteenth century the cloths for popular consumption were as in Corsica, local peasant woollen weaves.[131]

The highlands of Aragon, round Jaca, also seem to have been an inward-looking region. Self-sufficiency was both an ideal and a necessity: they produced wheat (both in the irrigated regions and the *montes*), vines (whether the site, the soil, and in particular the altitude were suitable or not), olives, in spite of the terrible frosts and ice on the mountains, and the essential vegetables whose quality and savour the economist Ignacio Asso praised two centuries later. For clothing there were peasant weaves, the famous Aragonese *cordelates*. Even in the eighteenth century in some of the mountainous districts wheat was still being bartered for oil. In the *Partido* of Huesca, both olive oil and sheep's butter were used in cooking.[132] Even the Castilian countryside, as it appears in the *Relaciones topo-*

---

[127] J. Albitreccia, in P. Leca, *Guide*, p. 16.
[128] A. Marcelli, *Interno al cosidetto* . . . p. 415–416; December, 1573.
[129] A. P. Filippini, *Istoria di Corsica*, 1st ed., Turnon, 1594; 2nd ed. Pisa, 1827–1831, 5 vols., Book XII, vol. 5, p. 382, quoted by F. Borlandi, *op. cit.*, p. 70, note 9.
[130] Hans Hochholzer, 'Kulturgeographie Siziliens' in *Geogr. Zeitschrift*, 1935, p. 290.
[131] E. Albèri, *op. cit.*, II, v, p. 477, 1574.
[132] Ignacio de Asso, *op. cit.*, p. 53 to 58.

gráficas,[133] the invaluable surveys carried out in 1575 and 1577 on Philip II's orders, offers some examples of independent local economies. These villages drew a livelihood from their own fields and called as little as possible on the oil, wine, and wheat of neighbouring villages. Research into the agrarian structures of Old Castile has shown that polyculture was practised and wherever the soil or a sheltered site allowed it, olive trees were grown in spite of the harsh climate.[134] Autarky was the ideal and money made only brief appearances vanishing again as quickly as it had come.

The more inward-looking these archaic economies were, the more likely it was that gold and silver, on their rare appearances there, would be over-estimated. The cost of living in Sardinia, noted a Venetian in 1558, is about a quarter or a fifth that of Italy,[135] that is for those with well-filled purses. Similarly, when a Venetian ship was obliged by unforeseen circumstances to put in, on Ascension Day, 1609, to Fasana, a little port near Pola on the Istrian coast, her passengers and crew went ashore and found provisions in abundant supply: veal at 3 *soldi* a pound, a kid for 40 *soldi*, oil at 3 *soldi*, bread and wine at very low prices, 'insomma', says one traveller, 'buonissimo vivere'.[136] Mediterranean countries, like other European countries, were checkered with low-cost regions, which in every case were separate worlds by-passed by the general economy.

In western Europe these cheap regions were usually small in area. In the east they might be very large, such as parts of the Balkans that lived very largely off their own produce, their harvests, salt and dried meats.[137] In Belgrade during the summer of 1555, Busbecq remarked:[138] 'This huge quantity of fish, enough to satisfy forty persons, cost less than half a thaler, and almost every other commodity is equally cheap there. . . .' So the Ragusans, Venetians, and others had every interest in buying their supplies from the large and profitable Balkan market. Foreign intrusion was resented. In January, 1582, a Venetian, Fabio Canal, complained bitterly

[133] On these see the general work by J. Ortega Rubio *Relaciones topográficas de España*, 1918, and especially the publications relating to the province of Guadalajara (J. C. Garcia and M. Villamil, 1903–1915) and the diocese of Cuenca (P. J. Zarcos Cueva, 1927). See also the important studies by Carmelo Viñas y Mey and Ramón Paz, *Relaciones de los pueblos de España ordeñadas por Felipe II*, I, Madrid, 1950; II, Toledo, 1951; III, Toledo, 1963. Of general relevance is the book by Noël Salomon, quoted above, note 122.
[134] Jesus Garcia Fernández, *Aspectos del paisaje agrario de Castilla la Vieja*, 1963, p. 4 ff.
[135] E. Albèri, *op. cit.*, I, III, p. 267.
[136] Tommaso Alberti, *Viaggio a Costantinopoli, 1609–1621*, Bologna, 1889, p. 6.
[137] For the Bulgarian countryside see I. Sakazov, *op. cit.*, p. 212.
[138] *Op. cit.*, trans Forster, p. 70. Almost a century later Tavernier noted the same abundance at Belgrade: two crowns a day for fourteen persons (although the cost of living must have risen, bread, wine, and meat, are all excellent 'and cost almost nothing in this town') *Histoire générale des Voyages de John Green*, ed. and trans. Abbé Prévost, X, p. 118.

to the Council of Ten of the steep rise in the price of horses in the region behind Spalato. Massive purchases by the French (because of the civil wars) were responsible for this deplorable new situation.[139] The existence of large numbers of these regions, great and small, entering very little into the monetary economy was by no means confined to the Mediterranean. In Germany, on the shores of the Baltic, at Reval, in Estonia, in Finland, it was a similar and sometimes even more striking feature. A Venetian travelling to Poland in December, 1590, bought all his supplies including candles[140] at Vienna, very wisely.[141] In France many revealing examples emerge from travellers' accounts. What more backward and uncomfortable province could there be than Brittany. In February, 1532, François I proposed to go there (and he did) 'against the wishes of all his Court, who detest this voyage as if it led to Hell'.[142] There were similar regions in England. Even in the time of Cromwell,[143] once the traveller left the main road he found himself in an ancient England of forest and heath, the haunt of vagabonds. The state of Scotland and Ireland must be left to the imagination.[144] This is evidence of the backwardness not of the Mediterranean but of the sixteenth century with its inadequate monetary economy and the powerlessness of men to order all things. It brings us face to face with an economic *ancien régime* that neither begins nor ends with the sixteenth century.

However a trickle of trade did escape from these economies, even from the most hermetically sealed. We should beware as Marc Bloch warned us, of hasty assertions about closed economies. Even the Corsican *pievi* exchanged goods with the outside world through their shepherds, and might barter pigs and chestnuts for oil, fabrics, or money. On the subject of islands, we have already noted, in another context, that the large island of Sardinia was not entirely cut off from the rest of the Mediterranean world.[145] And it is hardly necessary to point out that Sicily was a grain exporter and Castile an international wool market.

But it *is* worth pointing out that this could also be true of regions so isolated that they might appear to be totally self-contained, such as the district of Huesca, indeed the whole of Upper Aragon. How could we forget that through the *Partido* of Huesca passed the great Canfranc way, which from the Middle Ages had been the route taken by the wines of

[139] Fabio Canal to the Council of Ten, Spalato, 21st January, 1582, A.d.S., Venice, Lettere ai Capi del Consiglio dei Dieci, Spalato, Busta, 281, f° 67
[140] See above, p. 196, note 116.
[141] Leopold Chatenay, *Vie de Jacques Esprinchard Rochelais et Journal de ses voyages au XVIe siècle*, 1957, p. 148: travellers had to provide in the 'hostelries of Poland . . . their own beds . . . even their meat, drink and candles'.
[142] G. Antonio Venier to the Doge, Rouen, 22nd February, 1532, B.N., Paris, Ital., 1714, f° 189, copy; see also M. Sanudo, *op. cit.*, LVI, col. 244–245, 15th April, 1532.
[143] John Buchan, *Oliver Cromwell*, London, 1934, p. 22.
[144] P. Boissonade, 'Le mouvement commercial entre la France et les Iles Britanniques au XVIe siècle' in *Revue Historique*, May–Sept., 1920.
[145] See above, p. 150.

Guyenne and English woollen cloth,[146] and was still used by German merchants in the fifteenth and sixteenth centuries travelling to Saragossa for the saffron trade? That it was probably from Béarn, and therefore from beyond the Pyrenees that there came to the orchards of Jaca the *doyenne* pear and the *pomme d'api* known in the Béarn as the *pomme Dieu*;[147] that wheat from Aragon used to be taken down the Ebro towards Tortosa, and that Catalonia was still obtaining supplies from this source in the sixteenth century; that there was for a long time a separate currency in Jaca (the *sueldo jaqués*[148]); that the *cordelates*[149] were exported from Aragon to very distant places and, last but not least, that Aragon became Castilianized in the sixteenth century, that an Aragonese nobleman in the time of Philip II kept his family record book in Castilian?[150] So even Aragon, poor and barren as it was, had its channels of communication with the outside world only a few of which we know.

And above all there was the inevitable dialogue between advanced countries and underdeveloped regions. Then as now economic life was conditioned by differences in level or voltage. The Genoese merchant in the towns of Corsica obeyed an economic law by which he was the first to be bound and which indeed in a way excuses him, just as it does the Venetian merchant at Aleppo or Hormuz, the Ragusan at Üskub, Sofia, Temesvár, or Novi Pazar, the Nuremberg merchant in Bohemia or Saxony, all benefiting from the cheap labour and cost of living there.[151] For the towns could not do without these poor regions on their doorsteps (and which they maintained, whether deliberately or not, in their poverty). Every city however brilliant – and Florence was a brilliant city – had to draw its essential food supplies from an area contained within a radius of about 30 kilometres.[152] From the surrounding *contado*, Florence obtained her timber, oil, vegetables, poultry produce, fantastic numbers of casks of wine, game and birds which peasants sold in bunches at the city gates.[153] So the two economies met, the sophisticated and the backward. Valladolid[154] was well provided for by the rich Tierra de Campos outside her gates. Segovia had the red and white wine she needed brought from the countryside near Medina del Campo, Coca, and Zebreros, to the Thursday market when all the townsfolk bought their supplies. And so on . . . If Venice was a well-fed city, it was because her network of waterways enabled her to

---

[146] *Col. de doc. in ed. del Archivo General de la Corona de Aragon*, vol. XXXIX, p. 281; Ignacio de Asso, *op. cit.*, p. 384; Aloys Schulte, *op. cit.*, I, p. 308 ff.

[147] Ignacio de Asso, *op. cit.*, p. 57–58. [148] *Ibid.*, p. 263.

[149] Cloth was being manufactured at Jaca itself in the sixteenth century, I. de Asso, *op. cit.*, p. 208.

[150] F. Felda y Pérez de Nueros, *Felipe II, op. cit.*, p. 30 ff.

[151] Lazlo Makkai, 'Die Entstehung des gesellschaftlichen Basis des Absolutismus in den Ländern der österreichischen Habsburger' in *Études historiques*, published by National Committee of Hungarian Historians, 1960, vol. I, p. 627–668.

[152] Giuseppe Parenti, *Prime ricerche sulla rivoluzione dei prezzi in Firenze*, 1939, esp. p. 76: the normal supply zone of Florence did not extend further than 30 *miglia*, sometimes less, p. 94. [153] A.d.S., Florence, Misc. Medicea, 51.

[154] B. Bennassar, *op. cit.*, notably part 2, chapter 2, *Les moyens de l'économie*.

bring everyday foodstuffs and sheep cheese from as far off as Casalmaggiore in Lombardy;[155] and because her shipping routes were ideal for the transport of wheat, oil, wine, fish, meat on the hoof; and the firewood she needed in the winter cold was brought in boatloads from Istria and the gulf of Quarnero.[156]

The quadrilateral: Genoa, Milan, Venice, and Florence. We have looked at the advantages and the disadvantages, the factors that both encourage and at the same time restrict the economic organization of an area where distance is an obstacle: in other words, the geographical division of labour. This division can also be seen quite clearly within the Mediterranean as a whole.

This world, sixty days long, was, indeed, broadly speaking a *Weltwirtschaft*, a world-economy, a self-contained universe. No strict and authoritarian order was established, but the outlines of a coherent pattern can be discerned. All world-economies for instance recognize a centre, some focal point that acts as a stimulus to other regions and is essential to the existence of the economic unit as a whole. Quite clearly in the Mediterranean in the fifteenth and sixteenth centuries that centre was a narrow urban quadrilateral: Venice, Milan, Genoa, Florence, with conflicts and intertown rivalries as the relative weight of each city changed. The centre of gravity can gradually be seen to shift from Venice, where it still lay at the beginning of the century, to Genoa, where it was so brilliantly established between 1550 and 1575.

In the fifteenth century Venice was unquestionably the vigorous heart of the Mediterranean[157] and even of the double or triple unit born of the attachment of certain parts of Europe to the Mediterranean. It was the obvious, but by no means exclusive heart. Venice was seconded in her distant activities by Bruges, another decisive 'pole' which may or may not have been equal to the task – it has been questioned[158] – lying at the other end of the shipping routes that carried goods north as far as the Baltic, the North Sea, the hinterland of northwest Germany, and, most important, lying across the sea from England. Venice also had to rely on the powerful cities closest to her, to maintain her sovereignty – Milan, Genoa, and Florence. And if a single document would serve to prove this, the famous deathbed oration of the Doge Mocenigo[159] in 1423 would certainly do so: to the Levant, where her most prosperous trading connections lay, Venice dispatched the velvets of Genoa, the cloths of gold of Milan and the high-

[155] And had done so since 1444, A.d.S., Venice, Notatorio di Collegio, 8, f° 1, 10th July, 1444: boats, 'barchiele', '*veniunt Venetias cum caseo, ovis de Casali Maiori, Bessillo et aliis locis Lombardie.*
[156] Museo Correr, Donà delle Rose, 451.
[157] Alberto Tenenti, *Cristoforo da Canal*, 1962, p. 176.
[158] J. A. Van Houtte, 'Bruges et Anvers, marchés *nationaux* ou *internationaux* du XIVe au XVIe siècle?' in *Revue du Nord*, 1952.
[159] One of the classic texts of Venetian history, often reproduced, for example in *Bilanci Generali*, 1912, vol. 1, tome I, p. 577 ff.

quality woollen cloth of Florence; she lived off their industry and the trade that they sent her.

Such many-sided collaboration did not proceed without difficulties. This narrow strip at the centre of the world was torn by jealousy, rivalry, and war. And history has traced step by step the comedies, deceptions, and tragedies (not a few) of the relationship. Until 1454 [160] and the crucial turning point of the Peace of Lodi, the Italy of adventurers, city-states, and princes experienced in her own way the social and economic as well as political conflicts that we group together under the misleading title of the Hundred Years' War; with the general depression of all activity these were grim and sometimes savage times. City fought city, state tackled state. To view these conflicts as a search for Italian unity once glimpsed but then lost sight of by the most far-seeing statesmen is to accord too much honour to an inglorious chronicle. The merit of the Peace of Lodi, however, was that it marked a return to a calmer life and an immediate improvement in trade, which was to last until the untimely arrival of Charles VIII and his troops in September, 1494.

During this calm spell, the hegemony of the four 'great powers' remained uninterrupted. And Venice was sovereign. She was less concerned with matters of diplomatic policy than with money, bills of exchange, fabrics, spices, and shipping – in her usual, that is, almost incredible manner. In May, 1472,[161] the Council of Ten at Venice, held discussions every day without intermission, with 'the *zonta* of the 35'; as it had not done 'gran tempo fa'. The subject of debate was not the Turkish war, which had broken out again in 1470, but the depreciation and finally the proscribing of silver coins, *grossetti* and *grossoni*, in the first place those which had not been struck by the Zecca at Venice. A stop had to be put to the invasion by bad money, of which Venice suffered so many and with which she always dealt ruthlessly. Long before Thomas Gresham, Venetians already knew very well that 'bad money will chase out good', 'che la cativa cazarà via la bona', as the agent for Gonzaga writes in June, 1472.[162] The same source adds that 'there is nothing new to report here, except that no one seems to care any longer about the Turks. No steps are being taken against them.' So Venice, which had lost Salonica in 1430 and had just sacrificed to the Turks the wheat-growing island of Negropont in 1470, was entirely self-preoccupied, for her confidence in herself, her wealth, and her superiority was complete. The Turkish fleet was modelled after her own; her strongholds, armed with artillery and regularly maintained and supplied by the Arsenal, were unequalled. And business was good. Throughout the Mediterranean, and outside it as far as Flanders, the distributive system of the *galere da mercato* was functioning for the greater profit of the patricians who chartered these state-owned vessels.

---

[160] Corrado Barbagallo, *Storia Universale*, III, 1935, p. 1107.
[161] A.d.S., Mantua, A° Gonzaga. B 1431, Johannes de Strigys to the Marquis, Venice, 16th May, 1472 and following letters.
[162] *Ibid.*, the same to the same, 6th June, 1472.

The Signoria had lost, it is true, some vital positions: Salonica (1430), Constantinople (1453), 'truly our city', as a Senate text says; Negropont (1470), and we might add the Tana on the Sea of Azov (1475) from which galleys and roundships sailed to Venice, one of them according to a late document 'carga de schiave et salumi', carrying slave women and salt meat.[163] All these blows struck home, but the Republic's adaptable shipping system could always transfer its bases to other places, to Crete or Cyprus, where Venice was undisputed ruler after 1479. All comparisons are artificial, but it could be argued that Venice's occupation of Cyprus, from which she ousted the Genoese, was a sixteenth-century version of the occupation or attempted occupation, of India by the English, ousting the French after the battle of Plassey (1757). Besides, Venetian ships and merchants remained a presence at the end of the century and even later, both at Constantinople and in the Black Sea. They were present too in Syria and Egypt, two gateways to the trade of the Levant, the first crucial and the second important. In 1489 Alexandria represented possibly 3 million ducats in returns[164] for Venice. In 1497 the Signoria sent to Syria and Egypt, along with her precious wares, over 360,000 ducats in specie. Immediately the silver mark (for silver was already the metal used) rose more than 5 *grossi* in price.[165] Venice was sacrificing all her metal currency in order to bring back, as usual, pepper, spices, drugs, cotton, linens, and silks. This was a regular and established trade (who would yet have suspected the voyage Vasco da Gama was about to make) and, as it were, politically guaranteed. Syria and Egypt were united under the Mameluke state with its old commercial traditions. How could anyone have foreseen the victories of the Turks against the sultans of Cairo in 1516 and 1517? So Venice slept the sleep of the rich. She protested indeed against excessive luxury in women's dress, against the scandalous expenses incurred in festivities, and against embroidered coats for men. But who did not, like Sanudo, secretly admire the sumptuous dowries that were becoming the rule at patrician marriages, never less than 3000 ducats, sometimes over 10,000?[166] A few shouts in front of the Palace of the Doges from galley crews demanding their wages,[167]

[163] A.S.V. Venice, Brera 51, Cronaca Veneta f° 105 v°, 1st March, 1448. On the rundown condition of Tana, 22nd May, 1453, A.d.S., Venice, Senato Mar, f° 181. There was still a 'Consul Tane' appointed on 28th March, 1460, *ibid.*, 6, f° 163; notes on the trade in female slaves bought at Kaffa, 2nd July, 1474, A.d.S., Mantua, A° Gonzaga, Series E Levante e Corte Ottomana, 795.

[164] A. Guidoni to the Duke of Modena, Venice, 12th September, 1489, A.d.S. Modena, Venezia VII–54. II–8. These were hearsay figures. Some correspondence refers to 2,000,000 ducats being brought back by the Alexandria and Beirut galleys 'according to the Venetians' (*secondo loro*), Giovanni di Strigi to the Marquis of Mantua, Venice, 28th February, 1471, A.d.S., Mantua, Series E Venezia, B 1431.

[165] M. Sanudo, *op. cit.*, I, col. 734.

[166] *Ibid.*, I, 885–886. On luxury in masculine costume, Senato Terra 15, f°s 86 v° and 87, 7th January, 1506; against excessive table consumption, *ibid.*, f° 42, 21st November, 1504; against extravagance in feminine costume, *ibid.*, f°s 190 and 191, 4th January, 1508, against feasting, Sanudo, *op. cit.*, I, col. 822. But Sanudo lists with satisfaction the sumptuous dishes he had tasted at Venetian feasts.

[167] A.d.S., Venice, Senato Mar II, f° 126, 21st February, 1446.

a few complaints from the poor men of the *Arte della Seta* or *della Lana*, and a pessimistic senatorial decree on the crisis in large shipbuilding[168] cast the only shadows on an otherwise dazzling picture.

But the new century was to declare war on rich cities. Venice escaped by a miracle the storm of Agnadello in 1509. In turn, Genoa, Milan, and Florence suffered irreparable disasters. If the sack of Rome in 1527 had not surpassed all previous horrors, the sack of Genoa in 1522[169] would have the hideous reputation it deserves. Nothing was spared in the captured city, except – a significant detail – the bills of exchange of the merchants, which the soldiers respected on orders from above. Finally in 1528 Genoa went over to Charles V, sealing her fate. As for the Milanese, they shouted by turns, as they had to, 'Long live France',[170] or 'Long live the Emperor', then learned to live under the Spanish as they had learned to live under the Sforza and before them the Visconti. In any case, under the control of the Spanish authorities a local administrative aristocracy remained in charge of Milan and Lombardy.[171] All around might change, but their positions were safe.

In short the cities were not to be so easily eliminated from the land of the living and the powerful. Their position remained good at least until 1530. In the new constellation, in which Seville and Lisbon were in the ascendant, a chain of cities from Antwerp to Venice ruled the world, with Venice still maintaining her supremacy in the eastern Mediterranean, though not without difficulty, for there was only to be a lasting peace with the Turks after 1574. She also maintained her positions in Central Europe. On the other hand, her links with North Africa were swept away, or very nearly,[172] after the Spanish ventures of 1509–1511.[173] In the part of the sea nearest the Atlantic, Venice, situated too far to the east, never played a very important role.

Indeed, the balance sheet would have been a negative one, if Venice had not seen an expansion of her home industries – in silk and woollen manufacture, glassmaking and printing – above all if she had not had a full share in the general advance of the 'second sixteenth century', as the budget and customs figures show, until 1620.[174] Every year the Zecca minted about

---

[168] See above, p. 301 ff.

[169] Jacobo di Capo to the Marquis of Ferrara, Genoa, 31st May, 1522, A.d.S., Mantua, A° Gonzaga, Series E, Genova 758 and J. Tebaldi to the Duke of Modena, Venice, 8th June, 1522, A.d.S., Modena, Venezia 15–77, VI 67.

[170] Jean D'Auton, *Chronique*, I, p. 55, 1499, '*et n'y avoit ne Guelfe ne Gibelin qui pour l'heure ne fussent bons François*', Milan had just been captured.

[171] Federico Chabod, 'Stipendi nominali e busta paga effettiva dei funzionari dell'amministrazione milanese alla fine del Cinquecento' in *Miscellanea in onore di Roberto Cessi*, Rome, 1958, p. 187–363.

[172] F. Braudel, 'Les Espagnols et l'Afrique du Nord de 1492 à 1577' in *Revue Africaine*, 1928.

[173] See tables on p. 393; the Barbary voyages stopped in 1525; Jacques de Mas Latrie, *Traités de paix et de commerce*, 1868, p. 273 (22nd May, 1518); also on the decline of trade with the Barbary coast, M. Sanudo, *op. cit.*, XXV, col. 338.

[174] See below, vol. II, Fig. 57.

a 'million' ducats in gold coin and a 'million' in silver coin.[175] Her merchants were dispersed all over the world from Nuremberg to Hormuz, that is, in very far-off places. They preserved for their city a sort of 'capitalist empire' whose weight will be very hard to assess, but many surprises await us in this field. In 1555, on the occasion of the reorganization of a company, we find records of Venetian merchants active at Seville: Antonio Cornovi, Andrea Cornaro, Giovanni Correr, Lorenzo Aliprandi, Donato Rullo, and Bald. Gabiano.[176] In 1569 a Neapolitan document[177] gives us the names of *five hundred* Venetian merchants who bought wine and wheat in Apulia, principally at Bari; the unpublished documents of the French Consulate at Algiers record the presence in the year 1579[178] of an important money-lender, Bartholomeo Soma, 'merchant of Venice'. Towards 1600 the coffers of the Venetian state treasury were overflowing with money;[179] seven or eight hundred ships went in and out of her port every year if our calculations are correct.[180] And, above all, on the Rialto there was always an abundant supply of specie,[181] perhaps the best stock in Christendom: 'forse', says a Venetian document without exaggeration, 'in Europa, non si trova altra piazza più commoda'.[182] Of course faultfinders and would-be advisers were not satisfied. One of them suggested placing a tax on money-changing which represented 'four-fifths of the business in the piazza', 'quali sono li quattro quinti del traffego della piazza'.[183] So it is not surprising to find that during a three-month period, 24th May to 9th August, 1603, the books of one of the exchange banks, that of Bernardo Navagero, a native of Venice, record the no doubt partly artificial but nevertheless impressive turnover of nearly three million ducats.[184] Venice suffered several blows but remained wealthy, and during the final years of the sixteenth century and the opening years of the

[175] Museo Correr, Donà delle Rose, 26, f° 191 and 194 (1588). By way of comparison, on 6th July, 1671, (Marciana VII, MCCXVIII, 18) the Zecca minted over a million ducats in silver coins.
[176] Clemens Bauer, *op. cit.*, p. 151, note 47 on p. 48.
[177] A.d.S., Naples, Sommaria Partium, 591, f° 225–235, 22nd December, 1569.
[178] Archives of Bouches-du-Rhône, IX B 171, f° 6 v°, Algiers, 7th May, 1579.
[179] 6,000,000 ducats in 1605; 9,000,000 in 1609 in the coffers of the *Deposito Grande* of the *Zecca*. There are many references to the subject in the files of Senato Zecca, F. Braudel, in *La civiltà veneziana del Rinascimento*, Fondazione Giorgio Cini, 1958, p. 101.
[180] See above, p. 292.
[181] Possibly beginning in 1575–1580 if I have correctly interpreted an imprecise document, Museo Correr 161, f° 2, 14th December, 1593: the complexities of exchange and re-exchange are introduced to the Venetian piazza by foreign exchange dealers 'per il più fiorentini'.
[182] E. Magatti, 'Il mercato monetario veneziano alle fine del secolo XVI' in *Archivio Veneto*, 1914, p. 289–292.
[183] Museo Correr, Donà delle Rose, 42, f° 27 v° (undated, late sixteenth century).
[184] *Ibid.*, 181, f° 61 and 65 v°, according to an extract from the *zornal de ziri*, the total sum was 2,979,090 ducats and 71 denari. Another journal, the investigator was told contains a list of exchanges *che non girano*, in other words *secchi*.

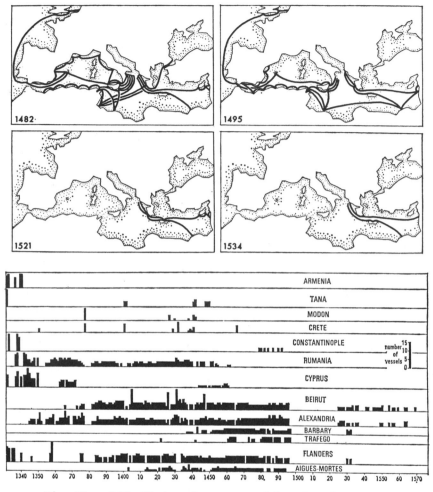

Figs. 31 and 32: *Venice: the voyages of the* galere da mercato

The four sketch maps above are taken from the long narrative by Alberto Tenenti and Corrado Vivanti in *Annales E.S.C.*, 1961, and summarize the stages by which the old system of convoys of *galere da mercato* declined (they had sailed to Flanders, Aiguesmortes, Barbary, the 'Trafego', Alexandria, Beirut, and Constantinople). All these lines were working in 1482. By 1521 and 1534 only the profitable links with the Levant survived. To simplify the map, all routes are shown from the entrance to the Adriatic only, not from Venice.

The table following is a summary of the quantitative history of these convoys (a gap in the documents interrupts the series at the end of the fifteenth century and beginning of the sixteenth century). The decline of the old system of convoys was however, compensated for by private shipping which had always existed, but which expanded over the years.

seventeenth, she abandoned herself once more to the pleasures of living and of thinking. Her late Renaissance is proof enough of this.

But this brilliant façade cannot entirely hide the truth. Venice, although she was perhaps even richer than during the fifteenth century, had declined in *relative* importance. She was no longer the centre of the Mediterranean. The commercial activity of the sea, concentrating more and more in the West, tipped the balance, spelling the inexorable decline of the eastern basin which had for so long been the source of wealth. The shift brought little joy to Milan, but brought Genoa and Florence to prominence. Genoa for her share, and a lion's share it was, acquired the Spanish and American trade; Florence promoted Lyons and took over France, without losing her position in Germany; she also had many representatives in Spain. These two cities were now the dominant forces in the quadrilateral, particularly since they did not confine their activity to commerce in the humble sense but became financial centres on a grand scale. In the second half of the century, Genoa took the lead. Geographers talk of a catchment area of a river; here there was a catchment of many trades by the quick-flowing rivers of money to the profit of financiers in Genoa and Florence. Internal catchment to begin with: in Florence, where as historians we can see a little more clearly now, credit was extended to the most humble levels of everyday life.[185] Foreign catchment was the most important, and it was by this means that Florence and Genoa gained control of all the economically backward regions, whether in Eastern Europe or southern Italy, in the Balkans, France,[186] or the Iberian peninsula. In the process even a city as leisurely and invulnerable as Venice could find itself caught up in the subtle tangles of foreign exploitation, as we have seen.[187]

There was nothing new about these activities, of course; but they were undertaken on an unprecedented scale. Never before had there flowed through Europe such a stream of currencies and credit bonds. This flow dominated the second half of the sixteenth century, swelling and maturing rapidly, then dwindling quickly away (even before the 1619–1622 crisis[188] which reversed the secular trend), as the result of some *structural* upheaval, or so it appears. At any rate, with the establishment of the great exchange fairs at Piacenza in 1579, the Genoese bankers became the masters of international payments, of the fortune both of Europe and of the world, the not unchallenged but well-entrenched masters of the political silver of Spain, from 1579 and perhaps even from 1577 on. They could reach out and take anything they pleased. It looked for a moment in 1590 as if they

[185] This is indicated by the present research of Maurice Carmona into seventeenth century Tuscany.
[186] Cf. the remark of a Florentine merchant in the fifteenth century, quoted by A. Monteil, *Histoire des Français*, VII, p. 424–425: 'You French merchants are nothing but retailers and shopkeepers.'
[187] See above, p. 322, note 232.
[188] Ruggiero Romano, 'Tra XVI e XVII secolo. Una crisi economica: 1619–1622' in *Rivista Storica Italiana*, 1962, p. 480–531 and 'Encore la crise de 1619–1622' in *Annales E.S.C.*, 1964, p. 31–37.

were going to pounce on the Portuguese pepper privileges which were up for sale. 'Indeed', wrote a Spanish merchant living in Florence on hearing this (he disliked the Genoese), 'they are a kind of people who would think the world itself but a small thing to take on.'[189] The 'age of the Fuggers', such a short one, was truly over and the age of the Genoese was belatedly beginning, not to end until the 1620s when the rise of the 'new Christians' of Portugal announced the hybrid capitalism of Amsterdam.

Today these broad stretches of history are more clearly visible.[190] It was during the decisive years 1575–1579,[191] after a spectacular trial of strength against Philip II and his advisers, that Genoese capitalism won the day. The fall of Antwerp, sacked by the army in 1576, difficulties and failure of the fairs of Medina del Campo, the increased weakness of Lyons after 1583, were all signs accompanying the triumph of Genoa and the Piacenza fairs. From then on there could be no question of equality between Venice and Genoa, Florence and Genoa and *a fortiori* between Milan and Genoa. All doors were open to Genoa,[192] all her neighbours dominated by her. They were only to take their revenge, if indeed at all, in the following century.

2. HOW MANY PEOPLE?

Most important of all and the clearest indication both of the measure and the trend of the century is the number of people. First, how big was the population – a difficult question. Second, was it increasing as all the evidence seems to suggest – no less difficult to answer, particularly if one sets out to distinguish different stages and percentages of growth and to compare one population with another.

A world of 60 or 70 million people. There are no definite figures. Only approximate numbers can be given, reasonably reliable ones for Italy and Portugal, and not too unrealistic for France, Spain, and the Ottoman Empire.[193] As for the other Mediterranean countries the lack of demographic data is complete.

[189] Baltasar Suárez to Simón Ruiz, Florence, 15th January, 1590, 'Cierto es gente que les parece todo el mundo es poco para barcarle', Archivio Provincial, Valladolid.

[190] On research into these questions of 'polarity' let me recommend the excellent article by Federigo Melis, 'Il commercio transatlantico di una compagnia fiorentina stabilitata a Siviglia a pochi anni dalle imprese di Cortes e Pizarro' in *V. Congreso de historia de la Corona de Aragon*, 1954, particularly p. 183 ff. My colleague is thinking of Florence, the centre of the world at the beginning of the sixteenth century, but why not Lyons? Also to be recommended the forthcoming studies by Felipe Ruiz Martín and J. Gentil da Silva.

[191] See below, p. 500 ff.

[192] A.d.S., Genoa, Materie politiche, privilegi, concessioni trattati diversi et negoziazioni 15–2734, no. 67. Trattato di commercio stipulato tra il Soltano Hacmet Han, Imperatore degli Ottomani e la Republica di Genova.

[193] The whole question of the demography of the Turkish Empire has been looked at afresh by Ömer Lütfi Barkan and his pupils. Their vast project of analysing the

In the West the probable figures *at the end of the century*[194] are the following: Spain, 8 million; Portugal, 1 million; France, 16 million; Italy, 13 million: a total population of 38 million. Then there are the Islamic countries. Konrad Olbricht accepted[195] 8 million as an estimate of the

---

documents relating to Turkish censuses in the sixteenth century is nearing completion. With the kind permission of my Turkish colleague at Istanbul, I am able to use the unpublished results which are summarized in the map in volume II, Fig. 55. For a description of aims and progress of this research, see Ömer Lütfi Barkan, 'La Méditerranée de F. Braudel' in *Annales E.S.C.*, 1954, 'Quelques observations sur l'organization économique et sociale des villes ottomanes des XVIe et XVIIe siècles' in *Recueils de la Société Jean Bodin*, VII, *La Ville*, 1st part, 1955, p. 289 ff. Further information in the typed transcript of Professor Barkan's lectures at the École des Hautes Études (1963).

[194] The best general guide is still Julius Beloch's article 'Die Bevölkerung Europas zur Zeit der Renaissance' in *Zeitschrift für Socialwissenschaft*, III, 1900. On Italy the same great German scholar's posthumous work *Bevölkerungsgechichte Italiens*, vol. I, 1937; vol. II, 1939; vol. III, 1961. On France, Levasseur's *La population française* has not yet been surpassed. For Portugal in the sixteenth century Lucio Azevedo and other Portuguese historians have accepted a population of a million, cf. G. Freyre, *Casa Grande*, 1946, p. 166; R. Konetzke, *op. cit.*, p. 271. Spain is a very difficult case: There is the study by Konrad Haebler *Die wirtschaftliche Blüte Spaniens*, 1888 (which is open to much criticism, more indeed than it received in J. Beloch's article); by Albert Girard there is 'Le chiffre de la population de l'Espagne dans les temps modernes' in *Revue d'Histoire moderne* 1928, which is clear, well-informed, but doubtful in its conclusions; by the same author, 'La répartition de la population en Espagne, dans les temps modernes' in *Revue d'Histoire écon. et soc.*, 1929, p. 347–362. I am not convinced of the merits of Fuentes Martiañez, *Despoblación y repoblación de España*, (*1482-1920*), Madrid, 1929, which seems to me to over-estimate the Spanish population in the time of the Catholic Monarchs. On the difficult question of the *vecinos*, I agree with J. Beloch that a coefficient of 4·5 is proper or at any rate defensible. Fuentes Martiañez suggests a figure of 8 million for the end of the sixteenth century. For Castile alone, there are the figures in Tomás González's classic study, which I have reproduced in the form of a table. I found at Simancas a document, (E° 166, *Consulta del Consejo de Guerra sobre la introduccion de la milicia de 30 U hombres en estos ryenos*, 13th January, 1589, copy) which gives an estimate of the population of the kingdom of Castile as 1,500,000 *Vecinos*, that is, using a coefficient of 4·5: 6,750,000 inhabitants. R. Konetzke's figures, *op. cit.*, p. 260–261, are too low.

There is very little solid foundation for such demographic estimates. Our calculations are probably scarcely more reliable than G. Botero's, *op. cit.*, II, a, p. 64–65, which are not to my knowledge frequently cited (Italy less than 9 million, France 15, Sicily 1·3, Germany 10, England 3, Italy higher than Spain). Botero in *Dell'isole* gives us two more figures: Corsica, 75,000, Cyprus, 160,000, and also points out the contrast between Christendom and Islam, (II, p. 119) the one with too many, the other with too few inhabitants.

Danger lies in accepting exaggerated estimates of the population in the good old days, for Milan in the fifteenth century for instance, as A. Fanfani has shown (*Saggi*, p. 135) taking issue with S. Pugliese, or Spain under Ferdinand and Isabella. It must also be remembered that most population counts were made for fiscal purposes, as K. J. Beloch pointed out, while nevertheless continuing his calculations. Then there was fraud: towards 1613, Antonio Serra, *Breve trattato delle cause che possono far abondare li Regni d'oro e argento . . . con applicatione al Regno di Napoli*, Naples, 1613, p. 38, thinks, 'giudicando all'in grosso' that there are a million households in Naples 'con li franchi e fraudati'.

[195] Konrad Olbricht, 'Die Vergrosstädterung des Abendlandes zu Beginn des Dreissigjährigen Krieges' in *Pet. Mit.*, 1939, p. 349, with bibliography and map.

population of the European part of Turkey in about 1600. Since the two parts of the Turkish empire, the Asian and the European, usually seem to have been equivalent (the latter if anything slightly superior),[196] a figure of 8 million for the Asian part of Turkey is a reasonable assumption. We are now left with the whole of North Africa. Can we attribute 2 or 3 million to Egypt and about the same to North Africa?[197] This would give us a maximum of 22 million for Islam and its dependent peoples on the shores of the Mediterranean. And the total population of the Mediterranean would be in the region of 60 million.

Of these figures, the first total, 38 million, is comparatively reliable, the second much less so. But the overall estimate is well within the bounds of probability. I would be inclined to lower the figure of the first group and raise that of the second. There seems, from population studies over the ages, to be a rough and ready rule to the effect that the population of Islam in the Mediterranean (and the peoples under its rule in the sixteenth century) was about double that of Italy. If this was so, in 1850,[198] when the countries of the first group yielded a total of 78.5 million (France, 35 million, Italy, 25 million, Spain, 15 million, Portugal, 3.5 million), Islam, or rather Islam plus the Balkans, ought to have numbered 50 million people.[199] A very summary check shows that this figure is not grossly inaccurate. In about 1930, in any case, there were 113 million in one group (42, 41, 24, 6) and 83 in the other: the ratio remains the same.[200] There is of course no reason to assume that this proportion was absolutely constant. But taking into account all possible variations, it does provide a rough guide. If it was the same in the sixteenth century, it would give a figure of 26 million, which is not very far from the 22 million of our previous estimate. We may still sympathise with Ömer Lütfi Barkan's sug-

[196] If the number of administrative areas is compared, or military recruitment both of sipahis and galley oarsmen. On the latter point, there were in 'Natolia' 478,000 households liable to be called on for oarsmen for the galleys, and 358,000 in Greece, 1594, E. Albèri, *op. cit.*, III, V, p. 402. Report by Matteo Zane. One text, Dispatches from Constantinople, 6–26th February, 1591, A.N., K 1675, refers to a million households, but does it refer to Greece alone or Greece and Asia combined?

[197] With absolutely no evidence to go on in North Africa (but I would stress that this region suffered greatly during the sixteenth century), and in the case of Egypt, taking the figures for the early nineteenth century, which must be regarded as a maximum: Richard and Quétin, *Guide en Orient*, 1852, p. 303 (2,213,015). Is it misleading to assume equality between Egypt and North Africa? In 1830, Algeria alone was said, without any solid proof, to have 2 million inhabitants; a proportional calculation would give a total population of between 4 and 5 million. J. C. Russell, 'Late ancient and medieval population' in *The American Philosophical Society*, June, 1958, p. 131, proposes a figure of 3½ million for the population of North Africa (of which one million represents Tunisia), basing his argument on the documents published by Elie de la Primaudaie in *Revue Africaine*, 1877.

[198] These figures are taken from Adolphe Landry, *Traité de démographie*, 1945, p. 57.

[199] A figure higher than that given in the *Guide* of Richard and Quétin, which I used for a very rough calculation, nearer 40 than 50.

[200] According to A. Landry, *op. cit.*, and various volumes by Vidal de la Blache and Gallois, *Géogr. Universelle*.

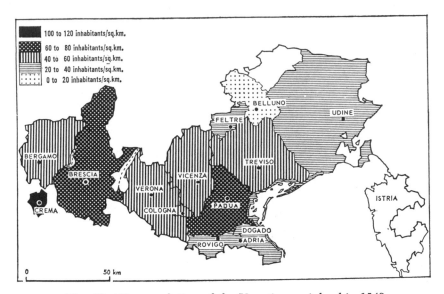

Fig. 33: *The population of the Venetian mainland in 1548*

After D. Beltrami, *Forze di Lavoro e proprietà fondiaria*, Rome, 1961, p. 3. Density calculated over fairly large areas. The *Dogado* was the territory immediately surrounding Venice which she possessed before the conquest of her mainland empire.

gestion[201] that Islam in the Mediterranean might have claimed a population of 30 or even 35 million, but this is an optimistic judgment. In any case, by lowering the figures for the West and raising those of the East, we still get a total of about 60 million inhabitants of the whole region, which seems to be to be an acceptable figure for the end of the sixteenth century, allowing a margin of error of about 10 per cent. What are the consequences?

In this world of 60 million people, the density per square kilometre was about 17, if the desert is not included in the Mediterranean region. This is an incredibly low figure. Of course there were large differences from region to region. In 1595 the average population density of the kingdom of Naples was 57 to the square kilometre;[202] it was as high as 160 in Campania, around Mount Vesuvius;[203] in about 1600 the population density in the area between the Ticino and the Mincio, the centre of gravity of the Italian population, was 100 to the square kilometre and sometimes even higher (117 in Cremona and the surrounding region; 110 in Milan and its rural districts and Lodi; 108 in the plain of Bergamo; 103 in the plain of Brescia); density decreased to the east and to the west (49 in Piedmont; 80 even in the rich region of Padua). The average density for the whole of

[201] *Art. cit.*, 'La Méditerranée . . .,' p. 193.
[202] J. Beloch, *Bevölkerungsgeschichte*, I, p. 234. In his earlier article the figure advanced was 54.
[203] *Ibid.*, p. 235.

Italy was 44,[204] a very high figure; in France there was an average of only 34 inhabitants to the square kilometre,[205] and in Spain and Portugal only 17.[206] These figures were published in the first edition of this book. Since then detailed research has been carried out, and new figures have been advanced. But we need not necessarily modify the calculations in the preceding paragraphs. The area most under discussion is of course the population of Islam. I am afraid I cannot agree with the estimation of the Moroccan population at 5 or 6 million, in 1500 it is true, despite my respect for its author.[207] An increase in the overall figure as suggested by Barkan[208] seems reasonable, but I am still not convinced that the two groups, Christendom and Islam, were equivalent. A further small proof is that the figures we have reached are also those of observant contemporaries, not only Botero[209] but also the enquiring mind of Rodrigo Vivero, whose papers are soon to be published.[210]

Mediterranean waste lands.[211] In fact population density was even lower than our figures suggest, since geographical space was so much vaster in relation to man than it is now. We must imagine a population only about a third or a quarter the size of today's, scattered over a far more unmanageable area.

And there were wastelands. The abnormal urban concentration and natural aridity contributed to give the distribution of population the oasis character that is still one of the features of the Mediterranean today.[212] Unwelcoming and hostile, these deserts, sometimes 'grandissimi', divided the lands of the Mediterranean. The borders of such regions were like the coasts of the sea, favoured zones of settlement where the traveller could

[204] J. Beloch, *op. cit.*, III, p. 379 ff.

[205] J. Beloch quotes a higher total figure for the French population, *art .cit.*, p. 783. Any estimate in this area must be *extremely* approximate.

[206] *Ibid.*

[207] Vitorino Magalhães Godinho, *Historia economica e social da expansão portuguesa*, I, 1947, p. 145 ff.

[208] *Art. cit.*, 'La Méditerranée . . .', p. 193, ' . . . the Ottoman Empire had a population not of 20 or 22 millions (F. Braudel's figures) but of 30 or possibly 35 million'.

[209] *Op. cit.*, II a, p. 64–65.

[210] B.M. Mss Add. 18287, Ps 5633.

[211] A few further notes and references beside the examples listed in this paragraph: in Turkey *deserti grandissimi*, E. Albèri, *op. cit.*, III, III, p. 387 (1594); wild beasts in North Africa in the fifteenth century, R. Brunschvig, *op. cit.*, I p. 267: the wastes of Syria, G. Berchet, *op. cit.*, p. 60 (16th April, 1574, 8/10 of the country was empty); I. de Asso, *op. cit.*, p. 176; *Actas de las Cortes . . .*, I, p. 312–313 (1548); G. Botero, *op. cit.*, p. 35, reference to Provence; G. Niemeyer, *op. cit.*, p. 51, 57, 62 (maps of the deserted regions of Andalusia in 1767); C. Bernaldo de Quirós, *Los reyes y la colonización interior de España desde el siglo XVI al XIX*, Madrid, 1929; Marc Bloch, 'Les paysages agraires: essai de mise au point' in *Ann. d'hist. éc. et soc.*, May, 1935, p. 47; Arqué, *op. cit.*, p. 172. Albitreccia, *op. cit.*, p. 18 . . . The renegade who reaches Toledo by way of '*montes y los despoblados*', Toledo Inquisition, L° 191, no. 1, quoted by F. Rodriguez Marín, *El ingenioso Don Quijote*, 1916, IV, p. 99, note 7.

[212] A. Siegfried, *op. cit.*, p. 106. Jules Sion, *France méditerranéenne*, p. 159 ff.

gather strength in the comfortable or at any rate unhurried atmosphere of the *fonduks* before tackling the obstacle before him. To list every one of these miniature Arabian deserts would take too long. Let us be content with a few images: for instance, not far from the Ebro with its irrigated fields, its toiling *fellahin*, and its avenues of trees, lay the miserable steppes of Aragon, where a monotonous wilderness of heather and rosemary stretched as far as the eye could see. Francesco Guicciardini, a Florentine envoy to Ferdinand the Catholic, travelled in the spring of 1512 across this '. . . paese desertissimo nel quale non si trova allogiamento alcuno, nè si vede pur un arbore: ma tutto è pieno di rosmarini e salvie, per esser terra aridissima'.[213] Similar descriptions come from other travellers, like the Venetian Navagero[214] in 1525. 'In Aragon, near the Pyrenean mountains', says a French account of 1617[215] 'one can walk for days on end without meeting a single inhabitant', and the poorest region in Aragon – for there were degrees – was the *partido* of Albarracin.[216] This was true of Aragon and of the whole Iberian peninsula. As Botero[217] notes, if Spain is so little cultivated it is because it is so thinly populated. Cervantes had nothing to invent – Don Quixote and Sancho Panza's journey must have led them through solitary wastes. Similarly in Portugal, the population thins out towards the south in the regions of Algarve, Alemtejo, and Beira.[218] There were deserts even around Lisbon, fragrant with the perfumes of wild herbs.[219] But every region in the Mediterranean, had its wildernesses, rang hollow. In Provence man has a 'quarter of the land, the low-lying basins which are oases with harvests, olive trees, vines, and ornamental cypresses. Nature has three quarters of the land, layered rocks, reddish-brown or silver grey'.[220] And from these rocks man had to wrest the narrow belt along the foothills, the terraced hillsides where he practised a kind of farming requiring agility and mobility;[221] little enough, but here as elsewhere, the peasant must live off narrow strips of land.

These depopulated lands yawn like gaping wounds to the south and east. Busbecq travelled through deserts in Asia Minor.[222] Leo Africanus on his way from Morocco to Tlemcen had to cross the Moulouya desert[223] where herds of gazelles fled away before the traveller.

No villages, no human dwellings. These territories were a haven of animal life. It is no surprise to find that the mountains were literally over-

---

[213] Francesco Guicciardini, *Diario del viaggio in Spagna*, Florence, 1932, p. 79; similar references on p. 54, 55, 56.

[214] *Op. cit.*, p. 5 v°.

[215] Davity, *Les estats, empires et principautez du monde*, Paris, 1617, p. 141.

[216] I. de Asso, *op. cit.*, p. 180 ff.

[217] *Op. cit.*, p. 232.

[218] Fortunato de Almeida, *História de Portugal*, III, p. 242–243.

[219] B. M. Sloane, 1572, f° 48 v°, 1633, (June or July).

[220] Louis Gachon, in *Nouvelles Littéraires*, 10th February, 1940.

[221] Roger Livet, *op. cit.*, notably p. 428.

[222] *Lettres*, 1748, I, p. 138–139.

[223] Leo Africanus, *Description de l'Afrique, tierce partie du monde*, 1896 ed., II, p. 308 ff.

run with wild creatures. In Bayard's native Dauphiné, bears abounded.[224] In Corsica in the sixteenth century huge boar-, stag-, and wolf-hunts had to be organized to protect the flocks, so the island exported wild beasts for the menageries of mainland princes.[225] Hares, rabbits, and partridges were plentiful in Spain and this game was carefully guarded by royal keepers around the woods of Aranjuez.[226] But the most plentiful game was foxes, wolves, and bears, even around Toledo[227] and Philip II in the very last days of his life went on a wolf hunt in the Sierra de Guadarrama.[228] There could be no more natural trick than that practised by the Andalusian peasants who, when they were about to attack some noblemen, cried wolf;[229] nor was there any more everyday accident than that which befell Diego Suárez,[230] when as a child he was guarding the sheep in the southern coastal region of Spain, depopulated as a result of the Barbary pirates and the fear they inspired. One day his donkey was devoured by wolves and the luckless shepherd ran off without waiting to see more or reporting to his master. In Granada the war of 1568–1570 aggravated the situation by creating in this countyside, formerly so prosperous, stretches of wasteland where wildlife multiplied at an incredible rate,[231] rabbits, hares, boars, stags, red and roedeer (the latter in 'great herds'), as well as wolves and foxes.

A similar but even more exotic sight could be seen in North Africa. In October, 1573, Don John of Austria went to hunt lions and wild bulls on the very site of Carthage.[232] A Spanish deserter trying to re-enter the *presidio* of La Goletta related that his travelling companion had been eaten by lions.[233] It was common for douars in North Africa in the sixteenth century to be surrounded by thorny barriers against hyenas and jackals.[234] Haëdo refers to great boar-hunts round Algiers.[235]

Even Italy, the image of prosperity in the sixteenth century, still had her wildernesses: forests, brigands, and wild beasts were plentiful in Bocaccio's

[224] *Le Loyal Serviteur*, p. 2.

[225] On wild beasts in Corsica, Giuseppe Micheli, 'Lettere di Mons. Bernardi (1569)' in *Arch. st. di Corsica*, 1926, p. 187.

[226] Fernand Braudel, 'Dans l'Espagne de Charles Quint et Philippe II' in *Annales E.S.C.*, 1951. For the Bosque of Segovia and the Prado, September, 1581, P.R.O., 30. 25. 57, f° 87.

[227] Carmelo Viñas and Ramón Paz, *op. cit.*, II, p. 90, at Menasalbas, '*los mas animales que hay son zorras y lobos*'; Charles V, in March, 1534, went on a hunting trip near Toledo lasting four or five days, '*havendo morto et porci et lupi*', A.d.S., Mantua, Spagna 587, Gio. Agnello to the Marquis, Toledo, 3rd April, 1534.

[228] In August, 1597, he went on a four-day wolf-hunt. A.d.S., Genoa, Spagna, 12, Cesare Giustiniano to the Signoria of Genoa, Madrid, 7th August, 1596.

[229] M. Alemán, *Guzmán de Alfarache, op. cit.*, I, 1st part, VIII, p. 140.

[230] MS at the Government General building at Algiers, f° 13, about 1574.

[231] Pedro de Medina, *op. cit.*, p. 172.

[232] B.N., Florence, Capponi Codice, V, f° 343 v° to 344 (account of the capture of Tunis).

[233] Alonso de la Cueva to Philip II, La Goletta, 16th May, 1561, Simancas, E° 486.

[234] G. Botero, *op. cit.*, I, p. 185. Or even better, Diego Suárez, *op. cit.*, p. 45, 49, 50.

[235] *Op. cit.*, p. 77.

time,[236] and the body of one of Bandello's characters is abandoned without burial near Mantua to the wolves and wild dogs.[237] In Provence, hares, rabbits, red deer, boars, and roedeer abounded; and foxes and wolves were hunted.[238] The latter did not disappear from the semi-desert wastes of the Crau until mid-nineteenth century.[239]

A large book could be written on animal life in the sixteenth century and no doubt every country would lay claim to the first place. Certainly the Mediterranean has no particular right to it. The many thousands of images it has to offer are neither original nor exclusive. In the Mediterranean as in other places man already had the upper hand, although he was not yet the absolute master he has virtually become today.

And as one would expect there was less open country in the more densely populated west than in Islam. Islam was the animal kingdom par excellence, with its great deserts both natural and man-made. On the borders of Serbia, 'the countryside is a desert', notes Lescalopier in 1574, 'which prevents Christian and other slaves from trying to escape'.[240] Wild life proliferated in these uninhabited lands. Busbecq, during his stay at Constantinople, took enormous pleasure in turning his house into a menagerie.[241]

The wide, uninhabited areas of Islam help to explain its reputation for horse-breeding and consequently its military strength, for the Balkans and North Africa were protected from Christian Europe in the first place by their immensity and in the second place by their abundant supply of horses and camels. Following the advance of the Turks, the camel successfully conquered the great flat spaces of the Balkan peninsula, as far as the foothills of the Dinaric Alps to the west and to the north as far as Hungary. Sulaimān's army, encamped before Vienna in 1529, was brought supplies by camel. 'Door-ships', with doors for the embarkation of animals, continually ferried camels and horses over from Asia to Europe. Their comings and goings were part of the daily sights of the port at Constantinople.[242] And we know that caravans of camels accomplished immense journeys in North Africa. Horses, donkeys, and mules took over in the mountains of the Balkans, Syria, Palestine, or on the routes from Cairo to Jerusalem.[243]

Facing Europe along the Hungarian border one of the great strengths of Islam and its immediate neighbours was long to be its outstanding cavalry, the object of much envy and admiration on the part of the Christians. The cavalry of any other country looked slow and clumsy in action against the Turks, of whom Botero wrote 'if they beat you, you cannot escape from them by flight, if they scatter under your attack, you

---

[236] *Decameron*, Novella III.
[237] *Op. cit.*, III, p. 337.
[238] Quiqueran de Beaujeu, *La Provence louée*, Lyons, 1614, p. 221, 225, 226, 261.
[239] F. Benoit, *op. cit.*, p. 180.
[240] P. Lescalopier, *Voyage . . .*, p. 27.
[241] *Op. cit.*, trans. Forster, p. 95 ff.
[242] Pierre Belon, *op. cit.*, p. 135.
[243] *Ibid.*

cannot follow them, for they are like hawks, they can either pounce upon you, or fly from you at great speed . . .'.[244]

Quality and quantity: this double wealth was well-known. When Don John's advisers were discussing a landing in Morea and Albania, in December, 1571, the prince was of the opinion that horses need not be shipped. It would be sufficient to take on board the requisite number of saddles and harnesses and enough money to buy the animals on landing.[245] In Christendom, by contrast, even in the famous horse-breeding regions, such as Naples and Andalusia, horses were treasures jealously guarded and notoriously the subject of smuggling. Philip II would delegate to no one the duty of dealing with applications for export licences for Andalusian horses, personally examining every request.

In short, on one side there were too many people and not enough horses; on the other too many horses and not enough people. This imbalance may have been a reason for the tolerance exercised by Islam, only too eager indeed to receive men, of any origin, whenever they came within reach.

A population increase of 100 per cent? Everywhere in the sixteenth century man was on the increase, suggesting once again that Ernst Wagemann[246] was right to insist that any large population increase must occur simultaneously throughout entire humanity. The sixteenth century, then, must have been one of these periods of general demographic advance. At any rate the rule certainly applies to all the populations around the shores of the Mediterranean. After 1450, or at latest 1500, numbers began to grow in France, Spain, and Italy as well as in the Balkans and Asia Minor. It was not until 1600 that this trend was reversed and the decline was not general and perceptible until after 1650, which we can take as the final limit. Within this broad movement there were of course individual failures to keep step and varying rates of increase. Progress was far from regular, if anything it was rather like a procession of penitents, who take two steps forward and one step back, but move nevertheless along the appointed route.

Stepping beyond the limit of prudence, for in this instance it is a bad counsellor, let us say that the population of the Mediterranean may by and large have doubled between 1500 and 1600. It rose from 30 or 35 million to 60 or 70 million, i.e., an *average* annual rate of increase of 7 per 1000. The very striking, and indeed revolutionary advance of the first sixteenth century (1450–1550) on the whole slowed down during the second (1550–1650) (approximate dates). This is the very general proposition I would make, without any guarantee at the outset of the discussion, hoping that the

[244] *Op. cit.*, II, p. 31.

[245] Lo que paresce a D. Juan de Austria, Messina, 4th December, 1571, Simancas E° 113.

[246] F. Braudel, 'La démographie et les dimensions des sciences de l'homme' in *Annales E.S.C.*, May–June, 1960, esp. p. 497.

reader will not lose sight of it amid the imperfect evidence and arguments that follow. Before he hears them he will be aware, then, that this increase was universal, that it was common to both rich regions and poor, the populations of the plains, the mountains, and the steppes, to all towns, whatever their size, and all rural districts. He will be prepared to accept that this biological revolution was the major factor in all the other revolutions with which we are concerned, more important than the Turkish conquest, the discovery and colonization of America, or the imperial vocation of Spain. Had it not been for the increase in the number of men, would any of these glorious chapters ever have have been written? This revolution is more important too than the 'price revolution', of which it may have been a contributory factor even before the massive arrivals of bullion from America.[247] This increase lay behind all the triumphs and catastrophes of a century during which man was first a useful worker and then, as the century wore on, a growing burden. By 1550 the turning-point had been reached. There were too many people for comfort. Towards 1600 this overload halted expansion in new directions and with the rise of banditry,[248] the latent social crisis whose effects were felt everywhere or almost everywhere, prepared the way for the bitter awakenings of the seventeenth century. All this by way of a brief foreword. Let us now look at the evidence, the signs of this rising tide.

Levels and indices. Ideally one should argue from serial figures. But there are none such available. So we shall have to use what imperfect material there is and be content with information from six or seven sources which is, however, fairly clear and consistent.

1. *Provence from the fourteenth to the sixteenth century* is one of our best sources of information, although even this is incomplete. Provence in the broadest sense, including the county of Nice, which later passed under the rule of Savoy, numbered 80,000 households, that is 350,000 to 400,000 inhabitants, at the beginning of the fourteenth century. Here, as in Languedoc, whose destiny was very similar, the Black Death (1348) struck brutally, killing a third or a half of the population. It was more than a hundred years before numbers at last began to rise after about 1470. 'The number of households [then] grew so rapidly that in 1540 it was three times what it had been in 1470.'[249] The population of Provence once more reached the level at which it stood on the eve of the Black Death. We do not know how this population fared during the 'second' sixteenth century and the seventeenth. It probably increased then declined as it did in other places, but there is no clear evidence. Mediæval and modern

---

[247] See the essay by René Grandamy, 'La grande régression, hypothèse sur l'évolution des prix réels de 1375 to 1875' in Jean Fourastié, *Prix de vente et prix de revient*, 13th series, Paris, 1964, p. 3–58.

[248] See below Vol II, Part II, ch. 5, *Societies*, section 3.

[249] Édouard Baratier, *La démographie provençale du XIIIe au XVIe siècle*, 1961, p. 121. The extent to which this increase was in fact a recovery is explained by Roger Livet, *op. cit.*, p. 147–148.

404 *Collective Destinies*

historians have, here as elsewhere, failed to bridge the gap. But this problem, though important, is not the crucial one, which is that the best part of the demographic advance of the sixteenth century was in fact a recovery of a previous level, a compensatory increase; that its progress which was rapid before 1540, probably slowed down with the second half of the sixteenth century.

2. *In Languedoc* we have a similar pattern. The fifteenth century offers the spectacle of a depopulated land, abandoned to wildlife and the spread of forests. The sixteenth century saw at first a rapid and revolutionary rise in population, which slowed down after 1550; towards 1600 the population was clearly stationary; dramatic and catastrophic decline set in after 1650. Such is the chronological sequence suggested by Le Roy Ladurie's recent invaluable research.[250]

3. *In Catalonia*, the same development recurs. A rise followed by a fall, the transition occurring in about 1620.[251]

4. *In Valencia*, the advance was slow, hardly noticeable from 1527 to 1563; but was very marked between 1563 and 1609 (over 50 per cent overall, and 70 per cent among the prolific Moriscos).[252]

5. *In Castile* there is clear evidence of substantial demographic advance during the sixteenth century, an advance that is even more striking if one discounts the exaggerated figures sometimes accepted for the population of Spain in the time of Ferdinand and Isabella (by Konrad Häbler and Albert Girard among others). In the sixteenth century there seems to have been a steady upward trend, as is clearly proved for the period 1530 to 1591 by the figures given by the nineteenth-century historian Tomás González,[253] although sometimes his figures are open to serious criticism.[254]

The errors in González' huge calculations—and there certainly are errors—do not invalidate the overall conclusions. In sixty-one years the population of Castile quite simply doubled (annual rate of increase over 11 per 1000) in spite of the burden of war and emigration to the New World, the importance of which should not be exaggerated.[255] In any case, two little-known contemporary estimates of the total population of Castile do not contradict this conclusion: the first, based on the census of the year 1541, puts the number of *vecinos* in Castile at 1,179,303,[256] which is higher than Tomás González' figure; the other, dated 13th January, 1589, the

[250] *Op. cit.*, Part II, ch. II.
[251] J. Nadal and E. Giralt, *La population catalane de 1553 à 1717*, 1960, p. 198.
[252] Henri Lapeyre, *Géographie de l'Espagne morisque*, 1959, p. 29 and 30.
[253] Tomás González, *Censo de la población de las provincias y partidos de la Corona de Castilla en el siglo XVI*, 1829.
[254] Particularly concerning the kingdom of Granada. So I have corrected the final figure of the table: instead of 71,904 *vecinos*, it now reads 48,021. This correction will be confirmed by the forthcoming studies by Felipe Ruiz Martín and Alvaro Castillo Pintado.
[255] See below p. 417 and notes 312, 313.
[256] *CODOIN*, XIII, p. 529–530.

Population of The Regions under The Crown of Castile

	1530	1541	1591
Burgos	83,440	63,684	96,166
Soria	29,126	32,763	38,234
Valladolid	43,749	43,787	55,605
León	28,788	59,360	97,110
Zamora	31,398	86,278	146,021
Toro	37,117	41,230	51,352
Salamanca	122,980	133,120	176,708
Avila	28,321	31,153	37,756
Segovia	31,878	33,795	41,413
Guadalajara	24,034	26,257	37,901
Madrid	12,399	13,312	31,932
Toledo	53,943	80,957	147,549
Murcia		19,260	28,470
Cuenca	29,740	33,341	65,368
Sevilla	73,522	80,357	114,738
Córdoba	31,735	34,379	46,209
Jaén	24,469	35,167	55,684
Granada		41,800	48,021
Vecinos	686,639	880,000	1,316,237
Inhabitants	3,089,875	3,960,000	5,923,066

The index of 4·5 has been used to obtain the total number of inhabitants, the *vecinos* corresponding to numbering by household.

source of which is the *Consejo de Guerra*, refers to 1,500,000 *vecinos*.[257] These figures, whose reliability is not of course beyond dispute, at least do not invalidate the general tenor of González' conclusions.

The results so far do not by any means either satisfy our curiosity or exhaust the possibilities of the documents at Simancas and elsewhere. In the course of research at Simancas I have frequently come across references to a vast census carried out in 1561, which probably gives the *padrón* of all the towns[258] and their *partidos*. If we knew its results it would make it easier to plot the graph of the demographic upswing between 1530 and 1591. There is no proof that the increase reached its peak in 1591 where we have situated it for lack of better evidence, and *a priori* Ramón Carande[259] would appear to be right. It is also quite clear that this high-water mark, whenever it occurred, was also a crucial turning-point in the fortunes of Spain. And finally it would be of value to know more about the distribution of the population throughout the different provinces of the Peninsula. It has been suggested that there was a general move to the South[260] of wealth certainly and undesirable elements too, but not of the solidly rooted

[257] Simancas E° 166, f° 3, 13th January, 1589.
[258] For Seville see Simancas, Expedientes de Hacienda, 170.
[259] *Op. cit.*, p. 43–44.
[260] Pierre Chaunu, *op. cit.*, I, p. 247 ff.

Fig. 34: *Population of Castile in 1541*

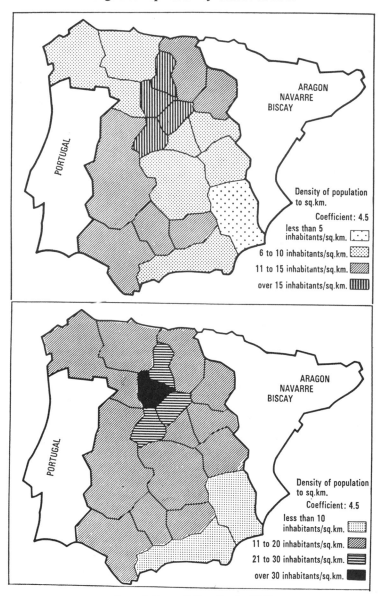

Population of Castile in 1591

A coefficient of 4·5 inhabitants to the *vecino* has been adopted. These maps and the two following are taken from the article by Alvaro Castillo Pintado, *Annales E.S.C.* The divisions correspond to the different provinces of Castile.

Fig. 35: *Increase in Population 1541-1591*

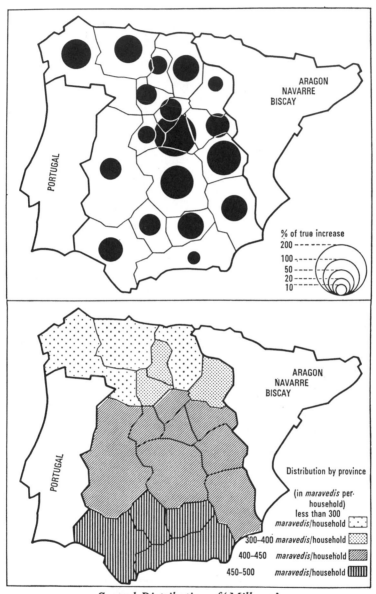

Second Distribution of 'Millones'

On the first map the greatest increase in population corresponds to the growth of the new capital, Madrid. On the second map, the adjusted scale of the 'millones', the newly introduced tax on consumption shows that the most populated regions were on the whole the least rich. It shows in fact not so much its 'distribution' as to how this tax was shared, its establishment.

northern population which was still well implanted at the end of the century.[261]

6. *Italy* also provides a significant contribution and an easily accessible one. The figures were all assembled and analysed by Karl Julius Beloch in his impressive study, the final volume of which was not published until 1961, thirty-two years after its author's death.[262] And the figures, both local and national, concur.

Here are the regional figures: Sicily[263] in 1501 had a population of a little over 600,000 inhabitants; in 1548 it was 850,000; in 1570 over 1,000,000; in 1583, 1,010,000; in 1607, 1,100,000. The population remained stationary throughout the seventeenth century and in 1713 rose again to 1,143,000. The population of Naples follows a similar curve;[264] and according to the count by household of the Spanish censuses, the population rises from 254,823 households (i.e., over 1,000,000 inhabitants) in 1505, to 315,990 in 1532; 422,030 in 1545; 481,354 in 1561; 540,090 in 1595 (the most reliable of the censuses), 500,202 by contrast in 1648,[265] and 394,721 in 1669.

If the 1505 figure = 100, the population of the kingdom of Naples rose to 124 in 1532; 164·9 in 1545; 187 in 1561; 212 in 1595, falling in 1648 to 190 and again in 1669 to 155. So over the fifty years that interest us (1545–1595) the index rose from 164·9 to 212, an increase of over 28 per cent with demographic decline only becoming apparent in the seventeenth century. If the population of Sicily remained stationary during the seventeenth century, in Naples this was a time of pronounced decline. The index falls from 190 in 1648 to 156 in 1669, bringing the level lower than that of 1545 (165 to 156). Numbers in the Papal State also rose from 1,700,000 in 1550 to 2,000,000 in 1600.[266] The population of Florence and her territory rose from 586,296 in 1551 to 646,890 in 1622.[267] There was an increase in Milan and the Milanese from 800,000 in 1542 to 1,240,000 in 1600. Piedmont numbered 800,000 inhabitants in 1571 and 900,000 in 1612.[268] The figures for Venice and her Italian possessions are: in 1548, 1,588,741;[269] in 1622, 1,850,000.[270]

The last local figure is that for Sardinia. Population counts carried out for purposes of taxation, although incomplete and leaving a large margin for error and fraud, nevertheless suggest a demographic upswing. In 1485

[261] According to current research by Alvaro Castillo Pintado.
[262] Karl Julius Beloch died in 1929. His *Bevölkerungsgeschichte Italiens* consists of three volumes: Vol. I, 1937; Vol. II, 1940; Vol. III, 1961.
[263] K. J. Beloch, *Bevölkerungsgeschichte*, I, p. 152.
[264] *Ibid.*, p. 215.
[265] I have found the same census at Simancas, S. P. Naples 268, but dated 1652.
[266] K. J. Beloch, *op. cit.*, III, p. 352.
[267] and [268] *Ibid.*, p. 351. For Florence and Tuscany, 870,000 in 1561, Vicenzo Fedeli, *Relatione di sua ambasciata in Firenze nell'anno 1561*, f° 15, Marciana.
[269] Daniele Beltrami, *Storia delle popolazione di Venezia dal secolo XVI alla caduta della Republica*, 1954, p. 69–70.
[270] K. J. Beloch, *op. cit.*, III, p. 352, gives the figure of 1,863,000 for 1557 and 1,821,140 for 1620. And (*art. cit.*, p. 178) of 1,650,000 for 1548.

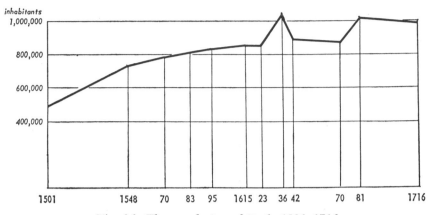

inhabitants
1,000,000
800,000
600,000
400,000

1501   1548   70 83 95   1615 23 36 42   70 81   1716

Fig. 36: *The population of Sicily 1501–1716*

After Julius Beloch. The official census figures indicate only a brief decline between 1636 and 1670.

the census records 26,163 hearths;[271] the lands owned by the Church represent 742 households, land owned by feudal landlords 17,431, and lands owned by the king 7990. The *donativo* of 15,000 *lire* was divided among the three categories as follows: 2500 from the Church lands, 7500 from the feudal lands and 5000 from the royal possessions. There can be no doubt that the total population was above the 100,000 or so corresponding to the number of households recorded. One historian has talked in terms of 150,000 inhabitants; the 1603[272] census, which records 66,769 households, undoubtedly reveals a very considerable increase, even if one accepts the very low coefficient of 4 to obtain the number of inhabitants. Between 1485 and 1603, if these figures are correct, the increase in the total population was in the order of about a hundred thousand, which must have been an extraordinary burden for the island to bear.

While all these figures indicate a general rise in the population, it is difficult to see a clear pattern of development. There was certainly a differential increase, but we know neither the course it followed nor what were its causes. Reviewing the general situation, I am aware of a certain number of doubts, the same doubts that occurred to Beloch himself[273] but which we might choose to resolve in a different manner. It is certainly true that the material for 1500 is very incomplete and what there is suggests a rather small total population for Italy, a total that worried Beloch (perhaps unnecessarily). Is a population of 9½ million too large or too small for the Peninsula that Charles VIII's invasion had just taken by

[271] Francesco Corridore, *Storia documentata della popolazione di Sardegna*, 1902, 2nd ed., p. 12.
[272] *Ibid.*, p. 19 and 20.
[273] K. J. Beloch, *op. cit.*, III, p. 352.

surprise? Our guide concludes that it is too small, and suggests that there must have been a population of at least 10 million. Towards 1550 the total would be 11,591,000 (marking an increase in spite of the so-called Italian Wars) and 13,272,000 towards 1600, falling to 11,545,000 in 1658. This would conform to the pattern of advance followed by a decline. But it does not conform to the rule that the population doubled in size, which we proposed at the beginning of this discussion. There is no reason why we should not assume that the increase was slower to take off in Italy than elsewhere. It was after all a country richer than most others to start with and in this context wealth is a poor indicator. But nothing authorizes us to accept Beloch's higher figure either. Nor do we know very much about the exact point at which the tide turned. Let us accept, *until we have further evidence*, that there were two turning points: 1630, when plague laid waste the north of the peninsula, and 1656, the year when plague struck Rome, Genoa, and Naples. But these are late dates, chosen simply because we have no better guide at the moment.

7. *The censuses of the Ottoman Empire* have been one of the most rewarding areas of recent historical research.[274] A population that in the time of Sulaimān (about 1520–1530) numbered 12 or 13 million, had risen to 17 or 18 million by 1580, and possibly to 30 or 35 million by 1600. These figures are open to discussion but by no means impossible. What is quite *beyond dispute* is that there was a substantial increase, although it may not have assumed the revolutionary proportions suggested by our colleague in Istanbul.

These are obviously approximations, but they are based on censuses at present under analysis, the provisional results of which I have their authors permission to quote. Once more the essential point is a correlation between East and West. By adding together the population of five big cities in about 1501–1509 – Venice, Palermo, Messina, Catania, and Naples – we obtain a total of 349,000 inhabitants. The same sum for the period 1570–1574 would produce a total of 641,000 inhabitants, i.e., an increase of 83·6 per cent. The population of twelve Turkish towns added together comes to 142,562 inhabitants before 1520, and 271,494 in about 1571–1580, i.e., an increase of something like 90 per cent.[275] So demographic trends in both halves of the Mediterranean are comparable.

Reservations and conclusions. The figures, then, all agree. *But these figures may be deceptive.* As was pointed out by Beloch in an article published back in 1900, the higher figures towards the end of the century may have been the result of an improved fiscal system that drew up more comprehensive lists of taxpayers than in the past and asked more of them. And in the seventeenth century they may be the consequences of an unquestionably more efficient census system.[276] Even with these reservations, and

---

[274] Ömer Lüfti Barkan, *art cit.*, p. 191–193.
[275] *Ibid.*, table I, p. 292.
[276] K. J. Beloch, *art. cit.*, p. 767.

accepting that it is just possible that errors of this nature may have magnified the rise in population of the sixteenth century and masked on the contrary the demographic decline of the seventeenth, the period 1500–1600 must still be seen as a time when the number of men increased. There is abundant evidence of this, some of it naive, some brutal. A naive judgment for instance was offered by the Toledan peasants in 1576.[277] There are certainly more people than there used to be in the village: the church is too small for the congregation; in neighbouring villages: 'If they have multiplied', said witnesses of the inhabitants of Puerto de San Vicente, 'it is because they have come into the world and married.'[278] More brutal was the report of the Venetian *provveditore* (not unlike the remark attributed to Napoleon on the evening of the battle of Eylau). 'Many Cretans were killed during the last war [1570–1573] in the service of the Signoria of Venice,' he said on returning from the island, 'but in a few years the gaps will be filled ['sera riffatto il numero'] for there are many children between the ages of ten and fifteen years, not to mention those who are younger . . . '.[279]

This is first-hand evidence and there is plenty of it. Second-hand evidence is no less important. From what we know of the Mediterranean countries between 1450 and 1550, it seems that with the years tension increased. Everywhere, in Castile, in Provence, and no doubt elsewhere as well, villages and small towns sprang up. Castile might appear empty in 1600, but in that case it must have been completely deserted between 1465 and 1467, when we can view it through the eyes of an observant traveller, the Bohemian nobleman Leon de Rosmithal.[280] Similarly to take wheat, cereal production, and the food supply of cities, the continual shortages we have noted in the period 1550–1600 are not found in preceding years. I am well aware that one cannot place absolute faith in an agricultural treatise, even G. Alonso de Herrera's, which appeared in 1513[281] and an edition of which was printed as late as 1620. Much of what he has to say comes straight from Roman works on agriculture. And the author is rather too inclined to speak well of the good old days. But the good old days were not altogether a myth, since Castile was then exporting wheat to the surrounding regions, not importing it. That the cost of living was lower is equally true, at least there are prices that date from before inflation. A comparable situation from the point of view of grain and food supplies in general can be assumed in Italy before 1550 or rather before 1500, when the population's mantle, as it were, still fitted comfortably.

[277] Carmelo Viñas and Ramón Paz, *Relaciones de los pueblos de España ordenados por Felipe II, Reino de Toledo*, part II, vol. II, Madrid, 1963, p. 766–767.
[278] Carmelo Viñas and Ramón Paz, *op. cit., passim* and II, p. 299.
[279] Luca Michiel, A.d.S., Venice, Relazioni B^a 63, f° 286 v°.
[280] Various editions. A useful collection is G. Garcia Mercadal's *Viajes de extranjeros por España y Portugal*, vol. I, 1952, p. 259 to 305: *Viaje del noble bohemio Leon de Rosmithal de Blatina por España y Portugal hecho de ano 1465 a 1467.*
[281] Alonso de Herrera, *Libro de Agricultura*, 1513, esp. f° 3 v° and f° 5. Other editions in 1538, 1598 – the 1620 edition (Madrid) is in B.N., Paris Res. 379.

Cities were already beginning to have problems with their food supply, but to the historian who is familiar with the dramatic crises of the second sixteenth century, they are fairly minor difficulties.[282]

Confirmations and suggestions. Recent important studies of Valladolid,[283] Palencia,[284] Pavia,[285] Bologna,[286] Udine,[287] and Venice[288] offer both confirmation and further suggestions. The most important confirmation is obviously that of the upward trend: the movement in rates of baptism, marriage, and death agrees with our estimates. One historian, B. Bennassar, has established that the population unquestionably increased in Valladolid and the surrounding villages, some of which were thriving and fertile, specifying however that the upward trend was halted between 1540 and 1570, that there was a pause about mid-century, and that the decline probably began in about 1580–1590, that is at an earlier date than that advanced in an older study by Earl Hamilton.[289] This decade, then, was the one that saw the biological turning-point in Spain's fortunes, before the sailing of the Invincible Armada and well before the recession in Sevilian trade (which did not occur until 1610–1620). It looks increasingly as if the 1580s marked the crucial turn of the tide in Spain's destiny, the decade when Portugal surrendered herself to her powerful neighbour, when the prosperity of Córdoba, Toledo, and Segovia began to slow down, when the *alcabalas*, taxes on consumption, *really* stopped rising, and when epidemics became more frequent.[290] Our problems would be over if it could be proved that Valladolid was typical of the rest of Spain, which is possible but as yet unproved.

Broadly similar pictures emerge from studies of Pavia, Bologna, or even Udine.[291] The sixteenth century witnessed a spectacular increase. The population of Pavia rose from 12,000 to 26,000 inhabitants between 1550 and 1600, then fell to 19,000 by 1650. The number of baptisms in Bologna stands at about 1000 in 1515, 3500 in 1585. But since quite clearly all these examples tend in the same direction, let us now move on to other more important general problems.

[282] The period 1550–1602 was characterized in Italy by wide fluctuations in the price of wheat. Dante Zanetti, *Problemi alimentari di una economia preindustriale*, 1964, p. 93.

[283] Bartolomé Bennassar, *Valladolid au siècle d'or*, Paris, 1967, Chapter VIII, *Les hommes du siècle*.

[284] Guilhermo Herrero Martinez de Azcoitia, *La poblacion palentina en los siglos XVI y XVII*, 1961.

[285] Giuseppe Aleati, *La popolazione di Pavia durante il dominio spagnuolo*, 1957.

[286] Athos Bellettini, *La popolazione di Bologna dal secolo XV all'unificazione italiana*, 1961.

[287] Ruggiero Romano, Frank Spooner, Ugo Tucci, *Les prix à Udine*, unpublished.

[288] D. Beltrami, *op. cit.*, see above note 369.

[289] Earl J. Hamilton, 'The decline of Spain' in *Economic History Review*, May, 1938, p. 169, 171, 177.

[290] *Ibid.*, p. 177, for the epidemics in Andalusia in 1560–1570, 1599, 1600, 1648–1649, 1677, G. Niemeyer, *op. cit.*, p. 51.

[291] *Op. cit.*, unpublished, by R. Romano, F. Spooner, U. Tucci.

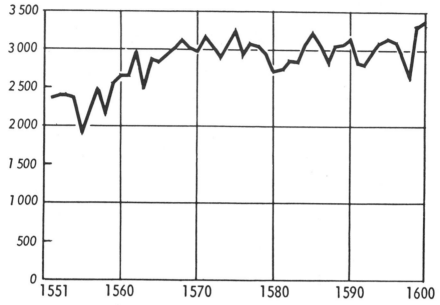

Fig. 37: *Baptisms at Florence, 1551–1600*
The curve rises until 1570, then remains at about the same level until 1600, at an annual birth rate of about 3000.

Some certainties. All the populations here under observation are what is known as *ancien régime* populations, that is, dating from before the improved balance of life brought by the eighteenth century. They are characterized by sharp fluctuations, mortality rates triumphing cruelly over birth rates, which patiently strove to right the balance. The curve followed by baptisms at Florence alone[292] adequately demonstrates the fluctuations of the 'natural' biological situation which even in a prosperous city were determined no doubt by fluctuations of a purely economic order. *Ancien régime*: the rates of birth and death, wherever they are known, broadly correspond to those of underdeveloped nations of the recent past and even of today – approximately 40 per thousand.

At Tudela de Duero, a large wine-growing village near Valladolid,[293] the birth rate between 1531 and 1579 varies (for the periods 1531–1542, 1543–1559, 1561–1570, 1572–1578, 1578–1591) from 42·7 per 1000 to 49·4; 44·5; 54·2; 44·7. The highest figure 54·2 (for the years 1572–1578) is 'artificial', but these figures are well above the 'natural' birth rate of 40 per thousand, a norm that is not however reached at Palencia,[294] in

[292] See Fig. 37.

[293] The following details are all taken from B. Bennassar, *Valadolid au siècle d'or*, *op. cit.*

[294] G. Herrero Martínez de Azcoitia, *La población palentina en los siglos XVI y XVII*, 1961, p. 39. After 1599, the birth rate following the plague shoots up to 50 or even 60, (maximum 66·87) per thousand.

Castile, between 1561 and 1595, where the birth rate varies between 34·81 and 37·48 per thousand, but it is true that Palencia was a town. Rates similar to those of Palencia are found in Bologna (1581, 37·6; 1587, 37·8; 1595, 35·8; 1600, 34·7; 1608, 36·4 per thousand) and slightly lower ones at Venice (1581, 34·1; 1586, 31·8). Lest we should be tempted to conclude that the birth rate increased in inverse proportion to wealth, the robust, almost rural birth rate at Florence is evidence to the contrary (1551, 41·1; 1559, 35·6; 1561, 46·7; 1562, 41·9).[295]

To return to the villages around Valladolid. The rate of marriage at Villabáñez (1570–1589) was 8 per thousand, intervals between births thirty-three months, the relation between births and marriages 4·2 'or a little below'. At Simancas (1565–1590) the mortality rate was 38·3 per thousand. The reason we already know. Here as elsewhere high infant mortality was responsible. During the period 1555–1590, there were 2234 baptisms and 916 burials of *criaturas*, that is, of very young infants, which represented 41 per cent of all deaths. The age of marriage, an indicator of the first importance, has been calculated for the village of Villabáñez, a small but usable sample: women married at just under 20, men between 23 and 25. I should add that these marriages seem to have been earlier than those for which we have records or can make guesses at elsewhere, although we cannot generalize from a survey that in this instance covers only about fifty cases.[296]

This was a world of precarious existence, and at birth life expectation was low. This we know even before looking at the figures. We also know that women tended to live longer than men, as the many widows recorded in the surveys of Castilian villages between 1575 and 1577 alone would tell us.[297] At Venice, in July 1552,[298] there were 55,422 women to 48,332 men (children of both sexes are counted together, 49,923). The demographer will no doubt prefer the more detailed figures for Zara[299] under their four headings: (Zara town; Zara, neighbouring islands; Zara, mainland; and Zara, Morlachian immigrants who had come 'da labrar in quel contado') 5648; 5419; 2374; 2000, a total, that is, of 15,441 *anime*. Only the first three figures are subdivided into *vecchi, homini da fatti, donne, putti*, and *putte*. There were few old people: 181, 190, and 94, that is 365 out of 13,441. The figures for boy-children are 1048, 559, 1170 and for girl-children 893, 553, and 1215, a total of 2777 boys to 2661 girls with boys slightly in the lead as one would expect. As for *homini da fatti* (between the ages of 18 and 50) they numbered 1156, 1023, and 505, a total of 2684 as against 4854 women (2370, 1821, and 663), women clearly being in the majority. The situation was very similar in Crete which we will take as our last example.[300] The population as a whole advanced as follows: 1525,

[295] Preceding percentages from Athos Bellettini, *op. cit.*, p. 136.
[296] Bennassar, *op. cit.*
[297] On the *Relaciones* in general, see N. Salomon, *op. cit. supra*, note 122.
[298] Reference mislaid.   [299] Correr, Donà delle Rose, 192.
[300] Sanudo, *op. cit.*, XL, 25, Constantinople, 24th August, 1525. Correr, Donà delle Rose, 21 (1542), A.d.S., Venice, Capi del Cons° dei X Lettere Ba 285 f° 88, Candia,

100,000 inhabitants (Sanudo's estimate, rather on the low side); 1538, 198,844; 1606, 212,000; 1608, 220,000; 1636, 176,684. But if we take just a part of the island, the territory of the town of Candia itself, we see that in 1636 it had a population of 98,114 of whom 23,169 were men (between the ages of 18 and 50), 21,362 boys and old men, as against 48,873 women. The total male population obtained from the addition of the first two figures was 44,531. This is the proportion found in the earliest *descrittione* of the population of Bologna in 1581: men, 19,083, women, 22,531. The female population was still in the majority fifteen years later in 1596.[301]

These figures indicate the high proportion of the active population. Men, women, and children all, or almost all, worked. It was the one redeeming feature of these young populations where the old and the unproductive, especially the old, had little place. Everyone earned his daily bread.

These few remarks and the few figures on which they are based are very far from solving the problem of the ratio of male to female population. We may assume that as a rule women were in the majority, but there are exceptions. Take Venice, for example, where we have just shown that this rule obtained in 1548, but the figures given in Daniele Beltrami's classic study[302] indicate just the contrary: in 1563, 1581, and in 1586, men were in the majority (51·6 per cent, 51·3 per cent, and 51 per cent of the total population). In 1643, however, and perhaps earlier, the male population was again in the minority (49·3 per cent). Is Venice, a city where the young (male) immigrant played such an important role, representative only of herself in this respect, or of all the cities where the birth rate was still rising and which would therefore have a predominantly male population? It is tempting to see this as a cause of swings in one direction then in another.

Another indicator: migration. If the Mediterranean had not been open on every side and particularly to the Atlantic in the west, it would have had to resolve the problem of a surplus population without recourse to the outside world, to absorb the extra mouths, by redistributing them throughout the area. And indeed this was partly what happened.

Proof of the overpopulation of Mediterranean Europe after the end of the fifteenth century is the frequent expulsion of the Jews, who were driven out of Castile and Portugal in 1492, from Sicily in 1493, from Naples in 1540 and 1541, from Tuscany in 1571, and finally from Milan in 1597.[303]

30th September, 1557, Duke, Captain, and Councillors t o the Ten, the population of Candia had considerably increased. Correr 1586; P.D. 975, 1636.

[301] Athos Bellettini, *op. cit.*, p. 9, n.9. The population of Bologna in 1596, Galiani *Cronaca di Bologna* (Marciana 6114. C III–5) was 58,941 of whom 4651 were men and women in religious communities, 15,595 men, 18,079 women, 7626 boys and 6166 girls, 2760 servants (male) and 4064 servants (female).

[302] *Op. cit.*, p. 80 ff.

[303] From Sicily on 31st January, 1492 (in execution of the decree of 18th September, 18th December); from Naples in 1539. Giovanni di Giovanni, *L'ebraismo della Sicilia*, Palermo, 1748, in-8°, 424 p., and above all Felipe Ruiz Martín, 'La expulsion de los judios del Reino de Napoles' in *Hispania*, vol. XXXV, 1952; Léon Poliakov, *Les banchieri juifs et le Saint-Siège du XIIIe au XVIIe siècle*, 1965.

The largest group of these involuntary exiles, the Iberian Jews, were to go as far as Turkey, to Salonica, and Constantinople, and North Africa, where they settled. In countries whose population was too great for their resources, as the Iberian peninsula under Ferdinand and Isabella may already have been, religion was as much the pretext as the cause of this persecution. The law of numbers was later to operate against the Moriscos in Spain under Philip III and later again, as George Pariset long ago noted,[304] against the Protestants in Louis XIV's France.

Further evidence is provided by the massive emigration from mountain regions to the plains and cities. We have already discussed this at some length. Another pointer is the flow of men from Christendom to Islam which seems to have obeyed some law of equilibrium. Algiers, the city that sprang up on the 'American' pattern was peopled almost entirely by immigrants. Emigration from Italy was responsible for the spread into northern Europe, the countries of Islam, and even the Indies, of a skilled labour force of artisans, artists, merchants, and artillerymen. Venice, at the end of the century claims that 4000 or 5000 Venetian families were living in the Middle East.[305] Here and there we find traces of these emigrations, such as the workers from Como who at the end of the sixteenth century left for Germany and Moravia;[306] or the agricultural day-labourers who left Liguria in about 1587[307] for the plains of Corsica; or the 'technicians'[308] whom one finds almost everywhere, particularly in France, bringing with them the manufacturing skills of the Italian peninsula, the weaving of gold and silk brocade, the secrets of glass-making from Murano[309] or of majolica from Albissola.[310] Italian inventors, artists, masons, and merchants travelled along every road in Europe.[311] But how does one begin to draw up a list of all these individual adventurers or estimate the size of the persistent immigration, in the opposite direction, from Germany

[304] G. Pariset, *L'État et les Églises de Prusse sous Frédéric-Guillaume Ier*, 1897, p. 785.
[305] See below, p. 560, notes 127–8, which does not mean to say that the figure is not excessive.
[306] G. Rovelli, *Storia di Como*, 1803, III, 2, p. 116–117, 145–147, quoted by A. Fanfani, *op. cit.*, p. 146.
[307] F. Borlandi, *Per la storia della popolazione delle Corsica*, 1940, p. 66, 67, 71, 74, 82; quoted by A. Fanfani, *op. cit.*, p. 146.
[308] U. Forti, *Storia della tecnica italiana*, 1940.
[309] Even in England, A. Fanfani, *op. cit.*, p. 146.
[310] Which lay behind the development of Nevers porcelain after 1550, Louis Guéneau, *L'organisation du travail à Nevers aux XVIIe et XVIIIe siécles*, 1919, p. 295.
[311] On the dispersion of Italian immigrants throughout the world there is a tremendous amount of literature both published and unpublished. Its extent can be judged from two studies, both remarkable, one of immigration to Lisbon, Peragallo, *Misc. di. st. ital.*, 1944, the other of emigration towards Geneva, Pascal, 'Da Lucca a Ginevra' in *Rivista storica italiana*, 1932. There have been as yet no studies of the emigration of soldiers; on the role of the Comaschi and the inhabitants of the Ticino valley in the art of the Baroque noted by J. Burckhardt, *Die Renaissance, op. cit.*, p. 16–17; on Italian engineer-architects, see index under Fratino or Jean-Baptiste Toriello for example in Douais, *op. cit.*, II, 110 etc.

into Italy? Historians have been inclined to assume that in both cases only small numbers of people were involved. But small numbers can add up to a large total in the end, at least in sixteenth-century terms. A hundred thousand Spaniards are said to have left the Peninsula for America during this period;[312] a hundred thousand spread over a century, about a thousand a year: not many by modern standards. But Vivero has strong words to say about it in 1632: 'The way things are going', he writes, 'Spain will soon be depopulated', and the Indies are in danger of being lost by these lazy newcomers (Vivero was born in New Spain and prejudiced). As soon as they arrive, 'Those who were cobblers want to be gentlemen of leisure and the labourers are unwilling to take up a pick . . .'.[313] Clearly the problem was exaggerated by contemporaries and by all those who having seen Seville have reflected on the destiny of Spain in their own times.

On the other hand, there has been almost total silence on the subject of the stream of French immigrants into Spain, the importance of which in the sixteenth century has been revealed in recent studies.[314] A typically overpopulated country, France continually dispatched artisans, itinerant merchants, water-carriers, and farm-workers to the neighbouring Peninsula. They came principally but not exclusively from the south of France. Catalonia received large contingents of these workers, who often settled there permanently; as early as August, 1536, a Spanish report notes that more than half the population of Perpignan was French,[315] as was the majority of the Catalan population at the beginning of the seventeenth century, 'ayant ouy assurer y avoir un tiers de plus de François que de naturalz', having heard it said that there are a third as many Frenchmen again as natives of the place, as a traveller[316] says in 1602. The same writer, Joly, also remarks that there were arriving 'every day' in Catalonia people from 'Rouergue, Auvergne, Gévaudan, and Gascony'.[317] Perhaps the nickname *Gavaches*[318] which the Catalans gave to poor French immigrants derives from the place name 'Gévaudan' though this is unlikely.[319] What is certain is that there was a steady stream of immigrants from France. The newcomers also went to Aragon, artisans attracted by the high wages 'because manufactured goods in Spain are dear',[320] unskilled men, taken on as pages and then 'clad in livery, for these gentlemen [their masters]

[312] Wilhelmy, in *Geographische Zeitschrift*, 1940, p. 209.
[313] B.M., Add. 18287.
[314] G. Nadal and E. Giralt, *La population catalane de 1553 à 1717*, 1960.
[315] A.N., K 1690, F. de Beaumont to the Empress, Perpignan, 20th August, 1536, '*Esta villa esta llena de franceses que son muchos mas que los naturales.*' The same is reported (B.M., Add 28368 f° 23 v°) F^co de Salablanca to H.M., Madrid 16th June, 1575: Perpignan is losing its inhabitants '*y son todos gente pobre y gran parte dellos franceses*'.
[316] 'Voyage de Barthélemy Joly en Espagne, 1603–1604', published by L. Barrau Dihigo, in *Revue Hispanique*, 1909, off-print, p. 29.
[317] *Ibid.*, p. 21 and 29.
[318] *Ibid.*, p. 21 and 29.
[319] Littre derives *gavache* from the Spanish *gavacho* which is no answer.
[320] 'Voyage de Barthélemy Joly . . .', p. 82.

take great pleasure in such vanity'[321] – or peasants who were even better received 'because of the indolence of the natives' – as our French informer tells us, adding 'they marry if they can their masters' widows',[322] all in any case fleeing from the crippling French *tailles* – and all much taken with the Spanish prostitutes, 'beautiful ladies, scented with musk, painted, and dressed like French princesses'.[323]

It was not only to Catalonia and Aragon that they came. In Valencia,[324] there were to be found among the shepherds and farmhands of the villages of the Old Christians, Frenchmen, arrived there who knows how. In Castile the Inquisition has plenty to tell us about the French artisans with their imprudent talk, the psalms they sing, their movements and the inns that are their regular rendezvous. If imprisoned, they will denounce each other. In this connection we find mention of every trade: weavers, cloth-croppers, tinkers, shovelmakers, blacksmiths, goldsmiths, locksmiths, cooks, roast-meat sellers, surgeons, gardeners, peasants, sailors, seacaptains, merchants or rather pedlars of books, professional beggars; often young men under twenty or twenty-five. One learns with astonishment of the journeys made right across France by these immigrants, like those printers of playing cards who left Rouen to meet a tragic fate at Toledo.[325]

If this flow of immigrants dried up in about the 1620s,[326] as has been suggested, it certainly started again later. From Béarn, says a text written in 1640,[327] 'there passes every year a great quantity of haymakers, reapers, cattle gelders, and other workers who relieve their households of the burden of feeding them and bring back some profit to their families . . .'. It was not only from Auvergne,[328] as was still thought only recently, that these immigrants, whether temporary or permanent, were attracted by the employment and high wages in Spain. I think we may take it that these immigrants amply compensated the Peninsula for its losses to Italy and the Indies.

3. IS IT POSSIBLE TO CONSTRUCT A MODEL OF THE MEDITERRANEAN ECONOMY?

Have we here enough material to measure the Mediterranean, to construct a comprehensive, quantitative 'model' of its economy? As a unit

[321] 'Voyage de Barthélémy Joly . . .', p. 82.
[322] *Ibid.*
[323] *Ibid.*
[324] T. Halperin Donghi, 'Les Morisques du Royaume de Valence au XVIe siècle' in *Annales E.S.C.*, 1956, p. 164.
[325] Ernst Schäfer, *Geschichte des spanischen Protestantismus*, 3 parts in 2 vols., 1902, Vol. I, part II, p. 137–139.
[326] J. Nadal and E. Giralt, *op. cit.*, p. 198.
[327] P. de Marca, *Histoire du Béarn*, 1640, p. 256–257, quoted by Henri Cavaillès, *La vie pastorale et agricole dans les Pyrénées des Gaves de l' Adour et des Nestes*, Bordeaux, 1932, p. 137–138.
[328] *Response de Jean Bodin à M. de Malestroict*, ed. Henri Hauser, *op. cit.*, p. 14.

it could then be compared to other 'world-economies' either bordering on or connected to the Mediterranean.

An attempt on this scale will provide at best some indication of orders of magnitude, the faintest of guide lines. To tell the truth it is one way of presenting the material. Such a model, if we can construct it, must aim to represent not any particular year or period but the century in its entirety looking beyond times of crisis or of plenty. What it should convey, if it is at all possible, is the mean, the water-line, so to speak, of the successive phases of the century. We shall fall far short of our aim, it is clear; but the effort will be worth while in spite of the difficulties ahead, not to mention the preliminary obstacles.

Can it be said for a start that the Mediterranean is an internally coherent zone? On the whole the answer is yes, in spite of the indefinite and above all changeable boundaries both on its continental and on its seaward sides: the Black Sea, the Red Sea, the Persian Gulf, the Straits of Gibraltar, and the Atlantic Ocean. These problems we have already discussed without reaching any hard and fast conclusion.[329]

It was my original idea, in the first edition of this book, that the many dimensions of the Mediterranean in the sixteenth century should be suggested through a series of examples, by selecting certain important and indicative details:[330] a city of 700,000 inhabitants, Constantinople; a grain fleet which every year, good or bad, ferried a million quintals of wheat or other cereals; the 3000 or so tons of wool which in 1580 lay on the quaysides of Leghorn;[331] the estimated 100,000 combatants, both Turks and Christians, assembled in the gulf of Lepanto on 7th October, 1571; the 600 vessels (totalling perhaps 45,000 tons) that participated in Charles V's expedition against Tunis in 1535; the highest recorded level of shipping at Leghorn, 150,000 tons entering the port in 1592–1593, probably an exaggerated figure; or two rather different annual totals at Naples: 1,300,000 ducats of business transacted on the exchanges, against 60,000 or 70,000 in insurance.[332] But this would mean leaving enormous blank spaces

[329] See above, Chapter III.
[330] *La Méditerranée* . . ., 1st edition, 1949, p. 342 ff.
[331] F. Braudel and R. Romano, *Navires et marchandises à l'entrée du port de Livourne*, p. 101. Hundreds of details of this kind are worth quoting: exports *extra regnum* of Neapolitan wine, of which the average volume between 1563 and 1566 was, for *vini latini*, 23,677 *busti*, for *vini grechi dulci et mangiaguerra*, 2319 *busti* (Sommaria Consultationum 2, f° 223, 2nd October, 1567); 'every year on average, there are sold in Apulia about 80,000 *rubii* of wool', *ibid.*, f° 75, 8th August, 1564; French trade in the Levant, estimated by Savary de Brèves at 30 million *livres* at the beginning of the seventeenth century, had by 1624 fallen by 50%, E. Fagniez, *op. cit.*, p. 324; some of the personal fortunes of the rich merchants of Genoa: many exceeded 500,000 ducats, Tomáso Marino was worth much more, Adamo Centurione almost a million, Museo Correr, Cicogna . . ., f° 2 and 2 v°; the total revenue of the Spanish Crown, 11 million ducats in 1572, Marciana 8360 CVIII-3, f° 11 v°; the amount of coined money in circulation in Europe at the end of the fifteenth century: a thousand million (*livres*), according to P. Raveau, *L'agriculture et les classes paysannes*, 1926, p. 11, n. 1 (the unit is not, alas, clearly indicated).
[332] A.d.S., Naples, Sommaria Consultationum, I, f° 216, 28th April, 1559.

between the specks of colour; at best, it would only give an impressionistic notion of the distance that separates our world from that of the sixteenth century.

Today, on the other hand, I am more attracted towards the language of what economists call 'national accounting'. I should like to try to draw up a tentative balance sheet of the Mediterranean in the sixteenth century, not in order to judge its relative mediocrity or modernity but to determine the relative proportions and relationships between the different sectors of its activity, in short, to form a picture of the major structures of its material life: a difficult and hazardous project. The risks involved will be apparent to any economist who has studied the economies of underdeveloped countries which have never been fully penetrated by the monetary economy. The same was true everywhere in the sixteenth century. And the variety of moneys, real and artificial, complicate any calculations, even when precise data[333] is available, which of course it usually is not. We also have to bear in mind the casual way in which contemporary records refer to ducats or crowns in Spain, ducats, crowns, or florins in Florence. So we find in Florence itself the following: 'Ducati 1000 d'oro di moneta di lire 7 per ciascun scudo'. The point to note here is the reference to the 7 *lire* piece.[334]

Agriculture, the major industry. It is generally admitted that the annual consumption per head of wheat (and other cereals) was of the order of two (present day)* quintals.[335] This figure obviously conceals wide variations in

* The modern quintal is equivalent to 100kg (220·5 lbs.).

[333] I hope the reader will not be shocked to find these approximate calculations expressed in 'ducats' with no further specification. There were of course many kinds of ducats, Venetian, Genoese, Florentine, Neapolitan, and Spanish. . . . Each had its own particular and by no means fixed value. These ducats were *all*, sooner or later to become moneys of account. It would be logical rather than to speak simply of ducats unspecified, to calculate the equivalent in gold or silver. Contemporary writers when estimating sums of money simply refer to 'millions of gold', that is millions of ducats. In the documents of the financial authorities of Spain, the abbreviation for the ducat is a triangle, the letter delta Δ, for the gold *escudo*, real money, a triangle upside down ∇. The relation of the ducat to the *escudo* in Spain was for a long time 350 *maravedis* (ducat) to 400 (*escudo*). Businessmen were of course well aware of the relative values of ducats (of different kinds) and crowns, especially since the exchange rates on the money market varied according to supply and demand. However, all this having been said, we can still accept the ducat for the purposes of our extremely approximate calculations as a valid unit without reference either to its local value or the exchange rate. Any errors this may contain will be absorbed by the highly approximate nature of all our figures.

[334] Maurice Carmona, 'Aspects du capitalisme toscan aux XVIe et XVIIe siècles' in *Revue d'histoire moderne*, 1964, p. 85, note 5.

[335] See in particular J. Gentil da Silva, 'Villages castillans et types de production aux XVIe siècle' in *Annales E.S.C.*, 1963, p. 740–741, where an annual consumption of two quintals is accepted for the Castilian villages. This average is open to much debate. According to Sundborg, in 1891–1893, *per capita* consumption in Italy was 1·2 quintals; 1·5 in Spain, 2·5 in France. Cf. Dr. Armand Gautier, *L'alimentation et les régimes chez l'homme sain et chez le malade*, 1908, p. 296; Andrzej Wyczanski refers to a consumption rate in 1571 of 2·2 quintals of rye in the Polish *starosty* of Korczyn,

actual consumption. But as an average it will do on the whole for the Mediterranean in the sixteenth century. If the population was 60 million, the total annual consumption of wheat or other *bread crops* must have been about 120 million quintals. Other foodstuffs, meat, fish, olive oil, and wine were merely complementary to the staple diet. If we take the average price of the quintal in about 1600 to be 5 or 4 Venetian ducats,[336] Mediterranean consumption (assumed equal to production) must have reached 480 or 600 million ducats every year, in other words a level out of all proportion to the odd 'six millions in gold' that arrived every year at Seville.[337] Grain alone establishes the overwhelming superiority of agricultural production over all others. Agriculture was the leading industry of the Mediterranean, and of course cereals accounted for only part of agricultural revenue.

The preceding estimate is no more than a lower limit. The figures one encounters in the course of research are often higher. Venice, for instance,[338] in about 1600 was consuming, both in good years and bad, about 500,000 *staia* of wheat (as well as rice, millet, and rye). The population of the city then stood at about 140,000, plus another 50,000 in adjoining territories (the *Dogado*), i.e., a total population of 200,000 inhabitants and an individual rate of consumption of 4 quintals if the figures refer only to the city and 3·1 quintals if the whole area is included. At two quintals per person, the supply would have fed 300,000 inhabitants. Perhaps the actual number of consumers was indeed higher than our figures suggest. Or perhaps Venice, a city with high wages, consumed more than another.

Take another example: some Venetian correspondence from Madrid[339] (February, 1621) passes on the report that a tax of two *reales* per *fanega* of wheat ('ch'è come un mezzo staio veneziano') was to be levied before the grain was ground at the mills, 'et fanno conto di cavar da questa impositione nove millioni d'oro l'anno'. Nine million in gold, that is nine million ducats (one ducat = 350 *maravedís*, one *real* = 35) which means that there were 45,000,000 *fanegas* for a total population of 6,000,000 inhabitants, each of whom could have consumed seven and a half *fanegas*, let us say seven *fanegas*, since the size of the population is conjectural: at 55·50 litres to the *fanega*, we reach the enormous figure of 388 litres per person, which proves either that the assessment of the tax return was

---

Kwartalnik historii Kultury materialej, VIII, 1960, p. 40–41; I. Bog, *Die bäuerliche Wirtschaft im Zeitalter des Dreissigjährigen Krieges*, Coburg, 1952, p. 48, a consumption rate of 2·5 quintals at Nuremberg, and of 1·9 at Naples in the sixteenth century, W. Naude, *Getreidepolitik der europäischen Staaten vom 13. bis 18. Jahrhundert*, Berlin, 1896, p. 156. For France, Vauban gives 3·4 quintals (3 *setiers*); the abbé Expilly (1755–1764) 2·7 quintals etc.

[336] See below p. 595 for wheat prices at Venice.

[337] According to the calculations of F. Ruiz Martín.

[338] Museo Correr, Donà delle Rose, 217, f° 131, 1st July, 1604. *Ibid.*, 218, f° 328 (1595), 468,000 *staia*.

[339] A.d.S., Venice, Dispacci Spagna, Alvise Correr to the Doge, Madrid, 11th February, 1621.

optimistic, or that there was a high rate of home consumption in Castile in the year 1621 when practically no grain was exported.

Another example, still in Castile: in 1576[340] ten villages in the Toledo region had a combined population of 2975 *vecinos*, or 12,000 to 13,000 inhabitants, the very great majority of whom were peasants; declared grain production was 143,000 *fanegas* (or about 64,000 quintals). The per capita average is about 5 quintals, so there must have been a margin for export to the towns and even the least favoured of these villages (since its land was mainly in vineyards) could boast two quintals per person.

These estimates are borne out by the following figures, although they cannot be regarded as decisive. The first are provided by the grain-producing provinces of the kingdom of Naples on the Adriatic and the Gulf of Taranto, the Abruzzi, Bari province, Capitanata and Basilicata in January, 1580; and the second by the famous 'Censo de la riqueza territorial e industrial de España en el año 1799',[341] the findings of which can be used as a yardstick in retrospect for the sixteenth century.

The Neapolitan provinces (an important section of the kingdom) figures for which are given in a precious document in the *Sommaria*, had a total population in the winter of 1579–1580 of 173,634 'hearths' or families (out of a total for the kingdom of 475,727)[342] therefore depending on the coefficient adopted (4 or 4·5) of 700,000 or 760,000 inhabitants. The harvest, according to official estimates, brought in over 100,000 *carra* of wheat. Since there were applications for *tratte* (export permits) for 8,500 *carra*, the amount available for the population's own needs must have been 92,000 *carra*, or 1,200,000 present-day quintals giving an individual quota clearly lower than 2 quintals. And from these quantities grain required for next year's sowing had yet to be deducted. However, the *Sommaria* which provides these figures says individual consumption is reckoned at 6 *tomoli* a year, that is about 220 kilogrammes. A contradiction? No, since 'per ordinario non si revela tutto il grano che effettivamento si raccoglie', and it was on this undeclared surplus that the Sommaria relied to make up the necessary food supply.[343]

The *Censo* of 1799 dates from much later than our period, of course, but its percentages are very nearly identical with those of the sixteenth century. In a Spain of 10·5 million inhabitants, wheat production totalled 14,500,000 quintals to the nearest round figure. If consumption equalled production, the annual individual quota would be rather less than 1·4 quintals. But if other cereals and pulses are included this would add over 13 million quintals to the original total[344] bringing it to double the size: even if these secondary cereals were not all used for human consumption,

[340] Carmelo Viñas and Ramón Paz, *op. cit.*, II, p. 99, 132, 140, 169, 272, 309, 397–398, 342–343, 348, 408, 426, 470.
[341] Re-edited in 1960.
[342] G. Coniglio, *op. cit.*, p. 24.
[343] A.d.S., Naples, Sommaria Consultationum, 7, f° 204, 18th January, 1580.
[344] *Censo*, p. XIII.

the projected level of 2 quintals per person would certainly be reached or exceeded. Pulses were undoubtedly very important (over 600,000 quintals[345]) even in the sixteenth century. Venetian documents constantly point out how disastrous it can be for certain villages to lose their crop of beans or lentils in a sudden summer storm.

These figures, while they support the general argument, cannot be taken as proof. Since we are at any rate reasonably certain of the overall total, let us turn to some of its consequences:

1. Wheat shipped overseas totalled at most 1 million quintals, or 8 per cent of consumption – which is a large volume of trade for the period (a million people might depend on it), but insignificant as a proportion of total consumption. So Gino Luzzatto[346] is justified in minimizing it and I was justified in giving it prominence in the early edition of this book.[347] The dramatic crisis of 1591, of which we shall have more to say, resulted in the arrival in Spain and Italy, even Venice, of between 100,000 and 200,000 quintals of northern wheat, a large quantity in terms of transport, very little in relation to everyday consumption. However it was enough to save whole towns from starvation.

But both before and after this crisis, the Mediterranean was able to live largely off its own agricultural produce. No pattern was to emerge here comparable to that developing in the Low Countries, in the case of Amsterdam, or which was much later to be wholeheartedly adopted by England under free trade. Urban centres did not rely on outside sources of food. 'Wheat from overseas' remained a last resort, to rescue the poor, rich consumers preferring the good grain of the nearby countryside: in Lisbon the reputed wheat of the Alemtejo;[348] in Marseilles the grain of the Provençal plains;[349] in Venice the grain they called *nostrale*. 'We are now being given', say the Venetian bakers in 1601, 'grain from outside that does not produce such good results as ours', by which they meant *padoan*, *trivisan*, *polesene*, and *friul* grain.[350] Even those grains accounted *forestieri* were most often produced in the Mediterranean.

2. Agriculture not only assured the Mediterranean of its everyday livelihood, but also provided a range of costly goods for export, sometimes in limited quantities, such as saffron and cumin, but sometimes amounting to a large volume, such as the so-called Corinth raisins, the *uve passe*, choice wines like malmsey that continued to be highly prized until the appearance of port, Malaga and Madeira; or the wines from the islands and ordinary table wines which a thirsty German market sent for every year, after the grape harvest, to the southern side of the Alps. Soon there were

---

[345] *Ibid.*
[346] G. Luzzatto, 'Il Mediterranean nella seconda metà del Cinquecento', in *Nuova Rivista Storica*, 1949.
[347] *La Méditerranée* . . ., 1st edition, 1949, p. 450 ff.
[348] L. Mendes de Vasconcellos, *Do sítio de Lisboa*, 1608, ed. Antonio Sergipe, p. 114.
[349] In the eighteenth century, R. Romano, *Commerce et prix du blé à Marseille au XVIIIe siècle*, 1956, p. 76–77.
[350] Museo Correr, Donà delle Rose, 217.

to be spirits,[351] not to mention olive oil, the fruits of the south, oranges, lemons, raw silk. This surplus combined with manufactured exports to pay for the purchases of grain, dried fish, or sugar from the Atlantic (as well as the lead, copper, and tin of the North) and as late as 1607 the balance of payments between Venice and Holland was still favourable to Venice, according to the *Cinque Savii*.[352]

3. So the Mediterranean remained a world of peasants and landlords, a world of rigid structures. Methods of farming, the balance maintained between different crops, or between crops in general and the meagre pasturelands and the vines and olives that were both making rapid progress (in Andalusia, Portugal, and Castile for instance, even more on the Venetian islands) changed very little unless there was persistent pressure from outside. It was the demand from the colonies that led to increased oil and wine production in Andalusia. And there was to be no 'internal' revolution until the introduction of maize, which arrived quite early it seems in the Basque provinces and in Morocco;[353] and took longer to reach other places. It did not appear in the Venetian countryside before 1600[354] or in the northern Tyrol before 1615.[355] The revolution of the more easily assimilated mulberry tree occurred earlier.

4. Land continued to be the most coveted of possessions. The whole countryside both inside and outside the Mediterranean region was a bewildering tangle of rents, *censos*, mortgages, tenancies, ground-rents, with numerous entailed properties, and a continual coming and going of money loans and repayments between town and countryside. Everywhere it was the same monotonous story. In the countryside around Geneva,[356] about which evidence has recently become available, it is possible to detect a very short-term circulation of money from the fifteenth century on, a decisive factor 'in a closed-circuit economy that was permanently out of breath', where the usury practised by townsfolk did not (in a Protestant country) have to be disguised under cover of rent and quit-rent. A sixteenth-century Spanish *arbitrista*, Miguel Caxa de Leruela,[357] refers to the natural tendency to invest money in land or vineyards near the town. 'As every man could see that a capital of 2000 ducats brought in 200 a year in return, and that the capital was repaid at the end of six years, it seemed to them a good investment.' Commerce and government loans

---

[351] On spirits from Candia, A.d.S., Venice, *Cinque Savii*, 1, f° 14, 6th October, 1601 and 14th March, 1602, aquavit and lemon juice, 'soliti condursi per Ponente'. Spirits do not appear on the customs registers of Venice until the final years of the sixteenth century.

[352] See above.

[353] V. Magalhães Godinho, 'O milho maiz – Origem e difusão' in *Revista de Economia*, vol. XV, no. 1.

[354] According to the unpublished study by R. Romano, F. Spooner and U. Tucci, *Les prix à Udine*.

[355] Hans Telbis, *Zur Geographie des Getreidebaues in Nord-Tirol*, 1948, p. 33.

[356] J. F. Bergier, *op. cit.*, p. 82 ff; quotation p. 83.

[357] Miguel Caxa De Leruela, *Restauración de la abundancia de España*. 1713, p. 50.

rarely offered lenders as good returns. So land competed with them for capital, land which was such a solid and visible guarantee (if the peasant could not pay the interest or did not repay the capital the land was seized). And the investor could always see with his own eyes how his money was bearing fruit on vine or in farmhouse. Such security was worth a great deal. And since agriculture was the greatest single source of revenue in the Mediterranean, an immense amount of wealth was tied up in this sector. So there is no reason to doubt Valle de la Cerda's statement in 1618 that there were in Spain over a hundred million ducats lent in *ducados a censos*.[358]

5. The enormous cereal bill of 400 or 600 million ducats may seem either too much or too little, depending on the angle from which it is viewed. Cereals can have represented only half of the agricultural 'product' if one accepts the proportions recently established for France (in the eighteenth century it is true),[359] and for Spain in 1799.[360] So it is possible to talk in very general terms of a total agricultural production of 800,000 to 1,200 million ducats. It must be stressed that this is a very tentative estimate. The prices on the Venetian market from which we started are high and representative only of the economy of a rich city. Second, and most important, not all the grain that was consumed went on to the market. So our estimate remains extremely theoretical and could hardly be otherwise. To return to the example quoted earlier of the Castilian villages in 1576, they must have consumed 26,000 quintals of the 60,000 they produced, that is about 50 per cent; but the other half did not necessarily go on to the market, some of it went straight into the tithe barns or granaries of urban landlords. So 60 per cent or perhaps 70 per cent of the overall production of the Mediterranean never entered the market economy to which our methods of accounting mistakenly seek to assimilate it.

6. The fact that a large percentage of the agricultural product remained outside the monetary economy with its comparative flexibility, increased the inelasticity of what was, in the Mediterranean and elsewhere the predominant economic activity. Techniques and yields, moreover, were undistinguished. Even in the eighteenth century in Provence,[361] the seed sown was still giving a yield of only 5 to 1, and this can probably be assumed as the average yield in the sixteenth century. To obtain an annual product of 120 million quintals, at least 24 million hectares of Mediterranean land must have been under the plough: an enormous area when one remembers that 24 million hectares in any one year meant, under a two-field system, an available area of 48 million hectares (one field lying fallow for every

[358] Luis Valle de la Cerda, *Desempeño del patrimonio de S.M. y de los reynos sin daño del Rey y vassalos y con descanso y alivio de todos*, 1618, quoted by J. Vicens Vives, *Historia economica de España*, 1st part, undated, p. 300.

[359] J. C. Toutain, 'Le produit de l'agriculture française de 1700 à 1958' in *Cahiers de l'Institut de Science Economique appliquée*, no. 115, July, 1961, esp. p. 212.

[360] See above, note 341.

[361] René Baehrel, *op. cit.*, p. 152. The following rapid calculations assume one quintal of seed-corn to the hectare.

one under crops), and when one is told that in 1600 the *total* arable surface in France was 32 million hectares.[362]

These calculations must be very tentative and the suggested figures are
probably too low, for wheat (and other cereals) were not always in biennial rotation. Some land was only cultivated every three, four, or even ten
years. And it is true that yields higher than 5 to 1 have been recorded.

In Cyprus, where 1/20th of the land was cultivated, the wheat yield was
6 to 1, barley 8 to 1.[363] In Apulia, on the new lands taken over from time to
time from sheep-farming, grain could give yields of 15 or 20 to 1. But these
were exceptional.[364] And there were bad harvests and catastrophes. Climatic conditions continued to be the principal factor and man's unaided
efforts, however determined, could not always bring him fortune. So there
was inelasticity in agriculture. The figures we have for agricultural exports, which bear a certain relation to production when they compose
fairly long series, generally show a constant level, whether of wool exported
from Spain to Italy or wheat and silk sent to outside markets by Sicily,[365]
graphically represented by a set of lines roughly parallel to the x-axis.

Progress was sometimes possible. Technically, the replacement of oxen
by mules in Castile[366] meant that ploughing could be done faster and the
wheat yield depended on the number of ploughings. But this replacement
was by no means general. The northern plough made its appearance in
the sixteenth century in Languedoc,[367] where its role remained modest,
and probably in northern Italy,[368] but the swing-plough, which neither
adequately turned nor aired the soil, continued in general use.

We have already discussed the improvements brought about by land
reclamation schemes.[369] There is no doubt that during the fifteenth century, when the population was small, new land became available to the
peasants of the Mediterranean. It was a time of expansion, or rather of
recovery of a former prosperity, that of the thirteenth century. An agricultural revolution undoubtedly preceded and supported all the expan-
sionist movements of the sixteenth century as Ruggiero Romano has
rightly argued. But in the end this forward movement was brought to a
halt by the very inelasticity of agriculture, under the same conditions as
in the thirteenth century. The reclaimed land often gave an inferior yield.
The number of mouths to feed was increasing more quickly than the
resources and the logic of later Malthusian arguments was already visible.

[362] J. C. Toutain, *art. cit.*, p. 36.
[363] Biblioteca Casanatense, Rome, MSS 2084, f° 45 ff.
[364] A.d.S., Naples, Sommaria, Consultationum, no. 2, f° 140, 13th March, 1563,
yield of 20 to 1.
[365] See graph Fig. 51, p. 598 and Fig. 52, p. 605.
[366] See above, p. 284.
[367] E. Le Roy Ladurie, *op. cit.*
[368] Carlo Poni's admirable book, *Gli aratri e l'economia agraria nel Bolognese dal
XVII al XIX secolo*, 1963, unfortunately only begins with the eighteenth century.
The *più* plough, which is recorded from 1664 (p. 4) must have appeared earlier, but
the text is unclear.
[369] See above, p. 66 ff.

The entire secular trend reversed direction perhaps as early as 1550, more certainly towards 1580. The foundations of a crisis were being laid, just as the improved circulation of silver (let us avoid for the moment calling it the silver revolution) was gathering speed. Historians of Spain are inclined to think that sooner or later agricultural investment ran into difficulties, peasants found it less easy to obtain credit, unpaid creditors seized the property,[370] and even the big landowners themselves were affected by the financial crisis of the years 1575–1579,[371] when the Genoese let their own creditors bear the brunt of their losses, as we shall see. These and other explanations (in the case of Languedoc, for instance[372]) are wholly credible and valid. But the basic explanation must lie in the inelasticity of agricultural production. It had reached its ceiling and the result of this impasse was to be the 'refeudalization' of the seventeenth century, an agricultural revolution in reverse.

An industrial balance sheet. John U. Nef,[373] writing of Europe at the beginning of the seventeenth century, reckoned that out of a total population of 70 million there must have been two or three million artisans. A similar figure could therefore in theory be advanced for the Mediterranean world with its 60 to 70 million inhabitants. But if the towns represent roughly 10 per cent of the population, that is about 6 or 7 million people, it is unlikely that two or three million of these, between a third and a half of the total, were actually artisans. In one particular example, Venice, it is not difficult to reach this kind of proportion: 3000 workers at the Arsenal,[374] 5000 *lanaioli*,[375] 5000 *setaioli*,[376] that is, 13,000 artisans, with their families 50,000 people, out of the total Venetian population of 140,000. And of course there were all the artisans in the many private shipyards whose names and occupations we know,[377] as well as the army of masons, the *muratori*, for the city was continually being built and rebuilt, wood was being replaced with stone and brick, and the *rii*, which were prone to silt up, had to be dredged. And we should include the fullers of cloth[378] near Venice at Mestre for example. A little further outside

[370] B. Bennassar, *op. cit.*

[371] This is the explanation suggested by Felipe Ruiz Martín in his important introduction to the *Lettres marchandes échangées entre Medina del Campo et Florence*, *op. cit.* As soon as the Genoese had the opportunity of settling with their creditors in *juros*, they shifted the burden of their losses on to other shoulders. Among their clients there were of course many landowners.

[372] E. Le Roy Ladurie, *op. cit.*

[373] John U. Nef, 'Industrial Europe', p. 5.

[374] R. Romano, 'Aspetti economici degli armamenti navali veneziani nel secolo XVI', in *Rivista Storica Italiana*, 1954.

[375] Museo Correr, Donà delle Rose, 42, f° 77 v° (1607) of whom 3300 were weavers, with a ratio of one master weaver to two men.

[376] Apparently equal in number to the *lanaioli* which must be an exaggeration.

[377] See R. Romano, 'La marine marchande vénitienne au XVIe siècle' in *Actes du IVe Colloque International d'Histoire Maritime*, 1962, p. 37.

[378] A.d.S., Venice, Senato Terra, 53, 7th May, 1569.

were the millworkers who ground the grain, tore up rags for paper, or sawed up planks and beams for the great city. One should also include the coppersmiths, blacksmiths, goldsmiths, workers in the sugar refineries, the glassmakers of Murano, stonecutters, and leather-workers,[379] the latter on the Giudecca. And there were many more. Not to mention the printers, for Venice in the sixteenth century produced a large proportion of European printed books.[380]

Perhaps one should accept Nef's estimate, while making it clear that the figure of 2 or 3 million must denote people *living off* artisan production: masters, workers, women and children, and not only the active artisan population. It was a way of counting in Venice itself: 20,000 people were commonly said, towards the end of the century, to be living off the many processes of woollen manufacture.[381]

To this figure the large number of rural artisans must be added. No village was without its artisans, however humble their work, or without its minor manufacturing activities. But the quantitative historian will find little joy here and, if he is guided by the habits of the past, he will tend to underestimate this obscure but vital labour in poor rural districts whose only access it might be to the flow of precious coined money. Until recently, historians have tended to concentrate on the impressive urban crafts, but there had always been rural crafts in Aragon, in the Pyrenees, around Segovia,[382] in the humble villages in Castile[383] or León,[384] or in the countryside around Valencia,[385] Their presence was obvious near Genoa.[386] Villages near Aleppo[387] worked silk and cotton. In fact there was hardly a single town that did not cause to spring up on her doorstep, or further away, the industries she needed and which could not, for lack of space, raw materials, or energy, be accommodated within her walls. This is the explanation of the foundries, mills, and paper-works in the mountains behind Genoa; of the various mines, foundries, and powder-mills throughout the kingdom of Naples and in particular near Stilo in Calabria;[388] of the sawmill at the gates of Verona,[389] on the Adige, where the boats

[379] A.d.S., Venice, Senato Terra, 2, 17th September, 1545.

[380] Lucien Febvre and Henri Jean Martin, *L'apparition du livre*, 1958, p. 280, 286, 287, 293.

[381] See note 384 and *Cinque Savii* 140, f°s 4–5, 11th March, 1598 'al numero di 20 (000) et più persone computando le famiglie et figlioli loro'.

[382] J. van Klaveren, *op. cit.*, p. 182 (1573).

[383] Carmolo Viñas and Ramón Paz, *op. cit.*, II, p. 217, for example at Peña Aguilera, a poor village, there were charcoal burners, quarrymen 'e algunos laborantes de lana'.

[384] Manufacture of peasant cloth and barrel staves in the villages of the Maragateria, cf. below p. 448, note 490.

[385] T. Halperin Donghi .*art. cit.*, in *Annales E.S.C.*, 1956, p. 162: industries consisted of silk-manufacture, pottery, the production of *espadrilles*, made of esparto grass for everyday use; finer ones were made of hemp.

[386] Jacques Heers, *op. cit.*, p. 218 ff.

[387] See below, p. 549, note 49.

[388] A.d.S., Naples, Sommaria Consultationum, innumerable references: 13, f[os] 389–390; 21, f[os] 51; 31, f[os] 139–146, 180–184; 37, f[o] 41 v[o], 42 . . . .

[389] A.d.S., Venice, Senato Terra 30, Verona, 1st March, 1559.

carrying planks and timbers were all the more likely to stop because it was also an ideal place for smuggling – and of all the mill-stones grinding the grain for a neighbouring town (over eighty outside Venice), the strings of mills along the Tagus and below Talavera de la Reyna[390] or, at the other end of the Mediterranean, the thirty windmills that were visible from the city of Candia alone.[391] Languedoc had its urban industries, but in the Cévennes and the Massif Central, one finds many manufacturing villages.[392] They are also found over a wide radius round Lyons.[393] The city lived off the cheap labour of its nearby or outlying rural districts.

However, it is unlikely that these rural industries in the Mediterranean ever attained anything like the importance they had already acquired in England (the manufacture of kerseys) or in northern Europe; they never took the form of a whole group of rural centres under the control of urban merchants as was so frequently the case in France in the eighteenth century.[394] I do not even think that the cluster of rural industries around Lyons had any equivalent in the Mediterranean in the sixteenth century, at least there is so far no evidence of it. If correct this observation would prove two things: first, that the Mediterranean countryside possessed an inherently better balance of resources than so many northern regions (and possibly this is true, for vines and olives were often the equivalent of rural industries of the northern countries[395] – arboriculture balanced the peasant budget); and, second, that urban industry in the large and medium-sized towns was able to meet, virtually unaided, the requirements of an immense market. But by the end of the sixteenth century and the beginning of the seventeenth, nine times out of ten industry was moving out to small towns and villages rather than into a big city.[396] These transfers underline the actual and potential strength of rural or semi-rural regions that was still a reality at the beginning of the nineteenth century. When Murat took possession of the kingdom of Naples, he clothed his army (in order to avoid buying expensive English red wool cloth) in black peasant wool cloth – the same as was worn by country people.[397]

If the kind of proportions one glimpses are accepted, the possibility must be envisaged that in the sixteenth century rural industry, *in terms of the number of people involved*, if not of quality or total revenue, was the equal of urban industry. This can neither be confirmed nor contradicted. The entire manufacturing community serving the Mediterranean market

[390] Carmelo Viñas and Ramón Paz, *op. cit.*, II, p. 448.
[391] S. Schweigger, *op. cit.*, (1581), p. 329.
[392] E. Le Roy Ladurie, *op. cit.*
[393] R. Gascon, *op. cit.*, forthcoming.
[394] For a clear example see François Dornic, *L'industrie textile dans le Maine et les débouchés internationaux 1650–1815*, 1955.
[395] Roger Dion, *Histoire de la vigne et du vin en France des origines au XIXe siècle*, 1959, p. 26.
[396] *La Méditerranée* . . ., 1st edition, p. 345 ff.; Giuseppe Aleati, *op. cit.*, p. 125, sees this as a crisis precipitated by the high cost of living in the cases of Pavia, Cremona, Como, and Milan.
[397] A detail I owe to R. Romano.

economy may have consisted of at most three million country people and three million poorly-off townsfolk. Of these perhaps 1,500,000 were active workers. Let us suppose that their average wages were equivalent to those received by the mine workers in the copper mines that Venice possessed at Agordo,[398] that is, 15 *soldi* a day or 20 ducats a year (feast-days were holidays but paid). The total wage-bill would be something like 30 million ducats. This is probably too low, for urban rates were much higher (and it was indeed from excessively high wages that urban industry sometimes collapsed). At Venice a worker in the *Arte della Lana* at the end of the century was earning 144 ducats a year and asking for more.[399] So our figures should or could be raised to 40 or 50 million. Finally, and this time it is practically a leap in the dark, if we reckon the value of industrial *production* as three or four times the total sum paid out in wages, we would get a maximum total of 200 million ducats.[400] Even if this figure were multiplied further, it would still remain far below the 860 or 1200 million at which we have *hypothetically* estimated agricultural production (not altogether surprisingly, perhaps, when in discussions of the Common Market, modern experts, in countries as overindustrialized as France, have said that the commercialization of meat is one of the world's biggest industries).

As far as sixteenth-century industry was concerned the bulk of its products were more frequently absorbed into the monetary economy than cereals, oil, and wine, although here too there was a degree of self-sufficiency. But it was tending to diminish. Thomas Platter[401] notes of Uzès in 1597: 'Each family spins its own wool at home, and then takes it to be woven and dyed and prepared for various uses. They use spinning wheels as we do, [in Basel; Platter was studying at Montpellier] but distaffs are never seen, for it is only the poorest people who spin hemp. The cloth may be bought from merchants and is sold at a lower price than that spun by hand.' We may seek the causes of the expansion of the textile industry and the sale of fabrics at once in the rising population, the concentration of workshops, and a probable decline in self-sufficiency.

The putting-out or 'Verlag' system and the rise of urban industry. From about 1520–1540 there began a decisive period of expansion of urban industry in the Mediterranean, as capitalism gained its second wind both in the Mediterranean and Europe. The first 'industrial revolution' with which Nef credited England alone from 1540,[402] or the rise of 'big industrial capi-

[398] Museo Correr, Cicogna, 2987, August, 1576, thirty men were employed there.
[399] A.d.S., Venice . *Cinque Savii*, I, 139, 20th April, 1603.
[400] *Censo*, table 3, the ratio of industrial to agricultural production in Spain in 1799 was 4·448 to 1.
[401] *Op. cit.*, p. 134.
[402] Cf. the new departure taken by the research of Felipe Ruiz Martín for Castile, *op. cit.*; John U. Nef, 'The progress of technology and the growth of large scale industry in Great Britain, 1500–1660' in *Economic History Review*, 1934, and comments by Henri Hauser in *Annales d'histoire économique et sociale*, 1936, p. 71 ff.

talism' that J. Hartung[403] long ago described as taking place in Germany after 1550,[404] were in fact, given their inadequate differentiation, trends representative of Europe and the Mediterranean as a whole. Future research will perhaps show that they compensated for the brutal reverse that was sooner or later to interrupt the expansion of the sixteenth century. Commercial capitalism, its heyday past, was being succeeded by an industrial capitalism that was to realise its full potential only with the latter, 'metallic' phase of the century. Industry compensated for recession elsewhere.

Almost everywhere (where it can be observed) this industry was of a capitalist nature, conforming to the familiar pattern of the *Verlaggsystem*[405] (the domestic or putting-out system): the merchant, the entrepreneur, or *Verleger*, puts out to the artisan the material to be worked on for a salary. This system was not new in the sixteenth century, but during the period it spread to places where it had previously been unknown (such as Castile apparently) or where it had been little practised (such as Venice). Wherever it was introduced it struck a blow against the guilds, the Italian *arti*, the Spanish *gremios*. Wherever it was introduced it benefited the merchant class which financed the slow production process and kept the profits from sales and exports. The role of these merchants 'qui faciunt laborare' was even more crucial in the relatively new process of silk manufacture than in the longer established production of woollens. Concentrations of silk looms were of course quite visible in the vast workshops, at Genoa for instance where no effort was apparently made to stop this concentration;[406] or even at Venice, where it was already provoking protests and government intervention. The law of 12th December, 1497, had forbidden any silk-manufacturer to employ more than six *tellari*.[407] The question was raised again in 1559, when attention was drawn to 'the greed of certain persons who since they have twenty or twenty-five looms working are causing evident inequalities'.[408]

The merchant then would advance the raw materials and money for wages, and handle sales of the finished product himself. The whole system can be reconstructed from the slightest significant detail. We are in Venice in the winter of 1530: Charles V's ambassador, Rodrigo Nino,[409] has been charged by his master to order silk fabrics; green, blue, red, and

J. Hartung, [03] 'Aus dem Geheimbuche eines deutschen Handelshauses im XVI. Jahrhundert' in *Z. für Sozial-und Wirtschaftsgeschichte*, 1898.
[404] Despite differences in technique (use of coal in England) and resources there are on the whole more points of resemblance than of divergence.
[405] See M. Keul in *Annales E.S.C.*, 1963, p. 836 note 3.
[406] *La Méditerranée . . .*, 1st edition, p. 342, following H. Sieveking, 'Die genueser Seiden-industrie im 15. und 16. Jahrhundert. Ein Beitrag zur Geschichte des Verlags-Systems' (remarkable article) in *Jahrbuch für Gesetzgebung Verwaltung und Statistik im Deutschen Reiche*, 1897, p[s]. 101–133.
[407] See following note.
[408] A.d.S., Venice, Senato Terra 30, 11th November, 1559, for a reminder of the *parte* of 12th December, 1497.
[409] Rodrigo Nino to Charles V, Venice, 1st December, 1530, Simancas E° 1308.

crimson damask, and crimson velvet. He will send some samples he says and negotiate about the price, but in any case once the order is placed 1000 ducats must be advanced and the balance will be paid when the work is finished. For the weaver must buy the silk from the merchant, who has it brought from Turkey in skeins and then made up at his expense. In this case, the purchaser is taking the merchant's place, so it is he who must advance the raw material, in the form of money. A minor incident at Cattaro in August, 1559, is even more revealing.[410] In this lonely corner of the sea the *filatogi* had taken to working raw silk which they bought directly, contravening the law of 1547 that forbade spinners to work *per conto suo*. Order must be reintroduced, decided the Senate: the *filatogi* must from now on spin only silk belonging to the merchants so that the latter will not have to buy spun thread at prices decided by these over-independent *filatogi* – a crystal-clear example. Or again: one artisan at Genoa is giving evidence about another[411] in 1582. 'Yes, he knows what he is saying, for he has been a fellow-worker of Agostino Costa *filatore* and has seen many times in the workshop of the said Agostino, the said Battista Montorio [the merchant] who brought him raw silk and took away finished silk.' Thirty years earlier in Spain, at Segovia, on the occasion of the arrival in 1570 of Queen Anne (Philip II's last wife) a procession of all the trades took place, first the workers of the mint, then the *tratantes en lana* (the wool merchants), then 'the clothmakers, whom the common people mistakenly call merchants [*mercaderes*]', says a seventeenth-century historian, 'when they are in fact the heads of huge families, who give a living to many people (sometimes two or three hundred) either in their own households or outside, and so by the work of so many hands manufacture a great variety of fine woollen cloths . . .'.[412]

The system prospered. We have to consider not only the predominant role of the merchant, the entrepreneur, but also the economic success of the system, the resistance it could offer when circumstances were no longer favourable. It led to the concentration and expansion of industry, a more rational division of labour, and increased production. Or so the evidence from places as far apart as Segovia, Córdoba, Toledo, Venice, and of course Genoa, suggests. Their vitality at the end of the century is in marked contrast to such old manufacturing centres as Florence, where the ancient arts of luxury woollen and silk cloth manufacture were to some extent suffering from old age, some said 'petty-mindedness'. Was this a structural failure? If so it would introduce an immensely interesting element to the argument – and it has been suggested by at least one well-informed historian.[413] Or possibly the more obvious reason is the correct one, that

[410] A.d.S., Senato Terra 29, 16th August, 1559.
[411] Archivio communale, 572, Genoa, 1582.
[412] Diego de Colmenares, *Historia de la insigne ciudad de Segovia*, 2nd edition, Madrid, 1640, p. 547.
[413] An explanation suggested by Felipe Ruiz Martín, in his introduction to the *Lettres marchandes . . ., op. cit.*

Florence was a victim of her high cost of living. Florence more than any other city (except Genoa) was affected by the arrival of precious metals and the sharp rise in prices that they brought. Banking and land competed with the *Arti* which in a Europe torn by war had difficulty finding customers, except in Spain, for their luxury goods. For whatever reason, after 1580, industrial activity at Florence was on the wane.

Other cities though, Venice in particular, continued to thrive until the following century. For this there were many reasons: plentiful labour, new techniques. Venetian woollen cloth was of medium quality, manufactured from second-grade Spanish wool and adapted to meet the tastes of the Levant which continued to be her chief customer, just as the woollen cloth of Segovia and the silks of Toledo and Córdoba were adapted both to the Spanish and American markets. A further factor was the character of the 'new men' who controlled production at the end of the century. In Venice at least these entrepreneurs were often foreigners who, after fifteen or twenty years of loyal service, would one day apply to the Signoria for Venetian citizenship, considering that they had amply earned it by their production of hundreds or thousands of pieces of cloth.[414] In short, there were many new elements: injections of new techniques and new men, both at the entrepreneur and the artisan level. For nothing was so mobile as industrial labour.

An itinerant labour force. The artisan community in the sixteenth century was made up of many races, rarely native to the area. Florentine crafts employed workmen from Flanders and Brabant in the fourteenth century.[415] In the sixteenth century the apprentices of the *Arte della Lana* at Florence were recruited over a large area extending well beyond the borders of Tuscany as we have already noted.[416] At Verona, which had obtained from the Signoria of Venice the right to manufacture *velluti neri* there were twenty-five master craftsmen in 1561:[417] not one of them was Venetian (something the Signoria would never have tolerated); fourteen came from Genoa, three from Mantua, two from Verona, two from Brescia, one from Vicenza, and one from Ferrara. As for the merchants 'che li fanno lavorare', there were only four of them: two from Verona and two from Genoa. This affords a glimpse of the mobility of both artisan and merchant classes.

The situation at Brescia was much the same: the *Arte della Ferrarezza* which manufactured armour, side-arms, and arquebuses, was continually

[414] For example, A.d.S., Venice, Senato Terra 74, 18th April, 1578; 106, 7th March, 1584, 112, 24th November, 1589. Negrin de Negrini, responsible for the manufacture of 1884 woollen cloths since 1564. Innovating spirit of some entrepreneurs, *ibid.*, *Cinque Savii* 15, f° 21, 7th February, (1609).
[415] Alfred Doren, *Wirtschaftsgeschichte Italiens im Mittelalter*, Ital. trans., 1936, p. 491.
[416] According to Maurice Carmona, see above, p. 342; n. 339. The labour force was decimated by an epidemic (of *petecchie*) in 1608 and workers had to be brought in from Milan to manufacture the very fine cloth needed for the marriage of the Prince, Haushof und Staatsarchiv, Vienna, Staatskanzlei Venedig, Faszikel 13, f° 359, Venice, 9th May, 1608.
[417] A.d.S., Venice, Senato Terra, 35, 15th December, 1561.

expanding and contracting according to circumstances, losing its workers to neighbouring towns, then recovering them, and so on. At the end of the century under the impulsion of the newly-appointed *Capitano* of the town, Francesco Molino,[418] it recalled one of the master armourers from Brescia who had gone to Saluzzo taking many *lavoranti* with him; workmen were recalled from Pistoia and Milan (thirty-one at Milan's expense), and the number of *botteghe* immediately rose to twenty-three. Then there was a fresh crisis because of problems in the supply of iron and the scarcity of merchants – one or two more were needed.

For industry followed the merchants, or rather their capital: Tommaso Contarini, who was travelling in the spring of 1610[419] to England as Venetian ambassador, stopped first at Verona, then on his way to Trent passed through Rovereto. He found to his astonishment in this little place an active *negocio delle sede* with a good number of *filatogi* and over 300 'telleri che lavorano ormesini': these workers had left Verona. Four years later, in May 1614, the Signoria of Venice accepted[420] the following extraordinary proposition. In return for the services of the anonymous person who had advanced it, in reporting to the authorities any workers or master craftsmen in important sectors of the city's industry, and in particular in the *Arte delle Seta*, 'che intendono partire', he would be granted the release of a *bandito*, an outlaw or a brigand who was, of course, in prison. Similarly, during the same period, Venice threatened reprisals on the persons or the possessions of any workers or master craftsmen in her sugar refineries ('practico o professore di raffinare zuccari') who left the city to exercise their trade elsewhere.[421]

These journeys or flights by artisans were governed by the general situation. Over long distances and short, a mobile labour force was constantly responding to variations in demand. The movement from big cities to medium-sized or small towns was typical of the end of the sixteenth century. Over an even larger area we have the example of the spread of the silk industry throughout Europe during the fifteenth and the entire sixteenth century. In Italy the seventeenth century saw the rise of the silk industry of the Mezzogiorno which experienced an industrial renaissance. Then quite abruptly during the 1630s[422] this prosperity ceased and one after the other the small towns of the North were smiled on by fortune, succeeding the southern towns as silk manufacturers. This shift was undoubtedly accompanied by artisan emigration.

General and local trends. There is no *a priori* reason to suppose that all these rapidly developing industries followed the same general pattern. It is

[418] Museo Correr, Donà delle Rose, 160, f⁰ˢ 53 and 53 v⁰.
[419] A.d.S., Venice, Senato Secreta Signori Stati, Tommaso Contarini to the Doge, Bolzano, 23rd March, 1610.
[420] A.d.S., Venice, *Cinque Savii*, 200, 27th May, 1614.
[421] *Ibid.*, 16, f⁰ 53, 15th November, 1611.
[422] According to J. Gentil da Silva, unpublished study of Italian fairs in the seventeenth century.

tempting to imagine that they did, with some exceptions and in some places with the recovery of a former level. But in fact the overall picture is still a mystery to us. We may quote in connection with the textile industries – and they were, alongside or even after the building industry, the most important, but by no means the only ones – some evidence of general relevance. For we know how much alum was exported from Spain and the Papal States and therefore know the total volume used of this mordant which was indispensable for the dyeing of fabrics or rather in the preparation for dyeing. It is a reliable barometer and provides an unequivocal answer. It rises and falls in time with the general situation, reaching its highest level between 1590 and 1602.[423]

But we do not know whether other industries conformed to this pattern, as is quite possible and indeed probable. Historians who are anxious to stress the connection between industrial activity and the demands of the merchant class have urged us to accept that they did; that the impetus to expansion came from the merchants.[424] But we shall have to accept that there may have been exceptions either in the short or the long run, for industry could also be a form of compensation, a replacement for something else. The building industry for instance could *sometimes* apparently move in the opposite direction to the general trend,[425] and there may have been particular local trends, about which first-hand evidence is becoming available. We know, for example, some of the curves of textile production. The interesting thing is that whatever the date they are all curiously alike. All industrial curves seem to take off vertically and to decline equally dramatically. The production of serge at Hondschoote[426] rockets up then falls sharply; textile production at Leyden follows a similar curve. At Venice (according to Pierre Sardella[427] and Domenico Sella[428]) it takes the classic form of a parabola. At Florence the incomplete figures we have would fit into a similar curve.[429] The rule is confirmed at Mantua,[430] a minor example, and is probably true of the woollen industry of Brescia and the Val Camonica.[431] It is quite unmistakable at Segovia, Córdoba, Toledo,[432] and Cuenca. Was this a general pattern?

[423] Jean Delumeau, *op. cit.*, esp. graph on p. 132–133.
[424] R. Gascon, *op. cit.*, p. 89; Clemens Bauer, *op. cit.*, p. 9, apropos of Antwerp, following Goris and Strieder.
[425] Andrzej Wyrobisz, *Budownictwo Murowane w Malopolsce w XIV i XV Wieku* (*The building industry in Little Poland in the fourteenth and fifteenth centuries*), 1963 summary in French, p. 166–170).
[426] Émile Coornaert, *op. cit.*, p. 493 ff. and diagram V *bis*.
[427] Pierre Sardella, *art. cit.*, in *Annales E.S.C.*, 1947.
[428] Domenico Sella, *art. cit.*, in *Annales E.S.C.*, 1957.
[429] Ruggiero Romano, 'A Florence au XVIIe siècle. Industries textiles et conjoncture' in *Annales E.S.C.*, 1952.
[430] Aldo de Maddalena, 'L'industrie tessile a Mantova nel 1500 e all'inizio del 1600' in *Studi in onore di Amintore Fanfani*, 1962.
[431] A. Zanelli, *Delle condizioni interne di Brescia*, p. 247, situates the peak of cloth production (18,000 pieces) in about 1550; I am more inclined to place it in 1555; everything turned on the customs measures enacted at Venice, Senato Terra I, 20th

It seems at any rate to be true even of the most humble industries. Venice, for instance, took care to eliminate all competition from the east coast of the Adriatic, whether from shipping, manufacture, or trade. She did not always succeed. The *galere da mercato* and other ships leaving Venice were in the habit of putting in to the little port of Pola in Istria to take on crews, oarsmen, and provisions. Pola became, for the benefit of the men already aboard or about to join the ships, the best-stocked market for cloth made from the coarse wool of the islands, the *rascie* and *grigie* which we have already mentioned[433] and which came from both the Istrian and the Dalmatian hinterland. In about 1512 these cloths were reaching the fairs of the *Sottovento*, Sinigaglia, Recanati, Lanciano, where they became so popular that Pola lost what had been her usual stock-in-trade. This was to last ten or fifteen years, until about 1525 when Venice stepped in to restore order. In the interval there had been time for a steep rise followed by a fall.

Similar trends can be detected in the Ottoman Empire, where manufacture was often in the hands of immigrants, Christian prisoners who, at Constantinople and elsewhere as well, frequently became master craftsmen[434] manufacturing precious fabrics;[435] even more numerous were Jewish artisans. The latter imported the textile industry to Constantinople and Salonica.[436] In Salonica, for instance, we know that production of woollen cloth began to fall off after 1564, and that many measures were taken by the rabbis, the leaders of the Jewish community, in an attempt to stop the rot (the prohibition of free purchase of wool, the obligation to buy clothing manufactured in the town). From this evidence the peak of an impressive production curve must have occurred in 1564. This pattern is confirmed by the little town of Safed, capital of Galilee on Lake Tiberias: between 1520 and 1560–1580, it was to become a prosperous wool-manufacturing town thanks to the Jewish immigrants and the crafts they imported.[437] A traveller noted in 1535, 'The manufacture of cloth prospers daily. It is said that over 15,000 kerseys have been made this year in Safed without prejudice to heavier fabrics. Some are equal in quality to those of Venice. Anyone, man or woman, who plies a trade to do with wool can make a very good living . . . I have bought a few kerseys and other cloths to sell and made a good profit from them . . .'. Turkish tax records confirm the rise of this small town: in 1525–1526 the tax paid by the dyers

May, 1545. The situation after that was irremediable – the master craftsmen who left did not return.
[432] According to the forthcoming study by Felipe Ruiz Martín.
[433] See above, p. 128 and Senato Mar 7, f° 26 v°, 18th August, 1461.
[434] Lectures given at École des Hautes Études by Ömer Lütfi Barkan.
[435] A.d.S., Florence, Mediceo 4279, a Jewish merchant seeking to buy in Tripoli Christian slaves who could work velvet or damask.
[436] I. S. Emmanuel, *Histoire de l'industrie des tissus des Israélites de Salonique*, 1935.
[437] S. Schwarzfuchs, 'La décadence de la Galilée juive du XVIe siècle et la crise du textile du Proche-Orient' in *Revue des Études juives*, January–June, 1962.

was 300 aspers; by 1533 it had risen to 1000; in 1555–1556 (for only four dye-works) it was 2236 aspers. It was at about this time that the tide turned, that is the decline of Safed *roughly* coincided with the decline of Salonica. In 1584 the Jews left Safed and its industry quickly collapsed (in 1587 a printing works, opened ten years earlier, closed down). By 1602 no cloth was manufactured there at all.

This is further evidence to add to the dossier on the probable pauperization of Jewish communities in the Near East as well as an indication of the general economic level of the Ottoman Empire in mid-century. In circumstances attributable to this decline difficulties arose in obtaining supplies of wool and in the 1580s cloth from England was being shipped direct to the Levant in English vessels. The rise of the Italian industry must also be taken into account, as well as the crucial economic and monetary crisis which was to launch the Ottoman Empire into the spiralling troubles of inflation.[438]

In any case, the peaks of industrial activity have their own particular interest.

1. It is important to note that in about 1520–1540 there began a period of general expansion almost everywhere;

2. that peaks of production occurred in about 1564, 1580, 1600;

3. that although industry was not of course the paramount economic force it was on the way to being in the eighteenth century and definitely became in the nineteenth, it was already exceptionally developed. Industrial success came rapidly;

4. that its decline was equally spectacular and relatively easier to chart than its rise. In Venice, for example, the woollen industry apparently made a brilliant debut in about 1458;[439] was clearly stagnating towards 1506,[440] at least on the mainland, and made a long-lasting recovery after 1520.[441] It was not until about 1600–1610 that this burst of activity began to run out of steam[442] and it was probably just then, in 1604 or so, that a period of expansion was opening in the Protestant Low Countries.[443]

There was a distinct relationship then between industrial expansion and decline in places often very far apart. Industry – or perhaps one should say pre-industry – was governed by a perpetual shifting of the balance, a continual new deal. When one hand had been played, the game began again. The loser might be lucky next time: Venice seems to prove this. But the last player to arrive was always the favourite, as the triumph of

---

[438] See below, p. 539 ff.

[439] A.d.S., Venice, Senato Terra 4, f° 71, 18th April, 1458: 'se ha principiado adesso el mester de la lana in questa città et lavorasse a grandissima furia de ogni sorte pani e principaliter garbi'.

[440] *Ibid.*, Senato Terra 15, f° 92, 23rd January, 1506, '. . . el mestier de la lana che soleva dar alimento a molte terre nostre et loci nostri hora è reducto in tanta extremità che piu esser non potria'.

[441] See note by P. Sardella and the much-quoted article by D. Sella; there were even difficulties at Venice, Senato Terra 15, f° 93 ff., 9th February, 1506 and even clearer A.d.S., Venice Consoli dei Mercanti, 128, 29th September, 1517.

[442] *Ibid.*   [443] Émile Coornaert, *op. cit.*, p. 48.

new towns in the sixteenth century in Italy and Spain was already proving. And the northern victory of the seventeenth century, although there had always been textile industry in the Low Countries, was that of a young rival.

Present everywhere, even in the humblest towns where the historian would never have suspected their existence, even in sun-baked cities with a reputation for idleness, like Naples, industries were springing up[444] like fitful fires[445] scattered over a wide plain of dry grass. Their flames might spread afield or die down perhaps to flare up again further away. A gust of wind in one direction or another and the flames might reach grass as yet untouched. Even today the same can still be true.[446]

The volume of commercial transactions. Commerce is a many sided activity. It will not fit easily into our calculations. 'Commerce' can mean the fruit that a peasant woman takes to market or the glass of wine which a poor man drinks at the door of the rich man's cellar (for the wealthy often indulged in this kind of retail trade) or it can mean the goods handled by the Venetian *galere da mercato* or the *Casa de la Contratación* at Seville. The range of activities it may embrace is immense. Besides, in the sixteenth century all goods were not commercially handled, far from it. The market economy covered only a fraction of economic life. More primitive forms – barter and autarky – rivalled it everywhere. If one accepts the view[447] that commerce is the final stage of the production process, in other words, that it adds surplus value to the goods it transports, one must recognize that this plus-value, and especially profits, are difficult to estimate, even in an example on which we are apparently well-informed. In the 1560s something like 20,000 quintals of pepper were annually transported to Europe from India and the East Indies. It was bought in Calicut for 5 *cruzados* per light quintal*, and sold at Lisbon for 64, that is at twelve times the price. It was clearly more than a simple matter of the same individual buying and selling: the cost of transport, taxation, and risks involved were both very great and variable and we do not know how much of the 1,300,000 *cruzados* selling price went into the merchant's pocket.

Handling merchandise was moreover only one of the occupations of the sixteenth century 'merchant', as is clear from his books, clearer still from the countless bankruptcy records. Every kind of operation and specula-

* The light quintal = about 50 Kg.

[444] A.d.S., Naples, Sommaria Consultationum, 7, f°s 33 to 39, 28th February, 1578: in 1576 there were produced 26,940 *canne* of silk cloth.
[445] The cloth industry at Brescia was also precarious, hampered by customs controls on wool; it was unable to obtain further supplies at Vercelli, Senato Terra 1, 20th May, 1545.
[446] Cf. the observations of François Simiand, *Cours d'économie politique*, 1928–1929, II, *passim* and p. 418 ff.
[447] L. F. de Tollenare, *Essai sur les entraves que le commerce éprouve en Europe*, 1820, p. 3, a product 'is not complete, it does not possess ts full potential exchange value until it is accessible to the purchaser. Commerce gives it its finishing touch . . . .'

tion appears there higgledy-piggledy: purchases of land or houses, industrial investment, banking, marine insurance, lotteries,[448] urban rents, peasants' quit-rents, stock-farming, advances from the loan banks (*Monti de Pietà*), speculation on the foreign exchanges. Actual transactions involving merchandise and artificial transactions on the money market figure side by side. The importance of purely financial transactions, with all their sophisticated ramifications, increases the further one goes up the scale of merchants and with the passing of the relatively prosperous years of the late sixteenth century. It was becoming widely known that commercial operations could be settled at the fairs almost *miraculously*. In 1550 de Rubis talks of the Lyons fairs where 'a million pounds can be paid sometimes in a morning without a single sou changing hands'.[449] Fifty years later, Giovan Battista Pereti, who kept the *giornale* of exchanges at the Banco di Rialto, explains in a report to the Signoria of Venice, that 3 or 4 million crowns' worth of business is transacted at every Piacenza fair, and that most of the time 'non vi è un quatrino de contanti'.[450] Exchange and re-exchange, the *ricorsa* bills[451] that were to extend their good and not always loyal services in the seventeenth century, had begun their career much earlier in the fifteenth century at Genoa,[452] by the end of the sixteenth century more or less everywhere,[453] and even at Lyons, where in January, 1584,[454] we find a typical example: two Italian merchants agreed to advance money to the Bishop of Langres and his two brothers, the sum being taken 'ad cambium et recambium' by a third merchant, 'a gentleman called Guicciardini'.

Let us however attempt an estimate. The results are certain to be wide of the mark but the exercise will be instructive.

Our first clue comes from the fiscal records of Castile. I need hardly dwell on their shortcomings. But the *alcabalas* or sales taxes, fluctuate according to the current economic situation and are not entirely negligible indicators. They also underline the varying degrees of activity, wealth, and income existing in the different cities and regions. At Valladolid[455] in 1576, a revenue of 22 million *maravedís* (the *alcabala* in theory representing

[448] Gambling held an important place not only in the life of the nobility (particularly towards the end of the century), but also in the lives of merchants. Any subject was a pretext for a wager, the number of cardinals to be promoted, the death or survival of famous men, the sex of unborn children. At Venice, when it was odds on that the French had captured Pavia, a Spaniard Calzeran insisted in wagering on the opposite. He was no doubt in touch with Lannoy or Pescara, in any case he won a fortune, A.d.S., Modena, Venezia 8.16.77. VIII, f° 66, J. Tebaldi to the Duke, Venice, 15th May, 1525.
[449] Quoted by R. Gascon, *op. cit.*, p. 177, Claude de Rubys, *Histoire véritable de la ville de Lyon*, 1604, p. 499.
[450] Museo Correr, Donà delle Rose, 181, July, 1603, f° 53.
[451] Giulio Mandich, *Le pacte de ricorsa et le marché italien des changes*, 1953.
[452] Jaques Heers, *op. cit.*, p. 75, 79 ff.
[453] F. Braudel, 'Le pacte de ricorsa au service du Roi d'Espagne' in *Studi in onore di Armando Sapori*, II, 1957.
[454] A.d.S., Florence, Mediceo 4745, unnumbered, January, 1589.
[455] Modesto Ulloa, *op. cit.*, p. 108.

one tenth of all sales) must correspond to an approximate turnover of
trade of 220 million *maravedís*, that is 5500 *maravedís*, or slightly over 15
ducats per head, of the city's 40,000 inhabitants, which does not of course
mean that every citizen could have made this sum in profits from commercial transactions. This was the total volume of business that theoretically flowed through the city. As the reader will realize, commercial
activity, often within a closed circuit, embraced a wide range of compensatory, speculative, and deceptive transactions. And the figure of 220
million is probably an underestimate. For the crown contracted with the
cities for fixed annual payments in lieu of *alcabalas*, letting them reimburse themselves afterwards, sometimes with interest. But after the 1580s
the towns no longer paid tax at a fixed rate, and the *alcabalas* which no
longer gave the old profits, reverted to central control.[456] But, in any case,
the figures of 220 million and 15 ducats per head denote a fairly high turnover in 1576. An even higher figure is found at Seville in 1597,[457] for this
was a far richer city than Valladolid and between 1576 and 1598 inflation
had also played its part. The resulting figure is 15,900 *maravedís* per head
of the Sevilian population (100,000 inhabitants and *alcabalas* of 159
million *maravedís*), that is triple the figure for Valladolid in 1576.

Let us now move on from these local figures (which provide a revealing
geographical picture of the wealth of Castile[458]) to the more general problem of estimating the total turnover of trade. For the whole of Castile
in 1598 the total income from the *alcabala* (unfortunately including the
tercias as well) amounts to a thousand million *maravedís* (the *tercias*
represent two-thirds of certain tithes paid to the church and must obviously be excluded from the calculation). But our hypothetical figure
of ten thousand million *maravedís* gives us some idea of the scale of the
total volume of internal trade. The per capita rate this yields is 1500 *maravedís*, or just 4 ducats. This figure is lower than that for Valladolid in 1576
or Seville in 1598, but that need not surprise us: urban economies are
always the most dynamic.

It is possible to base some calculations (though without certainty) on
the customs revenue for external trade. If the relation of customs duties
to total value of goods is arbitrarily assumed to be 1 to 10, it yields a
figure of 3·63 milliards of *maravedís* (imports). Although the balance of
payments was unfavourable to Spain, it is not totally arbitrary to assume
that exports also equalled 3·63 milliards; let us add 700 million for the
entry of precious metals, and without regarding it as in any way infallible,
we can then, by adding together the 1ι milliards (corresponding to the
alcabalas) and the 7,960,000,000 *maravedís* of external trade, reach a total
of nearly 18,000 million *maravedís*, or 9 ducats per head of the population
(Castile had a population of 5 million). As the reader will have noted

---

[456] According to Felipe Ruiz Martín.
[457] Modesto Ulloa, *op. cit.*, p. 132.
[458] Alvaro Castillo Pintado, 'El *servicio de millones* y la poblacion del Reino de
Granada in 1591' in *Saitabi*, 1961.

the relation of external trade (imports) to internal trade is something like 1 to 3.

Our second clue is provided by France between 1551 and 1556. Here we have only one certain figure, that of the total value of imports,[459] 36 million *livres tournois*, of which according to the source of the figures, 14 or 15 million represented luxury articles, superfluous *bifferies*. These 36 million (at 2 *livres* 6 *sous* to the *écu*) are the equivalent of 15·7 million crowns (*écus*). This figure can be doubled to obtain the total volume of imports and exports (31·4 millions) and can be multiplied by 3 to obtain the volume of internal trade (47·1 million). This would give an overall total of 78½ million crowns. If the population of France was 16 million (a figure generally accepted by historians, but by no means proved) the per capita rate would be nearly 5 *écus*, which expressed in Spanish ducats is about 5·6. This figure, applicable only to the years 1551–1556, is of course lower than the Spanish figure for the end of the century. But Castile was richer than France, the 1598 Spanish figure is swollen by inflation, and finally the divisor (16 million as the population of France) is by no means certain. But even the sum of these uncertainties cannot entirely deprive us of the satisfaction of seeing that the two 'indicators' can at least be mentioned in the same breath.

Can the lower figure be used as an index for the Mediterranean as a whole? There are good reasons for and against. Let us solve the problem by reducing the French result to the nearest round figure. We may then conclude *without any guarantee of certainty* that the total turnover of trade for the 60 million or so inhabitants of the Mediterranean was something like 300 'million in gold'.

This figure is far from reliable. No economist would accept it. But we can say in the first place that this volume is far superior to that of profits, the income of the merchant class – which might be 10, 20, or 30 per cent of all trade; second, that the volume of goods available for commercial transactions was, if our figures are correct, only about a third, if that, of production; third, that it is important to locate in this no doubt imperfect but revealing context, the part played by long distance trade, *Fernhandel*, the very life-blood of commercial capitalism. And this of course requires some comment.

The significance and limitations of long distance trade. The *raison d'être* of long distance trade is that it connects, sometimes with difficulty, regions where goods can be bought cheaply with others where they can be sold for high prices: buying kerseys or having them made in the Cotswolds, for example, and selling them in Aleppo or Persia; or buying linen cloth in Bohemia and selling it in Lisbon, Venice, or Lübeck. To make them worthwhile, these long journeys presupposed wide differences in economic levels, indeed enormous differences at the beginning of the sixteenth

[459] Albert Chamberland, 'Le commerce d'importation en France au milieu du XVIe siècle' in *Revue de Géographie*, 1894.

century, particularly at Lisbon, where commercial profits sprouted like tropical plants. As Porchnev[460] said of Baltic trade in the seventeenth century, what counted was not so much the volume of trade as the ultimate rate of profit. Capitalism in its agile youth (for it was now the most modern and wideawake economic force) was attracted by these high profits and their rapid rate of accumulation. In the long run of course all differences in price levels tend to be eliminated, particularly when business is good. Long distance trade then has to change its options. So there were periods when it was more or less profitable: very profitable was the first half of the sixteenth century;[461] profits levelled off in the second half; and there was renewed prosperity in the seventeenth century. It was the relative slump in trade that no doubt encouraged so many business men to invest their money in government loans and on foreign exchanges, culminating in a kind of financial capitalism in the second half of the sixteenth century. Let it be understood that there is no question of a drop in the volume of trade, which indeed continued to increase during this period. Our remarks apply exclusively to the *profits* obtained by the larger merchants.

The historian Jacques Heers[462] has protested against the exaggerated importance usually attributed to the spice and drug trades, which are sometimes spoken of as if they far outweighed any other traffic in the sixteenth century. 'When the history comes to be written not only of the alum trade[463] but of the trade in wine and grain, salt, cotton and even sugar and silk', he writes, 'we shall see a very different economic history of the Mediterranean world emerge, in which pepper and drugs will only play a very minor role, particularly after the fourteenth century . . . .' It all depends which way one looks at it. From the point of view of economic geography, Heers is right. From the point of view of the history of the rise of capitalism and of profits he is wrong. We should remember Porchnev's observation. In the area with which we are concerned the only thing that matters is the rate and facility of gain, the accumulation of capital. There is no doubt at all that in volume the grain trade far outweighed pepper. But Simón Ruiz was unwilling to commit himself to buying grain,

---

[460] B. Porchnev, Congress of historical sciences, Stockholm, 1960, vol. IV, 137.

[461] According to G. von Below, (*Über historische Periodisierungen mit besonderem Blick auf die Grenze zwischen Mittelalter und Neuzeit*, Berlin, 1925, p. 51–52) this period was outstanding both economically and artistically. Lucien Febvre considered it a happy age before the 'sad men' of the years after 1560, Franz Linder, 'Spanische Markt- und Börsen-wechsel' in *Ibero-amerikanisches Archiv*, 1929, p. 18, even claims that 1550–1600 was the age of *Ricorsa-Wechselschäft*.

[462] Jacques Heers, in *Revue du Nord*, January–March, 1964, p. 106–107.

[463] J. Finot, 'Le commerce de l'alun dans les Pays-Bas et la bulle encyclique du Pape Jules II en 1506' in *Bull. hist. et philol.*, 1902; Jean Delumeau, *L'alun de Rome, XVe–XIXe siècle*, 1962; 'The Alum Trade in the fifteenth and sixteenth centuries and the beginning of the Alum industry in England' in *The Collected papers of Rhys Jenkins*, Cambridge, 1936; L. Liagre, 'Le commerce de l'alun en Flandre au Moyen Age' in *Le Moyen Age*, 1955, vol. LXI, (4th series, vol. X); Felipe Ruiz Martín, *Les aluns espagnols, indice de la conjoncture économique de l'Europe au XVIe siècle* (forthcoming); G. Zippel, 'L'allume di Tolfa e il suo commercio' in *Arch. soc. Rom. Stor. patr.*, 1907, vol. XXX.

because it was riskier for the merchant. Grain was not like pepper or cochineal, a 'royal merchandise' and a relatively safe risk. When dealing in grain one had to reckon with the demands of transporters, and the vigilance of states and cities. Except when large sums of money were involved, as in 1521[464] or 1583[465] or on the occasion of the massive purchases of 1590–1591, large scale capitalism did not participate in any regular way in the train trade,[466] at least during the second half of the century; nor always in the closely supervised salt trade.

So long distance trade depended on a very fine balance. The entire economic history of Castile under Genoese influence provides clear evidence of this now that its workings have been analysed by Felipe Ruiz Martín.[467] It was when they had difficulty in exporting American bullion from Spain that the Genoese bought alum, wool, oil, and even wines from Andalusia in order to obtain from their sale the specie they needed either in the Netherlands or in Italy. The last wool boom in Venice seems to have been the result of one of these operations.[468] I am convinced that a similar system guided from above also operated in the kingdom of Naples, for the occasional purchase of saffron, silk, oil, or even Apulian wheat. A whole army of merchants, Milanese, Florentine, Genoese, and Venetians (especially merchants from Bergamo) was stationed in the towns of the kingdom of Naples, for the most part small traders, despite the airs of importance they gave themselves and the large stocks of oil or grain they possessed; they were only there to provide their masters or correspondents with the advantages of rights and privileges acquired locally over the year. And they operated only to order: just as the Marseilles merchants who squandered large quantities of specie at Aleppo or Alexandria[469] were only executing the orders of the merchants of Lyons, who manipulated the strings according to the state of the market. The Spanish merchants too were in the service of influential foreign businessmen.[470]

So at the top commercial capitalism consisted of a series of careful choices; or one might describe it as a system of supervision and control, intervening only when large profits were assured. An entire 'strategy' can be glimpsed, sometimes even emerging into broad daylight, intervening in one place then another according to variations in the price of commodities and also to the degree of risk involved. One often stood to gain more but also to lose more by handling merchandise than by playing

[464] Cf. the many documents A.d.S., Naples, Sommaria Partium, 96: *1521* f°s 131 v°, 133 v°, 150, 153, 'navis celeriter suum viagium exequi posset' (a Genoese ship), 166 v° (on Catalonia) 177 (Oran), 175; *1522*, f°s 186 v°, 199, 201, 221, 224–225, 228 v° and 229, 232, 244, 252 v°.
[465] According to Felipe Ruiz Martín, see below, p. 588, note 311.
[466] See below, p. 601–602.
[467] In a study to be published shortly.
[468] *Ibid.*
[469] See below, p. 566 and Micheline Baulant, *Lettres de négociants marseillais: les frères Hermite, 1570–1612*, 1953.
[470] Cf. Felipe Ruiz Martín, *Introduction, Lettres de Florence . . ., op. cit.,* p. XXXVI–XXXVII.

the money markets. Giovanni Domenico Peri, who is a reliable informant, tells us that 'there is often more profit to be made with 1000 crowns in merchandise than with 10,000 crowns on the exchanges'.[471] But we know that on the exchanges businessmen were more likely to risk other people's money than their own and that the transfer of huge sums of money was concentrated in a few hands. No doubt greater overall gains could be made on the 5 million ducats that the sea-borne grain trade represented in the Mediterranean at the end of the century than on the million ducats that pepper from Asia may have been worth on its arrival in Europe. But in the one case literally thousands of parties were involved, in the other a few powerful combines dominated the market. It was in their favour that the accumulation of capital operated. In 1627 the Portuguese *Marranos* who ousted the Genoese bankers were after all originally spice and pepper merchants.

And similarly the extremely powerful Genoese bankers and financiers even in their heyday controlled only one sector, and that by no means the most important, of the economic life of imperial Spain. But they derived great profit from it since their numbers were so small. Contemporaries were often aware of this relative importance. In June, 1598, the Genoese 'financiers' wanted to postpone the fairs of Medina del Campo, which would give them an opportunity to keep a little longer in their hands the money entrusted to them by investors. But the merchants of Burgos, formerly their liegemen and now their bitterest enemies, refused to co-operate. They explained that of the total business transacted at the fair, that of the *asentistas* who advanced loans to the king represented less than the dealings of the ordinary merchants, and was in fact hardly comparable. 'Indeed,' the plaintiffs explained, 'we may assure your Majesty that the sums to be paid at the fair by those who are not included in the decree are far superior to the payments due from those merchants who are mentioned in the same decree.'[472] The decree was that of 29th November, 1596, so as our text shortly puts it: 'es mucha más cantidad la que han de pagar en las ferias que no son decretados que los que lo son'. Clear evidence but it does not affect the main issue. The essential point is that in certain sectors concentration of business had become an established pattern.

Capitalist concentrations. This concentration of firms was a fairly frequent occurrence in the sixteenth century. But its progress might be accelerated or slowed down by the general situation. During the 'first' sixteenth century, when every sector was expanding, there arose the great family concerns, the empires of the Fuggers, Welsers, Hochstätters, and Affaitati.[473] After the mid-century recession a different situation began to emerge favouring the rise of larger numbers of small firms. At this point, the spread of information and the possibilities of speculation increased, as Wilfrid

[471] Quoted by Maurice Carmona, 'Aspects du capitalisme toscan aux XVIe et XVIIe siècles' in *Revue d'histoire moderne*, 1964, p. 96, note 2.
[472] Archivo Ruiz, 117, quoted by F. Ruiz Martín, in *El siglo de los Genoveses*.
[473] See the admirable book by Clemens Bauer for a discussion of these questions.

Brulez[474] stressed in his study of Flanders. In order to integrate these smaller firms into the outside world, transport had to become independent, work on a commission basis had to become generalized, the role of the broker had to be accepted and extended, and credit had to become easier to obtain and therefore more risky. And indeed a series of bankruptcies marks every flurry of change after 1550.

Little is known about the higher spheres of Mediterranean capitalism. The silence of the Genoese archives reduces us to incomplete explanations. It would be extremely interesting to see how far these higher sectors of commerce, finance, and banking depended on the lower strata of small merchants and large numbers of naïve investors. Without everyday affairs, the common or garden transactions of economic life, the banks at Naples or elsewhere would soon have been out of business. Without the cargoes they carried for very small clients, even the fleets of the New World would have been in difficulties. And finally without the savings of Spain and Italy, which they were the first to mobilize, the *asentistas* of Philip II would never have been able to engineer their enormous financial operations.

In the Mediterranean the usual pattern was the family firm at both upper and lower levels, and short-term associations that were rarely renewed. Close ties, divorces, and remarriages could be effective on a certain scale. The Genoese, for instance, who lent money to the king of Spain, were in fact a permanent association, although no formal legal constitution bound them together before the *medio general* of 1597. They operated in twos and threes, or all together in times of crisis or particularly favourable conjunctures. Their small numbers and class solidarity kept them firmly together. They were commonly known as the *contratación*, proof if one is required, that they were considered as a group. For firms that were not brought together by necessity, connections could be useful as appears from the genealogical research undertaken by Hermann Kellenbenz, which has shed much light on the network of marriages, family ties, friendships, and partnerships stretching from Amsterdam to Lisbon, Venice, and the Portuguese Indies. They prepared the way for, or followed the great geographical shift of world riches that marked the transition from the sixteenth to the seventeenth century.[475]

The availability of these networks may help to explain why the Mediterranean unlike the North never felt the need to set up large combines, the joint stock companies to whom the future was to belong.

The total tonnage of Mediterranean shipping.[476] We have little in the way of reliable figures to help us estimate the total tonnage of shipping in the

---

[474] *Op. cit.*, p. 580 ff.

[475] Notably the Hispano-Portuguese front against India and the role played by an information agency serving the interests of German and Flemish merchants: Hermann Kellenbenz, *Studia*, 1963, p. 263–290.

[476] For some useful comparisons, see R. Romano, 'Per una valutazione della flotta mercantile europea alla fine del secolo XVIII, in *Studi in onore di Amintore Fanfani*, 1962.

Mediterranean. England, France, the rebel provinces of the Netherlands, and Spain each possessed in about the 1580s 200,000 tons of shipping, the Netherlands probably more[477] (an estimated 225,000 tons in 1570), the three others certainly less, Spain something in the region of 175,000 (estimates in 1588);[478] France and England considerably less, but we do not know exactly how much. If we accept the total of 4000 ships given by Saint-Gouard[479] (he says between 4000 and 5000 ships) for the whole of the French fleet, and if we accept an average tonnage per vessel of 40 or 50 tons, the minimum estimate would be 160,000 tons. If we accept that in 1588[480] the English fleet consisted of 2000 ships, the highest possible figure would be 100,000 tons. It is true that according to the same source the figure in 1629[481] was 200,000 tons, following the expansion of English shipbuilding. So in the Atlantic there were perhaps 600,000 or 700,000 tons, not counting other northern navies and without subtracting the ships in Mediterranean ports in France and Spain. But we need go into no further detail since the tonnage of Atlantic shipping is only marginal to the central issue.

If we now try to calculate the tonnage of Mediterranean shipping during the last thirty years of the century, we can first of all include a third at most of the Spanish fleet, 60,000 tons. The Venetian shipping fleet in 1605[482] according to fairly reliable figures consisted of 19,000 tons in big ships only, and a total of 30,000 or 40,000 tons for all classes of ship. The same figure of 40,000 tons can be accredited to Ragusa, Genoa, and Marseilles, to the fleet of Naples and Sicily and double that for the Turkish empire i.e., a maximum of 280,000 tons which, added to Spain's 60,000, gives a total figure for the Mediterranean of rather under 350,000 tons. Even so the disproportion between the sea and the ocean is not too ludicrous: 300,000 or 350,000 on one side and 600,000 or 700,000 on the other, that is a ratio of 1 to 2. On one side the not insignificant Mediterranean, and on the other the Atlantic and the Seven Seas. And voyages within the Mediterranean were of course more frequent than those on the oceanic routes. A Ragusan vessel could easily make two or three voyages a year.

Should we include as 'Mediterranean' shipping the northern vessels that appeared there after the 1570s, possibly a hundred in number, that is at about 100 or 200 tons per ship, a total of 10,000 or 20,000 tons? It does not greatly signify: this tonnage is to the Mediterranean tonnage as 1 to 15 or 1 to 35; not much at most. Nor have we counted the hundred or so roundships of the Barbary corsairs, which may have totalled 10,000 tons at the beginning of the seventeenth century.

[477] According to J. Kulischer, *op. cit.*, II, p. 384.
[478] R. Konetzke, *op. cit.*, p. 203.
[479] Saint-Gouard to the king, Madrid, 21st May, 1572, B.N., Fr. 16104, f°s 88 ff.
[480] S. Lilley, *Men, Machines and History*, London, 1948, p. 72 and J. U. Nef, *The Rise of the British Coal Industry*, London, 1932, I, p. 173.
[481] S. Lilley, *ibid.*, p. 72.
[482] Museo Correr, Donà delle Rose, 271, f° 46 v°, 7th March, 1605. See also Alberto Tenenti, *Naufrages, corsaires et assurances*, p. 563 ff.

The figure of 300,000 or 350,000 thus reached is far from certain, but this calculation does establish: 1) that the Mediterranean was predominantly the province of Mediterranean vessels and their crews; 2) that the northerners were an anomaly, their presence did not drastically alter the structure of Mediterranean shipping, which as we have seen was solidly based; 3) that at least half of these northern ships were in any case in the service of Mediterranean cities and economies, sailing round the sea from port to port, picking up cargoes, leaving through the Straits of Gibraltar now and then, to return later the same way. So let us neither exaggerate nor minimize the role of these intruders which were in fact serving cities too rich to be self-sufficient.

May we extend to the Mediterranean as a whole the authoritative figures now available for the Ragusan shipping fleet:[483] 55,000 tons in 1570, 32,000 towards 1600; its crews: 3000 to 5000 men; its total value: 200,000 ducats towards 1540, 700,000 in 1570 and 650,000 in 1600; and finally its annual income, between 180,000 and 270,000 ducats – all well documented figures? If so, the total value of shipping in the Mediterranean would be something in the region of 6 million ducats, its income about 2 million ducats and the crews would number about 30,000 men. If, as was the case at Ragusa, at least half the income from freighting went to the crews, the rest going to the 'shareholders', the average annual income of a seaman would be 30 ducats, a modest sum. Nevertheless these wages made a dent in the profits of the shipowner, who also bore responsibility for the ship's maintenance and repair: one time it might be a rudder, another time a mast (never easy to obtain), sometimes merely a few barrels or a skiff. He had to provide food for the officers' table and for the sailors; and insurance on a ship's hull and freight might amount to 5 per cent or more of the capital investment. If the share taken by the officers and seamen increased, if the price per ton of construction (or purchase) was also rising, as it was at Lisbon[484] and Venice,[485] the capitalist merchant might have second thoughts about this expensive form of business: an income of two or three million ducats might seem a large sum, but shared among 10,000 ships it brought comparatively little to the individual shipowner. At Venice, if the norms on which our calculation is based are correct, ships brought in 180,000 to 200,000 ducats, a mouthful of bread but no more.

This is all guesswork. But we have only a few ships' accounts to work from, one or two inadequate pages, a notebook in the *Archivio di Stato* at Venice,[486] a late document (1638) concerning the great Venetian galleon *Santa Maria Torre di Mar*.[487] Although such documents must exist, one

---

[483] Iorjo Tadić, 'Le port de Raguse et sa flotte au XVIe siècle' in Michel Mollat, *Le navire et l'économie maritime du Moyen Age au XVIIIe siècle. Travaux du Deuxième Colloque International d'Histoire Maritime*, 1959, p. 15, 16.
[484] B.M. Add. 28478, fº 238, April, 1594: '. . . se deve ter consideração ao preço das cousas ser mayor'.
[485] See above, p. 308 ff.
[486] I am indebted to Ugo Tucci for looking through it for me.
[487] A.d.S., Venice, Senato Zecca, 39, 12th June, 1638.

Collective Destinies

has to be lucky to come across them. And lastly our figures are probably more indicative of long distance shipping than of the everyday coasting trade: this in itself is a serious omission. But one thing is certain. By the end of the sixteenth century the shipping business had been abandoned (except by a very few rich shipowners) to the small or very small business-man. If galleons are being fitted out at Naples, it will be sufficient to send a few recruiters to the ports of Apulia to find the necessary seamen.[488] When a ship comes to the end of her life, after at least twenty years of good service, her place is often taken by a poorer and smaller vessel.

Overland transport. We have already calculated[489] that according to the Spanish figures the ratio of goods carried by land to those carried by sea was possibly 1 to 3. If 3 million ducats represents the value of the shipping traffic, overland traffic alone in the Mediterranean would be worth about a million. I do not for a moment believe that this ratio was general. But even if we assumed an equal volume of traffic on land and sea, the total value, 6 million ducats, would still seem absurdly low. Somehow within this slight monetary framework we have to accommodate the busy flow of goods along all the Mediterranean routes, which as we have already seen is one (among many) of the major features of the inland sea.

Our calculations inevitably contain mistakes. But there can be no mistake about the poverty and meagre living of the transporters, on one hand the ordinary seamen and on the other peasants who divided their time between carrying and farming or a trade. We have, for instance, some circumstancial accounts of the *arrieros* of Maragateria near Astorga in the kingdom of León.[490] These *Maragatos* were poverty-stricken, and looked it even after they had made their fortunes later in the eighteenth and nineteenth centuries. At the end of the reign of Philip II they were occupied in loading fish, particularly sardines, in the Cantabrian ports, transporting them to Castile and bringing back wheat and wine. Their work would be done by truck drivers today. The distribution of fish throughout the towns of Castile was remarkable even in the sixteenth century.[491] The problem of how they lived becomes clearer when one examines the detailed population returns of 1561 and 1597, and sees that the transporter, *traginero*, also engaged in stock-raising, agriculture, crafts, and commerce. If he stuck to transporting he remained poor, like the young Juan Nieto who transported fish 'e mas vezes traia alquilado que por sus dineros', and 'was more often hired than paid in his own money'. The *traginero* who bought and sold the fish he carried was better off.

So the carrier, always on the verge of extreme poverty, was not only carrier but also peasant and artisan. This was so well after the sixteenth

footnote[488] A.d.S., Naples, Regia Camera della Sommaria, Reg. 14, 1594, 1623–1637.
[489] See above, p. 293 ff.
[490] José Luis Martín Galindo, 'Arrieros maragatos en el siglo XVIII' in *Estudios y Documentos*, no. 9, 1956.
[491] Pedro de Medina, *op. cit.*, p. 209 in the case of Alcalá de Henares.

century throughout the Mediterranean and Europe. The boats carrying salt up the Rhône from the marshes of Peccais to the Swiss cantons went no further than Seyssel. From there the salt went by cart to Geneva. But here transport depended on seed time and harvest, for the peasants undertook to carry goods only during slack periods of the farming year.[492] The transport trade cannot easily be separated from the rural community that provided its labour and even from that of the little towns that often derived a great deal of their income from it. Cartagena, at the beginning of Philip II's reign, appears to have been a town specializing in transport, *acarateo*.[493]

So the circulation of goods was assured by many activities, which brought little reward either by land or by sea, and were only attractive to the seaman or muleteer for the small profits to be made from constant exchange, for each travelled on his own account too. In this way, the transporter, who was often in touch with a primitive economy came into contact with a monetary economy; his position as middleman had its advantages of course when he returned to do business in his own village. Nevertheless, viewed in a general context, transport in the sixteenth century was cheap and this comparative cheapness was accentuated with the years, the sums received by the transporters failing to keep pace with the rise in prices.[494] This was undoubtedly a stimulus to trade.

The State: the principal entrepreneur of the century. The state in the sixteenth century was increasingly emerging as the great collector and redistributor of revenue; it derived income from taxation, the sale of offices, government bonds, and confiscation, an enormous share of the various 'national products'. This multiple seizure of funds was effective because state budgets on the whole fluctuated with the general situation and followed the rising tide of prices.[495] So the rise of the state is in the mainstream of economic development, neither an accident, nor an untimely force, as Joseph A. Schumpeter was perhaps a little too ready to believe.[496] Whether intentionally or not the state became the principal entrepreneur of the century. It was on the state that modern warfare depended, with its constantly increasing requirements in manpower and money; as did the biggest economic enterprises: the Seville-based *Carrera de Indias*, the shipping route between Lisbon and the East Indies, for which the *Casa da India*, in other words the king of Portugal, was responsible.

The *Carrera de Indias* worked, *mutatis mutandis*, on the same principle as the Venetian *galere da mercato*, proof that this form of state capitalism

---

[492] Brigue Archives, Stockalper Papers, Sch. 31, no 2939, Geneva, 10th July, 1650 and no. 2942, 14th July, 1650: there was a break for the harvest (information supplied by M. Keul). Cf. *ibid.*, no. 2966, 18–28th September, 1650 for a halt for the autumn sowing.

[493] Information supplied by Felipe Ruiz Martín.

[494] B. Bennassar, *op. cit.*

[495] See Vol. II, Figs. 56, 57, 58.

[496] *Op. cit.* (Italian edition) I, p. 174.

was beyond its initial stages. In the Mediterranean it was indeed to remain very active: the Arsenal at Venice[497] and its copy, the double arsenal at Galata, were the greatest centres of manufacture in the known world. Also dependent on the state were all the mints[498] that were at work both in Christendom and Islam, in Christendom often under direct state control. They were farmed out but strictly supervised in the Turkish Empire or the Regency of Algiers. Dependent on the state too were the public banks whose hour of glory came at the end of the century, as we shall see. Here it was the city-states, or at any rate states of a predominantly urban character that led the way. The territorial states had some time to wait, and the first of their banks was in fact to be the Bank of England in 1694.[499] Philip II paid no heed to the advice of the Fleming Peter van Oudegherste,[500] who tried in vain to persuade him to create a state bank.

This gap does not prevent the list of 'public' works from being very long. As a historian has pointed out, the huge installations set up by the Papal government at Tolfa and Alumiere for the extraction of alum were in fact an 'industrial complex'.[501] The Turkish government itself, outstandingly *dirigiste*, was responsible for many works; the rapid construction of the Sulaimāniye mosque[502] (and we now have an excellent recent study of work on the building site) is a good example. If we extended the label state capitalism in the west to such mixed enterprises, part public, part private, as the building of the Escorial,[503] with its remarkable constructional techniques, the list would be even longer. Through all these activities the state put back into circulation the money that arrived in its coffers, and in order to meet the demands of wars even overspent its income. War, public works, and state enterprises were therefore more of an economic stimulus than might be supposed. What was disastrous for the economy was when money piled up in the state coffers, in the treasury that Sixtus V amassed in the Castel Sant' Angelo,[504] in the coffers of the Zecca at Venice or in those of Sully at the Arsenal.

All this having been said, it will not be too difficult to calculate the wealth of the states. We already know a good deal about their budgets and we can fairly easily find out more. If we accept the following figures for the end of

[497] Ruggiero Romano, *art. cit.*, in *Rivista Storica Italiana*, 1954.

[498] Ali Sahili Oglu, unpublished study of currency minted in Turkey.

[499] The Banks of Stockholm (1672) and of Amsterdam (1609) had of course preceded it, but these were predominantly city banks. It is true that the headquarters of the Bank of England were in London.

[500] His first attempt was made in 1576, Felipe Ruiz Martín has drawn to my attention an important document in connection with this at Simancas E° 659, f° 103.

[501] Jacques Heers in *Revue du Nord*, 1964.

[502] Ömer Lütfi Barkan, 'L'organisation du travail dans le chantier d'une grande mosquée à Istanbul au XVIe siècle' in *Annales E.S.C.*, 1961, p. 1092–1106.

[503] For example, the stone-work, the use of lead, and of machines for lifting, details of which can be seen by visiting the Escorial and the Museum commemorating its construction.

[504] Cf. the remarks by Paul Herre, *Papsttum und Papstwahl im Zeitalter Philipps II*, Leipzig, 1907, p. 374.

the century: 9 million ducats for Castile,[505] 5 million for France under Henri IV,[506] 3·9 million for Venice and her Empire,[507] 6 million for the Turkish Empire,[508] that is 24 million for a population of about 30 million, and if we multiply this figure by two to correspond to the 60 million inhabitants of the Mediterranean as a whole, we arrive at the no doubt artificial total of 48 million. On this showing, a man contributed rather less than a ducat a year to his ruler (and a ducat to his landlord too, no doubt).

I am sure that this figure, after the huge sums we have been conjuring with, will appear very low. Was the mighty state, striding across the stage of history, no more than this? And yet these figures are probably the most reliable of any yet mentioned. But it must be borne in mind that all the states, even the Turkish Empire, had moved beyond the primitive economy. Their yearly tribute was exacted from the 'fast-flowing blood' of the circulation of metal currencies; whereas all the other estimates we have so far given are a translation into monetary terms of transactions which for a very large part escaped the market economy. The modern state had just been born, both fully armed and unarmed, for it was not yet sufficient to its task. In order to make war, collect taxes, administer its own affairs, and conduct justice, it was dependent on businessmen and the bourgeoisie hungry for social advancement. But even this is a sign of its new energy. In Castile (which is a particularly clear example) everyone participated in state enterprise; merchants, noblemen, and *letrados*. The competition for honours and profits had begun. And a competition for hard work too. From even the humblest secretaries of the *Consejo de Hacienda y Junta de Hacienda* we have reports, letters, proof of their devotion to the king and the public good, alongside requests and denunciations dictated by self-interest.

Whether the rise of the state was beneficial remains an open question. It was in any case inevitable, just as the sharp-eyed capitalism of the merchants was inevitable. An unprecedented concentration of resources operated to the advantage of the prince. Forty or fifty million ducats (an actual figure this time, not a tentative estimate) was an extraordinary lever to have at one's command.

Precious metals and the monetary economy. In history as in other scientific disciplines, classic explanations lose their force after a time. We no longer regard the sixteenth century as a period characterized by the uncontrolled competition of precious metals and prices, the view of François Simiand.[509]

[505] Calculations and graphs Vol. II, Fig. 58 by Alvaro Castillo Pintado.
[506] A. Poirson, *Histoire du règne de Henri IV*, 1866, IV, p. 610–611.
[507] *Bilanci Generali, op. cit.*, vol I, bk. 1, p. 466 and Museo Correr, Donà delle Rose, 161, f° 144.
[508] Ömer Lütfi Barkan, 'The Turkish budget in the year 1547–1548 and the Turkish budget in the year 1567–1568' (in Turkish) in *Iktisat Fakültesi Mecmuasi*, Istanbul, 1960.
[509] *Op. cit.*, p. 128.

Frank Spooner and I[510] put forward a tentative estimate of the total amount of metal money in circulation in Europe and the Mediterranean *before the discovery of America*. The figure we obtained, based on simple but unverifiable equations, was an approximate total of 5000 tons of gold and 60,000 of silver. The arrivals of bullion from America during the century and a half between 1500 and 1650 according to Hamilton[511] amount to 16,000 tons of silver and 180 of gold. Let us assume for the moment that these figures are roughly correct. They alter some problems and confirm others.

1. They paint a more optimistic picture of the situation before 1500, and therefore of the fifteenth century which already has its advocates among historians.[512] It is in this period that we can locate the considerable advance made *in the west* by the monetary economy: by 1500 it had taken over the entire sphere of government taxation, and part of the dues payable to the landed gentry and the Church.

2. Simiand thought American minerals were the decisive factor. The stock of bullion according to him doubled between 1500 and 1520, doubled again between 1520 and 1550, and more than doubled between 1550 and 1600. 'Over the whole sixteenth century,' he wrote, 'this stock therefore increased more than five-fold. In the seventeenth century by contrast, as well as the eighteenth and the first half of the nineteenth, stocks barely doubled over any hundred year period.'[513] We can no longer accept this interpretation. The sixteenth century did not loose unprecedented riches on the world. The rising population, currency devaluations, a relative economic expansion, and certainly the accelerated circulation of coined money and the means of payment are other explanations for the high levels and revolutions (or *pseudo-revolutions*) of the sixteenth century.[514] We shall have more to say about this.

3. In any case, the Mediterranean despite the expansion of credit, in the sixteenth century possessed neither the specie nor the paper equivalents sufficient to effect the annual balance of the exchanges and wages of a population of 60 million inhabitants. This shortage was endemic. At Venice, in 1603, although the city's coffers were well filled, there were not enough silver coins to pay the wages of the workers.[515] How much greater was the shortage in backward regions, where payments in kind had constantly to fill the gap. Not that payment in kind was altogether lacking in flexibility: it prepared the way for the monetary economy, but only payments in cash could make it work and prosper. On the shores of the Baltic, the small amounts of money invested by Hanseatic and western merchants helped to accelerate an economy that was still primitive. Towards the end

---

[510] Cf. our chapter in the *Cambridge Economic History*, vol. IV.
[511] *Op. cit.*, p. 42.
[512] J. A. Schumpeter, *op. cit.*, I, esp. p. 476, note 1; Jacques Heers, Raymond de Roover. . . .   [513] *Op. cit.*, p. 128.
[514] Carlo M. Cipolla, 'La prétendue révolution des prix. Réflexions sur l'expérience italienne' in *Annales E.S.C.*, 1955, p. 513 ff.
[515] Museo Correr, Donà delle Rose, 181.

of the century, of course, bills of exchange became more general and perhaps compensated for the slowdown (if there was one)[516] in arrivals of bullion from America during the second and third decades of the seventeenth century. In 1604[517] a Venetian tells us there was an annual turnover of 12 to 16 million crowns at the Piacenza fairs. Peri talks in terms of a turnover of 30 million towards 1630.[518] But these figures are unsupported. And such exchanges stimulated circulation only at the very pinnacle of economic life.

4. The monetary economy undoubtedly made progress. In the Turkish Empire this progress accompanied by a spate of currency depreciations virtually took on the dimensions of a revolution. Evidence of this is daily becoming available to historians. All prices were rising. All the old social patterns were breaking up and the dramatic upheavals of the West were prolonged there almost independently. They had the same causes and the same effects.[519]

5. But the important and unsurprising conclusion is the following. The circulation of money (here understood to mean every type of currency, even the lowest) only penetrated certain areas of human life. The natural flow of rivers is drawn by gravity towards low-lying regions. The flow of money on the other hand seems to have been restricted to the upper reaches of economic life. It thus created a series of inequalities: inequality between the most dynamic regions – the towns – and those where little or no money circulated – the countryside; inequality between advanced zones and backward zones, developed countries and under-developed countries (for this distinction already existed, the former constantly moving ahead, the latter even when making progress, like Turkey for example, never catching up with the leaders); inequality between forms of human activity, for only transport, industry, and above all commerce and government taxation had access to the flow of money; inequality between the very few rich (perhaps 5 per cent) and the great mass of poor and very poor, with the gap between the small minority and this huge majority continually widening. I believe that if the observable attempts at social revolution failed, were not even clearly formulated, it was because of the intense, relative pauperization of large numbers of the population.

Was one fifth of the population in great poverty? An estimate made with the help of parish priests in 1559 at Málaga,[520] which we shall take as an

---

[516] Evidence from Holland passed on to me by Morineau suggests that there may have been rather more clandestine imports during this crucial period than is usually thought.

[517] Museo Correr, Donà delle Rose, 181, f° 62, 3 to 4 million crowns per fair.

[518] Gino Luzzatto, *Storia economica dell'età moderna e contemporanea*, I, 1932, p. 179 ff.

[519] Verbal information supplied by Ömer Lütfi Barkan.

[520] Simancas, Expedientes de Hacienda, 122, 1559. I might equally well have taken Medina del Campo as an example and used the excellent article by B. Bennassar, 'Medina del Campo, un exemple des structures urbaines de l'Espagne au XVIe siècle'

example (a fairly well-off one), gave a total of 3096 households (*vecinos*), that is at four persons to a household, a little over 12,000 inhabitants. Three classes were distinguished according to income: the *razonables*, the *pequeños*, and finally the *pobres*. Of the latter there were over 700 widows and 300 workers (widows counted for a half-*vecino*, workers for a whole one), that is, about 2600 poor people, over 20 per cent of the whole. The 'reasonably well-off' (and this does not mean rich) numbered 300 *vecinos*, that is about 1200 people (10 per cent). The *pequeños* formed the immense majority, 70 per cent, about 8500 people. These proportions may well be representative. Twenty per cent of the population living in extreme poverty constitutes a large but quite credible percentage both inside and outside the Mediterranean region.[521] Contemporary observers, moreover, noted abject poverty at the heart of the most prosperous cities: in Genoa, where it was aggravated every winter,[522] at Ragusa, so rich and yet socially so unbalanced, where in 1595, according to one report, 'there is also much misery'.[523] We have no proof, of course, that the findings of Málaga are relevant to larger or less-favoured towns or above all that the same scale of measurement can be applied to peasant communities, whose income measured in money would be very small, but whose way of life though less sophisticated might be better balanced. If this percentage is accepted it would mean that 12 to 14 million Mediterranean inhabitants were living near the starvation level: it is a possibility that cannot be ruled out.[524]

For we are never dealing with full-employment economies. An ever-present pressure on the labour market was the mass of underemployed workers, vagrants, or semi-vagrants that had been a constant, indeed one might say a *structural*, feature of European and Mediterranean life since at least the twelfth century.[525] As for the standard of living of the peasantry, we know next to nothing about it, so we shall be obliged to make the most of a few surveys which cannot of course be considered universally representative.

A village in the Brescia region was destroyed by fire on 8th May, 1555.[526] A dependency of the Alpine commune of Collio de Valnopia, the small settlement at Tizzo nevertheless measured half a mile around, 260 houses, all burned, of which the investigator found only the walls standing. A point

in *Revue d'histoire économique et sociale*, 1961. At Venice, the official documents always distinguish between *poveri*, *mendicanti* and *miserabili*: there are degrees of destitution, Ernst Rodenwaldt, *Pest in Venedig*, art. cit., p. 16.
[521] For example, the estimates reproduced by Hektor Ammann, *Schaffhauser Wirtschaft im Mittelalter*, 1948, table on p. 306.
[522] See above, p. 255.   [523] Museo Correr, Donà delle Rose, 23, f° 23 v°.
[524] Heinrich Bechtel, *op. cit.*, p. 52, note 6, at Erfurt in 1511, 54 per cent of the population included in the census were in the lowest category of property-owners, possessing 0 to 25 florins, and 15 per cent were persons *ohne jedes Vermögen*.
[525] Cf. *L'Unterschicht*, Franco-German Colloquium of 1962.
[526] A.d.S., Venice, Senato Terra 22, Treviso, 22nd July, 1555; Treviso, 30th July, 1555; Brescia, 11th August, 1555 for the fire at Tizzo.

of detail: it paid 200 ducats annually in taxes to the Signoria of Venice. In these 260 houses, 274 families between them accounted for 2000 people, which means if the figures are accurate (and we have every reason to think they are) that each *household* contained seven people. Not counting the price of the houses, the total damage was valued at 60,000 ducats, or 30 ducats per person. A fire in July of the same year, 1555, destroyed two peasants' houses in Trevisano, in the plains; one was valued at 250 ducats, the other at 150. In the first, furniture, hay and grain amounted to 200 ducats, in the second, hay and grain amounted to about 90, without furniture (perhaps it have been saved). The two victims of the fire described themselves as *poveri* in their application for help, and say that they are now *nudi*, natural expressions no doubt from people asking for money, but which cannot have been in contradiction with the official estimate of their worldy goods. Now let us suppose that these individual figures can be used as a unit of measurement. Returning to Tizzo, let us complete the record of damage. Each house can be valued at 200 ducats, adding another 52,000 ducats to the bill, bringing the total damage to 112,000 and therefore the accumulated capital to 56 ducats, instead of 30, per head of the population. If we suppose that each family received a harvest similar to that of the poorer of the Trevisano fire victims, about 100 ducats, the total annual income of the village would have been about 27,400 ducats, or 13·7 ducats per head. This series of calculations brings us to the borderline of extreme poverty, perhaps it would be more correct to say of destitution. But we are never quite sure where this borderline lies.

I discovered too late to make full use of their extraordinary resources the documents of *Sommaria*, the accounts office of Naples. Through these fiscal records we are led along a multitude of paths into areas of extreme poverty and hardship. Pescara[527] on the Adriatic was a humble little town of 200 or 250 households, about 1000 inhabitants in all, and all foreigners, *romagnuoli, ferraresi, comachiesi, mantovani, milanesi,* and *slavoni*. Of these thousand immigrants, 'fifty families [200 people] own their own houses, vines, and ply a craft; the others have absolutely nothing but their huts or rather their piles of straw; they live from day to day, working at the salt-pans or digging the ground'. If only, the text goes on, the better-off peasants could afford to buy oxen to plough with, proof that they had none. This is utter poverty one would think. And yet the town had its port, its shops, and even its fair *della Annunziata* in March.

The *Sommaria* also gives details of the villages it sells and resells, according to the accidents of succession, to purchasers of seignorial revenues. Usually each inhabitant pays one ducat to the owner of the land, in one form or another, and this seignorial income is sold 'at five or ten per cent', that is at 10 or 20 ducats for every ducat of income. This rule of a ducat per head, a hasty calculation, is given for what it is worth. Another rule of thumb is that the per capita income of the peasant was

[527] A.d.S., Naples, Sommaria Consultationum, 2, f°s 68 v° and 69, 27th July, 1564.

approximately 10 ducats. But to take a particular case: Supertino[528] in the territory of Otranto was a village of 395 households, in May, 1549, a large village then, almost a small town. It had a higher population than Pescara. Its wealth lay principally in olive trees. The rule of a ducat per head rent to the landlord does not seem to work very well here. There were about 1600 inhabitants, and the landlord received 900 ducats. But this time we have a record of tithes paid to him in kind and therefore an opportunity to calculate the village's production and income in money (3000 kegs of wine, 11,000 *tomola* of wheat, 4000 *tomola* of barley, 1000 *tomola* of oats, 1250 *tomola* of beans, 50 *tomola* of chick peas and lentils, 550 *galatri* of flax, 2500 *staia* of olive oil – money value 8400 ducats). The income, if the list of incomes is complete and if the tithe was indeed one-tenth, must have been a little over 5 ducats per head of the population.

But the villages of Castile, according to the *Relaciones topográficas*[529] of the 1576 and 1578 enquiries, provide higher figures. The income level calculated from a selected sample[530] is 15,522 *maravedís* or 44 ducats per family; per capita income, supposing a family to consist of four people, is 11 ducats.

Further calculations are undoubtedly possible. The copious guild archives have not been seriously investigated. And tax records should surely make it possible to ascertain on a larger scale the 'national product' of each of the Venetian islands of Corfu, Crete, and Cyprus. There are exceptional series of documents on Sicily both at Palermo and Simancas. I think it ought to be possible, though by no means easy, to calculate the gross product of the Venetian or Tuscan states.

I did at one time think these problems could be solved by taking as a minimum level the price of slaves or galley men, or the wages of volunteers for the galleys, or even of soldiers, or the pay of domestic servants. But I am not convinced that these prices put on men were really *marginal*. A slave in Sicily or Naples could be sold for perhaps 30 ducats[531] in the first half of the century; after 1550 the price doubled.[532] One cannot conclude anything from this, for the slave market was very restricted; if there was a temporary influx of slaves, prices dropped sharply: in June, 1587, on his return from a pirate expedition with his galleys, Pietro di Toledo (the son of the famous viceroy of Naples) sold the slaves he had captured for a mere 30 ducats each.[533] We might add that it was possible to find slave-labour

[528] *Ibid.*, f° 59 v°, 22nd May, 1549.
[529] See the general study by Noël Salomon, quoted on p. 381.
[530] J. Gentil da Silva, 'Villages castillans et types de production au XVIe siècle' in *Annales E.S.C.*, 1963, no. 4, p. 729–744.
[531] A.d.S., Naples, Notai Giustizia 51, f° 5, 17th October, 1520, 36 ducats to be paid in new cloth; *ibid.*, f°s 177 v° and 178, 24th August, 1521, a black slave aged twelve, 36 ducats; *ibid.*, 66, f°s 141 v° and 152, the price of a horse was 33 ducats.
[532] *Ibid.*, Sommaria Partium, 595, f° 18, 28th January, 1569, a black slave aged thirty purchased at Lecce for 60 ducats.
[533] *Ibid.*, Sommaria Consultationum 9, f° 303–305, Naples, 18th June, 1587.

almost for nothing. At the end of the sixteenth century, we learn on the occasion of the liberation of the *ponentini* galley-slaves, who had been worked continuously for twelve years, that they had been sent to the galleys without ceremony by the *provveditore* of Cephalonia, and then passed from one galley to another, 'strabalzati di galera in galera'.[534] Equally disappointing from our point of view are the ransoms paid for prisoners.[535] The only ones recorded were those for the rich and influential, whose ransom did not reflect a standard selling price for men but what their captors thought they could afford. As for the voluntary oarsmen who were paid and fed aboard the galleys, a remark by the naval commander Giron[536] makes their situation plain. Also known as 'voluntary prisoners' (or not entirely voluntary) are those unfortunate men who have served their term and remain on board the galleys; they are then given a ducat a month, says our source, whereas in Italy they are given twice the sum. At this high wage he adds it would be easy to find many volunteers in Spain! So soldiers must always have been over-paid, attracted by the extra wages, for a soldier was already receiving three ducats a month in 1487.[537] In short, I have come to the conclusion that oarsmen in the galleys, even slaves, and certainly soldiers and domestic servants (at Ragusa for instance[538]) did not always come off worst in the division of men into those who were looked after by their society, assured of their keep however meagre, and the others. This dividing line runs below even these miserable classes and if anything moves downwards.

A provisional classification. Whatever the accuracy of the preceding calculations and others yet to be made, we shall not go far wrong in the scale

---

[534] A.d.S., Venice, Senato Mar 145, 24th March, 1600.
[535] See J. Mathiez, 'Trafic et prix de l'homme en Méditerranée aux XVIIe et XVIIIe siècles' in *Annales E.S.C.*, 1954, p. 157–164.
[536] Simancas Napoles Eº 1046, fº 25, Comᵒʳ Giron to H.M., Naples, 17th September, 1554.
[537] Museo Correr, Donà delle Rose, 46, fº 65, 11th March, 1487: these were *stradioti* employed in Morea. Cf. the remark attributed to Charles V, below Vol. II, ch. 5. In 1522, the janissaries were paid between 3 and 8 aspers a day, that is at 50 aspers to the ducat, between under 2 and under 5 ducats a month (Otto Zierer, *op. cit.*, III, p. 29). At Zara in 1533, a bombardier was paid 40 ducats a year. But bombardiers were specialists.
[538] The figures obtainable from the Archives at Ragusa make this quite plain. The many contracts between master and servant preserved in the registers of the Diversa di Cancellaria (for example, vol. 98, 122, 132, 146, 196) made it possible to conduct a brief survey. For apprentices, who came under a separate category, there was no formal payment specified at the end of their training, but according to the practice of the trade, the new artisan might receive clothing, new shoes, or his tools. The others were paid on expiry of the contract (which might be after two, five, six, seven, or ten years). This was in addition to payments in kind (board, lodging, clothing, and care during sickness). This payment which was graded according to the year of service gradually rose: from 1 to 2 gold ducats in 1505–1506 to 2·5 in 1535; to 3·4 and 4·5 in 1537 and 1547; to just above or below 3 in 1560–1561; to 4 in 1607; to 8 or 10 in 1608. But since the ducat was devalued, the situation scarcely improved over the years. There was a structural *ceiling.*

of retrospective values if we fix the following rates for the active members of the population: an income below 20 ducats a year was a subsistence wage; between 20 and 40 ducats 'small'; and between 40 and 150 'reasonable'. This scale does not allow either for local variations in the cost of living, or for variation over the years, which might be considerable during periods of inflation. It will do only as a very rough classification.[539]

So we know at once, when we learn that a professor at the University of Padua received a salary of 600 florins a year, that he was *ipso facto* a member of the privileged class, without needing to know that he held the first chair in civil law, 'primus locus lectionis ordinarie juris civilis' and was indeed Corrado del Buscio, and we need not take account of the generally high wage level in that summer of 1506.[540] It will be of some value to place any of the many wages mentioned in the documents against this elementary grid: to see that at the Zecca at Venice the wage pyramid began at the bottom with the beggarly sums paid to the boys who kept watch (20 ducats a year in 1554)[541] and went up to 60 ducats for the salary of a *partidor*[542] (1557), the official in charge of separating gold and silver, and only became really rewarding for an accountant at 180 ducats[543] (in 1590, it is true, after the known rise[544] in wages); to see that a workman in the Arsenal received only a modest wage in 1534[545] earning 24 *soldi* a day, from 1st March to 31st August, and 20 *soldi* from 1st September to the last day of February; the caulker, who was a skilled worker, was in the same year paid 40 *soldi* in summer and 30 in winter. So Venice's two great centres of power, the Arsenal and the Zecca,[546] depended on a poorly paid labour force. Even the secretaries appointed by the Council of Ten only drew an average of 100 ducats a year.[547] By contrast the 'inzegner' in the service of the Signoria, Zuan Hieronimo de San Michel, who was asking in March, 1556, for his salary to be increased from 20 to 25 ducats *a month*, seems to have been very comfortably off, earning in a month as much as a worker earned in a year.[548]

[539] See the table in Hektor Ammann, note 521 above.

[540] A.d.S., Venice, Senato Terra 15, f° 106.

[541] Museo Correr, Donà delle Rose 26, f° 46 v°.

[542] *Ibid.*, f° 48 v°.

[543] *Ibid.*, f° 100.

[544] Clearly established for the period 1572–1601 from the claims of the bakers: wages had doubled in the interval, Museo Correr, Donà delle Rose, 218, f° 302.

[545] A.d.S., Senato Mar 23, f°s 36 and 36 v°, 29th September, 1534, that is a little over 63 ducats a year.

[546] Museo Correr, Donà delle Rose, 161 f° 80, 1606, there were seventy-two workers employed at the Zecca (fifty-four for silver, eighteen for gold). The total wage bill was 5280 ducats, an average of almost 72 per worker. On average, workers in silver tended to be paid more. Sometimes one employee held two posts.

[547] Museo Correr, Donà delle Rose, 161, f° 208 v° 1586, 28 secretaries, total wage bill 2764 ducats.

[548] A.d.S., Venice, Senato Terra 23, Venice, 20th March, 1556.

In short, large sections of the community were either poor or very poor. They formed a huge proletariat whose existence historians are gradually beginning to recognize from the fragmentary evidence available, a proletariat whose presence was felt in every sector of the century's activity, increasingly so as years went by. It bred persistent outbreaks of brigandage, an endless, fruitless form of social revolution. The general impoverishment settled differences, relentlessly driving poor and possessionless alike towards the very bottom of the social ladder. In Spain the survival of ancient inherited wealth and a marked demographic decline contributed in the seventeenth century to produce a strange social category, a proletariat comparable to the plebeians of ancient Rome. Genuinely poor, rascals from the towns whom the picaresque novel has made famous, highwaymen, false or authentic beggars, all this *gente de hampa*, these *hampones*, tramps, had done with work maybe, but work and employment had done with them first. They had become entrenched, like the poor in Moscow under the last Tsars, in their poverty-stricken idleness. How would they have lived without the soup that was distributed at the doors of monasteries, these *sopistas*, eaters of *sopa boba*? Ragged folk playing cards or dice at street corners, they also provided the enormous numbers of domestic servants in rich houses. The young Count Olivares, when a student at Salamanca, had a tutor, twenty-one servants, and a mule to carry his books from his lodgings to the university.[549]

This was as typical of Spain as it was of France during the wars of religion, of Italy under Sixtus V, or even of Turkey at the end of the century. The growing burden of the poor was sufficient in itself to announce the impending violent economic change, from which the poor, on whatever shore of the Mediterranean, were to gain nothing.

Food, a poor guide: officially rations were always adequate. Our calculations and surveys will need revision: they can be much improved. By contrast we must not expect too much from an enquiry into sixteenth-century diets.[550] There is no shortage of documents. They are only too easily found. But they offer what seems very suspect evidence on the lower standards of living. According to them everything was for the best in the best of all possible worlds. That the Spinola family should have an abundant and varied diet is not surprising. Nor will it astonish us to find that the diet of the poor should consist very largely of cheap foodstuffs such as bread and biscuit. Cheese, meat and fish were also eaten. The gradual decline in meat consumption throughout Europe, and no doubt in the Mediterranean too, had begun, but was not yet far advanced. The unexpected element in these past diets is that when the rations allotted to

---

[549] Juan Regla, in J. Vicens Vives, *H. Social de España*, III, p. 300.
[550] Frank C. Spooner, 'Régimes alimentaires d'autrefois, proportions et calculs de calories' in *Annales E.S.C.*, 1961, no. 3, p. 568–574.

soldiers, seamen, galley-slaves, and poor-house inmates are measured for calorie content, they yield something like 4000 calories a day.

All would indeed be for the best if we did not know that official menus were always and without exception *officially* good. Everything on the menus posted up or sent to the authorities looks satisfactory, even very satisfactory. But we hardly need the evidence of a few disputes about the distribution of food on board the galleys to sow doubt in our minds. And yet there are the figures, or the comments for example of the *veedor* of the Naples galleys, who had been in charge of supplies for years and who speaks freely before the investigators from the *Sommaria*.[551] Even on board the Turkish galleys, ordinary rations included generous distributions of biscuit.[552] So we shall have to resign ourselves to accept what we find, that is, the balanced diet that is described and confirmed by so many documents, and which may simply mean that galley slaves and soldiers were servants precious enough to have their health cared for. And let us say at once and quite emphatically, for nothing that has gone before would suggest it: these menus were those of privileged people. Any man who had a regular ration of soup, *vaca salada*, *bizcocho*, wine, and vinegar was sure of his keep. Diego Suárez as a very young man worked on the building site of the Escorial, where he found that the rations were good: *el plato bueno*. The true poor were those who found no official provider, whether warlike or charitable. And they were legion. They form the dramatic background of the century of which we occasionally catch a violent glimpse: on 27th May, 1597, at Aix-en-Provence, according to a chronicle, 'the rectors and bursars of the Church of the Holy Spirit were giving out bread to the poor, and in the crush of the said poor, six or seven persons died, children, girls and a woman, having been pushed to the ground, trampled and suffocated, for there were more than 1200 poor people there'.[553]

Can our calculations be checked? If we add together all the different sources of income (although they are both indeterminate and partly overlapping) the gross annual product of the Mediterranean lies between 1200 million and 1500 million ducats, giving a per capita share of 20 or 35 ducats. These figures are by no means reliable and are certainly too high. The average income could hardly have reached this level. The error arises from the misleading process of estimating everything in terms of money, and it is impossible to proceed otherwise. This *would be* the average level if everything had passed through the market economy, which is not of course the case. But that need not cause us to dismiss all our hypothetical figures as meaningless, still less as irrelevant. Our object has been to make the necessary initial survey, to situate, as it were, the huge inaccessible regions of the Mediterranean landscape in relation to each other. Let us now turn the

---

[551] A.d.S., Naples, Sommaria Consultationum 3, f° 204 ff., 8th March, 1571.
[552] Piri Re'is, *Bahrije*, ed. Paul Kahle, 1926, *Introduction*, II, p. XLII.
[553] Foulquet Sobolis, *Histoire en forme de journal de ce qui s'est passé en Provence depuis l'an 1562 jusqu'à l'an 1607*, 1894, p. 245.

page and leave an area where as yet quantitative history is unrewarding, where all the valid statistics are hidden from our gaze. Ten years from now, if the paths suggested here are followed and explored with success, this chapter will have to be rewritten from start to finish.

Facsimile of the carpeta *of a letter from Philip II's ambassador in Lisbon, with dates of dispatch and arrival.*

Cf. p. 364, note 50.

CHAPTER II

Economies: Precious Metals, Money, and Prices

The role of precious metals has never seemed more important than in the sixteenth century. Contemporary writers unhesitatingly accord them pride of place and economists of the seventeenth century are even more emphatic. For one, they are 'the substance of the people';[1] another considers 'that we draw our living less from traffic in commodities than from gold and silver'. And a Venetian speaker goes so far as to say that precious metal, whether gold or silver is 'the sinews of all government, it gives it its pulse, its movement, its mind, soul, and it is its essence and its very life ["l'esser et la vita"]. . . . It overcomes all impossibilities, for it is the master, the *patron* of all: it carries with it the necessity of all things; without it all is weak and without movement.'[2]

Patron del tutto: now we are not so sure. Money was not the universal driving force it was so readily assumed to be. The role played by precious metals was determined not only by the stocks inherited from previous centuries, and therefore by accidents in the past, but equally by the velocity of circulation, by international relations, economic competition, the deliberate policies of states and mercantile communities, even by 'vulgar opinion'.[3] And often money acted merely as a screen, as an economist would say, masking the realities of goods, services, and exchanges. Finally, gold and silver (and even copper) did not simply add up to form a homogeneous stock of bullion. The metals used for currency were in constant collision and competition.[4]

So every time the value of gold coinage was raised (in relation to silver) it led to a run on gold, which immediately took on the role of *bad money*, arbitrarily in favour and chasing out the good, in this case silver coins. Such an event was never entirely fortuitous. If it occurred with obstinate regularity at Venice, might this not be because it facilitated the massive export of silver that was one of the mainstays of the republic's trade with the Levant? This was a deliberate attempt to force the market[5] with all its consequences and limitations: if gold went up, so did prices on all the exchanges, and the cost of living rose with them. Further con-

---

[1] Mathias de Saint-Jean, *Le Commerce honorable* . . . , 1646, p. 102; gold and silver constitute 'universal wealth' according to W. Petty, *Political Arithmetic*, 1699, p. 242.
[2] Museo Correr, Donà delle Rose, 161, f°s 239 v° and 240 about 1600.
[3] A. de Montchrestien, *op. cit.*, p. 94.
[4] J. van Klaveren, *art. cit.*, p. 3, quite unjustifiably argues the contrary.
[5] Museo Correr, Donà delle Rose, 161, f° 2, 14th December, 1593.

sequences were, for example, the unprecedented return of 250,000 sequins[6] from the Turkish Empire in 1603; or, at about the same time, currency speculation by the Grand Duke of Tuscany who, under an assumed name, sold 200,000 gold crowns to the Venetian Zecca, making a safe profit of 12,000 crowns 'as a result of our ignorance', says a Venetian who wanted gold to be put once and for all at a fixed ratio to silver, as the price of flour was related to that of wheat.[7] The rest of the story is easy to guess. The relative scarcity of silver coin opened the door wider than usual to clipped, lightweight silver pieces of low metallic content, which Venice was then obliged, not without some difficulty, to eliminate from circulation.[8] Did these troubles stem, in part at least, from the need to export silver to the Levant?

This explanation, which was not one suggested by contemporaries, might nevertheless account for the curious situation in Sicily, where, since at least 1531, gold had systematically been overvalued in relation to silver (1 to 15). Because of this 'disproportion', Sicily was constantly short of silver coin, which it was profitable to buy up in exchange for gold and then melt down, as the Naples mint frequently did to its advantage.[9] But some mystery still persists about this scandal, those whom it profited, and why it was allowed to continue.

Elsewhere, the relationship between gold and silver was more varied[10] in its effects, but did not go unobserved once men had become aware of the nature and reciprocal action of different currencies, strong against weak, good against bad, gold against silver or even 'black' money (vellon and before long pure copper coinage), later still metal against paper. 'Money' in the sense of wealth or fortune has never been of one single nature.

I. THE MEDITERRANEAN AND THE GOLD OF THE SUDAN

The flow of precious metal towards the East. And yet at first sight there could be nothing simpler than the circulation of precious metals in the

[6] An unexpected movement, running counter to the general trend at which Zuan Battᵃ Poreti, in his report to the Signoria expresses amazement, 1603, Museo Correr, 181, f° 53 v°.

[7] *Ibid.*, Cicogna 1999 (undated). Customs duties at Venice were paid in silver.

[8] *Ibid.*

[9] Antonio della Rovere, *La crisi monetaria siciliana (1531–1802)*, ed. Carmelo Trasselli, 1964, in general and esp. p. 30 ff. There was sustained pressure on gold as well as untimely issues of copper, between 1602 and 1606 for example, in the time of the Duke of Feria, L. Bianchini, *op. cit.*, p. 336.

[10] The higher price of gold might, for instance cause the demand for silver to fall, as is recognized and noted by Zuan Battᵃ Poreti (reference in note 6), and as a result *stop* ordinary prices from rising since they were tied to silver – a theory put forward by Frank Spooner in our joint contribution to Vol. IV of the *Cambridge Economic History*. Zuan Battᵃ Poreti argues that all exchange rates dependent on gold must and will rise along with it (f° 53): exchange rates in Venice for instance were based on the ducat, a money of account, which if gold (in this case the *sequin*) went up in price, would be devalued like a bank note, more ducats being required (thus raising the exchange rate) to buy a gold crown on the 'Besançon' fairs. Not only this but all commodities affected by prices on such exchanges (Spanish wool, dyes) would necessarily go up too.

Mediterranean. Centuries passed and nothing changed. Whatever their source: the silver mines of Old Serbia; the Alps; Sardinia; the gold-washing of the Sudan and Ethiopia, or even Sofala by way of North Africa and Egypt; from the silver mines of Schwaz in the Inn valley; of Neusohl in Hungary, Mansfeld in Saxony, Kuttenberg near Prague or the mines of the Erz-Gebirge;[11] from the mines in the New World after the first years of the sixteenth century – whatever their origin, precious metals once absorbed into Mediterranean life were fed into the stream that continually flowed eastward. In the Black Sea, Syria, and Egypt the Mediterranean trade balance was always in deficit. Trade with the Far East was only possible thanks to exports of gold and silver, which depleted Mediterranean bullion reserves. It has even been suggested, not unconvincingly, that the vitality of the Roman Empire was sapped by the haemorrhage of precious metals. It is a fact that coins from the Julio-Claudian era have been found as far away as Ceylon.[12]

The Mediterranean did, however, constantly try to stem this ruinous flow. Alexandria, in the time of the Roman Empire, paid for some of her purchases from the Far East with glassware.[13] In the Middle Ages western Europe exported slaves instead of gold and silver. Byzantium, by introducing the breeding of silkworms in the time of Justinian, succeeded in limiting her exports of money to the East.[14] These attempts merely underline the necessity, exhausting in the long run, of making repeated payments to the Far East, which exported a great deal to the Mediterranean and imported comparatively little in exchange.

So during the sixteenth and seventeenth centuries there circulated throughout the vast Asian continent, source of spices, drugs, and silk, the precious gold and above all silver coins minted at Venice, Genoa, or Florence, and later the famous Spanish silver pieces of eight. Away to the east flowed these currencies, out of the Mediterranean circuit into which it had often required so much patience to introduce them. The Mediterranean as a whole operated as a machine for accumulating precious metals, of which, be it said, it could never have enough.[15] It hoarded them only to lose them all to India, China, and the East Indies. The great discoveries may have revolutionized routes and prices, but they did not alter this fundamental situation, no doubt because it was still a major advantage to westerners to have access to the precious merchandise of the East, in particular pepper, which according to one Venetian 'brings with it all the other spices . . .'; no doubt also because in the sixteenth century, as in the past, the purchasing power of precious metals rose above that of Christian countries as soon as one crossed the border into the Orient. In about 1613, according to Antonio Serra, Venice was still annually export-

---

[11] For the last group, see John U. Nef, 'Industrial Europe . . . ', *art. cit.*, p. 7.
[12] André Piganiol, *Rome*, p. 389.
[13] G. I. Bratianu, *Études . . .* , p. 80.
[14] W. Heyd, *op. cit.*, I, p, 1 ff.
[15] See the just remarks on this subject by Giuseppe Mira, *Aspetti dell'economia comasca all'inizio dell'età moderna*, Como, 1939, p. 244 (1587).

ing over 5 million ducats in specie to the Levant,[16] although, in an effort to save her bullion reserves, she also sent cloth, glass trinkets, mirrors, hardware, and copper. The role of the *fattori* and resident agents whom the Venetian merchants employed 'on the quaysides' of the Levant[17] from Syria to the Persian Gulf was to keep informed, 'be advised',[18] and to keep an eye open for good business, but they were also daily engaged in bartering goods for other goods, *dar a baratto* or *barattare*, in other words buying and selling without using money. But it was always tempting to cut the process short and to pay in cash when this was profitable. The expert of the Banco di Rialto could still write in 1603[19]: 'di Levante e venuto sempre li capitale in mercancie, capital [that is money] has always returned from the Levant in the form of merchandise'. 'It is not customary,' writes Tavernier in about 1650, 'to bring back money from the Levant, but rather to invest it in good merchandise on which there is some profit to be made.'[20] A Venetian report of 1668 further notes that by introducing *pezze da otto di Spagna*[21] to Egypt, one could make a profit of 30 per cent.

These commercial practices which remained broadly the same both in the sixteenth and seventeenth centuries, indicate the pressures of a unilateral situation from which all trust was eliminated. The bill of exchange, which moved freely throughout Christendom, made only exceptional appearances in Islam, so exceptional indeed as to suggest that it was unknown in the East.[22] The Christian merchant, always pressed to find payment, could hardly ever borrow money in the Levant except at usurers' rates that might run to 40 per cent and more. Some Ragusan papers in 1573 refer to loans offered at this rate by Portuguese Jews in Egypt.[23] In Syria, Venetian merchants, hastening to buy up goods at any price in 1596, were led to borrow money from 'Turks' at 30 and 40 per cent. As a result, there was more than one bankruptcy, to the dishonour of the whole nation.[24] More-

[16] *Op. cit.*, p. 165. This figure is of course much exaggerated.
[17] Pierre Belon, *op. cit.*, p. 100 v°.
[18] *Ibid.*
[19] Museo Correr, Donà delle Rose, 181, f° 53 v°.
[20] Tavernier, *Les Six Voyages*, I, p. 270.
[21] Marciana 5729, *Relazione d'Egitto*, 1668.
[22] On this subject see the letter from Idiaquez to the Marquis of Mondejar, Venice, 26th March, 1579, A. N., K 1672, G 1, note 33, it is impossible to find a letter of credit on Constantinople at Venice, even for a straightforward ransom. There were no bills of exchange between the two cities except for very small sums: N. Iorga, *Ospiti . . .* , p. 38, 46, 62, 79, 80, 84–85, 88, 90, 92, 97–98, 100, 109, 121 (Wallachian exchange at Venice 1587–1590). The Ragusans paid their tribute to Constantinople by means of a system of bills of exchange accepted as payment for customs duties levied on Ragusan merchandise from the Balkans, at the gates of the city, the merchandise belonging to their compatriots scattered throughout the European half of the Turkish empire. It is the absence or scarcity of specie which explains the clearing-house operations at Medina del Campo or the Genoese fairs, J. Kulischer, *op. cit.*, II p. 345.
[23] Ragusa Archives, Diversa de Foris, XI, f° 75 ff. Record of payments made to Jewish money-lenders (twenty-five names) by G. Bonda and Stephan di Cerva. There were ten payments in all at intervals from 3rd March to 10th October, 1573. The loans were granted for periods of between one and four months.
[24] 16th February, 1596, G. Berchet, *op. cit.*, p. 87.

over there was from the start a black market in specie in western cities. In Venice, small banks, *banchetti*, handled clandestine currency dealings behind closed doors and windows[25] in spite of intermittent punitive measures by the Council of Ten.[26]

With the last quarter of the century, the French, English, and Flemish (or rather Dutch) came to occupy a leading position in Levantine trade, for they always paid cash. Inexperienced newcomers, they upset traditional habits, put old Venetian trading houses in difficulties and sent prices soaring. The French continued the practice of purchasing for cash,[27] but the English and Dutch soon arranged for exchange of their own goods: kerseys, lead, copper, tin; by 1583 the English were settling only a quarter of their business by money payments.[28]

And even this money had to be found. In the Mediterranean the great commercial centres such as Genoa, Leghorn, Venice, Ancona, and sometimes Naples would provide some of the precious coins in exchange for goods or services. In fact, these were secondary sources, whose silver came more or less directly from Spain, that is, from Seville. And if the English preferred to put in to Italian ports instead of to the latter, it was because between 1586 and 1604 they were not welcome in Spain.

It was through Seville and Spain, rich first in gold then in silver, in theory hoarding her treasure but in practice letting it escape, that the trade of the Mediterranean and indeed the known world was stimulated. This influx of precious metals was a new and revolutionary feature, of more recent origin than the chronology of the great discoveries would suggest.

Sudanese gold: early history. Before the sixteenth century – before the arrival of gold and silver from America – the Mediterranean had drawn on various sources, sometimes near at hand, more often far away, for the precious metals indispensable to her commercial activity. It is a long story and for the most part a familiar one. Only the last phase of this period, which came to an end in the middle of the sixteenth century – and which we may call for short the age of Sudanese gold – has perhaps received less attention, or had until recently.[29]

Audacious historians used to date the beginning of the Sahara gold traffic from the tenth century. But there is every reason to think that it

---

[25] A.d.S. Venice, Busta 105 C. 838, 24th November, 1585.

[26] Museo Correr, Donà delle Rose 26, f° 54, 26th May, 1562. Such exchanges were prohibited 'ni in bottega ni in casa' 2nd December, 1605, *Cinque Savii*, 12, f°s 105–106.

[27] J. B. Tavernier, *Les Six Voyages . . .* , Paris, 1681, I, p. 73

[28] John Newberie to Leonard Poore of London, Aleppo, 29th May, 1583; R. Hakluyt, *op. cit.*, II, p. 246–247.

[29] This problem has now been investigated in a remarkable study by V. Magalhães Godinho, *L'économie de l'Empire portugais aux XVIe et XVIIe siècles*, 1958 (typescript thesis, Sorbonne) vol I, p. 1–241.

began very much earlier, even preceding the arrival of the camel in the desert in the second century A.D., for before that date, 'the horses and oxen of the Garamantes pulled carts in the Libyan desert'.[30] It is probable that gold dust from the Sudan reached North Africa before the tenth century and led, after the year 1000,[31] to the emergence in the South of coherent and spectacular states in the loop of the Niger and in the North, in the Maghreb, to the founding of new towns like Algiers and Oran. Moorish Spain, whose masters in the tenth century held the key position of Ceuta,[32] found the gold to make its *dirhems* in North Africa.

But Sudanese gold provided more than a basis for the prosperity of North Africa and Moslem Spain, the Western Islamic bloc which its isolation in the twelfth century from the chief trade routes obliged to be self-sufficient. This gold played its part in the history of the Mediterranean as a whole, entering general circulation from the fourteenth century, perhaps after the spectacular pilgrimage to Mecca of Mansa Musa, King of Mali, in 1324.[33] North Africa with its supply of gold gradually became the driving force of the entire Mediterranean. In the fifteenth century it was invaded by Christian merchants[34] who settled without difficulty in Ceuta, Tangier, Fez, Oran, Tlemcen,[35] Bougie, Constantine,[36] and Tunis. Previous centuries had seen the arrival of soldier-adventurers, or pirate raids like Philip Doria's expedition in 1354[37] against Tripoli, 'the city rich in gold'; or grand schemes of conquest by Aragonese and Castilians alike.[38] In the fifteenth century it was the turn of the merchant: from now on, history records only commercial treaties, privileges, purchases, and exchanges. Handicapped in the East by the Turkish advance, Christian merchants found some compensation in North Africa.[39] The Maghreb had the advantage of being accessible not only to Catalonia but also to Mar-

[30] J. Carcopino, *Le Maroc antique*, 1943, p. 139.
[31] Roberto S. Lopez, *Studi sull'economia genovese nel medio evo*, 1936, reviewed by Marc Bloch in *Mélanges d'hist. soc.*, I, 1942, p. 114–115.
[32] In 931. Earlier, in 875, Ténès had been founded by sailors from Andalusia on the 'Algerian' coast.
[33] P. Béraud-Villars, *L'Empire de Gao . . .*, 1941, p. 220.
[34] The standard reference work is Jacques de Mas-Latrie, *Traités de paix et de commerce divers concernant les relations des Chretiens avec les Arabes, en Afrique septentrionale au Moyen Age*, 1866.
[35] E. Coudray, 'Les étrangers à Tlemcen' in *Journal de l'Algérie nouvelle*, 1897. I have also had the opportunity of reading and using a manuscript study by the same writer on the same subject.
[36] Such as Giorgio Gregorio Stella, a purchaser of wool and linen cloth at Constantine in 1470, Robert Brunschvig, *La Berbérie . . .*, I, p. 269.
[37] Laurent-Charles Féraud, *Annales tripolitaines*, 1927, p, 16.
[38] The plans of Sanchez IV of Castile and of Jaime of Aragon. Zones on either side of the Moulouya; plans of Henry III; destruction of Tetouan *circa* 1400 . . . , R. Konetzke, *op. cit.*, p. 84.
[39] Robert Brunschvig, *La Berbérie Orientale sous les Hafsides des origines à la fin du XVe siècle*, 1940, I, p. 269 notes this important connection. It is also worthy of note that Venice began sending the 'Barbary galleys' in about 1440, *ibid.*, I, p .253. This was peaceful infiltration, apart from Portuguese actions in Morocco.

seilles and Provence,[40] Ragusa,[41] and Sicily[42] as well as to Venice, whose galleys regularly put in at Tripoli, Tunis, Algiers, Bône, and Oran; accessible too to the Genoese – whose *fonduk* had vanished but its old cisterns still remained to be discovered by the victorious Spanish when they entered Tunis in 1573. At Tlemcen, 'the city of honest merchants', all the 'nations' of Christendom were represented. The agents of the Gonzaga, who bought thoroughbred horses, were as at home in Tunis and Oran as in Genoa or Venice, coming and going with bills of exchange on Barbary (on the credit of Christian merchants settled there) or returning with their horses, awkward travelling companions aboard the Venetian galleys.[43] In 1438 Alfonso the Magnanimous, who had supplied Tripoli and Tunis with Sicilian wheat during a famine, used the gold he received in payment to have 24,000 *Venetian* ducats minted in order to finance his struggle against Naples.[44]

With the help of the gold and slave trade, commercial penetration of the continent was far-reaching, extending south as far as the Tuat and the Niger.[45] All the merchandise of Christendom on sale in the commercial quarters of North Africa (textiles, kerseys, hardware, and trinkets), crossed the Sahara, the Maghreb lending itself the more easily to this invasion since it lacked political cohesion. In theory it was divided into three zones (the three geographical, cultural, and political zones of its history): Morocco under the Merinids, Tlemcenia under the abd al-Wadids, and Ifriqya (Tunisia) under the Hafsids. But each region had its enclaves, dissident regions, untamed mountain tribes, and independent towns. Oran and Ceuta were in fact city republics. It is an error (sometimes committed by the most knowledgeable) to consider North Africa as a rural complex. In the fourteenth and fifteenth centuries towns grew up sometimes out of all proportion to the surrounding countryside. They looked not only towards the Mediterranean but also to the South, the lands of Black Africa, the *Bled es Soudan*. From the edge of the Sahara to the

[40] R. Gandilhon, *op. cit.*, p. 29.

[41] There were in 1935, a number of unpublished documents in this connection in the Archives at Ragusa-Dubrovnik.

[42] G. La Mantia, 'La secrezia o dogana di Tripoli' in *Arch. st. sic.*, XLI, p. 476–477, note 1, with reference to the *duplae* or *duble* of Tripoli, 1438: 'Et quoniam merces et mercimonia pro maiore parte hodie apud Barbaros expediuntur ex quibus duplae veniunt quae ut videtis (this was a letter from King Alfonso to the 'stratigoto' of Messina) non possunt iuxta valorem suum facilem cursum habere, quo fit ut magnum populis nostris detrimentum sequatur'. So they are to be melted down 'per coniare moneta di ducati'. In Moslem countries, *duble* were still gold pieces in the sixteenth century in North Africa, R. Hakluyt, *op. cit.*, II, p. 176, 1584.

[43] See for example A.d.S. Mantua, A° Gonzaga, Genova 757, 5th January, 1485; 7th July, 1485; Spagna 585, 6th December, 1486; 7th November, 1486; Genova 757, 21st July, 1487 (bill of exchange of Federico Crivelli); 25th August, 1487 (bill of exchange on Tunis); 25th August, 1487; 11th September, 1487, 200 *dobie* of Tunis are worth 220 ducats; 15th October, 1487, etc.

[44] C. Trasselli, 'Transports d'argent à destination et à partir de la Sicile' in *Annales E.S.C.*, 1963, p. 883.

[45] Richard Hennig, *Terrae incognitae*, III, 1939; Lefèvre, 'Il Sahara nel Medioevo e il viaggio a Tuat del genovese Malfante' in *Riv. delle Colonie*, 1936; C. De La Roncière,

shores of the Gulf of Guinea, these links formed an ancient structured system 'of unchanging geo-economic conditions' as Vitorino Magalhães Godinho writes.[46]

Five commodities dominated the trade routes: gold dust (*tibar*[47]), black slaves, copper, salt, and textiles. The black Africans possessed the first two. Goods were exchanged at the point where the camel caravans from the North met the processions of bearers or the canoes of the South. On the whole the North, that is Islam, and behind Islam the western merchant, gained most from this trade. It was said that in Mali salt was exchanged for its weight in gold[48] in 1450. Certainly by 1515, according to Leo Africanus, Venetian cloth was being sold at exorbitant rates at Timbuktu and the local aristocracy was deep in debt to merchants from the Levant or the Maghreb.[49] This then was the wider economic context, but local economic conditions had a part to play as well. The gold supply ultimately depended upon elasticity of production in the three zones where gold-washing was carried out, about which there is no mystery and which are still known today[50]: Upper Senegal, Upper Niger, and the Guinea Coast.

The Portuguese in Guinea: gold continues to arrive in the Mediterranean. The advance of the Portuguese along the Atlantic coast of Africa was an event of major importance. At Cape Blanc there was a first contact between the explorers and the *Mouros brancos* of Barbary and a little gold dust found its way to the ocean. The Gulf of Guinea was reached in about 1440 and the *resgate* of slaves, gold, and ivory took place at the mouths of the rivers, at local fairs, in exchange for brightly coloured fabrics, usually of poor quality, rings, copper bracelets or bowls, coarse woollen cloth, as well as wheat and horses. In 1444 the first convoy of black slaves was landed at Lagos in Portugal. In 1447 the *cruzado*, Portugal's first national gold currency, was created. By the time of Henry the Navigator's death in 1460, commercial colonization of the coast of Guinea was virtually accomplished. The conquest was completed in January, 1482, by the unexpected construction, within the space of a few weeks, of the castle of São Jorge da Mina, built with materials brought from Portugal, particularly blocks of ready-cut stone.

The immediate prosperity of these trades (in gold, slaves, ivory, and malaguetta and other pepper substitutes) is beyond dispute. Gold extraction was conducted in the name both of the king and of private citizens.

'Découverte d'une relation de voyage du Touat décrivant, en 1447, le bassin du Niger', in *B. de la Section de Géogr. du Comité des Travaux Historiques*, 1919. On the same subject see the studies by G. Piersantelli, P. Schiarini, R. Di Tucci.

[46] *Op. cit.*, I, p. 194.

[47] To call it 'gold of Tibar' is a tautology, see below, note 81.

[48] R. Hennig, *op. cit.*, III, p. 286.

[49] Leo Africanus, *History and Description* . . . trans. Pory, 1896 ed., vol III, p. 827 and P. Béraud Villars, *op. cit.*, p. 90.

[50] G. Balandier, *L'Afrique ambiguë*, 1957, p. 67 ff.

During the period 1500–1520 about 700 kilos of gold were probably exported annually.[51] After 1520 there was a perceptible decline and in 1550 there opened a long period of crisis, lasting until at least 1580 and more likely until 1600; the Dutch made their appearance after 1605. So three phases can be distinguished in the African gold trade: a period of conspicuous activity from 1440 to 1520–1550, followed by a long recession between 1550 and 1600 and a fresh impetus in the new century.[52]

It is the long recession between roughly 1520 and 1600 which is the most difficult to explain. There are three possible causes: competition from England, France, and Spain during these years of decline (and of this there is plentiful evidence); the rising costs experienced by the Portuguese armadas and garrisons, so that gold became too costly (and this is quite plausible); and finally competition from American gold: the New World's earliest export to Europe was gold, 43 tons *officially* landed at Seville between 1551 and 1560, that is over 4 tons a year compared to 700 kilos at most from the Atlantic coast of Africa.

But the important point to note is that the Atlantic gold route did not, between 1440 and 1520, inhibit the passage of gold across the Sahara to North Africa, from where it passed into the Mediterranean. Proof of this is provided by coins minted in Sicily and the re-export of gold in both coins and ingots from the island. In 1489,[53] as in 1455, massive shipments of Sicilian wheat to Africa (75,000 quintals) brought in return half a ton of gold to the island. Further evidence is supplied by Venetian shipping. The *galere di Barberia* continued to frequent the ports of the Maghreb and loaded gold there. In December, 1484, two of these galleys were seized by the fleet of the Catholic Kings, 'et una cum ingenti auri quantitate', complained Venice.[54] We have records of the instructions given in 1505 and 1506 by a Venetian merchant, Michiel Da Leze,[55] to his factor aboard the Barbary galleys. On both occasions he gave him silver coins and cloth (the first time 2000 ducats in silver pieces, 'di moneda di Zeccha', and some scarlet cloth; the second time 3000 ducats 'in mocenigi di Zeccha' plus camlets from Aleppo and kerseys). They were to be exchanged for 'tanti hori boni, orj che sieno boni'. This was in fact gold dust that the factor was to have melted down at the Valencia mint, when the galleys reached Spain, and to use if possible to buy wool.

About ten years later the gold trade was still operating. On 15th July, 1519, three light galleys were ordered to leave Corfu and fetch from Tunis

[51] V. Magalhães Godinho, *op. cit.*, part II, chap. 1, p. 671 ff, typescript.
[52] Perhaps earlier, A.d.S. Venice, Senato Dispacci Spagna, Zane to the Doge, Madrid, 14th February, 1583, the Catholic King is having 'molto artigliare un navilio' with 150 soldiers on board to send it to the Mina to fetch a certain quantity of gold from there, 'di ragion della Corona di Portugallo'.
[53] Carmelo Trasselli, 'Un aureo barbaresco battuto in Sicilia', in *Numismatica*, 1963.
[54] Simancas, Venecia, E° 1308, f° 2, the Doge of Venice to the Catholic Kings, Venice, 23rd December, 1484.
[55] These valuable letters, 1497–1511, have been reclassified, A.d.S., Venice, *Lettere Commerciali*, XV, 9.

to Zara 'li ori de li mercadanti de le galie nostre de Barberia et altro haver sottile', both gold and expensive merchandise.[56] There is a similar reference in June, 1521. The merchants asked that there should be brought to Venice 'li ori che se trovarono haver de Tunis'.[57] The archives contain many other records of such voyages.[58] Were they merely surviving echoes of a dying trade? And yet it was almost three-quarters of a century since the Atlantic route had been opened up to Portuguese trade. For France this chronology is approximately the same. 'Le traficq de la Barbarie est fort perdu,' it was remarked at the mint at Montpellier but in 1518 a note says 'gold dust [*les pailloles*] from there is taken to other places than this mint'. 'No more gold comes from the Barbary quarter now because of the wars,' according to another writer, but this time the date is 10th October, 1526.[59] The last voyage of the *galere di Barberia* took place in 1525. So it must have been about then, in 1524, if I have correctly interpreted a subsequent decision by the Council of Ten,[60] that Venice witnessed a decline in shipments of gold or gold coins to be melted down. However, between 1524 and 1531,[61] 29,617 marks of gold, or 4321 a year, were being minted – three times the volume of Atlantic shipments of Sudanese gold. Venice was not dependent on North Africa alone for her supply of gold.

However, in the absence of clear documentary evidence, one wonders exactly what lay behind the changing fortunes of the ducat. In 1517 the ducat ceased to be a unit of real money represented by a gold piece, and became a money of account at the henceforward invariable rate of 6 *lire* 4 *soldi*. We should not jump to the conclusion – by assuming that money of account was similar to our bank notes (although this can sometimes be a helpful comparison) and that the situation in 1517 was comparable to one of our modern inflation crises – that Venetian currency went off the gold standard. The ducat, since it was an actual coin, simply passed into the same category, which it now headed, as the *soldo* and the *lira*, also moneys of account. The *sequin* which was a real coin, was in 1517 worth 6 *lire* 10 *soldi* (6 *soldi* more than the ducat); ten years later in 1526 it was worth 7 *lire* 10 *soldi*.[62] Was this simply a bonus to attract gold?

---

[56] A.d.S. Venice, Senato Mar 19, f° 101.

[57] *Ibid.*, f° 166 v°.

[58] *Ibid.*, f° 152 v°, 17th September, 1520.

[59] See the relevant notes in R. Gandilhon, *op. cit.*, p. 254; Jacques Raymond Collier, *Histoire du commerce de Marseille*, 1951, vol III, p. 123 on the concentration in the hands of a few merchants of the city's trade with North Africa.

[60] Museo Correr, Donà delle Rose, 26, f° 23 v° ff., 16th July, 1532 (in *Consiglio di X con le Zonta*), recalls the setting up in 1524 of the 'maestro di cecca' whose function was to increase the rate of coinage. On scarcity of silver for borrowing, A.d.S. Mantua, A° Gonzaga, Venezia, 1456, Venice, 14th September, 1533. Ziambattista Malatesta to the Marquis, gold had risen in price at Venice in 1526, A.d.S. Venice, Senato Zecca, 36.

[61] Museo Correr, Donà delle Rose, 26, see previous note.

[62] A.d.S. Venice, Senato Zecca, 36.

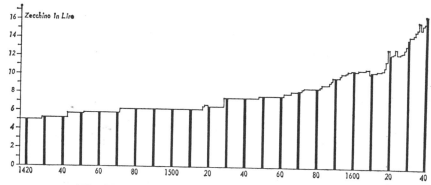

Fig. 38: *The exchange rate of the Venetian sequin*

The gold trade and the general economic situation. Prosperity and crisis within the gold trade were linked. When gold from Guinea reached Lisbon it was immediately launched on to the principal trade routes. At Antwerp it encountered silver from the German mines,[63] and in the Mediterranean it solved balance-of-payments problems. The gold from the first shipments arriving at Seville was also drawn into the accustomed channels and the Mediterranean received its share. Before the discovery of the New World, Seville had provided the Genoese merchants with their supplies of African gold; afterwards it provided them with American gold. It seems probable that the crisis of the 1520's observable on both coasts, the Atlantic and the Mediterranean, was a consequence of imports from America. The gold of Bambuk then lost some of its foreign customers, and found a market only in North Africa (in the widest sense) where its presence is recorded throughout the century.

But gold extraction in America, about which we now know so much more, thanks to two excellent studies, one published,[64] the other as yet unpublished,[65] could not remain indefinitely equal to its task and indeed collapsed before the middle of the century, possibly as early as 1530–1534. A probable consequence was the Castilian devaluation in 1537, when the *escudo* (or *corona* or *pistolete*) replaced the *excellente* of Granada.[66] The Castilian ducat now became a money of account as the Venetian ducat had twenty years earlier. So a crisis of which the first signs appeared in the 1520s was confirmed ten or twenty years later. It was at just about this time, according to Nef,[67] that silver production, in Germany this time,

[63] Vitorino Magalhães Godinho, *op. cit.*, H. van der Wee, *op. cit.*, II, p. 124–127.
[64] Jean-Pierre Berthe, 'Las minas de oro del Marqués del Valle en Tehuantepec (1540–1547) in *Historia Mexicana*, 1958, n. 29.
[65] Alvaro Jara, unpublished study.
[66] Henri Lapeyre, *op. cit.*, p. 257.
[67] John U. Nef, 'Silver production in Central Europe' in *Journal of Political Economy*, 49, 1951.

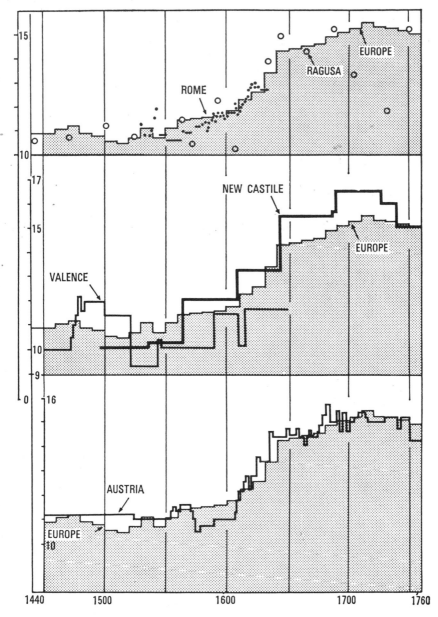

Fig. 39: *Gold versus silver*

This graph appears in Volume IV of the *Cambridge Economic History* (Ch. VII, by
F. Braudel and F. C. Spooner). The European *average* bi-metallic ratio (the relation
of gold to silver) on the whole deteriorated until the early eighteenth century, as can
be seen from the shaded area. It is in relation to this mean (Europe) that variations
in the individual quotations can be viewed – at Rome and Ragusa on which there is
some scattered information, in the first graph; in Valencia and New Castile on the
second; and in Austria on the third. The differences in level, whether spontaneous or
deliberate, led to speculative currency movements, of gold or silver as the case might
be. Note the steep rise of gold in the seventeenth century.

reached its peak, in about 1540. All these mining activities seem to have been connected; they rise and fall together. What happened? Until then, to paraphrase Spooner's arguments,[68] the economy had been stimulated by a *relative* inflation of gold. Its very abundance indirectly encouraged the development of the silver and copper-mining industry, since the value of silver and copper was increased in relation to gold. This was a strange inflation (and it would be a brave historian who would try to construct a model of it), benefiting only the rich, the privileged, and the powerful at the peak of the social and economic pyramid. But the phase during which gold was comparatively plentiful was to come to an end during the difficult years between 1530 or 1540 and 1560, with an intervening period of vacillation until the age of massive silver inflation with its predictable upheavals. A 'gold-dominated economy'[69] had, if one can use the expression, been succeeded by a 'silver-dominated economy' that was to last until the 1680's[70] and the first appearance of Brazilian gold.[71]

Sudanese gold in North Africa. Let us open a parenthesis. We do not know exactly what happened in North Africa during the crucial years 1520–1540, nor do we know exactly what interrupted the gold trade between the West and Barbary. One possible factor was Spanish intervention[72] (Oran was captured in 1509, Tripoli in 1510, and Tlemcen in 1518.[73] An even more likely cause was the 'wave' of Islamic reconquest spreading west from Egypt and Turkey, which prevented the Maghreb from becoming, as there was a real possibility it might, a 'European market'.[74] In any case, if exports of gold to the western Mediterranean practically ceased,[75] gold from the Sudan continued to supply the towns of North Africa, particularly once some order had been installed there, to the advantage of the Turks and Sharifs. Saharan gold was used to mint the *rubias*, *zianas*, *doblas*, *soltaninas* (or sequins) mentioned by Haëdo at the end of the sixteenth century.[76] The latter were coined at Algiers from refined metal, the others at Tlemcen from less pure gold, 'of course gold' according to

[68] *L'économie mondiale et les frappes monétaires en France 1493–1680*, 1956, p. 8–9.

[69] The expression is Jacob van Klaveren's, *op. cit.*, p. 3.

[70] *Ibid.*

[71] Roberto Simonsen, *Historia economica do Brasil, 1500–1820*, São Paolo, 1937, 2 vols.

[72] F. Braudel, 'Les Espagnols et l'Afrique du Nord, 1492–1577' in *Revue Africaine*, 1928.

[73] See previous note; R. B. Merriman, *The Rise of the Spanish Empire*, vol. III, *The Emperor*, p. 292. Francisco Lopez De Gomara, 'Cronica de los Barbarrojas' in *M.H.E.*, VI, p. 371–379.

[74] J. Denucé, *L'Afrique au XVIe siècle et Anvers*, p. 9.

[75] That there were still trade links between Venice for example and North Africa in 1533 (and later no doubt) is suggested by an incident noted by G. Cappelletti, *Storia della Repubblica di Venezia*, 1852, VIII, p. 119–120. But there was a gradual decline, visible in small details. A.d.S. Mantua, Genova 759, Genoa, 3rd March, 1534, Stefano Spinola to the Marquis, Barbary fruits are no longer to be found on the market at Genoa.

[76] D. de Haëdo, *op. cit.*, p. 24 and 24 v°.

an English observer,[77] the same *oro baxo con liga*[78] of which the Algerian women's bracelets were made. The Tlemcen gold had currency as far east as Tunis, and as far south as the Negro countries; it also penetrated into Kabylia; it circulated in 'Orania'. 'The gold coins in these provinces,' wrote Diego Suárez at the end of the century,[79] 'were formerly of higher carat than they have been since the Turks have occupied this kingdom.' It was with Sudanese gold too that the Moroccan *moticals* were minted, a currency in much demand in about 1580 among the bewildering variety offered by the money markets of Algiers.[80] In October, 1573, Don John took Tunis. Deciding to maintain the position, he sent back to Madrid a long report in which all the sources of income of the Hafsid rulers of Tunis are somewhat curiously listed. Alongside customs dues, taxes, and tolls there is mention of the 'gold dust of Tivar': the pleonasm of the expression is unimportant, and no doubt one should not take literally all the items listed by Don Juan, who was anxious to present Tunis in the most advantageous light. But it is unlikely that this detail was entirely fictitious.[81] Tripoli, at any rate, was a rendezvous not only for black slaves who were still arriving by the Sahara route (as recorded in 1586)[82] but also for gold dust.[83] There is no reason to suppose that it was not also, in the seventeenth century, brought to Tunis, the city of many fruitful encounters, the 'Shanghai' of the Mediterranean.[84] Indeed the contrary would be surprising.

One final proof. Expeditions into the Sahara, like those of the Sharifs in 1543, 1583, and 1591[85] (the last of which culminated in the capture of Timbuktu), or that of Salīh Re'īs in 1552 against Ouargla,[86] would be hardly comprehensible were it not for the lure of the gold and slaves of Black Africa. One appreciates the force of the argument put forward by Godinho that the rise of the Moroccan 'Chorfa' was linked to the revival of the gold trade. Towards the end of the sixteenth century gold from the Sudan reappeared on the Atlantic routes[87] as well as in the Maghreb, which may have found this an extra incentive to extend its links with Christendom, and indeed if all these signs are not misleading, was to some extent witnessing an economic recovery.[88]

[77] 1584, R. Hakluyt, *op. cit.*, II, p. 184.
[78] D. de Haëdo, *op. cit.*, p. 27 v°.
[79] B.N., Madrid, ch. 34.
[80] De de Haëdo, *op. cit.*, p. 27 v°.
[81] Relacion que ha dado el secretario Juan de Soto . . . copy, 20th June, 1574, Simancas E° 1142. *Tibar* or *tivar* of course means gold.
[82] 4th and 8th November, 1568, Simancas E° 1132.
[83] But during the Christian occupation, Tripoli had ceased to be a gold town. M. Sanudo, *op. cit.*, XI, col 112; Rossi, *op. cit.*, p. 17.
[84] The expression is Carmelo Trasselli's, 'Note preliminari sui Ragusei in Sicilia', forthcoming article.
[85] Emilio Garcia Gómez, 'Españoles en el Sudan' in *Revista de Occidente*, 1935.
[86] D. de Haëdo, *op. cit.*, p. 27 v°.
[87] D. de Haëdo, *op. cit.*, p. 27 v°; J. Gentil da Silva, *op. cit.*, p. 89, many Dutch vessels were engaged in *resgate* of gold along the Guinea coast.
[88] I am thinking of the trade links between Spain, Leghorn, Venice, and North

2. AMERICAN SILVER

America, which succeeded Africa as a source of gold for the Mediterranean, to an even greater extent displaced the German mines as a source of silver.

American and Spanish treasure. Everything the official figures and documents have to tell us about imports of American treasure to Spain has been made available by the studies of Earl J. Hamilton. The first quite modest shipments arrived in the sixteenth century. Until 1550 they included both gold and silver. It was not until the second half of the century that imports of gold became comparatively insignificant. From now on the galleons brought nothing but silver to Seville, though in huge quantities it is true. For in America the revolutionary amalgamation process in which silver ore was treated with mercury had been introduced in 1557 by the Spaniard Bartolomeo de Medina in the mines of New Spain; it was applied at Potosi[89] from 1571 on, increased exports ten-fold, and they reached their peak between 1580 and 1620, thus coinciding with the great age of Spanish imperialism.[90] In January, 1580, Don Juan de Idiáquez wrote to Cardinal Granvelle. 'The King is right to say that the Emperor . . . never amassed as much money as himself for his enterprises. . . .'[91] The Indies, in the words of Montchrestien,[92] were beginning to 'disgorge' their riches.

This flow of silver poured into a country traditionally protectionist, fenced around with customs barriers. Nothing could enter or leave Spain without the consent of a suspicious government, jealously guarding the arrival and departure of precious metals. So, in principle, the huge American treasure was being drawn into a sealed vessel. But Spain's insulation was not complete. If it had been, the Cortes would not have complained so frequently, in 1527, 1548, 1552, 1559, and again in 1563[93] of the drain of

---

Africa, for which there is much documentary evidence. Note for instance the negotiations between Algiers and Venice through the intermediary of the Venetian *bailo* at Constantinople, *Cinque Savii* 3, f° 721, 29th May, and 22nd June, 1600, the 'Viceroy' of Algiers proposes safe-conducts for eight or ten Venetian *marciliane* to be loaded with wool, wax, and hides. Commercial treaty between Tuscany and the king of Morocco, A.d.S., Florence, Mediceo 4274, 1604.

[89] Jean Cassou, *Les conquistadors*, p. 213–214. Before the new amalgamation technique the usual method was to use *huairas*, small furnaces pierced with holes, *ibid.*, p. 211. Gerolamo Boccardo, *Dizionario universale di economia politica e di commercio*, 1882, I, p. 160. P. Rivet, and H. Arsandaux, *La métallurgie en Amérique précolombienne* 1946, p. 21. For the date of 1571, the essential source is Lizárraga, *Hist. de Indias*, II, p. 556.

[90] An observation first made by L. von Ranke, quoted by Platzhoff, *op. cit.*, p. 17.

[91] *Correspondence de Granvelle*, ed. Piot, VII, p. 2, quoted by R. B. Merriman, *op. cit.*, IV, p. 438, note 2.

[92] *Op. cit.*, p. 159.

[93] *Actas*, I, p. 285.

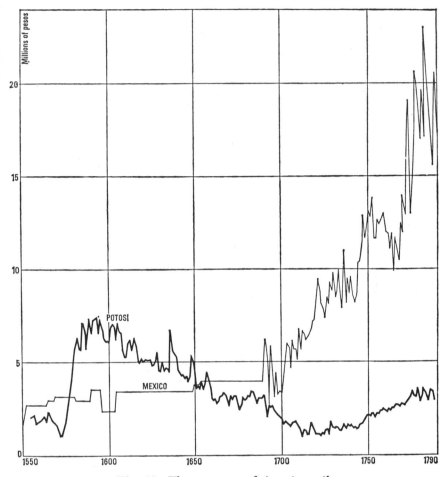

Fig. 40: *The two ages of American silver*

The Potosi curve taken from M. Moreyra Paz-Soldan, 'Calculo do los impuestos del Quinto et del Ensayamiento en la Mineria Colonial' in *Historia*, IX, 1945.

The curve showing moneys struck in Mexico is taken from W. Howe, *The Mining Guild of New Spain, 1770–1821*, 1949, p. 453 ff.

Potosi was the first important source of American silver. The production of the Mexican mines at the end of the eighteenth century attained heights previously unknown.

precious metals, which according to them, was impoverishing the nation. Nor would it have been so commonly remarked that the kingdoms of Spain are 'the Indies of other foreign kingdoms'.[94]

In fact, precious metals were all the time escapıng from Spanish coffers and travelling all over the world, the more so since every leakage led to

[94] B.N., Madrid, 9372, fᵒ 41.

their immediate revaluation.[95] And some suppliers could dictate their own terms. Montchrestien could write, even in the seventeenth century, thinking of Spanish dependence on France for the precious canvas for sails, 'they may have the ships, but we have their wings'.[96] And sail-canvas or wheat, to name but two, were commodities that could be obtained only by cash payment. Since merchants in the Mediterranean and elsewhere urgently needed specie, it is not surprising that there were innumerable cases of smuggling money. A French boat, *Le Croissant* of St.-Malo for instance, was seized in Andalusia [97] for illegal traffic in silver; another time, two Marseilles *barques* were stopped in the Gulf of Lions and found to be laden with Spanish coins.[98] Francés de Alava reported in 1567 that there was a substantial flow of silver into France. [99] 'They write me from Lyons,' he says, 'that by seeing the customs register of the city, a person has been able to establish that over 900,000 ducats have entered Lyons from Spain, of which 400,000 were in gold coins. . . . These coins came from Aragon, hidden in bales of leather. . . . And it all passes through Canfranc. Quantities of money are also arriving in Paris and Rouen without licence from your Majesty. . . .' In 1556, a Venetian, Soranzo, claimed that every year there entered France up to five and a half million gold crowns.[100] Foreign merchants resident in Spain were always sending home minted coins.[101] In 1554[102] the Portuguese ambassador reports that on the at first undisclosed orders of Prince Philip, Don Juan de Mendoza searched the passengers travelling on his galleys from Catalonia to Italy. The result was the confiscation of 70,000 ducats, most of it on Genoese merchants. So the treasure of Spain was not always too well guarded. And official checks (that are often the only evidence available to historians) do not tell us everything we want to know.

Silver could leave Spain legally as well as illegally.[103] Every shipment of cereals to Spain entitled the supplier to the explicit right to payment in coin, which he was then allowed to export. But for the greatest drain on silver reserves, the king himself and Spanish foreign policy in general were responsible. Instead of using their silver at home to set up new and profitable enterprises, as the Fuggers used the silver from their Schwaz

[95] *Circa* 1569, Paris, *op. cit.*, I, p. 339–340.

[96] *Op. cit.*, p. 66.

[97] P. de Ségusson de Longlée, *op. cit.*, p. 128, 129; Requête . . . , 1585, A.N., K 1563.

[98] 18th March, 1588, Simancas E° 336, f° 153 and (undated) E° 336, f° 154.

[99] F. de Alava to Philip II, Paris, 6th May, 1567, A.N., K 1508, B 21, note 6.

[100] E. Albèri, *op. cit.*, p. 405.

[101] As in the old days had the German *safraneros*, A. Schulte, *op. cit.*, I, p. 354. Smuggling in the direction of Lisbon.

[102] Rome, 20th June, 1554, *Corp. dip. port.*, VII, p. 360. Other cases of Genoese smuggling (1563). Simancas E° 1392; English smuggling, 10th June, 1578, *CODOIN*, XCI, p. 245–246.

[103] One could legally apply for permission to export, see for example the application from Giorgio Badoer, April, 1597, A.N., K 1676. Permission was usually granted for travelling expenses.

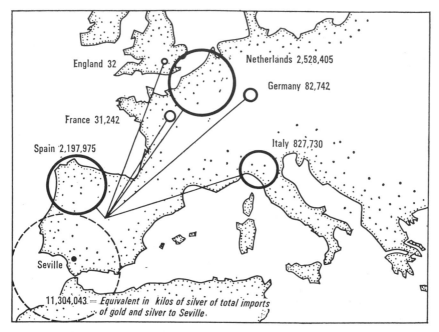

Fig. 41 : *Spanish 'political' silver in Europe 1580–1626*
The money referred to is that spent by his Catholic Majesty through the *asientos*
concluded with merchants. From this diagram it can be seen that the greatest expenditure, was, predictably, in the Netherlands. Less well known, in order of importance are:
expenditure on the Court and the defence of Spain (1580 saw the beginning of the war
in the Atlantic; the Peninsula had to be defended along its threatened coastline); the
relatively small sum spent in Italy; and the virtually nonexistent expenditure in France.
France did not sell herself to Spain, but was occupied with her own internal strife.
These payments were of course on behalf of the Spanish government and do not represent the total volume of precious metals leaving Spain for Europe. Map by F. C.
Spooner, from the figures and calculations of Alvaro Castillo Pintado.

mines at Augsburg, the Spanish Habsburgs let themselves be drawn into
foreign expense, already considerable in the time of Charles V and quite
extraordinary under Philip II – a thoughtless policy it has often been said.
But it may be that this was the price of empire, that its mere existence and
often its mere defence required sacrifices on this scale. The historian
Carlos Pereyra has called the Netherlands Spain's folly, swallowing up if
not all then a very large proportion of her American treasure. But Spain
could hardly abandon the Netherlands. It would have meant bringing the
war nearer home.

Be that as it may, the Peninsula, heavy with treasure, willingly or unwil-
lingly acted as a reservoir of precious metals to be tapped. The problem
for the historian, now that we know how the precious metals arrived in
Spain from the New World, is to see how they were redistributed.

American treasure takes the road to Antwerp. During the first half of the sixteenth century, treasure was exported from Spain to Antwerp, a city as much (if not more) the true capital of the Atlantic as Seville or Lisbon. Documents at Antwerp refer to links between the port on the Scheldt and the farthest regions of the ocean, West Africa and the early settlements in Brazil. The Schetz, for instance, owned an *engheno*, (sugar-mill) near São Vicente. In 1531 the Antwerp bourse was created. From this time on Spanish silver was sent to Antwerp and Bruges in the capacious *zabras* of Biscay. In 1544[104] it was still being carried in Biscayan ships, which in that year also transported Spanish infantry,[105] as they did in 1546-1548[106] and in 1550-1552.[107]

This traffic was common knowledge. The Venetian ambassadors informed the Signoria in the spring of 1551 that 800,000 ducats' worth of silver from Peru were to be minted in the Netherlands at a profit of 15 per cent. In exchange the Netherlands was to provide Spain with artillery and powder.[108] In 1552, the year of Innsbruck, Charles V's desperate situation opened the flood gates that caution usually kept closed.[109] So while the export of coin by individuals was reduced, exports from the public treasury were greatly increased. That did not prevent foreign firms established in Spain, for whom consignments of bullion were a matter of life and death, from continuing to dispatch them, taking advantage of the fact that they were often the agents for the government's own exports.[110] In 1553 silver arrived by official channels at Antwerp, for the Fuggers.[111]

Fortuitous circumstances brought a share even to England. The voyage of the future Philip II in 1554 brought large sums of money to the island. They helped restore the fortunes of an ailing currency which, in 1550, had reached its lowest level yet.[112] Between the year 1554 and his return to Spain in 1559, Philip, during his stay in England and the Netherlands, received a constant supply of silver by the Atlantic route.[113] During the difficult war years of 1557-1558 the arrival of the ships carrying bullion were the great events of the port of Antwerp. Today, 20th March, 1558, says one report, there arrived in Antwerp four vessels from Spain, after a voyage of ten days. They are carrying 200,000 crowns in coin and 300,000

[104] Cambios para Flandres, Simancas E° 500.
[105] *Ibid.*
[106] Simancas E° 502.
[107] Simancas E° 504.
[108] Morosini and Badoer to the Doge, 5th March, 1551, G. Turba, *Venet. Depeschen* . . . , vol I, 2, p. 517, note.
[109] As pointed out by R. Ehrenberg, *op. cit.*, I, p. 63, 160.
[110] K. Häbler, *Die wirtschaft. Blüte* . . . , p. 53, R. Ehrenberg, *op. cit.*, II, p. 63, 150, 155, 155 note 92, reference to the *Silberzüge* of the Fuggers in the Fugger Archives.
[111] R. Ehrenberg, *op. cit.*, I, p. 158.
[112] Salzman, *op. cit.*, p. 5.
[113] Moderacion de cambios, 1557, Simancas E° 514-515. Correspondancia del factor Juan Lopez del Gallo sobre cambios y provision de dineros, *ibid.*

in bills of exchange.[114] 'The last load of silver from Spain,' wrote Eraso to Charles V on June 13th[115] 'aboard the *zabras* of Pero Menéndez, arrived just in time to enable us to pay the German infantry and cavalry we are recruiting. . . .'

Any number of documents testify to the circulation of Spanish silver. The most instructive beyond question are the *asientos*, or '*partis*', as sixteenth-century Frenchmen called them, which Charles V and Philip II concluded with their moneylenders. After the Innsbruck crisis, first the Fuggers and then the Genoese bankers insisted that their contracts should be accompanied by *licencias de saca*, that is, permission to export from Spain the equivalent in specie of the sums they had advanced. For example the two *asientos* concluded in May, 1558,[116] with the Genoese bankers Nicolo Grimaldi and Gentile, stipulate among other conditions the transfer of silver from Laredo to Flanders.

This flow of coin and ingots overseas, steering well clear of the enemy nation France, is not only of great interest to the historian of the final struggles of the sixteenth century between the Valois and the House of Austria. It makes it plain that the Netherlands was not merely a parade ground for Charles V's Empire, but also a distribution centre from which American silver was passed to Germany, Northern Europe, and the British Isles. This distribution was crucial to European economic activity, which was after all not totally spontaneous. A system of exchange, circulation, and banking came into being, centred on the Scheldt port and extending as far as Germany, England, and even Lyons, which for years worked in liaison with the great bourse of the North.

To have a better idea of the importance of Antwerp as a distribution centre, one would need to follow in detail the variable and not always punctual flow of precious metals. In about 1554,[117] for instance, there was a marked scarcity, and the Peninsula was itself short of bullion. The war was not entirely responsible. Thomas Gresham, the power behind the throne in English finance, made a curious voyage to Spain in 1554 in search of precious metals. His requests, or his manoeuvres, contributed to the further deterioration of an already shaky credit situation. The Seville banks actually suspended payment. 'I fere,' wrote Gresham, 'that I shall be the occasione that they should play all bank-rowte.'[118] But the blame for the shortage must lie with the general economic situation rather than on Gresham's shoulders.

In any case, imperfect though it might be, this circulation, which was indispensable both to the English economy and to that of the Netherlands, possibly explains why relations between Spain and these northern countries were, for so long unusually peaceful. An entente between Philip II and

---

[114] H. van Houtte, 'Les avvisi du Fonds Urbinat', 1926, p. 369–370.
[115] Brussels, 13th June, 1558, A.E. Esp. 290, copy.
[116] B.N., fr. 15, 875, f°ˢ 476 ff.
[117] R. Gomez to F°° de Eraso, 6th October, 1554, A.E. Esp. 229, f° 85.
[118] May, 1554, R. Ehrenberg, *op. cit.*, II, p. 64.

Elizabeth was possible as long as the Crown and merchants of England could, by raising loans on the Antwerp bourse,[119] obtain their share of the American treasure. But this balance was upset by the crisis of 1566 and the Duke of Alva's ominous arrival in the Netherlands in 1567. In 1568, Gresham, the 'Queen's merchant' left Antwerp, where he had previously been residing. The situation in the Atlantic was then completely altered. Until that time English privateers had frequently attacked Spanish ships and possessions, but even more frequently they had been content with bloodless privateering, illicit trading rather than real piracy: Hawkins[120] had often reached agreements with the local Spanish authorities. But after 1568 there began an era of ruthless piracy.[121] English ships attacked the Biscay *zabras* carrying silver to the Duke of Alva.[122] From then on, of course, Elizabeth had to abandon any attempt to borrow on the Antwerp bourse, where her credit had collapsed, and adopt, with the aid of her national merchants,[123] a different financial strategy. How much this nationalist policy[124] was deliberately intended, by Gresham in particular, and how far dictated by circumstances we do not know.[125]

The capture of the Biscay *zabras* did not lead to war. England kept the bullion seized from these ships and used it to mint new coin.[126] She even took advantage of the fraudulent dealings of Spanish merchants who sent smuggled silver in ships nominally laden with wool. This black market was yet another windfall for the island.[127] Details of the affair, which had repercussions, could be pursued, but we need not here concern ourselves with the responsibility of William Cecil, nor subsequent fruitless discussions and recriminations,[128] nor Philip II's decisions, which in 1570 might have led to war had he not been restrained by the prudence of the Duke of Alva.[129] Diplomatic alarms should not blind us to the economic causes of the quarrel.

[119] *CODOIN*, LXXXIX, p. 32, 4th September, 1564. Elizabeth was still borrowing at Antwerp at the end of 1568, *CODOIN*, XC, p. 152, London, 6th November, 1568.

[120] As Antonio Rumeu De Armas has once more shown in his admirable book, *Piraterías y ataques navales contra las islas Canarias*, 1947, I, p. 335 ff.

[121] *Documents concerning English Voyages to the Spanish Main*, published by I. A. Wright, 1932, p. XVII.

[122] 18th December, 1568, *CODOIN*, XC, p. 160.

[123] Sir William Cecil placed his savings at Hamburg, *CODOIN*, XC, p. 227, London, 9th May, 1569.

[124] Gresham to Sir William Cecil, London, 14th August, 1569, R. Ehrenberg, *op. cit.*, II, p. 34. An analogous measure was the closing of the Steelyard in 1576–1577. But this nationalism did not rule out applications to foreign bourses, to Cologne at any rate in 1575, *CODOIN*, XCI, 10th December, 1575.

[125] *CODOIN*, XC, p. 184, 14th February, 1569.

[126] *Ibid.*, p. 185, 14th February, 1569.

[127] *Ibid.*, p. 254, 1st July, 1569.

[128] *CODOIN*, XC, p. 173 ff, p. 178 ff; *CODOIN*, XXXVIII, p. 11.

[129] O. de Törne, *Don Juan d'Autriche*, I, p. 109 ff. For details of trade, captured ships, the first blockade of Antwerp, 1568, and the second, 1572–1577, see V. Vázquez de Prada, *op. cit.*, I, p. 55 ff and 58 ff.

Possibly already disrupted after 1566,[130] with the outbreak of the revolt of the Netherlands, the traffic in bullion between Spain and the North was practically brought to a standstill between 1568–1569. That does not mean that none at all went north along the old route. But the transport of money was no longer effected on its former scale, nor was it as easy. It travelled now almost exclusively in specially assembled fleets like that commanded by the Duke of Medina Celi in 1572, and virtually had to run a blockade. The shipping route had become dangerous. Lazaro Spinola, the Genoese consul at Antwerp, and his advisers Gregorio di Franchi and Nicolò Lomellino wrote to this effect to the Republic of Genoa in July 1572:[131] the nation has debts and knows not how to pay them, 'attento il cativo temporale che corre alle mercantie per questi movimenti di guerra [in particular the strained situation with France] con quali non si può trater in Spagna restando chiusa la navigazione e per Italia dificilmente . . .'.

Medina Celi's fleet in 1572 had been fairly small. It was decided to assemble a larger one in Biscay in 1573–1574. It is hardly an exaggeration to call it the first Invincible Armada. It was placed under the command of a distinguished commander Pero Menéndez, but he died in 1574; then funds ran short, epidemics broke out, and the fleet was left fretting away in the harbour.[132] That year, 1574, struck a decisive blow at the vitality of Spain, from the Bay of Biscay to the distant Netherlands. There were a few subsequent shipments from the Peninsula to the Scheldt. In 1575 a small fleet under Recalde sailed from Santander to Dunkirk, where it arrived on 26th November, putting in on the way at the Isle of Wight, which suggests that relations with England had not yet reached breaking point. On the other hand there is no evidence that Recalde's fleet was carrying silver.[133]

In any case it would probably have been incapable of doing so. It is easy to ascertain how abnormal it had become to transport silver using the Atlantic route. Just after the state bankruptcy of 1575, declared to his advantage, Philip II found himself with several million crowns in liquid assets. Nothing could apparently be simpler, since they were needed in the Netherlands, than to convey the currency to Laredo or Santander and ship it north. But no merchant would touch it. Instead, he had to beg the

---

[130] It is symptomatic of the time that the Duke of Alva, in 1567, with his troops, his money and his bills of exchange, should have travelled to the Netherlands by way of Genoa, Savoy, and the Franche-Comté (Lucien Febvre, *Philippe II et la Franche-Comté*, p. 520 ff.), Lorraine and Luxemburg. A revealing detail: in 1568, 150,000 crowns on their way to the Duke of Alva were stopped on the Rhine by the Count Palatine. The Genoese responsible for conveying the money, Luciano Centurione and Constantino Gentile, obtained restitution of the sum seized on payment of an indemnity, Charles IX to Fourquevaux, 24th March, 1568, p. 169; Fourquevaux to Charles IX, Madrid, 6th April, 1568, C. Douais, *op. cit.*, I, p. 345; report from Brussels, 7th March, 1568, H. van Houtte, *art. cit.*, p. 437.

[131] Antwerp, 31st July, 1572, A.d.S., Genoa, Olanda, Lettere Consoli, 1265.

[132] *Armada reunida en Santander para ir a Flandes*, Simancas E° 561; C. Duro, *Armada española*, II, 288 ff.

[133] Antonio de Guaras to Zayas, London, 29th November, 1575, *CODOIN*, XCI, p. 108.

Fuggers to consent to convey 70,000 crowns (delivered to them in chests sealed with the royal seal to avoid trouble with the customs) to Lisbon, where they obtained in exchange good bills of exchange on Antwerp from local businessmen who needed the silver coins for their trade with the Portuguese Indies. Even for such relatively small sums, Thomas Müller, the Fuggers' agent in Spain, preferred to operate through Portugal because of the semi-neutrality of Portuguese merchants in the northern troubles. Thanks to this subterfuge, the money was transferred without leaving the Peninsula.[134]

Sometimes it really did leave. In the autumn of 1588, Baltazar Lomellini and Agustin Spinola risked, in order to assure their payments in Flanders to the Duke of Parma, 'una suma de dinero que ambian en tres zabras que han armado'.[135] A year later in 1589 a sum of 20,000 crowns that the Malvendas, Spanish merchants at Burgos,[136] had sent in a galleasse, was recorded at Le Havre.[137] In the same year, still on the Atlantic route, Spinola repeated his exploit of the previous year by sending two little galleasses, which he had fitted out himself and which were carrying silver on his account, to the Netherlands.[138] But these are exceptions that prove the rule. In fact, as a Venetian dispatch indicated in 1586, the Atlantic route had become extremely hazardous[139] and was little used. And to Spain this route had been vital.

The French detour. Since the route from Laredo and Santander was no longer usable, an alternative had to be found. Philip II resorted to the roads across France. Although shorter, they might at any time be interrupted by France's internal troubles, and transport required long convoys and a heavy escort. The transport of a mere 100,000 crowns, for example, from Florence to Paris at the end of the century[140] required seventeen wagons, escorted by five companies of cavalry and 200 foot soldiers. To reduce the weight, gold alone might be sent. This was tried several times in about 1576, using reliable carriers, men in the service of Spain, who carried up to 5000 gold crowns each, sewn into their garments, from Genoa to the Netherlands.[141] But such an expedient was only for exceptional, desperate, and dangerous occasions.[142]

---

[134] R. Ehrenberg, *op. cit.*, I, 180–181, p. 213, 215.

[135] Philip II to the Duke of Parma, S. Lorenzo, 7th September, 1588, A.N., K 1448, M.

[136] R. Ehrenberg's suggestion that they were out of action after 1577 is incorrect, *op. cit.*, I, p. 362–363.

[137] Philip II to B. de Mendoza, Madrid, 17th March, 1589, A.N., K 1449.

[138] *Ibid.*, the king to Mendoza, S. Lorenzo, 6th May, 1589 and 14th June, 1589.

[139] Bart. Benedetti, *Intorno alle relazioni commerciali . . . di Venezia e di Norimberga*, Venice, 1864, p. 30.

[140] L. Batiffol, *La vie intime d'une reine de France au XVIIe siècle*, Paris, 1931, p. 18.

[141] Idiáquez to the Marquis of Mondejar, Venice, 26th March, 1579, A.N., K 1672. G 38, copy. Idiáquez is recalling an incident from the time when he was ambassador at Genoa, hence the uncertainty of the date.

[142] In 1590 six couriers coming from Italy were robbed near Basle of 50,000 crowns intended for Ambrogio Spinola at Antwerp. Each courier could carry 10,000 crowns in gold pieces, V. Vázquez de Prada, *op. cit.*, I, p. 37.

It was at the end of 1572, after the St. Bartholomew Massacre, that the first large consignment of bullion from the Spanish crown passed through France.[143] The Duke of Alva, who had been short of money since his arrival in the Netherlands, was in desperate straits. It was rumoured at the beginning of 1569 that he had already spent 5 million ducats.[144] Two years later in 1571 the documents repeatedly insist on 'the tightness of money', 'la estrecheza del dinero', in which he found himself. Merchants were no longer willing to do business with him.[145] With no liquid currency, his credit diminished, the Duke saw that the possibility of using bills of exchange was receding, just as a bank never needs reserves so badly as when its customers suspect it has none. By 1572 the situation was so serious[146] that in April the Duke decided to appeal to the credit of the Grand Duke of Tuscany His approaches were successful, but the Spanish government was on poor terms with the Grand Duke, suspecting him of intriguing both inside and outside France against Spanish interests; Alva's request was disowned and the credit that had been granted was never used.[147]

Meanwhile, Philip II had sent through France 500,000 ducats in cash. 'We wish,' he wrote to his ambassador, Diego de Zuñiga,[148] 'to send to the Duke of Alva, from the Kingdom of Spain, a sum of 500,000 ducats in both gold and silver. Since they cannot now be transported by sea without great danger, for the route is closely guarded, it seems to us that the best and most convenient solution would be to send them through the kingdom of France, if my brother, the Most Christian King, would be good enough to give his permission and to issue orders that they may pass with the required security. . . .' Permission was granted and the money was transported in several loads. On 15 December, 1572, Zayas gave notice to the French ambassador, St. Gouard,[149] that in accordance with the authorized passage of 500,000 crowns, Grimaldi was sending 70,000 in reals (that is in silver) and Lorenza Spinola 40,000 in Castilian crowns (that is in gold). These were not the only consignments. In March, 1574, Mondoucet wrote from the Netherlands. 'If I am to believe what is publicly voiced here . . ., ducats from Castile are trotting through France to disturb all good plans.'[150] *Political* money was not moreover the only Spanish money

---

[143] Memorial de Ysoardo Capelo en que dize de la manera que se podra llevar a Flandes dinero de contado pasandolo por Francia, 1572, A.N., K 1520, B 33, note 49, copy.

[144] Fourquevaux to Charles IX, Madrid, 13th January, 1569, C. Douais, *op. cit.*, I, p. 46.

[145] Duke of Alva to Philip II, Brussels, 7th June, 1571, A.N., K 1523. B 31, note 78.

[146] C. de Montdoucet, *op. cit.*, I, p. 71–72, Brussels, 21st October, 1572.

[147] Del Caccia to the prince, Madrid, 21st September, 1572, A.d.S., Florence, Mediceo 4903. G. Mecatti, *op. cit.*, II, p. 750. Lavisse (*op. cit.*, VI, 1, p. 123) is therefore incorrect.

[148] Philip II to Diego de Zuñiga, Madrid, 25th September, 1572, A.N., K 1530, B 34, note 65.

[149] Saint-Gouard to Charles IX, Madrid, 26th September, 1572, B.N., Paris, fr. 16, 104.

[150] *Op. cit.*, II, p. 136, note 1, B.N., Paris, fr. 127, f^{os}, 181–182.

travelling along the roads of France. There was that sent by the merchants, not to mention smuggled silver (often one and the same thing).

In 1576 Philip II and his advisers examined the possibilities of the route from Nantes, where the solid credit of the Spanish merchant Andres Ruiz could be used as a pivot for transfers through 'Normandy and France'. It was a good opportunity for Zuñiga, who had made the suggestion, to point out French claims, notably their intention of 'freezing', as we should say, a third of the money in transit. It was also an opportunity for the Spanish ambassador to deplore the poor organization of *credito*, *trato*, and *comercio*[151] in France, about which he was certainly right.

At the same period, according to Richard Ehrenberg, silver was also sent from Saragossa through Lyons to Flanders.[152] Müller, the Fuggers' agent, used Florence and Lyons as intermediaries. In 1577 a Venetian letter[153] mentions the dispatch of 200,000 'couronnes' to Don John of Austria via Paris. In the same year the Malvenda of Burgos advanced 130,000 crowns, partly to Milan, partly to Paris, and all on Philip II's behalf.[154] In the same year, 1577, there is talk in France of a 'veritable invasion' of Spanish coins, both gold and silver – 'd'escudos de oro doblones y reales de plata d'Espagna', so great that the French government thought of controlling the value of this foreign currency,[155] which would be one way of retaining it in transit.

Transfers were continued during the following year. In July, 1578, Henri III gave permission for Spanish troops and silver (150,000 ducats[156]) to pass through France. But, a sign of the changed times, the ambassador, Vargas,[157] wondered whether it was prudent to continue to send them, when thieves in the pay of the Duke of Alençon were on the watch for it. It would be better, he added, to use 'the surveillance system of the merchants'.[158]

Spanish coins continued to circulate in France well after the year 1578, if only those sent directly by the king of Spain to Frenchmen, payments to the Guises,[159] and others. In 1582 one document[160] refers to the dispatch by Philip Adorno of 100,000 crowns each to Lyons and Paris, there to be made available to Alexander Farnese. In 1585 a remittance of 200,000 crowns to Lyons by Bartolomeo Calvo and Battista Lomellini is recorded.[161] But there is no proof that this money was sent in specie or

[151] Diego de Zuñiga to Philip II, Paris, 1st December, 1576, A.N., K 1542, B 41, orig. D.
[152] *Op. cit.*, II, p. 215.
[153] *C.S.P.*, *Venet.*, VII, p. 565, 19th October, 1577.
[154] R. Ehrenberg, *op. cit.*, I, p. 362–363.
[155] Vargas to Philip II, Paris, 12th December, 1577, received on 21st, A.N., K 1543, B 52, note 113, D.
[156] Vargas to Philip II, Paris, 11th July, 1578, A.N., K 1545, B 43, note 9, D.
[157] Vargas to Philip II, 27th July, 1578, *ibid.*, note 22, D.
[158] *Ibid.*
[159] O de Törne, 'Philippe II et les Guises' in *Revue Historique*, 1935.
[160] Philip II to J. B. de Tassis, Lisbon, 20th August, 1582, A.N., K 1447, p. 186.
[161] Longlée to Henri III, Saragossa, 3rd May, 1585, *Dépêches de M. de Longlée*, published by A. Mousset, p. 186.

that it travelled beyond Lyons to Flanders. Until there is more evidence, let us conclude that the Spanish only resorted to the routes across France until about 1578, and that this was never more than an emergency expedient. Perhaps it would have been abandoned even earlier had it not been for the difficulties that arose between 1575 and 1577 between Philip II and his Genoese creditors. The agreement they signed in 1577 – the *medio general* – was to lead to the predominance of the shipping route from Barcelona to Genoa.

The great route from Barcelona to Genoa and the second cycle of American treasure. It is not known exactly when this route assumed importance – perhaps during the 1570s, which marked the beginning of the great war against the Turk in the Mediterranean. As a result, Spanish capital was diverted towards Italy. This was certainly not an entirely new development. Well before 1570, American gold and silver had already been reaching the central Mediterranean, although never in quantities comparable to the steady stream that flowed to Antwerp. In October, 1532, Spanish galleys arrived at Monaco carrying 400,000 crowns bound for Genoa.[162] In 1546, Charles V borrowed 150,000 ducats from the Genoese[163] and this loan probably resulted in the export of bullion to the *Dominante* in compensation. A Portuguese correspondent[164] unequivocally refers to the remittance to Genoa of a sum of specie intended for the Pope in 1551. Ehrenberg says that in 1552 large quantities of silver were arriving in Genoa as well as in Antwerp.[165] In January, 1564, a letter from Baltazar Lomellini to Eraso refers to a payment made on the orders of Philip II, in November of the previous year, of 18,000 ducats on the Milan market into the account of Lomellini's father-in-law, Nicolò Grimaldi.[166] In 1565 some Florentine merchants agreed to a loan of 400,000 ducats, payable in Flanders. Did they demand in return that bullion should be sent to Florence?[167] In 1566, Fourquevaux, the French ambassador in Spain, mentions two Genoese loans, one of 150,000, the other of 450,000 crowns,[168] and the Tuscan ambassador Nobili refers, in May, to the dispatch of 100,000 crowns, this time to Genoa.[169] The Duke of Alva, travelling from Spain to Genoa in 1567, took with him both troops and silver.[170] And from time to time the need arose to supply Sicily and Naples with money, often indeed by means of *cambios* agreed on the Genoese or Florentine exchanges, naturally drawing some American treasure to these

---

[162] A.d.S. Mantua, Series E, Genova 759, 15th October, 1532.
[163] R. Ehrenberg, *op. cit.*, I, p. 343.
[164] C^{or} M^{or} to the king, Rome, 1st November, 1551, *Corpo dipl. port.*, VI, p. 38.
[165] *Op. cit.*, I, p. 155.
[166] Genoa, 28th January, 1564, Simancas E° 1393.
[167] Philip II to Pedro de Mendoza (1565). Simancas E° 1394.
[168] 4th February, 1566, C. Douais, *op. cit.*, I, p. 50.
[169] To the prince, Madrid, 11th May, 1566, A.d.S., Florence, Mediceo, 4897 *a*.
[170] The Duke of Alva to Philip II, Cartagena, 27th April, 1567, A.E. Esp. 4, f°
357.

cities in return.[171] 'In the last few days, eighteen loads of silver have been brought to Barcelona for Italy,' writes Fourquevaux in December, 1566.[172] During the summer of 1567 Nobili succeeded in sending some of the silver intended for the pay of the Tuscan galleys in the service of the Catholic King; not without some difficulty, however, for the assignment that had been promised to him out of church revenues was dispersed throughout the whole of Spain.[173] Of what he had assembled by May[174] Nobili proposed to send 25,000 'escudi'; in June he announced that eight chests containing 280,000 'reali' would be on their way;[175] finally in September, not having heard any certain news, he was hoping that it had all been safely loaded aboard the galleys.[176]

All these examples laid end to end do not give the impression of a regular flow: as long as the *dinero de contado*, coined money, travelled to Flanders (and this was where Genoese loans usually went), the Mediterranean only attracted a modest quantity. We have plenty of negative evidence.

It is possible, for instance, to log the currencies in circulation at Ragusa, where trading houses sometimes entered in the official registers of the *Diversa di Cancellaria*, a full record of the coins entrusted to their agents for purchases in the Balkans or the Levant, or paid in settlement of debts or as capital investment in a company. For many years gold coin, whether minted in Venice, Hungary, Rhodes, Chios, or Aleppo, was the principal if not the only currency. This places the monetary problem of Ragusa's relations with the Levant regarding gold in rather a special light.[177] On 5th June, 1551, Giugliano di Florio entrusted 650 crowns *d'oro in oro* to the master of a merchant vessel, Antonio Parapagno. The 650 crowns were made up of 400 *sultanini*, or Turkish sequins, and 250 *veneciani*, or Venetian sequins.[178] Another 100 crowns *auri in auro* were entrusted to Johannes de Stephano, a Ragusan, in November, 1558, for a voyage from Naples to Alexandria and from there to Genoa.[179] Hieronimus Johannes de Babalis in June, 1559, received 500 gold crowns from the same merchant for a voyage to Alexandria.[180] These gold coins were often Turkish sequins. And when silver eventually came into its own, it was a sum in Turkish aspers, *mille quingentos aspros*, 1500 small coins, that Giovanni di Milo,[181] a partner of Andrea di Sorgo, received for a voyage to the

---

[171] Garces to the Duke, Madrid, 13th June, 1565, Mediceo 4897, f° 122 v°. Viceroy of Naples to Philip II, 30th April, 1566. Sim. E° 1055, f° 116 and also f° 137 and 184.
[172] *Op. cit.*, I, p. 153.
[173] Nobili to the prince, Madrid, 18th June, 1567, A.d.S., Florence, Mediceo 4898, f° 68 v° and 69.
[174] Nobili to the prince, 30th May, 1567, *ibid.*, f° 60 v°.
[175] *Ibid.*, f° 64.
[176] *Ibid.*, 20th September, 1567, f° 99 v°.
[177] Ragusa Archives, Diversa di Cancellaria, 127, f°s 106 and 106 v°, 3rd October, 1539.
[178] Ragusa Archives, Div. di Cancellaria, 139, f°s 23 ff.
[179] *Ibid.*, 146, f° 34.   [180] *Ibid.*, 145, f° 23 v°.
[181] *Ibid.*, 146, f° 145, 20th August, 1560.

Levant in August, 1560. The usual silver coins, especially after 1564, were even more likely to be *talleri*, Turkish or Hungarian *thalers*,[182] since Spanish reals, *reali da otto*, did not reach Ragusa until later, between 1565 and 1570.[183]

In fact specie was scarce in the Mediterranean. In 1561, when Philip II wrote to the viceroy of Catalonia, Don Garcia de Toledo, at Barcelona asking him to obtain 100,000 ducats for the October and May fairs, the viceroy replied on 5th May that it was quite impossible:[184] 'Credit is so tight here and the merchants are very short of money! . . . I pray your Majesty will believe me that, when I have sometimes obtained 8 or 10,000 ducats here to aid our troops, I have had to name local merchants as guarantors and, what was more, pawn my silver plate. Even then I was charged 9 or 10 per cent interest.'

Something can be deduced too from the *partido* of 100,000 ducats *de oro di Italia* concluded in Genoa in April and under scrutiny in Naples later that year. This was an ordinary *asiento*, that is to say, it came under the heading of the contracts with many clauses that the monarchy often made with the bankers. Philip II, in return for the 100,000 ducats paid to him on the Genoa exchange, gave an assignment on the *donativo* of Naples, or if that should be insufficient, on a tax in the kingdom, to be paid back the following year. Since Naples was acting as the centre for reimbursement, the *partido* concluded at Genoa through the offices of the Spanish ambassador, Figueroa, was sent for the signature of the viceroy of Naples. The latter had his treasurer and an expert examine the clauses and terms of repayment; when everything had been checked, the money was lent at the enormous rate of 21⅔ per cent interest. 'I did not refuse to sign the capitulation,' wrote the Duke of Alcala, 'although it seems to me that the interest is excessive.' This is surely further proof of the 'tightness' of money at Genoa. A detail suggests what one would already suspect, that liquid money was more expensive in Genoa than in Spain, so a 2 per cent charge was deducted from the merchant's profits, according to observers, since payment was to be effected at Genoa. This higher price amounts to a little more than the cost of transport and insurance.[186]

Tight money prevailed then in 1566 at Genoa. The situation in Naples at the same period was even worse. At the beginning of that year, 1566, the question first arose of concluding an *asiento* of 400,000 or 500,000 ducats[187] to be assigned on the *donativo* of Naples, and it was this negotiation, if I am not mistaken, which finally culminated in the *cambio* of 100,000

[182] Vuk Vinaver, 'Der venezianische Goldzechin in der Republik Ragusa' in *Bolletino dell'Istituto della Società e dello stato veneziano*, 1962, p. 140–141.
[183] *Ibid.*, p. 141.
[184] Barcelona, 4th May, 1561, Simancas E° 328.
[185] Simancas E° 1055, f° 137.
[186] Freight charges for silver were 1·5 per cent in 1572. Gian Andrea Doria to the Republic of Genoa, Madrid, 27th April, 1572. A.d.S., Genoa, L. M. Spagna 5.2414.
[187] Viceroy of Naples to Philip II, Naples, 7th February, 1566; Simancas E° 1055, f° 29.

ducats just mentioned. The Duke of Alcala had only one recommendation
to make: that the *cambio* should not take place at Naples, for the money
market was in no state to provide loans even of the order of 100,000 ducats.
The merchants would act in concert and would increase their demands.
The operation had better take place in Spain or in Genoa.

But the 1570s brought a new situation. The Spanish treasury was obliged,
in order to pay for its arms requirements in the Mediterranean, to find new
routes for sending money whether in bills of exchange or specie.[188] Gian
Andrea Doria, in April, 1572, notified the republic of Genoa that he was
going to fetch from Cartagena the money which the Genoese merchants
preferred to ship from there rather than take it by land to Barcelona, since
the roads were unsafe.[189] These shipments were not interrupted even by
the second bankruptcy of the Spanish state in 1575, which shook Genoa
to its foundations, but also contributed to demolish what was left of the
Antwerp connection. In April, 1576, Philip II had 650,000 ducats *de
contado* sent to Genoa.[190] In the same year he offered to transport for the
Fuggers 10,000 crowns 'of gold in gold' in his galleys to Italy.[191] It was
along this same route that between 1575 and 1578 the Fuggers' agent
was to send up to 2 million *couronnes* intended for the Netherlands.[192]
When Philip II in July, 1577, ordered Gian Andrea Doria to go to Barcelona, it was to load silver for Italy. Once his vessel was loaded, the captain
was to weigh anchor quickly, with or without the Admiral of Castile, who
was supposed to be joining the ship, for the money was urgently required
in Italy, and it was important that 'the corsairs should not discover that
the money is being carried in a single galley'.[193] The new route did not of
course end at Italy; Genoa had become the clearing-house for money and
bills of exchange travelling north. But that did not prevent Italy from
receiving her share of Spanish treasure, on the contrary; and one of the
first to benefit was the Grand Duke of Tuscany, who by 1576 was back in
favour in Spain and from whom Philip II was in 1582 to request a loan of
400,000 ducats for Flanders.[194]

With the increase in imports of silver to Seville after 1580, this traffic
also increased. For an indication of its proportions during the years
1584–1586, rather than embark upon a confusing journey through the

---

[188] Philip II to Granvelle, Madrid, 25th March, 1572, Simancas E° 1061, f° 208.
Granvelle to Philip II, 21st April 1572, Simancas E° 1061, f° 27. G. de Caccia to the
prince, Madrid, 19th December, 1572, Mediceo 4903, 500,000 crowns in bills of exchange on Genoa.

[189] For reference see previous note, Mediceo 4903.

[190] R. Ehrenberg, *op. cit.*, II, p. 215.

[191] *Ibid.*, p. 214.

[192] *Ibid.*, p. 179. In 1576 a million was sent to Don John in the galleys from Barcelona
to Genoa, O. de Törne, *op. cit.*, II, p. 30.

[193] Philip II to the Prior D. Hernando de Toledo, S. Lorenzo, 16th July, 1577,
Simancas E° 335. The Almirante was to go on board the commander's galley which, in
the event, travelled in convoy with four other galleys. Prior D. H. de Toledo to Philip
II, Barcelona, 27th August, 1577 (received 31st). Simancas E° 335, f° 402.

[194] Philip II to the Grand Duke, Lisbon, 23rd December, 1582, Simancas E° 1451.

mass of known documents,[195] we could not do better than to read the well-informed letters of the French *chargé d'affaires* in Spain, the secretary, Longlée.

The year 1584, 18th January[196]: two galleys are to leave Barcelona taking silver to Genoa; 12th January: a million ducats is being sent 'to Milan for Flanders', and on its heels another million which will be kept in reserve in the *castello* of Milan;[197] 22nd March: a great quantity of silver is being sent to Italy for the affairs of Flanders;[198] 26th May: Gian Andrea Doria will sail from Barcelona on the 18th or 20th of June with twenty galleys and a few other vessels, and aboard this fleet will be 2 million for the Catholic King, one million in 'escus pistollets', the other in 'réalles', and approximately another million in bills of exchange of the 'Foucres' and of Genoese merchants; 1st June: the Genoese have made 'another contract for 400,000 crowns to be supplied in Italy' in four or five months;[199] Gian Andrea Doria is carrying in his galleys over $2\frac{1}{2}$ million for the Catholic King and 'about a million' belonging to private individuals, including the Grand Duke of Tuscany, as well as 300,000 crowns, the property of Gian Andrea Doria himself, 300,000 or 400,000 crowns for other Genoese citizens, to which must also be added 'what thirty or forty lords and gentlemen of Italy have withdrawn and are taking with them when they return to Italy on the galleys. Besides that there are 500,000 crowns for the house of the 'Foucres' in Germany, paid from the account of the king, as I have seen it written in the record of silver which is let out of Spain.'[200] In fact, we learn on 30th June, that this money for the Fuggers belonged to them: 'His Catholic Majesty made a loan to them in his name in order to let it out of Spain.'[201] The reserve fund in Milan was increased to 1,200,000 crowns; on 17th August, a loan of 80,000 crowns was agreed by Italian bankers, including J. B. Corvati, to the account of the Ambassador J. B. de Tassis.[202]

The year 1585, 4th April: a large sum of money is dispatched to Milan and Genoa, for the king;[203] 25th April, 400,000 crowns shipped from Barcelona to Italy, probably more;[204] 14th May: nineteen galleys of Genoa and Savoy, eight from Naples, and twenty-five from Spain, being undermanned, take on five thousand troops at Barcelona. They are to transport to Italy 1,200,000 crowns; 'besides that', seventy-six loads of silver have travelled from Saragossa to Barcelona;[205] 9th June: on the fleet of galleys there are 500,000 crowns belonging to the Duke of Savoy;[206] 15th June, the fleet carried 1,833,000 crowns for Italy, of which over

[195] For further details see Felipe Ruiz Martín, *Lettres marchandes. . . . op. cit.*, p. LXXXIV, ff.
[196] *Dépêches de M. de Longlée*, published by A. Mousset, Paris, 1912, p. 9.
[197] *Ibid.*, p. 19.   [198] *Ibid.*, p. 42.   [199] *Ibid.*, p. 77.
[200] *Ibid.*, p .76–77.   [201] *Ibid.*, p. 87.
[202] Then *veedor general* of the army in Flanders. 100,000 crowns were sent to J. B. Tassis of the 692,722 sent to Italy, 23rd July, 1585. A.N., K 1583.
[203] *Dépêches de M. de Longlée, op. cit.*, p. 120.
[204] *Ibid.*, p. 129.   [205] *Ibid.*, p. 139.   [206] *Ibid.*, p. 147.

1,000,000 were not registered;[207] on 20th September, another fleet of galleys leaves for Italy, carrying 400,000 crowns; 300,000 crowns have just arrived at Monzon, where Philip II is staying;[208] 18th September: an agreement is signed with the Fuggers 'to pay 500,000 crowns in Germany'.

The year 1586, 25th March: 1,200,000 crowns are sent to Italy for affairs in Flanders;[209] 31st May: seven galleys carry 600,000 crowns to Genoa, again for Flanders;[210] 29th September: a 'party' has been concluded, a week ago, with the 'Foucres' for 1,500,000 payable at Frankfurt, 250,000 at Besançon, and 250,000 at Milan;[211] on 11th October another 'party' is being negotiated to pay 700,000 to 800,000 crowns in Italy.[212]

In subsequent years, the flow of bullion swelled to even greater proportions, as can be seen simply from the level reached by the *asientos* during the last twelve years of the reign of Philip II. In 1586 the Fuggers must have lent him 1,500,000 gold crowns payable in Italy and Germany;[213] in 1587 Agostino Spinola gave him an advance of 1,000,000 *scudi*; in 1589 the Florentines lent him 600,000 crowns;[214] in the same year the Genoese merchants arranged a *cambio* of 2,000,000 for the Netherlands. The following year Ambrosio Spinola paid out 2,500,000 in the Netherlands,[215] In 1602 Ottavio Centurione advanced 9 million and even more – the large sum has been questioned by prudent historians[216] but without justification.[217] I have also found evidence of an agreement with Agostino Spinola in 1587, for 930,521 *escudos*, and contrary to what Ehrenberg, says, it was made out not for Italy but in the form of a bill of exchange on the Netherlands to the Duke of Parma.[218]

---

[207] *Dépêches de M. de Longlée, op. cit.*, p. 149.   [208] *Ibid.*, p. 175.
[209] *Ibid.*, p. 242.   [210] *Ibid.*, p. 269.   [211] *Ibid.*, p. 312.   [212] *Ibid.*, p. 315.
[213] The Genoese ambassador to the Republic, Madrid, 29th March, 1586, A.d.S., Genoa, L.M. 9–2418.
[214] Philip II to the Grand Duke, S. Lorenzo, 17th June, 1589, Simancas E° 1452.
[215] R. Ehrenberg, *op. cit.*, I, p. 351. To be compared with the reference to Spinola in Longlée's notes, 3rd March, 1590, *op. cit.*, p. 391.
[216] Antonio Domínguez Ortiz, 'Los estrangeros en la vida española durante el siglo XVII' in *Estudios de historia social de España*, 1960, p. 304, note 10.
[217] Formal evidence to be found in Ralph. de Turri, *Tractatus de cambiis*, Disp. 3. Qu. 13. No. 78; S. Contarini to the Doge, Valladolid, 16th December and 30th December, 1602, (A.d.S., Venice, Senato Dispacci Spagna); *Lettres missives de Henri IV*, VI, p. 16. The king to M. de Beaumont, 18th January, 1603, 'The King of Spain has obtained the contract[*party*] of eleven millions, to which I am informed another million has been added . . .' The '*party*' was a three-year agreement: 3 million every year to Flanders, plus two more for the Royal Household. These figures correspond quite closely to the facts. The *asiento* signed at Valladolid on 31st December, 1602 amounted to exactly 7,200,000 *escudos* (payable in Flanders in 36 *pagas*) and 2,400,000 *ducados* (payable in 36 *pagas* at Madrid, Seville, Lisbon) Simancas Contadurias Generales, 1° 96. It is in this series that the entire collection of *asientos* is housed. I examined them personally in 1951 and Alvaro Castillo Pintado has now completed his study of them. See below, Vol. II, fig. 59 which gives complete figures and therefore, I think, renders it unnecessary to provide a complete list of references here or to revise the original text of my book, which did no more than touch on this enormous problem.
[218] Philip II to Juan de Lastur, S. Lorenzo, 4th April, 1587, A.N., K 1448, minute.

These are mere details; the important point is the vastly increased traffic in specie and credit throughout the western Mediterranean, which had now been promoted to imperial silver route. No one would contest the historical importance of these repeated voyages by galleys laden with chests or barrels of money. When talking of American gold and silver we should remember not only the famous galleons of the Indies fleets, but also the Biscayan *zabras* and 'naves' and those galleys, which once peace had returned to the Mediterranean, were occupied in conveying to Italy no longer troops but passengers and mounds of silver pieces and on such an amazing scale.[219] There were accidents of course. In April, 1582, a galley sailing from Barcelona to Genoa was surprised by bad weather and had to throw some of her precious cargo overboard; fifty-six cases of *reales* were thrown into the sea, as well as a whole case of *escudos* and other gold pieces.[220] But such accidents were rare, as the insurance premium of 1·5 per cent clearly demonstrates. Accidents on land were equally if not more frequent. In January, 1614,[221] 140,000 crowns belonging to Genoese bankers were carried off, only six leagues from Barcelona, by about a hundred thieves.

The Mediterranean invaded by Spanish coins. This fortune of the Mediterranean exactly coincided with a drop in Atlantic traffic and the decline of Antwerp, along with all the other money markets and economic activities which had depended on the regular functioning of the Antwerp bourse. I am inclined to date the decline of Antwerp and the Netherlands before the great turning-point of the years 1584–1585, which was undeniably important, before even the sack of the town in 1576 and before the second Spanish state bankruptcy of 1575. I think it can be detected as early as 1567, as A. Goris suggested[222] or even better in 1569. There were even total stoppages in that year, for example in the woollen centre of Hondschoote, although it was still extremely prosperous and of world importance.[223] On the arrival of the Duke of Alva, such was the recession in the textile industry that he was unable to obtain locally enough blue cloth

[219] Amadeo Pellegrini, *Relaz. inedite di ambasciatori lucchesi . . .* , Rome, 1901, p. 13–14, on the voyage of Compagno Compagni in 1592, a winter voyage on which one galley was wrecked (with the loss of 120 oarsmen). The fleet was carrying between 600 and 800 thousand crowns and chests of coins. Note the accuracy of Cervantes' reference in *La Gitanilla* to the Genoese merchant who sends silver from Spain to Genoa by galley and to opportunities to sail in the galleys from Cartagena. Spanish silver was also transported, legally and otherwise, in roundships, on the *San Francisco* for example, loaded at Alicante and Ibiza and arriving at Leghorn on 3rd March, 1585, with 21,700 *reali* on board, A.d.S., Florence, Mediceo 2080.

[220] Simón Ruiz to B. Suárez, Medina del Campo, 17th April, 1583.

[221] A.d.S., Venice, Senato Dispacci Spagna, F^{co} Morosini to the Doge, Madrid, 18th January, 1614.

[222] For a different opinion, see the review by Émile Coornaert, *art. cit.*, in Revue du Nord.

[223] Émile Coornaert, *op. cit.*, p. 28–29, expansion until 1569, p. 30, 'in 1580, when many people had already left . . . .'

494

Collective Destinies

for the personnel of his palace.[224] The sack of Antwerp in November, 1576, certainly did not destroy a city at the height of its career.[225] A Portuguese report of 1573 indicates that since at least 1572 all trade with Flanders had been at a standstill.[226] As early as 1571 [227] a Spanish merchant returning to Antwerp felt he was in a different town. Even the Exchange 'no es . . . lo que solia', is not what it used to be.

The decline of Lyons dates from roughly the same time. What remained of its important financial functions were transferred to Paris between 1570 and 1580.[228] In 1577, on the Place aux Changes, once more a village square, the grass had begun to grow again.[229]

It was at about the same time that the great exchange fairs of Medina del Campo came to an end, an event usually dated by historians as contemporary with the second Spanish state bankruptcy in 1575. Less attention has been drawn to the more or less simultaneous decline of both Burgos and Bilbao to the north of Medina. To all intents and purposes, the large registers of marine insurance[230] at the consulate of Burgos were now closed. This signified the collapse of the long axis from Medina to Bilbao and through to Flanders which, at the beginning of Philip's reign, had been one of the main lines of the Spanish Empire.

So the Mediterranean was attracting away from the North a large share of the world's currency. A sign of the times was the renaissance of Barcelona, whose exchange fairs were re-opened in 1592, and whose ships by the end of the century were sailing out beyond Sardinia, Naples, and Sicily, which had previously marked the boundaries of her commercial zone, to Ragusa and Alexandria in Egypt.[231] In addition, the whole of Italy was

[224] R. B. Merriman, *op. cit.*, IV, p. 285–286. Can the currency changes in the Netherlands in 1585 be considered (Émile Coornaert, *op. cit.*, p. 46) a consequence, the last stage perhaps of the decline?

[225] In 1579, there remained in Antwerp only one Spanish firm of any importance, 4 Lucchese, 5 Genoese, 14 Italian, 10 Portuguese, R. Ehrenberg, *op. cit.*, II, p. 192.

[226] A. Vaticanes, Spagna 27, *Le cause per le quale il sermo Re di Portogallo . . .*, 1573, f⁰ˢ 161 to 162. Banking troubles at Seville in 1565–1567.

[227] V. Vázquez de Prada, *op. cit.*, I, p. 28, note 30.

[228] According to A. von Reumont, *op. cit.*, I, p. 355, it was in 1575 that the few Florentine firms remaining in Lyons left for Besançon, Chambéry, and Avignon. R. Ehrenberg, *op. cit.*, I, p. 306, says that by 1575 only a few Italians were still in Lyons, the rest having left for Paris. In 1592, the sole survivor was the Capponi bank, taken over in 1594 by the famous Lucchese Zametti. On this large topic see L'Hermite De Sollier, *La Toscane française*, Paris, 1661, on the Italian bankers settled in Paris. In a Tuscan context, the decline of Lyons may well have been one of the causes of the rapprochement between Spain and Tuscany after 1576. On the reorientation of the Tuscan economy towards Spain, see R. Galluzzi, *op. cit.*, III, p. 505 ff.

[229] R. Ehrenberg, *op. cit.*, II, p. 191.

[230] *Ordenanzas del Consulado de Burgos de 1538*, published by Eloy Garcia de Quevedo y Concellon, Burgos, 1905, with a long introduction, which suggests (p. 71) that decline set in after 1556, a date which seems to me too precise. In the view of Marie Helmer (confirmed in a note to me, 21st March, 1965) signs of decline began to appear in about 1566; there were crises in the years 1568, 1570, and 1572. By 1573 the downward trend and its effects were irreversible.

[231] A. de Capmany, *op. cit.*, IV, p. 337 (1594). Cf. the creation at Barcelona in 1609 of the Nuevo Banco 'per mes ampliar la Taula del Cambi', A. P. Usher, *op. cit.*, p. 437.

now flooded with precious metals. The ambassador du Ferrier, who for so long represented France in Venice and was well acquainted with both Italian and Levantine affairs, was disturbed in 1575[232] by rumours of war threatening the Peninsula. Would Spain take advantage of the internal troubles of Genoa to seize the city and along with it the rest of Italy? This Italy 'which has never been so wealthy', as he says in a letter to the king of France. What then would he have said of Italy in the subsequent decades? A man as well informed as the Duke of Feria could write in a long report in about 1595 that England's best course would still be to come to terms with Spanish authority 'following the example of Naples, Sicily, and Milan, which under their present regime flourish as they have never done before . . .'.[233] This quotation should perhaps be dedicated to those who have hastened to speak of the decline of the Mediterranean after the beginning of the sixteenth century.

In fact by degrees Spanish money invaded every part of the sea. It soon became a part of everyday life. Towards 1580 the coins in most common use on the Algiers markets were the Spanish gold *escudo*, silver *reales*, pieces of eight, six, and four, particularly pieces *de a ocho reales*. All these coins were at a premium on the market and were a commodity figuring largely in exports to Turkey, where *reales* were shipped by the chestful.[234] The registers of the French Consulate at Algiers, which go back to 1579[235] and of the French Consulate at Tunis[236] which begin in 1574 make frequent reference to the predominance of Spanish currencies. It was in Spanish coin that ransom prices were usually stated. In February, 1577, when the prisoners aboard an Algerian ship mutinied at Tetouan, the Turks hastily jumped overboard, unfortunately for them. Laden with *reales* and gold coins many sank straight to the bottom.[237]

Besides the large official shipments, small boats coming straight from Genoa or Spain to Leghorn carried among the bales of merchandise cases of 'reali'.[238] At the very end of the century, in 1599, of two cargoes of money registered at Ragusa whose destination was Rodosto and Alexandria, the first consisted of *talleri* and 'reali',[239] the second entirely of 'reali d'argento di Spagna a reali otto per pezza'.[240] The previous year, a Ragusan ship had been abandoned at Cerigo by her crew, who made for land in a boat to avoid falling into the hands of Cigala.[241] The master and his

---

[232] Du Ferrier to Henri III, Venice, 8–13th May, 1575, E. Charrière, *op. cit.*, III, p. 595.

[233] Simancas E° 343 (1595).

[234] D. de Haëdo, *op. cit.*, p. 24 and 24 v°; R. Hakluyt, *op cit.*, II, p. 176 (1584).

[235] R. Busquet, 'Les origines du consulat de la nation française à Alger' in *Inst. hist., Provence*, 1927.

[236] P. Grandchamp, *op. cit.*, for example, I, p. 17, 18, 23, 87, etc. Noted earlier by A. E. Sayous, *Le commerce des Européens à Tunis depuis le XIIe siècle*, 1929.

[237] D. de Haëdo, *op. cit.*, p. 177 v°.

[238] A.d.S., Florence, Mediceo 2080, 26th July, 1578, 3rd March, 1585.

[239] Ragusa Archives, D. de Foris, VIII, f° 172, 24th August, 1599.

[240] *Ibid.*, f°s 113 v° to 115 v°.

[241] A.N., K 1676, Iñigo de Mendoza to Philip III, 2nd January, 1599.

fleeing seamen took with them 17,000 *reales de a ocho*. Or to note another detail, in May, 1604, a Frenchman from Marseilles recognized at Ragusa that he owed a Florentine 'duo centum sexaginta tres peggias regaliorum de 8 regaliis pro qualumque pezzia'.[242] So Ragusa was by now affected by the invasion of Spanish money. What city or country indeed was not? Reals were arriving in Turkey as we have already seen, even from Poland in the heavy carts on the roads from Lwow to Constantinople.[243] There is no need to look far for examples in the Levant, where so much commercial correspondence, Italian, Ragusan, French, and English testifies to a predictable situation.

But these examples, which could easily be multiplied, should not distract us from the basic situation, which becomes plainer to see if it is recognized that after 1580 the true centre of distribution of Spanish silver, at least as much if not more than Spain herself, was Italy and her city-states. From this position Italy derived much benefit, her responsibility being to export to the Levant (and this was both easy and profitable) some of her surplus Spanish silver, and also to supply the rather more elusive gold coins, as well as silver and bills of exchange, to the tight corner in the Netherlands where Spain was fighting for her empire and for the future of the Catholic faith, and where the flow of coins pouring into the country sustained Protestant rebels as well as Spanish troops and loyal subjects. Italy then lay at the centre of a system that created its own liaisons, synchronization, and evident imbalances.

Italy, the victim of 'la moneda larga'. After 1580 the volume of bullion brought to Genoa by galley from Spain increased regularly, until what was no doubt the record consignment of June, 1598:[244] 2,200,000 crowns (200,000 in gold, 1,300,000 in ingots of silver, 700,000 in *reales*) in a single convoy. That is unless the record had been set up earlier, on 20th June, 1584, when twenty galleys under the command of Gian Andrea Doria arrived at Genoa carrying possibly three or four million crowns, as the evidence suggests but does not confirm.[245] At any rate there clearly were massive shipments. According to an estimate of *Contaduria Mayor* in 1594, ten million ducats' worth of bullion arrived in Spain every year, of which six million were exported, three by the king and three by private citizens. The remaining four million either stayed in Spain or were smuggled out by couriers, travellers, or seamen. One historian[246] has suggested that six million ducats were regularly reaching Italy every year towards the end of the century and were then dispersed in all directions both inside and outside the Peninsula. These massive loads of bullion were already operational even before they sailed into Genoa (or Villefranche, or Portofino, or

[242] Ragusa Archives, D. di Cancellaria, 192, f° 139, 30th May, 1604.
[243] See above p. 200.
[244] A.d.S., Florence, Mediceo 5032, Zanobi Carneschi to the Archbishop of Pisa, Genoa, 27th June, 1598.
[245] Felipe Ruiz Martín, *Lettres marchandes . . .* , p. 48.
[246] Tanteo general B.N., Madrid, 1004, quoted by Felipe Ruiz Martín, *ibid.*

Savona, or Leghorn). The mere news of their impending arrival was enough to create *largezza* on the Italian exchanges, just as the sighting of the Indies fleet did at Seville, Madrid, or Medina del Campo; these galleys were the second Indies fleet. It was not long before the *largezza* in Italy became insistent and sometimes damaging. Specie was cheap everywhere, that *moneda larga* which upset so many calculations. For the operation of credit suffers during a prolonged period of cheap money: it depends on fluctuations in the supply. Bills of exchange would be sold by those who wanted to borrow money, but when money is plentiful, borrowers are rare. Let me make this simple mechanism quite clear. When currency was easy to come by and everyone had more or less his share of it, less was seen of the borrower, that is, the seller of bills of exchange. Bills became scarce, so their price went up. In the reverse situation, when currency was scarce, bills of exchange were tendered from all directions and the lender was able to buy them at a low price. Simón Ruiz was uneasy and dissatisfied during these years that were apparently so prosperous. In addition to his ordinary occupation as a broker in big business, he acted as a money lender and buyer of bills on the Medina del Campo money market. Usually those who sold him bills were wool merchants who could not carry on their business without an advance, for wool which was bought in Spain was paid for only many months later at Florence. Ruiz bought for a low price the paper that represented his credit, and sent it to his compatriot and friend in Florence, Baltasar Suárez, who was to become the brother-in-law by marriage of the Grand Duke of Tuscany. On arrival, the bill of exchange would be converted into money at a profit. But this money had to be sent back to Medina del Campo through a new bill of exchange bought at Florence. If there was easy money, *largezza*, on the Florence market, the second bill could be bought only for a high price, so Ruiz would have made no profit on the second transaction. In other words, the banker stood to lose, or to be more accurate not to gain, over the six months the 5 per cent he was used to. Not to gain was to lose, to speculate dangerously with 'the firm's own money'. Nothing shows this more clearly than the complaints of the old man in Medina del Campo and the explanations and apologies of his ally in Florence.[247] 'As things are today,' writes the latter, 'whoever has money in hand must sell at the price the taker offers.'[248] Nothing could be more dangerous, the old friend in Florence goes on to say, than to try to swim against the stream, 'those who have tried to force the market at Florence [*violentar la plaza*] have made little profit from it,' he notes on 9th September 1591.[249] What was to be done against this tide of currencies and ingots of silver? The basic pattern on which all exchanges

[247] Cf. the letters exchanged between Simón Ruiz and his correspondents in Florence F. Ruiz Martín, *op. cit.* Of particular interest among the letters from Baltasar Suárez is one dated 24th February, 1590 (concerning the Bonvisi at Lyon) '*No querian creditos sino débitos . . . ; sta oy dia el cambio de manera que quien tiene el dinero lo a de dar a como quiere el tomador*', one dated 9th September, 1591, etc.
[248] *Ibid.*, letter dated 30th March, 1590.
[249] Baltasar Suárez to Simón Ruiz, Florence, 9th September, 1591.

worked was disturbed. To function properly it required fluctuations in the price of money which created profitable differences in level.

This invasion of Italy by '*contado*' can be viewed from another angle, simply by studying the money coined in the various mints of the Peninsula. Not one stood idle. It would undoubtedly be possible to reconstruct some of the purchases of the *Regia Zecca* at Naples from the documents in the *Sommaria*.[250] Between 1599 and 1628[251] 13 million ducats' worth were minted there. There was similar activity at Palermo and Messina[252] or Genoa.[253] The coins were no sooner minted than they were put into circulation and, particularly in the seventeenth century, rapidly left their place of origin. At Venice, the *Zecca*[254] worked uninterruptedly. On it the prosperity of the city depended. On average, about a million in gold and a million in silver was minted in a year. Since the usual line of supply, through merchants who brought currency or *verghe* to its counters, was not sufficient, the *Zecca* proceeded to buy on a contract basis. These contracts were often very large: in 1584, 500,000 ducats (2nd June, from the Capponis) 140,000 marks from the Otts, agents for the Fuggers at Venice; another million ducats from the Otts in 1585; a million in 1592 from Agostino Senestrato, Marcantonio and Giovanni Battista Giudici; 1,200,000 ducats in December, 1595, from Oliviero Marini and Vicenzo Centurione; a million on 26th March, 1597, from Hieronomo and Christoforo Ott. Subsequent contracts were smaller, but in March, 1605, we find a contract for 1,200,000 ducats being agreed with Giovanni Paolo Maruffo and Michel Angelo and Giovanni Steffano Borlotti. My intention here is not to compile a list of the purchases made by the *Zecca* at Venice, but to demonstrate the insatiable appetites of the Italian mints, which for the most part were met by Spanish silver.

We cannot indeed hope to obtain *a posteriori* the volume of money produced from American treasure merely by adding the totals of minted coins. That would be too simple, Coins melted down in one place might be remelted in another; a few months or a few years later they might turn up on the counter at a different mint. Between 1548 and the beginning of 1587 the *Zecca* at Naples coined about $10\frac{1}{2}$ million ducats and at the end of it all, 'in tutto il Regno non se siano settecento millia ducati', not 700,000

[250] A.d.S. Sommaria Consultationum 22, f[os] 9–10, 8th February, 1608.

[251] According to Turbolo, *Discorso* . . . , p. 3 and 4, Naples, B. di Storia Patria XXVIII, D. 8. And only 10,500,000 ducats between 1548 and 1587, or 260,000 a year to the nearest round figure (A.d.S. Naples, Sommaria Consultationum, 9, f° 168, 29th January, 1587) compared to 400,000, the annual average from 1599 to 1628, which, even taking into account the devaluation of the ducat, still signifies an increase.

[252] Antonio della Rovere, *op. cit.*, p. 43, note 40 *bis*.

[253] Ubaldo Meroni (ed.) *I 'libri delle usate delle monete' della Zecca di Genova, dal 1589 al 1640*, Mantua, 1957.

[254] The following references correspond to the figures mentioned in the rest of the paragraph: Marciana 7299 (2nd June, 1584); Correr, Donà delle Rose, 26, f° 93, 2nd June, 1584; *ibid.*, f° 93 v°, 13th July, 1584; *ibid.*, f° 95, 5th December, 1585; *ibid.*, f° 104, 14th June, 1591 A.d.S. Venice, Senato Zecca 2 (1591); *ibid.*, 4th December, 1595; 3rd January, 1596; *ibid.*, 5, 26th March, 1597; *ibid.*, 8th, 19th March, 1605.

were left.[255] Nevertheless, the fact that it circulated rapidly contributed to the abundance of metal in Italy.

It was not of course simply because it lay on the imperial route of Spanish silver that Italy was thus privileged. It was a useful coincidence, but a greater factor was the active Italian economy which has been persistently underestimated by historians, but which was healthy enough in these final years of the century to maintain a positive trade balance with Germany, Eastern Europe, the Netherlands, France, and Spain[256] (apart from Florence's deficit arising from her purchase of Castilian wool). These positive balances helped Italy to accumulate wealth and to pay off the deficit owed in the Levant and Turkey, of which we have spoken at such length, and the profitable returns from which stimulated the entire commercial and industrial activity of the Peninsula. Italy then found herself at the centre of a traffic in precious metals and bills of exchange, in effect mistress of an interdependent circuit. In a period of silver inflation gold became the safe investment, the metal that was hoarded and the one used for international payments. Unless specifying the contrary, bills of exchange were payable in gold. It was in gold coin too that the Flanders army demanded to be paid, if not in full then at least in part. And finally, gold was the only metal that could be carried by courier as we have seen. So if Italy depended on Spain, Spain depended on Italy for payments in the North, which frequently had to be made in gold at the Flanders end, through the good offices of Genoa. The Italian money markets alone were able to provide the gold coin and bills of exchange that were to end up in Antwerp in the hands of the paymasters of the Flanders army.

So Italy stood at the crossroads where the south–north axis maintained by Spanish policy and the Genoese *asientos* met the east–west axis running to the Levant and the Far East, where the golden road from Genoa to Antwerp met the silver road to the east.

On the eastern axis there were to be no surprises: silver was the favoured currency there, its value increasing once it reached the Levant (the Turkish empire being a gold zone drawing on Egypt and the African supplies); it increased even more the further east it travelled, crossing Persia and India finally to arrive perhaps in the Philippines or in China; Chinese gold was exchanged at 'two marks of gold to eight marks of silver', that is at 1 to 4, while the ratio in Europe was at least 1 to 12. This Italy–China axis, beginning in America and running right round the world either through the

---

[255] A.d.S., Naples, Sommaria Consultationum, 9, f° 168, 29th January, 1587.

[256] Which can be affirmed with virtual certainty: in the case of France see A. Chamberland's classic article, quoted above p. 441, note 459; in the case of Germany and the Netherlands there is the simple fact that in Venice and Florence bills on the north were available; on the unequal balance between Florence and Spain see F. Ruiz Martín, *Lettres marchandes* . . . The notion of a balance of payments was unfamiliar in the sixteenth century, but in the reply of the *hombres de negocios* to the Spanish government (1575, B.M. Harl. 3315, f° 155) there occurs this striking sentence: '. . . a estos reynos por ymportar mas las mercaderias que vienen a ellos que las que salen, y este inconveniente no es de poca consideracion'.

Mediterranean or round the Cape of Good Hope, can be considered a *structure*, a permanent and outstanding feature of the world economy which remained undisturbed until the twentieth century. The Genoa–Antwerp axis, by contrast, was dictated by a particular situation, though one that lasted some time. It would last as long as Spain held the Netherlands, that is until 1714, or as long as the silver inflation controlled by her persisted, that is until 1680.[257] So Italy remained at the intersection of these two axes throughout the seventeenth century. From the anchorage of Cadiz, English and Dutch vessels, boats from St.-Malo and sometimes Genoa, 'warships' or not, ferried to Genoa or Leghorn the pieces of eight commonly known then as 'piastres'.[258] This traffic all reached 'Alexandria, Great Cairo, Smyrna, Aleppo, and other places of the Levant'. Piastres 'are much sought after in all the said places and even in Persia . . .', writes Samuel Ricard[259] (the grandfather of the famous Ricardo), whose book was still being reprinted in 1706. Silver coins, that is, not gold. Of course, says a Venetian report dating from much earlier (1668),[260] one can spend in Egypt *ungari* or *zechini* 'senza perdervi cosa veruna; ma bisogna esser practico', without actually losing on it, but one must have one's wits about one. But with silver, one can make up to 30 per cent on pieces of eight. As for the south–north axis, it remained in position throughout the period we are concerned with. The predominance of Genoa undoubtedly declined after 1627,[261] but as late as 1650 her bankers were still making payments in the Netherlands on behalf of Spain.[262]

The age of the Genoese.[263] These preliminary observations will help us to situate the great age of Genoese finance, which takes its place in the history of capitalism between 1557 and 1627, following the brief age of the Fuggers and preceding the rise of the hybrid capitalism of Amsterdam. I confess that I would prefer to say 1640 or 1650 rather than 1627[264] but that is not

[257] The date suggested by J. van Klaveren, *op. cit.*, p. 3. Jean Meuvret, 'La conjuncture internationale de 1660 à 1715' in *Bulletin de la Société d'Histoire Moderne*, 1964, sees in this apparently only the start of a short-term inflation. 'Was this really a true revival?' Note that after 1604–1609, some of the silver from America was finding its way to northern Europe.

[258] The expression used by Samuel Ricard, see following note.

[259] Samuel Ricard, *Traité général du Commerce*, 2nd ed., 1706, p. 371.

[260] Marciana 5729, Relazione d'Egitto, 1668.

[261] In the opinion of F. Ruiz Martín, *Lettres marchandes.* . . .

[262] A.d.S. Genoa, Spagna 38, documents from 1647 to 1650.

[263] In the following pages I have drawn on two works by Felipe Ruiz Martín, *Lettres marchandes échangées entre Florence et Medina del Campo*, letters sent and received by Simón Ruiz and later by his nephew Cosme Ruiz to and from Florence, between 1577 and 1606, preceded by a long and magnificent introduction. The second work, to which I have had access before its forthcoming publication, is *El siglo de los Genoveses en Castilla (1528–1627): capitalismo cosmopolita y capitalismos nacionales*, in my opinion the best book on Spain in the sixteenth century since the classic studies by Ramón Carande.

[264] I have been struck by the enormous quantities of silver which continued to arrive at Genoa even at the end of the century. See after 1670 the correspondence of the

crucial. Obviously the fortune of the Genoese was not created by the wave of a magic wand in 1557, after the extraordinary bankruptcy of the Spanish state, nor did it end abruptly in 1627, the date of the fifth or sixth suspension of payments in Castile, when the Count Duke Olivares promoted the Portuguese *marranos* to the rank of principal money lenders to the Castilian crown. Genoa was for many years afterwards to remain a fulcrum of international finance.

Genoa's ancient wealth and her political about-face in 1528 prepared the way for her age of prosperity, as did her early merchant colonies in Andalusia and Seville,[265] her participation not only in the trade between Spain and the Indies, which is well known thanks to the work of André E. Sayous, but also between Seville and the Netherlands – the one trade supplying the other. According to Ehrenberg,[266] the Genoese did not gain control of Antwerp until 1555, but they had been on the scene since the beginning of the century and, between 1488 and 1514, were the most important Italian merchants on the Scheldt.[267] It is more than likely that they later financed north–south liaisons at least until 1566.

Their great opportunity was provided by the exhaustion and depleted resources of the Fuggers and their acolytes, who had been hard hit by the mid-century recession and who were to withdraw (apart from brief reappearances in 1575 and 1595) from the dangerous business of the *asientos*.

The *asientos* were contracts with multiple clauses drawn up between the government of Castile and the *hombres de negocios*. They consisted of short-term loans, repaid principally out of imports of treasure to Seville. Since the Indies fleets could not be relied upon to be punctual, the king required an alternative regular source of funds, in particular for the monthly payment *usually in gold* of the wages and other expenses of the Spanish army in Flanders. The astuteness of the Genoese in the period after 1557 lay in drawing not only on the various resources of the Catholic King inside and outside Castile, but also, in order to assemble and guarantee their enormous loans, on public savings, Spanish and even Italian. For the king (between 1561 and 1575) conceded to them *juros de resguardo*,[268]

French consul at Genoa, Compans, A.N., Affaires Étrangères, B 1 511, Gênes. See also the curve of money minted at the Genoa Zecca, in U. Meroni's publication, reference in note 253 above.

[265] Ramón Carande, 'Sevilla fortaleza y mercado' in *Anuario de Historia del Derecho español*, II, 1925 (off-print) p. 33, 55 ff. Jacques Heers, *op. cit.*, see the many references under *Seville* in the index.

[266] Frank Spooner has observed that the Genoese knew how to take advantage during these years of change of the increased value of gold, *op. cit.*, p. 21.

[267] Renée Doehaerd, *Études anversoises*, I, 1963, p. 33.

[268] Cf. F. Ruiz Martín, *Lettres marchandes. . . .* p. 29 ff and the excellent article by Alvaro Castillo Pintado, 'Los juros de Castilla apogeo y fin de un instrumento de credito' in *Hispania*, 1963. The *juros de caución* were not for sale. By obtaining the negotiable *juros* (*juros de resguardo*) or *resguardos* as they were known, the bankers had access to public savings, both inside and outside Spain, and particularly in Italy. The *resguardos* sold to investors were re-imbursed on settlement of the *asiento* (the

in theory state bonds handed over as a guarantee for the agreed loan, but which the *asentistas* were free to use as they pleased. They sold these bonds to their friends and acquaintances as well as to subscribers who flocked to buy them. Of course the Genoese would then have to buy back these *juros* to return them to the king, but only when he had reimbursed the loan. Second, *sacas* of specie were forbidden, between 1559 and 1566,[269] years during which the finances of Castile were reorganized, all outstanding debts being referred to the *Casa de la Contratación*, which became a sort of *Casa di San Giorgio*[270] using its resources to ensure the payment of *juros* 'situated' on the *Casa*. This was the object of the important Toledo ruling of November, 1560,[271] which is regarded by historians as a supplementary bankruptcy, decided, like the first in 1557, with the tacit consent of the business community, who received in *juros* the equivalent of most of the payments due to them, but were able to pay their own creditors in the same currency. In settlements of this nature the Genoese suffered less than the Fuggers. If they could no longer export their profits in the form of specie, they could easily invest them in Spanish commodities, alum, wool, olive oil, silk, etc., which could then be exported to Italy and the Netherlands, providing them with the liquid assets they required in these distant places. It was of course much more convenient when after 1566,[272] because of the troubles in Flanders, they were once more authorized to export silver coins and ingots more or less as they pleased.

But the crucial problem continued to be the transfer and payment of gold to the Low Countries. In order to solve it Philip II was obliged to apply to the international capitalists, the bankers of south Germany before the middle of the century, the Genoese after 1557. Philip was obliged to follow this course even more than Charles V had been. On the international market he controlled silver, but not copper, bills of exchange, and gold. Copper was really only a subsidiary. But this humble metal was unknown in the Iberian Peninsula, being obtained first from Germany and later, in the seventeenth century, from Sweden and Japan. Spain could easily obtain it on payment and the situation was only difficult in Portugal where copper fetched unprecedented prices until 1550[273] because of the demand from the East Indies. It was still said in 1640 that in the

---

finiquito) in bonds carrying the same interest. The Genoese therefore controlled the as yet uncoordinated market in government bonds which varied as to rate of interest, nature, and assignment. But there were risks: in 1575, the prince of Salerno, Nicolò Grimaldi went sensationally bankrupt through speculation in *resguardos*, Alvaro Castillo Pintado, *art. cit.*, p. 9.

[269] Felipe Ruiz Martín, *Lettres marchandes . . .*, p. XXXII.

[270] Simancas Consejo y Juntas de Hacienda, 37, Decreto sobre la paga de las mercedes y otras deudas, Toledo, 14th November, 1560.

[271] *Ibid.*

[272] Felipe Ruiz Martín, *Lettres marchandes*, p. XXXII.

[273] V. Magalhães Godinho, *op. cit.*, p. 420, in 1435 it stood at 3072 *réais* the quintal, in 1564 at 33,421. There was a sharp drop in 1568.

time of King Manuel copper was more expensive than gold in Portugal.[274] As for bills of exchange, a distinction should be made between those which were an instrument of credit, sometimes going beyond the bounds of reason, and those which went to make up for surpluses in the balance of trade. Spain, staggering under the weight of her American treasure, had a trade balance in deficit all around; the countries with surpluses were (or had been) the Netherlands and Italy (which continued in surplus). The latter countries' bills were therefore the ones to buy. For in theory payable in gold, bills of exchange governed the complicated movements of gold coins. Since Europe's gold supply was only meagrely replenished from the New World, these payments often depended on existing reserves.

In all these directions, Genoese capitalism was quickly to establish its superiority, but such an achievement would never have been possible, it should be stressed, without the cooperation of all Italy. This cooperation made success a certainty. The Genoese, when selling silver, found in their native city and to an even greater degree in the rest of Italy, the gold coins and bills they required. In 1607[275] the *Cinque Savii* refer only briefly to this phenomenon, since it was regarded as absolutely normal: the Genoese, since they provide stocks of silver (as well as credits for the purchase of sugar and pepper at Lisbon), 'hanno sicuro modo di estrazer da questa città quanto oro vogliono', are certain to be able to extract from Venice all the gold they desire – and as many bills on Germany and the Netherlands as they wanted too. Ambrosio Spinola and Giovanni Jacomo Grimaldi, explaining the situation after the state bankruptcy of 1596 to the Republic of Genoa, say that the problem with the money they have promised to provide in the Netherlands (on the request of Philip II and in the name of the other Genoese merchants of the *Contratación*, or as we should say the syndicate) 'is that the money markets of Florence and Venice through which such provision was usually made are convulsed from top to bottom'[276] by the violent consequences of the bankruptcy. Without them it was impossible to find such regular customers for *reales* and silver ingots and suppliers of the gold and bills that made it possible to avoid sending over-large bulky consignments of silver to the north – and at the same time to send the indispensable gold. And it really was indispensable. The soldiers in Flanders always demanded that part of their pay should be in gold coin, which was both profitable and convenient. Gold pieces were much sought after and they were easily transported in small quantities. So there was a continual exchange of silver pieces for gold. The merchants did, it is true, attempt to shake off this onerous obligation by trying to impose silver coins, or even better, pieces of cloth, as part of the soldier's pay. In this respect progress was slow. Silver was to become the regular currency for soldiers' pay only with the reign of Philip III and

[274] B.N., fr. 9093, f° 78 (1640).
[275] A.d.S., Venice, *Cinque Savii*, Riposte, 1602–1606, f°s 189 v° to 195, 16th January, (1607).
[276] 2nd April, 1597, A.d.S., Genoa Spagna 12.

the vellon inflation that marked its early years, and not before the slow promotion of Spanish reals to the rank of an internationally acceptable currency. More particularly, this change was not to be achieved before the return to a peaceful international situation at the end of the century and the beginning of the next, which reduced the soldiers' bargaining power and put an end to the pressure armies could exert on governments.

But until then, they demanded gold coin and with a vehemence that makes it one of the major features of currency circulation of the century, a structural feature, as Felipe Ruiz Martín has forcefully demonstrated.[277] From time to time some incident occurs to prove it. In February, 1569, for instance, the Duke of Alva was about to send an expeditionary force under Mansfeldt to the aid of the Catholics in France.[278] In order to provide enough gold pieces for the three-horse carriage of the detachment's paymaster, Diego de Gueines, it was necessary first to apply to the merchants of Rouen, Paris, and Lyons, and then, at some cost, to convert the 'monedas de plata como se rescibieron a los mercaderes a escudos de oro en oro', to change for gold crowns the silver currency received from the merchants. This trivial incident enables us to put our finger on something that was an everyday reality and to glimpse something of the wider context. The general system of the Genoese bankers, which received its finishing touch in 1579 with the creation of the Piacenza fairs and was to last until after the end of the century, viewed from the Netherlands, represented a vast gold-draining operation dependent upon the existence of a series of circuits in commodities, silver, bills of exchange, in a word all the wealth of the West. It was a winning game but it meant respecting certain imperative rules.

The Piacenza fairs. The triumph of the Genoese did not become apparent until after 21st November, 1579,[279] when the so-called Besançon fairs were moved by them to Piacenza, where they remained, except for a few brief interruptions until 1621[280] under continuous Genoese control. The Besançon fairs may have originated as far back as 1534.[281] The Genoese

---

[277] In particular in *Lettres marchandes* . . . , Chapter II, 'L'argent vassal de l'or', p. LIII ff.

[278] According to the account book, which he had printed, of Francisco de Lixalde, *pagador del exercito de Flandes*, of which the first entry is dated 12th March, 1567. This book has the manuscript title *Tanteos tomados en Flandes al pagador Francisco de Lixalde hoja de catorze meses antes que falleciese*, Simancas, p. 26. The same book was published, from a Latin copy, by M. F. Rachfahl, *Le registre de Franciscus Lixaldius, trésorier général de l'armée espagnole aux Pays-Bas, de 1567 à 1576*, 1902 187 p., in-8°.

[279] L. Goldschmidt, *Universalgeschichte des Handelsrechtes*, 1891, p. 127.

[280] G. Luzzatto, *op. cit.*, p. 180.

[281] Lucien Febvre passed on to me the information that according to the municipal records of Besançon (request made by Thomas Doria to the magistrates of the town, 27th July, 1566) it was in 1534–1535 that the imperial city first attracted the Genoese bankers 'who had given up their residence in the localities of Lyons and Monluel and were settled at the town of Lons-le-Saunier'. On these fairs see: Castan, 'Granvelle et

merchants had encountered such opposition at Lyons from the king of France who had not forgiven them for their treachery in 1528, and then, when they retreated to Chambéry, further opposition from the Duke of Savoy, who, under pressure from the French king, expelled them from his states, that they had to find another rendezvous for the financiers and their correspondents, first at Lons-le-Saunier, in January, 1535, at the Epiphany Fair, then at Besançon for the next Easter fair, the first of a long series. It was not Charles V but the Republic of Genoa itself that arranged this move, and favoured the new rendezvous all the more since the French occupied Savoy and Piedmont in 1536, and Besançon could be reached by way of Lombardy, the Swiss Cantons, and the Franche-Comté; since this distant meeting-place, 'inconvenient and tiresome' though it was, nevertheless had the advantage of being within striking distance of Lyons and the money and merchandise attracted there by its fairs, whose rhythm was for a long time closely followed at Besançon.[282] Lyons was still the true capital of world wealth, halfway between the Mediterranean and Antwerp, which explains why, when they encountered at Besançon difficulties about which we know very little, the Genoese transferred their fairs to Poligny, probably in 1568,[283] then to Chambéry, moving south all the time, but remaining within the orbit of Lyons. This proximity was vital, as is proved by the large number of payments recorded at Montluel, the first village of any size on the road from Lyons to Savoy.[284]

The transfer of the fairs to Piacenza, on the territory of the Duke of Parma, represented then a decisive step, the final break with Lyons, which was now separated from the new rendezvous by the width of the Alps. The establishment of the fairs at Piacenza was also the last act of the long crisis spread over the four previous years, whose true causes historians are only now beginning[285] to discover. This was the major episode in fortunes of the Genoese bankers.

The system of *asientos* associated with *juros de resguardo* had grown up, as the graph in Fig. 60 (in vol. II) shows, largely as a result of the troubles in Flanders since 1566 and the growing numbers of *licencias de saca*[286] and in spite of the Channel blockade. The insolent success of the Genoese, now openly installed in the new capital, Madrid, where all the

le Saint-Empire' in *R. Historique*, 1876, vol. I, p. 113, note; P. Huvelin, *Droit des marchés et des foires*, 1907; the speech by Contarini, 1584, in A. Lattes, *La libertà delle banche a Venezia*, Milan 1869, p. 121; R. Ehrenberg, *op. cit.*, I, p. 342, II, p. 227; Jacques Savary des Bruslons, *Dic. universel de Commerce*, Copenhagen, 1760, V, 'Foire', II, p. 679–680; L. Goldschmidt, *op. cit.*, p. 237.
[282] On the preceding, see Domenico Gioffré, *Gênes et les foires de change: de Lyons à Besançon*, 1960, p. 115–119.
[283] Lucien Febvre, *op. cit.*, p. 22, note 4, p. 110, note 3. I have found (in Doubs Archives, B. 563) the request made by the Genoese bankers for permission to hold their fairs at Poligny, 13th August, 1568; R. Ehrenberg, *op. cit.*, II, p. 227.
[284] J. Savary des Bruslons, *Dictionnaire universel de Commerce*, II, p. 227.
[285] In particular the studies of Felipe Ruiz Martín and Jose Gentil da Silva.
[286] The following paragraph is based on the explanations in Felipe Ruiz Martín's two studies quoted earlier (see note 263).

important contracts were signed, and where they had introduced an exchange linked with Alcalá de Henares, did not fail to arouse violent feelings of jealousy in Spanish public opinion, and, what was more serious, among Philip II's entourage. The Cortes, between 1573 and 1575, had reacted strongly against these foreigners.[287] But attacking them was one thing, replacing them another. Philip II's advisers and the king himself assumed rather too readily that it would be possible to apply instead to merchants in Spain and elsewhere. The decree of 1st September, 1575, then, was a blow struck at the entire fortunes of the Genoese. All *asientos* agreed since 14th November, 1560, were annulled, and considered 'illegal' and fraudulent. All accounts were to be settled according to the terms laid down unilaterally in the Pragmatic that appeared in December, 1575 (although bearing the date 1st September). To the Genoese this brought massive losses. They had discussions, applied for legal redress to the jurisdiction of the *Camara* of Castille, but above all they effectively blocked payments of gold to Flanders. It is even probable that they supported the Protestant rebels in the Netherlands. But in December of this dramatic year, the city of Genoa was convulsed by a political and social revolution of an extremely violent character (the underlying causes of which are unfortunately little known) with on one side the *Nobili Vecchi*, who dealt exclusively in finance, and on the other the *Nobili Nuovi* (*di San Pietro*), ordinary merchants supported by the *arti*, the craft guilds. The rebels won, seized the levers of command, and raised wages. The bankers retired to the outskirts of the city 'some to the estates of Battista Spinola, around Serravalle, near Novi, on the road to Milan',[288] or to Savoy. But the victorious party proved unequal to the administration of the city, still less to the restoration of the vast financial machine dislocated by Philip II's September decree, and the Buonvisi at Lyons, in October, 1575, were anxiously wondering 'whether the Easter Besançon fair would be held, and where it would be held.'[289] So everything still seemed very much in the balance at the end of 1575. The struggle in Genoa, the struggle in Spain, the competition between Genoese and non-Genoese merchants in every commercial centre in Europe were all part of a single campaign.

Total victory for the Genoese bankers did not come until two years later with what was for them the compromise agreement, the *medio general* signed with the king of Spain on 5th December, 1577, abrogating the draconian measures of 1575. It was a victory owed entirely to the incompetence and inexperience of the Castilian merchants and of all those, including the Fuggers, 'unconditional servants' of the Habsburgs, who sought to intervene. The capital they advanced was insufficient, it was recalled too soon and yet it moved too slowly. Moreover, the Genoese embargo on bills of exchange and gold was effective. They held all the best cards, leaving their would-be competitors little room for manoeuvre.

[287] *Actas*, IV, p. 225–226, 316, 411.
[288] J. Gentil da Silva, forthcoming publication, p. 24 of typescript.
[289] *Ibid.*, p. 21.

Whether it was sent through Florence, Lisbon, Lyons, or even Paris and the French roads, their rivals' money did not travel quickly enough. As a result, the unpaid Spanish troops mutinied and, after a series of disturbances, captured and violently sacked the city of Antwerp in November, 1576.[290] These dramatic events – in which it would be as naïve to assume that the Genoese had no hand as it would be to assume that Spain had nothing to do with the December uprising in Genoa – forced the king into a reconciliation. Until then he had shown 'poco voluntà di mitigare il rigore dil decreto', as a Genoese correspondent put it.[291] But how could he any longer pursue the unbending policy he secretly favoured? In March, 1577, serious talks began. Agreement was reached only on 5th December, 1577, when the *hombres de negocios* immediately made available to the Spanish king five million 'golden crowns in gold', payable at Genoa, Milan, and if necessary Naples or Sicily.

Meanwhile order was being restored in Genoa, and with the support of the merchant bankers of the Milanese and Tuscany, a new solution was envisaged: that the fairs should be held at Piacenza, on the territory of the Duke of Parma. Here, apart from a few interruptions (at Easter, 1580, they were held at Montluel, near Lyons, in Savoy), they were to remain along with the system they incarnated, and under Genoese control, until 1621. Through Genoa the Mediterranean long held the key to the control of world wealth.

At Piacenza[292] the spectacle resulting from this victory was an apparently modest one. These fairs in no way resembled either the tumultuous gatherings of Lyons or the popular fairs of Frankfurt and Leipzig. The watchword at Piacenza was discretion.

Four times a year – at the fairs of the Annunciation (1st February); Easter (2nd May); August (1st August) and All Saints (2nd November) – about sixty bankers would meet together. These were the *banchieri di conto*, a few Genoese, Milanese, Florentines, all members of a kind of club, to enter which one had to have the vote of the present members and a large sum of caution money (4000 crowns). These were the men who on the third day of the fairs would fix the *conto*, or official exchange rate, the importance of which need not be stressed. Alongside these *banchieri di conto* were the exchange-merchants or *cambiatori*, as they were often called, who were entitled on payment of caution (2000 crowns) to follow the fairs and present their payments (or *bilanci*). Into the third category came the *heroldi* (or *trattanti*), firm's representatives or brokers. In all then there were a maximum of two hundred people, bound by strict discipline, the final decision in cases of dispute lying with the all-powerful Senate of Genoa.

[290] Henri Pirenne, *Histoire de Belgique*, IV, 1927, p. 78.
[291] A.d.S., Genoa, Spagna 6.2415, Sauli and Lercaro to the Republic of Genoa, Madrid, 17th July, 1576.
[292] The following details are based on the description in Jose Gentil da Silva's forthcoming publication.

The fairs functioned as a clearinghouse – 'de virement ou de rencontre', in Savary's words,[293] the Italian says *riscontro*. Every merchant presented a bound volume, the *scartafaccio*, or market book, containing records of all the bills due to or from him, in other words his payments and withdrawals. The first step was to order all these accounts, to obtain recognition of the sums involved; then all the transactions to be settled at the fair were brought together in a series of cancellations or compensatory payments. The final result was a set of assets and liabilities bearing no relation to the fantastic sums originally quoted, which had all melted like snow in the sun. The regulations of the fair stipulated that all differences were to be paid in gold, but for this only a small quantity of specie was required and the creditor would often accept an extension of credit to another fair or exchange. So credit machinery was set up for the benefit of debtors. The details of these transactions were of course much more complicated; if one turns to the classic book by the Genoese Domenico Peri, *Il Negociante*, which was published in Genoa in 1638,[294] one sees that in practice there were often serious problems, in spite of the fact that exchange rates were fixed in advance. There were many disputes. For participants unacquainted with the rules, the organizers of the fairs would circulate on the fifth day model bills of exchange where the merchant had only to fill in the blank spaces.

Huge sums of money changed hands at these expeditious fairs. From about 1588, according to Davanzati,[295] over 37,000,000 *écus de marc* were handled and some years later, according to Domenico Peri,[296] the figure reached 48,000,000. The exchange rate quotations can be reconstructed from surviving commercial correspondence. But unless at least the accounts and correspondence of one of the Genoese bankers come to light, we shall never have more than an outsider's view of the fairs. The entire fortune of the Genoese depended upon a subtle mechanism, subtly operated. Their reign was the reign of paper, as the Fuggers' agent in Spain ill-temperedly said, accusing them in 1577 'of having more paper than hard cash', 'mehr Papier als Baargeld'.[297]

The reign of paper. The age of negotiable paper money did not begin in 1579 with the first Piacenza fairs. The whole century had prepared the way for it. But after 1566, or rather 1579, it assumed an importance that no one who came into the slightest contact with business could fail to observe. As different functions began to emerge, the occupation of banker began to be distinguished from other commercial activities, banker, or rather 'financier', since from the first, banking operations concerned the

[293] *Op. cit.*, under the article 'Foire', vol. II, Copenhagen, 1760, col. 68.
[294] At least the first volume. Cf. Catalogue of Kress Library, p. 23. I have used the Venetian edition (Gio: Giacomo Hertz) of 1682 in one volume.
[295] Gino Luzzatto, *op. cit.*, p. 180.
[296] *Ibid.*
[297] R. Ehrenberg, *op. cit.*, I, p. 350.

money of princes. It is essential to grasp how strange and new a profession it seemed at the time, if we are to understand the astonishment of contemporaries. Wise and honest men had always assumed that money followed trade in commodities; by 'real exchange' they meant what resulted from such straightforward dealing, but that money should lead an existence apart from commodities was difficult for them to accept; or that at Piacenza everything could apparently be settled by juggling with a set of figures. Philip II himself confessed that he understood nothing about exchange[298] and it may have been a contributory factor in his dislike of the Genoese.

In Venice, still half-immersed in the past, paper for some time remained only a discreet visitor. A Venetian document of 1575[299] estimates the total war loan granted at the time of the struggle against the Turk as over 5,500,000 ducats. Of this sum, only 216,821 ducats, or rather less than 4 per cent, was subscribed in *lettere di cambio*. In itself this is not conclusive: the loan was being raised on the spot and it was logical to pay it in gold ingots (57,772), or silver (1,872,342), or in coin (3,198,420). But there is always a Venetian ready to protest, whenever the occasion arises, against the spread of paper credit and the operations, honest or otherwise, to which it led. They could be severe judges, like the Venetian ambassador at Madrid, who wrote to the Signoria in 1573[300] that the Genoese *asentistas* neglected the true and honest trade in commodities, concerning themselves only with the *negoziatione dei cambi* and even declaring commodity trading 'cosa da bezarioto et da gente più bassa', an occupation fit only for paupers and men of low condition. In 1573 such sentiments were still comprehensible. But thirty years later in a Venice that was experiencing an all too brief 'age of enlightenment' where so many thinkers were interested in economic questions, Leonardo Dona, for instance, when one finds excellent 'discourses', a little florid perhaps but clearly argued on trade, politics, and money, it is less easy to understand the persistent astonishment of such men at the proliferation of paper, at the novelty of payments being made through the exchange, instead 'di farsi con denari', instead of being made in cash. As for re-exchange, which advanced by leaps and bounds and had also just been introduced to Venice on the initiative of foreign bankers, Florentine or Genoese, it appeared to them to be a 'pernicioso et perpetuo ziro tra mercante e mercante, godendo quali banchieri particolari le facultà de infiniti negocianti'.[301] So it was only under protest that the merchants and rich men of Venice were drawn into the strange world of the *fiere di Bizensone*.

And yet this world was really the 'reasonable' world because it held the key to the future and because its operations were intelligent operations,

[298] J. Gentil da Silva, 'Réalites économiques et prises de conscience' in *Annales E.S.C.*, 1959, p. 737 (11th February, 1580).
[299] Museo Correr, Donà delle Rose, 26.
[300] Quoted by Felipe Ruiz Martín, *Lettres marchandes* . . . p. XXXIX.
[301] Museo Correr, Donà delle Rose, 181, f° 53.

notwithstanding the criticisms of those who did not understand them. The coming of the age of paper, its extension if not its first appearance, in fact marked the beginning of a new economic structure, an extra dimension that had now to be reckoned with. The Genoese were pioneers in this respect and derived from it the usual advantages brought by progressive techniques. Their mistake was to stake everything on their superiority in this field and by devoting themselves to financial affairs to withdraw from the Atlantic trade where they were still very well placed in 1566. The Atlantic economy, more or less left to itself[302] was to develop and mature, producing its own merchants and before long its own financiers. The defeat of the Genoese did not, as it is often rather hastily assumed, represent the failure of pure finance and paper money and the triumph of the merchant who had remained faithful to traditional commerce; it signified rather the rise of a new capitalism with a different geographical centre of gravity, which had been in the making since the discovery of America, but which took over a century to reach completion. Ultimately it marked the victory of new financiers, the Portuguese moneylenders who were to intervene at Madrid in 1627 and, behind them, the heavy hand of the capitalists of the North. It was in fact one of the stages in the development of Dutch capitalism, the superstructures of which, including the most modern form of credit machinery, were in place by at least 1609: the force that was to replace Mediterranean capitalism. But the old model, patiently assembled over time, was in every respect a pattern for the new.

From the last state bankruptcy under Philip II to the first under Philip III. The last suspension of payments by Philip II in 1596 and the first by Philip III in 1607 bring us face to face with these problems of forbidding magnitude. Our aim must be not so much to describe the eventful history of these changes as to discover their underlying causes, the permanent factors at work, in order to test the explanatory schemas that have been so strikingly improved by recent research.

In our search for the right perspective, we must avoid being dazzled by the dramatic history of events which has regularly been viewed from too close up. We must constantly remind ourselves that any supremacy, whether political, economic, social, or cultural, has its beginnings, its apogee, and its decline, and that the stages in the rise of capitalism, that is, the points at which its course has been interrupted or altered, have parallels elsewhere. Like the age of the Fuggers, the age of the Genoese, and the later age of Amsterdam was to last barely the space of three generations.

Having said this, in order to go to the heart of the subject, it would be as well to note at once:

1. That the conflicts between the Castilian state and the bankers always contained two stages: first, the quarrel, then the reconciliation; in winter the quarrel might be prolonged (there was no urgency), as in 1596–1597,

---

[302] See the excellent article by H. van der Wee, *Annales E.S.C.*, vol. 22, 1967, p. 1067, 'Anvers et les innovations de la technique financière aux XVIe et XVIIe siècles'.

then with the coming of summer and the urgent needs of state, all parties hastened to reach agreement: the resulting compromise was known as the *medio general*. There was one *medio general* in 1577, one in 1597, two in 1607, one in 1627. The quarrel, or rather suspension of payments, was always known as the *decreto*.

2. That if the Castilian state lost every time, it was because it was no match for the *hombres de negocios*, who were centuries ahead of it. Philip II's raging against the Genoese was a sign of his obstinacy, his thwarted will, but not of his common sense. Had he been sensible he would have set up a state bank, as was suggested to him in 1582, or a number of *Monti*, on the Italian pattern, as was suggested to him in 1596; he would have embarked upon a deliberately inflationist policy (but could he have controlled it?) In fact Philip II seems to me to have been constantly placed in the position of a nineteenth-century South American state, rich in the product of its mines or its plantations, but hopelessly out of its depth in the world of international finance. Such a government might show its displeasure, even move to action, but in the end it would be forced to submit, to yield up its resources and its commanding posts, and show itself to be 'accomodating'.

3. That every time the state declared itself bankrupt, bringing contracts to a violent end, there were always some actors who lost, fell through a trap-door, or tiptoed away towards the wings: in 1557 it was the merchants of South Germany; in 1575, the Italian merchants apart from the Genoese; in 1596 and 1607 the Spanish merchants; in 1627 the Genoese merchants themselves, but they, like the Fuggers in 1577, did not leave the stage for good. The rule however still holds.

4. That in each case the brunt of the losses was borne by the taxpayers of Castile, already overburdened with a heavy fiscal load, and by small savers and investors in Spain and Italy. As long as there are bankers, there will always be people 'left holding Russian stocks'.

By about 1590 and even more clearly in 1593 and 1595 everything pointed towards another bankruptcy by the Crown of Castile. Its expenditure continued to rise above all reasonable limits while its income was declining, with a visible drop in fiscal revenues. The general economic depression was the cause of many bankruptcies and imprisonment for debts. Amid these difficulties only the imports of silver from America were on the increase, so that the circulation of precious metals at Seville and Barcelona, Genoa and Venice, or along the Rhine, which was used for transport to the Low Countries, was unaffected and functioning normally. The abundance of money could and did create illusions, a false sense of security even in hard-headed businessmen, despite the immense war in which Spain was engaged with much of the rest of Europe, despite their habitual prudence and despite the restraints brought once again by the suspension of the *sacas de plata* after 1589. The most alarming sign was undoubtedly fiscal tension in Castile which was becoming excessive; all taxpayers were being harried: the grandees, the nobility, the Church, the towns, and even the merchants if not the *hombres de negocios*, and enormous sums in *juros* were launched on a market that was still comparatively willing to buy. It was a situation that appears more explosive to historians with the benefit of hindsight than it did to the financiers of the day. They were literally astonished[303] by the royal *decreto* of mid-November by which Philip II suspended all payments and thereby recovered all the income and capital in the hands of the money-lenders.[304] An entirely unpredictable decision, it was thought at Lyons[305] at the end of November, since the Indies fleets had arrived after apparently crossing the Atlantic more rapidly than ever.[306] Predictable or not, the measure had immediate repercussions on all markets, beginning with Spain; in Europe, fears and errors of judgment at once even further complicated the situation. 'With this suspension', wrote Philip II's ambassador in Venice, Don Iñigo de Mendoza,[307] 'your Majesty without putting hand to sword will vanquish all his enemies whose sinews and strength came from the silver which Your Majesty has to cast out of his house. . . . It is this very same silver, as experience has shown . . . which is used by the Turks, the French and all other nations. . . .' The situation was of course far from as favourable as this to the king of Spain after his financial coup d'état and far from as simple as this would suggest. The king had by his own means arranged for enormous sums in specie (possibly four or five million ducats[308]) to be transported to Italy, but only with enormous difficulties and subject to the accidents such transport could involve. These difficulties were sometimes comical but no less real. The authorities at Valencia, for instance, objected to the shipment of a million ducats belonging to the king on the galleys for Italy, since they had not received the royal passport. It had to be sent off with all speed.[309] And speed was crucial if the system of payments was not to be dislocated in the explosive provinces of the Netherlands. It meant problems for the king, from which he did not and could not escape, despite the obstinacy, extremely revealing of his character, with which he continued to strike at the businessmen he disliked. But it caused problems for them too. The decree brought back to all of them memories of the hardships which the 1575 decree and its aftermath had brought to Genoa; then the 'old nobility' had had to sell 'the silver plate from their tables, the gold, pearls, and jewels of their wives. . . .'[310] And at the end of 1596,

[303] J. Gentil da Silva, *Stratégie des affaires à Lisbonne entre 1595 et 1607*, 1956, p. 50, 22nd November, 1596, at Lisbon, 27th at Lyons.
[304] Felipe Ruiz Martín, *El siglo de los Genoveses*, forthcoming, I have closely followed his excellent analysis which is both soundly based and original.
[305] J. Gentil da Silva, *op. cit.*, p. 51, 27th November, 1596.
[306] *Ibid.*, p. 50 and Victor von Klarwill, *The Fuggers News Letters*, London, 1926, II, p. 283, no. 573, 25th October, 1596.
[307] A.N., K 1676 (G.S.), Venice, 4th January, 1597, Iñigo de Mendoza to H.M.
[308] Felipe Ruiz Martín, *El siglo de los Genoveses*.
[309] A.d.S., Genoa, Spagna 11.2420, Cesare Giustiniano to the Doge, Madrid, 20th January, 1597.
[310] A.d.S., Genoa, *Relazione delle cose di Genova*, 1597, f° 26.

each of the *asentistas* had reason to fear that his financial operations over the last twenty years were in jeopardy, while he was daily harassed by payments to be honoured or obtained from others; postponement from week to week, the 'extension' of the fairs of Medina del Campo and elsewhere (there would not be a *real* to borrow[311]), could be no more than temporary solutions, constantly having to be renewed.

In the early stages of this trial of strength, Philip II's government, while unable to avoid contacts, pressures, and conversations, refused to make any promises. 'Not a single decision,' notes a Florentine, 'and everything is still in suspense and greatly confused [*molto confuso*].'[312] 'Up to now,' notes the Genoese ambassador at Madrid, '[there have been contacts] but no good news can yet be announced. . . .'[313] It seems clear that the king and his advisers were not out to 'metter per terra la contratatione',[314] to bring to the ground the system of *asientos* and the group of powerful businessmen known as the *contratación*. Their aim, and this was known before the decree, was to curb the demands of the financiers, to limit the profits of the *asentistas*, to obtain substantial long-term loans valid over a period of at least three years even if the 'Indies fleets did not arrive',[315] which was clearly too much to expect, for this source of bullion was vital to the circulation of bills of exchange and chests of silver. It was the banker who set in motion, accelerated, anticipated, and precipitated this circulation, and these were all expensive operations. The controllers, the royal *contadori* who had revised the accounts (in Spanish *tanteos*), declared that an *asiento* agreed with Ambrogio Spinola, for instance, for 400,000 crowns on Flanders, had cost the king 35 per cent in expenses.[316] The reply of the *asentistas*, while questioning the *tanteo*'s figures, recognized that these operations could be very costly, but denied that what the king lost went into the merchant's pockets, and on this point we must believe that the financiers were speaking at least half the truth.

In short, relations would soon have been established once more on a mutually suspicious footing no doubt (indeed how could it be otherwise between the king and his creditors?) if the Fuggers, had not intervened. They followed, if our chronology is correct, or at any rate accompanied the Portuguese, that is, the new Christians, who had advanced 250,000 crowns[317] to Philip II in the Netherlands on their commodity assets. They probably offered more, 4 million crowns according to some reports, but the negotiation fell through, either because they did not really possess so much (their heyday was yet to come) or because they attached too many

---

[311] J. Gentil da Silva, *op. cit.*, p. 52, 30th December, 1596.
[312] Exact reference mislaid.
[313] A.d.S., Genoa, Spagna 11.2420, H. Piccamiglio to the Doge, Madrid, 25th November, 1596. But there was hope of a rapid settlement in the letter from C. Giustiniano, 25th December, 1596, *ibid*.
[314] *Ibid*., the expression is Piccamiglio's 7th December, 1596.
[315] Cesare Giustiniano to the Doge, Madrid, 31st January, 1597.
[316] *Ibid*., Madrid, 20th January, 1597.
[317] *Ibid*., Madrid, 24th December, 1596.

conditions.[318] The Fuggers came to the rescue in early December, or rather one of their three agents in Spain, Thomas Carg, did. Without consulting the other two he reached an agreement with the Spanish king to advance twelve monthly payments of 300,000 crowns, payable 'through the local branch' in the Netherlands, against an advance of half the total in cash, plus corresponding assignments,[319] plus the promise that a monumental backlog of debts would be paid. The Genoese did not at first take this manoeuvre seriously. It was an 'artifice', an *asiento* '*aereo*', in the air.[320] Moreover they were themselves proposing to the king better terms spread over a longer period, or so they said with apparent sincerity.[321] By February the Genoese realized that the manoeuvre was serious, that all it now required to become reality was the consent of the Fuggers in Augsburg.[322] The subsequent disputes and dissension within this great banking family, divided against itself, would provide a fascinating excursion into biographical history, as would the eventful journey of Anton Fugger to Madrid in April, 1597.[323] In the present context, the Fuggers' intervention gave Philip II a year's breathing-space, and explains a discouraging series of fruitless talks, betrayals of some *trattanti* by others, some only projected, others actually carried out, as in the case of Battista Serra for instance.[324] But by the end of 1597 the Fugger interlude was over and agreement was to be reached fairly quickly. The Castilian government could no longer afford the luxury of putting it off.

Concluded between two of Philip II's 'ministers' and four representatives of the financiers, the agreement of 13th November, 1597, was to become the *medio general* of the 29th of the same month. The victims of the decree of 1596, the *decretados*, were to advance to the king, in eighteen monthly payments, 4,500,000 crowns in Flanders and 2,500,000 in Spain, between the end of January, 1598, and the end of June, 1599. For his part, the king agreed to grant them a series of substantial benefits, and in particular granted them an enormous sum in *juros*, over 7 million ducats. Concerning these *juros*, there had been sharp discussion over whether they were to be granted as life holdings or in perpetuity, and even more over the interest rate that the financiers would have liked to raise in order the better to be able to resell these bonds and other *libranzas* to the Spanish public. In this way they were to become even more entangled, if that was possible, in the complicated speculation in *juros*, of which the general rules are better known than how it worked in detail. To buy cheap and sell dear was easier said than done. The comparative stability of the market (accompanied

[318] J. Gentil da Silva, *op. cit.*, and references, p. 53, Rome, 25th January, 1597.
[319] A.d.S., Genoa, Spagna 11.2420, C. Giustiniano to the Doge, Madrid, 5th February and 22nd February, 1597. On the part played by Thomas Cherch (Carg) *ibid.*, Madrid, 2nd March, 1597.
[320] *Ibid.*, Madrid 5th January, 1597, and 22nd February, 1597.
[321] *Ibid.*, 22nd February, 1597.
[322] *Ibid.*
[323] For example, Ernst Hering, *Die Fugger*, Leipzig, 1940, p. 301 ff.
[324] J. Gentil da Silva, *op. cit.*, and references, p. 55, 12th June, 1597.

however by losses that in some cases are known to have been as much as 14 per cent on bonds at revised rates) made the enormous operation possible.[325] The Genoese and their financiers naturally paid their creditors in bonds, in spite of the protests of the latter, who having given cash wanted to be paid back in cash. But from the start, the bankers refused to pay 'di altra moneta che di quella che li darà S. Mta'.[326] This then was a banal crisis, the reader may think, in no way comparable to the violent shock of 1575. But it would be wrong to suppose that this painful year (almost to the day) of troubles was without consequences. For it ended by a closing of the ranks by the financiers, the 'syndicate' as they would be called today, the *decretados* of 1596, who had virtually constituted a company for several years under the directorship of four merchants, three Genoese (Ettore Piccamiglio, Ambrogio Spinola, Juan Jacomo de Grimaldi) and a Spaniard, Francisco de Malvenda. There can be no doubt that this led to a concentration of business to the advantage of the *decretados* and of the richest among them. The sums referred to in the decree itself in 1596 were divided as follows: Genoese, (in millions of *maravedís*), 2050; Florentines, 94; Germans, 4·5; Spaniards, 2523; in other words, a large, indeed the largest share belonged to the Spaniards. So they suffered more than the others and possibly did not succeed in passing on their losses to others as the Genoese did, to the detriment in particular of Venetian investors lured by the easy profits to be obtained by the *cambii*. After the *medio general* the new division was as follows (in *escudos* or *ducados*): Genoese, 5,581,000; Florentines 256,000; Germans 13,000; Spaniards, 2,200,000; as is perfectly reflected by the composition of the board of directors: three Genoese, one Spaniard, the former taking the lion's share.[327]

About ten years later the whole process began again, as if the system contained within it the structural necessity for bankruptcy at more or less regular intervals. I do not think I need describe in detail the decree of 9th November, 1607, and the *medio general* of 14th May, 1608, to show how Spain entered upon a new crisis only ten years after the last suspension of payments by Philip II, in spite of the pacific policy of the Duke of Lerma, but because of the extravagance of the new reign, the plundering of public funds and the general recession of the economy after 1595. The 1608 ruling created, to the sole advantage of the Genoese, a complicated but reliable system for paying off the floating debt, bonds for which were in the hands of their business associates. The latter formed a new syndicate under the titles of *Diputación del medio general de 1608*. The important

[325] I am here following Felipe Ruiz Martín, *op. cit.*

[326] On these settlements reference can be made to the entire correspondence of Cesare Giustiniano in detail.

[327] According to the information given by Felipe Ruiz Martín. On the state bankruptcy of 1607, Genoese correspondence (A.d.S., Genoa, Spagna 15.2424) is clearly of interest but it adds little or nothing to what we already know from Felipe Ruiz Martín's study which has the advantage of situating the crisis in the context of the economic and financial history of Castile.

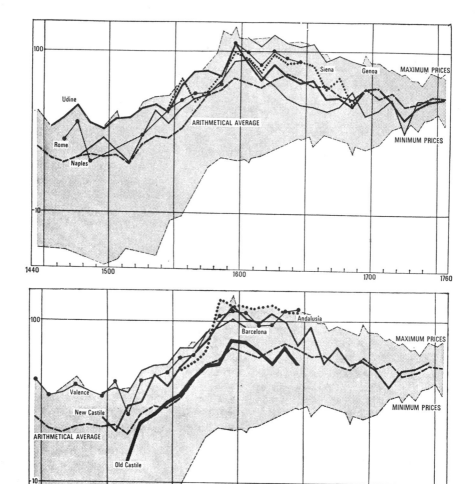

Fig. 42: *Wheat prices in the Mediterranean and Europe*

From F. Braudel and F. C. Spooner, Vol. IV of the *Cambridge Economic History*, (p. 470). From about fifty series of wheat prices, calculated in grams of silver per hectolitre, it has been possible to construct the range of cereal quotations (the shaded zone represents the range between maximum and minimum prices) for the whole of Europe and the arithmetical average (dotted line) of all these prices. Prices rose universally of course throughout the sixteenth century. On this 'envelope' I have superimposed, in two separate diagrams for the sake of clarity, various Mediterranean price-curves. It will be noted that the curve for Old Castile coincides almost exactly with the arithmetical average. All the other Mediterranean curves are well above average, at least until 1620 and in some cases even later. The Mediterranean or at least the Christian Mediterranean, since there are no price series available for the eastern part of the sea where prices were certainly lower, was a zone where bread was expensive, reaching almost the maximum price for the period. After the middle of the seventeenth century Mediterranean prices are much nearer the average, but it should be noted that during this period European prices in general were tending to converge as is clearly shown by the pronounced narrowing of the shaded zone. The distance between maximum and minimum was to decrease even further during the eighteenth century.

thing to note is that between one state bankruptcy and the next the degree of concentration had increased. The Spanish merchants disappeared from the *contratación* after a series of spectacular bankruptcies: in 1601[328] the failure of Aguilar and of Cosme Ruiz Embito, the nephew and successor of Simón Ruiz;[329] in 1607 that of Pedro de Malvenda.[330] So the Genoese held the field alone and were correspondingly detested and despised. And it was alone that in 1627 they were to meet the onslaught, engineered by the Count Duke Olivares, of the Portuguese financiers who had already been sounded out in 1596, applied to in 1607, and thrown into the fray in 1627, by which time they already occupied in the various cities of Castile (above all at Seville) a series of strong commercial positions. This triumph crowned their previous achievements and marked a turning-point in the history of international capitalism, as well as the immediate prelude to their endless difficulties with the frowning and implacable Inquisition.[331]

3. THE RISE IN PRICES

The general price rise of the sixteenth century was felt with force in the Mediterranean countries, especially after the 1570s, and was accompanied by its many familiar consequences. The violent character and the length of this 'revolution' – which in fact extended into the seventeenth century – could not fail to be noted by contemporary observers. For them it was an occasion to reflect on the complex problem of currency, the new and revolutionary power of money, and the general fortunes of men and states. Historians in their turn have looked for the culprit or culprits, and sometimes thought they have found the answer, but the truth appears more and more complex as fresh facts daily come to light and as economic history, why not admit it, is becoming a more scientific discipline.

Although it has come under much attack[332] I shall continue to use the term 'price revolution'. Opinions may differ as to its causes, its true dynamics and its extent, but not about its brutally novel character. One historian[333] has suggested that we in the twentieth century have experienced a greater price revolution in our own time. But this is no way to approach the problem. It must be judged by the universal astonishment of Philip II's contemporaries throughout this age of constantly rising prices which began well before 1500. To men of the sixteenth century it seemed that they were witnessing something quite unprecedented. The old days when goods changed hands for almost nothing had been succeeded by grim years during which the cost of living rose ever higher. One might possibly

[328] According to information given by Felipe Ruiz Martin.
[329] *Ibid.*   [330] *Ibid.*
[331] See below, Vol, II ch. 6, *Civilizations*, section 3.
[332] Of which the most readable is Carlo M. Cipolla, 'La prétendue "révolution des prix", réflexions sur l' "expérience italienne",' in *Annales E.S.C.*, October–December, 1955, p. 513–516.
[333] Gaston Zeller, *La Vie économique de l'Europe au XVIe siècle*, Lecture at Sorbonne, p. 3 ff.

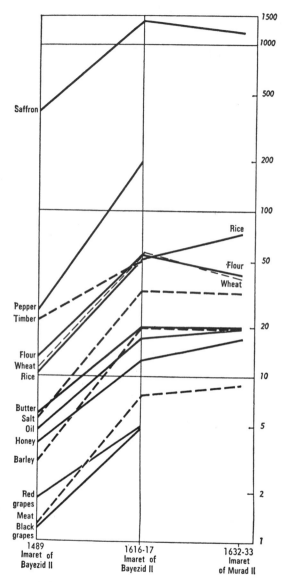

Fig. 43: *Prices at Bursa, 1489–1633*

I am indebted to Ömer Lütfi Barkan for these Turkish prices, which confirm that the price rise of the sixteenth century affected Turkey. The *imaret-s* were religious institutions where poor people and students were given food. The prices are given in aspers. There is still a possibility that the Turkish archives may yield price series which would vitally affect the assessment of general trends in the Mediterranean. N.B., these nominal prices do not allow for the devaluation of the asper.

question the use of the word revolution to describe the situation in Italy, for example, an established country with an advanced monetary economy, but faced with the chain of upheavals in the Balkans, Anatolia, the whole of the Turkish empire, how can one avoid using the term 'price revolution?' Dramatic situations require dramatic words.

Contemporary complaints. Evidence of the price increases comes from every source. The common factor is the stupefaction of all contemporary observers and their inability to comprehend the causes of a phenomenon always seen by them only in its local manifestations – which they were the more likely to contrast with the good old days since the end of the fifteenth century had been a period of high wages and the first thirty years of the sixteenth century a time of stability when the cost of living remained comparatively low, even in Poland.[334] As for France, a contemporary of Charles IX wrote in 1560: 'In my father's time, there was meat to eat every day, the meals were copious and the wine flowed like water.'[335] And similar complaints flow from the critical pen of the Spanish agriculturalist G. Alonso de Herrera: 'Today [1513] a pound of mutton costs as much as a whole sheep used to, a loaf as much as a *fanega* of wheat, a pound of wax or oil as much as an *arroba* did in those days and so on . . .'[336]

The grievances of the Cortes of Castile were reiterated many times during the century. But only rarely is this full-throated but parochial voice raised against the general situation. We find it continually complaining of the high price of grain, the disastrous export of gold, the indiscriminate slaughter of calves and lambs, which it blames for the higher prices; or speaking out against the export of leather to other countries, which is definitely responsible for the increased cost of shoes. And it rages against foreign speculators: they are to blame for the increased price of meat, horses, wool, cloth, silk . . .[337] The Cortes of 1548, alarmed by American demands, even suggested to the Emperor[338] that colonial industry should be developed and that exports from the Peninsula to the New World, which were considered damaging to home interests, should be discontinued. The Cortes of 1586 (at Valladolid) asked the king 'to tolerate no longer the importing of candles, glass trinkets, jewelry, cutlery and similar objects from foreign countries which are exchanged, although they are useless luxuries, for gold, as if Spaniards were Indians. . . .'[339] Such was the opinion of reasonable men, and they were not always wrong.[340]

[334] St. Hoszowski, *Les prix à Lwow* (*XVIe–XVIIe siècles*), 1954, p. 60: the cost of living was lower between 1521 and 1525 than it had been between 1451 and 1500.
[335] G. d'Avenel, *Hist. économique de la propriété* . . . , 1898, III, p. 246.
[336] C. Alonso Herrera, *op. cit.*, f° 353.
[337] A summary in Earl J. Hamilton, *op. cit.*, p. 283 ff.
[338] *Actas* . . . , V, p. 472–474, quoted by Earl J. Hamilton, *op. cit.*, p. 286.
[339] A detail quoted by Karl Marx in *Zur Kritik der politischen Oekonomie*, (Marx/ Engels *Werke*, Berlin, 1961, vol. 13, p. 107).
[340] Felipe Ruiz Martín, points out, apropos of the complaints from the Cortes, that the price rise was particularly marked in commodities purchased by the Genoese merchants.

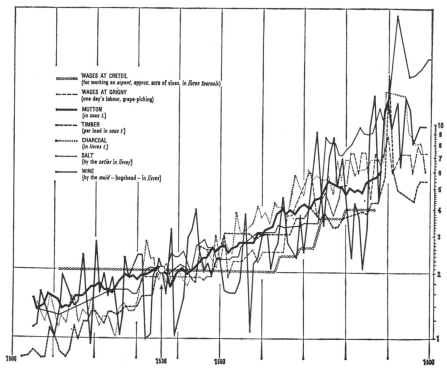

WAGES AT CRETEIL
(for working an *arpent*, approx. acre of vines, in *livres tournois*)

WAGES AT GRIGNY
(one day's labour, grape-picking)

MUTTON
(in *sous t.*)

TIMBER
(per load in *sous t.*)

CHARCOAL
(in *livres t.*)

SALT
(by the *setier* in *livres*)

WINE
(by the *muid* – hogshead – in *livres*)

1500   1530   1550   1600

Fig. 44: *Rising prices in Paris, from the archives of
charitable institutions*

Note the discrepancy between wages and price movements, the sharp rises in salt
prices. The price of mutton represents the average general rate of increase. From
archives of the Parisian *hôpitaux*, unpublished research by Micheline Baulant.

A Venetian notes in 1580 that prices at Naples have risen by almost two-
thirds. He has hardly pointed this out before he is attributing it to the
greed of government officials and the massive purchases and preparations
made by his Catholic Majesty for the conquest of Portugal.[341] In Viscaya
prices are rising too, and, says an official report of 1588, it is because
the people of the lowlands (the *tierra llana*) eat and drink to excess in the
taverns, where they pick up vicious and lazy habits, neglecting their fields
and orchards. So it is not to be wondered at if cider is scarce and sold at
exorbitant prices! Here high prices were blamed on the poor.[342]

Soetbeer[343], in a book written many years ago, cites no less than thirty-
three writers before 1600 and thirty-one between 1600 and 1621 who discuss, with varying degrees of comprehension, the rise in prices of which

[341] E. Albèri, *op. cit.*, II, V, p. 470.
[342] *Gobierno de Vizcaya*, II, p. 406.
[343] *Literaturnachweis über Geld und Münzwesen*, p. 9–14.

they were all witnesses and victims. To quote them would be tedious. To prolong the list which would not be difficult, would at least have the advantage of establishing that there was a widespread and moving awareness of the problem.

Was American treasure responsible? As far as I know, no general explanation was put forward before the second half of the sixteenth century. The two first examples of the *quantity theory*, advanced in 1557 and 1558, both passed virtually unnoticed by contemporaries: the works of Martín de Azpilcueta, professor at the University of Salamanca and a pupil of Vitoria, were not published until 1590, four years after his death, at Rome.[344] The same fate awaited the writings of Charles V's historiographer, Francisco López de Gomara, who also suspected a connection between the price rise and the arrival of bullion from America.[345] But his book had to wait until 1912 to find a publisher.

The problem was raised publicly only during the controversy between Jean Bodin and M. de Malestroict from 1566 to 1568.[346] Most contemporaries took Bodin's side, perhaps underestimating a little too hastily the devaluation of moneys of account to which his opponent drew attention. From then on the quantity theory became a commonplace. In 1585, Noël du Fail, in his *Contes et Discours d'Eutrapel*,[347] explains briefly '. . . and this is because of the lands newly discovered and the mines of gold and silver which the Spanish and Portuguese carry home and which they let pass finally into this perpetual mine of France, whose wheat and merchandise they can under no circumstances forego. . . .' Marc Lescabot in his *Histoire de la Nouvelle France* (1612) expresses it in even more concrete terms.[348] 'Before the voyages to Peru, one could keep much wealth in a little place, but now that gold and silver have been cheapened by abundance, great chests are required to transport what before could be carried wrapped up in a piece of drugget. A man could go a long way with a purse in his sleeve, but now he needs a trunk and a horse'. Gerard Malynes (1586–1641), the English merchant and commercial expert, notes for his part in 1601[349] that the general increase in prices is due to the 'Oceans of Monies' from the Indies. They 'caused the measure to be made lesser, whereby the number did increase to make up the tale'.

The quantity theory has come down to us more or less intact. It was restated in its modern form in the monumental work of Earl J. Hamilton,

---

[344] Josef Höffner, *Wirtschaftsethik und Monopole*, 1941, Berlin, 1892, p. 110.
[345] E. J. Hamilton, *op. cit.*, p. 292.
[346] Henri Hauser, ed., *La response de Jean Bodin à M. de Malestroit* . . . , (English translation in A. E. Monroe ed., *Early Economic Thought*, Cambridge, Mass., 1924) and *Paradoxes inédits du Sieur de Malestroit touchant les monnoyes*, ed. Luigi Einaudi, Turin, 1937.
[347] 1585, p. 125.
[348] P. 43 v°.
[349] Quoted by Eli F. Heckscher in his classic *Mercantilism* (Engl. translation M. Shapiro, London, New York, 1955, p. 225).

which accepts its basic validity. It has been defended more recently by Alexandre Chabert[350] who considers it useful in the explanation of some currency phenomena in the underdeveloped countries of today which bear a certain resemblance to past economies. In his eyes the weightiest argument is the correlation between the imports of bullion to Seville and the rise in prices both inside and outside Spain. Theoretically, François Simiand[351] was right to suggest that a cumulative curve would be preferable to a set of quinquennial averages for the arrival of precious metals – thus putting the problem in a slightly different light. But the fact that prices and quinquennial averages coincide proves that these arrivals did act as a series of stimuli to the mass of currency in circulation, increasing its velocity until the day when this mass had become too great and the stimulus insufficient to force it any higher. Every consignment of American silver was quickly dispersed in all directions, almost like an explosion.

Some arguments for and against American responsibility. President Luigi Einaudi[352] in his work on M. de Malestroict suggests that 299·4 per cent out of a total price rise of 627 per cent, calculated in France between 1471 and 1598, can be attributed to the influx of precious metals. The calculations cannot be verified. But the influx of precious metals is obvious. However would make a few reservations.

1. American mineral production, the instrument of inflation, was not necessarily a prime mover, functioning unaided. It was the economic development of Europe and the demand thus created which stimulated and dictated the labour of the gold-panners and the Indians in the silver mines. On this mass of gold and above all silver, let us quote what a text from the second half of the eighteenth century has to say of the immense riches of the New World, 'It is a fruit of America that would have remained buried in the ground if [European] trade, by the sale of commodities, had not forced the Americans to draw it out of the bowels of the earth'.[353] It is possible to argue then that the faraway European economy was, in the last analysis, responsible for the price revolution.

2. It must be recognized that European monetary reserves before 1500 were greater than has been suggested in the past. Many economic developments of the fifteenth century – the emergence of the modern state with its paid armies, salaried officials, taxes paid in money, the achievement of a monetary economy in favoured regions (for the most part maritime countries, Italy, Spain, Portugal, England, the Low Countries, in other words the active fringe of the continent) all presuppose a fairly substantial flow of currency. I would propose a very tentative figure of 5000 tons of

[350] 'Encore la révolution des prix au XVIe siècle' in *Annales E.S.C.* 1957, p 269 ff. and *Structure Économique et théorie monétaire*, 1956.
[351] *Recherches anciennes et nouvelles sur l'histoire des prix*, 1932, p. 403–420, 457–478, 492, 546.
[352] *Paradoxes inédits* . . . , p. 23.
[353] B.N., Paris, fr. 10766, f° 100 (undated).

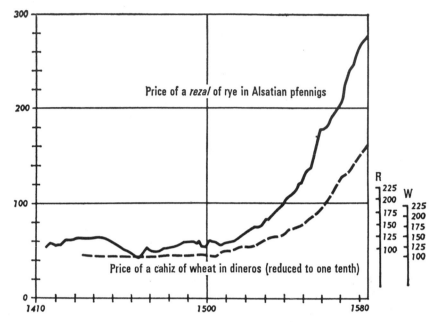

Fig. 45: *The price rise is felt at Strasbourg before Valencia*

After R. Grandamy in J. Fourastié, *Prix de vente et prix de revient*, 13th series, p. 26. The continuous line represents the price curve of rye at Strasbourg, and the dotted line the price of wheat at Valencia (mobile 30-year averages, 1451–1500 = 100). Scale of percentages on right. As can be seen, the Strasbourg curve rises more steeply than the curve for Valencia. Had American treasure been the sole cause of the price rise, the reverse would surely have occurred.

gold and 60,000 of silver, basing these estimates on the supposed balance between gold and silver and the slight shift of the bi-metallic ratio from 12 to 15[354] between 1500 and 1650. If one set out to calculate, as far as possible, on the basis of the known or presumed circulation in 1600, the stock of bullion inherited from previous centuries, one would be likely to discover results of fairly considerable magnitude[355] which the quantity

[354] If x and y represent the quantities of silver and gold in 1500 and there is bi-metallic equilibrium x (tons of silver) = 12y tons of gold. If the quantities added between 1500 and 1650 represent roughly 18,000 tons of silver and 200 tons of gold, the second equation will be:

$$x + 18{,}000 = 15 (y + 200).$$

[355] One would have to start with estimates, relate them to a given population and calculate proportionally an order of magnitude for other monetary stocks. At the beginning of 1587, Naples, which had a population of over 3,000,000 inhabitants, possessed a stock of 700,000 ducats; at this rate Europe would possess over 20 million and the Mediterranean 14. . . . This appears a low estimate, to start with. Monetary stocks are sometimes assumed by economists as equivalent to the total sum of coins minted over the previous thirty years. P. Boissonnade (*art. cit.*, p. 198) mentions the

theory would somehow have to accommodate. American metal, 'a free investment' did however increase the velocity of circulation at a rate closely corresponding to the price rise. The injection of this new bullion produced a multiplier effect.[356]

3. But other explanations may be admitted. The devaluation of moneys of account was partly responsible as the reader will see from the table on p. 529. Evidence of a different kind has been compiled by Jean Fourastié and his pupils.[357] Price levels began rising in Germany in 1470 and in many parts of France before the end of the fifteenth century well in advance that is of the privileged countries – Italy, the Iberian Peninsula, and England. If nominal prices only are considered, there can be absolutely no doubt on this point. Population growth in the poorer countries apparently advanced faster than in the others, faster above all than in the Mediterranean. In Central Europe the price revolution had begun before Columbus sailed. It did not reach the Mediterranean until about 1520 and did not become confirmed until about 1550.

4. A graph representing imports of silver to Seville resembles a typical industrial production curve, like that of Potosí, according to the figures of Paz y Soldan. It both rises and falls steeply, reaching its peak in 1601–1610: these years marked a turning point in world history, not merely in Mediterranean fortunes.

Wages. Inflation which was felt everywhere brought, its usual consequences.

Wages followed more slowly in the wake of the price rise, sometimes failing to move at all. That life was hard for the poor we have already seen. Nominal wages rose more or less rapidly along with prices and remained high temporarily at times of recession; but translated into real wages, these figures tell the same story and testify to the extreme poverty of the lower-paid workers. In Spain, taking the years 1571–1580 as 100, real wages which in 1510 had been at an index of 127·84, fell in 1530 to 91·35; after fluctuating for a while they reached 97·61 in 1550; 110·75 in 1560; 105·66 in 1570; 102·86 in 1580; 105·85 in 1590; 91·31 in 1600. It was not

---

sum of 4 million pounds sterling for England in the sixteenth century, René Baehrel ('Economie et histoire a propos des prix' in *Hommage à Lucien Febvre. Éventail de l'histoire vivante*, Paris, 1953, vol. I, p. 309, no. 72) talks of 2 million *livres* for France at the end of the eighteenth century. There are too few figures and those too unreliable to take us very far; all our calculations are insecurely founded, but they help us to build up a slightly better picture of a past economic system, to adjust our models of it and to come a little closer to reality. See the not entirely convincing but stimulating argument in R. Baehrel, *op. cit., passim* and p. 40, note 26. No valid model can be constructed without some study, quantitative if possible, of copper and vellon currencies, the money handled by the poor. The amount coined was insignificant compared to gold and silver. At Venice, where the annual total of coins minted was two million ducats, 60,000 ducats worth of *bezzi* were minted in 1604, 15,000 in *gazette* and *grossetti* in 1606, A.d.S., Venice, Senato Zecca, 9.

[356] Pierre Chaunu, *L'Amérique et les Amériques*, 1964, p. 93 ff.
[357] See below, Fig. 47, p. 526.

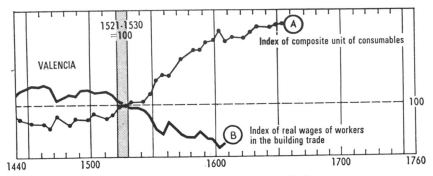

Fig. 46: *Prices and real wages at Valencia*

After E. H. Phelps Brown and Sheila Hopkins: the cost of living to the consumer went up and real wages fell correspondingly.

until after the crisis of 1600 and the widespread epidemics that reduced the population of the Peninsula, that wages, following vellon inflation, shot up to 125·49 in 1610, 130·56 in 1611. The price revolution brought little comfort to Spanish wage-earners,[358] although it treated them better than it did the artisans of France, England, Germany, or Poland.[359] The situation was equally depressing in Florence[360] where real wages tumbled during the price increase.

There were visible monetary signs of this, for the medium used for the wages of the poor and their everyday purchases was practically never gold, only occasionally silver, and was for the most part vellon and copper currency: what was called in Florence *la moneta nera* by contrast with the 'white' silver coinage. It is copper coin explains Davanzati, which interests the poor, and the agriculturalist Herrera spells it out for us: 'it is by the base metal currency that one can best judge the fertility and abundance of a country for it is with this money that all the necessities of daily life are bought every day from the shopkeepers.'[361] There follows his theory of base metal currency, which would lead us a long way from our subject.

In fact one should really speak of a tri-metallic rather than a bi-metallic ratio. In order to bring copper and vellon currencies into line, they were continually being recalled to the mints, where they were reminted as even lighter coins and put back into circulation. This constant devaluation of copper was out of all proportion to the necessary harmony of moneys. On each occasion the state profited, not the public, and least of all the poor. Such manipulation began early in Spain and Sicily, where the *piccioli* were being melted down and reminted as early as 1563 and 1568.[362]

Income from land. Inflation struck both rich and poor, but it affected some rich men more than others. It hit the 'industrialists', merchants, financiers

[358] J. Kulischer, *op. cit.*, I, p. 280–281.   [359] *Ibid.*, p. 281.
[360] G. Parenti, *op. cit.*, p. 224.   [361] *Op. cit.*, p. 351 v° to 352.
[362] L. Bianchini, *Della storia economico-civile di Sicilia*, Naples, 1841, I, p. 331 ff.

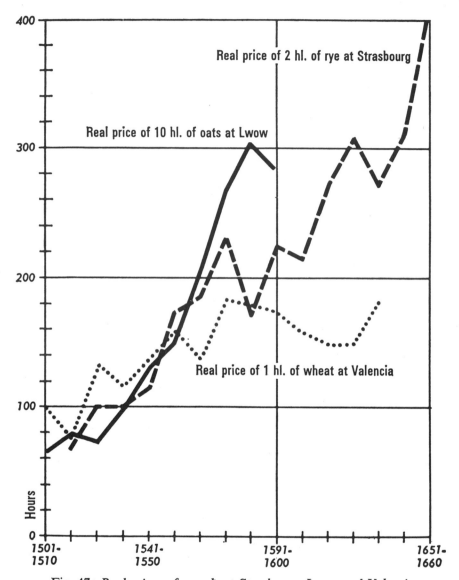

Fig. 47: *Real prices of cereals at Strasbourg, Lwow and Valencia*

After René Grandamy in J. Fourastié, *Prix de vente et prix de revient*, 13th series, p. 31. The prices are calculated in hourly rates for bricklayers' labourers. The drop in the standard of living is less marked at Valencia than in the two other continental towns.

(I should apologise for using these convenient but slightly anachronistic terms). It hit all those who were directly or indirectly caught up in the dangerous currents of money. It had much less effect upon landed proprietors. This is apparent from the detailed study by Carlo M. Cipolla, ('Finanze dei Borghi e Castelli sotto il dominio spagnuolo')[363] of the *castello* of Tegiole near Alessandria, the ancient fief of the bishop of Pavia, during the late sixteenth and early seventeenth century. In this particular instance, it appears that dues in kind and feudal labour had not all become money payments (and where money payments were customary, the lord or his representative always had the right to re-estimate the amount): so alongside feudal revenues worth comparatively little, the *castello* had other, as it were more modern sources of income, corresponding to rent from its tenants, which meant that it received from the *contadini* sacks of wheat, oats, and beans, casks of wine and cartloads of hay – a revenue providing the basis of the *castello*'s budget.

If, bearing this in mind, one thinks of the Spanish ambassador Bernardino de Mendoza,[364] whose sister administered his estates in his absence, selling his wheat every summer; of the Duke of Alcalá, viceroy of Naples, who in 1559 acquired 1500 vassals of the royal domains;[365] if one remembers those Aragonese nobles, landlords of small estates, or the grandees of Castile, owners of land, flocks, and wheatfields or the Sicilian lords who sold cereals, wine, or silk, one is everywhere impressed by the fact that to these noblemen, so very different from one another, land was a constant standby: during the insecure age of rising prices, it protected them from the abyss of inflation. If this seignorial class dominated Europe at the beginning of the seventeenth century, it was because it had lost much less ground than is commonly assumed. So it was no folly on the part of merchants, and *nouveaux riches* to buy up estates and property in the countryside. The relentless pursuit of land and titles in Naples by rich Florentines and super-rich Genoese may have been a form of vanity but it was also a far-seeing policy, a prudent and responsible course of action from their point of view.

Even the less well off were attracted by such safe investments. Towards the end of his life (he died in 1570) Benvenuto Cellini became the proprietor of a small estate near Florence which he bought in March, 1560, as a lifetime investment from some peasants whose honesty he suspected. Whether they really tried to poison him or not we shall never know, for Cellini had a vivid imagination and tended to exaggerate. But the interesting point is that he chose to provide security for his old age by investing in land.[366]

[363] In *Bollettino Stor. pavese*, VIII, 1945.
[364] Alfred Morel Fatio, *Études sur l'Espagne*, 4th series, 1925, p. 373.
[365] Princess Juana to Philip II, 13th July, 1559, Simancas E° 137, f° 22, 1, 500 vassals, near Seville, for 150,000 ducats.
[366] *The Life of Benvenuto Cellini* (tr. Symonds, London, 1949 ed. p. 407). In a completely different region, round Arles, there are examples of share-cropping at 50 and 25 per cent in the sixteenth century, Quiqueran De Beaujeu, *op. cit.*, p. 400–401.

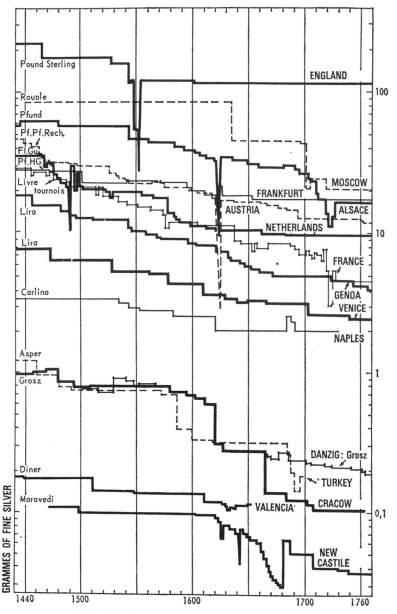

Fig. 48: *Devaluation of moneys of account*

This graph appears in the chapter by F. Braudel and F. C. Spooner in the *Cambridge Economic History*, vol. IV. The moneys are classified by their weights in grams of fine silver. Some were light, some heavy: some such as the pound sterling remained comparatively stable; others like the Polish *grosz*, the Turkish asper, and even the *livre tournois* were extremely unstable. Approximate values are given for the rouble and asper.

Pf. Pf. Rech = Pfund Pfennig Rechengulden.
Fl. Gu. = florin, after 1579 guilder.   Pf. HG. = Pfund Heller Gulden.

Banks and inflation. Except for land, every 'business' sector was affected, and in particular the banks.[367] All banking operations were conducted in moneys of account, not in real moneys and were therefore exposed to the perils of inflation. For these fictional moneys, Venetian and Genoese *lire*, Sicilian *oncie* and *tari*, Spanish *maravedis* and ducats, French *livres tournois*, were constantly losing their intrinsic value. The Sicilian ounce, which in 1546 still corresponded to 91·09 Italian *lire* of 1866, was worth only 20·40 in 1572–1573. Similarly the *livre tournois*, expressed in *francs Germinal*, fell from 4 in 1515 to 3·65 in 1521 (this devaluation was a method of attracting foreign currency, in particular Castilian gold, into France); to 3·19 in 1561; to 2·94 in 1573; to 2·64 in 1575; to 2·46 in 1602.[368] So the relationship of real money to money of account was continually being adjusted, and of the two the former was consistently better placed. Who bore the loss? If, after an interval of several years, a bank deposit registered in a money of account was repaid in the same terms as the original deposit, the depositor lost. If a banker's advance was repaid in the same terms, the banker lost. Time operated against money registered in units of account if it lay idle.

Mario Siri suggests that this was a constant strain on banking and business in the sixteenth century. Theoretically he is right. Losses whether on one side or the other all occurred within the single sector of commercial and financial affairs. Whether, as far as individuals were concerned, profits and losses balanced out is another question. In any case, given the usual rhythm of business (exchanges at the fairs, which came and went every three months for instance), given the exchange rates and the ever-rising spiral of inflation, it is unlikely that there would be any visible sign of the day-to-day process of exhaustion. No merchant's books mention it, but that does not mean that over a long period this gradual strain may not have had its effect. More commonly however, the failure of a merchant or a bank was likely to be the effect of short-term fluctuations. There were many banks and their position sometimes appeared astonishingly healthy – the Pisani-Tiepolo bank in March 1583,[369] the year preceding its collapse, had 200,000 ducats in Spanish reals brought to Venice in a single consignment. But they all made the mistake of granting loans and, what was more, of placing part of the money deposited with them in commercial ventures that took time. If a short term recession occurred, as it did in 1584, loans were not repaid, deposits were withdrawn, and crisis became irremediable. The Pisani-Tiepolo bank failed on 17th March, 1584.[370] The historian who wishes to pursue this question seriously will have to

[367] No historian has shown this better than Mario Siri, *La svalutazione della moneta e il bilancio del Regno di Sicilia nella seconda metà del XVI secolo*, Melfi, 1921 in-16, 22 p.
[368] According to Albert Despaux, *Les dévaluations monétaires dans l'histoire*, Paris, 1936, p. 362.
[369] A.d.S., Florence, Mediceo 3083, f° 417 v°, 27th March, 1583.
[370] Marciana, Chronicle of Girolamo Savina, f° 361 v°.

study the huge account books of the *banchieri antichi* preserved in the *Archivio di Stato* at Naples, take further the important research begun by A. Silvestri[371] and analyse the results: a Herculean labour.

For whatever reason the number of bank failures increased after 1550–1570, a trend aggravated by the 'royal cycle of money' which was also the royal cycle of inflation. The disease had such a hold that the only remedy was to come from the state banks which began to appear one by one at precisely this juncture. The only public foundation to receive its charter before this time had been the Bank of Palermo, organized under the protection and guarantee of the city's Senate, in 1551,[372] with headquarters in the premises known as *La Loggia*.[373] Its origins unquestionably lay in the *Tavola Communale o della Prefetia* of Trepani, which went back as far as the end of the fifteenth century[374]. This helps to explain why the Bank of Palermo, exceptional for its early appearance, was also exceptional in character. Like the public banks of the Mezzogiorno for which it often served as a model, it specialized in fiscal revenues, the management of public money and payments. It was finally crushed by the weight of these political and administrative burdens when, under the reign of Philip III, it was entrusted with the not very lucrative task of restoring Sicilian currency to health.

The great age of the creation of public banks was not to begin until thirty years after the foundation of the Palermo bank. In 1580 the *Casa di San Giorgio* resumed the banking functions it had abdicated over a century earlier in 1444 at the time of the gold crisis. On 23rd September, 1587, there was established the *Tavola della città di Messina*, whose statutes were not approved by Philip II until 1st July, 1596. Through this bank it was hoped – not unreasonably – that an end could be put both to the series of bank failures and to fraud on the part of the *collettori* of public revenue. This new bank naturally had the privilege of holding public funds in deposit. It was placed under the guarantee and control of the city of Messina.[375] In 1587[376] appeared the famous *Banco della Piazza di Rialto* at Venice, which was taken over in 1619 by the no less famous *Banco Giro*. In 1593, the *Banco di S. Ambrogio* was founded at Milan with an independent governing body as a *banco giro*. The same period saw the founding at Naples of the bank annexed to the *Monte di Pietà* and the Hospital of the *Santa Casa dell' Annunziata*, and at Rome the bank annexed to the Hospital of the Holy Ghost. The creation of so many banks, within

---

[371] A. Silvestri, 'Sui banchieri pubblici napoletani nelle prima metà del Cinquecento' in *Bollettino dell'Archivio storico del Banco di Napoli*, 1951, 'Sui banchieri pubblici napoletani dall'avvento di Filippo II al trono alla costituzione del monopolio', *ibid.*
[372] L. Bianchini, *op. cit.*, I, p. 340; G. Luzzatto, *op. cit.*, p. 183, gives 1553 as the date of its creation.
[373] G. Luzzatto, *ibid.*   [374] *Ibid.*
[375] L. Bianchini, *op. cit.*, p. 341.
[376] I have adopted the date 1587 given by G. Luzzatto. I note from my papers that the bank was given authorization by the Senate on 28th June, 1584.

a definite period of time and over a fairly widespread area, can be considered evidence in itself.

But it is far from simple evidence. Particularly in the north, the functions of the state banks were soon to extend beyond the strict limits of public finance. The *Banco della Piazza di Rialto*, for instance, in spite of prohibitions, from the start allowed overdrafts, using its customers' money. It had in fact widely issued 'bank money' which was in greater demand than metal currency. In so doing the banks were not innovating, merely imitating the practices of the old private banks. Their originality lay in the unprecedented scale of the loans they made. But it was clearly the failure, imperfection, and insecurity of the private banks that led to this sudden outcrop of public banks. Gino Luzzatto, from whose study much of the preceding information is taken, concludes: 'If these public banks created nothing new, they did at least afford the customers who flocked to them the peace of mind and security which had too often been denied them by the private banks. . . .'[377] And one has only to think of the long series of bank failures, from the bankruptcy of Priuli in 1552 to that of the second Pisani bank in 1584[378] or the long series of financial crashes at Naples, from that of the Genoese Ravasquez (a semi-failure to be more accurate) to the reduction (from eleven to four banks) so long discussed, if not realised, in 1580.[379]

Undoubtedly in both Naples and Venice these crashes were often caused by the untimely intervention of the public authorities. At Naples in 1552,[380] for example, the viceroy seized Ravasquez' gold reserves exchanging them for newly minted coins of lesser value. At Venice the Signoria had always compelled the banks to make loans on patriotic terms. But in both cases the secret evil was undoubtedly inflation. Everywhere it made state intervention necessary. A detail of the new banking organization of the *Casa di San Giorgio* gives food for thought: is it a vital clue or is that reading too much into it? In 1586, the bank opened to depositors its *cartulario-oro*, its gold-account; in 1606, its *cartulario-argento*; and in 1625, perhaps the most curious of all, an account for Spanish pieces of eight. What does this mean? That the depositor was credited in the currency which he had deposited and repaid in the same coin, if necessary, and therefore assured of a gold or silver guarantee against devaluation?[381] The bank was protecting itself as well as its customers from the risks of money of account, preferring the solid values of metal currency.

---

[377] G. Luzzatto, *op. cit.*, p. 188.
[378] H. Kretschmayr, *op. cit.*, III, p. 187, says 1582.
[379] Simancas, Napoles, S.P. 4, Madrid, 7th October, 1580.
[380] The Grand Commander to the King, Rome, 24th September, 1532, *Corpo dipl. port.*, VII, p. 172–173.
[381] G. Luzzatto, *op. cit.*, p. 186. In the same line of ideas, a small detail from some correspondence of a Marseillais, Gilles Hermite, to his brother, Genoa (April, 1593), Fonds Dauvergne, note 47, refers to a consignment of 300 pieces of eight sent with the master of a boat 'who must pay you in the same coin, pieces of eight or of four, and cannot pay the same sum in any other money, as we have agreed . . .'

The 'industrialists'. Other victims of the higher prices were the 'industrialists'. Some of our ignorance on their account has been dispelled by Giuseppe Parenti's book. What he has to say about Florence, and proceeds to apply to the whole of Italy during the late sixteenth and early seventeenth century, marks only a beginning but clearly a valuable one. The price rise in Florence and the industrial towns of Italy sent up the *nominal* wages of artisans. At Florence, taking the period 1520–1529 as the index 100, they fell to 99·43 in 1550–1559, rising to 162·63 in 1590–1599, and to 178·95 in 1610–1619. This increase falls far behind that of Spanish wages (100 in 1520–1529, 309·45 in 1610–1619), but is well above that of French wages (1550–1559, 100; 1610–1619, 107·4) or even English wages (1520–1529, 100; 1610–1619, 144) and is certainly much greater than that of Dutch wages. In Florence, with wage increases, that did not however improve the conditions of the workers, 'industrial' profits were curtailed – remaining stationary during the general inflation.[382] If they were higher than Spanish profits, which dropped sharply, they cannot be compared to French or English profits at the same period. So the price increase introduced an element of weakness to the very heart of Italian industrial activity. Was this the reason why it was to prove in the early seventeenth century no match for successful competition from the Low Countries, or later for equally dangerous competition from France?

States and the price rise. The states did better out of it. State finance comprised three sectors: receipts, expenditure, and debts. The third and by no means the least important was automatically alleviated by the rising tide of prices. Meanwhile, expenditure and receipts both increased at the same rate. The states all succeeded in increasing their revenues and floating with the current of inflation. They continued to spend on an impossible scale, of course, but they could draw on what were for the period extraordinary – and growing – resources.

Ehrenberg long ago warned historians – who ignored the warning – against trusting the budget estimates so frequently given by ambassadors (or indeed any others, I would be inclined to add). The word budget, with all its present day associations, is not strictly appropriate to the realities of the sixteenth century. But even inaccurate figures can provide an order of magnitude. They show that state budgets were steadily increasing. Take two Sicilian budgets a quarter of a century apart: in 1546, receipts: 340,000 *scudi*, expenditure: 166,000 *scudi*, which would leave a positive balance, but there were old debts to be paid off; in 1573 receipts were 750,194, expenditure, 211,032. But from this positive balance such a series of extraordinary expenses had to be deducted that the Spanish ministers of Sicily were obliged to borrow at 14 per cent and 16 per cent in order to balance expenditure and receipts.[383] There were similar increases

[382] G. Parenti, *op. cit.*, p. 235.
[383] M. Siri, *art. cit.*, note 367 above.

at Naples.[384] In Spain, Charles V's revenues tripled during his reign,[385] those of Philip II doubled between 1566 and 1573.[386] In 1566 they totalled 10,943,000 ducats,[387] in 1577, 13,048,000 ducats.[388] Jumping fifty years, we find that in 1619, Philip III's revenues totalled 26,000,000.[389]

In Philip II's budgets the enormous sum represented by debt, consolidated or otherwise, can be deduced and measured. In a budget of 1562,[390] whose absolute accuracy cannot be vouched for, the following items are listed: interest on *juros* of Castile, 500,000 ducats; interest on *juros* of Flanders, 300,000; of Aragon, 50,000; Sicily, 150,000; Milan, 200,000; the Atlantic islands, 30,000; in other words, a total of 1,230,000 ducats in interest, which must correspond to a nominal capital of between 12,000,000 and 24,000,000 ducats, depending on whether overall interest is calculated at 5 or 10 per cent.[391] Let us call this capital 20 million. Now in 1571–1573, the debt apparently amounted[392] to about 50 million, of which the different headings cannot be distinguished. In 1581[393] a Venetian mentions a total debt of 80,000,000; if these figures can be trusted Philip II's debt had quadrupled in twenty years.

More numerous and more accurate figures might be found among the many documents at Simancas. Once this material had been assembled, one could then calculate, from the balance sheets of the Prudent King, his total revenues, expenditure, debts, and the interest on his debts; establishing if possible the *real* budget curves. Here again, as with wages, the inflated figures are deceptive. Mario Siri in his studies of the Sicilian budgets has shown, by reducing the figures to quantities of refined metal, that there was not in fact an increase, but a reduction from one budget to another.

Descriptive studies of budgets however fail to tackle the true problems, which all require some measurement of the price increase. Broadly speaking, the states grew progressively more defenceless against the rising cost of living, hence their determination to create their own resources, to swim against the tide of rising prices. The clearest element of the history of the state in the sixteenth century is the fiscal struggle; the war of the Netherlands was not only a fight for freedom of conscience, for the defence of cherished liberties, it also represented an unsuccessful attempt to bring the Spanish state into a fruitful association with the economic fortune of the great commercial crossroads. . . .

It is a fact that Philip II's empire saw its European possessions one by

---

[384] L. Bianchini, *Della storia delle finanze del Regno di Napoli*, 1839, p. 315 ff.
[385] R. Konetzke, *op. cit.*, p. 197.
[386] R. B. Merriman, *op. cit.*, p. 443; Häbler, *op. cit.*, p. 122.
[387] R. Konetzke, *op. cit.*, p. 199.
[388] *Ibid.*
[389] J. de Salazar, *Politica Española*, 1617, p. 18.
[390] Memoria de las rentas y patrimonio del Rey de España de 1562, A.E.Esp. 234.
[391] The interest was lowered in 1563, 1608, 1621, *Nueva Recop, libr.* X, XIV.
[392] R. Merriman, *op. cit.*, IV, p. 443.
[393] E. Albèri, *op. cit.*, I, V, p. 294.

one cease to be positive sources of income. In the Netherlands, Milan, Naples and Sicily, the 'revenants bons', as they were called in France, were progressively absorbed by local needs. There remained Spain, or rather Castile. The presence of Philip II in the Peninsula meant, with the help of internal peace, until 1569, that taxpayers, including the grandees, could be brought to heel. 'His Catholic Majesty,' writes the bishop of Limoges in 1561,[394] 'is making more and more economies, desiring to provide for the future, giving orders concerning his finances and his domains; his vigilance is such that I would say any more might cause him to be accused of parsimony. . . .' In other words the king did not cease to consult his experts. He was never short of advice from them throughout his long reign, the financial aspects of which were so dramatic. I have already referred to the great assembly of Toledo and its decision of 14th November, 1560.[395] From then on the catalogue of taxes levied in Castile was constantly being lengthened and altered, by the addition of new items and the internal modification of existing taxes. The *alcabalas*, taxes on consumption for which towns contracted for fixed payments, in theory represented one-tenth of all sales. They were raised on four occasions by a hundredth, so the percentage rose to 14 per cent. Total revenue from the *alcabalas* which was 1,200,000 ducats in 1561, had reached 3,700,000 by 1574.[396] In 1577 it even had to be reduced by a million.

Naturally, the taxpayers complained. Cadiz in 1563[397] declared that all the taxes levied on commerce in the city since 1560 had ruined its trade. There were repeated protests from the Cortes, to whom however it never occurred to blame imports of American treasure for the disquieting price increases, rather seeing the cause in what was before their eyes, namely the growing monstrous burden of taxation imposed by the royal government. 'There have resulted from this,' say the Cortes of 1571,[398] 'so many charges, and the necessities of life have become so dear, that few men now can live without difficulty. . . .'

Unequally distributed, these enormous taxes were collected by the means available at the period. In other words, only a certain percentage ever reached the state coffers. Castile was certainly the empire's greatest source of taxation, through what was sometimes voluntary generosity on its part – patriotic gestures by the Cortes abound; but also because the royal will was too close at hand to be disobeyed. It is hardly to be wondered at if the Castilian economy suffered, if its industry was handicapped and the real cost of living rose even higher.[399] The contrary would be surprising. What was achieved by these efforts, by the noble gestures and the constant

[394] Madrid, 5th September, 1561, copy, B.N., Paris, fr. 16103, f° 45.
[395] See above, p. 502.
[396] R. Konetzke, *op. cit.*, p. 199.
[397] La Contaduria to Philip II, Madrid, 13th September, 1563, Simancas E° 143, f°ˢ 59 and 60.
[398] *Actas* III, p. 357.
[399] C. Pereyra, *Imperio español*, p. 27–31.

harassment? Any surplus, and this was often doubtful, was swallowed up in the general deficit of the Empire. Surpluses moreover quickly became a thing of the past: in Castile as in other parts of Europe ruled by Philip II, deficit was soon to become the rule.[400]

All national exchequers were in difficulties. In Florence, a state often considered a model of administration, the tax burden was so great that in 1582, according to contemporary accounts, it led to an exodus of population.[401] In Portugal, on the eve of the Spanish conquest, taxes of 20 per cent were levied on sales and of 50 per cent on fisheries.[402] In France the royal government at the beginning of 1587 was thinking quite simply of doubling taxation in Paris, a measure that would then be extended to all the cities in the kingdom, in spite of the terrible famine in which the country was gripped;[403] a step more associated with Turkish or Persian despots.

In these troubled times, the states had little choice as to their means. To return to Spain, the government adjusted interest rates at least three times in its own favour: in 1563, 1608, and 1621.[404] On countless occasions it postponed payment of its own debts, or as they said in the Netherlands, 'put an extension on the fairs';[405] it revalued gold in 1566. The gold *escudo* created by Charles V in 1573 was now worth 400 instead of 350 *maravedís*[406]; in 1609 it was raised again to 440[407]. And, finally, the Spanish government several times suspended payments on the short term debt: in 1557–1560, in 1575, in 1596, 1607, 1627, and 1647. It drew endlessly on the wealth of its cities, grandees, and the Church, shrinking from no exaction.

A complete study of the budgets of the sixteenth century, comparable to what is known of English receipts and expenditure during the period would provide the answer to one important question. Under the assault of prices, did Mediterranean or near-Mediterranean states suffer more than others? It seems probable, at least in the case of Spain, especially when one remembers the enormous sums of money that war cost this too-vast empire. 'War,' writes a French pamphleteer,[408] 'is extremely costly to him [Philip II], much more so than to any other prince, for example in his naval forces: he must take the greater part [of the crews] from foreign lands far away, which consumes a great quantity of his finances. And as for his wars on land, in the Low Countries for example, which is the principal, it

[400] In 1581, Philip II's revenue from the Peninsula totalled 6,500,000, his expenditure 7,000,000, E. Albèri, *op. cit.*, I, V, p. 294.
[401] A. Segre, *Storia del commercio*, I, p. 492, note 3.
[402] Jerónimo Conestaggio, *Dell'unione del regno di Portogallo alla corona di Castiglia*, Genoa, 1585, p. 14.
[403] Bº de Mendoza to Philip II, Paris, 8th January, 1587, A.N., K 1566.
[404] See above, note 268,A. Castillo, *art. cit.*, p. 14 ff. of off-print.
[405] H. Longchay, *art. cit.*, p. 945.
[406] Earl J. Hamilton, *op. cit.*, p. 62.
[407] *Ibid.*, p. 65.
[408] *Placcart et décret* . . . , 1597, B.N., Paris, Oc 241, in-12.

costs him six times as much as his enemies to wage them, for by the time he has levied a soldier in Spain and taken him to the frontier of Artois ready to fight a Frenchman, that man has already cost him 100 ducats, while the French soldier has cost his king only ten. . . .'

And from the point of view of naval equipment, which had to meet the requirements both of Atlantic warfare and Mediterranean battles, Spain was again at a disadvantage. Here too, prices were rising all the time. Tomé Cano, in his *Arte de Navegar*,[409] explains that a vessel of 500 tons which in the time of Charles V would have cost 4000 ducats is now worth 15,000; a quintal of sailcloth from Flanders which was formerly worth 2½ ducats now costs 8 ducats. I have carried merchandise, he says, from Cartagena to the Indies, at 14 ducats a ton: the asking price is 52 today, 'and even so ships do not earn as much now as they earned in the past'. With prices rising, wages, but also profits, were often much reduced, a factor that must have been partly responsible for the difficulties of Spain's Atlantic navy at the end of the sixteenth century. What was true of the great ships on the Atlantic was equally true of the narrow galleys in the Mediterranean. In 1538[410] it cost Spain 2253 ducats to fit a single galley without artillery (the hull of the galley costing about 1000 ducats). In 1582 there was some talk of Gian Andrea Doria selling his galleys at 15,000 crowns each – a figure merely thrown in the air. We do not know if it refers to galleys complete with oarsmen and artillery, but in any case the price difference is staggering.

The dwindling of American treasure. Imports of American treasure slowed down after the first and even more after the second decade of the seventeenth century. Whether symptom, consequence, or cause, this cessation marked a turning-point in world history. On the whole it would be wrong to attribute this 'event' to purely American causes as if America was the prime mover in this instance. It is said, for instance, that mining costs had risen, according to the law of diminishing returns; that larger amounts of bullion were now being kept in America, both through fraud and in order to meet local currency requirements.[411] Some of it may have been diverted by speculators from New Spain to the Far East and China on the Manila galleon.[412] And again in America the decimation of the indigenous population may have hindered and slowed down recruitment of the Indian labour necessary for silver extraction.[413]

There is some truth in all these explanations, but they have been advanced without the possible benefit of research still to be carried out not only in the archives at Seville but at Simancas and above all in Ameri-

[409] 1612, p. 43 v°.
[410] Simancas, *Guerra Antigua*, IV, f° 108 (*circa* 1538).
[411] Earl J. Hamilton, *op. cit.*, p. 36 ff for all the suggested causes.
[412] *Ibid.*, p. 37.
[413] François Chevalier, *La formation des grands domaines au Mexique. Terre et Société aux XVIe et XVIIe siècles*, 1952, p. 235.

can archives. There is no *a priori* reason to assume that a declining population cannot maintain a particular, privileged sector such as the mines; the active smuggling via the Rio de la Plata seems to have ended with the general mining recession of about 1623;[414] exports of bullion on the Manila galleon also stopped after about 1635.[415] But the basic short-coming of these explanations is obvious: they essentially concentrate on America, as if fraud, for example, was not equally commonplace on both sides of the Atlantic. Above all, such arguments neglect the economic ties which, through the Spanish Empire, associated the New World with the dynamic forces of Europe. In other words they make no reference to the overall economic situation, to the widespread recession observable in Europe after 1580, 1595, 1619–1622, before the great divide of the 1640's, and Spain's subsequent troubles in Catalonia and Portugal, later in 1647 with Naples, and the suppression in the same year of the Barlovento fleet,[416] the former protection of the West Indies.

Mention of the general economic situation means turning to prices, costs, wages, and profits. Vivero,[417] who knew the New World well, did not, in 1632, consider that the American machinery had broken down, and he was clearly mistaken; he was also mistaken in talking of an annual production of twenty-four million ducats, of which twenty were sent to Seville, but he was right when he described the mine owners as victims of the general recession, 'they are all in debt, since salt and maize are more expensive, the pay of the Indian workers has doubled and the masters have to go down on their knees to find them and to make up their contingents [*repartimentos*], and this is a labour force very little suited [*a proposito*] for work in the mines'. There were also the gaming tables and the 'bloodsuckers of the miners', the money lenders, who were eventually paying for silver with 'cloth and other merchandise on which they can make a profit, or what is worse, with wine'. But for a clearer picture, one would have to look to Spain and to Europe and tackle the problem in the widest possible context.

Devalued currency and false currency. In any case, by the middle of the seventeenth century the great age of American silver had come to an end. It was then that counterfeit money began to appear in large quantities. It had not been unknown in the sixteenth century. But by the seventeenth century, lightweight coins were entering the general circulation of the Mediterranean and were carried as far as the Levant, whereas during the previous fifty years they had been unknown in these waters.

Debased money had previously only been common in northern Europe

[414] Alice Piffer Cannabrava, *O commercio português no Rio de Plata 1580–1640*, São Paolo, 1944.
[415] Pierre Chaunu, *Les Philippines et le Pacifique des Ibériques XVIe-XVIIIe siècles*, 1960, p. 41.
[416] Albert Girard, *Le commerce français à Seville et à Cadix au temps des Habsbourgs*, 1932, p. 7.
[417] B.M., Add. 18287, PS 5633.

and in Islam, that is, on the outskirts of the Mediterranean world and even here had not appeared until fairly late. In the north, while English currency, once it had been put on a sound footing by Elizabeth, did not budge thereafter, the currency of the rebel provinces of the Netherlands underwent a series of fluctuations until the devaluation of November, 1585.[418] Even before this measure, since at least 1574, counterfeiters had been at work,[419] particularly at Liège, and in that year their coins reached the gates of Spain itself. To exchange this money by fraud for good money[420] was as good a way as any of opening a breach in the Spanish monopoly and of obtaining a share in American treasure. This traffic which was carried on in the very ports of Spain swelled to enormous proportions after the signature of the Twelve Years Truce in 1609. The Dutch then began to ship in vast quantities of small coin, a traffic previously only possible on ships from Lübeck or Hamburg, through the good offices of the English (England having made peace with Spain in 1604)[421], or even the French. This small coin, of low metallic content, arrived by the chest or barrelful. On the return journey, gold and silver coins would be concealed under salt or other merchandise. In 1607, in and around Bordeaux, four 'mints' were engaged on melting down Spanish coins obtained by every kind of subterfuge: they had only to be put in the melting-pot to bring an immediate profit of over 18 per cent.[422]

And for the time being, this was almost fair dealing. The age of relative honesty was short-lived however. From 1613 on, false *vellon* began to appear, in imitation of Spanish coins. Over two million *pesos* of this kind were manufactured a year and production increased later. According to experts this counterfeit coin could bring profits of over 500 per cent. Outside the Low Countries, similar false money was coined in Denmark, England, and Italy. *Quartillos falsos* would arrive by the boatload on the Cantabrian coast or at San Lucar de Barrameda.[423]

False money, which was already known on the Atlantic coast, later invaded the Mediterranean. In 1595 the Duchess of Piombino was allowing currency of *muy baxo quilate*[424] to be minted in her small territory. During the first decade of the seventeenth century, 'base money' reached the gates of the Levant. The corruption of the Mediterranean circulation was now complete. A Venetian report of 1611[425] indicates that in the extraordinary

---

[418] Émile Coornaert, *op. cit.*, p. 46; I have not read *Baja de la moneda*, 1591, Sim. E° 601.

[419] Philip to the Grand. Com. of Castile, 10th February, 1574, Sim. E° 561, f°ˢ 16 and 65.

[420] Sim E° 561, Moneda falsa que venja de Flandes en España.

[421] The Council of State to the King, 13th January, 1609, A.N., K 1426, A 37, no. 110.

[422] *Ibid.*, 27th November, 1607, A.N., K 1426.

[423] 26th April, 1613, A.N., K 1428, A 39, note 28; *ibid.*, K 1478, A 78, note 173; *ibid.*, K 1479, A 80, 1624; *ibid.*, K 1456, 1622; Sim. E° 628 Valor de la moneda en Flandes, 1614.

[424] B.N., Paris, Esp. 127, f°ˢ 8 v° and 9.

[425] G. Berchet, *op. cit.*, p. 133.

currency chaos at Aleppo, good coins which were usually worth 4 to 5 per cent more than the everyday currency, were fetching 30 to 35 per cent more that year. The rest of the story can be found in Paul Masson's *Le commerce français dans le Levant au XVIIe siècle.*[426]

During the period that concerns us, if Mediterranean internal trade was little affected by these extraordinary upheavals, a serious crisis was stirring in the Turkish empire, from Algiers to Egypt and Constantinople. Much has been written of the magnificent and unalterable Turkish finances. They may have been so during the long reign of Sulaimān the Magnificent (1522-1566). But in the very last year of this glorious reign, just after the unsuccessful siege of Malta, if the information contained in Hammer's book is correct,[427] in Cairo, the only Turkish 'mint' where gold coins were struck, these coins were devalued by 30 per cent. It is possible that this was an adjustment rendered necessary by the depreciation of silver. It would be interesting to know what it signified, and whether or not a devaluation in 1566, after the prolonged strain of the siege of Malta, marked the first sign of exhaustion of the Turkish empire.

By 1584 there is no room for doubt. There was a serious currency crisis.[428] The usual currency in Turkey was a small silver coin, more square than round in shape,[429] the asper (in Turkish *akce*, pronounced ak-che), made of pure silver 'not alloyed but purified', according to Pierre Belon.[430] They were assayed, says a traveller[431] by throwing them into a red hot pan. In weight they represented a quarter of a silver drachm; their value was 10 to 11 *deniers tournois*,[432] 7½ Venetian *quattrini*, 2 to 2¼ German *kreuzer*, and the equivalent of a Roman *bajocco* or the old Venetian *marchetto*.[433] The asper 'is worth as much as a Carolus is to us', writes Belon.[434] At the beginning of the century, it represented the 135th part of a sequin or *sultanin*, which was made of fine gold,[435] hardly inferior *di bontà* to the Venetian sequin, but equal and often superior to the best *ongari* of Germany.[436] On the accession of Selim I, the *sultanin* was worth 60 aspers, the official rate which does not appear to have been modified until 1584. So if there was a devaluation in 1566, it did not affect the equivalence in silver of the new style sequin. The Turkish *thaler*, a silver coin slightly inferior to the Austrian *Kronenthaler* or the Italian *escudo*, was

---

[426] P. 492, ff.
[427] *Op. cit.*, VI, p. 213.
[428] Ami Boué, *op. cit.*, III, p. 121; M. Siri, *art. cit.*, J. W. Zinkeisen, *op. cit.*, III, p. 798 ff.
[429] Philippe de Canaye, *op. cit.*, p. 42, note 4.
[430] *Op. cit.*, p. 158 v°.
[431] G. d'Aramon, *op. cit.*, p. 42.
[432] *Ibid.*
[433] Cantacuscino, *Commentaria*, II, p. 102, Luigi Bassano di Zara in Francesco Sansovino, *Dell'historia universale dell'origine et imperio de Turchi*, Bk 3, Venice, 1564, f° 43 r° and v°; S. Schweigger, *Reissbeschreibung . . .*, *op. cit.*, p. 267.
[434] *Op. cit.*, p. 158 v°.
[435] *Ibid.*
[436] Geminiano Montanari, *Zecca in consulta di stato . . .* (1683), p. 253.

worth 40 aspers, while the *Kronenthaler* and *escudo* were worth 50. These values are confirmed by the documents:[437] in 1547, 300 aspers were worth 6 crowns.[438] The Venetian *bailo* in 1564 indicates that his everyday expenses over three months amounted to 34,487 aspers, or 574 ducats and 47 aspers: which means the exchange rate was 60 to a ducat. He then made out a bill of exchange for 9,170 *scudi* and obtained an exchange rate of 50 aspers per *scudo*.[439] . . . In 1561, another *bailo* was only able to obtain 47 aspers to the *scudo* because of the tightness of money;[440] in 1580 the rate was back at 50 aspers.[441]

To complete the list of Ottoman coins we should include one more, Arabic this time, which was current in Egypt and Syria and the area between the Mediterranean, the Persian Gulf, and the Red Sea, the *maidin*, similar to the asper but containing one and a half times as much fine silver.[442] So about 40 of these *maidins* were equivalent to a sequin, and 35 to a crown or a *kronenthaler*.[443] As the English traveller Newberie said in 1583, '40 medins maketh a duckat'.[444]

The substantial devaluation of 1584,[445] followed a similar devaluation in Persia, the consequence of the enormous cost, made necessary by the war, of maintaining increased numbers of paid troops. The sultan, to whom Egypt in 1584 was supplying gold sequins at the rate of 43 *maidins*, forced the rate up to 85 in order to make his payments. So the sequin went up from 60 to 120 aspers. Since of course the sequin did not change, the aspers were made lighter and part of the refined silver was replaced by copper. By 1957, 10 or 12 aspers, instead of 4 were now being coined from one drachm of silver. After the troubles of 1590, the sequin went from 120 to 220 aspers. With the debasement of the currency, Turkey was now to experience an exact parallel of the vellon inflation in Castile, the mechanics of which and the havoc it caused between 1600 and 1650 have been described by Hamilton.[446] But the crisis, which was to last until the middle of the seventeenth century, had begun twenty years earlier. It was difficult to bring under control. Towards 1625–1630, further inflation occurred: the sequin reached 240 aspers, the *thaler* 120; an authoritarian devaluation of 50 per cent brought the sequin down in 1642 to 151–157 aspers (not 120), but inflation began again after 1561 and the long war of Candia against Venice brought chaos. If in 1660 the sequin was

[437] J. W. Zinkeisen, *op. cit.*, III, p. 800.
[438] J. von Hammer, *op. cit.*, VI, p. 5.
[439] Daniel Badoer to the Doge, Pera, 21st April, 1564, A.d.S., Venice, Senato Secreta, Cost. Filza 4/D.
[440] H. Ferro to the Doge, Pera, 6th May, 1561, A.d.S. Venice, Senato Secreta . . . 3/C.
[441] Undated document (1577) Simancas E° 1147, copy.
[442] Constantinople, 16th March, 1580, Simancas E° 1337.
[443] J. W. Zinkeisen, III, p. 800.
[444] R. Hakluyt, *op. cit.*, II, p. 247.
[445] See Part III, Chapter VI, section 1.
[446] *Op. cit.*, p. 211 ff.

still worth 240 aspers in Serbia, it was quoted at 310 aspers at Sofia in 1663.[447]

These devaluations had a prodigious effect on the economic health of the empire, where the asper did duty both as a real money and a money of account.[448] Such were the most obvious aspects of Turkish currency upheavals. There were others, notably the policy of base currency practised in Algiers, imposed by necessity. Spanish gold and silver were at a premium on the market there. It was a way of attracting and capturing the indispensable foreign currency. There was even a sort of sliding scale, and in 1580, Djafar Pasha, finding the exchange rate insufficient, raised the Spanish crown from 125 Algiers aspers to 130.[449] It is possible, as the Spanish scholar Manuel Gallardo y Victor suggested, that this devaluation affected the ransoming of Cervantes in 1580.[450] But before the devaluation of the Turkish sequin at Constantinople, when it was still being quoted at 66 Turkish aspers, it was worth 150 at Algiers, which indicates the astonishingly high store set by the gold coinage of the sultans, attracted to Algiers in the same way as Spanish crowns.[451] The latter, if our calculations are correct, were worth 30 per cent more than face value on the Algerian exchanges.

Three ages of metal. The reader will forgive me for stopping at this point. The diagrams and graphs complete a description already too long, although much abridged, and we shall have further cause to return to the difficult problems of the general economic situation. A fairly clear outline has nevertheless already emerged. Historians are now aware of three metallic ages following one upon the other: the age of Sudanese gold; the age of silver and gold from America; and the age of vellon or counterfeit currency, whether officially sanctioned or not, making its first timid appearance at the end of the sixteenth century, then swamping circulation in the first decades of the seventeenth. An over-simplified schema certainly; for these ages did not succeed one another in an orderly procession – there were overlaps, discrepancies, and periods of confusion which have yet of course to be charted and explained.

The age of gold: all payments were preferably made in gold coin. In 1503, Bayard seized a paymaster of the Spanish army near Barletta. 'When they arrived,' relates the Loyal Servant, 'their purses were opened and fine ducats found' – yet another piece of confirmation.[452] Then we find the king of France paying his soldiers (in 1524) 'with gold from Spain'.[453] Every battle in the early days of the conflict between Habsburgs

[447] According to B. Vinaver, 'La crise monétaire turque 1575–1650' in *Publications historiques de l'Académie des Sciences de Belgrade*, 1958.

[448] According to the unpublished thesis by Ali Sahili Oglu on Turkish minted currencies, French translation in preparation.

[449] D. de Haëdo, *op. cit.*, p. 24 v°.

[450] *Memoria escrita sobre el rescate de Cervantes . . .*, Cadiz, 1876, 8°, 23 p.

[451] R. Hakluyt, *op. cit.*, II, p. 176.   [452] *Le Loyal Serviteur, op. cit.*, p. 34.

[453] R. B. Merriman, *The Rise of the Spanish Empire*, vol. III, p. 207.

and Valois was fought with pieces of gold. A single messenger could carry enough money to make crucial payments. In May, 1526, Charles V's ambassador was anxious: 'four horsemen carrying the Pope's money' had passed through Mirandola; he had good cause for alarm.

Later, during the long reign of silver (from perhaps 1550 to 1650 or 1680) the transport of money became more obvious, for silver was a conspicuous traveller, requiring carts, ships, pack animals, not to mention the escort – at least fifty arquebusiers for the transport of silver from Genoa to Flanders in 1551.[454] The movement of large sums in gold was easily concealed and, apart from the parties involved, no one need be aware of them. But when it was learned in September, 1586, that Philip II had sent 100,000 gold crowns to Italy, there was much speculation as to the internal necessity that had obliged him to take this unusual step. For as a rule gold did not leave the Peninsula.[455] Being rare, it was highly valued and every time it was involved in a transaction, it dictated its own lordly terms. The masters of the mints and other experts covered many sheets of paper explaining to anyone who would pay attention that all would be well if only the gold mark were worth 12 marks of silver, as traditional wisdom decreed, but at Venice where gold was always being revalued, precise calculations show that the old ratio was out of date; as was explained without enthusiasm by the officials of the Venetian Zecca in November 1593.[456] A mark of gold, they explained, is worth 674 *lire*, 9 *soldi*, 12 marks of silver 633 *lire*, 16 *soldi*, in other words an advantage of gold over silver of 40 *lire*, 13 *soldi*, a slight but indisputable lead.

Years passed and European currency entered the age of copper. Its heyday coincided with the development of the copper mines in Hungary, Saxony, Germany, Sweden, and Japan. Portugal would have been flooded with copper coin through her proximity to Spain where the tide of inflation was rising, but Portugal could always pass it on to the Indies. Even during these disastrous years Portugal was always short of copper: indeed the third metal was so highly valued there that in 1622, not 12 but 13 reals had to be given for a ducat paid in small copper coins.[457]

But gold was soon to show its face again. Dispatched from Brazil, it reappeared at the end of the seventeenth century in Lisbon, England, Europe. . . . The Mediterranean too had its share, but was not to be the centre of gold inflation, as it had for so long been the centre of silver inflation.

[454] Simancas E° 504, 17th December, 1551.
[455] A.d.S., Venice, Senato Dispacci Spagna, 27th September, 1586.
[456] Mueso Correr, Donà delle Rose, 161, 26th November, 1593.
[457] V. Magalhães Godinho, *op. cit.*, typescript, p. 422.

CHAPTER III

Economies: Trade and Transport

My intention in this chapter is not to describe Mediterranean trade in all its complexity, but to discover a general pattern. I have therefore decided to consider three different problems: the pepper crisis, the wheat crisis, and the invasion of the Mediterranean by ships from the Atlantic. Between them these problems cover every dimension of the economic life of the sea: taken together they give some idea of its vast compass: stretching on one side to the Indian Ocean, and on the other to the Atlantic and the Mediterraneans of the north – the Channel, the North Sea, and the Baltic.

I. THE PEPPER TRADE

The circumnavigation of the Cape of Good Hope did not strike an immediate death-blow to the Mediterranean spice trade, as German historians[1] were the first to point out; it could not escape their attention that Germany continued to receive spices and pepper from Venice, and therefore that the Portuguese could not have established a permanent monopoly in this precious traffic.

But there is no doubt that news of the Portuguese achievement led to a serious crisis in Venice, and a wave of gloomy prophecies. The consequences of the Portuguese discoveries were envisaged with alarm; disaster appeared irremediable. To the city of St. Mark, the loss of the spice trade 'would be like the loss of milk to a new-born babe', wrote Girolamo Priuli in his journal in July, 1501.[2] Prices at once began to fluctuate wildly and countless difficulties arose, particularly after the king of Portugal, Dom Manuel, had fixed an official price for pepper in 1504 and two years later turned the 'spicery' concentrated at Lisbon into a Crown monopoly.[3] In 1504 the Venetian galleys found no spices at Alexandria or Beirut.[4]

[1] J. Kulischer, op. cit., II, p. 235; Johann-Ferdinand Roth, Geschichte des Nürnberger Handels, Leipzig, 1800–1802, I, p. 252; Carl Brinkmann, 'Der Beginn der neueren Handelsgeschichte', in Historische Zeitschrift, 1914; A. Schulte, op. cit., II, p. 117 ff; W. Heyd, op. cit., II, p. 525–526; J. Falke, Oberdeutschlands Handelsbeziehungen zu Südeuropa im Anfang des 16. Jahr., p. 610.
[2] Quoted by H. Kretschmayr, Geschichte von Venedig, II, p. 473.
[3] A. Schulte, op. cit., p. 118.
[4] According to Sanudo, no spices were loaded by the Venetians at Beirut and Alexandria because of the war between Turkey and Venice in 1499 and 1500, and there were none in 1504 or 1506. On the lack of spices in 1506, see J. Mazzei, op. cit., p. 41. As early as 1502, the galleys found only 4 bales of pepper at Beirut, according to W. Heyd, A. Fanfani, Storia del lavoro . . ., p. 38. On the reduced volume of the Venetian spice trade in 1512, A Fanfani, op. cit., p. 39. These difficult problems have usually been

It was not long before the new spice-dealers had captured part of the European market. They had little difficulty in promoting their products on the Atlantic coast of the continent. They reached the Netherlands in 1501[5] and England in January, 1504 when five Portuguese vessels docked at Falmouth, carrying 380 tons of pepper and spices from Calicut.[6] They also found markets in northern and southern Germany, where the old firm of Anton Welser and Konrad Vöhlin of Augsburg turned in 1503 towards the rising sun of Lisbon;[7] where the *Magna Societas* of Ravensburg decided in 1507 to buy pepper and spices henceforward at Antwerp, the northern centre of the Portuguese trade;[8] where Viennese merchants in 1512–1513, were complaining that supplies of pepper and spices from Venice were inadequate and asking the Emperor to authorize foreign merchants to bring spices from Antwerp, Frankfurt, or Nuremberg.[9] The new suppliers were successful too in western France and in Castile, where in 1524, according to an eyewitness, Portuguese pepper was on sale at Medina del Campo.[10] Nor can there be any doubt that this same pepper very soon penetrated the Mediterranean, where Portuguese sailing vessels played an important role, perhaps reaching Genoa as early as 1503: Venice closed her mainland frontiers in June of that year[11] to products coming from Genoa (and special mention was made of cloth of gold or silver, wool, *spices*, and sugar) or any other foreign place. She obliged the towns of the Terraferma to come to Venice for all their purchases. In order to increase imports of pepper and spices from the Levant, she granted permission in May 1514,[12] for spices to be transported in any vessel, instead of, as in the past, exclusively in the *galere da mercato* which now had to face stiff competition;[13] she also waived customs duties on their entry to Venice. Despite these measures, the Signoria was obliged in the following year, 1515, to send to Lisbon to replenish her own stocks.[14] In 1527 the Venetian Senate proposed to the king of Portugal, John III, that the sales contract for all pepper imported to Lisbon be farmed out to Venice, after allowing for Portuguese home consumption. The project never came to

---

unsatisfactorily posed and arbitrarily solved. In this paragraph I have used information, from the table drawn up by V. Magalhães Godinho, 'Le repli vénitien et égyptien de la route du Cap', in *Hommage à Lucien Febvre*, II, 1953, p. 287 ff.

[5] E. Prestage, *Portuguese Pioneers*, London, 1933, p. 295.

[6] Tawney and Power, *Tudor Economic Documents*, II, p. 19, quoted by L. F. Salzman, *English Trade in the Middle Ages*, Oxford, 1931, p. 445–446; Dr. Sottas, *op. cit.*, p. 135.

[7] A. Schulte, *op. cit.*, II, p. 118.

[8] *Ibid.*, I, p. 279.

[9] J. Kulischer, *op. cit.*, II, p. 234.

[10] A. Navagero, *op. cit.*, p. 36.

[11] A.d.S., Venice, *Cinque Savii alla Mercanzia*, Busta 2, 20th June, 1503.

[12] A.d.S., Venice, Senato Mar 18, 3rd May, 1514.

[13] Dr. Sottas, *op. cit.*, p. 136. In 1524, the state galleys' monopoly was reimposed for a further ten years, then permanently abolished.

[14] W. Heyd, *op. cit.*, I, p. 531, 538; Goris, *op. cit.*, p. 195 ff; J. Kulischer, *op. cit.*, II, p. 234.

anything. It is an indication of Venice's position in 1527 and proof of the great headway made by the Lisbon market.[15]

Mediterranean revenge: the prosperity of the Red Sea after 1550. At what point did the tide turn – for there is no doubt that turn it did – in favour of Venice and the Mediterranean?[16] It is hard to say. One factor was no doubt the movement of prices after the 1540s, which may be presumed to have disturbed the prosperous trade of Lisbon; and another the reputedly inferior quality of Portuguese commodities, whose aroma, according to connoisseurs, was diminished by the long sea voyage. The rumour, spread by Venice, was not without foundation; the same allegation appears in a Spanish document of 1574 otherwise hostile to Venice.[17] Mediterranean trade, with its intermediary Arab connections, was probably able by paying higher prices, to reserve superior products for itself. The Portuguese may have been going too far, when they insisted on offering extremely low purchasing prices in Asia.[18] True they had to meet the expenses of the long voyage, frequent loss of ships and deficits on the cargoes themselves, which were often damaged en route. The Mediterranean circuit, on the contrary, with its many intermediary stations along routes that were both shorter and more familiar, held less risk. For the Venetians the chief hazard was the sea voyage from Egypt and this was compensated by a high rate of return, the result of astonishing price differences between East and West. 'They make a profit,' noted Thénaud in 1512, 'of a hundred per cent or more, on merchandise which is of little value here.'[19] Even when pepper was in short supply (the only commodity that gave rise to a massive trade and the one the Portuguese were the most anxious to control), it was still possible to trade in luxury spices, drugs, and other produce of the East. For their part, eastern merchants urgently needed precious metals: gold from Egypt or silver from the West, which only reached the Indian Ocean in return for the spices and other goods travelling along the routes to the Mediterranean. India and the Far East welcomed coral and saffron from the Mediterranean, opium from Egypt, woollen cloth from the West, quick silver, madder from the Red Sea. These established trades were maintained by a series of powerful, organized companies all round the Indian Ocean, which the Portuguese arrival had disturbed but not eliminated; they were able to react fairly quickly.

Since Mediterranean trade with the East had not lost any of its attrac-

---

[15] Visconde de Soveral, *Apontamentos sobre as antiguas replaçoes politicas e commerciaes do Portugal com a Republica de Veneza*, Lisbon, 1893, p. 6, 7.

[16] According to V. Magalhães Godinho, there was a revival at least as early as 1514; there were semi-stoppages in 1517, 1519, 1523, 1529; good cargoes in 1531.

[17] Simancas E° 564, f° 10.

[18] R. Hakluyt, *op. cit.*, II, p. 223–224. Relation of Lorenzo Tiepolo, 1554, p. 21.

[19] Quoted by G. Atkinson, *op. cit.*, p. 131; Père Jean Thénaud, *Le voyage . . .*, undated, B.N., Rés. O², f° 998. See also Samuele Romanin, *Storia doc. di Venezia*, VI, p. 23 (1536); A.d.S., Venice, *Cinque Savii alla Mercanzia*, Busta 27, 26th January, 1536.

tions to the intermediaries, the only way to stop it would have been by force, in other words, a close guard over the sources of supply. The Portuguese succeeded in doing so several times, indeed whenever they tried, in the early days of their presence, for instance, when they dealt a blow to the privileged Red Sea[20] route, and even later. During the winter of 1545–1546, off the Malabar coast, 'the Portuguese squadron patrolled so effectively that all clandestine exports of pepper were prevented',[21] or at any rate smuggling was considerably reduced. But this close guard was maintained only for a while and Portuguese vigilance lapsed of its own accord. The Portuguese presence, which had spread quickly over a large area, throughout the Indian Ocean and beyond, as much the result of indispensable interregional traffic as of a spirit of adventure or gain, had culminated in the creation of an immense and fragile empire. Portugal was not rich enough to maintain this vast complex with its costly apparatus of fortresses, squadrons, and officials. The empire had to be self-supporting.

This lack of means very quickly turned the Portuguese into customs officials, but customs are profitable only when there is a plentiful flow of trade. The circumstances offered ample opportunity for smuggling, or what we may call smuggling and which was in fact necessity: a necessity first because it was impossible to occupy the vital crossroads of Hormuz in 1506 and immediately close it to all traffic. And secondly because the Turks were moving into Syria (1516), Egypt (1517), and Iraq (1534). Against them the Portuguese had to enlist the support of Persia, and therefore to maintain essential communications between India and Persia, to safeguard as far as possible the latter's trade with Syria and the Mediterranean. It was much more than a simple matter of corruption among the local Portuguese officials, greedy for gain and deaf to the distant commands of their government. Corruption certainly existed but was far from being the root of the trouble.

Such prudent and realistic policies did not however triumph overnight. It took time for the Portuguese Empire to become firmly established, time too for the Turkish Empire to take the measure of its weaknesses, limitations and what could be termed reasonable interests in the Indian Ocean, to abandon its original project of concentrating all the trade of the Levant at Constantinople, then to contemplate a serious advance southwards and eastwards, which was afterwards to all practical purposes abandoned, the Portuguese meanwhile doing everything within their means to avoid being the target of such a formidable enemy. The Turks were to wait another ten years before launching another offensive from occupied Egypt. It was not until 1529 that work began on a canal between the Nile and the Red Sea, but the preparations were interrupted by the need to face the enemy in the Mediterranean: 1532 was the year of Coron.[22] A further interval of

[20] See above, p. 181 ff.
[21] V. Magalhães Godinho raises these problems again in *Os descobrimentos e a economia mundial*, II, 1963, p. 487 ff.
[22] See R. B. Merriman, *op. cit.*, III, p. 299.

six years elapsed before Sulaimān Pasha led a naval expedition that captured Aden in 1538 but failed to take Diu in the same year.[23] In 1542,[24] the Portuguese only just managed to hold Christian Ethiopia; in 1546,[25] Diu, their fortress on the Gujarat peninsula, was once more besieged and only saved by a miracle. From every eastern horizon, even distant Sumatra, a constant stream of ambassadors arrived at Constantinople to solicit the sultan's aid against the Portuguese, bringing him the rarest gifts: brightly coloured parrots, spices, perfumes, balms, black slaves, and eunuchs.[26] But in 1551, at the mouth of the Red Sea, there was a fresh defeat – this time of the galleys commanded by Pīrī Re'īs;[27] in 1553, Sidi ʿAlī, the poet of the *Mirror of Lands*, was defeated at the entrance to the Persian Gulf.[28] However the following years saw a détente in relations between Turkey and Portugal and this détente favoured Mediterranean trade.

The old spice route was indeed once again busy and prosperous by the middle of the century. From then on Mediterranean pepper began to make inroads in the western half of the sea, pushing the pepper sold by the merchant-king of Lisbon further towards the Atlantic, but without there being any clear demarcation line. Mediterranean pepper had been arriving regularly at Antwerp, for instance, during the first half of the sixteenth century,[29] perhaps even later. In 1510 a ship sailed directly from Alexandria to Antwerp.[30] In 1540 Mediterranean pepper was influencing prices on the Scheldt market. In the same year, by trying to operate a pepper blockade against France,[31] the Iberians assisted the rival trade of Marseilles, which François I seemed anxious to protect, since he refused Portuguese proposals and promises of spices in May, 1541 wishing to give satisfaction, says a Venetian, *al Signor Turco*, and not wishing to aid Flanders, 'where Antwerp would, it seems, have become the first city of the world'.[32] In any case, a register of exports from Marseilles in 1543 indicates that pepper was being sent to Lyons – and probably beyond – as well as towards Toulouse.[33] By 1565 it had reached Rouen and Toulouse where it competed with pepper from Lisbon, bought at Bordeaux.[34] Towards mid-century,

[23] A. B. de Bragança Pereira, *Os Portugueses em Diu*, p. 2, 83 ff. N. Iorga, *op. cit.*, II, p. 365; A. S. de Souza, *Historia de Portugal*, Barcelona, 1929, p. 129; F. de Andrada, *O primeiro cerco que os Turcos puzerão na fortaleza de Dio, nas partes de India*, Coimbra, 1589.
[24] *Corpo diplomatico port.*, VI, p. 70–71.
[25] A. B. de Bragança Pereira, *op. cit.*, p. 2; J. Corte Real, *Successos do segundo cerco de Dio*, Lisbon, 1574; J. Tevins, *Commentarius de rebus in India apud Dium gestis anno MDXLVI*, Coimbra, 1548.
[26] 1547, J. von Hammer, *op. cit.*, VI, p. 7.
[27] *Ibid.*, p. 184–186.
[28] *Ibid.*, p. 186.
[29] J. Denucé, *L'Afrique et Anvers*, p. 71; M. Sanudo, *op. cit.*, LVIII, col. 678, September, 1533.
[30] J. Denucé, *op. cit.*, p. 71.
[31] Prohibicion de introducir especeria en Francia, Simancas Eº 497 and 498.
[32] Donato to the Doge, Amboise, 2nd May, 1541, B.N., Paris, Ital., 1715, copy.
[33] Archives of Bouches-du-Rhône, Amirauté de Marseille, IX *ter*.
[34] Paul Masson, *Les Compagnies du Corail*, 1908, p. 123–125.

French and English merchants were exchanging pepper, notably at Rouen, La Rochelle, and Bordeaux.[35] These must have been different products obtained from both sources. Circumstances favoured first one then the other. In 1559, for instance, the introduction of an *ad valorem* customs duty of 10 per cent discriminated against Portuguese pepper on the Castile market but, no doubt because of its proximity, this pepper does not seem to have vanished from the Peninsula.[36] Imports to Leghorn at the end of the century leave the same impression as the Anglo-French exchanges, that is that the two kinds of pepper were different commodities that competed with but did not exclude each other. In fact there was a single European pepper market[37] until the end of the sixteenth century and even later. Take for instance the chance remark of a Spanish merchant in Florence (29th November, 1591): at the news that the *naos de Yndias* are not coming to Lisbon that year, spices have gone up in price. 'Only pepper has remained the same,' he notes, 'since large supplies have arrived at Venice from the Levant.'[38]

What is quite clear is that the Mediterranean had recaptured a large portion of the pepper trade, indeed the lion's share. Trade with the Levant was flourishing, supplied by numerous caravans, some from the Persian Gulf, others from the Red Sea. And at the end of these routes, looking on to the Mediterranean, two double cities owed their prosperity to this trade: to the north, Aleppo and the active quays of Tripoli, to the south, Cairo and its port Alexandria, the latter as if drained of its substance by the over-sized capital. In the west the revival of the spice trade brought most benefit to the Venetians, the grand masters of trade, alongside whom the merchants of Marseilles and Ragusa cut a very modest figure. Venetian merchants even, rather curiously, moved inland, from Alexandria to Cairo in 1552[39] and from Damascus (now in decline and where moreover personal intrigue, *garbugli*, had brought the affairs of the Venetian colony to a sorry state)[40] to Aleppo, the terminus of the caravan routes from Babylonia. In Egypt the move was motivated by the desire to dispense with intermediaries, the Jewish wholesalers and traders of Cairo, opulent rivals who if left unchallenged would not be content with undisputed command of trade in the great caravan cities but would also seek to gain control of the seaborne traffic with Christian countries. In fact European merchants were usually obliged to work in collaboration with them.[41] Apart from these questions of local organization, the arrival of the Vene-

---

[35] P. Boissonade, 'France et Angleterre au XVIe siècle', *art. cit.*, p. 36.
[36] R. B. Merriman, *op. cit.*, IV, p. 441.
[37] Mediceo 2080 and also papers in Guicciardini Corsi archives.
[38] Baltasar Suárez to Simón Ruiz, Archivo Ruiz, Valladolid, 29th November, 1591.
[39] Wilken, p. 44, quoted by F. C. Lane, 'The Mediterranean Spice Trade' in *American Historical Review*, XLV, 1940, p. 582.
[40] Not to mention the Turco-Venetian War of 1538–1540. On the difficulties in Syria and Damascus, A.d.S., Venice, *Cinque Savii*, Busta 27, 23rd January, 1543, July 1543, 14th June, 1544, 7th December, 1548, 19th December, 1548.
[41] Lorenzo Tiepolo, *Relatione . . .*, (1554), published by Cicogna, p. 15–16.

tian merchants in Cairo and Aleppo signified the prosperity of these inland markets, of their capitalists, their caravan traffic and at the other end of the caravan routes, efficient buying by Arab merchants in India and the East Indies. The Mediterranean was recapturing the treasures of the Indian Ocean.

Routes taken by the Levant trade. Any number of documents will testify to this revival. But since the opposite view has generally been accepted, let me warn that some details can be misleading. To avoid confusion it must be realized that the two routes leading to Cairo and Aleppo had always been in competition. When one was closed, the other opened. Aleppo, during these years when trade was picking up again, had the disadvantage of being both on the road to Persia – particularly during the war of 1548–1555 – and on the route to Hormuz, the route to the Portuguese war. During the war between Turkey and Portugal (1560–1563) the caravans from Basra were very small.[42] It is not surprising then that Aleppo should be thriving one day,[43] and the next suffering from extraordinary price increases.[44] In July, 1557, Christofano Allegretti, a Ragusan factor, declared himself discouraged and decided to leave for Egypt: 'I do not believe this land of Aleppo has ever been as empty of merchandise, for there is nothing to be found but soap and ashes [*cenere*]. Gall-nuts cost about 13 to 14 ducats and since four French ships have arrived [at Tripoli], I do not doubt that the prices will reach the sky. For there are more than eight French ships here at the moment, ruining everyone by buying goods at any price.'[45] Two years earlier, in 1555, perhaps following the end of the Turco-Persian wars, many Moorish and Venetian merchants of Aleppo 'son passati in le Indie', went to the Indies.[46] Of course not all merchants followed the example of our Ragusan or these travellers and moved right away. In 1560, when Lorenzo Tiepolo[47] arrived at Aleppo, he was met by 250 merchants on horseback. In November, 1563 the Venetian *bailo* at Pera announced that the *galee grosse* had left Syria for Venice.[48] A Venetian report of the previous year indicates that Aleppo employed 5000 workers in the weaving industry.[49] Throughout the crises, the city remained a great industrial and commercial centre. And Aleppo's difficulties were personal. They did not always concern the whole of the eastern Mediterranean.

In particular they did not concern the Red Sea, which was often the only

[42] F. C. Lane, *art. cit.*, p. 580.
[43] For example in 1556, 1563–1564.
[44] For example in 1562, L. Tiepolo, *Relatione* . . . p. 40.
[45] Letter to Gozze and Andrea di Catharo at Messina, Tripoli in Syria, 15th September, 1557, Ragusa Archives, D. di Canc., f°s 37 ff.
[46] A.d.S., Venice, Relazioni, B. 31, Aleppo, 10th July 1557, G. Bª Basadona, consul of Syria, to the Signoria at Venice.
[47] L. Tiepolo, *op. cit.*, p. 30.
[48] A.d.S., Venice, Senato Secreta, Costant. Filza 4/D.
[49] L. Tiepolo, *op. cit.*, p. 39.

route – but what an important one – taken by the Far East trades. 'This Red Sea,' wrote Pierre Belon, who saw its shores towards the middle of the century,[50] 'is, if not a narrow channel, certainly no wider than the Seine between Harfleur and Honfleur, where one can navigate only with difficulty and much danger, for the rocks are very frequent.' A flotilla of little sailing vessels operated there, curious ships whose 'planks were held together, not with nails, but with cords made of cocoa-nut fibre, while the hull was caulked with the fibres of date-palms, soaked in fish oil'.[51] There were also great *houlques* and galleys,[52] the latter transported in pieces from Cairo to Suez, a bad and 'discommodious' port,[53] set among sandbanks and poorly protected from the winds.[54] Big ships and small, sailing by Aden or by the Abyssinian coast carried north the treasures of the Indies, of Sumatra and the Moluccas as well as pilgrims from all over Asiatic Islam. The need to take shelter during the sometimes catastrophic storms multiplied the number of ports along these difficult coasts: Suakin, Aden, Jiddah – the port for Mecca – Tor, the rival of Suez. It was at Jiddah, 'Juda' or even 'Ziden' as the texts call it, that the greatest number of long-distance ships called. And this brought to the port near Mecca enormous concourses of caravans, of up to 20,000 people and 300,000 animals at a time. Meat was never scarce in the holy city if wheat was often hard to come by.[55] From Jiddah ships and boats sailed to Tor, the starting-point for the caravans that took nine or ten days to reach Cairo.[56] Depending on the point of departure of the great shipping convoys of the Indian Ocean: Sumatra, Cambay (at the mouth of the Indus region), the Malabar coast, Calicut, Bul, Cannanore, and other leeward ports, spices reached the Red Sea in May or November every year.[57]

So the difficult gateway to the Red Sea stood wide open, and a huge volume of trade flowed through. The presence of costly porcelain, surely from China, although Belon refuses to believe that they really came from the far-off 'Indies', is proof enough of this,[58] for fragile porcelain would only be shipped along with a stream of other merchandise. As for spices, of which pepper was by far the most important, there was an annual flow of 20,000 to 40,000 light quintals[59] between 1554 and 1564. In 1554, the Venetians alone took 600 *colli*[60] of spices, about 6000 quintals, from Alexandria. Now the Venetians controlled only a part, half at most, of the Alexandrian trade, and to western trade must be added consump-

[50] Pierre Belon, *op. cit.*, p. 124.
[51] Sonia E. Howe, *In quest of spices*, London, 1946, p. 99.
[52] Pierre Belon, *op. cit.*, p. 131.
[53] *Ibid.*, p. 132 v°.
[54] *Ibid.*, p. 120.
[55] R. Hakluyt, *op. cit.*, II, p. 207–208, about 1586.
[56] L. Tiepolo, *op. cit.*, p. 21; D. Barbarigo, in E. Albèri, *op. cit.*, III, II, p. 3–4.
[57] *Ibid.*, p. 21.
[58] Pierre Belon, *op. cit.*, p. 134.
[59] About 50 kg (112 lbs.). All weights in this section are expressed in light (Portuguese) quintals.
[60] L. Tiepolo, *op. cit.*, p. 20.

tion of spices in the East, which was always considerable. Between 1560 and 1564 a copy of consular documents from Cairo gives an annual figure of 12,000 quintals for Venetian purchases alone,[61] a figure as high as in the old days before Vasco da Gama, and which tallies with the estimates of the Portuguese ambassador at Rome, who guessed that the total volume of the Alexandrian spice trade was 40,000 quintals.[62] In October 1564, a spy in the pay of Portugal estimated this traffic at 30,000 quintals of which 25,000 (2,800,000 lb. Eng.) were pepper[63] and the Venetian consul at Cairo, in May 1565 refers to 20,000 quintals of pepper unloaded at Jiddah;[64] and this was before the convoys from Gujarat, Calicut, and elsewhere (which usually docked in winter) had arrived. In the previous August twenty-three ships were unloading spices at Jiddah.[65] So once again, we find a figure of approximately 30,000 to 40,000 quintals for the Egyptian trade alone, that is not counting what came through Syria.

Let us say 30,000 or 40,000, then, a figure that has no claim to statistical value but which supports the conclusion that quite as much pepper and spice was passing through the Red Sea as there ever had in the past, a volume at least equal, and Frederic Lane thinks superior, to that arriving at Lisbon at the same period.[66] In short, enormous quantities of spices were reaching the Mediterranean. They represented 'millions in gold', as contemporaries said. And along with the pepper and spices came medicinal drugs such as opium, balm of mithridate, Lemnian earth, silk, perfumes, objects of decoration, the *pierres de besouard*, bezoar stones or antelope's tears mentioned by Belon,[67] precious stones, pearls. This was of course a luxury trade – but have not luxuries always been what instinctively 'seems the most necessary to man?'[68] Spices still dominated world trade in the seventeenth if not the eighteenth century.[69]

From then on big ships, with money or easily-exchanged goods in their holds hastened to Alexandria and Syria. In January, 1552 three Venetian ships sailed into Tripoli with 25,000 *doblas* and over 100,000 crowns on board. Rumours of such sums of money alerted the Portuguese ambassador in Rome.[70] He was well aware of the use to which it would be put. In the spring of 1554, a Ragusan ship was sighted at Alexandria.[71] In the

[61] F. C. Lane, *art. cit.*, p. 581.
[62] *Corp. dipl. port.*, IX, p. 110–111; F. de Almeida, *op. cit.*, III, p. 562; F. C. Lane, *art. cit.*, p. 581.
[63] F. C. Lane, *op. cit.*, p. 586.
[64] *Ibid.*,
[65] *Ibid.*
[66] R. Ehrenberg, *op. cit.*, I, p. 14, mentions a figure of 10,127 bales of pepper arriving at Lisbon for the Affaitati, who farmed the pepper contract.
[67] E. Charrière, *op. cit.*, II, p. 776 and note; Pierre Belon, *op. cit.*, p. 158 v°.
[68] Ernest Babelon, *Les origines de la monnaie considérées au point de vue économique et historique*, 1897, p. 248, quoted by Alfred Pose, *La Monnaie et ses institutions*, 1942, I, p. 4–5.
[69] J. Kulischer, *op. cit.*, II, p. 258.
[70] 23rd January, 1552, *Corp. dipl. port.*, VII, p. 108.
[71] L. Tiepolo to the Doge, Cairo, Collegio Secreta, Busta 31.

autumn of 1559 a Ragusan ship, one from Chios, and two Venetian, all laden with spices, were seized by the 'captain' of Alexandria.[72] One of them, the *Contarina*, returned to Venice in January laden with spices and pepper.[73] We know more or less what these vessels carried from the cargo of the *Crose*, a Venetian sailing ship of 540 tons, which in 1561 transported to the Levant copper in bars, manufactured copper, woollen cloth, silk cloth, kerseys, caps, coral, amber, various trinkets, paper, and coin (*contadi*). On the return journey, she brought back pepper, ginger of various origins, cinnamon, nutmeg, cloves, frankincense, gum Arabic, sugar, sandalwood, and a host of other exotic goods.[74]

Anxiety soon gripped Lisbon, where both true and false reports abounded. In the same year, 1561, it was learned that the Turks, as if the natural flow of traffic into their ports was not sufficient, had seized about twenty thousand quintals of Portuguese pepper on the Indian Ocean and sent them to Alexandria.[75] It was even rumoured that the viceroy of the Portuguese Indies had rebelled against his sovereign and was sending the pepper of the royal fleets to Egypt.[76] From the reports he received from his informers, the Portuguese ambassador at Rome, who was experienced in such matters, concluded in November 1560, that with such enormous quantities of pepper and spice arriving at Alexandria it was hardly surprising that so little reached Lisbon.[77] The French ambassador in Portugal, Jean Nicot, openly rejoiced in April, 1561:[78] 'If this flow of spices through the Red Sea is restored,' he writes, 'the stores of the King of Portugal will be much reduced, which is the thing he fears most and to prevent which his arms have been employed so long.'

There was now a real shortage of pepper in the countries served by the Portuguese spice trade. An extreme case perhaps was the English attempt to push forward from Moscow to the Caspian Sea and on to Persia. Jenkinson's first voyage took place in 1561.[79] As for France, seeing the impossibility of forcing entry to the Portuguese 'magazine', which remained firmly closed to them,[80] Nicot advised his countrymen to go to the coast of Guinea in search of malaguetta, the pepper substitute that continued to find buyers for some time, particularly in Antwerp.[81] The Fuggers after 1559 dispatched a factor to Alexandria and organized a trade route via Fiume and Ragusa.[82] In Spain, the price of spices rose sharply. After

[72] 14th November, 1559, Senato Secreta, Cost. Filza 2/A, f° 190 v°.
[73] G. Hernandez to Philip II, Venice, 3rd January, 1560, Simancas E° 1324, f° 27.
[74] F. C. Lane, *art. cit.*, p. 581–583.
[75] Jean Nicot, *Sa correspondance diplomatique*, pub. by Ed. Falgairolle, 1897, 12th April, 1561, p. 127.
[76] F. C. Lane, *art. cit.*, p. 585.
[77] *Corp. dipl. port.*, VII, p. 215, 238, 258, 277; VIII, p. 79, 97, 115, 250, 297, 327; IX, p. 110–111, quoted by F. C. Lane, *art. cit.*, p. 585.
[78] J. Nicot, *op. cit.*, p. 127, 12th April, 1561.
[79] See above, p. 194 ff.
[80] J. Nicot, *op. cit.*, p. 31, p. 107–108, XXXIII ff.
[81] J. Nicot, *op. cit.*, 12th December, 1559, p. 39.
[82] F. C. Lane, *op. cit.*, p. 588.

remaining fairly stable between 1520 and 1545, then rising regularly with other prices between 1545 and 1558, it suddenly shot up between 1558 and 1565, much faster than any other commodity, tripling in New Castile.[83] This abnormal price increase was first observed by Earl J. Hamilton who pointed out the possible connection between the high price of pepper and the motives behind Legazpi's expedition to the Philippines in 1564.[84] As early as 1558, complaints were being voiced in Genoa about the excessive price of 'drugs' from Portugal.[85]

Was the Turco-Portuguese war (1560–1563) a reaction by Portugal against this state of affairs? Or was it on the contrary a sign of weakness? The standard histories seem unable to provide an answer. This war, once again a rather inconclusive affair, took place off Bab el Mandeb and Hormuz, at the entrance to the two gulfs controlled by Turkish galleys. This time the Turks concentrated their efforts on the Persian Gulf,[86] while there were rumours of treachery by Turkish agents collaborating with the Portuguese in the Yemen.[87] Meanwhile at Constantinople, for reasons still obscure to us, ambassadors from India and the kingdom of Assi (Sumatra) formed a constant procession, bearing handfuls of rare pearls.[88] One of these delegations, arriving by way of Egypt, reached the capital in Turkish galleys.[89]

These details are not easy to relate to one another. It is true that the Turco-Portuguese war cannot really be called an orthodox war, with a beginning and an end. With hostilities scattered over such a wide area it could take months or years to carry out an offensive and then to find out what had been achieved. Giovanni Agostino Gilli, a Genoese secret agent at Constantinople, was probably right when he spoke of the sultan's reluctance to become embroiled in these distant troubles. To each of the Indian envoys he gave a coat of cloth of gold and 20,000 aspers, but not the artillery and master gunners they wanted.[90] At the end of 1563 there was serious talk of peace with the Portuguese, reported in letters sent on 7th and 8th December, 1563, to the viceroy of Naples by a Spanish secret agent at Constantinople, 'a usually reliable source'. 'The Portuguese ambassador,' this correspondent writes, 'has sued for peace with the Turks, seeking to obtain for the Portuguese the right to transport their merchandise from India through the Red Sea and then by land to Cairo, Alexan-

[83] E. J. Hamilton, *op. cit.*, p. 232–233.
[84] *Ibid.*, p. 233, note 2.
[85] R. di Tucci, *Relazioni* . . ., p. 639.
[86] J. Nicot, *op. cit.*, 28th July, 1561, p. 63–64.
[87] H. Ferro to the Doge, Pera, 16th September, 1561, Senato Secreta, Cost., Filza 3/D.
[88] Gio: Agostino Gilli to the Republic of Genoa, Constantinople, 5th July, 1563, A.d.S., Genoa, Costantinopoli, 1558–1565, 1–2169. G. Hernandez to Philip II, Venice, 10th July, 1563, Simancas E° 1324, f° 221; Pétrémol to Charles IX, Constantinople, 11th February, 22nd April, 1564, E. Charrière, *op. cit.*, II, p. 748–750; Daniel Badoaro to the Doge, Pera, 6th May, 1564, A.d.S., Senato Secreta, Filza 4/D.
[89] E. Charrière, *op. cit.*, II, p. 748–750.
[90] See note 88.

dria, and Syria where it can be sold. But nothing has yet been agreed.' And the ambassador has asked not to be troubled further by visits from the customs officials 'which has not yet been granted him'.[91]

These negotiations, which caused some anxiety in Venice, are worth pondering for a moment, although they came to nothing. At the end of the year 1563, scarcely sixty-five years after Vasco da Gama's voyage, they form a somewhat curious sequel to the unsuccessful overtures by Venice in 1527. They represent the triumph of the Red Sea route, the revenge of Venice, and the Mediterranean.

The revival of the Portuguese pepper trade. We do not know the circumstances under which the war of the Indian Ocean ended. The answer may lie in Lisbon. But the troubles of the Portuguese spice trade were far from over even then.

In Europe the disturbances in the Netherlands, around Antwerp, did it great damage. In 1566, the firm of Welser, which had Portuguese connections, suffered considerably from speculation in pepper and the Indies contracts. With their Italian associate Rovalesca, the Fuggers bore the consequences.[92] In 1569 some rather curious negotiations opened over the projected transfer of the Portuguese spice trade from Antwerp to London.[93]

At the same time the coasts of the Indian Ocean remained unsafe, and this time the Turks were as much affected as their opponents. In 1567 when he learned that forty galleys were being fitted at Suez, Fourquevaux, at Madrid,[94] already saw them sailing as far as Sumatra. If the Turks were to interrupt shipping with the East Indies, 'that would reduce the arrogance of the Portuguese. And in France one could buy spices cheaper from Alexandria and other ports in Syria if in the future none travelled to Portugal.' In 1568 it was reported from Venice that twenty Turkish galleys were preparing to launch an attack on the Portuguese from Basra and to capture the island of Bahrein and its pearl fisheries.[95] But in the same year, 1568, Arabia rose up in arms. A long series of disturbances began, particularly in the Yemen.[96] Apart from some unlikely political gossip there is little to tell us what became of Aden, the gateway to the Red Sea. Order was restored only in 1573 by that Sinān Pasha who later became Grand Vizier.[97]

Portugal no doubt took advantage of Turkish difficulties although she had her own as well (Goa was besieged for fourteen months in 1570;[98] the fortress of Ternate was to fall in 1575). The threat from the sultan's

[91] Simancas E° 1053, f° 10.
[92] H. Fitzler, *art. cit.*, p. 265–266.
[93] Philip II to the Duke of Alva, 21st November, 1569 and 23rd November, 1569, Simancas E° 542, f°ˢ 9 and 22.
[94] 13th November, 1567, C. Douais, *op. cit.*, I, p. 288; report from Corfu, 27th September, 1567, Simancas E° 1056, f° 86.
[95] J. de Cornoça to Philip II, Venice, 22nd May, 1568, Simancas E° 1326.
[96] See below, vol. II, part III, ch. 3, section 2.
[97] *Ibid.*, part III, ch. 5, notes 19 and 20.
[98] R. Hakluyt, *op. cit.*, II, p. 219.

galleys was receding. And the far-reaching reorganization of the Portuguese spice trade in 1570 was an improvement. By the *regimento* of 1st March, 1570,[99] the king, Dom Sebastian, in effect abandoned the Crown monopoly to his vassals, a reform which some people, Pires[100] in particular, had been advocating for some time. In the same year the viceroy, Dom Luis de Ataide, boasted of having patrolled the sea so effectively that only two ships, instead of sixteen or eighteen as in previous years, had been able to sail from Calicut to Mecca.[101]

A fresh swing of the pendulum can perhaps be dated from 25th November, 1570, when Venice removed the obligation on foreign shippers to bring spices to Venice exclusively in Venetian ships,[102] although several meanings can be attached to this measure, which was in any case a fairly mild one. But the situation was soon to turn against Venice. The war with Turkey (1570–1573) was extremely damaging. All her rivals, Ragusa, Ancona, and above all Marseilles, took advantage of it. Bills of lading from July to September, 1573, show that the French (Mannlich the Elder on at least one occasion) were carrying off from Alexandria in Egypt, entire cargoes of 'zimbre' and pepper 'of Assy'.[103] It is not so much the drop in imports of bales of silk to Aleppo (because of the war or rather the threat of war with Persia) that is disquieting, says a Venetian consul in April, 1574,[104] as the ruinous competition from French merchants who have flocked here since the war. There were no complaints on the other hand about spices, which now seemed to be taking the route through Syria. In October, 1574, a rich vessel, the *Ludovica*, left Venice with 150,000 ducats' worth of merchandise aboard. A storm obliged her to put in to Ancona, where the governors of the town found her to be laden with copper and declared her legitimate spoil since she was carrying contraband merchandise. They seized the ship and her cargo and imprisoned master and mariners.[105] From chance references in some commercial correspondence in 1574[106] and little else to go on, it appears that there were either leaving or lying in Syrian ports some French ships (30th January, 1574), a French boat (3rd April), a Venetian *nave*, the *Moceniga*, which was at Tripoli in March and again in November, the *saëtte Altana*, probably from Venice. And they piled on board mace, *chotoni*, arsenic, spun cotton, spices, ginger, a chest of *mirobolani*; on 12th May, 1575,[107] the merchantman *Girada* carried away cotton, *peladi*, silks, drugs, and spices.

[99] *Leis e provisões de el Rei D. Sebastião*, Coimbra, 1816, p. 68 ff., quoted by F. de Almeida, *op. cit.*, III, p. 562.
[100] 14th February, 1560, *Corp. dipl. port.*, VIII, p. 355.
[101] B.N., Paris, Fonds portugais, n° 8, f° 197.
[102] A.d.S., Venice, *Cinque Savii*, Busta 3, 25th November, 1570.
[103] Fonds Dauvergne n° 113, 115 (reference to Mannlich le Vieux 117, 118, 122–125. '*Zimbre belladin*' or '*méquin*'.
[104] G. Berchet, *op. cit.*, p. 61.
[105] G. da Silva to Philip II, Venice, 5th November, 1574, Simancas E° 1333.
[106] Lettere commerc., 12 *ter*, A.d.S., Venice.
[107] Simancas, E° 1331.

So the flow of goods from the Levant was not interrupted either on the Syrian or the Egyptian route. Meanwhile Portuguese pepper was making headway in the Mediterranean. A deliberation of the Council of the Pregadi, on 13th September, 1577, makes this clear.[108] From a report by the *Cinque Savii alla Mercanzia* the Council learned that at Lisbon four ships had taken on board for Venice *una buona suma di pevere*, but that their owners changed their minds when they heard that they would have to pay a duty of 3 per cent at Venice, according to an old ruling of 1519 (the date is significant), which imposed the duty on spices coming from the western Mediterranean only, not from the Levant. It was decided to postpone the shipment in the hope of obtaining the suppression of this duty, a request duly granted for a period of two years, 'seeing that this merchandise [the Portuguese pepper]' said the experts, 'might be sent to other places, to the loss of this city and export duties'. It would be better then '*since only a little pepper is arriving from Alexandria*, to grant free entry to pepper from the West'. Two years later, Christobal de Salazar was writing to Philip II, 'At Alexandria, trade and traffic are quite destroyed, especially in spices, for the route is abandoned,' *porque se ha dexado el camino*.[109]

Portuguese pepper: deals and projects. This helps to explain three attempts to capture the profits of the pepper trade in the Mediterranean.

The first attempt was Portuguese. It is outlined in a letter written to Philip II on 10th November, 1575, by Friar Mariano Azaro, a Discalced Carmelite and former student at Padua, who was a great expert in these matters.[110] He proposed introducing Portuguese pepper to the Spanish dominions in Italy, Milan, Naples, Sicily, and Sardinia, ousting Venetian pepper, which was commonly sold there; he also proposed enlisting the support of the Pope and other Italian rulers and establishing either at Puerto de Santa Maria or Cartagena or some other peninsular port a distribution centre for Italy, another Antwerp so to speak. The pepper would be transported in the royal galleys. That this project should incidentally suggest that Portuguese pepper had conquered the Spanish markets by 1516 does not increase its credibility. Who knows with what fantastic information we should be inundated if all the pamphlets of the *arbitristas* of Spain had survived! But behind this barefoot friar were two, possibly three, important people: first, Ruy Gómez da Silva, a Portuguese as we know, and who 'shortly before his death had taken it upon him to propose to Your Majesty a certain suggestion I had made to him concerning the spiceries of the Levant'; the secretary Antonio Graciano, to whom the friar had written in the first place; and, finally, the king, who was by now preoccupied with the pepper trade and the Portuguese monopoly, and who, when informed by his secretary of the suggestion, asked for a second report, which is what we have here. So it was a serious project, an attack

[108] A.d.S., Venice, Busta 538, f° 846 and v°.
[109] Venice, 8th July, 1679, A.N., K 1672, Gl, n° 84.
[110] Seville, 10th November, 1575, Simancas E° 564, f° 10.

upon Venice in the grand manner. Since Venice was dependent upon the Turk for her spices and wheat and had therefore out of vile self-interest betrayed Christendom, why should she not be punished, in the name of morality and respectable Portuguese pepper! Besides, as everyone knew (and this is a counterblast to disparaging remarks about the quality of the pepper from Lisbon) the Turks first steeped their spices in infusions to manufacture their beverages and hydromel, and then unscrupulously sold them in the Syrian markets.

The second attempt came from Tuscany, or rather the Medici. Grand Duke Francesco made great efforts between 1576 and 1578,[111] to obtain the *appalto* of the spices that came from the Indies to Portugal. To this effect he dangled the prospect of money in front of that strange descendant of the kings of Lisbon, the last of the crusaders, Dom Sebastian, who, fired with dreams of fighting the Infidel in Morocco, was preoccupied with raising the necessary funds for an adventure that was to prove suicidal to himself, his nobility, and his kingdom. The Grand Duke was extremely ambitious: he was negotiating simultaneously with the sultan and his aim was nothing less than the world monopoly of pepper, according to the Venetians, whose judgment could be as shrewd as their gossip was malicious.[112] These grandiose schemes were finally limited to the negotiation of a loan of 200,000 crowns between the merchants of Florence, the Medici, and the Portuguese ambassador, Antonio Pinto,[113] which was undoubtedly the pretext for a massive shipment of Portuguese pepper to Leghorn in return. By a narrow margin certainly, the Grand Duke nevertheless failed to capture the monopoly in 1587.[114] But after these discussions, closer links were maintained between Florence and Lisbon.

The third and last attempt was made by Philip II himself. His aims were at once to increase his hold over the neighbouring kingdom, to blockade the rebels in the Netherlands (plans to deprive them of salt, grain or spices had been suggested at various times) and finally to establish an active Hispano-Portuguese salt and spice trade.[115] In this he was ceding to pressure from influential businessmen eager to capture the rich Asian trades, a Roth or a Nathaniel Jung, both Germans, who by 1575, were thinking of applying for the Portuguese spice contract.

What had only been a project became a reality when Philip II annexed Portugal. 1580 marked for him, as 1547 had for Charles V, the high point of his reign. If Portugal surrendered to him, as she did, it was in order to receive the threefold protection of Philip II's money, armies, and fleets, and with this three-pronged weapon to strengthen her hold on the Indian Ocean. After 1580 it was natural that the king should want to block the

---

[111] G. Vivoli, *op. cit.*, III, p. 155. On the role played in this episode by Jacomo Bardi and his agent Ciro Allidosio, B.N., Paris, Fonds Portugais, n° 23, f°s 570 and 571 v°.
[112] Ch. de Salazar to the king, Venice, 11th September, 1577, Simancas E° 1336.
[113] Abbe Brizeño to the king, Florence, 26th November 1576, Simancas E° 1450.
[114] R. Galluzzi, *op. cit.*, IX, p. 108; G. Parenti, *op. cit.*, p. 80 and 90.
[115] Philip II to Requesens, 23rd January, 1576, Simancas E° 569, f° 60.

channels through which the Levant trade was supplied, thus destroying with a single blow the fortunes of the Turks and of Venice in the interests of his own empire. But in his determination to organize Asia and the New World and to link them together, Philip II encountered far less resistance in the Indian Ocean than he did around the shores of the Atlantic, particularly the North Atlantic. So it was against the Protestants, the rebels in the Netherlands and England, that he took action rather than against the Turk, with whom he remained unofficially at peace. Here then lies the explanation of the strange policy pursued by the Prudent King who now that he was master of Portugal did his best to promote and place in Mediterranean markets the pepper he had just acquired. He hoped in this way to redistribute the precious manna along channels more secure than the Atlantic routes; and above all to thwart his enemies of it. This policy, which was only formulated after much planning and hesitation, took even longer before being implemented in 1585. It represented nothing less than the mobilization of Spanish resources against the Atlantic and northern Europe.

Portuguese pepper is offered to Venice. The proposal that Venice should take the contract for sales of Portuguese pepper was not then a sensational development. It had been in the air for four or five years. In its original form it consisted of an offer, of Spanish inspiration no doubt, which was transmitted to the Signoria at the end of 1581 by the Venetian ambassador Morosini, and the Venetian consul at Lisbon, Dall'Olmo, that a fleet of '*galee*' be sent to the Portuguese capital.[116] In December, the Collegio debated the question with the evidence before it. Should the ships be sent? In theory Venice was willing, but there were practical objections. In the first place, who would underwrite the venture? No private individual had the necessary capital for fitting out the vessels and for the purchase of spices in Portugal, where 'the Venetians have no credit', in other words where they had few commercial connections and could therefore make little use of bills of exchange. The second problem was what merchandise to send in return, since glass, glassware, vases, and other similar goods were prohibited in Portugal. And finally, since the situation in Portugal was still unsettled, the galleys might be attacked on the way by English, 'Norman', or other corsairs, all enemies of Philip II. To these objections, those in favour of the expedition replied that credit would be found somehow, that the Signoria could offer its own guarantees, that the Catholic King would lift the ban on the merchandise, that an escort of two or three galleys would be sufficient to protect the convoy. Finally it was decided to wait for Morosini's next report before taking further action. Such is the account given by the Spanish ambassador at Venice, Christobal de Salazar, in his letter of 8th December, 1581.[117] The matter was still under discussion in 1584, since the Venetian consul Dall'Olmo sent back to

[116] Cf. Dall'Olmo's report in 1584, see note 118.
[117] Simancas E° 1339.

Venice a copious document on ways of restoring trade between the republic and Lisbon.[118]

So a series of talks had preceded the proposal made to the Signoria in 1585. This proposal was nonetheless singular in itself, marking as it did a curious reversal of roles. There is no better way of examining it than by studying the report made at the end of the year 1585 by the 'experts' Antonio Bragadino and Jacopo Foscarini.[119] Spain proposed that 30,000 cantars (about 15,000 quintals) of pepper should be made available at Lisbon every year, at a rate of 30 ducats per cantar, one third to be paid down, the other two thirds staggered over a period of six months, plus several by no means negligible advantages: an escort by the Spanish royal galleys from the Peninsula as far as Sicily: *tratas* of wheat for the galleys on their arrival at the island; and, finally, a reduction in favour of Venice of the *gabelle*, which were so heavy in Portugal.

But there were disadvantages too. To accept the Spanish proposal, said the experts, would mean acquiescing in the decline of trade with the Levant, which had been and still was the livelihood of the republic; it would deal a bitter blow to the *arti* of wool and silk to which this trade was vitally important and which employed a large number of Venice's population; and, finally, there was the danger of being swamped by the 30,000 cantars. Would this not be more pepper than the Venetians would know what to do with? Even the price (30 ducats instead of the 36 or 38 usually charged to the *contrattatori*) might be a trap. These were the arguments against the project which the rapporteurs exposed, only to dismiss them one by one.

What if the trade with the Levant came to an end? As far as spices and pepper were concerned it already had. 'It is clearly visible that every day the traffic with the Levant is reduced. . . . Not only do our ships return from Syria and Alexandria without spices, but it is learnt that the Levant itself, and in particular Constantinople, lacks spices for its own consumption and comes to Venice to seek spices and pepper arriving there from Lisbon.'[120] And the Catholic King was quite capable of carrying out an effective blockade which would cut off all supplies from the Levant. He would send where he pleased the spices that he now controlled. So if Venice did not accept his proposal, he might make it to Tuscany instead. In any case, while there might be less spice in Syria and Egypt, the Levant trade in general was still flourishing: the voyages continued, and Venetian cloth was exchanged for silks, camlets, cottons, gall-nuts, and ashes.[121] As for the quantity, it was very unlikely to be too much, for pepper had doubled in price,[122] the present farmers had sold their stocks not at 100 ducats, the

[118] *Informazione sul commercio dei Veneziani in Portogallo e sui mezzi di ristorarlo,* 1584, pub. by B. Cecchetti, *Nozze Thiene da Schio,* 1869.
[119] A. Bragadino and J. Foscarini, *Parere intorno al trattato fra Venezia e Spagna sul traffico del pepe e delle spezierie delle Indie Orientali,* 1585, pub. by Fr. Stefani, *Nozze Correr-Fornasari,* 1870.
[120] *Ibid.,* 1, 12–13.
[121] *Ibid.,* p. 14.   [122] *Ibid.,* p. 15.

usual price, but at 180.[123] So the proposal should be accepted, concluded the writers.

It is a far from objective report. That the situation of the spice and pepper trade from the usual sources in the Levant was, in 1585, under some strain is true. But this trade still existed. And Portuguese pepper was also in difficulty. From the very same report, we discover that if Philip II was in search of new *contrattatori* it was because the old ones were unsatisfactory, they did not take the stipulated quantities and forced prices up. As for those who went to the Indies, they left stocks there, 'exposed to smuggling and export by the Levant'.[124]

The wonderful deal never came off. The reason is not wholly to be sought in Venetian petty-mindedness, in the political passions, and Hispanophobia prevalent in Venice, although all these entered into it; since 1582–1583, the Senate had been particularly hostile to the Catholic King[125] and his suddenly increased power. Was it political folly on Venice's part to turn down the offer? Some thought so, like the ambassador Lippomano who, after the Signoria's refusal, did his best to develop commercial links between Lisbon and Venice.[126] Or was it occasioned by the desire to avoid trouble with the Turks and to safeguard the 4000 Venetian families living in the Levant, in Damascus, Aleppo, Alexandria, Cairo, even in Baghdad?[127] I think this argument has been a little exaggerated, although it is true that the presence of Venetian merchants has been recorded as far away as Hormuz.[128]

In any case, Venice was not alone in refusing the contract. Milan, Genoa, and Florence,[129] were all approached and all turned it down. This general rejection by Italy, at first sight hard to explain, cannot have been the result of collective madness. Capitalism frowned on the scheme. Why this was so becomes clearer in the light of the subsequent large contract agreed with the Welsers and Fuggers between 1586 and 1591, and of the double history of the spice trade, Portuguese and Levantine, two streams of pepper and spices flowing along very different routes from the Moluccas, the Sunda Islands or the Malabar coast, to the countries of Europe and the Mediterranean.

The Welser and Fugger contract: 1586–1591. The Portuguese pepper trade consisted of one minor and two major contracts. The minor one was for Portuguese domestic sales. The two major ones were the Asian contract for buying spices and pepper in the Indies and transporting them to Lisbon,

[123] A. Bragadino and J. Foscarini, *op. cit.*, p. 10.
[124] *Ibid.*
[125] H. Kretschmayr, *op. cit.*, III, p. 179.
[126] *Ibid.*
[127] *Ibid.*
[128] U. Tucci, 'Mercanti veneziani in India alla fine del secolo XVI', in *Studi in onore di Armando Sapori*, 1957, II, p. 1091–1111.
[129] P. Ricardi to Cardinal Medici at Rome, Naples, 12th March, 1587, *Archivio storico italiano*, vol. IX, p. 246–247.

and the European contract for handling sales in Europe. The monarchy, with its enormous warehouses at the *Casa da India*, was the hinge on which everything turned: it received pepper from the farmers of the Asian concession at a certain price; to the farmers of the European concession it sold the pepper at clear double the price.

It was the European contract that Philip II was hawking around Italy, hoping thus to deprive the Dutch and the English of their pepper and spices, which they had been in the habit of buying at Lisbon. As for the Asian contract, a draft project was presented to Philip II by a German, Giraldo Paris, at Monzon on 29th November, 1585. It was signed by the king at Valencia on 15th February, 1586[130] and delivered to a consortium of capitalists, among whom were the Welsers and Fuggers. The details of the agreement are unimportant. The net result was that the pepper, transported from the east at the risk of the farmers, was sold to the king at 16 *cruzados* and resold by him at 37.

Matthaus Welser, who is found negotiating at Madrid in 1587, was deeply implicated in this affair; he had also accepted the European contract and tried to involve the Fuggers as well. At first they, like the Italians, dragged their feet. 'It is no business for us,' they wrote in November, 1587; 'What should we do in such a labyrinth?'[131] But in 1591, in the somewhat forlorn hope of bringing some order into their difficult agreements with Spain, they allowed themselves to be drawn into the European contract.[132] This was at the time in the hands of a vast international consortium, the Welsers and Fuggers for Germany, Rovalesca and Giraldo Paris for Italy, Francisco and Pedro Malvenda for Spain, and Andrès and Thomas Ximenez for Portugal. The association was divided into thirty-two shares, of which the Fuggers held seven, the Welsers five, the Rovalesca four, the Malvenda four, and the Ximenez and their associates eleven. It was represented at Antwerp, Middleburg, Zeeland, Hamburg, Lübeck, and Venice, where the Welsers had opened a thriving new branch in 1588. By 1591 it was handling enormous quantities of pepper: 14,000 quintals were sent to Lübeck for instance. Huge cargoes travelled to Venice, the Signoria having agreed to protect all merchandise addressed there and to obtain safe-conducts for the English.[133] But this massive mobilization of capital and capitalists produced disappointing results. Only the king of Spain made anything out of it. In 1591, the same year that it was formed, the Fuggers prudently withdrew, selling their shares on 7th July, to the Evora, Portuguese *marranos* associated with the Ximenez, and the Caldeira.[134]

The reason for this failure was that shipping routes in the Atlantic after

---

[130] R. Konetzke, *op. cit.*, p. 126; F. Dobel, 'Über einen Pfefferhandel der Fugger und Welser, 1586–1591', in *Zeitschrift des hist. Vereins f. Schwaben u. Neuburg*, XIII, p. 125–138; Hedwig Fitzler, *art. cit.*, p. 248–250.
[131] 8th November, 1587, H. Fitzler, *art. cit.*, p. 266.
[132] *Ibid.*, p. 267.
[133] The Fuggers to the Otts, Augsburg, 24th August, 1591, *ibid.*, p. 268.
[134] *Ibid.*, p. 274.

the defeat of the Spanish Armada were more dangerous than ever. The defeat of Spain meant the rout of her allies and in more than one place a drop in the Atlantic pepper trade. With the rise in selling prices, the consortium's pepper came to be dearer in Venice than pepper shipped from the Levant, an astonishing fact which is made plain in a letter from the Fuggers to their agent in Lisbon, dated 9th November and 7th December, 1587.[135] Many customers were turning back to the Venetian market.

In conclusion, if Italy systematically refused to meet the terms offered by Philip II, who, under his new title of Philip I had become the merchant-king of Lisbon, it was because supplies were once more getting through, to some extent at least, on the Syrian and Egyptian routes. The threat to Atlantic shipping inevitably brought renewed activity to the shorter routes through the Near East. Even Atlantic pepper had now to be brought to Italy as a merchant of Florence noted a little later in a letter to Simón Ruiz, dated 4th May, 1589, and his explanation is equally true of the preceding years: 'as it is impossible to send pepper to Flanders, to England or Germany from Lisbon, the merchants will be obliged to send it to Italy in any ship they can lay hands on, since the Germans buy theirs in Florence and Venice . . . '.[136] Even the Atlantic pepper trade was drawn towards the Mediterranean.

The survival of the Levantine spice routes. From the 1580s to the end of the century the spice routes of the Levant remained active, until the total capture of the Indian Ocean by the Dutch. They appeared there for the first time in 1596 with Cornelius Houtmann's voyage; by 1625 they had imposed their rule throughout the ocean and were now looking to America for fresh worlds to conquer. It is somewhere about this time, either just before or just after 1625, that we must date the irremediable decline of the Levant trade.[137] The first warning had been the Twelve Years Truce of 1609, which officially opened the Indian Ocean to the trading ventures of these new arrivals. And in 1614 the appearance of the first large Dutch vessel in the Red Sea had been another hint of what was to come.[138] This capture from the rear, partly by land, partly by sea, of the traffic of the East (including Persian silk[139]), the spread throughout the area of Dutch textiles, the belligerent arrival of the English[140] and the French[141] marked the beginning of a second European age in the Indian Ocean that was to be more catastrophic to the Levant than the imperfect domination of the Portuguese.

[135] Letter to Krel, mentioned by H. Fitzler, *ibid.*, p. 265.
[136] Municipal Library Valladolid, Ruiz Archives.
[137] B.N., Paris, Fonds Dupuy, n° 22, f° 89 ff, 1610. Portuguese revenues had been decreasing over the previous 12 or 13 years 'because of the traffic the Dutch have had with the Indies'.
[138] Cl. Heerringa, *op. cit.*, I, p. 154–155, quoted by J. Denucé, *op. cit.*, p. 71.
[139] G. Berchet, (1625), *op. cit.*, p. 163.
[140] *Ibid.*, p. 162.
[141] G. Atkinson, *op. cit.*, p. 128.

Within this huge context and with the aid of the imperfect documentary evidence, let us trace year by year the chronicle of at least the last twenty years of the century. While the particular examples we find may not be in any way decisive, at least they support the conclusion that basically traditional trade survived, although it certainly had its ups and downs.

Some Marseilles papers dating from the summer of 1578 refer to purchases of nutmeg in Syria.[142] In January, 1579 a commercial letter from Aleppo[143] mentions the departure of two Venetian *navi* (and a Venetian *nave* always of considerable capacity, would at the end of the century quite frequently be carrying 500,000 ducats' worth of merchandise): the *Balbiana et Costantina*, master Marcho Fachinetto, and the *Gratarola*, master Candido di Barbari. A third spent the winter at the Cyprus saltworks and was planning to reach the 'beach' of Tripoli in the course of January. The arrival of fresh supplies brought down the price of woollen cloths as usual, and more provision of good quality cloth was requested by the next ships: woollen cloth from Bergamo in particular, as well as *perlete* and *paternostri* from Murano, and a *gropo* of Venetian coin. In the same year another Venetian ship is recorded as having some trouble with the Turkish galleys of Modon, on her way to Alexandria.[144] A letter dated 12th May, from Aleppo,[145] announces the arrival of a caravan with 200 loads of silk and 250 of spices, accompanied by Persian and Christian merchants, all subjects of the Sophy. On the Saturday of Holy Week there was a great market. In August the Venetian consul in Syria announced the departure of two Venetian *navi*, 'rich with silks and spices'.[146] Finally in the same year, on 4th July, the list of goods captured by the San Stefano galleys of Tuscany included seventeen pieces of ebony (weight 205 pounds), sugar (936 pounds), one *balleta* of silk (102 pounds), frankincense (1185 pounds), ginger (150), cloves (1114), nutmeg (236) and finally pepper (7706 pounds in various bales the weights of which varied between 260 and 522 pounds).[147]

There followed a crisis during the years 1582–1583. A letter from Aleppo[148] in December 1582 says that trade is scarce and what little there is is disastrous. Only the silk trade maintained its position. In July, 1583 business was so bad that instead of making a profit, capital was returning with a loss of 8 per cent and according to the latest information from Egypt, the same was true in Alexandria.[149] Was this why the Englishman Newberie wrote from Baghdad in July 1583: 'I think cloth, kersies and tinne have never bene here at so low prices as they are now'.[150]

[142] Fonds Dauvergne, n° 111, 23rd July, 1578.
[143] Sent to Marco Rubbi, January 1579, A.d.S., Venice, lett. com., 12 *ter*.
[144] J. de Cornoça to Philip II, Venice, 18th June, 1579, A.N., K 1672, Gl, n° 73.
[145] *Ibid.*, Venice, 10th July, 1579.
[146] *Ibid.*, Venice, 9th September, 1579.
[147] Mediceo 2077, f° 590.
[148] Addressed to Zuane Balbiani, A.d.S., Venice, Lettere Com., 12 *ter*.
[149] Ch. de Salazar to Philip II, Venice, 30th July, 1583, Simancas E° 1341.
[150] R. Hakluyt, *op. cit.*, II, 347.

But after 1583 it was a different story. A wholesale merchant of Marseilles writes on 10th April that pepper prices are rising fast, 'although from Aleppo there come many spices'. It is beyond all understanding, he complains, 'and I assure you that there is no merchant in the district however experienced, but does not have his plans thrown into confusion'.[151] For himself, by the following year he was thinking of leaving for the Indies, together with a Venetian wholesaler, to risk 2000 crowns 'of our own'. John Eldred, in 1583, describes Tripoli in Syria as the port most frequented by Christian merchants[152] and Aleppo as very populous. He refers to a large volume of traffic between Baghdad and Aleppo. At Basra, where he notes the presence of twenty-five fine Turkish galleys, there put in every month he says, several ships of 40 to 60 tons from Hormuz, 'laden with all sorts of Indian marchandise, as spices, drugs, Indico, and Calicut cloth'. He does not give precise details. But during the summer of 1584 when John Eldred returned to Aleppo, he joined a caravan of 4000 camels, 'laden with spices and other rich marchandises'. And at Alexandria in 1584, one could buy 'all sorts of spices'.[153]

In 1587, according to another source, ships were leaving Sumatra every year for Mecca.[154] And we are told that in about 1586 the customs duties at Mecca brought in 150,000 ducats (half to the sultan, half to the Sharif of the city), and that every year about forty or fifty great ships landed there laden with spices. More was to come. In the face of Portuguese interference in the Indian Ocean, there occurred after the 1590s a corresponding expansion of the trading centres outside Portuguese control. The port of Chaul for instance, expanded at the expense of Diu and Goa. Since all the merchants who had dealings with Mecca and Hormuz were settled there, it cost the king of Portugal up to 150,000 *fardãos* in customs duties every year.[155] Further evidence[156] comes from an Augustinian friar, Frey Augustinho d'Azevedo, himself Portuguese, who had returned overland from the Indies, and made his report to Philip II, between 1584 and 1587, according to the historians[157] who discovered this precious document, in my guess about 1593.[158] In any case, it clearly dates from the last decades of the century. Thanks to this report we have an unforgettable picture of Hormuz, a port open to every kind of immigrant, every kind of

---

[151] Fonds Dauvergne, n° 28, Gilles Hermitte to his brother, also contains a reference to cinnamon of high quality, *belle robe* ('good stuff'). On his plans for a voyage to the Indies in 1584, *ibid.*, n°s 32, 34, 35.

[152] R. Hakluyt, *op. cit.*, II, p. 268.

[153] *Ibid.*, I, p. 176–177.

[154] *Ibid.*, II, p. 250–265, 1583–1591.

[155] A. B. de Bragança Pereira, *Os Portugueses em Diu* (undated) p. 277 ff.

[156] B.N., Madrid, Ms 3015, f° 149 ff., Apontamentos para V. Mag. ver sobre as cousas do Estado da India e Reyno de Monomotapa, por frey Augustinho Dazevedo, da Ordem de Santo Agostinho que veyo por terra da India, undated.

[157] The document was discovered by J. Gentil da Silva and brought to my notice by V. M. Godinho. The suggested date (1584–1587) is based on details concerning the Portuguese Indies contained in the text.

[158] Since it refers to the Venetians using the port of Alexandretta.

commerce, and every kind of smuggling, whether by Venetians, Armenians, the Turks themselves, or the Portuguese renegades who left in astonishing numbers for Turkey, where their knowledge of the Indies was a valuable asset in the clandestine trade in pearls, rhubarb, benjamin, and sandalwood in one direction, and contraband goods, munitions, and modern armaments in the other. Thus it was that 'o melhor da India', the best of India, reached Venice, which in return sent a varied assortment of shoddy goods, glass trinkets, mirrors, false pearls, and wallpaper. And it was for Venice, always ready to compromise with the heretical Turks or English, that the pious Augustinian saw up to six thousand camels laden with treasures travelling through the desert, and with his own eyes watched five big Venetian ships leave Alexandretta. Does this mean that after the visible difficulties of the 1580s in Venetian affairs, there was a revival in trade?

In the Levant, towards the end of the century, the Aleppo route was restored to favour, because it was shorter, because it was an overland route (piracy was rife in the Indian Ocean after the 1590s), and above all because of silk and its increasingly important position in the European economy. Every single letter from Venetian or Marseilles merchants in Aleppo, Tripoli, or Alexandretta, carries a reference to silk,[159] local silk from the region surrounding Tripoli, or fine silks of Persia brought to Aleppo by the usual merchants, Armenians, or Tartars. For several years Aleppo was handicapped by the Turco-Persian war (which ended in 1590). Most of the fighting was of course in the north, round Tabriz, and along the routes that led from both sides of the Caucasus down to the Caspian Sea. But the war was sometimes carried suddenly south as far as Baghdad. And in any case it led to a series of monetary crises in both Turkey and Persia, which naturally had repercussions in Aleppo[160] where it grew increasingly difficult to find money, so that in June, 1586 it became necessary to raise the customs duties on merchandise arriving in Venice from Syria[161] from 1 per cent to 1·5 per cent, to the benefit of the *cottimo*. In spite of these problems trade survived, as we have already seen. Venice in 1593 admitted to trade worth a million ducats in Syria,[162] and in 1596 announced that it was worth two million.[163] The principal commodities were silks and spices. The figure of two million refers to Venetian exports – the cloths, silk-stuffs, trinkets, and glass left in the *souks* at Aleppo; but the cargoes that were loaded in exchange on board four or five big ships increased miraculously in price as they approached Venice.

After 1593 the Levant traffic no longer left from Tripoli but from Alexandretta, which the Venetians now made their shipping headquarters and where they were followed by other Christian shippers. The new port was

---

[159] Lettres marseillaises, series HH, 29th March, 5th April, 1591, 7th May, 11th May, 1594, A. Com., Marseilles.
[160] Alvise Cucina to A. Paruta, Venice, 24th December, 1588, Lettere Com. 12 *ter*.
[161] A.d.S., Venice, *Cinque Savii* . . ., Busta 27, June 1586.
[162] G. Berchet, *op. cit.*, p. 77.
[163] *Ibid.*, p. 79–80.

free from the vexations of the old one; although certainly unhealthier, it was nearer Aleppo. But the lack of buildings to house the stocks of merchandise was an inconvenience for the Venetians (who retained their policy of commerce *a baratto* and were therefore encumbered with bundles of goods) far more than for the merchants of Marseilles who arrived with money in their pockets.[164] The increase in trade probably resulted less from the change of port than from the end of the war between Turkey and Persia.

It also owed something to the end of hostilities between Turkey and Portugal, which between 1584 and 1589 had been a quarrel not so much over the pepper as over the gold of the East African coast. The defeat of the fleet of 'Alī Beg in 1589[165] brought the war to an end and comparative peace reigned as far as the East Indies, troubled only by local princes and corsairs.

An entire intelligence network, with direct links between Spain – or rather the Portuguese government – and the Indies, operated through the Spanish embassy at Venice, what a document calls 'las nuevas de India por tierra'.[166] The intermediaries were Jews, agents for trading houses, the factors of the Welsers for example[167] or the Bontempelli brothers, Antonio and Hieronymo, who were in the service of a wealthy Venetian merchant, Augustino Da Ponte.[168] After 1589 these sources reported all quiet in the Indies, in spite of the appearance of Malabar pirates in the centre and on the borders of the ocean.[169] The peace was to be rudely shattered a few years later by the invasion of the Dutch after 1596.

Another determining factor was the threat to Atlantic shipping. There were English privateers working round all the key islands, the Cape Verde Islands, the Canaries, the Azores and sometimes they sailed down as far as St. Helena, where the ships returning from the Indies put in for fresh water and their crews hunted mountain goats to enliven their diet. There was a shipping crisis in the ocean. And to the vessels captured by pirates must be added the many shipwrecks. The huge ships used on the Indies run became, with the general rise in prices, luxury objects, and their owners economized on timber and on the quality of the crews. In their enormous hulls the weight of the cargoes became dangerous. They put to sea without enough sail, with worm-eaten rudders; as in the Mediterranean, ships were careened in the Italian manner, without bringing the monsters into dry dock. Hence in the course of their long and eventful voyages a series of 'tragico-maritime' disasters, the long catalogue of which, drawn up by

---

[164] G. Berchet, *op. cit.*, p. 32 (1611).
[165] H. Fitzler, *art. cit.*, p. 254–255.
[166] 10th April and 10th August, 1589, A.N., K 1674.
[167] J. de Cornoça to the King, Venice, 8th February, 1589, A.N., K 1674.
[168] F. de Vera to the king, Venice, 12th May, 1590, *ibid.*
[169] On these letters sent through Venice, 16th May, 4th July, 1598, Memoria para las cartas . . ., 1598, 25th July, 24th August, 1598, Hormuz, 15th May, 1599, Venice, 14th August, 1601, A.N., K 1678; March, 6th June, 28th November, 1609, 19th February, 27th March, 4th June, 1610, A.N., K 1679.

G. de Brito, marks the line followed after the 1580s by the Portuguese decline which soon became inexorable. Between 1592 and 1602 there were lost, sometimes in fine weather, as a result of leaks or other technical accidents, thirty-eight ships on the Indies run.[170] Reckoning them at the same price as the Venetian ships, 20 million ducats and maybe more must have gone to the bottom.

These huge losses, the repeated blockades of Lisbon (during the winter 1597–1598 for instance) as well as captures by the pirates of Algiers, were all blows to the Portuguese pepper trade. In New Castile between 1595 and 1599, the price of pepper doubled.[171] These blows and price increases opened the door wider to the old firm of the Mediterranean. A letter from some German merchants on 17th February, 1593, announces that the *muda de Suez* has arrived with 30,000 cantars 'which means', writes one historian, 'that the Alexandrian market was providing as much pepper as Lisbon'.[172]

So the Levant trade was still very much alive. We have mentioned the progress made by the Venetians. This was clearly revealed in 1596, when the rates of the *cottimo* of Aleppo were reduced from 5 per cent to 2 per cent.[173] Three years later, in 1599, there was a drop in turnover, but Venetian trade was still reaching the respectable figure of a million and a half ducats, the total figure for the whole of Christendom being in the region of 3 million, of which half a million was handled by the French, or by merchants trading under the French flag.[174] In the same year, after stormy discussions, the Venetians obtained some privileges in Egypt (including freedom to load leather and linen) and unofficial permission to smuggle wheat from Damietta and Rosetta, the providential sources of Crete's food supply.[175] In 1600, the sixteen Venetian trading houses at Aleppo mentioned in the consular report of 1593 were still active.[176] In 1603 Venetian trade in the city was still worth a million and a half ducats.[177] In 1599 further evidence comes from Marseilles bills of lading at Alexandretta, which refer to cargoes of indigo, nutmeg, and cloves.

So in 1600 as far as pepper and spices are concerned the predominance of the ocean route was far from established. With ups and downs, the rivalry between the two routes lasted over a century and, on both sides, crisis alternated with prosperity. The end of the story falls outside the period of our survey which stops in about 1600. The dates and the circumstances

---

[170] *Op. cit.*, II, p. 530 ff, p. 556.

[171] E. J. Hamilton, *op. cit.*, p. 347.

[172] H. Kellenbenz, *art. cit.*, p. 447.

[173] G. Berchet, *op. cit.*, p. 81.

[174] *Ibid.*, 12th December, 1599, p. 103.

[175] A. Paruta, *Relazione di Andrea Paruta . . .*, pub. by L. Baschiere, Venice, 1893, p. 9 ff.

[176] A.d.S., Venice, *Cinque Savii . . .*, Busta 26, 21st April, 1600.

[177] G. Berchet, *op. cit.*, 17th February, 1603, p. 122. As late as 1609 there is a report of a Venetian ship, with a cargo of 500,000 ducats belonging to the nobility, being lost at sea. Alonso de la Cueva to Philip III, Venice, 1st May, 1609, A.N., K 1679.

of the ultimate eclipse of the Mediterranean have yet to be ascertained. It cannot have been very far off as the seventeenth century began, but it was by no means yet accomplished – a hundred years after the date usually suggested as that of the death of the old queen of the world, the Mediterranean, dethroned by the new king, the Atlantic.

Possible explanations. The preceding account, incomplete and like all chronological accounts prone to mistake appearance for reality, cannot be said to have resolved all the problems. Three or four recent books have made it easier to see what was happening at the other end of the interminable passage to India, in the Far East.[178] The rapacity and lack of foresight of the Portuguese in the East Indies, in the 'drug islands', diverted the flow of luxury spices that had previously been drawn towards Malacca. An independent current became established with the Javanese junks, the drugs of the East Indies and the high quality pepper of the islands of Java and Sumatra. During the last twenty years of the century, these currents, freed from Portuguese control, centred around Atjeh, in Sumatra, the rendezvous of Moslem ships which sailed from there to the Persian Gulf or the Red Sea. Even the fine cinnamon of Ceylon was also transported to Atjeh, to be loaded on board ships bound for the Mediterranean. The fortune of Atjeh, where a thriving Turkish trading-station existed by the beginning of the seventeenth century, is the more significant in that during the same period sales of spices to China, Indochina and (apart from the Malabar coast) India were increasing by leaps and bounds, thus reducing the amount available for the Portuguese to ship around the Cape. That is not to say that Portuguese exports were not substantial, even during the early years of the seventeenth century. But it is here that we shall at last find an explanation for the continued prosperity of the Mediterranean route.

It does not by any means provide the whole answer though. For in fact all these explanations we have so patiently assembled: the naïveté of the Portuguese; the sagacity of the Turks; the great expansion eastward to the Malay Archipelago of Islam and of the spice and pepper trade dependent on it; the brutal sorties by the Portuguese squadrons at the beginning of the century; or the war between Turkey and Venice (1570–1573) which both promoted Marseilles and stimulated the secondary route between Tabriz and Poland, Lwow and Danzig – all these explanations which are in fact so many *events* in the pepper and spice war, tend to obscure the problem in its entirety, a problem that is best appreciated when viewed

---

[178] A. P. Meilink Roelofsz, *Asian trade and European influence in the Indonesian Archipelago between 1500 and about 1640*, The Hague, 1963. C. R. Boxer, *The great ship from Amacon, Annals of Macao and the old Japan trade, 1555–1640*, Lisbon 1959; F. Glamann, *Dutch Asiatic Trade, 1620–1740*, The Hague, 1958; V. Magalhães Godinho, *L'économie de l'Empire portugais aux XVe et XVIe siècles. L'or et le poivre, route de Guinée et route du Cap*, publications of École Pratique des Hautes Études, Paris, 1969; and by the same author, *Les finances de l'État portugais des Indes orientales au XVIe et au début du XVIIe siècle*, typed thesis, Paris, 1958, Sorbonne library.

in a world context – from the American silver mines to the Moluccas or the western tip of Sumatra. Viewed in this context, how does the problem emerge? Above all as a steady flow of gold and silver coins of every description, travelling from west to east, following the rotation of the earth, carrying along with them a wide range of commodities as a kind of supplementary currency and loosing in the opposite direction a rich and varied stream of different commodities and precious goods from east to west.

Within this circulatory system sweeping through the Mediterranean in both directions, every change had repercussions. If, between the roughly fixed limits of 1550 and 1620, pepper and spices were passing through the Mediterranean, was this not because the Mediterranean was for many years the destination of American silver? This was the stimulus that set trade in motion. A Venetian, Piero Zen, pointed out to the Turks at Constantinople in 1530 that 'l'arzento va dove e il piper', silver goes where the pepper is.[179] But the reverse was equally true. Details can be important here. Historians are still debating for example the date of the initial revival of the Levant trade. Kellenbenz has suggested 1540; I prefer 1550 and Godinho agrees.[180] But this is merely guesswork; none of us can claim to know for certain. It is my impression that the precise date would become evident if we ever discovered exactly when the chronic shortage of specie in the Mediterranean of the early sixteenth century was transformed into the relative abundance of the latter half[181] (with occasions, like 1583–1584 for instance, when money was so plentiful as to exceed the usual avenues of investment). From Venice's point of view I think the turning-point must have occurred somewhere between 1545 and 1560. On 9th June, 1545,[182] the workers of the Zecca were unemployed because so little gold and silver was arriving in the city. To relieve their *grandissima povertà* and give them work, a thousand ducats was minted in very small coin. In 1551,[183] incentives were offered to encourage people to bring gold to the Zecca. They would not have to pay the usual 3·5 per cent charge for coining. By 1554[184] those who wanted *cechini per navegar* were so numerous that the 3 per cent duty was reimposed. In 1561[185] so much silver (not gold) was brought to the Zecca that it could not all be minted in the small existing coins – that would have taken over a year. It was therefore decided to take the unprecedented step of minting large silver coins *ducati d'argento*. Finally in 1566 anyone who wanted to have gold minted in the Zecca had to fulfil a whole set of conditions![186] In short, we need to locate the moment at which American silver, which was flooding into

[179] M. Sanudo, XL, cols. 530–1, 7th August, 1530.
[180] *Op. cit.*, typescript, p. 1035 ff.
[181] F. Ruiz Martín, *op. cit.*
[182] Museo Correr, Donà delle Rose, 26, f° 38.
[183] *Ibid.*, 26, f° 45 v°, 46.
[184] *Ibid.*, 26, f° 48.
[185] *Bilanci Generali*, serie seconda, vol. I, Venice, 1912, p. 595–596.
[186] Museo Correr, Donà delle Rose, 26, f° 56.

Antwerp for example from 1550 on,[187] arrived in the Italian zone of the Mediterranean in sufficient quantities to restore trade with the Levant. Importance can be attached to coincidences: the crisis of the 1580s in the Levant, seems to me to correspond to a short-term fluctuation in the general economic situation, which went into a clear recession throughout the Mediterranean when Spanish silver flowed back towards the Atlantic at the time of the annexation of Portugal and the great cereal crisis of the Peninsula.

2. EQUILIBRIUM AND CRISIS IN THE MEDITERRANEAN GRAIN TRADE

The Mediterranean has never had a superabundance of grain: the scarcity of home-grown cereals and the constant search for substitutes has bred a kind of ingenuity. The study of the grain problem takes us to one of the most vulnerable areas of Mediterranean life and at the same time to a greater understanding of that life in all its complexity. The pepper and spice trade was one of luxury foodstuffs, and the names associated with it are those of the great merchant families of the sixteenth century: the Affaitati, the Ximenez, the Malvenda, the Welsers, and the Fuggers. The grain trade, although less spectacular, represented an enormous volume of business. As well as the several main supply routes, it fed a network of secondary arteries and capillaries which it would be most unwise to dismiss lightly.

Typically grain purchases were made locally, within a closed economy and a small radius. Towns drew on the granaries of the surrounding countryside. Only large cities could afford the luxury of importing such a bulky commodity over long distances.

The cereals. Traffic in grain, whether over large or small distances, was not confined merely to wheat or the grains of high commercial quality which in Sicily went by the name of *grani forti* or *grani di Rocella*.[188] In Florence three categories were distinguished: *cima delle cime, mezzano, debole.* Grain described as *cima* had had all impurities removed, and weighed 52 pounds to the *staio* or 72·500 kilograms to the hectolitre. The prices of the different categories were respectively 7, 6, and 5 *lire* per *staio* at the 1590 tariff.[189] *Deboli* referred to small grain, from the Levant (usually of rather poor quality); from the Abruzzi[190] or the Duchy of Urbino (scarcely better although Venice was not above eating it); or the grain produced in Spain and elsewhere from irrigated land exhausted by overcultivation.

Besides wheat other cereals appeared every day on Mediterranean tables,

---

[187] J. van Klaveren, *op. cit.*, p. 74.
[188] Viceroy of Sicily to Philip II, Palermo, 8th January, 1563, A.N., AB IX, 596, copy.
[189] G. Parenti, *op. cit.*, p. 78 and 79.
[190] *Arch. st. ital.*, vol. IX, p. 251.

especially barley and millet. In 1550 ten ships carrying barley and wheat arrived at Naples from Apulia.[191] Verona in 1559 complained of a disastrous millet crop[192] and was proposing to sell her reserve stocks at one ducat per Venetian *staro*. In 1562, following a catastrophic drought, there was another bad harvest. The entire millet crop was lost – 'and that is what the poor people eat', wrote the Spanish ambassador.[193] In the villages of Zante only black barley-bread was eaten.[194] Near Troy in Asia Minor, Philippe de Canaye observed that for lack of wheat the Turkish villagers ate bread made from oatmeal,[195] which in view of the rarity of oats in the Mediterranean was in its way a luxury. In Corsica the usual substitute was chestnut bread, known as tree-bread. Rice, much eaten in the East of course, as well as in the Po valley and in Valencia, occasionally replaced bread elsewhere. Pulses, chick peas from Spanish overseas territories, or beans, especially Egyptian, were also considered as bread substitutes. Alonso de Pimentel, the new captain of La Goletta, on receiving a large quantity of wheat and barley writes, 'What a misfortune that we have been sent no chick peas!'[196]

There were cereals and cereals then, and a multitude of foodstuffs are concealed behind the plural term *los panes* frequently encountered in Spanish documents. There was a bread for the rich and a bread for the poor; only the former was made from wheat. In Lisbon, grain from the north, when intended for rich men's tables, was first carefully sieved to remove stones and other impurities and the women of Lisbon could be seen on their doorsteps engaged upon this task.[197]

Some rules of the grain trade. It is only through small clues (a particular deal, the supplying of a particular city, an isolated speculation or account) that as historians we can glimpse something of the complicated life of the grain merchant. And everything conspired to make that life an anxious one: the unreliability of the harvests, the vigilant watch kept by states and above all cities, speculation by other merchants down to the humblest shopkeeper, the huge outlay involved and the risk of seeing an entire cargo lost through the actions of unscrupulous sailors. And there was no shortage of middlemen. To complicate matters even further, the profession of grain merchant was often exercised alongside other activities.

From the registers of Jacopo and Bardo Corsi, for example, we can see that these wealthy Florentine merchants were at one moment advancing money to Galileo and selling silk and long pepper on credit, the next

[191] 7th May, 1550, *ibid.*, p. 217.

[192] H. Zane to the Council of Ten, Verona, 19th September, 1559, A.d.S., Venice, B 594, f° 139.

[193] G. Hernández to Philip II, Venice, 25th August, 1562, Simancas E° 1324, f° 156.

[194] Philippe de Canaye, *op. cit.* .p. 184, famine on Zante in 1573.

[195] *Ibid.*, p. 166–167.

[196] Lo que D. Alonso Pimentel scrive . . ., 30th November, 1570, Simancas E° 1133.

[197] A. Fortunato de Almeida, *op. cit.*, III, p. 313.

handling massive wheat purchases at Palermo on behalf of the Grand Duke of Tuscany. The registers contain a record of all the transactions, completed or still under negotiation, of one of the Corsi's agents, Bartolomeo Corsini. After a series of purchases in 1595 the Florentines owed 11,766 ducats. Further transactions in 1596 concerned 3500 *salme* of wheat bought at Palermo which was to be embarked in two Ragusan ships at the *caricatore* of Girgenti, at a total cost of 10,085 ducats, or just under 3 ducats per *salma*, to be paid at Leghorn. There follows a series of accounts referring to 2000, 7000, and 6000 *salme* of grain standing in various *caricatori* awaiting shipment. Then come financial details of various settlements and transactions, followed by statements of assets and liabilities.[198] The mechanics of grain speculation would be more comprehensible if we knew more about the kind of operation described by the same agent for the Corsi in 1598. For unspecified reasons, a *nave* carrying wheat belonging to the Corsi unloaded at Messina 3700 *salme*, quite a large quantity that had somehow to be disposed of. For this wheat was left over from purchases made in 1595 and it was likely to be in no condition to use for bread or even for biscuit, and scarcely fit to be thrown to the chickens. Some of this grain was then sold on credit, the rest turned into biscuit, which seems to have been difficult to sell. Of 2500 cantars, 564 were sold in June; in August 620 were delivered to the Tuscan galleys; 1316 were left in the warehouse. As time went on the price fell from 37 *tari* to 30 then to 16.[199] And the agent complains of the bad faith of the buyers and the bakers who undertook to make the biscuit.[200] That was one side of the story. The Neapolitans who in the time of Osuna assassinated a grain hoarder, or so-called, Starace,[201] must have had their own opinion of wholesale grain merchants.

Many jealous eyes kept a careful watch over the grain trade, and not least those of governments. Every state was concerned, even the very smallest, even the Duchy of Savoy or Transylvania. Grain was responsible for more espionage, writes the nineteenth-century historian Bianchini, than the affairs of the Inquisition itself. There was good cause. Fiscal greed was as insatiable over grain as it was over salt. And the grain trade opened the door to a series of graces and favours. It was an instrument of power, a means of pressure, a way of repaying services and granting privileges. The consul of the Spanish nation at Venice, Thomas Cornoça, who according to the experts did his job well and whom Portuguese documents show to have been in the service of the merchant-king of Lisbon, asked as a reward in 1573 that wheat should be allowed free transit from Piedmont to the Grisons, through the state of Milan: a small favour among the many that were asked and granted.[202] In Sicily concessions on

[198] *Arch. Guicciardini-Corsi*, V, VII, 7.
[199] *Ibid.*, letters of 4th, 23rd, 25th June, 21st October, 1588 and 2nd July, 1599.
[200] Letter dated 2nd July, 1599.
[201] *Arch. storico italiano*, IX, p. 218, note 1.
[202] Silva to the king, Venice, 23rd May, 1573, Simancas E° 1322.

export duties were an accepted procedure.[203] A register of *tratas* in 1578
shows that Gian Andrea Doria was granted '6000 *tratte*', in other words the
right to export 6000 *salme* of Sicilian grain, that is at 2 crowns a time, a
concession of 12,000 crowns,[204] an increase on the 4500 *salme* that he had
been granted in 1566.[205] In order to supply the bases at Nice and Villefranche, where the Spanish garrisons and the Savoy galleys in the service
of Spain were stationed, the Duke of Savoy in 1566 requested from Philip
II a *tratta perpetua* of 6000 *salme* of Sicilian wheat.[206] Let him be granted
a single concession of 1500 *salme* decided the king. No details were available, but we know that Emmanuel Philibert in fact trafficked in this grain
supposedly intended for the Spanish guard on his territory.[207] The same
policy was followed by the 'lord of Monaco', Carlo Grimaldi, who had
long been the beneficiary of a concession of 6000 *salme* in Sicily. A letter
from Philip II, dated 13th October, 1584, withdrew this privilege, for he
had been selling the export licences instead of using them for supplying
Monaco, and what was more had been selling them for less than the
standard Sicilian rate.[208] In the other half of the Mediterranean world it
was the same story: on the occasion of an export licence granted to the
Ragusans in 1562 for about 1600 *salme* to be taken from Valona, we
learn that this came under the particular patronage of the Dowager
Sultana.[209]

These are small details in an episodic history. That grain export licences
should be a source of income and a means of payment for governments
constitutes yet another link between governments and the grain trade,
making the latter no easier to follow either in Turkey or in Christendom.
And the watchfulness of the states was insignificant compared to the mor-
bid vigilance of the towns.[210]

Grain was a preoccupation simply because it was always scarce: Mediterranean harvests usually verged on the inadequate. Richer kinds of farming,
vines, and livestock were in constant competition with cereal growing[211]
– an important factor but not the only one. Wheat in the Mediterranean
took up a great deal of room, requiring large areas for not very high yields,
particularly since the same land could not be sown every year. In Sicily
the two-field system (one year crops, one year fallow) usually operated[212]

[203] The reward granted to Hugo de Moncada in 1522, J. E. Martiniz Ferrando,
Privilegios ortogados por el Emperador Carlos V . . ., 1943, p. 172, n° 1543.
[204] Notamento di tratte . . ., 1578, Simancas E° 1148, the *tratas* cost 32 *tari*.
[205] Nobili to the prince, Madrid, 20th February, 1566, Medicco 4897 a.
[206] 28th February, 1566, Simancas S. R. Napoles I.
[207] P. Egidi, *op. cit.*, p. 135–136.
[208] Consulta, Palermo, 10th January, 1586, B. Com. Palermo, 3 Qq E 70.
[209] Andrea Dandolo to the Doge, Pera, 1st May, 1562, A.d.S., Venice, Senato
Secreta, Cost. Filza 3/C.
[210] See above, p. 328 ff.
[211] I de Asso, *op. cit.*, p. 108 ff. On the progress made by vine-growing in Andalusia
and New Castile, see E. J. Hamilton, *op. cit.*, p. 242; K. Häbler, *op. cit.*, p. 40.
[212] Philip II to the viceroy of Sicily, Toledo, 12th October, 1560, B. Com. Palermo,
3 Qq Z 34, f° 7.

and the same system was also used in the Apulian Tavoliere.[213] In Spain triennial rotation (three *hojas*) was the ideal, since the land was too quickly exhausted under the two-field system. The practice of dry-farming required ploughing the same land at different times, first with a deep then a shallow furrow, to compensate for the lack of rainfall.[214] And all government measures – taxes on grain, the regulation of sales – were so many blows on the back of a peasantry that could only groan under the burden, or, in Spain, allow itself to be tempted by the life of the muleteers or the American colonists.

And then there were the recurrent tragedies of winter floods and summer droughts that devotional processions were powerless to avert.[215] The final result was extreme instability of price levels which fluctuated with the slightest news. It was not until the eighteenth century that a serious attempt was made to discover the cause of these fluctuations, and few books are as enlightening on this subject as one published anonymously (possibly by Sestrini) at Florence in 1793.[216] It abounds with intelligent reflections on the disparity of wheat prices in the various regions of the Mediterranean. In the eighteenth as in the sixteenth century, there was a visible difference between the east, where bread was cheap, and the west where bread was expensive. It also explains how a poor harvest in any one region can create a zone of dear grain with prices even higher on the periphery of this zone than at the centre.[217] The same was true in the sixteenth century. As soon as scarcity became apparent in a particular area, merchants flocked towards it, dispatched their boats, and cleared their stocks. Prices over an area sometimes extending well beyond the original zone were affected by this movement. But as more ships raced to the zone of shortage, the influx of grain brought prices down again – a perfect lesson in political economy.

This was precisely what happened at Constantinople in 1561, a bad year throughout the Mediterranean, in Portugal where the spring had been 'unusually dry',[218] in Spain where the harvest had been disastrous,[219] in Sicily where the price of the *salma* after the harvest rose to $2\frac{1}{2}$ ducats,[220] and in the east, where the gap between the two harvests was difficult to bridge and there was anxiety as early as spring.[221] A Venetian *nave*, the *Colomba*, was diverted to Nicomedia to load wheat for the capital.[222]

---

[213] L. Bianchini, *op. cit.*, I, p. 359.
[214] I. de Asso, *op. cit.*, p. 77.
[215] 1540, at Naples, *Arch. st. ital.*, vol. IX, p. 105.
[216] *Confronto della ricchezza dei paesi* . . ., 1793.
[217] *Ibid.*, p. 17.
[218] J. Nicot, *op. cit.*, p. 127, 12th April, 1561.
[219] Philip to the viceroy of Sicily, Madrid, 19th August, 1561, B. Com., Palermo, 3 Qq E 34.
[220] Viceroy of Sicily to the king, Palermo, 16th October, 1561, Simancas E° 1126.
[221] H° Ferro to the Doge, Pera, 27th August, 1561, A.d.S., Venice, Dispacci Sen° Secreta Cost. Filza III/C.
[222] *Ibid.*, 3rd March, 1561.

Four other *navi*, also Venetian, which were loading grain at Vólos, were captured by the galleys on guard at Salonica and taken to Constantinople.[223] Here at the centre of the crisis the massive arrival of ships soon met the deficit and prices came tumbling down, the *chilo* (equivalent to one ninth of a *salma*,) fell to $17\frac{1}{2}$ aspers, less than three ducats per *salma*.[224] In the following year, the price of wheat went down, in the Greek ports, to 12 aspers a *chilo* or less than two ducats a *salma*.

Take another example: when a terrible famine struck Spain in 1578, the viceroy of Sicily, Marcantonio Colonna, wanted to send ships to the, rescue. The merchants loaded 24,000 *salme* and undertook to transport 6000 to Spain. As for the rest, they were unwilling to commit themselves in advance, 'for it may happen', they explained, 'that everyone hastens to the place where he thinks there is most profit and then there is an overabundance of grain' and of course commercial disaster.[225] This was the situation envisaged in 1584 by the writer of the report quoted above. He warned the government which was willing to handle the transport, of the risk they might run if the merchants rushed to Spain attracted by the smell of profit, 'el olor de la ganancia'.[226]

The ultimate catastrophe for a merchant was to have one of his ships on her way to some region in difficulties, seized by a town, which would always pay in its own time and at far below the expected price. It is easy to understand the rage of the Genoese merchants whose ship, laden with wheat from Apulia, was sailing in 1578 towards the *altissimi* prices of Spain when it was requisitioned – by the Republic of Genoa herself![227]

In theory, the merchant's aim was a simple one: to carry over from a good year to a bad one (or rather, since grain did not keep well and could not be stored for long) from a region where there was a good harvest to a region where there was a poor harvest, the surplus grain he had bought. Then, depending on the fortunes of the harvest, the currents of exchange might flow back in the opposite direction. In the grain trade anything was possible. There was not a cereal-growing region, on or near a coast, not a port that did not at one time or another have a surplus to offer. We need only go back to the fifteenth century to find that Corfu was then exporting *formento grosso*,[228] and to the first half of the sixteenth century to find Cyprus sending wheat and in particular barley to Venice.[229] In 1570 Spalato found Turkish wheat from the surrounding regions flowing into

[223] Corfu, 10th April, 1561, Simancas E° 1051, f° 51.
[224] H° Ferro to the Doge, 29th May, 1561, G. Hernandez to the king, Venice, 8th September, 1561, Simancas E° 1324, f° 15 and 16.
[225] See next note.
[226] Simancas E° 1087, f° 209, 5th December, 1584.
[227] The consul Garbarino to the Republic of Genoa, Naples, 11th September, 1578, A.d.S., Genoa, Lettere Consoli Napoli, 2.2635.
[228] A 'commodity of high quality', sold at Venice, Julianus de Picernardis to the Marquis of Mantua, Venice, 20th May, 1473, Arch. Gonzaga, B 1431.
[229] M. Sanudo, *op. cit.*, II, col. 87: 301, Cyprus, 9th November, 1498, wheat is loaded for Pisa, A.d.S., Venice, Senato Mar, f°ˢ 54 (1515), 116 v° (1516). Museo Correr, Donà delle Rose, 46, f° 43 v° (1519), 47 (1535).

her warehouses, and allowed it to be exported to Venice, until she became aware of the Turkish preparations for war[230] and, in sudden panic, forbade export of all the grain still within her walls. In some years there were extraordinary anomalies: in 1555, Spanish grain was sent to Rome;[231] in 1564 Andalusia sent grain to Genoa with formal authorization from the Catholic King;[232] Castile opened up her granaries in 1571;[233] in 1587 the viceroy of Sardinia congratulated himself on his achievements: 4000 *salme* of grain had been sent to Genoa under his administration.[234] Anything could happen: even Oran could become an export centre for African grain,[235] as Diego Suárez explains:[236] around the *presidio* local grain was only a quarter or a fifth the price of Spanish grain. The difference was appreciable when, that is, this grain existed – which was certainly not every year.[237] Algiers too might find herself either very rich or extremely poor, from year to year.[238]

But even the merchants' store of grain was not always able, unfortunately, to meet the needs of the population during the frequent, violent, and deadly famines. In 1554 there was one *horribilissima in tutta Italia*.[239] And relief cannot have come quickly from abroad, since tens of thousands of people died and in Florence the price of grain rose to 8 *lire* the *stagio*.[240]

The grain trade and the shipping routes. Grain was a transportable but a bulky commodity. However precious it might be, it could not support heavy transport costs. On the overland routes, except of course in cases of famine or very high prices, grain was only sent on very short distances.

A plan to send grain from Italy to Spain is recorded in 1584.[241] Embarcation was to take place at the *presidios* on the Tuscan coast: Orbetello, Talamona, or 'Puerto Hercules'. The grain (70,000 *fanegas*, Castile measure) was actually to be purchased from Corneto and Toscanella, on papal territory; from Grosseto and the Sienese Maremma, which came under the jurisdiction of the Grand Duke of Tuscany; and from Castro and Montalto, possessions of the Duke of Parma. Some of these places were fifteen, twenty-five, or thirty miles inland. As a result, to the

---

[230] Andrea Michiel, count and captain to the Ten, Spalato, 10th March, 1570, A.d.S., Venice, Lettere di Capi del Consiglio dei Dieci, Spalato, 281, f° 60.

[231] 7th March, 1555, B.N., Paris, Esp. 232, f° 89.

[232] Simancas E° 1293, *Sobre los capitulos que dieron las personas* . . . (1564).

[233] *Actas*, III, p. 373–374.

[234] 21st August, 1587. V. Riba y Garcia, *op. cit.*, p. 317–318.

[235] *Ibid.*, p. 288–289.

[236] Manuscript in former Government-General of Algeria, p. 471.

[237] Purchase of local grain at Mers-el-Kebir, 12th March, 1565, Simancas E° 486.

[238] R. Hakluyt, *op. cit.*, II, p. 176, about 1584. In 1579 the shortage was so great that the oarsmen had to be dismissed. J. de Cornoça to Philip II, Venice, 7th July, 1579, A.N., K 1672.

[239] G. Mecatti, *op. cit.*, II, p. 693.

[240] *Ibid.*; cf. the war of Siena and the belligerents' habit of *tagliare il grano*, *ibid.*, p. 683.

[241] Naples, 5th October, 1584, Simancas E° 1087.

purchasing price of 10 Spanish reals per *fanega*, cost of transport overland to the sea-port had to be added: 3 crowns per *moggio* or 3 reals per *fanega*. This grain had increased in price by 30 per cent in the course of a fairly short journey. So it is easy to understand the scepticism of the viceroy of Naples about the proposed improvement of the road from Apulia to Naples (29th July, 1562). 'As for the preparation of carriageable roads to bring supplies to the city of Naples, it is being carried forward as quickly as possible. But I dare say that seeing the enormous sum of money it will cost to bring grain by cart from Apulia, few people will care to take the risk'.[242] Wheat could not cross Italy by road. Grain sometimes travelled across the kingdom of Naples but there is no indication that it went all the way from the Adriatic to the Tyrrhenian coast. It hardly seems likely, since in Tuscany transport over a radius of only four to thirteen miles around Florence was sufficient to increase the cost of grain by 4·24 per cent in 1570 and 3·35 per cent in 1600[243] (which apparently indicates that the price of the commodity itself increased more than the cost of overland transport, but it would be imprudent to generalize from this example, since other percentages, also in Florence, indicate the contrary). In January, 1559 it was decided not to send barley from the villages of Santa Ella and La Rambla to Málaga, since the cost of wagon transport was as much as the barley itself.[244]

We may feel some sympathy then for the Venetian secretary, Marco Ottobon,[245] who travelled to Poland during the winter of 1590–1591 and enquired on the way, both at Innsbruck and Vienna, about the likely price of grain in Cracow and Hungary, then calculated for the *Provveditori alle Biave* how much a *staio* would cost by the time it reached Venice. He had to convert currencies and measures, take into account all duties and commissions, and was almost always forced to conclude that the operation was impossible. The equivalent of a Venetian *staio* could be bought at Cracow for the equivalent of 8 Venetian *lire*. Transport between Cracow and Vienna would cost 7 *lire* 12 *soldi*; from Vienna to Villach, 7 *lire* 10; from Villach to Venzone, 3 *lire*; from Venzone to Porto Gruaro, 1 *lira* 4; from Porto Gruaro (by boat) to Venice 3 *soldi*. On top of this there were duties and commissions to pay, not to mention the cost of sacks or barrels. The total cost would be 30 *lire* 19 *soldi*, almost 31 *lire*: in the course of its travels the merchandise would have quadrupled in price. Transport costs were the greatest single factor in variations in the price of commercialized grain.[246]

[242] Simancas, Secretarias Provincales, Napoles I.

[243] G. Parenti, *op. cit.*, p. 82.

[244] F. Verdugo to Philip II, Málaga, 21st January, 1559, Simancas E° 138, f° 264.

[245] A.d.S., Venice, Secreta Archivi Propri Polonia, Marco Ottobon to the Provveditori alle Biave, Vienna, 24th November, 1590.

[246] E. Levasseur, 'Une méthode pour mesurer la valeur de l'argent' in *Journal des Économistes*, 15th May, 1856; 'in our own day (1856) in Algeria, a hectolitre of wheat can be sold for 29 francs in Algiers and 21 francs 10 centimes in Oran, while it costs only 10 francs at Tiaret and Setif . . .'

So it is easy to understand why grain was more readily sent by water-way. The expansion southwards of Burgundian grain would have been impossible without the boats travelling down the Rhône. When foreign cereals, naturally expensive, were sent to Florence, they were ferried up the Arno as far as possible, to Signa, the river port of the capital.[247] The wealth of the territory of Lentini (Leontinoi) in Sicily was the result both of its agricultural resources and of its fortunate situation: it was not far from the coast, and its *fiume grande*, the San Leonardo was navigable to within a few leagues of the town; at least it was in 1483.[248]

Transport by sea was comparatively cheap. To return to our earlier example of Italian grain travelling to Spain, the buying price per *fanega* was 10 Castilian reals, transport to the coast 3 reals, export duty 5 reals, transport (in a good Ragusan *nave*) only $3\frac{1}{2}$ reals. There was a fairly heavy insurance premium to pay, since the season was late (9 per cent *ad valorem*) which added another 30 *maravedís* per *fanega*. So the cost of shipping amounted to only about 4 reals per *fanega*, whereas the price of a *fanega* at Alicante or Cartagena was 22 reals, 3 *maravedís* (the *real* is here reckoned at 54 *maravedís*). In the export of grain then, transport by sea was the cheapest operation involved, proportionately cheaper than carriage overland, transport by pack animal, or export licence. And shipping costs did not increase automatically with the distance travelled; it cost the same to ship from Italy to Barcelona or Valencia; whether one left from Sicily or Tuscany. Seacaptains even considered it more advantageous to sail to Spain across the 'Gulf' from Sicily, than to cross further to the north, from the *presidios* in Tuscany: from Sicily, they said, they could 'tener el golfo mas lançado', be better placed for a direct crossing.

So it was the inner region of the Mediterranean, with easy access to shipping routes, which could best afford the luxury of a grain trade. This in itself would suffice to explain why only those cities with direct sea links (apart from certain privileged towns like Milan) grew and developed. If the Mediterranean islands were often able to devote their energies to a rich and pervasive monoculture, it was because they had the sea and the grainships on their doorstep. Although constantly on the verge of food shortage, they were always able to rescue themselves from the brink, a gymnastic feat that the sea alone made possible or inspired. Grain covered extraordinary distances by water – Egyptian or Aegean grain was eaten in Valencia, in Spain,[249] in Genoa and Rome. The bishop of Dax wrote from Ragusa to Charles IX in January, 1572: 'In this city not a single grain of wheat is eaten which does not have to be fetched from five hundred miles away,'[250] a situation dating from well before the sixteenth century. This was how grain travelled in antiquity, in boats sometimes without decks.

[247] G. Parenti, *op. cit.*, p. 83; A. Doren, *Storia econ. dell' Italia* . . ., 1936, p. 366.
[248] Matteo Gaudioso, 'Per la storia . . . di Lentini' in *A. st. per la Sicilia Orientale*, 1926–27, p. 83.
[249] E. J. Hamilton, *op. cit.*, p. 257, note 4.
[250] E. Charrière, *op. cit.*, III, p. 244–249.

In the eleventh century, wheat from Aragon went down the Ebro then from Tortosa travelled the long diagonal route across the sea to relieve extreme hardship in Syria.[251]

Ports and countries that exported grain. All the chief markets of the grain trade were situated on the coast or on a waterway, like the little ports whose boats converged on Leghorn: Grosseto, Montalto, Corneto[252] or the harbours in the Abruzzi which a surviving insurance policy shows to have engaged in a lively traffic with Venice: Grottamare, Sinagaglia.[253] It was even more true of the larger markets: the towns of the Danube plains, linked by the great river with the Black Sea (a report from the Levant in December, 1575[254] indicates that the tribute of grain from Wallachia and Bogdiana was, on Turkish orders, to be made into biscuit and deposited on the banks of the Danube, where it would be collected); the Aegean markets which served the wheat-growing coastal regions; Gallipoli serving Thrace, Patmos near the Asian coast, Salonica at the entrance to Macedonia[255] and Vólos, the great resource for western buyers, which exported the wheat from the plains of Thessaly.[256] In Egypt, the Nile, like the Danube, carried huge quantities of wheat as well as rice, beans, and chick peas down to the sea. In the West, the great grain exporters were Apulia and Sicily – the latter a sort of sixteenth-century Canada or Argentina.

For this reason alone the case of Sicily would repay study. It also has the advantage of being clearer than any other. The administration and government of Sicily by the viceroys was first and foremost a question of handling the grain. Their letters abound in references to harvests, prices, export licences, deals to be made with foreign merchants at Palermo where the Sicilian nobles, enriched by the island's great cereal production, also had their residences.[257] Sicily had played the vital role of grain-supplier for many centuries, since antiquity in fact, with varying degrees of prominence but without interruption. The contract signed between Genoa and Manfred, king of Sicily in 1261, for the export of 10,000 *salme* a year (20,000 quintals) could with a little exaggeration (for Genoa had grown

---

[251] I de Asso, *op. cit.*, p. 108–109.
[252] Mediceo 2079 and 2080.
[253] Ragusa Archives, Diversa de Foris, XI, f°s 56 ff; many references to short-distance traffic, grain from Fiume and Spalato being taken to Venice; insurance registers dealt with by Pasqual Cerva (1601–1602).
[254] G. da Silva to the king, Venice, 10th December, 1575, Simancas E° 1334.
[255] Not a single Venetian ship in the grain port of Salonica, notes H° Ferro, letter to the Doge, 16th February, 1561, A.d.S., Venice, Senato Secreta Cost. Filza 2/B f° 334.
[256] Ragusa Archives, Lettere di Levante, 33, f°s 11 v° to 13 v°, Rector and Council of Ragusa, Biaggio Vodopia, *sopracarico* of the ship belonging to Gio. Pasquale sent to the Levant. Full list of the *caricatori* in the Aegean: Metelino, the Gulf of Marga, Kavalla, Salonica, Vólos, Zotone. But everywhere 'se ne trovano sempre caramusali con li grani da vendere'.
[257] E. Albèri, *op. cit.*, 1574, II, V, p. 477.

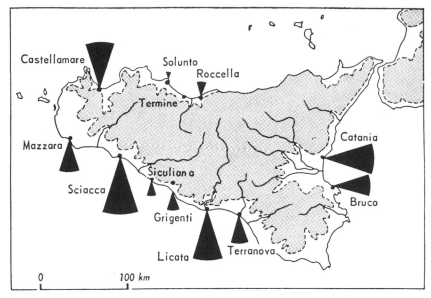

Fig. 49: *The Sicilian* caricatori *in 1532*

After L. Bianchini, *op. cit.*, p. 241. The ports exporting wheat correspond to the plains and hills of the island. Apart from Castellamare, there was no export port to the north; they were chiefly concentrated along the south coast. Sciacca held the record for exports (40,000 *salme* out of a total volume of 260,000 *salme*, that is 520,000 quintals). For Grigenti, Termine, Bruco, read Girgenti, Termini, Bruca.

in the meantime) be mistaken for a sixteenth-century contract.[258] The entire West, and the neighbouring Barbary coast most of all, dreamed of Sicilian grain. Leo Africanus relates that the Arabs handed over their children as pledges to obtain Sicilian wheat.[259] When Tripoli was recaptured by the Christian troops, there was immediate concern in Sicily about the duties to be levied on wheat sent to Africa. Only the 2500 *salme* reserved for the fortress itself were to be exempted.[260]

By the time of Ferdinand the Catholic, the list of *caricatori*, the Sicilian grain wharves, was already established: Solunto, Termini, Roccella, Catania, Bruca, Terranova, Licata, Girgenti, Siculiana, Mazzara, and Castellammare. The record of exports for 1532[261] reveals the leading position of the south with its hills. The official total of exports for that year (1532) was almost 260,000 *salme* or 520,000 quintals of grain, four times the requirement of Genoa according to an estimate of 1577.[262] Genoa annually imported 60,000 to 70,000 *salme* of Sicilian wheat.[263] But there was hardly

[258] L. Bianchini, *op. cit.*, I, p. 346.
[259] G. M. Amari, *op. cit.*, III, 3, p. 831.
[260] La Mantia, *art. cit.*, p. 487.
[261] L. Bianchini, *op. cit.*, I, p. 241.
[262] Relatione di quel che occorre al Duca di Terranova . . . 1577, Simancas E° 1146.
[263] *Ibid.*

a city in the west that had not been eating the island's excellent grain for centuries.

This long-standing trade was very highly organized. The commercial centre was Palermo, which did not however handle loading or transport but dealt with everything to do with the *negozio frumentario*,[264] no doubt because the landowners who sold the grain lived there themselves; more to the point, so did the agents for the wealthy Florentine or Genoese merchants, in order to be within reach of the viceroy (who it is true divided his time between Messina and Palermo) or at any rate his offices and the *portolano*, the official who complicated even further the red tape and procedures necessary for obtaining the *tratas*, the precious export licences. These licences were not free of charge and their prices varied according to a sliding scale, which Mario Siri[265] has reconstructed in the table reproduced below:

Sliding scale of Sicilian export duties
(after Mario Siri)

Price per salma	Duty per salma
18 to 22 tari	6 tari
22 to 26 tari	10 tari
26 to 30 tari	12 tari
over 30 tari	16 tari

These duties naturally affected Sicilian prices. Did this fact contribute in 1550[266] to the increased demand for wheat from the Levant which was cheaper, according to the nineteenth century historian Bianchini? If so, the decline of the Sicilian grain fleet might have been a consequence of this competition. Or perhaps, as seems more likely, the decline of the fleet coincided with the growing importance of Venetian and Ragusan cargo vessels capable of carrying thousands of *salme* of grain. The ships loading wheat in Sicily for Venice in the year 1573 had a capacity of respectively 4800, 4000, 4000, 4000, 2500, 2000, 1800, 1500, 1000 and 1000 *salme*.[267] A new fleet had grown up, specializing in the transport of bulky goods like grain, salt and wool. This fleet completed the equipment of the Sicilian grain market, which also possessed vast warehouses in the *caricatori* – sixteenth-century grain elevators – and operated a system of warehouse warrants, for which a receipt was given to the depositor. The history has yet to be written of the *cedola*, the receipt given to a landowner who did not wish to sell his grain immediately but did want an advance payment. To whom did he sell the *cedola* when the need arose?

[264] E. Albèri, *op. cit.*, II, V, p. 243 (1574).
[265] M. Siri, *art. cit.*
[266] L. Bianchini, *op. cit.*, I, p. 337.
[267] Relatione delle navi venute a carricar di formenti in Sicilia per Veneciani le quali sono state impedite, Simancas E° 1139.

All this has a strangely modern sound about it. But to judge it better, we would need to know more about these grain stores and their accounts and about the money-lenders who accepted the *cedole* than is to be found in Bianchini's history.[268] We would need to know more too about the administrative and capitalist system embracing both the production and the sale of grain, a system which always led back to the men who controlled the movement of money. If grain prices fell, the peasants (known curiously as the *borghesi*) could not pay their debts and had to sell their oxen or even leave their land. In effect they borrowed money at the beginning of every year in order to buy seed-corn and the oxen for ploughing and to take the chance of cultivating new ground. 'Even the nobles and the *caballeros*,' says a Spanish report at the beginning of the seventeenth century, 'borrow money in this way intending to repay it in grain, and if they cannot do so, they are exposed to pay high interest, so that they rush to the viceroys to beg that the debt be lessened and sometimes their request is granted. . . .'[269] This is exactly the same situation, both for peasants and noblemen, as is found in the early seventeenth century, near Valladolid in Castile.[270]

During the sixteenth century one has the impression that this system was gradually being destroyed. Curious speculation in the *cedole* began to occur, for example. Forgeries were put into circulation with the connivance of the *magazinieri*, and non-existent wheat was sold; when the time came to settle up, the seller would plead damage or theft from the *caricatori*. Some *magazinieri* went bankrupt. The government in vain tried to defend public honesty, threatening offenders with the galleys, demanding sincere declarations, forbidding advance selling or buying of grain, and the usurious contracts 'alla voce e secondo le mete' as they were called, or wagers on the price of the merchandise.[271] But the scandals persisted and some landowners preferred to let their grain rot in the trenches where they stored it, rather than let it fall into the hands of the swindlers and speculators in the ports. Unless, that is, this was another way of speculating in a commodity that was in short supply, even in Sicily, towards the end of the sixteenth century. So serious did the situation become that the municipal authorities and even the government itself did not hesitate to seize wheat from the *caricatori*.[272]

In Apulia, where there was a flourishing export trade based on the ports of Manfredonia, Foggia, and Trani and carrying grain to Ragusa, Venice, and Naples, a similar system operated: the *tratte*, export licences for cus-

---

[268] *Op. cit.*, I, p. 337.
[269] *Memoria del governo del Reyno di Sicilia* (undated), Biblioteca Comunale, Palermo, Qq F 29.
[270] B. Bennassar, Valladolid, *op. cit.*
[271] Pragmatic of 26th August, 1559, item 61, n° 4. On the 'voce' also practised at Naples see the fuller description in G. Coniglio, *op. cit.*, p. 21 ff. The merchant advanced money to the peasant, who undertook to sell him his wheat – 'alla voce' – at the future market price.
[272] L. Bianchini, *op. cit.*, I, p. 356.

toms purposes, were sold in advance and in large numbers by the royal tax officials. These licences depreciated and could be bought up at a low price. According to the merchants, Venice was saving up to 32 per cent in customs payments in this way.[273]

Eastern Grain. But the West could not survive on internal exchange alone. During the middle years of the century, in particular, western stocks were replenished by shipments from the Levant, which with its smaller population had more grain available for export, usually at lower prices. The three principal sources of grain in the East were: Egypt; the plains of Thessaly, Macedonia, Thrace, and Bulgaria; and the Rumanian lowlands. Rumanian wheat soon disappeared from the Mediterranean circuits and was appropriated for the insatiable appetite of Constantinople. There remained the Greek and Bulgarian export markets and the granaries of Egypt. From the latter, the consul Lorenzo Tiepolo estimated in 1554 that the sultan was obtaining 600,000 *ribebe* of wheat, barley, and beans (curiously there is no mention of rice).[274] These 600,000 *ribebe* (at 100 Sicilian *salme* to 165 *ribebe*[275]) correspond to 363,636 *salme* or 720,000 quintals: a gigantic supply, much more than Sicily could provide.[276] While a large part of this grain was destined for Constantinople, some was left in Egypt for the rations of Turkish soliders and some was sent to Mecca. Besides, the sultan's 'wheat' was not necessarily all the wheat in Egypt. Tiepolo's figures (including the 1,200,000 ducats which this trade was worth to the sultan) are only estimates. In fact, as he himself adds, everything varies according to the height of flooding along the Nile, the incidence of epidemics and the price situation. The report gives two prices for a *ribeba* of beans and three for grain.[277]

Moreover, at Alexandria as well as at Vólos, Salonica, Valona, La Prevesa, or Santa Maura, Turkish grain was loaded on to westbound ships, legally, with the consent of the Grand Turk, as is reported frequently in Ragusan or Venetian commercial papers. In Constantinople there was a constant refrain of requests from western countries: from Tuscany as early as 1528;[278] from Genoa in 1563;[279] in 1580, all such requests were refused, even those of the French,[280] but a flourishing black market nevertheless continued to export Turkish grain westwards even during the prohibition. The headquarters of this black market was the Aegean,

---

[273] Karl Otto Müller, *Welthandelsbräuche, 1480–1540,* 2nd impression Wiesbaden, 1962, p. 54.
[274] *Relatione,* pub. by Cicogna, p. 24.
[275] According to the table of measurements given by A. de Capmany, *op. cit.,* IV appendix, p. 63 which is itself taken from Pegolotti.
[276] See Fig. 51, p. 598.
[277] 32 and 45 *maidini* for a *ribeba* of beans; 41, 48, and 60 for grain, that is in ducats per *salma,* 1.2; 1.7; and 2.4.
[278] K. O. Müller, *op. cit.,* p. 275.
[279] E. Charrière, *op. cit.,* II, p. 717, note.
[280] The sultan to the king, 15th July, 1580, *Recueil,* p. 21.

certain islands of which, Patmos for example,[281] grew excellent wheat, but where there was usually to be found contraband grain brought from the mainland, especially Greece, in the light *caramusalis*, the marauding ships without which the Venetian islands, from Crete to Corfu, would often have gone short of bread. Sometimes it was difficult to obtain supplies from these sources[282] and large sums of money had to change hands. But in good years they had plenty of grain to sell. In 1564 the cargoes of the *caramusalis* bought up by the Venetian governors of Crete provided more grain than was needed for the island's food supply. The surplus, of which part was made into biscuit, was transported to Venice.[283]

But the Aegean trade was always a risky affair, at the mercy of the displeasure or demands of a *sandjak-beg*, or the appearance of the Turkish galleys patrolling the grain ports.[284] So the appointment of the Turkish 'officers' in the Aegean was always an important event in Venice. In March, 1562 a certain Suil Pasha (if I have correctly transcribed his name) was appointed to the *sanjak* of Metelino (Mitilíni) through the influence of the Sultana and Muḥammad Pasha and was about to take up his post; 'I was tempted,' writes the Venetian *bailo*, Andrea Dandolo, 'not to make him the usual present, because of the harm he had recently done the Signoria; but remembering that it was but a short way from the *sandjak-beg's* residence to the grain ports where the best grain is being sold at the moment at 12 aspers the *chilo*, I was afraid he might take it himself.' And the *bailo* preferred to comply.[285] The Archipelago remained even in the eighteenth century the centre of a black market in grain, using the same marauding Greek ships.[286]

Equilibrium, crisis, and vicissitudes in the grain trade. After this rather long introduction we are now in a better position to tackle the problem of the vicissitudes of the grain trade in the sixteenth century. There is always a risk of overdramatizing in an area where contemporary judgments were rarely dispassionate. On the whole, however, it would be true to say that the food problem grew steadily worse towards the end of the century and the 'peasant situation' became increasingly alarming. Famines increased, not in number – they had always been frequent – but in gravity. Their effects were felt more deeply. Six *carestie* hit Naples between 1560 and 1600; in 1560, 1565, 1570, 1584, 1585, 1591; the last three were more serious than the first three.[287] It is not that 'the harvests are worse than in the past', writes an experienced observer of Neapolitan affairs in 1608,[288] 'but the

[281] R. Hakluyt, *op. cit.*, II, p. 308, 1594.
[282] Pera, 6th October, 1560, A.d.S., Venice, Senato Secreta, 2/B, f° 274.
[283] To the Council of Ten, Candia, 4th January, 1563 (f° 102, 7th January, (f° 103)); Capi del Cons° dei X, Lettere Bª 285.
[284] Zante, 31st March – 6th April, 1563, A.d.S., Venice, Senato Secreta, 3/C.
[285] A.d.S., Venice, the *bailo* to the Doge, Pera, 22nd March, 1562.
[286] Baron de Tott, *Memoirs*, Eng. trans., vol. II (part IV) p. 148-9.
[287] Giuseppe Pardi, *art. cit.*, p. 85.
[288] B.N., Paris, Esp., 127, f°. 52.

number of people has increased, as the population counts show: 95,641 more hearths in 1545, 53,739 in 1561; the count now in progress will, it is thought, reveal an increase of 100,000. When grain is in short supply or scarcely sufficient to go round, every one seeks to conceal it'. The shortage was unfortunately not confined to the kingdom or city of Naples. Throughout the Mediterranean man's resources were failing to keep pace with his numbers.

It is therefore tempting to envisage a single Mediterranean situation, to talk of *the* grain crisis but let us not jump too hastily to conclusions. The only criteria available for measuring the overall situation relate to the large scale international grain trade. Considerable quantities of grain were concerned, but:

1. this was an atypical pattern of exchange, as we have already seen;[289]
2. on closer observation, the history of this specifically commercialized grain reveals at least four major landmarks – indications of crisis: the arrival of northern grain in the ports and towns on the Atlantic coast of the Iberian peninsula from the beginning of, and throughout the sixteenth century; the Turkish wheat boom between 1548 and 1564, in effect a measure of the crisis in Italian cereal production; Italian self-sufficiency – the agricultural miracle between 1564 and 1590; and during the 1590s and thereafter, the arrival in Italy of grain from the north;
3. in every case these crises were finally met by some solution or compromise, even the last, the extent and relative character of which should not be misjudged.

Even to talk of crisis and equilibrium is to oversimplify. There was what an economist would call a marginal crisis, leaving unaffected a fundamental equilibrium that limited the extent of catastrophe and tension. In mid-crisis, at Venice on 16th June, 1591, the Senate was able to say, correctly, 'experience has shown that there is usually harvested within our state, of wheat and other cereals, a little less than is required for our needs', 'un pocho men che bastevoli al bisogno'.[290]

It would be as well then to consider each of these four crises in turn and, as a second precaution, to beware of painting too black a picture of a situation that was never, it is true, altogether happy. The extreme step of importing grain, from far or very far away, was a measure of men's hunger, a measure too of the wealth of the buyers.

The first crises: northern grain at Lisbon and Seville. This is demonstrated by the arrival of northern grain in Portugal and Andalusia. Portugal began importing very early, at the beginning of the sixteenth century; Andalusia, still rich in her own wheat was not affected until much later,

[289] See above, p. 423.
[290] A.d.S., Venice, Senato Terra 120, 16th June, 1591.

in the 1550s or even 1570–1580. There were two separate crises, in fact, the Portuguese and the Spanish, following similar courses and foreshadowing later developments in Italy.

In Portugal maritime expansion had created a curiously modern state. With a little exaggeration it could be described as an earlier version of England, centred like England, on its capital; Lisbon, standing head and shoulders above the multitude of small towns and villages active in its service, especially after the accession of the House of Aviz in 1386. A patriarchal, underpopulated Portugal, producing its own cereals and even exporting some to England,[291] drinking its own wine, was giving way to a Portugal increasingly uncertain of its daily bread. Orchards, olives, and vines were taking up more and more room. Considerable efforts to increase cereal production can be detected in the south in Alemtejo for example, where different varieties of grain were acclimatized. The need for grain, grain 'imperialism',[292] drove the Portuguese to seize control of the markets of the wide Moroccan plains, to introduce cereals briefly to Madeira and later to implant them successfully in the Azores. But the most satisfactory solution was to buy grain from outside, to abandon what was basically an unprofitable domestic activity.

Lisbon was very soon eating foreign grain, imported for many years from Andalusia and Castile and dispatched (though not always) from Sicily. In 1546, the ambassador of the king of Portugal at Rome, Simão de Veiga, made a hasty, but fruitless journey to Palermo.[293] The Portuguese, who had long-standing connections first with Bruges, then with Antwerp, also turned to Flanders, possibly as early as the fifteenth century; in 1508 at any rate they were buying very good grain there, *o muito bom* at 10 *pataques*, and the best, *o melhor* for 11.[294] These purchases continued throughout the century. Usually northern grain, whether from the Baltic or elsewhere, was carried in the tiny Breton boats which arrived at Lisbon hundreds at a time. Poorest of the poor, how could the Breton sailors resist the temptation of payment in gold which they received in Portugal and were legally allowed to carry away? They 'arrive here every day', writes the French ambassador Jean Nicot, from Lisbon on 4th September, 1559, 'carrying great quantities of corn and without any permission [from the King of France]. I follow after to try to restore order.'[295] But he was not very successful. For Portugal was, according to his own description, 'a country . . . marvellously lacking in every kind of cereal'. And almost a century later, in 1633, a hundred of the same little boats are recorded at Lisbon, being first sequestered then released by the Portuguese authorities. In order to survive, these sailors would sell sails, rudder, the boat itself

[291] Gilberto Freyre, *Casa Grande e Senzala*, 1946, I, p. 411–412.
[292] Vitorino Magalhães Godinho's expression.
[293] Rome, 18th April, 1546, in *Corpo dipl. Port.*, VI, p. 35, 36.
[294] Braacamp Freire, 'Maria Brandoa' in *Archivo historico portuguez*, VI, 1908, p. 427.
[295] *Correspondance de Jean Nicot, op. cit.*, p. 5.

and still die of hunger in the end.[296] This half-illicit traffic carried on by the Breton boats laid a burden 'el qual es muy fuerte'[297] on the Portuguese economy and policy. For all that, it made use of the trade circuits without which none of this apparently spontaneous traffic would be possible. It was the merchants of Bilbao and Burgos, Simón Ruiz at Medina del Campo, who in 1558 were making these movements possible.[298]

By this date the grain carried in these Breton *barques* had already reached Castile, to whose economy it was 'harto dañoso' extremely harmful.[299] By Castile, let us understand, although it is not quite accurate, the ports of Biscay and Galicia. We do not know exactly when it first appeared in Andalusia. But it is possible that the Frenchman, Guion Soliman, who in August, 1557 sold the boat in which he had brought grain to Cadiz, was a Breton.[300] In any case, from then on voyages by Breton ships became more frequent, giving them an opportunity to bring back, depending on their port of call, either the 'red gold' of Portugal or the silver of Spain.

In Cadiz, Seville, Andalusia, and the south of Spain as far as Málaga and Alicante, a pattern of development similar to that in Portugal began to emerge as the wealth of the New World reached Seville. This newly acquired wealth encouraged the planting of vines and olive trees. But the region was so rich in wheat that this development was slow. Seville was short of grain while neighbouring towns – Puerto de Santa Maria, the rich Jerez de la Frontera, and above all Málaga had no difficulty in obtaining food supplies. At Málaga the *proveedores* of the armadas found their task an easy one for a long time. By paying one or two more reals for a *fanega*[301] they could obtain a ready supply of grain. Prices were much lower than in Catalonia[302] almost down to the level of Naples or Sicily.[303] There was no lack of grain then, but there was a lack of pack animals to transport it. The government had only to requisition the animals for the price of wheat to be at the mercy of its officials.[304] All was well then until mid-century. As late as 1551 the Fuggers obtained leave to export from Andalusia and the *partido* of Calabrava 36,000 *fanegas*, of which 16,000 were for Barcelona.[305] Two years later, in August 1553, the Count of Tendilla[306] claimed the concession (*ayuda de costa*) of an export

[296] British Museum, Sloane, 1572.
[297] Simancas E° 171, Portugal, D. J. de Mendoza to H. M., Lisbon, 30th March, 1558.
[298] Archivo Simón Ruiz, Valladolid, Legajo I, f° 75–76, for example Benedito Ugonchery to Simón Ruiz, 27th August, 1558 and many other letters.
[299] See note 297.
[300] A.N., K 1490, Cadiz, 4th August, 1557.
[301] Mondejar to Charles V, Alhambra, 19th July, 1541, Simancas *Guerra Antigua*, XX, f° 96.
[302] R. Carande, *Carlos V y sus banqueros*, p. 24–25.
[303] Mondejar to Charles V, Alhambra, 2nd December, 1539, Simancas *Guerra Antigua*, XVI, f° 145.
[304] *Ibid.*
[305] Valladolid, May 1551, Simancas *Guerra Antigua*, XLI, f° 247.
[306] The Count of Tendilla to Juan Vazquez de Molina, Málaga, August 1553, Simancas, *Guerra Antigua*, LIII, f° 43.

licence for 4000 to 5000 *cahizes* of grain from Málaga. Since the market was glutted, he could have been granted even more, but it would have been worth no more than 'the ink on the paper', 'sin poner en ello mas que tinta y papel'. And the peasants had to be relieved of their surplus harvest. 'We have now had six or seven fertile years' writes one of the *proveedores* of Málaga,[307] 'perhaps we shall not fare so well in the years to come.'

In fact, the situation did not deteriorate until about the 1560s. In 1561,[308] Seville protested loudly against the Genoese who controlled her customs and were pressing for payment on the grain (both wheat and barley) that the city had imported in large quantities from France, Flanders and the Canaries. Did they want the poor to die of hunger? These were by no means the first shipments of foreign grain to Seville, but the turning-point had not yet been reached: in 1564,[309] for instance, there were plans to export Andalusian wheat to Genoa (although never carried out, the plans reached a fairly advanced stage). Some time between 1561 and 1569, a lean year, this transformation must have taken place. Andalusia, with more oil, wine, and silver than she needed, was from now on habitually importing foreign wheat. By 1560 at the latest[310] the evolution was complete. Flour from Andalusia was no longer sufficient to make the biscuit for the fleets, and the Spanish Crown had to go in search every year, good or bad, of 100,000 *fanegas* of grain from the North (55,000 quintals) which was at once a little and a great deal. In 1583 the shortage spread to the whole of Spain, disrupting the entire economy.[311]

The problem is to know whether or not this deficit (henceforward permanent) can be regarded as a fundamental clue to the Spanish economy and its 'peasant situation'. It is a question that the historian is ill-equipped to answer. There exists no general study of the complex agricultural situation of the Peninsula (including Portugal) even remotely comparable to Marc Bloch's book on the original features of French agriculture[312] or Emilio Sereni's recent description of rural Italy.[313] The sum of our knowledge is very small. The Peninsula has always been remarkable for its extreme diversity: it possesses many poor and backward regions. During the invasion of Navarre, in 1522, French soldiers died of hunger in this land of millet bread and on their return to Bayonne after their defeat, some gorged themselves to death.[314] Galicia too, in 1581, was a barren region, where the coarse rye-bread seemed, to a wealthy Venetian traveller, unfit for human

---

[307] F^{co} de Diego to F^{co} de Ledesma, Málaga, 23rd November, 1553, Simancas, *Guerra Antigua*, LIII, f° 40.

[308] The city of Seville to H. M. ,7th August, 1561, Simancas Consejo y Juntas de Hacienda, 28.

[309] Sobre los capitulos que dieron las personas . . ., Simancas E° 1389 (1564).

[310] J. van Klaveren, *op. cit.*, p. 155, note 1.

[311] F. Ruiz Martín, *op. cit.*, p. CXXXV and note 4.

[312] *Les caractères originaux de l'histoire rurale française*, 1931.

[313] Emilio Sereni, *Storia del paesaggio agrario italiano*, Bari, 1961.

[314] *Loyal Serviteur, op. cit.*, p. 102.

consumption.[315] And yet we know that there was an agricultural revival, whose roots went back a long way and which was still spreading during the first half of the sixteenth century. The increased numbers of mules in harness, their comparatively low price,[316] the energy with which they pulled the light swing-plough for surface ploughing,[317] the increased cultivation of new ground, the extension of olives and vines, especially the latter, wherever the soil and climate would allow or tolerate them, the obvious reduction of sheep farming in so many areas (even for fine wool) – all point to expansion and progress in agriculture. Investigation of notarial documents in Valladolid[318] has brought to light *censos* drawn up on the occasion of land purchase. Urban capitalism with its high interest rates was instrumental in this revival.

It was an expansion accomplished at the expense of the *montes blancos*, or *albales*, the white 'mountains', stripped of their trees and intended for crop cultivation, plantations, or temporary enclosures for animals. Between the *Candelaria* (Candlemas), and Midsummer Day following, any peasant could appropriate a piece of this unoccupied land (and the temporary provision became permanent) and plant trees, olives, a few rows of vines, perhaps enclose a piece of grazing land for his animals. Countless documents bear witness to this long struggle against the barren stony land and a series of words from the past (*escalias*, newly broken ground; *escaliar* to break the ground, *artigar* to clear the undergrowth; *presuras*, taking possession; *baldios*, uncultivated lands; *dehesas*, common pasture; *ejidos*, common lands and waste ground at the entrance to the village, where any peasant had the right to thresh his harvest under the feet of animals) all these words, taken from low Latin, and found with variants in Catalonia or in Andalusia, as well as in their native land, Castile, apparently take us straight to the heart of problems broadly common to all western rural communities. Or so it seems. But it would be worth trying to measure this expansion, to see if it was maintained (for the demographic advance in Spain had reached its peak before the end of the century) trying too to gauge the prosperity of the peasant community which was exaggerated by observers. The much-vaunted 'rural bourgeoisie' was a fragile thing.[319] Crisis reached the countryside soon after the middle of the century. Was the land exhausted? A curious letter written by Philip II, dated 12th October, 1560, maintains the contrary.[320] Perhaps even more than by the feudal yoke, which grew no lighter, the peasant was crushed by the burden of usury: it had helped him during the 'first' sixteenth century, but after

[315] Public Record Office, 30, 25, 157, Giornale autografo di Francesco Contarini da Venezia a Madrid, Lisboa . . .

[316] Noël Salomon, *La Campagne de la Nouvelle Castille à la fin du XVIe siècle d'après les Relaciones Topograficas*, 1964, p. 95, note 2.

[317] *Ibid.*

[318] According to Bartolomé Bennassar, *op. cit.*, from which all the information in this paragraph concerning Valladolid is taken.

[319] N. Salomon, *op. cit.*, p. 302 ff.

[320] Philip II to the Viceroy of Naples, Biblioteca Comunale Palermo, 3 Qq Z, 34, f 7.

1550 it was to turn against him, driving him off his land, and bad times soon followed. In 1571, 12,452 families recruited in the Asturias, Galicia, Burgos, and León, were resettled in 400 villages on land formerly belonging to the Moriscos expelled from Granada. Twenty years later the official survey of 1593 revealed how unsuccessful this operation had been: some peasants had sold their inheritances, others had left theirs in the hands of their creditors and emigrated no-one knew where; a few lucky ones had taken advantage of these misfortunes, bought up a few olive trees here, half a property there and now passed as *villanos ricos*.[321] Surveys of the villages of New Castile (1575–1580) also convinced one historian, who studied the whole of this extraordinary dossier,[322] that the shadows were lengthening in these hard-working villages: there were too many people for the land which could no longer be extended, too many underpaid day-labourers, emigration to the towns and to the Indies was beginning; the villages were declining.

There can be no doubt that the Spanish economy as a whole took a turn for the worse about the years 1580–1590[323] and that agriculture was the first sector to show signs of trouble although we do not know how, or why or exactly when it became clear that recession was on the way. The participants and the elements of the problem are clear enough: migrant flocks, settled flocks, the regular cultivation of the *regadios*, the irrigated gardens with their orange, mulberry, and other fruit trees; the *secanos*, dry lands on which vines and olive trees grew; sown fields (one year in two or three, they were sown half with wheat, half with barley) the fallow land, the *barbechos*, growing beans. But often on the *montes* peasants risked growing anything, 'algunos años labrase aqui algo' as a survey made in 1492 says of some parts of Gibraltar.[324] By the end of the sixteenth century it was becoming a losing battle.[325]

Foreign grain cannot be blamed for this state of affairs. At most it was a warning sign of approaching trouble. In Portugal, where the trouble had deep roots, unusual consequences were noted by contemporaries. The Spanish ambassador at Lisbon noted on 1st October, 1556 that 'the country is sick and in numerous regions many people are dying, it is said, from illnesses provoked by the bad food they have eaten and are still eating. The present year has provided even less bread than in the past and all are terrified at the thought of the future, unless God sends a remedy. Here in Lisbon, there is at present a little bread made from the grain which came by sea from France, but it all disappears quickly. . . .'[326]

---

[321] Joachim Costa, *Colectivismo agrario en España* (Buenos Aires edition, 1944), p. 214 ff.

[322] N. Salomon, *op. cit.*, p. 48 ff.

[323] This is the central argument of Felipe Ruiz Martín's forthcoming book.

[324] F. de Zafra to the Catholic Kings, 20th June, 1492 (or 1494), *CODOIN*, LI, p. 52–53.

[325] On this 'battle', see the admirable studies by Spanish geographers, for example Alfredo Floristan Samanes, *La Ribera tudelana de Navarra*, 1951.

[326] D. Luys Sarmiento to Juan Vazquez de Molina, Lisbon, 1st October, 1556, Simancas, Diversos de Castilla, n° 1240.

It was a country rotten at the core, an enormous deadweight of which Philip was to find himself master in 1580, upon the conquest of Portugal. Let us remember in particular the connection between undernourishment and illness, for it was no coincidence. The epidemics that were to strike Spain at the end of the century – before the recession hit any other part of Europe – find an explanation here. This crisis disturbed a fundamental equilibrium.

The Turkish wheat boom: 1548–1564. With the middle of the century crisis loomed in Italian agricultural production.[327] There began a period of bad harvests, of obvious food shortages, and high prices throughout the peninsula. The causes of these hardships are not clear: over-population, poor meteorological conditions, a decline in agricultural investment, foreign wars – all these are possible or rather contributory causes and the situation deteriorated even further following 'una carestia di formento et altri grani' that did not spare even such a well-protected city as Venice.[328] In any case, Italy quickly discovered a remedy for her often serious difficulties: a few payments in silver and her capacious grain ships, or those of Ragusa, were on their way to the ports of the Levant and the Turkish market.

This departure was sufficiently marked to bring about an increase in average tonnages to about 600 tons and before long even more. Among these big ships, it was typical to find certain Turkish roundships specializing in the long voyage from Constantinople to Alexandria in Egypt. One of these, owned by the Grand Vizier Rustem Pasha, arrived in Venice in December, 1551 with a cargo charged to the account of Zuan Priuli, and the Signoria exempted it from anchorage duty.[329] There was, indeed, during these years active complicity from important Turkish dignitaries who possessed land and crops and were eager for money. Turkey, especially at first, found herself in a begging position, as if she did not know what to do with her surpluses. 'The more reserved our merchants are,' wrote the Venetian *bailo* on 4th September, 1551, 'the better terms they will find, for there is plenty of grain, belonging both to the nobles and to the people and, because of the war with the Emperor, there are no possible buyers except the Venetians and the Ragusans.'

In this year 1551, which saw the victorious expedition of Sinān Pasha against Tripoli, Venice imported from these grain ports between 300,000 and 400,000 *staia* (240,000 to 320,000 hectolitres or 180,000 to 240,000 quintals). If other cargoes are added, in particular those of the Genoese ships, about which unfortunately no details are available, perhaps 500,000

---

[327] This section is largely based on Marcel Aymard's book, *Venise, Raguse et le commerce du blé dans la seconde moitié du XVIᵉ siècle*, Paris, publication of École Pratique des Hautes Études, 1966. I have borrowed the title of one of his chapters. Full references to any documents quoted in this section without footnotes will be found in his work.
[328] Marciana, Italian Manuscript, 8386, 1550.
[329] A.d.S., Venice, Senato Mar 31, f° 153, 23rd December, 1551.

quintals of grain were imported from Turkey that year. At this rate all the ports in the Ottoman Empire must have been involved, not so much the Egyptian but certainly the Greek ports and fairly often the ports of the Sea of Marmara, sometimes even Varna on the Black Sea. Ragusan merchantmen, ostensibly sailing to Rodosto to load hides or wool, would make clandestine calls at Vólos to pick up grain. It meant very good business especially for a few Venetian merchants settled in Constantinople, foremost among whom was Antonio Priuli. The difference was so great, between the buying price in the Levant and the selling price in Italy – which could be twice, two and a half, or three times as much – that the merchants 'could not lose'.

But both in Venice and Ragusa – and elsewhere too no doubt – this profitable trade, which was accompanied on the part of the Italian cities by advances in silver and bounties for the merchants, with guaranteed selling prices (evidence that there was at first great difficulty in collecting enough of the coined money necessary for these purchases) could bring unpleasant surprises. In the Turkish ports this much-demanded grain soon rose in price. It was still profitable, but was perhaps attracting fewer Venetian buyers, since on 24th October, 1554, the Signoria stopped asking for higher anchorage dues from foreign ships than from Venetian vessels, provided they were carrying grain alone,[330] a measure that at least indicates that Venice in spite of the size of her fleet was finding some difficulty in arranging transport of cereals from the Levant.

After 1555, grain was in short supply, at one time in Egypt, at others in Constantinople, or Syria. Prices continued to rise: from 51–55 aspers the *chilo* in 1550–1551, they rose to 63–65 in 1554–1555; and reached 100 in 1557–1559.[331] At this time, in 1555, the first Turkish export ban was issued, a move that explains the frequent attacks by Turkish galleys on western sailing ships near the usual embarcation points.[332] The black market immediately took over and opened a breach in the Turkish cordon at Canea on Crete, which developed into a thriving smuggling centre, with its own specialists like Stefano Tarabotto or Marchio di Poggio. *Caïques* and *caramusalis* carried the contraband grain out to the big western merchantmen. Gold and silver coins were the answer to many problems that at first sight seemed insoluble. Piero de' Medici went so far as to write to Cosimo I, on 14th October, 1559, that he had 'heard from a reliable source that these *Signori* [the Venetians] are on the point, with their manoeuvres, of receiving Negropont as a fief from the Turk: they are offering to pay a huge tribute, so great that it is doubtful whether the island would yield so much revenue. And all this in order to have enough grain for their needs, without passing through France or Spain.'[333] This was

[330] Museo Correr, Donà delle Rose, 46, f° 45 v° and 46.
[331] M. Aymard, *op. cit.*, p. 177, 4th April, 1561.
[332] Report from Zante, 31st March – 6th April, 1563, Simancas E° 1052, f° 148.
[333] A.d.S., Florence, Mediceo 2972, f° 551, quoted by A. Tenenti, *Cristoforo da Canal*, p. 113, note 52.

pure calumny in the aftermath of Cateau-Cambrésis, when the second Turkish prohibition on exports was issued, a warning shot that did not put an end to the interlopers' activity. In 1562, 1563, and 1564, Venetian merchants, more often than not backed up by a Signoria attentive to the common interest and to that of her business community, continued to travel to the Levant to trade, even 'at peril of their lives'.[334]

However these difficulties seem to have increased after 1561. There were several incidents: ships either laden or still empty were seized, some returned without their cargoes. In 1564 the Signoria appointed Tarabotto to Canea to organize clandestine exports, but without much success. When all else failed, the Venetian galleys seized Ragusan roundships (in December, 1563; March, 1565; January, 1566). Six known captures resulted in a total of just under 37,000 *staia* or about 22,000 quintals over more than two years.[335] These hauls were far from enough to restore a compromised situation; the Turkish boom had been short lived.

If Italy was now obliged to look elsewhere for her daily bread, it was because Turkey was in turn entering an age of scarcity. One historian has classified certain periods as catastrophic: from 1564 to 1568; 1572 to 1581, and 1585 to 1590 which is not to say that the intervening years were by any means prosperous. Constantinople, the swollen city, suffered every kind of evil: poverty, high prices, spectacular famines and finally plague. 'Between 1561 and 1598', according to the dispatches of the Venetian *bailo*, 'there were reckoned to be 94 months of plague (almost eight years in all) and this figure is probably an underestimate'.[336] Such reports have their value but can sometimes conceal the true situation. Through its military victories, which brought it into contact with the rest of the world (Syria, 1516; Egypt, 1517; Rhodes, 1522; Belgrade, 1540; Hungary, 1541) and through the grain boom which lasted several years, a previously backward country, whose social structures were almost 'Carolingian' based on life-tenure of property ('beneficia' as it were) was drawn into the orbit of a powerful monetary economy already sufficiently strong to disrupt old patterns but not yet strong enough to create new and truly modern structures. This monetary economy with its devaluations, price increases, arbitrary accumulation, and the luxury of importation was superimposed onto an archaic economy, creating within the latter, as it were, aberrant islands and pockets.

The grain crisis, combined with the money crisis, was largely responsible for encouraging the development of inherited property, the transition as it would be called in the west from 'beneficium' to 'fief', from a precarious system of property dependent on the goodwill of the state, to full ownership as exemplified by the contemporary estates of Hungary and Poland. If historians talk of 're-feudalization', an ambiguous word (but what else can one call it), in the west between the sixteenth and eighteenth

---

[334] M. Aymard, *op. cit.*, p. 178.
[335] *Ibid.*, p. 185.
[336] *Ibid.*

centuries, a very similar pattern was developing in Turkey, though what one is to call it will depend on the results of research still to be done. Busch-Zantner in his pioneer work[337] has described (but at the very end of the sixteenth and early seventeenth century) the *čiftliks*, estates created, he thinks, under the impetus of land improvement and particularly in grain-producing regions. Ömer Lütfi Barkan and his pupils in the course of an extensive research programme have confirmed this spread of the modern estate to the advantage of the Sultanas and Pashas whom we know to have been engaged in the grain boom: with a few exceptions, they reserved to themselves the right to sell grain to western buyers, a trade forbidden to the 'people'. One suspects that this transformation was very far reaching. Turkey like western Europe was living through the 'price revolution' and the agricultural revolution imposed upon her, as upon other countries, by population growth.

These are implications so important for a comparative history that I hesitate to suggest a general conclusion applicable to the Mediterranean as a whole, until the Turkish problem has been thoroughly investigated. Until then we shall know little about the reasons for opening and closing of the Turkish markets to the West: population growth was certainly one; war along the frontiers – armies, like cities devoured grain surpluses;[338] economic and social disturbances. Only further research can decide. But great changes were certainly on the way after the 1560s.[339]

Eating home-produced bread: Italy's situation between 1564 and 1590. 'A virtual certainty by 1560, and beyond any doubt by 1570, the closure of the Levant threw back on her own resources an Italy obliged to feed a growing population.'[340] And despite the dramatic, or dramatized examples recorded between 1564 and 1590, Italy survived. Or rather a certain Italy did, the Italy of the great parasite cities – Rome, Genoa, Florence, Venice – which although the only places threatened, or rather the most threatened, came through the crisis. There are three possible explanations:

1. This Italy could draw on the surplus crops of another Italy which was still well-provided: Sicily, Apulia, the Romagnuola, the Romagnas, the Abruzzi, Corsica,[341] even Sardinia from time to time – that archaic Italy, parts of which had not yet been fully exploited by commerce. The cases of Genoa, Rome, and Venice are proof enough of this. Venice could also draw on minor supplementary sources. There was the possibility of grain from Bavaria, of purchases in the Turkish ports on the Adriatic, the slight

[337] R. Busch-Zantner, *op. cit.*, see below chapter on *Societies*.
[338] One of the arguments of M. Aymard's book.
[339] The remark for instance of Andrea Malipiero, Consul of Syria, Aleppo, 20th December, 1564, A.d.S., Venice, Relazioni . . ., B 31, 'Quivi si sente penuria grande di fromento, cosa molto insolita . . .', appears to me significant.
[340] M. Aymard, *op. cit.*
[341] The Abbondanza of Genoa to Agostino Sauli and Gio: Battista Lercaro, Com^rl Generali in Corsica, Genoa, 30th April, 1589, A. Civico, Genoa.

but providential contribution of Albania, providential despite the small supply and the inferior quality of the grain, generally considered rather too sweet. In Albania buyers found favourable terms, the local nobles played a role similar to that of Polish landowners, and since the monetary economy had not yet penetrated the region, prices remained stable: a classic pattern of colonial exchange.

2. More use was made than in the past of cereals other than wheat. If this could be proved it would be of capital importance but precise evidence is hard to find. One frequently finds mention of supplementary cereals in descriptive history: in Venice, in July, 1604, for example, on the eve of the harvest there remained in the city granaries as much millet as wheat.[342] It was poor man's food, like the meat imported on the hoof from Hungary, the pulses, broad beans, peas, lentils, or rye, a discreet standby over the ages. Since millet kept better than wheat (often for over ten years)[343] it was much used for military stores, on the mainland, in Dalmatia, or the Levant. And it had been cultivated in northern Italy for centuries. In 1372[344] during the dramatic war of Chioggia, Venice, hard pressed by the Genoese, was saved by the 10,000 *staia* of millet in her municipal stores. In the sixteenth century rather than a subsidiary cereal, millet was the poor man's only bread. Next door to Venice, in Vicenza, during the winter of 1564–1565, since no wheat had been harvested, 'almost the entire population is living off millet'.[345] At Venice during the extreme food shortage which began in October, 1569, and lasted until the fortunately abundant harvest of 1570, the *Fondego* of Flour, at St. Mark's and at the Rialto, daily distributed flour from the municipal reserves. The ration tickets allotted two loaves to each person per day, 'mezo formento, mezo miglio'.[346] Twenty years later, still at Venice, the price of wheat, just after the harvest of 1589, quickly rose to 5, 6, or 7 ducats. The bakers were given permission to make rice-bread, with three parts of wheat flour to one of rice. But 'the solution was soon abandoned, for this bread being too savoury whetted the appetite. In order to safeguard the true interests of the poor, the Signoria ordered that millet bread should be baked and sold to the poor: it was execrable.'[347] In 1590–1591, there was an éven greater shortage and in 1592, wheat from the Levant, England, and Bavaria had to be brought in to save the situation. And yet during that year the emergency had been less acute since the Signoria from the start, schooled by the experience of the previous years, allowed the bakers to make bread with any cereal, 'millet, rye, and other mixtures, without any

---

[342] Museo Correr, Donà delle Rose, 217, f° 131.
[343] A.d.S., Venice, Senato Terra, 120, 6th June, 1591, to the Rectors of Bergamo: some millet is on the point of going rotten, having been purchased *'fino l'anno* 1579 . . .'. On the Venetian millet-producing areas, Museo Correr, D. delle Rose, 42, f° 39 v°, 1602.
[344] Marciana, 9611, f° 222.
[345] A.d.S., Venice, Senato Terra 43, 14th January, 1565.
[346] Marciana, Chronicle of Girolamo Savina, f° 325 ff.
[347] Marciana, *ibid.*, f° 365 ff.

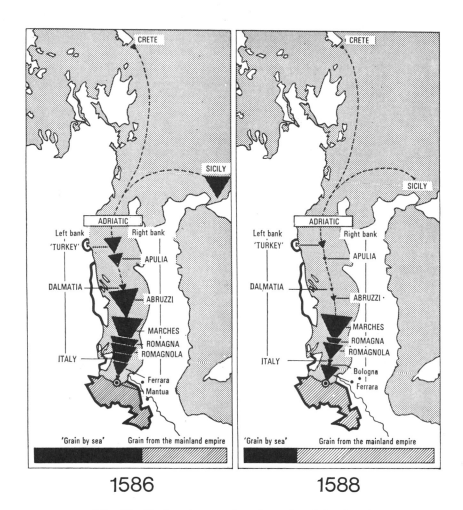

Fig. 50: *Venice: imported grain and mainland grain*

From Museo Correr 217. Venice had always eaten both home-grown grain and grain brought in by sea. At the end of the sixteenth century, the latter was no longer the chief source of supply (in 1588, for instance). There can be no doubt that increased cereal production in the Venetian mainland empire which was to continue during the sixteenth century, was one of the major features of the Venetian economy. Note the importance among the sources of imported grain of northern Italy, north of the Abruzzi. The role played by wheat from Naples and Sicily progressively diminished. By these dates no more grain was being shipped from the Levant and none from the western Mediterranean. (The Romagnola is north of the Romagna, more precisely the *Romagna estense*, the territory of Lugo and Bagnacavallo).

weight limit . . . so that throughout the city there were sold loaves of mixed composition and all sizes, for every baker sought to make them good and big in order to sell them better'.[348]

So secondary cereals were eaten in Venice during bad times. Would it be rash to assume that there was a more or less permanent market for them among the poor? To *suppose* that this was a growing market would help to reconcile some figures we have concerning the Venetian food supply, which although apparently contradictory may well be correct. The source of the first is Marino Sanudo. Between October, 1511 and the end of August, 1512 that is for eleven months, Venice received over a million *staia* of wheat into the city granaries (1,080,721); if the monthly average of these eleven months is added to make a complete year the figure comes to about 1,200,000: in all nearly 700,000 quintals 'che è sta un grandissimo numero'.[349] But records for the years 1548, 1552, 1555, and 1556 give an annual figure, year in year out, of 656,970 *staia* of flour (corresponding to a larger volume of grain) and in 1604, the city's consumption was apparently 515,257 *staia* of grain.[350] Since the population had not fallen in the meantime, on the contrary it had increased, either bread consumption had fallen, or cereals other than wheat were being more extensively used, and I incline towards the latter explanation.

3. Finally the most important explanation of all: Italy survived by increasing home production. This was a long term phenomenon, possibly beginning as far back as 1450. The increase was the result of methods we have already studied: the cultivation of the hillsides, the conquest of the mountain slopes, the reclamation of plains of every size, a fresh division of land between crops and pasture as agriculture continually displaced the grazing lands and the herds they supported, and man's need for room constantly grew. This need brought about the destruction of trees and wild animals, and the reduction of domestic flocks. It was an old process. In Lombardy, land reclamation during the thirteenth century had reduced the number of sheep. Franco Borlandi[351] has rightly diagnosed this as one of the causes of the wool crisis and the success of fustians, a woollen-cotton mixture, one of the first ersatz products.

In the course of this expansion, the rural landscape was transformed.[352] Hillsides abandoned to nature and pasture land during antiquity were converted during the land explosion of the middle ages into series of terraces, planted with trees that protected the vines and whose leaves provided fodder for the flocks. In the sixteenth century agriculture moved further up the hillside. I have already quoted Guicciardini's comment that

---

[348] Marciana, *ibid.*

[349] M. Sanudo, *op. cit.*, vol. XV, col. 164, 30th September, 1512.

[350] Museo Correr, Donà delle Rose, 217, f° 131; 218, f° 328.

[351] 'Futainiers et futaines dans l'Italie du Moyen Age' in *Hommage à Lucien Febvre, Éventail de l'histoire vivante*, 1953, vol. II, p. 133 ff.

[352] E. Sereni, *op. cit.*, and the long review of this book by Georges Duby, 'Sur l'histoire agraire de l'Italie' in *Annales E.S.C.*, 1963, p. 352 ff.

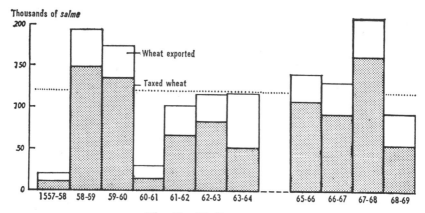

Thousands of *salme*

Fig. 51: *Sicilian exports*

According to documents in the archives at Simancas. The shaded area represents the exported grain on which the *tratte* had been paid, the white area that on which the *tratte* had not been paid. The average figure (dotted line) is about 120,000 *salme*. Variations were more a function of differences in the harvest than of varying demand. Every three or four years Sicily had a poor harvest. Exports were maintained at the same level during the seventeenth century and with the same periodic fluctuations.

Italy was cultivated up to the mountain tops.[353] In 1580 Michel de Montaigne was astonished by what he saw at the Springs of Lucca. 'Mountains all well cultivated and green to their summits, planted with chestnut and olive trees and elsewhere with vines, which they grow all around the mountains, encircling them with rings or terraces. On the outer edge of the terrace raised up a little are the vines; on the inner depression grows wheat. . . .'[354] But it was also towards the low-lying marshy plains that the Italians systematically extended their improvements.

' It was a process demanding ever more men and ever more money. It led to increased investment on the part of the towns. Urban landowners, recently ennobled, found land by turns a profitable or a safe investment. In so doing, they came up against the key problem: how to train and utilize the peasant masses, to acquire what would today be called the plus-value added by their labour. Unfortunately we have very little information about this widespread movement. In an article to which I am much indebted, Ruggiero Romano[355] argues that investment in land brought high profits in the fifteenth century and early sixteenth century. A small stake could bring a high return in the early days, a pattern very similar in fact to the beginnings of commercial capitalism in Lisbon, after the return of Vasco

---

[353] See *La historia d'Italia, op. cit.*, (Venice, 1587), p. 1 v°.

[354] *Journal de voyage d'Italie*, 'Collection Hier', p. 227.

[355] R. Romano, 'Rolnictwo i chlopi we Wloszech w XV i XVI wieku', in: *Przeglad historyczny*, LIII, n° 2, p. 248–250; see also C. M. Cipolla, 'Per la storia della terra in Bassa Lombardia' in *Studi in onore di Armando Sapori*, 1957, I, p. 665 ff.

da Gama.[356] These were the palmy days of land capitalism, coinciding with that first phase of commercial capitalism that reached its peak at the time of the Welsers and Fuggers. The situation was later to deteriorate.

All this is hypothetical of course. In the case of Venice (but Venice, where the evidence is clearer than elsewhere may have lagged behind the rest of Italy) large-scale investment in the area of the *beni inculti*, chiefly low-lying and marshy land, did not begin much before the 1550s if the documents are to be trusted. It was not until then that social tensions, between peasants and landlords, first became apparent. Political crimes, the province of the upper classes, were now succeeded by agricultural crimes involving the lower strata of society. Towards the end of the century these troubles amounted to a social revolution in disguise, for such was the true nature of banditry, a problem to which we shall be returning[357] and one which swelled to ever greater proportions as the century drew to a close. It is at this point, one has the impression, that the huge fortune of Venice was being withdrawn from commercial enterprise and invested for good or ill in loans at interest on the Besançon exchanges and above all in the countryside and costly land improvement schemes. A classic pre-capitalist cycle was coming to an end.

This then is the probable, though by no means proven background to the history of Italian grain. It provides us with some perspective on the problem and suggests possible lines of development. Unfortunately, the evidence tails off at the crucial moment. The turning-point in the economic situation of the *peasantry* certainly occurred after 1550 and possibly not until 1600. And the situation of the landed proprietors was very different. They triumphed because the peasants lost, rather as they did in Castile. However there can be no doubt that the widespread efforts of the Italian peasants and the ruthless determination of the landlords ensured, despite many anxious moments, the equilibrium, real or apparent, of the grain supply during the years 1564-1590.

The last crisis: imports from the north after 1590. All the problems of the Mediterranean food supply had long prepared the way for the massive importation of grain from the north, carried in Dutch, Hanseatic, and English sailing ships from the Baltic to the Mediterranean after the 1590s. This was by no means the first grain to arrive from the north. Besides the Iberian peninsula, Genoa was already importing grain by the middle of the fifteenth century.[358] In 1527 Venice had grain brought from Flanders or England.[359] The Strozzi apparently did the same in 1530 for Rome.[360]

[356] E. J. Hamilton, 'American treasure and the rise of capitalism', in *Economica*, November, 1929.

[357] See below, Vol II, ch. 2, *Societies*

[358] See Jacques Heers, 'L'expansion maritime portugaise', *art. cit.*, p. 7: two Basque ships, each with a capacity of 5,000 cantars (total 470 tons) carrying grain to Genoa from Middelburg.

[359] W. Naudé, *Die Getreidehandelspolitik der europäischen Staaten vom 13, bis zum 18. Jahrhundert*, Berlin, 1896, p. 167.

[360] R. Ehrenberg, *op. cit.*, I, p. 299: 'from Flanders or Brittany'.

In October 1539, a correspondent of the Gonzaga in Antwerp referred to the departure for Italy (Genoa, Florence, and Lucca) of 16 *nave grosse* laden with wheat, which he predicted would not keep well.[361] Cosimo de' Medici probably imported Flemish grain as early as the 1540s and in 1575 Tuscany at least tried to buy Breton grain.[362] For every one of these little-known cargoes ten or twelve others probably went unrecorded.

But the movement became widespread only after a series of bad harvests which befell Italy after 1586,[363] producing a cumulative effect. By 1590 the situation was desperate: the Grand Duke of Tuscany was the first Italian ruler to dispatch agents to Danzig,[364] and Venice followed suit when winter came.[365] In 1590 and 1591 ships are *definitely* recorded arriving at Leghorn[366] and Genoa.[367] In 1591, the Venetian secretary Ottobon sent five from Danzig. In June of the same year, 'it has rained so much', wrote a merchant from Florence, 'that it is feared the harvest will be as bad as last year's; the wheat, at least in the plains, is lying on the ground, and it is so wet that, instead of drying, it is rotting away'.[368] Here we may once again note that the climate was partly responsible. In September the same merchant wrote categorically: 'We are having a difficult year because of the lack of grain; the best and surest remedy is awaited from Hamburg and Danzig.'[369]

Thus began the voyages of the northern grain ships. Really large cargoes were not received before the winter of 1592–1593. Harbour records at Leghorn indicate that in 1593 nearly 16,000 tons of northern wheat and rye were imported,[370] of which almost half had been ordered by the Grand Duke and the rest by merchants, the Buonvisi of Lucca, the Lucchini of Bologna, and the Vernagalli, Buonacorsi, Biachorali, Biachinelli, Capponi, Lanfranchi, Berzighelli, Orlandini, Mendes, Ximenez, Ricasoli, Melinchi, Bardi, Guardi, Taddi, and Massei . . . of Florence. If proof were needed this list of names from the harbour records[371] (subject to errors in transcrip-

[361] Baptista Cortese to the Marquis of Mantua, Antwerp, 12th October, 1539, A.d.S., Mantua, Gonzaga Archives, Series E, Fiandra 568.

[362] *Méditerranée*, 1st edition, p. 469, reference mislaid.

[363] W. Naudé, *op. cit.*, p. 142.

[364] Ricardo Ricardi and Hier° Giraldi, who arrived in Danzig on 3rd September, 1590, Relatione de negotii tanto di mercantie che cambi di Danzica (December, 1590) under the signature of Ambrosio Lerice, A.d.S., Venice, Secreta Archivi Propri Polonia 2.

[365] *Ibid.*, and see above p. 195 ff.

[366] B. Suárez to Simón Ruiz, Florence, 26th February and 28th December, 1591, Ruiz Archives Valladolid (the situation was most grave in Rome).

[367] At least at the end of the year 1591. Baltasar Suárez to Simón Ruiz, Florence, 29th May, 1591, *Ibid.*, 'En Génova del grano que va llegando de Osterdam y Amburgo se a vendido a 24 (escudos) la salma que es preçio jamas oydo; pero como llegue la gran cantidad que se espera, no pongo duda sino que abajarà', Ruiz Archives.

[368] Camillo Suárez to Simón Ruiz, Florence, 17th June, 1591, *ibid.*

[369] 9th September, 1591, *ibid.*

[370] F. Braudel and R. Romano, *Navires et marchandises à l'entrée du port de Livourne*, p. 106 and 117.

[371] A. d. Stato, Florence, Mediceo 2080.

tion) would confirm the dispersion of the grain trade. Between 1590 and 1594 the demand from Leghorn was so great that it led to payments to England, Danzig, and the Dutch of over two million crowns.[372] In 1596 there was still an active demand, the Grand Duke was sending another representative to Poland and Danzig, and was attempting to gain control of all purchases in the North.[373] Thus there was becoming established a massive grain trade of which the Grand Duke gradually became master thanks to his huge capital resources. Leghorn profited greatly from this boom in grain; as a port it had many advantages over the other Italian ports. It was only a week's distance from Gibraltar, said the Danzig mariners, and lay on the same course as the wind that took them through the straits; they could load alum there for the return journey and pick up salt a week or two later in Spain. Going to Venice was quite a different kettle of fish.

But the voyage to Leghorn undertaken by entire fleets was not altogether free from dangers, obstacles and even temptations. Sailing down the Channel or around the British Isles by Scotland could mean an encounter with the English who might or might not allow the ships to pass – and with bad weather; in Spanish ports there was always the risk of an embargo; Barbary pirates prowled the Mediterranean. So at Lisbon, Cadiz, or Seville if the grain showed signs of perishing, and if the competent consular authorities were willing, there was a great temptation to unload and sell the grain and return home with all speed. In the end it was with silver, half of it paid in advance, that Leghorn and other Italian towns could force the hand of the poorer towns of the North. Of course, Tuscany and its surrounding regions were not the only places in need of the new supply. The whole of Italy was soon accustomed to it and depending on local ports and needs, the entire western Mediterranean, including North Africa.

And the trade born of necessity before long revealed itself to be quite profitable. Simón Ruiz, the merchant of Medina del Campo was very sceptical at first. 'I am much grieved,' he wrote on 24th April, 1591 to his correspondent in Florence, 'by the lack of bread in Italy. May it please God to bring a remedy! The grain which is carried from Flanders and Danzig cannot in my opinion arrive in good condition since it is already spoilt when it reaches Seville. What must it be like by the time it gets to Italy! Shipping grain is not usually worth the risk. I know what I am talking about, and it has cost me dear in the past. If anyone at all gains any benefit from it, it is the mariners who sail in the grain ships. I have seen men lose much money in that venture.'[374] Simón Ruiz was speaking from experience, since as a young man he had been concerned in shipping grain to Lisbon. But in this case he was wrong. Of the five boats sent to Venice

---

[372] W. Naudé, *op. cit.*, p. 142.
[373] *Ibid.* See also G. Vivoli, *op. cit.*, III, p. 182, 317, 350.
[374] Ruiz Archives, Valladolid.

by Ottobon, only three finally reached Venice,[375] one had to unload at Lisbon and the fifth was lost. But even so, from a commercial point of view, the operation was still worthwhile. In large contracts, the Ximenez – in particular Fernando Ximenez of Antwerp who made sure that his associates, the Veiga and the Andrade, were restricted to the contracts negotiated by the Grand Duke of Tuscany – could in the early stages make profits of up to 300 per cent.[376] For the transport of grain from the north was not merely a matter of ships, freighting, and grain purchases, it meant enormous transfers of funds to Antwerp (at first) and other northern cities, as we have seen in connection with Marco Ottobon's journey, and as is testified by the copies of bills of exchange drawn by the *Abbondanza* of Genoa. There were always profits to be made from these operations.[377]

But the crisis that opened in 1590 did not last indefinitely. It seems to have been alleviated as the world moved into the new century and Italy and the Mediterranean after resorting to northern grain during the emergency, apparently regained their self-sufficiency: after 1600, maize was to prove of great assistance.[378] But the problem cannot yet be considered solved. Further research is needed into the grain from the north. Its history has yet to be pursued well into the seventeenth century and the entire import curve, which I *assume* to have moved downwards, perhaps after 1607–1608, has yet to be plotted; it could then be set in a historical context, which is to some extent what we shall be doing in a moment, for grain was not the only import from the north.

Sicily: still the grain store of the Mediterranean. Let us now consider not simply the grainships of the North, but the Mediterranean itself, its structure and its vital centre – Italy – instead of an episode in its history, a temporary situation. In the first edition of this book,[379] I was persuaded both by documentary evidence and the statements of historians to magnify this episode into a symptom of the decline of the Mediterranean. This decline now seems to me, especially in Italy, to have become apparent only very much later. I would now consider that the great economic turning-point did not occur before 1620–1621 and the great biological turning-point – the wave of epidemics – not before 1630.[380]

When I was writing the first edition, the decisive argument in my eyes

[375] Correspondence quoted earlier (see above p. 196) of Marco Ottobon, and A.d.S., Venice, Papadopoli, Codice 12, f° 18, 16th October, 1591.

[376] Baltasar Suárez to Simón Ruiz, Florence, 26th February, 1591, 'en que ganan larguisimo pues tengo por cierto açen con uno mas de tres', Ruiz Archives, Valladolid. On the enormity of the sums of money involved: Venice in 1590 invested over 800,000 ducats from the Public Treasury, Marciana, Memorie di Malatie . . ., 8235 CVIII, 5, f° 198 v° ff.

[377] Archivio Civico Genoa, Abbondanza Lettere 1589–1592.

[378] Unpublished work by R. Romano, F. Spooner, and U. Tucci on prices at Udine.

[379] 1st edition, 1949, p. 466–467.

[380] See above, p. 334.

was what I called the failure of Sicily and Sicily's wheat. I had every reason to be convinced of it at the time. But Sicilian wheat did not fail the Mediterranean.

Two series of arguments had led me to suppose that it had. In the first place the poor harvests and famines in Sicily after 1590. By 1591 it is clear that there was real famine. Unprecedented prices were being charged, wheat being sold at 78 *tari* 10 at Palermo; everywhere *si trovanno le persone morte nelle strade per la fame.* According to contemporaries, this was the result both of unreasonable taxation and bad harvests. The *salma* finally reached 40 crowns, a price unknown in living memory. There were rich men to be found selling wheat for its weight in gold, 'a peso di sangre' as it was said. Palermo and Messina, which sold grain below the inflated rates were deep in debt, Messina to the tune of over 100,000 ducats.[381] The situation did not improve until 1595.

This was one reason to fear the worst. It was at this point in my research that I became acquainted with an article by Hans Hochholzer, combining history and geography and devoted to Sicily.[382] And he had a contribution to offer on this very question: some retrospective statistics found in the Archives at Vienna and dating from 1724, when the island was briefly in Austrian possession. They concerned *imports* of grain to Messina, beginning in 1592, rising to a peak in 1640, and declining to almost nothing by 1724. This document settled the matter: if Sicily was regularly importing grain from the end of the sixteenth century, this could only mean that she had ceased to be the granary of the western Mediterranean. But Sicilian documents – and this was to be proved after the publication in 1951 of the Simancas Catalogue devoted to the series *Sicilia* – indicated the contrary. A study of the documents relating to the seventeenth century[383] yielded categorical results: Sicily was still exporting wheat in the seventeenth century. There was only one solution: to find and examine closely the key document at Vienna.[384] On receiving the photocopy I was shocked to discover that the interpretation of this list of figures was based on an almost unbelievable series of misunderstandings: the word *introyte*, which means income, revenue, in this case customs duties, had been taken to refer to incoming goods, while *grani* (which in this context indicates a subdivision of the monetary unit the *taro*) was translated by cereals; as a result, wheat was deduced to be entering Sicily, when in fact the document quite clearly refers to *exports* of *silk*, raw and blanched, as can be seen from the first lines of the facsimile.

Once this doubt had been removed, everything became clear. Even during the period of greatest prosperity, the Sicilian market experienced wide fluctuations depending on the quality of the harvest. Between 1590

---

[381] 'Carestia di frumenti del 1591', B. Comunale Palermo, Qq N 14 a, f°s 144–147.
[382] 'Kulturgeschichte Siziliens' in *Geogr. Zeitschrift*, 1935.
[383] A close study of the documents concerning the sixteenth and seventeenth centuries has been made for me by my friend and colleague, Felipe Ruiz Martín.
[384] Vienna Archives, Collectanea Siciliana, fasc. 6.

and 1677 there were several bad patches: 1550–1554; 1575–1580; 1605–1608; 1634–1641; 1668–1677.[385] In this context, the depressed period 1590 to 1595 was merely one of the recurrent troughs. Apart from these periods, which were by no means typical, Sicilian wheat continued to be exported both to the Adriatic and the western Mediterranean and, unless I am much mistaken, exports for some time remained fairly near the old level of 150,000 *salme* a year or 300,000 quintals. The exact figures must exist in full somewhere in the Sicilian archives. At Simancas they are unfortunately only intermittently recorded.

But at least our problem is solved. Sicily throughout the seventeenth century remained the island of wheat, prevented by her merchant community from abandoning cereal production (barley which has not been mentioned was exported both to Naples and Spain, food for horses and sometimes for men) and from giving up too much land to stockfarming or orchards. In Sicily the fields were defended by a system of administrative and capitalist control of which I have given only the barest outline and which may itself one day tempt an historian. There could hardly be a better example of 'national income' to study in the sixteenth and seventeenth century than that of Sicily. There are figures for everything: population, animals used for ploughing, rents, fiscal revenues. For January to June, 1694 all exports of wheat from Sicily are recorded by *caricatore* with ports of destination, names of the transport ships, prices, customs duties, and the names of the merchants, an opportunity to observe that trade concentration benefited certain among them. Each controlled a port as if it were his own private property. These were the true grain barons. That in 1699 grain should be exported from Sicily to France is amusing; that some was sent to Flanders in the same year is even more ironic.[386]

But these are mere details. Sicily as a whole, both in the sixteenth century and late into the following century, had a healthy balance of trade, in spite of the hazards inherent to all material existence under the *ancien régime*. In the seventeenth century silk exports did not decline until after 1619;[387] wheat continued to be a principal commodity; an active shipping fleet frequented the coast of Sicily, sailing to the Levant and even more to nearby Tunisia, leaving in the Sicilian ports, at least until 1664, some part of the considerable sums of silver it was carrying; the silk industry was flourishing, or rather reviving in Messina and Catania. In Sicily, the decline of the Mediterranean cannot on any reckoning be said to have occurred prematurely.

On grain crises. To sum up, all the wheat crises present similar features. They would be even more similar if there was more documentary evidence of the course they took in Islam, where they are for the most part concealed

[385] According to the records analysed by Felipe Ruiz Martín (see note 383).
[386] According to the records analysed by Felipe Ruiz Martín.
[387] Vienna Archives, Collectanea Siciliana, fasc. 6. I deliberately say 1619, not 1640 like Hochholzer, since variations in the export dues must be taken into account.

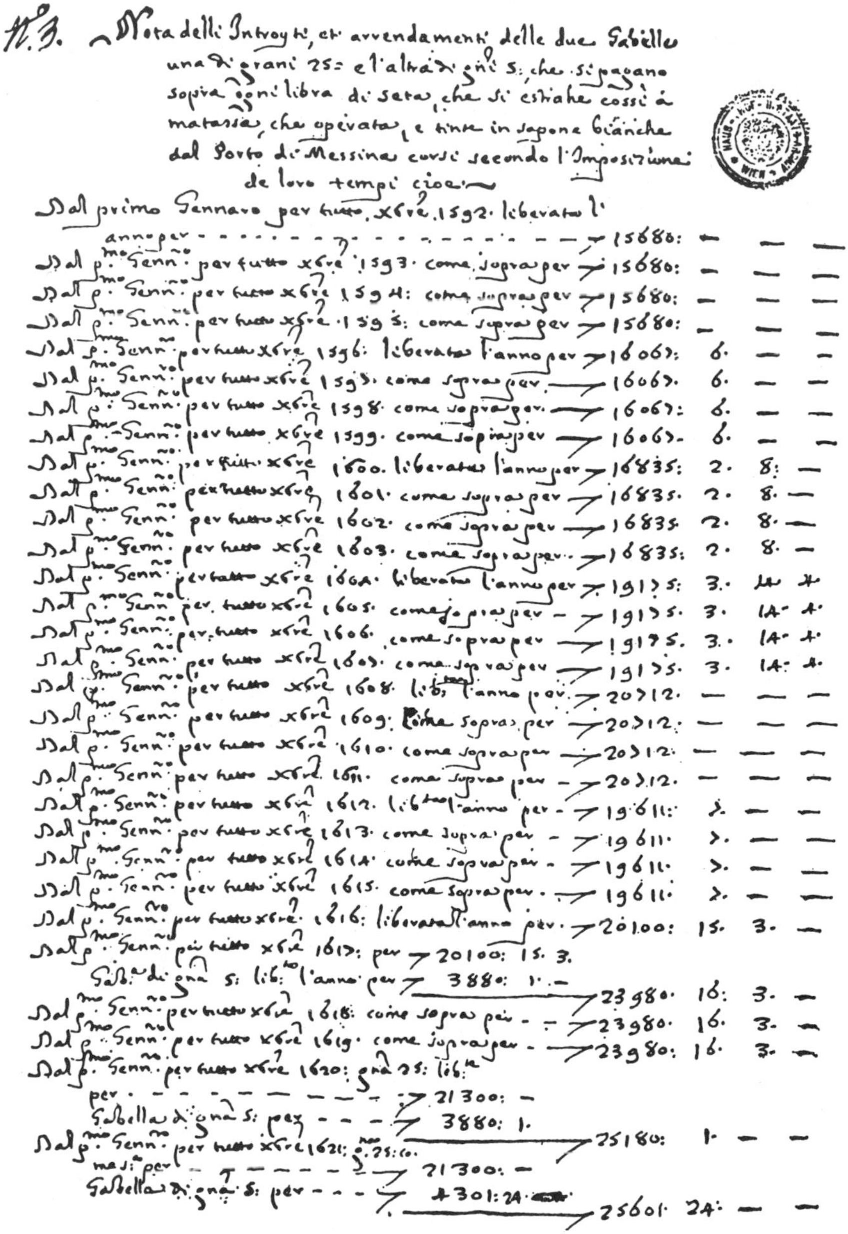

N.3. Nota delli Introyti, et arrendamenti delle due Gabelle una di grani 25: e l'altra di g.ni 5: che si pagano sopra ogni libra di seta, che si estrahe cossi à matassa, che operata, e tinte in sapone bianche dal Porto di Messina corsi secondo l'Impositioni de loro tempi cioè

Dal primo Gennaro per tutto Xbre 1592 liberato l'anno per	15680:	—	—	—
Dal p.mo Genn.ro per tutto Xbre 1593 come sopra per	15680:	—	—	—
Dal p.mo Genn.ro per tutto Xbre 1594: come sopra per	15680:	—	—	—
Dal p.mo Genn.ro per tutto Xbre 1595: come sopra per	15680:	—	—	—
Dal p.mo Genn.ro per tutto Xbre 1596: liberato l'anno per	16067:	6.	—	—
Dal p.mo Genn.ro per tutto Xbre 1597 come sopra per	16067.	6.	—	—
Dal p.mo Genn.ro per tutto Xbre 1598 come sopra per	16067:	6.	—	—
Dal p.mo Genn.ro per tutto Xbre 1599 come sopra per	16067.	6.	—	—
Dal p.mo Genn.ro per tutto Xbre 1600 liberato l'anno per	16835:	2.	8:	—
Dal p.mo Genn.ro per tutto Xbre 1601 come sopra per	16835.	2.	8.	—
Dal p.mo Genn.ro per tutto Xbre 1602 come sopra per	16835	2.	8.	—
Dal p.mo Genn.ro per tutto Xbre 1603 come sopra per	16835:	2.	8.	—
Dal p.mo Genn.ro per tutto Xbre 1604 liberato l'anno per	19175:	3.	14	4
Dal p.mo Genn.ro per tutto Xbre 1605 come sopra per	19175.	3.	14.	4.
Dal p.mo Genn.ro per tutto Xbre 1606 come sopra per	19175.	3.	14.	4.
Dal p.mo Genn.ro per tutto Xbre 1607 come sopra per	19175.	3.	14:	4.
Dal p.mo Genn.ro per tutto Xbre 1608 lib.to l'anno per	20312.	—	—	—
Dal p.mo Genn.ro per tutto Xbre 1609: come sopra per	20312.	—	—	—
Dal p.mo Genn.ro per tutto Xbre 1610 come sopra per	20312.	—	—	—
Dal p.mo Genn.ro per tutto Xbre 1611 come sopra per	20312.	—	—	—
Dal p.mo Genn.ro per tutto Xbre 1612 lib.to l'anno per	19611:	7.	—	—
Dal p.mo Genn.ro per tutto Xbre 1613 come sopra per	19611.	7.	—	—
Dal p.mo Genn.ro per tutto Xbre 1614 come sopra per	19611.	7.	—	—
Dal p.mo Genn.ro per tutto Xbre 1615 come sopra per	19611.	7.	—	—
Dal p.mo Genn.ro per tutto Xbre 1616: liberato l'anno per	20100:	15.	3.	—
Dal p.mo Genn.ro per tutto Xbre 1617: per 20100: 15. 3. Gab.a di g.na 5: lib.to l'anno per 3880: 1.	23980.	16:	3.	—
Dal p.mo Genn.ro per tutto Xbre 1618: come sopra per	23980.	16.	3.	—
Dal p.mo Genn.ro per tutto Xbre 1619 come sopra per	23980:	16.	3.	—
Dal p.mo Genn.ro per tutto Xbre 1620: g.na 25: lib.ta per 21300: — Gabella di g.na 5: per 3880: 1.	25180:	1.	—	—
Dal p.mo Genn.ro per tutto Xbre 1621: g.na 25: ... per 21300: — Gabella di g.na 5: per 4301: 24	25601.	24.	—	—

Fig. 52: *Sicily after 1593: a document which proves not that grain was imported but that silk was exported*

Document from the Archives of Vienna (Haus-Hof- und Staats-Archiv), col. Siciliana 6, Dogana di Messina, Messina, 1st January, 1724).

from the historian. They clearly correspond to patterns of population growth, whose effects were on the whole benign until about 1550 or 1560. The more people there were the more grain was produced. Thereafter, the law of diminishing returns began to operate. The fairly untroubled abundance of the fifteenth and 'first' sixteenth century gave way sooner or later to increasingly serious difficulties of supply. In the west, this was partly the result of the ousting of cereal-growing by more profitable and more reliable crops – vines and olives. Other causes were the growth of trade, increased human demand, differential price increases, and sometimes social factors.[388] To meet such problems 'never before encountered', as a document says with reference to Syria,[389] the solutions envisaged varied according to the amount of wealth available. The purchase of grain from distant sources was, it is hardly necessary to point out, an obvious indication of general prosperity – despite the fact that it was at the same time, catastrophic for the poor.

3. TRADE AND TRANSPORT: THE SAILING SHIPS OF THE ATLANTIC

A unique gauge of Mediterranean trade as a whole is provided by the successive waves of Atlantic shipping that entered the sea. For there were two massive invasions (with some differences, some similarities) the first roughly between 1450 and 1552, the second after 1570 or rather 1572–1573: with the second invasion, consisting exclusively of northern ships, the route to the Mediterranean with all its advantages was permanently opened up to the North.

I have already suggested an explanation for these major developments in Mediterranean history:[390] that the arrival of foreign ships corresponded to the creation of new opportunities resulting from an economic revival, quite as much as to commercial competition from the North (although this obviously existed); in short the newcomers bore witness to a certain level of prosperity. In a period of economic expansion, the Mediterranean had better things to do than transport commodities, particularly bulky ones. If this really was the case, with the arrival of foreign transport ships, narrative history provides the statistician with a magnificent yardstick. For the stream of ocean vessels was interrupted for a period of about twenty years. Does this mean that Mediterranean prosperity was also interrupted during the middle years of the century?

I. BEFORE 1550: THE FIRST ARRIVALS

It is not easy to discover the routes taken by the first Atlantic vessels to enter the Mediterranean, partly because they were often poor wretches

---

[388] I am thinking in particular of the taste of the rich for white bread.
[389] A.d.S., Venice, Relaz. Ambasciatori, B. 31. 20th December, 1564.
[390] See above. p. 298, 312.

who left few traces of their passage, partly because in the early days Iberians and northerners came in side by side, making it hard for us to distinguish one from the other or to establish the exact date of each voyage.

Basque, Biscayan, and even Galician ships. The mariners of the Atlantic Iberian coast entered Mediterranean waters possibly as early as the end of the thirteenth century. When their numbers increased, after 1450, they were already well known in the Mediterranean for their services to both Barcelona and Genoa and were frequent visitors to both the south and north coasts of the western basin. They acted simply as carriers, nothing more.[391] The few Basque merchants recorded at Genoa handled only small transactions (for the most part in wool); their principal function was to answer for the masters of ships, whose reputation was never very good, and to borrow on their behalf the sums of money necessary for the fittings of their ships.

And then, one day, these sturdy sailing vessels left their usual haunts and, in the service of various western cities, reached the waters of the eastern Mediterranean. By about 1495 they were sailing straight from Genoa, Málaga and above all Cadiz, to Chios, carrying Atlantic sugar to the island.[392] They continued to do so for many years. We must also remember their voyages to England and in particular to Flanders. In 1532,[393] a Venetian says that Biscay (in the widest sense) is a jewel in Charles V's crown, the secret of his maritime power, 'from Biscay he can have all the ships he desires'. In fact these ships were to monopolize the Flanders route until 1569[394] and before this date their galleons were sailing on the long *Carrera de Indias*.[395] For many years these 'vagabonds' were active in every kind of Mediterranean trade, and between 1480 and 1515 they were as likely to be carrying 'wine from Marseilles to London as Irish skins to Marseilles'.[396]

The first to arrive from beyond the Straits of Gibraltar, they remained a long time in the Mediterranean concentrating round Genoa, Marseilles, and Barcelona[397] and along the long Spanish coast. They crop up in sixteenth-century documents when one expects them to be rare or to have already left. There is a record of a Biscay captain anchoring his vessel at Marseilles in February, 1507 preparing to carry wine to Flanders and England;[398] and of another, in 1510, sailing from Bari to Antwerp for Hans Paumgartner;[399] in 1511, a Biscayan ship brought kerseys to Ra-

[391] J. Heers, 'Le commerce des Basques en Méditerranée au XVe siècle' in *Bulletin Hispanique*, n° 57, 1955, pp. 292–320.
[392] J. Heers, *Gênes au XVe siècle, op. cit.*, p. 496.
[393] E. Albèri, *op. cit.*, I, p. 1, Relation de Nicolo Tiepolo 1532.
[394] See above, p. 228.
[395] Pierre Chaunu, *op. cit.*, vol. VIII, p. 254–256.
[396] R. Collier, *H. du Commerce de Marseille, op. cit.*, III, p. 118.
[397] A de Capmany, *op. cit.*, IV, appendix, p. 43, 1526.
[398] R. Collier, *op. cit.*, III, p. 155.
[399] K. O. Müller, *op. cit.*, p. 55, a cargo of cumin, profit realized: 69 per cent.

gusa;[400] in 1521, during the acute grain shortage in Spain, Neapolitan documents refer to Biscay merchants and mariners among those supplying the Peninsula with grain from Apulia;[401] we meet them again in 1526,[402] or January 1527 on the way to Messina with a cargo of sardines and tunny from Portugal;[403] in 1530, two Biscay ships laden with salt were sunk by Barbarossa;[404] in 1532, one of their sailing ships reached Alicante after rough treatment from the Barbary corsairs.[405] On the routes from Spain to Italy, in 1531, 1535 and 1537, when one would have thought their role in the Mediterranean was finished, a port register contains mention of no less than twelve Biscay ships;[406] and they were not the last.[407] Perhaps it was not until the middle of the sixteenth century and the end of the first wave of Atlantic shipping that they entirely disappeared from the active routes of the Mediterranean.

The Portuguese. After the capture of Ceuta which opened wide the door of the Mediterranean, Portuguese ships were soon both as numerous and as active as the Biscayans in these waters. Even before the arrival of their armadas,[408] Portuguese merchant vessels were offering their services and Portuguese pirates imposing theirs: they seized a Venetian merchantman carrying Cretan wine in November 1498;[409] in October, 1501 they captured a Genoese ship off the Barbary coast; any Moorish passengers they captured had to leave rich booty in their hands in order to buy their freedom.[410] They naturally entered the service of the great commercial cities. They are found around Valencia and the Balearics, at Marseilles, employed more often by Florence than by Genoa, although the latter did not reject their offers.[411] Throughout the western basin of the Mediterranean, Portuguese sailing ships were soon carrying hides loaded at Lisbon – a sign of the still backward Portuguese economy – Andalusian wheat, salt from

[400] S. Razzi, *op. cit.*, p. 116.

[401] A.d.S., Naples, Sommaria Consultationum, 96, f° 136, 3rd September, 1521, and f° 151 v°, 24th October, 1521.

[402] *Ibid.*, 121, f° 160, 1st November, 1526.

[403] *Ibid.*, 123, f° 36 v° and 37, 18th January, 1527.

[404] A.d.S., Mantua, A. Gonzaga, Series E, Genova 759, Giovambattista Fornari to the Marquis of Mantua, Genoa, 25th July, 1530.

[405] M. Sanudo, *op. cit.*, LVI, col. 238. Palermo, 5th April, 1532.

[406] Domenico Gioffrè, 'Il commercio d'importazione genovese, alla luce dei registri del dazio, 1495–1537' in *Studi in onore di Amintore Fanfani*, 1962, V, p. 164.

[407] The sardine boats of Galicia, for instance, taking their catch to Barcelona, Valencia or Seville. The *corregidor* of Galicia to H. M., 20th February, 1538, Simancas, *Guerra Antigua*, XI, f° 200.

[408] A.d.S., Mantua, A. Gonzaga, Series E, Spagna, 588, Gio. Agnello to the Marquis of Mantua, Barcelona, 3rd May, 1535; the Portuguese fleet entered Barcelona on 28th April: '*fece l'entrata con molte cerimonia alla portoghese . . .* '

[409] M. Sanudo, *op. cit.*, II, col. 138, 18th November, 1498.

[410] A.d.S., Mantua, A. Gonzaga, Series E. Venezia 1439, F°° Trevisano to the Marquis of Mantua, Venice, 1st October, 1501.

[411] Jacques Heers, 'L'expansion maritime portugaise à la fin du Moyen Age: la Méditerranée' in *Revista da Faculdade de Letras de Lisboa*, n° 2, 1956, p. 18.

Ibiza, alum from Spain and Italy, sugar from Madeira and other Atlantic islands after 1480 or 1490, above all after the ordinance issued by Dom Manuel (on 21st August, 1498) forbidding any but Portuguese subjects to engage in the sugar trade.[412] Every year towards the end of the fifteenth century there were exported according to the official concessions 40,000 *arrobe* of Portuguese sugar to Flanders, 7000 to England, 6000 to Leghorn, 13,000 to Genoa, 2000 to Rome, 15,000 to Venice, 25,000 to Constantinople and Chios.[413] Sugar arrived in Venice in *caravelle grosse*.[414] Gradually, it seems, Portuguese ships were built bigger in order to handle trade over the whole sea, since they were from very early on sailing to Chios, Constantinople, the Levant, and Egypt. Sugar and the light ships used by the Portuguese together account for their success in the Mediterranean, long before Vasco da Gama's voyage around the cape.

As in the case of the Biscáyans, we do not know exactly when the Portuguese disappeared from the Mediterranean. There are some random mentions of them: as late as 1535 two of their caravels were noted off Minorca, one of them captured by Barbarossa and the other probably lost with all her cargo;[415] at Marseilles on 15th January, 1536, an English merchant bought a ship from a Portuguese citizen, John Ribere;[416] in 1549, two Portuguese vessels arrived at Venice.[417] But we should not allow these incidents and a few others to mislead us. The Portuguese episode was undoubtedly almost over by the middle of the sixteenth century. Other ships and seamen had arrived to offer their services and Portuguese shipping must have become a more lucrative business to the west of the Pillars of Hercules than to the east. Unless, that is, there were now fewer opportunities in the Mediterranean.

Normans and Bretons. The succession did not immediately fall upon the Normans and Bretons, who were latecomers to the Mediterranean although both had appeared quite early off the Atlantic coasts of Spain and Portugal: from 1466 on there may have been a Breton quarter in San Lucar de Barrameda;[418] it is quite possible, although the word *berton* in Spanish, like *bertone* in Italian, was applied throughout the sixteenth

[412] Vincente Almeida d'Eça, *Normas economicas na colonizacão portuguesa*, Lisbon, 1921, p. 24.
[413] Domenico Gioffrè, *art. cit.*, p. 130, note 38, and by the same author, 'Le relazioni fra Genova e Madera nel 1° decennio del secolo XVI' in *Pubblicazioni del civico Istituto Colombiano, Studi Colombiani*, 1951, p. 455, note 25. 1 *arroba* = 11.5 kg.
[414] This development of the sugar trade is well described by D. Gioffrè, *art. cit.*, p. 130 ff; 9 caravels carrying sugar to Venice, M. Sanudo, *op. cit.*, I, col. 640, 4th June, 1497; *ibid.* on the Portuguese, I, 1032 and II, 138.
[415] Luis Sarmiento to Charles V, Evora, 5th December, 1535, Simancas, *Guerra Antigua*, VII, f° 42.
[416] J. Billioud, *H. du commerce de Marseille*, III, p. 228.
[417] A.d.S., Venice, *Cinque Savii*, 3, 1549.
[418] Michel Mollat, 'Aspect du commerce maritime breton à la fin du Moyen Age', in *Mémoire de la Société d'Histoire et d'Archéologie de Bretagne*, vol. XXVIII, 1948, p. 16–17.

century, to all northerners indiscriminately. But if piracy is a sign of recent arrival, there can be no doubt that the Italian Wars brought them in their wake, in 1496–1497 for example or 1502.[419] In January 1497, certain *navi bertone* were engaged in active piracy off Majorca.[420] But apparently trade did not follow them, especially in the case of the Bretons who, when questioned about Venice, in 1500 replied that 'they have hardly navigated in those waters'.[421] It is another forty years before there is a reference to two of their ships at Gibraltar in 1540.[422] A puff of wind would have taken them into the Mediterranean, but they did not enter the sea until just before the second wave of Atlantic invaders, and, as far as we know, even then they only reached the ports on the east coast of Spain. In 1567 a Breton ship was at Alicante;[423] in November, 1570 or 1571, another was at Málaga, the *Baron* with on board her the master, Guillaume Potier, and the merchants Étienne Chaton and François Pin, plus a cargo of canvas and a few thousand quintals of fish. When they had sold it all, they bought 4000 crowns' worth of raisins and other goods and were preparing to return to Brittany when the *proveedor* of Málaga laid an embargo on the vessel, threw one of the merchants into jail, and was intending to send the ship on the king's business either to Oran or Peñon de Velez. This flagrantly contravenes the treaty between the two countries, writes the French ambassador, and 'it is not the first time a French ship like this has been requisitioned at Málaga'.[424] And it was not until 1571 that the first ship from St. Malo arrived at Civitavecchia.[425]

Among these humble and discreet visitors, the Normans are mentioned more frequently. In 1499, one of their big ships, the *Magdeleine*, was captured by a Portuguese corsair at Almeria.[426] Ten years later Norman sailing ships were regularly fetching alum from the Mediterranean for the Rouen weaving trade; this mineral came either from Spain, in which case it was picked up at Mazarron, or from the Papal states, loaded at Civitavecchia. In 1522, 1523, 1527, 1531, 1532, 1534, 1535, 1536, 1539,[427] their visits to the Mediterranean can easily be checked: dozens of these little sailing boats figure in the registers of Norman tabellions [clerks] and in the harbour records of Civitavecchia. There was no lack of incidents at the ports. On 3rd February, 1535 at Cartagena, three little Norman ships carrying herring, salt fish and 'otras muchas mercaderias' were requisitioned before they could leave for Leghorn and Civitavecchia. Two of

[419] R. Collier, *H. du commerce de Marseille*, III, p. 146–147.
[420] M. Sanudo, *op. cit.*, I, col. 471.
[421] M. Mollat, *art. cit.*, p. 10.
[422] *Saco de Gibraltar, op. cit.*, p. 93.
[423] *Correspondance de Fourquevaux*, I, p. 178–179, 13th February, 1567.
[424] Representation made by the Ambassador of France to His Catholic Majesty (1570 or 1571), A.N., K 1527, B 33 n° 41.
[425] Jean Delumeau, *L'alun de Rome XVe–XIXe siècle*, 1962, p. 241.
[426] E. Gosselin, *Documents authentiques et inédits pour servir à l'histoire de la marine marchande et du commerce rouennais pendant les XVIe et XVIIe siècles*, Rouen, 1876, p. 8–11.
[427] M. Mollat, *op. cit.*, p. 241.

them were called *Maria*, one from Dieppe and the other from St.-Valéry-en-Caux, and the third ship also from Dieppe was *La Louve*.[428] The usual route was that taken by the *Fleur de Lys* of Dieppe[429] (80 tons, 22nd May, 1536) sailing to 'Ligorne et Civitegie' and unloading alum at Le Havre de Grâce, London, Antwerp, or Rouen; or that followed by the *Françoise* of Rouen (2nd October, 1535) which put in to Marseilles, Villefranche, Leghorn, Naples, Messina, and Palermo.[430]

Inevitably, in the long run, Norman ships were drawn by contract or by accident, on to other routes, to North Africa for instance, where they loaded coral near Cape Negro and, finally, though not before 1535 or 1536, they reached the eastern Mediterranean, as all the incoming vessels did sooner or later. In 1539,[431] the *Grande Martine* of Dieppe made the trip to Marseilles, Cyprus, Constantinople, and Salonica.

Comparatively late arrivals, the Normans prolonged their stay in the Mediterranean. Civitavecchia could always provide them with cargoes between 1545 and 1552. And longer voyages called them east and south. In 1560, a ship from Dieppe, captured by Euldj 'Alī,[432] turned up in the Black Sea, where she was eventually lost in the service of the Turk. In 1561 another fell prey to the Spanish off the Balearics. It was learned that the said vessel had left Dieppe for the Barbary coast, that she had taken a pilot at Toulon and that the said pilot – this is the French version – had, unknown to everyone else, brought on board oars, which were contraband goods for ships travelling to the countries of Islam; that lead and shot were also found on board, but these, according to the Admiral of France, were intended for Dieppe, not for Africa, an explanation considered highly improbable by the sceptical Chantonnay who was perhaps right for once.[433] More fortunate were the voyages made by other vessels from Dieppe, the *Coq*, master Le Prieur, for instance which entered Leghorn on 4th January, 1574, carrying lead, barrels of herring, hides, tin, a few kerseys and, a reminder of Dieppe's days of glory, 20,880 logs of brazil-wood;[434] or the *St.-Paul*, master Gérard, which sailed into Leghorn on 22nd February, 1578, bringing for the merchants of Lucca barrels of herring, peas, salmon, flax, hemp, linen cloth, and, again, brazil-wood (4700 logs). But these were late appearances and very much an exception. They would not withstand the 'second' English invasion, which cannot of course be adequately dealt with until we have considered the earlier impressive entry of the English to the Mediterranean.[435]

[428] 4th February, 1535, Simancas, *Guerra Antigua*, VII, f° 59.
[429] E. Gosselin, *op. cit.*, p. 43.
[430] *Ibid.*, p. 42–43, 2nd October 1535.
[431] *H. du Commerce de Marseille*, III, p. 221.
[432] E. Charrière, *Négociations dans le Levant*, II, p. 631–632, Constantinople, 30th October, 1560.
[433] Chantonnay to Philip II, Moret, 16th March, 1561, A.N., K 1494, B 12, n° 60; the same to the same, 23rd March, 1561, *ibid.*, n° 62.
[434] A.d.S., Florence, Mediceo 2080.
[435] Cf. below p. 613–614.

Flemish ships. A few words will suffice for the 'Flemish' (in fact, nine times out of ten, Dutch) vessels, which arrived in fairly large numbers in the Mediterranean in the armadas sent by Charles V against Tunis in 1535 and Algiers in 1541. One of their ships is mentioned at Barcelona in 1535. After 1550 they became rare. What is one to make of the hooker, the *Santa Pietà*, which was quite clearly sold at Venice in 1560 and was lying in the harbour? She can hardly have come on her own.[436] A 'Flemish' (or Dutch?) ship brought a hundred pieces of ordnance to Cartagena in June, 1566.[437] In 1571 on the one occasion we can actually trace a Dutch ship, with her master, Joan Giles, *natural de Holanda*, leaving Antwerp for Cadiz and Leghorn, carrying Italian merchandise and Italian merchants (mostly if not all Florentine), the said master sailed into La Rochelle, and pillaging his own ship, sold the entire cargo.[438]

The first English sailing ships. Following Richard Hakluyt, the date of English entry to the Mediterranean has usually been given as 1511. In fact this year saw the beginning of a series of prosperous voyages to the Levant, preceded by a long and not always brilliant apprenticeship. Nor does the English ship mentioned in the port of Genoa by two notarial documents[439] (30th August, and 6–7th October, 1412) necessarily signify the beginning of an enterprise that was spread over a period of centuries, any more than the two ventures launched by Robert Sturmy,[440] merchant of Bristol, in 1446 and 1456, at ten years' interval from each other. On the first occasion the cog *Ann*, chartered by him, carried 160 pilgrims to the Holy Land as well as a cargo of wool, woollen cloth and sheets of tin. She reached Jaffa, where the pilgrims disembarked, to make their return journey either overland or in another ship. On 23rd December, the cog *Ann*, surprised by a storm, was wrecked off Modon and her crew of thirty-seven perished with her. Ten years later, Sturmy himself journeyed to the Levant in the *Katharine Sturmy*. His voyage was to last over a year. In 1457 after having stayed in 'divers parts of the Levant' (we have no further details), he apparently procured 'some green pepper and other spices to have set and sown in England, (as the fame went)'. But the expedition ended tragically, not in ship-wreck this time, but as a result of Genoese jealousy.[441] They were waiting for the Englishman off Malta and pillaged his ship. Sturmy himself disappeared in the incident.

In 1461 the English opened a joint consulate at Naples together with

[436] Ragusa Archives, D. di Cancellaria, 146, fᵒˢ 27 to 29, 17th June, 1960. If described as a hooker it must have been from the North.
[437] Nobili to the Prince, Madrid, 6th June, 1566, Mediceo 4897 a. Cf. C. Douais, *op. cit.*, I, p. 90 and 92.
[438] The Duke of Alva to F. de Alava, Antwerp, 13th February, 1571, A.N., K 1519, B 29, n° 18.
[439] R. Doehaerd and Ch. Kerremans, *op. cit.*, 1952, p. 139 and 143.
[440] Eleonora Carus-Wilson, *Mediaeval Merchant Venturers*, 1954, p. 64 ff.
[441] Jacques Heers, 'Les Génois en Angleterre: la crise de 1458–1466' in *Studi in onore di Armando Sapori*, II, p. 810.

the French and Germans;[442] in the same year they also opened one on their own in Marseilles.[443] Twenty years later they were setting up their vital consulate at Pisa, clear proof that they hoped, by using Pisa, Florence, and Tuscany as a base, to challenge the dual monopoly in the Levant of Genoa and Venice. It may be noted in retrospect that Sturmy had also used Pisa as a stopping place.[444]

Nevertheless the progress of the English was slow; and had no doubt to be paid for, like that of all the newcomers, by entering the employ of other states. The precious records of the *Caratorum Maris* of Genoa seem to suggest this.[445] But there is little evidence that there was a long period during which they served other powers, transporting bulky, low-priced merchandise over long distances. It is possible that the English won their way more quickly and at less expense than other newcomers, to the Levant, with its spices, and Crete with her precious wines. But it certainly did not happen overnight: they did not appear at Barcelona, for example until 1535[446] and it was not until the beginning of the sixteenth century that English commodities – lead, tin, salted fish, peasant cloth – really penetrated the Mediterranean, and in greater quantities than has hitherto been thought.[447]

The period of prosperity (1511–1534). The names and histories of the ships, and the incidents of the voyages to the Levant between 1511 and 1534 are well known to us.[448] The *Christopher Campion*, the *Mary George*, the *Mary Grace*, the *Trinity*, the *Matthew* of London, and several other ships from Bristol and Southampton, sailed regularly to Sicily, Crete, Chios, sometimes to Cyprus, as well as Tripoli in Syria and Beirut. They carried to the Mediterranean woollen cloth and 'kersies of divers colours'; they brought back pepper, spices, silks, camlets, malmseys, muscatels, sweet oils, cotton wool, and carpets. They were frequent visitors: fortunately, write the masters of the *Mahonna* at Chios to Genoa, in January and February, 1531 we have received some merchandise from an English vessel coming from Egypt and Syria (the goods were not, incidentally, in very good condition).[449] The English did not only use their own ships, but often entrusted their merchandise to Venetian 'galleasses' or to Ragusan, Cretan, Spanish, and even Portuguese roundships.[450]

[442] Hektor Ammann, *art. cit.*, in *Vierteljahrschrift für S. u. W. G.*, vol. 42, 1955, p. 266.
[443] *Ibid.*
[444] Domenico Gioffrè, 'Il commercio d'importazione genovese alla luce dei registri del dazio, 1495–1537' in *Studi in onore di Amintore Fanfani*, 1962, V, p. 113 ff. W. Cunningham, *The growth of English Industry and Commerce*, 1914, I, p. 373.
[445] D. Gioffrè, *art. cit.*, p. 121–122.
[446] A. de Capmany, *op. cit.*, III, p. 225–226; IV, appendix, p. 49.
[447] D. Gioffrè, *art. cit.*, p. 122–123, NB their use of Cadiz.
[448] R. Hakluyt, *op. cit.*, II, p. 96 ff.
[449] Philip Argenti, *Chius vincta*, 1941, p. 13.
[450] R. Hakluyt, *op. cit.*, II, p. 96.

On Chios, their rallying point at the far end of the sea, the English had a 'factor' until 1552.[451] In 1592,[452] Hakluyt, the collector of relations of voyages and discoveries, was to hear from John Williamson, who went as cooper aboard the *Mathew Gonson* of London, in 1534, the story of the voyage he made in that year to Crete and Chios. The ship (300 tons burden and a hundred men on board) a large vessel for the time, sailed with the *Holy Cross* a 'short shippe' of 160 tons burden. After a full year at sea, they returned from this long voyage with a cargo of oil and wine in casks that were found to be so weak on arrival that they had to be drawn as they lay and the wine and oil transferred into new vessels. But the cargo was nevertheless of excellent quality, particularly the muscatels and red malmsey, 'the like whereof were seldom seen before in England'. She also carried Turkish carpets, spices, and cotton. The *Holy Cross* had been so badly shaken by the voyage that she was laid up in dock and never sailed again.

The large number of papers and letters collected by Hakluyt and the usually precise character of his accounts are proof enough of the frequency of English shipping, in the age of the Renaissance, in the Mediterranean and as far as the gateways to the east. It prospered during the years 1511 to 1534 and continued until 1552, 'and somewhat longer', then was suddenly interrupted, 'given over'.[453] The last voyage recorded in Hakluyt's collection is that of the 'great Barke *Aucher*' (1550), as told by her captain, Roger Bodenham,[454] and an eventful voyage it was too. She left England in January and in spring arrived in the ports of Crete, where she met many Turkish boats laden with grain. Accompanied by a number of small boats carrying their goods to Chios, the English ship reached the island, which was still one of the most active commercial centres of the East, with its Genoese merchants, its mastic plantations, its production of silk bedcovers, and its many ships. She left the island in haste, to avoid the Turkish galleys preceding the victorious fleet on its way back from Tripoli in Barbary. The *Aucher* went on to Crete, where there were 'many banished men' in the mountains, ready to come down to fight in the island's defence, wild men, booted to the thigh, each with his bow and arrow, sword, and dagger, and drinking wine 'out of all measure'. Then on to Zante, Messina, Cadiz, and England. An interesting detail: on this voyage sailed the same Richard Chamberlain who was two years later to lead the expeditions to the mouth of the Dvina in northern Russia. But one looks in vain in this account for any valid reason why voyages by English ships should have stopped. We have few details concerning the *Jesus* of Lübeck and the *Mary Gonson*, which were chartered in 1552 for a voyage to the Levant.[455]

[451] R. Hakluyt, p. 98. English merchants at Constantinople, 1544. *Itinéraire* . . . of Jérôme Maurand, ed. Dorez, p. 126.
[452] R. Hakluyt, II, p. 98.
[453] *Ibid.*, II, Epistle dedicatorie to Sir Robert Cecil, unnumbered.
[454] *Ibid.*, II, p. 99–101.
[455] James A. Williamson, *Maritime Enterprise*, Oxford, 1913, p. 233.

The account of John Locke's voyage to Jerusalem in 1553, although of great interest, concerns only a lone traveller who, when dropped by an English vessel at Cadiz, travelled on to Venice; and there took passage aboard a pilgrim ship that was to carry him to the Holy Land. The return journey took him to many ports, of which he gives a vivid description, as he does of the band of northern pilgrims, Flemish and German, whose daggers were often raised in quarrels after heavy drinking of the Mediterranean wines.[456]

Hakluyt explains the English withdrawal from the Mediterranean by the fall first of Chios, in 1566, and then of Cyprus in 1571, an explanation accepted by English historians. But how is one to explain their absence between 1552 and 1566?[457] The absence of English shipping (1552–1573) does indeed broadly correspond to the period of Turkish ascendancy (1538–1571) but was not necessarily its effect.

In the first place, the English withdrawal had economic reasons. For one thing there was the general recession in the world economy of the years 1540–1545 and an economic crisis undoubtedly occurred in England towards mid-century, as is well known since it is unfailingly quoted as a reason for the formation of the Merchant Adventurers' Company, a venture first conceived towards the middle of the century and probably realized in 1552[458] on the occasion of Chancellor's voyage of discovery. This voyage was originally intended to reach Cathay and the spices of the East by way of the dangerous north-east passage. As it turned out, it inaugurated the Russian commercial episode,[459] through which it was hoped to circumvent the Mediterranean trade with the Levant. The enterprise was from the first a response to economic malaise, to the falling price of English goods and the drop in overseas demand, which led in turn to a recession in trade and a shortage of the precious colonial commodities. Perhaps by studying the conditions of trade in English commercial centres one might be able to discover why voyages to the Mediterranean ceased to be worthwhile for London merchants, for this was clearly basically why they were discontinued. To blame the Turks does not seem very logical. The English were more likely discouraged by competition from Mediterranean shipping as well as from the overland routes across Europe and by the generally unfavourable conjuncture of these difficult years.

II. FROM 1550 TO 1573: THE MEDITERRANEAN LEFT TO MEDITERRANEAN SHIPS

Along with the English, all the other intruders from beyond the straits vanished as if swept from the Mediterranean, and if a few laggards were

---

[456] R. Hakluyt, *op. cit.*, II, p. 101–102.

[457] Alfred C. Wood, *A History of the Levant Company*, London, 1935, p. 3, wrongly dates the capture of Chios by the Turks in 1570, the same year as Cyprus (another error).

[458] Inna Lubimenko, *op. cit.*, p. 20 and 27.

[459] R. Hakluyt, *op. cit.*, I, p. 243.

left behind, a ship from Dieppe, a Breton fishing-smack or the odd boat from St.-Malo, there can be no doubt that the sea was suddenly empty of northerners. The Mediterranean once again took over all the duties of internal transport, for a good twenty years, from 1553 to 1573. All the bulky commodities – salt, grain, wool, cumbersome hides – were carried in Ragusan ships, whose importance was increasing – in 1535 and 1541 for instance, in the fleets that Charles V led against Tunis and Algiers; in Venetian merchantmen whose numbers undoubtedly rose (total tonnage in 1498 was 26,800 *botti*; in 1560 it was 29,000 and, by 1567, 54,400),[460] figures that tell their own story. Venice filled the gap left by the departure of the Atlantic ships. The same was true of Ragusa: the merchant fleet in 1540 totalled 20,000 *carri*; it had risen to 35,000 between 1560 and 1570, the decade that marked its apogee.[461] All these new roundships appeared when the times called for them. They also explain why large Mediterranean ships were once again seen on the distant Atlantic and even North Sea routes.

In fact, these routes had never been totally abandoned by the southerners.[462] In 1533 only the state-sponsored fleets stopped using them, not the private vessels. A French correspondent refers to the imminent departure in December, 1547, of 'grandes naufs vénitiennes'.[463] In March, 1548 the same writer announces the arrival of 'quelques naufs arragonsoyes' [Ragusan] 'ou vénitiennes' at *Antone* [Southampton].[464] After 1550, or rather the 1560s, references to such voyages become more frequent. In about 1551,[465] 'some of the first gentlemen of Venice', Alessandro and Giustiniano Contarini and Alvise Foscarini complained that the king of France had seized one of their ships on her way to England. In the Netherlands in May, 1552 ten or twelve ships 'some Biscayan, some Portuguese, and Ragusan, in good order and well equipped . . . are to join the principal fleet' then being prepared.[466] On 17th October, 1552, there is good news from the *consoli veneziani a Londra*.[467] Between 1553 and 1565, thirteen Genoese ships (some of which had a capacity of 500 tons), carried alum from Civitavecchia to Flanders.[468] On 20th June, 1566, merchants 'who travel to London' were called together to discuss how best to elect

[460] R. Romano, 'La marine marchande vénitienne au XVIe siècle' in *Les sources de l'histoire maritime en Europe du Moyen Age au XVIIIe siècle*, 1962.

[461] I. Tadić, *art. cit.*, p. 15.

[462] Several references in Ragusa Archives, Diversa di Cancellaria 106, f° 247, 17th November, 1516, to a Ragusan ship travelling between London and Ragusa; *ibid.*, f° 180, Genoa, 10th March, 1515, a Ragusan ship sailing direct from Chios to England; *ibid.*, 122, f° 24, Cadiz, 21st February, 1538, a Ragusan ship loaded at Southampton and bound for Cadiz, Palermo, and Messina.

[463] Selve to the king, 12th December, 1547, *Correspondance* . . . ed. G. Lefevre-Portalis, p. 252.

[464] *Ibid.*, p. 321.

[465] Moscow Archives, Fonds Lamoignon, 3, f° 128.

[466] R. Häpke, *op. cit.*, I, p. 512.

[467] A.d.S., Venice, Senato Terra 67, f° 8.

[468] J. Delumeau, *op. cit.*, p. 241.

their consul.[469] On 3rd December, Genoa herself complained of the dishonesty of the Genoese master of a hooker, who, coming from the West to Cadiz, sailed straight to Naples instead of returning to Leghorn and Genoa as he should have done.[470] In May, 1558, some Frenchmen seized a Venetian ship off Le Havre.[471] Between 18th December, 1562, and 15th February, 1563, a Florentine vessel, the *Santa Maria de la Nunziata*, sailed from Antwerp to Leghorn.[472] The unpublished journal of Francesco de Molin shows him leaving Venice on 21st March, 1566, aboard a big ship owned by Jacomo Foscarini and Jacomo Ragazoni; she sailed to Zante where she took on an entire cargo of raisins (*uve passe*), 'which seemed a most remarkable thing to me', he says 'to fill a whole ship of a thousand *botte* with such a commodity'. The voyage continued by Malta, Majorca, Málaga, Cadiz, and Lisbon before the ship finally put in at 'Margata'[473] where the cargo was unloaded and sent to London and the ship left again in October. Her adventures at sea, in particular in the service of Spain, which put an embargo on her and sent her to Flanders on Spanish business, are of no interest to us. At Málaga in July 1567 a 'big Venetian *nave*' laden with merchandise for Cadiz and Cretan wines for England was also on the point of being requisitioned. In 1569, six Venetian *navi* are simultaneously recorded on the route to the north.[474] From what we know of their tonnage, the importance of this southern traffic may be imagined. In the same year (1569) two ships were seized by Huguenot pirates off La Rochelle (the *nave Giustiniana*, 1200 tons, with a cargo of 130,000 crowns and seventy pieces of artillery concealed under piles of salt, and the small ship *Vergi*).[475] It was the occasion of an official complaint and some exchange of correspondence and provides us with further evidence of the uninterrupted traffic between Venice and England. One learns without surprise that kerseys were to have figured in the return cargo,[476] a detail that did not go unnoticed by the services of the Duke of Alva in the Netherlands.[477] In August he writes that the English, threatened by war with Spain, are exporting their woollen cloth in Venetian and Ragusan ships, which both in the Atlantic and in the Mediterranean, apart from isolated accidents and pirate raids, had the privileges of neutrals. In May, 1569 the Spanish ambassador in London was urging the Venetian ships to leave England as soon as possible,[478] for in order to put pressure on England difficulties had to be put in the way of the Venetian and

[469] A.d.S., Venice, *Cinque Savii*, 17, f° 10.
[470] A. d. Stato, Genoa, Spagna, Negoziazioni, 2747, 3rd December, 1557.
[471] M. François, *Le Cardinal François de Tournon*, 1951, p. 366.
[472] A.d.S., Florence, Mediceo 2080.
[473] Marciana, Ital., 8812, CVI, 3, f° 10 v°: Margate at the mouth of the Thames.
[474] *CODOIN*, XC, p. 288.
[475] *Calendar of State Papers, Venetian*, VII, p. 430, 441, 445–447, 454, 456; *CODOIN*, XC, p. 236–237, 254, 288, 327.
[476] *CODOIN*, XC, p. 236–237, 23rd May, 1569.
[477] The Duke of Alva to the king, Brussels, 8th August, 1569, *CODOIN*, XV, p. 170.
[478] *CODOIN*, XC, p. 236–237.

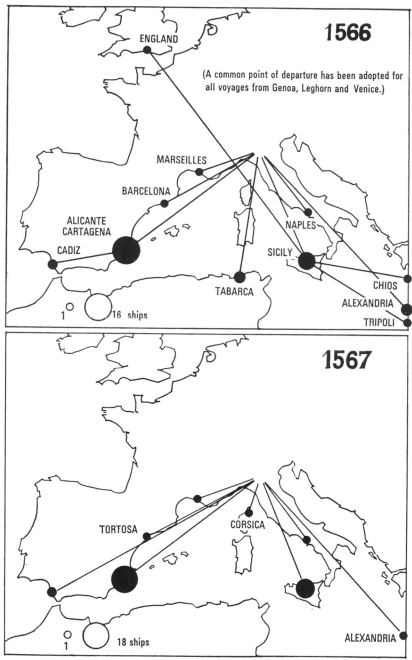

1566

(A common point of departure has been adopted for all voyages from Genoa, Leghorn and Venice.)

ENGLAND

MARSEILLES

BARCELONA

ALICANTE
CARTAGENA

CADIZ

NAPLES

SICILY

TABARCA

CHIOS

ALEXANDRIA

TRIPOLI

1 ○ ◯ 16 ships

1567

TORTOSA

CORSICA

ALEXANDRIA

○
1 ◯ 18 ships

Fig 53: *A register of marine insurance at Genoa*

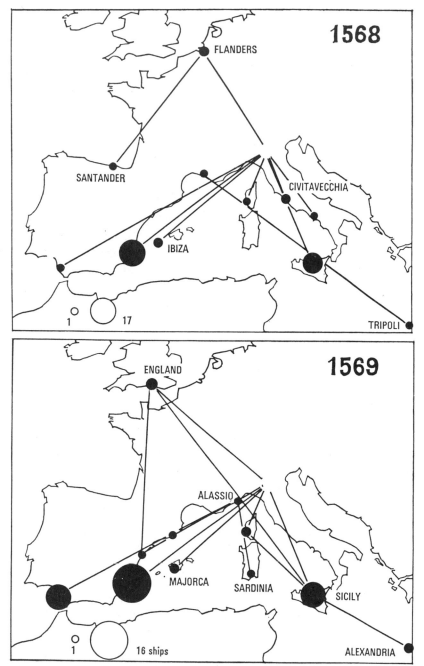

1568

FLANDERS

SANTANDER

CIVITAVECCHIA

IBIZA

1   17

TRIPOLI

1569

ENGLAND

ALASSIO

MAJORCA   SARDINIA

SICILY

1   16 ships

ALEXANDRIA

Fig 53: *A register of marine insurance ot Genoa*

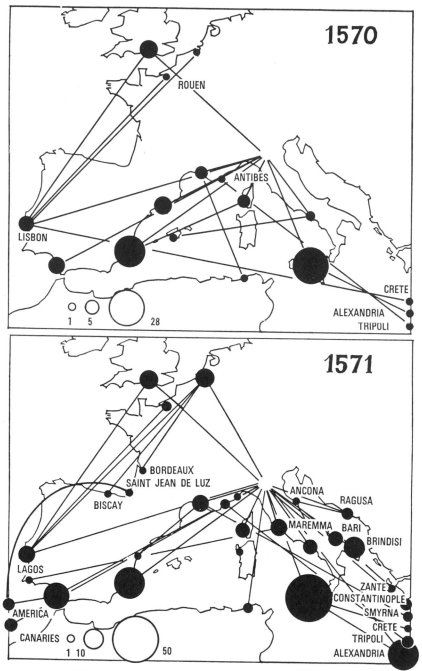

1570

ROUEN

ANTIBES

LISBON

CRETE
ALEXANDRIA
TRIPOLI

○ ○ ⬤
1 5   28

1571

BORDEAUX
SAINT JEAN DE LUZ

BISCAY

ANCONA

RAGUSA

MAREMMA   BARI
BRINDISI

LAGOS

ZANTE
CONSTANTINOPLE
SMYRNA
CRETE

AMERICA

CANARIES ○ ○   ○
1 10   50

TRIPOLI
ALEXANDRIA

Fig 53 : *A register of marine insurance at Genoa*

Ragusan roundships. It is curious to find the Huguenots lending a hand.[479]

But this revival in Mediterranean shipping was born of the general situation. Between roughly 1550 and 1570, or rather 1575, there was an obvious recession. Business was bad for everybody. But every state had to see to its own needs. And the richer states, because they rode out the storm while others sank, appeared prosperous. In spite of the usual disastrous accidents which befell the great ships of the Mediterranean, they continued to hold their own, maintaining both internal and external communications. And then fine economic weather returned. If we resist the temptation of the over-simple solution, it was the return of prosperity that brought an end to the Mediterranean voyages to the north, or at any rate made them a rare occurrence. During the extraordinary boom at the end of the century, the rich could once again afford the luxury of delegating certain tasks to others. First English and then Dutch ships once more entered the Mediterranean, this time in larger numbers than they had during the early years of the century.

The return of the English in 1572–1573. The English ships reappeared at least as soon as 1573. It is in this year that we find what seems to be their first appearance at Leghorn. Perhaps they returned even earlier? An

---

Fig. 53: *A register of marine insurance at Genoa*

From the register in A.d.S Genoa, San Giorgio Securitatum, 1565–1571. This record of all marine insurance registered at Genoa provides material for six consecutive maps (1566–1571) one for each year. One's immediate impression is of a growing volume of traffic. The Genoese insurers found their clientele enlarged, particularly in 1571 when the war of Cyprus and other Venetian difficulties enabled them to take over some of the business of their old rival. The 1571 map is sensational: this shows Genoese shipping as well as some Venetian and provides evidence of voyages in the Adriatic, the Levant, to the Atlantic, the English Channel, and the North Sea. These insurance records of course both over- and under-represent the total volume of shipping from Genoa, whose chief ports of call, Alicante and Palermo, do however emerge clearly, as well as the rather less active route to the Levant. The need to simplify the detailed information provided in the register made it necessary to conflate the three ports of departure (Genoa, Leghorn, and Venice). Two points stand out: the progress made by Genoese capitalism in the sector of Venetian marine insurance, and the Mediterranean vessels that linked Genoa, Venice, and Leghorn to northern and Atlantic Europe. (The Maremma marked on the last map is the Tuscan Maremma).

---

[479] A disappointment: I could only find mention by name (in the series *Noli e Sicurtà* in Ragusa Archives) two Ragusan ships making the voyage, one in April, 1563, from Zeeland to Leghorn, the other on 4th July, 1565, leaving Antwerp for Ragusa. But many insurance policies taken out for six or twelve month periods do not state the ship's itinerary; and there are cases of Ragusan ships being insured elsewhere than in their native port. On the other hand there is a rewarding crop in the series *Securitatum 1564–1571*, A.d.S., Genoa: both sailing to and from the Mediterranean, three voyages from Lisbon, 10 voyages to Cadiz, five voyages to the North (Rouen, Antwerp, England, Flanders); after 1569–1570, these voyages to the North become more frequent, to the advantage in particular of Venetian ships insured at Genoa. Did Genoa benefit from Venice's difficulties when she was at war with the Turk?

English Newfoundland fishing boat may have arrived at Civitavecchia in 1572.[480] A ship certainly arrived at Leghorn on 25th June, 1573: '*La Rondine*',[481] (the *Swallow*) master *Giovanni Scotto, inglese*, loaded at London and Southampton and carrying three bales of *carisee* (kerseys), two barrels of wrought tin, a few cotton fabrics, thirty-seven casks of broken bells, five whole bells, 380 pigs of lead and a keg of salt tongue – in all a modest cargo. The *St. Mary of Grief*, master Sterlich, arrived on 20th July, carrying goods taken on board at Cadiz. The *Kite*, which sailed into Leghorn on 16th December, 1573, brought lead, soda, woollen cloth, and tin from London, all of which, a detail worth noting, had been ordered by merchants of Genoa. These three ships alone point the way to what was to be the chief commodity traffic with England: woollen cloth, lead, and tin. Later additions were to be the countless barrels of herring, cod, and preserved salmon. Once re-established the link was never broken again. In 1573 our Leghorn registers mention three English ships, in 1574, nine; two only (but the evidence is incomplete for this year) in 1575; three in 1576; five in 1578; nine in 1579; two in 1580; thirteen in 1581; ten in 1582; four in 1583; six in 1584; eight in 1585; six in 1590–91; three in 1591–1592; sixteen in 1592–1593. The English had found their way back to the Mediterranean.

Nothing at the gateway to the Mediterranean, in Spain, seems to offer any explanation for this return and very little in the sea itself. Can it be attributed to the improvements in the sail and rigging of roundships which occurred towards mid-sixteenth century and made these ships easier to handle in a sea of varying moods? Or if one takes the evidence of the Leghorn *portate* (the unloading of barrels of white herring, lead, and tin) was there an increased demand in the Mediterranean for English commodities that satisfied two kinds of hunger, the hunger of fast days and Lent and the hunger for armaments? It was at about this time of course that bronze artillery was beginning to replace cast iron. There can be no doubt at any rate that the demand for tin and lead was general throughout the Mediterranean, in Moslem countries, and in Russia as well as in the Christian West. By 1580 the English ships that called at Sicily were suspected of being on their way to Constantinople with tin for the casting of artillery.[482] They also supplied Naples[483] and were welcomed at Malta, after the initial, rather unfortunate contacts made in 1581 by the *Roe*, an English bark, master Peter Baker, carrying iron, steel, bronze, and tin and in 1582 by the bark *Reynolds*.[484] The Knights of Malta, in July of that year granted a safe-conduct to the English, provided they did not carry contraband, to

[480] Jean Delumeau, *L'alun de Rome, op. cit.*, p. 241.
[481] The *Swallow*, Mediceo 2080. The same reference for all the ships mentioned in this paragraph.
[482] Marcantonio Colonna to the king, Palermo, 26th February, 1580, Simancas E° 1149, passes on information given to him by Bernardino de Mendoza.
[483] An indispensable supply, as the Count of Miranda was to tell Philip II, Naples, 13th July, 1591, Simancas E° 1093.
[484] R. Hakluyt, *op. cit.*, II, p. 145–146.

trade freely with the island and pass on to the Levant. This favour was naturally an opportunity to place several specific orders, powder for cannon and arquebus, saltpetre, tin, steel, iron, copper, common white kerseys, coarse canvas, balls of iron for shot, fine millstones, and trees and masts for galleys; and also the *carboni di petra rosetta*, which the English called 'cole of Newcastle' – a detail in the history of English coal.

But the return of the English to the Mediterranean appears above all to have been in reply to explicit invitations, such as those of the Grand Duke of Tuscany between 1576 and 1578,[485] seeking to attract the English to Leghorn; or, in 1578–1579, those of Horatio Pallavicino, the Genoese turned Protestant, who was one of the last great Italian bankers and business men in England.[486] In 1578, in partnership with another Genoese, Battista Spinola of Antwerp, he agreed a loan of 350,000 florins to the provinces of Flanders (who had by then broken with Philip II), the loan to be guaranteed by the city of London. In exchange, Pallavicino obtained for a six-year period the monopoly of imports of alum, which was bound to prejudice sales of alum from Philip II's states. It was therefore doubly in Spain's interests to react: both to safeguard her own trade and to prevent the rebels from doing good business, the profits from which would be used against Spain, as she knew only too well. Pallavicino, foreseeing difficulties, thought of bringing north at once the alum he possessed at Genoa, Milan, and the Spanish ports. At the end of the summer he sent the ship *Santa Maria Incoronata*, of 7000 cantars, south as far as Alicante, Cartagena, and Cadiz to pick up some of his stocks.[487] His Catholic Majesty, forewarned of this move, prepared to make enquiries at Milan and to stop any ships entering Spanish ports carrying alum.[488] The trap was set, but the Genoese was warned of the danger from Alicante. So he decided to entrust the task of transporting the precious alum to English ships. These, seven in number, in fact reached Alicante on their return journey without incident, and, brought to London in March, 1579, 14,000 cantars (an average of 2000 cantars per ship, indicating an average capacity of about 100 tons). The entire shipment was worth the good sum of 60,000 crowns. In addition, if another document is to be taken at face value, it seems that Pallavicino also sent 2000 more cantars to Flanders by way of Germany.[489]

Further evidence on the English arrival is provided by a decree of the Venetian Senate dated 26th January, 1580,[490] and blaming once again the post-Lepanto crisis. 'Before the last war,' say the Senators, 'our merchants of Venice were in the habit of engaging in trade and traffic to

[485] G. Vivoli, *op. cit.*, III, p. 155.
[486] Cf. L. Stone, *An Elizabethan: Sir Horatio Palavicino*, 1956.
[487] 23rd September, 1578, *CODOIN*, XCI, p. 287–288.
[488] *CODOIN*, XCI, p. 297
[489] *Ibid.*, p. 398. On the episode as a whole see p. 275, 287–288, 360, 375, 387–388, 393.
[490] *Bilanci generali*, Second series, vol. I, tome I, p. 439, note 1.

the western waters [that is England] and our ships served the islands of Cephalonia, Zante, and Candia [Crete] where they would take on raisins and wines to be shipped to the west, and on their return they would bring to this city *carisee*, woollen cloth, tin, and other goods.' In this way five or six ships had regularly been sailing to the North Sea every year. But since the war (in other words since 1571–1573) 'il detto viaggio e del tutto levato' the said voyage has been completely abandoned. 'Foreign' ships now went directly to the Venetian islands and took on board raisins and new wines, with the complicity of certain Venetian subjects resident in these islands and brought in exchange the *carisee*, cloth, tin, and silver of the north.

So we are brought back yet again to the Venetian crisis of 1571–1573, which was apparently responsible not only for the visible but short-lived fortune of Marseilles, in the Levant, but also for the return of English shipping to the Mediterranean. Here, as in the Levant, Venice could quickly have recovered her position. If she did not so do, it was because the economic situation was once more becoming favourable by 1575, with the result that responsibilities were more readily delegated, as we have already suggested. Certainly, there were still Venetian ships to be seen in the north, up to the end of the century. In 1582, for instance, in the trivial incident of the repatriation of a hundred poor Portuguese 'who had come quite naked' from Terceira to England, mention is made of two Venetian *navi*.[491] In October, 1589 the *Santa Maria di Gracia* (either Venetian or Ragusan) was loading wine for England at Candia and Rethimnon. Or so her freight contract tells us.[492] But on the whole, as we have already explained, Venice, like the other great Mediterranean cities, was ready to offer employment to 'foreign' ships and mariners. This employment provides the most acceptable explanation for the return of the northern ships to the Mediterranean.[493]

[491] 29th November, 1582, *CODOIN*, XCII, p. 436.
[492] A.d.S., Venice, Lettere Com., 12 *ter*, 20th October, 1589.
[493] I have left aside two minor considerations: 1. The mariners of Dieppe and Marseilles may have acted as guides for the English on their first return voyages. It is true that English ships reached Leghorn between 1573 and 1584 and are indicated as having taken on cargo at Dieppe (one reference, 4th February, 1574), Calais (five references, 3rd February, 1574, 25th January, 1576, 2nd February, 1576 – twice – 14th January, 1579), 'in France' (one reference, 12th January, 1579), in Flanders (one reference (10th January, 1584), in Zeeland (one reference, 24th October, 1581). A text by A. de Montchrestien *op. cit.*, 1615, p. 226–227, seems (but is not) conclusive: 'Forty years ago (i.e., in 1575) the former [the English] had no trade either with Turkey or Barbary but frequented only Hamburg and Stade, where they had their staple. The captain, Anthoine Girard, who is still living and Jean Durant, when young men from Marseilles, gave them their first opening at London; what is more, they guided and piloted their first ships. At that time, it was the ships of Marseilles which brought them spices and all other manner of goods through the Straits; but now . . .' 2. The quarrel between Venice and England over the *uve passe* was to last for more than a quarter-century (*C.S.P. Venetian*, VII, p. 542, 544, 545, 548, 549, 550, 552). It began in 1576, when a Lucchese merchant in London was granted the monopoly of imports of *uve passe* to England. There followed discussions and customs reprisals: 1580, 1591,

Anglo-Turkish negotiations: 1578–1583[494]. The English had yet to conquer the markets of the Levant. Richard Hakluyt[495] claims that this was the work of two merchants of London, Sir Edward Osborne and Richard Staper who decided to embark upon this course in 1575. At their own expense they sent to Constantinople two agents, John Wight and Joseph Clements, who travelled through Poland and at Lwow, in September, 1578 joined the party of the Turkish ambassador Aḥmad Chā'ūsh, who brought them safely to their destination on 28th October. They obtained a letter from the sultan for the queen of England, dated 15th March, 1579. Bernardino de Mendoza, who from London followed the operation more closely than the Spanish agent in Constantinople, Giovanni Margliani, noted in November, 1579 that the queen had received by way of France, a letter full of promises from the sultan, enjoining her in order to preserve and make even closer her ties with the king of France, to marry (no doubt the French had something to do with the insertion of this advice) the Duke of Anjou. The letter adds that English merchants whether coming by land or sea would receive a cordial welcome. The truth is, writes Mendoza, that the Turks could not care less about the marriage; what interests them is tin, 'which the English began a few years ago to transport to the Levant', the tin without which they cannot 'cast their cannon'. And five ships with over 20,000 crowns' worth of this metal were on the point of leaving London for the Levant. The queen's reply, dated 25th September, 1579, was entrusted to Richard Stanley aboard the *Prudence*.[496] The time was ripe. With the Portuguese succession open, Philip II had embarked upon massive preparations, which gave Elizabeth in particular cause for alarm. The only course open to her was an alliance with the Turk. She even asked during the negotiations that the Ottoman armada should be sent out.

The final outcome was that England obtained in June, 1580, the thirty-five articles of her original capitulation, including unrestricted trading facilities for her subjects under her own flag, all of which was obtained in the teeth of the French (whose prestige and influence were diminishing in the Levant, according to the English), and by bribing 'the defunct Mehemet Pasha' according to the French,[497] who were deceived[498] by certain promises made by the Turk into thinking that the newcomers were to sail under the French flag. Once the English merchant had obtained his privileges he would not surrender them. In November 1580, a Turkish

---

1592, 1602 and there may have been a reconciliation in 1609 (cf. *La Méditerranée . . .*, 1st edition, p. 482, 487–488). In spite of this, Venetian ships continued to sail to England.

[494] Bibliographical references in R. B. Merriman, *op. cit.*, IV, p. 154, note 3.
[495] R. Hakluyt, *op. cit.*, II, p. 136–137.
[496] *CODOIN*, XCI, p. 439, 28th November, 1579.
[497] Berthier's instructions, 5th September, 1580, *Recueil . . .*, p. 36.
[498] They acted in league with the Venetians against the English, Hérault de Maisse to the king, 27th July, 1583, A.E., Venice 31, f° 103 v° ff.

ambassador, probably an Italian renegade, arrived in England.[499] On 11th September, 1581, the Levant Company was set up by Elizabeth, to the greater gain of Sir Edward Osborne, Richard Staper, Thomas Smith, William Garret, and a few others. Its constitution caused some friction with the English merchants who had been trading more or less on their private account in the Levant, and with those who were informally associated in the Venice trade. But the advantages of the new trading facilities, with a large-scale organization, came at a timely moment, just as affairs, in Moscow were becoming complicated and risky and the Danish ships in 1582 were beginning to use force to prevent ships trading with St. Nicholas Bay.[500] In November, 1582, the *Susan* of London sailed for Constantinople, with presents and a letter for the sultan from the queen.[501] The letter was carried by the new ambassador appointed to Turkey by Elizabeth, William Hareborne,[502] the 'Guillaume Harbron' who appears in French dispatches[503] and who was to be a sturdy pioneer of the English cause. Sicily only learned of the passage of the ship on 15th March, 1583,[504] by which time she had already reached the Aegean.

On 3rd May, William Hareborne was kissing the sultan's hands 'and he has been done as much honour', writes De Maisse,[505] 'as any other king's ambassador who has ever been there before'. Against him and the consuls he appointed in the East, both the French and the Venetians those 'malicious and dissembling peoples' with whom, according to Hareborne, one had to 'walk warily', were finally powerless.[506]

The success of English shipping. The Levant Company prospered from the start. In its original form, that of the charter granted on 11th September, 1581, it realized profits of up to 300 per cent.[507] Its progress was even more dazzling after 1592 in its second incarnation after the merger in January with the so-called Venice Company founded in 1583.[508] By 1595 the Levant Company had fifteen ships and 790 seamen[509] at its disposal. It was trading with Alexandretta, Cyprus, Chios, Zante, and to a lesser extent with Venice and Algiers.[510] In 1599 it had twenty ships in Italian waters alone. In 1600 it increased its fleet by sixteen extra ships.[511] This success did not

---

[499] *CODOIN*, XCI, 13th November, 1580, p. 523.

[500] *CODOIN*, XCI, p. 334, 396, 399, 409; R. Hakluyt, *op. cit.*, I, p. 453–454; I. Lubimenko, *op. cit.*, p. 51.

[501] R. Hakluyt, *op. cit.*, II, p. 165.

[502] *Ibid.*, II, p. 157.

[503] *Recueil . . .*, p. 36.

[504] 15th March, 1583, Simancas E° 1154.

[505] Venice, 2nd June, 1583, A.E., Venice, 31, f° 15 and 15 v°.

[506] Hareborne to Richard Forster, Pera, 5th September, 1583, R. Hakluyt, *op. cit.*, II, p. 172–173.

[507] A. C. Wood, *op. cit.*, p. 17.

[508] *Ibid.*, p. 20.

[509] *Ibid.*, p. 23.

[510] *Ibid.*, p. 23.

[511] *Ibid.*, p. 23.

prevent the company from pleading great difficulty, as if by coincidence on the eve of the renewal of its charter on 31st December, 1600,[512] that is in Elizabeth's lifetime, and again on 14th December, 1605,[513] at the beginning of the reign of her successor James I. There were indeed problems: the length of the voyages; the hostility of Spain until 1604; the threat from the Barbary corsairs; the violent rearguard action fought by Marseilles and Venice, who did not yield their positions willingly, not to mention trouble with the Turks and the burden that the maintenance of an embassy at Constantinople and a series of consulates in Barbary and the Levant placed upon the Company. But the perseverance of the English merchants, the excellence of their ships, the low price of their cloth, and the quality of their organization was rewarded by success. A few dozen of their ships could accomplish more in the Levant and the Mediterranean than the hundreds of cockleshells sent out by Marseilles.[514] Among the reasons for their success were the ingenious convoy system insisted upon by the English; the money they obtained through the favourable balance of trade in Constantinople; and the greater honesty of their merchants (compared to the Venetians and French who were always ready to cheat over the quantity or quality of fabrics).

All these arguments which were first advanced by Hakluyt and repeated by later historians have a certain force. But there was more to it than this. The English were helped on their way by the revival of trade with the Levant, mentioned earlier in connection with the spice trade. The old firm of the Mediterranean gained once more from the terrible battles of the Atlantic.[515] Between 1583 and 1591 it was no coincidence that English agents should have made their way along the roads through Syria to the Indian Ocean, Persia, the Indies, and Sumatra. These wanderers have left us their fantastic travellers' tales of the routes in the Near and Far East. In Egypt, a hot country, the English whose stock-in-trade was thick cloth were obliged to pay cash for their purchases. So here they were outmanoeuvred by skilful and persistent competition from the French.[516] The English therefore turned their attention to Syria and the roads through it; in this area they were able to organize the exchange of commodities for other commodities, a trade that the second circumnavigation of the Cape (by the Dutch) did not immediately disrupt. After all, the East India Company, founded in 1600, was an offshoot of the Levant Company.[517]

In the central Mediterranean, at Leghorn, the figures testify to the increasing success of the northerners, for example the register of *portate*

[512] A. C. Wood, *op. cit.*, p. 36.
[513] *Ibid.*, p. 39.
[514] Marseilles was still considered to have about a thousand ships working in 1610, Paul Masson, *Histoire du commerce français dans le Levant au XVIIe siècle, op. cit.*, p. 31.
[515] Paul Masson, *ibid.*, p. XVI.
[516] A. C. Wood, *op. cit.*, p. 33–35.
[517] *Ibid.*, p. 31.

of ships from the 'western waters' [the text gives no further details and lumps Dutch and English ships together]:[518] for the period from October to December, 1598, there arrived 5000 casks of lead, 5613 casks of smoked herring, 268,645 *pesci merluzzi*, and 513 *fardi* of *pesci stockfiss*.

The situation at the end of the century. By the end of the century the English were everywhere in the Mediterranean, in Moslem, or Christian countries, and travelling along all the overland routes that led to it or away from it to Europe or the Indian Ocean. In 1588 they were attracted to Moldavia and Wallachia.[519] For several years London had been formulating grand designs.[520] In 1583 there was a symbolic success when the *Hercules* (which had already made at least one previous voyage) brought back from Tripoli the richest cargo any English merchant had yet shipped to an English port.[521] Spanish, Greek, and Marseilles pilots helped the newcomers to accomplish the conquest of the sea, port by port, but it is not always possible to date these successive victories, particularly since entry to a port for the first time was usually discreet and cautious. Marseilles, for instance, decided on 26th November, 1590 to allow two English vessels to enter the port. 'It has been . . . resolved and ordered that since the town has need of lead and tin, in the calamitous times in which we find ourselves, the merchandise carried aboard the two vessels will enter the city together with the masters and clerks, in order to sell them, trade and negotiate freely with the inhabitants of the said city and to buy other goods if they so desire, to be laden into the said vessels, except they be prohibited or forbidden goods.'[522] This was certainly not the first time that English ships had put into Marseilles, for connections had existed since 1574, but now they were legally and officially granted entry.

They had come a long way in a few years. As early as 1589, a Genoese note refers[523] to the key points in an English intelligence network covering every sector of the sea: at Constantinople, William Hareborne (who was in fact at this date in London);[524] in Algiers, John Tipton; in Malta, John Lucas; and in Genoa, Richard Hunto. The last mentioned, whose surname has been Italianized gives the Genoese the impression of being an enemy to all Catholics, 'a most malicious and perverse enemy', and is reputed to be a spy (*inteligencero* says the document, which is written in Spanish) in the pay of Horatio Pallavicino – whom we have already met. In January, 1590, the English were congratulating themselves on having prevented a new Spanish agent, Juan Estefano Ferrari, from concluding a deal. They were now sufficiently integrated into Mediterranean trade to have their

[518] A.d.S., Florence, Mediceo, 2079, f° 210 and 210 v°.
[519] R. Hakluyt, *op. cit.*, II, p. 290.
[520] *CODOIN*, XCII, p. 455–456.
[521] R. Hakluyt, *op. cit.*, II, p. 271.
[522] A. Com., Marseilles, BB 52, f° 24 v°.
[523] A.d.S., Genoa, L. M. Spagna 10 2419 (undated).
[524] R. Hakluyt, *op. cit.*, II, p. 289–290.

own policy. It was certainly not based on power and force: the English approach was usually one of subtlety not to say guile (but they were by no means alone in this). They had two strings to their bow, Islam and Christendom, and sometimes fell back on a third – piracy.

The English had been pirates from the very beginning and of the worst kind.[525] In 1581 one of their sailing ships was making raids upon Turkish vessels.[526] Twenty years later, in 1601, a report from London mentions complaints by Genoa, Venice, and others that English ships had been robbing their merchantmen and disposing of their booty in the towns of Barbary.[527] Leghorn became, after the Anglo-Spanish peace of 1604, the favourite haunt of retired English pirates.[528] It is true that piracy can be a sign of weakness. English piracy, during these last years of the century, shows that their place was far from assured in this sea of rich cities and rich ships. It was not until later that that paradox, an English-dominated Mediterranean came to pass. It was not until 1620 that English warships first sailed into the Mediterranean and not until 1630 or 1640 that branches of English trading houses opened at Genoa.[529]

The arrival of the Hansards and the Dutch. The return of the English was connected with the tin trade. The first massive entry of Hanseatic and Dutch shipping was the result of grain purchases by Mediterranean states – grain, rather than the clumsy and ineffectual policies of the Spanish, who in theory controlled the gateway to the Mediterranean, although these too were partly responsible.

It was the bad Italian harvests of the years 1586 to 1590[530] that first alerted the Dutch and Hanseatic merchants, with possible assistance from Jewish wholesalers and middlemen as has been assumed not without some reason by Luzac,[531] de Jonge,[532] and Wätjen.[533] These are details of execution, as is the fact that the initiative came from Danzig, Lübeck, and Hamburg. Nothing could be more natural than that these towns standing

---

[525] Any number of references: piracy against the French, P. Masson, *op. cit.*, p. XXIV; against the Ragusans, Archives of Ragusa, D. de Foris, VII, f° 36 (Messina, 26th May, 1598), capture and burning of the ship *Our Lady of Loreto*; another attack made by the English off Cagliari, 8th March, 1594, D. de Foris, II, f°, 127 v° ff; capture of the ship *Holy Trinity and Saint John the Baptist*, near Zante, D. de Foris, V, f° 88, 12th May, 1595.

[526] *Recueil* . . ., p. 53; R. Hakluyt, *op. cit.*, II, p. 145–146; *CODOIN*, XCII, p. 60–61 (24th June, 1581).

[527] 22nd February, 1601, A.N., K 1630. The strange episode of the Englishman, Richard Cocaine, who in 1601 hired his ship the *Royal Merchant* to a Ragusan at Genoa: the captain then went off on a pirate raid against the Turks. Mediceo 1829, f° 258.

[528] R. Galluzzi, *op. cit.*, III, p. 270.

[529] A.d.S., Genoa, *Giunta di Marina*, note on the English consulate, undated.

[530] W. Naudé, *op. cit.*, pp. 142–143, 331.

[531] Élie Luzac, *Richesse de Hollande*, I, *op. cit.*, p. 63.

[532] Johannes Cornelis de Jonge, *Nederland en Venetie*, s'Gravenhage, 1852, p. 299–302.

[533] H. Wätjen, *op. cit.*, II, p. 5.

Northern grain at Leghorn in 1593

Record of transport ships (from Mediceo 2079, f°s 150 v° to 169 v°)

	Amsterdam and Zeeland	England	Lübeck	Hanseatic Ports		Danzig	Antwerp and Flanders	Norway	Riga	Unknown origin
				Emden	Hamburg					
Ships whose port of origin was ...	12	7	4	5	16	9	4	2	1	13
Ships loaded at ...	28*	7	3	3	12	11	0	0	1	8

(Row 1 Lübeck + Emden + Hamburg bracketed: 34; Row 2 bracketed: 29)

* Of which only one in Zeeland.

The seventy-three ships arrived at Leghorn as follows: 6th January (2), 9th January (1), 12th January (5), 13th January (37), 14th January (4), 16th January (1), 20th January (8), 26th January (3), 31st January (1), 11th March (1), 14th March (2), 1st April (1), 29th April (1), 3rd May (1), 5th May (1), 6th May (2), 12th May (1), 15th May (1). As for the length of voyage, there is no record for the year 1593, but in 1609–1611 (Mediceo 2097) real lengths of voyage in weeks are as follows: A. Amsterdam–Leghorn (12, 6, 5, 5, 8, 5, 32 days, 16) B. Danzig–Leghorn (14). C. London–Leghorn (4, 8). D. Bristol–Leghorn (12). E. Plymouth–Leghorn 28 days.

The conclusions to be drawn from this table are self-evident (variable length of voyage, predominance of winter voyages, clear indication that Amsterdam acted as a centre for the redistribution of grain), and the reader will be able to work them out for himself. It is however worth noting that 1. In this year 1593, six English ships brought their usual cargoes of lead, tin, and herring, but that there had slipped into their convoy one Dutch ship (loaded in England) and a ship from Emdem, the *Black Eagle*, loaded at Lisbon. 2. That in all, counting both wheat and rye, the northerners landed over 15,000 tons of grain at Leghorn that year, which gives an average tonnage per ship of about 200 tons; 3. That the list of names of ships shows the heavy predominance of non-religious names.

at the gateway to the great prairies and experienced specialists in the bulk transport of grain should have heard the appeal of the Mediterranean. It was to Danzig in fact that the Grand Duke of Tuscany sent his agent Ricardo in 1590, along with his aides, with instructions to send 'granajo della Polonia' to Lübeck and then on to Holland, France and England.[534] There is no doubt that the enormous order placed with the North by the Grand Duke that year – worth a million ducats it was rumoured – was entirely responsible for the original appearance of the northern fleets. Thereafter this traffic needed no external impetus. In 1591 some historians have claimed that thirteen sailing ships were placed under embargo in Spain on their way through, in spite of the passports granted them by the Catholic King.[535] Forty arrived at Leghorn.[536] So many appeals were made that it is hardly surprising to find all the northern countries[537] rallying to the call. Dutch, Hansard, and English ships combined to form the grain fleets, as can be seen from the list of *portate* at Leghorn in 1593.

From grain to spices: The Dutch conquer the Mediterranean. Although the Hansards and the Dutch arrived together in the Mediterranean, only the latter found themselves a permanent place. Ludwig Beutin's book[538] suggests that competition between the two northern peoples was responsible. By the beginning of the seventeenth century, the Hansards had been eliminated and their ships hardly ever went any further than Málaga.[539]

What were the causes of this defeat? Probably the Hansards, who had remained profitably neutral during the wars between Iberians and other northern nations, found that this advantage was automatically cancelled out after the peace treaties of 1604 and 1609. In the eighteenth century they were again, thanks to European wars, to extend their trade links with the Mediterranean. But at the end of the sixteenth century there could have been many other reasons. Was it because the Hansards had Spanish connections, therefore found employment in the Atlantic, and did not need

[534] G. Vivoli, *op. cit.*, III, p. 181.
[535] *Ibid.*, p. 317, references to Galluzzi and Rondinelli, p. 318.
[536] *Ibid.*
[537] On the entry of German ships to the Mediterranean, there are three documents at Ragusa (Diversa de Foris, XV, f° 123 v° to 124): Venice, 24th October, 1596, details of the insurance of the ship the *Crescent*, master Hans Emens of Hamburg, which had brought grain from Hamburg to Venice; Venice, 28th November, 1596, insurance for the ship *Holy Trinity* registered at Hamburg, master Antinio (?) Luder, which had carried grain to Venice; Venice, 24th December, 1596, similar details of the ship *Fortuna Volante*, master Girardo Vestrevuola, which again had brought grain from Hamburg. On the long trip between the North and Venice various incidents occurred: in 1597, two ships (Masters Luca and Giacomo Neringhia) having taken on grain at Danzig were unloaded at Lisbon; they took on a fresh cargo of goods there and carried it to Venice, where they asked to be exempted from anchorage dues, as grain ships were, having come so far, which request was granted, A.d.S., Venice, *Cinque Savii*, Busta 3, 29th July, 1597.
[538] *Der deutsche Seehandel im Mittelmeergebiete bis zu den napoleonischen Kriegen*, Neumünster, 1933.
[539] Ships from Hamburg are mentioned in Italy in 1600, Simancas E° 617.

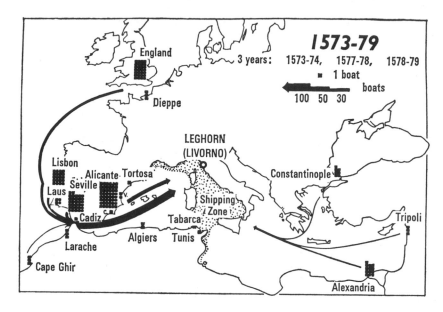

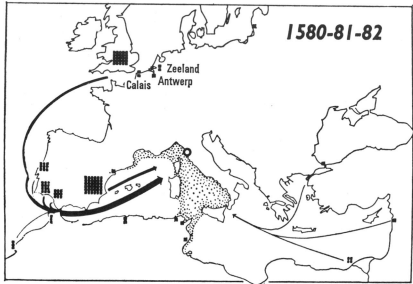

Fig. 54: *The increasing numbers of northern boats at Leghorn 1573–93*

From F. Braudel and R. Romano, *Navires et marchandises à l'entrée du port de Livourne.* The four maps show the rapid increase of traffic entering Leghorn (each map shows the combined shipping of three years).

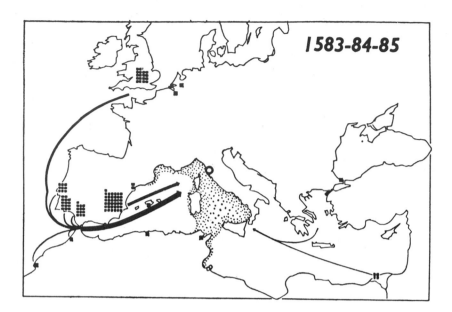

1583-84-85

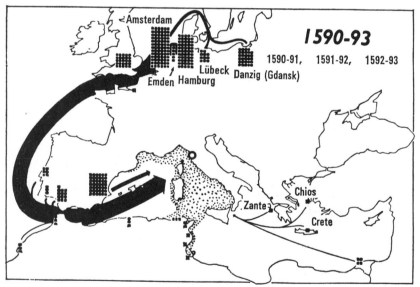

1590-93

Amsterdam

1590-91,   1591-92,   1592-93

Emden Hamburg Lübeck Danzig (Gdansk)

Chios

Zante

Crete

The importance of the Levant, which was never very great, was to decrease even further, despite the great value of some cargoes.

The numerically more important western shipping at first came mostly from Spain and Portugal, with a few boats arriving from the English Channel and the North Sea. This pattern was disrupted by the massive arrival of the northern grain ships in 1590–1593.

the spices and pepper that might have drawn them to the Levant? Ot was it because behind these maritime cities there was no thriving industry, if only because of the preferential links between southern Germany and Genoa and Venice? Or was it lack of money? By some paradox which must have an explanation, it was the Dutch who in 1615 and no doubt earlier,[540] transported to Syria certain German commodities: amber, mercury, cinnabar, copper wire, and iron. I do not believe the blame can be laid on the outdated organization of the Hanse. There were quite as many ship-owners and insurers to be found there as throughout the Mediterranean. Was it a question of ships? But the Hansards had vessels of every tonnage.

For whatever reason, then, the Dutch were successful and in about 1597 reached the eastern end of the sea. In that year, Balthasar Moucheron, enemy of Spain, sent a ship to Tripoli in Syria under the French flag.[541] In the following year all Dutch shipping obtained permission from Henry IV to trade under the French flag in the Turkish ports[542] (they received their first capitulations only in 1612). In 1599 the Venetian consul reported[543] that that year 'there had again come' a 'Flemish' ship, with over 100,000 crowns in ready money, which had done no little damage to Venetian trade. He was anxious to know whether the merchants of the Netherlands would remain in Syria, since the Dutch 'consul' had declared they would leave if their compatriots continued to make progress in the Indian Ocean. The Venetians would gladly have wished them godspeed. But the Dutch remained, in spite of Houtmann's circumnavigation of the Cape in 1595, the occupation of Java in 1597, the reconnaissance of the Comores, the capture of Mauritius in 1598[544] and the return of the second fleet in 1598. For it was to take years for the conquest of the Indian Ocean and the diversion of its currents of trade to become effective and for the Company of Distant Territories (*Van Verne*) to be converted into the triumphant Company of the East Indies in 1602. And besides, even if they had been able to intercept the precious drug trade, they would still have been attracted to the Levant by the silk trade (which they were soon, without immediate success to try to divert towards the Persian Gulf) and by spun cotton.

So the Dutch swarmed into the Mediterranean like so many heavy insects crashing against the window panes – for their entry was neither gentle nor discreet. Was it simply that they were the cruellest of pirates, the opinion of the Portuguese who, after the looting 'da nossa cidade' of Faro were certainly in a position to know?[545] Or was it because they had to force their way into the Mediterranean as they had in the Atlantic,

[540] G. Berchet, *op. cit.*, p. 157–159.
[541] J. Denucé, *op. cit.*, p. 17.
[542] *Ibid.*, p. 71. But 'consulage' was exercised by the English.
[543] G. Berchert, *op. cit.*, p. 103.
[544] J. Denucé, *op. cit.*, p. 68.
[545] Bernardo Gomez De Brito, *Historia tragico-maritima*, Lisbon, 1904–1905, II, pp. 506–507, about 1604.

elbowing others out of their way? Those other latecomers, in the thirteenth and fourteenth centuries, the Catalans, had also been obliged to force an entry by piracy. The English were no better. Their cannons were not merely used to force a passage through the Straits and in defence against the Spanish galleys. They were fired indiscriminately at anything considered worth taking – Turkish, French, or Italian, it was all the same to the English and they rapidly acquired a bad reputation. The Dutch too frequently resorted to freebooting in the Mediterranean.[546] They were soon associating with the Barbary corsairs whose tactics they transformed (as we shall see later), organizing both this activity and their illegal exploits in the Atlantic from the great port of Leghorn.[547] In 1610[548], in any case, two ships sailed into the Tuscan port from the Indian Ocean. Were they Mediterranean or Dutch? We are not told, but the clerk covered a whole page with the inventory of the riches they carried. Not only this but a curious relationship sprang up between the Signoria of Venice and Amsterdam (sometimes using the king of France as an intermediary), the complexities of which are not easy to unravel. There is a tantalizing reference in Venice at this time to marine insurance covering all quarters of the globe, including the Indies.[549] Was this the work of the Dutch? The documents are silent on this point.

Dutch history on the small Mediterranean stage and elsewhere is far from entirely intelligible. Holland did not become a world power until the end of the century. Why was the victory of Elizabeth's ships over Philip II's clumsy armadas not followed by the English supremacy that would have seemed logical? England won and Holland immediately sent her citizens, trade, and ships to the far corners of the earth, to the East Indies and China and continued to do so until the middle of the seventeenth century. There is only one plausible explanation: Holland, by her proximity to the Catholic provinces of the Netherlands and by her persistence in forcing the coffers of Spain, had better access than England to the Peninsula and the American treasure upon which her commerce depended. For without the pieces of eight patiently extracted from Spain, Dutch shipping could not have sailed the seven seas. In England at the beginning of the seventeenth century, the affairs of the Levant Company were considered more advantageous since they were balanced by large exports of commo-

[546] H. Wätjen, *op. cit.*, p. 55.

[547] R. Galluzzi, *op. cit.*, III, p. 270; G. Vivoli, *op. cit.*, IV, p. 7–10. A curious detail is the arrival at Leghorn on 29th November, 1581, of a ship which was probably Portuguese (the *Santo Antonio*, captain Baltasar Dias) loaded in Brazil and carrying notably 460 cantars of *pau brasil*. On Tuscan attempts at 'colonization' in Brazil, see the intriguing but too short note by G. G. Guarnieri, *art. cit.*, p. 24, note 1.

[548] A.d.S., Florence, Mediceo 2079, f°ˢ 337 and 365, the first ship, *Nuestra Señora do Monte del Carmine*, from Goa, had a cargo of 4000 cantars of pepper and her arrival is dated merely 1610 without details; on 14th August, 1610, arrived *Nostra Signora di Pietà*, from the East Indies, carrying 4170 cantars of pepper, precious stones and 145 cantars of Indian fabrics . . .

[549] A.d.S., Venice, *Cinque Savii*, Busta 6, 15th November, 1596, copy.

dities to Turkey, than those of the East India Company which required the export of considerable sums of money.[550] Between Spain and Holland there was the link of silver, reinforced by peace between 1609 and 1621, a link that was to be broken, along with Spain's entire fortunes in the middle of the seventeenth century just as – by coincidence? – the wheel of fate turned against Holland.

How the Dutch took Seville after 1570 without firing a shot. The brilliant victory in the seventeenth century of the English and Dutch can only adequately be explained on a world scale. In the first place it was the result of a series of technical improvements in the design and handling of ships, as we have already noted.[551] The appearance of the northern sailing vessel of 100 to 200 tons, well armed and easily manoeuvred, marks a turning-point in maritime history. More progress was made in shipping in the northern seas between 1500 and 1600 than was achieved between the year of the Spanish Armada and Trafalgar.[552] The northerners gave their ships stronger defences, increased the size of their crews and added to their artillery, clearing the upper decks for better manoeuvrability, as Ralph Davis has pointed out, to my mind quite conclusively.[553] Wherever figures are available, the average size of the crew in relation to the ship's tonnage is superior in the north to that in the Mediterranean.[554] The disadvantage of carrying smaller cargoes was balanced by greater security and therefore less expensive insurance rates.[555] The costly Mediterranean galleys could sometimes of course, even in the seventeenth century, make startling comebacks: a sailing vessel was only the stronger when there was enough wind to fill her sails.[556] In a dead calm the agile galley could move to the blind spots of the immobilized fortress and carry off the victory.

But such occasions were exceptional. The military and commercial superiority of the North cannot seriously be questioned. And the English and Dutch were well aware of this before 1588. They considered the Portuguese navigators 'bedraggled hens'.[557] The Portuguese in return described their conquerors as the scum of the earth. The Dutch, they were still saying in 1608,[558] are content when at sea with 'a morsel of biscuit,

[550] A. C. Wood, *op. cit.*, p. 43.

[551] See above, p. 300.

[552] L. von Pastor, *op. cit.*, German edition, vol. X, p. 306.

[553] 'Influences de L'Angleterre sur le déclin de Venise au XVIIe siècle' in *Decadenza economica veneziana nel secolo XVII*, Giorgio Cini Foundation, Venice, 1961, p. 183–235.

[554] On this point see above, p. 304; *C. S. P.*, *East Indies*, I, p. 107, October, 1600, five boats are sent to the Indies: 1500 tons, 500 crew. R. Davis, *art. cit.*, p. 215: in 1628, according to the Venetian *bailo*, 'the English carry more seamen and gunners leaving much space free for combat'.

[555] R. Davis, *art. cit.*, p. 215 (*C. S. P.*, Venetian, 2nd October, 1627).

[556] F. Braudel, 'L'économie de la Méditerranée au XVIIe siècle' in *Economia e Storia*, April–June, 1955, reproduced in *Cahiers de Tunisie*, 1956, p. 175 ff.

[557] B. M. Sloane, 1572 (about 1633).

[558] Quoted by C. R. Boxer, *op. cit.*, p. 76, note 150. The text is by Pedro de Baeza.

a scraping of butter, salt pork, fish, and beer; on such fare they will spend months on the high seas'. The southerners they say, expect better food 'since we are not like these men bred to poverty'. There were of course other explanations for the northerners' success.

Let us, for a start deal, with some reasons frequently advanced: that the Iberians were poor defenders of the Mediterranean gateway, for instance; by trying to ward off the storm, they in fact unleashed it by adopting an Atlantic policy beyond their means in competition with the North. There is certainly a grain of truth in this. It was in 1586 that the Spanish, who were now rulers of Lisbon as well as Seville, multiplied their embargoes and prohibitions of northern ships.[559] But these measures did not prevent an active Iberian trade with the enemy: as a 'continental blockade' it was ineffective.[560] And everything continued much the same as before. And then the chronology should make us suspicious. The English returned to the Mediterranean in 1572–1573, that is ten years before the Spanish embargoes and the Dutch in 1590–1593, that is several years after them. . . . Clearly, the major explanation for an economic reversal of this magnitude must lie in or be deduced from the general economic situation.

The north and south had been enemies well before the end of the century. The Netherlands rebelled in 1566, the English severed Spanish shipping routes after 1569. But these 'complementary enemies'[561] could not live without each other. They fought, then made it up or compromised, depending on whether agreement was reached openly or unofficially. As a result the war in the Atlantic would flare up, die down, and break out again, and was for ever being tempered by informal solutions. Then, between 1566 and 1570 came an important turning-point. Until then Atlantic trade had been three-fold: the northerners (the Dutch in the front line,[562] the Bretons soon in second position,[563] the English, later the Hansards and Scandinavian fishing boats,[564] all maintaining links between the north and the Peninsula, supplying grain, timber, dried or salted fish, lead, tin, copper, canvas, woollen cloth, ironware); the Iberians, with the *Carrera de Indias* based on Spain, and the ocean link with the East Indies based on Portugal; and lastly the Italians, chief among whom were the Genoese at Seville who financed this commodity trading, the gap in the trade balance being made good, though always with some delay, by American silver.

Then the system suffered two heavy blows: after 1566, the Genoese merchants, who were now obtaining *sacas de plata* from the king, lost

[559] For references see *La Méditerranée*, 1st edition, p. 493.
[560] J. H. Kernkamp, *Handel op den vijand 1572–1609*, 2 vols, Utrecht, 1931–1934, is still the standard work. On the frequent inefficacy of these measures see V. Vázquez de Prada, *op. cit.*, (1596–1598), I, p. 63.
[561] The expression is borrowed from Germaine Tillion, *Les ennemis complémentaires*, 1960 (of the French and the Algerians between 1955 and 1962).
[562] After 1550, V. Vázquez de Prada, *op. cit.*, I, p. 48.
[563] *Ibid.*
[564] A.N., K 1607 B (B. 89).

interest in exporting the commodities which had until then been facilitating their payments to the North. And after 1569 the flow of silver from Laredo to Antwerp was interrupted.[565] But the Atlantic trade did not suffer from these setbacks, indeed it prospered and this astonishing fact is a key explanation.

There can be no question of totally interrupting the Atlantic trade, said Spanish economic experts to the king's advisers; that would be the ruin of shipping and the Indies trade and would drain the resources of the treasury. Their arguments appear in a long report issued in 1575.[566] Abandoned by Genoese capitalism, the export trade from Seville found other sponsors. Firms in the Netherlands, enriched by previous years, were to advance their own goods and to wait for payment until the Indies fleets returned with silver. In other words, the merchants of Seville now became merely commission agents: they saw goods pass through and took their percentage, but practically never risked their own property. From now on, their capital was to go into buying land and villages, *juros*, or settling entails. From this passive role, it was only a step to total inactivity, a prospect they viewed with equanimity. In this way Seville was conquered, eaten away from the inside by the obscure gnawing of termites, and all to the advantage of Holland. Antwerp, in the running war that began in 1572, remained the capital of political money: like Saigon before 1953 during the traffic in piastres. But Amsterdam attracted the merchants of Antwerp and, through Seville, drew the huge prize of Spanish America into her net. It was a victory that would never have been achieved without years of patient work, alliances, covered deals, the slow corruption of the Seville market, the cooperation for instance of the Duke of Medina Sidonia if only for the transmission of silver from San Lucar de Barrameda, of which he was the overlord.[567]

Towards the end of the century this infiltration of the trade of Seville became known and during the summer of 1595 the king decided to strike a blow at such clandestine traffic which had by now gone too far to escape a full official enquiry. The orders were executed by the licenciate Diego de Armenteros, assisted by Luis Gaytan de Ayala. They visited sixty-three trading houses in Seville, owned by Castilians, Portuguese, Flemings, Frenchmen, Germans, all suspect because of their relations with Holland, Zeeland, and England.[568] Needless to say not a single Englishman, Dutchman, or Zeelander was found on the scene. 'It is well known,' wrote Armenteros, 'that they only trade in Spain through trusted intermediaries.' The two *visitadores* confiscated papers and account books, when there were any books to be found, some merchants having gone to the lengths of hiding them under their mattresses. All the papers were examined by

[565] See above, p. 482.
[566] Simancas E° 569, f° 84, undated.
[567] This gradual 'Passivierung' of Seville is admirably explained by J. van Klaveren, *op. cit.*, esp. p. 111 ff, from which much of my information is drawn .
[568] 1594, Simancas E° 174.

the five *contadores*, expert accountants placed at the disposition of the investigators. The wealth of the evidence made their task complicated and difficult: it was not easy to establish who the true owners of the merchandise really were. For the provinces remaining loyal to Spain exchanged goods with the rebel islands. And short of instituting special safe-conducts to be issued by the governor of the Netherlands, or making this system compulsory and general between the two warring zones of Flanders, it was difficult to find out whether goods belonged to one half or the other. The confusion arose from the fact that it was impossible to send goods from the loyal provinces through Dunkirk or Gravelines. With the rebel islands nearby and Dover across the straits, how long would that have taken, not to mention the absence of the king's ships? Should the investigators hold an enquiry and hear witnesses? No one could or would tell the truth. A merchant held for questioning who lets certain of his goods be confiscated knows quite well that his correspondent will reimburse himself out of merchandise belonging to him. Such are the conclusions of the joint letter sent on 12th July, on behalf of the Duke of Medina Sidonia and the two investigators and penned by Diego Armenteros.[569]

The situation is made even clearer in a letter from the same Armenteros written a month later, probably to one of Philip II's secretaries, his friend or protector, at any rate an important political figure.[570] In the confiscated papers, Armenteros had found any number of entries proving that the incriminated merchants were trading quite calmly with the rebels in the Netherlands or with the English, corresponding with them and sending them sums of money. Among others, a whole series of papers concerns Francisco de Conique, Pedro Leymieri, and Nicolas Baudaert, all three resident in England, and David Leymieri, the latter living in Amsterdam. A letter written to Pedro Leymieri in England informs him 'that our fleet has returned in such disarray that if it were to leave here again it could quite easily be captured whole with only a few ships'. This company (Leymieri and partners) was, according to what he had been told, the richest in Seville. Six ships had arrived at San Lucar carrying merchandise belonging to the firm and the Duke of Medina Sidonia had allowed them to land. It is true, added Armenteros, that this was worth 12,000 ducats to him. . . . 'There is not a foreigner entering San Lucar,' he says, 'who is not fêted and favoured, even helped to export silver.' When he had a reliable person at hand, he would send on the papers concerning the Leymieri affair. Meanwhile he urged secrecy, 'that I may not add to the number of enemies I have already made by serving His Majesty'. . . .

There is evidence even more cruelly revealing. In the following year, 1596,[571] sixty ships lying in Cadiz harbour laden for the 'Indies' were surprised by the English fleet which sacked the town. They contained a total

[569] Simancas E° 174.
[570] 18th August, 1595, *ibid.*
[571] Here I am following Jacob van Klaveren, *op. cit.*, p. 116–117.

of 11 million ducats' worth of merchandise. The English offered not to burn them for a payment of 2 million. The Duke of Medina Sidonia refused the deal and the ships went up in flames – but it was not the Spanish who suffered this enormous loss, for the merchandise did not belong to them. A whole book could be written on Seville, the city of corruption, of vicious denunciation, of prevaricating officials, a city in which silver had wrought havoc.

These harsh facts help us, if not to reach a conclusion, at least to glimpse something of the true explanations. The balance of world history was tipped not by the incompetence of Philip II's agents, nor by the obvious inadequacy of the guard on the Straits of Gibraltar, but quite clearly by the bankruptcy of the Spanish state, a self-evident fact by 1596 and which even before it was finally established had raised once more the problems of silver circulation and the division of world wealth. Holland, now in a period of sudden expansion, towards the Mediterranean on one hand with the grain and other trades, and towards the spice islands on the other, was looking for and finding compensation.

One curious detail: the advance of the Dutch, especially in the Mediterranean but towards the Indies and America too, was preceded by the arrival of Portuguese merchants, for the most part new Christians, coming either from Lisbon or from the cities of the North where they had taken refuge. Was there a 'Lisbon takeover' parallel to the 'Seville takeover'?

New Christians in the Mediterranean. This immense infiltration by northern, Atlantic, international capitalism, based on Amsterdam, could hardly ignore the rich Mediterranean. Like Spain, which was shamelessly looted, it was a tempting prize for a young, sharp-toothed capitalism that soon discovered how to find accomplices on the spot. Preparing and easing the way for the Dutch, sometimes involuntarily, the rich Portuguese *marranos* came on to the scene, the Ximenez of Lisbon and Antwerp, for example, and their associates the Andrade and the Veiga, who arranged deliveries of northern grain for the Grand Duke of Tuscany after the 1590s, making considerable profits for themselves out of it, and who also had a hand in the spice trade with Italy. In 1589 they began sending loads of spices to Baltasar Suárez in Florence. Then they transferred their goodwill from the Castilian to Antonio Gutierrez, who had just come to Florence and, being himself Portuguese, soon found himself in relation with other merchants from his homeland, Manuel da Costa, for instance, who sent him chests of sugar in May 1591.[572] Simón Ruiz' correspondence with Florence tells us about these Portuguese who controlled everything, 'en esto de especierias',[573] according to Baltasar Suárez, who wanted his friend to intercede on his behalf with the powerful Ximenez. The latter had sent 500 quintals of

---

[572] Correspondence of Simón Ruiz, Archivo Provincial de Valladolid, Antonio Gutierrez to Simón Ruiz, Florence, 20th May, 1591.
[573] Florence, 20th May, 1591, *ibid.*

pepper in a single consignment to Italy.[574] The previous year, they had
had a ship come from Brazil to Leghorn with 600 chests of sugar.[575] And
all their ventures were successful. Pepper from Alexandria was in short
supply at just the right moment. 'They have luck in everything they turn
their hand to,' exclaims Baltasar Suárez.[576] 'Son afortunados en cuanto
ponen mano.'

Other Portuguese merchants arrived in Italy close on their heels. In
February, 1591 two of them, Fernández and Jorge Francisco are about
to settle at Pisa. If they do 'there is no doubt that they will draw all the
trade of Portugal towards them'.[577] In August of the same year, 'if what I
hear is true', writes Baltasar Suárez, 'the Ximenez are sending someone to
open up a business in their name and are even sending to Pisa Sebastian
Ximenez Penetiques, who is at present their agent in Cadiz. A son of Rui
Nuñez is coming from Antwerp and, since these are all rich people, the
Grand Duke wants to attract them and is preparing to grant them many
privileges.'[578]

These details betray a certain change in the economic situation: since
pepper had become difficult to sell by the Atlantic routes, it was naturally
diffused towards Italy and from there to Germany, and it was therefore
to Italy that for a while Portuguese emigrants flocked. In Venice Philip II's
ambassador refers to these Portuguese Jews whom he has seen arriving
dressed in the Christian fashion, then declaring themselves *por judios* and
'putting on the red hat which is the distinctive sign they wear in this
state'.[579] Venice became once more tolerant towards them, welcomed,
supported, and protected them and benefited from their competition. A few
names emerge, not necessarily well-known: two brothers, 'Rui Loppes
and Diego Rodrighes', who, after twenty-four years' residence in the city,
applied in May, 1602 for Venetian *cittadinanza*,[580] or the Rodrigo di
Marchiano, a Jew from Portugal, who initiated the sugar trade from Cape
Ghir in Barbary,[581] or the other *marranos* from Flanders and Hamburg
who passed through Venice on their way to the Levant. There then seems
to have been set up, whether discreetly or openly, effectively or apparently,
a prosperous chain of Jewish, Levantine, and western merchants working
together from Constantinople to Salonica, Valona, Venice, and west as far
as Seville, Lisbon and Amsterdam. It was not for nothing that Spanish,
Tuscan, or Maltese pirates were during these years so attentive to 'scouring' merchant vessels and seizing any merchandise belonging to Jews, the

[574] Florence, 17th June, 1591.
[575] Florence, 31st December, 1590.
[576] Florence, 9th September, 1591, *ibid.*
[577] Florence, 26th June, 1591.
[578] Florence, 12th August, 1591.
[579] Don Alonso de la Cueva to H. M., Venice, 30th May, 1608, A.N., K 1678,
43 b.
[580] A.d.S., Venice, *Cinque Savii*, 141, f° 44, 22nd May, 1602.
[581] *Ibid.*, 22, f° 52, 20th November, 1598 and 16th August, 1602.

ropa de judios mentioned in Spanish texts. These cargoes were often worth having.[582]

One is therefore tempted to ask. Was this prosperity the result of a formal or informal agreement between the Dutch and the new Christians? If so, then the Atlantic was responsible. We have not enough evidence to say so with certainty but it is quite possible. Published anonymously in 1778, *La Richesse de Hollande*, [*The Wealth of Holland*] is an impressive book if not necessarily an accurate one. Among several erroneous statements one finds the following claim, 'It was only in 1612, in imitation of certain Jews who had taken refuge among them, and who had it was said set up counting houses everywhere, that the Dutch began to set up their own and to send their ships all over the Mediterranean.'[583]

[582] See below, Vol II, part II ch. 6 and 7.

[583] *Op. cit.*, vol. I, p. 63 and 501. The book is in fact by Elie Luzac, or to be more accurate, it is a version by him of the earlier work by Jacques Accarias de Serionne, which appeared in Amsterdam in 1765.

ABOUT THE AUTHOR

Fernand Braudel (1902–1985) received his degree in history in 1923 and subsequently taught in Algeria, Paris and São Paulo. He spent five years as a prisoner of war in Germany, during which time he wrote his grand thesis, *The Mediterranean and the Mediterranean World in the Age of Philip II*, which was published in 1949. In 1946 he became a member of the editorial board of *Annales*, the famous journal founded by Marc Bloch and Lucian Febvre, whom he succeeded at the Collège de France in 1949. He was a member of the Ecole Pratique des Hautes Etudes, and from 1962 until his death he was chief administrator of the Maison des Sciences de l'Homme. Professor Braudel held honorary doctorates from universities all over the world.

Abbreviations

A.C.	Archives Communales
A. Dep.	Archives Départementales
A.d.S.	Archivio di Stato
A.E.	Affaires Étrangères (Foreign Affairs) Paris
A.H.N.	Archivo Historico Nacional, Madrid
A.N. K.	Archives Nationales, Paris, Series K
B.M.	British Museum
B.N.	Bibliothèque Nationale, Paris
B.N. F.	Biblioteca Nazionale, Florence
B.N. Madrid	National Library, Madrid
CODOIN	*Coleccion de documentos ineditos para la historia de España*
Correr	Museo Correr, Venice
C.S.P.	Calendar of State Papers
G.G.A.	Former Government-General Building Algiers
Instructions Nautiques	Service hydrographique de la marine française
Marciana	Marciana Library, Venice
P.R.O.	Public Record Office, London
Sim.	Simancas
Simancas E°	Simancas, Series Estado